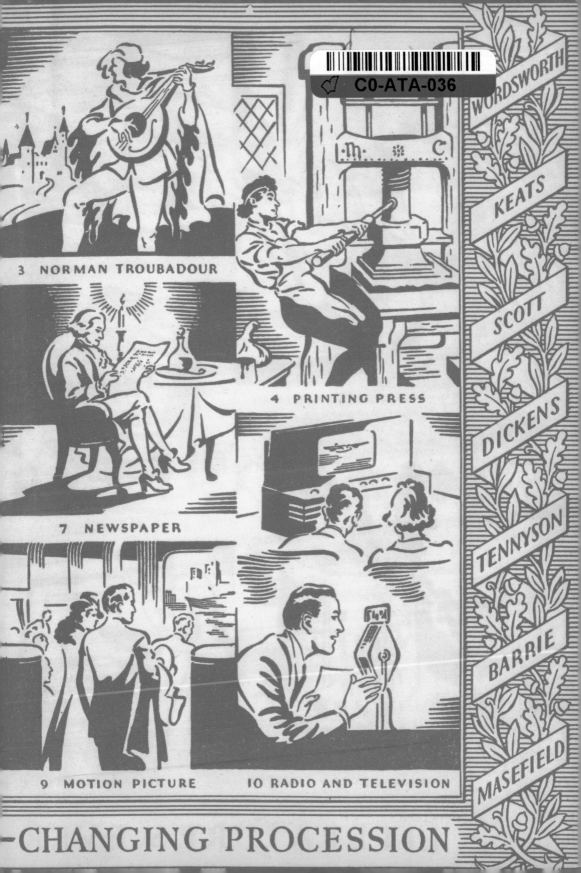

3 NORMAN TROUBADOUR

4 PRINTING PRESS

7 NEWSPAPER

9 MOTION PICTURE 10 RADIO AND TELEVISION

—CHANGING PROCESSION

C0-ATA-036

WORDSWORTH

KEATS

SCOTT

DICKENS

TENNYSON

BARRIE

MASEFIELD

ENGLISH WRITERS

REVISED EDITION

✶✶✶✶ ✶✶✶✶ ✶✶✶✶ ✶✶✶✶ ✶✶✶✶ ✶✶✶✶ ✶✶✶✶

BY

TOM PEETE CROSS
Professor of English and Comparative Literature, University of Chicago

REED SMITH
Professor of English, University of South Carolina

ELMER C. STAUFFER
Teacher of English, Herzl Junior College, Chicago
Formerly Teacher of English, Crane Technical High School, Chicago

AND

ELIZABETH COLLETTE
Teacher of English, Peabody High School, Pittsburgh

✶✶✶✶ ✶✶✶✶ ✶✶✶✶ ✶✶✶✶ ✶✶✶✶ ✶✶✶✶ ✶✶✶✶

GINN AND COMPANY
BOSTON · NEW YORK · CHICAGO · LONDON
ATLANTA · DALLAS · COLUMBUS · SAN FRANCISCO

COPYRIGHT, 1951, BY GINN AND COMPANY

COPYRIGHT, 1945, BY GINN AND COMPANY
COPYRIGHT, 1940, BY TOM PEETE CROSS, REED SMITH, ELMER C. STAUFFER, AND
ELIZABETH COLLETTE
PHILIPPINES COPYRIGHT, 1940, BY TOM PEETE CROSS, REED SMITH, ELMER C. STAUFFER, AND
ELIZABETH COLLETTE
COPYRIGHT, 1931, BY TOM PEETE CROSS, REED SMITH, AND ELMER C. STAUFFER
PHILIPPINES COPYRIGHT, 1937, BY TOM PEETE CROSS, REED SMITH, AND ELMER C. STAUFFER

ALL RIGHTS RESERVED

752.11

☆ ☆ ☆   ☆ ☆ ☆ ☆   ☆ ☆ ☆ ☆   ☆ ☆ ☆ ☆   ☆ ☆ ☆ ☆   ☆ ☆ ☆ ☆   ☆ ☆ ☆ ☆

Preface

BOTH in its selection of material and in its editorial equipment, the revised edition of *English Writers* combines the most valuable results of past experience and of present theory, and is at the same time an anthology and a history of English literature. The editors have consulted city and state courses of study. Besides, and of even greater importance, all the selections, recent as well as those written before our time, have been taught many times in high-school classes, with inclusion in *English Writers* in mind.

Because of its freshness and directness recent literature makes a strong appeal to young readers. Through its use many teachers have achieved gratifying results in arousing unresponsive classes and enlivening a dull literature hour. No time, trouble, or expense has been spared to make the recent-literature section in this book full, fresh, and attractive. The editors believe that nowhere else will be found gathered in a single volume for use in high school the variety and the charm of the present-day selections in the fields of the new poetry, the recent personal essay, the modern short story, and the drama.

In preparing the revised edition of *English Writers* the editors have kept constantly in mind the intimate connection between English history and English literature. The growth of English ideals and of the English tradition has been indicated in the discussions of the social and historical backgrounds that precede each period. Each introduction is followed by a special table showing the correlation between English literature and events in Europe and America, thus making a pervasive and fundamental integration between literature and history.

The lives of the writers and an estimate of their writings have been so presented as not only to make the authors real persons instead of mere names, but also to show their relation to their periods as well as their influence upon contemporary and later literature.

At the same time individual selections of merit and charm — the inspired single poem, the old scrapbook favorite — find a place, whether or not their writers have any other claim to literary importance.

In addition to abundant examples of the short story, English prose fiction is represented by short but interesting selections from three of the greatest English novels, *Robinson Crusoe*, *David Copperfield*, and *Henry Esmond*.

As regards editorial equipment, in the very nature of things no small part of the sympathetic interpretation of literature for young students must consist of the intelligent clearing away of difficulties by such means

v

as definition of words, glossing of phrases, explanation of references, and analysis of ideas. Emotional enjoyment is dependent on intellectual insight; or, more simply, to appreciate, one must first understand.

To remove initial barriers, therefore, and to open the way for a direct, personal contact between the pupil's mind and the masterpiece, the following editorial aids have been provided:

1. Concise summaries of historical periods and stimulating discussions of the chief literary types and tendencies.

2. Skillfully selected reading lists for use in the outside reading course and the library. These lists are of three kinds: (1) background work for each historical period; (2) further reading of the more important individual authors; and (3) additional worth-while reading in the various literary types, such as the short story, the personal essay, the one-act play, and the like.

3. Unusually numerous and attractive illustrations which serve both to interpret and to vivify the selections.

4. Carefully planned brief headnotes giving the character, occasion, purpose, significance, and general emotional background of the various selections, — story, essay, poem, — headnotes giving just the bit of essential information that every reader should have before beginning the selection. In the main they consist of information that few immature readers could get for themselves.

5. Footnotes explaining difficult words or phrases.

6. Discussion hints in the form of fresh, stimulating questions to provoke class discussion and to point the way to a more thorough comprehension both of the leading ideas of each selection and of its chief parts or subdivisions.

7. Carefully written sketches of the life and literary significance of each of the ninety writers represented in the text, accompanied by photographs. These biographies, together with the historical summaries and type discussions throughout the book, form a fresh and full history of English literature.

8. A dictionary of names and phrases, arranged alphabetically, to explain important historical, literary, mythological, and Biblical references of wide range and repeated application. Asterisks throughout the text indicate the names or the key words of the phrases explained in the dictionary.

Acknowledgments

Grateful acknowledgment is due to the following publishers for permission to use selections from their publications:

D. APPLETON-CENTURY COMPANY: "On a Piece of Chalk," from *Lay Sermons, Addresses, and Reviews,* by THOMAS H. HUXLEY.

ERNEST BENN, BROTHERS: "The Lagoon," from *Tales of Unrest,* by JOSEPH CONRAD.

BURNS, OATES & WASHBOURNE, LTD.: "Lepanto," from *Collected Poems,* by G. K. CHESTERTON; "Daisy" and "To a Snow-flake," from the *Works* of FRANCIS THOMPSON; "Sheep and Lambs," from *Innocencies,* by KATHARINE TYNAN.

JONATHAN CAPE, LTD.: "The Fog," "Nature's Friend," "The Rain," and "Sheep," from *The Poems of W. H. Davies.*

CASSELL & COMPANY, LTD.: "The Master," from *London River*, by H. M. TOMLINSON.

THE CLARENDON PRESS: "Triolet" and "The Windmill," from *The Shorter Poems of Robert Bridges*, CLARENDON PRESS, Oxford (1931), by permission of the publishers.

CONSTABLE & CO., LTD.: "Old Susan," from *Selected Poems*, and "Peeping Tom," from *Fleeting and Other Poems*, by WALTER DE LA MARE.

THOMAS Y. CROWELL COMPANY: quotation from *The Cuchulainn Saga*, edited by ELEANOR HULL.

J. M. DENT & SONS, LTD.: "The Donkey," from *Collected Poems*, by G. K. CHESTERTON.

DODD, MEAD & COMPANY, INC.: "The Soldier" and "The Great Lover," from *Collected Poems*, by RUPERT BROOKE. Copyright, 1915, by DODD, MEAD & COMPANY, INC. "Lepanto," from *Collected Poems*, by G. K. CHESTERTON. Used by permission of the publishers, DODD, MEAD & COMPANY, INC.

DOUBLEDAY, DORAN & COMPANY, INC.: "The Ballad of East and West" and "Mandalay," from *Barrack Room Ballads*, copyright 1892 and 1899 by RUDYARD KIPLING, and "Rikki-tikki-tavi," from *The Jungle Book*, by RUDYARD KIPLING, copyright 1893, 1921, reprinted by permission from DOUBLEDAY, DORAN & COMPANY, INC.; "The Market," from *Harbours of Memory*, by WILLIAM McFEE, copyright 1921 by DOUBLEDAY, DORAN & COMPANY, INC.; "The Man Who Could Work Miracles," from *The Short Stories of H. G. Wells*, copyright 1929 by DOUBLEDAY, DORAN & COMPANY, INC.

GERALD DUCKWORTH & CO., LTD.: "Courtesy," from *Sonnets and Verse*, by HILAIRE BELLOC.

E. P. DUTTON & CO., INC.; "The Spires of Oxford," taken from WINIFRED M. LETTS'S *Hallow-e'en and Poems of the War* by permission of the publishers, E. P. DUTTON & CO., INC., New York City.

GINN AND COMPANY: "Johnie Cock," from *Old English Ballads*, edited by FRANCIS B. GUMMERE; the selection from Cædmon, from *English Literature*, by WILLIAM J. LONG; "Alysoun" and "Springtime," and interpretative outlines from *English Prose and Poetry*, by J. M. MANLY.

GEORGE G. HARRAP & COMPANY, LTD.: quotation from *The Cuchulainn Saga*, edited by ELEANOR HULL.

WILLIAM HEINEMANN, LTD.: "The Garden of Proserpine," from *Poems and Ballads*, by ALGERNON CHARLES SWINBURNE.

HENRY HOLT & COMPANY, INC.: "Old Susan," from *Selected Poems*, by WALTER DE LA MARE.

ALFRED A. KNOPF, INC.: "On Drawing," reprinted from *The Borzoi*, by A. P. HERBERT; "The Master," reprinted from *London River*, by H. M. TOMLINSON, by permission of and special arrangement with ALFRED A. KNOPF, INC., authorized publishers.

JOHN LANE, THE BODLEY HEAD, LTD.: "The Story-Teller," from *The Short Stories of Saki*.

LONGMANS, GREEN & CO.: "The Little Waves of Breffny," from *The One and the Many*, by EVA GORE-BOOTH.

McCLELLAND AND STEWART, LTD.: "The Soldier" and "The Great Lover," from *Complete Poems*, by RUPERT BROOKE.

MACMILLAN AND COMPANY, LTD.: "Blackbird" and "Invictus," from *Poems*, by WILLIAM ERNEST HENLEY.

THE MACMILLAN COMPANY OF CANADA, LTD.: "Blackbird" and "Invictus," from *Poems*, by WILLIAM ERNEST HENLEY; "The Ballad of East and West" and "Mandalay," from *Barrack-Room Ballads*, and "Rikki-tikki-tavi," from *The Jungle Book*, by RUDYARD KIPLING; "Crossing the Bar" and "Merlin and the Gleam," by ALFRED LORD TENNYSON.

METHUEN & CO., LTD.: "On Drawing," from *The Borzoi*, by A. P. HERBERT.

JOHN MURRAY: "The Spires of Oxford," by WINIFRED M. LETTS.

OXFORD UNIVERSITY PRESS, New York: "The Fog," "The Rain," "Sheep," from *The Poems of W. H. Davies*.

Punch: "On Drawing," by A. P. HERBERT. Reprinted by permission of the Proprietors of *Punch*.

SCOTT, FORESMAN AND COMPANY: selections from *Beowulf*, from *Twelve Centuries of English Poetry and Prose*, edited by ALFONSO G. NEWCOMER.

CHARLES SCRIBNER'S SONS: *Shall We Join the Ladies?* by JAMES M. BARRIE; "Quality," from *The Inn of Tranquillity*, by JOHN GALSWORTHY; "The Last Words of Juggling Jerry," from *Poems*, by GEORGE MEREDITH; "Parted" and "The Shepherdess," from *The Poems of Alice Meynell*; "Heather Ale," "The Philosophy of Umbrellas," "Requiem," and "The Sire de Malétroit's Door," from *New Arabian Nights*, by ROBERT LOUIS STEVENSON; "Daisy" and "To a Snow-flake," from the *Works* of FRANCIS THOMPSON.

THE VIKING PRESS, INC.: "The Story-Teller," from *The Short Stories of Saki* (H. H. MUNRO), copyright 1930 by THE VIKING PRESS, INC., New York.

Grateful acknowledgment is also due to the following authors and their representatives:

G. K. CHESTERTON: "Lepanto," from *Collected Poems*.

W. H. DAVIES: "The Fog," "Nature's Friend," "The Rain," and "Sheep," from *The Poems of W. H. Davies*.

The Executors of WILLIAM ERNEST HENLEY: "The Blackbird" and "Invictus," from *Poems*.

A. P. HERBERT: "On Drawing," from *The Borzoi*.

VYVYAN BERESFORD HOLLAND, Administrator of the estate of OSCAR WILDE: "The Ballad of Reading Gaol," by OSCAR WILDE.

The Executors of A. E. HOUSMAN: "Loveliest of Trees," "Reveille," "When I Was One-and-Twenty," and "With Rue My Heart Is Laden," from *A Shropshire Lad*, by A. E. HOUSMAN.

MRS. RUDYARD KIPLING: "The Ballad of East and West," "Mandalay," and "Rikki-tikki-tavi."

The Estate of ERIC KNIGHT: "Cockles for Tea," from *Sam Small Flies Again*, copyright 1939, by ERIC KNIGHT. HARPER & BROTHERS. Reprinted by permission of the Author's Estate.

WILFRED MEYNELL: "To a Snow-flake," from the *Works* of FRANCIS THOMPSON.

SIEGFRIED SASSOON: "Aftermath," from *Picture Show*; "The Rear-Guard" and "Suicide in the Trenches," from *Counter-Attack*.

H. M. TOMLINSON: "The Master," from *London River*.

Contents

The Beginnings of English Literature (55 B.C.–1400 A.D.)

ix

The Elizabethan Period (1400–1616)

CONTENTS

The Puritan Period (1603–1660)

CONTENTS

The Age of Classicism (1660–1744)

The Transition from Classicism to Romanticism (1744–1798)

The Romantic Period (1798–1832)

CONTENTS

CONTENTS

The Victorian Period (1852–1892)

Recent and Contemporary Literature (1892–   )

CONTENTS

CONTENTS

D

CONTENTS

THE SHORT STORY

THE DRAMA

☆ ☆ ☆ ☆   ☆ ☆ ☆ ☆   ☆ ☆ ☆ ☆   ☆ ☆ ☆ ☆   ☆ ☆ ☆ ☆   ☆ ☆ ☆ ☆   ☆ ☆ ☆ ☆

List of Colored Illustrations

☆☆☆☆   ☆☆☆☆   ☆☆☆☆   ☆☆☆☆   ☆☆☆☆   ☆☆☆☆   ☆☆☆☆

To the Pupil

IF YOU enjoy good literature, you will find the book that you hold in your hands especially attractive. It contains selections from the best that has been produced in the literature of England. In it you may trace the history of English civilization straight through from the earliest period to the present day. From it you may learn much about the ways of living, the traditions, and the social ideals which have marked the progress of the English people through more than twelve centuries. In *English Writers* you may follow sympathetically the hopes, the fears, the defeats, and the triumphs of the English people as seen through the eyes of poets and other writers; for, in the case of England, as of other countries, the deepest truths of history are to be found not so much in material things as in the lives and ideals of the people mirrored in literature and other forms of art.

If you read *English Writers* intelligently, you cannot but be impressed with the high idealism which has characterized the best English thought from ancient times down to the present day. Respect for women, personal loyalty, and fidelity to one's plighted word are virtues which are lauded in every period of English literature. You may learn from *Beowulf* that even in the comparatively primitive times of the Anglo-Saxons courage, truthfulness, and fidelity were regarded as fundamental virtues. At a later period Chaucer's knight is characterized by "trouthe and honour, fredom and curteisye," virtues which appear again in Spenser's Redcross Knight, which are reflected in some of Shakespeare's best characters, and which are still admired by all representatives of the English-speaking race, wherever they are found.

Aside from its special appeal to us as citizens of an English-speaking country, *English Writers* has a more general interest which it shares with all other good literature: it brings us pleasure, companionship, experience, and instruction. Like all other good books, *English Writers* should help us to realize that reading is one of the greatest pleasures in life. Here, as elsewhere, whatever may be your main purpose in reading, your contact with good books should never fail to give you enjoyment and satisfaction.

With a book such as *English Writers* in your hands you need never be bored or lonely. Whether the characters portrayed are taken from real life or are purely imaginary, they may become your companions and friends. The people you meet in books may please you either because they resemble human friends whom you esteem or because they present unfamiliar types whom you are glad to welcome as new acquaintances.

There are also many other pleasant and profitable experiences offered in the pages of *English Writers*. If you have read the selections from English authors given in the revised editions of *Adventure* and *Achievement* of this series, you will be all the more eager to broaden your horizon still further by reading the present volume. Indeed, reading *English Writers* should help you not only to be a better citizen, but also to bring together and unify all that you have ever studied or experienced in the past. You will get far more from the selections in this volume if, as you read, you try to associate them with whatever you already know of practical living, of history, of literature, of civics, of science, and of all other subjects with which you have become acquainted inside or outside of your school course.

As your teacher directs, you will, of course, read some of the selections in *English Writers* more carefully than you do others; but, whatever your assignment, you should always read with enthusiasm, and you should continue to read until you understand the message that the author of each selection has to convey. Whether you read for pure amusement Hood's "Faithless Sally Brown" or whether you follow with serious interest Newman's "Definition of a Gentleman" or Huxley's lecture "On a Piece of Chalk," you should derive pleasure and profit from your occupation. In *English Writers* you may enjoy the varied music of poetry written by Chaucer, Spenser, Milton, Gray, Keats, Masefield, and other distinguished English poets, the smoothly flowing style of Addison, the sonorous language of Samuel Johnson, and the quaint phraseology of Lamb. Here you may savor to your heart's content the simplicity of the old ballads, of Blake, Katharine Tynan, and Winifred Letts, the pathos of Thomas Moore, the delicate grace of Herrick and Lovelace, and the high seriousness of Milton. Here you may range from writers who, like Spenser and Scott, follow the older poetic traditions to representatives of the newer movements in literature, such as Gilbert Keith Chesterton and Siegfried Sassoon.

In the pages of *English Writers* you will also meet attractive and stimulating persons. Here you will find authors who, as in the cases of Byron, Scott, and Stevenson, led varied and interesting lives, or who, like Coleridge, had a special genius for conversation. Hasten to make their acquaintance and you will never have cause to regret it. Not only the authors of the various selections, but also many of the characters who appear in the text, are well worth knowing. Here you will meet the genial Chaucer, sometimes called "the father of English poetry"; the learned Johnson, with his mighty vocabulary; and other real persons who cannot but impress you with their intellect, their personal charm, their wit, their moral courage. Among the purely imaginary characters you will find such well-known figures as King Arthur, Lady Macbeth, Robinson Crusoe, and David Copperfield. You will enjoy meeting the Canterbury pilgrims, you will like Sir Roger de Coverley and the other members of the Spectator's Club, and you will find something worth remembering in even such humble persons as the shoemakers in Galsworthy's "Quality." Whether your mood is cheerful or pensive, whether you prefer humor or pathos, comedy or tragedy, you will find in *English Writers* characters who are both interesting and stimulating.

From the selections in *English Writers* you may also derive many and varied experiences. Here, with only the effort of turning a page, you may visit the most fascinating places and take part in the most thrilling actions. Here you may travel at will from the lonely glens of Scotland to the crowded coffeehouses of London and from the chalk cliffs of Dover to the gloomy scene of Arthur's last battle in the west. Do you long for exciting adventures? You may find them as you dive with Beowulf beneath the water in search of Grendel's lair or visit Arsat in his lonely tropical retreat. Do you desire romance? You may experience it with the Redcross Knight as he rides abroad righting wrongs, with Gulliver as he visits the court of the Lilliputian king, with Porphyro as he flees through the storm with his beloved Madeline on St. Agnes's Eve, with the lone adventurer as he wanders into the crumbling palace of the Lady of the Land, with the youthful Denis as he finds an unexpected bride behind the Sire de Malétroit's door. Are you fond of historical writing? You may enjoy it in *Henry Esmond* and in Macaulay's picture of England in 1685. If you admire heroism, you may find it in the behavior of Christian and Faithful in the town of Vanity Fair and in Stevenson's noble "Requiem." Or, if you prefer the quietude of simple country scenes, you may enjoy it in Burns's "Cotter's Saturday Night" and Yeats's "Lake Isle of Innisfree." If you are fond of nature, you may cultivate your powers of observation and your faculty for enjoyment by reading the poems of Blake, Wordsworth, Shelley, Tennyson, William Henry Davies, Alfred Edward Housman, and numerous other individual selections. To many of you the greatest single experience to be enjoyed in *English Writers* will be the opportunity of reading, with adequate helps, Shakespeare's great tragedy *Macbeth*.

Finally, you will enjoy *English Writers* because it illustrates one of the most characteristic English traits, the love of humor. Here you may pass at will from the subtle humor of Chaucer to the sheer nonsense of Hood. In most of the selections containing humorous elements you will find the humor connected with something else, as, in the *Sir Roger de Coverley Papers* and *David Copperfield*, with character; in *Gulliver's Travels*, with satire; in "Tam o' Shanter," with situation; in "The Philosophy of Umbrellas" and "On Drawing," with the author's own whimsical way of looking at his subject. Whether the interest of the selection is primarily humorous or not, you should be constantly on the alert to recognize and enjoy any humorous features it may contain. Finally, do not forget that *English Writers* contains examples of the work of two of the greatest English humorists, Chaucer and Dickens.

☆ ☆ ☆   ☆ ☆ ☆ ☆   ☆ ☆ ☆   ☆ ☆ ☆ ☆   ☆ ☆ ☆   ☆ ☆ ☆ ☆   ☆ ☆ ☆ ☆

To the Teacher

IN GUIDING classes through the wide field of English literature most teachers will probably prefer to follow the plan of development around which this book is organized, that is, the study of types set in a framework of chronology and history. Both the type method and the historical method possess undoubted advantages for attaining clear comprehension and intelligent appreciation, and a combination of the two, such as is effected in the revised editions of *American Writers* and *English Writers* of this series, affords an ideal approach.

Other teachers, however, may be more concerned with the personal and social experiences of their pupils as these experiences are mirrored and idealized in literature. To such teachers it would seem better to direct the reading along the lines of the pupils' own developing interests and experiences, and at times along the lines of the other activities and departments in the school. For these purposes, therefore, the editors suggest an alternative organization of the contents of *English Writers*. The plan is merely suggestive; but it indicates not only the possibilities in the case but also the flexibility of the material. For example, teachers who wish to emphasize both the types of literature and the social interests of the boys and girls should find it relatively easy to do so. The list of proposed topics might well be varied to conform to departmental preferences or personal wishes.

One plan that has met with gratifying success is to go through the assigned material once, stressing the historical development of English literature according to types and setting, with particular reference to the backgrounds and the authors, and then to hold a rapid, appreciative review according to the following emotional and experiential themes, reinforced and enlivened by a selected program of class readings in the more beautiful and significant selections.

In the suggested groupings there is some justifiable duplication.

"THE PARLIAMENT OF MAN"

Of Travel, *Francis Bacon* (p. 175)
The Spectator's Club, *Richard Steele* (p. 255)
Elegy Written in a Country Churchyard, *Thomas Gray* (p. 298)
From "The Deserted Village," *Oliver Goldsmith* (p. 305)
A Man's a Man for A' That, *Robert Burns* (p. 333)
London, 1802, *William Wordsworth* (p. 342)

"OH, TO BE IN ENGLAND"

"FAR–OFF THINGS, AND BATTLES LONG AGO"

ADVENTURE, ACHIEVEMENT, ROMANCE

"MAN SHALL NOT LIVE BY BREAD ALONE"

"AND THE GREATEST OF THESE IS LOVE"

THE ADVANCE OF LIBERAL THOUGHT

"LEST WE FORGET"

From the *Morte d'Arthur, Sir Thomas Malory* (p. 49)
On Shakespeare, *John Milton* (p. 198)
Elegy Written in a Country Churchyard, *Thomas Gray* (p. 298)
Auld Lang Syne, *Robert Burns* (p. 331)
Scots, Wha Hae wi' Wallace Bled, *Robert Burns* (p. 332)
London, 1802, *William Wordsworth* (p. 342)
The Harp That Once through Tara's Halls, *Thomas Moore* (p. 349)
'Tis the Last Rose of Summer, *Thomas Moore* (p. 349)
Break, Break, Break, *Alfred Lord Tennyson* (p. 463)
From *In Memoriam, Alfred Lord Tennyson* (p. 471)
Crossing the Bar, *Alfred Lord Tennyson* (p. 475)
Shakespeare, *Matthew Arnold* (p. 495)
Requiem, *Robert Louis Stevenson* (p. 499)
The Charge of the Light Brigade, *Alfred Lord Tennyson* (p. 523)
The Spires of Oxford, *Winifred M. Letts* (p. 594)
The Soldier, *Rupert Brooke* (p. 595)
Suicide in the Trenches, *Siegfried Sassoon* (p. 597)
The Rear-Guard, *Siegfried Sassoon* (p. 598)
Aftermath, *Siegfried Sassoon* (p. 598)
Recessional, *Rudyard Kipling* (p. 608)

★★★★ ★★★★ ★★★★ ★★★★ ★★★★ ★★★★ ★★★★

ENGLISH
WRITERS

55 B.C.–1400 A.D.

❁

The Beginnings
of English Literature

D

Lord Thomas and Fair Annet (p. 59)

HISTORICAL BACKGROUND OF OLD-ENGLISH LITERATURE

THE RACES OF ENGLAND

LIKE the people of our own country, the population of England is composed of various racial elements. Each race has contributed social customs, traditions, historical facts, or other materials out of which literature is made. As centuries passed, these various elements gradually became mingled together, so that we have at last come to speak of our civilization as American or English, without remembering how many of our ideas and how much of our culture were imported from sources that were originally foreign. It is in the literature which our ancestors have left that we can trace most clearly the fascinating story of the civilization of England and America. In English literature we not only find recorded the hopes, the aspirations, the ideals, of the various races that have gone to make up the complex English people, but we get also, if we read intelligently, a better estimate of the various contributions that Celts, Saxons, Danes, Normans, and other peoples have made to the national ideals of the English.

Just as the English people is composed of various races, so the literature of the country has at various times been written in several different languages. The oldest literature known as English was written in a Germanic language called Anglo-Saxon; later a kind of French called Anglo-Norman was used for literary purposes by the aristocracy, while the older Anglo-Saxon, mixed with many words from Norman French, was used by the lower classes; and throughout the early history of England — indeed, for more than a thousand years — Latin was used for composing serious and dignified literature.

The Earliest Inhabitants. The earliest inhabitants of Britain left no written literature or history. From research we learn that they lived during what is known as the Stone Age. We should probably be safe in saying that these ancient people worshiped the sun and said prayers and sang hymns to the weather and the other forces of nature; but we unfortunately know nothing of just what language they spoke, what thoughts flashed through their minds as they wandered through the dark woods and dangerous bogs, or what songs they sang and what tales they told as they crouched together around their fires.

The Celts. Later than the Stone Age people, but still several centuries

© Aerofilms, Ltd.

Stonehenge, a prehistoric ruin on Salisbury Plain

before the birth of Christ, there came to the British Isles a group of tribes speaking various forms of a language known as Celtic. Those who went to Ireland are known as Goidels (goi′dĕlz) or Gaels; those who invaded Britain are called Britons or Cymry (kĭm′rĭ). These invaders drove the earlier settlers into the back country or mixed with them.

The ancient Celts of Britain were in general rude and primitive. They did not live in towns, but in small groups of huts surrounding the strongholds of the chieftains. Their social organization was tribal, each tribe having its own chief, to whom the lower classes were entirely subservient. The tribes were frequently at war with each other, and seldom united except against a common foe.

The Celts had many classes of poets, of which the most famous, the bards,* sang songs in praise of their chiefs, accompanying themselves on a small harp with five strings. During the Middle Ages Irish and Welsh bards were well known throughout Europe. They told many tales and sang many lays (songs) that afterward served to enrich the great stream of English literature.

Though the Celts, like the early Germans and Scandinavians, were in many respects barbarous, their literature was richer in tone and content and more artistic in form than that of their neighbors. An ancient author tells us that the Celts had two passions, — to fight well and to talk cleverly, — and their literature shows, not only that they were fierce in battle, but that they cultivated the art of poetry. Their literature also proves that they held women in great respect and had a high sense of personal honor. They were, moreover, keenly appreciative of the beauties of nature. The fairy charm, or magic, of flower, leaf, fountain, and stream is everywhere present in early Celtic poetry. Just how much the literature of England and America owes to this "natural magic" of the Celts we cannot tell exactly, but certainly our debt is great.

In the following passage the richly poetic language with which the ancient Celtic writer adorns his description of a beautiful and lovable maiden illustrates both the charm of Celtic nature poetry and the loving admiration bestowed upon woman.

The maiden was clothed in a robe of flame-coloured silk, and about her neck was a collar of ruddy gold, on which were precious emeralds and rubies. More yellow was her head than the flower of the broom, and her skin was whiter than the foam of the wave, and fairer were her hands and her fingers than the blossoms of the wood anemone amidst the spray of the meadow fountain. The eye of the trained hawk, the glance of the three-mewed[1] falcon, was not brighter than hers. Her bosom was more snowy than the breast of the white swan, her cheek was redder than the reddest roses. Whoso beheld her was filled with her love. Four white trefoils[2] sprung up wherever she trod. — From *The Mabinogion*, translated by Lady Charlotte Guest

The wild and reckless bravery and the heroic deeds of ancient Celtic warriors are often described with truly epic grandeur. When, for example, Cu Chulainn (kōō kŭl'ĭn), one of the greatest heroes of early Celtic romance, had been wounded to death in his last battle, we are told that he asked permission of his enemies to go as far as a neighboring lake to drink.

"We will give thee leave," said they, "provided that thou come to us again."
"I will return if I am able," answered Cu Chulainn, "and if I am too weak, I will bid you come to me."
And he went to the lake and drank his drink, and washed himself, and came forth to die, calling on his foes to come to meet him. And since he was too weak to stand, he went to a tall stone which was upright in the plain, and he bound himself to it with his girdle, that he might not die seated nor lying down, but that he might die standing up. Thus he died, but, though his foes came all around him, they durst not go to him for fear, since they thought he was still alive.

To the ancient Celts we owe also a large body of charming tales about lovely fairy ladies who fell in love with and married mortals, or who lured men away to islands of eternal summer beyond the sea or to gorgeous underground palaces surrounded by gardens of never-fading flowers and

---

[1] Thrice-molted; that is, full-grown.　　　[2] Clover leaves.

© Photochrom Co., Ltd.

A Roman bath in Britain

fruit that was always ripe. The Celts were the first to tell the stories of Saint Brendan's marvelous voyage, of King Arthur's[1] passing to Avalon, and of Sir Tristram's love for the beautiful Isolt,[2] all of which have been repeated in English and have delighted readers young and old for nearly a thousand years.

Many of the ancient Celtic tales were not written down till late in the Middle Ages, but we know that they existed even in ancient times.

The Romans. Shortly before the birth of Christ there came to Britain still another band of invaders. In 55 B.C. the great Roman general Julius Caesar* crossed the English Channel with an army, and for four hundred years thereafter a large part of Britain was occupied and ruled by the Romans. The Roman conquerors of Britain established law and order throughout most of the island. They erected great walls to protect the country from the barbarous tribes of the north. They built roads, walled towns, stone forts, and other structures, such as temples and baths. *Castra* (kăs′trȧ), the Roman word for "camp," has left traces of its use in numerous

---

[1] See "Arthur."*   [2] *Or* Isolde (ē zōl′dĕ).

modern English names of places, such as Doncaster and Winchester. The Romans also introduced their language, their social customs, and their religion; and although we find few traces of these in later times, it is interesting to note that if the Romans had not been forced to leave Britain, we today should probably be speaking a language derived largely from Latin, as are French and Spanish.

About 410 A.D. the Roman government, hard pressed by tribes of barbarians crowding down into Italy and Gaul from the north, was forced to withdraw the Roman troops from Britain. Left without their Roman protectors, the Britons, who had lived for so long under Roman rule, fell an easy prey to the fierce northern tribes and other barbarians who now invaded their country. Hence the early literature of Britain shows few traces of the Roman occupation.

The Anglo-Saxons. About the middle of the fifth century after Christ (449 A.D.) there landed in England several tribes who came from Denmark and from the parts of Germany that lie along the coast of the Baltic Sea and the North Sea. They were the Angles, the Saxons, and the Jutes. They are usually referred to as Anglo-Saxons. From the Angles the island got a new name, "England" ("Angleland").

The Anglo-Saxons were tall and fair-haired. They wore shirts of mail called "byrnies" (bûr'nĭz), sometimes adorned with gold; their helmets were crowned with figures of boars' heads or other decorations; and they fought with swords and spears or with bows and arrows. Next to war, one of their chief passions was love of freedom. Each chieftain was surrounded by a band of freemen who, though they ate at their lord's table and were ready to defend him with their lives, were proud of their independence. The freemen owned the land which they occupied, and held on to it tenaciously. Thus for generation after generation the same Anglo-Saxon family might be found in the same village cultivating the same field.

The Anglo-Saxons lived, not in towns built and walled with stone as the Romans had done, but in groups of wooden houses surrounded by a wooden stockade. The Anglo-Saxon words for such communities were *tun, ham,* or *wic.* The words *tun* and *ham* have remained in modern English as "town" and "home," and are preserved in place-names such as Wilton and Buckingham. Though large towns and cities have grown up in England in recent times, for more than a thousand years most of the population, like their Anglo-Saxon forefathers, continued to live in small settlements. Each Anglo-Saxon community was governed by a court made up of freemen, who administered a rude kind of justice that became the basis of modern English common law.

At first the Anglo-Saxon invaders plundered and destroyed; later they settled down and became part of what we call the English people. Living, as they had done, near the seacoast, they had become skillful sailors, and in

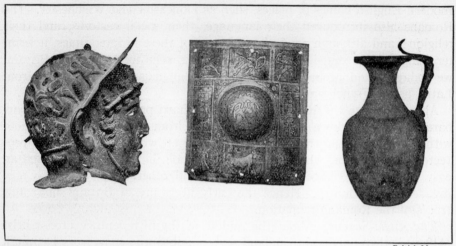

British Museum

A Roman helmet, part of a Roman shield, and a Roman jug found in Britain

their long boats, smeared with tar to keep out the water, they rowed fear-lessly through the northern seas, occasionally increasing their speed by setting sails made of skins or coarse cloth. At first they had the reputation of being pirates and were greatly dreaded by the Britons; but after the Anglo-Saxon conquest most of them settled down and became farmers attached to the soil.

The Celtic tribes of Britain, who had become used to letting the Romans do their fighting for them, fell easy victims to the fierce Anglo-Saxon in-vaders, who had been trained to plunder and war from childhood. The Anglo-Saxons killed the Britons wholesale or drove them back into the mountainous districts of Wales, Devonshire, and Cornwall.[1] They doubt-less married some of the British women; but they took no trouble to learn the British language, and adopted only a few words from the Celtic tongue or from the Latin language as it was spoken in Britain.

OLD-ENGLISH LITERATURE

The pagan Anglo-Saxons had a rude alphabet made up of signs called runes,* but it was not until after the introduction of the Roman alphabet by Christian missionaries that anything properly called literature was written down. Soon after the coming of Christianity to Britain,[2] Chris-tian authors and copyists (or scribes, as they are called) began to translate the Bible, and to compose literature both in Latin and in Anglo-Saxon.

[1] For the location of these and other places referred to in this introduction see the map on page 11.
[2] See page 10.

British Museum

Anglo-Saxon weapons

They wrote entirely by hand on parchment made of skins. The first Anglo-Saxon, or Old-English, literature was written down in the northern, or Northumbrian, monasteries,* so called from the fact that they were located in a district known as Northumbria, which included parts of Scotland and England north of the Humber River. During most of the seventh and eighth centuries (600–800) Christianity and literature flourished in Britain, especially in the north.

In 787, new invaders, this time from Scandinavia, began to make raids into England. As they were still pagans they cared nothing for Christianity or learning; and, being attracted by the rich vestments and gold ornaments in the monasteries, they robbed wholesale, especially in Northumbria. They destroyed many valuable libraries, and literature did not appear again until after Alfred the Great became king in 871.

All the Anglo-Saxon literature that has been preserved was composed or copied by Christian writers. Christian poets not only wrote down and revised the older poetry, but they composed new poems on religious or worldly subjects.

Epic and War Poetry. The longest and best of the Anglo-Saxon pagan poems is *Beowulf* (bā′ŏ wŏŏlf), the most interesting parts of which are given on pages 20–28. There are also a few fragments of other pagan Anglo-Saxon epics, and several complete short poems, written during the eighth or ninth century in England, but reflecting conditions before the Anglo-Saxons came from the Continent. The joy that the Anglo-Saxons took in battle is well illustrated in several poems which were by good luck copied into the manuscripts of the *Anglo-Saxon Chronicle*, our earliest English history.

The Coming of Christianity. Christianity has always been a powerful force leading men to gentler manners, to better morals, and to a more civilized life. Upon literature too it has had an immense influence. Especially is this true of the influence that Christianity has exercised upon the literature of England.

Christianity was first brought to Britain during the Roman occupation, but it was later stamped out as far as possible by the pagan Anglo-Saxons in those parts of the island occupied by them, and for a hundred and fifty years the conquerors remained pagans. When Christian missionaries finally came to Britain, they arrived from two directions — from Ireland and from Rome.

In 563 A.D. the great Irish statesman and preacher Saint Columba, or Columkille (kŏl'ŭm kĭl), founded the monastery of Iona on a little island off the west coast of Scotland. The Irish, who had been Christians for more than a century, were enthusiastic missionaries. Under the leadership of Columba and his successors they preached the gospel of Christianity throughout most of Scotland and the northern parts of England.

In 597 A.D. another great missionary, Saint Augustine, landed in the south of England. There is a beautiful story of how Pope Gregory, by whom Augustine was sent, came to be interested in converting the English. One day, before he became Pope, his attention was called to the white bodies, fair faces, and golden hair of some boys who were being sold as slaves in the marketplace of Rome. "From what country do these children come?" he asked. "They are Angles," answered the slave-traders. "Not Angles, but angels, since they have faces so angel-like," said Gregory, making a pious pun. He then asked from what country they came. "From Deira [a kingdom of northern England]," replied the merchants, and Gregory again answered with a pun. "Their country," said he, "is well called Deira, for it shall be saved *de ira*[1] [that is, from the wrath of God]. And what is the name of their king?" "Aella," he was told. "'Aella' is a fitting name for him," said the future Pope, "for Alleluia shall be sung in his land." And so when Gregory became Pope he remembered his prophecy and sent Augustine to preach Christianity in England. Augustine was received by King Ethelbert (ĕth'ĕl bûrt) of Kent and was allowed to preach Christianity to the Anglo-Saxons. He founded a church near the spot where the great cathedral of Canterbury[2] now stands. From this center the new religion spread northward until it met that of the Irish missionaries who had come down from Iona.

Christian Literature. One of the most charming stories in English literature is told of Cædmon (kăd'mŏn), who lived in one of the northern monasteries and is the earliest English poet whose name has been preserved. Cædmon was a poor, ignorant servant in the monastery of Whitby,[3] on

[1] dā ē'rȧ.   [2] See picture on page 41.   [3] See picture on page 292.

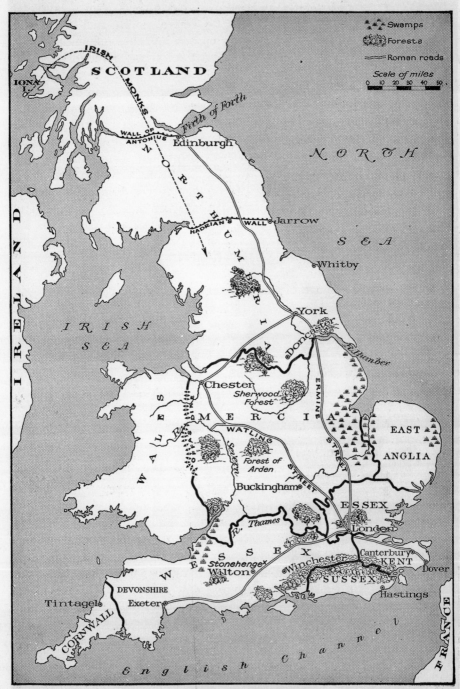

Early England

A Christian scribe at work in an early English monastery

the coast of the North Sea in Northumbria. Until late in life he lived
without being able to compose verses. When the monks, according to
custom, met together and each in turn sang to the accompaniment of the
harp, Cædmon would always rise from the table and slip away ashamed
when he saw the harp approaching him. One evening when this had
happened and he had gone out to attend to the horses, he fell asleep in
the stable. In a dream an angel appeared to him and said, "Cædmon,
sing some song to me." "I cannot sing," answered the poor horse boy.
The angel, however, insisted and told Cædmon to sing "the beginning of
created things." Thus inspired, Cædmon immediately composed a poem
nine lines long, of which the records give both the original and a Latin
translation. This poem, the oldest piece of verse in the English language,
is usually known as Cædmon's "Hymn." Translated out of Anglo-Saxon
into modern English, it is as follows:

> Now shall we praise the Master of heaven,
> The might of the Maker, the thought of His heart,
> The deeds of the Father. How He, Lord everlasting,
> Established of old the source of all wonders.
> Creator all-holy, He hung the heavens,
> A roof high upreared, o'er the children of men;
> The King of mankind then created for mortals'
> The world, the earth spread beneath them,
> He, Lord everlasting, omnipotent God.

When Cædmon awoke, he not only remembered all that he had sung
during his sleep, but immediately added much more on the same subject
in verse worthy of God. He was then taken into the presence of the abbess,
the head of the monastery, who heard his story with wonder and gave him
opportunity to use his divine gift of poetry.

The tone of Anglo-Saxon literature is generally dignified and rather
gloomy. It is seldom humorous except in a grim way. The stories to
which the poets allude are usually of the tragic loves and hates of ancient
heroes and of "old, unhappy, far-off things, and battles long ago."

The Christian monks and scholars to whom we owe the earliest English
literature were well acquainted with Latin; they spoke the Latin language
on formal occasions, their church services were in Latin, and it was natural
that they should write in Latin when they had anything serious to record.
The greatest of the Latin writers of Anglo-Saxon England was the "Venerable Bede." Bede (673(?)–735 A.D.) spent most of his life in the monastery of Jarrow, in the north of England. He was a great reader, possessed
wide learning, and wrote many books, the most important of which is the
Church History of the English People, written in Latin and afterward
translated into Anglo-Saxon.

Alfred the Great. Alfred the Great (ruled 871–901 A.D.), affectionately called "England's darling," was one of the greatest kings that ever sat on the English throne. He was not only

a great general; he was also a great lawmaker and patron of literature. He labored long and earnestly to restore order and to encourage education after his country had been laid waste by the Scandinavian invaders. In one of his writings Alfred tells us that when he came to the throne of his own kingdom, Wessex (871 A.D.), illiteracy was so widespread that few priests could understand the church service, even in the English language. To improve the situation, he invited scholars to take up their residence at his court; he urged the importance of popular elementary education; and he translated or caused to be translated various instructive Latin works, in order that his people might be able to read them.

Galloway

Alfred the Great
A statue at Winchester, England

The Anglo-Saxon Chronicle. The *Anglo-Saxon Chronicle*, which began before the time of Alfred the Great as a series of rough notes jotted down by the monks of various monasteries, is our oldest English history in the native tongue. Sometime during the ninth century the notes in various monasteries were gathered together, and an effort was made at writing a continuous history. This work has been attributed to Alfred the Great. The *Chronicle* was kept up until the year 1154, nearly a century after the Norman Conquest. *The Anglo-Saxon Chronicle* and Bede's *Church History of the English People* are the chief sources of our knowledge of the earliest English history.

The Northmen. As we have already seen, England suffered an invasion of the northern peoples near the end of the eighth century. The newcomers were Scandinavians. They are known as Northmen or vikings (vī'kĭngz). They were pagan barbarians much like what the Anglo-Saxons had been three or four hundred years before. They conquered district

A battle between Anglo-Saxons and viking invaders

after district, and for more than a century they threatened to overrun all England, but they were finally compelled to make peace. Of the English kings who fought against the Northmen, the most famous was Alfred the Great.

Though most of England was at one time in the hands of the Northmen, they seem to have had little influence upon written literature during the Anglo-Saxon period. Nevertheless we know that they brought with them some of their literary traditions, for hundreds of years later several of our finest romantic tales came, at least in part, from Norse sources.

Correlation of English Literature with Historical Events during the Old-English Period

HISTORICAL EVENTS		LITERARY LANDMARKS
JULIUS CAESAR'S *first invasion of* BRITAIN	55 B.C.	
End of ROMAN *rule in* BRITAIN	*About* 410 A.D.	
SAINT PATRICK'S *mission to* IRELAND	432	
ANGLO-SAXON *invasion of* BRITAIN	449	
	500–600	*Traditional period of* KING ARTHUR
SAINT AUGUSTINE'S *mission to* ENGLAND	597	
	673 (?)	BEDE *born. Died 735*
	600–800	*Period of* NORTHUMBRIAN *literature*
	About 680	CÆDMON'S Hymn
	About 700	Beowulf
	731	BEDE, Church History of the English People (*in Latin*)
SCANDINAVIAN *invasions*	787–871	*Destruction of literary culture*
Reign of ALFRED THE GREAT	871–901	*Restoration of literary culture in the west and south of* ENGLAND
	About 890	The Anglo-Saxon Chronicle (*compiled by* ALFRED THE GREAT(?)). *Ends 1154*
Battle of BRUNANBURH	937	
Reign of EDWARD THE CONFESSOR	1042–1066	
KING HAROLD; *battle of* HASTINGS	1066	

THE OLD-ENGLISH PERIOD IN SONG AND STORY

To many people the cold, dry facts of history mean little, and even literary works written in the long-gone past are often difficult to understand. For most of us one of the best introductions to the life and literature of earlier times is through the writings of modern authors who, by means of their knowledge and imaginative powers, have retouched the faded picture of the past and made it live again. The following works were written by modern authors, but deal with the medieval period. Read the titles and see which you prefer. Then try to get the books and read them.

POETRY AND DRAMA

CHESTERTON, GILBERT K. "Ballad of the White Horse," in *Collected Poems*. Dodd, Mead & Company, Inc.

KIPLING, RUDYARD. "The Roman Centurion's Song," "The Land," "Puck's Song," "Eddi's Service," "The Pirates in England," "Dane-geld," and "The Return," in *Verse: Inclusive Edition, 1885–1932*. Doubleday, Doran & Company, Inc.

LONGFELLOW, HENRY WADSWORTH. "The Skeleton in Armor."

MILLAY, EDNA ST. VINCENT. *The King's Henchman*. Harper & Brothers.

SHAKESPEARE, WILLIAM. *Macbeth* and *King Lear*.

PROSE

BISHOP, FARNHAM, and BRODEUR, ARTHUR G. *The Altar of the Legion*. Little, Brown & Company.

BULWER-LYTTON, SIR EDWARD. *Harold, the Last of the Saxon Kings*.

KIPLING, RUDYARD. *Puck of Pook's Hill*. Doubleday, Doran & Company, Inc.

WRIGHT, SYDNEY FOWLER. *Elfwin*. George G. Harrap & Co., Ltd.

EPIC POETRY

An EPIC is a long narrative poem written in a noble, dignified style and telling of heroic exploits performed by great heroes. It differs from other narrative poems by the fact that it has greater dignity and sweep and presents more lifelike characters than they do; that is, an epic deals with great national events and with characters who are interesting aside from the story. In the Iliad,* for example, Achilles is as important as the story of the fall of Troy.* In a romance,* as contrasted with an epic, our interest is concentrated on the story, the reader being satisfied if the heroes fight well and the ladies are beautiful. You can usually tell a genuine epic from a romance or other narrative poem by asking this question: "Does the story deal with important events in legend or history and are the characters interesting aside from the things they do?"

The most famous epics of ancient times are the Iliad and the Odyssey *[1] and Vergil's Aeneid,* all of which deal with heroes who fought at the siege of Troy. In medieval times several European nations produced epics that celebrated some great event in their history. Just as the Old-French epic called the *Song of Roland* told of how Roland, one of Charlemagne's* Twelve Peers, died while fighting bravely against overwhelming odds, so the ancient Germans and Scandinavians sang of the exploits of their gods and heroes. *Beowulf* (p. 20) is the epic of the Anglo-Saxons. It tells how a great national hero, Beowulf, slew monsters in defense of his fellow men and lived a life of honesty and nobility till he fell a victim to the rage of a fire-breathing dragon. The romances describing the exploits of King Arthur's* knights are generally lacking in the lifelikeness necessary to make them true epics; but they are often referred to as epics, and some of them deserve the title. Spenser's *Faerie Queene* (p. 166), though partly a romance, has many epic traits, and the term "epic" is also sometimes applied to the Arthurian poems composing Tennyson's *Idylls of the King.*[2] Matthew Arnold's [3] "Sohrab and Rustum," which describes an episode in the life of a Persian hero, is a modern narrative poem of true epic dignity. Some of our longer popular ballads deal with events or personages in national history and are marked by a high and dignified style that gives them a distinctly epic quality. A poem which, like Milton's *Paradise Lost,* treats a religious theme in an exalted style is called a religious epic.

---

[1] An episode from the Odyssey is given in the revised edition of *Adventure* of this series.
[2] The "Passing of Arthur" (given in the revised edition of *Achievement* of this series) may be called an epic fragment.　　　　　[3] For biography see page 729.

18

HWÆT WE GARDE
na ingear dagum. þeod cyninga
þrym ge frunon huda æþelingas ellen
fremedon. oft scyld scefing sceaþe
na þreatum monegū mægþum meodo setla
of teah egsode eorl syððan ærest
wearð feasceaft funden he þæs frofre gebad
weox under wolcnum weorð myndum þah
oðþ him æghwylc þara ymbsittendra
ofer hron rade hyran scolde gomban
gyldan þ wæs god cyning. ðæm eafera wæs
æfter cenned geong ingeardum þone god
sende folce tofrofre fyren ðearfe on
geat þ hie ær drugon aldor lease lange
hwile him þæs lif frea wuldres wealdend
worold are forgeaf beowulf wæs bren
blæd wide sprang scyldes eafera scede
landum in.
þ biþ in eorl...

British Museum

A page from the parchment manuscript containing the epic "Beowulf"

These examples should help you to understand the difference between a true epic and a narrative poem[1] such as Burns's "Tam o' Shanter" (p. 388) or Tennyson's "Lady of Shalott" (p. 520).

From *Beowulf*

Beowulf (bā′ṓ wōōlf) was written in England about 700 A.D., and is the oldest of the Germanic epics, or poems telling of great deeds of ancient heroes belonging to the Germanic peoples. It is full of the interest of ancient times when men lived rudely but nobly, and when heroes who feared no man cowered before imaginary creatures such as demons and dragons. *Beowulf* is a little more than three thousand lines long. Of the poet who wrote *Beowulf* we know nothing except that he was an Anglo-Saxon, a Christian, and a man of genius. He wrote in a noble, dignified style, and he was fond of emphasizing courtly manners and high moral standards.

Beowulf is written in the most common Anglo-Saxon verse form, which is alliterative; that is, the music of the poetry depends, not upon rhymes at the end of the lines, but upon similar sounds at the beginnings of words (alliteration*) and upon a complicated arrangement of accented and unaccented syllables.

The style of Anglo-Saxon poetry as illustrated in *Beowulf* is abrupt; we are apt to be confused by the frequent use of a pronoun where we should expect a noun. One of the most striking traits of the Anglo-Saxon poetical style is the use of "kennings," a kind of metaphor* common both in Germanic and in Celtic poetry. Thus, "earl's raiment" is used for "armor," "whale's road" for "sea," "peace-weaver" for "wife," and "ring-giver" for "chieftain."

[*Beowulf* is based on ancient traditions brought by the Anglo-Saxons from their home on the Continent. It consists of at least three separate stories, each recounting an exploit of the hero Beowulf. After a short introduction the poet tells how Hrothgar (hrŏth′gär), the king of a Danish tribe called the Scyldings (shĭl′dĭngz), built a palace, or "folk-hall," called Heorot (hĕ′ṓ rŏt), between the seashore and the border of a dark and marshy forest believed to be inhabited by wicked spirits and demonic creatures. We must think of Heorot as a large, four-sided wooden building having a roof with high gables like horns. Not long after Hrothgar and his court had occupied the new palace, there came one night a gigantic monster called Grendel, a descendant of Cain,* the first murderer. Larger than human size was this "demon of death," "grim and greedy," and no sword could injure him. One after another, Grendel carried off or ate thirty of Hrothgar's thanes, or warriors. The monster returned again and again until the hall was abandoned by the court, and for twelve years stood empty and silent. Meanwhile the story of Grendel's doings was told abroad by traveling poets, or scops (skŏps), and singers (gleemen) until it was heard by Beowulf, a young noble at the court of Hygelac (hĭg′ĕ läk), king of the Geats (gā′äts), who probably lived in southern Sweden, across the water from Hrothgar's kingdom. Beowulf determined to rid Heorot of the man-eating monster. Accompanied by fourteen picked warriors he crossed the sea, a day's journey, to Denmark. On arriving he was met by a courteous coast guard and conducted to Hrothgar's court. Here he was graciously received by the king, and he and his companions were refreshed with pleasant drinks and entertained with songs. In introducing himself to Hrothgar, Beowulf spoke frankly of his own great deeds, whereupon Hunferth (ōōn′fârth), the king's official spokesman, or orator, attempted to humble the pride of the young hero. But Beowulf got the better of him in argument and proceeded with the business on which he had come. He offered to meet Grendel singlehanded.

After the festivities, in which Hrothgar's gracious queen, Wealhtheow (wĕ älh′thā ṓ), took part, the king and his followers left the hall while Beowulf and his men remained to guard the place against possible attacks by the fiendish monster. Now read the following translation. If it seems at first a little hard to follow, remember that much of the effectiveness of this ancient poem would be lost if it were translated into ordinary modern English.]

---

[1] For a discussion of narrative poetry see page 36.

BEOWULF'S WATCHING

THEN Hrothgar departed,[1] the Scyldings' protector,
out of the hall with his band of warriors;
the martial leader would seek his consort,
Wealhtheow the queen. The glory of
kings
had set against Grendel, as men have
heard tell,
a hall-ward[2]; he held a special office
about the Dane-prince, kept guard
'gainst the giant.
But the chief of the Geats well trusted in
his own proud might and the Creator's
favor. 9
He doffed from him then his iron byrnie,[3]
the helm[4] from his head, and gave to a
henchman
his sword[5] adorned, choicest of irons,
bade him take charge of the gear of war.
 Some words of pride then spake the
good chief,[6]
Beowulf the Great, ere he mounted his
bed:
"I count myself no feebler in martial
vigor
of warlike works than Grendel himself.
Therefore I will not, tho' easy it would be,
with sword destroy him or lull him to rest.
'Tis a warfare he knows not — to strike
against me 20
and hew my shield, renowned tho' he be
for hostile works; but we two to-night
shall do without sword, if he dare seek

war without weapon. And afterward
God,
the wise, the holy, shall glory adjudge
to whichever hand it seemeth meet to
him."
 Then lay down the brave man, — the
bolster received
the warrior's cheek; and around him
Seamen keen reclined on hall-beds.
Not one of them thought that he should
thence 30
seek ever again the home he loved,
the folk or free burg where he was
nurtured:[1]
since erst[2] they had heard how far too
many
folk of the Danes a bloody death
o'ertook in that wine-hall. But to them
the Lord
gave woven victory,[3] to the Weders'
people[4]
comfort and succor, so that they all
by the might of one, by his single powers,
their foe overcame. Shown is it truly 39
that mighty God ruleth the race of men.

THE COMING OF GRENDEL

[The following episode tells of Grendel's attack and Beowulf's victory. It is one of the
most famous passages in the poem. Even in
the modern translation it is a thrilling piece
of epic narration. Literature contains many
stories about haunted houses rendered un-
inhabitable by demons or witches, but finally
cleansed of their foul inmates by a hero who
watched at night and met the monsters single-
handed; none is told more impressively
than this.]

NOW in the murky night came stalking
the shadow-walker.[5] All the warriors

---

[1] Since the beginning of Grendel's visits, Hrothgar and his followers have not been sleeping
in the hall of Heorot.
[2] Warden, or guardian, of the hall.
[3] Shirt of mail.
[4] Helmet.
[5] *He . . . sword.* Since Grendel makes no use of
mortal weapons, and since he wears no armor,
Beowulf, wishing to fight on equal terms,
removes his shirt of mail and his helmet and
gives his sword to one of his followers.
[6] *Some . . . chief.* In early times a warrior was
permitted to boast, provided he made good
his words. Later, after the establishment of
chivalry in England (p. 30), modesty was
praised and boastfulness frowned upon.

[1] *Not . . . nurtured.* They all expected to be
killed, but they bravely kept their places.
[2] Formerly.
[3] *woven victory.* As the Greeks thought that a
man's fate was spun out for him in the form
of a thread by certain goddesses, so the
ancient Germanic peoples thought it was
woven for him as a fabric.
[4] The Geats, Beowulf's companions.
[5] Prowler by night, Grendel.

who should defend that pinnacled mansion
slept, save one.

Then came from the moor, under the
mist-hills,
Grendel stalking; he bore God's anger.
The wicked spoiler thought to ensnare
many a man in the lofty hall.
He strode 'neath the clouds until the
wine-house,
the gold-hall of men, he readily saw,   10
richly adorned; . . .
but ne'er in his life, before nor since,
found he a bolder man or hall-thanes.

So then to the mansion the being
bereft
of joys[1] came journeying; soon with his
hands
undid the door, tho' with forged bands
fast;
the baleful-minded, angry, burst open
the mansion's mouth. Soon thereafter
the fiend was treading the glittering
floor,
paced wroth[2] of mood; from his eyes
started   20
a horrid light, most like to flame.
He in the mansion saw warriors many,
a kindred band, together sleeping,
fellow-warriors. His spirit exulted.
The fell[3] wretch expected that ere day
came
he would dissever the life from the body
of each, for in him the hope had risen
of a gluttonous feast. Yet 'twas not his
fate
that he might more of the race of men
eat after that night. The mighty kinsman
of Hygelac watched how the wicked
spoiler   31
would proceed with his sudden grasping.

Nor did the monster mean to delay;
for he at the first stroke quickly seized
a sleeping warrior, tore him unawares,
bit his bone-casings,[4] drank his veins'
blood,

in great morsels swallowed him. Soon
had he
devoured all of the lifeless one,
feet and hands. He stepped up nearer,
took then with his hand the doughty-
minded   40
warrior at rest; with his hand the
foe
reached towards him. He instantly
grappled
with the evil-minded, and on his arm
rested.

Soon as the criminal realized
that in no other man of middle-earth,
of the world's regions, had he found
a stronger hand-grip,[1] his mind grew
fearful.
Yet not for that could he sooner escape.
He was bent on flight, would flee to his
cavern,
the devil-pack[2] seek; such case had never
in all his life-days befallen before.   51
Then Hygelac's good kinsman remembered
his evening speech; upright he stood,
and firmly grasped him; his fingers
yielded.
The giant was fleeing; the earl stept
further.
The famed one considered whether he
might
more widely wheel and thence away
flee to his fen-mound[3]; he knew his
fingers' power
in the fierce one's grasp. 'Twas a dire
journey
the baleful spoiler made to Heorot.   60
The princely hall thundered; terror was
on all the Danes, the city-dwellers,
each valiant one, while both the fierce
strong warriors raged; the mansion resounded.

Then was it wonder great that the
wine-hall

---

[1] Grendel is without joy because he is a descendant of Cain* and hence cursed by God.
[2] Angry.   [3] Cruel.   [4] Flesh (a kenning).

[1] Beowulf's grip was as strong as that of thirty
men.
[2] Band of devils. The poet thinks of Grendel as
living with other demonic creatures.
[3] Underground dwelling in the marshes (fens).

Beowulf's fight with Grendel

withstood the brave ones, nor fell to the
    ground,
the fair earthly dwelling; yet was it too
    fast,
within and without, with iron bands,
cunningly forged, though where the
    fierce ones
fought, I have heard, many a mead-
    bench,   70
with gold adorned, from its sill started.[1]
Before that, expected not the Scyldings'
    sages
that any man ever, in any wise,
in pieces could break it, goodly and bone-
    decked,[2]
or craftily destroy — only the flame's
    clutch
in smoke could devour it. Startling
    enough

the noise uprose. Over the North Danes
stood dire terror, on every one
of those who heard from the wall the
    whoop,
the dread lay sung by God's enemy,   80
the triumphless song of the thrall[1] of
    hell,
his pain bewailing. He[2] held him fast, —
he who of men was strongest of might,
of them who in that day lived this life.

    Not for aught would the refuge of
        earls[3]
leave alive the deadly guest;
the days of his life he counted not useful
to any folk. There many a warrior
of Beowulf's drew his ancient sword; 89
they would defend the life of their lord,

[1] *from . . . started.* Was broken from the floor,
  to which it was fastened.
[2] Adorned with antlers, here called bones.

[1] Servant.
[2] Beowulf. Anglo-Saxon poets often use pronouns whose reference is, from the stand-
  point of modern composition, not clear.
[3] *refuge of earls.* Beowulf. A common kenning
  for "chieftain."

of the great prince, if so they might.
They knew not, when they entered the
      strife,
the bold and eager sons of battle,
and thought to hew him on every side,
his life to seek, that not the choicest
of irons on earth, no battle-falchion,
could ever touch the wicked scather,[1]
since martial weapons he had forsworn,
every edge whatever. Yet on that day
of this life was his life-parting   100
wretched to be, and the alien spirit
to travel far into power of fiends.[2]

Then he who before in mirth of mood
(he was God's foe) had perpetrated
many crimes 'gainst the race of men,
found that his body would not avail him,
for him the proud kinsman of Hygelac
had in hand; each was to the other
hateful alive. The cruel wretch suffered
bodily pain; a deadly wound   110
appeared on his shoulder, his sinews
      started,
his bone-casings burst. To Beowulf was
the war-glory given; Grendel must
      thence,
death-sick, under his fen-shelters flee,
seek a joyless dwelling; well he knew
that the end of his life was come, his
      appointed
number of days. For all the Danes,
that fierce fight done, was their wish ac-
      complished.

So he then, the far-comer, the wise
      and strong
of soul, had purified Hrothgar's hall, 120
saved it from malice; his night's work re-
      joiced him,
his valor-glories. The Geatish chieftain[3]
had to the East-Danes his boast fulfilled,
had healed, to-wit, the preying sorrow
that they in that country before had
      suffered

and had to endure for hard necessity,
no small affliction. A manifest token
it was when the warrior laid down the
      hand —
arm and shoulder, Grendel's whole
      grappler   129
together there — 'neath the vaulted roof.[1]

[Next morning, when Beowulf's exploit was
known, people came from far and wide to see
Grendel's track and the bubbling water red
with blood, where he had sunk to his home
beneath the marshy wilderness. One man composed a song praising Beowulf and sang it on
the spot. He also sang a lay about characters
in the story of Siegfried, another famous
Germanic hero. His story is known to us
today through Wagner's opera and William
Morris's[2] Sigurd the Volsung, and is charmingly retold in Sons of the Volsungs, by
Dorothy Grant Hosford (The Macmillan
Company). After Hrothgar had congratulated Beowulf and thanked God for the victory, the warriors held a feast to celebrate the
event.

During the feast Hrothgar bestowed upon
Beowulf a gold-adorned helmet and eight
horses with decorated bridles, and upon each
of Beowulf's followers an old, and hence
valuable, sword. The king's official poet then
recited a lay telling part of an ancient tale of
feud and battle in which Hrothgar's people
were involved.

Some time afterward Grendel's mother, a
terrible water demon, visited the hall in order
to avenge her son's defeat. She came during
Beowulf's temporary absence; but, finding the
place occupied by other defenders, fled, carrying with her Grendel's arm and one of
Hrothgar's most valued retainers. When Beowulf hastily returned, Hrothgar told him of
his new misfortune and added that Grendel's
mother lived at the bottom of a gloomy,
haunted pool not far from the hall. Beowulf
replied that he would dare to attack the
demon, even in her terrible watery home. Accordingly, next morning, accompanied by
Hrothgar and a band of chosen fighting men,
he sought out the pool, on the edge of which
they found the head of the warrior who had
been carried off by Grendel's mother. Then
Beowulf put on his armor and took in his hand

---

[1] They . . . scather. "Scather" means "injurer."
      Grendel could not be injured with ordinary
      weapons, but Beowulf's companions did not
      know this fact.
[2] power of fiends. When Grendel died, he had to
      go to hell and be tortured by the fiends.
[3] Beowulf.

[1] Beowulf proved that he had conquered Grendel
      by laying down (or, perhaps better, setting
      up) the monster's arm in the hall.
[2] For biography see page 734.

a famous sword called Hrunting the Thruster, which had been lent him by Hunferth. Before diving beneath the water he requested Hrothgar to dispose of his possessions in case he did not return.]

BEOWULF'S VISIT TO GRENDEL'S LAIR UNDER THE WATER

A. The Fight beneath the Waves

After these words the Weder-Geats' lord[1]
with ardour hastened, nor any answer
would he await. The sea-wave received
the warrior-hero.[2] It was a day's space
ere he the bottom could perceive.
Forthwith she[3] found — she who the flood's course
had blood-thirsty held a hundred years,
grim and greedy — that a man from above
was there exploring the realm of strange creatures.
Then at him she grasped, the warrior seized   10
in her horrible claws. Nevertheless she crushed not
his unhurt body; the ring-mail guarded him,
so that she might not pierce that war-dress,
the lock-linked sark,[4] with her hostile fingers.
  Then when the sea-wolf[5] reached the bottom,
she bore to her dwelling the prince of rings
so that he might not, brave as he was,
his weapons wield; for many strange beings
in the deep oppressed him, many a sea-beast
with its battle tusks his war-sark broke;

[1] Beowulf.
[2] Beowulf here dives under the water to seek Grendel's mother.
[3] Grendel's mother.
[4] *lock-linked sark.* A shirt made of links of metal locked together.
[5] Grendel's mother.

the wretches pursued him. Then the earl found   21
he was in he knew not what dread hall,
where him no water in aught could scathe,[1]
nor because of the roof could the sudden grip
of the flood reach him; he saw a fire-light,
a brilliant beam brightly shining.
The hero perceived then the wolf of the deeps,
the mighty mere-wife[2]; a powerful onslaught
he made with his falchion, the sword-blow withheld not,
so on her head the ringed sword sang   30
a horrid war-song.[3] The guest then discovered
how that the battle-beam[4] would not bite,
would not scathe life, but that the edge failed
its lord at his need; formerly had it endured
hand-conflicts many, slashed often the helm,
war-garb of the doomed; then was the first time
for the precious gift that its power failed.
  Still was he resolute, slacked not his ardour,
of great deeds mindful was Hygelac's kinsman.
Flung he the twisted[5] sword, curiously bound,   40
the angry champion, that stiff and steel-edged
it lay on the earth; in his strength he trusted,
his powerful hand-grip. So shall man do,

[1] *no water . . . scathe.* The cave is under the water, but does not itself contain any water.
[2] Sea-woman.
[3] The poet refers to the clash of the sword as a "war-song."
[4] The sword, thus referred to because of its glittering.
[5] Applied to the sword because of the winding ornaments with which it was decorated.

when he in battle thinks of gaining
lasting praise, nor cares for his life.

By the shoulder then seized he (cared
not for her malice),
the lord of the war-Geats, Grendel's
mother;
the fierce fighter hurled, incensed as he
was,
the mortal foe,[1] that she fell to the
ground.
She quickly repaid him again in full   50
with her fierce grasps, and at him caught;
then stumbled he weary, of warriors the
strongest,
the active champion, so that he fell.
She pressed down the hall-guest, and
drew her dagger,
the broad gleaming blade, — would
avenge her son,
her only child. On his shoulder lay
the braided breast-net[2] which shielded
his life
'gainst point, 'gainst edge, all entrance
withstood.

Then would have perished Ecgtheow's[3]
son
'neath the wide earth, champion of the
Geats,   60
had not his war-byrnie help afforded,
his battle-net hard, and holy God
awarded the victory. The wise Lord,
Ruler of Heaven, with justice decided it
easily, when he again stood up.

B. Victory

Then he saw 'mongst the arms a victorious falchion,[4]
an old gigantic sword, of edges doughty,
the glory of warriors; of weapons 'twas
choicest,
save it was greater than any man else

to the game of war could carry forth,
good and gorgeous, the work of giants.

The knotted hilt seized he, the Scyldings' warrior, —
fierce and deadly grim, the ringed sword
swung;
despairing of life, he angrily struck,   9
that 'gainst her neck it griped her hard,
her bone-rings[1] brake. Thro' her fated
carcass
the falchion passed; on the ground she
sank.
The blade was gory, the man joy'd in his
work.

The sword-beam shone bright, light
rayed within,
even as from heaven serenely shines
the candle of the firmament. He looked
down the chamber,
then turned by the wall: his weapon up-
raised
firm by the hilt Hygelac's thane,
angry and resolute. Nor was the edge
to the war prince useless; for he would
forthwith   20
Grendel requite for the many raids
that he had made upon the West Danes,
and not on one occasion only,
when he Hrothgar's hearth-companions
slew in their rest, sleeping devoured
fifteen men of the folk of the Danes,
and as many others conveyed away,
hateful offerings. He had so repaid
him
for that, the fierce champion, that at rest
he saw,
weary of contest,[2] Grendel lying   30
deprived of his life, as he had been
scathed by
the conflict at Heorot; the corpse
bounded[3] far
when after death he suffered the stroke,
the hard sword-blow, and his head it
severed.

Forthwith they saw, the wise men,

<hr>

[1] mortal foe. Grendel's mother, who hated Beowulf with mortal hatred.
[2] the braided breast-net. The body armor, made
of braided, or interlocked, rings of metal.
[3] Ecgtheow (ĕj'thā ō). The father of Beowulf.
As the poet tells us elsewhere, he was a distinguished chieftain.
[4] Sword. A gigantic supernatural weapon which
Beowulf sees among the arms in the cave.

[1] Vertebrae of the neck.
[2] weary of contest. War-weary; here, dead.
[3] Bounded because of the stroke with which
Beowulf cut off Grendel's head.

those who with Hrothgar kept watch by
the water,
that the surge of the waves was all com-
mingled,
the deep stained with blood. The grizzly
haired
old men[1] together spake of the hero,
how they of the atheling[2] expected no
more   40
that, victory-flush'd, he would come to
seek
their famous king, since this seemed a
sign
that him the sea-wolf had quite destroyed.
The noon-tide came, they left the nesses,[3]
the Scyldings[4] bold; departed home
thence
the gold-friend[5] of men. The strangers sat,
sick at heart, and gazed on the mere,
wished but weened not that they their
dear lord
himself should see.[6]
   Then that sword, the war-blade,   50
with its battle-gore like bloody icicles,
began to fade.[7] A marvel it was,
how it all melted, most like to ice
when the Father relaxes the bands of
the frost,
unwinds the flood-fetters, He who has
power
over seasons and times; true Creator is
that!
More treasures he took not, the Weder-
Geats' lord,
within those dwellings (though many he
saw there)
except the head, and the hilt also,

with jewels shining; — the blade had all
melted,   60
the drawn brand was burnt, so hot was
the blood,
so venomous the demon, who down there
had perished.
Afloat soon was he that at strife had
awaited
the slaughter of foes; he swam up
through the water.
The ocean surges all were cleansed,
the dwellings vast, when the stranger
guest
her life-days left and this brief existence.
Then came to land the sailors' protector[1]
stoutly swimming, rejoiced in his sea-
spoil,
the mighty burden of what he brought
with him.   70
Then toward him they went, with thanks
to God,
the stout band of thanes, rejoiced in their
lord,
because they beheld him safe and sound.
From the vigorous chief both helm and
byrnie
were then soon loosed. The sea sub-
sided —
the cloud-shadowed water with death-
gore spotted.
   Thence forth they went retracing their
steps
happy at heart, the high-way measured,
the well-known road. The nobly bold
men
up from the sea-shore bore the head,   80
not without labor for each of them,
the mightily daring. Four undertook
with toil to bear on the battle-spear,
up to the gold-hall, the head of Grendel;
until straightway to the hall they came,
resolute, warlike, four and ten of them,
Geats all marching with their lord.
Proud amid the throng, he trod the
meadows.
   Then entering came the prince of
thanes,   89

---

[1] Hrothgar and his followers, who were waiting
for Beowulf on the shore above the cave.
[2] *atheling* (ăth'ĕl ing). Prince; here applied to
Beowulf.
[3] Headlands. Here, the promontory above Grendel's lair.   [4] Danes.   [5] Hrothgar.
[6] *The strangers . . . see.* Though the Danes gave
up the watch, Beowulf's companions still
waited on, wishing, but not expecting, the
return of their chief.
[7] The magic sword with which Beowulf had just
cut off Grendel's head melted away because
of the heat of the blood.

[1] Beowulf, whose men might be spoken of as
sailors. since they had come across the sea.

the deed-strong man with glory honored,
the man bold in battle, Hrothgar to greet.
And into the hall, where men were drink-
        ing,
Grendel's head by the hair was borne,
a thing of terror to nobles and lady.
'Twas a wonderful sight men looked upon.

[Having returned to Hrothgar's hall, Beowulf
told about his encounter, displayed his trophies,
and was praised by Hrothgar. Again we have
a description of a feast, with its ceremony and
dignified speeches.

Next morning Beowulf and his companions took their leave and, loaded with treasures, returned home in their "foamy-necked
ship, most like to a bird." On his arrival
Beowulf recounted his adventures and presented his gifts to the young king Hygelac
and his queen Hygd (hĭgd). Again the poet
lays great stress on the importance of etiquette.

When at last Hygelac fell in battle, Beowulf
acted for a time as guardian of the kingdom.
Finally he himself became king of the Geats
and ruled wisely for fifty years. Meanwhile
a fire dragon fifty feet long guarded a treasure
in a cave under a barrow, or earth mound,
near the sea. When Beowulf was an old man,
the dragon became angry because part of its
treasure had been stolen, and with its breath
it burned houses and villages far and wide.
In spite of his age Beowulf put on his armor,
and with twelve companions went to the
mouth of the dragon's cave. Here he bade a
long and affectionate farewell to his followers,
closing with the assurance that he would do
his duty, leaving Fate, or Wyrd* (wērd), the
ruler of men, to determine the outcome. He
then approached the mouth of the cave and
fought stoutly against the dragon, but gradually got the worst of it. After the monster
was slain by the only one of Beowulf's retainers who did not flee, Beowulf, mortally
wounded, commanded his follower to bring
forth the treasure that he might look upon it,
ordered his tomb to be built on the headland
called the "Whale's Ness," and bade farewell
to life. And "his soul went forth from his body
to find the ward of the steadfast in right."]

Discussion Hints

1. From suggestions given in the story,
describe an ideal Anglo-Saxon warrior.

2. What is a "kenning"? Point out several.

3. What evidence do you find that the poet
was a Christian?

4. What do you learn as to household customs, such as sleeping arrangements, eating,
and drinking?

5. What do you learn about the relation of
a chief or king to his subjects?

6. Pick out examples of alliteration.*

7. What passages seem to you most like
what you would call poetry? Give reasons
for your answer.

8. A craft project. Construct from cardboard or other suitable material a model of
Hrothgar's hall as conceived by the author of
Beowulf. The interior of the building is depicted on page 23; the exterior is suggested
on page 20. The hall was built of wood and
more or less resembled a barn with a gabled
roof having points resembling horns; hence
the name "Heorot" (hart, deer). Pupils who
have Scandinavian ancestors or who have
visited Scandinavian countries may have pictures of somewhat similar structures. If so,
they should bring them to class as illustrations.

Suggestions for Reading in the
Old-English Period

1. If you have enjoyed the selections from
Beowulf, you may wish to read more of the
poem. Extensive selections, translated into
modern English, are to be found in Twelve
Centuries of English Prose and Poetry (Scott,
Foresman and Company), edited by A. G.
Newcomer. An excellent verse translation of
the entire poem, along with numerous other
translations from Anglo-Saxon poetry, is
given in The Oldest English Epic (The Macmillan Company), by Francis B. Gummere.

2. The old Germanic love of war is everywhere present in Anglo-Saxon poetry. One
of the finest Anglo-Saxon war poems is the
"Battle of Brunanburh." If possible, read
Tennyson's modern rendering, which gives
an idea of the style and spirit of the original.

3. Modern versions of some of the best
Anglo-Saxon prose are given in Select Translations from Old English Prose (Harvard University Press), edited by A. S. Cook and C. B.
Tinker. An especially interesting selection
entitled "The Farthest North in the Time of
Alfred" may well be compared with Longfellow's poem "The Discoverer of North
Cape: a Leaf from King Alfred's Orosius,"
which deals with the same theme.

HISTORICAL BACKGROUND
OF MIDDLE-ENGLISH LITERATURE

THE NORMAN CONQUEST

THE year 1066 was marked by an event that brought about widespread changes in English life and English literature. In that year an army of Normans, led by William the Conqueror, crossed to England from the north of France and overcame the English king, Harold, in the great battle of Senlac, or Hastings, on the southeast coast of England. The Normans were descendants of Northmen (Scandinavians) who had settled in France about the time their kinsmen were ravaging England, but they had soon learned the French language and had become more refined and civilized by adopting French manners. Hence the influences which they introduced into England were as much French as Scandinavian.

CHANGES AFTER THE NORMAN CONQUEST

The Norman conquerors brought with them a love of law and order which the Saxons and Danes had not known. William the Conqueror drew up a code of laws and prepared the *Domesday Book*, which, in the form of two great volumes, includes a gigantic survey of all the real estate and other taxable property of England, as well as the population. It lists every piece of property and states the amount of taxes to be paid on it.

Under Norman rule there was also a great increase in the growth and importance of towns in England. Except for a few towns, such as London and York, which had existed as far back as Roman times, Anglo-Saxon settlements consisted of comparatively small villages. Under the Normans many businessmen moved to England from the Continent, settled in locations that offered opportunity for trade, and so laid the foundations for modern English towns as commercial centers. Yet at best the towns of medieval England were little like modern cities: the houses were mostly of wood, there were practically no building codes, the streets were narrow, and the sanitation, from our point of view, was very poor. The Normans also built castles, each of which became the center of a community composed of servants and other retainers.[1] Some of these cultivated the neighboring fields, which, for the most part, were not enclosed by hedges or fences.

[1] See the picture on page 30.

A Norman castle and feudal estate in England during the Middle Ages

Under the Norman kings, especially Henry I (1100–1135) and Henry II (1154–1189), there came into being the institution known as chivalry. A kind of rude sense of honor and of respect for women and religion had existed among the ancient Celts and among the Anglo-Saxons, but it was not until the twelfth century that these social and moral forces were organized into a fixed and elaborate set of rules and regulations. The knight of the period after the Conquest was expected to be always ready to fight for God and his overlord and to defend his own and his lady's honor with his life. Thus chivalry was closely connected with feudal obligations, with the Church, and with social relations between men and women. The romances of the Middle Ages and many historical novels, such as Sir Walter Scott's, depend for their charm largely upon their artistic use of chivalry.

The Normans and the Anglo-Saxons were completely united into one people only after much bloodshed, cruelty, and hard feeling; yet the general tone of literature after the Conquest was far more cheerful than it had ever been before. Not until after the Conquest did English literature begin to show those traits suggested by the term "merry," that is, generally pleasant as well as happy. When we speak of "Merry England," we are thinking not of the hard, gloomy life described in Anglo-Saxon literature, but of the England depicted in the literature of chivalry; in the ballads of Robin* Hood and his merry men in Sherwood Forest; in charming little poems about spring and love, such as those printed below (p. 55); and in Chaucer (p. 37).

Again, with the Norman Conquest came a great change in the language of England. The conquerors, who had long since ceased to use their old Scandinavian tongue, spoke a form of French known as Anglo-Norman, a language which, as we know, was based on Latin. Being the rulers, they naturally despised English and used their own language whenever they could. Hence Norman French was the language of the English court and of the aristocracy in general. It was the language of chivalry and of love. Such words as *chivalry, virtue, honor, courtesy, devotion,* came into English from French sources. French, along with Latin, was also the language in which much of the literature of England was composed. So despised was English from the Norman Conquest until after the year 1200 that it was seldom used for composing literature. At last, however, toward the close of the Middle Ages, the English language triumphed. Of the many changes that took place in the English language during the Middle Ages, partly as a result of Norman-French influence, we should recall the following:

1. Many new words were introduced.
2. English grammar was simplified.
3. The order of words gradually became that of modern English. As can be seen from *Beowulf,* the Anglo-Saxon order was often different from that of today.
4. There came to be a standard English language. Before the Conquest the people of England spoke various dialects. There was no generally accepted vocabulary or pronunciation; and although the various tribes could in most cases understand each other, none of them consciously imitated their neighbors. The dialect which finally triumphed and which forms the basis of modern English was the Midland (the dialect of the London district), mixed with many words and expressions from the north and a few from Kent, in the southeast.

MEDIEVAL LITERATURE IN ENGLAND

Remembering that the literature of medieval England after 1066 was written in three languages, Latin, French, and English, let us see what that literature was like.

To begin with, it was much more varied and abundant than it had ever been before. Then for the first time appeared in England most of the kinds of literature composed today, and, besides, some varieties that we of the twentieth century lack. After the Norman Conquest the people of

Consulting the "Domesday Book"

England had, in addition to literary forms unfamiliar to us, histories, romances* (p. 49), tales (p. 37), dramas,[1] lyric poetry (p. 55), and ballads (p. 57).

Histories, or chronicles, which before the Conquest had been little more than brief, disconnected notes, now became long, continuous narratives. Of the various histories composed in England during this period the most important for us is the *History of the Kings of Britain*, written in Latin about 1136 by a monk known as Geoffrey of Monmouth. Geoffrey's *History* pretends to give the story of the English people from the earliest times, but it is largely imaginary and contains many stories that were afterward taken up and retold as literature. The most important part of Geoffrey's *History* is that in which the author records some of the traditions about King Arthur* and his knights.

Some of the most interesting stories in medieval English literature are told in the form of romances.* The romances of the Middle Ages are a combination of romantic fiction and society novel; that is, the scenes are

---

[1] See page 82.

laid in the past, but the dress, manners, and language of the characters are those of the age of chivalry. The romances were composed originally in French, but they were soon translated into other languages and spread all over Europe. We have a number of romances in English, mostly translations from French sources. Many romances are in prose; many others are in verse and hence are called metrical romances.

The romances were divided into four groups, or "matters," as they were called, according to the sources from which the stories were thought to have come. (1) The "Matter of France" consists of poems about Charlemagne* and his Twelve Peers; (2) the "Matter of England" includes stories derived largely from Anglo-Saxon, Danish, or general Germanic traditions; (3) a third group is based on themes derived from Greek and Roman literature or from the Orient; (4) a fourth is known as the "Matter of Britain."

Of all the "matters," or groups of romances, by far the largest and most popular was the "Matter of Britain." This includes all the stories which recount the adventures of King Arthur's knights of the Round* Table. Most of the Arthurian romances were written in French, but a few were translated into English. One of the best of these, *Sir Gawain and the Green Knight*, was written about 1375 in a difficult dialect used in the northern part of England. Aside from the works of Chaucer, who was a contemporary of the unknown author, this is the most readable of all Middle-English narrative poems.

The best English literature of the medieval period was composed during the fourteenth century (1300–1400). Here belongs Chaucer (p. 37), the most famous Middle-English poet and one of the world's greatest humorists. The fourteenth century has often been called the Age of Chaucer. Here too belongs *The Vision of Piers Plowman*, a long poem giving a vivid and satirical* picture of the evils of society. To the fourteenth century also belongs the work of the great religious reformer John Wycliffe (wĭk'lĭf), who made the first complete translation of the Bible into the English language.

After Chaucer's death (1400) England became involved in the long civil struggle known as the Wars of the Roses* and in the religious disturbances that led to the Reformation.[1] As a result literature declined. Aside from Sir Thomas Malory (p. 49), no writer of sufficient importance to claim our attention appeared until after the beginning of the Renaissance.[2]

In the year 1476 William Caxton* set up the first printing press in England. The laborious and expensive hand-copying of the medieval scribes gave place to the easy, fast, and comparatively cheap duplication of books by the press, and a wider public could now possess and enjoy the treasures of literature.

[1] Page 71. [2] Page 71.

D

Correlation of English Literature with Historical Events during the Middle-English Period

HISTORICAL EVENTS		*LITERARY LANDMARKS*
Battle of HASTINGS; NORMAN CONQUEST	1066	
Reign of WILLIAM THE CONQUEROR	1066–1087	
The Domesday Book	1086	
The FIRST CRUSADE	1096	
The AGE OF CHIVALRY	1100–1200	Early romances in ANGLO-NORMAN
Reign of HENRY I	1100–1135	
	About 1136	GEOFFREY OF MONMOUTH, History of the Kings of Britain (in Latin)
Reign of HENRY II	1154–1189	
Reign of RICHARD I (RICHARD THE LIONHEARTED)	1189–1199	
Reign of KING JOHN	1199–1216	
Signing of MAGNA CARTA (or the GREAT CHARTER)	1215	
Reign of EDWARD I	1272–1307	
	1300–1400	Romances, lyric poetry, mystery plays, miracle plays
Battle of BANNOCKBURN	1314	
Beginning of the HUNDRED YEARS' WAR	1338	
	1340(?)	CHAUCER born. Died *1400*
First appearance of the plague known as the BLACK DEATH	1348	
Battle of POITIERS	1356	
	About 1360	Beginning of WYCLIFFE's translation of the Bible
	About 1365	First version of The Vision of Piers Plowman
	About 1375	Sir Gawain and the Green Knight
	1370–1400	CHAUCER, Canterbury Tales
Reign of RICHARD II	1377–1399	
Reign of HENRY IV	1399–1413	
	1400–1500	Morality plays and other early dramas
Reign of HENRY V	1413–1422	
Battle of AGINCOURT	1415	
	1430(?)	SIR THOMAS MALORY born. Died *1471*
Fall of CONSTANTINOPLE	1453	
Beginning of WARS OF THE ROSES*	1455	
	1476	First PRINTING PRESS set up in ENGLAND by CAXTON*
	About 1480	MALORY, Morte d'Arthur
Reign of HENRY VII	1485–1509	
Discovery of AMERICA by COLUMBUS	1492	

The Middle-English Period also includes chronicles (histories), short as well as long prose narratives, and popular ballads.

THE MIDDLE-ENGLISH PERIOD IN SONG AND STORY

Read again the introduction to "The Old-English Period in Song and Story" (p. 17). Next run through the following titles and see which you prefer. Then try to get the books and read them.

POETRY AND DRAMA

Many English poems, especially since the beginning of the Romantic Period (p. 313), deal with themes borrowed from the Middle Ages. Among the most suitable of the longer narrative poems to begin with are Sir Walter Scott's *Lady of the Lake* (part of which is given in the revised edition of *Adventure* of this series), *The Lay of the Last Minstrel*, and *Marmion*. For modern imitations of the medieval popular ballads see pages 335, 401, and 628, and the revised editions of *Adventure* and *Achievement* of this series.

Of Shakespeare's historical plays dealing with events or personages between the Norman Conquest and the end of the Middle Ages, three of the most readable are *Richard II*, *Henry IV, Part I*, and *Henry V*. *Sherwood* (Frederick A. Stokes Company), by Alfred Noyes, is a modern play dealing sympathetically with traditions about Robin* Hood.

PROSE

BULWER-LYTTON, SIR EDWARD. *The Last of the Barons.*

CERVANTES, MIGUEL. *Don Quixote.*

DOYLE, SIR A. CONAN. *Sir Nigel* and *The White Company.*

GREENE, F. N. *Legends of King Arthur and His Court.* Ginn and Company.

KINGSLEY, CHARLES. *Hereward the Wake.*

KIPLING, RUDYARD. "The Anvil," "Norman and Saxon," "The Reeds of Runnymede," in *Verse: Inclusive Edition, 1885–1932.* Doubleday, Doran & Company, Inc.

LANIER, SIDNEY. *The Boys' King Arthur.* Charles Scribner's Sons.

PORTER, JANE. *The Scottish Chiefs.* Charles Scribner's Sons.

PYLE, HOWARD. *Men of Iron* (Harper & Brothers), *The Merry Adventures of Robin Hood, The Story of King Arthur and His Knights, The Story of the Companions of the Round Table, The Story of Sir Lancelot and His Companions, The Story of the Grail and the Passing of Arthur.* The last five, beautifully illustrated by the author, are published by Charles Scribner's Sons.

SCOTT, SIR WALTER. *Ivanhoe.*

TENNYSON, ALFRED LORD. *The Idylls of the King.* (Two of Tennyson's Arthurian poems, "Gareth and Lynette" and "The Passing of Arthur," are given in the revised edition of *Achievement* of this series. Tennyson's "Lady of Shalott," another poem connected with Arthurian legend, is given on page 520.)

TWAIN, MARK. *A Connecticut Yankee in King Arthur's Court* and *The Prince and the Pauper.* Harper & Brothers.

NARRATIVE LITERATURE

NARRATIVE poetry, that is, poetry which tells a story, is one of the oldest forms of literature. Indeed, narratives in verse are known to have existed in such remote times that some scholars have even believed that poetry is older than prose. As far back as history takes us, men have been fond of recording both history and fiction in poetic form; and although the fashion of writing long historical accounts in verse is no longer popular, many shorter verse narratives still continue to be composed in the form of ballads.

In the earliest English literature three classes of narrative poetry were especially important: (1) epics — long, dignified poems telling of the brave deeds of ancient heroes; (2) romances* — long, imaginative accounts of the loves and adventures of fair ladies and brave knights; (3) ballads — shorter narrative poems, simple in plot and intended to be sung.

Medieval literature includes many other sorts of narratives told in poetic form. Chaucer's *Canterbury Tales* is a collection of narratives which include not only metrical romances, but also legends about saints and tales told in verse form. Chaucer's tales are among the best narrative poems ever written.

During the Renaissance[1] (1400–1616), the Puritan Period[2] (1616–1660), and the Age of Classicism[3] (1660–1744) English narrative poetry yielded in popularity to the lyric[4] and the drama.[5] The most important narrative poems of these periods are Spenser's *Faerie Queene* (p. 166), Milton's *Paradise Lost*, and certain long satirical* or religious poems by Dryden, Pope, and other writers. Here also belong Pope's famous translations of the Iliad* and the Odyssey.*

From the beginning of the transition from classicism to romanticism[6] (1744) on through the Romantic Period[7] (1798–1832) and throughout a considerable part of the nineteenth century, narrative poetry enjoyed constant popularity. Many narrative poems of the eighteenth and nineteenth centuries, such as Burns's "Tam o' Shanter" (p. 388), Scott's *Lady of the Lake*,[8] Byron's "Destruction of Sennacherib" (p. 409), Tennyson's "Lady of Shalott" (p. 520), Kingsley's "Sands of Dee" (p. 525), and Morris's "Lady of the Land" (p. 529), are metrical stories told chiefly for the sake of the narrative. In many other modern poems, however, the narrative is interspersed with passages which, on the one hand, are either purely descriptive or

---

[1] Page 71. [2] Page 184. [3] Page 213. [4] Page 150. [5] Page 81. [6] Page 289. [7] Page 313.
[8] Given in part in the revised edition of *Adventure* of this series.

which, on the other hand, express the poet's feelings and hence are lyric. Goldsmith's "Deserted Village" (p. 305), Burns's "Cotter's Saturday Night" (p. 383), and Keats's "Eve of St. Agnes" (p. 411), contain, along with a certain amount of narration, numerous passages that describe scenes or express the author's own feelings. In *Childe Harold* (p. 352), Byron, in the course of a long narrative poem, frequently turns aside from his account of the hero's travels to indulge in lyric outbursts on the majesty of the ocean, the fallen grandeur of Rome, and a host of other subjects that arouse his anger, his pity, or his enthusiasm. If we are interested in a poem chiefly because of what happens, it is a narrative; if our interest arises chiefly from the pictures of individual scenes, it is descriptive; if we find our interest in the story shared by passages that serve only to express feeling, the poem is at least partly lyrical. Since the beginning of the Transition Period (1744) much of our purest narrative poetry has been found in the form of popular ballads, taken down from the lips of uneducated people or in poems written more or less in imitation of the popular ballads. In recent years Kipling (p. 628),[1] Yeats (p. 632), Noyes,[2] Masefield,[3] and other writers have written narrative poetry of merit.

Narrative poetry has been composed in many forms. Most of Chaucer's *Canterbury Tales* is written in heroic* couplets, Spenser invented a stanza of his own,[4] Milton's *Paradise Lost* and Tennyson's *Idylls of the King*[5] are in blank* verse, and the simple four-line ballad stanza has been popular for hundreds of years.

GEOFFREY CHAUCER[6] (1340?-1400)

From the Prologue to *The Canterbury Tales*

The Canterbury Tales is the masterpiece of Chaucer, the greatest poet of early England. Written when the author was past middle life, it reveals a keenness of humor, a breadth of human sympathy, and a perfection of literary artistry to be found nowhere else in Middle-English literature.

The Canterbury Tales is an unfinished collection of stories, mostly in verse, fitted into a literary framework. Chaucer imagines a group of people brought together by the fact that all of them intend to make a pious pilgrimage to the shrine of the famous saint Thomas à Becket, at Canterbury.* Just outside of London they meet by chance at an inn* kept by a jovial fellow named Harry Bailly (bā'lĭ). Bailly, finding that they are all bound for the same place, proposes that they travel together and pass the time along the road in telling stories, each to tell two on the way to Canterbury and two more on the way back. He further suggests that each try to tell the best story, proposes a supper in honor of the one who does best, and offers to

---

[1] See the revised edition of *Adventure* of this series.
[2] See the revised editions of *Adventure* and *Achievement* of this series.
[3] See the revised editions of *Adventure* and *Achievement* of this series.
[4] See "Spenserian* stanza."
[5] See the revised edition of *Achievement* of this series.
[6] For biography see page 697.

ride with them and act as judge of this impromptu storytelling contest. The pilgrimage is the framework into which the tales are fitted.

Had Chaucer carried out his plan we should have had more than a hundred tales, but he actually wrote only about two dozen. He did, however, write enough to show how great was his own genius as a narrator and how rich and varied a supply of story plots existed in medieval England. The tales told by the Canterbury pilgrims form a collection almost unparalleled for variety and charm in the history of literature.

In the Prologue to *The Canterbury Tales* Chaucer tells us how the pilgrims came to meet at the Tabard Inn, and describes a number of the company. The descriptions are interesting for several reasons : (1) They form a series of character sketches of various classes of society in fourteenth-century England. They range all the way from the dignified and aristocratic Knight to the unconventional and lowborn Wyf (wēf) of Bath. (2) Each picture is so carefully drawn that we can see before us the person described. (3) The various characters are depicted with a combination of sympathy and gentle humor that has never been surpassed. Though a genuine lover of humanity, Chaucer never fails to take a mildly satirical * dig at various little human faults and shortcomings of his characters. (4) The language and versification are admirably adapted to the poet's purpose.

HOW TO READ CHAUCER

Even persons who know little or nothing about the Middle-English language need have no difficulty in deriving both pleasure and profit from reading Chaucer. All you need is a little perseverance. If you read only one line, you may not get the meaning, but do not be discouraged ; read ten or twenty lines, and even though you may find some unfamiliar words and peculiar spellings, in the end you are pretty sure to get the drift of the story. Try this experiment several times, each time rereading the passage you have just finished. It will not be long before you discover that reading Chaucer, instead of being a difficult task, is a real delight.

The National Council of Teachers of English have for sale ($1.50) a phonograph record on Chaucer. On one side is a talk by Dr. Harry

Morgan Ayres of Columbia University, on Chaucerian pronunciation; on the other is a reading by Dr. Ayres of the Prologue to *The Canterbury Tales* and the "Nun's Priest's Tale."

The pronunciation of Chaucer's English. In pronouncing Middle English remember that the English language of Chaucer's time was in general rounder and fuller in tone and hence was more musical than modern English. Or, to put it another way, in Chaucer's day vowels were pronounced more as they are in modern French, German, or Italian than as they are in modern English. In general, pronounce as follows :

accented *a* like *a* in "father," not like *a* in "bat"
o and *oo* like *o* in "lord"
ou and *ow* like *oo* in "boot," not like *ow* in "now"
y like *i* in "pin" or *i* in "police"

Be careful not to slur or slide over any vowels, as we often do in modern English. In Chaucer most vowels are to be pronounced so as to mark a separate syllable.

Pronounce the consonants about as you do in modern English, remembering to trill the *r*'s.

Chaucer's versification. Most of the lines in the Prologue are written in iambic * pentameter.* The lines rhyme in pairs, each pair forming what is known as a heroic * couplet, as in the following, where the accented syllables are marked (*ı*), the unaccented syllables (×).

"A knight there was, and that a worthy man,
That fro the tyme that he first began."

Note that in Chaucer's day vowels might be pronounced which we no longer pronounce or even write. For example,

"Hire over lip|pe wyp|ed she | so clen|e
That in | hir cop|pe was | no fer|thyng sen|e
Of gre|ce, whan | she dronk|en hadde|hir
  draught|e."

Here you will notice that in "lippe," "wyped," "coppe," and "grece" the rhythm * requires the sounding of a vowel not now sounded. It is usual also to sound an *e* at the end of a line. These "final" *e*'s are pronounced like *a* in "Emma." But not all *e*'s at the end of a word are sounded, as you can see with "hire" in the first line and "hadde" in the last, where

A portrait of Chaucer in a manuscript

the words following begin with a vowel or an almost silent *h*. But the two chief points are those mentioned above: the changed accent and the sounding of vowels now silent. If you get a feeling for the rhythm, you cannot go wrong.

In order to make the start easier, the first eighteen lines of the Prologue are given below in modern English. After reading them try the original, which follows, and you will soon find it easy to go on alone, and you will come to like it.

"When that April with his showers sweet
The drought of March has piercèd to the root,
And bathèd every vein in such liquor
That from its gentle virtue springs the flower;
And when that Zephyr with his soft, sweet breath
Has called to life in every wood and heath
The tender foliage, and the young spring sun
In April half his monthly course has run,
And little birds do make their melody,
That sleep throughout the night with open eye
(Because they are so stirred by nature sage):
Then folk do long to go on pilgrimage,
(And palmers for to visit far-off strands,)
To distant shrines, well known in sundry lands;
And specially, from every county's end
Of Engèland to Canterbury they wend,
The holy blessed martyr for to seek
Who them has helpèd when that they were sick."

WHAN that Aprille* with his shoures soote
The droghte of Marche hath perced to the roote,
And bathed every veyne in swich licour,
Of which vertu engendred is the flour;
Whan Zephirus eek with his swete breeth
Inspired hath in every holt and heeth

The tendre croppes, and the younge sonne
Hath in the Ram his halfe cours y-ronne,[1]
And smale fowles maken melodye,
That slepen al the night with open ye, 10
(So priketh hem nature in hir corages):
Than longen folk to goon on pilgrimages,
And palmers[2] for to seken straunge strondes,
To ferne halwes,[3] couthe[4] in sondry londes;
And specially, from every shires[5] ende
Of Engelond, to Caunterbury[6] they wende,
The holy blisful martir for to seke,
That hem hath holpen,[7] whan that they were seke.[8]
Bifel that, in that sesoun on a day,
In Southwerk at the Tabard[9] as I lay[10]
Redy to wenden[11] on my pilgrimage 21
To Caunterbury with ful devout corage,[12]
At night was come in-to that hostelrye[13]
Wel nyne and twenty in a compaignye,
Of sondry folk, by aventure y-falle[14]
In felawshipe, and pilgrims were they alle,
That toward Caunterbury wolden[15] ryde;
The chambres and the stables weren wyde,[16]

[1] *the younge . . . y-ronne.* Chaucer, using the language of medieval astronomy, means that it was after the middle of April. The Ram is one of the constellations, in which the sun seemed to be during late March and the first half of April. Chaucer was fond of astronomy and used it in his poetry more than a modern poet would be likely to do.
[2] See "Pilgrim."*
[3] *ferne halwes.* Distant shrines.
[4] Known.   [5] County's.
[6] See "Canterbury."*
[7] Helped.   [8] Sick.
[9] An inn,* or hotel, that had as its sign a picture of a tabard, a kind of jacket without sleeves.
[10] *as I lay.* We would say "As I was staying (or stopping)."
[11] Go, wend.
[12] Heart.
[13] Inn.
[14] *by . . . y-falle.* Happened by chance.
[15] Would.   [16] Roomy.

Taylor

Canterbury Cathedral

And wel we weren esed atte beste.[1]
And shortly, whan the sonne was to[2]
   reste,   30
So hadde I spoken with hem everi-
   chon,[3]
That I was of hir felawshipe anon,
And made forward[4] erly for to ryse,
To take our wey, ther as I yow devyse.[5]

[1] *esed . . . beste.* Made unusually comfortable.
[2] At.
[3] Everyone.
[4] Agreement.
[5] *ther . . . devyse.* To the place I tell you of.

But natheles,[1] whyl I have tyme and
   space,
Er that I ferther in this tale pace,[2]
Me thinketh it acordaunt[3] to resoun,
To telle yow al the condicioun
Of ech of hem, so as it semed me,
And whiche[4] they weren, and of what
   degree,[5]   40
And eek in what array[6] that they were
   inne:
And at a knight than wol I first biginne.

[1] Nevertheless.   [2] Pass on.   [3] According.
   [4] Who.   [5] Social rank.   [6] Dress.

THE KNIGHT

[As the highest in rank among the Canterbury pilgrims, the Knight stands first in the description of the various members of the group. Though he has traveled far and seen service in many wars, he has never lost the high ideals of truth and honor, liberality, courtesy, and humility that marked the medieval gentleman at his best.]

A KNIGHT there was, and that a worthy
   man,
That fro the tyme that he first bigan
To ryden out,[1] he loved chivalrye,[2]
Trouthe and honour, fredom[3] and cur-
   teisye.
Ful worthy was he in his lordes werre,[4]
And therto hadde he riden (no man
   ferre[5])
As wel in cristendom as hethenesse,[6]
And evere honoured for his worthinesse.
At Alisaundre he was, whan it was
   wonne[7];
Ful ofte tyme he hadde the bord bi-
   gonne[8]   10
Aboven alle naciouns in Pruce.[9]
In Lettow hadde he reysed[10] and in Ruce,
No cristen man so ofte of his degree.[1]
In Gernade at the sege[2] eek hadde he be
Of Algezir, and riden in Belmarye.
At Lyeys was he, and at Satalye
Whan they were wonne; and in the
   Grete See[3]
At many a noble aryve[4] hadde he be.
At mortal[5] batailles hadde he been
   fiftene,
And foughten for our feith at Tramis-
   sene   20
In listes thryes,[6] and ay[7] slayn his foo.
This ilke[8] worthy knight hadde been also
Somtyme[9] with the lord of Palatye,
Ageyn[10] another hethen in Turkye:
And evermore he hadde a sovereyn prys.[11]
And[12] though that he were worthy, he
   was wys,[13]
And of his port[14] as meek as is a mayde.
He nevere yet no vileinye[15] ne sayde
In al his lyf, un-to no maner wight.[16]
He was a verray[17] parfit[18] gentil knight.
But for to tellen yow of his array,   31
His hors were goode, but he was nat gay.[19]

[1] *ryden out.* Ride out seeking adventures.
[2] Read again what is said above about chivalry (p. 30).
[3] Liberality.
[4] *his lordes werre.* His lord's war. Under the feudal system a knight was required to serve on horseback in the wars of his overlord.
[5] Farther.
[6] *in . . . hethenesse.* In Christian as well as in heathen countries.
[7] *Alisaundre . . . wonne.* When Chaucer wrote this line, everybody remembered the capture of the famous city of Alexandria by the king of Cyprus in 1365.
[8] *hadde . . . bigonne.* Had sat at the head of the table (a position of great honor).
[9] Prussia. Chaucer goes on to give a list of the other countries and places where the Knight had traveled or fought: Lettow (Lithuania), Ruce (Russia), Gernade (Granada, in Spain), Algezir (in Spain), Belmarye (in Africa), Lyeys (in Armenia), Satalye, Tramissene, Palatye (all three in Asia Minor), Turkye (Turkey). English knights often went to the Continent and fought under foreign lords when there was nothing to do at home.
[10] Made an expedition.

[1] *No . . . degree.* No other Christian man of his rank had ever engaged in so many foreign campaigns.
[2] Siege.
[3] The Mediterranean.
[4] Landing of troops. The Knight had been present at many noble landings of armies in the eastern Mediterranean Sea. It was here that many of the crusaders* disembarked.
[5] Deadly, fierce.
[6] *In . . . thryes.* He had fought three battles to the death in the lists, or enclosure where tournaments were held.
[7] Always.   [8] Same.   [9] Formerly.
[10] Against.
[11] *sovereyn prys.* Exceedingly great fame.
[12] Lines 26–30 give a picture of an ideal knight in Chaucer's day. After you get the meaning of the passage, learn it by heart.
[13] Wise.
[14] Behavior.
[15] Discourteous language.
[16] *no maner wight.* No kind of person.
[17] True.
[18] Perfect.
[19] *hors . . . gay.* The horses used by him and his attendants were good, but he himself was not gaily dressed. In Chaucer's day the word *hors* had the same form in the plural as in the singular.

Of fustian he wered a gipoun
Al bismotered with his habergeoun.
For he was late y-come from his viage,[1]
And wente for to doon his pilgrimage.

THE SQUIRE*

[The Squire is the Knight's son and is in training for his father's profession. Though still young, rather dandified in dress, and skilled in the art of love-making, he is courteous to his elders, is a trained athlete, and has already seen service in war abroad.]

WITH him ther was his sone, a yong Squyer,
A lovyer, and a lusty[2] bacheler,[3]
With lokkes crulle, as they were leyd in presse.[4]
Of twenty yeer of age he was, I gesse.
Of his stature he was of evene lengthe,[5]
And wonderly delivere,[6] and greet of strengthe.
And he hadde been somtyme in chivachye,[7]
In Flaundres, in Artoys, and Picardye,[8]
And born him wel,[9] as of so litel space.[10]
In hope to stonden in his lady grace.[11] 10

[1] *Of fustian . . . viage.* The Knight wore a short coat (gipoun) of coarse, durable cloth (fustian), which was all smutted (bismotered) by rubbing against his coat of mail (habergeoun), for he had but lately come from his journey (viage) and had hastened to make his pilgrimage (without stopping to change his clothes).
[2] Gay-hearted.
[3] A youth in training for knighthood.
[4] *lokkes . . . presse.* Locks (of hair) curled as if they had been placed in a press.
[5] *evene lengthe.* Average height.
[6] Active.
[7] *in chivachye.* On cavalry expeditions.
[8] *Flaundres . . . Artoys . . . Picardye.* Flanders, Artois, and Picardy, provinces of northern France. The passage simply means that the Squire, though a young man, had already seen foreign service, though not in regions so far away as his father had.
[9] *born nim wel.* Behaved bravely.
[10] *as . . . space.* Considering how young he was.
[11] *stonden . . . grace.* Stand well in his lady's favor. Note that chivalry required the lover to make himself worthy of his lady by feats of arms.

Embrouded was he, as it were a mede[1]
Al ful of fresshe floures, whyte and rede.
Singinge he was, or floytinge,[2] al the day;
He was as fresh as is the month of May.
Short was his goune,[3] with sleves longe and wyde.[4]
Wel coude he sitte on hors, and faire ryde.[5]
He coude songes make and wel endyte,[6]
Iuste[7] and eek daunce, and wel purtreye[8] and wryte.[9]
So hote he lovede, that by nightertale
He sleep namore than doth a nightingale.[10]   20
Curteys he was, lowly, and servisable,[11]
And carf[12] biforn his fader at the table.

THE PRIORESS

[The Prioress, a nun,* is the head of a young ladies' seminary, or convent, near London. She is the highest in social rank among the women of the company. No one of Chaucer's characters is described with a finer blending of sympathy and humor. The author does full justice to her amiability and her tenderness of heart, but delights also in her harmless little refinements and affectations.]

THER was also a Nonne, a Prioresse,
That of hir smyling was ful simple and coy;[13]

[1] *Embrouded . . . mede.* Gaily dressed (embroidered) like a meadow.
[2] Whistling.
[3] Gown.
[4] In Chaucer's day long, wide sleeves were the extreme of fashion.
[5] *faire ryde.* Ride well.
[6] Compose. Composing verses used to be a favorite pastime among people of the upper class.
[7] Fight with a lance in a tournament.
[8] Draw.
[9] In Chaucer's day the ability to write was not common, even among the upper classes.
[10] *So hote . . . nightingale.* He was such an ardent lover that he sat up most of the night singing love songs like a nightingale.
[11] Anxious to be of service.
[12] Carved the roast and acted as waiter to his father.
[13] *That . . . coy.* Whose smile was very modest and quiet.

Hir grettest ooth was but by sëynt
  Loy:[1]
And she was cleped[2] madame Eglentyne.
Ful wel she song the service divyne,
Entuned[3] in hir nose ful semely[4];
And Frensh she spak ful faire and fetisly,[5]
After the scole of Stratford atte Bowe,[6]
For Frensh of Paris was to hir unknowe.
At mete wel y-taught[7] was she with-
  alle;   10
She leet[8] no morsel from hir lippes falle,
Ne wette hir fingres in hir sauce depe.
Wel coude she carie[9] a morsel, and wel
  kepe,
That no drope ne fille[10] up-on hir brest.
In curteisye[11] was set ful moche[12] hir
  lest.[13]
Hire over lippe wyped she so clene,
That in hir coppe[14] was no ferthing[15]
  sene
Of grece, whan she dronken hadde hir
  draughte.
Ful semely after hir mete she raughte,[16]
And sikerly she was of greet disport,[17] 20
And ful plesaunt, and amiable of port,[18]
And peyned hir to countrefete chere
Of court, and been estatlich of manere,

And to ben holden digne of reverence.[1]
But, for to speken of hir conscience,
She was so charitable and so pitous,[2]
She wolde wepe, if that she sawe a mous
Caught in a trappe, if it were deed or
  bledde.
Of smale houndes had she,[3] that she
  fedde
With rosted flesh, or milk and wastel
  breed.[4]   30
But sore weep she if oon of hem were
  deed,
Or if men smoot it with a yerde[5] smerte[6]:
And al was conscience and tendre herte.
Ful semely hir wimpel[7] pinched[8] was;
Hir nose tretys[9]; hir eyen[10] greye as
  glas;
Hir mouth ful smal, and ther-to[11] softe
  and reed;
But sikerly[12] she hadde a fair forheed.
It was almost a spanne brood, I trowe[13];
For, hardily,[14] she was nat undergrowe.[15]
Ful fetis[16] was hir cloke, as I was war.[17]
Of smal coral aboute hir arm she bar
A peire of bedes, gauded al with grene;[18]
And ther-on heng a broche of gold ful
  schene,[19]   43
On which ther was first write a crowned
  A,
And after, *Amor vincit omnia.*[20]

---

[1] Saint Eligius, the patron saint of goldsmiths. To swear by him was regarded as a very mild oath.
[2] Called.
[3] Intoned.
[4] Properly.
[5] Skillfully.
[6] *Stratford atte Bowe.* A convent near London.
[7] *wel y-taught.* Well instructed. Note the Prioress's elegant table manners.
[8] Let.
[9] Lift to her mouth. People in medieval times were generally far less careful in their table manners than we are today, and forks were not used at the table.
[10] *ne fille.* Might not fall.
[11] Etiquette, manners.
[12] Much.
[13] Pleasure.
[14] Cup.
[15] Particle. She always wiped her upper lip so clean that no grease was left in her cup after she had drunk.
[16] Reached.
[17] *sikerly . . . disport.* Surely she was very full of lively spirits.
[18] Behavior.

[1] *peyned . . . reverence.* She took pains to imitate (countrefete) the manners (chere) of the court, and to have dignified manners, and to be regarded as worthy (digne) of respect.   [2] Compassionate.
[3] *Of . . . she.* She had some small (pet) dogs.
[4] *wastel breed.* Fine white bread.
[5] Stick.   [6] Sharply.
[7] A kind of veil covering the head and neck.
[8] Gathered.   [9] Shapely.   [10] Eyes.
[11] Besides.   [12] Surely.
[13] *I trowe.* I should say.
[14] Certainly.
[15] Undersized.
[16] Neat.   [17] *was war.* Perceived.
[18] *A peire . . . grene.* A string of beads having a large green one (gaud) at intervals of ten.
[19] Bright.
[20] *crowned . . . omnia.* Marked on the Prioress's brooch was a capital *A* with a crown above it, and, below (in Latin), "Love conquers all." *A* stands for the Latin word *amor,* which means "love." or "charity."

THE MONK*

[Chaucer's Monk is an official of a large monastery;* it is his special business to ride out and inspect the manors, farms, and other landed property belonging to his establishment. He is also in charge of a "cell," one of the branches of the monastery. Chaucer's description, though containing a few satirical touches, is, on the whole, kindly.]

A MONK ther was, a fair for the maistrye,[1]
An out-rydere,[2] that lovede venerye,[3]
A manly man, to been an abbot able.
Ful many a deyntee[4] hors hadde he in stable:
And, whan he rood, men mighte his brydel here
Ginglen in a whistling wynd as clere,
And eek[5] as loude as doth the chapelbelle.
There-as[6] this lord was keper of the celle,
The reule of seint Maure or of seint Beneit,[7]
By-cause that it was old and som-del streit,[8]   10
This ilke monk leet olde thinges pace,[9]
And held after the newe world the space.[10]
He yaf nat of that text a pulled hen,[11]
That seith, that hunters been nat holy men;
Ne that a monk, whan he is recchelees,[12]
Is likned til a fish that is waterlees;

[1] *fair . . . maistrye.* A very fine one indeed.
[2] See "monk."*
[3] Hunting.
[4] Fine.
[5] Also.
[6] Where.
[7] *Maure . . . Beneit.* Saint Maur and Saint Benedict were two distinguished monks who formulated the set of monastic rules named for Saint Benedict. Chaucer's monk was a Benedictine.
[8] *som-del streit.* Somewhat strict.
[9] Pass.
[10] *held . . . space.* Followed the new fashion instead of living according to the strict Benedictine discipline, which required monks to labor with their hands and to study.
[11] *yaf . . . hen.* Did not give a plucked hen; didn't care a rap.
[12] Careless of his duties.

This is to seyn, a monk out of his cloistre.
But thilke[1] text held hen nat worth an oistre;
And I seyde his opinioun was good.
What[2] sholde he studie, and make him selven wood,[3]   20
Upon a book in cloistre alwey to poure,
Or swinken[4] with his handes, and laboure,
As Austin[5] bit[6]? How shal the world be served?
Lat Austin have his swink[7] to him reserved.
Therefor he was a pricasour[8] aright;
Grehoundes he hadde, as swifte as fowel in flight;
Of priking[9] and of hunting for the hare
Was al his lust,[10] for no cost wolde he spare.
I seigh[11] his sleves purfiled[12] at the hond
With grys,[13] and that the fyneste of a lond;   30
And, for to festne his hood under his chin,
He hadde of gold y-wroght a curious pin:
A love-knot in the gretter ende ther was.
His heed was balled,[14] that shoon as any glas,
And eek his face, as[15] he hadde been anoint.
He was a lord ful fat and in good point[16];
His eyen stepe,[17] and rollinge in his heed,
That stemed as a forneys of a leed,[18]
His botes souple, his hors in greet estat.
Now certeinly he was a fair prelat;   40
He was nat pale as a for-pyned goost.[19]
A fat swan loved he best of any roost.[20]
His palfrey was as broun as is a berye.

[1] That same.   [2] Why.   [3] Crazy.   [4] Work.
[5] Saint Augustine, a famous North African bishop of the early church, from whose writings the Augustinian friars derived their rules.   [6] Bids, commands.   [7] Work.
[8] Hard rider.   [9] Tracking game.
[10] Pleasure.   [11] Saw.   [12] Edged.
[13] Gray fur.   [14] Bald.   [15] As if.
[16] *in good point.* Fleshy; French, *en bon point.*
[17] Large.
[18] *stemed . . . leed.* Shone like a fire under a pot.
[19] *for-pyned goost* (gôst). Tormented ghost.
[20] *roost* (rôst). Roast.

THE CLERK

[The Clerk (*English pronunciation* klärk) is a student from Oxford University who is preparing for the priesthood. He has completed the elementary courses and has long since taken up the study of "logic"; that is, he has entered upon what we should call graduate study. Medieval students were by no means all so studious as this clerk. Many were idle, careless, lazy, and fun-loving.]

A CLERK ther was of Oxenford also,
   That un-to logik hadde longe y-go.[1]
As lene was his hors as is a rake,
And he nas nat[2] right fat, I undertake[3];
But loked holwe,[4] and ther-to[5] soberly.[6]
Ful thredbar was his overest courtepy,[7]
For he had geten him yet no benefice,
Ne was so worldly for to have office.[8]
For him was levere[9] have at his beddes heed
Twenty bokes, clad in blak or reed   10
Of Aristotle* and his philosophye,
Than robes riche, or fithele,[10] or gay sautrye.[11]
But al be that he was a philosophre,[12]
Yet hadde he but litel gold in cofre;

[1] *un-to . . . y-go.* Had long since gone to logic (one of the branches of medieval philosophy); that is, he had finished his undergraduate course and entered the higher realms of medieval education.
[2] *nas nat.* Was not.   [3] Affirm.
[4] Hollow, hungry.   [5] Besides.   [6] Solemn.
[7] *overest courtepy.* Outer short coat.
[8] *he . . . office.* He had not yet obtained a position as a priest, nor was he worldly-minded enough to get a place in the business world. In Chaucer's day an ambitious young scholar might rise by becoming a secretary or clerk in the service of the government or of some rich man.
[9] *him was levere.* He had rather. Compare the phrase "I had as lief." "Lief" is the positive of the adjective; "liever" is the comparative.
[10] A fiddle.
[11] A stringed instrument something like a small harp. Now spelled psaltery.
[12] The word meant both a philosopher and an alchemist (medieval chemist). Chaucer humorously says that though the clerk was a learned man, he could not, as the alchemists tried to do, turn the baser metals into gold.

But al that he mighte of his frendes hente,[1]
On bokes and on lerninge he it spente,
And bisily gan for the soules preye
Of hem that yaf him where-with to scoleye.[2]
Of studie took he most cure[3] and most hede.
Noght o[4] word spak he more than was nede,   20
And that was seyd in forme and reverence.
And short and quik, and ful of hy sentence.[5]
Sowninge in[6] moral vertu was his speche,
And gladly wolde he lerne, and gladly teche.[7]

THE WYF OF BATH

[Chaucer's picture of the Wyf (wēf) of Bath is one of the best in the Prologue. The Wyf of Bath was engaged in clothmaking, an important occupation employing many women in Chaucer's day. She is a rather large woman, somewhat over forty years old, slightly deaf, conspicuous in dress, and coarse in speech, but good-natured, friendly, and possessed of much worldly wisdom. She is anxious to seem pious and has made many pilgrimages. She comes from the neighborhood of the town of Bath. She is so clearly portrayed that we cannot but conclude that Chaucer had in mind a particular person when he drew her picture.]

A GOOD Wyf[8] was ther of bisyde Bathe,
   But she was som-del[9] deef, and that was scathe.[10]
Of cloth-making she hadde swiche an haunt,[11]
She passed hem of Ypres and of Gaunt.[12]

[1] Get.   [2] Go to school.   [3] Care.
[4] One; a single.   [5] Meaning.
[6] *Sowninge in.* Tending to.
[7] *gladly . . . teche.* This is a beautiful and often-quoted line. It has been applied to more than one great teacher since Chaucer's day.
[8] Woman.   [9] Somewhat.
[10] A misfortune.   [11] Skill.
[12] *Ypres, Gaunt.* Towns in Flanders (now Belgium) famous for the manufacture of cloth.

In all the parisshe wyf ne was ther noon
That to the offring bifore hir sholde
    goon;[1]
And if ther dide, certeyn, so wrooth was
    she,
That she was out of alle charitee.
Hir coverchiefs[2] ful fyne were of ground[3];
I dorste[4] swere they weyeden ten pound[5]
That on a Sonday were upon hir heed.
Hir hosen[6] weren of fyn scarlet reed,   12
Ful streite y-teyd, and shoes ful moiste[7]
    and newe.
Bold was hir face, and fair, and reed of
    hewe.
She was a worthy womman al hir lyve,
Housbondes at chirche-dore[8] she hadde
    fyve,
Withouten[9] other compaignye in youthe;
But thereof nedeth nat to speke as
    nouthe.[10]
And thryes hadde she been at Ierusa-
    lem[11];
She hadde passed many a straunge
    streem;   20
At Rome she hadde been, and at Bo-
    loigne,
In Galice at seint Iame, and at Coloigne.
She coude[12] moche of wandring by the
    weye.
Gat-tothed was she, soothly for to seye.[13]

---

[1] *In al . . . goon.* She so felt her own worth that
    she would allow no other woman in the par-
    ish to go ahead of her at church when the
    congregation went up to the altar to kiss the
    relics of some saint and make an offering.
[2] Coverings for the head.
[3] Texture.   [4] Durst.
[5] Medieval headdresses were often heavy with
    gold and silver network.
[6] Stockings.   [7] Soft.
[8] In medieval England marriages were usually
    celebrated at the church door.
[9] Besides.   [10] *as nouthe.* At present.
[11] Jerusalem, where many pilgrims went to visit
    the sepulcher of Jesus. The places mentioned
    in the next few lines were also famous for their
    sacred relics or images. Because of her sins
    and her natural desire for travel, the Wyf
    of Bath had made pilgrimages to all these
    places.   [12] Knew.
[13] *Gat-tothed . . . seye.* To tell the truth, her
    teeth were set wide apart. According to
    an old superstition people whose teeth are
    wide apart will do much traveling.

Up-on an amblere[1] esily she sat,
Y-wimpled wel,[2] and on hir heed an hat
As brood as is a bokeler or a targe[3];
A foot-mantel[4] aboute hir hippes large,
And on hir feet a paire of spores sharpe.
In felaweschip wel coude she laughe and
    carpe.[5]   30
Of remedies of love she knew per-chaunce,
For she coude of that art the olde
    daunce.[6]

THE PARSON

[The Parson represents the parish priesthood
of the Roman Catholic Church of England
in Chaucer's day. He is the true shepherd
of his flock, a genuinely unselfish minister
of God. He not only teaches his people
the way of truth, but he practices what he
preaches. He is tireless in visiting his parishioners. Though a learned man (a clerk), he
did not leave his people in the care of a strange
priest while he himself sought at St. Paul's in
London the easy and well-paid position of a
chantry or joined a religious brotherhood in
order to save living expenses. A more beautiful and appealing literary portrait of Christian devotion and self-sacrifice has never been
drawn. It shows that Chaucer recognized
and reverenced the spirit of true religion when
he found it.]

A GOOD man was ther of religioun,
    And was a povre Persoun[7] of a
        toun[8];
But riche he was of holy thoght and werk.
He was also a lerned man, a clerk,
That Cristes gospel trewely wolde
    preche;
His parisshens[9] devoutly wolde he teche.
Benigne he was, and wonder diligent,
And in adversitee ful pacient;

---

[1] A horse with an easy, rocking gait.
[2] *Y-wimpled wel.* Her neck and head well cov-
    ered with a wimple, or veil.
[3] *bokeler . . . targe.* Kinds of shields.
[4] A riding skirt.
[5] Chat playfully.
[6] *she . . . daunce.* She knew the whole art of
    love-making.
[7] Parson.
[8] Farmstead, or small settlement.
[9] Parishioners.

And swich[1] he was y-preved[2] ofte
sythes.[3]
Ful looth were him to cursen for his
tythes,[4]   10
But rather wolde he yeven, out of doute,
Un-to his povre parisshens aboute
Of his offring,[5] and eek[6] of his sub-
staunce.[7]
He coude in litel thing han suffisaunce.
Wyd was his parisshe, and houses fer
a-sonder,
But he ne lafte nat,[8] for reyn ne thonder,
In siknes nor in meschief[9] to visyte
The ferreste[10] in his parisshe, moche and
lyte,[11]
Up-on his feet, and in his hand a staf.
This noble ensample to his sheep he yaf,
That first he wroghte, and afterward he
taughte;   21
Out of the gospel he tho[12] wordes
caughte;
And this figure he added eek ther-to,
That if gold ruste, what shal yren[13] do?
For if a preest be foul, on whom we truste,
No wonder is a lewed[14] man to ruste;
And shame it is, if a preest take keep,[15]
A [filthy] shepherde and a clene sheep.
Wel oghte a preest ensample for to yive,
By his clennesse, how that his sheep
shold live.   30
He sette nat his benefice to hyre,[16]
And leet his sheep encombred in the
myre,[17]

[1] Such.
[2] Proved, shown to be.
[3] ofte sythes. Oftentimes.
[4] Ful . . . tythes. He hated to excommunicate
(cursen) his parishioners when they failed to
pay their tithes, or church dues.
[5] Gifts made to him.
[6] Also.
[7] His own property.
[8] he . . . nat. He did not fail.
[9] Trouble.
[10] Farthest off.
[11] moche and lyte. Rich and poor.
[12] Those.
[13] Iron.
[14] Ignorant.
[15] Heed.
[16] sette . . . hyre. Did not sublet his parish.
[17] Mire, mud.

And ran to London, un-to sëynt Poules,[1]
To seken him a chaunterie[2] for soules,
Or with a bretherhed to been withholde,[3]
But dwelte at hoom, and kepte wel his
folde,
So that the wolf ne made it nat mis-
carie;[4]
He was a shepherde and no mercenarie.[5]
And though he holy were, and vertuous,
He was to sinful man nat despitous,[6] 40
Ne of his speche daungerous[7] ne digne,[8]
But in his teching discreet and benigne,
To drawen folk to heven by fairnesse
By good ensample, this was his bisy-
nesse:
But it were[9] any persone obstinat,
What so he were, of heigh or lowe estat,
Him wolde he snibben[10] sharply for the
nones.[11]
A bettre preest, I trowe that nowher
non is.
He wayted after[12] no pompe and rever-
ence,
Ne maked him a spyced[13] conscience, 50
But Cristes lore, and his apostles twelve,
He taughte, but first he folwed it him-
selve.

[1] sëynt Poules. St. Paul's Cathedral.
[2] Chantry, an establishment founded by wealthy
people, in which priests were paid to say
prayers for the souls of the founders.
Priests connected with a chantry were supposed to lead an easy life.
[3] with . . . withholde. To be supported as a member of a religious brotherhood.
[4] So . . . miscarie. Jesus, the Good Shepherd,
referred to his people as sheep and to the
temptations of the world as wolves.
[5] Hireling. Jesus said that when his sheep
(people) were placed in the care of a false
shepherd or hireling, the sheep were sure to
fall a prey to the wolf (John 10: 12–13).
[6] Merciless.   [7] Overbearing.
[8] Haughty, proud.
[9] it were. If there were.   [10] Rebuke.
[11] for the nones. Extremely. Literally, "for the
once," on that occasion.
[12] wayted after. Looked for, expected.
[13] Overscrupulous. The Parson did not make
fussy, overfine moral distinctions, but followed the simple teaching of Jesus and the
Twelve Apostles. Quite aside from their
religious significance, lines 51–52 are well
worth remembering for their poetic beauty.

The pilgrims on the road to Canterbury

FROM A PAINTING BY HAROLD SICHEL

Discussion Hints

1. If you read any of the conventional romances of chivalry, you get the impression that the typical knight spent most of his time in slaying monsters or rescuing distressed ladies or riding through dark forests seeking romantic adventures. Chaucer gives a realistic picture of a fourteenth-century knight to whom war was a business. In what respects is Chaucer's knight individualized?

2. In what respects does the Squire resemble his father? In what respects is he different?

3. Compare the picture of the Parson with the description of an eighteenth-century clergyman which is given by Goldsmith in "The Deserted Village" (pp. 306–307, ll. 21–72). Both of these descriptions are famous and should be remembered together.

4. If you were describing a group of nine typical Americans, what trades, professions, and classes would you include? Which of these would lend themselves best to poetic treatment? Give reasons for your answer.

5. Point out illustrations of Chaucer's gentle, kindly humor.

6. Write in modern English the description of the Squire or the Clerk.

7. Write in dramatic form a dialogue between Chaucer (who was a good mixer, as we learn from page 41, ll. 31–34) and Harry Bailly, the proprietor of the inn (who has already become acquainted with his guests), on the evening before the beginning of the pilgrimage.

8. Read again what is said about "Chaucer's versification" (p. 38). Then scan lines 1–25 (pp. 43–44), making a list of all the words with a final *e* that should be pronounced to make the lines scan properly.

SIR THOMAS MALORY[1] (1430?–1471)

From the *Morte d'Arthur*, Book XXI

The *Morte d'Arthur* (môrt dår tür') ("Death of Arthur") is the most celebrated Arthurian romance* of the Middle Ages. It is a great compilation translated from various French sources and so arranged as to give a complete history of the Knights of the Round* Table from Arthur's* birth till his last battle. Taken as a whole, the book exemplifies the finest ideals of chivalry and the best traditions of old romance. Many passages, such as that given below, are marked by rapid action and are written in a dignified, simple, picturesque style. When the passage opens, Arthur has left his kingdom in the hands of Modred (Mordred) and has gone abroad on a military expedition against Lancelot (Launcelot), the lover of his wife, Guenever. The text has been considerably modernized.

As SIR MORDRED was ruler of all England, he had letters written as though that they came from beyond the sea, and the letters specified that King Arthur was slain in battle with Sir Launcelot. Wherefore Sir Mordred made a parliament, and called the lords together, and there he made them to choose him king; and so was he crowned 10 at Canterbury,* and afterward he drew him unto Winchester,[1] and there he took the Queen Guenever, and said plainly that he would wed her. And so he made ready for the feast, and a day set that they should be wedded; wherefore Queen Guenever was sorrowful. But she durst not discover her heart, but spake fair, and agreed to Sir Mordred's will. Then she desired of Sir Mordred for to go to London, to buy all manner 20 of things that belonged unto the wedding. And because of her fair speech Sir Mordred trusted her well enough, and gave her leave to go. And so when she came to London she took the Tower of London, and suddenly in all haste possible she filled it with all manner of victuals, and well supplied it with men, and so kept it. Then when Sir Mordred understood how he was beguiled, he was 30 passing angry out of measure. But all might not prevail Sir Mordred, for Queen

---

[1] For biography see page 697.

[1] The early capital of England.

D

Guenever would never for fair speech nor for foul trust to come in his hands again.[1]

And so as Sir Mordred was at Dover with his host, there came King Arthur with a great navy of ships, and galleys, and carracks.[2] And there was Sir Mor-
40 dred ready awaiting upon his landing, to let his own father to land[3] upon the land that he was king over. Then there was launching of great boats and small, and full of noble men of arms; and there was much slaughter of good knights, and many a full bold baron was laid full low, on both parties. So when this battle was done, King Arthur caused to be buried his people that were dead. Then was it
50 told the king that Sir Mordred had pight a new field[4] upon Barham Down.[5] And upon the morn the king rode thither to him, and there was a great battle betwixt them, and much people was slain on both parties; but at the last Sir Arthur's party stood best, and Sir Mordred and his party fled unto Canterbury.

And then King Arthur marched with his host down by the seaside, westward
60 toward Salisbury; and there was a day set betwixt King Arthur and Sir Mordred, that they should meet upon a down[6] beside Salisbury, and not far from the seaside; and this day was set on a Monday after Trinity Sunday, whereof King Arthur was passing glad, that he might be avenged upon Sir Mordred. So then [King Arthur and his army] departed, and came to Sir Mordred, where he had a
70 grim host of an hundred thousand men.

Then were they agreed that King Arthur and Sir Mordred should meet betwixt both their hosts, and each of them should bring fourteen persons; and they came with this word unto Arthur. Then said he: "I am glad that this is done": and so he went into the field. And when Arthur should depart, he warned all his host that if they see any sword drawn:
80 "Look ye come on fiercely, and slay that traitor, Sir Mordred, for I in no wise trust him." Likewise Sir Mordred warned his host: "If ye see any sword drawn, look that ye come on fiercely, and so slay all that before you stand; for in no wise I will not trust for this treaty, for I know well my father will be avenged on me." And so they met as their appointment was, and so they were agreed and accorded thoroughly; and wine was
90 fetched, and they drank. Right soon came an adder out of a little heath bush, and stung a knight on the foot. And when the knight felt himself stung, he looked down and saw the adder, and then he drew his sword to slay the adder, and thought of none other harm. And when the host on both parties saw that sword drawn, then they blew trumpets, and horns, and shouted grimly. And so both
100 hosts attacked each other. And King Arthur took his horse, and said: "Alas, this unhappy day!" and so rode to his party. And Sir Mordred likewise. And never was there seen a more dolefuller battle in no Christian land. And thus they fought all the long day, and never ceased till the noble knights were laid to the cold earth; and ever they fought still
110 till it was near night, and by that time was there an hundred thousand laid dead upon the down. Then was Arthur madly angry out of measure, when he saw his people so slain from him. Then the king looked about him, and then was he aware, of all his host and of all his good knights, were left no more alive but two knights; that one was Sir Lucan the Butler, and his brother Sir Bedivere, and they were
120 full sore wounded. "Alas that ever I

[1] *But . . . again.* Neither entreaties nor threats could make Guenever give herself up to Mordred.

[2] Large vessels.

[3] *to . . . land.* To prevent his own father (King Arthur) from landing. Here, as often in the later romances, Mordred is represented as both Arthur's nephew and his son.

[4] *pight . . . field.* Prepared for battle on a new field.

[5] *Barham Down.* A hill near Dover.

[6] Hill.

And never was there seen a more dolefuller battle in no Christian land

should see this doleful day, for now," said Arthur, "I am come to mine end. But would to God that I knew where were that traitor Sir Mordred, that hath caused all this mischief." Then was King Arthur aware where Sir Mordred leaned upon his sword among a great heap of dead men. "Now give me my spear," said Arthur unto Sir Lucan, "for yonder 130 I have espied the traitor that hath wrought all this woe. Tide me death, betide me life,"[1] saith the king, "now I see him yonder alone he shall never escape mine hands, for at a better advantage shall I never have him." Then the king took his spear in both his hands, and ran toward Sir Mordred, crying: "Traitor, now is thy death-day come." And when Sir Mordred heard King Arthur, he ran 140 toward him with his sword drawn in his hand. And there King Arthur smote Sir Mordred under the shield with a thrust of his spear, throughout the body, more than a fathom. And when Sir Mordred felt that he had his death wound, he thrust himself with the might that he had up to the bur[2] of King Arthur's spear. And just so he smote his father Arthur, with his sword held in both his hands, 150 on the side of the head, that the sword pierced the helmet and the brain-pan, and therewithal Sir Mordred fell stark dead to the earth; and the noble Arthur fell in a swoon to the earth, and there he swooned ofttimes. And Sir Lucan the Butler and Sir Bedivere ofttimes lifted him up. And thus weakly they led him betwixt them both, to a little chapel not far from the seaside. And when the king 160 was there he thought him well eased.[3] "By my advice," said Sir Lucan, "it is best that we bring you to some town." "I would it were so," said the king; "but I may not stand, mine head aches so."

[1] *Tide . . . life.* Come death or life.
[2] A broad iron ring surrounding the handle of the spear to prevent the hand from slipping.
[3] *thought . . . eased.* Felt relieved.

Then Sir Lucan took up the king on one side, and Sir Bedivere on the other, and in the lifting the king swooned; and Sir Lucan fell in a swoon with the lift, and therewith the noble knight's heart 170 burst. And when the king awoke, he beheld Sir Lucan, how he lay foaming at the mouth. Then Sir Bedivere wept for the death of his brother. "Leave this mourning and weeping, for all this will not avail me; but my time hurries fast," said the king. "Therefore," said Arthur unto Sir Bedivere, "take thou Excalibur, my good sword, and go with it to yonder waterside, and when thou comest there I 180 charge thee throw my sword in that water, and come again and tell me what thou there seest." "My lord," said Bedivere, "your commandment shall be done, and I will quickly bring you word again." So Sir Bedivere departed, and by the way he beheld that noble sword, that the pommel and the haft was all of precious stones; and then he said to himself: "If I throw this rich sword in the water, 190 thereof shall never come good, but harm and loss." And then Sir Bedivere hid Excalibur under a tree. And so, as soon as he could, he came again unto the king, and said he had been at the water, and had thrown the sword in the water. "What saw thou there?" said the king. "Sir," he said, "I saw nothing but waves and winds." "That is untruly said by thee," said the king, "therefore go thou 200 quickly again, and do my commandment; as thou art to me beloved and dear, spare not, but throw it in." Then Sir Bedivere returned again, and took the sword in his hand; and then it seemed to him a sin and shame to throw away that noble sword, and so again he hid the sword, and returned again, and told to the king that he had been at the water, and done his commandment. 210 "What sawest thou there?" said the king. "Sir," he said, "I saw nothing but the waters wappen[1] and waves wanne.[2]

[1] Lap.   [2] Become dark (wan).

"Ah, traitor untrue," said King Arthur, "now hast thou betrayed me twice. Who would have believed that, thou that hast been to me so beloved and dear? and thou art named a noble knight, and would betray me for the richness of the 220 sword. But now go again quickly, for thy long tarrying putteth me in great danger of my life, for I have taken cold. And unless thou do now as I bid thee, if ever I may see thee, I shall slay thee with mine own hands; for thou wouldst for my rich sword see me dead." Then Sir Bedivere departed, and went to the sword, and quickly took it up, and went to the waterside; and there he bound 230 the girdle about the hilt, and then he threw the sword as far into the water as he might; and there came an arm and an hand above the water and met it, and caught it, and so shook it thrice and brandished, and then vanished away the hand with the sword in the water. So Sir Bedivere came again to the king, and told him what he saw. "Alas," said the king, "help me hence, for I fear I have 240 tarried too long." Then Sir Bedivere took the king upon his back, and so went with him to that waterside. And when they were at the waterside, even fast by the bank hoved[1] a little barge with many fair ladies in it, and among them all was a queen, and all they had black hoods, and all they wept and shrieked when they saw King Arthur. "Now put me into the barge," said the king. And so he did 250 softly; and there received him three queens with great mourning; and so they set them down, and in one of their laps King Arthur laid his head. And then that queen said: "Ah, dear brother, why have ye tarried so long from me? alas, this wound on your head hath caught over-much cold." And so then they rowed from the land, and Sir Bedivere beheld all those ladies go from him. 260 Then Sir Bedivere cried: "Ah, my lord Arthur, what shall become of me, now

[1] Hovered, stood.

ye go from me and leave me here alone among mine enemies?" "Comfort thyself," said the king, "and do as well as thou mayest, for in me is no trust for to trust in; for I will into the vale of Avilion* to heal me of my grievous wound: and if thou hear never more of me, pray for my soul." But ever the queens and ladies wept and shrieked, that it was 270 pity to hear. More of the death of King Arthur could I never find, but that ladies brought him to his burials. Yet some men say in many parts of England that King Arthur is not dead, but taken by the will of our Lord Jesu into another place; and men say that he shall come again, and he shall win the holy cross.

Discussion Hints

1. What features of the story might lead the reader to suppose that the events described were historical rather than pure fiction? What features indicate that the account is fiction? What features remind you of a fairy tale? What features justify calling the *Morte d'Arthur* a romance* (pp. 18, 32)?

2. Does the episode of the adder make the story seem more probable? Explain your answer.

3. Was Sir Bedivere justified in not throwing Excalibur into the lake until he was forced to do so? Discuss in class.

4. Do you find in the story any evidence that Malory knew more than one account of Arthur's fate?

5. Find examples of words or phrases that are uncommon or are used differently in modern English.

6. After reading Malory's account, read Tennyson's "Passing of Arthur" (given in the revised edition of *Achievement* of this series). What differences between the two accounts do you find?

Suggestions for Reading in Narrative Literature

1. Chaucer, sometimes called "the father of English poetry," was the first great literary genius who wrote in the English language.

Among the *Canterbury Tales* you will enjoy especially the following:

"The Knight's Tale." A romance of the days of chivalry, in which two dear friends become rivals for the hand of the beautiful Emelie.

"The Clerk of Oxford's Tale." A touching version of the famous story of Patient Griselda.

"The Squire's Tale." A narrative filled with the charm of Oriental magic and romance, but unfortunately left unfinished by the author.[1]

These are all given in modern English translation by Frank E. Hill in *Chaucer's Canterbury Tales* (Longmans, Green & Co.), an unusually faithful modern verse-rendering of the Prologue, four tales, and other poems by Chaucer. An excellent prose translation is given in *The Complete Poetical Works of Geoffrey Chaucer* (The Macmillan Company), by John S. P. Tatlock and Percy Mackaye.

Pupils who, after reading the samples given in *English Writers*, prefer the original will find an excellent edition of all Chaucer's poetry and prose in the *Complete Works* (Houghton Mifflin Company), by Fred Norris Robinson. Among the most interesting of Chaucer's shorter poems included in these editions are "The Book of the Duchess" and "The Legend of Good Women."

[1] Don't forget this fact when you come to read Milton's famous reference to the story (see page 195).

2. There are several modern plays based on the *Canterbury Tales*, parts of which may be used for class reading or presentation. One of these, *The Canterbury Pilgrims* (The Macmillan Company), is by Percy Mackaye. Another, based on "The Pardoner's Tale" and entitled *Under the Oak*, by Douglas Wight, is given in *Short Plays for Modern Players* (D. Appleton-Century Company, Inc.), edited by Glenn Hughes.

3. The romances are the chief glory of medieval literature. You should read as much of Sir Thomas Malory's *Morte d'Arthur* as possible. The complete text, with modernized spelling and punctuation, is easily accessible in Everyman's Library, published by E. P. Dutton & Co., Inc.

A version of the most readable parts of *Sir Gawain and the Green Knight*, made by Jessie L. Weston, is reprinted in *Readings in the Literature of England*, Volume I (D. C. Heath and Company), edited by T. P. Cross and C. T. Goode.

4. Those who wish to pursue further their reading in Middle-English literature will find abundant examples of narrative material, romances, ballads, books of travel, and so on presented in modern form in two easily available volumes: *The Chief Middle English Poets* (Houghton Mifflin Company), edited by Jessie L. Weston; and *The Chief British Poets of the Fourteenth and Fifteenth Centuries* (Houghton Mifflin Company), edited by W. A. Neilson and K. G. T. Webster.

LYRIC POETRY[1]

Alysoun[2]

The adjective most often applied to England of the Middle-English Period is "merry." To readers of literature "Merry England" is the England of gorgeous courts, of gay knights, of fair ladies, of colorful tournaments, of gentlemanly outlaws, of peasants dancing on the village green, of the cuckoo and the nightingale, and of romantic literature preserved in time-stained manuscripts for later generations to read and enjoy. Among the most precious of the literary treasures reflecting the brighter side of English medieval life are the poetic expressions of personal emotion called lyrics. Unfortunately few Middle-English lyrics have come down to us, but enough, by good luck, have been preserved to show how merry England really was in spite of famine, poverty, and war. Middle-English poets, like their Norman conquerors, wrote of love, of flowers, and of springtime, but they often wrote of these familiar themes so freshly and sincerely that their work is distinctly English. The meter of Middle-English lyric poetry is usually simple and thus suited to the themes treated.

The two following poems were composed about 1300, a little before the birth of Chaucer. As the original Middle English is rather difficult, they are given here in a simple literal translation.

Betwixt old March and April gay,
  When sprays begin to spring,
The little bird in her own way
  Follows her will to sing.
  But I must live in love longing
  For one who is the fairest thing.
  'Tis she who may to bliss me bring,

[1] For a general discussion of English lyric poetry,
  see page 150.
[2] *Alysoun* (ăl'ĭ sūn).

For she my love hath won.
  A blessed fortune is my lot,   9
  'Tis sent to me from Heaven, I wot,
  To other women my love turns not
But lights on Alysoun.

Fair enough in hue her hair,
  Her brows are brown, and black her
    eyne.
She smiled on me with lovesome air;
  Trim is her waist and neat and fine.
  Unless thou'lt take me to be thine,
  Thy own dear love, O lady mine,
  Of longer living shall I pine,
By death shall be undone.   20
  A blessed fortune is my lot, etc.

Often at night I toss and wake;
  For this my cheeks are pale and wan.
Lady, 'tis all for thy dear sake
  Longing has fallen me upon.
  In world is none so wise a man
  That all her goodness tell he can.
  Her neck is whiter than the swan;
My heart she has undone.   29
  A blessed fortune is my lot, etc.

Weary as water in weir I wake,
  And woo thee more and more,
Lest some one rob me of my make.[1]
  For I have heard of yore,
  Better to suffer a while full sore,
  Than go a-mourning evermore.
  Gayest under gore,
Hear my orison!
  A blessed fortune is my lot, etc.

[1] Mate.

Springtime

WITH love is come to town the spring,
   With blossoms and birds' whisper-
     ing;
  That all this bliss now bringeth.
There are daisies in the dales,
Pipings sweet of nightingales,
  His song each warbler singeth.
The throstlecock doth strutting go;
Away is all their winter woe
  When up the woodruff springeth.
A thousand birds are singing gay   10
Of winter's sadness passed away,
  Till all the woodland ringeth.

The rose puts on her ruddy hood,
The leaves within the greening wood
  With a will are growing.
The moon is brightening her face;
Here is the lily in her grace,
  With thyme and fennel blowing;
A-wooing go the wilding drakes,
Beasts are courting now their mates;
  The stream is softly flowing;   21
Many a wretch bemoans his lot;
I am one of them, I wot,
  My love for naught bestowing.

The moon now mendeth fast her light,
So doth the seemly sun shine bright,
  When birds are bravely chaunting;
The dews are falling on the hill;
For pleas of love in whispers still
  Sweethearts are not wanting;   30
The worm is wooing in the clod;
Women wax now wondrous proud,
  Their joy in life a-vaunting.
If love of one I may not know,
This blissful boon I will forgo,
  Lonely the wild wood haunting.

Discussion Hints

1. Can you form a clear picture of the lady in "Alysoun"? Do you think the poet had a particular lady in mind? Give reasons for your answer.

2. After reading "Springtime" do you conclude that the poet got his knowledge of nature from books or from actual observation? Give reasons for your answer.

3. After reading "Springtime" what should you say was the medieval attitude toward winter? What could a modern writer find to say in praise of winter?

4. The music for one of the most famous Middle-English lyrics, "Summer Is Icumen In," is given on RCA Victor record No. 4316. If the record is available, by all means play it in class.

Suggestions for Reading in Lyric Poetry

Medieval lyric poetry includes not only poems of springtime and love such as those given above, but also many beautiful hymns, carols, and other less-known forms of lyric poetry.

Examples of the lyric poetry of medieval England may be found in the following books:

The Oxford Book of English Verse (Oxford University Press).

The Oxford Book of Carols (Oxford University Press).

The Chief Middle English Poets (Houghton Mifflin Company), edited by Jessie L. Weston.

The Golden Treasury of English Lyrics, edited by F. T. Palgrave.

BALLADS[1]

A BALLAD is a song that tells a story. Ballads are usually short and are intended to be sung. The poems printed below belong to a special class called popular ballads. By "popular" we mean that the ballads referred to are written in simple meter and language, deal with subjects that interest the uncultured and lowly, and are anonymous. Just as the romances of the Middle Ages[2] were written for the entertainment of the aristocracy, so the popular ballads reflect the lives and thoughts of the lower classes. Most of the early English ballads that have come down to us appear to have been composed during the fifteenth century. There are also many ballads that were composed in more recent times; and, indeed, ballads may appear today wherever there is a group of simple folk, such as lumberjacks, field laborers, or mountaineers, with a common stock of simple stories and traditions. We do not know who were the authors of the popular ballads; but this does not matter, for the poet who composes a popular ballad is little more than the mouthpiece of the community to which he belongs. Whatever deeply affects the thoughts and emotions of an unlettered community may be taken up by the ballad poet and turned into verse. For example, after the Norman Conquest the English were profoundly stirred by the oppression of the invaders. Their sentiments were expressed in the ballads of Robin* Hood, the noble English outlaw who defended the rights of the common people and robbed the rich and proud only to give to the poor and humble. There were also numerous ballads dealing with the endless raids back and forth across the Scottish Border.* Unfaithful lovers, faithless sweethearts, shocking murders, dead people returned from the grave, and other mysterious happenings, almost anything that touched the lives and thoughts of the common people, might be turned into a ballad. The story the ballad poet tells is so well known to his audience that he does not need to relate *all* the facts; hence many popular ballads leave much to the memory and imagination of the hearers.

Many ballads have been handed down from generation to generation by word of mouth, and thus have become an essential part of the literary inheritance of the English people. The English colonists who came to America brought with them ballads, some of which have survived and are sung down to the present day. For more than two centuries after the

---

[1] Discussion hints for the ballads are grouped together on page 67. Ballads are also discussed and examples given in the revised editions of *Adventure, Achievement,* and *American Writers* of this series.
[2] Page 32.

close of the Middle Ages the popular ballads were regarded by the upper classes as beneath their notice, and consequently few ballads found their way into books; but early in the Transition Period (1744–1798) (p. 291) educated people began to appreciate folk literature, and the enthusiasm has continued till the present day. Within the last two hundred years many poets, such as Wordsworth (p. 335), Coleridge (p. 395),[1] and Scott (p. 401), have been glad to imitate the ancient popular ballads. In recent years the term "ballad" has come to be applied to almost any comparatively simple narrative poem,[2] such as Kipling's "Ballad of East and West" (p. 628). Though many popular ballads are commonplace in theme and vulgar in style, some reveal a simple directness, a native vigor, and a tragic pathos that appeal to the whole world.

Ballads are usually composed in a simple stanza* form consisting of four lines, of which the first and third have four accents* each and do not rhyme, and the second and fourth have three accents each and rhyme. The rhythm* is iambic.* The following, taken from page 60, is a typical ballad stanza. It is scanned by marking the accented syllables (ı), and the unaccented syllables (x). The rhyme* scheme is indicated by placing the same letter opposite the lines that rhyme, and different letters opposite the lines that do not rhyme.

> And whan she cam into the kirk,   *a*
>
> She shimmered like the sun;   *b*
>
> The belt that was about her waist,   *c*
>
> Was a' wi pearles bedone.   *b*

Because folk ballads were intended to be sung, many of them contain extra syllables that can easily be slurred over, or they shift the accent from time to time. For the same reason many ballads contain one or more stanzas in which the second and fourth lines end in imperfect instead of perfect rhymes. The following stanza, taken from page 59, will illustrate:

> "My maides, gae to my dressing-room,   *a*
>
> And dress to me my smock;   *b*
>
> The one half is o the holland fine,   *c*
>
> The other o needle-work."   *b*

[1] Coleridge's "Ancient Mariner" (in the revised edition of *Achievement* of this series), as well as several of his other poems, owes much of its charm to the influence of the early English ballads.

[2] See, for example, Masefield's "Ballad of John Silver" (in the revised edition of *Adventure* of this series).

Lord Thomas and Fair Annet

The rapid succession of the dramatic scenes, the singing quality of the ballad stanzas, and the tragic culmination of the story make "Lord Thomas and Fair Annet" as good literature today as it was hundreds of years ago. It has been called one of the most beautiful of all ballads. As you read, note the repetition and parallelism* of ideas and phrases, remembering that this, like all other genuine popular ballads, was meant to be sung to a company, not read to oneself.

The ballad of "Lord Thomas and Fair Annet" is one of the most popular of all the English ballads that survive in America.

LORD THOMAS and Fair Annet
　Sate a' day on a hill;
Whan night was cum, and sun was sett,
　They had not talked their fill.

Lord Thomas said a word in jest,
　Fair Annet took it ill:
"A, I will nevir wed a wife
　Against my ain friends' will."

"Gif¹ ye wull nevir wed a wife,
　A wife wull neir wed yee."　　　　10
Sae he is hame to tell his mither,
　And knelt upon his knee.

"O rede,² O rede, mither," he says,
　"A gude rede gie to mee:
O sall I tak the nut-browne bride,
　And let Fair Annet bee?"

"The nut-browne bride haes gowd³ and
　gear,⁴
Fair Annet she has gat nane;
And the little beauty Fair Annet haes,
　O it wull soon be gane."　　　　20

And he has till⁵ his brother gane:
　"Now, brother, rede ye mee;
A, sall I marrie the nut-browne bride,
　And let Fair Annet bee?"

"The nut-browne bride has oxen, brother,
　The nut-browne bride has kye¹;
I wad hae ye marrie the nut-browne bride,
　And cast Fair Annet bye."

"Her oxen may dye i the house, billie,²
　And her kye into the byre,³　　　　30
And I sall hae nothing to mysell
　Bot a fat fadge⁴ by the fyre."

And he has till his sister gane:
　"Now, sister, rede ye mee;
O sall I marrie the nut-browne bride,
　And set Fair Annet free?"

"I'se rede ye tak Fair Annet, Thomas,
　And let the browne bride alane,
Lest ye sould sigh, and say, Alace,
　What is this we brought hame!"　　40

"No, I will tak my mither's counsel,
　And marrie me owt o hand;
And I will tak the nut-browne bride:
　Fair Annet may leive the land."

Up then rose Fair Annet's father,
　Twa hours or it were day,
And he is gane into the bower
　Wherein Fair Annet lay.

"Rise up, rise up, Fair Annet," he says,
　"Put on your silken sheene⁵;　　　50
Let us gae to St. Marie's kirk,
　And see that rich weddeen."

"My maides, gae to my dressing-room,
　And dress to me my hair;
Whaireir yee laid a plait before,
　See yee lay ten times mair."

"My maides, gae to my dressing-room,
　And dress to me my smock;
The one half is o the holland fine,
　The other o needle-work."　　　60

¹ If.　　² Advice.　　³ Gold.
⁴ Property.　　⁵ To.

¹ Cows, cattle.　　² Comrade, pal.
³ Cow house.　　⁴ *fat fadge.* A squat, fat person
⁵ Shoes.

The horse Fair Annet rade upon,
  He amblit like the wind;
Wi siller[1] he was shod before,
  Wi burning gowd behind.

Four and twenty siller bells
  Wer a' tyed till his mane,
And yae tift[2] o the norland wind,
  They tinkled ane by ane.

Four and twenty gay gude knichts
  Rade by Fair Annet's side,   70
And four and twenty fair ladies,
  As gin[3] she had bin a bride.

And whan she cam to Marie's kirk,
  She sat on Marie's stean[4];
The cleading[5] that Fair Annet had on,
  It skinkled[6] in their een.[7]

And whan she cam into the kirk,
  She shimmered like the sun;
The belt that was about her waist,
  Was a' wi pearles bedone.[8]   80

She sat her by the nut-browne bride,
  And her een they wer sae clear,
Lord Thomas he clean forgat the bride,
  When Fair Annet drew near.

He had a rose into his hand,
  He gae it kisses three,
And reaching by the nut-browne bride,
  Laid it on Fair Annet's knee.

Up than spak the nut-browne bride,
  She spak wi meikle[9] spite: 90
"And whair gat ye that rose-water,
  That does mak yee sae white?"

"O I did get the rose-water
  Whair ye wull neir get nane,
For I did get that very rose-water
  Into my mither's wame."[1]

The bride she drew a long bodkin
  Frae out her gay head-gear,
And strake Fair Annet unto the heart,
  That word spak nevir mair.   100

Lord Thomas he saw Fair Annet wex
  pale,
  And marvelit what mote bee;
But when he saw her dear heart's blude,
  A' wood-wroth[2] wexèd hee.

He drew his dagger, that was sae sharp,
  That was sae sharp and meet,
And drave it into the nut-browne bride,
  That fell deid at his feit.

"Now stay for me, dear Annet," he
  sed,
  "Now stay, my dear," he cry'd;   110
Then strake the dagger until his heart,
  And fell deid by her side.

Lord Thomas was buried without kirk-wa,
  Fair Annet within the quiere[3];
And o the tane[4] thair grew a birk,[5]
  The other a bonny briere.

And ay they grew, and ay they threw,[6]
  As they wad faine be neare;
And by this ye may ken right weil
  They were twa luvers deare.   120

Lord Randal

Here, as in many popular ballads, the story is hinted at rather than told in full. A lover has been poisoned by his lady, but why?

"Lord Randal" is one of the most widely known and often-sung English ballads. It was popular in Great Britain long ago, and according to a recent authority it is still "sung very freely from one end of the island to the other." It is a special favorite in America, where more than twenty versions have been recorded.

[1] Silver.   [2] *yae tift*. One puff.   [3] If.
[4] *Marie's stean*. A stone seat at the door of Saint
  Mary's Church.   [5] Clothing.   [6] Sparkled.
[7] Eyes.   [8] Ornamented.   [9] Much.

[1] Womb.
[2] As angry as if he were crazy (wood (wōd)).
[3] Choir. A part of the church.
[4] *the tane*. The one.
[5] Birch.   [6] Throve, flourished.

O WHERE hae ye been, Lord Randal,
   my son?
O where hae ye been, my handsome
   young man?"
"I hae been to the wild wood; mother,
   make my bed soon,
For I'm weary wi hunting, and fain wald
   lie down."

"Where gat ye your dinner, Lord Randal,
   my son?
Where gat ye your dinner, my handsome
   young man?"
"I din'd wi my true-love; mother, make
   my bed soon,
For I'm weary wi hunting, and fain wald
   lie down."

"What gat ye to your dinner, Lord
   Randal, my son?
What gat ye to your dinner, my hand-
   some young man?"   10

"I gat eels boiled in broo; mother, make
   my bed soon,
For I'm weary wi hunting, and fain wald
   lie down."

"What became of your bloodhounds,
   Lord Randal, my son?
What became of your bloodhounds, my
   handsome young man?"
"O they swell'd and they died; mother,
   make my bed soon,
For I'm weary wi hunting, and fain wald
   lie down."

"O I fear ye are poison'd, Lord Randal,
   my son!
O I fear ye are poison'd, my handsome
   young man!"
"O yes! I am poison'd; mother, make
   my bed soon,
For I'm sick at the heart and I fain wald
   lie down."   20

Sir Patrick Spence

"Sir Patrick Spence" is a brief, compact tale of a common English or Scottish experience, a shipwreck. History does not record the name of Sir Patrick, but the vividness of the pictures in the poem suggests that the story has a basis in fact. Much to the delight of all lovers of ballad literature, two versions of "Sir Patrick Spence" have recently been discovered in America.

THE king sits in Dumferling* toune,
   Drinking the blude-reid wine:
"O whar will I get a guid sailor,
   To sail this schip of mine?"

Up and spak an eldern knicht,
   Sat at the kings richt kne;
"Sir Patrick Spence is the best sailor
   That sails upon the se."

The king has written a braid letter,
   And signd it wi his hand,   10
And sent it to Sir Patrick Spence,
   Was walking on the sand.

The first line that Sir Patrick red,
   A loud lauch lauchèd he;
The next line that Sir Patrick red,
   The teir blinded his ee.

"O wha is this has don this deid,
   This ill deid don to me,
To send me out this time o' the yeir,
   To sail upon the se!   20

"Mak haste, mak haste, my mirry men
   all,
Our guid schip sails the morne":
"O say na sae, my master deir,
   For I feir a deadlie storme.

"Late late yestreen I saw the new moone,
   Wi the auld moone in hir arme,[1]
And I feir, I feir, my deir master,
   That we will cum to harme."

[1] It is a common superstition among sailors that when the dark part of the moon (the old moon) can be seen inside the horns of the new moon, a storm will follow.

O our Scots nobles wer richt laith   29
  To weet their cork-heild schoone[1];
Bot lang owre a' the play wer playd,
  Thair hats they swam aboone.[2]

O lang, lang may their ladies sit,
  Wi thair fans into their hand,
Or eir they se Sir Patrick Spence
  Cum sailing to the land.

O lang, lang may the ladies stand,
  Wi thair gold kems in their hair,
Waiting for thair ain deir lords,
  For they'll se thame na mair.   40

Haf owre, haf owre to Aberdour,
  It's fiftie fadom deip,
And thair lies guid Sir Patrick Spence,
  Wi the Scots lords at his feit.

The Gay Goshawk

"The Gay Goshawk" is a love story of olden times brought down to us in the form of a popular ballad. It deals with the ever-interesting theme of devotion triumphant over seemingly insurmountable obstacles. A lady in the "southen land" receives from her absent lover a letter sent by his pet hawk. As a result she deceives her kinsfolk by pretending to die and, by her own request, is carried to Scotland, where she and her lover are united. It is just the sort of romantically sentimental tale to catch and hold the imagination of the folk and to be made into a popular ballad. Read it aloud, with other members of the class, or, better still, sing it if the music is available.

O WALY, waly, my gay goss-hawk,
  Gin your feathering be sheen!'
'O waly, waly, my master dear,
  Gin ye look pale and lean![3]

'Whether is it for the gold sae rid,[4]
  Or is it for the silver clear?
Or is it for the lass in southen land,
  That she cannot win[5] here?'

'It is not for the gold sae rid,
  Nor is it for the silver clear,   10
But it is for the lass in southen land,
  That she cannot win her[e].'

'Sit down, sit down, my master dear,
  Write a love-letter hastily,
And put it in under my feathern gray,
  And I'll away to southen land as fast
    as I can flee.

'But how shall I your true-love ken?[1]
  Or how shall I her know?
I bear the tongue never wi her spake,
  The eye that never her saw.'   20

'The red that is in my love's cheek
  Is like blood spilt amang the snaw;
The white that is on her breast-bone
  Is like the down on the white sea-maw.

'There's one that stands at my love's gate
  And opens the silver pin,[2]
And there ye may safely set ye on
  And sing a lovely song.

'First ye may sing it loud, loud, loud,
  And then ye may sing it clear,   30
And ay the oerword[3] of the tune
  Is, Your love cannot win here.'

He has written a love-letter,
  Put it under his feathern gray,
And he's awa to southen land,
  As fast as ever he may.

---

[1] Shoes with cork heels — expensive shoes.
[2] *swam aboone.* Floated on the water.
[3] Talking birds (and talking animals) are a common feature in ballads and folk tales.
[4] Red.
[5] Succeed in arriving.

[1] Recognize.   [2] Bolt or lock.   [3] Refrain.

When he came to the lady's gate,
　There he lighted down,
And there he sat him on the pin
　And sang a lovely song.　　　　40

First he sang it loud, loud, loud,
　And then he sang it clear,
And ay the oerword of the tune
　Was, Your love cannot win here.

'Hold your tongues, my merry maids all,
　And hold them a little while:
I hear some word from my true-love,
　That lives in Scotland's isle.'

Up she rose, to the door she goes,
　To hear what the bird woud say,　　50
And he's let the love-letter fall
　From under his feathern gray.

When she looked the letter on,
　The tear blinded her eye,
And when she read it oer and oer
　A loud laughter took she.

'Go hame, go hame, my bonny bird,
　And to your master tell,
If I be nae wi him at Martinmass,[1]
　I shall be wi him at Yule.'[2]　　60

The lady 's to her chamber gane,
　And a sick woman grew she;
The lady 's taen a sudden brash,
　And nathing she'll do but die.

'An asking, an asking, my father dear,
　An asking grant to me!
If that I die in southen land,
　In Scotland bury me.'

'Ask on, ask on, my daughter dear,
　That asking is granted thee;　　70
If that you die in southen land,
　In Scotland I'll bury thee.'

[1] November 11.　　[2] Christmas.

'Gar call to me my seven bretheren,
　To hew to me my bier,
The one half of the beaten gold,
　The other of the silver clear.

'Go call to me my seven sisters,
　To sew to me my caul[1];
Every needle-steik that they put in
　Put by a silver bell.'　　80

The first Scots kirk that they came to,
　They heard the mavis[2] sing;
The next Scots kirk that they came to,
　They heard the dead-bell ring.

The next Scots kirk that they came to,
　They were playing at the foot-ball,
And her true-love was them among,
　The chieftain amangst them all.

'Set down, set down these corps,' said he,
　'Let me look them upon;'　　90
As soon as he lookd the lady on,
　The blood sprang in her chin.

'One bite of your bread, my love,
　And one glass of your wine!
For I have fasted these five long days,
　All for your sake and mine.

'Go hame, go hame, my seven brothers,
　Go hame and blaw your horn,
And ye may tell thro southen land
　How I playd you the scorn.'[3]　　100

'Woe to you, my sister dear,
　And ane ill death may you die!
For we left father and mother at hame
　Breaking their heart for thee.'

[1] Here, shroud.
[2] Thrush.
[3] *playd . . . scorn.* Deceived you.

The Three Ravens

True love stronger than death is the theme of the ballad of "The Three Ravens." There are numerous survivals of this ballad in America, some of them humorous.

THERE were three ravens sat on a tree,
  Downe a downe, hay downe, hay downe;[1]
There were three ravens sat on a tree,
  With a downe;

There were three ravens sat on a tree,
They were as blacke as they might[2] be,
  With a downe derrie, derrie, derrie, downe, downe.

The one of them said to his mate,
"Where shall we our breakefast take?"

"Downe in yonder greene field   10
There lies a knight slain under his shield.

"His hounds they lie downe at his feete,
So well they can their master keepe.

"His haukes they flie so eagerly
There's no fowle dare him come nie."

Downe there comes a fallow doe,
As great with yong as she might goe.

She lifted up his bloudy hed,
And kist his wounds that were so red.

She got him up upon her backe,   20
And carried him to earthen lake.[1]

She buried him before the prime,[2]
She was dead herselfe ere even-song time.

God send every gentleman,
Such haukes, such hounds, and such a leman.[3]

Edward

Like numerous other ballads, "Edward" owes its popularity principally to its grim tragic theme, a family feud that results in hatred and murder. Such domestic tragedies often make a profound impression upon small communities of simple folk, and hence are likely to find their way into popular ballad tradition. "Edward" is also noteworthy because it illustrates admirably the parallelism* which is so characteristic of genuine folk poetry. The ballad was brought to America and has flourished here.

WHY dois your brand[3] sae drap wi bluid,
      Edward, Edward,
Why dois your brand sae drap wi bluid,
  And why sae sad gang[4] yee O?"
"O I hae killed my hauke[5] sae guid,
      Mither, mither,
O I hae killed my hauke sae guid,
  And I had nae mair bot hee O."

"Your haukis bluid was nevir sae reid,
      Edward, Edward,   10
Your haukis bluid was nevir sae reid,
  My deir son I tell thee O."
"O I hae killed my reid-roan steid,
      Mither, mither,
O I hae killed my reid-roan steid,
  That erst was sae fair and frie O."

"Your steid was auld, and ye hae got mair,
      Edward, Edward,
Your steid was auld, and ye hae got mair,
  Sum other dule[4] ye drie[5] O."   20
"O I hae killed my fadir deir,
      Mither, mither,
O I hae killed my fadir deir,
  Alas, and wae is mee O!"

---

[1] *Downe . . . downe.* A meaningless refrain common in the popular ballads.   [2] Could.
[3] Sword.   [4] Go.   [5] Hawk, falcon.

[1] Pit, grave.
[2] About nine o'clock in the morning.
[3] Sweetheart.
[4] Grief.
[5] Suffer, undergo.

"And whatten penance wul ye drie for
that,
      Edward, Edward?
And whatten penance will ye drie for
that?
    My deir son, now tell me O."
"Ile set my feit in yonder boat,
      Mither, mither,   30
Ile set my feit in yonder boat,
    And Ile fare ovir the sea O."

"And what wul ye doe wi your towirs
and your ha,[1]
      Edward, Edward?
And what wul you doe wi your towirs and
your ha,
    That were sae fair to see O?"
"Ile let thame stand tul[2] they doun
fa,
      Mither, mither,
Ile let thame stand tul they doun fa,
    For here nevir mair maun I bee O." 40

"And what wul ye leive to your bairns
and your wife,
      Edward, Edward?
And what wul ye leive to your bairns and
your wife,
    Whan ye gang ovir the sea O?"
"The warldis room, late them beg thrae
life,
      Mither, mither,
The warldis room, late them beg thrae life,
    For thame nevir mair wul I see O."

"And what wul ye leive to your ain
mither deir,
      Edward, Edward?   50
And what wul ye leive to your ain mither
deir?
    My deir son, now tell me O."
"The curse of hell frae me sall ye beir,
      Mither, mither,
The curse of hell frae me sall ye beir,
    Sic counseils ye gave to me O."

Get Up and Bar the Door

Rollicking humor characterizes the lines
of "Get Up and Bar the Door." The reader
forgets his surprise at seeing the intruders
dispose of the Martinmas cheer, in astonishment at their bold proposal to kiss the housewife, only to join in the wife's hilarity at her
husband's loss of his wager. Versions of this
ballad are known in America as well as in
England.

IT FELL about the Martinmas[3] time,
    And a gay time it was then,
When our good wife got puddings to
make,
    And she's boild them in the pan.

The wind sae cauld blew south and
north,
    And blew into the floor;
Quoth our goodman to our goodwife,
    "Gae out and bar the door."

"My hand is in my hussyfskap,[1]
    Goodman, as ye may see;   10
An it should nae be barrd this hundred
year,
    It's no be barrd for me."[2]

They made a paction[3] tween them twa,
    They made it firm and sure,
That the first word whaeer shoud speak,
    Shoud rise and bar the door.

Then by there came two gentlemen,
    At twelve o'clock at night,
And they could neither see house nor hall,
    Nor coal nor candle-light.   20

"Now whether is this a rich man's house,
    Or whether is it a poor?"
But neer a word wad ane o them speak,
    For barring of the door.

[1] Hall   [2] Till.
[3] A church festival held on November 11.

[1] Housewifery. (She is making puddings.)
[2] for me. So far as I am concerned.
[3] Bargain, agreement.

D

And first they ate the white puddings,
　And then they ate the black;
Tho muckle[1] thought the goodwife to
　　hersel,
　Yet neer a word she spake.

Then said the one unto the other,
　"Here, man, tak ye my knife;　　30
Do ye tak aff the auld man's beard,
　And I'll kiss the goodwife."

"But there's nae water in the house,
　And what shall we do than?"

"What ails ye at the pudding-bree,[1]
　That boils into the pan?"

O up then started our goodman,
　An angry man was he:
"Will ye kiss my wife before my een,
　And scad[2] me wi pudding-bree?"　　40

Then up and started our goodwife,
　Gied three skips on the floor:
"Goodman, you've spoken the foremost
　　word,
　Get up and bar the door."

Johnie Cock

In true ballad fashion, simply, swiftly, and directly, "Johnie Cock" relates a bit of grim tragedy that happened in Scotland when game laws were cruel and poaching punishable by death. The hero of the ballad was a gallant youth who loved hunting so much that, in spite of his mother's entreaties and warnings of danger from the foresters, he took his hunting dogs, went to the slope of his favorite hill, and killed a deer. He and his dogs ate bountifully of the good venison and lay down to sleep and rest. A talkative old palmer * spied them and carried word to the seven foresters of Pickeram, Johnie's deadly foes. The ballad then tells with rare restraint and pathos how they fell upon Johnie while he was still asleep and what a brave defense he made.

UP JOHNIE raise in a May morning,
　Calld for water to wash his hands,
And he has calld for his gude gray
　　hounds
　That lay bound in iron bands,
　　bands,
　That lay bound in iron bands.

2. "Ye'll busk,[2] ye'll busk my noble
　　dogs,
　Ye'll busk and mak them boun,[3]
For I'm going to the Braidscaur hill
　To ding[4] the dun[5] deer doun.[6]"

　　　　¹ Much.　　² Make ready.
　³ boun (bōōn). Ready.　　⁴ Strike.
　⁵ Dull brown.　⁶ doun (dōōn). Down.

3. Johnie's mother has gotten word o that,
　And care-bed she has taen:[3]　　11
"O Johnie, for my benison,[4]
　I beg you'l stay at hame;
For the wine so red, and the well-
　　baken bread,
　My Johnie shall want nane.

4. "There are seven forsters at Pick-
　　eram Side,
　At Pickeram where they dwell,
And for a drop of thy heart's bluid
　They wad ride the fords of hell."

5. But Johnie has cast off the black velvet,
　And put on the Lincoln twine,[5]　　21
And he is on to gude greenwud
　As fast as he could gang.

6. Johnie lookit east, and Johnie lookit
　　west,
　And he lookit aneath the sun,
And there he spied the dun deer
　　sleeping
　Aneath a buss o whun.[6]

¹ What . . . pudding-bree. What is the matter with the liquor in which the pudding is being boiled?　² Scald.
³ care-bed . . . taen. Gone to bed sick with anxiety.
⁴ Blessing.　⁵ Cloth (green in color).
⁶ buss o whun. Bush of furze, a kind of prickly bush.

7. Johnie shot, and the dun deer lap,[1]
   And she lap wondrous wide, 29
   Until they came to the wan water,
   And he stemd[2] her of her pride.

8. He 'as taen out the little pen-knife,
   'Twas full three quarters long,
   And he has taen out of that dun deer
   The liver bot and the tongue.[3]

9. They eat of the flesh, and they drank
     of the blood,
   And the blood it was so sweet,
   Which caused Johnie and his bloody
     hounds
   To fall in a deep sleep.

10. By then came an old palmer,* '40
    And an ill death may he die!
    For he's away to Pickeram Side
    As fast as he can drie.[4]

11. "What news, what news?" says the
      Seven Forsters,
    "What news have ye brought to
      me?"
    "I have noe news," the palmer said,
    "But what I saw with my eye.

12. "As I cam in by Braidisbanks,
    And down among the whuns,
    The bonniest youngster eer I saw 50
    Lay sleepin amang his hunds.

13. "The shirt that was upon his back
    Was o the holland[5] fine;
    The doublet[6] which was over that
    Was o the Lincoln twine."

14. Up bespake the Seven Forsters,
    Up bespake they ane and a':
    "O that is Johnie o Cockleys Well,
    And near him we will draw." 59

15. O the first stroke that they gae him,
    They struck him off by the knee;
    Then up bespake his sister's son:
    "O the next'll gar[7] him die!"

16. "O some they count ye well-wight[1]
      men,
    But I do count ye nane;
    For you might well ha wakend me,
    And askd gin I wad be taen.

17. "The wildest wolf in aw this wood
    Wad not ha done so by me;
    She'd ha wet her foot ith wan water,
    And sprinkled it oer my brae,[2] 71
    And if that wad not ha wakend me,
    She wad ha gone and let me be.

18. "O bows of yew, if ye be true,
    In London, where ye were bought,
    Fingers five, get up belive,[3]
    Manhuid shall fail me nought."

19. He has killd the Seven Forsters,
    He has killd them all but ane,
    And that wan[4] scarce to Pickeram
      Side, 80
    To carry the bode-words[5] hame.

20. "Is there never a [bird] in a' this
      wood
    That will tell what I can say;
    That will go to Cockleys Well,
    Tell my mither to fetch me away?"

21. There was a [bird] into that wood,
    That carried the tidings away,
    And many ae[6] was the well-wight man
    At the fetching o Johnie away.

Discussion Hints

1. What succession of dramatic scenes do
you find in "Lord Thomas and Fair Annet"?
Note that ballad poets are fond of presenting
a story by describing a series of striking incidents, depending upon the audience to fill
out the complete narrative from their knowledge of the events referred to. This is one
reason why you may have to read some ballads
more than once before you get the complete
story. As you study the ballads in *English
Writers*, look for other examples of ballads in
which the story is suggested by a series of
dramatic incidents rather than told from beginning to end as in an ordinary narrative.

[1] Leaped. [2] Stopped.
[3] *The liver . . . tongue.* Only the liver and also
the tongue, the choice parts.
[4] *can drie.* Is able.
[5] Linen. [6] Tight-fitting coat. [7] Make.

[1] Very brave. [2] Brow. [3] Quickly.
[4] Won: that is, arrived. [5] News. [6] A one.

2. In "Lord Randal" the story is built up by the use of parallelism.* Do any other of the ballads given here use this device?

3. Act out the ballad of "Sir Patrick Spence" in pantomime in class. (While the actors go through the necessary motions, let someone read the ballad aloud.)

4. If possible compare "Sir Patrick Spence" with Longfellow's imitation ballad, "The Wreck of the *Hesperus*" (in the revised edition of *Adventure* of this series). What similarities do you find? Which ballad do you prefer?

5. With the help of the text and the suggestions given in the headnote tell the story of "The Gay Goshawk" in full. What, for example, do you think caused the separation of the lover and the lady?

6. In the last stanza of "Edward" why do you suppose the son curses his mother?

7. Read aloud again stanzas 4 and 17 of "Johnie Cock." Stanza 4 is one of the grimmest in ballad poetry and stanza 17 one of the most pathetic.

8. Pick out passages that show what qualities in a man were most admired by the ballad authors.

9. Pick out examples of characteristic ballad words and phrases that occur more than once. How many of these words or phrases are archaic, that is, out of date?

10. Pick out the leading themes, such as revenge, jealousy, family discord, murder, etc. What themes occur more than once?

11. It should never be forgotten that the popular ballads are intended to be sung, each to its tune, instead of being recited only or read aloud. The class may well devote at least one period to the singing of ballads. If anybody in the class knows a ballad, let him sing it. Do not mind whether or not you have what is called a "good" voice; many of the most effective ballad singers have had no formal musical training. If you can get the music department to co-operate, so much the better; but sing, anyway. If there is a piano in your home, try singing ballads. Words and tunes for many English popular ballads may be found in the following:

English Folk-Songs for Schools (John Curwen & Sons, Ltd.), edited by S. Baring-Gould and Cecil J. Sharp.

One Hundred English Folksongs (Oliver Ditson Company, Inc.), edited by Cecil J. Sharp.

American Anthology of Old-World Ballads (J. Fischer and Brothers), words and piano settings of famous ballads, edited by Reed Smith and Hilton Rufty.

Words and music of several English ballads recorded in the United States are in the revised edition of *American Writers* of this series.

12. Inquire in the community where you live whether the older people have heard any of the ballads given in *English Writers* or any other ballads which they have learned from oral tradition rather than from books. Bring to class any such that you may find, and sing them or read them aloud. Discuss any differences you may notice between different versions of the same ballad. (If you succeed in getting hold of any ballads through your inquiries, send in both the words and the music to Reed Smith, care of Ginn and Company, Boston, Massachusetts. He will be glad to see that any contribution is filed permanently with one of the state folklore societies, and that you receive due credit for it. If you make your investigation a class project so as to cover the whole community, you may succeed in rescuing some fine old version of a ballad that might otherwise be lost.)

13. Craft projects. Pupils who like to do things with their hands will find pleasure and profit in carrying out one or more of the following projects:

a. Construct a model of a medieval castle. If you do not know just what a castle looked like, you may get help from the picture on page 30, from picture post cards collected by yourself or your friends, or from illustrations in books on history or architecture in your school or community library.

b. Dress a collection of dolls in costumes such as you imagine were worn by the Canterbury pilgrims. You may get suggestions from the picture facing page 48 or, if you can find a copy, from the famous picture by the eighteenth-century poet and artist William Blake.[1]

Suggestions for Reading in Ballads

Many collections of popular ballads are now available. The best one-volume edition is entitled *English and Scottish Popular Ballads* (Houghton Mifflin Company), edited by G. L. Kittredge and H. C. Sargent. Selections are given in *The Oxford Book of Ballads* (Oxford University Press), edited by Sir Arthur Quiller-Couch, and in numerous collections issued by other publishers.

[1] For biography see page 714.

1400-1616

❀

The
Elizabethan Period

Shakespeare and friends at the Mermaid Tavern

THE RENAISSANCE

ABOUT the time of the death of Chaucer (1400) a great change began to take place in the life of England. This change had originated about a century before in Italy, and had swept over the whole of civilized Europe. As a result people found the world more beautiful and life more rich in joy than ever before. They reached out in all directions for new experiences and new knowledge. So complete and profound was this change from the medieval to the modern world that the new awakening is called the Renaissance (rĕn ĕ säns') ("new birth").

In England the Renaissance includes roughly the years from 1400 till the death of Shakespeare, in 1616. The second half of the sixteenth century and the early part of the seventeenth are especially important in the history of the English Renaissance, because during these years the great Queen Elizabeth occupied the English throne (1558–1603) and Shakespeare (1564–1616) composed his immortal dramas.

THE REFORMATION

One of the chief differences between the Renaissance and the preceding period lay in the effort of the individual to liberate himself from the bonds of feudalism * and other rigid institutions of the Middle Ages. In religious matters there appeared a new interpretation of the relation of the individual Christian to the church and to God. This movement, though not altogether free from undesirable elements, finally resulted in a further liberation of the human spirit, and is often referred to as the Reformation. In science also a new spirit began to show itself. Astronomers, physicists, chemists, and physicians began to substitute direct, personal investigation for a blind acceptance of many old explanations of the causes of things. It was Francis Bacon[1] (1561–1626) who laid the foundations of what may be called the modern laboratory method of research in natural science.

HUMANISM

One of the most powerful influences during the Renaissance came from a vastly increased knowledge of ancient classical literature. Literary treasures found in Greek manuscripts, which had been largely unknown during the Middle Ages, found their way into western Europe, especially

[1] For biography see page 702.

71

after the capture of Constantinople by the Turks in 1453. About the year 1500 the teaching of Greek was introduced into England, and Oxford University soon became so famous as a center of Greek learning that the great Dutch scholar Erasmus went there to study instead of going to Italy, which had formerly been more important. Many scholars were so profoundly affected by the beauty and value of the ancient literature and philosophy that they sought to impress the Greek view of life upon the world. Those who labored during the Renaissance to make the ancient classics prevail came to be known as humanists, and their teachings as humanism. They are called humanists because they advocated studies and other interests that tend to broaden and humanize people. Not only did they emphasize the importance of beauty and perfection in art, but they preached the Greek doctrine of a well-rounded life as the ideal toward which men should strive. To the humanists the "complete" gentleman was well trained both in body and in intellect. Thus, with a sound mind in a sound body, he was prepared to appreciate and enjoy the world to the fullest extent. Sir Philip Sidney,[1] who was perhaps the finest product of Renaissance culture in England, was an excellent scholar, a trained athlete, a brave soldier, an accomplished courtier, and a great poet. The gradual broadening of human knowledge that accompanied humanism is often referred to as the Revival of Learning.

ENGLAND BECOMES A WORLD POWER

The Renaissance in England was also stimulated by political conditions. With the accession of Henry VII to the throne in 1485 the Wars of the Roses * ended, and England was at peace for almost the first time in two hundred years. The people had become so weary of the long wars with France and the destructive conflicts at home that they welcomed enthusiastically the return of peace. Under the next king, Henry VIII (who ruled from 1509 to 1547), and under Elizabeth, England began to attain higher and higher rank as a world power. Englishmen became proud of their country and boasted of her prowess, especially after the defeat of the great Spanish Armada,* in 1588. Many Elizabethan writings, notably the historical plays of Shakespeare, were composed under the influence of the popular pride and enthusiasm over the accomplishments of the English people.

There was also a tremendous increase in internal wealth and prosperity. English ships imported valuable cargoes, especially from the New World. Foreign trade grew rapidly, and London merchants became rich and powerful.

[1] For biography see page 700.

❁

A performance of a play in an Elizabethan theater,
showing the audience as well as the stage
and the upper platform, which represented
a balcony, the second story of a house,
the top of a wall, or other place raised
above the level of the main action

FROM A PAINTING BY HAROLD SICHEL

❁

EFFECT ON ENGLAND OF WORLD EXPANSION

An important effect of England's foreign contacts was a quickening of the imagination of English writers. When the Italian discoverer Christopher Columbus, financed by Spanish capital, sailed forth into the unknown western sea in 1492, he was yielding to the thirst for new knowledge and new experiences that characterized the whole Renaissance. Sir Francis Drake, who sailed round the world in 1577–1580, and Sir Walter Raleigh,[1] who founded colonies in the New World a few years later, were only two of a host of Englishmen who visited strange and far-off lands during the reign of Elizabeth.

Returning sailors brought back marvelous accounts of countries whose wonders confirmed or surpassed the wild tales contained in medieval books of travel. When explorers told of lands where there was no king or where the king was elected by the people, thoughtful Englishmen began to question whether in truth their own sovereign ruled by divine right, as they had been taught to believe. When travelers described nations that seemed to get along very well with social systems and ideas of right and wrong which were quite different from those of the English, these same thinkers began to investigate the whole question of human relationships and the basis of morality. Thus the foundations were laid for later and more democratic theories of government and a new interpretation of the duties and rights of man. These Renaissance theorists also helped to create a background for the modern study of primitive society and of sociology in general.

Of all the newly discovered countries the one that especially fascinated the English was America. Englishmen felt that a new world had been opened up to them. They looked upon America as a land of marvels and of untold possibilities. The Spaniard Ponce de León imagined that the Fountain of Youth was located somewhere in America; the English were not far behind him in the wonders that they attributed to the land beyond the Atlantic. To the people of the Renaissance, America was not only a new world; it was a new Eden.*

This feeling about America was intensified by unsettled conditions in England. During the sixteenth and seventeenth centuries religious intolerance increased; large tracts of country were absorbed by great landed estates; and many poor people, driven from their homes, were forced to become wanderers. Thus religious, economic, and social conditions at home were largely responsible for the fact that many English people, well-to-do as well as poor, emigrated to the New World, carrying with them their religious and political beliefs and their literary traditions. The idea of America as a land of freedom, plenty, and opportunity began to take shape during the Renaissance.

[1] For biography see page 699.

ENGLISH LITERATURE DURING THE RENAISSANCE

The Renaissance was accompanied by an enormous increase in the production and quality of English literature. In England the latter part of the Renaissance was especially an age of poetry. Both lyric and dramatic poets took up the new views, beautified them, and sang of them in a vast number of compositions. Many lyric poems of the English Renaissance deal with love, a theme the Elizabethans never tired of treating. They wrote in praise of peace, of springtime, and of the simple life ; but, above all, of love — heavenly love and earthly love, love between God and man, love between friends, and love between man and woman. Following Italian and French models, they idealized the relations between men and women until love became pure and beautiful like the Platonic * love of ancient Greece. Indeed, the Elizabethans left little for modern poets to say on the subject of love.

Elizabethan lyric poetry was composed in many forms, the most important of which is the sonnet.* Sir Philip Sidney (p. 157), Spenser (p. 158), Shakespeare (p. 159), and numerous other writers composed long series of sonnets telling of their love for real or imaginary ladies.

English narrative poetry of the Renaissance is best represented by Spenser's *Faerie Queene* (p. 166), which, though based largely on medieval themes, reflects the general spirit of the Renaissance.

English prose also made a distinct advance during the Renaissance. The Reformation was marked by several English translations of the Bible. Thanks to these and to the introduction of printing,[1] common men could now read the Scriptures in their own tongue, a thing they had never been able to do before. The most important translations are those known as the King James [2] Bible (p. 161), used by Protestants, and the Douay * (Douay-Reims) Version, used by Roman Catholics. There were also translations of foreign nonreligious works into English prose. Collections of short stories and anecdotes were widely read, and there were many long pastoral * narratives dealing with the loves and adventures of shepherds and shepherdesses. Plots taken from these translations were used frequently by Shakespeare and other dramatists. They also helped to lay the foundation for the modern novel.

The most important fact concerning Elizabethan prose is that the authors began to pay more attention to style. The style known as euphuism,* used by John Lyly * and other writers, was, it is true, self-conscious, artificial, and often obscure, but it nevertheless marks a forward step in the history of English prose. The style of Bacon's *Essays* (p. 175) shows a distinct advance in the arrangement of the words and sentences. The prose of the English Bible (p. 161) is a model of simplicity and clearness.

[1] See page 33.   [2] See "James* I."

Queen Elizabeth visits Sir Francis Drake on board his ship after his return from circumnavigating the globe

The crowning glory of the English Renaissance is the drama. Never before or since have English plays been so abundant or so excellent.

By the time Shakespeare began writing plays English playwrights had before them all the necessary raw materials out of which to compose great dramas. Many of their plays have been lost, and little is known of the lives of the dramatists themselves; but enough of their work remains to convince us of their industry as playwrights and their skill as dramatic writers.

THE LONDON THEATERS OF SHAKESPEARE'S DAY

When Shakespeare came up to London from his native village of Stratford, the capital was still like a medieval town. It was enclosed by stone walls, and its population, including the inhabitants of the little suburbs outside the walls, hardly amounted to two hundred thousand people. The houses were mostly of wood, and the sanitation and policing were wretched; but the streets, though narrow, were gay with bright-colored costumes and filled with people of all kinds and conditions. Here Shakespeare saw many types of characters who afterward appeared in his plays.

The city authorities of London discouraged theatrical performances as evil influences; hence the earliest theaters, the oldest of which was erected in 1576, had to be built outside the city walls. Many of Shakespeare's plays were acted at the Globe, a theater situated on the south side of the Thames in a rather disreputable district frequented largely by underworld characters.

The Elizabethan theater was a wooden structure either round or having six or eight sides, but without a roof. Around the walls were balconies containing the higher-priced seats, while the ground floor, called the pit, was simply an open space where the poorer spectators stood to watch the play unless they had brought stools to sit on. The stage consisted of a wooden platform extending out into the audience without the great arch and heavy drop-curtain that separate the modern stage from the body of the theater. As there was no adequate police protection, the audience made fun of the actors whenever they felt inclined, and pickpockets (called "cutpurses") plied their trade, even during the performances. Both actors and playwrights were generally looked down upon socially. Women's parts were taken by boys, and there were several theatrical companies composed entirely of children.

After the death of Shakespeare the drama became rapidly less important until the Puritan Period (p. 184), when the London theaters were closed by act of Parliament.

England in Shakespeare's time

Correlation of English Literature with Historical Events during the Elizabethan Period

HISTORICAL EVENTS		LITERARY LANDMARKS
End of WARS OF THE ROSES*	1485	
Reign of HENRY VII	1485–1509	
Discovery of AMERICA	1492	
	About 1500	Beginning of HUMANISM in ENGLAND
Reign of HENRY VIII	1509–1547	
	1552(?)	SPENSER born. Died 1599
	1552	RALEIGH born. Died 1618
	1553	LYLY born. Died 1606
	1554	SIDNEY born. Died 1586
	1557	TOTTEL'S Miscellany (see Sonnet*)
Reign of ELIZABETH	1558–1603	
	1561	BACON born. Died 1626
	1564	SHAKESPEARE born. Died 1616
		MARLOWE born. Died 1593
	1573(?)	JONSON born. Died 1637
	1576	First LONDON theater
FRANCIS DRAKE first circumnavigates the globe	1577–1580	
	1577	HOLINSHED, Chronicles
	1579	LYLY, Euphues
MARY QUEEN OF SCOTS executed	1587	
Defeat of the SPANISH ARMADA	1588	MARLOWE, Doctor Faustus
	1590	SPENSER, Faerie Queene (Books I–III)
	1590–1616	SHAKESPEARE'S works
	1591	RALEIGH, The Revenge[1]
	1597	BACON, Essays (First Series)
	About 1600	SHAKESPEARE, As You Like It
	About 1601	SHAKESPEARE, Julius Cæsar
Death of ELIZABETH	1603	
	About 1606	SHAKESPEARE, Macbeth
First settlement of the ENGLISH in AMERICA	1607	
	1611	King James Bible
	1616	Death of SHAKESPEARE

The Elizabethan Period also includes the writings of Thomas Dekker (1570?–1641?), Francis Beaumont (1584–1616), and John Fletcher (1579–1625).

[1] Tennyson's poem, based in part on Raleigh's account of the last fight of the *Revenge*, is given in the revised edition of *Adventure* of this series.

The Globe Theater, where many of Shakespeare's plays were performed

THE ELIZABETHAN PERIOD IN SONG AND STORY

Read again the introduction to "The Old-English Period in Song and Story" (p. 17). Next run through the following titles and see which you prefer. Then try to get the books and read them.

POETRY

ALDRICH, THOMAS BAILEY. "Guilielmus Rex" and "At Stratford-upon-Avon," in *Poems.* Houghton Mifflin Company.

BURTON, RICHARD. "Across the Fields to Anne," in Stevenson's *Home Book of Verse.* Henry Holt and Company.

KEATS, JOHN. "Lines on the Mermaid Tavern."

KIPLING, RUDYARD. "The Looking Glass," "With Drake in the Tropics," "Together," and "The Craftsman," in *Verse, Inclusive Edition, 1885–1932.* Doubleday, Doran & Company, Inc.

MILTON, JOHN. "On Shakespeare" (p. 198).

NEWBOLT, SIR HENRY. "Drake's Drum," in *Poems, New and Old.* John Murray.

NOYES, ALFRED. *Tales of the Mermaid Tavern,* "The Admiral's Ghost," and *Drake.* Frederick A. Stokes Company.

TENNYSON, ALFRED LORD. "The *Revenge*" (in the revised edition of *Adventure* of this series).

DRAMA

ANDERSON, MAXWELL. *Elizabeth the Queen, a Play in Three Acts* and *Mary of Scotland, a Play in Three Acts.* Samuel French, Inc.

DRINKWATER, JOHN. *Mary Stuart.* Houghton Mifflin Company.

MASEFIELD, JOHN. *End and Beginning.* The Macmillan Company.

PEABODY, JOSEPHINE PRESTON. *Fortune and Men's Eyes,* a play based on Shakespeare's Sonnet XXIX (p. 159), and *Marlowe.* Houghton Mifflin Company.

PROSE

AINSWORTH, HARRISON. *The Tower of London* and *Windsor Castle.* Everyman's Library (E. P. Dutton & Co., Inc.).

BENNETT, JOHN. *Master Skylark: A Story of Shakespeare's Time.* D. Appleton-Century Company, Inc.

CLARKE, MRS. MARY COWDEN. *Girlhood of Shakespeare's Heroines.* 3 vols. Everyman's Library (E. P. Dutton & Co., Inc.).

IRVING, WASHINGTON. "Stratford on Avon," in *The Sketchbook.*

KINGSLEY, CHARLES. *Westward Ho!*

KIPLING, RUDYARD. *Rewards and Fairies.* Doubleday, Doran & Company, Inc.

LAMB, CHARLES and MARY. *Tales from Shakespeare.*

MAJOR, CHARLES. *Dorothy Vernon of Haddon Hall* and *When Knighthood Was in Flower.* Grosset & Dunlap.

SABATINI, RAPHAEL. *The Sea Hawk.* Houghton Mifflin Company.

SCOTT, SIR WALTER. *The Fortunes of Nigel.*

STEVENSON, ROBERT LOUIS. *The Black Arrow.*

DRAMA

A DRAMA is a story intended to be spoken and acted on the stage. When we read a play or see one performed, we are interested primarily in finding out what the characters will do under certain circumstances. Or, to put it a little differently, a drama reveals action resulting from human character.

Though no two plays develop in exactly the same way, the plots of all typical dramas of five acts may be conveniently divided into several parts, each of which has its own particular dramatic purpose. Since few plays open at the very beginning of the story, the dramatist usually starts by giving one or more scenes which inform the audience regarding the time, the place, the chief characters and their relations to one another, and whatever else is necessary to an intelligent understanding of the remainder of the play. This part is known as the *introduction*, or *exposition*. In *Macbeth*, the Shakespearean play given below, the exposition is contained in Act I, Scenes i and ii. After the introduction comes the *complication*, or *rising action*. During the complication we see the tying of the knot that is to be untied at the end of the play. In *Macbeth* we see the chief character, spurred on by the Witches' prophecy and his wife's ambition, sweep upward in his career of unbridled crime toward apparent success. The rising action usually comes to an end about the middle of the third act, at a point known as the *pivot*, *climax*, or *turning-point*. At the turning-point the forces working for and against the chief character are about evenly balanced. Up to the turning-point a comedy looks as if it would end badly for the chief character, but at the turning-point the action turns toward a happy ending. The case of a tragedy is just the opposite. Up to the turning-point a tragedy looks as if it would end in success, but at the turning-point the action turns definitely toward a tragic ending.

In *Macbeth* the turning-point is the murder of Banquo in Act III, Scene iii. Up to then Macbeth has been successful; there his downfall begins. After the turning-point comes the *resolution*, often called the *falling*, or *descending*, *action*, leading to the final *conclusion*, which may be either comic or tragic. During the resolution of a tragedy (which in *Macbeth* begins with the escape of Fleance, Act III, Scene iii), the chief character is overcome by the forces that have opposed him. Thus a typical drama, like a typical novel (p. 432), holds our attention because it represents human beings face to face with the wills of other human beings or with other forces that may or may not be too much for them. It is this ebb and flow of conflict that forms the chief source of interest in both the novel and the drama.

A performance of a scene from a mystery play in England during the Middle Ages

THE ENGLISH DRAMA BEFORE SHAKESPEARE

The English drama began in the Middle Ages after the Norman Conquest (1066 A.D.). The earliest plays in England were given in connection with the services of the church. They represented scenes from Bible stories, and are known as mystery plays, or mysteries. One of the oldest mystery plays that we know of represented the meeting between the Marys and the angels at the tomb of Jesus (Luke 24 : 1–10), and was performed in connection with the church service on Easter morning. Later other well-known Bible stories were dramatized, until there was a long series of little plays or scenes representing the whole Biblical history of mankind from the creation of Adam, as described in Genesis, down to the Last Judgment.

These mystery plays were at first performed by monks, in the church itself, but they were later taken over by the trade guilds, or crafts (unions of merchants and tradesmen), and were given at least once a year in most of the large towns of England. Each guild, or craft, presented the scene which it could depict best, the water merchants representing Noah's Flood; the butchers, the sacrifice of Isaac; and so on. Each scene was mounted on a "pageant" wagon, or float, the various wagons moving in order through the streets and stopping at certain points so that the crowd might see the performance. Though crude in many respects, the mystery plays contained not only the germs of the later serious drama, but also a certain amount of comedy, as in the scene where Noah's wife boxes her husband's ears when he tries to force her to go into the ark.

Side by side with the later mystery plays there existed another type of medieval drama known as the miracle play, which represented the legend of a saint or martyr.

A third type of play was the morality play, or morality. A morality play is a dramatized allegory,* presenting a story that illustrates some underlying abstract truth or life lesson. In one of the most impressive morality plays, entitled *Everyman*, a character representing the soul and called Everyman appears in a succession of scenes that depict human life. Everyman is summoned by a character impersonating Death to appear before God and give an account of himself. He is accompanied by various companions, — Youth, Friendship, Wealth, etc., — to whom he appeals for help; but as he approaches the grave they all forsake him except Good Deeds, whom he has despised. There were also many other morality plays representing religious or political conditions in allegorical form.[1]

Besides the mysteries, miracle plays, and moralities there were plays about Saint* George, Robin* Hood, and other folk characters, and short plays known as interludes. Interludes were usually light and humorous.

Before Shakespeare's time we also find plays written in imitation of ancient Roman tragedy or the comedies of the Latin dramatists Plautus * and Terence.* These imitations of Latin plays made the English public familiar with several dramatic features, such as having a ghost as a character, a device afterward to become famous through Shakespeare's use of it in *Julius Cæsar*, in *Hamlet*, and in *Macbeth*.

THE ENGLISH DRAMA OF THE ELIZABETHAN PERIOD

The classical influences, together with the mysteries, miracle plays, moralities, and interludes, led up to and made possible the wonderful outburst of dramatic production that marked the Age of Shakespeare. Between the year 1580 and the appearance of Shakespeare's earliest plays about ten years later, John Lyly* (lĭl'ĭ) learned to write clever comedies in a graceful though often artificial style,[2] and Christopher Marlowe,[3] in his *Doctor Faustus* and other dramas, established blank* verse as the accepted form of poetry for dignified drama. These and other playwrights prepared the public to understand and appreciate the best that dramatic genius could produce.

As Shakespeare progressed in plot and character portrayal he also

---

[1] About two hundred years later Bunyan's *Pilgrim's Progress* (p. 205) presents in narrative form an allegory such as might have been made the subject of a medieval morality play.

[2] See "euphuism."*   [3] For biography see page 699.

Galloway

Shakespeare's birthplace, Stratford on Avon

learned how to use blank* verse more skillfully and how to combine it successfully with rhyme and prose.

Among Shakespeare's greatest contemporaries in the drama were Marlowe,[1] Dekker, Ben Jonson,[2] and Beaumont and Fletcher, the last two usually mentioned together because they frequently collaborated in writing plays.

THE ENGLISH DRAMA AFTER SHAKESPEARE

During the Puritan Period (p. 183) the drama became less and less important and more and more sensational and corrupt till an act of Parliament closed the theaters in 1642. After the restoration of Charles II to the English throne in 1660, the theaters reopened and plays became abundant; but the comedies were generally cynical and unpleasantly realistic, and the tragedies were far-fetched in plot and bombastic in language. During the Transition Period (p. 289) Goldsmith, in *She Stoops to Conquer* (1773), and Sheridan, in *The Rivals* (1775), introduced a more wholesome spirit into

---

[1] For biography see page 699.   [2] For biography see page 700.

Keystone

Trinity Church at Stratford on Avon, where Shakespeare is buried

English comedy and led the way to the clever, mildly satirical* comedies of the nineteenth century.

In general the drama declined during the Romantic and Victorian periods (pp. 313 and 425), and the interest in poetry[1] and the novel [2] increased. Late in the nineteenth century the drama took on renewed life. Playwrights, like other authors, began to take their work more seriously and to strive after greater realism.[3] Their plays often dealt with unconventional themes and reflected new points of view regarding society and human institutions, especially marriage. Whereas the older love dramas had frequently ended with the happy wedding, recent playwrights, such as George Bernard Shaw, show a fondness for writing plays that deal with the problems that arise after marriage. To them marriage is the beginning of a human problem rather than its solution. Contemporary dramatists, especially those who have written since the World War (1914–1918), often treat social problems far more frankly than their predecessors did. Some plays go so far as to present human life and society as a complicated puzzle arousing only cynicism or despair. On the other hand, some of our most

[1] Pages 317 and 428.   [2] Pages 318 and 432.   [3] Page 569.

popular contemporary English dramatists seek to present plays that are amusing and inspiring to the audience, rather than depressing and discouraging. Barrie[1] has won a high place in recent literature largely by writing plays that mingle realism with sentiment in such a way as to avoid, on the one hand, Victorian mawkishness and, on the other, gross materialism and dark pessimism. Other dramatic writers of the present day produce movies or stage plays based on fairy tales or romances, or on the lives of favorite historical personages, such as Queen Victoria and Abraham Lincoln. Indeed, recent English drama, both on the screen and on the stage, shows a strong tendency toward introducing some romance and idealism into even the most realistic and gloomy plots.

Not long after Shakespeare's time, prose began to take the place of rhyme and blank verse in the drama. For the last two hundred years all plays intended to be acted rather than to be read in private, with a few exceptions, have been written in prose.

Throughout all the changes which the drama has undergone in tone, technique, and response to public taste, Shakespeare has constantly retained his pre-eminence as the greatest dramatic poet of the English race.

WILLIAM SHAKESPEARE[2] (1564-1616)

Macbeth

Shakespeare's *Macbeth* has many features that make it an especially good Shakespearean play for reading and study. (1) It contains an easily detected underlying theme; (2) the characters are clearly drawn; (3) the dramatic conflicts of will and other forces are intense and are superbly presented in setting, words, and actions; (4) the play is based on historic facts, but, (5) as it stands, it is almost entirely the work of Shakespeare's powerful creative imagination.

The Plot

The underlying theme of *Macbeth* is the destruction wrought by misdirected ambition. Macbeth, a gallant general, the commander in chief of the armies of Scotland, finds himself a popular hero. Inspired by the prophecy of three Witches, he is fired with the ambition to make himself king. His wife, knowing her husband's mind and heart, determines to aid him. The way to the throne lies through the murder of the reigning king. Then, having gained the throne, Macbeth finds he can hide this first crime only by murdering all who suspect his guilt. He even goes so far as to cause the needless butchery of the wife and children of the honest and noble-hearted Macduff. Finally, the revolt of the people and the suicide of Lady Macbeth leave the guilty Macbeth alone and friendless, to fall before the vengeance of the mighty thane Macduff.

[1] For biography see page 747. [2] For biography see page 698.

The Characters

MACBETH

The principal character is Macbeth, a man so dauntless in battle that single-handed he slew the "merciless Macdonwald," and showed no more fear of the powerful "Norweyan lord" than an eagle does of a sparrow. Yet he is a man whose wife declares him to be

> "too full of the milk of human kindness
> To catch the nearest way"

to the throne by murdering the king. He is a man who can face an army, but who wilts before a witch; who is a hero in battle, but a coward at the thought of his own crimes; who allows a vague prophecy to lead him from his high estate and from murder to murder until he is

> "in blood
> Stepp'd in so far that, should I wade no more,
> Returning were as tedious as go o'er,"

and ends his life deserted and unhonored, slain by one whom he had most grievously injured.

LADY MACBETH

Next to Macbeth is Lady Macbeth, a keenly intellectual, proud, aspiring woman who risks all to help her husband to realize his ambition. She is his complement. When he falters, she urges him on; when remorse threatens to undo him, she comforts him; but, left alone, she broods over their crimes until her reason fails and she dies, probably by her own hand.

BANQUO (băng'kwō)

In direct contrast to Macbeth and Lady Macbeth is Banquo. He too is a soldier, the equal of Macbeth in prowess and honor; but, unlike Macbeth, he resists the temptation to act unworthily. To him also the Witches promise exaltation; but he merely laughs at them and goes his own way, rejoicing that he has kept his life pure and his honor unsullied. It is by Banquo's nobility of nature that Macbeth feels himself rebuked until the exasperated tyrant causes the murder of his former companion and friend.

MACDUFF

Of all the prominent characters in *Macbeth* the most likable is Macduff. He is a valiant soldier who loves his country more than anything else. He has no use for fine speeches or for those who make them. He suspects Macbeth, and he says what he thinks. He can fight, and he does so until, finally, through great courage, he beheads Macbeth in battle.

THE WITCHES

The dramatic action is dominated by three weird sisters, the Witches of the heath. They enter as the play begins; they speed Macbeth on his upward path; they open the way for his final downfall. In conflict with their power is the will of Macbeth. He musters all his courage to thwart them, but to no purpose. Their dark sayings and their hell broth, with its ghostly apparitions, prevail, and the great leader goes to his doom. In Banquo, on the other hand, the Witches produce the opposite effect. Because he is innocent in heart and mind, he laughs at their riddles and keeps his "bosom franchis'd, and allegiance clear."

The scene of "Macbeth" in Scotland

Where Shakespeare Got His Plot

As in the case of most of his plays, Shakespeare did not invent the essentials of the plot, but took old material and breathed into it the breath of life. The basis of *Macbeth* is found in a book which was one of Shakespeare's favorites, Holinshed's *Chronicles*. This book is a history of England, Scotland, and Ireland, containing a mixture of legend and historic truth. According to Holinshed there was a Macbeth who, with the help of his wife, did murder a king. In the *Chronicles* Shakespeare found also the names of Macduff and certain other characters of the play. The moving wood and the great strength of a child of unnatural birth are devices as old as literature itself.

These are the elements that William Shakespeare took and, about the year 1606, shaped, by the power of his incomparable genius, into the play of *Macbeth*, a "tempest set to music."

Preliminary Hints

1. Locate on the map above the following places: Forres, Inverness, Scone, Birnam Wood, Dunsinane, Fife.

2. As you read the play, make a note of all the references which seem to indicate that Shakespeare had really visited Scotland. See, for example, I, vi.

3. Notice what scenes of the play are all or partly in prose. In each case try to find a good reason for Shakespeare's use of prose.

DRAMATIS PERSONAE

DUNCAN, king of Scotland.
MALCOLM, } his sons.
DONALBAIN,
MACBETH, } generals of the king's army.
BANQUO,
MACDUFF,
LENNOX,
ROSS, } noblemen of Scotland.
MENTEITH,
ANGUS,
CAITHNESS,
FLEANCE, son to Banquo.
SIWARD, earl of Northumberland, general of
  the English forces.
YOUNG SIWARD, his son.
SEYTON, an officer attending on Macbeth.
Boy, son to Macduff.

An English Doctor.
A Scotch Doctor.
A Captain.
A Porter.
An Old Man.

Lady MACBETH.
Lady MACDUFF.
Gentlewoman attending on Lady Macbeth.
HECATE.
Three Witches.
Apparitions.

Lords, Gentlemen, Officers, Soldiers, Murderers, Attendants, and Messengers.

SCENE: *Scotland; England.*

ACT I

SCENE I. *A desert place*

[Short as this scene is, it sounds the keynote
for the entire play. The Witches, the wild-
ness of place and weather, and the solemn
words of line 7 fill the scene with the promise
of tragic events.]

Thunder and lightning. Enter three
WITCHES

1 WITCH.] When shall we three meet
  again
In thunder, lightning, or in rain?

2 WITCH. When the hurlyburly's done,
When the battle's lost and won.
3 WITCH. That will be ere the set of
  sun.
1 WITCH. Where the place?
2 WITCH.   Upon the heath.
3 WITCH. There to meet with Macbeth.
1 WITCH. I come, Graymalkin.[1]
2 WITCH. Paddock[1] calls: — Anon!
ALL. Fair is foul, and foul is fair;[2] 10
Hover through the fog and filthy air.
                              [*Exeunt*]

SCENE II. *A camp near Forres*

[This scene reveals Macbeth's courage, his
prowess in battle, and the honor in which he
is held at court. The progress of the battle
is reported by a Captain and by Ross.]

Alarum[1] within. Enter DUNCAN, MAL-
COLM, DONALBAIN, LENNOX, *with* Attendants, *meeting a bleeding* CAPTAIN

DUNCAN. What bloody man is that?
He can report,

  ¹ Alarm, a trumpet call.

As seemeth by his plight, of the revolt
The newest state.
    MALCOLM.   This is the sergeant
Who like a good and hardy soldier
  fought
'Gainst my captivity. Hail, brave friend!

  ¹ *Graymalkin, Paddock.* Graymalkin, a cat, and
    Paddock, a frog or toad, are devils in the form
    of animals attending on two of the Witches.
  ² *Fair . . . fair.* To witches fair things seem
    ugly, and ugly things seem fair.

Say to the king the knowledge of the broil
As thou didst leave it.
    CAPTAIN.   Doubtful it stood,
As two spent swimmers that do cling together
And choke their art.[1] The merciless Macdonwald —
10 Worthy to be a rebel, for to that[2]
The multiplying villainies of nature
Do swarm upon him — from the western isles
Of kerns and gallowglasses[3] is supplied;
And fortune, on his damned quarrel smiling,
Show'd like a rebel's whore:[4] but all's too weak;
For brave Macbeth — well he deserves that name —
Disdaining fortune, with his brandish'd steel,
Which smok'd with bloody execution,
Like valour's minion[5] carv'd out his passage
20 Till he fac'd the slave;
Which[6] ne'er shook hands, nor bade farewell to him,
Till he unseam'd[7] him from the nave[8] to the chaps,[9]
And fix'd his head upon our battlements.
    DUNCAN. O valiant cousin! worthy gentleman!
    CAPTAIN. As whence the sun 'gins his reflection
Shipwrecking storms and direful thunders break,
So from that spring whence comfort seem'd to come

Discomfort swells.[1] Mark, king of Scotland, mark:
No sooner justice had, with valour arm'd,
Compell'd these skipping kerns to trust their heels, 30
But the Norweyan[2] lord, surveying vantage,[3]
With furbish'd arms and new supplies of men,
Began a fresh assault.
    DUNCAN.   Dismay'd not this
Our captains, Macbeth and Banquo?
    CAPTAIN.   Yes;
As sparrows eagles,[4] or the hare the lion.
If I say sooth, I must report they were
As cannons overcharg'd with double cracks[5];
So they doubly redoubled strokes upon the foe:
Except[6] they meant to bathe in reeking wounds,
Or memorize another Golgotha,[7] 40
I cannot tell —
But I am faint, my gashes cry for help.
    DUNCAN. So well thy words become thee as thy wounds;
They smack of honour both. Go get him surgeons.

              [*Exit* CAPTAIN, *attended*]

Enter ROSS *and* ANGUS

Who comes here?
    MALCOLM. The worthy thane[8] of Ross.
    LENNOX. What a haste looks through his eyes! So should he look
That seems to speak things strange.
    ROSS.   God save the king!
    DUNCAN. Whence cam'st thou, worthy thane?

---

[1] *choke their art.* Interfere with each other.
[2] *for to that.* Because to that end.
[3] *kerns and gallowglasses.* Light-armed and heavy-armed troops, probably Irish who had settled in the "western isles" of Scotland.
[4] *Show'd . . . whore.* Appeared at first favorable, then unfavorable.
[5] *valour's minion.* The favorite of valor.
[6] Macbeth.
[7] Ripped open.
[8] Navel.
[9] Jaws.

[1] *As . . . swells.* As destructive storms sometimes come at sunrise, so at the moment of victory comes news of another attack.
[2] Norwegian.
[3] *surveying vantage.* Seeing a good chance.
[4] *As sparrows eagles.* As much as sparrows dismay (that is, terrify) eagles.
[5] Shot.   [6] Whether.
[7] *memorize . . Golgotha.* Make another scene of bloodshed as famous as the scene of the crucifixion of Jesus.   [8] Lord.

Ross.   From Fife, great king;
Where the Norweyan banners flout the
    sky
50 And fan our people cold.
Norway himself, with terrible numbers,
Assisted by that most disloyal traitor,
The thane of Cawdor, began a dismal
    conflict;
Till that Bellona's bridegroom,[1] lapp'd
    in proof,[2]
Confronted him with self-comparisons,[3]
Point against point,[4] rebellious arm
    'gainst arm,
Curbing his lavish[5] spirit; and, to
    conclude,
The victory fell on us.

Duncan.   Great happiness!
Ross.   That now
Sweno, the Norways' king, craves com-
    position[1];
Nor would we deign[2] him burial of his
    men   60
Till he disbursed, at Saint Colme's inch,[3]
Ten thousand dollars to our general use.
Duncan. No more that thane of
    Cawdor shall deceive
Our bosom interest.[4] Go pronounce his
    present[5] death,
And with his former title greet Macbeth.[6]
Ross. I'll see it done.
Duncan. What he hath lost, noble
    Macbeth hath won.   [Exeunt]

Scene III. *A heath near Forres*

[The Witches increase the feeling of horror.
Macbeth is introduced. The Witches greet
him and urge on his ambition. Left alone,
he speaks of murder. He begins to yield to
temptation. He resolves to seek the king.]

Thunder. Enter the three Witches

1 Witch. Where hast thou been,
    sister?
2 Witch. Killing swine.
3 Witch. Sister, where thou?
1 Witch. A sailor's wife had chest-
    nuts in her lap,
And munch'd, and munch'd, and
    munch'd. "Give me," quoth I:
"Aroint thee,[6] witch!" the rump-fed[7]
    ronyon[8] cries.
Her husband 's to Aleppo[9] gone, master
    o' the Tiger:
But in a sieve[10] I'll thither sail,

And, like[7] a rat without a tail,[8]
I'll do, I'll do, and I'll do.[9]   10
2 Witch. I'll give thee a wind.
1 Witch. Thou 'rt kind.
3 Witch. And I another.
1 Witch. I myself have all the other;
And the very ports they blow,
All the quarters that they know
I' the shipman's card.[10]
I'll drain him dry as hay.
Sleep shall neither night nor day
Hang upon his pent-house lid[11];   20
He shall live a man forbid[12]:
Weary se'nnights[13] nine times nine
Shall he dwindle,[14] peak, and pine:

---

[1] Macbeth, referred to poetically as the husband
    of Bellona, an ancient goddess of war.
[2] *lapp'd in proof.* Clad in tested armor.
[3] *Confronted . . . self-comparisons.* Opposed to
    him someone as good as he was.
[4] Sword to sword.   [5] Unrestrained.
[6] *Aroint thee.* Go away, begone.   [7] Fat.
[8] A term of abuse with no special meaning.
[9] A town of Turkey in Asia, the most remote
    place the dramatist could think of.
[10] Witches were said to be able to sail in a sieve
    (sifter).

[1] Terms of peace.
[2] Allow.
[3] Inchcolm, isle of Saint Columba in the Firth
    of Forth.
[4] *bosom interest.* Intimate affection.
[5] Immediate.
[6] *Go . . . Macbeth.* Sentence him to immediate
    death and make Macbeth Thane of Cawdor.
[7] In the form of.
[8] *rat . . . tail.* According to an old superstition,
    when a witch took the form of an animal, the
    animal was imperfect.
[9] *I'll . . . do.* I'll do something terrible.
[10] A compass.
[11] *pent-house lid.* Here, eyelid.
[12] Under a curse.
[13] A "se'nnight" is a week.   [14] Grow thin.

Though his bark cannot be lost,
Yet it shall be tempest-tost.
Look what I have.
2 WITCH. Show me, show me.
1 WITCH. Here I have a pilot's thumb,
Wreck'd as homeward he did come.

[*Drum within*]

30 3 WITCH. A drum, a drum!
Macbeth doth come.
ALL. The weird sisters, hand in hand,
Posters[1] of the sea and land,
Thus do go about, about:
Thrice to thine, and thrice to mine,
And thrice again, to make up nine.
Peace! the charm's wound up.

Enter MACBETH *and* BANQUO

MACBETH. So foul and fair a day I
have not seen.
BANQUO. How far is 't call'd to Forres? What are these
40 So wither'd, and so wild in their attire,
That look not like th' inhabitants o' the
earth,
And yet are on 't? Live you? or are you
aught
That man may question? You seem to
understand me,
By each at once her choppy [2] finger laying
Upon her skinny lips: you should be
women,
And yet your beards [3] forbid me to interpret
That you are so.
MACBETH. Speak, if you can: what
are you?
1 WITCH. All hail, Macbeth! hail to
thee, thane of Glamis!
2 WITCH. All hail, Macbeth! hail to
thee, thane of Cawdor!
50 3 WITCH. All hail, Macbeth, that
shalt be king hereafter!
BANQUO. Good sir, why do you start,
and seem to fear
Things that do sound so fair? — I' the
name of truth,

Are ye fantastical,[1] or that indeed
Which outwardly ye show? My noble
partner
You greet with present grace and great
prediction
Of noble having and of royal hope,
That he seems rapt withal[2]; to me you
speak not.
If you can look into the seeds of time,
And say which grain will grow and which
will not,
Speak, then, to me, who neither beg nor
fear   60
Your favours nor your hate.
1 WITCH. Hail!
2 WITCH. Hail!
3 WITCH. Hail!
1 WITCH. Lesser than Macbeth, and
greater.
2 WITCH. Not so happy, yet much
happier.
3 WITCH. Thou shalt get[3] kings,
though thou be none:
So all hail, Macbeth and Banquo!
1 WITCH. Banquo and Macbeth, all
hail!
MACBETH. Stay, you imperfect
speakers, tell me more: 70
By Sinel's [4] death I know I am thane of
Glamis;
But how of Cawdor? the thane of Cawdor lives,
A prosperous gentleman; and to be king
Stands not within the prospect of belief[5]
No more than to be Cawdor. Say from
whence
You owe this strange intelligence?[6] or why
Upon this blasted heath you stop our way
With such prophetic greeting? Speak, I
charge you.   [WITCHES *vanish*]
BANQUO. The earth hath bubbles as
the water has,
And these are of them. Whither are they
vanish'd?   80

---

1 Rapid travelers.
2 Chapped.
3 Witches were said to wear beards.
1 Imaginary.
2 *rapt withal.* Entranced with it.
3 Beget, be the father of.
4 Sinel was the father of Macbeth.
5 *Stands . . . belief.* Is unbelievable.
6 *owe . . . intelligence.* Got this strange news.

MACBETH. Into the air; and what seem'd corporal[1] melted

As breath into the wind. Would they had stay'd!

BANQUO. Were such things here as we do speak about?

Or have we eaten on the insane root[2]

That takes the reason prisoner?

MACBETH. Your children shall be kings.

BANQUO.　　　　You shall be king.

MACBETH. And thane of Cawdor too: went it not so?[3]

BANQUO. To th' selfsame tune and words. Who's here?

Enter ROSS *and* ANGUS

ROSS. The king hath happily receiv'd, Macbeth,

90　The news of thy success: and, when he reads

Thy personal venture in the rebels' fight,

His wonders and his praises do contend

Which should be thine or his;[4] silenc'd with that,[5]

In viewing o'er the rest o' the selfsame day,

He finds thee in the stout Norweyan ranks,

Nothing afeard of what thyself didst make,

Strange images of death.[6] As thick as hail[7]

Came post[8] with post; and every one did bear

Thy praises in his kingdom's great defence,

100 And pour'd them down before him.

ANGUS.　　　　　　　We are sent

To give thee from our royal master thanks;

Only to herald thee into his sight,[1]

Not pay thee.

ROSS. And, for an earnest[2] of a greater honour,

He bade me, from him, call thee thane of Cawdor;

In which addition,[3] hail, most worthy thane!

For it is thine.

BANQUO.　　　　[*Aside*] What, can the devil speak true?

MACBETH. The thane of Cawdor lives: why do you dress me

In borrow'd robes?

ANGUS.　　　　Who[4] was the thane lives yet;

But under heavy judgment bears that life 110

Which he deserves to lose. Whether he was combin'd[5]

With those of Norway, or did line[6] the rebel

With hidden help and vantage, or that with both

He labour'd in his country's wreck,[7] I know not;

But treasons capital, confess'd and prov'd,

Have overthrown him.

MACBETH.　　　　[*Aside*] Glamis, and thane of Cawdor!

The greatest is behind. [*To* ROSS *and* ANGUS] Thanks for your pains.

[*To* BANQUO] Do you not hope your children shall be kings,

When those that gave the thane of Cawdor to me

Promis'd no less to them?

BANQUO.　　　　　That trusted home 120

Might yet enkindle[8] you unto the crown,[9]

---

1 Made of flesh and blood.

2 *on . . . root.* Of a root that deprives one of his reason.

3 *went . . . so?* Was not that the Witches' prediction?

4 *His . . . his.* The king does not know whether he ought to wonder at or praise you.

5 That contention.

6 *Nothing . . . death.* Not afraid of the death you were causing.

7 *As . . . hail.* As fast as hailstones follow each other.　　　　8 Messenger.

1 *herald . . . sight.* Conduct thee to the king.

2 Pledge, promise.　　　　3 Title.

4 He who.

5 Allied.　　　6 Re-enforce.

7 *in . . . wreck.* To ruin his country.

8 Here, encourage.

9 *That . . . crown.* That partly fulfilled prophecy, if trusted to the end, might elevate you to the throne.

Besides the thane of Cawdor. But 'tis
  strange;
And oftentimes, to win us to our harm,
The instruments of darkness tell us
  truths,
Win us with honest trifles, to betray 's[1]
In deepest consequence.[2]
Cousins, a word, I pray you.
  MACBETH.   [Aside] Two truths are
    told,
As happy prologues to the swelling
  act
Of the imperial theme.[3] — I thank you,
  gentlemen.—
130 [Aside] This supernatural soliciting[4]
Cannot be ill; cannot be good: if ill,
Why hath it given me earnest[5] of
  success,
Commencing in a truth? I am thane of
  Cawdor:
If good, why do I yield to that sugges-
  tion[6]
Whose horrid image doth unfix my
  hair
And make my seated[7] heart knock at my
  ribs,
Against the use of nature?[8]   Present
  fears[9]
Are less than horrible imaginings.
My thought, whose murder yet is but
  fantastical,[10]
140 Shakes so my single state of man[11] that
  function

Is smother'd in surmise,[1] and nothing is
But what is not.
  BANQUO.   Look, how our partner's
    rapt.
  MACBETH. [Aside] If chance will have
    me king, why, chance may crown me,
Without my stir.[2]
  BANQUO.   New honours come upon
    him,
Like our strange garments,[3] cleave not to
  their mould
But with the aid of use.
  MACBETH.   [Aside] Come what
    come may,
Time and the hour runs through the
  roughest day.[4]
  BANQUO. Worthy Macbeth, we stay
    upon your leisure.[5]
  MACBETH. Give me your favour:[6] my
    dull brain was wrought
With things forgotten.[7] Kind gentle-
  men, your pains   150
Are register'd where every day I turn
The leaf to read them.[8] Let us toward
  the king.
Think upon what hath chanc'd; and, at
  more time,
The interim having weigh'd it, let us
  speak
Our free hearts each to other.
  BANQUO.   Very gladly.
  MACBETH. Till then, enough. Come,
    friends.   [Exeunt]

[1] Betray us.
[2] deepest consequence. Most serious results.
[3] As . . . theme. As introductions to the climax
  of my making myself king.
[4] Urging (toward something evil).
[5] A pledge.
[6] Temptation.
[7] Firmly placed.
[8] Whose . . . nature. The horrible idea of which
  doth make my hair stand on end, and my
  heart beat unnaturally.
[9] Objects of fear.
[10] Imaginary; in the mind.
[11] my . . . man. My weak human nature.

[1] function . . . surmise. Power of action ("function") is destroyed by thoughts of the future.
[2] Without my stir. Without my taking action.
[3] Like . . . garments. Like new clothes that have
  not been worn long enough to fit well.
[4] Come . . . day. Our lives are controlled by
  fate, even under the most unfavorable circumstances.
[5] we . . . leisure. We are ready when you are.
[6] Give . . . favour. I beg your pardon.
[7] wrought . . . forgotten. Troubled with things I
  had forgotten.
[8] your . . . them. I shall always remember the
  trouble you have taken on my account.

Scene IV. *Forres. The palace*

[A large part of the dramatic interest of this scene lies in the contrast between the king's confidence in Macbeth's loyalty and Macbeth's own treacherous thoughts.]

Flourish. Enter DUNCAN, MALCOLM, DONALBAIN, LENNOX, *and* Attendants

DUNCAN. Is execution done on Cawdor? Are not
Those in commission[1] yet return'd?
MALCOLM.   My liege,
They are not yet come back. But I have spoke
With one that saw him die; who did report
That very frankly he confess'd his treasons,
Implor'd your highness' pardon, and set forth
A deep repentance: nothing in his life
Became him like the leaving it; he died
As one that had been studied in his death[2]
10 To throw away the dearest thing he ow'd,[3]
As 'twere a careless trifle.
DUNCAN.   There's no art
To find the mind's construction in the face:[4]
He was a gentleman on whom I built
An absolute trust.

Enter MACBETH, BANQUO, ROSS, *and* ANGUS

                        O worthiest cousin!
The sin of my ingratitude even now
Was heavy on me. Thou art so far before,
That swiftest wing of recompense is slow
To overtake thee. Would thou hadst less deserv'd,

That the proportion[1] both of thanks and payment
Might have been mine! Only I have left to say,   20
More is thy due than more than all can pay.
MACBETH. The service and the loyalty I owe,
In doing it, pays itself. Your highness' part
Is to receive our duties; and our duties
Are to your throne and state children and servants;
Which do but what they should, by doing every thing
Safe toward your love and honour.[2]
DUNCAN.   Welcome hither:
I have begun to plant thee, and will labour
To make thee full of growing. Noble Banquo,
That hast no less deserv'd, nor must be known   30
No less to have done so, let me infold thee
And hold thee to my heart.
BANQUO.   There if I grow,
The harvest is your own.
DUNCAN.   My plenteous joys,
Wanton[3] in fulness, seek to hide themselves
In drops of sorrow. Sons, kinsmen, thanes,
And you whose places are the nearest, know,
We will establish our estate upon
Our eldest, Malcolm, whom we name hereafter
The Prince of Cumberland; which honour must
Not unaccompanied invest him only,[4]   40
But signs of nobleness, like stars, shall shine

---

[1] *Those in commission.* Those who were commissioned to execute Cawdor.
[2] *studied . . . death.* Carefully instructed how to die.
[3] Owned.
[4] *There's . . . face.* One cannot tell a man's character by his looks.

[1] Here, the larger amount.
[2] *Safe . . honour.* To assure you the love and honor we owe you.
[3] Uncontrolled.
[4] *which . . . only.* Which honor must not be given to him alone.

On all deservers. From hence to Inverness,
And bind us further[1] to you.

MACBETH. The rest is labour, which is not us'd for you.[2]
I'll be myself the harbinger,[3] and make joyful
The hearing of my wife with your approach;
So humbly take my leave.

DUNCAN. My worthy Cawdor!

MACBETH. [Aside] The Prince of Cumberland! that is a step
On which I must fall down, or else o'erleap,
For in my way it lies.[1] Stars, hide your fires; 50
Let not light see my black and deep desires;
The eye wink at[2] the hand; yet let that be
Which the eye fears, when it is done, to see.   [Exit]

DUNCAN. True, worthy Banquo; he is full so valiant,
And in his commendations I am fed;
It is a banquet to me. Let's after him,
Whose care is gone before to bid us welcome.
It is a peerless kinsman.

[Flourish. Exeunt]

SCENE V. Inverness. MACBETH'S castle

[Lady Macbeth's soliloquy is strained and tense with ambition for Macbeth. When he arrives, she urges him to take advantage of the king's visit.]

Enter LADY MACBETH, *alone, with a letter*

LADY MACBETH. [Reads]

They[4] met me in the day of success; and I have learn'd by the perfect'st report, they have more in them than mortal knowledge. When I burn'd in desire to question them further, they made themselves air, into which they vanish'd. Whiles I stood rapt in the wonder of it, came missives from the King, who all-hail'd me "Thane of Cawdor"; by which title, before, these weird sisters saluted
10 me, and referr'd me to the coming on of time, with "Hail, king that shalt be!" This have I thought good to deliver[5] thee, my dearest partner of greatness, that thou mightst not lose the dues[6] of rejoicing, by being ignorant of what greatness is promised thee. Lay it to thy heart, and farewell.

Glamis thou art, and Cawdor, and shalt be

What thou art promis'd. Yet do I fear thy nature;
It is too full o' the milk of human kindness[3]
To catch the nearest way:[4] thou wouldst be great; 20
Art not without ambition, but without
The illness[5] should attend it: what thou wouldst highly,
That wouldst thou holily; wouldst not play false,
And yet wouldst wrongly win: thou'ldst[6] have, great Glamis,
That which cries, 'Thus thou must do,' if thou have it;
And that which rather thou dost fear to do

---

[1] *that . . . lies.* Note how these words foreshadow Macbeth's fate.
[2] *wink at.* Pretend not to see.
[3] *too . . . kindness.* This is a troublesome phrase. Lady Macbeth seems to mean that her husband is too full of the ordinary unheroic qualities of human nature to do anything requiring hardness in order to gain the object of his ambition. She does not mean that he is too gentle and kindhearted.
[4] *the nearest way.* "The nearest way" is the murder of King Duncan.
[5] Wickedness.
[6] Thou wouldst.

---

[1] *bind us further.* Put me under further obligation.
[2] *The rest . . . you.* Leisure is work unless I use it for you.
[3] Advance agent, or messenger.   [4] The witches.
[5] Report.   [6] Here, satisfaction.

Than wishest should be undone. Hie thee
　　hither,
That I may pour my spirits in thine ear,
And chastise with the valour of my
　　tongue
30 All that impedes thee from the golden
　　round[1]
Which fate and metaphysical[2] aid doth
　　seem
To have thee crown'd withal.

　　　　　Enter a MESSENGER
　　　　　　　　What is your tidings?
MESSENGER. The king comes here to-
　　night.
LADY MACBETH.　　　　Thou'rt mad to
　　say it:
Is not thy master with him? who, were't
　　so,
Would have inform'd for preparation.
MESSENGER. So please you, it is true;
　　our thane is coming.
One of my fellows had the speed of him,[3]
Who, almost dead for breath, had
　　scarcely more
Than would make up his message.
LADY MACBETH.　　Give him tending;
40 He brings great news.
　　　　　　　　　[*Exit* MESSENGER]
　　　　　　The raven himself is hoarse
That croaks the fatal entrance of Duncan
Under my battlements. Come, you
　　spirits
That tend on mortal[4] thoughts, unsex me
　　here;
And fill me from the crown to the toe
　　top-full
Of direst cruelty! make thick my blood;
Stop up th' access and passage to re-
　　morse,
That no compunctious visitings of na-
　　ture[5]
Shake my fell[6] purpose, nor keep peace
　　between

The effect and it![1] Come to my woman's
　　breasts,
And take my milk for gall,[2] you mur-
　　d'ring ministers,[3]　　　　　　　　50
Wherever in your sightless[4] substances
You wait on nature's mischief! Come,
　　thick night,
And pall thee[5] in the dunnest smoke of hell,
That my keen knife see not the wound it
　　makes,
Nor heaven peep through the blanket of
　　the dark,
To cry, "Hold, hold!"

　　　　　　Enter MACBETH
　　　　Great Glamis! worthy Cawdor!
Greater than both, by the all-hail here-
　　after!
Thy letters have transported me beyond
This ignorant present, and I feel now
The future in the instant.
MACBETH.　　　　　　My dearest love, 60
Duncan comes here to-night.
LADY MACBETH.　　　　And when goes
　　hence?
MACBETH. To-morrow, as he pur-
　　poses.
LADY MACBETH.　　　　　O, never
Shall sun that morrow see!
Your face, my thane, is as a book where
　　men
May read strange matters. To beguile
　　the time,
Look like the time;[6] bear welcome in
　　your eye,
Your hand, your tongue; look like the
　　innocent flower,
But be the serpent under't. He that's
　　coming
Must be provided for; and you shall put
This night's great business into my dis-
　　patch,[7]　　　　　　　　　　　　70

---

[1] The crown.　　　　　　　　　[2] Supernatural.
[3] *had . . . him.* Outstripped him.
[4] Deadly, murderous.
[5] *compunctious . . . nature.* Natural feelings of
　　pity.　　　　　　　　　[6] Cruel.
D

[1] *keep . . . it.* Prevent my cruel purpose from at-
　　taining its result.
[2] *take . . . gall.* Make me hardhearted.
[3] *murd'ring ministers.* Evil spirits of murder.
[4] Invisible.　　[5] *pall thee.* Cover thyself.
[6] *To beguile . . . time.* To deceive other men, look
　　as other men expect you to look.
[7] Care and execution.

Which shall to all our nights and days to
  come
Give solely sovereign sway and master-
  dom.

MACBETH. We will speak further.
LADY MACBETH. Only look up clear;
To alter favour[1] ever is to fear.
Leave all the rest to me.   [*Exeunt*]

SCENE VI. *Before* MACBETH's *castle*

[In perhaps no other scene in Shakespeare is
dramatic irony* better illustrated than in this
short scene. The castle breathes quiet and
peace, but in this deceptive atmosphere move
forces of treachery and death.]

Hautboys[1] *and torches. Enter* DUNCAN,
MALCOLM, DONALBAIN, BANQUO,
LENNOX, MACDUFF, ROSS, ANGUS,
and Attendants

DUNCAN. This castle hath a pleasant
  seat[2]; the air
Nimbly and sweetly recommends itself
Unto our gentle senses.
BANQUO.   This guest of summer,
The temple-haunting martlet,[3] does ap-
  prove,
By his lov'd mansionry,[4] that the
  heaven's breath
Smells wooingly here: no jutty,[5] frieze,
Buttress, nor coign of vantage,[6] but this
  bird
Hath made his pendent bed and pro-
  creant cradle:[7]
Where they most breed and haunt, I
  have observ'd
10 The air is delicate.

Enter LADY MACBETH

DUNCAN.   See, see, our honour'd
  hostess!
The love that follows us sometime is our
  trouble,[8]

Which still we thank as love. Herein I
  teach you
How you shall bid God 'ild[2] us for your
  pains,
And thank us for your trouble.
LADY MACBETH.   All our service
In every point twice done and then done
  double
Were poor and single[3] business to con-
  tend
Against those honours deep and broad
  wherewith
Your majesty loads our house: for those
  of old,
And the late dignities heap'd up to them,
We rest your hermits.[4]
DUNCAN.   Where's the thane
  of Cawdor?   20
We cours'd him at the heels,[5] and had a
  purpose
To be his purveyor[6]: but he rides well,
And his great love, sharp as his spur, hath
  holp him
To his home before us. Fair and noble
  hostess,
We are your guest to-night.
LADY MACBETH.   Your servants ever
Have theirs, themselves, and what is
  theirs, in compt,
To make their audit at your highness'
  pleasure,
Still to return your own.[7]

---

[1] The hautboy (hō'boi) is a musical instrument,
  the modern oboe.   [2] Location.
[3] Martin, a kind of swallow.
[4] Building; here, the bird's nest.
[5] Projection.
[6] *coign of vantage.* Convenient corner.
[7] *pendent . . . cradle.* Hanging nest for its young.
[8] *The love . . . trouble.* Just as we honor those we
  love, so also do we give them trouble by
  seeking favors from them, favors which are
  excusable on the basis of our affection.

---

[1] Countenance, expression.
[2] Reward.
[3] Small.
[4] *We . . . hermits.* We shall not fail to pray for
  you as hermits pray for their benefactors.
[5] *cours'd . . . heels.* Followed close upon his heels.
[6] Forerunner.
[7] *Your servants . . . own.* As your servants we
  hold ourselves and our possessions subject to
  account ("in compt") and ready to be delivered to you at your call.

DUNCAN.   Give me your hand; And shall continue our graces towards
Conduct me to mine host: we love him   him.   30
    highly,   By your leave, hostess.   [*Exeunt*]

SCENE VII. *Within* MACBETH's *castle*

[Macbeth soliloquizes on the results of his
deed, and seems to suggest all the horrors of
the rest of the play. He is tormented, not by
moral scruples or tenderheartedness, but by
the consciousness that here in this world evil
deeds recoil upon the doer. Lady Macbeth
tries to hearten him.]

Hautboys and torches. Enter a Sewer,[1]
and divers Servants *with dishes and
service, over the stage. Then enter*
MACBETH

MACBETH. If it were done when 'tis
    done, then 'twere well
It were done quickly: if th' assassination
Could trammel up[2] the consequence, and
    catch
With his surcease success[3]; that but[4]
    this blow
Might be the be-all and the end-all here,
But[5] here, upon this bank and shoal of
    time,
We'd jump[6] the life to come. But in
    these cases
We still have judgment here, that we but
    teach
Bloody instructions, which, being taught,
    return
10 To plague th' inventor: this even-
    handed justice
Commends th' ingredients of our poi-
    son'd chalice
To our own lips.[7] He's here in double
    trust:
First, as I am his kinsman and his sub-
    ject,

Strong both against the deed; then, as
    his host,
Who should against his murderer shut
    the door,
Not bear the knife myself. Besides, this
    Duncan
Hath borne his faculties[1] so meek, hath
    been
So clear[2] in his great office, that his
    virtues
Will plead like angels, trumpet-tongu'd,
    against
The deep damnation of his taking-off[3]; 20
And pity, like a naked new-born babe
Striding the blast, or heaven's cherubin
    hors'd
Upon the sightless[4] couriers of the air,[5]
Shall blow the horrid deed in every eye,
That tears shall drown the wind. I have
    no spur
To prick the sides of my intent,[6] but
    only
Vaulting ambition, which o'erleaps itself
And falls on th' other.[7]

Enter LADY MACBETH

                    How now! what news?
LADY MACBETH. He has almost
    supp'd: why have you left the
    chamber?
MACBETH. Hath he ask'd for me?
LADY MACBETH.   Know you not
    he has?   30
MACBETH. We will proceed no further
    in this business:
He hath honour'd me of late; and I have
    bought
Golden opinions from all sorts of people,

---

[1] A headwaiter.   [2] *trammel up*. Prevent.
[3] *catch . . . success*. Be successful from the mo-
    ment the assassination was over.
[4] *that but*. If.   [5] Only.
[6] Take a chance on.
[7] *even-handed . . . lips*. Impartial justice presents
    to our lips the poisoned cup ("chalice") we
    are preparing for another.

[1] Powers.   [2] Honorable.
[3] Murder.   [4] Invisible.
[5] *couriers of the air*. Winds.
[6] Intention.   [7] *th' other*. The other side.

Which would be worn now in their new-
est gloss,
Not cast aside so soon.[1]
LADY MACBETH. Was the hope drunk
Wherein you dress'd yourself? hath it
slept since?
And wakes it now, to look so green and
pale
At what it did so freely? From this time
Such I account thy love. Art thou afeard
40 To be the same in thine own act and
valour
As thou art in desire? Wouldst thou
have that
Which thou esteem'st the ornament of
life,[2]
And live a coward in thine own esteem,
Letting "I dare not" wait upon "I
would,"
Like the poor cat i' the adage?[3]
MACBETH.   Prithee, peace:
I dare do all that may become a man;
Who dares do more is none.
LADY MACBETH.   What beast was 't,
then,
That made you break[4] this enterprise to
me?
When you durst do it, then you were a
man;
50 And, to be more than what you were,
you would
Be so much more the man. Nor time nor
place
Did then adhere,[5] and yet you would
make both:

[1] *I have . . . soon.* Many people think well of
me, and I should not cast their good opinion
aside so soon.
[2] *the ornament of life.* The crown. The whole
passage means "Do you wish to have the
good opinion of others, and at the same
time sacrifice your own esteem by being
too cowardly to take what you want
(the crown)?" Read again Lady Macbeth's estimate of her husband in I, v,
ll. 19–27.
[3] *cat . . . adage.* The adage (proverb) says, "The
cat would eat fish, but she will not wet her
feet."
[4] Propose.
[5] *Nor time . . . adhere.* Neither time nor place
seemed to be suitable for the deed.

They have made themselves, and that
their fitness now
Does unmake you. I have given suck,
and know
How tender 'tis to love the babe that
milks me;
I would, while it was smiling in my face,
Have pluck'd my nipple from his bone-
less gums,
And dash'd the brains out, had I so
sworn as you
Have done to this.
MACBETH.   If we should fail?
LADY MACBETH.   We fail.
But screw your courage to the sticking-
place,   60
And we'll not fail. When Duncan is
asleep —
Whereto the rather shall his day's hard
journey
Soundly invite him — his two chamber-
lains
Will I with wine and wassail[1] so con-
vince,[2]
That memory, the warder of the brain,
Shall be a fume, and the receipt of
reason
A limbeck only:[3] when in swinish sleep
Their drenched natures lie as in a death,
What cannot you and I perform upon
Th' unguarded Duncan? what not put
upon   70
His spongy officers, who shall bear the
guilt
Of our great quell[4]?
MACBETH.   Bring forth men-children
only;
For thy undaunted mettle should com-
pose
Nothing but males. Will it not be re-
ceiv'd,[5]
When we have mark'd with blood those
sleepy two

[1] Revelry.   [2] Overpower completely.
[3] *That . . . only.* That memory, the watchman
of the brain, shall be a mere vapor, and the
brain, the receptacle of reason, a mere empty
vessel like a limbeck (the cap of a still for
distilling liquor).
[4] Murder.   [5] Believed.

Of his own chamber and us'd their very
    daggers,
That they have done 't?
    LADY MACBETH.   Who dares receive it
    other,[1]
As we shall make our griefs and clamour
    roar
Upon his death?[2]
    MACBETH.   I am settled, and bend
    up
80 Each corporal agent[3] to this terrible
    feat.
Away, and mock the time with fairest
    show;[4]
False face must hide what the false heart
    doth know.   [*Exeunt*]

Discussion Hints

ACT I, SCENE I

1. What time of day do you think it is?

2. What are the weather conditions?

3. Are any noises heard except that of the thunder?

4. Where is Macbeth at this moment?

5. What lines of this scene point forward to what is coming later?

6. Compare this opening scene with the opening scene of each of the plays by Shakespeare you have already studied; for example, *As You Like It* (in the revised edition of *Adventure* of this series), *Julius Cæsar* (in the revised edition of *Achievement* of this series), and so on. How does it compare in length? in the number of facts told? in the suggestion of atmosphere?

7. The whole action of this scene will not take over five minutes, yet much longer time will be required to set the stage for it. Do you think it should be retained? You may answer No, but be sure to consider the matter again after you have read the whole play.

[1] Otherwise.
[2] *As we . . . death.* As we shall grieve loudly over his death.
[3] *bend . . . agent.* Bring to bear every bodily power.
[4] *mock . . . show.* Deceive people with pleasant behavior.

SCENE II

1. Imagine yourself a reporter writing for a Scottish newspaper. Write an account of the battle as you have heard it told to King Duncan.

2. Would this scene have been as effective dramatically if Macbeth had been introduced and allowed to tell Duncan of the battle? Give reasons for your answer.

3. What impression of the king and of his son Malcolm do you get from this scene? Do their characteristics in any way add to the interest you feel in Macbeth?

4. What impression of Macbeth do you get from this scene?

SCENE III

1. Let three members of the class take the parts of the Witches here and act out each speech that precedes the entrance of Macbeth and Banquo. Be careful to keep them "weird," with the horror of their actions attaining its climax as the last line is reached. Don't let them overact, or they will be merely ridiculous.

2. What do you think Macbeth means when he says, "So foul and fair a day I have not seen"? Who had used "foul" and "fair" together earlier in the play? Is this just chance, or do you think Shakespeare had any purpose in the repetition? If so, can you explain it?

3. Restate the promises of the Witches to Macbeth; to Banquo.

4. Explain Banquo's question in line 107.

5. Contrast Macbeth and Banquo in their reactions to the Witches' prophecies.

6. In lines 153–155 suppose that, instead of agreeing to wait, Macbeth and Banquo had spoken then their "free hearts each to other." Do you think Macbeth would have revealed to Banquo any designs against King Duncan? If so, would Banquo have joined him in these plans or would he have restrained Macbeth? Discuss in class.

SCENE IV

In this scene the king makes two decisions, each of which tends to strengthen Macbeth's evil purpose with regard to him. What are they?

SCENE V

1. When did Macbeth write the letter to his wife? Notice that we hear only that part of the letter which carries on the plot. Of course "they" refers to whom?

2. In Lady Macbeth's soliloquy memorize the words which show she is determined that her husband shall be king of Scotland.

3. Discuss Lady Macbeth's interpretation of her husband's character in the light of what you have already seen of it from the preceding pages. Can you quote any lines in the text which seem to confirm or contradict her estimate of him?

4. What different side of Lady Macbeth's character do lines 43–57, beginning "Come, you spirits," disclose? Do you think it is ambition for herself or for her husband that makes her try to cover up this side?

5. Show that Lady Macbeth's first greeting to her husband is in keeping with the resolve she has made.

6. Is Macbeth still vacillating, or has he decided on his course? Give a reason for your answer.

SCENE VI

1. Quote specific passages that illustrate the dramatic irony* of this scene.

2. Why did Lady Macbeth alone greet the king? Do you think she overdid the hypocritical words of welcome?

SCENE VII

1. Write out a clearly expressed prose paraphrase of Macbeth's soliloquy in lines 1–12.

2. What reason does Macbeth give his wife for abandoning the plot against Duncan? Is it the reason that influences him most strongly?

3. Different actresses have expressed many meanings by the tone of voice used for the two words "We fail" (l. 59). How do you think they should be read and punctuated? Give reasons for your answer.

General Questions or Assignments on Act I

1. Using these two topics, "Introduction" (or "Exposition") and "Rising Action," write two unified and coherent paragraphs summarizing the story of the play as far as it is told in Act I.

2. Four personages (Macbeth, Lady Macbeth, Duncan, and Banquo) have now been sufficiently portrayed to make possible a preliminary estimate of their characters. Write one well-chosen sentence descriptive of the character of each. The sentence should contain at least three descriptive words or phrases.

3. If your class were going to produce this first act upon the stage and you were in charge of the costuming, describe in detail the plans you would make for the costumes in each scene.

4. Assuming that you have been made property man for this production, make a complete list of the "props" you would need for Act I.

5. Draw a plan of the stage for each scene, indicating on it all entrances and exits of the characters during the scene. Plan also where each should stand or sit during the scene.

6. Would the stage electrician have any special problems to meet in this act? If so, what?

ACT II

SCENE I. *Inverness.* Court of MACBETH'S *castle*

[Anxiety and fear fill the air. Banquo's short, nervous questions show his disturbed state of mind. Macbeth cannot bear the strain of suspense. He sees a vision of a bloody dagger. An ominous bell gives the signal for the murder.]

Enter BANQUO, *and* FLEANCE *with a torch before him*

BANQUO. How goes the night, boy?
FLEANCE. The moon is down; I have not heard the clock.

BANQUO. And she goes down at twelve.
FLEANCE.   I take 't, 'tis later, sir.
BANQUO. Hold,   take   my   sword.
   There's husbandry[1] in heaven;
Their candles are all out.[2] Take thee
   that[3] too.
A heavy summons lies like lead upon
   me,[4]
And yet I would not sleep. Merciful
   powers,
Restrain in me the cursed thoughts[5] that
   nature
Gives way to in repose!

Enter MACBETH, *and a* Servant *with
a torch*

                 Give me my sword.
10 Who's there?
   MACBETH. A friend.
   BANQUO. What, sir, not yet at rest?
   The king's a-bed:
He hath been in unusual pleasure, and
Sent forth great largess to your offices:[6]
This diamond he greets your wife
   withal,
By the name of most kind hostess; and
   shut up
In measureless content.[7]
   MACBETH.   Being unprepar'd,
Our will became the servant to defect;
Which else should free have wrought.[8]
   BANQUO.   All's well.
20 I dreamt last night of the three weird
   sisters:
To you they have show'd some truth.
   MACBETH.   I think not of them;
Yet, when we can entreat an hour to
   serve,[9]

We would spend it in some words upon
   that business,
If you would grant the time.
   BANQUO.   At your kind'st leisure.
   MACBETH. If you shall cleave to my
   consent,[1] when 'tis,[2]
It shall make honour for you.
   BANQUO.   So[3] I lose none
In seeking to augment it, but still keep
My bosom franchis'd,[4] and allegiance
   clear,
I shall be counsell'd.
   MACBETH.   Good repose the while!
   BANQUO. Thanks, sir; the like to you! 30.
         [*Exeunt* BANQUO *and* FLEANCE]
   MACBETH. Go bid thy mistress, when
   my drink is ready,
She strike upon the bell. Get thee to
   bed.
               [*Exit* Servant]
Is this a dagger which I see before me,
The handle toward my hand? Come, let
   me clutch thee.
I have thee not, and yet I see thee still.
Art thou not, fatal vision, sensible
To feeling as to sight?[5] or art thou but
A dagger of the mind, a false creation,
Proceeding from the heat-oppressed
   brain?
I see thee yet, in form as palpable   40
As this which now I draw.
Thou marshall'st[6] me the way that I was
   going;
And such an instrument I was to use.
Mine eyes are made the fools o' the other
   senses,
Or else worth all the rest: I see thee still;
And on thy blade and dudgeon[7] gouts[8]
   of blood,
Which was not so before. There's no
   such thing:
It is the bloody business which informs[9]

---

[1] Economy.
[2] *Their candles ... out.* The stars are not shining.
[3] Probably Banquo's dagger or helmet. On the
   stage the action would explain.
[4] *A heavy ... me.* I am very sleepy.
[5] *cursed thoughts.* Evil dreams.
[6] *largess ... offices.* Gifts for your servants.
[7] *shut ... content.* Is completely satisfied.
[8] *Being ... wrought.* Being unprepared, we could
   not do as much as we might have wished;
   otherwise our entertainment would have
   been more liberal.
[9] *entreat ... serve.* Find a spare hour.

[1] Counsel.
[2] *cleave ... 'tis.* Support me when the time
   comes.   [3] Provided.
[4] *bosom franchis'd.* Conscience clear.
[5] *sensible ... sight.* Capable of being felt as well
   as seen.
[6] Guidest.   [7] Handle.
[8] Large drops.   [9] Gives false information.

Thus to mine eyes. Now o'er the one half-world
50 Nature seems dead, and wicked dreams abuse
The curtain'd sleep; witchcraft celebrates
Pale Hecate's* offerings; and wither'd murder,
Alarum'd[1] by his sentinel, the wolf,
Whose howl's his watch, thus with his stealthy pace,
With Tarquin's* ravishing strides, towards his design
Moves like a ghost. Thou sure and firm-set earth,
Hear not my steps, which way they walk, for fear
Thy very stones prate[1] of my where-about,
And take the present horror from the time,[2]
Which now suits with it. While I threat, he lives: 60
Words to the heat of deeds too cold breath gives.[3]   [A bell rings]
I go, and it is done; the bell invites me.
Hear it not, Duncan; for it is a knell
That summons thee to heaven or to hell.
                                        [Exit]

SCENE II. *The same*

[The murder is not enacted on the stage, but, as in Greek plays, is merely described. Critics are not in agreement as to whether Lady Macbeth's self-control comes from a hard heart or from a determination to help her husband. A knock at the gate calls the guilty pair to their senses.]

Enter LADY MACBETH

LADY MACBETH.   That which hath made them drunk hath made me bold;
What hath quench'd them hath given me fire. Hark! Peace!
It was the owl[2] that shriek'd, the fatal bellman,[3]
Which gives the stern'st good-night. He is about it:
The doors are open; and the surfeited grooms
Do mock their charge with snores:[4] I have drugg'd their possets,[5]
That death and nature do contend about them,
Whether they live or die.

Enter MACBETH

MACBETH.   Who's there? what, ho!
LADY MACBETH.   Alack, I am afraid they have awak'd,
And 'tis not done. Th' attempt and not the deed 10
Confounds us.[4] Hark! I laid their daggers ready;
He[5] could not miss 'em. Had he[6] not resembled
My father as he slept, I had done 't. My husband!
MACBETH.   I have done the deed. Didst thou not hear a noise?
LADY MACBETH.   I heard the owl scream and the crickets cry.
Did not you speak?
MACBETH.   When?
LADY MACBETH.   Now.
MACBETH.   As I descended?
LADY MACBETH. Aye.
MACBETH. Hark!
Who lies i' the second chamber?
LADY MACBETH.   Donalbain.

[1] Warned.
[2] The owl was a bird of evil omen.
[3] Besides performing other duties at night, the bellman visited condemned criminals just before their execution.
[4] *the surfeited . . . snores.* The drunken servants, by snoring, show that they are not on guard.
[5] Drinks.

[1] Prattle.
[2] *take . . . time.* Prevent the deed by taking away from the present time the awful silence which fits it.
[3] *Words . . . gives.* Talking tends to prevent action.
[4] *Confounds us.* Utterly ruins us.
[5] Macbeth.   [6] Duncan.

20 MACBETH. This is a sorry sight.

    [*Looking on his hands*]

LADY MACBETH. A foolish thought, to say a sorry sight.

MACBETH. There's one did laugh in's sleep, and one cried "Murder!"

That[1] they did wake each other: I stood and heard them:

But they did say their prayers, and address'd them

Again to sleep.

LADY MACBETH.   There are two lodg'd together.

MACBETH. One cried "God bless us!" and "Amen" the other,

As[2] they had seen me with these hangman's hands:

Listening[3] their fear, I could not say "Amen,"

When they did say "God bless us!"

30 LADY MACBETH. Consider it not so deeply.

MACBETH. But wherefore could not I pronounce "Amen"?

I had most need of blessing, and "Amen" Stuck in my throat.

LADY MACBETH.   These deeds must not be thought

After these ways: so, it will make us mad.

MACBETH. Methought I heard a voice cry "Sleep no more!

Macbeth does murder sleep," — the innocent sleep,

Sleep that knits up the ravell'd sleave[4] of care,

The death of each day's life, sore labour's bath,

Balm of hurt minds, great nature's second course,

40 Chief nourisher in life's feast, —

LADY MACBETH. What do you mean?

MACBETH. Still it cried "Sleep no more!" to all the house:

"Glamis hath murder'd sleep, and therefore Cawdor

Shall sleep no more; Macbeth shall sleep no more!"

LADY MACBETH. Who was it that thus cried? Why, worthy thane,'

You do unbend your noble strength, to think

So brainsickly of things. Go get some water,

And wash this filthy witness from your hand.

Why did you bring these daggers from the place?

They must lie there: go carry them, and smear

The sleepy grooms with blood.

MACBETH.   I'll go no more: 50

I am afraid to think what I have done;

Look on 't again I dare not.

LADY MACBETH.   Infirm of purpose!

Give me the daggers: the sleeping and the dead

Are but as pictures; 'tis the eye of childhood

That fears a painted devil.[1] If he do bleed,

I'll gild[2] the faces of the grooms withal;

For it must seem their guilt.

    [*Exit. Knocking within*]

MACBETH. Whence is that knocking?

How is 't with me, when every noise appals me?

What hands are here? ha! they pluck out mine eyes!

Will all great Neptune's* ocean wash this blood

Clean from my hand? No; this my hand will rather

The multitudinous seas incarnadine,[3]

Making the green one red.

Re-enter LADY MACBETH

LADY MACBETH. My hands are of your colour, but I shame

To wear a heart so white. [*Knocking within*] I hear a knocking

---

[1] So that.   [2] As if.   [3] Listening to.
[4] *knits ... sleave.* Straightens out worry ("care") as though it were a tangled skein of floss ("ravell'd sleave")

[1] *painted devil.* Picture of the devil
[2] Make red by smearing with blood.
[3] *The ... incarnadine.* Dye the ocean red.

At the south entry: retire we to our
  chamber.
A little water clears us of this deed:
How easy is it, then! Your constancy
Hath left you unattended.[1] [*Knocking
  within*] Hark! more knocking.
Get on your night-gown,[2] lest occasion
  call us,

And show us to be watchers.[1] Be not
  lost
So poorly in your thoughts.
  MACBETH. To know my deed, 'twere
  best not know myself.

                    [*Knocking within*]
Wake Duncan with thy knocking! I
  would thou couldst!   [*Exeunt*]

SCENE III. *The same*

[The drunken Porter's soliloquy gives the
audience relief from the strain caused by the
murder. In the interval Macbeth and Lady
Macbeth prepare for the discovery of the
deed. At the alarm Macbeth murders the
grooms. Malcolm and Donalbain, sons of
the murdered Duncan, suspect Macbeth and,
fearing for their lives, flee from Scotland.]

Enter a PORTER. *Knocking within*

  PORTER. Here's[3] a knocking indeed!
If a man were porter of hell-gate, he
should have old turning the key.[4]
[*Knocking*] Knock, knock, knock!
Who's there, i' the name of Beelzebub?*
Here's a farmer, that hang'd himself
on the expectation of plenty.[5] Come
in time; have napkins[6] enough about
you; here you'll sweat for 't. [*Knocking*]
Knock, knock! Who's there, in the
other devil's name? Faith, here's an

equivocator[2] that could swear in both
the scales against either scale; who committed treason enough for God's sake,
yet could not equivocate to heaven. O,
come in, equivocator. [*Knocking*] Knock,
knock, knock! Who's there? Faith,
here's an English tailor[3] come hither
for stealing out of a French hose.[4]
Come in, tailor; here you may roast your 20
goose. [*Knocking*] Knock, knock; never
at quiet! What are you? But this place
is too cold for hell. I'll devil-porter it no
further: I had thought to have let in
some of all professions, that go the primrose way to the everlasting bonfire.
[*Knocking*] Anon, anon! I pray you, remember the porter.   [*Opens the gate*]

Enter MACDUFF *and* LENNOX

  MACDUFF. Was it so late, friend, ere
    you went to bed,
That you do lie so late?[6]   30
  PORTER. Faith, sir, we were carousing
till the second cock.[7]
  MACDUFF. I believe drink gave thee
the lie last night.

---

1 *Your ... unattended.* Your courage has deserted
  you.
2 Dressing-gown.
3 *Here's .. key.* The Porter, half drunk, imagines
  he is the doorkeeper of hell and is greeting
  new arrivals.
4 *should ... key.* Would be busy turning the
  key.
5 *farmer . . . plenty.* One of the complaints
  of the common people was that farmers
  hoarded produce in the hope of getting high
  prices during seasons of scarcity. The
  Porter imagines that the first person to knock
  at the gate of hell is one of these grasping
  farmers, who committed suicide when he
  found that a plentiful crop was expected
  and that hence he would have to sell at
  a loss.
6 Handkerchiefs. The Porter tells the farmer
  that he will need plenty of handkerchiefs to
  wipe away the sweat.

---

1 Awake.
2 One who tells a falsehood while seeming to tell
  the truth. Equivocators in certain religious
  matters were especially detested in Shakespeare's day. The Porter imagines he is opening the gate of hell to one of these.
3 Tailors had the reputation of stealing part of
  their customers' cloth.   4 Breeches.
5 *roast your goose.* The Porter is making a pun.
  What is it? If you don't know, look up the
  word *goose* in an unabridged dictionary.
6 *do . . . late.* Are so late in getting up.
7 *the second cock.* About three in the morning.

"Give me the daggers"

PORTER. That it did, sir, i' the very throat on me : but I requited him for his lie; and, I think, being too strong for him, though he took up my legs sometime, yet I made a shift to cast him.

Enter MACBETH

40 MACDUFF. Is thy master stirring?
Our knocking has awak'd him; here he comes.
  LENNOX. Good morrow, noble sir.
  MACBETH.   Good morrow, both.
  MACDUFF. Is the king stirring, worthy thane?
  MACBETH.   Not yet.
  MACDUFF. He did command me to call timely[1] on him.
I have almost slipp'd the hour.
  MACBETH.   I'll bring you to him.
  MACDUFF. I know this is a joyful trouble to you;
But yet 'tis one.
  MACBETH. The labour we delight in physics pain.[2]
This is the door.
  MACDUFF.   I'll make so bold to call,
50 For 'tis my limited service.[3]   [*Exit*]
  LENNOX. Goes the king hence today?
  MACBETH.   He does; — he did appoint so.
  LENNOX. The night has been unruly: where we lay,
Our chimneys were blown down; and, as they say,
Lamentings heard i' the air, strange screams of death,
And, prophesying with accents terrible
Of dire combustion[4] and confus'd events
New hatch'd to th' woeful time, the obscure bird[5]
Clamour'd the livelong night : some say, the earth
Was feverous and did shake.
  MACBETH.   'Twas a rough night.

  [1] Early.
  [2] *physics pain.* Makes trouble less.
  [3] *limited service.* Especial duty.
  [4] Uproar.
  [5] *the obscure bird.* The owl.

LENNOX. My young remembrance cannot parallel 60
A fellow[1] to it.

Re-enter MACDUFF

MACDUFF. O horror, horror, horror! tongue nor heart
Cannot conceive nor name thee!
  MACBETH. } What's the matter?
  LENNOX. }
  MACDUFF. Confusion now hath made his masterpiece!
Most sacrilegious murder hath broke ope
The Lord's anointed temple,[2] and stole thence
The life o' the building.
  MACBETH.   What is 't you say? the life?
  LENNOX. Mean you his majesty?
  MACDUFF. Approach the chamber, and destroy your sight
With a new Gorgon.* Do not bid me speak; 70
See, and then speak yourselves.
        [*Exeunt* MACBETH *and* LENNOX]
                Awake, awake!
Ring the alarum-bell. Murder and treason!
Banquo and Donalbain! Malcolm! awake!
Shake off this downy sleep, death's counterfeit,[3]
And look on death itself! up, up, and see
The great doom's image![4] Malcolm! Banquo!
As from your graves rise up, and walk like sprites,
To countenance this horror.[5] Ring the bell.   [*Bell rings*]

  [1] Equal.
  [2] *Lord's anointed temple.* The body of the king (who was said to be the Lord's anointed).
  [3] *death's counterfeit.* An imitation of death.
  [4] *The great . . . image.* A sight as terrible as the Last Judgment.
  [5] *As . . . horror.* As the dead will rise at the Last Judgment, so you, to be in keeping with this horror, must rise and walk like spirits.

Enter LADY MACBETH

LADY MACBETH.　What's the business,
80 That such a hideous trumpet calls to
　　parley
The sleepers of the house? speak, speak!
　MACDUFF.　　　　O gentle lady,
'Tis not for you to hear what I can
　speak:
The repetition, in a woman's ear,
Would murder as it fell.[1]

Enter BANQUO

　　　　　　O Banquo, Banquo,
Our royal master's murder'd!
　LADY MACBETH.　　　Woe, alas!
What, in our house?
　BANQUO.　　　Too cruel anywhere.
Dear Duff, I prithee, contradict thyself,
And say it is not so.

Re-enter MACBETH *and* LENNOX,
with ROSS

MACBETH.　Had I but died an hour
　before this chance[2]
90 I had liv'd a blessed time; for, from this
　instant,
There's nothing serious in mortality:[3]
All is but toys[4]; renown and grace is
　dead;
The wine of life is drawn, and the mere
　lees[5]
Is left this vault to brag of.

Enter MALCOLM *and* DONALBAIN

DONALBAIN.　What is amiss?
MACBETH.　　　　　You are,
　and do not know't:
The spring, the head, the fountain of
　your blood
Is stopp'd, the very source of it is stopp'd.
　MACDUFF.　Your royal father's mur-
　der'd.

MALCOLM.　　　　O! by whom?
LENNOX.　Those of his chamber, as it
　seem'd, had done't:
Their hands and faces were all badg'd
　with blood;　　　　　　　　　　100
So were their daggers, which unwip'd we
　found
Upon their pillows:
They star'd, and were distracted; no
　man's life
Was to be trusted with them.
　MACBETH.　O, yet I do repent me of
　my fury,
That I did kill them.
　MACDUFF.　　Wherefore did you so?
　MACBETH.　Who can be wise, amaz'd,
　temperate and furious,
Loyal and neutral, in a moment? No
　man:
The expedition[1] of my violent love
Outrun the pauser, reason. Here lay
　Duncan,　　　　　　　　　　　110
His silver skin lac'd with his golden
　blood;
And his gash'd stabs look'd like a breach
　in nature
For ruin's wasteful entrance; there, the
　murderers,
Steep'd in the colours of their trade,[2]
　their daggers
Unmannerly breech'd[3] with gore: who
　could refrain,
That had a heart to love, and in that
　heart
Courage to make's[4] love known?
　LADY MACBETH.　Help me hence, ho!
　MACDUFF.　Look to the lady.
　MALCOLM.　　[*Aside to* DONALBAIN]
　　　　Why do we hold our tongues,
That most may claim this argument for
　ours?[5]
　DONALBAIN.　　[*Aside to* MALCOLM]
What should be spoken here, where our
　fate,　　　　　　　　　　　　120

---

[1] *The repetition . . . fell.* The news of the murder,
　if repeated in the ears of a woman, would kill
　her.　　　　　[2] Occurrence.
[3] *There's . . . mortality.* There is nothing worth
　while in life.
[4] Mere nothings.　　　[5] Dregs.

[1] Haste, urgency.
[2] *colours . . . trade.* The blood of murder.
[3] Covered (as with breeches).
[4] *make's.* Make his.
[5] *That . . . ours.* Who are most concerned.

Hid in an auger-hole,[1] may rush, and
  seize us?
Let's away.
Our tears are not yet brew'd.[2]
  MALCOLM.   [*Aside to* DONALBAIN]
                    Nor our strong sorrow
Upon the foot of motion.[3]
  BANQUO.   Look to the lady;
     [LADY MACBETH *is carried out*]
And when we have our naked frailties
  hid,[4]
That suffer in exposure, let us meet
And question this most bloody piece of
  work,
To know it further. Fears and scruples
  shake us:
In the great hand of God I stand, and
  thence
130 Against the undivulg'd pretence I fight
Of treasonous malice.[5]
  MACDUFF.   And so do I.
  ALL.   So all.
  MACBETH. Let's briefly put on manly
  readiness,[6]
And meet i' the hall together.

ALL.   Well contented.
[*Exeunt all but* MALCOLM *and* DONAL-
                                   BAIN]
  MALCOLM. What will you do? Let's
  not consort with them:
To show an unfelt sorrow is an office
Which the false man does easy. I'll to
  England.
  DONALBAIN. To Ireland I: our sepa-
  rated fortune
Shall keep us both the safer: where we
  are,
There's daggers in men's smiles: the
  near in blood
The nearer bloody.[1]
  MALCOLM.   This murderous shaft[2]
  that's shot   140
Hath not yet lighted; and our safest way
Is to avoid the aim. Therefore, to horse;
And let us not be dainty of[3] leave-
  taking,
But shift away: there's warrant in that
  theft
Which steals itself, when there's no mercy
  left.   [*Exeunt*]

SCENE IV. *Outside* MACBETH'S *castle*

[A quiet scene follows the tragic incidents.
The burial of the dead monarch and the flight
of the princes are discussed. News is brought
that Macbeth has gone to Scone* to be
crowned.]

Enter ROSS *and an* OLD MAN

  OLD MAN. Threescore-and-ten I can
  remember well:
Within the volume of which time I have
  seen

Hours dreadful and things strange; but
  this sore night
Hath trifl'd former knowings.[4]
  ROSS.   Ah, good father,
Thou see'st the heavens, as[5] troubl'd
  with man's act,
Threatens his bloody stage: by th'
  clock 'tis day,
And yet dark night strangles the travel-
  ling lamp.[6]

---

[1] Any small and unsuspected hiding-place.
[2] *Our . . . brew'd.* This is no time for weeping.
  The princes see through the insincere grief
  of Macbeth and Lady Macbeth.
[3] *Nor . . . motion.* Nor has the time arrived for
  our sorrow to make us take vengeance.
[4] *our . . . hid.* Put on our clothes.
[5] *Against . . . malice.* Banquo declares himself the
  foe of the treason and of the unrevealed intention (pretence) behind it.
[6] *put . . . readiness.* Clothe ourselves properly.

[1] *near . . . bloody.* "Near" means "nearer."
  Donalbain says, "The nearer one of these
  persons is to us in blood [that is, kinship], the
  more interested he is in our death." Macbeth
  is the cousin of the dead king and the next
  heir to the throne after Malcolm and
  Donalbain.   [2] Arrow.
[3] *dainty of.* Particular about.
[4] *trifl'd . . . knowings.* Made my former experiences seem trifles.
[5] As if.
[6] *the travelling lamp.* The sun.

Is 't night's predominance, or the day's
  shame

That darkness does the face of earth
  entomb,

10 When living light should kiss it?

OLD MAN.   'Tis unnatural,

Even like the deed that's done. On
  Tuesday last,

A falcon, tow'ring in her pride of place,

Was by a mousing owl hawk'd at and
  kill'd.[1]

ROSS. And Duncan's horses — a thing
  most strange and certain —

Beauteous and swift, the minions[2] of
  their race,

Turn'd wild in nature, broke their stalls,
  flung out,

Contending 'gainst obedience, as[3] they
  would make

War with mankind.

OLD MAN.   'Tis said they eat each
  other.

ROSS. They did so, to th' amazement
  of mine eyes,

20 That look'd upon 't.

Enter MACDUFF

        Here comes the good Macduff.

How goes the world, sir, now?

MACDUFF.   Why, see you not?

ROSS. Is 't known who did this more
  than bloody deed?

MACDUFF. Those that Macbeth hath
  slain.

ROSS.   Alas, the day!

What good could they pretend[4]?

MACDUFF.   They were suborn'd[5]:

Malcolm and Donalbain, the king's two
  sons,

Are stol'n away and fled; which puts
  upon them

Suspicion of the deed.

ROSS.   'Gainst nature still![1]

Thriftless ambition, that will ravin up

Thine own life's means![2] Then 'tis most
  like[3]

The sovereignty will fall upon Macbeth. 30

MACDUFF. He is already nam'd; and
  gone to Scone*

To be invested.

ROSS.   Where is Duncan's body?

MACDUFF. Carried to Colmekill,*

The sacred storehouse of his predecessors,

And guardian of their bones.

ROSS.   Will you to Scone?

MACDUFF. No, cousin, I'll to Fife.[4]

ROSS.   Well, I will thither.

MACDUFF. Well, may you see things
  well done there, — adieu! —

Lest our old robes sit easier than our new!

ROSS. Farewell, father.

OLD MAN. God's benison[5] go with you;
  and with those   40

That would make good of bad, and
  friends of foes!   [*Exeunt*]

Discussion Hints

ACT II. SCENE I

1. What causes Banquo's nervousness? Is
it fear of yielding to the Witches' prophecies
or is he suspicious of Macbeth's actions?

2. Explain the meaning of the two speeches
in lines 26–29.

3. According to the source from which
Shakespeare got his material for the play,
Banquo was equally guilty with Macbeth.
Does Shakespeare add anything to the
dramatic value of the play by making him
innocent? Can you think of any other reason
why Shakespeare made him so?

4. Plan the stage action for the speech
beginning "Is this a dagger" (l. 33). Would
you have the audience see a dagger at all?
If so, where would it be?

---

[1] *falcon . . . kill'd.* It was unnatural that such a
  noble bird as a falcon, just at the moment
  when it was "towering" (ready to strike),
  should be killed by such an ignoble bird as
  an owl.

[2] Favorites; hence, most valuable.

[3] As if.   [4] Intend.   [5] Bribed.

[1] *'Gainst nature still.* It is also unnatural for a son
  to kill a father.

[2] *Thriftless . . . means.* It would be wasteful
  ambition that would greedily devour ("ravin
  up") the means by which one lives.

[3] Likely.

[4] Macduff's home.

[5] Blessing.

SCENE II

1. To whom does the "them" in line 1 refer? Evidently, then, Lady Macbeth has just come from what room?

2. Contrast Lady Macbeth with her husband here. Which is apparently the more calm and practical? Is this natural or is it partly assumed? Note the significance of the last four words of the scene.

SCENE III

1. Try to give a clear description of the Porter. Is he old or young? What kind of voice has he? Would you have his movements quick and nervous, slow and doddering, or what?

2. Why is the Porter's speech in prose?

3. Does Lennox's speech (ll. 52–59) remind you in any way of parts of *Julius Cæsar*? If so, point out the similarities (*Julius Cæsar* is given in the revised edition of *Achievement* of this series).

4. Study carefully Macbeth's words and actions through this scene. Compare them with his words and actions in Scene ii.

5. Was Lady Macbeth's fainting real or pretended? This is a much-disputed point. Give the evidence on both sides and defend your own opinion (in this connection see Scene ii and its headnote). Did her fainting, whether real or not, help her husband?

SCENE IV

Does this scene develop the plot in any way? Could it be omitted?

General Questions or Assignments on Act II

1. Imagine yourself to be Banquo, knowing what he does of the Witches' prophecies and the events that followed. Set down, as he might have done in his diary, all the arguments for and against the guilt of Macbeth. Then draw the conclusion that you think he would have reached.

2. This act has shown you Macduff and Ross. Briefly give your idea of the characteristics of each.

3. Historically, what is the significance of Scone*? Tell the tradition concerning the "stone of Scone."

4. Identify each of the following quotations; that is, tell which character is speaking, to whom he is speaking, and what the circumstances are:

a.   "for it is a knell
That summons thee to heaven or to hell."

b.   "Had he not resembled
My father as he slept, I had done 't."

c. "All professions, that go the primrose way to th' everlasting bonfire."

d.   "This murderous shaft that's shot
Hath not yet lighted; and our safest way
Is to avoid the aim."

5. The present queen of England is a daughter of Baron Glamis, Earl of Strathmore. If possible find out something of the history of this family and its present position in Scotland. Is there a claim that the family is descended from Macbeth?

ACT III

SCENE I. *Forres. The palace*

[Banquo suspects Macbeth. Since he is an obstacle to Macbeth's success, Macbeth feels himself to be in danger. Macbeth, tormented by the thought that Banquo's descendants shall rule, determines to have him murdered.]

Enter BANQUO

BANQUO. Thou hast it now: king, Cawdor, Glamis, all,

As the weird women promis'd, and, I fear,
Thou play'dst most foully for 't: yet it was said
It should not stand[1] in thy posterity,
But that myself should be the root and father
Of many kings. If there come truth from them,

[1] Remain.

As upon thee, Macbeth, their speeches
  shine,[1]
Why, by the verities[2] on thee made good,
May they not be my oracles as well,
10 And set me up in hope? But hush! no
  more.

Sennet[3] *sounded. Enter* MACBETH, *as king*;
  LADY MACBETH, *as queen*; LENNOX
  ROSS, Lords, Ladies, *and* Attendants

MACBETH. Here's our chief guest.
LADY MACBETH.   If he had been
  forgotten,
It had been as a gap in our great feast,
And all-thing[4] unbecoming.
MACBETH. To-night we hold a solemn[5]
  supper, sir,
And I'll request your presence.
BANQUO.   Let your highness
Command upon me; to the which my
  duties
Are with a most indissoluble tie
For ever knit.
MACBETH. Ride you this afternoon?
BANQUO.   Ay, my good lord.
20 MACBETH. We should have else de-
  sir'd your good advice,
Which still[6] hath been both grave and
  prosperous,[7]
In this day's council; but we'll take to-
  morrow.
Is 't far you ride?
BANQUO. As far, my lord, as will fill
  up the time
'Twixt this and supper[8]: go not my horse
  the better,
I must become a borrower of the night
For a dark hour or twain.[9]

MACBETH.   Fail not our feast.
BANQUO. My lord, I will not.
MACBETH. We hear, our bloody cou-
  sins are bestow'd
In England and in Ireland, not confess-
  ing   30
Their cruel parricide,[1] filling their hearers
With strange invention[2]: but of that
  to-morrow,
When therewithal[3] we shall have cause
  of state
Craving us jointly.[4] Hie you to horse;
  adieu,
Till you return at night. Goes Fleance
  with you?
BANQUO. Ay, my good lord: our time
  does call upon 's.
MACBETH. I wish your horses swift
  and sure of foot;
And so I do commend you to their backs.
Farewell.   [*Exit* BANQUO]
Let every man be master of his time   40
Till seven at night; to make society
The sweeter welcome, we will keep our-
  self
Till supper-time alone: while[5] then, God
  be with you!
  [*Exeunt all but* MACBETH *and an*
          ATTENDANT]
Sirrah,[6] a word with you: attend those
  men
Our pleasure?
ATTENDANT. They are, my lord, with-
  out the palace-gate.
MACBETH. Bring them before us.
          [*Exit* ATTENDANT]
          To be thus[7] is nothing,
But to be safely thus. Our fears in
  Banquo
Stick deep; and in his royalty of nature
Reigns that which would be fear'd.
  'Tis much he dares;   50

[1] Are clearly fulfilled.
[2] Truths.
[3] A set of notes on a trumpet, announcing the
  approach of royal personages.
[4] Entirely, altogether.
[5] Formal, official.
[6] Always. This was a common meaning of "still"
  in Shakespeare's day.
[7] *grave and prosperous.* Weighty and sound.
[8] That is, seven o'clock. See line 41.
[9] *go . . . twain.* If my horse does not travel faster,
  I shall have to ride for an hour or two after
  nightfall.

D

[1] Murder of a near relative; here, their father.
[2] *invention.* False statements.
[3] In addition to that.
[4] *cause . . . jointly.* State matters requiring the
  attention of both of us.
[5] Till.
[6] Sir, used in addressing an inferior.
[7] *To be thus.* Being king.

And, to[1] that dauntless temper of his
   mind,
He hath a wisdom that doth guide his
   valour
To act in safety. There is none but he
Whose being I do fear; and, under him,
My Genius[2] is rebuk'd, as, it is said,
Mark Antony's was by Caesar.[3] He chid
   the sisters,
When first they put the name of king
   upon me,
And bade them speak to him; then
   prophet-like
They hail'd him father to a line of kings:
60 Upon my head they plac'd a fruitless
   crown,
And put a barren sceptre in my gripe,
Thence to be wrench'd with[4] an un-
   lineal[5] hand,
No son of mine succeeding. If 't be so,
For Banquo's issue have I fil'd[6] my
   mind;
For them the gracious Duncan have I
   murder'd;
Put rancours[7] in the vessel of my peace
Only for them; and mine eternal jewel[8]
Given to the common enemy of man,
To make them kings, the seed of Banquo
   kings!
70 Rather than so, come, fate, into the list,
And champion me to th' utterance![9] —
   Who's there?

Re-enter ATTENDANT, *with two*
MURDERERS

Now go to th' door, and stay there till we
   call. —

                [*Exit* ATTENDANT]
Was it not yesterday we spoke together?

[1] In addition to.
[2] Guardian spirit.
[3] *under him . . . Caesar.* Just as Mark Antony
   (lacking the nobility of Caesar) felt inferior
   in his presence, so also do I seem to myself
   inferior in the presence of Banquo.
[4] By.
[5] Not in the direct line of descent.
[6] Defiled.   [7] Hatred.
[8] *mine . . . jewel.* My immortal soul.
[9] *come . . . utterance.* Let fate fight against me to
   the uttermost, as in mortal combat.

1 MURDERER. It was, so please your
   highness.
MACBETH.   Well then, now
Have you consider'd of my speeches?
   Know
That it was he, in the times past, which
   held you
So under fortune; which you thought
   had been
Our innocent self:[1] this I made good to
   you
In our last conference, pass'd in proba-
   tion[2] with you,
How you were borne in hand,[3] how   80
   cross'd, the instruments,
Who wrought with them, and all things
   else that might
To half a soul and to a notion[4] craz'd
Say, "Thus did Banquo."
   1 MURDERER.   You made it known
   to us.
   MACBETH. I did so, and went further,
   which is now
Our point of second meeting. Do you
   find
Your patience so predominant in your
   nature
That you can let this go? Are you so
   gospell'd[5]
To[6] pray for this good man and for his
   issue,
Whose heavy hand hath bow'd you to the
   grave
And beggar'd yours for ever?
   1 MURDERER. We are men, my liege. 90
   MACBETH. Ay, in the catalogue[7] ye
   go for men;
As hounds and greyhounds, mongrels,
   spaniels, curs,

[1] *Know . . . self.* The Murderers are men whom
   Macbeth has wronged. He makes them believe that it is Banquo who has kept them
   from being fortunate ("held" them "under
   fortune").
[2] *pass'd in probation.* Went over the proofs, one
   by one.
[3] *borne in hand.* Deceived with false hopes.
[4] Mind.
[5] Filled with the spirit of the Gospels — forgiveness.
[6] As to.   [7] General list.

Shoughs, water-rugs, and demi-wolves,[1]
　are clept[2]
All by the name of dogs: the valued file[3]
Distinguishes the swift, the slow, the
　subtle,
The housekeeper,[4] the hunter, every one
According to the gift which bounteous
　nature
Hath in him clos'd; whereby he does
　receive
Particular addition,[5] from the bill
100 That writes them all alike; and so of
　men.
Now, if you have a station in the file,
Not i' the worst rank of manhood,
　say 't;
And I will put that business in your
　bosoms,
Whose execution takes your enemy off,
Grapples you to the heart and love
　of us,
Who wear our health but sickly in his life,
Which in his death were perfect.[6]
　　2 MURDERER.　　　I am one, my liege
Whom the vile blows and buffets of the
　world
Hath so incens'd, that I am reckless what
110 I do to spite the world.
　　　1 MURDERER.　　　　And I another
So weary with disasters, tugg'd with
　fortune,
That I would set my life on any chance,
To mend it, or be rid on 't.
　　MACBETH.　　　　　Both of you
Know Banquo was your enemy.
　　BOTH MURDERERS.　　True, my lord.
　　MACBETH. So is he mine; and in such
　bloody distance,[7]
That every minute of his being thrusts

Against my near'st of life;[1] and though
　I could
With barefac'd power sweep him from
　my sight
And bid my will avouch[2] it, yet I must
　not,
For[3] certain friends that are both his and
　mine,　　　　　　　　　　　　　　120
Whose loves I may not drop, but wail his
　fall
Who I myself struck down;[4] and thence
　it is,
That I to your assistance do make love,
Masking the business from the common
　eye
For sundry weighty reasons.
　　2 MURDERER.　　　We shall, my lord,
Perform what you command us.
　　1 MURDERER.　　　Though our lives —
　　MACBETH. Your spirits shine through
　you. Within this hour at most
I will advise you where to plant your-
　selves;
Acquaint you with the perfect spy o' the
　time,[5]
The moment on 't; for 't must be done
　to-night,　　　　　　　　　　　　130
And something[6] from the palace; al-
　ways thought
That I require a clearness:[7] and with
　him —
To leave no rubs nor botches in the
　work[8] —
Fleance his son, that keeps him com-
　pany,
Whose absence is no less material to
　me

---

[1] *Shoughs . . . demi-wolves.* Breeds of dogs.
[2] Called.
[3] *valued file.* List in which the dogs are graded
　according to their worth.
[4] Watchdog.
[5] *Particular addition.* Special title or distinction.
[6] *And I . . . perfect.* And I will offer you an
　opportunity to get rid of your enemy and
　to make a friend of me, to whom he is also
　dangerous.
[7] *such bloody distance.* The distance between two
　swordsmen who are fighting to the death.

[1] *near'st of life.* My most vital parts.
[2] Take the responsibility for.
[3] Because of.
[4] *wail . . . down.* Am obliged to bewail the fall
　of the man I have killed.
[5] *the perfect . . . time.* The meaning is not clear.
　Some think it refers to a Third Murderer,
　"the perfect spy." Others think it means
　"the sure means of knowing the right time
　to act."
[6] Somewhat, some distance.
[7] *always . . . clearness.* It being always borne in
　mind that I must be kept free of suspicion.
[8] *To leave . . . work.* Not to botch the job.

Than is his father's, must embrace the
    fate
Of that dark hour. Resolve yourselves[1]
    apart;
I'll come to you anon.
    BOTH MURDERERS.   We are re-
solv'd, my lord.

MACBETH. I'll call upon you straight[1]:
    abide within.
                [*Exeunt* MURDERERS]
It is concluded: Banquo, thy soul's
    flight,   140
If it find heaven, must find it out to-
    night.   [*Exit*]

SCENE II. *The palace*

[The evil effects of sin become apparent.
Macbeth no longer confides fully in the queen.
The two are drifting apart. Macbeth's hint of
a new crime, however, stimulates his wife to
control the situation at the banquet.]

Enter LADY MACBETH *and a* SERVANT

LADY MACBETH. Is Banquo gone from
    court?
SERVANT. Ay, madam, but returns
    again to-night.
LADY MACBETH. Say to the king, I
    would attend his leisure
For a few words.
    SERVANT.   Madam, I will.   [*Exit*]
    LADY MACBETH.   Nought's had,
all's spent,
Where our desire is got without content:
'Tis safer to be that which we destroy
Than by destruction dwell in doubtful joy.

Enter MACBETH

How now, my lord! why do you keep
    alone,
Of sorriest fancies your companions
    making;[2]
10 Using those thoughts which should in-
    deed have died
With them they think on? Things with-
    out all remedy
Should be without regard: what's done
    is done.
MACBETH. We have scotch'd[3] the
    snake, not kill'd it:

She'll close and be herself,[2] whilst our
    poor malice
Remains in danger of her former tooth.
But let the frame of things disjoint, both
    the worlds suffer,[3]
Ere we will eat our meal in fear, and
    sleep
In the affliction of these terrible dreams
That shake us nightly: better be with
    the dead,
Whom we, to gain our peace, have sent
    to peace,   20
Than on the torture of the mind to
    lie
In restless ecstasy.[4] Duncan is in his
    grave;
After life's fitful fever he sleeps well;
Treason has done his[5] worst: nor steel,
    nor poison,
Malice domestic, foreign levy,[6] nothing,
Can touch him further.
    LADY MACBETH.   Come on;
Gentle my lord,[7] sleek o'er your rugged
    looks;
Be bright and jovial among your guests
    to-night.
    MACBETH. So shall I, love; and so, I
    pray, be you:
Let your remembrance apply to Ban-
    quo;[8]   30

---

[1] *Resolve yourselves.* Make up your minds.
[2] *Of . . . making.* Indulging in the most despi-
    cable thoughts.
[3] Slashed; that is, merely wounded.

[1] Immediately.
[2] *She'll . . . herself.* The parts will reunite and
    she will be a snake again.
[3] *let . . . suffer.* Let the universe fall apart, and
    both this world and the next perish.
[4] Here, intense mental suffering.
[5] Its.
[6] Here, invasion.
[7] *Gentle my lord.* My dear lord.
[8] *Let . . . Banquo.* Treat Banquo kindly.

Present him eminence,[1] both with eye and tongue:
Unsafe the while, that we
Must lave our honours in these flattering streams,
And make our faces vizards to our hearts,
Disguising what they are.[2]

LADY MACBETH.   You must leave this.

MACBETH. O, full of scorpions is my mind, dear wife!
Thou know'st that Banquo and his Fleance lives.

LADY MACBETH. But in them nature's copy's not eterne.[3]

MACBETH. There's comfort yet; they are assailable;
40 Then be thou jocund: ere the bat hath flown
His cloister'd flight,[4] ere to black Hecate's* summons
The shard-borne beetle with his drowsy hums

Hath rung night's yawning peal,[1] there shall be done
A deed of dreadful note.

LADY MACBETH. What's to be done?

MACBETH. Be innocent of the knowledge, dearest chuck,
Till thou applaud the deed. Come, seeling[2] night,
Scarf up[3] the tender eye of pitiful day,
And with thy bloody and invisible hand
Cancel and tear to pieces that great bond
Which keeps me pale! Light thickens,[4]   50
and the crow
Makes wing to th' rooky[5] wood:
Good things of day begin to droop and drowse,
Whiles night's black agents to their preys do rouse.
Thou marvell'st at my words, but hold thee still;
Things bad begun make strong themselves by ill.
So, prithee, go with me.   [Exeunt]

SCENE III. *A park near the palace*

[The murder of Banquo is the pivot, or turning-point (climax), of the play, because it marks the highest point of Macbeth's success. The escape of Fleance is the first step in the falling action (see page 81).]

Enter three MURDERERS

1 MURDERER. But who did bid thee join with us?

3 MURDERER.   Macbeth.

2 MURDERER. He needs not our mistrust;[5] since he delivers
Our offices, and what we have to do,

To the direction just.[6]

1 MURDERER.   Then stand with us.
The west yet glimmers with some streaks of day:
Now spurs the lated[7] traveller apace
To gain the timely inn; and near approaches
The subject of our watch.

3 MURDERER.   Hark! I hear horses.

BANQUO. [*Within*] Give us a light there, ho!

---

[1] *Present him eminence.* Treat him with especial honor.

[2] *Unsafe . . . are.* The time is perilous indeed, when we must try to cleanse our honor in these streams of flattery and make our faces masks to disguise our real character.

[3] *But . . . eterne.* But they will not live forever.

[4] *ere . . . flight.* That is, before nightfall.

[5] *He . . . mistrust.* We need not distrust him.

[1] *ere . . . peal.* That is, before bedtime. "Yawning peal" means summons to sleep.

[2] A term used in falconry. Falcons' eyes were seeled (the lids sewed together by a thread of fine silk) to keep them blinded until they were trained.

[3] *Scarf up.* Bind up as with a scarf.

[4] *Light thickens.* Darkness comes.

[5] Misty, gloomy.

[6] *delivers . . . just.* Reports what we have to do in accordance with the exact instructions.

[7] Belated.

10 2 MURDERER. Then 'tis he: the rest
That are within the note of expectation[1]
Already are i' the court.
1 MURDERER. His horses go about.[2]
3 MURDERER. Almost a mile: but he
does usually,
So all men do, from hence to th' palace
gate
Make it their walk.[3]

Enter BANQUO, *and* FLEANCE *with a torch*

2 MURDERER. A light, a light!
3 MURDERER. 'Tis he.
1 MURDERER. Stand to 't.
BANQUO. It will be rain to-night.

1 MURDERER.   Let it come down.
[*They set upon* BANQUO]
BANQUO. O, treachery! Fly, good
Fleance, fly, fly, fly!
Thou mayst revenge. O slave! [*Dies.*
FLEANCE *escapes*]
3 MURDERER. Who did strike out the
light?
1 MURDERER.   Was't not the way[1]?
3 MURDERER. There's but one down;
the son is fled.
2 MURDERER.   We have lost 20
Best half of our affair.
1 MURDERER. Well, let's away, and
say how much is done.   [*Exeunt*]

SCENE IV. *Hall in the palace*

[Macbeth gives a state dinner. The murderers of Banquo tell Macbeth of the escape
of Fleance. Macbeth's apprehension grows
into acute horror when Banquo's ghost comes
to the table. Macduff's absence disturbs Macbeth, who fears it means that Macduff is suspicious of him. Macbeth determines to visit
the Witches to obtain further information.]

A banquet prepared. Enter MACBETH,
LADY MACBETH, ROSS, LENNOX,
LORDS, *and* Attendants

MACBETH. You know your own de-
grees[4]; sit down: at first
And last the hearty welcome.
LORDS.   Thanks to your majesty.
MACBETH. Ourself will mingle with
society,
And play the humble host.
Our hostess keeps her state,[5] but in best
time

We will require her welcome.
LADY MACBETH. Pronounce it for me,
sir, to all our friends,
For my heart speaks they are wel-
come.
[*First* MURDERER *appears at the
door*]
MACBETH. See, they encounter thee
with their hearts' thanks.
Both sides are even: here I'll sit i' the
midst.   10
Be large in mirth; anon[2] we'll drink a
measure
The table round. — [*Goes to the door*]
There's blood upon thy face.
MURDERER. 'Tis Banquo's then.
MACBETH. 'Tis better thee without
than he within.[3]
Is he dispatch'd?
MURDERER. My lord, his throat is
cut; that I did for him.
MACBETH. Thou art the best o' the
cut-throats; yet he's good
That did the like for Fleance: if thou
didst it,
Thou art the nonpareil.[4]

[1] *note of expectation.* List of expected guests.
[2] *go about.* Turn aside, do not come this way.
In order to avoid bringing horses on the
stage, Shakespeare represents the riders as
dismounting before they are seen by the
spectators in the theater.
[3] *Almost . . . walk.* Though from here to the
palace is almost a mile, Banquo, as is the
custom, usually walks the distance instead
of going on horseback.
[4] Ranks according to which you are to be seated.
[5] *keeps . . . state.* Remains enthroned in her chair
of state.

[1] Plan for the murder.
[2] Immediately.
[3] *'Tis . . . within.* It is better outside thee than
inside him.
[4] One without an equal.

MURDERER.   Most royal sir,
20 Fleance is scap'd.
    MACBETH. Then comes my fit again:
        I had else been perfect,
Whole as the marble, founded as the
        rock;
As broad and general as the casing[1]
        air:
But now I am cabin'd, cribb'd, confin'd,
        bound in
To saucy doubts and fears.[2] But Ban-
        quo's safe?
    MURDERER. Ay, my good lord; safe
        in a ditch he bides,
With twenty trenched gashes on his
        head,
The least a death to nature.
    MACBETH.   Thanks for that.
There the grown serpent lies; the worm[3]
        that's fled
30 Hath nature that in time will venom
        breed,
No teeth for th' present. Get thee gone:
        to-morrow
We'll hear ourselves again.[4]
                    [Exit MURDERER]
    LADY MACBETH.   My royal lord,
You do not give the cheer[5]: the feast is
        sold
That is not often vouch'd, while 'tis
        a-making,
'Tis given with welcome: to feed were
        best at home;
From thence the sauce to meat is cere-
        mony;
Meeting were bare without it.[6]

---

[1] Surrounding.
[2] *But now . . . fears.* But now I am shut up like a
    prisoner by doubts and fears that insolently
    assail me. "Saucy" here means "inso-
    lent."
[3] Serpent.
[4] *We'll . . . again.* We'll talk with each other
    again.
[5] Hearty welcome.
[6] *the feast . . . it.* The feast that is not given
    with welcome is like a feast that is sold
    at an inn. If food alone is wanted, one had
    best eat at home. Away from home the
    "sauce" to a dinner is the host's hearty
    welcome.

Enter the Ghost of BANQUO, *and sits in*
        MACBETH'S *place*

    MACBETH.   Sweet remembrancer![1]
Now, good digestion wait on appetite,
And health on both!
    LENNOX.   May't please your
        highness sit.
    MACBETH. Here had we now our
        country's honour roof'd,[2]   40
Were the grac'd person of our Banquo
        present;
Who may I rather challenge for un-
        kindness
Than pity for mischance.
    ROSS.   His absence, sir,
Lays blame upon his promise. Please 't
        your highness
To grace us with your royal company?
    MACBETH. The table's full!
    LENNOX.   Here is a
        place reserv'd, sir.
    MACBETH. Where?
    LENNOX. Here, my good lord. What
        is 't that moves your highness?
    MACBETH. Which of you have done
        this?
    LORDS.   What, my good lord?
    MACBETH. Thou canst not say I did
        it: never shake   50
Thy gory locks at me.
    ROSS. Gentlemen, rise; his highness
        is not well.
    LADY MACBETH. Sit, worthy friends:
        my lord is often thus,
And hath been from his youth: pray you,
        keep seat;
The fit is momentary; upon a thought[3]
He will again be well: if much you note
        him,
You shall offend him, and extend his
        passion:
Feed[4] and regard him not. [*Aside to*
        MACBETH] Are you a man?

---

[1] Reminder.
[2] *our country's . . . roof'd.* All the highest nobles
    of our country under one roof.
[3] *upon a thought.* In a moment.
[4] Eat.

MACBETH. Ay, and a bold one, that dare look on that

60 Which might appal the devil.

LADY MACBETH. [Aside to MACBETH] O proper stuff![1]

This is the very painting of your fear:

This is the air-drawn dagger which, you said,

Led you to Duncan. O, these flaws[2] and starts,

Impostors to[3] true fear, would well become

A woman's story at a winter's fire,

Authoriz'd by her grandam. Shame itself!

Why do you make such faces? When all's done,

You look but on a stool.[4]

MACBETH. Prithee, see there! behold! look! lo! how say you?

70 Why, what care I? If thou canst nod, speak too.

If charnel-houses and our graves must send

Those that we bury back, our monuments

Shall be the maws of kites.[5]

[Ghost vanishes]

LADY MACBETH. [Aside to MACBETH] What, quite unmann'd in folly?

MACBETH. If I stand here, I saw him!

LADY MACBETH. [Aside to MACBETH] Fie, for shame!

MACBETH. Blood hath been shed ere now, i' the olden time,

Ere humane statute purg'd the gentle weal;[6]

Ay, and since too, murders have been perform'd

---

[1] O proper stuff! O nonsense! (Used here contemptuously.)

[2] Sudden outbursts of emotion.

[3] In comparison with.

[4] Here, chair (a common meaning in Elizabethan English).

[5] If charnel-houses . . . kites. If morgues and graves give up their dead, we had better let our bodies be devoured by kites (a kite is a kind of hawk).

[6] Ere . . . weal. Before human laws established order in society.

Too terrible for the ear. The time has been,

That, when the brains were out, the man wouid die,

And there an end; but now they rise again, 80

With twenty mortal murders[1] on their crowns,

And push us from our stools: this is more strange

Than such a murder is.

LADY MACBETH. My worthy lord,

Your noble friends do lack[2] you.

MACBETH. I do forget.

Do not muse[3] at me, my most worthy friends;

I have a strange infirmity, which is nothing

To those that know me. Come, love and health to all;

Then I'll sit down. Give me some wine; fill full.

Re-enter the Ghost

I drink to th' general joy o' the whole table,

And to our dear friend Banquo, whom we miss; 90

Would he were here! to all and him we thirst,[4]

And all to all.

LORDS. Our duties, and the pledge.

MACBETH. Avaunt! and quit my sight! let the earth hide thee!

Thy bones are marrowless, thy blood is cold;

Thou hast no speculation[5] in those eyes

Which thou dost glare with!

LADY MACBETH. Think of this, good peers,

But as a thing of custom: 'tis no other;

Only it spoils the pleasure of the time.

MACBETH. What man dare, I dare:

Approach thou like the rugged Russian bear, 100

---

[1] mortal murders. Deadly wounds.   [2] Miss.

[3] Wonder.   [4] Wish to drink a toast.

[5] Power of sight.

The arm'd rhinoceros, or the Hyrcan
    tiger[1];
Take any shape but that, and my firm
    nerves
Shall never tremble: or be alive again,
And dare me to the desert with thy
    sword;
If trembling I inhabit then, protest[2] me
The baby of a girl.[3] Hence, horrible
    shadow!
Unreal mockery,[4] hence!
                    [*Ghost vanishes*]
                Why, so: being gone,
I am a man again. Pray you, sit still.
    LADY MACBETH.   You have displac'd
        the mirth, broke the good meeting,
110 With most admir'd[5] disorder.
        MACBETH.   Can such things be,
And overcome[6] us like a summer's cloud,
Without our special wonder? You make
    me strange
Even to the disposition that I owe,[7]
When now I think you can behold such
    sights,
And keep the natural ruby of your
    cheeks,
When mine is blanch'd with fear.
    ROSS.   What sights, my lord?
    LADY MACBETH.   I pray you, speak
    not; he grows worse and worse;
Question enrages him. At once, good
    night:
Stand not upon the order of your going,[8]
120 But go at once.

LENNOX.   Good night; and better
    health
Attend his majesty!
    LADY MACBETH.   A kind good night
        to all!
    [*Exeunt all but* MACBETH *and* LADY
                                MACBETH]
    MACBETH. It will have blood; they
        say blood will have blood:
Stones have been known to move and
    trees to speak;
Augures[1] and understood relations[2] have
By magot-pies and choughs and rooks
    brought forth
The secret'st man of blood.[3] What is the
    night?[4]
    LADY MACBETH. Almost at odds with
        morning, which is which.
    MACBETH. How say'st thou, that
        Macduff denies his person
At our great bidding?[5]
    LADY MACBETH.   Did you send to
        him, sir?
    MACBETH. I hear it[6] by the way,[7] but
        I will send: 130
There's not a one of them[8] but in his
    house
I keep a servant fee'd. I will to-morrow,
And betimes[9] I will, to the weird
    sisters:
More shall they speak; for now I am
    bent to know,
By the worst means, the worst. For mine
    own good
All causes shall give way: I am in
    blood

---

[1] *Hyrcan tiger.* A kind of fierce tiger said to live in southwestern Asia.

[2] Declare.

[3] *If . . . girl.* Though the specific meaning of this passage is much disputed, the general sense is clear enough. Macbeth means that if he remains trembling in fear before the most terrible living enemy as he does before the Ghost, he is willing to be called a coward or weakling ("baby of a girl," meaning either a "doll-baby" or a "weak, puny infant").

[4] Counterfeit; illusion.

[5] Much to be wondered at.

[6] Come over.

[7] *You make . . . owe.* You make me a stranger even to myself.

[8] *Stand . . . going.* Do not insist upon leaving in order of rank.

[1] Auguries, omens.

[2] *understood relations.* Secret relations between things which are unknown to ordinary people.

[3] *magot-pies . . . blood.* Magpies ("magot-pies"), choughs, and rooks are birds that can be taught to talk. They were supposed to be able to reveal secrets.

[4] *the night.* The time of night.

[5] *How . . . bidding?* What do you think of Macduff's failure to accept our royal invitation?

[6] The fact of Macduff's failure to obey Macbeth's summons.

[7] *by the way.* Indirectly.

[8] The nobles whom Macbeth suspects.

[9] Early.

Stepp'd in so far that, should I wade no
   more,
Returning were as tedious as go o'er :
Strange things I have in head that will
   to hand,
140 Which must be acted ere they may be
   scann'd.[1]

LADY MACBETH. You lack the season[1]
   of all natures, sleep.
MACBETH. Come, we'll to sleep. My
   strange and self-abuse
Is the initiate fear that wants hard
   use :[2]
We are yet but young in deed. [*Exeunt*]

SCENE V. *A heath*

[The Witches prepare for the ruin of Macbeth.]

Thunder. Enter the three WITCHES,
meeting HECATE*

1 WITCH. Why, how now, Hecate!
   you look angerly.
HECATE. Have I not reason, beldams[2]
   as you are,
Saucy and overbold? How did you dare
To trade and traffic with Macbeth
In riddles and affairs of death;
And I, the mistress of your charms, •
The close[3] contriver of all harms,
Was never call'd to bear my part,
Or show the glory of our art?
10 And, which is worse, all you have done
Hath been but for a wayward son,
Spiteful and wrathful; who, as others do,
Loves for his own ends, not for you.
But make amends now : get you gone,
And at the pit of Acheron* [4]
Meet me i' the morning : thither he
Will come to know his destiny :
Your vessels and your spells provide,
Your charms, and every thing beside.
20 I am for th' air; this night I'll spend
Unto a dismal and a fatal end :

Great business must be wrought **ere**
   noon :
Upon the corner of the moon
There hangs a vaporous drop profound ;[3]
I'll catch it ere it come to ground :
And that distill'd by magic sleights[4]
Shall raise such artificial sprites[5]
As by the strength of their illusion
Shall draw him on to his confusion[6] :
He shall spurn fate, scorn death, and
   bear   30
His hopes 'bove wisdom, grace, and fear;
And you all know security[7]
Is mortals' chiefest enemy.
         [*Music, and a Song*]
Hark! I am call'd; my little spirit, see,
Sits in a foggy cloud, and stays for me.
         [*Exit*]
   [*Sing within :* "Come away, come
         away," etc.]
1 WITCH. Come let's make haste;
   she'll soon be back again. [*Exeunt*]

[1] Seasoning, that which preserves.
[2] *My . . . use.* My strange self-deceptions are
   those of a beginner in crime, whose conscience
   needs to be hardened by custom.
[3] *vaporous drop profound.* A drop of vapor full
   of magic power.
[4] Devices.
[5] Spirits.
[6] Destruction.
[7] Overconfidence.

[1] Examined carefully.   [2] Hags.   [3] Secret.
[4] Here, some place on the heath supposed to be
   the entrance to hell.

Scene VI. *Forres. The palace*

[This scene contains no action and is often omitted in modern productions. It serves, however, to carry along the interest in the falling action. It also supplies comment on Macbeth's doings. Lines 1-20 of Lennox's opening speech are, of course, ironical.*]

Enter LENNOX *and another* LORD

LENNOX. My former speeches have but hit[1] your thoughts,
Which can interpret farther : only, I say
Things have been strangely borne.[2] The gracious Duncan
Was pitied of[3] Macbeth : marry,[4] he was dead :
And the right-valiant Banquo walk'd too late ;
Whom, you may say, if 't please you, Fleance kill'd,
For Fleance fled : men must not walk too late.
Who cannot want[5] the thought, how monstrous
It was for Malcolm and for Donalbain
10 To kill their gracious father? damned fact!
How it did grieve Macbeth! did he not straight,[6]
In pious rage, the two delinquents tear,
That were the slaves of drink and thralls[7] of sleep?
Was not that nobly done? Ay, and wisely too;
For 'twould have anger'd any heart alive
To hear the men deny 't. So that, I say,
He has borne all things well: and I do think
That, had he Duncan's sons under his key —
As, and 't please heaven[8] he shall not — they should find
20 What 'twere to kill a father; so should Fleance.

But, peace! for from broad words,[1] and 'cause he fail'd
His presence at the tyrant's feast,[2] I hear,
Macduff lives in disgrace. Sir, can you tell
Where he bestows himself?
LORD.   The son of Duncan,
From whom this tyrant holds the due of birth,[3]
Lives in the English court; and is receiv'd
Of[4] the most pious Edward[5] with such grace
That the malevolence of fortune nothing
Takes from his high respect. Thither Macduff
Is gone to pray the holy king, upon his aid   30
To wake Northumberland and warlike Siward[6];
That by the help of these, with Him above
To ratify the work, we may again
Give to our tables meat, sleep to our nights;
Free from our feasts and banquets bloody knives,[7]
Do faithful homage and receive free honours;[8]
All which we pine for now: and this report

[1] *from broad words.* On account of talking too freely.
[2] *'cause . . . feast.* Because he did not attend Macbeth's banquet. "Tyrant" here means "usurper," not necessarily a tyrant in the modern sense.
[3] *holds . . . birth.* Withholds the throne.   [4] *By.*
[5] Edward the Confessor, a king of England (1042–1066) noted especially for his piety.
[6] According to Holinshed's *Chronicles*, Shakespeare's source (see page 88), Siward was earl of Northumberland, a large district just south of Scotland.
[7] *Free . . . knives.* Free our feasts and banquets from bloody knives; that is, from murder.
[8] *free honours.* Honors such as free citizens receive from their lawful king.

[1] Agreed with.   [2] Conducted, carried out.
[3] By.   [4] Indeed.   [5] Lack, be without.
[6] Immediately.   [7] Slaves.   [8] *and 't.* If it.

Hath so exasperate the king, that he
Prepares for some attempt of war.
　　LENNOX.　　　　Sent he to Macduff?
40　LORD. He did: and with an absolute
　　"Sir, not I,"
The cloudy[1] messenger turns me his
　　back,[2]
And hums, as who should say, "You'll
　　rue the time
That clogs[3] me with this answer."
　　LENNOX.　　　　And that well might
Advise him to a caution,[4] to hold what
　　distance
His wisdom can provide. Some holy
　　angel
Fly to the court of England and unfold
His[5] message ere he come; that a swift
　　blessing
May soon return to this our suffering
　　country
Under a hand accurs'd!
　　LORD. I'll send my prayers with him.
　　　　　　　　　　　　　　　[Exeunt]

Discussion Hints

ACT III, SCENE I

1. Is it the sound of the trumpet that causes
Banquo to say "But hush! no more"? Or
is it something else that stops his soliloquy?
How does this speech agree with the decision
you reached in answering the first general
question under Act II (p. 112)?

2. Who are meant by "our bloody cousins"
(l. 29)? Does this reference to them indicate any change in Macbeth during the
time that has elapsed?

3. Paraphrase, sentence by sentence, Macbeth's speech (ll. 47–59).

4. Study the brief speeches of the First and
Second Murderers. Can you see any difference between the two men? Shakespeare generally made even his minor characters indi-

vidual. For which part would you select the
older man? What differences would be shown
by their voices? movements? features? See if
you can find somewhere pictures of two men
who seem suited to the two parts. Perhaps
you may think of two present-day actors who
seem to you suited to the parts.

SCENE II

1. What feeling has begun to work upon
both Macbeth and Lady Macbeth? Quote
the lines in which each expresses this feeling.

2. Memorize the speech beginning "Duncan is in his grave" (ll. 22–26).

3. Do you think Lady Macbeth realized
that Macbeth was definitely planning the
murder of Banquo and Fleance? Quote any
line that justifies your answer.

4. "Things bad begun make strong themselves by ill" (l. 55). Using this as the topic
sentence, write a paragraph showing how **it**
is true of the deeds of Macbeth.

SCENE III

1. Plan the staging of this scene to make it
as dramatic as possible. Consider the lighting
particularly. How would you arrange the
escape of Fleance so as to make it plausible?

2. Two theories have been brought forward
at this point by different critics: (1) that
the Third Murderer was Macbeth himself;
(2) that it was Ross. Study carefully the text
of this scene and the next, and list your arguments for and against each theory. If time
permits, the question at issue will make an
excellent subject for an expository theme or
for a class debate.

3. To Macbeth the murder of Fleance was
even more important than that of Banquo.
Why?

SCENE IV

1. Make a diagram showing how you
would seat the guests in this banquet scene.
How was the room lighted?

2. Compare the appearing and disappear-
ing of the Ghost here with that of the dagger
in the earlier scene. Why does the Ghost
usually appear on the stage? Does anyone
except Macbeth see it? If you have ever
seen Shakespeare's *Hamlet* performed, describe the appearance of the Ghost. From

---

[1] Frowning, sullen.
[2] *turns me ... back.* Turns his back. "Me" means
　"for me" and is an example of the ethical
　dative, used here, as often elsewhere in
　Elizabethan English, for slight emphasis.
[3] Burdens.
[4] *Advise ... caution.* Suggest that Macduff be
　cautious.　　　　　　[5] Macduff's.

what you know of *Julius Cæsar* (in the revised edition of *Achievement* of this series), *Hamlet*, and *Macbeth*, do you think Shakespeare's audience expected the ghosts to appear visibly on the stage?

3. Would it not have been better for Lady Macbeth to allow the guests to leave when Ross first suggested it? Give a reason for your answer. But notice how later ("At once, good night," etc., l. 118) she interrupts quickly to dismiss them all. Explain the change.

4. What reason other than sympathy might have caused Ross's question "What sights, my lord?" (l. 116)?

5. "There's not a one . . . fee'd" (ll. 131–132). Just what does this mean? What does it show of Macbeth's state of mind?

6. "More shall they speak" (l. 134). What does Macbeth hope or fear the Witches will tell him?

7. What is your own feeling toward Macbeth at the end of this scene?

SCENE V

Many critics believe that this scene was not written by Shakespeare, but by some hack-writer in later times to meet the demands of a stage manager. These critics point out, for example, that the scene has no dramatic purpose; that it lacks entirely the weird and gloomy atmosphere of the other witch scenes; and that it is written in iambic* couplets* of eight syllables each, a metrical form not characteristic of Shakespeare. On the other hand, many critics point out that Shakespeare's audience believed in witches and would be interested in seeing them presented on the stage. On the basis of these arguments would you omit the scene from your production? The same arguments are applied to IV, i, ll. 39–43 and 125–132.

SCENE VI

1. Lennox and the other lord may be taken as representing public opinion concerning Macbeth in Scotland and outside. Notice what they call Macbeth. Give a brief statement summing up the state of things.

2. Summarize the information given here of plans to oppose Macbeth.

General Questions or Assignments on Act III

1. The turning-point, pivot, or climax (p. 81) of the play is reached in this act. What deed marks it? Beginning with the inciting force (that is, the event which started the action of the play), list in order each step in the rising action up to the climax.

2. The falling action begins immediately after the turning-point. What is the first event in it?

3. The suggestion has been made that Shakespeare intended that the first ghost to appear in Scene iv should be Duncan's, not Banquo's. Quote any words in the text that would bear out this view. What is your opinion?

4. Which part in this act calls for the greater skill in acting, Macbeth's or Lady Macbeth's? Give specific illustrations to support your answer.

ACT IV

SCENE I. *A cavern. In the middle, a boiling cauldron*

[Macbeth visits the Witches. Their equivocal prophecies at first please him and then anger him. When we hear his plan to wipe out Macduff's family, we realize how low he has fallen.]

Thunder. Enter the three WITCHES

1 WITCH. Thrice the brinded cat[1] hath mew'd.

[1] *brinded cat*. A brindled (brown streaked with black) cat, associated with witchcraft.

2 WITCH. Thrice, and once the hedge-pig[1] whin'd.

3 WITCH. Harpier[2] cries; 'tis time, 'tis time.

1 WITCH. Round about the cauldron go;

In the poison'd entrails throw.

[1] Hedgehog. The hedgehog is a creature of ill omen because it can disappear almost before one's eyes.

[2] A "familiar," a spirit attendant on witches.

Toad, that under cold stone
Days and nights has thirty-one
Swelter'd[1] venom sleeping got,[2]
Boil thou first i' the charmed pot.

10   ALL. Double, double toil and trouble;
Fire burn and cauldron bubble.

    2 WITCH. Fillet of a fenny snake,[3]
In the cauldron boil and bake;
Eye of newt[4] and toe of frog,
Wool of bat and tongue of dog,
Adder's fork[5] and blind-worm's sting,
Lizard's leg and howlet's[6] wing,
For a charm of powerful trouble,
Like a hell-broth boil and bubble.

20   ALL. Double, double toil and trouble;
Fire burn and cauldron bubble.

    3 WITCH. Scale of dragon, tooth of wolf,
Witches' mummy,[7] maw and gulf[8]
Of the ravin'd[9] salt-sea shark,
Root of hemlock[10] digg'd i' the dark,
Liver of blaspheming Jew,
Gall of goat, and slips of yew[11]
Sliver'd in the moon's eclipse,
Nose of Turk and Tartar's lips,
30 Finger of birth-strangled babe
Ditch-deliver'd by a drab,
Make the gruel thick and slab[12]:
Add thereto a tiger's chaudron,[13]
For th' ingredients of our cauldron.

[1] Exuded, sweated.
[2] *Toad . . . got.* Toads were believed to secrete poison. A toad that had slept under a stone for a time was supposed to be particularly deadly.
[3] *Fillet . . . snake.* Slice of a marsh snake. Each ingredient of the Witches' mixture is part of some creature associated with magic and witchcraft.
[4] A water lizard.
[5] Forked tongue.   [6] Young owl's.
[7] Part of an embalmed corpse. In Shakespeare's day powdered mummy was used as medicine. A mummy of a witch would naturally be associated with evil magic.
[8] *maw and gulf.* Stomach and throat.
[9] Ravenous.
[10] A plant associated with witchcraft.
[11] The yew tree was often planted in graveyards and was regarded as poisonous. Like other plants used in witchcraft, it was thought to be more effective if it was gathered during an eclipse of the moon.
[12] Slimy.   [13] Entrails.

    ALL. Double, double toil and trouble;
Fire burn and cauldron bubble.

    2 WITCH. Cool it with a baboon's blood,
Then the charm is firm and good.

Enter HECATE *to the other three* WITCHES

    HECATE. O, well done! I commend your pains[1];
And every one shall share i' th' gains: 40
And now about the cauldron sing,
Like elves and fairies in a ring,
Enchanting all that you put in.
    [*Music, and a Song*, "Black spirits," etc.]
    [*Exit* HECATE]

    2 WITCH. By the pricking of my thumbs,
Something wicked this way comes:
Open, locks,
Whoever knocks!

Enter MACBETH

    MACBETH. How now, you secret, black, and midnight hags!
What is 't you do?
    ALL.   A deed without a name.
    MACBETH. I conjure you, by that which you profess   50
Howe'er you come to know it, answer me:
Though you untie the winds and let them fight
Against the churches; though the yesty[2] waves
Confound and swallow navigation up;
Though bladed corn[3] be lodg'd,[4] and trees blown down;
Though castles topple on their warders' heads;
Though palaces and pyramids do slope

[1] The trouble you have taken.
[2] Frothy, like yeast.
[3] *bladed corn.* Young grain not yet in the ear Here, as generally in England, "corn" means wheat, rye, barley, or some other small grain, not "maize" (Indian] corn), as in America.
[4] Beaten down.

"Macbeth! beware Macduff"

Their heads to their foundations; though
    the treasure
Of nature's germens tumble all together,[1]
60 Even till destruction sicken; answer me
To what I ask you.
  1 WITCH.   Speak.
  2 WITCH.   Demand.
  3 WITCH.   We'll answer.
  1 WITCH. Say, if thou'dst rather hear
    it from our mouths,
Or from our masters?
  MACBETH.   Call 'em, let me see 'em.
  1 WITCH. Pour in sow's blood, that
    hath eaten
Her nine farrow[2]; grease that's sweaten[3]
From the murderer's gibbet[4] throw
Into the flame.
  ALL.   Come, high or low;
Thyself and office deftly show!

Thunder. First APPARITION, *an*
    armed Head[5]

MACBETH. Tell me, thou unknown
    power, —
  1 WITCH.   He knows thy thought:
70 Hear his speech, but say thou nought.
  1 APPARITION. Macbeth! Macbeth!
  Macbeth! beware Macduff;
Beware the thane of Fife. — Dismiss me:
  enough.   [*Descends*]
  MACBETH. Whate'er thou art, for thy
  good caution, thanks;
Thou hast harp'd my fear aright: but
  one word more, —
  1 WITCH. He will not be commanded:
  here's another,
More potent than the first.

Thunder. Second APPARITION, *a*
    bloody Child[6]

2 APPARITION. Macbeth! Macbeth!
  Macbeth!

---

[1] *the treasure . . . together*. The treasury containing all the seeds or elements of nature be utterly destroyed
[2] *nine farrow*. Litter of nine pigs.
[3] Sweated.   [4] Gallows.
[5] Head wearing a helmet. This foretells the beheading of Macbeth (V, viii, l. 55).
[6] Macduff.

MACBETH. Had I three[1] ears, I'd hear
  thee.
  2 APPARITION. Be bloody, bold, and
  resolute; laugh to scorn
The power of man, for none of woman
  born   80
Shall harm Macbeth.[2]   [*Descends*]
  MACBETH. Then live, Macduff: what
  need I fear of thee?
But yet I'll make assurance double sure,
And take a bond of fate: thou shalt not
  live;[3]
That I may tell pale-hearted fear it
  lies,
And sleep in spite of thunder.

Thunder. Third APPARITION, *a Child*
    crowned,[4] *with a tree in his hand*

                  What is this,
That rises like the issue of a king,
And wears upon his baby brow the round
And top of sovereignty?[5]
  ALL.   Listen, but speak not to 't.
  3 APPARITION. Be lion-mettl'd, proud;
  and take no care   90
Who chafes, who frets, or where conspirers are:
Macbeth shall never vanquish'd be until
Great Birnam* wood to high Dunsinane
  hill
Shall come against him.[6]   [*Descends*]
  MACBETH.   That will never be:

---

[1] Macbeth says "three" probably because the Apparition has just called his name three times. He doubtless means "If I had three ears, I'd listen with them all."
[2] *none . . . Macbeth*. Remember this prophecy; it will be important later.
[3] *take . . . live*. To make the promise of fate certain, I'll kill Macduff.
[4] *Child crowned*. Malcolm, who became king after the death of Macbeth. In the final assault upon Macbeth's forces, Malcolm's soldiers carry branches (V, iv).
[5] *round . . . sovereignty*. Crown.
[6] *until . . . him*. Until Birnam* wood (forest) move twelve miles away to Dunsinane castle, a seeming impossibility. Dunsinane is the stronghold where Macbeth makes his last stand. "Dunsinane" is here pronounced dŭn sĭn'ăn; elsewhere in the play it is pronounced dŭn'sĭ nān.

Who can impress[1] the forest, bid the tree
Unfix his earth-bound root? Sweet bodements[2]! good!
Rebellion's head, rise never till the wood
Of Birnam rise, and our high-plac'd Macbeth
Shall live the lease of nature,[3] pay his breath
100 To time and mortal custom.[4] Yet my heart
Throbs to know one thing: tell me, if your art
Can tell so much: shall Banquo's issue ever
Reign in this kingdom?
ALL.   Seek to know no more.
MACBETH. I will[5] be satisfied: deny me this,
And an eternal curse fall on you! Let me know:
Why sinks that cauldron? and what noise in this?   [Hautboys]
1 WITCH. Show!
2 WITCH. Show!
3 WITCH. Show!
110 ALL. Show his eyes, and grieve his heart;
Come like shadows, so depart!

A show of eight Kings,[6] *the last with a glass*[7] *in his hand;* BANQUO's Ghost *following*

MACBETH.   Thou art too like the spirit of Banquo; down!
Thy crown does sear mine eyeballs. And thy hair,
Thou other gold-bound brow, is like the first:
A third is like the former. Filthy hags!

Why do you show me this? A fourth! Start, eyes![1]
What, will the line stretch out to th' crack of doom?
Another yet! A seventh! I'll see no more:
And yet the eighth appears, who bears a glass[2]
Which shows me many more; and some I see   120
That twofold balls and treble sceptres[3] carry:
Horrible sight! Now I see 'tis true;
For the blood-bolter'd[4] Banquo smiles upon me,
And points at them for his. [*Apparitions vanish*] What, is this so?
1 WITCH. Ay, sir, all this is so; but why
Stands Macbeth thus amazedly?
Come, sisters, cheer we up his sprites,[5]
And show the best of our delights:
I'll charm the air to give a sound,
While you perform your antic round[6];   130
That this great king may kindly say
Our duties did his welcome pay.
[*Music. The* WITCHES *dance, and vanish with* HECATE]
MACBETH. Where are they? Gone? Let this pernicious hour
Stand aye[7] accursed in the calendar!
Come in, without there!

Enter LENNOX

LENNOX.   What's your grace's will?
MACBETH. Saw you the weird sisters?
LENNOX.   No, my lord.

---

[1] Compel into service in his army.
[2] Predictions.
[3] *lease of nature.* Normal length of life.
[4] *pay . . . custom.* Die a natural death.
[5] Am determined to.
[6] *A show . . . Kings.* The eight Scottish kings of the Stewart* line, — Robert II (1371–1390), Robert III, and the six Jameses, — who were said to be the descendants of the traditional Banquo.
[7] Here, a magic looking-glass revealing the future.

D

[1] *Start, eyes!* That is, Start, eyes, out of your sockets!
[2] A magic looking-glass, which, it was believed, could reveal future events.
[3] *twofold . . . sceptres.* James* I of England (1603–1625), who was also James VI of Scotland, was the first of the traditional descendants of Banquo to sit on the English throne. The twofold ball represents his double coronation, as king both of England and of Scotland. The treble scepter probably symbolizes the three kingdoms of England, Scotland, and Ireland.
[4] With hair matted with blood.   [5] Spirits.
[6] *antic round.* Fantastic dance.
[7] *aye* (ā). Forever.

MACBETH. Came they not by you?

LENNOX.   No, indeed, my lord.

MACBETH. Infected be the air whereon they ride,

And damn'd all those that trust them! I did hear

140 The galloping of horse: who was't came by?

LENNOX. 'Tis two or three, my lord, that bring you word

Macduff is fled to England.

MACBETH.   Fled to England!

LENNOX. Ay, my good lord.

MACBETH. [*Aside*] Time, thou anticipat'st[1] my dread exploits:

The flighty[2] purpose never is o'ertook[3]

Unless the deed go with it: from this moment

The very firstlings of my heart shall be

The firstlings of my hand.[1] And even now,

To crown my thoughts with acts, be it thought and done:

The castle of Macduff I will surprise;   150

Seize upon Fife; give to the edge o' the sword

His wife, his babes, and all unfortunate souls

That trace him in his line.[2] No boasting like a fool;

This deed I'll do before this purpose cool:

But no more sights! Where are these gentlemen?

Come, bring me where they are.

          [*Exeunt*]

SCENE II. *Fife.* MACDUFF'S *castle*

[The peaceful home life of Macduff's family is brutally cut short by the Murderers. The dialogue between the little boy and his mother serves as a relief from the stark intensity of the main tragedy and contrasts strikingly with the brutal murder that is to follow. This needless crime brings on revolt in the kingdom and arouses Macduff and Malcolm to revenge.]

Enter LADY MACDUFF, *her* SON, *and* ROSS

LADY MACDUFF. What had he[4] done, to make him fly the land?

ROSS. You must have patience, madam.

LADY MACDUFF.   He had none;

His flight was madness: when our actions do not,

Our fears do make us traitors.

ROSS.   You know not

Whether it was his wisdom or his fear.

LADY MACDUFF. Wisdom! to leave his wife, to leave his babes,

His mansion, and his titles, in a place

From whence himself does fly! He loves us not;

He wants the natural touch:[3] for the poor wren,

The most diminutive of birds, will fight, 10

Her young ones in her nest, against the owl.

All is the fear and nothing is the love;

As little is the wisdom, where the flight

So runs against all reason.

ROSS.   My dearest coz,[4]

I pray you, school[5] yourself: but, for[6] your husband,

He is noble, wise, judicious, and best knows

The fits o' the season.[7] I dare not speak much further:

But cruel are the times, when we are traitors

And do not know ourselves[8]; when we hold rumour

---

[1] *from . . . hand.* In the future I am determined to put my thoughts into immediate action.
[2] *That . . . line.* Who are descended from him.
[3] *wants . . . touch.* Lacks the ordinary natural feelings toward his family.
[4] Cousin. In Shakespeare's day this form of address did not necessarily imply any close kinship.   [5] Control.   [6] As for.
[7] *fits . . . season.* Disorders of the present time.
[8] *do . . . ourselves.* That is, are not conscious of being traitors.

---

[1] Dost prevent.   [2] Swift.
[3] Achieved.   [4] Macduff.

20 From what we fear, yet know not what
    we fear,
But float upon a wild and violent sea
Each way and move. I take my leave of
    you;
Shall not be long but I'll be here again.
Things at the worst will cease, or else
    climb upward
To what they were before. My pretty
    cousin,
Blessing upon you!
  LADY MACDUFF. Father'd he is, and
    yet he's fatherless.
  ROSS. I am so much a fool, should I
    stay longer,
It would be my disgrace and your dis-
    comfort :[1]
30 I take my leave at once.   [*Exit*]
  LADY MACDUFF.   Sirrah,[2] your
    father 's dead :
And what will you do now? How will you
    live?
  SON. As birds do, mother.
  LADY MACDUFF.   What, with
    worms and flies?
  SON. With what I get, I mean; and
    so do they.
  LADY MACDUFF. Poor bird! thou'dst
    never fear the net nor lime,[3]
The pitfall nor the gin.[4]
  SON. Why should I, mother? Poor
    birds they are not set for.[5]
My father is not dead, for all your say-
    ing.
  LADY MACDUFF. Yes, he is dead: how
    wilt thou do for a father?
  SON. Nay, how will you do for a
    husband?
40 LADY MACDUFF. Why, I can buy me
    twenty at any market.

[1] *should . . . discomfort.* Were I to stay any
  longer I should disgrace myself and make
  you uncomfortable by my weeping.
[2] *Sirrah,* etc. The playful yet pathetic dialogue
  between the little boy and his mother is one
  of Shakespeare's best scenes dealing with
  children.
[3] A sticky substance used for catching small
  birds.   [4] Snare.
[5] *Poor . . . for.* Traps are not set for poor birds
  such as I am.

  SON. Then you'll buy 'em to sell
again.
  LADY MACDUFF. Thou speak'st with
    all thy wit; and yet, i' faith
With wit enough for thee.
  SON. Was my father a traitor,
mother?
  LADY MACDUFF. Ay, that he was.
  SON. What is a traitor?
  LADY MACDUFF. Why, one that
swears and lies.[1]   50
  SON. And be all traitors that do so?
  LADY MACDUFF. Every one that does
so is a traitor, and must be hang'd.
  SON. And must they all be hang'd
that swear and lie?
  LADY MACDUFF. Every one.
  SON. Who must hang them?
  LADY MACDUFF. Why, the honest
men.
  SON. Then the liars and swearers are 60
fools; for there are liars and swearers
enow[2] to beat the honest men and hang
up them.
  LADY MACDUFF. Now, God help thee,
poor monkey! But how wilt thou do for
a father?
  SON. If he were dead, you'd weep for
him; if you would not, it were a good sign
that I should quickly have a new
father.   70
  LADY MACDUFF. Poor prattler, how
thou talk'st!

Enter a MESSENGER

  MESSENGER. Bless you, fair dame! I
    am not to you known,
Though in your state of honour I am
    perfect.[3]
I doubt[4] some danger does approach you
    nearly :
If you will take a homely man's advice,
Be not found here; hence, with your
    little ones.

[1] *swears and lies.* Breaks his oath of allegiance
  to his king or his marriage vow, as her husband has done.   [2] Enough.
[3] *Though . . . perfect.* I have perfect knowledge
  of your rank.   [4] Fear.

To fright you thus, methinks I am too
    savage;
To do worse to you were fell[1] cruelty,
80 Which is too nigh your person. Heaven
    preserve you!
I dare abide no longer.   [*Exit*]
    LADY MACDUFF.   Whither should
    I fly?
I have done no harm. But I remember
    now
I am in this earthly world; where to do
    harm
Is often laudable, to do good sometime
Accounted dangerous folly: why then,
    alas,
Do I put up that womanly defence,
To say I have done no harm?

Enter MURDERERS

             What are these faces?
1 MURDERER. Where is your husband?
LADY MACDUFF. I hope, in no place
    so unsanctified
Where such as thou mayst find him.
1 MURDERER.   He's a traitor. 90
SON. Thou liest, thou shag-ear'd[1] vil-
    lain!
1 MURDERER. [*Stabbing him*] What,
    you egg!
Young fry[2] of treachery!
SON.   He has kill'd me, mother:
Run away, I pray you!   [*Dies*]
    [*Exit* LADY MACDUFF, *crying* "Mur-
      der!" *Exeunt* MURDERERS, *fol-
      lowing her*]

SCENE III. *England. Before the King's palace*

[Macduff, in England, tries to persuade
Malcolm to return and claim his throne. Malcolm, at first suspicious of Macduff's motives
and sentiments, at last agrees and reveals his
intention to invade Scotland. Macduff is told
of the murder of his family. The storm of war
is ready to break.]

Enter MALCOLM *and* MACDUFF

MALCOLM. Let us seek out some deso-
    late shade, and there
Weep our sad bosoms empty.
    MACDUFF.   Let us rather
Hold fast the mortal[2] sword, and, like
    good men,
Bestride our down-fall'n birthdom.[3] Each
    new morn
New widows howl, new orphans cry,
    new sorrows
Strike heaven on the face, that it re-
    sounds
As if it felt with Scotland, and yell'd out
Like syllable of dolour.[4]
    MALCOLM. What I believe, I'll wail;

What know, believe; and what I can re-
    dress,
As I shall find the time to friend,[3] I will. 10
What you have spoke, it may be so per-
    chance.
This tyrant, whose sole name[4] blisters our
    tongues,
Was once thought honest: you have
    lov'd him well;
He hath not touch'd you yet. I am
    young; but something
You may deserve of him through me, and
    wisdom
To offer up a weak, poor, innocent lamb
T' appease an angry god.[5]
    MACDUFF. I am not treacherous.
    MALCOLM.   But Macbeth is.
A good and virtuous nature may recoil
In an imperial charge.[6] But I shall crave
    your pardon;   20

---

[1] Deadly.
[2] Deadly.
[3] *Bestride . . . birthdom.* Stand astride our fallen
    native land to defend it.
[4] *Like . . . dolour.* A similar cry of grief.

[1] Shaggy-haired.   [2] Offspring.
[3] *to friend.* Favorable.
[4] *whose sole name.* The mere mention of whose
    name.
[5] *something . . . god.* Malcolm suggests that Mac-
    duff might win the royal favor by betraying
    him to Macbeth.
[6] *recoil . . . charge.* Turn (to evil) under a king's
    command.

That which you are, my thoughts cannot
   transpose:
Angels are bright still, though the brightest fell:
Though all things foul would wear the
   brows of grace,
Yet grace must still look so.[1]
    MACDUFF.   I have lost my hopes.
    MALCOLM. Perchance even there
   where I did find my doubts.
Why in that rawness[2] left you wife and
   child,
Those precious motives, those strong
   knots of love,
Without leave-taking? I pray you,
Let not my jealousies be your dishonours,
30 But mine own safeties:[3] you may be
   rightly just,
Whatever I shall think.
    MACDUFF.   Bleed, bleed,
   poor country!
Great tyranny, lay thou thy basis sure,
For goodness dare not check thee; wear
   thou thy wrongs;
The title is affeer'd[4]! Fare thee well,
   lord:
I would not be the villain that thou
   think'st
For the whole space that's in the tyrant's
   grasp,
And the rich East to boot.
    MALCOLM.   Be not offended:
I speak not as in absolute fear of you.
I think our country sinks beneath the
   yoke;
40 It weeps, it bleeds; and each new day a
   gash
Is added to her wounds: I think withal

---

[1] *That . . . so.* What I think of you cannot
change you: though the brightest of the
angels (Lucifer*) fell, angels are still bright;
though all foul things should assume the
lovely appearance of grace, it would not do
for grace to look foul merely on that account.
(Read again I, iv, ll. 11–12, and Malcolm's
general meaning will be clear.)

[2] Unprepared state.

[3] *Let . . . safeties.* Do not regard my suspicions
(jealousies) as intended to discredit you, but
to safeguard myself.

[4] Confirmed.

There would be hands uplifted in my
   right;
And here from gracious England have I
   offer
Of goodly thousands: but, for all this,
When I shall tread upon the tyrant's
   head,
Or wear it on my sword, yet my poor
   country
Shall have more vices than it had before;
More suffer, and more sundry[1] ways
   than ever,
By him that shall succeed.
    MACDUFF.   What should he be?
    MALCOLM. It is myself I mean; in
   whom I know   50
All the particulars of vice so grafted,
That, when they shall be open'd, black
   Macbeth
Will seem as pure as snow; and the poor
   state
Esteem him as a lamb, being compar'd
With my confineless harms.[2]
    MACDUFF.   Not in the legions
Of horrid hell can come a devil more
   damn'd
In evils to top Macbeth.
    MALCOLM.   I grant him bloody,
Luxurious, avaricious, false, deceitful,
Sudden, malicious, smacking of every sin
That has a name: but there's no bottom,
   none,   60
In my voluptuousness; your wives, your
   daughters,
Your matrons, and your maids, could not
   fill up
The cistern of my lust, and my desire
All continent[3] impediments would o'er-
   bear,
That did oppose my will. Better Mac-
   beth
Than such an one to reign.
    MACDUFF.   Boundless intemperance
In nature is a tyranny; it hath been
Th' untimely emptying of the happy
   throne,

---

[1] Various.

[2] *my confineless harms.* The boundless evils that
I shall do.   [3] Restraining.

And fall of many kings. But fear not yet
70 To take upon you what is yours: you
　　may
Convey[1] your pleasures in a spacious
　　plenty,
And yet seem cold, the time you may so
　　hoodwink.[2]
We have willing dames enough; there
　　cannot be
That vulture in you, to devour so many
As will to greatness dedicate themselves,
Finding it so inclin'd.
　　MALCOLM.　　　With this there grows
In my most ill-compos'd affection[3] such
A stanchless[4] avarice that, were I king,
I should cut off the nobles for their lands,
80 Desire his jewels and this other's[5] house:
And my more-having would be as a
　　sauce
To make me hunger more, that I should
　　forge
Quarrels unjust against the good and
　　loyal,
Destroying them for wealth.
　　MACDUFF.　　　　　　This avarice
Sticks deeper, grows with more per-
　　nicious root
Than summer-seeming[6] lust, and it hath
　　been
The sword of our slain kings:[7] yet do not
　　fear;
Scotland hath foisons[8] to fill up your will
Of your mere own:[9] all these are port-
　　able,[10]
90 With other graces weigh'd.[11]
　　MALCOLM.　But I have none: the
　　king-becoming graces,

As justice, verity, temperance, stable-
　　ness,
Bounty, perseverance, mercy, lowliness,
Devotion, patience, courage, fortitude,
I have no relish[1] of them; but abound
In the division of each several crime,[2]
Acting it many ways. Nay, had I power,
　　I should
Pour the sweet milk of concord into hell,
Uproar the universal peace, confound
All unity on earth.
　　MACDUFF.　　　　O Scotland, Scotland![100]
　　MALCOLM.　If such an one be fit to
　　govern, speak:
I am as I have spoken.
　　MACDUFF.　　　　　　Fit to govern!
No, not to live. O nation miserable,
With an untitled tyrant bloody-scepter'd,
When shalt thou see thy wholesome days
　　again,
Since that the truest issue of thy throne
By his own interdiction[3] stands ac-
　　curs'd,
And does blaspheme his breed? Thy
　　royal father
Was a most sainted king: the queen that
　　bore thee,
Oftener upon her knees than on her feet,[110]
Died every day she liv'd.[4] Fare thee well!
These evils thou repeat'st upon thyself
Hath banish'd me from Scotland. O my
　　breast,
Thy hope ends here!
　　MALCOLM.　　　　Macduff, this noble
　　passion,
Child of integrity, hath from my soul
Wip'd the black scruples, reconcil'd my
　　thoughts
To thy good truth and honour. Devilish
　　Macbeth
By many of these trains[5] hath sought to
　　win me
Into his power; and modest wisdom
　　plucks[6] me

---

[1] Indulge.
[2] the time . . . hoodwink. You may so deceive the world.
[3] ill-compos'd affection. Evil disposition.
[4] Not capable of being satisfied.
[5] his, this other's. This one's, that one's.
[6] Befitting youth (the summer of life).
[7] The sword . . . kings. That which hath slain our kings.
[8] Plenty.
[9] your mere own. That which belongs to you alone.
[10] Bearable.
[11] With . . . weigh'd. Counterbalanced by the virtues you possess.

[1] Flavor, smack.
[2] In . . . crime. In every form of each separate offense.　　[3] Decree.
[4] Died . . . liv'd. Lived a life of pious self-sacrifice. "I die daily" (1 Corinthians 15 : 31).
[5] Plots.　　　　　　[6] Restrains.

120 From over-credulous haste: but God above
Deal between thee and me! for even now
I put myself to thy direction, and
Unspeak mine own detraction; here abjure
The taints and blames I laid upon myself,
For strangers to my nature. I am yet
Unknown to woman, never was forsworn,
Scarcely have coveted what was mine own,
At no time broke my faith, would not betray
The devil to his fellow, and delight
130 No less in truth than life: my first false speaking
Was this upon myself. What I am truly,
Is thine and my poor country's to command;
Whither, indeed, before thy here-approach,
Old Siward, with ten thousand warlike men,
Already at a point,[1] was setting forth:
Now we'll together; and the chance of goodness
Be like our warranted quarrel![2] Why are you silent?
    MACDUFF. Such welcome and unwelcome things at once
'Tis hard to reconcile.

Enter a DOCTOR

140 MALCOLM. Well; more anon. — Comes the king forth, I pray you?
    DOCTOR. Ay, sir; there are a crew of wretched souls
That stay his cure:[3] their malady convinces
The great assay of art[4]; but at his touch,
Such sanctity hath heaven given his hand,
They presently[1] amend.
    MALCOLM.   I thank you, doctor.
        [*Exit* DOCTOR]
    MACDUFF. What's the disease he means?
    MALCOLM.   'Tis call'd the evil*:
A most miraculous work in this good king;
Which often, since my here-remain in England,
I have seen him do. How he solicits[2] heaven,
Himself best knows: but strangely-visited[3] people,   150
All swoln and ulcerous, pitiful to the eye,
The mere despair[4] of surgery, he cures,
Hanging a golden stamp[5] about their necks,
Put on with holy prayers: and 'tis spoken,
To the succeeding royalty he leaves
The healing benediction. With this strange virtue,
He hath a heavenly gift of prophecy,
And sundry blessings hang about his throne,
That speak[6] him full of grace.

Enter ROSS

    MACDUFF.   See, who comes here?
    MALCOLM. My countryman; but yet
I know[7] him not.   160
    MACDUFF. My ever-gentle cousin, welcome hither.
    MALCOLM. I know him now. Good God, betimes[8] remove
The means that makes us strangers!
    ROSS.   Sir, amen.
    MACDUFF. Stands Scotland where it did?
    ROSS.   Alas, poor country,
Almost afraid to know itself! It cannot

---

[1] *at a point.* Prepared.
[2] *the chance . . quarrel.* May the chances of success be as sure as the justness of our cause.
[3] *stay . . . cure.* Wait to be healed.
[4] *convinces . . . art.* Overcomes the best efforts of physicians.
[1] Immediately.   [2] Prevails upon.
[3] Strangely afflicted.
[4] *mere despair.* Absolute, utter despair.
[5] Coin.   [6] Show him to be.
[7] Recognize.   [8] Speedily.

Be call'd our mother, but our grave:
where nothing,
But who knows nothing, is once seen to
smile;[1]
Where sighs and groans and shrieks that
rend the air,
Are made, not mark'd[2]; where violent
sorrow seems
170 A modern ecstasy[3]: the dead man's knell
Is there scarce ask'd for who; and good
men's lives
Expire before the flowers in their caps,
Dying or ere[4] they sicken.
    MACDUFF.   O, relation
Too nice,[5] and yet too true!
    MALCOLM.   What's the newest grief?
    ROSS. That of an hour's age doth hiss
the speaker[6];
Each minute teems[7] a new one.
    MACDUFF.   How does my wife?
    ROSS. Why, well.
    MACDUFF.   And all my children?
    ROSS.   Well too.
    MACDUFF. The tyrant has not bat-
ter'd at their peace?
    ROSS. No; they were well at peace
when I did leave 'em.[8]
180   MACDUFF. Be not a niggard of your
speech:[9] how goes 't?
    ROSS. When I came hither to trans-
port the tidings
Which I have heavily borne, there ran a
rumour
Of many worthy fellows that were out[10];
Which was to my belief witness'd[11] the
rather,

[1] *where . . . smile.* Where nobody but a fool is
seen to smile.
[2] Noticed.
[3] *modern ecstasy.* Trivial excitement.
[4] *or ere.* Before.
[5] *relation . . . nice.* Story too detailed.
[6] *That . . . speaker.* In Scotland griefs come so
fast that one but an hour old is ancient history, and therefore the narrator is hissed at
by those who are up to date.
[7] Brings forth.
[8] *No . . . 'em.* Ross's words, with their puns
on "well" and "at peace," are, of course,
intentionally ambiguous.
[9] *a niggard . . . speech.* Stingy with your words.
[10] In arms, in rebellion.   [11] Made believable.

For that[1] I saw the tyrant's power[2] a-foot:
Now is the time of help; your eye[3] in
Scotland
Would create soldiers, make our women
fight,
To doff[4] their dire distresses.
    MALCOLM.   Be 't their comfort
We are coming thither: gracious Eng-
land hath
Lent us good Siward and ten thousand
men;   190
An older and a better soldier none
That Christendom gives out.[5]
    ROSS.   Would I could answer
This comfort with the like! But I have
words
That would be[6] howl'd out in the desert
air,
Where hearing should not latch[7] them.
    MACDUFF.   What concern they?
The general cause? or is it a fee-grief
Due to some single breast?[8]
    ROSS.   No mind that's honest
But in it shares some woe; though the
main part
Pertains to you alone.
    MACDUFF.   If it be mine,
Keep it not from me, quickly let me have it.200
    ROSS. Let not your ears despise my
tongue for ever,
Which shall possess them with[9] the
heaviest sound
That ever yet they heard.
    MACDUFF.   Hum! I guess at it.
    ROSS. Your castle is surpris'd; your
wife and babes
Savagely slaughter'd: to relate the man-
ner,
Were, on the quarry[10] of these murder'd
deer,
To add the death of you.

[1] *For that.* Because.   [2] Army.
[3] Presence.   [4] Throw off; literally, do off.
[5] *gives out.* Proclaims.
[6] *would be.* Ought to be.   [7] Catch.
[8] *The general . . . breast.* Is it a general or an individual grief?
[9] *possess them with.* Make them possessors of.
[10] The heap of slain animals killed in a hunt;
here, Macduff's family.

MALCOLM.　　　　　　Merciful heaven!
What, man! ne'er pull your hat upon
　your brows;
Give sorrow words: the grief that does
　not speak
210 Whispers[1] the o'er-fraught[2] heart and
　bids it break.
　　MACDUFF. My children too?
　　ROSS.　　Wife, children, servants, all
That could be found.
　　MACDUFF.　　　And I must be from
　thence!
My wife kill'd too?
　　ROSS.　　　I have said.
　　MALCOLM.　　　Be comforted:
Let's make us medicines of our great
　revenge,
To cure this deadly grief.
　　MACDUFF. He has no children. — All
　my pretty ones?
Did you say all? O hell-kite! All?
What, all my pretty chickens and their
　dam[3]
At one fell swoop?
220　MALCOLM. Dispute[4] it like a man.
　　MACDUFF.　　　I shall do so;
But I must also feel it as a man:
I cannot but remember such things
　were,
That were most precious to me. Did
　heaven look on,
And would not take their part? Sinful
　Macduff,
They were all struck for thee! naught[5]
　that I am,
Not for their own demerits, but for
　mine,
Fell slaughter on their souls. Heaven
　rest them now!
　　MALCOLM. Be this the whetstone of
　your sword: let grief
Convert[6] to anger; blunt not the heart,
　enrage it.
230　MACDUFF. O, I could play the woman
　with mine eyes,
And braggart with my tongue! But,
　gentle heavens,

Cut short all intermission[1]; front to front
Bring thou this fiend of Scotland and
　myself;
Within my sword's length set him; if he
　scape,
Heaven forgive him too!
　　MALCOLM.　　This tune goes manly.
Come, go we to the king; our power[2]
　is ready;
Our lack is nothing but our leave.[3]
　Macbeth
Is ripe for shaking, and the powers above
Put on[4] their instruments. Receive
　what cheer you may:
The night is long that never finds the
　day.　　　　　　[Exeunt] 240

Discussion Hints

ACT IV, SCENE I

1. Since there was no drop curtain in the
theater of Shakespeare's day to mark the end
of the different acts and scenes, it was necessary to have the beginning of each scene
marked by the entrance of one or more actors.
For modern production would it not be more
effective to have the three Witches on the
stage when the curtain goes up? Write a
theme describing the most effective setting
for the opening of this scene. Include in it
the action for the first three speeches. Would
you have these speeches follow each other
without a pause? Would you have the audience hear the sounds the Witches refer to?

2. Why did Macbeth visit the Witches?
Did he get all the information he wished?
What did he get?

3. Compare the attitude of Macbeth and
the Witches toward each other with that in
the first meeting between them. What do the
differences indicate concerning Macbeth?

4. Describe briefly each of the Apparitions
and its significance to Macbeth.

5. Compare Macbeth's swift decision to
murder Lady Macduff and her children with
his earlier hesitation and dread before the
murder of Duncan. Refer to act and scene.
What does the comparison show of the change
in Macbeth? Which seems to you worse, the

---

[1] Whispers to.　　[2] Overburdened.　　[3] Mother.
[4] Strive against.　[5] Worthless person.　[6] Turn.

[1] Delay.　　　　　　　　[2] Army.
[3] *Our . . . leave.* All that we have left to do is to
　take our leave of King Edward.
[4] *Put on.* Incite.

murder of Duncan or that of Lady Macduff and her children? Why?

Scene II

1. Is this scene necessary to the plot? What would be the advantage or disadvantage of omitting it?

2. Who might perhaps have sent the Messenger to Lady Macduff?

Scene III

1. What is it that Malcolm fears from Macduff? Has he any ground for this fear?

2. How does Malcolm test Macduff's loyalty? Does this scene seem plausible to you? What might have been Shakespeare's reasons for putting it in?

3. In which scene, this one or the preceding one, do you get the more favorable picture of Macduff? Which do you think is the truer picture?

4. If you have read Shakespeare's *Julius Cæsar* (in the revised edition of *Achievement* of this series), compare Macduff's manner of receiving the news of his wife's death with that of Brutus under similar circumstances in *Julius Cæsar*, IV, iii. Which of the two men seems the more natural in his feelings and words? Can you give any reason for the difference?

5. The meaning of Macduff's words "He has no children" (l. 216) has been much discussed. Some critics believe that "he" refers to Macbeth, in which case the meaning would be, "If Macbeth had any children, he could not have been so brutal as to cause the murder of the child of another." Other critics believe that Macduff is referring to Malcolm and that the meaning is, "Malcolm has no children; if he had, he would not urge me coldly to be comforted, as he has just done." According to tradition Macbeth had a son, but Shakespeare does not mention his name. Does anything in the play suggest that Macbeth had a child? Would Macduff be so discourteous as to talk at, instead of to, the royal prince? Which of the two interpretations given above do you prefer? Give reasons for your answer.

General Questions or Assignments on Act IV

1. How does the length of this act compare with that of the preceding ones?

2. Make a list of the events that carry on the plot.

3. What do you learn from the text, the notes, and the correlation table (p. 16) about Edward the Confessor and "touching for the king's evil"?*

ACT V

Scene I. *Dunsinane. Ante-room in the castle*

[Lady Macbeth, at the mercy of her grief-disordered mind, walks in her sleep and acts her part and her husband's in the murder of Duncan. The violent end of her now hopeless life can be foreseen.]

Enter a Doctor *of Physic and a* Waiting-Gentlewoman

Doctor. I have two nights watch'd with you, but can perceive no truth in your report. When was it she last walk'd?

Gentlewoman. Since his majesty went into the field, I have seen her rise from her bed, throw her night-gown[1] upon her, unlock her closet,[2] take forth

[1] Dressing-gown.
[2] Private, personal room; boudoir. Not a closet in the modern sense.

paper, fold it, write upon 't, read it, afterwards seal it, and again return to bed; yet all this while in a most fast sleep. 10

Doctor. A great perturbation in nature, to receive at once the benefit of sleep, and do the effects of watching![1] In this slumbery agitation, besides her walking and other actual performances, what, at any time, have you heard her say?

Gentlewoman. That, sir, which I will not report after her. 20

Doctor. You may to me; and 'tis most meet you should.

[1] *effects of watching*. The things one does when awake.

GENTLEWOMAN. Neither to you nor any one; having no witness to confirm my speech.

Enter LADY MACBETH, *with a taper*

Lo you, here she comes! This is her very guise; and, upon my life, fast asleep. Observe her; stand close.[1]

DOCTOR. How came she by that light?

30 GENTLEWOMAN. Why, it stood by her: she has light by her continually; 'tis her command.

DOCTOR. You see, her eyes are open.

GENTLEWOMAN. Ay, but their sense is shut.

DOCTOR. What is it she does now? Look, how she rubs her hands.

GENTLEWOMAN. It is an accustom'd action with her, to seem thus washing 40 her hands; I have known her continue in this a quarter of an hour.

LADY MACBETH. Yet here's a spot.

DOCTOR. Hark! she speaks: I will set down what comes from her, to satisfy my remembrance the more strongly.

LADY MACBETH. Out, damned spot! out, I say! — One, two; why, then 'tis time to do 't. — Hell is murky! — Fie, my lord, fie! a soldier, and afeard? 50 What need we fear who knows it, when none can call our power to account? — Yet who would have thought the old man to have had so much blood in him?

DOCTOR. Do you mark that?

LADY MACBETH. The thane of Fife had a wife; where is she now? — What, will these hands ne'er be clean? — No more o' that, my lord, no more o' that: you mar all with this starting.

60 DOCTOR. Go to, go to;[2] you have known what you should not.

GENTLEWOMAN. She has spoke what she should not, I am sure of that: heaven knows what she has known.

LADY MACBETH. Here's the smell of the blood still: all the perfumes of Arabia will not sweeten this little hand. Oh, oh, oh!

DOCTOR. What a sigh is there! The heart is sorely charg'd.[1]   70

GENTLEWOMAN. I would not have such a heart in my bosom for the dignity of the whole body.

DOCTOR. Well, well, well, —

GENTLEWOMAN. Pray God it be, sir.

DOCTOR. This disease is beyond my practice: yet I have known those which have walk'd in their sleep who have died holily in their beds.

LADY MACBETH. Wash your hands; 80 put on your night-gown; look not so pale. I tell you yet again, Banquo's buried; he cannot come out on 's[2] grave.

DOCTOR. Even so?

LADY MACBETH. To bed, to bed; there's knocking at the gate: come, come, come, come, give me your hand: what's done cannot be undone: to bed, to bed, to bed.   *[Exit]*

DOCTOR. Will she go now to bed?   90

GENTLEWOMAN. Directly.

DOCTOR. Foul whisperings are abroad: unnatural deeds
Do breed unnatural troubles: infected minds
To their deaf pillows will discharge their secrets:
More needs she the divine than the physician.
God, God forgive us all! Look after her;
Remove from her the means of all annoyance,[3]
And still[4] keep eyes upon her. So, good night:
My mind she has mated,[5] and amaz'd my sight:
I think, but dare not speak.

GENTLEWOMAN.   Good night, good doctor.   *[Exeunt]* 100

---

[1] *stand close.* Keep concealed.
[2] Come, come!
[1] Burdened.
[3] Injuring (herself).
[5] Rendered powerless.
[2] Of his.
[4] Constantly.

SCENE II. *The country near Dunsinane*

[The Scottish nobles and their soldiers show their intention of joining Malcolm and the English army.]

Drum and colours. Enter MENTEITH, CAITHNESS, ANGUS, LENNOX, *and* Soldiers

MENTEITH. The English power[1] is near, led on by Malcolm,
His uncle Siward, and the good Macduff:
Revenges burn in them; for their dear[2] causes
Would to the bleeding and the grim alarm
Excite the mortified man.[3]
ANGUS. Near Birnam* wood
Shall we well meet them; that way are they coming.
CAITHNESS. Who knows if Donalbain be with his brother?
LENNOX. For certain, sir, he is not: I have a file
Of all the gentry: there is Siward's son,
10 And many unrough[4] youths, that even now
Protest their first of manhood.[5]
MENTEITH. What does the tyrant?
CAITHNESS. Great Dunsinane he strongly fortifies:
Some say he's mad; others, that lesser hate him,

Do call it valiant fury: but, for certain,
He cannot buckle his distemper'd cause
Within the belt of rule.[1]
ANGUS. Now does he feel
His secret murders sticking on his hands;
Now minutely revolts[2] upbraid his faith-breach;
Those he commands move only in command,
Nothing in love: now does he feel his title 20
Hang loose about him, like a giant's robe
Upon a dwarfish thief.
MENTEITH. Who then shall blame
His pester'd senses to recoil and start,[3]
When all that is within him does condemn
Itself for being there?
CAITHNESS. Well, march we on,
To give obedience where 'tis truly ow'd:
Meet we the medicine of the sickly weal;[4]
And with him pour we in our country's purge
Each drop of us.[5]
LENNOX. Or so much as it needs
To dew the sovereign flower and drown the weeds. 30
Make we our march towards Birnam.
[*Exeunt, marching*]

SCENE III. *Dunsinane. A room in the castle*

[Macbeth learns of the enemies who beset him and of the illness of the queen. He arouses pity for his loneliness and admiration for the courage that springs up in him.]

Enter MACBETH, *the* DOCTOR, *and* Attendants

MACBETH. Bring me no more reports; let them fly all:

[1] Army. [2] Very personal.
[3] *the mortified man.* A holy man.
[4] Beardless, therefore smooth-faced.
[5] *Protest . . . manhood.* For the first time show themselves to be men (by taking arms).

Till Birnam wood remove to Dunsinane
I cannot taint[6] with fear. What's the boy Malcolm?

[1] *cannot . . . rule.* Cannot manage his ill-regulated affairs.
[2] *minutely revolts.* Revolts occurring every minute. Note the pronunciation of "minutely" (mĭn'ĭt lĭ).
[3] *pester'd . . . start.* Irritated sensibilities for recoiling and starting.
[4] *medicine . . weal.* That which is to cure the sickly country; probably Malcolm.
[5] *pour . . . us.* Shed every drop of our blood to cleanse our country of its sickness.
[6] Be infected.

Was he not born of woman? The spirits that know
All mortal consequences have pronounc'd me[1] thus:
"Fear not, Macbeth; no man that's born of woman
Shall e'er have power upon thee." Then fly, false thanes,
And mingle with the English epicures:
The mind I sway[2] by and the heart I bear
10 Shall never sag with doubt nor shake with fear.

Enter a SERVANT

The devil damn thee black, thou cream-fac'd[3] loon[4]!
Where got'st thou that goose look?
SERVANT. There is ten thousand —
MACBETH.　　　　Geese, villain?
SERVANT.　　　　　　Soldiers, sir.
MACBETH. Go prick thy face, and over-red thy fear.[5]
Thou lily-liver'd[6] boy. What soldiers, patch[7]?
Death of thy soul! those linen cheeks of thine
Are counsellors to fear.[8] What soldiers, whey-face?
SERVANT. The English force, so please you.
MACBETH. Take thy face hence.
　　　　　　　　[*Exit* SERVANT]
　　　　　　　Seyton! — I am sick at heart,
20 When I behold — Seyton, I say! — This push[9]
Will cheer me ever, or disseat me now.
I have liv'd long enough: my way of life

Is fall'n into the sear, the yellow leaf;[1]
And that which should accompany old age,
As honour, love, obedience, troops of friends,
I must not look to have; but, in their stead,
Curses, not loud but deep, mouth-honour, breath,
Which the poor heart would fain deny,[2] and dare not.[3]
Seyton!

Enter SEYTON

SEYTON. What's your gracious pleasure?
MACBETH.　　　　What news more? 30
SEYTON. All is confirm'd, my lord, which was reported.
MACBETH. I'll fight, till from my bones my flesh be hack'd.
Give me my armour.
SEYTON.　　　　'Tis not needed yet.
MACBETH. I'll put it on.
Send out moe[4] horses, skirr[5] the country round;
Hang those that talk of fear. Give me mine armour.
How does your patient, doctor?
DOCTOR.　　　Not so sick, my lord,
As she is troubled with thick-coming fancies,
That keep her from her rest.
MACBETH.　　　　Cure her of that.
Canst thou not minister to a mind diseas'd,　　40
Pluck from the memory a rooted sorrow,

[1] To me.　　　[2] Am directed.
[3] Pale-faced.
[4] Lout, rascal. Note the coarse, violent speech of the desperate Macbeth.
[5] *over-red thy fear.* Smear with red, redden thy fear; that is, take courage. Macbeth carries on the idea of the bloodless countenance of the cowardly servant by referring to his "whey-face" and his "linen cheeks."
[6] Cowardly.　　　[7] Fool.
[8] *Are . . . fear.* Incite others to fear.
[9] Attack.

[1] *Is . . . leaf.* Has become old and withered ("sear") like an autumn leaf.
[2] *fain deny.* Gladly refuse.
[3] *I have . . . dare not.* Read these lines until the utter loneliness of the speaker becomes clear to you. Note too throughout the scene the distracted state of Macbeth's mind as revealed by his sudden alternations between courage and fear, his pettish outburst at the servant, and his broken and disconnected discourse.
[4] More.
[5] Scour.

Raze out[1] the written troubles of the brain,
And with some sweet oblivious[2] antidote
Cleanse the stuff'd bosom of that perilous
    stuff
Which weighs upon the heart?
    DOCTOR.   Therein the patient
Must minister to himself.
    MACBETH. Throw physic[3] to the dogs;
    I'll none of it.
Come, put mine armour on; give me my
    staff.
Seyton, send out. Doctor, the thanes fly
    from me.
50 Come, sir, dispatch.[4] If thou couldst,
    doctor, cast
The water of my land, find her disease,
And purge it to a sound and pristine
    health,[5]

I would applaud thee to the very echo,
That should applaud again. Pull 't off,[1] I
    say.
What rhubarb, senna, or what purgative
    drug,
Would scour these English hence?
    Hear'st thou of them?
    DOCTOR. Ay, my good lord; your
    royal preparation
Makes us hear something.
    MACBETH.   Bring it[2] after me.
I will not be afraid of death and
    bane,[3]
Till Birnam forest come to Dunsinane. 60
    DOCTOR. [*Aside*] Were I from Dun-
    sinane away and clear,
Profit again should hardly draw me
    here.   [*Exeunt*]

SCENE IV. *Country near Birnam wood*

[Malcolm gives the command that makes
    true what seemed impossible.]

Drum and colours. Enter MALCOLM, *old*
  SIWARD *and his* Son, MACDUFF,
  MENTEITH, CAITHNESS, ANGUS, LEN-
  NOX, ROSS, *and* Soldiers, *marching*

MALCOLM. Cousins, I hope the days
    are near at hand
That chambers will be safe.
    MENTEITH.   We doubt it nothing.
    SIWARD. What wood is this before
    us?
    MENTEITH.   The wood of Birnam.
    MALCOLM. Let every soldier hew him
    down a bough,
And bear 't before him : thereby shall we
    shadow
The numbers of our host, and make dis-
    covery
Err in report of us.

    SOLDIERS.   It shall be done.
    SIWARD. We learn no other but the
    confident tyrant
Keeps still in Dunsinane, and will endure
Our sitting down before 't.[4]
    MALCOLM.   'Tis his main hope: 10
For, where there is advantage to be given,
Both more and less have given him the
    revolt,[5]
And none serve with him but con-
    strained things,
Whose hearts are absent too.
    MACDUFF.   Let our just censures
Attend the true event,[6] and put we on
Industrious soldiership.
    SIWARD.   The time approaches
That will with due decision make us
    know

---

[1] *Raze out.* Erase.
[2] Causing forgetfulness.
[3] Medicine.
[4] Hurry (spoken to Seyton).
[5] *cast . . . health.* Diagnose my country's disease
  and restore her to her former good health.

[1] *Pull 't off.* That is, pull the armor off.
[2] The armor.
[3] Destruction.
[4] *sitting down before 't.* Laying siege to it.
[5] *where . . . revolt.* Wherever there has been a
  chance, both nobles and common people have
  revolted against him.
[6] *Let . . . event.* Let us wait for the outcome
  ("event") before we form our final judgment
  ("censure") regarding the state of things.

What we shall say we have and what we owe.

Thoughts speculative their unsure hopes relate,

But certain issue strokes must arbitrate;[1]   20

Towards which advance the war.

[Exeunt, marching]

SCENE V. *Dunsinane. Within the castle*

[The lament of women tells Macbeth that Lady Macbeth is dead.]

Enter MACBETH, SEYTON, *and* Soldiers, *with drum and colours*

MACBETH. Hang out our banners on the outward walls;

The cry is still, "They come." Our castle's strength

Will laugh a siege to scorn; here let them lie

Till famine and the ague eat them up.

Were they not forc'd[1] with those that should be ours,

We might have met them dareful, beard to beard,

And beat them backward home.

[A cry of women within]

What is that noise?

SEYTON. It is the cry of women, my good lord.   *[Exit]*

MACBETH. I have almost forgot the taste of fears:

10 The time has been, my senses would have cool'd

To hear a night-shriek, and my fell of hair[2]

Would at a dismal treatise[3] rouse and stir

As life were in 't: I have supp'd full with horrors;

Direness, familiar to my slaughterous thoughts,

Cannot once start[4] me.

Re-enter SEYTON

Wherefore was that cry?

SEYTON. The queen, my lord, is dead.

MACBETH. She should have died hereafter;[2]

There would have been a time for such a word.

To-morrow, and to-morrow, and to-morrow,

Creeps in this petty pace from day to day,   20

To the last syllable of recorded time;

And all our yesterdays have lighted fools

The way to dusty death. Out, out, brief candle!

Life's but a walking shadow; a poor player

That struts and frets his hour upon the stage

And then is heard no more. It is a tale

Told by an idiot, full of sound and fury,

Signifying nothing.

Enter a MESSENGER

Thou com'st to use thy tongue; thy story quickly.

MESSENGER. Gracious my lord,   30

I should report that which I say I saw,

But know not how to do 't.

MACBETH.   Well, say, sir.

[1] *Thoughts . . . arbitrate.* Speculation regarding the future is useless; the true result must be determined by blows.

[2] *She should . . . hereafter.* Here and throughout the remainder of the speech Macbeth is talking to himself. In his utter misery he feels that life is a failure and nothing makes any difference. His thoughts run somewhat as follows: Lady Macbeth would have had to die some day; the time would have come ultimately "for such a word" as death. Therefore, why put it off? Postpone death as long as you will, one tomorrow keeps following another at the same slow, meaningless pace until "all our yesterdays" carry us at last, fools that we are, to "dusty death."

[1] Reinforced.   [2] *fell of hair.* Pelt; here, scalp.
[3] Story, or discourse   [4] Startle.

MESSENGER. As I did stand my watch upon the hill,
I look'd toward Birnam, and anon, me-thought,
The wood began to move.
MACBETH.   Liar and slave!
MESSENGER. Let me endure your wrath, if 't be not so:
Within this three mile may you see it coming;
I say, a moving grove.
MACBETH.   If thou speak'st false,
Upon the next tree shalt thou hang alive,
40 Till famine cling[1] thee: if thy speech be sooth,[2]
I care not if thou dost for me as much.
I pull in resolution,[3] and begin

To doubt[1] th' equivocation[2] of the fiend
That lies like truth: "Fear not, till Bir-nam wood
Do come to Dunsinane"; and now a wood
Comes toward Dunsinane. Arm, arm, and out!
If this which he avouches does appear,
There is nor flying hence nor tarrying here.
I 'gin to be a-weary of the sun,
And wish th' estate o' the world were now undone.   50
Ring the alarum-bell! Blow, wind! come, wrack[3]!
At least we'll die with harness on our back.   [Exeunt]

SCENE VI. *Dunsinane. Before the castle*

[This scene shows the spirit of Macbeth's foes.]

Drum and colours. Enter MALCOLM, *old* SIWARD, MACDUFF, *and their* Army *with boughs*

MALCOLM. Now near enough; your leavy screens throw down,
And show like those you are. You, worthy uncle,
Shall, with my cousin, your right noble son,

Lead our first battle[4]: worthy Macduff and we
Shall take upon 's what else remains to do,
According to our order.
SIWARD.   Fare you well.
Do we but find the tyrant's power tonight,
Let us be beaten, if we cannot fight.
MACDUFF. Make all our trumpets speak; give them all breath,
Those clamorous harbingers of blood and death.   [Exeunt] 1c
[Alarums continued]

SCENE VII. *Another part of the field*

[In the confidence that no man "born of woman" shall hurt him, Macbeth fights valorously against tremendous odds.]

Enter MACBETH

MACBETH. They have tied me to a stake; I cannot fly,
But, bear-like,[4] I must fight the course. What's he
That was not born of woman? Such a one Am I to fear, or none.

Enter young SIWARD

YOUNG SIWARD. What is thy name?
MACBETH.   Thou'lt be afraid to hear it.
YOUNG SIWARD. No; though thou call'st thyself a hotter name
Than any is in hell.
MACBETH.   My name's Macbeth.

---

[1] Wither, shrivel.   [2] Truth.
[3] *pull in resolution.* Check the confidence I have felt.   [4] As in bear-baiting.*

[1] Suspect.
[2] Here, a saying that sounds like truth but really is a lie.
[3] Wreck, destruction.
[4] Division of an army.

YOUNG SIWARD. The devil himself could not pronounce a title
More hateful to mine ear.
MACBETH. No, nor more fearful.
10 YOUNG SIWARD. Thou liest, abhorred tyrant; with my sword
I'll prove the lie thou speak'st.
[They fight, and young SIWARD *is slain]*
MACBETH. Thou wast born of woman.
But swords I smile at, weapons laugh to scorn,
Brandish'd by man that's of a woman born. *[Exit]*

Alarums. Enter MACDUFF

MACDUFF. That way the noise is. Tyrant, show thy face!
If thou be'st slain, and with no stroke of mine,
My wife and children's ghosts will haunt me still.

I cannot strike at wretched kerns,[1] whose arms
Are hir'd to bear their staves: either thou,[2] Macbeth,
Or else my sword, with an unbatter'd edge,
I sheathe again undeeded.[3] There thou shouldst be; 20
By this great clatter, one of greatest note
Seems bruited.[4] Let me find him, fortune!
And more I beg not. *[Exit. Alarums]*

Enter MALCOLM *and old* SIWARD

SIWARD. This way, my lord. The castle 's gently render'd[5]:
The tyrant's people on both sides do fight;
The noble thanes do bravely in the war;
The day almost itself professes yours,[6]
And little is to do.
MALCOLM. We have met with foes
That strike beside us.[7]
SIWARD. Enter, sir, the castle.
[Exeunt. Alarum]

SCENE VIII. *Another part of the field*

[Macbeth resists the temptation to commit suicide. He learns that fate has toyed with him, but he battles dauntlessly. He is a noble fighter to the end.]

Enter MACBETH

MACBETH. Why should I play the Roman fool, and die
On mine own sword?[1] whiles I see lives.[2] the gashes
Do better upon them.[3]

Enter MACDUFF

MACDUFF. Turn, hell-hound, turn!
MACBETH. Of all men else I have avoided thee:
But get thee back; my soul is too much charg'd
With blood of thine already.

MACDUFF. I have no words,
My voice is in my sword, thou bloodier villain
Than terms can give thee out![8]
[They fight]
MACBETH. Thou losest labour:
As easy mayst thou the intrenchant[9] air
With thy keen sword impress as make me bleed: 10
Let fall thy blade on vulnerable crests;

[1] Light-armed foot soldiers, usually, as here, from Ireland.
[2] Thou (shalt meet me in battle).
[3] Without having accomplished a deed.
[4] Announced with noise.
[5] *gently render'd.* Surrendered without resistance.
[6] *almost . . . yours.* Is almost won.
[7] *strike beside us.* Intentionally miss us (because they are really our friends).
[8] *terms . . . out.* Words can describe thee.
[9] Not capable of being cut.

[1] *play . . . sword.* Commit suicide, as many Romans did when there seemed no longer any reason for living. [2] Living men.
[3] *Do . . . them.* Look better on them than on me.
D

I bear a charmed life, which must not
  yield
To one of woman born.
  MACDUFF.   Despair thy charm;[1]
And let the angel[2] whom thou still hast
  serv'd
Tell thee, Macduff was from his mother's
  womb
Untimely ripp'd.
  MACBETH. Accursed be that tongue
  that tells me so,
For it hath cow'd my better part of man!
And be these juggling fiends no more be-
  liev'd,
20 That palter[3] with us in a double sense,
That keep the word of promise to our ear,
And break it to our hope. I'll not fight
  with thee.
  MACDUFF. Then yield thee, coward,
And live to be the show and gaze o' the
  time:
We'll have thee, as our rarer monsters are,
Painted upon a pole,[4] and underwrit,
"Here may you see the tyrant."
  MACBETH.   I will not yield,
To kiss the ground before young Mal-
  colm's feet,
And to be baited with the rabble's curse.
30 Though Birnam wood be come to Dun-
  sinane,
And thou oppos'd, being of no woman
  born,
Yet I will try the last[5]: before my body
I throw my warlike shield: lay on, Mac-
  duff;
And damn'd be him that first cries,
  "Hold, enough!"
          [Exeunt, fighting. Alarums]

Retreat. Flourish. Enter with drum and
  colours, MALCOLM, old SIWARD, ROSS,
  the other Thanes, and Soldiers

  MALCOLM. I would the friends we miss
  were safe arriv'd.

1 Despair thy charm. Do not hope that thy
  charm will protect thee.   2 Here, fiend, devil.
3 Equivocate, speak with double meaning.
4 Painted . . . pole. Painted on a cloth hung from
  a pole.   5 Last resort.

  SIWARD. Some must go off[1]; and yet,
  by these I see,
So great a day as this is cheaply bought.
  MALCOLM. Macduff is missing, and
  your noble son.
  ROSS. Your son, my lord, has paid a
  soldier's debt:
He only liv'd but till he was a man;   40
The which no sooner had his prowess
  confirm'd[2]
In the unshrinking station where he
  fought,[3]
But like a man he died.
  SIWARD.   Then he is dead?
  ROSS. Ay, and brought off the field:
  your cause of sorrow
Must not be measur'd by his worth, for
  then
It hath no end.
  SIWARD.   Had he his hurts before[4]?
  ROSS. Ay, on the front.
  SIWARD.   Why then,
  God's soldier be he!
Had I as many sons as I have hairs,
I would not wish them to a fairer death:
And so his knell is knoll'd.
  MALCOLM.   He's worth more sorrow, 50
And that I'll spend for him.
  SIWARD.   He's worth no more:
They say he parted well,[5] and paid his
  score;
And so God be with him! Here comes
  newer comfort.

Re-enter MACDUFF, with MACBETH'S
          head

  MACDUFF. Hail, king! for so thou art:
  behold, where stands
Th' usurper's cursed head: the time is
  free.[6]

1 go off. Die.
2 Proved.
3 unshrinking . . . fought. Place where he fought
  bravely.
4 In front.
5 parted well. Departed well; that is, died
  bravely.
6 the time . . . free. The world is free (from
  tyranny).

I see thee compass'd with thy kingdom's
  pearl,[1]
That speak my salutation in their minds;
Whose voices I desire aloud with mine:
Hail, King of Scotland!
   ALL.   Hail, King of Scotland!
                    [*Flourish*]
60   MALCOLM. We shall not spend a large
  expense of time
Before we reckon with your several loves,
And make us even with you. My thanes
  and kinsmen,
Henceforth be earls, the first that ever
  Scotland
In such an honour nam'd. What's more
  to do,
Which would be planted newly with the
  time,
As calling home our exil'd friends abroad
That fled the snares of watchful tyranny;
Producing forth the cruel ministers
Of this dead butcher and his fiend-like
  queen,
70 Who, as 'tis thought, by self and violent
  hands[2]
Took off her life; this, and what needful
  else
That calls upon us, by the grace of Grace,
We will perform in measure, time, and
  place:
So, thanks to all at once and to each one,
Whom we invite to see us crown'd at
  Scone.*
              [*Flourish. Exeunt*]

Discussion Hints

ACT V. SCENE I

1. In what scene did Lady Macbeth last appear? Briefly review the events of that scene and the state of Lady Macbeth's mind at its close.

2. Write a short theme telling what you think has been happening to Lady Macbeth during the interval between that scene and this one.

---

[1] *thy kingdom's pearl.* The ornament, the best men, of thy kingdom.
[2] *by . . . hands.* By her own violent hands.

3. Account for the writing of the letter, the washing of her hands, the counting of the strokes of the bell ("One, two," l. 47), the reference to the knocking at the gate. Pick out other words that recall past scenes.

4. Explain the Doctor's meaning in lines 99–100:

"My mind she has mated, and amaz'd my
  sight:
I think, but dare not speak."

SCENE II

Lines 13–14. "Some say he's mad" etc. What is your opinion? Follow the story through this act and see if your opinion strengthens or changes.

SCENE III

1. Line 7. Give the names of four of the "false thanes" Macbeth is thinking of.

2. Point out in this scene as many indications as possible that Macbeth is completely unnerved.

3. Compare, in their effect upon the Doctor, this scene with Lady Macbeth's sleepwalking scene. For which one has the Doctor the more sympathy?

SCENE IV

Quote the prophecy of the Witches which is now about to be fulfilled.

SCENE V

1. Paraphrase, sentence by sentence, lines 19–28. Memorize the lines as Shakespeare wrote them.

2. Can you recall other passages where Shakespeare has made the player on the stage comment upon life and its changes? An especially famous passage occurs in *As You Like It* (II, vii, 138–165) (given in the revised edition of *Adventure* of this series).

General Questions or Assignments on the Entire Play

1. Read again the headnote to *Macbeth* (p. 86), and then, by means of the summaries at the beginning of the scenes, trace (1) the *introduction*, or *exposition*; (2) the *complication*, or *rising action*; (3) the *pivot*, or *climax*, or *turning point*; (4) the *resolution*, or *falling action*; and (5) the *conclusion*. Write out your results in the form of an outline.

2. Now that you have read the play, which of the five statements made in the first paragraph of the headnote (p. 86) can you illustrate from your own study? Give reasons for your answer.

3. The word *tragedy* as applied to a drama means more than merely an exceedingly unfortunate event or series of events. If the central character comes to grief in the end, the event may be tragic, but the play is not necessarily a tragedy. In a real tragedy such as those of Shakespeare the downfall of the central figure usually results from one or more of the following causes: (1) some inherent weakness of character, (2) the influence of some other person or persons, or (3) the influence of supernatural forces. In your opinion do any or all of these causes contribute toward making *Macbeth* a tragedy? Give reasons for your answer.

4. Show that plot, character, and setting in *Macbeth* all contribute toward bringing out the tragedy. Give specific evidence for your answer.

5. Defend the way in which Macbeth and Lady Macbeth die. Why would it be inappropriate for the play to end happily for them?

6. Go through the play and indicate the scenes that might be omitted in a modern production. Explain your choice.

7. In what scenes is prose used? In each case try to find a good explanation.

8. Prove the importance of some one of the minor characters.

9. In tragedies such as Shakespeare's the central character is usually called upon to make some important decision that is destined to affect his future action. Show that this is true of *Macbeth*, stating the nature of the question to be decided, how the character decides it, and how his future is affected by his decision.

10. Answer again question 7 on page 101. Is your answer the same now as it was before?

11. In III, i, 27–28, Macbeth, addressing Banquo, says, "Fail not our feast," and Banquo replies, "My lord, I will not." The dramatic effect of Banquo's reply depends largely upon the fact that the audience knows something that Banquo does not; namely, that he will not be alive to keep his promise. Whenever, as here, the audience can say of a character, "Ah! if he knew what we know, he would not speak or act as he does," the situation is a case of what is known as dramatic irony.* Find other cases of dramatic irony in *Macbeth*.

12. Discuss the changes in Macbeth's character between I, iii, and III, v.

13. In what scenes do Witches appear? Read these scenes again, and summarize what information you gain from them in regard to witchcraft. Belief in the reality of witchcraft was widespread in Shakespeare's time. Can you find in your community anybody who still believes in witchcraft or knows any witch lore?

14. Explain the following passages:

a. The deep damnation of his taking-off.
                                    I, vii, 20

b.   There's husbandry in heaven;
   Their candles are all out. II, i, 4–5

c.   in his royalty of nature
   Reigns that which would be fear'd.
                                    III, i, 49–50

d.   Thou hast harp'd my fear aright.
                                    IV, i, 74

e. I
Unspeak mine own detraction.
                                    IV, iii, 122–123

f.   infected minds
   To their deaf pillows will discharge their
   secrets.   V, i, 93–94

g.   The time approaches
   That will with due decision make us
   know
   What we shall say we have and what
   we owe.   V, iv, 16–18

15. The meter of most of the play is unrhymed iambic* pentameter. Pick out examples of the normal iambic pentameter line. Pick out iambic pentameter lines that rhyme in couplets. Where do such lines usually occur? What scenes contain most examples of rhyming trochaic* tetrameter*?

16. Commit to memory I, vi, 1–10; II, ii, 35–40; V, v, 19–28.

17. Subjects for themes:

a. Banquo's connection with the story of *Macbeth*.

b. The unsettled state of Scotland as reflected in *Macbeth*.

c. Witches and witchcraft in *Macbeth*.

Paraphrasing

1. Write a paraphrase of V, i, 91–100, that will make clear the meaning of each difficult word or phrase.

2. Write in modern prose the thought expressed in the passage beginning "If it were done" and ending "to come" (I, vii, 1–7).

3. Give the substance of IV, i, 144–153, sentence by sentence, in your own words. Compare this speech with some earlier utterance of Macbeth's, to show whether he has gained in promptness of resolve and capacity for crime. How does Macbeth suffer for his crimes otherwise than by meeting death at the hands of Macduff?

4. Give the substance of the following passages in your own language, using, wherever possible, literal instead of figurative language (I, vii, 60–72; III, ii, 13–26).

A Craft Project

Using the information derived from a study of the picture of the Globe Theater (p. 79) and the picture of the interior of an Elizabethan playhouse (facing page 72), construct out of cardboard or other suitable material a model of an Elizabethan theater and an Elizabethan stage.

Suggestions for Reading

1. Two others of Shakespeare's plays, *As You Like It* (a joyous comedy) and *Julius Cæsar* (a gripping tragedy), are given, respectively, in the revised editions of *Adventure* and *Achievement* of this series. Several of his historical plays are referred to on pages 17 and 35. Of Shakespeare's remaining plays, among the most readable are these:

COMEDIES	TRAGEDIES
Comedy of Errors	*Romeo and Juliet*
Midsummer Night's Dream	*Hamlet*
Twelfth Night	
The Tempest	
A Winter's Tale	

You should not miss the charming summaries of Shakespeare's plays given in *Tales from Shakespeare*, by Charles Lamb[1] and his sister Mary.

There are many editions of Shakespeare's works. Among the most authoritative and, at the same time, easily available are the one-volume editions by George Lyman Kittredge (Ginn and Company) and William Allan Neilson (Houghton Mifflin Company). A handy edition, with interlinear glosses, by Reed Smith and George Coffin Taylor, is published by Ginn and Company.

A great many books have been written about Shakespeare's life and work. Suitable introductions to Shakespeare are given in the following:

ALDEN, RAYMOND M. *A Shakespeare Handbook.* F. S. Crofts and Company.

BLACK, E. CHARLTON and AGNES KNOX, and FREEMAN, JENNIE YOUNG. *An Introduction to Shakespeare.* Ginn and Company.

MASEFIELD, JOHN. *William Shakespeare.* Henry Holt and Company.

2. For those interested in acting:

BARKER, FRED G. (ED.). *Forty-Minute Plays from Shakespeare.* The Macmillan Company.

GRAY, ISABEL M. *Short Scenes from Shakespeare and How to Act Them.* The Macmillan Company.

3. Collections of plays suitable for reading in the early English drama aside from Shakespeare:

ADAMS, JOSEPH Q. (ED.). *Chief Pre-Shakespearean Dramas.* Houghton Mifflin Company.

NEILSON, WILLIAM A. (ED.). *Chief Elizabethan Dramatists.* Houghton Mifflin Company.

RHYS, ERNEST (ED.). *Everyman and Other Interludes.* Everyman's Library.

THORNDYKE, A. H. (ED.). *Minor Elizabethan Drama.* 2 vols. Everyman's Library.

[1] For biography see page 721.

LYRIC POETRY[1]

LYRIC poetry includes one of the oldest, most extensive, and most generally interesting bodies of literature. A lyric may be defined as a poem that expresses some personal feeling or emotion of the author; or, as the literary critics put it, the lyric is subjective.* In this respect it is contrasted with the drama[2] and with the narrative,[3] which are primarily objective.* In the drama our interest arises from the characters and what they do and say; in a narrative our interest arises usually from the story itself; but in a lyric the poet allows us to look into his own heart and see how he feels, and why, and it is his personal reactions and emotions that interest us.

All of us have feelings, but few of us can express our feelings coherently and beautifully. The chief value of poets to those of us who are not poets lies in the following facts: they are more sensitive than other people; they see into the heart of nature and human life more deeply than the average run of men do; they know how to produce in themselves feelings and mental states which the rest of us experience only vaguely or not at all; and they know how to express their feelings in language that interprets to us our own hearts and the world about us in terms of truth and beauty. It is for these reasons that simple lyric poetry appeals even to untrained readers.

So interested does the poet frequently become in his own emotions and those of his characters, and in conveying these emotions to his readers, that even when, as in some of the narrative poems of Byron (p. 409), Tennyson (p. 520), and other writers, he is telling a story, he may weave into his narrative his own thoughts; or when he is writing a play, he may, as Shakespeare often does, delay the action, in order to put lyric poems into the mouths of his characters.

Since lyric poetry often expresses emotions too delicate, too subtle, or too powerful to last long, lyric poems are usually short. This fact is closely connected with another: the oldest lyrics were intended to be sung, and therefore, like all good songs, are not too long. In fact, the word *lyric* is derived from the Greek word for a lyre, an ancient stringed instrument something like a small harp. Although many modern lyrics are not intended to be sung, the term *lyric*, in its broadest sense, includes all hymns and many songs. Marlowe's "Passionate Shepherd to His Love" (p. 153), Raleigh's "Nymph's Reply to the Shepherd" (p. 153), the little songs in-

[1] General discussion hints for the lyric poetry of the Elizabethan Period are grouped together on page 160.   [2] Page 81.   [3] Page 36.

150

cluded in Shakespeare's plays (p. 154), Ben Jonson's "To Celia" (p. 154), Cowper's hymn "God Moves in a Mysterious Way" (p. 303), and many short poems of the Romantic Period[1] and the nineteenth century are lyrics written to be sung. The most famous song-writers in modern English literature are Robert Burns (p. 328) and Thomas Moore (p. 349). Burns's songs are irresistibly appealing because they express powerful emotion simply and sincerely and because the poet adapted them to the beautiful tunes to which they were sung.

Thus, to put the matter briefly, we may say that lyric poetry includes not only songs and hymns, but all verse that expresses an emotional or reflective mood, whether the lyric passage forms a part of a longer poem or is written in some special form such as the sonnet,* the ode,* or the elegy.*

Of the many moods expressed in lyric poetry, two of the most common are sorrow and love. Landor's "Rose Aylmer" (p. 348) and Tennyson's "Break, Break, Break" (p. 463) are exquisite examples of tender, sorrowful emotion caught and crystallized forever in lyric form. One of the oldest and best-known kinds of lyric poem is the elegy,[2] which usually laments the death of someone.

Many English poets have sung of love. In Burns's "Cotter's Saturday Night" (p. 383) the poet intersperses his narrative with lyric passages expressing the love of home and country. Patriotism is also the inspiration of Burns's "Scots, Wha Hae wi' Wallace Bled" (p. 332). Many of the finest English lyrics are addressed to a real or an imaginary sweetheart. During the Elizabethan Period numerous poets, including Sidney (p. 157), Spenser (p. 158), and Shakespeare (p. 159), composed long series, or "sequences," of love lyrics in the form of sonnets. Love between husband and wife is the theme of Burns's "John Anderson My Jo" (p. 332) and of numerous lyrics of the nineteenth century, including Mrs. Browning's *Sonnets from the Portuguese* (p. 490).

English poetry is especially rich in lyrics expressing the love of nature. During the Middle Ages (p. 29) and the Elizabethan Period (p. 71), poets sang of spring, flowers and sunshine, but they showed little or no enthusiasm for autumn or winter. Milton and other poets of the seventeenth century take a mild pleasure in country landscapes during pleasant weather, but in general they show no enthusiasm for the sterner aspects of nature. As a rule the writers of the Age of Classicism (p. 213) prefer artificial landscapes under sunny skies to the untrimmed countryside under less smiling conditions. With the Transition Period (p. 289), however, poets began to see new beauties in external nature. Collins, in his "Ode

---

[1] Page 313.

[2] Three great English elegies should be remembered together: Milton's "Lycidas," Shelley's "Adonais," and Matthew Arnold's "Thyrsis." These are all written in the form of pastoral* elegies. A fourth great English lament is Tennyson's *In Memoriam* (p. 471), which consists of a series of lyrics.

to Evening" (p. 296), and Gray, in his "Elegy" (p. 298), are among the earliest English poets to express pleasure in the calm repose of evening, and a few other poets of the first half of the eighteenth century celebrate the pleasures of autumn and winter. As we pass on from this period into the Romantic Period (p. 313) we find a constantly increasing stream of lyric poems on new aspects of nature. Mountain scenery, storms, winter, and wild nature in general came to be favorite themes with the romantic poets. Byron (p. 355) was thrilled by the roaring ocean, which still remains full of romantic associations. Wordsworth and later poets found in nature an escape from the sorrows of the world or a revelation of the goodness of God. During the Romantic Period children, wild animals, and even the modest flower by the roadside were treated in literature with a tenderness and love never expressed before. Wordsworth found poetry in the common English daisy (p. 340); Burns wrote lyrics on a field mouse (p. 328) and a mountain daisy (p. 330); and Blake sought beauty even in the savage tiger (p. 327). In recent poetry almost any aspect of nature may be the subject of a lyric poem.

Besides the host of lyric poems expressing feeling there are many that are reflective or philosophic rather than merely emotional. To this group belong Pope's "Universal Prayer" (p. 230) and much of Gray's "Elegy" (p. 298). Tennyson's "Crossing the Bar" (p. 475) and Browning's "Prospice" (p. 484) express the poets' feelings at the approach of death.

Finally, it must not be supposed that a poem, in order to express emotion, must necessarily be serious. Many lyrics express moods which are so light, happy, and joyous that their chief impressions are of gaiety and mirth. Such are the two charming Middle-English lyrics on love and spring (p. 55), Marlowe's "Passionate Shepherd to His Love" (p. 153) and Raleigh's "Nymph's Reply" (p. 153); Shakespeare's songs (p. 154); Herrick's "To the Virgins, to Make Much of Time" (p. 200); and Leigh Hunt's "Jenny Kissed Me" (p. 350).

English lyric poets of today (and their name is legion) write on many subjects and in many ways. Some, like A. E. Housman (p. 579), are content most of the time with conventional verse forms and traditional subject matter. The Irish poets, led by Yeats (pp. 581 and 632), have revived interest in Irish legends and in everyday Irish life. One group of poets has been interested in the age-old religious themes. Others depict the challenging and terrific way of life and death created by the World War. Most modern in outlook are those who sing (some in old forms and some in new) of the themes of democracy. To men like James Stephens (p. 601), W. W. Gibson (p. 604), and John Masefield (p. 611) any human matters, be they heroic or prosaic, are suitable for poetry. Suitable too is it that John Masefield, commoner born, for long a brilliant writer of realistic narrative and lyric verse, should be poet laureate of democratic England.

CHRISTOPHER MARLOWE[1] (1564-1593)

The Passionate Shepherd to His Love

"The Passionate Shepherd to His Love" is a dainty love lyric of more than three hundred years ago; yet we still enjoy its playful message and its sweet music when we read it aloud. It should be read in connection with "The Nymph's Reply to the Shepherd," which follows it here.

COME live with me and be my love,
  And we will all the pleasures prove,[2]
That valleys, groves, hills, and fields,
Woods, or steepy mountain yields.

And we will sit upon the rocks,
Seeing the shepherds feed their flocks,
By shallow rivers, to whose falls
Melodious birds sing madrigals.

And I will make thee beds of roses,
And a thousand fragrant posies,   10

A cap of flowers and a kirtle
Embroider'd all with leaves of myrtle:

A gown made of the finest wool,
Which from our pretty lambs we pull;
Fair linèd slippers for[1] the cold,
With buckles of the purest gold;

A belt of straw and ivy buds,
With coral clasps and amber studs;
And if these pleasures may thee move,
Come live with me and be my love.   20

The shepherd swains shall dance and
    sing
For thy delights each May morning;
If these delights thy mind may move,
Then live with me and be my love.

SIR WALTER RALEIGH[3] (1552-1618)

The Nymph's Reply to the Shepherd[4]

"The Nymph's Reply to the Shepherd," which is an answer to the passionate shepherd of Marlowe's poem, is fully as playful and almost as dainty and musical as the poem to which it replies. The girl's answer contains a great deal of common sense as well as humor.

IF ALL the world and love were young,
  And truth in every shepherd's tongue,
These pretty pleasures might me move,
To live with thee and be thy love.

Time drives the flocks from field to fold,
When rivers rage, and rocks grow cold,
And Philomel* becometh dumb;
The rest complains of cares to come.

The flowers do fade, and wanton[2] fields
To wayward Winter reckoning yields;
A honey tongue, a heart of gall,[3]   11
Is fancy's spring, but sorrow's fall.

Thy gowns, thy shoes, thy beds of roses.
Thy cap, thy kirtle, and thy posies
Soon break, soon wither, soon forgotten,—
In folly ripe, in reason rotten.

Thy belt of straw and ivy buds,
Thy coral clasps and amber studs,
All these in me no means can move,
To come to thee and be thy love.   20

But could youth last, and love still breed,[4]
Had joys no date,[5] nor age no need,
Then these delights my mind might move
To live with thee and be thy love.

[1] For biography see page 699.
[2] Experience, enjoy.
[3] For biography see page 699.
[4] There is some doubt whether the poem is really
    by Sir Walter Raleigh.

[1] Against, to keep out.   [2] Luxuriant.
[3] Bitterness.   [4] Increase.   [5] End.

BEN JONSON[1] (1573?–1637)

To Celia

For three hundred years the soft music and the delicate compliment to a woman contained in the song "To Celia" have made it a favorite with the English-speaking world. The tune to which this song is sung is as beautiful as the words.

Drink to me only with thine eyes,
　And I will pledge with mine;
Or leave a kiss but in the cup,
　And I'll not look for wine.
The thirst that from the soul doth rise
　Doth ask a drink divine;
But might I of Jove's* nectar[2] sup,
　I would not change for thine.

I sent thee late[3] a rosy wreath,[4]
　Not so much honouring thee　　　10
As giving it a hope, that there
　It could not wither'd be.
But thou thereon didst only breathe,
　And sent'st it back to me;
Since when it grows, and smells, I swear,
　Not of itself, but thee.

Discussion Hints

1. In connection with "The Passionate Shepherd to His Love" (p. 153) read "The Nymph's Reply to the Shepherd," on the same page. Which do you prefer? Why?

2. Point out pastoral* elements in these two poems.

3. Give in your own words the shepherd's arguments and the nymph's objections.

4. Try writing parodies of the two poems, using words and ideas of the present day and representing the passionate shepherd as a salesman or clerk and the nymph as a salesgirl or stenographer.

5. If the music is available, sing Jonson's song "To Celia." Ask the music department to co-operate. "To Celia" is available in recordings 1238 and 22081 by the RCA (Victor) Manufacturing Company, Inc.

6. In "To Celia" why will the speaker not ask for wine in the cup?

SHAKESPEARE'S[5] LYRICS

Shakespeare was a great dramatist; but in reading his plays we are apt to forget that, above everything else, he was a poet. As is stated on page 150, he was fond of putting lyrical passages into the mouths of his characters. He also composed numerous lyrics suitable for singing, which he introduced here and there into his dramas for the purpose of pleasing his audience and bringing them into the proper mood for enjoying the play. It is possible that neither Shakespeare nor his audience took these songs very seriously; but they have kept the sweetness of their original flavor far better than some of his more serious works, and several of them are still sung and enjoyed by people who know little of the plays in which they occur. Shakespeare's sonnets* (p. 159), being far more complicated in form and often more subtle in meaning, are less widely understood and appreciated than his songs.

---

[1] For biography see page 700.　　[2] The drink of the gods.　　[3] Lately.
[4] *rosy wreath*. Wreath of roses.　　　　[5] For biography see page 698.

Winter

[From *Love's Labour's Lost*]

"Winter" is realistic rather than romantic in tone. It is one of Shakespeare's most attractive short poems.

WHEN icicles hang by the wall,
  And Dick the shepherd blows his nail,[1]
And Tom bears logs into the hall,
  And milk comes frozen home in pail,
When blood is nipped, and ways be foul,[2]
Then nightly sings the staring owl,
    Tu-who;
Tu-whit, tu-who — a merry note,
While greasy Joan[3] doth keel[4] the pot.

When all aloud the wind doth blow, 10
  And coughing drowns the parson's saw,[1]
And birds sit brooding[2] in the snow,
  And Marian's[3] nose looks red and raw,
When roasted crabs[4] hiss in the bowl,
Then nightly sings the staring owl,
    Tu-who;
Tu-whit, tu-who — a merry note,
While greasy Joan doth keel the pot.

Come Away, Come Away, Death!

[From *Twelfth Night*]

COME away,[5] come away, Death,
  And in sad cypress[6] let me be laid;
Fly away, fly away, breath;
  I am slain by a fair cruel maid.
My shroud of white, stuck all with yew,
    O, prepare it!
My part of death, no one so true
    Did share it.

Not a flower, not a flower sweet,
  On my black coffin let there be strown;
Not a friend, not a friend greet 11
  My poor corpse, where my bones shall be thrown.
A thousand thousand sighs to save,
    Lay me, O, where
Sad true lover never find my grave,
    To weep there!

Hark, Hark! the Lark at Heaven's Gate Sings

[From *Cymbeline*]

HARK, hark! the lark[7] at heaven's gate sings,
  And Phoebus* gins[8] arise,
His steeds to water at those springs
  On chaliced[9] flowers that lies;

And winking Mary-buds[5] begin
  To ope their golden eyes:
With everything that pretty is,
  My lady sweet, arise!
    Arise, arise!

[1] *blows his nail.* Blows on his fingernails to warm his fist.   [2] *ways be foul.* Roads are bad.
[3] A typical serving maid.
[4] Cool by stirring.   [5] Hither.   [6] A kind of crape.
[7] The English skylark, which "singing still dost soar, and soaring ever singeth" (see Shelley's "To a Skylark," p. 361, l. 10).
[8] Begins to.   [9] Cup-shaped.

[1] Proverb, saying.
[2] *sit brooding.* Sit quiet, with feathers fluffed out to keep warm.
[3] A typical serving maid.
[4] Crab apples, which made a hissing sound when they were dropped into a bowl of hot drink.
[5] Buds of marigold.

Full Fathom Five Thy Father Lies

[From *The Tempest*]

FULL fathom five thy father lies,
 Of his bones are coral made:
Those are pearls that were his eyes:
 Nothing of him that doth fade,
But doth suffer a sea-change
Into something rich and strange.
Sea-nymphs hourly ring his knell;
                        Ding-dong.
Hark! now I hear them, — Ding-dong,
 bell.

Discussion Hints

1. What realistic features, as opposed to purely romantic ones, do you find in "Winter" (p. 155)? If you wished to write a romantic poem about winter, what features would you include?

2. Give the first stanza of "Come Away, Come Away, Death!" (p. 155) in the form of prose.

3. Remember that "Hark, Hark! the Lark at Heaven's Gate Sings" (p. 155), like the other songs from Shakespeare's plays, was not merely recited or spoken, but was sung to its own tune.

4. Name several cuplike flowers that might accurately be called "chaliced" ("Hark, Hark! the Lark at Heaven's Gate Sings," l. 4).

5. If you have access to a copy of Shakespeare's *Tempest*, look up the song "Full Fathom Five Thy Father Lies," and be prepared to tell the class by whom and under what circumstances it is sung.

6. What features of "Full Fathom Five Thy Father Lies" help to make the account of the supposed drowning gently sentimental rather than really tragic?

7. Remember especially lines 4–6 of "Full Fathom Five Thy Father Lies." They have become famous, and are quoted on the tombstone of the poet Shelley (p. 719).

8. If you have read *Macbeth* (p. 86), point out at least one passage in which Shakespeare puts into the mouth of a character a speech that is really a lyric.

9. If possible let the class give a program of Shakespearean music. Ask the music department to co-operate. "Hark, Hark! the Lark" and "Who Is Sylvia?" are available in recording 6926 by the RCA (Victor) Manufacturing Company, Inc. "I Know a Bank Where the Wild Thyme Grows" is available in recording 4085, by the same company.

ELIZABETHAN SONNETS

THE SONNET* is one of the most characteristic forms of Elizabethan lyric poetry. Thousands of sonnets were composed during the Elizabethan Period, either in the form of individual poems or in series, or sequences. The sonnet has been used to express many emotions, such as joy, sorrow, love of nature, and love of friends; but poets have never used it more effectively to express the love between men and women than did the Elizabethans. Of the many Elizabethan writers who composed sonnets, the best-known are Sidney, Spenser, and Shakespeare.

SIR PHILIP SIDNEY[1] (1554-1586)

From *Astrophel and Stella*

Astrophel and Stella is a sequence, or series, of sonnets* addressed by the handsome and gifted Sir Philip Sidney to Lady Penelope Devereux (děv'ĕr ōō), a beautiful and charming young woman who, unfortunately for Sir Philip, married somebody else.

Sidney's sonnets are important because of their influence on other writers as well as because of their own beauty. They are typical of their age in their use of such poetical devices as rhyme, alliteration,* and word melody. Though they also occasionally contain examples of artificial and obscure language (conceits*), they deserve our admiration because they are truly sincere and because they reveal the noble character of the knightly and high-minded author. After the fashion of the time, Sidney calls both himself and his loved one by assumed names. Astrophel (ăs'trŏ fĕl) (Star-lover) is Sidney; Stella (Star) is Lady Penelope Devereux.

I

LOVING in truth, and fain[2] in verse my
 love to show,
That she, dear she, might take some
 pleasure of my pain, —
Pleasure might cause her read. reading
 might make her know,
Knowledge might pity win, and pity
 grace obtain, —

[1] For biography see page 700.
[2] Eager, desirous.

I sought fit words to paint the blackest
 face of woe,
Studying inventions[1] fine, her wits to
 entertain,
Oft turning others' leaves, to see if thence
 would flow
Some fresh and fruitful showers upon my
 sunburnt brain.
But words came halting out, wanting
 Invention's stay[2];
Invention, Nature's child, fled step-
 dame Study's blows;[3]   10
And others' feet still seemed but strangers
 in my way.
Thus, great with child to speak, and help-
 less in my throes,
Biting my truant pen, beating myself for
 spite;
"Fool," said my Muse to me, "look in
 thy heart, and write."

XXXI

With how sad steps, O Moon, thou
 climb'st the skies!
How silently, and with how wan a face!

[1] Imaginative ways of treating the subject.
[2] *Invention's stay.* The support of natural imaginative power.
[3] *Invention . . . blows.* Imagination, being the spontaneous result of nature, could not be forced to operate by artificial means such as intensive thought (study).

What, may it be that even in heavenly
    place
That busy archer[1] his sharp arrows tries!
Sure, if that[2] long-with-love-acquainted
    eyes
Can judge of love, thou feel'st a lover's
    case;   20
I read it in thy looks; thy languished
    grace,
To me that feel the like, my state descries.[3]

Then, even of fellowship,[1] O Moon, tell
    me,
Is constant love deemed there but want
    of wit?
Are beauties there as proud as here they
    be?
Do they above love to be loved, and yet
Those lovers scorn whom that love doth
    possess?
Do they call virtue there ungratefulness?

EDMUND SPENSER[4] (1552?-1599)

From *Amoretti*

Spenser's *Amoretti* is a collection of love son-
sets* celebrating his courtship. They illustrate the Elizabethan fondness for pretty
compliments to women; but, unlike many
other Elizabethan lyrics, they are known to be
sincere, for Spenser afterward married the
lady to whom they are addressed. They are
characteristic of Spenser in their rich beauty
of language and in their pure and harmonious
atmosphere of true love.

XXXVII

WHAT guile is this, that those her
    golden tresses
She doth attire under a net of gold,
And with sly skill so cunningly them
    dresses
That which is gold or hair may scarce be
    told?
Is it that men's frail eyes, which gaze too
    bold,
She may entangle in that golden snare,
And, being caught, may craftily enfold
Their weaker hearts, which are not well
    aware?
Take heed, therefore, mine eyes, how ye
    do stare
Henceforth too rashly on that guileful net,
In which if ever ye entrappèd are,   11
Out of her bands ye by no means shall get.
Fondness[5] it were for any, being free,
To covet fetters, though they golden be!

LXI

The glorious image of the Maker's
    beauty,[2]
My sovereign saint, the idol of my
    thought,
Dare not henceforth, above the bounds
    of duty,
T' accuse of pride, or rashly blame for
    ought.
For being, as she is, divinely wrought,
And of the brood of angels heavenly
    born,   20
And with the crew of blessed saints up-
    brought,
Each of which did her with their gifts
    adorn —
The bud of joy, the blossom of the
    morn,
The beam of light, whom mortal eyes
    admire;
What reason is it then but she should
    scorn
Base things that to her love too bold
    aspire!
Such heavenly forms ought rather wor-
    shipt be
Than dare be loved by men of mean[3]
    degree.

[1] *even of fellowship.* Because you seem to be a
    lover, as I am.
[2] *The glorious . . . beauty.* My sweetheart. Ac-
    cording to Genesis 1 : 26, man is made in the
    image of God.
[3] Low.

[1] Cupid.*   [2] *if that.* If.
[3] Makes known.
[4] For biography see page 701.   [5] Folly.

WILLIAM SHAKESPEARE[1] (1564-1616)

When in Disgrace with Fortune and Men's Eyes

Although the individual sonnets of Shakespeare's collection, or sequence, vary greatly in poetic excellence, the two given here are so filled with mellowed sweetness of rhythm* and meter, with richness and beauty of imagery,* and with deep thought and powerful feeling, that they rank among the finest products of Shakespeare's lyrical genius. In the first sonnet the poet says that no matter how downcast or despondent he may feel when he compares his poor self and his poorer fortunes with those of other and more favored men, if he happens to think about his loved one his heart overflows with joy like that of a singing lark. The identity of the person addressed in Shakespeare's sonnets is a matter of dispute.

XXIX

WHEN in disgrace with fortune and men's eyes,
I all alone beweep my outcast state,
And trouble deaf heaven with my boot-
    less[1] cries,
And look upon myself, and curse my fate,
Wishing me like to one more rich in hope,
Featured like him,[2] like him with friends
    possessed,
Desiring this man's art, and that man's
    scope,[3]
With what I most enjoy contented least;
Yet in these thoughts myself almost de-
    spising,   10
Haply[4] I think on thee, — and then my
    state,
Like to the lark at break of day arising
From sullen earth, sings hymns at
    heaven's gate;[5]
For thy sweet love remembered such
    wealth brings
That then I scorn to change my state
    with kings.

Tired with All These, for Restful Death I Cry

LXVI

The following sonnet* strikes a note that is rare in Elizabethan lyric poetry. Here the lover is tired of everything and would willingly die were it not for the fact that he would have to leave his loved one behind. The mood which the sonnet expresses may be compared to that of Hamlet's famous soliloquy, beginning "To be or not to be." Read especially *Hamlet*, III, i, 70–74.

TIRED with all these, for restful death
    I cry, —
As,[2] to behold desert a beggar born,
And needy nothing[3] trimm'd in jollity,
And purest faith unhappily forsworn,
And gilded honour shamefully misplaced,
And maiden virtue rudely strumpeted,
And right perfection wrongfully dis-
    graced,
And strength by limping sway[6] disablèd,
And art made tongue-tied by authority,[7]
And folly doctor-like[8] controlling skill,
And simple truth miscall'd simplicity,[9]
And captive good attending captain ill:
Tired with all these, from these would I
    be gone,
Save that, to die, I leave my love alone.

[1] Unavailing.
[2] *Featured ... him.* With his (good) looks. "He" is a rival for the favor of the person addressed.   [3] Opportunity.
[4] Perhaps; by chance.
[5] *the lark ... gate.* This line suggests the beginning of Shakespeare's "Hark, Hark! the Lark at Heaven's Gate Sings" (p. 155).
[6] *limping sway.* Weak, incompetent persons in power.
[7] *art ... authority.* Artistic genius prevented from expressing itself by those in authority.
[8] *folly doctor-like.* Folly acting as though it were wise.   [9] Foolishness, folly.

[1] For biography see page 698.
[2] *Tired ... As.* I am so tired when I consider such situations as the following that I long to die.
[3] *needy nothing.* Here, a needy person of no merit.

Discussion Hints

1. In *Astrophel and Stella* (p. 157) pick out three or four repeated words, a characteristic of Sidney. Select several examples of Sidney's use of alliteration.* Find groups of words that seem to you especially melodious.

2. What are the "fetters" of *Amoretti*, XXXVII, l. 14 (p. 158)?

3. Examine the rhyme scheme of the *Amoretti*. Do the two sonnets* have the same rhyme scheme? Compare them in the matter of rhyme scheme with Sidney's sonnets (p. 157), with Shakespeare's (p. 159), and with Milton's (p. 198).

4. Are Shakespeare's two sonnets* (p. 159) English or Italian in form? Explain how you can tell.

General Discussion Hints on Lyric Poetry of the Elizabethan Period

1. Using the words and phrases descriptive of woman found in the preceding lyrics, describe a beautiful woman as an Elizabethan poet saw her.

2. From the trees, plants, and birds referred to, should you say that in general the Elizabethan poets were careful to describe nature in detail? Before answering read, if possible, Shakespeare's Sonnet XVIII (in the revised edition of *Achievement* of this series).

3. Elizabethan and earlier English poets were fond of speaking of love (1) as caused by a dart or arrow from the lady's eye, and (2) as entering the lover through his eyes. In how many of the preceding lyrics do you find either or both of these ideas?

4. Paraphrase *Astrophel and Stella*, I (p. 157), and *Amoretti*, XXXVII (p. 158).

5. Put into one sentence each of the two stanzas of Jonson's song "To Celia" (p. 154).

Suggestions for Reading in Lyric Poetry

AULT, NORMAN (ED.). *Book of Elizabethan Lyrics.* Longmans, Green & Co.

CHAMBERS, SIR EDMUND K. *Oxford Book of Sixteenth Century Verse.* Oxford University Press.

For those who wish to read or sing Shakespeare's lyrics:

BROOKE, TUCKER (ED.). *Shakespeare's Songs; being a Complete Collection of the Songs Written by or Attributed to William Shakespeare.* J. M. Dent & Sons, Ltd.

EDWARDS, EDWARD (arranger and decorator). *Book of Shakespeare's Songs, with Musical Settings by Various Composers.* G. Schirmer and Company.

VINCENT, CHARLES JOHN (ED.). *Fifty Shakespeare Songs.* The Oliver Ditson Company. Contains both words and music.

THE BIBLE

IN ADDITION to the fact that it is a sacred document, the Bible owes its place in literature (1) to its noble theme, God, man, and the universe; (2) to its superb but simple language; (3) to the majestic music of its style.

The translation here followed is the work of forty-seven scholars appointed by King James* I, and is consequently known as the King James Bible. It is the most famous book in the world.

Job[1]

Job, the eighteenth book of the Old Testament, is a record of marvelous religious experience expressed in language of great poetic beauty. To the casual reader the Book of Job tells of the misfortunes, doubts, and final restoration to prosperity and faith of a certain rich and pious man. To the more serious reader it opens up the great question of how far misfortune is the result of individual wrongdoing. The following chapter is selected because of its deep truth and its rich imagery,* and because it contains many passages frequently alluded to in other English literature.

CHAPTER 38

1 *God challengeth Job to answer.* 4 *God, by enumerating his mighty works, convinceth Job of ignorance,* 31 *and of imbecility.*

THEN the Lord answered Job out of the whirlwind, and said,

2 Who *is* this that darkeneth counsel by words without knowledge?

3 Gird up now thy loins like a man; for I will demand of thee, and answer thou me.

4 Where wast thou when I laid the foundations of the earth? declare, if thou hast understanding.

5 Who hath laid the measures thereof, if thou knowest? or who hath stretched the line upon it?[2]

6 Whereupon are the foundations thereof fastened? or who laid the corner stone thereof;

7 When the morning stars sang together, and all the sons of God shouted for joy?

8 Or *who* shut up the sea with doors, when it brake forth, *as if* it had issued out of the womb?

9 When I made the cloud the garment thereof, and thick darkness a swaddling band for it,

10 And brake up for it my decreed *place*, and set bars and doors,

11 And said, Hitherto shalt thou come, but no further: and here shall thy proud waves be stayed?

12 Hast thou commanded the morning since thy days; *and* caused the dayspring to know his place;

13 That it might take hold of the ends of the earth, that the wicked might be shaken out of it?

14 It is turned as clay *to* the seal; and they stand as a garment.

15 And from the wicked their light is withholden, and the high arm shall be broken.

16 Hast thou entered into the springs of the sea? or hast thou walked in the search of the depth?

[1] *Job* (jōb).   [2] *stretched . . . it.* Measured it.

17 Have the gates of death been opened unto thee? or hast thou seen the doors of the shadow of death?

18 Hast thou perceived the breadth of the earth? declare if thou knowest it all.

50 19 Where *is* the way *where* light dwelleth? and *as for* darkness, where *is* the place thereof,

20 That thou shouldest take it to the bound thereof, and that thou shouldest know the paths *to* the house thereof?

21 Knowest thou *it*, because thou wast then born? or *because* the number of thy days *is* great?

22 Hast thou entered into the treas-
60 ures of the snow? or hast thou seen the treasures of the hail,

23 Which I have reserved against the time of trouble, against the day of battle and war?

24 By what way is the light parted, *which* scattereth the east wind upon the earth?

25 Who hath divided a watercourse for the overflowing of waters, or a way
70 for the lightning of thunder;

26 To cause it to rain on the earth, *where* no man *is*; *on* the wilderness, wherein *there is* no man;

27 To satisfy the desolate and waste *ground*; and to cause the bud of the tender herb to spring forth?

28 Hath the rain a father? or who hath begotten the drops of dew?

29 Out of whose womb came the ice?

and the hoary frost of heaven, who hath 80 gendered it?

30 The waters are hid as *with* a stone, and the face of the deep is frozen.

31 Canst thou bind the sweet influences of the Pleiades, or loose the bands of Orion?

32 Canst thou bring forth Mazzaroth in his season? or canst thou guide Arcturus with his sons?[1]

33 Knowest thou the ordinances of 90 heaven? canst thou set the dominion thereof in the earth?

34 Canst thou lift up thy voice to the clouds, that abundance of waters may cover thee?

35 Canst thou send lightnings, that they may go, and say unto thee, Here we *are*?

36 Who hath put wisdom in the inward parts? or who hath given under- 100 standing to the heart?

37 Who can number the clouds in wisdom? or who can stay the bottles of heaven,

38 When the dust groweth into hardness, and the clods cleave fast together?

39 Wilt thou hunt the prey for the lion? or fill the appetite of the young lions,

40 When they couch in *their* dens, *and* 110 abide in the covert to lie in wait?

41 Who provideth for the raven his food? when his young ones cry unto God, they wander for lack of meat.

The Psalms

The Book of Psalms, popularly ascribed to King David,* is highly poetical, is rich in imagery,* and is characterized by an abundance of parallelism,* a poetical device which is found in the Hebrew original and is preserved in the English translation. The following psalms embody deep truths, and are filled with phrases that are used time and again in English literature and have passed into everyday speech. Millions of people have quoted the Psalms from memory, and probably an even greater number have used in

their speech Biblical phrases the source of which they did not know.

PSALM 1

1 *The happiness of the godly.* 4 *The unhappiness of the ungodly.*

BLESSED *is* the man that walketh not in the counsel of the ungodly, nor

[1] *Canst . . . sons?* Hast thou power to control the heavenly bodies?

standeth in the way of sinners, nor sitteth in the seat of the scornful.

2 But his delight *is* in the law of the LORD; and in his law doth he meditate day and night.

3 And he shall be like a tree planted by the rivers of water, that bringeth
10 forth his fruit in his season; his leaf also shall not wither; and whatsoever he doeth shall prosper.

4 The ungodly *are* not so: but *are* like the chaff which the wind driveth away.

5 Therefore the ungodly shall not stand in the judgment, nor sinners in the congregation of the righteous.

6 For the LORD knoweth the way of
20 the righteous: but the way of the ungodly shall perish.

PSALM 23

David's confidence in God's grace.

A Psalm of David.

THE LORD *is* my shepherd; I shall not want.

2 He maketh me to lie down in green pastures: he leadeth me beside the still waters.

3 He restoreth my soul: he leadeth me in the paths of righteousness for his name's sake.

4 Yea, though I walk through the
10 valley of the shadow of death, I will fear no evil: for thou *art* with me; thy rod and thy staff they comfort me.

5 Thou preparest a table before me in the presence of mine enemies: thou anointest my head with oil; my cup runneth over.

6 Surely goodness and mercy shall follow me all the days of my life: and I will dwell in the house of the LORD for
20 ever.

PSALM 24

1 *God's lordship over the world.* 3 *The citizens of his spiritual kingdom.* 7 *An exhortation to receive him.*

A Psalm of David.

THE EARTH *is* the LORD'S, and the fulness thereof; the world, and they that dwell therein.

2 For he hath founded it upon the seas, and established it upon the floods.

3 Who shall ascend into the hill of the LORD? or who shall stand in his holy place?

4 He that hath clean hands, and a pure heart; who hath not lifted up his 30 soul unto vanity, nor sworn deceitfully.

5 He shall receive the blessing from the LORD, and righteousness from the God of his salvation.

6 This *is* the generation of them that seek him, that seek thy face, O Jacob. Selah.

7 Lift up your heads, O ye gates; and be ye lifted up, ye everlasting doors; and the King of glory shall come in. 40

8 Who *is* this King of glory? The LORD strong and mighty, the LORD mighty in battle.

9 Lift up your heads, O ye gates; even lift *them* up, ye everlasting doors; and the King of glory shall come in.

10 Who is this King of glory? The LORD of hosts, he *is* the King of glory. Selah.

PSALM 100

1 *An exhortation to praise God cheerfully,* 3 *for his greatness,* 4 *and for his power.*

A Psalm of praise.

MAKE a joyful noise unto the LORD, all ye lands.

2 Serve the LORD with gladness: come before his presence with singing.

3 Know ye that the LORD he *is* God: *it is* he *that* hath made us, and not we ourselves; *we are* his people, and the sheep of his pasture.

4 Enter into his gates with thanksgiving, *and* into his courts with praise: 10 be thankful unto him, *and* bless his name.

5 For the LORD *is* good; his mercy *is* everlasting; and his truth *endureth* to all generations.

PSALM 121

The great safety of the godly, who put their trust in God's protection.

A Song of degrees.

I WILL lift up mine eyes unto the hills, from whence cometh my help.

2 My help *cometh* from the LORD, which made heaven and earth.

3 He will not suffer thy foot to be moved: he that keepeth thee will not slumber.

4 Behold, he that keepeth Israel shall neither slumber nor sleep.

5 The LORD *is* thy keeper: the LORD *is* thy shade upon thy right hand. 10

6 The sun shall not smite thee by day, nor the moon by night.

7 The LORD shall preserve thee from all evil: he shall preserve thy soul.

8 The LORD shall preserve thy going out and thy coming in from this time forth, and even for evermore.

Ecclesiastes

"Ecclesiastes," one of the "wisdom books" of the Old Testament and popularly regarded as the work of King Solomon, is a collection of poetical discourses and observations on the general theme "Vanity of vanities; all is vanity." The following chapter emphasizes especially the importance of wisdom. As you read it note the passages that have found their way into everyday modern English.

CHAPTER 12

1 *The Creator is to be remembered in due time.* 8 *The Preacher's care to edify.* 13 *The fear of God is the chief antidote of vanity.*

REMEMBER now thy Creator in the days of thy youth, while the evil days come not, nor the years draw nigh, when thou shalt say, I have no pleasure in them;

2 While the sun, or the light, or the moon, or the stars, be not darkened, nor the clouds return after the rain:

3 In the day when the keepers of the house shall tremble, and the strong men shall bow themselves, and the grinders cease because they are few, and those that look out of the windows be darkened,

4 And the doors shall be shut in the streets, when the sound of the grinding is low, and he shall rise up at the voice of the bird, and all the daughters of music shall be brought low;

5 Also *when* they shall be afraid of *that which is* high, and fears *shall be* in the way, and the almond tree shall flourish, and the grasshopper shall be a burden, and desire shall fail: because man goeth to his long home, and the mourners go about the streets:

6 Or ever the silver cord be loosed, or the golden bowl be broken, or the pitcher be broken at the fountain, or the wheel broken at the cistern. 30

7 Then shall the dust return to the earth as it was: and the spirit shall return unto God who gave it.

8 ¶ Vanity of vanities, saith the Preacher; all *is* vanity.

9 And moreover, because the Preacher was wise, he still taught the people knowledge; yea, he gave good heed, and sought out, *and* set in order many proverbs. 40

10 The Preacher sought to find out acceptable words: and *that which was* written *was* upright, *even* words of truth.

11 The words of the wise *are* as goads, and as nails fastened *by* the masters of assemblies, *which* are given from one shepherd.

12 And further, by these, my son, be admonished: of making many books 50 *there is* no end; and much study *is* a weariness of the flesh.

13 ¶ Let us hear the conclusion of the

whole matter: Fear God, and keep his commandments: for this *is* the whole *duty* of man.

14 For God shall bring every work into judgment, with every secret thing, whether *it be* good, or whether *it be* evil.

Philippians[1]

The following verse is well worth learning by heart. It outlines a philosophy of life that is as good today as it was two thousand years ago, when Saint Paul recommended it in his famous letter to the Christians of Philippi.

FINALLY, brethren, whatsoever things are true, whatsoever things *are* honest, whatsoever things *are* just, whatsoever things *are* pure, whatsoever things *are* lovely, whatsoever things *are* of good report; if *there be* any virtue, and if *there be* any praise, think on these things.

Discussion Hints

1. Why are so many questions asked in the passage from Job (p. 161)?

2. Point out several questions asked of Job that seem to have come from a poet rather than from a scientist.

3. Point out the similes* in Psalm 1 (p. 162).

4. Point out a metaphor* in Psalm 23 (p. 163).

5. It has been said that the simple directness of the prose of the Bible is largely the result of the use of the active voice. How often is the passive voice used in the psalms given here?

[1] The passage is the eighth verse of the fourth chapter of Philippians.

6. What phrases used in the selections from the Bible do you recognize as occurring in everyday modern English? Make a list and compare it with the lists made by other members of the class.

7. Point out the passages with which you are familiar.

8. Select half a dozen striking illustrations of parallelism.*

9. Memorize Job 38:4-13 (p. 161) and Psalm 23 (p. 163).

10. Learn by heart Ecclesiastes 12:8 (p. 164), and remember it when you come to read the account of Vanity Fair (p. 205).

Passages to be Explained

... Hitherto shalt thou come, but no further: and here shall thy proud waves be stayed (Job 38:11, p. 161)

... I walk through the valley of the shadow of death (Psalm 23:4, p. 163)

Suggestions for Reading

The Book of Ruth
"The Sermon on the Mount" (Matthew 5-7)
"The Good Samaritan" (Luke 10:30-37)
"The Prodigal Son" (Luke 15:11-32)
"Charity" (1 Corinthians 13)
"The Millennium" (Revelation 21 and 22)

AN ALLEGORICAL ROMANCE

EDMUND SPENSER[1] (1552?–1599)

From *The Faerie Queene*

The following passages are taken from the first book of Spenser's great allegory,* *The Faerie Queene*. They have delighted thousands of readers by the quiet, melodious movement of the verse, by the perfect adaptation of the sound to the sense, and by the series of vivid pictures that they present.

The Faerie Queene is Spenser's masterpiece. He worked at it for twenty years, and left it unfinished at his death. It is an epic (p. 18) in that it has for its theme the greatness of a nation (England), the virtues of its rulers, and their struggles against their enemies. It is a romance (p. 32) in that it tells of the exploits of noble knights who fight with dragons and enchanters to protect fair ladies. It is an allegory* in that, beneath the surface, it suggests the struggles of good against evil and of England against her enemies. The Redcross Knight, for example, represents Holiness; Una, the perfection of holiness (Truth); and so on. The allegory is elaborate and not always easy to understand. Fortunately, however, we can enjoy much of the beauty of the poem by reading it simply as a tale of old romance told in beautiful verse that makes us feel the dreamy charm of fairyland. Read it aloud, and see for yourself. A striking feature of *The Faerie Queene* is the stanza form, known as the Spenserian* stanza because Spenser invented it.

Each book of *The Faerie Queene* recounts the exploits of a different knight. In the first book, from which our selections are taken, the brave and virtuous Redcross Knight (Saint* George), who represents Holiness, sets out with the beautiful maiden Una (Truth) and her attendant dwarf to free the lady's parents from a terrible dragon. On the way the Redcross Knight, through the magic of a wicked sorcerer, is induced to abandon Una. He then meets the lovely but wicked Duessa* (daughter of Deceit and Shame), or

[1] For biography see page 701.

Fidessa, as she calls herself, accompanied by a heathen Saracen knight named Sansfoy (Faithless). The Redcross Knight slays Sansfoy and becomes the champion of Duessa. Meanwhile Una, while seeking for her lost lover, falls into the hands of Sansfoy's brother, Sansloy (Lawless). At the magnificent but crumbling castle of Pride the Redcross Knight meets Sansjoy (Joyless), a brother of the two Saracens, and challenges him to mortal combat. The story then goes on as follows:

THE BATTLE BETWEEN THE REDCROSS KNIGHT AND SANSJOY. FROM BOOK I, CANTO V[1]

II

At last the golden oriental[2] gate
Of greatest heaven gan to open fair,
And Phoebus* fresh, as bridegroom to
    his mate,
Came dancing forth, shaking his dewy
    hair,
And hurls his glist'ring beams through
    gloomy air.
Which when the wakeful Elf[3] perceiv'd,
    straightway
He started up, and did himself prepare,
In sunbright arms, and battailous[4] array:
    For with that Pagan[5] proud he com-
    bat will that day.

[1] For the sake of uniformity of style and ease of reading, the spelling of the passages from *The Faerie Queene* has been modernized.
[2] Eastern.
[3] A poetical name for the Redcross Knight.
[4] Warlike.
[5] Sansjoy.

166

IV

Soon after comes the cruel Sarazin,* 10
In woven mail all armèd warily,[1]
And sternly looks at him, who not a pin
Does care for look of living creature's
eye.[2]
They bring them wines of Greece and
Araby,*
And dainty spices fetch'd from furthest
Ind,*
To kindle heat of courage privily:
And in the wine a solemn oath they bind
T' observe the sacred laws of arms,
that are assign'd.

V

At last forth comes that far renownèd
Queen,[3]
With royal pomp and princely majesty;
She is ybrought unto a palèd green,[4] 21
And placèd under stately canopy,
The warlike feats of both those knights
to see.
On th' other side in all men's open view
Duessa* placèd is, and on a tree
Sansfoy his shield[5] is hang'd with bloody
hue;
Both those the laurel girlonds[6] to the
victor due.

VI

A shrilling trumpet sounded from on high,
And unto battle bade themselves address[7]:
Their shining shields about their wrists
they tie, 30

[1] Craftily.
[2] Here pronounced ē.
[3] The queen here referred to is Pride, mistress
of the crumbling castle where the Redcross
Knight and Sansjoy are staying.
[4] *a palèd green*. A grassy space enclosed by a
fence. With "palèd" compare our "paling."
[5] *Sansfoy his shield*. Sansfoy's shield (which the
Redcross Knight had carried off as a trophy
after slaying the owner).
[6] *laurel girlonds*. Laurel garlands (given as prizes
of a combat); here applied to Duessa and
the shield.
[7] *themselves address*. Prepare for.

And burning blades about their heads do
bless,[1]
The instruments of wrath and heaviness;
With greedy force each other doth assail,
And strike so fiercely, that they do im-
press
Deep dinted furrows in the batter'd mail;
The iron walls to ward their blows are
weak and frail.

VII

The Sarazin was stout, and wondrous
strong,
And heapèd blows like iron hammers
great;
For after blood and vengeance he did
long.
The knight was fierce, and full of youthly
heat, 40
And doubled strokes, like dreaded thunder's threat:
For all for praise and honour he did fight.
Both stricken strike, and beaten both do
beat,
That from their shields forth flieth fiery
light,
And helmets hewen deep show marks of
either's might.

X

At last the Paynim[2] chanc'd to cast his
eye,
His sudden eye, flaming with wrathful
fire,
Upon his brother's shield, which hung
thereby:
Therewith redoubled was his raging ire,
And said, "Ah, wretched son of woeful
sire,[3] 50
Dost thou sit wailing by black Stygian*
lake,
Whilst here thy shield is hang'd for
victor's hire,[4]

[1] Here, brandish.
[2] Pagan.
[3] *Ah . . . sire*. These words are spoken to his
brother, who has been slain.
[4] Prize.

And, sluggish german, dost thy forces
    slake
    To after-send his foe, that him may
      overtake?[1]

XI

"Go, caitive[2] Elf, him quickly overtake,
And soon redeem from his long wand'ring
    woe;
Go, guilty ghost, to him my message
    make,
That I his shield have quit[3] from dying
    foe."
Therewith upon his[4] crest he stroke him
    so,   59
That twice he reelèd, ready twice to fall;
End of the doubtful battle deemèd tho[5]
The lookers on, and loud to him gan[6]
    call
    The false Duessa, "Thine the shield,
      and I, and all!"

XII

Soon as the Faery[7] heard his Lady[8]
    speak,
Out of his swooning dream he gan awake,
And quick'ning faith, that erst was
    woxen[9] weak,
The creeping deadly cold away did shake:
Tho[10] mov'd with wrath, and shame, and
    Lady's sake,
Of all attonce[11] he cast[12] aveng'd to be,

[1] *sluggish german . . . overtake.* Sluggish brother
(here Sansjoy is speaking to himself), do you
slacken your efforts to send your foe (the
Redcross Knight) after your brother to the
land of the dead? In a large dictionary
look up the meaning of "german," "brother-
german," and "cousin-german."
[2] Caitiff, despicable. This and the next three
lines are addressed to the Redcross Knight.
[3] Redeemed.
[4] The Redcross Knight's.
[5] Then.
[6] Did. Literally, began to.
[7] The Redcross Knight.
[8] Duessa, whom he does not yet know to be false.
[9] *erst . . . woxen.* Formerly had waxed; that is,
    previously had become.
[10] Then.
[11] At once.   [12] Resolved.

And with so exceeding fury at him
    strake,   70
That forcèd him to stoop upon his knee;
    Had he not stoopèd so, he should have
    cloven be.[1]

XIII

And to him said: "Go now, proud mis-
    creant,[2]
Thyself thy message do to german dear[3];
Alone he, wand'ring, thee too long doth
    want:
Go say, his foe thy shield with his doth
    bear."
Therewith his heavy hand he high gan
    rear,[4]
Him to have slain; when lo! a darksome
    cloud
Upon him fell: he nowhere doth appear,
But vanish'd is. The Elf him calls aloud,
    But answer none receives: the dark-
    ness him does shroud.[5]   81

XIV

In haste Duessa from her place arose,
And to him running said: "O prowest[6]
    knight,
That ever lady to[7] her love did chose,
Let now abate the terror of your might,
And quench the flame of furious despite
And bloody vengeance; lo! th' infernal
    powers,
Covering your foe with cloud of deadly
    night,
Have borne him hence to Pluto's* bale-
    ful bowers.[8]
    The conquest yours, I yours, the shield
      and glory yours!"   90

XVI

Wherewith he goeth to that sovereign
    Queen,
And falling her before on lowly knee,
To her makes present of his service seen:

[1] *Cloven be.* Been cut in two.
[2] Unbeliever and scoundrel.
[3] *german dear.* Thy dear brother.
[4] *gan rear.* Did raise.   [5] Conceal.
[6] Most valiant.   [7] For, as.
[8] *baleful bowers.* Cruel dwelling.

Which she accepts, with thanks, and
    goodly gree,[1]
Greatly advancing[2] his gay chivalree.
So marcheth home, and by her takes the
    knight,
Whom all the people follow with great
    glee,
Shouting, and clapping all their hands on
    height,
    That all the air it fills, and flies to
      heaven bright.

[The Redcross Knight, after being healed of
his wounds, escapes with the dwarf from
the house of Pride, leaving Duessa behind.
While resting by a fountain the Knight
is suddenly taken prisoner by the giant
Orgoglio (ôr gōl′yō). Meanwhile Una escapes
from Sansloy, meets the dwarf, and learns
what has happened. Just then Arthur, seeking the court of the Faerie Queene, appears
on the scene. He fights with Orgoglio and
frees the Redcross Knight. The Redcross
Knight and Una proceed on their way,
finally reaching the wasted kingdom of Una's
father and the brazen tower where Una's
parents are imprisoned by the dragon. The
Knight fights a desperate battle with the
dragon and finally succeeds in slaying it.]

THE DRAGON SLAIN. THE BETROTHAL
OF UNA. FROM BOOK I, CANTO XII

II

Scarcely had Phoebus* in the glooming
    east   100
Yet harnessèd his fiery-footed team,
Ne[3] rear'd above the earth his flaming
    crest,[4]
When the last deadly smoke aloft did
    steam,
That sign of last outbreathèd life did
    seem
Unto the watchman on the castle wall,

[1] Favor.
[2] Praising.
[3] Nor.
[4] *Scarcely . . . crest.* Spenser is here saying in
beautiful but high-flown poetic language suitable for an epic that dawn had come but
that the sun had not yet risen above the
horizon.

Who thereby dead that baleful Beast
    did deem,[1]
And to his Lord and Lady[2] loud gan call,
    To tell how he had seen the Dragon's
      fatal fall.

IV

Then gan triumphant trumpets sound
    on high,   109
That sent to heaven the echoèd report
Of their new joy, and happy victory
'Gainst him, that had them long oppres'd
    with tort,[3]
And fast imprisonèd in siegèd fort.
Then all the people, as in solemn feast,
To him assembled with one full consort,
Rejoicing at the fall of that great beast
    From whose eternal bondage now
      they were releas'd.

V

Forth came that ancient Lord and aged
    Queen,
Array'd in antique robes down to the
    ground,   119
And sad habiliments right well beseen;[4]
A noble crew[5] about them waited round
Of sage and sober peers, all gravely
    gown'd;
Whom far before did march a goodly
    band
Of tall young men, all able arms to
    sound,[6]
But now they laurel branches bore in
    hand;
    Glad sign of victory and peace in all
      their land.

[1] *Who . . . deem.* Who therefore (seeing that the
smoke had ceased to rise from the dragon's
body) judged the creature to be dead. The
Dragon had just been slain by the Redcross
Knight.
[2] *his Lord and Lady.* The father and mother of
Una.
[3] Wrong.
[4] *sad . . . beseen.* Well dressed in sober and dignified clothes.
[5] Company.
[6] Here, wield.

VI

Unto that doughty Conqueror[1] they came,
And him before themselves prostrating
  low,
Their Lord and Patron loud did him
  proclaim,
And at his feet their laurel boughs did
  throw.   130
Soon after them all dancing on a row
The comely virgins came, with girlonds
  dight,[2]
As fresh as flowers in meadow green do
  grow,
When morning dew upon their leaves
  doth light:
And in their hands sweet timbrels all
  upheld on height.

[After the outdoor celebration Una's father
and mother conduct the Redcross Knight and
Una to the palace, where meats and drinks
of every kind are served. Una's father now
offers the Redcross Knight his daughter's
hand; but the Knight declares that the wedding must be postponed until he has fulfilled
a promise formerly made by him to serve
the Faerie Queene for six years.]

XIX

"Unhappy fall that hard necessity
(Quoth he[3]), the troubler of my happy
  peace,
And vowèd foe of my felicity;
Ne[4] I against the same can justly
  preace[5]:
But since that bond ye cannot now re-
  lease,   140
Nor doen undo[6] (for vows may not be
  vain),
Soon as the terms of those six years shall
  cease,
Ye then shall hither back return again,
  The marriage to accomplish vow'd be-
  twixt you twain.

[1] The Redcross Knight.
[2] Decorated.
[3] The king, Una's father.
[4] Nor.
[5] Press, insist.
[6] doen undo. Cause to be undone.

XX

"Which for my part I covet to perform,
In sort as[1] through the world I did pro-
  claim,
That whoso kill'd that monster most
  deform,
And him in hardy battle overcame,
Should have mine only daughter to his
  dame,[2]   149
And of my kingdom heir apparent be:
Therefore since now to thee pertains[3]
  the same,
By due desert of noble chivalry
  Both daughter and eke kingdom, lo! I
  yield to thee."

[Just as the solemn betrothal of the Redcross Knight and Una is about to take place,
a messenger arrives bearing a letter which forbids the ceremony on the ground that the
Redcross Knight is already betrothed to
Fidessa (Duessa). Fortunately the Redcross
Knight is able to prove Fidessa's true character and the falsity of the charge, whereupon the messenger is seized and bound,
and the betrothal is completed with great
ceremony.]

Discussion Hints

1. Tell the story of the selections from
The Faerie Queene that you have just read.

2. See if you can learn more about the story
of Saint * George and the dragon than is given
in the "Dictionary of Names and Phrases";
for example, look under "Saint George" in an
encyclopedia if one is accessible.

3. Spenser is noted for the vividness with
which he paints pictures with words. Which of
the descriptions in the selections given above
do you think illustrate best his genius in this
respect?

4. Spenser is fond of describing persons
and events in exalted, high-sounding, dignified language suitable for epic poetry (p. 18).
An example is noted in Book I, Canto XII,
stanza II (p. 169). Can you point out other
illustrations?

[1] *In sort as.* Just as.
[2] *to his dame.* For his wife.
[3] Belongs.

*Forth came that ancient Lord and aged Queen
Arrayed in antique robes down to the ground*

5. Does the language of the selections from *The Faerie Queene* seem to you more archaic than that of the selections from Spenser's *Amoretti* and the other Elizabethan sonnets (pp. 157–159)? Give evidence to prove your answer. What words in *The Faerie Queene* suggest that Spenser is consciously imitating the language of an earlier time? Does his language in *The Faerie Queene* resemble that of Chaucer (p. 37)? Be ready to report in class.

6. Scan Book I, Canto V, stanza II (p. 166), and Canto XII, stanza V (p. 169), marking the accented and unaccented syllables and giving the rhyme* scheme.

7. Read Book I, Canto V, stanza IV (p. 167), and Canto XII, stanza V (p. 169), several times, trying to appreciate the dreamy, musical effect of Spenser's verse. Do you feel that the Alexandrine at the end of each stanza receives additional emphasis from its exceptional length (see "Spenserian* stanza")?

8. Examine the alliterative* lines. Do you find an unusual number of *l*'s, *m*'s, and *n*'s (liquid consonants)? If so, what effect do they have upon the quality of the verse?

Suggestions for Reading

1. Spenser never finished *The Faerie Queene*. Even the six books which he has left are more than most of us can find time to read entire. Read Book I, Canto I, and, if you like Spenser, Books II and III.

2. *The Faerie Queene* is based largely on medieval romance ; hence the most interesting supplementary reading is to be found in romances such as Sir Thomas Malory's *Morte d'Arthur* (p. 49). For readings in the medieval romances see page 54. The first book of *The Faerie Queene* tells a story much like that of the "Fair Unknown," given in Malory's *Morte d'Arthur* (Book VII, Chapters 1–21), and retold in Tennyson's "Gareth and Lynette" (in the revised edition of *Achievement* of this series).

ESSAYS

AN ESSAY is a piece of prose writing in which the author tries to explain something or to express his own thoughts or feelings about a subject; in fact, the word *essay* means "a trial, an attempt." According to the author's intention and method we usually divide essays into two classes: (1) formal; (2) informal, or familiar.

Formal essays are essays which are intended to explain or interpret something, rather than simply to entertain or amuse. In a strictly formal essay the author generally avoids expressions of merely personal opinion, and sticks closely to the exposition of facts, which he presents in logical order. Formal essays which attempt to explain the value of literary works are called critical. The essays of Dryden and of Samuel Johnson (p. 238) are typical examples of formal critical essays. Some essays attempt to explain both a writer and his works, and hence are both critical and biographical. Parts of Macaulay's *History of England* (p. 513) are much like formal essays. There are also many formal essays which, like Huxley's (p. 540), deal with scientific matters. In fact, nearly all scientific textbooks intended for use in schools consist of a series of formal expository essays. But formal essays are not confined to critical, biographical, historical, or scientific subjects. Any essay the purpose of which is to inform rather than to amuse is likely to be formal. Though many formal essays are apt to be hard reading unless we are interested in the subject beforehand, some, such as Cardinal Newman's (p. 508), are written in such a delightful style that the way the subject is treated interests us almost as much as the subject itself.

As the word *informal* suggests, the informal, or familiar, essay is much less apt to be strictly logical in structure and formal in treatment than the formal essay. In a familiar essay the chief interest lies in the author's way of looking at and treating his material rather than in the material itself. We read familiar essays to see what new and original ideas the author expresses; what fanciful and even fantastic combinations of old ideas he makes; what fun or pathos he reveals in human life by the power of his genius. He may deal with almost any subject, important or trivial, large or small, sad or humorous; all we require is that he enable us to look at the world through his eyes, and that the glimpse make our own enjoyment or sympathy greater.

The familiar essay developed relatively late in the history of literature. The father of the familiar essay was the great French author Montaigne (mŏn tān') (1533–1592), whose essays were translated into English the year Queen Elizabeth died (1603) and were read and admired by Bacon and Shakespeare. Though not the first writer who ever wrote essays, Montaigne was the first to make the essay thoroughly familiar in tone and literary in style. In simple, almost conversational, language he gives us his kindly, philosophical views on many aspects of human life, often turning aside into pleasant bypaths that lead him away from the main subject. The first author to write essays in the English language was Francis Bacon (p. 175), who is also famous as one of the first to use modern methods of scientific investigation. Bacon's essays consist of a collection of memoranda, "dispersed meditations," as the author calls them. They do not wander pleasantly like those of Montaigne; but they are so closely packed with striking phrases and laden with the author's own practical wisdom, especially on the art of achieving success in the world, that they are still widely read and admired in spite of Bacon's rather cold and selfish philosophy of life.

About a century after Bacon's time the familiar essay reached a high degree of perfection in the papers written by Addison (p. 261) and Steele (p. 255) for two periodicals, *The Tatler** and *The Spectator.** In smooth-flowing, clear, graceful language the authors comment interestingly on the morals, manners, whims, and affectations of their day. *The Sir Roger de Coverley Papers*, written by Addison and Steele, consist of a series of essays which not only give the authors' views on English life in town and country, but also are connected with each other in such a way as to form a narrative containing the seeds of the modern novel (see page 432). These essays were widely read and imitated both in England and in America, and helped to form the style of Washington Irving[1] and a host of other writers. Following the example of Addison and Steele, many authors of the later eighteenth century expressed their opinions on politics, religion, literature, or society in the form of familiar essays.

In keeping with its emphasis upon the importance of personal feelings, the Romantic Period was especially rich in essays reflecting the writer's own point of view. Charles Lamb (p. 375), one of the gentlest and most lovable of English writers, has left us a collection of witty or romantic observations which have brought smiles and tears to thousands of readers. Lamb's *Essays of Elia* include the best familiar essays in English literature.

As the nineteenth century progressed, the informal, personal essay gradually gained in popularity over the heavy, formal variety. Among those who wrote familiar essays during the last half of the nineteenth century Stevenson (p. 509) deserves special attention. The delicate humor, the cheerful courage, and the adventurous spirit that appear in

[1] See the revised editions of *Adventure* and *American Writers* of this series.

many of his essays reveal him as just the man to have written two of the best modern romantic novels, *Kidnapped* and *Treasure Island*.[1]

Within the last twenty years or so the English essay, like the American essay, has "shortened up, lightened up, and brightened up." Instead of being long, leisurely, and often impersonal, it has tended more and more to become swift, suggestive, and highly personal. So directly and intimately do many recent essays reflect the whim, the mood, the feeling, of the man behind the pen that they may be truly termed lyric.[2] In many recent English essays we almost get the impression that we are listening to a cultured gentleman talking intimately to a group of friends. The modern personal essay at its best is well illustrated by the work of A. P. Herbert (p. 616), H. M. Tomlinson (p. 618), and William McFee (p. 623).

As we can see by this time, the familiar essay is not a literary form that follows certain definite rules as to length, construction, and outward form. Its increasing popularity is largely owing to the freedom of treatment which it allows. In fact, many little sketches which might be called essays are included in longer pieces of writing. For example, Izaak Walton included in his *Complete Angler* (p. 202) many passages that are really informal essays.

FRANCIS BACON[3] (1561-1626)

Shrewd, pithy, worldly-wise observations upon man, nature, and life in general are the chief features of Bacon's *Essays*. Bacon's style is simple and straightforward, but his habit of using words of Latin origin in the Latin sense makes a careful study of his vocabulary necessary to a complete understanding of his thought. His essays are merely the by-product of his more serious thinking, which was chiefly along the lines of science and philosophy; but, as has been well said, "Even in the dust of his writings there is gold." Almost every sentence is an epigram* that could be amplified into a good-sized magazine article. This compression of thought, however, makes the reader stop frequently and reflect before he can grasp the full meaning of some of Bacon's sentences. Yet many of these sentences are among the clearest and most quotable in English literature. Take, for example, the following: "Virtue is like a rich stone, best plain set"; "He that hath wife and children, hath given hostages to fortune"; "Truth, which only doth judge itself, is the sovereign good of human nature." They all go straight to the point. Bacon's *Essays* are among the earliest and best-known classics of English prose.

Of Travel

TRAVEL, in the younger sort,[4] is a part of education; in the elder, a part of experience. He that travelleth into a country before he hath some entrance into[1] the language, goeth to school, and not to travel. That young men travel under some tutor, or grave servant, I allow well;[2] so that he be such a one that hath the language, and hath been in the country before; whereby he may be able 10

[1] Given in the revised edition of *Adventure* of this series.
[2] That is, they set forth the author's feelings about the facts rather than the facts themselves (see page 150).
[3] For biography see page 702.
[4] Here, persons, people.

[1] *Entrance into.* Knowledge of.
[2] *I . . well.* Is, in my opinion, advisable.

to tell them[1] what things are worthy to be seen in the country where they go; what acquaintances they are to seek; what exercises or discipline the place yieldeth. For else young men shall go hooded,[2] and look abroad little. It is a strange thing, that in sea voyages, where there is nothing to be seen but sky and sea, men should make diaries; but in land-travel, wherein so much is to be observed, for the most part they omit it;[3] as if chance were fitter to be registered than observation. Let diaries therefore be brought in use. The things to be seen and observed are, the courts of princes, specially when they give audience to ambassadors; the courts of justice, while they sit and hear causes; and so of consistories ecclesiastic;[4] the churches and monasteries, with the monuments[5] which are therein extant; the walls and fortifications of cities and towns, and so the havens and harbours; antiquities and ruins; libraries; colleges, disputations, and lectures, where any are; shipping and navies; houses and gardens of state and pleasure, near great cities; armories; arsenals; magazines[6]; exchanges; burses[7]; warehouses; exercises of horsemanship, fencing, training of soldiers and the like; comedies, such whereunto the better sort of persons do resort; treasuries of jewels and robes; cabinets and rarities[8]; and, to conclude, whatsoever is memorable in the places where they go. After all which the tutors or servants ought to make diligent inquiry. As for triumphs, masks,* feasts, weddings, funerals, capital executions, and such shows, men need not to be put in mind of them; yet are they not to be neglected. If you will have a young man to put his travel into a little room, and in short time to gather much, this you must do. First as was said, he must have some entrance into the language before he goeth. Then he must have such a servant or tutor as knoweth the country, as was likewise said. Let him carry with him also some card or book describing the country where he travelleth; which will be a good key to his inquiry. Let him keep also a diary. Let him not stay long in one city or town; more or less as the place deserveth, but not long; nay, when he stayeth in one city or town, let him change his lodging from one end and part of the town to another; which is a great adamant[1] of acquaintance. Let him sequester[2] himself from the company of his countrymen, and diet[3] in such places where there is good company of the nation where he travelleth. Let him upon his removes from one place to another, procure recommendation to some person of quality residing in the place whither he removeth; that he may use his favour in those things he desireth to see or know. Thus he may abridge his travel with much profit. As for the acquaintance which is to be sought in travel; that which is most of all profitable, is acquaintance with the secretaries and employed men of ambassadors: for so in travelling in one country he shall suck the experience of many. Let him also see and visit eminent persons in all kinds, which are of great name abroad; that he may be able to tell how the life agreeth with the fame.[4] For[5] quarrels, they are with care and discretion to be avoided. They are commonly for mistresses, healths, place, and words. And let a man beware how he keepeth company with choleric and quarrelsome persons; for

---

[1] The young men whom he accompanies.
[2] As if blindfolded.
[3] That is, making diaries.
[4] *consistories ecclesiastic.* Church courts.
[5] Tombs and other relics of the past.
[6] Storage places for arms and ammunition.
[7] Banks.
[8] *cabinets and rarities.* Such things as are exhibited in museums.

[1] Used in the old sense of something that attracts.
[2] Hide.
[3] Eat.
[4] *how . . . fame.* Whether the man lives up to his reputation.
[5] As regards.

they will engage him into their own quarrels. When a traveller returneth home, let him not leave the countries where he hath travelled altogether behind him; but maintain a correspondence by letters with those of his acquaintance which are of most worth. And let his travel appear rather in his discourse than in his apparel or gesture; and in his discourse let him be rather advised in his answers, than forward to tell stories; and let it appear that he doth not change his country manners[1] for those of foreign parts; but only prick in some flowers of that he hath learned abroad into the customs of his own country.

Of Revenge

REVENGE is a kind of wild justice; which the more man's nature runs to, the more ought law to weed it out. For as for the first wrong, it doth but offend the law; but the revenge of that wrong putteth the law out of office. Certainly, in taking revenge, a man is but even with his enemy; but in passing it over, he is superior; for it is a prince's part to pardon: and Solomon,[1] I am sure, saith, *It is the glory of a man to pass by an offence.* That which is past is gone, and irrevocable; and wise men have enough to do with things present and to come; therefore they do but trifle with themselves, that labour in past matters. There is no man doth a wrong for the wrong's sake; but thereby to purchase himself profit, or pleasure, or honour, or the like. Therefore why should I be angry with a man for loving himself better than me? And if any man should do wrong merely out of ill-nature, why, yet it is but like the thorn or briar, which prick and scratch, because they can do no other. The most tolerable sort of revenge is for those wrongs which there is no law to remedy; but then let a man take heed the revenge be such as there is no law to punish; else a man's enemy is still beforehand, and it is two for one. Some, when they take revenge, are desirous the party should know whence it cometh. This is the more generous. For the delight seemeth to be not so much in doing the hurt as in making the party repent. But base and crafty cowards are like the arrow that flieth in the dark.[2] Cosmus,[3] Duke of Florence, had a desperate saying against perfidious or neglecting[4] friends, as if those wrongs were unpardonable; *You shall read* (saith he) *that we are commanded to forgive our enemies,*[5] *but you never read that we are commanded to forgive our friends.* But yet the spirit of Job was in a better tune: *Shall we* (saith he) *take good at God's hands, and not be content to take evil also?*[6] And so of friends in a proportion. This is certain, that a man that studieth revenge keeps his own wounds green, which otherwise would heal and do well. Public revenges are for the most part fortunate; as that for the death of Caesar;* for the death of Pertinax;[7] for the death of Henry the Third[8] of France; and many more. But in private revenges it is not so. Nay rather, vindictive persons live the life of witches; who, as they are mischievous, so end they infortunate.

---

[1] *change . . . manners.* Exchange the manners of his own land for those of another.

[2] Compare Psalms 91 : 5.

[3] Cosmo de'Medici (1389–1464). A banker and statesman of Florence who was a famous patron of the arts.

[4] Neglectful.   [5] Compare Matthew 6 : 12.

[6] *Shall . . . also.* Compare Job 2 : 10.

[7] A Roman emperor notorious for his cruelty. He became emperor in 192 A.D., and the next year was slain by his own guards.

[8] King of France, assassinated in 1589 by Jacques Clément, a Jacobin monk.

[1] Compare Proverbs 19 : 11.

D

Of Studies

STUDIES serve for delight, for ornament, and for ability. Their chief use for delight, is in privateness and retiring; for ornament, is in discourse; and for ability, is in the judgment and disposition of business. For expert men can execute, and perhaps judge of particulars, one by one; but the general counsels, and the plots[1] and marshalling of affairs, come best from those that are learned. To spend too much time in studies is sloth; to use them too much for ornament, is affectation; to make judgment wholly by their rules, is the humour[2] of a scholar. They perfect nature, and are perfected by experience: for natural abilities are like natural plants, that need pruning by study; and studies themselves do give forth directions too much at large, except they be bounded in by experience. Crafty[3] men contemn studies, simple men admire[4] them, and wise men use them; for they teach not their own use; but that[5] is a wisdom without[6] them, and above them, won by observation. Read not to contradict and confute; nor to believe and take for granted; nor to find talk and discourse; but to weigh and consider. Some books are to be tasted, others to be swallowed, and some few to be chewed and digested; that is, some books are to be read only in parts; others to be read, but not curiously[7]; and some few to be read wholly, and with diligence and attention.[8] Some books also may be read by deputy, and extracts made of them by others; but that would be only in the less important arguments,[9] and the meaner[10] sort of books; else distilled books are like common distilled waters,[1] flashy[2] things. Reading maketh a full man; conference[3] a ready man; and writing an exact man.[4] And therefore, if a man write little, he had need have a great memory; if he confer little, he had need have a present wit[5]; and if he read little, he had need have much cunning, to seem to know that[6] he doth not. Histories make men wise; poets,[7] witty[8]; the mathematics, subtle; natural philosophy,[9] deep; moral, grave[10]; logic and rhetoric, able to contend. *Abeunt studia in mores.*[11] Nay there is no stond[12] or impediment in the wit, but may be wrought out[13] by fit studies: like as diseases of the body may have appropriate exercises. Bowling is good for the stone[14] and reins[15]; shooting for the lungs and breast; gentle walking for the stomach; riding for the head; and the like. So if a man's wit be wandering, let him study the mathematics; for in demonstrations, if his wit be called away never so little, he must begin again. If his wit be not apt to distinguish or find differences, let him study the schoolmen*; for they are *cymini sectores.*[16] If he be not apt to beat over matters,[17] and to call up one thing to prove and illustrate another, let him study the lawyers' cases: so every defect of the mind may have a special receipt.

[1] Liquors, essences.
[2] Tasteless, insipid.
[3] Conversation.
[4] *Reading . . . man.* A frequently quoted sentence. Memorize it.
[5] *a present wit.* An alert mind.
[6] That which.   [7] Poetry.
[8] Highly imaginative.
[9] *natural philosophy.* Science.
[10] *moral, grave.* The study of moral philosophy makes men serious and dignified.
[11] *Abeunt . . . mores.* "Studies influence our characters and lives."   [12] Obstacle.
[13] *wrought out.* Removed.
[14] A disease of the bladder.   [15] Kidneys.
[16] *cymini sectores.* "Hairsplitters."
[17] *apt . . . matters.* Skilled in analysis.

[1] Plans.   [2] See "humours."*   [3] Practical.
[4] Wonder at.   [5] Their own use.
[6] Beyond, outside of.
[7] With great care.
[8] *Some books are to be tasted . . . attention.* Memorize this sentence. It is often quoted.
[9] Subject matter.   [10] Less important.

Discussion Hints

1. Make an outline of "Of Travel." How much can you omit? What does this suggest about the compression of Bacon's essays?

2. Select several sentences that seem good topic sentences for paragraphs or even for themes.

3. What, referred to by Bacon, would a modern traveler try to see?

4. What experiences referred to by Bacon would a modern traveler omit?

5. Would "Of Travel" lose in coherence if the order of the paragraphs were changed? Explain your answer.

6. Explain in your own words the argument set forth in the first paragraph.

7. A critic once said that Bacon could be read backward as easily as forward. Does "On Revenge" bear out this assertion?

8. What do Bacon's comments on the deaths of certain rulers suggest as to his political ideas?

9. A frequent comment on Bacon's essays is, "They are in reality collections of topic sentences." Is that the case with "On Revenge"? Give reasons for your answer.

10. Which of Bacon's arguments in favor of studies would be most effective today? Select two and state them as forcibly as you can in your own language.

11. Bacon says that "crafty men contemn studies." Write a theme giving the ordinary businessman's reasons for his attitude toward studies.

12. Select the six epigrams* of Bacon's which you consider best.

13. From the essays given here pick out two or three sentences that make the reader stop and reflect in order to grasp Bacon's thought. Explain briefly the meaning of the sentences in your own words.

Suggestions for Reading

1. Besides the essays given above, you may well read those entitled "Of Truth," "Of Gardens," "Of Friendship," "Of Adversity," "Of Youth and Age," "Of Riches," as well as any others whose titles strike your fancy.

2. The essays of the great French essayist Montaigne (see page 173) have been read and admired by thousands of English readers from the time of Shakespeare to the present day. By all means sample Montaigne's essays if you get a chance.

1603-1660

❀

The
Puritan Period

Piscator exhibits the trout he has caught (p. 202)

PURITANISM

PURITANISM may be described as a great moral and political reform that swept over Great Britain at the close of the Renaissance (p. 71). Even during the Elizabethan Period many people felt that an unrestrained enjoyment of the world, the Renaissance desire to drink every cup of pleasure to the dregs, was morally wrong and should be frowned upon. Moreover, soon after the beginning of the Reformation (p. 71) there arose in the Church of England a movement toward greater strictness of life and simplicity of church organization and worship. This movement is called Puritanism. It led eventually to the formation of a large number of sects, each of which claimed to hold the only correct views on religion and government. Though belonging to various religious groups, the Puritans had this in common: they were all determined to resist tyranny in Church and State, and were filled with a passion for liberty and righteousness such as the world had never known.

The more fanatical Puritans went so far as to maintain that not only the Church, but also the State, should be like the heavenly kingdom. Many believed that the king ruled, not by divine right, but by the will of the people, and that he might be dethroned if he failed in the performance of his office. Charles* I (1625–1648) ruled unjustly, and civil war followed. So powerful did the Puritans become that in 1649 they actually tried the king for his life, convicted him, cut off his head, and proceeded to found a republic, or commonwealth, modeled, as they imagined, on the brotherhood of the saints in heaven. They established what they believed to be a real "kingdom of God upon earth." As Lord Protector, Oliver Cromwell* conducted the new government to the best of his ability; but in 1660, after his death, the English people were weary of the Commonwealth, welcomed Charles II (son of Charles I) back from exile, and restored the monarchy. Nevertheless the spirit of Puritanism persisted. It lived on in England and was transplanted by emigrants to America, where it has ever since exercised a tremendous influence upon government, religion, social life, and literature. It must not be supposed that the Puritans were all fanatics; many were intelligent persons whose desire for reform never ran away with their common sense.

SOCIAL AND POLITICAL BACKGROUND

The Puritan Period was one of great social and economic unrest. Under Charles I many Englishmen were forced to leave the country by reason of losing their lands or by reason of the severity of the law courts, which were presided over by unjust and unscrupulous judges. After the establishment of the Commonwealth the followers of the king were often persecuted, their estates were confiscated by the government, and many were forced to take refuge abroad. Thus at one time or another both aristocrats and commoners suffered from loss of freedom or property. Yet in spite of these obstacles England, especially under Cromwell's rule, advanced in wealth at home and in respect abroad. English colonies grew, and English merchants prospered. During the Puritan Period the foundations of the British colonial empire were laid. Education also progressed, and the reading public increased. Meanwhile London remained much like a medieval town that had outgrown its walls. The streets were dirty and ill paved and were less gay and colorful than they had been during the Elizabethan Period; but the population had increased to about five hundred thousand, and the city was well on the way to becoming the great metropolis it is today.

To all outward appearances the social and economic changes that took place during the Puritan Period had comparatively little effect upon England outside the towns. While the kings were in power the central part of the country was largely occupied by forests and deer parks owned by the sovereign or by the nobility, and gradually increased by additions from land that had been once open to the common people but was enclosed by the rich and powerful for their own use. Under the Commonwealth many large estates were confiscated by the government; but after the return of Charles II in 1660, they were generally returned to their original owners or passed into the hands of other members of the upper classes.

LITERATURE

Literature during the Puritan Period shows the effect of the social and religious conflicts of the day, but it is far from being a direct reflection of life. In such troubled times men often turn deliberately from the strife and uncertainty around them to worldly dissipation or to the comfort of religion. The Puritans were opposed to the corruptness of the theater; and, as a result, in 1642 they forced the theaters to close. During the next twenty years few plays were composed or performed. Such literature as was written during the Puritan Period differed in several important respects from that of the freer times of Elizabeth. It was no longer unified by a common poetic spirit, and hence shows the greatest variety of mood, of

Oliver Cromwell visiting Milton

From a painting by David Neale in the Cleveland Museum of Art

form, and of artistic purpose. Elizabethan literature is full of the joy of living; that of the Puritan Period is often either gloomy and pessimistic or worldly and frivolous. The most cheerful writings, which were usually in the form of verse, are in many cases uninspired and have little to recommend them but prettiness. Naturally, much of what was written during the period deals with political or religious controversies, and hence has little value as literature and is forgotten. Nevertheless, among the productions that have survived are to be found some of the finest products of the English literary genius.

In spite of some confusion the poets of the Puritan Period fall into several fairly definite groups. One group of writers composed poems which frequently deal with love and other Renaissance themes, but which reveal skill rather than genius, and are often marred by artificial and obscure comparisons and language. The poets who were especially fond of expressing such far-fetched ideas were later called in derision the "metaphysical school."

Another group, known as Cavalier* poets because they were for the most part gentlemen at the court of Charles I, reacted against the intense seriousness of the Puritans by writing in gay or frivolous mood fanciful and charming verses on love and other worldly themes. Others, known as the religious group, found their escape from the troubles of life by taking as their themes the joy and comfort to be found in religion. Still others wrote pastoral* poetry, as Spenser and other Elizabethans had done, but they usually made their shepherds and country scenes more lifelike than their predecessors had done. Robert Herrick (p. 200) is especially noteworthy because he began as a rather artificial imitator of Ben Jonson,[1] and ended as a genuinely sympathetic and gifted portrayer of the pleasures of country life in the remote Devonshire parish where he spent his last years as a clergyman. The following lines, quoted from the versified summary of one of his volumes, give a fair idea of the variety of subjects treated by the poets of the period, even by the great Milton himself.

> I sing of brooks, of blossoms, birds and bowers,
> Of April, May, of June, and July-flowers;
> I sing of May-poles, hock-carts,[2] wassails,[3] wakes,[4]
> Of bridegrooms, brides, and of their bridal-cakes;
> I write of Youth, of Love, and have access
> By these, to sing of cleanly wantonness;
> I sing of dews, of rains, and piece by piece,
> Of balm, of oil, of spice, and ambergris[5];
> I sing of times trans-shifting[6]; and I write
> How roses first came red, and lilies white.
> I write of groves, of twilights, and I sing
> The court of Mab,* and of the Fairy King.
> I write of Hell; I sing, and ever shall,
> Of Heaven, and hope to have it after all.

Prose flourished during the Puritan Period; but the prose writings consisted mostly of sermons, controversial tracts, and historical documents that are not important enough to claim our attention here. The greatest prose-writer of the period was John Bunyan (p. 205), whose *Pilgrim's Progress*, an allegory* of a Christian's life, is written in simple but highly

---

[1] For biography see page 700.
[2] The hock-cart, or hackney cart, was the last loaded wagon to leave the field at harvest time, the harvest-home cart.
[3] Festivities.
[4] All-night watches and merrymakings. A wake was originally a church festival.
[5] A substance highly valued for making perfumery.
[6] Changing.

imaginative prose, and has been read more than any other book in the English language except the Bible. Undisturbed by the religious and political troubles of the time, Izaak Walton (p. 202) wrote charmingly of country scenes and fishing excursions. During this period also the reading public grew larger, always a good sign, and there began to appear a few periodical publications, which were the literary ancestors of *The Tatler** and *The Spectator** (pp. 220, 255) and of our modern newspapers.

JOHN MILTON

The crowning glory of the Puritan Period is John Milton, who, next to Shakespeare and possibly Chaucer, is the greatest of English poets. He has been called *the* poet of Puritanism; but, like all other great geniuses, he is not completely typical of his age. He wrote both in prose and in verse, and his works include most of the literary types popular at the time; but his ideas and his style are in general far above those of his contemporaries. His *Paradise Lost*, which is only one of numerous long narrative poems composed during the seventeenth century, is the greatest religious epic in the English language, and one of the greatest poems of all time.

Correlation of English Literature with Historical Events during the Puritan Period

HISTORICAL EVENTS		*LITERARY LANDMARKS*
Reign of JAMES I	1603–1625	
Founding of JAMESTOWN	1607	
	1608	MILTON *born. Died 1674*
	1616	SHAKESPEARE *died. Born 1564*
Sailing of the "Mayflower" from PLYMOUTH, ENGLAND, *to* PLYMOUTH, MASSACHUSETTS	1620	
Reign of CHARLES I	1625–1648	
	1628	BUNYAN *born. Died 1688*
	1632	MILTON, L'Allegro *and* Il Penseroso
	1634	MILTON'S Comus *acted*
Founding of HARVARD COLLEGE	1636	
	1637	MILTON, Lycidas
Beginning of CIVIL WAR *in* ENGLAND	1642	*Theaters closed by Parliament*
Dethronement of CHARLES I; *establishment of the* COMMONWEALTH	1648	
Execution of CHARLES I	1649	
CROMWELL *created* LORD PROTECTOR	1653	WALTON, The Complete Angler
Return of CHARLES II; *Restoration of the* MONARCHY	1660	
Reign of CHARLES II	1660–1685	
The GREAT PLAGUE *in* LONDON	1665	
The GREAT FIRE *in* LONDON	1666	
Ceding of NEW NETHERLAND (NEW YORK) *by* HOLLAND *to* ENGLAND	1667	MILTON, Paradise Lost
	1678	BUNYAN, Pilgrim's Progress

The Puritan Period also includes the work of Herrick (1591–1674) and Lovelace (1618–1658). Note that the Puritan Period slightly overlaps the Elizabethan Period (see page 69).

THE PURITAN PERIOD IN SONG AND STORY

POETRY

KIPLING, RUDYARD. "James I" and "Edgehill Fight." In *Verse: Inclusive Edition, 1885–1932*. Doubleday, Doran & Company, Inc.

MACAULAY, THOMAS BABINGTON. "Battle of Naseby, 14th June, 1645" and "The Cavaliers March to London, 1642."

NOYES, ALFRED. "A Roundhead's Rallying Song." In *Collected Poems*. Frederick A. Stokes Company.

DRAMA

DRINKWATER, JOHN. *Oliver Cromwell.* Houghton Mifflin Company.

PROSE

BLACKMORE, RICHARD DODDRIDGE. *Lorna Doone: A Romance of Exmoor.*

DEFOE, DANIEL. *A Journal of the Plague Year.*

DUMAS, ALEXANDER. *Twenty Years After.*

LE GALLIENNE, RICHARD. *There Was a Ship.* Doubleday, Doran & Company, Inc.

MARRYAT, FREDERICK. *Children of the New Forest.*

MASEFIELD, JOHN. *Martin Hyde, the Duke's Messenger.* Little, Brown & Company.

QUILLER-COUCH, SIR ARTHUR THOMAS. *The Splendid Spur: Being Memoirs of the Adventures of John Marvel, a Servant of His Late Majesty King Charles I, in the Years 1642–1643.* Doubleday, Doran & Company, Inc.

SCOTT, SIR WALTER. *Woodstock* and *Peveril of the Peak.*

PASTORAL POETRY

JOHN MILTON[1] (1608–1674)

"L'Allegro" and "Il Penseroso"

"L'Allegro" and "Il Penseroso" are among the most famous companion poems in English literature. They were written by John Milton when he was a young man twenty-four years old and had been out of college less than a year. *L'Allegro* (lal lā′grō) is an Italian expression meaning "the merry (or light-hearted) man"; *il penseroso* (ēl pĕn sĕ rō′sō) means "the thoughtful (or serious-minded) man."

Both poems are pastoral,* and the plans of both are the same: (1) an introduction banishing the opposite mood; (2) a description of how the mood of the poem came about; (3) the pleasures of an ideal day or days lived in that mood; (4) the poet's attitude toward the mood. Thus the contrast in the poems is not so much of two unlike persons as it is of two unlike moods of the same person (who, of course, is Milton himself).

The mood of "L'Allegro" is light-hearted and carefree. The typical day (or series of days) begins with the singing of the lark on an early, sunny morning in the country; it continues with haying time and harvest, the simple dinner of the country people, followed by country sports and tales; and it ends with such scenes as evening life in cities, social gatherings, marriages, comedies, and secular music.

The mood of "Il Penseroso" is quieter and more serious. The typical day (or series of days) begins at evening with the singing of the nightingale, a quiet, moonlight walk, the study of astronomy and philosophy; then follows the reading of elevated poetry, such as tragic dramas and romances; next comes a rainy, stormy morning, followed by a walk in the woods; the day ends with listening to beautiful religious music in a great cathedral.

As you read the two poems trace the changes of scene and mood in each by means of the interpretative outlines printed in brackets at intervals throughout each poem. Notice how closely the poems resemble each other in structure. Make faithful use of the footnotes and the "Dictionary of Names and Phrases" in order to get the meaning of Milton's difficult language and his rich and varied classical references. In these matters the poems are far from easy, and will call for your best thought and effort. Then, after such difficulties are mastered, read the poems aloud, section by section, for the pleasure of enjoying the beautiful phrasing, happy imagery,* and exquisite music of two of the best-known poems in English literature.

L'Allegro

[The banishment of Melancholy.]

HENCE,[2] loathèd Melancholy,
 Of Cerberus* and blackest Midnight born,
In Stygian* cave forlorn,
'Mongst horrid shapes, and shrieks, and sights unholy,

Find out some uncouth cell,[1]
Where brooding Darkness spreads his jealous wings,
And the night-raven sings;
There under ebon shades and low-browed rocks,
As ragged as thy locks,   9
In dark Cimmerian* desert ever dwell.

---

[1] For biography see page 702.
[2] Begone.

[1] *uncouth cell.* Unknown and ugly place of retirement.

[The invocation to Mirth.]

But come, thou Goddess fair and free,
In heaven ycleped[1] Euphrosyne,*
And by men, heart-easing Mirth,
Whom lovely Venus* at a birth
With two sister Graces* more
To ivy-crownèd Bacchus* bore;
Or whether (as some sager[2] sing)
The frolic Wind that breathes the spring,
Zephyr[3] with Aurora* playing,
As he met her once a-Maying,   20
There on beds of violets blue,
And fresh-blown roses washed in dew,
Filled her with thee, a daughter fair,
So buxom,[4] blithe, and debonair.[5]
     Haste thee, Nymph, and bring with
          thee
Jest,[6] and youthful Jollity,
Quips, and Cranks,[7] and wanton Wiles,[8]
Nods, and Becks,[9] and wreathèd Smiles,
Such as hang on Hebe's* cheek,
And love to live in dimple sleek[10];   30
Sport that wrinkled Care derides,
And Laughter holding both his sides,
Come, and trip it as ye go,
On the light fantastic toe;
And in thy right hand lead with thee
The mountain Nymph,[11] sweet Liberty;
And, if I give thee honour due,
Mirth, admit me of thy crew,
To live with her, and live with thee,
In unreprovèd[12] pleasures free;   40

---

[1] *ycleped* (ĭ clĕpt'). Called.
[2] Wiser ones. Perhaps Milton himself, as we
know of no "wiser ones" from whom he could
certainly have got the idea that Mirth was
the daughter of Zephyr and Aurora.
[3] The west wind of spring.
[4] Merry, lively.
[5] *debonair* (dĕb ō nâr'). Gay and elegant.
[6] The abstract qualities which Milton (lines 26–
36) bids Euphrosyne bring are personified
as a group of young people gathering for a
festivity.
[7] *Quips . . . Cranks.* Smart and odd sayings.
[8] *wanton Wiles.* Playful tricks.
[9] Beckonings.
[10] Soft.
[11] *mountain Nymph.* Liberty was believed to live
in the mountains. Mountain people are
noted for their love of liberty.
[12] Unreprovable, innocent.

[The delights of dawn and forenoon
in the country.]

To hear the lark begin his flight,
And singing startle the dull night,
From his watch-tower in the skies,
Till the dappled Dawn doth rise;
Then to come, in spite of[1] sorrow,
And at my window bid good-morrow,
Through the sweet-briar or the vine,
Or the twisted eglantine[2];
While the cock with lively din,
Scatters the rear of Darkness thin;   50
And to the stack, or the barn-door,
Stoutly struts his dames before:
Oft listening how the hounds and horn
Cheerly rouse the slumbering Morn,
From the side of some hoar[3] hill,
Through the high wood echoing shrill:
Sometime walking, not unseen,
By hedgerow elms, on hillocks green,
Right against the eastern gate,[4]   59
Where the great Sun begins his state,[5]
Robed in flames and amber light,
The clouds in thousand liveries dight[6];
While the ploughman, near at hand,
Whistles o'er the furrowed land,
And the milkmaid singeth blithe,
And the mower whets his scythe,
And every shepherd tells his tale[7]
Under the hawthorn in the dale.

[The pleasures of an idealized country day.]

Straight[8] mine eye hath caught new
          pleasures,   69
Whilst the landskip round it[9] measures[10]:
Russet lawns[11]; and fallows[12] gray;

---

[1] *in spite of.* To do spite to.
[2] Probably honeysuckle.
[3] Ancient and gray.
[4] *Right . . . gate.* Directly toward the place where
the sun rises.
[5] Stately progress.   [6] Dressed.
[7] *tells his tale.* Counts his "tale," or tally (the
number of his sheep).
[8] Immediately.   [9] The eye.
[10] If you put this line in its natural prose order,
with "it" as the subject, you will understand it.
[11] *Russet lawns.* Sun-dried fields. not lawns about
a house.
[12] Uncultivated fields.

Where the nibbling flocks do stray;
Mountains on whose barren breast
The labouring clouds do often rest;
Meadows trim with daisies pied,[1]
Shallow brooks, and rivers wide.
Towers and battlements it sees
Bosomed high in tufted trees,
Where perhaps some Beauty lies,[2]   79
The Cynosure[3] of neighbouring eyes.
Hard by, a cottage chimney smokes
From betwixt two agèd oaks,
Where Corydon and Thyrsis[4] met
Are at their savoury dinner set
Of herbs and other country messes,[5]
Which the neat-handed Phillis[6] dresses;
And then in haste her bower she leaves,
With Thestylis[6] to bind the sheaves;
Or, if the earlier season lead,
To the tanned[7] haycock in the mead. 90
   Sometimes with secure[8] delight
The upland hamlets[9] will invite,
When the merry bells ring round,
And the jocund rebecks[10] sound
To many a youth and many a maid
Dancing in the chequered shade;
And young and old come forth to play
On a sunshine holiday,
Till the livelong daylight fail:

[Social gatherings in the country, stories,
   and early to bed.]

Then to the spicy nut-brown ale,   100
With stories told of many a feat,
How fairy Mab* the junkets[11] eat:
She was pinched and pulled, she said;
And he, by Friar's lanthorn led,[12]

[1] Variegated.   [2] Lives.
[3] *Cynosure* (sĭ'nō shōōr). Center of attraction.
[4] *Corydon, Thyrsis.* Names for shepherds in pastoral* poetry.   [5] Dishes.
[6] *Phillis, Thestylis.* Names for shepherdesses in pastoral poetry.
[7] Browned from the sun and rain.
[8] Carefree.   [9] Villages.
[10] A rebeck is a kind of rude fiddle.
[11] Cream cheese and other country delicacies set out by the peasants for the fairies to eat.
[12] *She . . . led.* One of the party tells how she was annoyed by the fairies; another how he was led astray by friar's lantern, the will-o'-the-wisp, sometimes called jack-o'-lantern.

Tells how the drudging Goblin[1] sweat
To earn his cream-bowl duly set,
When in one night, ere glimpse of morn,
His shadowy flail hath threshed the corn
That ten day-labourers could not end;
Then lies him down the lubber[2] fiend,
And, stretched out all the chimney's
   length,   111
Basks at the fire his hairy strength,
And crop-full[3] out of doors he flings,[4]
Ere the first cock his matin[5] rings.
Thus done the tales,[6] to bed they creep,
By whispering winds soon lulled asleep.

[Evening pleasures in cities — marriages,
   comedies, Lydian (secular) music.]

Towered cities please us then,[7]
And the busy hum of men,
Where throngs of Knights and Barons
   bold,   119
In weeds[8] of peace, high triumphs[9] hold,
With store of[10] Ladies, whose bright eyes
Rain influence,[11] and judge the prize
Of wit or arms,[12] while both[13] contend
To win her grace whom all commend.[14]
There let Hymen* oft appear
In saffron[15] robe, with taper clear,
And pomp, and feast, and revelry,
With mask* and antique pageantry;
Such sights as youthful Poets dream
On summer eves by haunted stream.   130

[1] Robin* Goodfellow.
[2] Clumsy.
[3] Stomach-filled.
[4] Rushes clumsily.
[5] Morning song.
[6] *Thus . . . tales.* When the tales are done.
[7] We now leave the country and turn to the city.
[8] Clothes.
[9] *high triumphs.* Splendid shows, such as court assemblies or tournaments.
[10] *store of.* Many.
[11] *Rain influence.* Milton compares the eyes of the ladies to the stars, which were supposed to "rain" influence upon men.
[12] *judge . . . arms.* Select the winners in contests of wit or in feats of arms.
[13] Those who take part in the contests of wit and those who take part in the contests of arms.
[14] *her . . . commend.* The favor of the lady who presides at the contest.
[15] Orange-yellow, the color of Hymen's dress in the masks of Milton's day.

❀

Many a youth and many a maid
Dancing in the chequered shade

FROM A PAINTING BY HAROLD SICHEL

❀

Then[1] to the well-trod stage anon,
If Jonson's[2] learnèd sock* be on,
Or sweetest Shakespeare, Fancy's child,
Warble his native wood-notes wild.
And ever, against eating cares,
Lap me in soft Lydian airs,[3]
Married to immortal verse,
Such as the meeting[4] soul may pierce,
In notes with many a winding bout[5]
Of linkèd sweetness long drawn out   140
With wanton heed and giddy cunning,[6]
The melting voice through mazes run-
ning,

Untwisting all the chains that tie
The hidden soul of harmony;
That Orpheus'* self may heave his head
From golden slumber on a bed
Of heaped Elysian* flowers, and hear
Such strains as would have won the ear
Of Pluto* to have quite set free
His half-regained Eurydice.*[1]   150

[The poet's attitude: the resolve to live
with Mirth.]

These delights if thou canst give,
Mirth, with thee I mean to live.

Il Penseroso

[The banishment of Folly and vain Joys.]

HENCE, vain deluding Joys,
    The brood of Folly without father
bred!
How little you bested,[7]
Or fill the fixèd mind with all your toys[8]!
Dwell in some idle brain,
And fancies fond[9] with gaudy shapes
possess,
As thick and numberless
As the gay motes that people the sun-
beams,
Or likest[10] hovering dreams,
The fickle pensioners of Morpheus'*
train.[11]   10

[The invocation to Melancholy.]

But, hail! thou Goddess sage and holy!
Hail, divinest Melancholy[12]!

Whose saintly visage is too bright
To hit the sense of human sight,[2]
And, therefore to our weaker view
O'erlaid with black, staid Wisdom's hue;
Black, but such as in esteem
Prince Memnon's sister[3] might beseem,[4]
Or that starred Ethiop queen[5] that strove
To set her beauty's praise above   20
The Sea-Nymphs, and their powers
offended.
Yet thou are higher far descended;
Thee bright-haired[6] Vesta* long of yore
To solitary Saturn* bore;[7]
His daughter she; in Saturn's reign,
Such mixture was not held a stain.
Oft in glimmering bowers and glades
He met her, and in secret shades

[1] Next; at another time.
[2] Ben Jonson wrote comedies showing much
    learning (for biography see page 700).
[3] *Lydian airs.* A kind of gentle, pleasing music.
[4] Responsive.   [5] Turn (in the music).
[6] *With . . . cunning.* Done with great art, yet in
    such a way as to appear spontaneous or
    natural.   [7] *bested* (bĕ stĕd'). Help, profit.
[8] Trifles.   [9] Foolish.   [10] Most like.
[11] *The fickle . . . train.* The ever-changing followers
    of the god of sleep.
[12] Thoughtfulness, pensive contemplation, not
    sadness or depression in the modern meaning
    of the word. Contrast this mood with that
    suggested by calling Melancholy "loathèd"
    ("L'Allegro." l. 1).
    D

[1] *That . . . Eurydice.* Airs so sweet that even
    Orpheus,* though in a heavenly slumber,
    would lift his head and listen, and Pluto, had
    he heard them, would have "quite set free"
    Eurydice.
[2] *To hit . . . sight.* To be perceived by the naked
    eye.
[3] *Memnon's sister.* Memnon was an Ethiopian
    prince referred to in classical mythology. He
    was dark and noted for his beauty; hence
    his sister presumably would be also dark
    and beautiful.
[4] Become, suit.   [5] Cassiopeia.*
[6] Vesta is called "bright-haired" because of her
    connection with the fire on the domestic
    hearth.
[7] *Thee . . . bore.* Milton's Melancholy is here the
    daughter of Retirement (Vesta) and Culture
    (Saturn).

Of woody Ida's* inmost grove,[1]   29
Whilst yet there was no fear of Jove.*
Come, pensive Nun, devout and pure,
Sober, steadfast, and demure,
All in a robe of darkest grain,[2]
Flowing with majestic train,
And sable stole[3] of cypress lawn[4]
Over thy decent[5] shoulders drawn.
Come; but keep thy wonted state,[6]
With even step, and musing[7] gait,
And looks commercing with[8] the skies
Thy rapt[9] soul sitting in thine eyes:
There, held in holy passion still,   41
Forget thyself to marble,[10] till
With a sad[11] leaden downward cast
Thou fix them on the earth as fast.[12]
And join with thee calm Peace and Quiet,
Spare[13] Fast, that oft with gods doth diet,
And hears the Muses* in a ring
Aye round about Jove's altar sing;
And add to these retirèd Leisure,   49
That in trim gardens[14] takes his pleasure;
But, first and chiefest, with thee bring
Him that yon soars on golden wing,
Guiding the fiery-wheelèd throne,
The cherub* Contemplation;
And the mute Silence hist[15] along,
'Less Philomel* will deign a song,

---

[1] *Ida's inmost grove.* The quietest place on lofty
    Mount Ida, in Crete.
[2] Color, probably violet.   [3] Scarf or hood.
[4] *cypress lawn.* Crape.
[5] Shapely, beautiful.
[6] *wonted* (wŭnt'ĕd) *state.* Accustomed dignified
    attitude and behavior.   [7] Thoughtful.
[8] *commercing with.* Holding intercourse with;
    looking intently at.   [9] Enraptured.
[10] *to marble.* Until thou seemest to turn to a
    marble statue.
[11] Here, serious, not sorrowful.
[12] *fix . . . fast.* Fix your eyes as constantly on
    the earth as you formerly fixed them on the
    heavens.   [13] Lean.
[14] *trim gardens.* In Milton's day and throughout
    the Age of Classicism (see page 213) people
    came more and more to admire gardens that
    were "trim" (well kept). Streams were
    made to flow in straight channels through
    them, and flower beds and shrubbery were
    laid off in geometrical figures. See illustra-
    tion on page 216.
[15] *Silence hist.* Summon Silence by whispering
    "Hist."

In her sweetest saddest plight,
Smoothing the rugged brow of Night,
While Cynthia* checks her dragon yoke
Gently o'er the accustomed oak.   60

[Evening pleasures: listening to the night-
    ingale, a moonlight walk.]

Sweet bird,[1] that shunn'st the noise of
    folly,
Most musical, most melancholy!
Thee, Chauntress,[2] oft the woods among
I woo, to hear thy even-song;
And missing thee, I walk unseen
On the dry smooth-shaven green,
To behold the wandering Moon,
Riding near her highest noon,
Like one that had been led astray
Through the heaven's wide pathless way,
And oft, as if her head she bowed,   71
Stooping through a fleecy cloud.
Oft, on a plat of rising ground,
I hear the far-off curfew* sound,
Over some wide-watered shore,
Swinging slow with sullen roar:
Or, if the air will not permit,
Some still removèd[3] place will fit,
Where glowing embers through the room
Teach light to counterfeit a gloom,[4]   80
Far from all resort of mirth,
Save the cricket on the hearth,
Or the Bellman's[5] drowsy charm[6]
To bless the doors from nightly harm.

[Evening pleasures of a student: astronomy,
    philosophy, tragedy, romantic poetry.]

Or let my lamp, at midnight hour,
Be seen in some high lonely tower,

---

[1] The nightingale. The Cheerful Man loves the
    lark.
[2] Singer.
[3] Remote.
[4] *Where . . . gloom.* Where the dying fire no longer
    gives much light in the room.
[5] The bellman, or night watchman, went through
    the streets ringing a bell, calling the hour,
    announcing the weather, and, at times,
    singing.
[6] *drowsy charm.* The bellman's voice singing
    hymns or other songs that charmed people
    to sleep.

Where I may oft outwatch the Bear,[*1]
With thrice great Hermes,[2] or un-
sphere
The spirit of Plato,[*3] to unfold   89
What worlds or what vast regions
hold
The immortal mind that hath forsook
Her mansion in this fleshly nook;
And of those Daemons that are found
In fire, air, flood, or underground,
Whose power hath a true consent[4]
With planet or with element.
Sometime let gorgeous Tragedy
In sceptred pall[5] come sweeping by,
Presenting Thebes,* or Pelops* line,
Or the tale of Troy* divine,[6]   100
Or what (though rare) of later age
Ennobled hath the buskined* stage.[7]
But, O sad Virgin! that thy power
Might raise Musaeus from his bower;
Or bid the soul of Orpheus*[8] sing
Such notes as, warbled to the string,
Drew iron tears down Pluto's* cheek,
And made Hell grant what love did
seek;

Or call up him[1] that left half-told
The story of Cambuscan* bold,   110
Of Camball, and of Algarsife,
And who had Canacè[2] to wife,
That owned the virtuous[3] ring and glass,
And of the wondrous horse of brass
On which the Tartar King did ride;
And if aught else great Bards* beside
In sage and solemn tunes have sung,
Of turneys, and of trophies hung,
Of forests, and enchantments drear,
Where more is meant than meets the
ear.[5]   120

[The pleasures of a stormy morning.]

Thus, Night, oft see me in thy pale
career,
Till civil-suited[6] Morn appear,
Not tricked and frounced[7] as she was
wont
With the Attic boy[8] to hunt,
But kerchieft in a comely cloud,[9]
While rocking winds are piping loud,
Or ushered with a shower still,[10]
When the gust hath blown his fill,
Ending on the rustling leaves,   129
With minute-drops[11] from off the eaves.

[A retired walk in the forest.]

And, when the sun begins to fling
His flaring beams, me, Goddess, bring

---

[1] *outwatch the Bear.* Sit up until the constellation of the Great Bear, which never sets in the latitude of England, disappears with the morning light; that is, sit up all night. In America we call the Great Bear the "Big Dipper." Look for it.

[2] *thrice great Hermes.* Hermes Trismegistus was a fabled Egyptian scientist of ancient times. He is called "thrice great" because he was famous as a king, as a priest, and as a philosopher, or scientist. To read him would imply a deep interest in the most ancient philosophy and science.

[3] *unsphere . . . Plato.* Bring down the spirit of Plato from the stars and make him reveal the secrets of his philosophy. Plato's works deal with the immortality of the soul and with daemons, or spirits, that were thought to inhabit earth, air, fire, and water.

[4] Sympathetic connection

[5] *sceptred pall.* Kingly robes.

[6] *Thebes. . divine.* All these are famous subjects of ancient tragedy.

[7] *what . . . stage.* More recent great tragedies, especially the plays of Shakespeare.

[8] Musaeus and Orpheus were famous mythical or semimythical poets of ancient Greece whose lost works Milton longs to recover and read in his thoughtful hours.

[1] Chaucer, who left unfinished his "Squire's Tale" (one of *The Canterbury Tales*) (p. 37), in which occur the names that follow.

[2] *Canacè* (kăn′á sē). The heroine of the "Squire's Tale." Two men were in love with her.

[3] Possessing magical power.

[4] Tournaments.

[5] *more . . . ear.* That is, in allegories* such as Spenser's *Faerie Queene* (p. 166).

[6] In plain citizen dress.

[7] *tricked and frounced.* Adorned and with hair curled.

[8] *Attic boy.* Cephalus,* who was loved by Aurora,* the goddess of dawn.

[9] *kerchieft . . . cloud.* Wearing a becoming cloud as a kerchief, or head-covering.

[10] Gentle.

[11] Small drops falling every minute.

To archèd walks of twilight groves,
And shadows brown,[1] that Sylvan[2] loves,
Of pine, or monumental oak.
Where the rude axe with heavèd stroke
Was never heard the Nymphs* to daunt,
Or fright them from their hallowed
　　haunt.
There in close covert, by some brook,
Where no profaner[3] eye may look,　　140
Hide me from Day's garish[4] eye,
While the bee with honeyed thigh,
That at her flowery work doth sing,
And the waters murmuring,
With such consort[5] as they keep,
Entice the dewy-feathered Sleep.
And let some strange mysterious dream
Wave at his wings, in airy stream
Of lively portraiture displayed,
Softly on my eyelids laid.　　150

[Pleasures of religious music: the cathedral.]

And as I wake, sweet music breathe
Above, about. or underneath,
Sent by some spirit to mortals good,
Or the unseen Genius[6] of the wood.
But let my due[7] feet never fail
To walk the studious cloister's pale,[8]
And love the high embowèd[9] roof,
With antick pillars massy proof,[10]
And storied windows richly dight,[11]
Casting a dim religious light.　　160
There let the pealing organ blow,
To the full-voiced Quire[12] below,

In service high and anthems clear,
As may with sweetness, through mine
　　ear,
Dissolve me into ecstasies,
And bring all Heaven before mine eyes.

[Retirement in old age to a hermitage.]

And may at last my weary age
Find out the peaceful hermitage,
The hairy gown[1] and mossy cell,
Where I may sit and rightly spell　　170
Of[2] every star that Heaven doth shew,
And every herb that sips the dew;
Till old experience do attain
To something like prophetic strain.

[The poet's attitude: the resolve to live
with Melancholy]

These pleasures, Melancholy, give,
And I with thee will choose to live.

Discussion Hints

1. Make a list of the things that the Light-hearted Man likes. Compare it with a list of the things that the Serious-minded Man likes. Do the two men like anything in common?

2. Judging by any evidence that you can find, which mood would you say Milton himself preferred, that of "L'Allegro" or that of "Il Penseroso"? Discuss in class.

3. Select three or four of Milton's striking phrases, old ideas expressed in new ways.

4. Does Milton appeal to all five senses (sight, hearing, smell, taste, and touch)? Does he appeal more to one sense than to the others?

5. If you can draw or paint, make a picture of the Light-hearted Man and of the Serious-minded Man, each with his followers, or make a word picture.

6. If you were going to illustrate "L'Allegro" and "Il Penseroso," showing each change of scene, how many different pictures should you need for each poem? See, for example, the illustration facing page 192.

[1] Dark.
[2] In classical mythology Silvanus (Sylvan) was a supernatural being associated with woods and forests.
[3] Too profane.
[4] Glaring.
[5] Harmony.
[6] Guardian spirit.
[7] Dutiful.
[8] let . . . pale. May I always tread the enclosure (pale) formed by the cloisters, or covered walks surrounding the quadrangles of a college.
[9] Arched.
[10] massy proof. Able to bear an enormous weight.
[11] storied . . . dight. Stained-glass windows which tell stories by means of pictures.
[12] Choir.

[1] hairy gown. A hermit's gown made of woven hair.
[2] spell Of. Learn about.

7. Read Johnson's "On Certain Poems" (p. 238) and discuss his criticism of "L'Allegro" and "Il Penseroso."

8. Comment briefly on the meter of the two poems, noting particularly the change in rhythm* between the first ten lines and the rest of the poem. Before examining the meter look up the words *iambic,** *tetrameter,** and *trimeter** in the "Dictionary of Names and Phrases."

9. Select lines in which the sound or the rhythm, or both, are especially adapted to the sense.

10. Point out parallel passages in the two poems.

11. Many critics think that in "L'Allegro" Milton was drawing a character sketch of the Cavaliers* of his day, and that in "Il Penseroso" he was describing the Puritans (see page 183). Do you think the poems have this underlying reference? Give reasons for your answer.

12. Pick out lines that you have heard quoted.

13. What have you read by
> "him that left half-told
> The story of Cambuscan bold"

("Il Penseroso," ll. 109–110)?

14. What have you read by the poet who is probably referred to in lines 118–120 of "Il Penseroso"?

15. Read the headnote to "L'Allegro" and "Il Penseroso" and the biography of Milton (p. 702), and then decide why the poems may be regarded as at least partly autobiographical.

16. What pleasures of the present day do you think would appeal to (1) the Light-hearted Man? (2) the Serious-minded Man?

17. Identify Zephyr, Aurora,* Orpheus,* Morpheus,* Vesta,* and Plato.*

18. In lines 81–116 of "L'Allegro" Milton gives a picture of a farmer's daily life as viewed by a poet who has little or no first-hand knowledge of farming. How does it compare with a farmer's real life? Discuss

in connection with the definition of "pastoral"* given in the "Dictionary of Names and Phrases." What differences does your comparison suggest between real life and life as presented in certain types of literature?

19. Point out passages in "L'Allegro" and "Il Penseroso" that bring out the charm of the English landscape.

20. Another famous pair of companion poems consists of "The Passionate Shepherd to His Love" and "The Nymph's Reply to the Shepherd" (p. 153). What pastoral* elements connect these two poems with Milton's "L'Allegro" and "Il Penseroso"? How do the two pairs of poems differ?

21. Passages to be explained:

1. In "L'Allegro," ll. 1–2, 8, 18, 77–78, 96, 119–121.

2. In "Il Penseroso," ll. 10, 31–32, 58, 63–64, 92, 165.

22. Memorize "L'Allegro," ll. 25–34, 135–144; "Il Penseroso," ll. 155–166.

23. Paraphrase "L'Allegro," ll. 38–48, 117–128; "Il Penseroso," ll. 31–44.

24. Write a summary (précis) of "L'Allegro," ll. 69–90, 91–116; of "Il Penseroso," ll. 63–96.

Suggestions for Reading

Everybody should, if possible, read at least part of *Paradise Lost*, especially Book I. Of Milton's minor poems the best known are "Lycidas" (a lament for the death of a college mate), "Comus" (a mask*); the beautiful ode* "On the Morning of Christ's Nativity"; and certain of the sonnets, especially "To the Lord General Cromwell," "On the Late Massacre in Piedmont," and "On His Deceased Wife."

Of the many essays on Milton two of the most popular are those by James Russell Lowell, in *Among My Books*, and by Thomas Babington Macaulay.[1]

[1] For biography see page 732.

LYRIC POETRY[1]

JOHN MILTON[2] (1608-1674)

On Shakespeare

Milton's poems "On Shakespeare" and "On His Blindness" are important for two reasons: (1) In both poems nobility of theme and grandeur of language are so admirably blended as to give the impression of "high seriousness" that is characteristic of the greatest poetry. (2) The first shows how one of the world's greatest poets esteemed another; the second expresses in unforgettable language Milton's resignation under the tragic affliction of blindness.

WHAT needs my Shakespeare for his honoured bones
The labor of an age in pilèd stones[3]?
Or that his hallowed reliques[4] should be hid
Under a star-ypointing pyramid?
Dear son of memory,[5] great heir of fame.
What need'st thou such weak witness of thy name?

Thou in our wonder and astonishment
Hast built thyself a livelong[1] monument.
For whilst to the shame of slow-endeavouring art,
Thy easy numbers flow,[2] and that each heart　　　　10
Hath from the leaves of thy unvalued[3] book
Those Delphic[4] lines with deep impression took;
Then thou, our fancy of itself bereaving,
Dost make us marble with too much conceiving;[5]
And so sepulchred[6] in such pomp dost lie,
That kings for such a tomb would wish to die.

On His Blindness

When Milton was about forty years old and had been writing pamphlets and laboring in behalf of the Commonwealth for almost ten years, his sight began to fail. He was warned to stop using his eyes or he would go blind. However, because of his devotion to what he felt to be his duty, he not only refused to stop but worked harder and harder over his books and manuscripts. The result was that in 1652, when he was in his forty-fifth year, he went totally blind, and his "one talent" (the ability to write) was, as he imagined, "lodged useless" with him. How he felt over his sad affliction is told in this famous sonnet,* one of the noblest in literature.

[1] Enduring.
[2] *to the shame . . . flow.* You composed with such ease that you make other writers such as I ashamed of their slowness.　　[3] Priceless.
[4] Inspired, oracular. Delphi, in Greece, was the seat of the famous oracle of Apollo.*
[5] *thou . . . conceiving.* You turn us into marble by the effort of thought you compel us to make in order to understand your full meaning.
[6] Buried in a sepulcher, or tomb. "Sepulchred" is here pronounced sĕ pŭl′kĕrd, one of the accepted pronunciations in Milton's day.

[1] Discussion hints for lyric poetry of the Puritan Period are grouped together on page 201. For discussion of lyric poetry see page 150.
[2] For biography see page 702.
[3] *pilèd stones.* A stone monument.
[4] Remains.
[5] *son of memory.* One who will always be remembered.

Milton dictating "Paradise Lost" after his blindness

From a painting by Michael Munkácsy

WHEN I consider how my light is spent[1]
Ere half my days,[2] in this dark world and
wide,
And that one talent[3] which is death to
hide
Lodged with me useless, though my soul
more bent
To serve therewith my Maker, and
present
My true account, lest he returning
chide;
"Doth God exact day-labour, light
denied?"

I fondly[1] ask. But Patience, to prevent[2]
That murmur, soon replies, "God doth
not need
Either man's work or his own gifts.
Who best   10
Bear his mild yoke, they serve him best.
His state
Is kingly: thousands[3] at his bidding
speed,
And post o'er land and ocean without
rest;
They also serve who only stand and
wait."[4]

[1] *light . . . spent.* Sight is gone.
[2] *Ere . . . days.* Before I have lived half the
length of a normal life.
[3] The ability to write.

[1] Foolishly.
[2] Forestall.
[3] Heavenly messengers, angels.
[4] *They . . . wait.* This is a famous line; remember it.

ROBERT HERRICK[1] (1591–1674)

To the Virgins, to Make Much of Time

"To the Virgins" is one of the best English lyrics written during the Puritan Period. In it Herrick shows his ability to express in light, graceful, musical language a piece of homely advice as old as civilization. Youth is short and time is fleeting; therefore let maidens marry and settle down while they are still young instead of frittering away their time in mere pleasure until it is too late to get a husband.

I

GATHER ye rosebuds while ye may,
    Old time is still a-flying[2];
And this same flower that smiles to-
    day,
    To-morrow will be dying.

II

The glorious lamp of heaven, the sun,
    The higher he's a-getting,
The sooner will his race be run,
    And nearer he's to setting.

III

That age is best which is the first,   9
    When youth and blood are warmer;
But being spent, the worse and worst
    Times still succeed the former.

IV

Then be not coy, but use your time,
    And while ye may, go marry;
For, having lost but once your prime,
    You may forever tarry.

RICHARD LOVELACE[3] (1618–1658)

To Lucasta, Going to the Wars

Graceful expression, musical rhythm,* and chivalrous feeling combine to place the two following lyrics among the most popular songs in English literature. They show greater sincerity and contain fewer far-fetched conceits* than most of Lovelace's poems.

In the first the poet soldier, like a true Cavalier,* addresses his lady in light, graceful verse.

I

TELL me not, sweet, I am unkind,
    That from the nunnery

Of thy chaste breast and quiet mind
    To war[1] and arms I fly.

II

True, a new mistress now I chase,
    The first foe in the field;
And with a stronger faith embrace
    A sword, a horse, a shield.

III

Yet this inconstancy is such
    As you, too, shall adore;   10
I could not love thee, dear, so much,
    Loved I not honour more.

[1] For biography see page 703.
[2] *Gather . . . a-flying.* Even while you may be gathering rosebuds, that is, indulging in the most attractive pleasures, do not forget that time is flying.
[3] For biography see page 704.

[1] One of the campaigns of the English Civil War (1642–1649), which resulted in the execution of Charles* I and the establishment of the Puritan Commonwealth. Lovelace fought on the side of the Royalists, or Cavaliers.

To Althea, from Prison[1]

"To Althea, from Prison" is an exquisite, though fanciful, expression of the power of love to give freedom to a lover, even though he is in physical confinement.

I

WHEN Love with unconfinèd wings
   Hovers within my gates,
And my divine Althea brings
   To whisper at the grates[2];
When I lie tangled in her hair
   And fettered to her eye,
The birds that wanton in the air
   Know no such liberty.

II

When flowing cups run swiftly round
   With no allaying Thames,[3]   10
Our careless heads with roses bound,
   Our hearts with loyal flames;
When thirsty grief in wine we steep,
   When healths[4] and draughts go free[5]—
Fishes that tipple in the deep
   Know no such liberty.

III

When, like committed[6] linnets, I
   With shriller throat shall sing
The sweetness, mercy, majesty,
   And glories of my King;   20
When I shall voice aloud how good
   He is, how great should be,[7]
Enlargèd[8] winds, that curl the flood,
   Know no such liberty.

IV

Stone walls do not a prison make,
   Nor iron bars a cage;

Minds innocent and quiet take
   That for an hermitage[1];
If I have freedom in my love
   And in my soul am free,   30
Angels alone, that soar above,
   Enjoy such liberty.

Discussion Hints

1. Why, in Milton's opinion, does Shakespeare need no monument of stones?

2. Does line 14 of "On Shakespeare" impress you as too much like a conceit*? Give a reason for your answer.

3. Where does the thought change and the contrast begin between the first and second parts of "On His Blindness"?

4. How does the parable of the talents in the Bible (Matthew 25:14–30) help to explain lines 3–6?

5. How does the story in the Bible (Matthew 8:5–10; Luke 7:2–10) help to explain lines 11–13? See also Matthew 26:53.

6. What connection has this sonnet* with Milton's life?

7. Can any of the lyrics given here be called puritanical in the modern sense of the word? Do not forget that during the Puritan Period, as elsewhere in history, society was characterized by many moods, some grave, some gay. Recall the variety of subjects treated by the poet Herrick (p. 186).

8. Which of these lyrics reflect those social conditions among the aristocracy that resulted from the reign of Charles* I?

9. Select several epigrams* from this collection of lyrics.

10. What epigrams* do you find that refer to the shortness of life?

11. Is any subject treated more frequently than others? If so, what is it?

12. What examples of conceits* do you find in these lyrics? Explain as clearly as you can why you regard each example as undesirable in poetry?

13. Point out the apparent inconsistencies in the language of the poems by Lovelace and show that they are not real.

[1] Lovelace wrote this poem after he had been imprisoned for sympathizing with Charles* I in his quarrel with Parliament.
[2] Prison bars.
[3] *With . . . Thames.* Not diluted with water.
[4] Toasts.   [5] *go free.* Are drunk freely.
[6] Imprisoned, caged.
[7] *how great . . . be.* Lovelace here expresses the hope that Charles I may receive complete recognition as king. He was disappointed, for Charles was beheaded in 1649.
[8] Unrestrained, blowing freely.

[1] A place of retirement.

PROSE

IZAAK WALTON[1] (1593-1683)

From *The Complete Angler*

While many other Englishmen of the Puritan Period were busy quarreling and fighting over politics and religion, a retired merchant named Izaak Walton went fishing, and when he had moments of leisure he wrote down his observations upon his favorite pastime and upon human life. His work, which appeared first in 1653 under the title *The Complete Angler*,[2] has remained ever since, to the delight of thousands of readers, many of whom never caught a fish in their lives.

Among the many features that help to make *The Complete Angler* one of the most charming books in English literature, several should be remembered (1) It is written in an unusually simple and natural style. (2) It reflects the author's kindly, philosophic personality. (3) It presents characters who walk briskly, talk vigorously, fish, eat, and drink humanly, and think the world going pretty well in spite of all the tumult. *The Complete Angler* is written in the form of a dialogue, chiefly between two characters called Piscator (Fisherman) and Venator (Hunter). In the following passage Piscator addresses Venator.

CHAPTER IV

Observations of the Nature and Breeding of the Trout

THE trout is a fish highly valued both in this and foreign nations: he may be justly said, as we English say of venison, to be a generous fish: a fish that is so like the buck[3] that he also has his seasons; for it is observed, that he comes in and goes out of season with the stag and buck. He is a fish that feeds clean and purely, in the swiftest streams, and on the hardest gravel; and he may 10 justly contend with all fresh-water fish for precedency and daintiness of taste, and that being in right season, the most dainty palates have allowed precedency to him.

And before I go further in my discourse, let me tell you, that you are to observe, that as there be some barren does[1] that are good in summer, so there be some barren trouts that are good in 20 winter; but there are not many that are so, for usually they be in their perfection in the month of May, and decline with the buck. Now you are to take notice that in several countries, as in Germany and in other parts, compared to ours, fish differ much in their bigness and shape, and other ways, and so do trouts: it is well known that in the Lake Leman, the Lake of Geneva, there are 30 trouts taken of three cubits[2] long. And you are further to know that there be certain waters that breed trouts remarkable both for their number and smallness. I know a little brook in Kent that breeds them to a number incredible, and you may take them twenty or forty in an hour, but none greater than about the size of a gudgeon[3]: there are also in divers rivers, especially that be near to 40 the sea, as Winchester or the Thames about Windsor, a little trout called a samlet or skegger trout (in both which places I have caught twenty or forty at

---

[1] For biography see page 704.
[2] Fisherman.
[3] The male deer.

[1] Female deer.
[2] *three cubits.* Four and one-half feet.
[3] A small minnow, seldom over three inches long.

a standing), that will bite as fast and as freely as minnows; these be by some taken to be young salmons; but in those waters they never grow to be bigger than a herring.

50 There is also in Kent, near to Canterbury, a trout called there a Fordidge trout, a trout that bears the name of the town where it is usually caught, that is accounted the rarest of fish: many of them near the bigness of salmon, but known by their different color; and in their best season they cut very white; and none of these have been known to be caught with an angle.[1] Many have
60 been curious to search into their bellies, what the food was by which they lived, and have found out nothing by which they might satisfy their curiosity.

Concerning which you are to take notice that it is reported by good authors that grasshoppers and some fish have no mouths, but are nourished and take breath by the porousness of their gills, man knows not how: and this may be
70 believed, if we consider that when the raven hath hatched her eggs, she takes no further care, but leaves her young ones to the care of the God of nature, who is said, in the Psalms, "to feed the young ravens that call upon him."[2] And they be kept alive and fed by dew, or worms that breed in their nests, or some other ways that we mortals know not; and this may be believed of the Fordidge
80 trout, which, as it is said of the stork (Jeremiah 8: 7), that "he knows his season," so he knows his times, I think almost his day of coming into that river out of the sea, where he lives, and, it is like, feeds nine months of the year, and fasts three in the river of Fordidge. And you are to note that those townsmen are very punctual in observing the time of beginning to fish for them, and boast
90 much that their river affords a trout that

exceeds all others. And just so does Sussex boast of several fish: as namely, a Shelsey cockle, a Chichester lobster, an Arundel mullet, and an Amerly trout.

And now for some confirmation of the Fordidge trout: you are to know that this trout is thought to eat nothing in the fresh water; and it may be better believed, because it is well known that 100 swallows and bats and wagtails, which are called half-year birds, and not seen to fly in England for six months in the year, but about Michaelmas[1] leave us for a better climate than this; yet some of them that have been left behind their fellows, have been found many thousands at a time, in hollow trees, or clay caves; where they have been observed to live and sleep out the whole winter without 110 meat; and there is [said to be] one kind of frog that hath her mouth naturally shut up about the end of August, and that lives so all the winter; and though it be strange to some, yet it is known to too many among us to be doubted.

And so much for these Fordidge trouts, which never afford an angler sport, but either live their time of being in the fresh 120 water, by their meat formerly got in the sea (not unlike the swallow or frog), or by the virtue of the fresh water only; or, as the birds of Paradise and the chameleon are said to live by the sun and the air.

Now the next thing that I will commend to your consideration is that the trout is of a more sudden growth than other fish. Concerning which, you are 130 also to take notice that he lives not so long as the perch and divers other fishes do.

And next you are to take notice that he is not like the crocodile, which if he lives never so long, yet always thrives

[1] Fishhook.
[2] *to feed . . . him.* The passage is not quoted exactly. See Psalms 147: 9.

[1] The feast of Saint Michael and All Angels, a church festival celebrated on the twenty-ninth of September.

till his death; but 'tis not so with the trout; for after he is come to his full growth, he declines in his body, and 140 keeps his bigness or thrives only in his head till his death. And you are to know that he will, especially before the time of his spawning, get almost miraculously through weirs and flood-gates against the streams; even through such high and swift places as is almost incredible. Next, that the trout usually spawns about October or November, but in some rivers a little sooner or later; 150 which is the more observable, because most other fish spawn in the spring or summer, when the sun hath warmed both the earth and the water, and made it fit for generation. And you are to note, that he continues many months out of season; for it may be observed of the trout, that he is like the buck or the ox, that will not be fat in many months, though he go in the very same pasture 160 that horses do, which will be fat in one month; and so you may observe that most other fishes recover strength, and grow sooner fat and in season, than the trout doth.

And next you are to note that till the sun gets to such a height as to warm the earth and the water, the trout is sick and lean, and lousy, and unwholesome; for you shall in winter find him to have 170 a big head, and then to be lank, and thin, and lean; at which time many of them have sticking on them sugs, or trout-lice, which is a kind of worm, in shape like a clove or pin, with a big head, and sticks close to him and sucks his moisture: those I think the trout breeds himself, and never thrives till he free himself from them, which is when warm weather comes; and then, as he grows 180 stronger, he gets from the dead, still water, into the sharp streams and the gravel, and there rubs off these worms or lice; and then as he grows stronger, so

he gets him into swifter and swifter streams, and there lies at the watch for any fly or minnow that comes near to him; and he especially loves the May-fly; and these make the trout bold and lusty, and he is usually fatter and better meat at that end of that month [1] than 190 at any time of the year.

Now you are to know that it is observed that usually the best trouts are either red or yellow; though some (as the Fordidge trout) be white and yet good; but that is not usual: and it is a note observable, that the female trout hath usually a less [2] head and a deeper body than the male trout, and is usually the better meat. 200

And you are to note that there are several kinds of trouts; but these several kinds are not considered but by very few men; for they go under the general name of trouts; just as pigeons do in most places; though it is certain there are tame and wild pigeons; and of the tame, there be helmets and runts, and carriers and cropers, and indeed too many to name. Nay, the Royal* Society have 210 found and published lately that there be thirty and three kinds of spiders. And it is so with many kinds of fish, and of trouts especially, which differ in their bigness and shape and spots and color. And, doubtless, there is a kind of small trout, which will never thrive to be big, that breeds very many more than others do, that be of a larger size; which you may rather believe if you consider that 220 the little wren and titmouse will have twenty young ones at a time, when usually the noble hawk or the musical thras-sel or blackbird exceed not four or five.

And now you shall see me try my skill to catch a trout; and at my next walking, either this evening or to-morrow morning, I will give you direction how you yourself shall fish for him.

[1] May.   [2] Smaller.

Discussion Hints

1. If you know anything about fishing, comment upon Walton's knowledge of trout. Give your comments authority by quoting actual words from *The Complete Angler*.

2. Look up the word *trout* in an encyclopedia. Remembering that Walton's use of the word may be different from ours, what can you say in regard to the accuracy of his information?

3. What evidence do you find that Walton was superstitious?

4. Walton speaks of a "Shelsey cockle," a "Chichester lobster," etc. How many varieties of sea food do you know that are named after special places or districts?

5. Why should Walton refer to the Royal* Society as an authority?

6. Do you find any of Walton's science incorrect? Discuss in class.

7. What evidence do you find that Walton was familiar with the Bible?

8. In what respects does the selection resemble an essay (see page 173)?

9. Write a theme of two hundred words on the Fordidge trout or any other fish you know about.

10. Words and expressions to be explained or defined:

    a. divers (p. 202, l. 40)
    b. half-year birds (p. 203, l. 102)
    c. chameleon (p. 203, l. 125)
    d. weirs (p. 204, l. 144)

Suggestions for Reading

No one who is fond of fishing or of the outdoors will be content with the sample of Walton given here. Read here and there in *The Complete Angler*.

JOHN BUNYAN[1] (1628-1688)

Vanity Fair

[From *The Pilgrim's Progress*]

In November, 1660, a daring Puritan preacher delivered a sermon to a small congregation in a lone farmhouse in Bedfordshire, England. What he said in his sermon is forgotten, but the results will probably be remembered as long as English literature lives. For the sermon brought about the imprisonment of the preacher, John Bunyan, and his prison cell became a hermitage in which the lowly preacher beheld his vision of the trials and tribulations that beset a typical Christian on his way through life, and gave to the world Bunyan's masterpiece, *The Pilgrim's Progress from This World to That Which is to Come.*

The Pilgrim's Progress describes the experiences of an imaginary hero, Christian, as he journeys through life, striving to reach the Celestial* City. The story is composed in a direct, simple, vivid style that appeals to people of all kinds, young and old, ignorant and learned. The deep religious feeling revealed in its pages and the reality of the characters portrayed also help to give the

[1] For biography see page 704.

book a high place in literature. It has been called "the most genuine work of Puritan England."

The Pilgrim's Progress was published in 1678. During the next hundred years it ran through more than sixty editions. It was reprinted in America in 1681, and there have been many later editions on this side of the Atlantic Ocean. It is still a best seller. It has been translated into over a hundred different languages and dialects, and in all of them it still instructs and delights. It is one of the greatest allegories* in literature.

[The author falls asleep, and in his dream sees Christian, the hero, leave his worldly-minded family and neighbors in the City of Destruction and set out on his way to the Celestial City. On the road he is joined by a companion named Faithful, with whom he travels successfully through the wilderness of dejection.]

THEN I saw in my dream, that when they were got out of the wilderness, they presently saw a town before them, and the name of that town is Vanity; and at the town there is a fair kept, called Vanity* Fair: it is kept all the year long; it beareth the name of Vanity Fair, because the town where it is kept is lighter than vanity; and also because all that is there sold, or that cometh thither, is vanity. As is the saying of the wise, "All that cometh is vanity."[1]

This fair is no new-erected business, but a thing of ancient standing; I will show you the original[2] of it.

Almost five thousand years agone,[3] there were Pilgrims walking to the Celestial* City as these two honest persons are: and Beelzebub,* Apollyon, and Legion,* with their companions, perceiving by the path that the Pilgrims made, that their way to the city lay through this town of Vanity, they contrived here to set up a fair; a fair wherein should be sold all sorts of vanity, and that it should last all the year long: therefore at this fair are all such merchandise sold, as houses, lands, trades, places, honours, preferments, titles, countries, kingdoms, lusts, pleasures, and delights of all sorts, as wives, husbands, children, masters, servants, lives, blood, bodies, souls, silver, gold, pearls, precious stones, and what not.

And, moreover, at this fair there is at all times to be seen juggling, cheats, games, plays, fools, apes, knaves, and rogues, and that of every kind. Here are to be seen, too, thefts, murders, adulteries, [and] false swearers.

Now, as I said, the way to the Celestial City lies just through this town where this lusty fair is kept; and he that will go to the City, and yet not go through this town, must needs "go out of the world."[4] The Prince of princes himself, when here, went through this town to his own country, and that upon a fair day too; yea, and as I think, it was Beelzebub, the chief lord of this fair, that invited him to buy of his vanities; yea, would have made him lord of the fair, would he but have done him reverence as he went through the town. Yea, because he was such a person of honour, Beelzebub had him from street to street, and showed him all the kingdoms of the world[1] in a little time, that he might if possible, allure the Blessed One to cheapen[2] and buy some of his vanities; but he had no mind to the merchandise, and therefore left the town, without laying out so much as one farthing[3] upon these vanities. This fair, therefore, is an ancient thing, of long standing, and a very great fair.

Now these Pilgrims, as I said, must needs go through this fair. Well, so they did; but, behold, even as they entered into the fair, all the people in the fair were moved, and the town itself as it were in a hubbub about them; and that for several reasons; for

First, The Pilgrims were clothed with such kind of raiment as was diverse[4] from the raiment of any that traded in that fair. The people, therefore, of the fair, made a great gazing upon them: some said they were fools, some they were bedlams,[5] and some they were outlandish[6] men.

Secondly, And as they wondered at their apparel, so they did likewise at

---

[1] See Ecclesiastes 11:8.

[2] Origin.

[3] *Almost . . . agone.* That is, almost from the beginning of the world. In Bunyan's day the world was believed to be about five thousand years old.

[4] *go . . . world.* Die.

[1] *showed . . . world.* According to the New Testament the devil took Jesus "up into an exceeding high mountain" and showed him "all the kingdoms of the world, and the glory of them," adding, "All these things will I give thee, if thou wilt fall down and worship me." Jesus refused. (Matthew 4:8–10.)

[2] Ask the price of, bargain for.

[3] The smallest English coin, equal to one fourth of a penny.

[4] Here, different.

[5] Lunatics.

[6] Foreign.

"What will ye buy?"

their speech; for few could understand what they said; they naturally spoke the language of Canaan,* but they that kept the fair were the men of this world; so that, from one end of the fair to the other, they seemed barbarians each to 90 the other.

Thirdly, But that which did not a little amuse the merchandisers was, that these Pilgrims set very light by[1] all their wares; they cared not so much as to look upon them; and if they called upon them to buy, they would put their fingers in their ears, and cry, "Turn away mine eyes from beholding vanity,"[2] and look upwards, signifying that their trade and 100 traffic was in heaven.

One chanced mockingly, beholding the carriage of the men, to say unto them, "What will ye buy?" But they, looking gravely upon him, answered, We "buy the truth."[3] At that there was an occasion taken to despise the men the more: some mocking, some taunting, some speaking reproachfully, and some calling upon others to smite them. At 110 last things came to a hubbub, and great stir in the fair, insomuch that all order was confounded. Now was word presently brought to the great one of the fair, who quickly came down, and deputed some of his most trusty friends to take these men into examination, about whom the fair was almost overturned. So the men were brought to examination; and they that sat upon 120 them,[4] asked them whence they came, whither they went, and what they did there in such an unusual garb? The men told them, that they were pilgrims and strangers in the world, and that they were going to their own country, which was the heavenly Jerusalem; and that they had given no occasion to the men of the town, nor yet to the merchandis-

ers, thus to abuse them, and to let[1] them in their journey, except it was, for that, 130 when one asked them what they would buy, they said they would buy the truth. But they that were appointed to examine them did not believe them to be any other than bedlams and mad, or else such as came to put all things into a confusion in the fair. Therefore they took them and beat them, and besmeared them with dirt, and then put them into the cage, that they might be 140 made a spectacle to all the men of the fair. There, therefore, they lay for some time, and were made the objects of any man's sport, or malice, or revenge, the great one of the fair laughing still at all that befell them. But the men being patient, and not rendering railing[2] for railing, but contrariwise, blessing, and giving good words for bad, and kindness for injuries done, some men in the fair 150 that were more observing, and less prejudiced than the rest, began to check[3] and blame the baser sort for their continual abuses done by them to the men; they, therefore, in angry manner, let fly at them again, counting them as bad as the men in the cage, and telling them that they seemed confederates, and should be made partakers of their misfortunes. The others replied, that for 160 aught they could see, the men were quiet, and sober, and intended nobody any harm; and that there were many that traded in their fair, that were more worthy to be put into the cage, yea, and pillory too, than were the men that they had abused. Thus, after divers words had passed on both sides, the men behaving themselves all the while very wisely and soberly before them, they 170 fell to some blows among themselves, and did harm one to another. Then were these two poor men brought before their examiners again, and there charged as

---

[1] *set ... by.* Cared little for.

[2] *Turn ... vanity.* See Psalms 119: 37.

[3] *buy the truth.* See Proverbs 23: 23.

[4] *sat ... them.* Examined them as judges.

[1] Hinder.

[2] Abusive language.

[3] Reproach.

being guilty of the late hubbub that had been in the fair. So they beat them pitifully, and hanged irons upon them, and led them in chains up and down the fair, for an example and a terror to others,
180 lest any should speak in their behalf, or join themselves unto them. But Christian and Faithful behaved themselves yet more wisely, and received the ignominy and shame that was cast upon them, with so much meekness and patience, that it won to their side, though but few in comparison of the rest, several of the men in the fair. This put the other party yet into greater rage, insomuch
190 that they concluded[1] the death of these two men. Wherefore they threatened, that the cage nor irons should serve their turn, but that they should die, for the abuse they had done, and for deluding the men of the fair.

[Christian and Faithful are tried before a law court in Vanity Fair. Faithful is condemned to death and executed, but Christian escapes and proceeds on his way to the Celestial City.]

Discussion Hints

1. Do you know of any cases where the phrase "Vanity Fair" is used today? If so, to what is it applied? One of our most famous English novels is entitled *Vanity Fair*. It was written by the great nineteenth-century novelist William Makepeace Thackeray.[2]

2. Write a theme of one hundred words describing a modern Vanity Fair.

3. What sort of persons are represented by the citizens of Vanity Fair who were "less prejudiced than the rest" (p. 208, ll. 151–152)?

4. Which do you find more difficult to understand: the allegory* of *The Pilgrim's Progress* or that of *The Faerie Queene* (p. 166)? Explain your answer.

1 Determined on.
2 For biography see page 725.

5. Which uses more learned references and allusions, Bunyan or Bacon (p. 175)?

6. List the passages that you recognize as suggested by the Bible. When Bunyan wrote *The Pilgrim's Progress*, how long had it been since the King James* Bible (p. 161) had appeared?

7. In what respects is the style of *The Pilgrim's Progress* like that of the Bible?

8. Why is *The Pilgrim's Progress* to be regarded as a product of the Puritan spirit (see page 183)?

9. Point out several of Bunyan's quaint turns of phrase that are different from the English of today.

10. A critic compares Bunyan and Walton (p. 202) as follows: "Each had abundant humour, each was a keen observer of Nature and of human nature, each was a lover of peace, each had a modest little fount of poetry within him . . . each . . . is such a friendly writer." How do the two men compare in the selections given here?

11. Explain the underlying or allegorical* meaning of the following passages:

a. This fair is no new-erected business, but a thing of ancient standing (p. 206, ll. 13–14)

b. The way to the Celestial City lies just through this town (p. 206, ll. 41–42)

c. Few could understand what they said (p. 208, ll. 84–85)

12. Words to be explained:

a. allure (p. 206, l. 59)
b. pillory (p. 208, l. 166)
c. ignominy (p. 209, l. 183)

Suggestions for Reading

Nobody can afford to admit that he has not read *The Pilgrim's Progress*, called, next to the Bible, "the best seller of the ages." Of the many essays on Bunyan, perhaps the best-known is the one written by Thomas Babington Macaulay.[1]

1 For biography see page 732.

D

being guilty of the late hubbub, that had been in the fair. So they beat them pitifully, and hanged irons upon them, and led them in chains up and down the fair, for an example and a terror to others, lest any should speak in their behalf, or join themselves unto them. But Christian and Faithful behaved themselves yet more wisely, and received the ignominy and shame that was cast upon them, with so much meekness and patience, that it won to their side (although but few in comparison of the rest) several of the men in the fair. This put the other party into greater rage, insomuch that they concluded the death of these two men. Wherefore they threatened that the cage nor irons should serve their turn, but that they should die, for the abuse they had done, and for deluding the men of the fair.

[Christian and Faithful are tried before a low court in Vanity Fair. Faithful is condemned to death and executed, but Christian escapes and presses on his way to the Celestial City.]

Discussion Hints

1. Do you know of any cases where the phrase "Vanity Fair" is used today? If so, to what is it applied? One of the most famous English novels is entitled "Vanity Fair." It was written by the great nineteenth-century novelist, William Makepeace Thackeray.

2. Write a theme of one hundred words describing a modern Vanity Fair.

3. What sort of persons are represented by the criminals in Vanity Fair who were "less prejudiced" than the rest. (p. 208, ll. 15–17)

4. Which do you find more difficult to understand: the allegory of The Pilgrim's Progress or that of the Faerie Queene (p. 169)?

To be continued on ...

For biography see page 226.

3. Which has more learned reference and allusions, Bunyan or Bacon? (p. ...)

6. List the passages that you recognize as suggested by the Bible. When Bunyan wrote The Pilgrim's Progress, how long had it been since the King James Bible (p. 161) had appeared?

7. In what respects is the style of The Pilgrim's Progress like that of the Bible?

8. Why is The Pilgrim's Progress to be regarded as a product of the Puritan spirit (see page 163)?

9. Point out several of Bunyan's major traits of character that are different from the English of today.

10. A full comparison [Bunyan and Walton] may be made as follows: Walton had a calm, serene, each was a keen observer of Nature and of human nature; each was a lover of peace; each had a modest little fund of poetry within him; each ... is such a homely writer. How, while, the two men compare in the selections given, how ...

11. Explain the connotation or suggested meaning of the following passages:

a. This Slough is no amended boundary ...

b. The way is the Celestial City, etc.

c. Fair-ground understood what he would ... (p. 208, ll. 81–83)

18. Words to be explained:

a. allure (p. 205, l. 5)

b. deluding (p. ...)

c. ignominy (p. 205, l. 182)

Suggestions for Reading

Nobody can afford to admit that he has not read The Pilgrim's Progress, called, next to the Bible, "the best-seller" of the ages. Of the many essays on Bunyan, perhaps the best-known is the one written by Thomas Babington Macaulay.

12th Century ... — page 226

1660-1744

❀

The
Age of Classicism

The knight walks . . . between a double row of his tenants (p. 263, ll. 92–94)

IN 1660 the Commonwealth came to an end and the monarchy was restored, with Charles II as king. Charles was succeeded in 1685 by his brother, James. Both were immoral and corrupt. In 1688 James II was overthrown by a popular revolution and was succeeded by his daughter Mary and her husband, William III. Anne (1702–1714), Mary's sister, and the last of the Stewarts,* followed. From the time of William and Mary the English sovereigns have ruled, not by "divine right," but by the will of the people as expressed through their representatives in Parliament. The years between the Restoration and the death of Alexander Pope, in 1744, are usually referred to as the Age of Classicism.

CHANGING STANDARDS

The years immediately following 1660, known as the Restoration Period, were marked by great changes in the literature and life of England. Charles II and his court, returning from exile in France, brought back French dress, French ideas, and French social customs, many of which shocked the staid and pious Puritans. People in general, especially the upper classes, were weary of the restraints imposed upon them by the Puritan government, and gladly imitated the court. Hence moral standards were relaxed, and respect for decency, law, and authority declined.

This lowering of old standards in morals and manners was very different from the expansion of life that had characterized the Renaissance.[1] Instead of feeling the mystery of life, the English people turned their attention to what seemed more practical matters of everyday living. A sense of fact dominated the public thinking, and the popular slogans were "Reason" and "Common Sense." There was a general feeling that "everything is for the best in this, the best of all possible worlds." "Whatever is," wrote Pope, "is right." Men distrusted emotion and enthusiasm and depended more upon what they called "reason" as a test of human conduct. Hence the age was one of prose and of practical scientific investigation rather than of poetry and abstract philosophy. Satire* and burlesque* flourished, and great attention was devoted to literary criticism.

SOCIAL AND POLITICAL BACKGROUND

Throughout the Age of Classicism, London became more and more the cultural and literary center of England. People who wished to be "smart" hurried to the city, and even gentlemen owning country estates were apt

[1] Page 71.

to be looked upon as boorish unless they also had residences in town. In London, country squires were usually regarded with amusement or contempt. Coffeehouses * and clubs became popular social centers, and London drawing rooms were filled with polished and witty ladies and gentlemen who discussed politics and literature. Yet the London streets were poorly lighted, policing was inadequate, and in both town and country highwaymen were common and travel was slow and dangerous. After the Great Fire of 1666 a new and more modern London began to grow up in place of the old medieval town. Streets were widened; avenues were opened; and magnificent palaces and churches were erected, many in the new classical style.[1] By the year 1700 London had a population of three quarters of a million.

Though many of the upper classes were satisfied with things as they were, costly foreign wars, mounting taxes, incompetent clergy, and political corruption caused gradually increasing discontent, especially among the lower and middle classes. As education became more common the reading public grew rapidly, and the man in the street took a more intelligent interest in politics and religion and demanded a larger share in public affairs. Disgusted with the corruption and incompetence of their rulers, the common people, by means of the ballot, assumed a larger part in the government. With increased political power came increased self-respect. When the ordinary citizen demanded and received a better deal in society and government, modern democracy was born.

THE CLASSICAL SCHOOL

Between 1660 and the death of Pope (1744) there grew up a generation of writers known as the Classical or Neoclassical School. The term "classical" is used in at least two important senses, which we should be careful to distinguish : (1) it is applied to the literatures of ancient Greece and Rome; (2) it is used, as it is here, of the late seventeenth century and early eighteenth century because the writers of that period composed literature according to a set of fixed rules and critical theories which, as they believed, were those followed by ancient authors. They are sometimes called pseudoclassicists, because they frequently misunderstood the principles of literary art illustrated in ancient masterpieces. The chief doctrines of the Classical School in English literature are the following :

1. Poetry should be composed according to fixed rules. Form was regarded as more significant than content; the way a thing was said was more important than the thing itself. The classicists disliked anything that was irregular. They believed it more important to follow the rules

[1] See the illustration on page 217.

Cheapside, London, in the eighteenth century

© *Country Life*, London

A formal Italian garden in England

than to try to be an "original genius." In their opinion the world is at its best when nature, both animate and inanimate, is "methodized"; that is, arranged, and governed by laws and restrictions. Influenced by this love of whatever is orderly and normal, the classicists admired the average cultivated man of drawing-room society rather than the simple, unlearned peasant; they preferred the carefully trimmed hedges of a formal Italian garden to the tangled woods and wandering lanes of the countryside; and they thought the balanced architecture of a Greek temple superior to the irregular construction of a Gothic cathedral. This attitude toward man and nature is one of the most marked characteristics of the classical point of view as opposed to the romantic.[1]

2. Poetry should be witty and clever rather than profoundly emotional. Instead of showing passion or other deep feeling, the poet should be calm and critical. In the opinion of the classicists, Shakespeare, who had paid scant attention to the classical rules, was little better than an inspired barbarian.

3. The established verse form was the heroic* couplet. This had been used as far back as the time of Chaucer, but was revived by the classicists and brought to perfection by Alexander Pope.

[1] Page 313.

© *Country Life*, London

Blenheim Palace, built in 1705-1716

A good example of the carefully balanced style of architecture popular in England
during the Classical Period

4. Poetry should use a special diction, or vocabulary. According to the classicists certain words and phrases were "elegant," and hence suitable for use in poetry; others were not and were called "low," that is, vulgar. In the poetry of the Age of Classicism a woman is apt to be referred to as a "female" or, better still, a "fair"; a hunter does not aim a gun, he "poises the levelled tube."

This desire on the part of the classicists to exclude from the vocabulary of poetry many common words made the literature, especially the poetry, of the period more artificial. Like thousands of writers and readers of the present day, they thought that an idea is more poetical if it is expressed in high-flown language. Many classicists also carried too far the use of personification.* For example, we often find in the poetry of the period such phrases as "dread Solitude," "horrid Desolation," "comfortless Despair," and "pallid Fear," which show little sign of personification except that the nouns are capitalized. In spite of all their faults, however, the classicists performed a real service to literature by emphasizing the importance of order and care in literary composition.

DRAMA

With the return of Charles II to England the theaters were reopened, and plays were written in abundance; but, influenced as they were by the court, the comedies were often cynical, satirical,* and indecent in their portrayal of life. They were more realistic* than the plays of Shakespeare's time, but they lacked Shakespeare's spontaneity and vigor. The tragedies, moreover, were often bombastic and far-fetched. In general the drama of the Age of Classicism made few contributions to great literature.

POETRY

As emotion and originality became more and more subordinated to intellect and imitation, lyric poetry became less abundant, the most popular form being the ode.*[1] In accordance with the practical temper of the period, poetry usually took the form of social, political, religious, or literary satire* or criticism. Much of the verse composed during the Age of Classicism was intended to instruct the intellect rather than to stir the emotions. It appealed to the mind rather than to the heart. Many poems treated of subjects that belong properly to the domain of prose.[2] There was also much "occasional" verse, poems dashed off on the spur of the moment to celebrate some society scandal or special occasion. The greatest poets of the period are Pope (pp. 223 and 230) and Dryden (p. 226), both of whom were distinguished as critics as well as poets. Pope is now remembered for having expressed many truths, some of them old, in striking and unforgettable form, and for having brought the heroic* couplet to a state of perfection.

THE AGE OF PROSE

The Age of Classicism is especially noteworthy for its prose. Prose was the medium used for a large number of critical, satirical, and controversial works, some of which rank high in English literature. To this period belong Dryden's critical essays, Swift's *Gulliver's Travels* (p. 274) and other satires,* and Johnson's prose works (p. 238). Prose was also used in the "newsletters," which had begun to appear before 1650, and which may be regarded as the earliest English newspapers. The beginnings of the modern novel and of the "familiar" essay also fall within the limits of the Age of Classicism.

During this period, English prose developed greatly in style. Addison's (p. 261) style is a model of simple, polished English. The carefully balanced sentences of Johnson's most characteristic prose, though some-

---

[1] See the ode of Dryden (p. 226).   [2] For example, Pope's *Essay on Criticism* (p. 223).

what long and ponderous, represent a marked improvement over the rude style of most earlier English writers.

Johnson, who died in 1784, has often been called the last of the eighteenth-century classicists; but the influence of classicism persisted long after Johnson's day and, indeed, has never completely disappeared from English literature.

THE BEGINNINGS OF THE NOVEL

As the Age of Classicism advanced, the lower and middle classes of English society became better educated and more influential than they had ever been before. Heretofore those of the common people who could read at all and who liked fiction had had to be satisfied with romances * and tales of knights and fair ladies, literature written by and for aristocrats. The newly educated reading public desired literature better suited to their tastes and dealing with people more like themselves. As usually happens in such cases, their desires were met by literary men, who are always on the alert to give the public what it wants. The result was a new type of literature, the novel. The modern realistic novel, as contrasted with other types of fiction such as the romance (p. 32), began as a narrative written for readers of the lower classes and depending for its appeal not upon thrilling plot or romantic setting so much as upon characters taken from real life.

Between 1700 and 1725 Daniel Defoe, best known for his *Robinson Crusoe* (p. 265), became popular by writing narratives that depicted realistically the fortunes of characters drawn from the lower classes. He was especially gifted in giving to pure fiction an air of convincingness and truth. Defoe was followed by Samuel Richardson,* a rather commonplace London printer who began by writing love letters for servant girls and ended by being the most successful novelist of his day. His first story, *Pamela, or Virtue Rewarded* (1740), tells of the temptations and final triumph of a prudent and virtuous servant girl, and has been called the first real English novel. In *Clarissa Harlowe, or the History of a Young Lady* (1747), sometimes referred to as Richardson's masterpiece, the author traces for humble readers the tragic history of a heroine of the upper classes, whose downfall is caused by a fascinating, aristocratic villain. In order to make his novels more convincing, Richardson carried on the narrative by means of long letters exchanged between the characters, who are often made to write sentimentally and to set forth their emotions at great length as many eighteenth-century letter-writers actually did, features which pleased Richardson's readers immensely. In his effort to get to the very bottom of his characters' emotions and mental reactions, Richardson is a predecessor of the modern psychological novelists. Another important early writer of novels was Henry Fielding.* Fielding, disgusted with the exaggerated sentimentalism and overdone morality of Richardson's characters, wrote *Joseph Andrews* (1742), *Tom Jones* (1749), and other novels designed to show how people, both of the upper and the lower classes, actually talked and acted in his day. Avoiding moralizing and sentimentality, he was remarkably successful in giving an honest and forthright portrayal of human life as it was lived in England during the first half of the eighteenth century. The hero of *Tom Jones* is a young man who, unlike Richardson's overvirtuous men and women, is a very human mixture of good and bad qualities. Both Richardson and Fielding continued to write until after the close of the Age of Classicism.

THE BEGINNINGS OF THE FAMILIAR ESSAY

Urged on by their new self-consciousness, the lower and middle classes sought to improve their manners and their subjects of conversation. Here too literature came to their aid. Soon after 1700 there appeared the "familiar" essay,[1] a type of literature which, though it grew out of older forms, was first perfected by Addison[2] and Steele[3] in their two periodicals, *The Tatler** and *The Spectator.** In their essays (pp. 261 and 255) these two writers, in a charmingly simple and informal style, discussed social etiquette, art, literature, politics, morals, and other matters likely to interest the new reading public. *The Tatler* and *The Spectator* were among the first of a long series of periodicals, extending even to the present day, devoted wholly or in part to subjects of general cultural interest, and intended to amuse and educate the public.

[1] For a discussion of the essay as a literary type see page 173.
[2] For biography see page 709.   [3] For biography see page 709.

Correlation of English Literature with Historical Events during the Age of Classicism

HISTORICAL EVENTS		LITERARY LANDMARKS
The RESTORATION	1660	
REIGN *of* CHARLES II 1660–1685		
	1661(?)	DEFOE *born. Died 1731*
The GREAT PLAGUE *in* LONDON	1665	
The GREAT FIRE *in* LONDON	1666	
	1667	SWIFT *born. Died 1745*
	1672	ADDISON *born. Died 1719*
		STEELE *born Died 1729*
Founding of PENNSYLVANIA	1682	
REIGN *of* JAMES II 1685–1688		
Revolution in ENGLAND	1688	POPE *born. Died 1744*
WILLIAM III *and* MARY	1689	RICHARDSON *born. Died 1761*
Battle of the BOYNE	1690	
	1697	DRYDEN, Alexander's Feast
	1700	DRYDEN *died. Born 1631*
REIGN *of* ANNE 1702–1714		
Battle of BLENHEIM *won by the* DUKE OF MARLBOROUGH*	1704	
Union of ENGLAND *and* SCOTLAND	1707	FIELDING *born. Died 1754*
	1709	JOHNSON *born. Died 1784*
		First number of the Tatler
	1711	*First number of the* Spectator
		POPE, Essay on Criticism
End of the WAR *of the* SPANISH SUCCESSION	1713	
REIGN *of* GEORGE I 1714–1727		
	1719	DEFOE, Robinson Crusoe, *Part I*
The SOUTH SEA BUBBLE	1720	
ROBERT WALPOLE, *prime minister*	1721	
	1726	SWIFT, Gulliver's Travels
REIGN *of* GEORGE II 1727–1760		
	1740	BOSWELL *born. Died 1795*
		RICHARDSON, Pamela
	1742	FIELDING, Joseph Andrews
	1744	*Death of* POPE

The Age of Classicism also includes the chief writings of Samuel Pepys (1633–1703) and the Earl of Chesterfield (1694–1773).

THE AGE OF CLASSICISM IN SONG AND STORY

POETRY

DOBSON, AUSTIN. "A Dialogue to the Memory of Alexander Pope." In *Complete Poetical Works*. Oxford University Press.

KIPLING, RUDYARD. "Brown Bess." In *Verse: Inclusive Edition, 1885–1932*. Doubleday, Doran and Company, Inc.

NOYES, ALFRED. "Dick Turpin's Ride," "Forty Singing Seamen," and "The Highwayman." In *Collected Poems*. Frederick A. Stokes Company. The last two are given in the revised edition of *Achievement* of this series.

SOUTHEY, ROBERT. "The Battle of Blenheim."

DRAMA

BALDERSTON, JOHN LLOYD. *Berkeley Square*. Samuel French. Also in *Best Plays of 1929–1930*, edited by Burns Mantle. Dodd, Mead & Company, Inc.

CHESTERTON, GILBERT KEITH. *The Judgment of Doctor Johnson*. G. P. Putnam's Sons.

FAGAN, JAMES BERNARD. "*And So to Bed*": *A Comedy in Three Acts*. Henry Holt & Company, Inc. A play about Samuel Pepys.

MACKAY, CONSTANCE D'ARCY. *Beau Nash and Other One-Act Plays of Eighteenth-Century Life*. D. Appleton-Century Company, Inc. Good for amateur performance.

PROSE

DEFOE, DANIEL. *Journal of the Plague Year*. An imaginative account of the great plague of 1665.

MASEFIELD, JOHN. *Martin Hyde, the Duke's Messenger*. Little, Brown & Company.

SABATINI, RAFAEL. *Captain Blood, Fortune's Fool*, and *Mistress Wilding: A Romance of the Time of Monmouth's Rebellion*. All are published by Houghton Mifflin Company.

TARKINGTON, BOOTH. *Monsieur Beaucaire*. Grosset and Dunlap.

THACKERAY, WILLIAM MAKEPEACE. *The History of Henry Esmond, Esq., a Colonel in the Service of Her Majesty Queen Anne; Written by Himself*. (Given in part on page 447.)

DIDACTIC VERSE

ALEXANDER POPE[1] (1688–1744)

Epigrams* from *An Essay on Criticism*

Pope's *Essay on Criticism*, published when the author was only twenty-three years old, is an exposition, in heroic* couplets, of the literary rules of the Age of Classicism (see page 214). If the subject appears to you more adapted for treatment in prose than in verse, you should remember that much of the verse written by the classicists "was intended to instruct the intellect rather than to stir the emotions" (p. 218). Most of the critical rules set forth in the *Essay* were familiar in Pope's time, and are now generally accepted as commonplaces or are regarded as partly false. However, they are expressed in such mechanically perfect form and are so epigrammatic* and so quotable that several of them have found their way into ordinary modern English speech and are repeated by thousands of people who have never read the *Essay* through in their lives.

'TIS hard to say, if greater want of skill
Appear in writing or in judging ill.

. . .

A fool might once himself alone expose,
Now one in verse makes many more in prose. . . .

Nature to all things fix'd the limits fit,
And wisely curb'd proud man's pretending wit. . . .

First follow Nature, and your judgment frame
By her just standard, which is still the same. . . .

For wit and judgment often are at strife,
Tho' meant each other's aid, like man and wife. . . . 10

Those Rules of old discovered, not devis'd,
Are Nature still, but Nature methodiz'd.

. . .

Be Homer's* works your study and delight,
Read them by day, and meditate by night. . . .

Those oft are stratagems which error seem,
Nor is it Homer nods, but we that dream.

. . .

A little learning is a dang'rous thing;
Drink deep, or taste not the Pierian spring.[1] . . .

A perfect Judge will read each word of Wit
19
With the same spirit that its author writ.

. . .

Whoever thinks a faultless piece to see,
Thinks what ne'er was, nor is, nor e'er shall be. . . .

And if the means be just, the conduct true,
Applause, in spight of trivial faults, is due. . . .

Neglect the rules each verbal Critic lays,
For not to know some trifles, is a praise.

. . .

[1] *Pierian spring.* A spring in ancient Greece sacred to the Muses.* Here, a symbol of learning, particularly literary learning.

Pope's house at Twickenham

From an aquatint, 1793. Courtesy of Professor George Sherburn

True Wit[1] is Nature to advantage
   dress'd,
What oft was thought, but ne'er so well
   express'd.
        . . .

Words are like leaves; and where they
   most abound,
Much fruit of sense beneath is rarely
   found.   30
        . . .

In words, as fashions, the same rule will
   hold;
Alike fantastic, if too new, or old:
Be not the first by whom the new are
   try'd,
Nor yet the last to lay the old aside.

        . . .

[1] Note that Pope, like most other classicists, uses
wit, not to mean a form of humor, but
imagination or the ability to perceive the
similarity between ideas.

Avoid Extremes; and shun the fault of
   such,
Who still are pleas'd too little or too
   much.
At ev'ry trifle scorn to take offence,
That always shows great pride, or little
   sense.
        . . .

Regard not then if Wit be old or new,
But blame the false, and value still the
   true.   40
        . . .

Some praise at morning what they blame
   at night;
But always think the last opinion right.

        . . .

We think our fathers fools, so wise we
   grow,
Our wiser sons, no doubt, will think us so.

        . . .

Unhappy Wit, like most mistaken things,
Atones not for that envy which it brings.

. . .

Good-nature and good-sense must ever
  join;
To err is human, to forgive, divine.

. . .

All seems infected that th' infected spy,
As all looks yellow to the jaundic'd eye.

. . .

'Tis not enough, taste, judgment, learning, join;   51
In all you speak, let truth and candour
  shine.

. . .

Be silent always when you doubt your
  sense;
And speak, though sure, with seeming
  diffidence.

. . .

Men must be taught as if you taught
  them not,
And things unknown propos'd as things
  forgot.

. . .

Fear not the anger of the wise to raise;
Those best can bear reproof, who merit
  praise.   58

. . .

Fools rush in where angels fear to tread.

. . .

Discussion Hints

1. Which of the epigrams* given here have
you ever heard quoted or misquoted?

2. Point out several of the epigrams that
apply to the present day. Explain how they
apply.

3. In the epigram beginning "In words, as
fashions" (l. 31), Pope's statement in the first
two lines is as true today as it was when he
wrote it. The last two lines contain one of
the best rules ever given for forming a vocabulary. Can you name any old words
that we are too apt to neglect? What sort of
new words are we apt to adopt too quickly?
Discuss in class.

4. Remember that when Pope urges his
readers to imitate nature he is using the
term "nature," not in the modern sense, but
in the sense of nature as imitated and methodized by the ancients, such as Homer* (see
page 216).

5. In what respect might the phrase
"Nature methodiz'd" be applied to the formal garden illustrated on page 216?

6. Point out the epigrams in which Pope
implies that an author may sometimes neglect
the rules.

7. Learn by heart three of the epigrams
that seem to you most worth remembering.

LYRIC POETRY[1]

JOHN DRYDEN[2] (1631-1700)

Alexander's Feast; or, The Power of Music

In 1697 the Saint Cecilia Society of London asked Dryden to write an ode* for them, recalling, doubtless, the fact that ten years before he had written "A Song for Saint Cecilia's Day," which everyone had liked greatly. Dryden consented, and wrote "Alexander's Feast" in a single night.

The theme of the poem is the power of music. The scene is the military banquet that Alexander* the Great gave in Persepolis to celebrate his conquest of Persia. By his side sits Thais* (thā′ĭs), one of the loveliest women of her time. Timotheus, the musician and poet, stands forth to play. He sings of ambition, wine, pity, love, and revenge. As he sounds these notes, Alexander and Thais show the effect the music is having upon them. Finally, on the note of revenge, Alexander leaps up and, with Thais and the other banqueters, seizes the torches from the walls and sets fire to Persepolis. Thus, the poet seems to say, music conquers the conqueror of the world.

A SONG IN HONOUR OF SAINT
CECILIA'S DAY, 1697

I

'TWAS at the royal feast for Persia won
By Philip's warlike son:[3]
  Aloft in awful[4] state
  The godlike hero sate
    On his imperial throne.
His valiant peers were placed around;
Their brows with roses and with myrtles
    bound:
  (So should desert in arms be crowned.)

The lovely Thais,* by his side,
Sate like a blooming Eastern bride,   10
In flower of youth and beauty's pride.
  Happy, happy, happy pair!
    None but the brave,
    None but the brave,
  None but the brave deserves the **fair**.

CHORUS

Happy, happy, happy pair!
    None but the brave,
    None but the brave,
  None but the brave deserves the **fair**.

II

Timotheus,[1] placed on high   20
  Amid the tuneful quire,
With flying fingers touched the lyre:
  The trembling notes ascend the sky,
  And heavenly joys inspire.
The song began from [2] Jove,*
Who left his blissful seats above,
(Such is the power of mighty love.)
A dragon's fiery form belied [3] the god:
Sublime on radiant spires [4] he rode,
When he to fair Olympia [5] pressed: 30
And while he sought her snowy breast,
Then round her slender waist he curled,
And stamped an image of himself, a
    sovereign of the world.
The listening crowd admire the lofty
    sound,
A present deity, they shout around;
A present deity, the vaulted roofs re-
    bound:

---

[1] Discussion hints for lyric poetry of the Age of Classicism are grouped together on page 231. For a discussion of lyric poetry see page 150.   [2] For biography see page 706.
[3] *Philip's . . . son.* Alexander* the Great.
[4] Awe-inspiring.

[1] Musician to Alexander.   [2] With.
[3] Disguised.   [4] Coils of the dragon.
[5] Olympias, the mother of Alexander.

With ravished ears
The monarch hears,
Assumes the god,
Affects to nod,   40
And seems to shake the spheres.[1]

CHORUS

With ravished ears
The monarch hears,
Assumes the god,
Affects to nod,
And seems to shake the spheres.

III

The praise of Bacchus* then the sweet
    musician sung,
  Of Bacchus ever fair, and ever young.
  The jolly god in triumph comes;
  Sound the trumpets, beat the drums;
    Flushed with a purple grace   51
    He shows his honest face:
Now give the hautboys[2] breath; he
    comes, he comes.
Bacchus, ever fair and young,
  Drinking joys did first ordain;
Bacchus' blessings are a treasure,
Drinking is the soldier's pleasure;
  Rich the treasure,
  Sweet the pleasure,
Sweet is pleasure after pain.   60

CHORUS

Bacchus' blessings are a treasure,
Drinking is the soldier's pleasure;
  Rich the treasure,
  Sweet the pleasure,
Sweet is pleasure after pain.

IV

Soothed with the sound the king grew
    vain;
Fought all his battles o'er again;
And thrice he routed all his foes, and
    thrice he slew the slain.

The master[1] saw the madness rise,   69
His[2] glowing cheeks, his ardent eyes;
And while he heaven and earth defied,
Changed his hand, and checked his
    pride.
  He chose a mournful Muse,*
  Soft pity to infuse;
He sung Darius* great and good,
  By too severe a fate,
Fallen, fallen, fallen, fallen,
  Fallen from his high estate,
And weltering in his blood;
Deserted at his utmost need   80
By those his former bounty fed;
On the bare earth exposed he lies,
With not a friend to close his eyes.

With downcast looks the joyless victor
    sate,
  Revolving in his altered soul
    The various turns of chance below;
  And, now and then, a sigh he stole,
  And tears began to flow.

CHORUS

Revolving in his altered soul   89
    The various turns of chance below;
  And, now and then, a sigh he stole,
  And tears began to flow.

V

The mighty master smiled to see
That love was in the next degree;
'Twas but a kindred-sound to move,
For pity melts the mind to love.
  Softly sweet, in Lydian measures,[3]
  Soon he soothed his soul to pleasures.
War, he sung, is toil and trouble;
Honour but an empty bubble;   100
  Never ending, still beginning,
Fighting still, and still destroying:
  If the world be worth thy winning,
Think, O think it worth enjoying:
  Lovely Thais sits beside thee,
  Take the good the gods provide thee.

[1] Timotheus.
[2] What are the antecedents of the pronouns in
    lines 70–75?
[3] *Lydian measures.* A kind of gentle, pleasing
    music.

[1] *Assumes . . . spheres.* Acts the part of his
    father, Jove, whose nod shook the universe.
[2] *Hautboy.* A musical instrument with a high
    tone, now called an oboe.

The many rend the skies with loud applause;
So Love was crowned, but Music won
the cause.
  The prince, unable to conceal his
pain,
    Gazed on the fair [1]   110
    Who caused his care,
  And sighed and looked, sighed and
looked,
Sighed and looked, and sighed again;
At length, with love and wine at once
oppressed,
The vanquished victor sunk upon her
breast.

Chorus

  The prince, unable to conceal his
pain,
    Gazed on the fair
    Who caused his care,
  And sighed and looked, sighed and
looked,
Sighed and looked, and sighed again;
At length, with love and wine at once
oppressed,   121
The vanquished victor sunk upon her
breast.

VI

Now strike the golden lyre again;
A louder yet, and yet a louder strain.
Break his bands of sleep [2] asunder,
And rouse him, like a rattling peal of
thunder.
  Hark, hark, the horrid sound
    Has raised up his head;
    As awaked from the dead,
  And amazed, he stares around. 130
"Revenge! revenge!" Timotheus cries,
  "See the Furies * arise;
  See the snakes that they rear,
  How they hiss in their hair,
And the sparkles that flash from their
eyes!

---

[1] Thais.
[2] *his . . . sleep.* The bands of sleep that bind him
(Alexander).

Behold a ghastly band,
Each a torch in his hand!
Those are Grecian ghosts, that in battle
were slain,
  And unburied remain
  Inglorious on the plain: [1]   140
  Give the vengeance due
  To the valiant crew.
Behold how they toss their torches on
high,
  How they point to the Persian
abodes,
And glittering temples of their hostile
gods."
The princes applaud with a furious
joy;
And the king seized a flambeau [2] with
zeal to destroy;
  Thais led the way,
  To light him to his prey,
And, like another Helen,* fired another
Troy.*   150

Chorus

And the king seized a flambeau with
zeal to destroy;
  Thais led the way,
  To light him to his prey,
And, like another Helen, fired another
Troy.

VII

  Thus long ago,
Ere heaving bellows [3] learned to
blow,
  While organs yet were mute, [4]
Timotheus, to his breathing
flute
  And sounding lyre,
Could swell the soul to rage, or kindle
soft desire.   160

---

[1] *unburied . . . plain.* According to an ancient
and widespread belief the spirit of an unburied corpse can never find rest.
[2] A kind of torch.
[3] That is, of the organ.
[4] *Ere . . . mute.* Before the organ was invented
(by Saint Cecilia).

The king seized a flambeau with zeal to destroy

At last divine Cecilia came,
Inventress of the vocal frame [1];
The sweet enthusiast, from her sacred
    store,
Enlarged the former narrow bounds,
And added length to solemn sounds, [2]
With Nature's mother-wit, and arts un-
    known before.
Let old Timotheus yield the prize,
    Or both divide the crown:
He raised a mortal to the skies;
She drew an angel down.   170

GRAND CHORUS

At last divine Cecilia came,
Inventress of the vocal frame;
The sweet enthusiast, from her sacred
    store,
Enlarged the former narrow bounds,
And added length to solemn sounds,
With Nature's mother-wit, and arts un-
    known before.
Let old Timotheus yield the prize,
    Or both divide the crown:
He raised a mortal to the skies;
    She drew an angel down.   180

ALEXANDER POPE [3] (1688-1744)

The Universal Prayer

Influenced by his own religious convictions as well as by the theological controversies that marked a large part of the eighteenth century, Pope undertook to write a prayer that would suit all races and all creeds. The result was "The Universal Prayer." It owes its place in English literature not only to its underlying theme, but also to its simple, dignified language.

FATHER of all! in ev'ry age,
    In ev'ry clime adored,
By saint, by savage, and by sage,
    Jehovah, Jove, or Lord!

Thou Great First Cause, least under-
    stood,
Who all my sense confined
To know but this, that thou art good,
    And that myself am blind;

Yet gave me, in this dark estate,
    To see the good from ill;   10
And binding Nature fast in Fate,
    Left free the human Will.

What Conscience dictates to be done,
    Or warns me not to do;
This teach me more than Hell to shun,
    That more than Heav'n pursue.

What blessings thy free bounty gives
    Let me not cast away;
For God is paid when man receives;
    T' enjoy is to obey.   20

Yet not to earth's contracted span
    Thy goodness let me bound,
Or think thee Lord alone of man,
    When thousand worlds are round.

Let not this weak unknowing hand
    Presume thy bolts to throw,
And deal damnation round the land
    On each I judge thy foe.

If I am right, thy grace impart,
    Still in the right to stay;   30
If I am wrong, O teach my heart
    To find that better way.

Save me alike from foolish Pride,
    Or impious Discontent,
At aught thy wisdom has denied,
    Or aught thy goodness lent.

[1] *vocal frame*. The organ. A good illustration of the classicists' fondness for using artificial instead of simple names (see page 217).
[2] *And added . . . sounds*. Note how well this line describes the notes of an organ.
[3] For biography see page 705.

Teach me to feel another's woe,
  To hide the fault I see;
That mercy I to others show,
  That mercy show to me.   40

Mean tho' I am, not wholly so,
  Since quickened by thy breath;
O lead me, wheresoe'er I go,
  Thro' this day's life or death.

This day be bread and peace my lot:
  All else beneath the sun
Thou know'st if best bestowed or not,
  And let thy will be done.

To Thee, whose temple is all Space,
  Whose altar earth, sea, skies,   50
One chorus let all Being raise,
  All Nature's incense rise!

Discussion Hints

1. Why is the poem by Dryden called an ode*?

2. Do Dryden and Milton agree as to the quality of Lydian music? (See "L'Allegro," p. 193, l. 136.)

3. In a hundred words tell the story of Bacchus* from the third stanza of "Alexander's Feast."

4. What traditions regarding Saint Cecilia are referred to by Dryden?

5. Point out striking examples of onomatopoeia* in Dryden's poem.

6. Explain lines 179–180 of "Alexander's Feast."

7. Assuming that "Alexander's Feast" is typical of Dryden, what should you say about his fondness for illustrations drawn from ancient history and Greek and Roman mythology?

8. In what sense did Helen* "fire" Troy? (See "Alexander's Feast.")

9. What are the metrical scheme and the rhyme* scheme of Pope's "Universal Prayer"? The same arrangement of accents and rhymes is found in many hymns and is therefore appropriate for a poem such as Pope's.

A DIARY

BIOGRAPHY, AUTOBIOGRAPHY, AND DIARIES

BIOGRAPHY has always had a special fascination for the reading public. In reading a biography we say to ourselves: "Here I am learning about a real human being, not an imaginary character such as appears in plays, novels, and short stories. This is real life." But it is not so easy as it seems to present a picture of a real person on the printed page, and it has taken a long time for English biographers to discover how to make their subjects really live before the eyes of the reader. Most of the early English biographies are now forgotten because they record little except the big superficial facts in the lives of their subjects. Boswell alone among the older English biographers gives us a close-up view of his subject. His *Life of Johnson* (p. 244) is still widely read because it furnishes an intimate, detailed picture of the daily life of the great man and because it was written by one who knew Johnson well and observed him carefully. Some of the other older English biographies, such as Johnson's *Lives of the Poets* (p. 238), are so prejudiced that they throw as much light on the writers as they do on their subjects.

During the Romantic Period and the nineteenth century the writing of biography improved greatly. As the years passed, biographers succeeded more and more in piercing beneath the outward facts and in revealing to the reader the true personalities of their subjects.

In recent years biographers and historians have tried more earnestly than ever before to make the personages they portray realities, not mere figures stalking across the stage of life. Like the modern novelists, they have come to realize that all men and women, even the greatest, are mixtures of good and evil and are often actuated by motives that are complex and conflicting. Thus there has come into existence the modern imaginative or impressionistic biography. Before beginning the work of composition, the modern biographer gathers all the outward facts that the older biographers used, and more; but when he comes to the actual writing, he avoids swamping the reader with a mass of details and records only the evidence that is really significant. The modern biographer is far more than a mere chronicler: he is both a historian and a student of human character. He not only takes us into the past and lets us live again in some interesting, perhaps half-forgotten period, but also reveals to us many hidden springs of character that explain the lives of the great or

HAROLD
SICHEL

Mr. Pepys, always careful in his dress,
leaves home on business

FROM A PAINTING BY HAROLD SICHEL

the near great. This new method of writing biography goes far toward explaining why more people read biographical writings today than ever before. Lytton Strachey's *Life of Queen Victoria*, which appeared in 1921, is perhaps the best-known example of the new type of English biography.

The deep interest which we all have in the lives of our fellow men is also responsible for the great popularity of autobiographic works of all sorts. Any piece of writing which is, or even pretends to be, a true confession or revelation of the thoughts or private life of the writer is sure to find many readers if it is at all well written. Moreover, lives which would seem commonplace enough today sometimes become interesting if they were lived long ago. It is for these reasons that we still read with enthusiasm the diary of Samuel Pepys, although he died more than two hundred years ago. We seldom get such intimate glimpses into the lives of even our nearest neighbors today as we do into the thoughts and actions of this seventeenth-century Englishman. Rarely, if ever, in the history of the world has anyone dared to set down on paper so frank a statement of all his doings, important and petty, noble and mean, as did Samuel Pepys. Pepys's *Diary* is probably nearer to a record of real life than any other diary ever written. This is owing to the fact that Pepys wrote it for his own pleasure and satisfaction, not for publication.

SAMUEL PEPYS[1] (1633–1703)

From Pepys's *Diary*

For nine years Samuel Pepys,[2] a government official under Charles II, recorded daily everything that came to his orderly and active mind. His quarrels with his wife, his contrition after these quarrels, his resolutions to do better, his lapses from his resolutions; his political dishonesty and his gifts; his impressions of plays and sermons; his observations during the Great Fire in London — all these he set down in his own system of shorthand. And there they remained until 1825, when a student, after seven years of labor, deciphered them. They are now one of the most trustworthy sources of information on the activities, thoughts, and opinions of a "gentleman of worth and virtue of the days of the carefree King Charles II."

[An accident at home.]

January 1st., 1662. Waking this morning out of my sleep on a sudden, I did with my elbow hit my wife a great blow over her face and neck, which waked her with pain, at which I was sorry, and to sleep again. We went by coach to see the play of the Spanish Curate;[1] and a good play it is, only Diego the Sexton did overdo his part too much.

[Gossip.]

April 1st, [1663]. I went to the Temple,* to my Cozen Roger Pepys, to see and talk with him a little; who tells me that, with much ado, the Parliament do agree to throw down Popery: but he says it is with so much spite and passion, and an endeavour of bringing all Nonconformists into the same condition, that he is afeard matters will not yet go so well as he could wish. To my office all the afternoon: Sir J. Minnes like a mad 20

---

[1] For biography see page 707.

[2] Pronounced pēps, pĕp'ĭs, pĕps, or even pīps.

[1] A comedy by Fletcher and Massinger, two Elizabethan dramatists.

coxcomb did swear and stamp, swearing that Commissioner Pett hath still the old heart against the King that ever he had, and all the damnable reproaches in the world, at which I was ashamed, but said little; but, upon the whole, I find him still a fool, led by the nose by stories told by Sir W. Batten, whether with or without reason. So, vexed in my mind 30 to see things ordered so unlike gentlemen or men of reason, I went home.

[A little graft.]

3d. To White Hall[1] and to Chapel, which being most monstrous full, I could not go into my pew, but sat among the quire. Dr. Creeton, the Scotchman, preached a most admirable, good, learned, and most severe sermon, yet comicall. He railed bitterly ever and anon against John Calvin,* and his brood, the Presby-40 terians, and against the present terme, now in use, of "tender consciences." He ripped up Hugh Peters[2] (calling him the execrable skellum[3]), his preaching stirring up the maids of the city to bring in their bodkins and thimbles. I met Captain Grove, who did give me a letter directed to myself from himself. I discerned money to be in it, and took it, knowing as I found it to be, the pro-50 ceeds of the place I have got him to be, the taking up of vessels for Tangier. But I did not open it till I came home — not looking into it till all the money was out, that I might say I saw no money in the paper, if ever I should be questioned about it. There was a piece of gold, and 4£ in silver.

[An excellent dinner.]

4th. Very merry at, before, and after dinner, and the more for that my dinner

was great, and most neatly dressed by 60 our own only mayde. We had a fricasee of rabbits, and chickens, a leg of mutton boiled, three carps in a dish, a great dish of a side of lamb, a dish of roasted pigeons, a dish of four lobsters, three tarts, a lamprey pie, a most rare[1] pie, a dish of anchovies, good wine of several sorts, and all things mighty noble, and to my great content.

[Church-going and good resolutions.]

5th. (Lord's day). Up and spent the 70 morning, till the Barber came, in reading in my chamber part of Osborne's[2] Advice to his Son, which I shall not never enough admire for sense and language, and being by and by trimmed,[3] to Church, myself, wife, Ashwell,[4] etc. Home and, while dinner was prepared, to my office[5] to read over my vows with great affection and to very good purpose. So to dinner, and very well pleased with it. Then to 80 church again, where a simple bawling young Scot preached.

19th (Easter-day). Up, and this day put on my close-kneed coloured suit, which, with new stockings of the colour, with belt, and new gilt-handled sword, is very handsome. To church, where the young Scotchman preaching, I slept awhile. After supper, fell in discourse of dancing, and I find that Ashwell hath a 90 very fine carriage, which makes my wife almost ashamed of herself to see herself so outdone, but to-morrow she begins to learn to dance for a month or two. Will[6] being gone, with my leave, to his father's this day for a day or two, to take physique these holydays.

---

[1] White Hall. Whitehall, in Pepys's day a palace of the English kings.
[2] Hugh Peters. A native of Cornwall who, after being expelled from college, became an actor and later a preacher. As a preacher he was widely known for his buffoonery in the pulpit.
[3] Villain, scoundrel.

[1] Especially fine.
[2] Francis Osborne was a popular writer who died in 1659. He was the author of several books of advice to young people. His Advice to His Son was one of Pepys's favorite books.
[3] being . . . trimmed. Having had my beard trimmed soon afterward.
[4] Mary Ashwell, Mrs. Pepys's maid. She is often referred to in Pepys's Diary.
[5] Here, private room.
[6] William Hewer, a young protégé of Pepys's.

23d. St. George's day and Coronation, the King and Court being at Windsor, 100 at the installing of the King of Denmarke by proxy, and the Duke of Monmouth. Spent the evening with my father. At cards till late, and being at supper, my boy being sent for some mustard to a beef's tongue, the rogue staid half an hour in the streets, it seems at a bonfire, at which I was very angry, and resolve to beat him to-morrow.

[A whipping.]

24th. Up betimes, and with my salt 110 eele[1] went down into the parlor and there got my boy and did beat him till I was fain to take breath two or three times, yet for all I am afeard it will make the boy never the better, he is grown so hardened in his tricks, which I am sorry for, he being capable of making a brave man, and is a boy that I and my wife love very well.

[The great fire in London.]

September 2d, 1666. (*Lord's day*). 120 Some of our maids sitting up late last night to get things ready against our feast to-day, Jane called us up about three in the morning, to tell us of a great fire they saw in the City. So I rose, and slipped on my night-gown, and went to her window; and thought it to be on the back-side of Marke-lane at the farthest; but, being unused to such fires as followed, I thought it far enough off; and 130 so went to bed again, and to sleep. About seven rose again to dress myself, and there looked out at the window, and saw the fire not so much as it was, and further off. By and by Jane comes and tells me that she hears that about 300 houses have been burned down to-night by the fire we saw, and that it is now burning down all Fish Street, by London Bridge. So I made myself ready presently, and walked to the Tower; and 140 there got up upon one of the high places, Sir J. Robinson's little son going up with me; and there I did see the houses at that end of the bridge all on fire, and an infinite great fire on this and the other side the end of the bridge. So I down to the waterside, and there got a boat, and through [the] bridge, and there saw a lamentable fire. Every body endeavouring to remove their goods, and flinging 150 into the river, or bringing them into lighters that lay off; poor people staying in their houses as long as till the very fire touched them, and then running into boats, or clambering from one pair of stairs, by the waterside, to another. And, among other things, the poor pigeons, I perceive, were loth to leave their houses, but hovered about the windows and balconys, till they burned 160 their wings, and fell down. Having staid, and in an hour's time seen the fire rage every way; and nobody, to my sight, endeavouring to quench it, but to remove their goods, and leave all to the fire; and having seen it get as far as the Steele-yard, and the wind mighty high, and driving it into the City: and everything, after so long a drought, proving combustible, even the very stones of 170 churches; I to White Hall, and there up to the King's closet in the Chapel, where people come about me, and I did give them an account dismayed them all, and word was carried in to the King. So I was called for, and did tell the King and Duke of York what I saw; and, that unless his Majesty did command houses to be pulled down, nothing could stop the fire. They seemed much troubled, 180 and the King commanded me to go to my Lord Mayor from him, and command him to spare no houses, but to pull down before the fire every way. Here meeting with Captain Cocke, I in his coach, which he lent me, and Creed with me to Paul's; and there walked along Watling street, as well as I could, every creature

[1] *salt eele*. A whip made of rope and shaped like an eel.

coming away loaden with goods to save, 190 and, here and there, sick people carried away in beds. At last met my Lord Mayor in Canning Street, like a man spent, with a hankercher about his neck. To the King's message, he cried like a fainting woman, 'Lord! what can I do? I am spent: people will not obey me. I have been pulling down houses; but the fire overtakes us faster than we can do it.' So he left me, and I him, 200 and walked home: seeing people almost distracted, and no manner of means used to quench the fire. The houses, too, so very thick thereabouts, and full of matter for burning, as pitch and tar, in Thames Street; and warehouses of oyle, and wines, and brandy, and other things. And to see the churches all filling with goods by people who themselves should have been quietly there at this time. 210 By this time, it was about twelve o'clock; and so home. Soon as dined, I and Moone away, and walked through the City, the streets full of nothing but people; and horses and carts loaden with goods, ready to run over one another, and removing goods from one burned house to another. We parted at Paul's; he home, and I to Paul's Wharf, where I had appointed a boat to attend me, 220 and took in Mr. Carcasse and his brother. And again to see the fire, which was now got further, both below and above, and no likelihood of stopping it. Met with the King and Duke of York in their barge, and with them to Queenhithe, and there called Sir Richard Browne to them. Their order was only to pull down houses apace, and so below bridge at the waterside; but little was or could be 230 done, the fire coming upon them so fast. Good hopes there was of stopping it at the Three Cranes above, and at Buttulph's Wharf below bridge, if care be used; but the wind carries it into the City, so as we know not, by the waterside, what it do there. River full of lighters and boats taking in goods, and

good goods swimming in the water; and only I observed that hardly one lighter or boat in three that had the goods of a 240 house in, but there was a pair of Virginall's [1] in it. Having seen as much as I could now, I away to White Hall by appointment, and there walked in St. James's Park; and there met my wife, and Creed, and Wood, and his wife, and walked to my boat; and there upon the water again, and to the fire up and down, it still encreasing, and the wind great. So near the fire as we could for 250 smoke; and all over the Thames, with one's faces in the wind, you were almost burned with a shower of fire-drops. This is very true: so as houses were burned by these drops and flakes of fire, three or four, nay, five or six houses, one from another. When we could endure no more upon the water, we to a little ale-house on the Bankside, over against the Three Cranes, and there staid until it was dark 260 almost and saw the fire grow; and, as it grew darker, appeared more and more; and in corners and upon steeples, and between churches and houses, as far as we could see up the hill of the City, in a most horrid, malicious, bloody flame, not like the fine flame of an ordinary fire. We staid till, it being darkish, we saw the fire as only one entire arch of fire from this to the other side of the bridge, 270 and in a bow up the hill for an arch of above a mile long: it made me weep to see it. The churches, houses, and all on fire, and flaming at once; and a horrid noise of flames made, and the cracking of houses at their ruin. So home with a sad heart, and there find every body discoursing and lamenting the fire; and poor Tom Hater come with some few of his goods saved out of his house. I 280 invited him to lie at my house, and did receive his goods; but was deceived in his lying there, the news coming every moment of the growth of the fire; so as

[1] *a pair of Virginall's.* An ancestor of the modern piano.

we were forced to begin to pack up our own goods, and prepare for their removal; and did by moonshine, it being brave, dry, and moonshine and warm weather, carry much of my goods into 290 the garden; and Mr. Hater and I did remove my money and iron chests into my cellar, as thinking that the safest place. I got my bags of gold into my office, ready to carry away, and my chief papers of accounts also there, and my tallies into a box by themselves.

5th. I lay down in the office again upon W. Hewer's quilt, being mighty weary, and sore in my feet with going 300 till I was hardly able to stand. About two in the morning my wife calls me up,[1] and tells me of new cryes of fire, it being come to Barking Church, which is the bottom of our lane. I up; and finding it so, resolved presently to take her away, and did, and took my gold, which was about 2350 £, W. Hewer and Jane down by Proundy's boat to Woolwich[2]; but, Lord! what a sad sight it was by 310 moone-light, to see the whole City almost on fire, that you might see it as plain at Woolwich, as if you were by it. There, when I come, I find the gates shut, but no guard kept at all; which troubled me, because of discourses now begun, that there is a plot in it, and that the French had done it. I got the gates open, and to Mr. Sheldon's, where I locked up my gold, and charged my wife and W. Hewer 320 never to leave the room without one of them in it, night or day. Home, and whereas I expected to have seen our house on fire, it being now about seven o'clock, it was not. But to the fire, and there find greater hopes than I expected. By the blowing up of houses, and the great help given by the workmen out of the King's yards, sent up by Sir W. Pen, there is a good stop given to it, as well

at Marke Lane End as ours; it having 330 only burned the dyall[1] of Barking Church, and part of the porch, and was there quenched. To Sir W. Pen's, and there eat a piece of cold meat, having eaten no thing since Sunday, but the remains of Sunday's dinner. Here I met Mr. Young and Whistler; and, having removed all my things, and received good hopes that the fire at our end is stopped, they and I walked into the town. Into Moore-fields, 340 our feet ready to burn, walking through the town among the hot coles, and find that full of people, and poor wretches carrying their goods there, and every body keeping his goods together by themselves; and a great blessing it is to them that it is fair weather for them to keep abroad night and day. Thence homeward, having passed through Cheapside, and Newgate market, all burned; 350 and seen Anthony Joyce's house in fire; and took up, which I keep by me, a piece of glass in the Mercers' chapel in the street, where much more was, so melted and buckled with the heat of the fire like parchment. I also did see a poor cat taken out of a hole in a chimney, joyning to the wall of the Exchange, with hair all burnt off the body, and yet alive. So home at night, and find there good hopes 360 of saving our office; but great endeavours of watching all night, and having men ready; so we lodged them in the office, and had drink and bread and cheese for them. And I lay down and slept a good night about midnight: though, when I rose, I heard that there had been a great alarm of French and Dutch[2] being risen, which proved nothing. But it is a strange thing to see how long this time did look 370 since Sunday, having been always full of variety of actions, and little sleep, that it looked like a week or more, and I had forgot almost the day of the week.

---

[1] Awakes me.
[2] A marine arsenal on the Thames near London. Pepys was an official in the Navy Department.

[1] Sundial.
[2] The French and the Dutch were often suspected of making trouble in England during the reign of Charles II.

[Last words.]

May 31st, 1669. Up very betimes, and continued all the morning with W. Hewer, upon examining and stating my accounts, in order to the fitting myself to go abroad beyond sea, which the ill condi-
380 tion of my eyes, and my neglect for a year or two hath kept me behind-hand in, and so as to render it very difficult now, and troublesome to my mind to do it.

And thus ends all that I doubt I shall ever be able to do with my own eyes in the keeping of my Journal, I being not able to do it any longer, having done now so long as to undo my eyes almost every time that I take a pen in my hand; and,
390 therefore, whatever comes of it, I must forbear: and, therefore, resolve, from this time forward, to have it kept by my people in long-hand, and must be contented to set down no more than is fit for them and all the world to know.

And so I betake myself to that course, which is almost as much as to see myself go into my grave: for which, and all the discomforts that will accompany my
400 being blind, may the good God prepare me! S[amuel] P[epys].

Discussion Hints

1. Point out evidence which justifies the claim that Pepys's *Diary* is astonishingly frank in revealing the most intimate thoughts and actions of the writer. Why did Pepys feel safe in giving such a full account?

2. What evidence does the *Diary* furnish as to the state of political and religious feeling in England after the Restoration? How does the picture you get compare with that given in your English history?

3. What do you learn from Pepys's *Diary* concerning the personal habits, likes, and dislikes of the writer?

4. Supposing yourself to be a special reporter assigned to cover the Great Fire in London, what observations made by Pepys would you regard as especially good "copy"?

5. In Pepys's account of his dinner do you notice the absence of any kinds of food that would be regarded as a natural part of a modern well-balanced meal?

6. What part of speech does Pepys omit most often from his sentences? How do you account for the omission?

7. Does Pepys use any expressions that are not regarded as good grammar today? Explain your answer.

8. Some of our cleverest modern newspaper columnists amuse their readers occasionally by imitating Pepys's style. Have you ever seen any of these modern imitations? If so, give an account of one or more of them.

Suggestions for Reading

Suitable selections from Pepys's *Diary* are given in *Everybody's Pepys*. Harcourt, Brace and Company, Inc.

PROSE CRITICISM

SAMUEL JOHNSON[1] (1709–1784)

On Certain Poems

"On Certain Poems," taken from Johnson's life of Milton in his *Lives of the Poets*, shows Johnson's style at its best. As contrasted with the long, mouth-filling words and the involved, carefully balanced sentences that characterize his more typical prose writings,

[1] For biography see page 707.

the style is comparatively simple and natural. Though Johnson's prejudices prevented him from judging Milton's work as a whole with entire fairness, we cannot help admiring the justness with which he appreciates the companion poems "L'Allegro" (p. 190) and "Il Penseroso" (p. 193), and the dignified and noble language in which he sets forth the plan and merits of Milton's great epic, *Paradise Lost*. A reading of the following selections or any other equally long passages from the *Lives of the Poets* is a literary tonic for the boy or girl who is blessed with the mental vigor to master the words and follow the meaning of the sentences.

OF THE two pieces, "L' Allegro" and "Il Penseroso," I believe opinion is uniform; every man that reads them, reads them with pleasure. The author's design is not, what Theobald[1] has remarked, merely to shew how objects derived their colours from the mind, by representing the operation of the same things upon the gay and the melancholy
10 temper, or upon the same man as he is differently disposed; but rather how, among the successive variety of appearances, every disposition of mind takes hold on those by which it may be gratified.

The *chearful*[2] man hears the lark in the morning; the *pensive* man hears the nightingale in the evening. The *chearful* man sees the cock strut, and hears the
20 horn and hounds echo in the wood; then walks "not unseen" to observe the glory of the rising sun or listen to the singing milk-maid, and view the labours of the plowman and the mower; then casts his eyes about him over scenes of smiling plenty, and looks up to the distant tower, the residence of some fair inhabitant: thus he pursues rural gaiety through a day of labour or of
30 play, and delights himself at night with the fanciful narratives of superstitious ignorance.

The *pensive* man at one time walks "unseen" to muse at midnight, and at another hears the sullen curfew.* If the weather drives him home he sits in a room lighted only by "glowing embers"; or by a lonely lamp outwatches the

North Star to discover the habitation of separate souls, and varies the shades 40 of meditation by contemplating the magnificent or pathetic scenes of tragic and epic poetry. When the morning comes, a morning gloomy with rain and wind, he walks into the dark trackless woods, falls asleep by some murmuring water, and with melancholy enthusiasm expects some dream of prognostication or some musick played by aërial performers. 50

Both Mirth and Melancholy are solitary, silent inhabitants of the breast that neither receive nor transmit communication; no mention is therefore made of a philosophical friend or a pleasant companion. The seriousness does not arise from any participation of[1] calamity, nor the gaiety from the pleasures of the bottle.

The man of *chearfulness* having ex- 60 hausted the country tries what "towered cities" will afford, and mingles with scenes of splendour, gay assemblies, and nuptial festivities[2]; but he mingles a mere spectator as, when the learned comedies of Jonson or the wild dramas of Shakespeare are exhibited, he attends the theatre.

The *pensive* man never loses himself in crowds, but walks the cloister[3] or fre- 70 quents the cathedral. Milton probably had not yet forsaken the Church.[4]

Both his characters delight in musick; but he seems to think that chearful notes would have obtained from Pluto* a compleat dismission of Eurydice,* of whom solemn sounds only procured a conditional release.

For the old age of Chearfulness he makes no provision; but Melancholy he 80 conducts with great dignity to the close of life. His Chearfulness is without

---

[1] Lewis Theobald (thē′ō bōld *or* tĭb′ăld), a contemporary of Johnson, now best known as an editor and critic of Shakespeare.
[2] What is the modern spelling?

[1] In.
[2] *nuptial festivities.* Marriage feasts.
[3] The covered walk surrounding the quadrangle of a college.
[4] Here, the Established Church, as opposed to Nonconformists, including the Puritans.

levity, and his Pensiveness without asperity.[1]

Through these two poems the images are properly selected and nicely[2] distinguished, but the colours of the diction seem not sufficiently discriminated. I know not whether the characters are 90 kept sufficiently apart. No mirth can, indeed, be found in his melancholy; but I am afraid that I always meet some melancholy in his mirth. They are two noble efforts of imagination.

[After discussing other works by Milton, Johnson proceeds as follows.]

I am now to examine *Paradise Lost*; a poem, which, considered with respect to design, may claim the first place, and with respect to performance, the second, among the productions of the human 100 mind.

By the general consent of critics, the first praise of genius is due to the writer of an epic poem, as it requires an assemblage of all the powers which are singly sufficient for other compositions. Poetry is the art of uniting pleasure with truth, by calling imagination to the help of reason. Epic poetry undertakes to teach the most important truths by the 110 most pleasing precepts, and therefore relates some great event in the most affecting manner. History must supply the writer with the rudiments of narration, which he must improve and exalt by a nobler art, must animate by dramatic energy, and diversify by retrospection and anticipation; morality must teach him the exact bounds and different shades of vice and virtue; from policy, and the 120 practice of life, he has to learn the discriminations of character, and the tendency of the passions, either single or combined; and physiology must supply him with illustrations and images. To put these materials to poetical use, is required an imagination capable of paint-

ing nature, and realizing fiction. Nor is he yet a poet till he has attained the whole extension of his language, distinguished all the delicacies of phrase, 130 and all the colours of words, and learned to adjust their different sounds to all the varieties of metrical modulation.

[The best modern critics are] of opinion, that the poet's first work is to find a moral, which his fable[1] is afterwards to illustrate and establish. This seems to have been the process only of Milton; the moral of other poems is incidental and consequent; in Milton's only it is 140 essential and intrinsic. His purpose was the most useful and the most arduous; "to vindicate the ways of God to man"; to show the reasonableness of religion, and the necessity of obedience to the Divine law.

To convey this moral there must be a fable, a narration artfully constructed, so as to excite curiosity, and surprise expectation. In this part of his work, 150 Milton must be confessed to have equalled every other poet. He has involved in his account of the fall of man the events which preceded, and those that were to follow it; he has interwoven the whole system of theology with such propriety, that every part appears to be necessary; and scarcely any recital is wished shorter for the sake of quickening the progress of the main action.   160

The subject of an epic poem is naturally an event of great importance. That of Milton is not the destruction of a city, the conduct of a colony, or the foundation of an empire. His subject is the fate of worlds, the revolutions of heaven and of earth; rebellion against the supreme King, raised by the highest order of created beings;[2] the overthrow of their host, and the punishment of their crime; 170 the creation of a new race of reasonable[3]

---

[1] Moroseness, sourness.
[2] Exactly, discriminatingly.

[1] Plot.
[2] *highest ... beings.* In *Paradise Lost* certain of the angels.
[3] Capable of reasoning.

creatures, their original happiness and innocence, their forfeiture of immortality, and their restoration to hope and peace.

Great events can be hastened or retarded only by persons of elevated dignity. Before the greatness displayed in Milton's poem, all other greatness 180 shrinks away. The weakest of his agents are the highest and noblest of human beings, the original parents of mankind; with whose actions the elements consented; on whose rectitude, or deviation of will, depended the state of terrestrial nature, and the condition of all the future inhabitants of the globe.

Discussion Hints

1. Read Johnson's summaries, beginning with "The *chearful* man" (p. 239, l. 16), in connection with "L'Allegro" (p. 190) and with "The *pensive* man" (p. 239, l. 33) in connection with "Il Penseroso" (p. 193), and point out what lines in the two poems correspond to the successive parts of the summary. For example, "The *chearful* man sees the cock strut" ("L'Allegro," l. 52) "and hears the horn and hounds echo in the wood" (ll. 53–56). Judged by the outline provided in the headnote (p. 190), do Johnson's summaries give a fair account of the contents of the two poems?

2. Read what is said in the introduction to "The Age of Classicism" (p. 216) regarding the classicists' attitude toward Shakespeare. How does this compare with Johnson's attitude as implied in the adjective "wild" (p. 239, l. 66)?

3. Is Johnson right in asserting that both the cheerful man and the pensive man are "solitary" (p. 239, l. 51)? Discuss in class.

4. Notice that on page 240, l. 86, Johnson uses the word *nicely* in the rare, though correct, sense of "exactly, discriminatingly," the opposite of inexactly, carelessly. Look up the word *nice* in a large dictionary and see how many meanings it has and what they are. As you continue your reading look for further cases of *nice* or *nicely* used in the senses indicated by Johnson.

5. Does your study of "L'Allegro" and "Il

Penseroso" (pp. 190, 193) cause you, with Johnson, to find "no mirth . . . in his [Milton's] melancholy; but . . . some melancholy in his mirth" (p. 240, ll. 90–93)? Give reasons for your answer.

6. Johnson calls *Paradise Lost* "with respect to performance" second "among the productions of the human mind." What long poems would you compare to *Paradise Lost?*

7. Commit to memory Johnson's definition of poetry (p. 240, ll. 106–108). What other definitions of poetry do you know? If you can think of any or find any, compare them with Johnson's.

8. What epic poem has Johnson probably in mind when he refers to "the destruction of a city"? when he refers to "the conduct of a colony, or the foundation of an empire"?

Phrases and Passages to be Explained

fanciful narratives of superstitious ignorance (p. 239, ll. 31–32)
some dream of prognostication (p. 239, l. 48)
The seriousness does not arise from any participation of calamity, nor the gaiety from the pleasures of the bottle (p. 239, ll. 56–59)
His Chearfulness is without levity, and his Pensiveness without asperity (p. 239, l. 82 — p. 240, l. 84)
diversify by retrospection and anticipation (p. 240, ll. 116–117)
essential and intrinsic (p. 240, l. 141)
forfeiture of immortality (p. 241, l. 173)
the original parents of mankind (p. 241, l. 182)

Suggestions for Reading

If you have access to a copy of Johnson's *Lives of the Poets,* you should read not only the remainder of the life of Milton, but also, if time permits, at least samples of the lives of Addison, Collins, and Gray. Johnson's style and his manner of treating his subjects should especially interest and stimulate you. An easily accessible edition of the *Lives* is given in Everyman's Library (E. P. Dutton & Co., Inc.).

A long-recognized standard essay on Samuel Johnson is that written by Thomas Babington Macaulay for the Encyclopaedia Britannica.

6. To fix to one's interest.

The great and rich depend on those whom their power or their wealth *attaches* to them.   *Rogers.*

ATTA′CHMENT. *n. ſ.* [*attachement*, Fr.]

1. Adherence; attention; regard.

The Jews are remarkable for an *attachment* to their own country.   *Addiſon. Freeholder,* N° 5.

The Romans burnt this laſt fleet, which is another mark of their ſmall *attachment* to the ſea.
Arbuthnot on Coins.

2. An apprehenſion of a man to bring him to an-ſwer an action; and ſometimes it extends to his moveables.

3 *Foreign attachment*, is the attachment of a for-eigner's goods found within a city, to ſatisfy creditors within a city.

To ATTACK. *v. a.* [*attaquer*, Fr.]

1. To aſſault an enemy; oppoſed to *defence*.

The front, the rear
Attack, while Yvo thunders in the center.
A. Philips's Briton.

Thoſe that *attack*, generally get the victory, though with diſadvantage of ground.
Cane's Campaigns.

2. To impugn in any manner, as with ſatire, con-futation, calumny; as, the declaimer *attacked* the reputation of his adverſaries.

ATTA′CK. *n. ſ.* [from the verb.] An aſſault upon an enemy.

Hector oppoſes, and continues the *attack*; in which, after many actions, Sarpedon makes the firſt breach in the wall
Pope's Iliad, argum. b. xii.

If appriz'd of the ſevere *attack*,
The country be ſhut up.   *Thomſon.*

I own 'twas wrong, when thouſands call'd me back,
To make that hopeleſs, ill-adviſed *attack*.
Young.

ATTA′CKER. *n. ſ.* [from *attack*.] The perſon that attacks.

To ATTA′IN. *v. a.* [*atteindre*, Fr. *attineo*, Lat.]

1. To gain; to procure; to obtain.

Such knowledge is too wonderful for me; it is high; I cannot *attain* unto it.   *Pſ.* cxxxix. 6.

Is he wiſe who hopes to *attain* the end without the means, nay by means that are quite contrary to it?   *Tillotſon.*

2. To overtake; to come up with: a ſenſe now little in uſe.

The earl hoping to have overtaken the Scot-tiſh king, and to have given him battle; but not *attaining* him in time, ſet down before the caſtle of Aton.   *Bacon's Henry* VII.

3. To come to; to enter upon.

Canaan he now *attains*; I ſee his tents
Pitch'd above Sichem.
Milton's Paradiſe Loſt, b. xii.

4. To reach; to equal.

So the firſt precedent, if it be good, is ſeldom *attained* by imitation.   *Bacon's Eſſays.*

Government is an art above the *attainment* of an ordinary genius.   *South.*

If the ſame actions be the inſtruments, both of acquiring fame and procuring this happineſs, they would nevertheleſs fail in the *attainment* of this laſt end, if they proceeded from a deſire of the firſt.   *Addiſon. Spectator,* N° 257.

The great care of God for our ſalvation muſt appear in the concern he expreſſed for our *attain-ment* of it.   *Rogers.*

To ATTA′INT. *v. a.* [*attenter*, Fr.]

1. To *attaint* is particularly uſed for ſuch as are found guilty of ſome crime or offence, and eſpe-cially of felony or treaſon. A man is *attainted* two ways, by appearance, or by proceſs. Attainder by appearance is by confeſſion, battle, or verdict. Confeſſion is double; one at the bar before the judges, when the priſoner, upon his indictment read, being aſked guilty or not guilty, anſwers guilty, never putting himſelf upon the verdict of the jury. The other is before the coroner in ſanctuary, where he, upon his confeſſion, was in former times conſtrained to abjure the realm; which kind is called attainder by abjuration. At-tainder by battle is, when the party appealed, and chooſing to try the truth by combat rather than by jury, is vanquiſhed. Attainder by verdict is, when the priſoner at the bar, anſwering to the indictment not guilty, hath an inqueſt of life and death paſſing upon him, and is by the verdict pro-nounced guilty. Attainder by proceſs is, where a party flies, and is not found till five times called publickly in the county, and at laſt outlawed upon his default.   *Cowel.*

Were it not an endleſs trouble, that no traitor or felon ſhould be *attainted*, but a parliament muſt be called.   *Spenſer on Ireland.*

I muſt offend before I be *attainted*.
Shakeſp. Hen. VI.

2. To taint; to corrupt.

My tender youth was never yet *attaint*
With any paſſion of inflaming love.
Shakeſp. Henry VI.

ATTA′INT. *n. ſ* [from the verb.]

1. Any thing injurious, as illneſs, wearineſs. This ſenſe is now obſolete.

Nor doth he dedicate one jot of colour
Unto the weary and all-watched night;
But freſhly looks, and overbears *attaint*
With chearful ſemblance.   *Shakeſp. Henry* V.

2. Stain; ſpot; taint.

No man hath a virtue that he has not a glimpſe of; nor any man an *attaint*, but he carries ſome ſtain of it.   *Shakeſp. Troilus and Creſſida.*

3. In horſemanſhip. A blow or wound on the hinder feet of an horſe.   *Farrier's Dict.*

ATTA′INTURE. *n. ſ* [from *attaint*]. Reproach; im-putation.

Hume's knavery will be the ducheſs's wreck,
And her *attainture* will be Humphry's fall.
Shakeſpeare's Henry VI.

A page from Doctor Johnson's "Dictionary"

A DICTIONARY

SAMUEL JOHNSON[1] (1709–1784)

From the *Dictionary of the English Language*

Johnson's great work is his *Dictionary of the English Language,* upon the preparation of which he spent seven years. It appeared in 1755. It differed from all its predecessors (1) in including a large number of dialect words and excluding many common words of French origin, (2) in giving the pronunciation of difficult words, (3) in giving full-sentence quotations to illustrate the use of certain words, and (4) in asserting that it is the use of a word and not its history that determines its meaning; in short, it was the first real dictionary of the English language. In a number of cases the author obscured the meaning of words by involved definitions. In a few cases he let his personal feelings govern his phrasing. Some of his definitions, of which the following are examples, have become famous.

Network, *n.s.* [*net* and *work*] Any thing reticulated or decussated, at equal distances, with interstices between the intersections.

[1] For biography see page 707.

Oats, *n.s.* [*azen,* Saxon] A grain which in England is generally given to horses, but in Scotland supports the people.[1]

Pastern, *n.s.* [*pasturon,* French] The knee of an horse.[2]

Pension, *n.s.* [*pension,* Fr.] An allowance made to any one without any equivalent. In England it is generally understood to mean pay given to a state hireling for treason to his country.[3]

Purl, *n.s.* [I know not whence derived.] A kind of medicated malt liquor, in which wormwood and aromaticks are infused.

---

[1] Johnson's inveterate scorn of Scotland and Scotsmen emerges here.

[2] When a lady once asked Johnson why he defined "pastern" in this way, he replied simply, "Ignorance, madam, pure ignorance."

[3] It is characteristic of Johnson's sturdy honesty that when he was later (1762) granted a pension by the government, he declined to change this definition.

BIOGRAPHY[1]

JAMES BOSWELL[2] (1740–1795)

From the *Life of Johnson*

During more than twenty years a little hero-worshiping Scotsman named James Boswell spent a considerable part of his time in the company of Samuel Johnson,[3] constantly observing and making notes on what the great man said and did. From his notes he composed in a clear, flexible style a life of Johnson which stands today as one of the most detailed, picturesque, and readable biographies in the English language. Though a lifelong admirer of Johnson, Boswell refrained from idealizing the picture or concealing the great man's shortcomings. The result is a biography that comes about as near giving a complete and unprejudiced account of its subject as is humanly possible. It is for this reason that thousands of readers today enjoy Boswell's *Life of Johnson* who never read a line of the great classicist's own writings.

JOHNSON AT SCHOOL

HE WAS first taught to read English by Dame Oliver, a widow, who kept a school for young children in Lichfield. He told me she could read the black letter,[4] and asked him to borrow for her, from his father, a Bible in that character. When he was going to Oxford, she came to take leave of him, brought him, in the simplicity of her kindness, a present of gingerbread, and said he was the best scholar she ever had. He delighted in mentioning this early compliment: adding, with a smile, that "this was as high a proof of his merit as he could conceive." His next instructor in English was a master whom, when he spoke of him to me, he familiarly called Tom Brown, who, said he, "published a spelling-book, and dedicated it to the Universe; but I fear no copy of it can now be had."

He began to learn Latin with Mr. Hawkins, usher, or undermaster, of Lichfield school — "a man" (said he) "very skilful in his little way." With him he continued two years, and then rose to be under the care of Mr. Hunter, the head master, who according to his account, "was very severe and wrong-headedly severe. He used" (said he) "to beat us unmercifully; and he did not distinguish between ignorance and negligence; for he would beat a boy equally for not knowing a thing, as for neglecting to know it. He would ask a boy a question, and if he did not answer it, he would beat him, without considering whether he had an opportunity of knowing how to answer it. For instance, he would call up a boy and ask him Latin for a candlestick, which the boy could not expect to be asked. Now, Sir, if a boy could answer every question, there would be no need of a master to teach him."

However, Johnson was very sensible how much he owed to Mr. Hunter. Mr. Langton[1] one day asked him how he had acquired so accurate a knowledge of

[1] For discussion of biography see page 232.
[2] For biography see page 708.
[3] For biography see page 707.
[4] *black letter.* Old English letters.

[1] Bennet Langton (1737–1801), a distinguished Greek scholar, a member of the Literary Club, and a friend of Johnson's for many years. The occasion of his introduction to Johnson is referred to below (p. 245).

Latin, in which I believe he was exceeded by no man of his time; he said, "My master whipped me very well. Without that, Sir, I should have done nothing." He told Mr. Langton that while Hunter was flogging his boys unmercifully, he used to say, "And this I do to save you from the gallows." Johnson, upon all occasions, expressed his approbation of enforcing instruction by means of the rod. "I would rather" (said he) "have the rod to be the general terror to all, to make them learn, than tell a child, if you do thus, or thus, you will be more esteemed than your brothers or sisters. The rod produces an effect which terminates in itself. A child is afraid of being whipped, and gets his task, and there's an end on't: whereas, by exciting emulation and comparisons of superiority, you lay the foundation of lasting mischief; you make brothers and sisters hate each other."

That superiority over his fellows, which he maintained with so much dignity in his march through life, was not assumed from vanity and ostentation, but was the natural and constant effect of those extraordinary powers of mind, of which he could not but be conscious by comparison; the intellectual difference, which in other cases of comparison of characters, is often a matter of undecided contest, being as clear in his case as the superiority of stature in some men above others. Johnson did not strut or stand on tiptoe; he only did not stoop. From his earliest years, his superiority was perceived and acknowledged. He was from the beginning *anax andrōn*, a king of men. His schoolfellow, Mr. Hector, has obligingly furnished me with many particulars of his boyish days; and assured me that he never knew him corrected at school but for talking and diverting other boys from their business. He seemed to learn by intuition; for though indolence and procrastination were inherent in his constitution, whenever he made an exertion he did more than any one else. In short, he

is a memorable instance of what has been often observed, that the boy is the man

© McLeish

The house in Lichfield where Dr. Johnson was born

in miniature; and that the distinguishing characteristics of each individual are the same through the whole course of life. His favourites used to receive very liberal assistance from him; and such was the submission and deference with which he was treated, such the desire to obtain his regard, that three of the boys, of whom Mr. Hector was sometimes one, used to come in the morning as his humble attendants, and carry him to school. One in the middle stooped while he sat upon his back, and one on each side supported him, and thus he was borne triumphant. Such a proof of the early predominance of intellectual vigour is very remarkable, and does honour to human nature.

JOHNSON'S FRIENDS, 1752–1753

His acquaintance with Bennet Langton, Esq., of Langton, in Lincolnshire, another much valued friend, commenced

120 soon after the conclusion of his *Rambler*,* which that gentleman, then a youth, had read with so much admiration, that he came to London chiefly with the view of endeavouring to be introduced to its author. By a fortunate chance he happened to take lodgings in a house where Mr. Levett[1] frequently visited; and having mentioned his wish to his landlady, she introduced him to Mr. Levett, who 130 readily obtained Johnson's permission to bring Mr. Langton to him; as, indeed, Johnson, during the whole course of his life, had no shyness, real or affected, but was easy of access to all who were properly recommended, and even wished to see numbers at his *levee*, as his morning circle of company might, with strict propriety, be called. Mr. Langton was exceedingly surprised when the sage first 140 appeared. He had not received the smallest intimation of his figure, dress, or manner. From perusing his writings, he fancied he should see a decent, well-drest, in short, a remarkably decorous philosopher. Instead of which, down from his bed-chamber, about noon, came, as newly risen, a huge uncouth figure, with a little dark wig which scarcely covered his head, and his clothes hanging loose 150 about him. But his conversation was so rich, so animated, and so forcible, and his religious and political notions so congenial with those in which Langton had been educated, that he conceived for him that veneration and attachment which he ever preserved.

One night when Beauclerk[2] and Langton had supped at a tavern in London, and sat till about three in the morning, 160 it came into their heads to go and knock up Johnson, and see if they could prevail on him to join them in a ramble. They rapped violently at the door of his chambers in the Temple,* till at last he appeared in his shirt, with his little black wig on the top of his head, instead of a nightcap, and a poker in his hand, imagining, probably, that some ruffians were coming to attack him. When he discovered who they were, and was told 170 their errand, he smiled, and with great good humour agreed to their proposal: "What, is it you, you dogs! I'll have a frisk with you." He was soon dressed, and they sallied forth together into Covent-Garden,* where the greengrocers and fruiterers were beginning to arrange their hampers, just come in from the country. Johnson made some attempts to help them; but the honest gardeners 180 stared so at his figure and manner, and odd interference, that he soon saw his services were not relished. They then repaired to one of the neighbouring taverns, and made a bowl of that liquor called *Bishop*,[1] which Johnson had always liked: while, in joyous contempt of sleep, from which he had been roused, he repeated the festive lines,

"Short, O short, then be thy reign,   190
And give us to the world again!"

They did not stay long, but walked down to the Thames, took a boat, and rowed to Billingsgate.* Beauclerk and Johnson were so well pleased with their amusement that they resolved to persevere in dissipation for the rest of the day: but Langton deserted them, being engaged to breakfast with some young ladies. Johnson scolded him for "leav- 200 ing his social friends, to go and sit with a set of wretched *un-idea'd* girls." Garrick being told of this ramble, said to him smartly, "I heard of your frolic, t'other night. You'll be in the *Chronicle*." Upon which Johnson afterwards observed, "*He* durst not do such a thing. His *wife* would not *let* him!"

He entered upon this year, 1753, with

[1] Robert Levett, a man whom Johnson befriended. He was originally a waiter, but learned a little about medicine and practiced among the poor.

[2] One of Johnson's friends and a member of the Literary * Club.

[1] A drink made by mixing port wine, oranges or lemons, and sugar.

210 his usual piety, as appears from the following prayer, which I transcribed from
that part of his diary which he burned a
few days before his death :

"Jan. 1, 1753, *N.S.*,[1] which I shall use
for the future.

"Almighty GOD, who hast continued
my life to this day, grant that, by the assistance of thy Holy Spirit, I may improve the time which thou shalt grant
220 me, to my eternal salvation. Make me
to remember, to thy glory, thy judgments
and thy mercies. Make me so to consider the loss of my wife, whom thou hast
taken from me, that it may dispose me
by thy grace, to lead the residue of my
life in thy fear. Grant this, O LORD, for
JESUS CHRIST'S sake. Amen."

JOHNSON AND GOLDSMITH, 1773

He and Mr. Langton and I went together to the Club,[2] where we found Mr.
230 Burke,[3] Mr. Garrick,[4] and some other
members, and amongst them our friend
Goldsmith,[5] who sat silently brooding
over Johnson's reprimand[6] to him after
dinner. Johnson perceived this, and said
aside to some of us, "I'll make Goldsmith
forgive me"; and then called to him in a
loud voice, "Dr. Goldsmith — something
passed today where you and I dined : I
ask your pardon." Goldsmith answered
240 placidly, "It must be much from you,
Sir, that I take ill." And so at once the
difference was over, and they were on as
easy terms as ever, and Goldsmith rattled
away as usual.

In our way to the club to-night,
when I regretted that Goldsmith would,
upon every occasion, endeavour to shine,
by which he often exposed himself,

[1] *N.S.* New Style; the new Gregorian calendar,
adopted in England about 1752.
[2] See "Literary * Club."
[3] Edmund Burke.*
[4] David Garrick (1717–1779), a famous actor.
[5] For Oliver Goldsmith's biography see page 713.
[6] Goldsmith had suggested that Johnson stop
talking long enough to let someone else speak,
whereupon Johnson called him impertinent.

Mr. Langton observed that he was not
like Addison, who was content with the 250
fame of his writings, and did not aim also
at excellency in conversation, for which
he found himself unfit : and that he said
to a lady who complained of his having
talked little in company, "Madam, I
have but nine-pence in ready money, but
I can draw for a thousand pounds." I
observed that Goldsmith had a great deal
of gold in his cabinet, but not content
with that, was always taking out his 260
purse. JOHNSON. "Yes, Sir, and that so
often an empty purse!"

Goldsmith's incessant desire of being
conspicuous in company was the occasion
of his sometimes appearing to such disadvantage as one should hardly have
supposed possible in a man of his genius.
When his literary reputation had risen
deservedly high, and his society was
much courted, he became very jealous of 270
the extraordinary attention which was
everywhere paid to Johnson. One evening, in a circle of wits, he found fault
with me for talking of Johnson as entitled
to the honour of unquestionable superiority. "Sir, (said he,) you are for making a
monarchy of what should be a republic."

He was still more mortified, when talking in a company with fluent vivacity,
and, as he flattered himself, to the admi- 280
ration of all who were present; a German
who sat next him, and perceived Johnson
rolling himself as if about to speak, suddenly stopped him, saying, "Stay, stay
— Toctor Shonson is going to say something." This was, no doubt, very pro-
voking, especially to one so irritable as
Goldsmith, who frequently mentioned it
with strong expressions of indignation.

It may also be observed that Gold- 290
smith was sometimes content to be
treated with an easy familiarity, but
upon occasions would be consequential
and important. An instance of this occurred in a small particular. Johnson
had a way of contracting the names of his
friends : as Beauclerk, Beau; Boswell,

Bozzy; Langton, Lanky; Murphy, Mur; Sheridan,[1] Sherry. I remember one day, 300 when Tom Davies[2] was telling that Dr. Johnson said, "We are all in labour for a name to *Goldy's* play," Goldsmith seemed displeased that such a liberty should be taken with his name, and said, "I have often desired him not to call me *Goldy*." Tom was remarkably attentive to the most minute circumstance about Johnson. I recollect his telling me once, on my arrival in London, "Sir, our great 310 friend has made an improvement on his appellation of old Mr. Sheridan. He calls him now *Sherry derry*."

Goldsmith was often very fortunate in his witty contests, even when he entered the lists with Johnson himself. Sir Joshua Reynolds[3] was in company with them one day, when Goldsmith said, that he thought he could write a good fable, mentioned the simplicity 320 which that kind of composition requires, and observed, that in most fables the animals introduced seldom talk in character. "For instance," said he, "the fable of the little fishes, who saw birds fly over their heads, and, envying them, petitioned Jupiter* to be changed into birds. The skill," continued he, "consists in making them talk like little fishes." While he indulged himself in this fanciful 330 reverie, he observed Johnson shaking his sides, and laughing. Upon which he smartly proceeded, "Why, Dr. Johnson, this is not so easy as you seem to think: for, if you were to make little fishes talk, they would talk like whales."

TALK AT THE CLUB. 1778

On Friday, April 3, I dined with him[4] in London, in a company where were present several eminent men, whom I shall not name, but distinguish their parts in the conversation by different letters. 340

F.[1] "I have been looking at this famous antique marble dog of Mr. Jennings,[2] valued at a thousand guineas, said to be Alcibiades's[3] dog." JOHNSON. "His tail then must be docked. That was the mark of Alcibiades's dog." E.[4] "A thousand guineas! The representation of no animal whatever is worth so much. At this rate a dead dog would indeed be better than a living lion." JOHN- 350 SON. "Sir, it is not the worth of the thing, but of the skill in forming it, which is so highly estimated. Everything that enlarges the sphere of human powers, that shows man he can do what he thought he could not do, is valuable. The first man who balanced a straw upon his nose; Johnston[5] who rode upon three horses at a time; in short, all such men deserved the applause of mankind, not on account 360 of the use of what they did, but of the dexterity which they exhibited." BOSWELL. "Yet a misapplication of time and assiduity is not to be encouraged. Addison, in one of his *Spectators*,* commends the judgment of a King, who as a suitable reward to a man that by long perseverance had attained to the art of throwing a barley-corn through the eye of a needle, gave him a bushel of barley." 370 JOHNSON. "He must have been a King of Scotland, where barley is scarce." F. "One of the most remarkable antique figures of an animal is the boar at Florence." JOHNSON. "The first boar that is well made in marble, should be preserved as a wonder. When men arrive at a facility of making boars well, then the workmanship is not of such value,

---

[1] Thomas Sheridan, the father of Richard, the dramatist.

[2] A London actor and bookseller, a friend of Johnson's. It was at his shop that Boswell first met Johnson.

[3] A celebrated portrait painter. He lived from 1723 to 1792.   [4] Johnson.

[1] Lord Upper Ossory; his family name was Fitzpatrick.

[2] Henry C. Jennings, a collector of antiques.

[3] According to Plutarch's * *Lives* the Greek politician Alcibiades had a valuable dog whose tail he caused to be cut off.

[4] Edmund Burke.

[5] An Irishman who, in 1762, became well known in London for his feats of horsemanship.

A literary gathering

From left to right: Boswell, Johnson, Reynolds, Garrick, Burke, Paoli, Burney, Warton, Goldsmith

380 but they should however be preserved as examples, and as a greater security for the restoration of the art, should it be lost."

E. "From the experience which I have had — and I have had a great deal — I have learnt to think *better* of mankind." JOHNSON. "From my experience I have found them worse in commercial dealings, more disposed to cheat than I had 390 any notion of; but more disposed to do one another good than I had conceived." J.[1] "Less just and more beneficent." JOHNSON. "And really it is wonderful, considering how much attention is necessary for men to take care of themselves, and ward off immediate evils which press upon them, it is wonderful how much they do for others. As it is said of the greatest liar, that he tells 400 more truth than falsehood; so it may be said of the worst man, that he does more good than evil." BOSWELL. "Perhaps from experience men may be found *happier* than we suppose." JOHNSON. "No, Sir; the more we enquire we shall find men the less happy." P.[2] "As to thinking better or worse of mankind from experience, some cunning people will not be satisfied unless they have put men to the 410 test, as they think. There is a very good story told of Sir Godfrey Kneller,[3] in his character of a justice of the peace. A gentleman brought his servant before him, upon an accusation of having stolen some money from him; but it having come out that he had laid it purposely in the servant's way in order to try his honesty, Sir Godfrey sent the master to prison." JOHNSON. "To resist tempta-120 tion once is not a sufficient proof of hon-

esty. If a servant, indeed, were to resist the continued temptation of silver lying in a window, as some people let it lie, when he is sure his master does not know how much there is of it, he would give a strong proof of honesty. But this is a proof to which you have no right to put a man. You know, humanly speaking, there is a certain degree of temptation which will overcome any virtue. Now, in 430 so far as you approach temptation to a man, you do him an injury; and, if he is overcome, you share his guilt."

Discussion Hints

1. What traits of Johnson's character are illustrated in the selections from Boswell's *Life of Johnson*? Compare them with the traits given in the biography of Johnson on page 707.

2. What evidence do you find of Johnson's humor?

3. Judging by the selections given here, why do you think Boswell admired Johnson?

4. Point out some of the details that seem to justify the claim that Boswell's *Life of Johnson* is a remarkably detailed biography.

5. What did Goldsmith mean when he charged Boswell with wishing to make "a monarchy of what should be a republic" (p. 247, ll. 276–277)?

6. What bearing on Johnson's literary style has the story about the little fishes (p. 248, ll. 324–335)?

7. Do you find in the selections any evidence of Johnson's fondness for long words?

8. What would we think today of Johnson's ideas of educating children?

9. Judging by what you read here, what was Boswell's attitude toward Goldsmith?

Suggestions for Reading

There are numerous editions of Boswell's *Life of Johnson* or of selections from it. Suitable selections are given in *Everybody's Boswell*. Dodd, Mead & Company, Inc.

---

[1] Probably Sir Joshua Reynolds.
[2] Probably Edward Gibbon (1737–1794), a famous historian, best known for his *History of the Decline and Fall of the Roman Empire*.
[3] A famous portrait painter (1646–1723) of the time of Charles II.

LETTERS

IN THESE days of telephones, telegraphs, rapid transit, radio, hurry, and bustle few of us feel the need of giving much time or attention to the composition of letters. In fact, letter-writing is sometimes referred to as one of the lost arts. It is therefore interesting to see what sort of letters people sent to each other two centuries ago, when communication was difficult and postage expensive, and when men and women made more of letter-writing than we do now. The following letters, written more than a century and a half ago, might serve in at least one respect as a model to those of us who write letters today: they say what they have to say in clear, simple English.

SAMUEL JOHNSON[1] (1709–1784)

To the Right Honourable the Earl of Chesterfield

Johnson, just before beginning his *Dictionary* (see page 243), appealed to the Earl of Chesterfield[2] for his patronage, but the earl contemptuously refused his support. When, after seven years, Chesterfield saw that Johnson was about to succeed in his great undertaking, he let it be known that he would be glad to have the book dedicated to him. The result was Johnson's famous letter, which may be called the declaration of independence of English literature from the institution of patronage (see "patron" *).

February 7, 1755

My Lord,

I have lately been informed, by the proprietor of *The World*, that two papers, in which my Dictionary is recommended to the public, were written by your Lordship. To be so distinguished, is an honour, which, being very little accustomed to favours from the great, I know not 10 well how to receive, or in what terms to acknowledge.

When, upon some slight encourage-

ment, I first visited your Lordship, I was overpowered, like the rest of mankind, by the enchantment of your address;[1] and could not forbear to wish that I might boast myself *Le vainqueur du vainqueur de la terre*;[2] — that I might obtain that regard for which I saw the world contending; but I found my attendance 20 so little encouraged, that neither pride nor modesty would suffer me to continue it. When I had once addressed your Lordship in public, I had exhausted all the art of pleasing which a retired and uncourtly[3] scholar can possess. I had done all that I could; and no man is well pleased to have his all neglected, be it ever so little.

Seven years, my Lord, have now past 30 since I waited in your outward rooms,[4] or was repulsed from your door; during

1 *enchantment . . . address.* Your charm of manner.
2 *Le vainqueur . . . terre.* "The conqueror of the conqueror of the earth."
3 Unaccustomed to the ways of courts.
4 See illustration on page 252.

1 For biography see page 707.
2 For biography see page 708.

National Gallery

Johnson waiting in the Earl of Chesterfield's antechamber

which time I have been pushing on my work through difficulties, of which it is useless to complain, and have brought it, at last, to the verge of publication, without one act of assistance, one word of encouragement, or one smile of favour. Such treatment I did not expect, for I 40 never had a Patron* before.

The shepherd in Virgil grew at last acquainted with Love, and found him a native of the rocks.

Is not a Patron, my Lord, one who looks with unconcern on a man struggling for life in the water, and, when he has reached ground, encumbers him with help?[1] The notice which you have been pleased to take of my labours, had it 50 been early, had been kind; but it has been delayed till I am indifferent, and cannot

[1] *Is not ... help?* Note the biting irony* of this sentence.

enjoy it; till I am solitary, and cannot impart it; till I am known, and do not want it. I hope it is no very cynical asperity not to confess obligations where no benefit has been received, or to be unwilling that the Public should consider me as owing that to a Patron, which Providence has enabled me to do for myself. 60

Having carried on my work thus far with so little obligation to any favourer of learning, I shall not be disappointed though I should conclude it, if less be possible, with less; for I have been long wakened from that dream of hope, in which I once boasted myself with so much exultation,

My Lord,

Your Lordship's most humble 70

Most obedient servant,

Sam. Johnson

THE EARL OF CHESTERFIELD[1] (1694-1773)

From a Letter to His Son, Philip Stanhope

The following letter is one of many written by the famous Earl of Chesterfield to his son. Chesterfield's letters reflect the cold and calculating personality of the writer, but they are still read and admired because of their elegant and graceful style and because of the practical advice scattered through their pages. Lord Chesterfield's low estimate of women should not be taken as representing the best opinion of his day.

September 5, 1748

Dear Boy,

As women are a considerable, or at least a pretty numerous, part of company, and as their suffrages[2] go a great way toward establishing a man's character in the fashionable part of the world — which is of great importance to the fortune and figure he proposes to make in it
10 — it is necessary to please them. I will therefore, upon this subject, let you into certain *arcana*,[3] that will be very useful for you to know, but which you must with the utmost care conceal, and never seem to know. Women, then, are only children of a larger growth; they have an entertaining tattle and sometimes wit, but for solid, reasoning good sense, I never in my life knew one that had it,
20 or acted consequentially[4] for four-and-twenty hours together. Some little passion or humour always breaks in upon their best resolutions. Their beauty neglected or controverted, their age increased, or their supposed understandings depreciated instantly kindles their little passions, and overturns any system of consequential conduct that in their most reasonable moments they might have

[1] For biography see page 708.
[2] Votes, opinions.
[3] Secrets.
[4] Logically.

been capable of forming. A man of sense 30 only trifles with them, plays with them, humours and flatters them, as he does with a sprightly, forward child; but he neither consults them about, nor trusts them with, serious matters, though he often makes them believe that he does both — which is the thing in the world that they are proud of; for they love mightily to be dabbling in business — which, by the way, they always spoil — 40 and, being justly distrustful that men in general look upon them in a trifling light, they almost adore that man who talks more seriously to them, and who seems to consult them — I say, who seems, for weak men really do, but wise ones only seem to do it. No flattery is either too high or too low for them. They will greedily swallow the highest, and gratefully accept of the lowest; and you may 50 safely flatter any woman, from her understanding down to the exquisite taste of her fan. Women who are either indisputably beautiful or indisputably ugly are best flattered upon the score of their understandings; but those who are in a state of mediocrity are best flattered upon their beauty, or at least their graces; for every woman who is not absolutely ugly thinks herself handsome, 60 but, not hearing often that she is so, is the more grateful and the more obliged to the few who tell her so; whereas a decided and conscious beauty looks upon every tribute paid to her beauty only as her due, but wants to shine and to be considered on the side of her understanding; and a woman who is ugly enough to know that she is so, knows that she has nothing left but her understanding, which 70 is consequently — and probably in more senses than one — her weak side.

But these are secrets that you must keep inviolably, if you would not, like Orpheus,* be torn to pieces by the whole sex. On the contrary, a man who thinks of living in the great world must be gallant, polite, and attentive to please the women. They have, from the weakness of men, more or less influence in all courts; they absolutely stamp every

80

man's character in the *beau monde*,[1] and make it either current or cry it down and stop it in payments. It is, therefore, absolutely necessary to manage, please, and flatter them, and never to discover the least marks of contempt, which is what they never forgive. Adieu.

[1] *beau monde*. Fashionable world.

ESSAYS[1]

RICHARD STEELE[2] (1672–1729)

Addison[3] and Steele should be remembered together as the originators of the familiar essay in English literature. Their essays appeared in several early periodicals or newspapers, of which the most important were *The Tatler** and *The Spectator.** Taking for their theme any subject that might interest the great rising middle class (see page 220), they wrote charmingly of manners, morals, literature, and many other subjects. Sometimes they satirize* existing customs or opinions, but their humor is kindly, and their advice is practical and homely. In an age when dishonesty, brutality, and bad manners were common, Addison and Steele did a great service to their fellow men by teaching the value of honesty, geniality, and politeness.

The Spectator's Club[4]

[From *The Sir Roger de Coverley Papers*]

Along with numerous disconnected essays on various subjects, a number of *The Spectator* papers describe the doings of an imaginary society more or less like the many clubs[5] which formed the centers of political and social life in London during the early eighteenth century. In this way the famous *Sir Roger de Coverley Papers* came into existence. In the imaginary character of Sir Andrew Freeport the authors found a convenient means of expressing their views on the commercial life of the time; Will Honeycomb represents fashion and society; other members stand for the law, the church, and military life, the country gentry being depicted in the benevolent, patriotic, prejudiced, lovable old knight Sir Roger de Coverley. The *Sir Roger de Coverley Papers* give an excellent view of English life during the early eighteenth century.

Aside from their value as essays on manners, they helped to lay the foundation for the modern novel by the fact that they present in the form of a continuous story characters and settings drawn from real life.

*Ast alii sex
Et plures uno conclamant ore.*[1]

JUVENAL

THE first of our society[2] is a gentleman of Worcestershire, of ancient descent, a baronet, his name Sir Roger de Coverley. His great-grandfather was inventor of that famous country-dance which is called after him.[3] All who know that shire are very well acquainted with the parts and merits of Sir Roger. He is a 10 gentleman that is very singular in his behaviour, but his singularities proceed from his good sense, and are contradictions to the manners of the world only as he thinks the world is in the wrong. However, this humour[4] creates him no ene-

---

[1] For discussion of the essay see page 173.
[2] For biography see page 709.
[3] For biography see page 709.
[4] Discussion hints on *The Sir Roger de Coverley Papers* are grouped together on page 263.*
[5] See "Literary* Club" and "coffeehouses."*

[1] "But six others and more cry out with one voice."
[2] The group that met at some particular coffeehouse.*
[3] "Sir Roger de Coverley" is the name of an English dance corresponding to the Virginia reel.
[4] Peculiarity, or oddity, of character or behavior.

255

mies, for he does nothing with sourness or obstinacy; and his being unconfined to modes and forms, makes him but the readier and more capable to please and oblige all who know him. When he is in town, he lives in Soho Square.[1] It is said he keeps himself a bachelor by reason he was crossed in love by a perverse, beautiful widow of the next county to him. Before this disappointment, Sir Roger was what you call a fine gentleman; had often supped with my Lord Rochester[2] and Sir George Etherege,[3] fought a duel upon his first coming to town, and kicked Bully Dawson[4] in a public coffee-house for calling him "youngster." But being ill-used by the above-mentioned widow, he was very serious for a year and a half; and though, his temper being naturally jovial, he at last got over it, he grew careless of himself, and never dressed afterwards. He continues to wear a coat and doublet of the same cut that were in fashion at the time of his repulse, which, in his merry humours, he tells us, has been in and out twelve times since he first wore it. He is now in his fifty-sixth year, cheerful, gay, and hearty; keeps a good house in both town and country; a great lover of mankind; but there is such a mirthful cast in his behaviour that he is rather beloved than esteemed. His tenants grow rich, his servants look satisfied, all the young women profess love to him, and the young men are glad of his company. When he comes into a house, he calls the servants by their names, and talks all the way up-stairs to a visit. I must not omit that Sir Roger is a justice of the quorum;[5] that he fills the chair at a quarter session[6] with great abilities; and, three months ago, gained universal applause by explaining a passage in the Game Act.[1]

The gentleman next in esteem and authority among us is another bachelor, who is a member of the Inner Temple[*2]; a man of great probity, wit, and understanding; but he has chosen his place of residence rather to obey the direction of an old humoursome[3] father, than in pursuit of his own inclinations. He was placed there to study the laws of the land, and is the most learned of any of the house in those of the stage. Aristotle[*] and Longinus[4] are much better understood by him than Littleton or Coke.[5] The father sends up, every post, questions relating to marriage-articles, leases, and tenures, in the neighbourhood; all which questions he agrees with an attorney to answer and take care of in the lump. He is studying the passions themselves, when he should be inquiring into the debates among men which arise from them. He knows the argument of each of the orations of Demosthenes[6] and Tully[7] but not one case in the reports of our own courts. No one ever took him for a fool, but none, except his intimate friends, know he has a great deal of wit.[8] This turn makes him at once both disinterested and agreeable; as few of his thoughts are drawn from business, they are most of them fit for conversation. His taste of[9] books is a little too just for the age he lives in; he has read all, but approves of very few.

[1] *Game Act.* A law regulating the hunting of game. The author implies, with mild sarcasm, that to explain the Game Act required more than ordinary ability.

[2] One of the four societies of law students and lawyers in London; also one of the buildings where the members of the society have their chambers.

[3] Eccentric, whimsical.

[4] A Greek philosopher and literary critic.

[5] *Littleton ... Coke.* Sir Thomas Littleton (1422–1481) and Sir Edward Coke (1552–1634), famous authorities on English law.

[6] A famous Greek orator.

[7] Cicero.[*]

[8] Intellectual acuteness.

[9] In.

[1] A section of London fashionable in Steele's day.

[2] A noted wit, a friend of Charles II.

[3] A famous dramatist of the Restoration Period.

[4] A well-known sharper and bully of the time.

[5] *justice of the quorum.* A county judge; hence a man of importance.

[6] *quarter session.* The general criminal court of the county, which met quarterly.

His familiarity with the customs, manners, actions, and writings of the ancients makes him a very delicate observer of what occurs to him[1] in the present world. He is an excellent critic, and the time of the play is his hour of business; exactly 100 at five he passes through New Inn,[2] crosses through Russell Court, and takes a turn at Will's[3] till the play begins;[4] he has his shoes rubbed and his periwig powdered at the barber's as you go into the Rose.[5] It is for the good of the audience when he is at a play, for the actors have an ambition to please him.

The person of next consideration is Sir Andrew Freeport, a merchant of great 110 eminence in the city of London; a person of indefatigable industry, strong reason, and great experience. His notions of trade are noble and generous, and — as every rich man has usually some sly way of jesting which would make no great figure were he not a rich man — he calls the sea the British Common. He is acquainted with commerce in all its parts, and will tell you that it is a stupid and 120 barbarous way to extend dominion by arms; for true power is to be got by arts and industry. He will often argue that if this part of our trade were well cultivated, we should gain from one nation;· and if another, from another.[6] I have heard him prove that diligence makes more lasting acquisitions than valour, and that sloth has ruined more nations than the sword. He abounds in several fru-130 gal maxims, amongst which the greatest

favourite is, "A penny saved is a penny got." A general trader of good sense is pleasanter company than a general scholar; and Sir Andrew having a natural, unaffected eloquence, the perspicuity of his discourse gives the same pleasure that wit would in another man. He has made his fortunes himself, and says that England may be richer than other kingdoms by as plain methods as he him-140 self is richer than other men; though at the same time I can say this of him, that there is not a point in the compass but blows home a ship in which he is an owner.

Next to Sir Andrew in the club-room sits Captain Sentry, a gentleman of great courage, good understanding, but invincible modesty. He is one of those that deserve very well, but are very awkward 150 at putting their talents within the observation of such as should take notice of them. He was some years a captain, and behaved himself with great gallantry in several engagements and at several sieges; but having a small estate of his own, and being next heir to Sir Roger, he has quitted a way of life in which no man can rise suitably to his merit who is not something of a courtier as well as a sol-160 dier. I have heard him often lament that in a profession where merit is placed in so conspicuous a view, impudence should get the better of modesty. When he has talked to this purpose I never heard him make a sour expression, but frankly confess that he left the world because he was not fit for it. A strict honesty and an even, regular behaviour are in themselves obstacles to him that must press through 170 crowds who endeavour at the same end with himself — the favour of a commander. He will, however, in this way of talk, excuse generals for not disposing according to men's desert, or enquiring into it. "For," says he, "that great man who has a mind to help me, has as many to break through to come at me as I have to come at him"; therefore he will con-

[1] *occurs to him.* Comes before him.
[2] A building where law students and lawyers had their chambers.
[3] A famous coffeehouse. See "coffeehouses."*
[4] *till . . . begins.* In Steele's day theatrical performances usually began about five o'clock in the afternoon; people who wished to be regarded as fashionable generally entered the theater late.
[5] A noted London tavern which stood near Drury Lane Theater.
[6] *if another, from another.* If another part of our trade were well cultivated, we should gain from another nation.

D

180 clude that the man who would make a figure, especially in a military way, must get over all false modesty, and assist his patron against the importunity of other pretenders by a proper assurance in his own vindication.[1] He says it is a civil cowardice to be backward in asserting what you ought to expect, as it is a military fear to be slow in attacking when it is your duty. With this candour does 190 the gentleman speak of himself and others. The same frankness runs through all his conversation. The military part of his life has furnished him with many adventures, in the relation of which he is very agreeable to the company; for he is never overbearing, though accustomed to command men in the utmost degree below him; nor ever too obsequious from an habit of obeying men 200 highly above him.

But that our society may not appear a set of humorists[2] unacquainted with the gallantries and pleasures of the age, we have among us the gallant Will Honeycomb, a gentleman who, according to his years, should be in the decline of his life, but having ever been very careful of his person, and always had a very easy fortune, time has made but very little 210 impression either by wrinkles on his forehead or traces in his brain. His person is well turned and of a good height. He is very ready at that sort of discourse with which men usually entertain women. He has all his life dressed very well, and remembers habits[3] as others do men. He can smile when one speaks to him, and laughs easily. He knows the history of every mode,[4] and can inform you from 220 which of the French king's wenches our wives and daughters had this manner of curling their hair, that way of placing their hoods; and whose vanity to show her foot made that part of the dress so short in such a year. In a word, all his conversation and knowledge has been in the female world. As other men of his age will take notice to you[1] what such a minister said upon such and such an occasion, he will tell you when the Duke 230 of Monmouth[2] danced at court such a woman was then smitten, another was taken with him[3] at the head of his troop in the Park.[4] In all these important relations, he has ever about the same time received a kind glance or a blow of a fan from some celebrated beauty, mother of the present Lord Such-a-one.[5] If you speak of a young commoner that said a lively thing in the House, he starts up: 240 "He has good blood in his veins; that young fellow's mother used me more like a dog than any woman I ever made advances to." This way of talking of his very much enlivens the conversation among us of a more sedate turn; and I find there is not one of the company but myself, who rarely speak at all, but speaks of him as of that sort of man who is usually called a well-bred, fine gentle- 250 man.[6] To conclude his character, where women are not concerned he is an honest, worthy man.

I cannot tell whether I am to account him whom I am next to speak of as one of our company, for he visits us but seldom; but when he does, it adds to every man else a new enjoyment of himself. He is a clergyman, a very philosophic man, of general learning, great 260 sanctity of life, and the most exact good breeding. He has the misfortune to be of a very weak constitution, and con-

---

[1] *in . . . vindication.* In pressing his claims.
[2] Freaks, peculiar fellows.
[3] Clothes.
[4] Style.

[1] *will . . . you.* Will call your attention to.
[2] A son of Charles II, noted for his bad morals and his good looks.
[3] *was taken with him.* Fell in love with him.
[4] Probably the parade ground in Hyde Park, a fashionable suburb of London in Steele's day.
[5] *In all these . . . Lord Such-a-one.* When telling these things he recounts his own imaginary flirtations.
[6] *a well-bred, fine gentleman.* Many fashionable men of Steele's day had moral standards that were low.

sequently cannot accept of such cares and business as preferments[1] in his function would oblige him to; he is therefore among divines what a chamber-counsellor[2] is among lawyers. The probity of his mind and the integrity of his life 270 create him followers, as being eloquent or loud advances others. He seldom introduces the subject he speaks upon; but

we are so far gone in years that he observes, when he is among us, an earnestness to have him fall on[1] some divine topic,[2] which he always treats with much authority, as one who has no interests in this world, as one who is hastening to the object of all his wishes, and conceives hope from his decays and infirmities. 280 These are my ordinary companions.

The Coverley Household

[From *The Sir Roger de Coverley Papers*]

A greater sense of responsibility on the part of the upper classes and a more tolerant attitude toward the lower classes grew up in England during the eighteenth century. It is this new social spirit that Steele seeks to impress upon his readers in his delightful essay on the Coverley household.

Aesopo ingentem statuam posuere Attici
Servumque collocarunt aeterna in basi,
Patere honoris scirent ut cuncti viam.[3]

PHAEDRUS

THE reception, manner of attendance, undisturbed freedom and quiet, which I meet with here in the country, has confirmed me in the opinion I always had, that the general corruption of manners in servants is owing to the conduct 10 of masters.[4] The aspect of every one in the family carries so much satisfaction that it appears he knows the happy lot which has befallen him in being a member of it. There is one particular which I

have seldom seen but at Sir Roger's: it is usual in all other places that servants fly from the parts of the house through which their master is passing; on the contrary, here, they industriously place themselves in his way; and it is on both 20 sides, as it were, understood as a visit, when the servants appear without calling. This proceeds from the humane and equal temper of the man of the house, who also perfectly well knows how to enjoy a great estate with such economy as ever to be much beforehand. This makes his own mind untroubled, and consequently unapt to vent peevish expressions, or give passionate or inconsistent orders to those 30 about him. Thus respect and love go together; and a certain cheerfulness in performance of their duty is the particular distinction of the lower part of this family. When a servant is called before his master, he does not come with an expectation to hear himself rated for some trivial fault, threatened to be stripped, or used with any other unbecoming language, which mean masters 40 often give to worthy servants: but it is often to know what road he took that he came so readily back according to order; whether he passed by such a ground; if the old man who rents it is

---

[1] A preferment is a superior position, especially, as here, in the church.
[2] A lawyer who gives advice only in private.
[3] "The Athenians erected a large statue to Aesop,* and placed him, though a slave, on a lasting pedestal, to show that the way of honor lies open to all."
[4] *conduct of masters.* One of our most trustworthy historians tells us that during the early eighteenth century servants were, as a rule, "treated like dogs by their masters, and were caned mercilessly for trivial faults."

[1] *fall on.* Happen upon.
[2] *divine topic.* A subject connected with religion.

in good health; or whether he gave Sir Roger's love to him, or the like.

A man who preserves a respect founded on his benevolence to his dependents lives
50 rather like a prince than a master in his family; his orders are received as favours, rather than duties; and the distinction of approaching him is part of the reward for executing what is commanded by him.

There is another circumstance in which my friend excels in his management, which is the manner of rewarding his servants. He has ever been of opinion that giving his cast[1] clothes to be
60 worn by valets has a very ill effect upon little minds, and creates a silly sense of equality between the parties, in persons affected only with outward things. I have heard him often pleasant on this occasion,[2] and describe a young gentleman abusing his man in that coat which a month or two before was the most pleasing distinction he was conscious of in himself. He would turn his discourse
70 still more pleasantly upon the ladies' bounties of this kind; and I have heard him say he knew a fine woman who distributed rewards and punishments in giving becoming or unbecoming dresses to her maids.

But my good friend is above these little instances of good-will, in bestowing only trifles on his servants; a good servant to him is sure of having it in his choice
80 very soon of being no servant at all. As I before observed, he is so good an husband,[3] and knows so thoroughly that the skill of the purse is the cardinal virtue of this life, — I say, he knows so well that frugality is the support of generosity, that he can often spare a large fine when a tenement falls, and give that settlement to a good servant who has a mind to go into the world, or make a stranger
90 pay the fine to that servant, for his more

[1] Cast off.
[2] *heard . . . occasion* Often heard him crack jokes on this subject.
[3] *so . . . husband.* So economical.

comfortable maintenance, if he stays in his service.[1]

A man of honour and generosity considers it would be miserable to himself to have no will but that of another, though it were of the best person breathing, and for that reason goes on as fast as he is able to put his servants into independent livelihoods. The greatest part of Sir Roger's estate is tenanted by persons 100 who have served himself or his ancestors. It was to me extremely pleasant to observe the visitants from several parts to welcome his arrival into the country; and all the difference that I could take notice of between the late servants who came to see him and those who stayed in the family, was that these latter were looked upon as finer gentlemen and better courtiers. 110

This manumission[2] and placing them in a way of livelihood I look upon as only what is due to a good servant, which encouragement will make his successor be as diligent, as humble, and as ready as he was. There is something wonderful in the narrowness of those minds which can be pleased, and be barren of bounty to those who please them.

One might, on this occasion, recount 120 the sense that great persons in all ages have had of the merit of their dependants, and the heroic services which men have done their masters in the extremity of their fortunes, and shown to their undone[3] patrons that fortune was all the difference between them; but as I design this my speculation only as a gentle admonition to thankless masters, I shall not go out of the occurrences of common 130 life, but assert it, as a general observa-

[1] *he can . . . service.* A fine was a fee paid to the owner of a piece of property when a lease changed hands ("a tenement falls"). The author means that in such a case Sir Roger can afford either to give the property to a good servant who wants to make his way in the world or he can give to his servant the fee paid by the stranger who takes the lease, if the servant would rather stay in his employ.
[2] Liberation, emancipation.   [3] Ruined.

tion, that I never saw, but in Sir Roger's family and one or two more, good servants treated as they ought to be. Sir Roger's kindness extends to their children's children, and this very morning he sent his coachman's grandson to prentice.[1] I shall conclude this paper with an account of a picture in his gallery, where 140 there are many which will deserve my future observation.

At the very upper end of this handsome structure I saw the protraiture of two young men standing in a river, — the one naked, the other in a livery. The person supported seemed half dead, but still so much alive as to show in his face exquisite joy and love towards the other. I thought the fainting figure resembled 150 my friend Sir Roger; and, looking at the butler, who stood by me, for an account of it, he informed me that the person in

the livery was a servant of Sir Roger's, who stood on the shore while his master was swimming, and observing him taken with some sudden illness, and sink under water, jumped in and saved him. He told me Sir Roger took off the dress[1] he was in as soon as he came home, and by a great bounty at that time, followed by 160 his favour ever since, had made him master of that pretty seat[2] which we saw at a distance as we came to this house. I remembered indeed Sir Roger said there lived a very worthy gentleman, to whom he was highly obliged, without mentioning anything further. Upon my looking a little dissatisfied at some part of the picture, my attendant informed me that it was against Sir Roger's will, and at the 170 earnest request of the gentleman himself, that he was drawn in the habit[3] in which he had saved his master.

JOSEPH ADDISON[2] (1672–1719)

Sir Roger at Church

[From *The Sir Roger de Coverley Papers*]

Like the essays of Steele, Addison's contributions to *The Spectator** consisted partly of disconnected essays, partly of papers dealing with Sir Roger de Coverley. Addison's essays mark a new era in English prose. Gone are the laborious, clumsy sentences of most earlier English prose. Gone also is the old excessively involved, confusing phraseology. Far less common are the quotations from Greek and Latin, though Addison, like his educated contemporaries, was a great admirer of Greek and Roman literature. Simple and straightforward, yet dignified in vocabulary and phraseology, Addison's prose style has been a model of good English for more than two hundred years. Instead of making bitter attacks on the faults of his age, he gives his readers kindly humor and pleasant instruction in manners and morals. He laughs at himself and at his contemporaries as reflected in

Sir Roger and his associates, but his satire* is never ill-natured. He writes of eighteenth-century England, and he finds his world a pretty good place to live in.

In order to appreciate the contrast between the usual situation in the English Church of Addison's day and the idealized picture given in "Sir Roger at Church," we should remember one or two important facts. The Church of England was a powerful institution, closely connected not only with the religious life of the nation, but also with its social and political life. Every tenant of a landlord such as Sir Roger was required to pay tithes; that is, contribute one tenth of his produce to the support of the church. The landlord had the right to appoint the minister who cared for the spiritual welfare of his tenants. Many landlords paid little regard to the religious life of their tenants, quarreled with the parson.

[1] *to prentice.* To a position as apprentice to a master who would teach him a trade.
[2] For biography see page 709.

[1] Livery.
[2] Dwelling and the surrounding grounds.
[3] Dress, livery.

or treated their private chaplains as mere servants.

'Αθανάτους μὲν πρῶτα θεοὺς, νόμῳ ὡς διάκειται, Τίμα.[1]   PYTHAGORAS

I AM always very well pleased with a country Sunday, and think, if keeping holy the seventh day were only a human institution, it would be the best method that could have been thought of for the polishing and civilizing of mankind. It is certain the country people
10 would soon degenerate into a kind of savages and barbarians, were there not such frequent returns of a stated time, in which the whole village meet together with their best faces, and in their cleanliest habits,[2] to converse with one another upon indifferent[3] subjects, hear their duties explained to them, and join together in adoration of the Supreme Being. Sunday clears away the rust of
20 the whole week, not only as it refreshes in their minds the notions of religion, but as it puts both the sexes upon[4] appearing in their most agreeable forms, and exerting all such qualities as are apt to give them a figure in the eye of the village. A country fellow distinguishes himself as much in the churchyard, as a citizen does upon the 'Change,[5] the whole parish-politics being generally discussed in that
30 place either after sermon or before the bell rings.

My friend Sir Roger, being a good churchman, has beautified the inside of his church with several texts of his own choosing. He has likewise given a handsome pulpit-cloth, and railed in the communion-table at his own expense. He has often told me, that at his coming to his estate he found his parishioners very
40 irregular; and that in order to make

1 "First, in obedience to thy country's laws,
   Worship the immortal gods."
2 Clothes.
3 Various.
4 *puts . . . upon.* Makes both sexes desirous of.
5 *upon the 'Change.* In the Exchange; that is, in business.

them kneel and join in the responses, he gave every one of them a hassock and a common prayer-book; and at the same time employed an itinerant singing-master, who goes about the country for that purpose, to instruct them rightly in the tunes of the psalms: upon which they now very much value themselves, and indeed outdo most of the country churches that I have ever heard.   50

As Sir Roger is landlord to the whole congregation, he keeps them in very good order, and will suffer nobody to sleep in it besides himself; for if by chance he has been surprised into a short nap at sermon, upon recovering out of it he stands up and looks about him, and if he sees anybody else nodding, either wakes them himself, or sends his servant to them. Several other of the old knight's 60 peculiarities break out upon these occasions. Sometimes he will be lengthening out[1] a verse in the singing of psalms, half a minute after the rest of the congregation have done with it; sometimes when he is pleased with the matter of his devotion, he pronounces Amen three or four times to the same prayer: and sometimes stands up when everybody else is upon their knees, to count the congregation, or 70 see if any of his tenants are missing.

I was yesterday very much surprised to hear my old friend in the midst of the service calling out to one John Matthews to mind what he was about, and not disturb the congregation. This John Matthews it seems is remarkable for being an idle fellow, and at that time was kicking his heels for his diversion. This authority of the knight, though exerted in that 80 odd manner which accompanies him in all circumstances of life, has a very good effect upon the parish, who are not polite[2] enough to see anything ridiculous in his behaviour; besides that the general good sense and worthiness of his character make his friends observe these little sin-

1 *lengthening out.* Continuing to sing.
2 Well taught, polished.

gularities as foils that rather set off than blemish his good qualities.

90 As soon as the sermon is finished, nobody presumes to stir till Sir Roger is gone out of the church. The knight walks down from his seat in the chancel between a double row of his tenants, that stand bowing to him on each side: and every now and then inquires how such an one's wife, or mother, or son, or father do, whom he does not see at church; which is understood as a secret repri-
100 mand to the person that is absent.

The chaplain has often told me, that upon a catechising day, when Sir Roger has been pleased with a boy that answers well, he has ordered a Bible to be given him next day for his encouragement; and sometimes accompanies it with a flitch[1] of bacon to his mother. Sir Roger has likewise added five pounds a year to the clerk's[2] place[3]; and, that he may encour-
110 age the young fellows to make themselves perfect in the church service, has promised upon the death of the present incumbent, who is very old, to bestow it according to merit.

The fair understanding between Sir Roger and his chaplain, and their mutual concurrence in doing good, is the more remarkable, because the very next village is famous for the differences and con-
120 tentions that rise between the parson and the squire, who live in a perpetual state of war. The parson is always preaching at the squire; and the squire, to be revenged on the parson, never comes to church. The squire has made all his tenants atheists and tithe-stealers[4]; while the parson instructs them every Sunday in the dignity of his order, and insinuates to them almost in every sermon that he is
130 a better man than his patron. In short,

matters are come to such an extremity, that the squire has not said his prayers either in public or private this half year; and that the parson threatens him, if he does not mend his manners, to pray for him in the face of the whole congregation.

Feuds of this nature, though too frequent in the country, are very fatal[1] to the ordinary people; who are so used to be dazzled with riches, that they pay as 140 much deference to the understanding of a man of an estate, as of a man of learning; and are very hardly brought to regard any truth, how important soever it may be, that is preached to them, when they know there are several men of five hundred[2] a year who do not believe it.

Discussion Hints

The Spectator's Club

1. The members of the club represent the chief groups, or classes, of English polite society during the early eighteenth century. If you were describing an imaginary club representing the various professions and classes of well-to-do American life today, would you include any professions or classes not represented in the club described by Steele?

2. After reading the account of Sir Andrew Freeport, write a theme of two hundred words describing a big-business man of today.

3. Remembering that in England a "common" is a tract of land belonging, not to any one individual, but to the whole community, what do you think Sir Andrew Freeport means when he calls the sea "the British Common" (p. 257, l. 117)?

4. What is Sir Andrew Freeport's attitude toward war?

5. What are Captain Sentry's views on getting ahead in the world?

6. Have you ever heard the proverb "A penny saved is a penny got" (p. 257, ll. 131–132) expressed in any other form?

7. Make an outline showing the structure of the essay.

---

[1] Side.

[2] A clerk was a member of the church appointed to read the responses and assist in other ways in the church service.

[3] Here, the salary that went with the place, or position, of clerk.

[4] Persons who neglect to pay their church dues.

---

[1] Damaging.

[2] *of . . . hundred.* With an income of five hundred pounds ($2500) a year, the equivalent of about $10,000 now.

The Coverley Household

1. What lesson is implied in this essay?

2. Do you agree with the opinion expressed in the first sentence? Give reasons for your answer.

3. What is meant by "it would be miserable . . . another" (p. 260, ll. 94–95)?

4. Why did Sir Roger's former servant wish to be "drawn in the habit in which he had saved his master" (p. 261, ll. 172–173)? Why did Sir Roger object?

Sir Roger at Church

1. What lesson is implied in this essay?

2. What are the reasons assigned in the first paragraph for attending church? Can you add any others?

3. If an author of today had written "everybody else is upon their knees" (p. 262, ll. 69–70), what should you say of the grammar?

4. What means does Sir Roger use to make churchgoing attractive? Would the same means probably be effective today?

General Questions on "The Sir Roger de Coverley Papers"

1. Write a two-hundred-word character sketch of Sir Roger.

2. Imitating as nearly as you can the manner of *The Spectator*, write an essay in which Sir Roger visits some place or scene of the present day, such as a summer resort, a large city, an automobile show, or a fair.

3. What is Sir Roger's most marked trait? Do his peculiarities add to the general impression or detract from it?

4. Sir Roger is a Tory*; Sir Andrew Freeport is a Whig.* Do you find any indications of these facts in the essays?

5. Do you find in the essays any evidence of plot, character portrayal, and setting; that is, anything that makes them look like chapters in a novel?

6. Find examples of words or phrases now obsolete.

7. The name "Captain Sentry" suggests the fact that this personage belongs to the military profession. Do the names of any other personages in the essays suggest their occupations or personal peculiarities?

THE NOVEL

DANIEL DEFOE[1] (1661?–1731)

From *Robinson Crusoe*

Robinson Crusoe, by Daniel Defoe, is one of the most remarkable books ever written. At the time of its composition the author was known chiefly as a clever and unscrupulous political agent and journalist; yet his book was astonishingly popular in its own day, it has been read and enjoyed by hundreds of thousands of readers since then, it is still the delight of old and young in all English-speaking countries, and it has been translated into most of the languages of the civilized world. It owes its widespread fame to various features, of which the following are especially important. (1) It answers a question of universal interest; namely, How would a man fare if thrown entirely upon his own resources, without human companionship and without the conveniences of civilization? In *Robinson Crusoe* we see an uneducated adventurer, weak and alone, struggle successfully against the pitiless forces of nature in a far-off uninhabited island, and we watch with breathless interest to find out how, solely by his wits, he solves one by one the problems upon which his very life depends. Each time he succeeds, we say to ourselves, "Would *I* have thought of that?" (2) Like others of Defoe's writings, *Robinson Crusoe* illustrates the author's skill in giving to pure fiction the impression of undoubted fact. He represents Crusoe as telling his own story, and he introduces many circumstantial details which help to persuade us for the moment that the events really happened. Though the narrative is based to a slight extent upon the experiences of adventurers such as Alexander Selkirk,* essentially it is almost entirely the work of Defoe's powerful creative imagination. Here, as elsewhere in his writings, Defoe's experience as a reporter served him well. (3) The style is simple and homely but effective. It is also intimate: the author frequently introduces such remarks as "It

would make the reader pity me," "You may be sure," and so on. Defoe was writing primarily for the relatively humble readers of his own time, but his style appeals to everybody.

Many critics regard Defoe as the real father of the English novel, in the sense that he was the first to write a truly convincing story about realistic* characters. In composing *Robinson Crusoe* he shows himself a great writer of fiction with a keen sense of what the public wants.

[The narrator, Robinson Crusoe, born in Yorkshire, England, was early filled with a desire to roam. At the age of nineteen he ran away from home and started for London by sea, but was shipwrecked almost immediately. Instead of returning home, he went on to London, where he embarked with a friendly sea captain on a trading voyage to the coast of Guinea. This voyage resulted profitably, and he set out on another, but was captured by a Turkish pirate and was carried to Sallee, on the coast of Morocco, where he remained a slave for two years. He at last escaped in a small boat, along with a boy named Xury, and after further adventures on the coast of Africa was picked up by a Portuguese ship and carried to Brazil. Here he became a prosperous planter; but after four years he was induced to embark on an expedition to the coast of Guinea. Early in the voyage his ship was caught in a tropical hurricane and was wrecked on the shore of an uninhabited island near the mouth of the Orinoco River. All the crew were drowned except Crusoe, who barely escaped with his life. He succeeded in bringing ashore various miscellaneous articles from the wrecked vessel and gradually established himself on the island. By long, patient labor he constructed a storehouse for his goods beside a rock some distance from the shore, and later, a "bower,"

---

[1] For biography see page 710.

265

or "country place," surrounded by a hedge farther inland. He found the island occupied only by a few harmless creatures such as goats, some of which he domesticated for food. Besides these, his only companions were a dog, some cats, and a parrot. His food at first consisted of goat's flesh, sea turtles, melons, and grapes (which he found on the island), and a few supplies that he had been able to rescue from the wreck.

After spending two years in establishing himself, he ventured to make a tour of the island, after which he was glad to return home. The narrative then proceeds as follows.]

I CANNOT express what a satisfaction it was to me, to come into my old hutch,[1] and lie down in my hammock-bed.

The rainy season of the autumnal equinox was now come, and I kept the thirtieth of September in the same solemn manner as before, being the anniversary of my landing on the island, having now been there two years, and no more pros- pect of being delivered than the first day I came there. I spent the whole day in humble and thankful acknowledgments of the many wonderful mercies which my solitary condition was attended with, and without which it might have been infinitely more miserable. I gave humble and hearty thanks that God had been pleased to discover to me, even that it was possible I might be more happy in this solitary condition than I should have been in a liberty of society, and in all the pleasures of the world.

Thus, and in this disposition of mind, I began my third year; and though I have not given the reader the trouble of so particular account of my works this year as the first, yet in general it may be observed, that I was very seldom idle; but having regularly divided my time, according to the several daily employ- ments that were before me, such as, first, my duty to God, and the reading the Scriptures, which I constantly set apart some time for thrice every day; secondly,

the going abroad with my gun for food, which generally took me up three hours in every morning, when it did not rain; thirdly, the ordering, curing, preserving, and cooking what I had killed or catched for my supply; these took up great part of the day. Also it is to be considered that the middle of the day when the sun was in the zenith, the violence of the heat was too great to stir out; so that about four hours in the evening was all the time I could be supposed to work in; with this exception, that sometimes I changed my hours of hunting and work- ing, and went to work in the morning, and abroad with my gun in the afternoon.

I was now, in the months of November and December, expecting my crop of barley and rice. The ground I had manured or dug up for them was not great; for my seed of each was not above the quantity of half a peck. About the latter end of December, which was our second harvest of the year, I reaped my crop.

I was sadly put to it for[1] a scythe or a sickle to cut it down, and all I could do was to make one as well as I could out of one of the broadswords, or cutlasses, which I saved among the arms out of the ship. However, as my first crop was but small, I had no great difficulty to cut it down. I cut nothing off but the ears, and carried it away in a great basket which I had made, and so rubbed it out[2] with my hands. At the end of all my harvesting, I found that out of my half- peck of seed I had near two bushels of rice, and above two bushels and a half of barley; that is to say, by my guess, for I had no measure at that time.

However, this was a great encourage- ment to me, and I foresaw that in time it would please God to supply me with bread. And yet here I was perplexed again, for I neither knew how to grind or make meal of my corn,[3] or indeed how

---

[1] The "bower" referred to above.

[1] *I was . . . for.* I badly needed.
[2] *rubbed it out.* Threshed it.   [3] Here, grain.

to clean it and part it; nor if made into meal, how to make bread of it; and if how to make it, yet I knew not how to bake it. These things being added to my desire of having a good quantity for store, and to secure a constant supply, I resolved not to taste any of this crop, but to preserve it all for seed against the 90 next season, and in the meantime to employ all my study and hours of working to accomplish this great work of providing myself with corn and bread.

First, I had no plough to turn up the earth, no spade or shovel to dig it. Well, this I conquered by making a wooden spade, but this did my work in but a wooden manner, and though it cost me a great many days to make it, yet, for 100 want of iron it not only wore out the sooner, but made my work the harder, and made it be performed much worse. When the corn was sowed, I had no harrow, but was forced to go over it myself, and drag a great heavy bough of a tree over it, to scratch it, as it may be called, rather than rake or harrow it.

When it was growing and grown, I wanted many things to fence it, secure it, 110 mow or reap it, cure and carry it home, thrash, part it from the chaff, and save it. Then I wanted a mill to grind it, sieves to dress it, yeast and salt to make it into bread, and an oven to bake it. But as I resolved to use none of the corn for bread till I had a greater quantity by me, I had the next six months to apply myself wholly by labour and invention to furnish myself with utensils proper 120 for the performing all the operations necessary for the making the corn (when I had it) fit for my use.

But first I was to prepare more land, for I had now seed enough to sow above an acre of ground. Before I did this, I had a week's work at least to make me a spade, which when it was done was but a sorry one indeed, and very heavy, and required double labour to work with it. 130 However, I went through that, and

sowed my seed in two large flat pieces of ground, as near my house as I could find them to my mind, and fenced them in with a good hedge, the stakes of which were all cut of that wood which I had set before, and knew it would grow; so that in one year's time I knew I should have a quick or living hedge, that would want but little repair. This work was not so little as to take me up less than three 140 months, because great part of that time was of the wet season, when I could not go abroad.

I had long studied, by some means or other, to make myself some earthen vessels, which indeed I wanted sorely, but knew not where to come at them. However, considering the heat of the climate, I did not doubt but if I could find out any such clay, I might botch up some 150 such pot, as might, being dried in the sun, be hard enough and strong enough to bear handling, and to hold anything that was dry, and required to be kept so; and as this was necessary in the preparing corn, meal, &c., which was the thing I was upon, I resolved to make some as large as I could, and fit only to stand like jars, to hold what should be put into them. 160

It would make the reader pity me, or rather laugh at me, to tell how many awkward ways I took to raise this paste.[1] What odd, misshapen, ugly things I made; how many of them fell in, and how many fell out, the clay not being stiff enough to bear its own weight; how many cracked by the over-violent heat of the sun, being set out too hastily; and how many fell in pieces with only remov- 170 ing, as well before as after they were dried; and in a word, how after having laboured hard to find the clay, to dig it, to temper it, to bring it home, and work it, I could not make above two large earthen ugly things, I cannot call them jars, in about two months' labour.

[1] *raise . . . paste.* Prepare this clay (for making pots, dishes, etc.).

However, as the sun baked these two very dry and hard, I lifted them very 180 gently up, and set them down again in two great wicker baskets, which I had made on purpose for them, that they might not break, and as between the pot and the basket there was a little room to spare, I stuffed it full of the rice and barley straw, and these two pots being to stand always dry, I thought would hold my dry corn, and perhaps the meal, when the corn was bruised.[1]

190   Though I miscarried so much [2] in my design for large pots, yet I made several smaller things with better success; such as little round pots, flat dishes, pitchers, and pipkins, and any things my hand turned to; and the heat of the sun baked them strangely hard.

But all this would not answer my end, which was to get an earthen pot to hold what was liquid, and bear the fire, which 200 none of these could do. It happened after some time, making a pretty large fire for cooking my meat, when I went to put it out after I had done with it, I found a broken piece of one of my earthenware vessels in the fire, burnt as hard as a stone, and red as a tile.

This set me to studying how to order my fire, so as to make it burn me some pots. I had no notion of a kiln, such as 210 the potters burn in, or of glazing them with lead, though I had some lead to do it with; but I placed three large pipkins, and two or three pots, in a pile one upon another, and placed my fire-wood all round it with a great heap of embers under them. I plied the fire with fresh fuel round the outside, and upon the top, till I saw the pots in the inside red hot quite through, and observed that they 220 did not crack at all. When I saw them clear red, I let them stand in that heat about five or six hours, till I found one of them, though it did not crack, did melt or run, for the sand which was mixed with the clay melted by the violence of the heat and would have run into glass if I had gone on. So I slacked my fire gradually till the pots began to abate of the red colour; and watching them all night that I might not let the fire abate 230 too fast, in the morning I had three very good, I will not say handsome, pipkins, and two other earthen pots, as hard burnt as could be desired; and one of them perfectly glazed with the running of the sand.

No joy at a thing of so mean a nature was ever equal to mine, when I found I had made an earthen pot that would bear the fire; and I had hardly patience 240 to stay till they were cold, before I set one upon the fire again, with some water in it, to boil me some meat, which it did admirably well; and with a piece of a kid I made some very good broth, though I wanted oatmeal, and several other ingredients, requisite to make it so good as I would have had it been.

It need not be wondered at, if all these things took me up most part of the third 250 year of my abode here; for it is to be observed, that in the intervals of these things I had my new harvest and husbandry[1] to manage; for I reaped my corn in its season, and carried it home as well as I could, and laid it up in the ear, in my large baskets, till I had time to rub it out.

And now indeed my stock of corn increasing, I really wanted to build my 260 barns bigger. I wanted a place to lay it up in; for the increase of the corn now yielded me so much, that I had of the barley about twenty bushels, and of the rice as much, or more; insomuch, that now I resolved to begin to use it freely; for my bread had been quite gone a great while; also I resolved to see what quantity would be sufficient for me a whole year, and to sow but once a year.   270

All the while these things were doing, you may be sure my thoughts run many

---

[1] Ground.

[2] *miscarried so much.* Made so many mistakes.

[1] Farm work.

times upon the prospect of land which I had seen from the other side of the island, and I was not without secret wishes that I were on shore there. But I made no allowance for the dangers of such a condition, and how I might fall into the hands of savages, and perhaps such as I 280 might have reason to think far worse than the lions and tigers of Africa. That if I once came into their power, I should run a hazard more than a thousand to one of being killed, and perhaps of being eaten; for I had heard that the people of the Caribbean coasts were cannibals, or man-eaters, and I knew by the latitude that I could not be far off from that shore. All these things, I say, which I 290 ought to have considered well of, and did cast up[1] in my thoughts afterwards, yet took up none of my apprehensions at first; but my head run mightily upon the thought of getting over to the shore.

This at length put me upon thinking whether it was not possible to make myself a canoe, or *periagua*, such as the natives of those climates make, even without tools, or, as I might say, without 300 hands, *viz.* of the trunk of a great tree. This I not only thought possible, but easy, and pleased myself extremely with the thoughts of making it, and with my having much more convenience for it than any of the negroes or Indians; but not at all considering the particular inconveniences which I lay under, more than the Indians did, *viz.* want of hands to move it, when it was made, into the 310 water, a difficulty much harder for me to surmount, than all the consequences of want of tools could be to them.

[As a result] I went to work upon this boat the most like a fool that ever man did, who had any of his senses awake. I pleased myself with the design, without determining whether I was ever able to undertake it; not but that the difficulty of launching my boat came often into 320 my head; but I put a stop to my own

---

[1] *cast up.* Take account of.

inquiries into it, by this foolish answer which I gave myself, "Let's first make it; I'll warrant I'll find some way or other to get it along, when 'tis done."

This was a most preposterous method; but the eagerness of my fancy prevailed, and to work I went. I felled a cedar-tree. I question much whether Solomon* ever had such a one for the building of the Temple at Jerusalem. It was five foot 330 ten inches diameter at the lower part next the stump, and four foot eleven inches diameter at the end of twenty-two foot, after which it lessened for a while, and then parted into branches. It was not without infinite labour that I felled this tree. I was twenty days hacking and hewing at it at the bottom. I was fourteen more getting the branches and limbs, and the vast spreading head of it 340 cut off, which I hacked and hewed through with axe and hatchet, and inexpressible labour. After this, it cost me a month to shape it and dub[1] it to a proportion, and to something like the bottom of a boat, that it might swim upright as it ought to do. It cost me near three months more to clear the inside, and work it so as to make an exact boat of it. This I did indeed without fire, by 350 mere[2] mallet and chisel, and by the dint of hard labour, till I had brought it to be a very handsome *periagua*, and big enough to have carried six and twenty men, and consequently big enough to have carried me and all my cargo. But all my devices to get it into the water failed me; though they cost me infinite labour too. It lay about one hundred yards from the water, and not more. 360 This grieved me heartily, and now I saw, though too late, the folly of beginning a work before we count the cost.

In the middle of this work, I finished my fourth year in this place, and kept my anniversary with the same devotion, and with as much comfort as ever before; for by a constant study, and serious ap-

---

[1] Shape, as with a tool.   [2] Nothing but.

plication of the Word of God, and by the
370 assistance of His grace, I gained a different knowledge from what I had before.

In the first place, I was removed from
all the wickedness of the world here. I
had neither the lust of the flesh, the lust
of the eye, or the pride of life.[1] I had
nothing to covet[2]; for I had all that I
was now capable of enjoying. I was lord
of the whole manor; or if I pleased, I
might call myself king, or emperor over
380 the whole country which I had possession of. There were no rivals. I had no
competitor, none to dispute sovereignty
or command with me.

I had now been here so long, that
many things which I brought on shore
for my help, were either quite gone, or
very much wasted and near spent.

My ink had been gone for some time,
all but a very little, which I eked out
390 with water, a little and a little, till it
was so pale it scarce left any appearance
of black upon the paper. As long as it
lasted, I made use of it to minute[3] down
the days of the month on which any remarkable thing happened to me.

The next thing to my ink's being
wasted, was that of my bread; I mean the
biscuit which I brought out of the ship.
This I had husbanded to the last degree,
400 allowing myself but one cake of bread a
day for above a year, and yet I was quite
without bread for near a year before I
got any corn of my own, and great reason
I had to be thankful that I had any at
all, the getting it being, as has been already observed, next to miraculous.

My clothes began to decay, too,
mightily. As to linen, I had none a good
while, except some chequered shirts
410 which I found in the chests of the other
seamen, and which I carefully preserved,
because many times I could bear no other
clothes on but a shirt; and it was a very
great help to me that I had among all

the men's clothes of the ship almost three
dozen of shirts. There were also several
thick watch-coats of the seamen's, which
were left indeed, but they were too hot to
wear; and though it is true, that the
weather was so violent hot, that there 420
was no need of clothes, yet I could not
go quite naked; no, though I had been
inclined to it, which I was not, nor could
abide the thoughts of it, though I was
all alone. The reason why I could not
go quite naked, was, I could not bear
the heat of the sun so well when quite
naked, as with some clothes on; nay, the
very heat frequently blistered my skin;
whereas with a shirt on, the air itself 430
made some motion, and whistling under
that shirt, was twofold cooler than without it.

Upon those views I began to consider
about putting the few rags I had, which
I called clothes, into some order; I had
worn out all the waistcoats I had, and
my business was now to try if I could not
make jackets out of the great watch-
coats which I had by me, and with such 440
other materials as I had; so I set to work
a-tailoring, or rather indeed a-botching,
for I made most piteous work of it. However, I made shift to make two or three
new waistcoats, which I hoped would
serve me a great while. As for breeches
or drawers, I made but a very sorry shift
indeed, till afterward.

Had any one in England been to meet
such a man as I was, it must either have 450
frightened them, or raised a great deal of
laughter; and as I frequently stood still
to look at myself, I could not but smile
at the notion of my travelling through
Yorkshire[1] with such an equipage, and
in such a dress. Be pleased to take a
sketch of my figure as follows:

I had a great high shapeless cap, made
of a goat's skin, with a flap hanging
down behind, as well to keep the sun 460
from me, as to shoot the rain off from
running into my neck; nothing being so

---

[1] the lust . . . life. See 1 John 2:16.
[2] I had . . . covet. See Exodus 20:17.
[3] To note briefly, as in the minutes of a meeting.

[1] Crusoe's native county in England.

I was exceedingly surprised with the print of a man's naked foot on the shore

hurtful in these climates as the rain upon the flesh, under the clothes.

I had a short jacket of goatskin, the skirts coming down to about the middle of my thighs; and a pair of open-kneed breeches of the same; the breeches were made of the skin of an old he-goat, whose 470 hair hung down such a length on either side, that like pantaloons, it reached to the middle of my legs; stockings and shoes I had none, but had made me a pair of somethings, I scarce know what to call them, like buskins, to flap over my legs, and lace on either side like spatterdashes; but of a most barbarous shape, as indeed were all the rest of my clothes. . . . Over my head [I carried] 480 a great, clumsy, goat's-skin umbrella.

[After spending many years alone on the island, engaged in occupations such as are described above, Crusoe had the following remarkable experience.]

It happened one day, about noon, going towards my boat, I was exceedingly surprised with the print of a man's naked foot on the shore, which was very plain to be seen in the sand. I stood like one thunderstruck, or as if I had seen an apparition. I listened, I looked round me, I could hear nothing, nor see anything; I went up to a rising ground to look 490 farther; I went up the shore and down the shore, but it was all one, I could see no other impression but that one. I went to it again to see if there were any more, and to observe if it might not be my fancy; but there was no room for that, for there was exactly the very print of a foot, toes, heel, and every part of a foot; how it came thither I knew not, nor could in the least imagine. But after 500 innumerable fluttering thoughts, like a man perfectly confused and out of myself, I came home to my fortification, not feeling, as we say, the ground I went on, but terrified to the last degree, looking behind me at every two or three steps, mistaking every bush and tree, and fancy-

ing every stump at a distance to be a man. Nor is it possible to describe how many various shapes affrighted imagination represented things to me in, how 510 many wild ideas were found every moment in my fancy, and what strange, unaccountable whimsies came into my thoughts by the way.

When I came to my castle, for so I think I called it ever after this, I fled into it like one pursued; whether I went over by the ladder as first contrived, or went in at the hole in the rock, which I called a door, I cannot remember; no, 520 nor could I remember the next morning; for never frightened hare fled to cover, or fox to earth, with more terror of mind than I to this retreat.

[As the result of his alarm caused by seeing the footprint, Crusoe spent some time in great terror and anxiety. Finally his worst fears were realized by the arrival of a number of canoes loaded with naked savages and their prisoners. On landing the savages proceeded to kill and cook the prisoners and then to eat them piecemeal. On a similar, later occasion one of the prisoners escaped from the cannibals and was rescued by Crusoe, who took him as a servant and named him Friday after the day on which the event took place. Some years after these occurrences Crusoe and Friday rescued from the cannibals a Spaniard and an old savage who turned out to be Friday's father. Finally the island was visited by a ship, on which Crusoe and Friday returned to civilization after having lived on the island for more than twenty-eight years. On arriving in Europe, Crusoe found that during his absence his affairs had prospered. He accordingly married and settled down in England.]

Discussion Hints

1. It has been said that *Robinson Crusoe* is an experiment in representing "man in a state of nature." Read the headnote again, and then explain what you think this expression means.

2. Illustrate from the text the reasons given in the headnote for the book's popularity.

3. Describe a typical day in Crusoe's life on the island.

4. Describe some of Crusoe's substitutes for tools and other devices used in civilized society for getting a living.

5. List as many as possible of the experiences in which you can participate imaginatively through the pages of *Robinson Crusoe*.

6. Find in an atlas as many as possible of the places referred to.

7. How does the position of Crusoe's island help to explain the fact that barley and rice could be harvested in winter?

8. What evidence do you find that Crusoe (or Defoe) had a sense of humor?

9. If you have read Robert Louis Stevenson's *Treasure Island* (given in the revised edition of *Adventure* of this series), point out any respects in which it resembles *Robinson Crusoe*. Do you conclude that Stevenson imitated Defoe in any way?

10. Defoe's book is based slightly upon the experiences of Alexander Selkirk.* Compare the selection from *Robinson Crusoe* with Cowper's poem "The Solitude of Alexander Selkirk" (p. 303).

11. Perhaps you have read *The Swiss Family Robinson*, one of the best-known of the many imitations of *Robinson Crusoe*. If so, which do you regard as the better and more convincing work? Give reasons for your answer.

12. The episode of the mysterious footprint on the sand, coming as it does after so many years of solitude, is famous as an example of romantic suggestiveness. If possible read the complete account, which is here considerably abbreviated.

13. Defoe at times uses the word *want* in the older sense of "lack" or "be without." Find examples. Point out other examples of differences between Defoe's use of words and that of more recent times.

Words and Phrases to be Explained

autumnal equinox (p. 266, ll. 4–5)
zenith (p. 266, l. 43)
botch (p. 267, l. 150)
pipkins (p. 268, l. 194)
preposterous (p. 269, l. 325)

Suggestions for Reading

You will enjoy especially the first part of *Robinson Crusoe*, down to the time Crusoe leaves the island. Another interesting and instructive book by Defoe is his *Journal of the Plague Year*, which gives a powerful, imaginative account of the great plague in London in 1665. "The Apparition of Mrs. Veal," a short story by Defoe, is one of the best ghost stories ever written. It is given in *The Book of the Short Story*, edited by Alexander Jessup and Henry S. Canby (D. Appleton-Century Company, Inc.).

A SATIRICAL ROMANCE

JONATHAN SWIFT[1] (1667-1745)

From "A Voyage to Lilliput"

[From *Gulliver's Travels*, Part I]

Gulliver's Travels is one of the few great books of the world that appeal equally to the young and to the mature reader. To the beginner it is a fascinating account of the adventures of an imaginary hero, Lemuel Gulliver, during a series of voyages to far-off lands of strange peoples and preposterous marvels. As we read we are transported to one country where horses rule and men are disgusting brutes; to another where the inhabitants are of gigantic size; and, in "A Voyage to Lilliput," to a country where the people are less than six inches tall and everything else is in proportion. Moreover, all is told so convincingly that for the moment we are actually persuaded that the stories are really true.

But the trained reader, while enjoying the narrative no less, sees also, in *Gulliver's Travels*, a deeper meaning. Beneath the apparently simple, inoffensive yarns lies hidden a bitter satire.* In "A Voyage to Lilliput," Swift, ever the hater of insincerity and sham, voices indirectly his suspicion of the false science of his day, his dislike for the schemings and corruption of courtiers and government officials, and his contempt for the pettiness of mankind in general. To his brilliant though embittered mind the civilized nations of Europe seemed much like pygmies, whose quarrels and social formalities were as ridiculous as those of the Lilliputians.

Here, as elsewhere in Swift's prose writings, the author expresses his views, not in high-sounding phrases and hard words, but in language so simple and clear that it seems almost like ordinary conversation. Though published in 1726, more than two centuries ago, *Gulliver's Travels* remains today a model of straightforward, unadorned English.

[The supposed narrator, Lemuel Gulliver, born in England and educated as a physician, went to sea as a ship's doctor. On one of his voyages his ship was wrecked in a remote region of the South Seas, and all hands except Gulliver were apparently lost. He, however, succeeded in swimming ashore, where, weary and sleepy, he found himself on an unknown coast.]

CHAPTER I

I LAY down on the grass, which was very short and soft, where I slept sounder than ever I remembered to have done in my life, and, as I reckoned, above nine hours; for, when I awaked, it was just daylight. I attempted to rise, but was not able to stir; for as I happened to lie on my back, I found my arms and legs were strongly fastened on each side to the ground; and my hair, which was long and thick, tied down in the same manner. I likewise felt several slender ligatures[1] across my body, from my armpits to my thighs. I could only look upwards; the sun began to grow hot, and the light offended my eyes.

I heard a confused noise about me; but, in the posture I lay, could see nothing except the sky. In a little time I felt something alive on my left leg, which, advancing gently forward over my breast, came almost up to my chin; when, bending my eyes downward as much as I could, I perceived it to be a human creature, not six inches high, with

[1] For biography see page 711.

[1] Bindings.

I attempted to rise, but was not able to stir

a bow and arrow in his hands, and a quiver at his back. In the meantime I felt at least forty more of the same kind (as I conjectured) following the first.

I was in the utmost astonishment, and roared so loud that they all ran back in a fright; and some of them, as I was afterwards told, were hurt with the falls they got by leaping from my sides upon the ground. However, they soon returned, and one of them, who ventured so far as to get a full sight of my face, lifting up his hands and eyes by way of admiration, cried out in a shrill but distinct voice — *Hekinah degul!* The others repeated the same words several times, but I then knew not what they meant.

I lay all this while, as the reader may believe, in great uneasiness. At length, struggling to get loose, I had the fortune to break the strings, and wrench out the pegs, that fastened my left arm to the ground; for by lifting it up to my face, I discovered the methods they had taken to bind me, and, at the same time, with a violent pull, which gave me excessive pain, I a little loosened the strings that tied down my hair on the left side, so that I was just able to turn my head about two inches.

But the creatures ran off a second time, before I could seize them; whereupon there was a great shout in a very shrill accent, and after it ceased, I heard one of them cry aloud, *Tolgo phonac*; when, in an instant, I felt above an hundred arrows discharged on my left hand, which pricked me like so many needles; and, besides, they shot another flight into the air, as we do bombs in Europe, whereof many, I suppose, fell on my body (though I felt them not), and some on my face, which I immediately covered with my left hand.

When this shower of arrows was over, I fell a-groaning with grief and pain, and then striving again to get loose, they discharged another volley larger than the first, and some of them attempted with spears to stick me in the sides; but by good luck I had on me a buff jerkin,[1] which they could not pierce. I thought it the most prudent method to lie still, and my design was to continue so till night, when, my left hand being already loose, I could easily free myself; and as for the inhabitants, I had reason to believe I might be a match for the greatest armies they could bring against me, if they were all of the same size with him that I saw.

But fortune disposed otherwise of me. When the people observed I was quiet, they discharged no more arrows; but, by the noise I heard, I knew their numbers increased; and about four yards from me, over against my right ear, I heard a knocking for above an hour, like that of people at work; when, turning my head that way, as well as the pegs and strings would permit me, I saw a stage erected, about a foot and a half from the ground, capable of holding four of the inhabitants, with two or three ladders to mount it; from whence one of them, who seemed to be a person of quality, made me a long speech, whereof I understood not one syllable.

Being almost famished with hunger, having not eaten a morsel for some hours before I left the ship, I found the demands of nature so strong upon me, that I could not forbear showing my impatience (perhaps against the strict rules of decency) by putting my finger frequently to my mouth, to signify that I wanted food. The *hurgo* (for so they call a great lord, as I afterwards learned) understood me very well. He descended from the stage, and commanded that several ladders should be applied to my sides; on which above an hundred of the inhabitants mounted, and walked towards my mouth, laden with baskets full of meat, which had been provided and sent thither by the king's orders, upon the first intelligence he received of me.

[1] *buff jerkin.* A thick, close-fitting leather jacket.

I observed there was the flesh of several animals, but could not distinguish them by the taste. There were shoulders, legs, and loins, shaped like those of mutton, and very well dressed, but smaller than the wings of a lark. I ate them by two or three at a mouthful, and took three 130 loaves at a time, about the bigness of musket bullets. They supplied me as they could, showing a thousand marks of wonder and astonishment at my bulk and appetite. I then made another sign that I wanted drink.

They found by my eating that a small quantity would not suffice me; and being a most ingenious people, they slung up, with great dexterity, one of their largest 140 hogsheads, then rolled it towards my hand, and beat out the top: I drank it off at a draught; which I might well do, for it did not hold half a pint, and tasted like a small[1] wine of Burgundy, but much more delicious. They brought me a second hogshead, which I drank in the same manner, and made signs for more; but they had none to give me.

When I had performed these wonders, 150 they shouted for joy, and danced upon my breast, repeating, several times, as they did at first, *Hekinah degul*. They made me a sign that I should throw down the two hogsheads, but first warning the people below to stand out of the way, crying aloud, *Borach mivola*; and, when they saw the vessels in the air, there was an universal shout of *Hekinah degul*.

Soon after, I heard a general shout, 160 with frequent repetitions of the words, *Peplom selan*, and I felt great numbers of people on my left side, relaxing the cords to such a degree, that I was able to turn upon my right, and so get a little ease. But, before this, they had daubed my face and both my hands with a sort of ointment very pleasant to the smell, which, in a few minutes, removed all the smart of their arrows. These circum-170 stances, added to the refreshment I had

received by their victuals and drink, which were very nourishing, disposed me to sleep. I slept about eight hours, as I was afterwards assured; and it was no wonder, for the physicians, by the emperor's order, had mingled a sleepy potion[1] in the hogsheads of wine.

It seems that, upon the first moment I was discovered sleeping on the ground, after my landing, the emperor had early 180 notice of it by an express[2]; and determined in council, that I should be tied in the manner I have related (which was done in the night, while I slept), that plenty of meat and drink should be sent to me, and a machine prepared to carry me to the capital city.

This resolution, perhaps, may appear very bold and dangerous, and I am confident would not be imitated by any 190 prince in Europe on the like occasion. However, in my opinion, it was extremely prudent, as well as generous; for, supposing these people had endeavoured to kill me with their spears and arrows, while I was asleep, I should certainly have awaked with the first sense of smart, which might so far have roused my rage and strength, as to have enabled me to break the strings wherewith I was tied; 200 after which, as they were not able to make resistance, so they could expect no mercy.

Five hundred carpenters and engineers were immediately set at work to prepare the greatest engine[3] they had. It was a frame of wood, raised three inches from the ground, about seven feet long and four wide, moving upon twenty-two wheels. The shout I heard was upon the 210 arrival of this engine, which, it seems, set out in four hours after my landing. It was brought parallel to me as I lay. But the principal difficulty was to raise and place me in this vehicle.

---

[1] *sleepy potion*. A drink intended to cause sleep.
[2] A special messenger.
[3] The word *engine* was formerly applied to any sort of mechanical contrivance.

[1] Light.

Eighty poles, each of one foot high, were erected for this purpose, and very strong cords, of the bigness of packthread, were fastened by hooks to many 220 bandages, which the workmen had girt round my neck, my hands, my body, and my legs. Nine hundred of the strongest men were employed to draw up these cords by many pulleys fastened on the poles; and thus in less than three hours I was raised and slung into the engine, and there tied fast.

All this I was told; for, while the whole operation was performing, I lay 230 in a profound sleep, by the force of that soporiferous[1] medicine infused into my liquor. Fifteen hundred of the emperor's largest horses, each about four inches and a half high, were employed to draw me towards the metropolis, which, as I said, was half a mile distant.

We made a long march the remaining part of that day, and rested at night with five hundred guards on each side of me, 240 half with torches, and half with bows and arrows, ready to shoot me, if I should offer to stir. The next morning, at sunrise, we continued our march, and arrived within two hundred yards of the city gates about noon. The emperor, and all his court, came out to meet us; but his great officers would by no means suffer his majesty to endanger his person by mounting on my body.

250 At the place where the carriage stopped there stood an ancient temple, esteemed to be the largest in the whole kingdom; which, having been polluted some years before by an unnatural murder, was, according to the zeal of those people, looked upon as profane, and therefore had been applied to common use, and all the ornaments and furniture carried away. In this edifice it was determined 260 I should lodge. The great gate, fronting to the north, was about four feet high, and almost two feet wide, through which I could easily creep. On each side of the

[1] Sleep-producing.

gate was a small window, not above six inches from the ground; into that on the left side the king's smith conveyed four score and eleven chains, like those that hang to a lady's watch in Europe, and almost as large, which were locked to my left leg with six-and-thirty padlocks. 270

Over against this temple, on the other side of the great highway, at twenty feet distance, there was a turret at least five feet high. Here the emperor ascended, with many principal lords of his court, to have an opportunity of viewing me, as I was told, for I could not see them. It was reckoned that above an hundred thousand inhabitants came out of the town upon the same errand; and, in 280 spite of my guards, I believe there could not be fewer than ten thousand, at several times, who mounted my body, by the help of ladders. But a proclamation was soon issued, to forbid it, upon pain of death.

When the workmen found it was impossible for me to break loose, they cut all the strings that bound me; whereupon I rose up, with as melancholy a disposi- 290 tion as ever I had in my life. The chains that held my left leg were about two yards long, and gave me not only the liberty of walking backwards and forwards in a semicircle, but, being fixed within four inches of the gate, allowed me to creep in, and lie at my full length in the temple.

CHAPTER II

When I found myself on my feet I looked about me, and must confess I 300 never beheld a more entertaining prospect. The country around appeared like a continued garden, and the enclosed fields, which were generally forty foot square, resembled so many beds of flowers. These fields were intermingled with woods of half a stang,[1] and the tall-

[1] *half a stang.* About an eighth of an acre.

est trees, as I could judge, appeared to be seven foot high. I viewed the town on my left hand, which looked like the painted scene of a city in a theatre.

The emperor was already descended from the tower, and advancing on horseback towards me, which had like to have cost him dear; for the beast, though very well trained, yet wholly unused to such a sight, which appeared as if a mountain moved before him, reared up on his hinder feet. But that prince, who is an excellent horseman, kept his seat, till his attendants ran in and held the bridle, while his majesty had time to dismount.

When he alighted, he surveyed me round with great admiration, but kept without the length of my chain. He ordered his cooks and butlers, who were already prepared, to give me victuals and drink, which they pushed forward in a sort of vehicles upon wheels, till I could reach them. I took these vehicles, and soon emptied them all; twenty of them were filled with meat, and ten with liquor; each of the former afforded me two or three good mouthfuls; and I emptied the liquor of ten vessels, which was contained in earthen vials, into one vehicle, drinking it off at a draught; and so I did with the rest. The empress and young princes of the blood of both sexes, attended by many ladies, sat at some distance in their chairs[1]; but upon the accident that happened to the emperor's horse, they alighted, and came near his person, which I am now going to describe. He is taller, by almost the breadth of my nail, than any of this court, which alone is enough to strike an awe into the beholders. His features are strong and masculine, with an Austrian lip and arched nose, his complexion olive, his countenance erect, his body and limbs well proportioned, all his motions grace-

ful, and his deportment majestic.[1] He was then past his prime, being twenty-eight years and three-quarters old, of which he had reigned about seven in great felicity, and generally victorious. For the better convenience of beholding him, I lay on my side, so that my face was parallel to his, and he stood but three yards off. However, I have had him since many times in my hand, and therefore cannot be deceived in the description.

His dress was very plain and simple, and the fashion of it between the Asiatic and the European; but he had on his head a light helmet of gold, adorned with jewels, and a plume on the crest. He held his sword drawn in his hand, to defend himself, if I should happen to break loose; it was almost three inches long; the hilt and scabbard were gold, enriched with diamonds. His voice was shrill, but very clear and articulate, and I could distinctly hear it, when I stood up.

The ladies and courtiers were all most magnificently clad; so that the spot they stood upon seemed to resemble a petticoat spread on the ground, embroidered with figures of gold and silver. His imperial majesty spoke often to me, and I returned answers, but neither of us could understand a syllable. There were several of his priests and lawyers present (as I conjectured by their habits[2]), who were commanded to address themselves to me; and I spoke to them in as many languages as I had the least smattering of, which were, High and Low Dutch, Latin, French, Spanish, Italian, and Lingua Franca[3]; but all to no purpose.

[1] *His features . . . majestic.* In describing the Emperor of Lilliput, Swift is supposed to have had in mind King George I, though the portrait is in many points unlike. George I had been Elector of Hanover, in Germany, before he became king of England.

[2] Clothes.

[3] *Lingua Franca.* A jargon made up of several languages mixed and used mostly in commercial relations with the peoples of the Orient.

[1] Sedan chairs, chairs for carrying a single person, covered with canopies, and borne on poles by two men.

After about two hours the court retired, and I was left with a strong guard, to prevent the impertinence, and probably the malice of the rabble, who were very impatient to crowd about me as 400 near as they durst; and some of them had the impudence to shoot their arrows at me, as I sat on the ground by the door of my house, whereof one very narrowly missed my left eye.

Towards night, I got with some difficulty into my house, where I lay on the ground, and continued to do so about a fortnight, during which time the emperor gave orders to have a bed prepared 410 for me. Six hundred beds, of the common measure, were brought in carriages and worked up in my house; an hundred and fifty of their beds, sewn together, made up the breadth and length; and these were four double, which, however, kept me but very indifferently from the hardness of the floor, that was of smooth stone. By the same computation, they provided me with sheets, blankets, and 420 coverlets, tolerable enough for one who had been so long inured to hardships as I.

In the meantime, the emperor held frequent councils, to debate what course should be taken with me; and I was afterwards assured by a particular friend, a person of great quality, who was looked upon to be as much in the secret as any, that the court was under many difficulties concerning me. They apprehended 430 my breaking loose; that my diet would be very expensive, and might cause a famine. Sometimes they determined to starve me, or at least to shoot me in the face and hands with poisoned arrows, which would soon dispatch me: but again they considered that the stench of so large a carcase might produce a plague in the metropolis, and probably spread through the whole kingdom.

440 In the midst of these consultations, several officers of the army went to the door of the great council-chamber, and two of them being admitted, gave an account of my behaviour which made so favourable an impression in the breast of his majesty and the whole board in my behalf, that an imperial commission was issued out, obliging all the villages nine hundred yards round the city to deliver in, every morning, six beeves, forty sheep, 450 and other victuals, for my sustenance; together with a proportionable quantity of bread and wine, and other liquors; for the due payment of which his majesty gave assignments upon his treasury. For this prince lives chiefly upon his own demesnes,[1] seldom, except upon great occasions, raising any subsidies upon his subjects, who are bound to attend him in his wars at their own expense. 460 An establishment was also made of six hundred persons, to be my domestics, who had board-wages allowed for their maintenance, and tents built for them very conveniently on each side of my door.

It was likewise ordered that three hundred tailors should make me a suit of clothes, after the fashion of the country; that six of his majesty's greatest scholars 470 should be employed to instruct me in their language; and lastly, that the emperor's horses, and those of the nobility and troops of guards, should be frequently exercised in my sight, to accustom themselves to me.

All these orders were duly put in execution, and in about three weeks I made a great progress in learning their language; during which time the emperor 480 frequently honoured me with his visits, and was pleased to assist my masters in teaching me. We began already to converse together in some sort; and the first words I learnt were to express my desire that he would please to give me liberty, which I every day repeated on my knees. His answer, as I could apprehend it, was, that this must be a work of time, not to be thought on without the advice of his 490

[1] *his own demesnes.* Here, the income derived from his own property.

council, and that first I must *lumos kelmin pesso desmar lon emposo*; that is, swear a peace with him and his kingdom.

He desired I would not take it ill if he gave orders to certain proper officers to search me. I said his majesty should be satisfied, for I was ready to strip myself and turn up[1] my pockets before him. This I delivered, part in words, and part 500 in signs.

He replied, that by the laws of the kingdom I must be searched by two of his officers; that he knew this could not be done without my consent and assistance; that he had so good an opinion of my generosity and justice, as to trust their persons in my hands; that whatever they took from me should be returned when I left the country, or paid 510 for at the rate which I should set upon them. I took up the two officers in my hands, put them first into my coat-pockets, and then into every other pocket about me, except my two fobs[2] and another secret pocket I had no mind should be searched, wherein I had some little necessaries that were of no consequence to any but myself. In one of my fobs there was a silver watch, and in the other 520 a small quantity of gold in a purse.

These gentlemen having pen, ink, and paper about them, made an exact inventory of everything they saw; and, when they had done, desired I would set them down, that they might deliver it to the emperor. This inventory I afterwards translated into English, and is word for word as follows:

Imprimis.[3] In the right coat-pocket of 530 the great man-mountain (for so I interpret the words *quinbus flestrin*), after the strictest search, we found only one great piece of coarse cloth, large enough to be a foot-cloth for your majesty's chief room

of state. In the left pocket we saw a huge silver chest, with a cover of the same metal, which we the searchers were not able to lift. We desired it should be opened, and one of us stepping into it, found himself up to the mid-leg in a sort 540 of dust, some part whereof flying up to our faces, set us both a sneezing for several times together. In his right waist-coat pocket we found a prodigious bundle of white thin substances folded one over another, about the bigness of three men, tied with a strong cable, and marked with black figures; which we humbly conceive to be writings, every letter almost half as large as the palm of our hands. 550 In the left, there was a sort of engine, from the back of which were extended twenty long poles, resembling the palisadoes before your majesty's court; wherewith we conjecture the man-mountain combs his head, for we did not always trouble him with questions, because we found it a great difficulty to make him understand us. In the large pocket on the right side of his middle 560 cover (so I translate the word *ranfu-lo*, by which they meant my breeches), we saw a hollow pillar of iron, about the length of a man, fastened to a strong piece of timber, larger than the pillar; and upon one side of the pillar were huge pieces of iron sticking out, cut into strange figures, which we know not what to make of. In the left pocket, another engine of the same kind. In the smaller 570 pocket on the right side were several round flat pieces of white and red metal, of different bulk; some of the white, which seemed to be silver, were so large and heavy that my comrade and I could hardly lift them. In the left pocket were two black pillars irregularly shaped; we could not without difficulty reach the top of them, as we stood at the bottom of his pocket. One of them was covered, and seemed all of a 580 piece; but at the upper end of the other there appeared a white round substance, about twice the bigness of our heads.

---

[1] *turn up.* We would say "turn inside out."

[2] A fob is a little pocket, made in the waistband of men's breeches or trousers, for a watch or valuables.

[3] Latin for "in the first place."

Within each of these was enclosed a prodigious plate of steel, which, by our orders, we obliged him to show us, because we apprehended they might be dangerous engines. He took them out of their cases, and told us that in his own 590 country his practice was to shave his beard with one of these, and to cut his meat with the other. There were two pockets which we could not enter: these he called his fobs. Out of the right fob hung a great silver chain, with a wonderful kind of engine at the bottom. We directed him to draw out whatever was fastened to that chain, which appeared to be a globe, half silver, and half of some 600 transparent metal; for on the transparent side we saw certain strange figures, circularly drawn, and thought we could touch them till we found our fingers stopped by that lucid substance. He put this engine to our ears, which made an incessant noise, like that of a water-mill; and we conjecture it is either some unknown animal, or the god that he worships; but we are more inclined to the 610 latter opinion, because he assured us (if we understood him right, for he expressed himself very imperfectly), that he seldom did anything without consulting it. He called it his oracle, and said it pointed out the time for every action of his life. From the left fob he took out a net almost large enough for a fisherman, but contrived to open and shut like a purse, and served him for the same use; 620 we found therein several massy pieces of yellow metal, which, if they be real gold, must be of immense value.

Having thus, in obedience to your majesty's commands, diligently searched all his pockets, we observed a girdle about his waist, made of the hide of some prodigious animal, from which, on the left side, hung a sword of the length of five men; and on the right, a bag or pouch, 630 divided into two cells, each cell capable of holding three of your majesty's subjects. In one of these cells were several globes, or balls, of a most ponderous metal, about the bigness of our heads, and required a strong hand to lift them; the other cell contained a heap of certain black grains, but of no great bulk or weight, for we could hold about fifty of them in the palms of our hands.

This is an exact inventory of what 640 we found about the body of the man-mountain, who used us with great civility and due respect to your majesty's commission. Signed and sealed, on the fourth day of the eighty-ninth moon of your majesty's auspicious reign.

Clefren Freloc,
Marsi Freloc.

When this inventory was read over to the emperor, he directed me, although in 650 very gentle terms, to deliver up the several particulars.

He first called for my scimitar, which I took out, scabbard and all. In the meantime, he ordered three thousand of his choicest troops (who then attended him) to surround me at a distance, with their bows and arrows just ready to discharge; but I did not observe it, for mine eyes were wholly fixed upon his majesty. 660 He then desired me to draw my scimitar, which, although it had got some rust by the sea-water, was in most parts exceeding bright. I did so, and immediately all the troops gave a shout between terror and surprise; for the sun shone clear, and the reflection dazzled their eyes, as I waved the scimitar to and fro in my hand. His majesty, who is a most magnanimous prince, was less daunted than 670 I could expect; he ordered me to return it into the scabbard and cast it on the ground as gently as I could, about six foot from the end of my chain.

The next thing he demanded was one of the hollow iron pillars, by which he meant my pocket-pistols. I drew it out, and at his desire, as well as I could, expressed to him the use of it; and charging it only with powder, which, by the 680 closeness of my pouch, happened to escape wetting in the sea (an inconvenience against which all prudent mariners take special care to provide), I first cautioned the emperor not to be afraid, and then I let it off in the air.

The astonishment here was much greater than at the sight of my scimitar. Hundreds fell down as if they had been 690 struck dead; and even the emperor, although he stood his ground, could not recover himself in some time.

I delivered up both my pistols, in the same manner as I had done my scimitar, and then my pouch of powder and bullets, begging him that the former might be kept from the fire, for it would kindle with the smallest spark, and blow up his imperial palace into the air.

700 I likewise delivered up my watch, which the emperor was very curious to see, and commanded two of his tallest yeoman of the guards to bear it on a pole upon their shoulders, as draymen in England do a barrel of ale. He was amazed at the continual noise it made and the motion of the minute-hand, which he could easily discern (for their sight is much more acute than ours), and asked 710 the opinions of his learned men about it, which were various and remote, as the reader may well imagine without my repeating; although, indeed, I could not very perfectly understand them.

I then gave up my silver and copper money, my purse, with nine large pieces of gold, and some smaller ones; my knife and razor, my comb and silver snuff-box, my handkerchief and journal-book. My 720 scimitar, pistols, and pouch were conveyed in carriages to his majesty's stores; but the rest of my goods were returned to me.

CHAPTER III

My gentleness and good behaviour had gained so far on the emperor and his court, and indeed upon the army and people in general, that I began to conceive hopes of getting my liberty in a short time. The natives came by degrees to be less apprehensive of any danger 730 from me. I would sometimes lie down, and let five or six of them dance on my hand; and at last the boys and girls would venture to come and play at hide-and-seek in my hair. I had now made a good progress in understanding and speaking their language.

The horses of the army, and those of the royal stables, having been daily led before me, were no longer shy, but would 740 come up to my very feet without starting. The riders would leap them over my hand as I held it on the ground; and one of the emperor's huntsmen, upon a large courser, took my foot, shoe and all, which was indeed a prodigious leap.

I had the good fortune to divert the emperor one day after a very extraordinary manner. I desired he would order several sticks of two feet high, and the 750 thickness of an ordinary cane, to be brought me; whereupon his majesty commanded the master of his woods to give directions accordingly; and the next morning six woodmen arrived with as many carriages, drawn by eight horses to each.

I took nine of these sticks, and fixing them firmly in the ground in a quadrangular figure, two foot and a half 760 square, I took four other sticks and tied them parallel at each corner, about two foot from the ground; then I fastened my handkerchief to the nine sticks that stood erect, and extended it on all sides, till it was as tight as the top of a drum; and the four parallel sticks, rising about five inches higher than the handkerchief, served as ledges on each side.

When I had finished my work, I de- 770 sired the emperor to let a troop of his best horse, twenty-four in number, come and exercise upon this plain. His majesty approved of the proposal, and I took them up one by one in my hands, ready mounted and armed, with the proper offi-

The emperor was pleased to be lifted up and give the word of command

cers to exercise them. As soon as they got into order, they divided into two parties, performed mock skirmishes, dis-780 charged blunt arrows, drew their swords, fled and pursued, attacked and retired, and, in short, discovered the best military discipline I ever beheld. The parallel sticks secured them and their horses from falling over the stage: and the emperor was so much delighted that he ordered this entertainment to be repeated several days, and once was pleased to be lifted up and give the word of command; and, 790 with great difficulty, persuaded even the empress herself to let me hold her in her close chair within two yards of the stage, from whence she was able to take a full view of the whole performance.

It was my good fortune that no ill accident happened in these entertainments; only once a fiery horse, that belonged to one of the captains, pawing with his hoof, struck a hole in my handkerchief, and his 800 foot slipping, he overthrew his rider and himself; but I immediately relieved them both, and covering the hole with one hand, I set down the troop with the other, in the same manner as I took them up. The horse that fell was strained in the left shoulder, but the rider got no hurt, and I repaired my handkerchief as well as I could; however, I would not trust to the strength of it any more in such dangerous enterprises.   810

I had sent so many memorials and petitions for my liberty, that his majesty at length mentioned the matter, first in the cabinet, and then in a full council.

[It was finally decreed that Gulliver should be set free, provided he agreed to certain "articles and conditions." These were brought to him in writing.]

After ... [the "articles and conditions"] were read, I was demanded to swear to the performance of them, first in the manner of my own country, and afterwards in the method prescribed by their

820 laws; which was, to hold my right foot in my left hand, and to place the middle finger of my right hand on the crown of my head, and my thumb on the tip of my right ear.

I swore and subscribed to these articles with great cheerfulness and content.

[After further adventures Gulliver escaped from Lilliput and made his way back to England.]

Discussion Hints

1. One of the early editors of Swift's works says, "Swift makes the stature of the Lilliputians one twelfth of the human stature; and in all things he has observed the same proportion." The editor points out that the hogshead which Gulliver drank at one draft, holding hardly half a pint, would contain about 108 gallons if the hogshead were of normal size; the beds allowed him are in number 600, placed four deep and 150 side by side, a close approach to 144, the square of 12; and the amount of food the emperor agrees to allow him corresponds to that of 1728 Lilliputians, the cube of 12. Do you find any indications that Swift worked out his other measurements according to any scale?

2. What conclusions do you draw from the story as to Swift's attitude toward high government officials and their regulations?

3. From the descriptions of Gulliver's various possessions given in the Lilliputians' report (p. 281) can you tell just what objects are meant?

4. As the result of Swift's use, the word *Lilliputian* has become a part of the English language. Look it up in an unabridged dictionary. Look up also *Brobdingnag, Yahoo,* and *Houyhnhnm,* report on the meanings, and find out what you can about the pronunciations.

5. What passages show that Swift is satirizing (see "satire"*) not only human governments, but also humanity in general?

Suggestions for Reading

The sample of *Gulliver's Travels* given here must surely have made you wish to read more in this famous book. A convenient edition, illustrated by Wuanita Smith, is published by Grosset & Dunlap. If time is limited, read at least Books I and II. The "Voyage to Brobdingnag," which gives an account of a country where everything is on a gigantic scale, forms an excellent basis for contrast with "A Voyage to Lilliput."

1744-1798

❀

The Transition
from Classicism
to Romanticism

While words of learned length and thundering sound,
Amazed the gazing rustics ranged around (p. 307, ll. 93–94)

As WE HAVE seen (p. 214), before the death of Pope (1744) new influences were beginning to affect English society and English literature. During the next fifty years the growth of democracy and popular education was supplemented by other forces destined to produce far-reaching and revolutionary changes. The period during which these forces were in conflict with the ideals of classicism is called the Transition Period. In literature the Transition Period begins somewhat before the death of Pope and extends to the year 1798, which marks the appearance of the *Lyrical Ballads*, an epoch-making collection of poems by the romantic poets Wordsworth and Coleridge. The period to which the Transition Period led is known as the Romantic Period (p. 313). During the Transition Period some writers followed the classical rules, while others yielded more or less to the new influences. The same writer (for example, Gray[1] or Goldsmith[2]) might at one time show himself a classicist, at another a romanticist; for then, as now, writers worked without a full consciousness of the significance of the great changes that were taking place in themselves and in others.

REACTION AGAINST FORMALISM IN LIFE AND LITERATURE

The Transition Period was marked not only by a growing democratic spirit in life and literature, but also by an increasing dissatisfaction with the classical standard of "reason" as the only true test of human behavior (see page 213). Men began to feel that life was becoming too formal and mechanical. Gradually they became convinced that by suppressing their natural feelings, and appealing only to cold, formal logic, they were missing much that was fine and inspiring. Hence they began to give freer scope to such emotions as pity and tenderness, and talked much about "the language of the heart." This change was accompanied by a vast religious revival. Multitudes wept as the two great preachers Whitefield and Wesley * unfolded the mysteries of divine love, and assured their hearers that God spoke through the heart, not through the coldly reasoning head. Even people who were not especially religious believed that by listening to "the language of the heart" rather than to reason ("the language of the head") one becomes more benevolent; that is, more generally well-wishing and kindly disposed toward all mankind. The upper classes became sentimental over the woes of the poor and the degraded; but unfortunately

[1] For biography see page 712.   [2] For biography see page 713.

the modern social conscience was not yet thoroughly awake, and little was done toward improving the condition of the lower classes. Criminal laws were still strict and even cruel, and banditry and general lawlessness were all too common.[1]

As a result of improved moral influences the bribery and low practices that had characterized English politics during the latter part of the Age of Classicism decreased under the leadership of William Pitt, who rose to power early in the Transition Period and who based his political appeal upon patriotism, honor, and idealism.

ECONOMIC AND OTHER SOCIAL CHANGES

As had been the case during the Elizabethan Period (p. 71), so, during the latter half of the eighteenth century, the life of England was greatly stimulated by increased knowledge of new countries. Between 1750 and 1760 Robert Clive was laying the foundations of British power in India. In 1759 General Wolfe, by his victory over the French at the battle of Quebec, established British supremacy in America. Geographical discoveries made by various navigators, including Captain Cook, whose earliest voyage to the Pacific dates from 1768, began to make known the romantic South Seas. These and other exploits opened the way for a long line of English adventurers and theorists who found in far-off lands new opportunities for trade or new sources of knowledge regarding primitive society.

Though many conservative thinkers during the Transition Period were still contented with the social standards of the Age of Classicism (p. 213), an increasingly large number of people were becoming dissatisfied with the growing complication of civilized society. These latter believed that society would be greatly improved if men would imitate the simple living which was supposed to have prevailed during the best part of the Middle Ages and was still to be found in remote country communities or among the kindly natives of far-off islands of the sea. Meanwhile industrialism was gradually developing (see page 319); more and more land was being enclosed (see pages 184 and 305); and many country people, the "bold peasantry" referred to by Goldsmith in "The Deserted Village" (p. 305, 1. 15), were being forced to move to the new industrial towns or to emigrate to foreign countries. From these and other signs it was clear that some great social change was on the way; and, indeed, those who lived long enough saw a revolution in America, another in France, and a social upheaval in England which, though not accompanied by actual civil war, was none the less revolutionary.

---

[1] If you have read Dickens's *Tale of Two Cities* (in the revised edition of *Achievement* of this series), you should at this point read again in Book the First, Chapter 1, and in Book the Second, Chapters 2 and 14, which describe conditions in England during the latter part of the Transition Period.

CHANGING TASTES IN LITERATURE

The new influences gradually found expression in the literature of the period. Lyric poetry became more spontaneous. Poets were less restrained and formal in expressing their emotions. The religious revival resulted in many hymns (p. 303) of tenderness and beauty. The drama too underwent a change. In contrast to the cynical, satirical,* and realistic* plays of the Restoration Period (p. 218), there came into popularity a type of drama in which the characters express fine sentiments, faults turn out to be virtues, mistakes result in blessings, and goodness always triumphs. Here, too, belong better and less sentimental plays, especially Goldsmith's wholesome comedy *She Stoops to Conquer* (1773) and the sparkling dramas of Sheridan (see page 294), including the well-known *Rivals* (1775).

Hand in hand with the reaction against the cold rationalism of the classicists went a growing distaste for the hard-and-fast rules imposed upon poetry by Pope and his followers. The conviction grew that a writer might express himself in verse that did not follow all the classical rules. Polish in literary composition gradually came to be less esteemed than naturalness. Radical critics even agreed that if a poet were only an "original genius" he might disregard many of the principles of the classicists.

As a part of the general reaction against classical standards (p. 214), English philosophers and literary men began to take a broader and more appreciative view of nature. In 1726 James Thomson* published his "Winter," the first of a series of noteworthy poems dealing sympathetically with the four divisions of the year and called *The Seasons*, and Collins (p. 296) and Gray (p. 298) are only two of a group of poets, known as the "Graveyard School," who wrote of the pleasures of solitude and twilight.

There were also other important evidences that the domain of poetry was gradually broadening. Among these the most significant was a renewed interest in the popular ballads (p. 57) because of their supposed simplicity and naturalness. Before the end of the Transition Period several collections of old ballads were published. Of these the most important was the *Reliques of Ancient English Poetry*, published by Bishop Percy in 1765. Percy's *Reliques* did more than any other one book to stimulate the enthusiasm for folk poetry that has marked the English-speaking public ever since.

During this period people began to appreciate the architecture and literature of the Middle Ages, which formerly had been called "Gothic" in contempt, because they were supposed to be the products of a rude, uncultured age. In contrast with the formal, balanced structures admired by the classicists,[1] medieval castles, churches, and other ancient buildings[2] began to be appreciated because of their picturesque and irregular beauty. The admiration for the popular ballads was largely due to the fact that they

---

[1] See illustration on page 217.   [2] See illustration on page 292.

© Dixon-Scott

Whitby Abbey, a typical example of a medieval ruin such as came to be admired during the Transition and Romantic periods had come down from the Middle Ages. English critics and poets also began to find beauty in Chaucer (p. 37) and in the medieval romances (p. 32), as well as in Spenser's *Faerie Queene* (p. 166), with its wandering knights, fair ladies, dark forests, and crumbling ruins. Since, however, little medieval literature had been printed, there was much guesswork and much faking of medieval ballads and other writings. Especially important were the Ossianic* prose poems published in 1760 to 1763 by a young Highland Scot named James Macpherson. Macpherson's *Poems of Ossian*, which was really a forgery, was accepted by most people, though not by Johnson,[1] as a collection of genuine translations of poems composed by an ancient Celtic bard,* and hence was read, admired, and imitated by many poets.

During the Transition Period the vocabulary of poetry also became less stilted than was required by the standards of the classicists. The heroic* couplet gradually became less artificial during the second half of the eighteenth century. The Spenserian* stanza, blank* verse, and other older forms began to appear again, especially the ballad stanza (see page 58), which had long been used in the simple poetry of the common people. In short, during the Transition Period we find the beginnings of another great emancipation of art and life from the fetters of tradition.

THE NOVEL

Richardson (see page 219) and Fielding, who had begun writing novels during the Age of Classicism, continued their work during the Transition Period. The next important English writer of fiction was Laurence Sterne, whose *Tristram Shandy* (1759) combines whimsical, sentimental characters based on life with a humorous narrative, and has come to be regarded as one of the great landmarks of English literature. The chief objections to Sterne's work are his fondness for becoming sentimental over things that are too trivial to arouse any deep emotion, and his habit of letting his story wander on in the same way as events do in life. In 1766 Goldsmith[2] published *The Vicar of Wakefield*, a narrative of family life in which gentle sentimentalism accompanies acute portrayal of human character in a novel that became enormously popular, has been translated into many languages, and still retains its charm. Accompanying the growth of interest in the Middle Ages during the Transition Period was the appearance of the Gothic romance, portraying romantic and often sentimental characters, against a setting of gloomy castles, moldering dungeons, and ghostly apparitions. The Gothic romances prepared the public to appreciate the novels of medieval life with which Sir Walter Scott was to delight thousands of readers during the Romantic Period (see page 313). The Gothic romances were to some extent forerunners of the modern spooky mystery story.

[1] For biography see page 707.   [2] For biography see page 713.

Correlation of English Literature with Historical Events during the
Transition from Classicism to Romanticism

HISTORICAL EVENTS		LITERARY LANDMARKS
Beginning of RELIGIOUS REVIVAL	1739	
Rising of the YOUNG PRETENDER*	1745	
Battle of CULLODEN*	1746	COLLINS, Ode to Evening
	1747	RICHARDSON, Clarissa Harlowe
	1748	THOMSON died. Born 1700
	1749	FIELDING, Tom Jones
Beginning of CLIVE's work in INDIA	1751	GRAY, Elegy published
		SHERIDAN born. Died 1816
	1754	FIELDING died. Born 1707
BRADDOCK'S defeat during the FRENCH AND INDIAN WAR	1755	JOHNSON, Dictionary of the English Language
Ministry of WILLIAM PITT	1757	
Battle of QUEBEC	1759	COLLINS died. Born 1721
		STERNE, Tristram Shandy
		BURNS born. Died 1796
Reign of GEORGE III 1760–1830		
	1760	MACPHERSON's first Ossianic* Poems
	1761	RICHARDSON died. Born 1689
	1764	First GOTHIC romance
STAMP ACT; early form of STEAM ENGINE invented	1765	PERCY, Reliques of Ancient English Poetry
	1766	GOLDSMITH, Vicar of Wakefield
SPINNING MACHINE invented; first of CAPTAIN COOK's voyages	1768	
	1770	GOLDSMITH, The Deserted Village
	1771	GRAY died. Born 1716
BOSTON TEA PARTY	1773	GOLDSMITH, She Stoops to Conquer
	1774	GOLDSMITH died. Born 1728
Beginning of the AMERICAN REVOLUTION; battle of BUNKER HILL	1775	SHERIDAN, The Rivals
DECLARATION OF INDEPENDENCE	1776	
	1779	COWPER, Olney Hymns
		JOHNSON, Lives of the Poets
Surrender of CORNWALLIS at YORKTOWN	1781	
PITT, prime minister	1783	
	1786	BURNS, Poems Chiefly in the Scottish Dialect (Kilmarnock Edition)
The FRENCH REVOLUTION; fall of the BASTILLE; WASHINGTON, first president of the UNITED STATES	1789	BLAKE, Songs of Innocence
	1791	BOSWELL, Life of Johnson
		JOHN WESLEY died. Born 1703
Beginning of the REIGN OF TERROR in FRANCE	1793	
	1794	BLAKE, Songs of Experience
Rebellion in IRELAND	1798	WORDSWORTH and COLERIDGE, Lyrical Ballads

Within the Transition Period also fall the work of William Cowper (1731–1800); some of the later publications of the classicists, such as Samuel Johnson (1709–1784) and James Boswell (1740–1795); and some of the earlier publications of the romanticists, such as William Blake (1757–1827), whose major work falls between the years 1783 and 1794. Both the life and the work of Burns (1759–1796), who also belongs primarily to the romanticists, fall within the Period of Transition.

THE PERIOD OF TRANSITION IN SONG AND STORY

POETRY

BROWNING, ELIZABETH BARRETT. "Cowper's Grave."

BURNS, ROBERT. "Charlie, He's My Darling," "The Chevalier's Lament," "It Was A' for Our Rightfu' King," "O'er the Water to Charlie," and "There'll Never be Peace till Jamie Comes Hame."

CAMPBELL, THOMAS. "Lochiel's Warning."

HOGG, JAMES. "Flora Macdonald's Farewell" and "The Stuarts of Appin."

MACAULAY, THOMAS BABINGTON. "A Jacobite's Epitaph" ("A broken heart lies here").

NOYES, ALFRED. "The Highwayman" (in the revised edition of *Achievement* of this series). In *Collected Poems*. Frederick A. Stokes Company.

PROSE

BARRIE, JAMES M. *Farewell, Miss Julie Logan*. Charles Scribner's Sons.

CHURCHILL, WINSTON. *Richard Carvel*. The Macmillan Company.

IRVING, WASHINGTON. "Christmas Sketches" (two are given in the revised edition of *Adventure* of this series), from the *Sketch Book* and *Bracebridge Hall*.

MARSHALL, ARCHIBALD. *The Old Order Changeth* and *The Squire's Daughter*. Dodd, Mead & Company, Inc.

MASEFIELD, JOHN. *Jim Davis.*

MOORE, FRANK F. *The Jessamy Bride*. Garden City Publishing Company, Inc. Goldsmith is the chief character.

SCOTT, SIR WALTER. *The Bride of Lammermoor, The Heart of Midlothian, The Pirate, Redgauntlet, Rob Roy*, and *Waverley*.

STEVENSON, ROBERT LOUIS. *David Balfour, Kidnapped, The Master of Ballantrae*, and *Treasure Island* (in the revised edition of *Adventure* of this series).

THACKERAY, WILLIAM MAKEPEACE. *The Newcomes.*

LYRIC POETRY[1]

WILLIAM COLLINS[2] (1721–1759)

Ode to Evening

Not only is the "Ode to Evening" one of the earliest English poems in praise of evening; it is one of the best of Collins's odes and also one of the most beautiful poems in English literature. It is simple in theme and dignified and polished in diction. Its charm lies in the soft, musical tone, the exquisite imagery,* and the harmonious feeling of calm enjoyment with which the poet surrounds twilight. Several lines and phrases suggest Milton's poetry (see page 190), and the personified[3] abstractions, such as "Pleasures" (l. 27) and "Fancy" (l. 50), are in the manner of the classicists; but the mood of the poem is chiefly romantic. It is romantic also in its use of an unrhymed stanza. Thus it is not only a lovely poem, but an important landmark in the period of transition from classicism to romanticism. As you read it remember how new its sentiments were in its day.

IF[4] AUGHT of oaten stop,[5] or pastoral*
    song,
May hope, chaste Eve,[6] to soothe thy
    modest ear,
    Like thy own solemn springs,
    Thy springs, and dying gales,

O nymph reserved, while now the bright-
    haired sun

Sits in yon western tent, whose cloudy
    skirts,
With brede ethereal wove,[1]
    O'erhang his wavy bed:

Now air is hushed, save where the weak-
    eyed[2] bat
With short, shrill shriek,[3] flits by on
    leathern wing;   10
    Or where the beetle winds
    His small but sullen horn,

As oft he rises 'midst the twilight path,
Against the pilgrim borne in heedless
    hum:
    Now teach me, maid[4] composed,
    To breathe some softened strain,

Whose numbers, stealing through thy
    darkening vale,
May, not unseemly, with its stillness suit,
    As, musing slow, I hail
    Thy genial loved return!   20

For when thy folding star[5] arising shows
His paly circlet, at his warning lamp
    The fragrant Hours,* and elves
    Who slept in flowers the day,

---

[1] For a discussion of lyric poetry see page 150.
[2] For biography see page 711.
[3] See "personification."*
[4] *If . . . hum.* The conclusion of this conditional clause begins with line 15.
[5] *oaten stop.* One of the openings (stops) in the pipes on which shepherds play in pastoral* poetry; here used by metonymy* for simple music or poetry.
[6] Evening, or Twilight, personified as a beautiful female figure.

[1] *With . . . wove.* Woven with braid (or embroidery) made of exceedingly thin ("ethereal") clouds.
[2] The bat is called "weak-eyed" because it cannot see well by day.
[3] *With . . . shriek.* Note the intentionally harsh (onomatopoetic*) effect of this phrase, which imitates the harshness of the bat's cry.
[4] Eve.
[5] *folding star.* The star whose appearance warns the shepherd to lead his flock to the fold.

And many a nymph who wreathes her
    brows with sedge,
And sheds the freshening dew, and, love-
    lier still,
    The pensive Pleasures sweet
    Prepare thy shadowy car.

Then lead, calm votaress,[1] where some
    sheety lake [2]
Cheers the lone heath, or some time-
    hallowed pile,[3]   30
    Or upland fallows [4] grey
    Reflect its last cool gleam.

But when chill blustering winds, or driv-
    ing rain,
Forbid my willing feet, be mine the hut,
    That from the mountain's side,
    Views wilds, and swelling floods,

And hamlets brown, and dim-discovered
    spires;
And hears their simple bell, and marks
    o'er all
    Thy dewy fingers draw
    The gradual dusky veil.[5]   40

While Spring shall pour his showers, as
    oft he wont,[6]
And bathe thy breathing tresses, meekest
    Eve!
    While Summer loves to sport
    Beneath thy lingering light;

While sallow Autumn fills thy lap with
    leaves;
Or Winter, yelling through the troublous
    air,
    Affrights thy shrinking train,
    And rudely rends thy robes;[7]

So long, sure-found beneath the sylvan
    shed,
Shall Fancy, Friendship, Science, rose-
    lipped Health,   50
    Thy gentlest influence own,
    And hymn thy favourite name![1]

Discussion Hints

1. Of what English poet of the Puritan
Period (p. 183) do lines 11, 12, and 31 of the
"Ode to Evening" remind you? Do you find
other lines that might have been inspired by
the same poet?

2. Note that the "Ode to Evening," in
contrast to typical poems of the Age of Classicism (p. 214), is unrhymed. Note also that
in spite of the absence of rhyme much the
same effect is produced by (1) the balance between the first two long lines of each stanza
and the last two short lines, and (2) the perfect rhythm* throughout the poem.

3. What examples of personification* do
you find in the poem?

4. In what respects does Collins's conception of evening suggest Milton's conception
of melancholy (p. 193)?

5. Explain "dying gales" (l. 4), "dim-
discovered spires" (l. 37), "sallow Autumn"
(l. 45), "sylvan shed" (l. 49).

Suggestions for Reading

"The Passions, an Ode for Music."
"Ode on the Popular Superstitions of the
    Highlands."
"Dirge in Cymbeline."
"Ode Written in the Beginning of the Year
    1746" ("How sleep the brave who sink to
    rest").
All in *Minor Poets of the Eighteenth Century.*
Everyman's Library.

---

[1] Eve.
[2] What picture is called up by "sheety lake"?
[3] Here, ancient building.   [4] Uncultivated fields.
[5] Read this stanza aloud several times and note
    its exquisite cadence.*
[6] Is wont (accustomed).
[7] *Or . . . robes.* An imaginative way of saying that
    winter shortens the evenings and hastens
    night.

[1] *So . . . name!* The poet means that evening fos-
    ters imagination, friendship, etc. Note the
    personification* of the abstract qualities.

THOMAS GRAY[1] (1716–1771)

Elegy Written in a Country Churchyard

Gray's "Elegy" is probably the most widely read and deeply loved poem in the English language. Thomas Gray, the author of the "Elegy," was a shy, thoughtful, studious man who might have served as the original of Milton's Il Penseroso (p. 193). Gray began the "Elegy" at the age of twenty-six, but kept it with him for the next eight years, revising, polishing, and perfecting it. The churchyard that served as the first inspiration of the poem is that of Stoke Poges,[2] a little village near London. Here Gray spent much time, and here he and his mother are buried.

The poem owes its tremendous popularity chiefly to three facts: (1) Its form is simple, yet even the untrained reader feels at once that he is in the presence of something supremely beautiful. (2) The music of its verse is irresistibly wistful and melancholy. (3) It emphasizes the importance of simple people. Buried in the humble country churchyard lie some who but for handicaps of birth and station might have been as great as Milton, Hampden, or Cromwell. Even the most honored of England's dead, those interred in some great cathedral or church, such as Westminster Abbey, are leveled in death with the poor village clodhopper buried under a misspelled epitaph. The theme of tne poem, "the short and simple annals of the poor," appeals to all human hearts.

Gray's "Elegy" is an unusually instructive example of the poetry of the period of transition from classicism to romanticism. The scene, like that of Collins's "Ode to Evening" (p. 296), is twilight, here twilight in a melancholy churchyard far from the artificial social whirl which the writers of the Age of Classicism loved to depict. Though dignified in language and highly polished in form, it avoids the excessive artificiality of the typical classicist. It is romantic in its democratic sentiments, in its use of country scenes as a background for human emotion, and in its gentle melancholy; but it never yields to the unchecked display of feeling found in the writings of some of the later romantic poets. To get the best effect, you should read the poem slowly aloud.

[1] For biography see page 712.
[2] See illustration on page 299.

THE curfew* tolls the knell of parting day,
The lowing herd wind slowly o'er the lea,
The plowman homeward plods his weary way,
And leaves the world to darkness and to me.

Now fades the glimmering landscape on the sight,
And all the air a solemn stillness[1] holds,
Save where the beetle wheels his droning flight,
And drowsy tinklings lull the distant folds;[2]

Save that from yonder ivy-mantled tower
The moping owl does to the moon complain   10
Of such as, wandering near her secret bower,
Molest her ancient solitary reign.

Beneath those rugged elms, that yew-tree's shade,
Where heaves the turf in many a mouldering heap,
Each in his narrow cell forever laid,
The rude forefathers of the hamlet sleep.

The breezy call of incense-breathing Morn,[3]
The swallow twittering from the straw-built shed,[4]
The cock's shrill clarion, or the echoing horn,
No more shall rouse them from their lowly bed.   20

[1] "Stillness" is the subject of the sentence.
[2] *Now . . . folds.* In these lines what onomatopoetic* words help to emphasize the stillness?
[3] *The breezy . . . Morn.* Is the poet thinking of "L'Allegro" (p. 190)?
[4] *straw-built shed.* Thatched shed (in which the swallow's nest is built).

Taylor

The churchyard at Stoke Poges, with the yew tree under which Gray is said to have written his famous "Elegy"

For them no more the blazing hearth
  shall burn,
  Or busy housewife ply her evening
  care;
No children run to lisp their sire's return,
  Or climb his knees the envied kiss to
  share.

Oft did the harvest to their sickle
  yield,
  Their furrow oft the stubborn glebe[1]
  has broke;
How jocund[2] did they drive their team
  afield!
  How bowed the woods beneath their
  sturdy stroke!

Let not Ambition mock their useful
  toil,
  Their homely joys, and destiny obscure;   30
Nor Grandeur hear, with a disdainful
  smile,
  The short and simple annals of the
  poor.

The boast of heraldry, the pomp of
  power,
  And all that beauty, all that wealth
  e'er gave,
Awaits alike the inevitable hour:
  The paths of glory lead but to the
  grave.

Nor you, ye proud, impute to these the
  fault,
  If Memory o'er their tomb no trophies
  raise,
Where through the long-drawn aisle and
  fretted vault
  The pealing anthem swells the note of
  praise.[3]   40

[1] Soil.
[2] jocund (jŏk'ŭnd). Happy.
[3] Where . . . praise. In some great cathedral or
  church, such as Westminster Abbey, where
  there are many magnificent tombs with inscriptions in memory of the dead.

Can storied urn[1] or animated[2] bust
  Back to its mansion[3] call the fleeting
  breath?
Can Honour's voice provoke[4] the silent
  dust,
  Or Flattery soothe the dull cold ear of
  Death?

Perhaps in this neglected spot is laid
  Some heart once pregnant with celes-
  tial fire;
Hands that the rod of empire might have
  swayed,
  Or waked to ecstasy the living lyre.[5]

But Knowledge to their eyes her ample
  page
  Rich with the spoils of time did ne'er
  unroll;   50
Chill Penury repressed their noble rage,[6]
  And froze the genial current of the soul.

Full many a gem of purest ray serene
  The dark unfathomed caves of ocean
  bear;
Full many a flower is born to blush unseen,
  And waste its sweetness on the desert
  air.

Some village Hampden that with dauntless breast
  The little tyrant of his fields withstood;[7]
Some mute inglorious Milton[8] here may
  rest,
  Some Cromwell guiltless of his country's blood.[9]   60

[1] storied urn. An urn with a picture or story
  portrayed on its sides.   [2] Lifelike.
[3] Dwelling; here, body.   [4] Call forth.
[5] Perhaps . . . lyre. Here may be buried someone who might have become a great statesman or a great poet.
[6] Poetic enthusiasm. Gray gives the two reasons
  why the people buried here never became
  famous; namely, ignorance and poverty.
[7] Some . . . withstood. Someone to defend local
  rights as John Hampden, in 1636, defended
  the rights of the people against Charles* I.
[8] mute . . . Milton. Someone with Milton's poetic
  genius and love of freedom, but without his
  power to express himself in great poetry, and
  hence "mute" and "inglorious."
[9] Cromwell . . . blood. A statesman who had
  Cromwell's genius but not, as Gray believed,
  his guilt. See "Cromwell."*

The applause of listening senates to
command,
The threats of pain and ruin to despise,
To scatter plenty o'er a smiling land,
And read their history in a nation's
eyes,

Their lot forbade; nor circumscribed
alone
Their growing virtues, but their crimes
confined;
Forbade to wade through slaughter to a
throne,
And shut the gates of mercy on mankind,

The struggling pangs of conscious truth
to hide,
To quench the blushes of ingenuous
shame,   70
Or heap the shrine of Luxury and Pride
With incense kindled at the Muse's
flame.

Far from the madding[1] crowd's ignoble
strife,
Their sober wishes never learned to
stray;
Along the cool sequestered vale of life
They kept the noiseless tenor of their
way.

Yet ev'n these bones from insult to pro-
tect
Some frail memorial still erected nigh,
With uncouth rhymes and shapeless
sculpture decked,   79
Implores the passing tribute of a sigh.

Their name, their years, spelt by the un-
lettered Muse,[2]
The place of fame and elegy supply;
And many a holy text around she strews,
That teach the rustic moralist to die.

For who, to dumb Forgetfulness a prey,
This pleasing anxious being e'er resigned,
Left the warm precincts of the cheerful
day,
Nor cast one longing, lingering look
behind?[1]

On some fond breast the parting soul
relies,
Some pious drops the closing eye requires;   90
Ev'n from the tomb the voice of Nature
cries,
Ev'n in our ashes live their wonted[2]
fires.

For thee,[3] who mindful of the unhon-
oured dead
Dost in these lines their artless tale
relate;
If chance, by lonely Contemplation led,
Some kindred spirit shall inquire thy
fate,

Haply some hoary-headed swain[4] may
say,
"Oft have we seen him at the peep of
dawn
Brushing with hasty steps the dews away
To meet the sun upon the upland
lawn.   100

"There at the foot of yonder nodding
beech,
That wreathes its old fantastic roots
so high,
His listless length at noontide would he
stretch,
And pore upon the brook that babbles
by.

---

[1] Notice that this word is "madding" (raving,
furious), not "maddening."
[2] spelt . . . Muse. Misspelled by some rustic
writer. Some of the inscriptions in Stoke
Poges churchyard are spelled incorrectly.

[1] who . . . behind. Who ever willingly resigned
this pleasing, though anxious, life to be a
prey to death ("dumb Forgetfulness"), or
desired to leave no memorial behind?
wonted (wŭn'tĕd). Accustomed.
[3] The poet himself, Thomas Gray, who, in the
rest of the poem, imagines he has died and
tells what he thinks people would say of him
[4] hoary-headed swain. White-haired old man.

"Hard by yon wood, now smiling as in
      scorn,
   Muttering his wayward fancies he
      would rove,
Now drooping, woeful wan, like one for-
      lorn,
   Or crazed with care, or crossed in hope-
      less love.

"One morn I missed him on the customed
      hill,
   Along the heath, and near his favourite
      tree;   110
Another came; nor yet beside the rill,
   Nor up the lawn, nor at the wood was
      he;

"The next with dirges due in sad array
   Slow through the church-way path we
      saw him borne.
Approach and read (for thou canst read[1])
      the lay,
   Graved on the stone beneath yon aged
      thorn."

THE EPITAPH[2]

Here rests his head upon the lap of Earth
   A youth to Fortune and to Fame un-
      known.
Fair Science frowned not on his humble
      birth,
   And Melancholy marked him for her
      own.   120

Large was his bounty, and his soul sin-
      cere,
   Heaven did a recompense as largely
      send:
He gave to Misery all he had, a tear,
   He gained from Heaven ('twas all he
      wished) a friend.[3]

[1] for . . . read. By this phrase the "hoary-headed
   swain" implies that he cannot read.
[2] This epitaph is engraved on Gray's tomb in
   Stoke Poges churchyard.
[3] Presumably Horace Walpole, the son of the
   prime minister Sir Robert Walpole, and an
   early friend of Gray's.

No farther seek his merits to disclose,
   Or draw his frailties from their dread
      abode,
(There they alike in trembling hope repose,)
   The bosom of his Father and his God.

Words and Passages to be Explained

drowsy tinklings (l. 8)
rude forefathers (l. 16)
stubborn glebe (l. 26)
short and simple annals of the poor (l. 32)
frail memorial (l. 78)
pore (l. 104)

Discussion Hints

1. Describe in your own words the setting
of the poem.

2. In the first four stanzas what words or
phrases help most to suggest the picture?

3. Do you agree with Gray's explanation
(ll. 49–52) of the causes why those buried in
the churchyard never became famous? Give
reasons for your answer.

4. What are some of the "spoils of time"
(l. 50), inventions or discoveries, that modern
science could "unroll" to the astonishment of
Gray and his contemporaries?

5. Lines 53–56 have two meanings: one
literal, the other symbolical, or allegorical.*
Make clear that you understand both
meanings.

6. Write a précis (summary) of lines 1–44.

7. Paraphrase lines 61–72.

8. Memorize the first stanza and the stanza
beginning with line 53.

9. What is the meter of Gray's "Elegy"?
What is the rhyme* scheme?

10. Read the headnote again and then
point out features that help to make the poem
(a) classical, (b) romantic.

11. What picture of himself does Gray draw
in the poem? Point out the passages on which
your answer is based.

12. Make a list of passages that you have
heard or seen quoted or that are suitable for
quotation.

13. Subjects for themes:
   a The meaning of Gray's "Elegy."

b. "The short and simple annals of the poor."

c. A picture representing the subject of the poem.

d. Why I regard Gray's "Elegy" as a great poem.

Suggestions for Reading

1. "Ode on a Distant Prospect of Eton College," "Ode on the Death of a Favourite Cat," "William Shakespeare," "The Progress of Poesy."

2. Gray was a delightful letter-writer. *Poems: with a Selection of Letters and Essays,* with an introduction by John Drinkwater, is published in Everyman's Library (E. P. Dutton & Co., Inc.).

3. If possible read in connection with Gray's "Elegy" Gilbert Keith Chesterton's "Elegy in a Country Churchyard" (given in the revised edition of *Achievement* of this series).

WILLIAM COWPER [1] (1731–1800)

From the *Olney Hymns*

Cowper's hymns are true lyrics in that they are the spontaneous expression of the poet's deep religious feelings. Many of them are still sung today. Historically, these poems, with their pleas for personal instead of mass religious experience, are thoroughly in keeping with the general revolutionary emphasis upon the importance of the individual that marked the latter part of the eighteenth century. The example here given is a beautiful personal appeal justifying the ways of God to men, a theme which Milton also chose as the subject of his great religious epic, *Paradise Lost.*

The *Olney Hymns* are so called because they were composed at Olney, in Buckinghamshire.

I

GOD moves in a mysterious way
   His wonders to perform;
He plants his footsteps in the sea,
   And rides upon the storm.

II

Deep in unfathomable mines
   Of never-failing skill
He treasures up his bright designs,
   And works his sovereign will.

III

Ye fearful saints, fresh courage take,
   The clouds ye so much dread   10
Are big with mercy, and shall break
   In blessings on your head.

IV

Judge not the Lord by feeble sense,
   But trust him for his grace:
Behind a frowning providence
   He hides a smiling face.

V

His purposes will ripen fast,
   Unfolding every hour;
The bud may have a bitter taste,
   But sweet will be the flower.   20

VI

Blind unbelief is sure to err,
   And scan his work in vain:
God is his own interpreter,
   And he will make it plain.

The Solitude of Alexander Selkirk

By the power of his creative genius Cowper was able to imagine Alexander Selkirk,* the original of Defoe's Robinson Crusoe, as writing poems about his experiences and emotions in his lonely island home. "The Solitude of Alexander Selkirk," which is one of a collection of poems on the same subject, is marked by simple directness, fondness for moralizing, and the success with which the poet puts himself in Selkirk's place.

[1] *Cowper* (kōō′pĕr *or* kou′pĕr). For biography see page 712.

I AM monarch of all I survey;
My right there is none to dispute;
From the centre all round to the sea
I am lord of the fowl and the brute.
O Solitude! where are the charms
That sages have seen in thy face?
Better dwell in the midst of alarms,
Than reign in this horrible place.

I am out of humanity's reach,
I must finish my journey alone,　　　　10
Never hear the sweet music of speech;
I start at the sound of my own.
The beasts that roam over the plain
My form with indifference see;
They are so unacquainted with man,
Their tameness is shocking to me.

Society, Friendship, and Love
Divinely bestow'd upon man,
Oh, had I the wings of a dove
How soon would I taste you again!　　20
My sorrows I then might assuage
In the ways of religion and truth,
Might learn from the wisdom of age,
And be cheer'd by the sallies of youth.

Ye winds that have made me your sport,
Convey to this desolate shore
Some cordial endearing report
Of a land I shall visit no more:
My friends, do they now and then send
A wish or a thought after me?　　　　30
O tell me I yet have a friend,
Though a friend I am never to see.

How fleet is a glance of the mind!
Compared with the speed of its flight,
The temper itself lags behind,
And the swift-wingèd arrows of light.
When I think of my own native land
In a moment I seem to be there;
But alas! recollection at hand
Soon hurries me back to despair.　　　40

But the sea-fowl is gone to her nest,
The beast is laid down in his lair;
Even here is a season of rest,
And I to my cabin repair.

There's mercy in every place,
And mercy, encouraging thought!
Gives even affliction a grace
And reconciles man to his lot.

Discussion Hints

From the *Olney Hymns*

1. What, according to Cowper, are some of the evidences of God's "mysterious way"?

2. What is the meaning of "fearful" (l. 9)?

3. Explain the allegory* of lines 19–20.

4. How does the selection from the *Olney Hymns* illustrate the belief that all parts of nature, even the most awe-inspiring, are the work of a wise and loving God? In stanza IV, with what is "feeble sense" (that is, "reason") contrasted?

The Solitude of Alexander Selkirk

1. Were the feelings of Robinson Crusoe like those of Cowper's Alexander Selkirk? In the selection from *Robinson Crusoe* (p. 265) point out passages that suggest any of Cowper's phrases.

2. Reread what is said on page 216 about the classicists' fondness for cultivated society, and then decide whether "The Solitude of Alexander Selkirk" reflects better this attitude or some other. Quote passages to prove your answer.

3. If you were cast on a desert island, how do you think your reaction would compare with that of the castaway in the poem?

4. Learn by heart the first stanza.

5. In the lyric poems given on pages 296–304 pick out illustrations of ordinary objects called by fanciful names in imitation of the poets of the Age of Classicism.

Suggestions for Reading

1. "The Diverting History of John Gilpin," "On the Loss of the *Royal George*," "On the Receipt of My Mother's Picture." From *Poems of William Cowper*. Everyman's Library.

2. Cowper, like Gray, was a charming letter-writer. Some of his best letters are given in *Selected Letters of William Cowper*, edited by William Hadley. Everyman's Library.

3. "Robinson Crusoe's Story," a clever little poem by Charles Edward Carryl.

NARRATIVE POETRY[1]

OLIVER GOLDSMITH[2] (1728-1774)

From "The Deserted Village"

"The Deserted Village" is not only one of the best-known of Goldsmith's poems, it is one of the greatest poems in the English language. It is also worth reading because of its connection with important economic and social problems of the eighteenth century. It reflects the country-bred Goldsmith's sorrow at the changes in rural life caused by the growth of industrialism and wealth, by emigration, and by the constantly increasing concentration of land in the hands of a few rich owners. The charm of the poem lies in its genuinely human pictures, in its natural humor and pathos, in its delightful though idealized descriptions of rural scenes, and in the perfection of its workmanship.

In its praise of rural life and its enthusiastic admiration of simple, humble folk as the real backbone of the nation, "The Deserted Village" is romantic.* On the other hand, such phrases as "smiling spring" (l. 3) and "vagrant train" (l. 29) belong more to the artificial language of classical poetry than to the vocabulary of romantic poetry. The poem also resembles much verse of the Age of Classicism in that it is to some extent didactic, that is, intended to teach a lesson.

SWEET Auburn,[3] loveliest village of the
   plain,
Where health and plenty cheered the
   labouring swain,
Where smiling spring its earliest visit
   paid,
And parting summer's lingering blooms
   delayed.

Sweet smiling village, loveliest of the
   lawn,
Thy sports are fled, and all thy charms
   withdrawn;
Amidst thy bowers the tyrant's[1] hand is
   seen,
And desolation saddens all thy green:
One only master grasps the whole domain.
And half a tillage stints thy smiling plain.[2]

Ill fares the land, to hastening ills a
   prey,   11
Where wealth accumulates, and men decay:
Princes and lords may flourish, or may
   fade;
A breath can make them,[3] as a breath has
   made;
But a bold peasantry, their country's
   pride,
When once destroyed, can never be supplied.[4]

Near yonder copse, where once the
   garden smiled,
And still where many a garden-flower
   grows wild;
There, where a few torn shrubs the place
   disclose,
The village preacher's modest mansion
   rose.   20

---

[1] For discussion of narrative poetry see page 36.
[2] For biography see page 713.
[3] Auburn is probably no particular village, although some of the details might apply to the village of Lissoy in Ireland, where Goldsmith spent part of his childhood.

[1] Tyrant here means the landowner who enclosed ground formerly used by the peasants.
[2] *half . . . plain.* Only half the ground was cultivated.
[3] *A breath . . . them.* A man can be created a noble merely by the king's order.
[4] *Ill . . . supplied.* This is one of the first bits of eighteenth-century English poetry that glorifies humble peasant folk.

D

A man he was to all the country dear,
And passing rich with forty pounds a
    year;
Remote from towns he ran his godly race,
Nor e'er had changed, nor wished to
    change his place;
Unpractised he to fawn, or seek for
    power,
By doctrines fashioned to the varying
    hour;
Far other aims his heart had learned to
    prize,
More skilled to raise the wretched than
    to rise.
His house was known to all the vagrant
    train,[1]
He chid their wanderings, but relieved
    their pain;   30
The long-remembered beggar was his
    guest,
Whose beard descending swept his aged
    breast;
The ruined spendthrift, now no longer
    proud,
Claimed kindred there, and had his
    claims allowed;
The broken soldier, kindly bade to stay,
Sat by his fire, and talked the night
    away;
Wept o'er his wounds, or tales of sorrow
    done,
Shouldered his crutch, and showed how
    fields were won.
Pleased with his guests, the good man
    learned to glow,
And quite forgot their vices in their
    woe;   40
Careless their merits or their faults to
    scan,
His pity gave ere charity began.

  Thus to relieve the wretched was his
    pride,
And even his failings leaned to Virtue's
    side;
But in his duty prompt at every call,
He watched and wept, he prayed and
    felt, for all.

            [1] vagrant train. Tramps.

And, as a bird each fond endearment
    tries
To tempt its new-fledged offspring to the
    skies,
He tried each art, reproved each dull
    delay,
Allured to brighter worlds, and led the
    way.[1]   50

  Beside the bed where parting life was
    laid,
And sorrow, guilt, and pain by turns dis-
    mayed,
The reverend champion [2] stood. At his
    control
Despair and anguish fled the struggling
    soul;
Comfort came down the trembling wretch
    to raise,
And his last faltering accents whispered
    praise.

  At church, with meek and unaffected
    grace,
His looks adorned the venerable place;
Truth from his lips prevailed with double
    sway,
And fools, who came to scoff, remained
    to pray.[3]   60
The service passed, around the pious
    man,
With steady zeal, each honest rustic
    ran;
Even children followed with endearing
    wile,
And plucked his gown,[4] to share the good
    man's smile.
His ready smile a parent's warmth ex-
    pressed,
Their welfare pleased him, and their
    cares distressed;
To them his heart, his love, his griefs
    were given,
But all his serious thoughts had rest in
    Heaven.

[1] Allured . . . way. A line often quoted.
[2] reverend champion. A striking metaphor.*
[3] Truth . . . pray. Learn these two lines.
[4] The clergyman's gown, or cassock.

As some tall cliff, that lifts its awful
    form,
Swells from the vale, and midway leaves
    the storm,   70
Though round its breast the rolling
    clouds are spread,
Eternal sunshine settles on its head.[1]

Beside[2] yon straggling fence that skirts
    the way,
With blossomed furze unprofitably gay,[3]
There, in his noisy mansion, skilled to
    rule,
The village master taught his little
    school;
A man severe he was, and stern to view;
I knew him well, and every truant knew;
Well had the boding tremblers learned to
    trace
The day's disasters in his morning face;
Full well they laughed, with counterfeited
    glee,   81
At all his jokes, for many a joke had he;
Full well the busy whisper, circling round,
Conveyed the dismal tidings when he
    frowned;
Yet he was kind, or if severe in aught,
The love he bore to learning was in
    fault;
The village all declared how much he
    knew;
'Twas certain he could write, and cipher
    too;
Lands he could measure, terms and tides
    presage,
And even the story ran that he could
    gauge.[4]   90
In arguing too, the parson owned his
    skill,
For even though vanquished, he could
    argue still;[5]

While words of learned length and thun-
    dering sound,
Amazed the gazing rustics ranged
    around;
And still they gazed, and still the won-
    der grew,
That one small head could carry all he
    knew.[1]

But past is all his fame. The very spot,
Where many a time he triumphed, is
    forgot.
Near yonder thorn, that lifts its head on
    high,
Where once the sign-post caught the
    passing eye,   100
Low lies that house where nut-brown
    draughts inspired,
Where gray-beard Mirth and smiling
    Toil retired,
Where village statesmen talked with
    looks profound,
And news much older than their ale went
    round.
Imagination fondly stoops to trace
The parlour splendours of that festive
    place;
The white-washed wall, the nicely sanded
    floor,
The varnished clock that clicked behind
    the door;
The chest contrived a double debt to pay,
A bed by night, a chest of drawers by
    day;   110
The pictures placed for ornament and
    use,[2]
The twelve* good rules, the royal game
    of goose,[3]
The hearth, except when winter chilled
    the day,
With aspen boughs, and flowers, and
    fennel gay;
While broken tea-cups, wisely kept for
    show,
Ranged o'er the chimney, glistened in a
    row.

[1] *As . . . head.* A famous simile.*
[2] Here begins Goldsmith's justly praised descrip-
    tion of the village schoolmaster.
[3] The furze bush bears an abundance of gay
    flowers, but in other respects is of little value.
[4] Estimate the number of gallons in a cask, a
    hard thing to do.
[5] *For even . . . still.* Learn this line; it is often
    quoted.

[1] *And still . . . knew.* Two lines often quoted.
[2] To cover stains on the walls.
[3] A game played on a board which pictured geese.

Yes! let the rich deride, the proud
disdain,
These simple blessings of the lowly train;
To me more dear, congenial to my heart,
One native charm, than all the gloss of
art.   120

Where then, ah! where, shall poverty
reside,
To 'scape the pressure of contiguous
pride[1]?
If to some common's[2] fenceless limits
strayed,
He drives his flock to pick the scanty
blade,
Those fenceless fields the sons of wealth
divide,
And even the bare-worn common is
denied.

If to the city sped — What waits him
there?

The dome where Pleasure holds her midnight reign,
Here, richly decked, admits the gorgeous
train;
Tumultuous grandeur crowds the blazing
square,   130
The rattling chariots clash, the torches
glare.
Sure scenes like these no troubles e'er
annoy!
Sure these denote one universal joy!
Are these thy serious thoughts? — Ah,
turn thine eyes
Where the poor houseless shivering
female lies.

Do thine, sweet Auburn, thine, the
loveliest train,
Do thy fair tribes participate her pain?
Even now, perhaps, by cold and hunger
led,
At proud men's doors they ask a little
bread!

Ah, no! To distant climes,[1] a dreary
scene,   140
Where half the convex world intrudes
between,
Through torrid tracts with fainting steps
they go,
Where wild Altama[2] murmurs to their
woe.
Far different there from all that charmed
before,
The various terrors of that horrid shore;
Those blazing suns that dart a down-
ward ray,
And fiercely shed intolerable day;
Those matted woods where birds forget
to sing,
But silent bats in drowsy clusters cling;
Those poisonous fields with rank luxu-
riance crowned,   150
Where the dark scorpion gathers death
around;
Where at each step the stranger fears to
wake
The rattling terrors of the vengeful
snake;
Where crouching tigers wait their hap-
less prey,
And savage men more murderous still
than they;
While oft in whirls the mad tornado
flies,
Mingling the ravaged landscape with the
skies.
Far different these from every former
scene,
The cooling brook, the grassy-vested
green,
The breezy covert of the warbling grove,
That only sheltered thefts of harmless
love.   161

Even now the devastation is begun,
And half the business of destruction
done;
Even now, methinks, as pondering here
I stand,
I see the rural Virtues leave the land:

[1] *Contiguous pride.* Proud people who live near by.
[2] A common was a tract of land belonging to all
the people of a community in common. In
Goldsmith's day such land was often enclosed
by landowners for their own use (see page 290).

[1] *distant climes.* Here, America.
[2] The Altamaha River in Georgia.

Down where yon anchoring vessel spreads
   the sail,
That idly waiting flaps with every gale,
Downward they move, a melancholy
   band,
Pass from the shore, and darken all the
   strand.   169
Contented Toil, and hospitable Care,
And kind connubial Tenderness are
   there;
And Piety with wishes placed above,
And steady Loyalty, and faithful Love.
And thou, sweet Poetry, thou loveliest
   maid,
Still first to fly where sensual joys invade;
Unfit in these degenerate times of shame,
To catch the heart, or strike for honest
   fame;
Dear charming nymph,[1] neglected and
   decried,
My shame in crowds, my solitary pride;
Thou source of all my bliss, and all my
   woe,   180
That found'st me poor at first, and
   keep'st me so;
Thou guide by which the nobler arts
   excel,
Thou nurse of every virtue, fare thee
   well!

Discussion Hints

1. Goldsmith is one of the earliest English poets to glorify simple countryfolk. As you read further in *English Writers*, look for other cases.

2. What contrast do you find between the first four lines and the remainder of the selection?

3. The famous picture of the village preacher (ll. 21–72) is said to have been modeled on Goldsmith's own father. Assuming this to be true, what features of the description do you think are taken from the original?

[1] Poetry, which Goldsmith did not believe was properly appreciated.

4. Which parson do you prefer: Goldsmith's (ll. 21–72) or Chaucer's (p. 47)? Why?

5. Lines 99–116 give a remarkably clear picture of the bar of an eighteenth-century inn. Point out details that make the picture vivid.

6. Point out passages in which Goldsmith laments the effects of wealth, city life, enclosures, and emigration.

7. Is Goldsmith's description of Georgia accurate (ll. 143–157)? What mistakes does the description contain?

8. Write the following lines in current English: 1–2, 17–20, 29–42.

9. Memorize the following passages: lines 1–10, 21–24, 39–42, and 95–96.

10. Illustrate from the selection the relation of "The Deserted Village" to English poetry of the Age of Classicism (p. 214). Point out also passages that illustrate the qualities of simplicity and naturalness as opposed to artificiality.

11. Compare lines 11–16 with Burns's "A Man's a Man for A' That" (p. 333, ll. 25–32).

Passages to be Explained

parting summer's lingering blooms delayed
   (l. 4)
The village preacher's modest mansion rose
   (l. 20)
He chid their wanderings, but relieved their pain
   (l. 30)
even his failings leaned to Virtue's side
   (l. 44)
parting life (l. 51)
Pleasure holds her midnight reign (l. 128)
torrid tracts (l. 142)
connubial Tenderness (l. 171)

Suggestions for Reading

"The Traveller"; "Retaliation"; "Elegy on the Death of a Mad Dog."

You will, of course, also wish to read at some future time, if not now, Goldsmith's well-known comedy *She Stoops to Conquer* and his equally well-known novel *The Vicar of Wakefield.*

1798-1832

❀

The
Romantic Period

The Cotter's Saturday Night

THE period of English literature marked by the triumph of the forces which had begun during the transition from classicism to romanticism (p. 289) is known as the Romantic Period. It extends roughly from the publication of the *Lyrical Ballads* (p. 335), by Wordsworth and Coleridge, in 1798 to the death of Sir Walter Scott (p. 401) in 1832.

To appreciate the literature of the Romantic Period we should remember, first of all, that the term "romantic" as applied to the late eighteenth and early nineteenth centuries includes more than it does in the ordinary usage of the present day. Today most of us apply the term to scenes or happenings that are strange or unusual, especially those involving love or adventure. "Romantic" is the term we also apply to ancient moss-covered ruins, vine-clad cottages, bodies of water seen by moonlight, the ocean in a storm, lofty mountains, and beautiful sunsets. Some of us even go so far as to use the term to describe anything that fills us with an indescribable pleasure or ecstasy.

In literary criticism the term "romantic" is used in a more extended sense to describe a large and complicated body of ideas and tendencies that characterized English life and English literary works during the late eighteenth century and the early nineteenth. In general the Romantic Period was marked by the abandonment of old, accepted rules in society, in politics, in religion, and in literature, and the establishment of new standards. It brought into English life not only a new freedom and a new feeling for truth and beauty, but also new responsibilities and new dangers. The movement revealed itself in a multitude of ways, of which the following are the most important.

A NEW ATTITUDE TOWARD MAN

The common man was respected and idealized as never before. The classicists had admired especially the cultivated city man of courtly and conventional manners (p. 216); the romanticists preferred the humble peasant, who, though possessing little outward polish, was by nature kindly, simple, and noble. When Burns[1] declared that

> The rank is but the guinea's stamp,
> The man's the gowd for a' that,[2]

and when, in "The Cotter's Saturday Night" (p. 383), he pictured the sterling virtues and noble lives of obscure countryfolk, he was only express-

[1] For biography see page 714.   [2] Page 333.

ing boldly the idea that Goldsmith had suggested in the preceding period when he wrote of "a bold peasantry" as "their country's pride" (p. 305).

Admiration for the common man and for the simple life was only one aspect of a larger faith in the essential goodness of humanity that marked the Romantic Period. By means of the French Revolution, which began in 1789, the oppressed people of France sought to rectify the social injustice from which the lower classes had suffered since the Middle Ages.[1] Their motto, "Liberty, equality, fraternity," became the slogan of romantic democracy throughout western Europe and America. The ideals of the French Revolution affected English thinkers profoundly. Wordsworth,[2] a young man at the time of the outbreak of the Revolution, was enthusiastic over the downfall of tyranny and the promise of liberty for the common people of France; and even after the excesses of the revolutionists and the high-handed policy of Napoleon* had caused him to lose much of his faith in the revolutionary principles, he still continued to write in praise of freedom and in condemnation of bigotry and oppression. Shelley[3] wrote both prose and verse in support of political freedom, and Byron[4] was an avowed enemy of tyranny in every form. Even before the French Revolution the people of America, filled with the romantic spirit, expressed their faith in democracy by establishing in 1776 a new government "of the people, by the people, for the people," founded upon the great principle that "all men are created free and equal."

The new admiration for simplicity, naturalness, and unaffectedness caused the romanticists to include in their love and sympathy little children and even many of the lower animals. Before the Transition Period children had seldom been treated with any great understanding and sympathy in English literature; the romanticists regarded childhood reverently, largely because children were looked upon as too young to have been spoiled by the artificializing influences of society. Wordsworth was especially fond of writing about the sweet simplicity and naturalness of children (p. 335). In his ode "Intimations of Immortality" he takes as his theme the old idea that children still preserve recollections of the pure and beautiful heavenly realm from which they have recently come, and that only as they grow older is their vision of truth and goodness gradually blurred by the conventional world in which they are forced to grow up. Burns's "To a Mouse" (p. 328) is one of the best of many romantic writings which express sympathy for dumb animals.

---

[1] The horrors of the French Revolution are graphically depicted in Dickens's *Tale of Two Cities* (given in the revised edition of *Achievement* of this series). The Revolution is also the subject of Carlyle's *French Revolution* (see page 350, footnote 3).

[2] For biography see page 715. [3] For biography see page 719. [4] For biography see page 718.

THE RETURN TO NATURE

Coupled with the new romantic attitude toward man went a new feeling for nature. To the classicist the ideal landscape had consisted of a carefully planned and orderly garden with clipped hedges and trimmed walks;[1] to the romanticist such artificial scenes were inferior to wild country landscapes where the natural loveliness of woods and streams was untouched by the hand of man. Looking thus upon the outer world with new eyes, the romanticists discovered in wild nature beauties that had never before been perceived. The classicists had found little or nothing to admire in winter or storm or lofty mountain or raging sea; the romanticists found in them the inspiration for some of their best poetry. The typical classicist preferred smooth plains to mountains because they were easier to cross; he disliked the ocean because sea voyages were uncomfortable and dangerous. The romantic poets praised inclement weather, storms, and the wild ocean because they revealed the power of God or were otherwise beautiful or awe-inspiring. Byron's famous lines beginning "Roll on, thou deep and dark blue Ocean — roll!" (p. 355) form one of the finest lyric passages written in praise of the sea during the Romantic Period.

It is important to remember that, whatever aspect of nature the romanticists chose to admire, they usually found in the outer world something more than a mere superficial pleasure. Some romantic poets, for example, Byron, sought the solitude of wild nature as an escape from their fellow men. Many others, however, found in nature a comforting and strengthening influence or even a revelation of the perfect wisdom and goodness of God. Wordsworth asserts that nature "never did betray the heart that loved her," and in one of his best sonnets (p. 343) he upbraids his contemporaries because they saw so little of the poetry to be found in the world about them. To Wordsworth nature was a link uniting him on the one hand to his fellow men and on the other to God. To Shelley nature served merely as a starting point for poetic flights into exalted realms of myth-making and lofty imagination. As seen through his eyes the west wind (p. 358) and the cloud (p. 360) cease to be inanimate things and become possessed of a life of their own. To Keats[2] nature as exemplified by the song of the nightingale (p. 369) became the symbol of immortal beauty and pure romance. Many romantic poets, in their new enthusiasm for nature, included in their sympathy not only more impressive things, such as storms and mountains, but even the humblest weed by the roadside, To Wordsworth

> the meanest flower that blows can give
> Thoughts that do often lie too deep for tears.

[1] See illustration on page 216.   [2] For biography see page 720.

Burns composed one of his most touching lyrics on a lowly mountain daisy (p. 330)[1] accidentally uprooted by his plow. Indeed, the romanticists found so many new attractions in the outdoor world that some critics of literature regard the new attitude as the very essence of romanticism, and define the romantic movement as "the return to nature."

The new attitude toward man and nature inevitably led to the conviction that life among simple country surroundings is more natural and wholesome than life in cities. When, during the Period of Transition, the poet Cowper[2] wrote "God made the country, and man made the town," he was expressing a belief that became widespread during the Romantic Period. Romantic poets and theorists sought to persuade their fellow men that if they would only get "back to nature," and thus escape from the conventionalizing and soul-stifling influences of organized society, they would become more natural, more open to the appeals of religion, and in every way more admirable.

THE LYRIC SPIRIT

The importance of personal feeling and emotion, which had been recognized during the Transition Period, was an even more marked characteristic of the romantic point of view. The classicist had sought as his ideal the general, the impersonal, the typical; the romanticist, on the other hand, strove to express his own personality and to give voice to his own reactions on life, regardless of whether he followed the established rules of literature or of society. In other words, whereas the classicist had sought to view the world objectively,* the romanticist was apt to be highly subjective* in his attitude toward himself and his fellows. His test of things was more often his heart than his head, his emotions than his reason. In short, he was likely to be an individualist. As a result romantic poetry and prose are frequently most interesting for the view they give us of the writer's own opinions, prejudices, hopes, fears, joys, or sorrows.

During the Romantic Period many ordinary men, as well as poets, were easily moved to tenderness, sometimes to tears, by things that appear to have affected their ancestors but little. William Blake, in his "Auguries of Innocence" (p. 325), gives a list of the things that stirred the emotions of the romantic sentimentalist; Burns grew tender over a field mouse; and Wordsworth was only one of a large number of romantic poets whose hearts were stirred by the poetry and pathos of childhood. The emotional appeal of poverty and of hard, grinding labor was also voiced in many poems and prose writings during the Romantic Period. These humanitarian feelings were brought to America and have influenced American literature even to the present day.

[1] See also Wordsworth's "To the Daisy," p. 340. [2] For biography see page 712.

THE RETURN TO THE MIDDLE AGES

The interest in the Middle Ages which had begun during the Transition Period (p. 289) increased greatly during the Romantic Period. The enthusiasm of the romanticists for naturalness, simplicity, and spontaneity went hand in hand with an increased admiration for the popular ballads (p. 57) and for medieval literature in general. Percy's *Reliques*, which had appeared in 1765, during the Transition Period, was widely read and admired, and many other collections of ancient ballads and songs were made, including *Minstrelsy of the Scottish Border*, edited by Sir Walter Scott. A host of poets, chief among whom was Scott,[1] wrote imitations of the popular ballads. Much of Coleridge's[2] poetry[3] owes its charm, at least in part, to the influence of the ballads. In addition to the ballads, ancient Scandinavian and Celtic themes also became popular during the Romantic Period. Especially influential were the Ossianic* poems, which had appeared during the Transition Period. Among the romanticists, Scott, in his poems and novels, and Moore, in his *Irish Melodies* (p. 349), did much to arouse interest in the poetry and traditions of the Gaelic Celts. The whole age of chivalry, including the medieval romances, was idealized and admired as never before. Themes drawn from the life of the Middle Ages, especially the age of chivalry, became favorite subjects with both poets and prose-writers. Of the many poems dealing with medieval subjects written during the late eighteenth century and the early nineteenth, Keats's "La Belle Dame sans Merci" (p. 368) and Coleridge's "Christabel" (p. 395) are deservedly among the most famous.

The romantic enthusiasm for earlier literature also embraced many writings of the Elizabethan (p. 71) and Puritan periods (p. 183). Shakespeare, Spenser, and Milton were especially admired. Shakespeare, no longer regarded as merely "an inspired barbarian" (p. 216), was looked upon as England's greatest dramatic writer and as one of the world's most inspired original geniuses.

THE REVOLT AGAINST CLASSICISM

POETRY

From what has been said above, it is clear that the Romantic Period represented a complete revolt against the view, both of society and of literature, held by the classicists (p. 214).

Though both lyric and narrative poetry flourished during the Romantic Period, it was in the domain of the lyric that the romantic spirit found

---

[1] For biography see page 722. [2] For biography see page 721.

[3] Coleridge's *Ancient Mariner*, written in imitation of the old ballads, is given in the revised edition of *Achievement* of this series.

its most characteristic expression. The best lyric poems of Burns, Wordsworth, Shelley, and Keats represent the high-water mark of English lyric poetry. As **narrative** poets Scott and Byron also rank high in English literature.

The poetry of the Romantic Period was as new in form as it was in subject matter. The heroic* couplet, though still employed occasionally, now revealed a flexibility more like that found in the poetry of Chaucer (p. 37) than in the verses of the school of Pope. Romantic poets were especially fond of using old and long-neglected verse forms such as blank* verse, the sonnet,* and the Spenserian* stanza. Because of its use in the much-admired poetry of the folk, the ballad stanza (see page 58) was especially popular. The ode* also took on new life, especially in the hands of Wordsworth and Keats (p. 366). In their desire to make use of striking and unfamiliar forms, some poets invented new ones, as Coleridge did in "Christabel" (p. 395), or went entirely outside English literature and adopted Continental verse forms, as Shelley did when he used *terza* rima*, an Italian form, in his "Ode to the West Wind" (p. 358).

In language as well as in verse forms romantic poetry represents a revolt against the rules of the classicists. Avoiding the indiscriminate use of personified* abstractions and abandoning the artificial, high-flown vocabulary of early-eighteenth-century verse, poets began to use a vocabulary more closely resembling that of everyday speech. This tendency was, of course, quite in keeping with the general desire for greater naturalness and simplicity which characterized the whole Romantic Period. Wordsworth, in his famous preface to the second edition of the *Lyrical Ballads*, stated the extreme case for the friends of simplicity when he maintained that the vocabulary of poetry should be selected from the language of common men.

THE NOVEL

The Romantic Period was marked by a great increase in the number of novels written and in the extent of the novel-reading public. The Gothic romances, which had begun during the Transition Period (p. 289), continued to flourish and culminated in the novels of Sir Walter Scott. Scott took the old, familiar themes of Gothic romance, breathed into them the breath of life, and changed them from more or less cheap melodrama into real literature. From 1814, the date of the appearance of *Waverley*, almost until his death in 1832, Scott was busy writing and publishing a long series of novels, most of which reveal the same wholesome love of nature and the same vital interest in the past that are to be found in his poetry.[1] Scott's historical novels are romantic because they tell of thrilling adventures,

---

[1] *The Lady of the Lake*, a part of which is in the revised edition of *Adventure* of this series, is a poem of Scott's that resembles his novels closely except that it is shorter and is written in verse.

beautiful and distressed ladies, brave and handsome heroes, and chivalrous outlaws, and the scenes are laid amid wild mountain scenery, in dark forests, in gorgeous palaces, or in gray and moss-grown castles of a bygone age. Scott's work illustrates, above all, the enthusiasm of the romanticists for the past of Britain, especially for the age of chivalry. Scott is also noted for his use of local color. His novels were enormously popular in their day, they are still widely read, and they have been imitated by many later novelists.

Along with Scott we should also remember Jane Austen, whose novels, published between 1811 and 1818, reflected English middle-class society in small communities more perfectly than had ever been done before. Jane Austen uses the language of everyday English life. Her painstaking realism * represents a decided step in advance of the realism of Defoe (p. 265) and other novelists of the early eighteenth century.

THE ESSAY

In keeping with the general tendency of the age, the Romantic Period was rich in essays which present the essayist's personal reaction. Charles Lamb (p. 375), with his fondness for the past, his gentle humor, and his quaint style, has left us a collection of charming familiar essays that reflect the author's unusually lovable personality and possess a flavor all their own. The Romantic Period is also rich in essays that seek to interpret literature in a humane and appreciative spirit. Instead of applying the dogmatic and rather narrow critical standards of Johnson (p. 238) and other classical writers, romantic critics approached the works of others with sympathy and tried to understand the personality and intention of the writer before they attempted to interpret his work.

Taken altogether, the various characteristics of English romanticism may be conveniently summed up in a phrase applied to it years ago by a distinguished critic, who called it the "Renaissance of Wonder."

THE INDUSTRIAL REVOLUTION

During the Transition and Romantic periods the industrial life of England underwent a change which in effect amounted to a peaceful revolution. The Industrial Revolution began a little after 1700, during the Age of Classicism (p. 213), and continued until the middle of the nineteenth century. During its progress England ceased to be mainly an agricultural country, the chief exports of which were grain, hides, and raw materials, and became mainly an industrial country dotted with towns and cities whose people lived chiefly by manufacturing goods for sale at home or abroad.

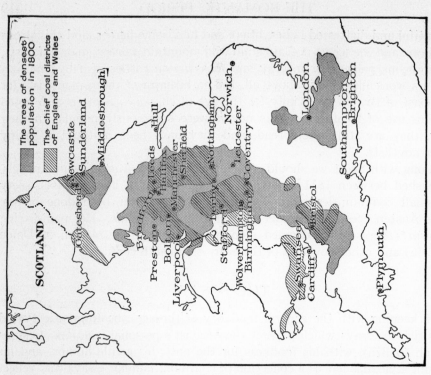

England after the Industrial Revolution

England before the Industrial Revolution

The change was hastened by the invention of machinery and the increased use of coal for smelting iron. In 1765 James Watt invented an early form of the steam engine, in 1768 Richard Arkwright constructed an improved machine for spinning yarn, in 1785 Edmund Cartwright made a usable power loom for weaving cloth, and other new machines were invented for knitting stockings and making lace. Transportation was greatly improved by the construction of better roads, by the digging of canals, and, finally, by the building of railroads. The first English railway was opened in 1825, a few years before the beginning of the first railroad in America. The first steamboat in England is said to have been operated soon after 1800, about the same time that Fulton's *Clermont* made its trial run on the Hudson River in America. In 1825 the first steamship reached Liverpool from America, thus uniting the two countries more closely than ever before.

The Industrial Revolution also resulted in a rapid growth of English towns, especially in those districts where manufacturing could be carried on to advantage. The growth of the towns brought with it housing problems, slum areas, and, in many cases, poverty and discontent among the laboring classes. The social problems of the industrial centers were rendered more difficult by an enormous increase in the population of England. During the early years of the Industrial Revolution the population of the whole country was not much more than ten millions; by the latter part of the nineteenth century it had increased to more than forty millions.[1]

---

[1] The influence of the Industrial Revolution upon America is discussed on pages 48–49 of the revised edition of *American Writers* of this series.

Correlation of English Literature with Historical Events during the Romantic Period

HISTORICAL EVENTS		LITERARY LANDMARKS
	1770	WORDSWORTH *born. Died 1850*
	1771	SCOTT *born. Died 1832*
	1772	COLERIDGE *born. Died 1834*
	1774	SOUTHEY *born. Died 1843*
The AMERICAN REVOLUTION	1775	LAMB *born. Died 1834.* LANDOR *born. Died 1864.* JANE AUSTEN *born. Died 1817.* BURKE,* Speech on Conciliation with America
DECLARATION OF AMERICAN INDEPENDENCE	1776	
First iron bridge in ENGLAND	1779	MOORE *born. Died 1852*
Surrender of CORNWALLIS *at* YORKTOWN	1781	
Invention of a loom for weaving cloth by steam power	1785	
	1786	BURNS, Poems Chiefly in the Scottish Dialect (Kilmarnock Edition)
	1788	BYRON *born. Died 1824*
The FRENCH REVOLUTION; *fall of the* BASTILLE; WASHINGTON, *first President of the* UNITED STATES	1789	BLAKE, Songs of Innocence
	1792	SHELLEY *born. Died 1822*
Execution of LOUIS XVI *of* FRANCE; REIGN OF TERROR; *Invention of the cotton gin in* AMERICA *by* WHITNEY	1793	
	1795	KEATS *born. Died 1821*
	1796	BURNS *died. Born 1759*
	1797–1798	COLERIDGE, Christabel *begun*
Rebellion in IRELAND	1798	WORDSWORTH *and* COLERIDGE, Lyrical Ballads
First steamboat in ENGLAND *About*	1800	
	1802	SCOTT, Minstrelsy of the Scottish Border
NAPOLEONIC WARS	1803–1815	
NAPOLEON,* *Emperor of* FRANCE	1804	
Battle of TRAFALGAR*	1805	SCOTT, Lay of the Last Minstrel
Abolition of the SLAVE TRADE	1807	MOORE, Irish Melodies (*continued to* 1834)
Beginning of the PENINSULAR WAR; *battle of* CORUNNA	1808	
	1810	SCOTT, Lady of the Lake
War between GREAT BRITAIN *and the* UNITED STATES	1812–1815	
	1812	BYRON, Childe Harold's Pilgrimage (Cantos I and II) AUSTEN, Pride and Prejudice
Battle of NEW ORLEANS	1814	SCOTT, Waverley
Battle of WATERLOO	1815	
	1816	BYRON, The Prisoner of Chillon

GEORGE III *died*	1820	KEATS, Eve of St. Agnes; SCOTT, Ivanhoe
Reign of GEORGE IV 1820–1830		
	1821	SHELLEY, Adonais
The MONROE DOCTRINE *formulated in* AMERICA; *beginning of social reforms in* ENGLAND	1823	LAMB, Essays of Elia
First steam railway in ENGLAND; *first steamship between* AMERICA *and* ENGLAND	1825	
	1827	BLAKE *died. Born 1757*
Emancipation of CATHOLICS	1829	
Reign of WILLIAM IV 1830–1837		
	1832	*Death of* SCOTT

The Romantic Period also includes Leigh Hunt (1784–1859), whose literary work began soon after 1800 and lasted almost until his death, and Thomas Hood (1799–1845), whose literary work began in 1826 and lasted for nearly twenty years.

Notice that the Transition Period (p. 289) and the Romantic Period overlap, so that poets such as Blake and Burns wrote truly romantic poetry, though they were born during the Transition Period. Your attention should also be called to the fact that certain historical events, such as the American Revolution (1775) and the French Revolution (1789), actually began during the Transition Period, although they are historically associated most closely with the Romantic Period.

THE ROMANTIC PERIOD IN SONG AND STORY

POETRY

BROWNING, ROBERT. "Home Thoughts from the Sea."

HARDY, THOMAS. "At the Pyramid of Cestius near the Graves of Shelley and Keats"; "On a House in Hampstead, sometime the Dwelling of John Keats"; "Shelley's 'Skylark.'" In *Collected Poems*. The Macmillan Company.

KIPLING, RUDYARD. "Jane's Marriage"; "'Poor Honest Men'"; "The American Rebellion"; "The Secret of the Machines." In *Verse: Inclusive Edition, 1885–1932*. Doubleday, Doran & Company, Inc.

MASEFIELD, JOHN. "A Ballad of Cape St. Vincent." In *Collected Works*. The Macmillan Company.

SWINBURNE, ALGERNON CHARLES. "In Memory of Walter Savage Landor." In *Collected Poetical Works*. Harper & Brothers.

TENNYSON, ALFRED, LORD. "England and America in 1782"; "Buonaparte."

VAN DYKE, HENRY. "Keats"; "Shelley"; "Wordsworth." In *Works*. Charles Scribner's Sons.

WATSON, WILLIAM. "Wordsworth's Grave." In *Poems*. Harrap & Co., Ltd.

WOLFE, CHARLES. "The Burial of Sir John Moore" (in the revised edition of *Adventure* of this series).

DRAMA

DRINKWATER, JOHN. *Robert Burns: A Play*. Houghton Mifflin Company.

FITCH, CLYDE. *Beau Brummell*. Samuel French, Inc.

FICTION

AUSTEN, JANE. *Pride and Prejudice*; *Sense and Sensibility*; *Persuasion*.

BRONTË, CHARLOTTE. *Shirley*.

DICKENS, CHARLES. *A Tale of Two Cities* (in the revised edition of *Achievement* of this series).

DOYLE, SIR ARTHUR CONAN. *The Great Shadow*. Harper & Brothers.

FARNOL, JEFFERY. *The Broad Highway*. Little, Brown & Company.

GEORGE ELIOT. *Adam Bede*; *Silas Marner*.

HARDY, THOMAS. *The Trumpet Major*. Harper & Brothers.

LEVER, CHARLES JAMES. *Charles O'Malley*. A. L. Burt Company, Inc.

MARRYAT, CAPTAIN FREDERICK. *Mr. Midshipman Easy*.

MULOCK, DIANA MARIA (MRS. D. M. CRAIK). *John Halifax, Gentleman*.

SABATINI, RAFAEL. *The Snare*. Grosset & Dunlap.

STEVENSON, ROBERT LOUIS, and QUILLER-COUCH, A. T. *St. Ives*. Charles Scribner's Sons.

THACKERAY, WILLIAM MAKEPEACE. *Vanity Fair*.

LYRIC POETRY[1]

WILLIAM BLAKE[2] (1757–1827)

Piping down the Valleys Wild

One of Blake's most striking characteristics is his ability to look upon the world with the eyes of an inspired child, to see fairy elves in the trees and fields, and to catch glimpses of angels and devils riding on clouds or hiding under hedges. "Piping down the Valleys Wild" is typical of Blake's work at its best. In an age when affectation and formality were only too common, it is noteworthy for its simple language, its simple meter, and its simple, almost childlike imagery.* Though it appeared in 1789, when the forces of the Romantic Period were still struggling against artificiality, it is truly romantic.

PIPING down the valleys wild,
 Piping songs of pleasant glee,
On a cloud I saw a child,
 And he laughing said to me:

"Pipe a song about a Lamb!"
 So I piped with merry cheer.
"Piper, pipe that song again";
 So I piped: he wept to hear.

"Drop thy pipe, thy happy pipe;
 Sing thy songs of happy cheer!" 10
So I sang the same again,
 While he wept with joy to hear.

"Piper, sit thee down and write,
 In a book, that all may read."
So he vanished from my sight;
 And I plucked a hollow reed,

And I made a rural pen,
 And I stained the water clear,
And I wrote my happy songs
 Every child may joy to hear. 20

Auguries of Innocence

William Blake's "Auguries of Innocence" is a poem worth reading again and again for the broad sympathy which it teaches to the understanding reader. The plea for kindness to animals was a comparatively new note in English literature and is completely in the spirit of the Romantic Period. Blake, like many other poets of the Romantic Period with deeply religious natures, embraced all created things in his affection because of his love for the Creator.

TO SEE a world in a grain of sand,
 And a heaven in a wild flower;
Hold infinity in the palm of your hand,
 And eternity in an hour.

A Robin Redbreast in a cage
Puts all Heaven in a rage;
A dove-house filled with doves and
 pigeons
Shudders hell through all its regions.
A dog starved at his master's gate
Predicts the ruin of the state; 10
A game-cock clipped and armed for fight
Doth the rising sun affright;
A horse misused upon the road
Calls to Heaven for human blood.
Every wolf's and lion's howl
Raises from hell a human soul;
Each outcry of the hunted hare
A fibre from the brain doth tear;
A skylark wounded on the wing
Doth make a cherub cease to sing. 20

[1] For discussion of lyric poetry see page 150.
[2] For biography see page 714.

He who shall hurt the little wren .
Shall never be beloved by men ;
He who the ox to wrath has moved
Shall never be by woman loved ;
He who shall train the horse to war
Shall never pass the Polar Bar.[1]
The wanton boy that kills the fly
Shall feed the spider's enmity ;
He who torments the chafer's[2] sprite[3]
Weaves a bower in endless night.   30
The caterpillar on the leaf
Repeats to thee thy mother's grief ;
The wild deer wandering here and there
Keep the human soul from care ;
The lamb misused breeds public strife,
And yet forgives the butcher's knife.
Kill not the moth nor butterfly,
For the last judgment draweth nigh ;
The beggar's dog and widow's cat,
Feed them and thou shalt grow fat.   40
Every tear from every eye
Becomes a babe in eternity ;
The bleat, the bark, bellow, and roar,
Are waves that beat on heaven's shore.

The bat that flits at close of eve
Has left the brain that won't believe ;
The owl that calls upon the night
Speaks the unbeliever's fright.
The gnat that sings his summer song
Poison gets from Slander's tongue ;   50
The poison of the snake and newt
Is the sweat of Envy's foot ;
The poison of the honey-bee
Is the artist's jealousy ;
The strongest poison ever known[4]
Came from Caesar's* laurel crown.
Nought can deform the human race
Like to the armourer's iron brace ;
The soldier armed with sword and gun
Palsied strikes the summer's sun.   60
When gold and gems adorn the plough,
To peaceful arts shall Envy bow,
The beggar's rags fluttering in the air
Do to rags the heavens tear ;

The prince's robes and beggar's rags
Are toadstools on the miser's bags.
One mite wrung from the labourer's
      hands
Shall buy and sell the miser's lands,
Or, if protected from on high,
Shall that whole nation sell and buy ; 70
The poor man's farthing[1] is worth more
Than all the gold on Afric's shore.
The bawd and gambler, by the state
Licensed, build that nation's fate ;
The harlot's cry from street to street
Shall weave old England's winding sheet ;[2]
The winner's shout, the loser's curse,[3]
Shall dance before dead England's hearse.

He who mocks the infant's faith
Shall be mocked in age and death ;   80
He who shall teach the child to doubt
The rotting grave shall ne'er get out ;
He who respects the infant's faith
Triumphs over hell and death.
The babe is more than swaddling-bands
Throughout all these human lands ;
Tools were made, and born were hands,
Every farmer understands.
The questioner who sits so sly
Shall never know how to reply.   90
He who replies to words of doubt
Doth put the light of knowledge out ;
A puddle, or the cricket's cry,
Is to doubt a fit reply.
The child's toys and the old man's
      reasons
Are the fruits of the two seasons.
The emmet's[4] inch and eagle's mile
Make lame philosophy to smile.
A truth that's told with bad intent
Beats all the lies you can invent.   100
He who doubts from what he sees
Will ne'er believe, do what you please ;
If the sun and moon should doubt,
They'd immediately go out.

[1] A coin worth only a fourth of an English penny.
[2] *weave . . . sheet.* Cause the death of the English nation. A winding sheet is a sheet in which a corpse is wound or wrapped.
[3] *winner's . . . curse.* The allusions are to the evils of gambling.
[4] "Emmet" is an old word for "ant."

[1] *pass the Polar Bar.* Enter Heaven.
[2] A cockchafer, a kind of beetle.
[3] Spirit.
[4] *The strongest . . . known.* Envy.

Every night and every morn
Some to misery are born;
Every morn and every night
Some are born to sweet delight;
Some are born to sweet delight,
Some are born to endless night.   110
Joy and woe are woven fine,
A clothing for the soul divine;
Under every grief and pine
Runs a joy with silken twine.
It is right it should be so;
Man was made for joy and woe;

And, when this we rightly know,
Safely through the world we go.

We are led to believe a lie
When we see *with* not *through* the eye,   120
Which was born in a night to perish in a
  night
When the soul slept in beams of light.
God appears and God is light
To those poor souls who dwell in night;
But doth a human form display
To those who dwell in realms of day.

The Tiger

Blake's gift of seeing things hidden from the eyes of ordinary mortals enabled him to perceive the mystical power of God revealed in all nature, from the lowly lamb to the grim tiger. In "The Tiger," as elsewhere in his work, the clearness of the picture is doubtless due in part to the fact that Blake was an artist as well as a poet.

TIGER, Tiger, burning bright
In the forest of the night,
What immortal hand or eye
Framed thy fearful symmetry?

In what distant deeps or skies
Burned that fire within thine eyes?
On what wings dared he aspire?
What the hand dared seize the fire?

And what shoulder, and what art,
Could twist the sinews of thy heart?   10
When thy heart began to beat,
What dread hand formed thy dread feet?

What the hammer, what the chain,
Knit thy strength and forged thy brain?
What the anvil? What dread grasp
Dared thy deadly terrors clasp?

When the stars threw down their spears,
And watered heaven with their tears,
Did he smile his work to see?   19
Did he who made the lamb make thee?

Huntington Library

Blake's original drawing to illustrate
"The Tiger"

Discussion Hints

Piping down the Valleys Wild

1. Describe in your own words the picture given in the poem.

2. What is a "rural pen" (l. 17)?

Auguries of Innocence

1. Define the word *auguries* and explain the title in the light of the first four lines of the poem.

2. In connection with the famous first four lines of "Auguries of Innocence" read also "Flower in the Crannied Wall" (p. 473), Tennyson's better-known but less effective poem on the same theme. Try to express in your own words what general idea Blake is trying to express.

3. Does the expression "To see a world in a grain of sand" (l. 1) suggest to you any fact of modern science? Did Blake intend to make such a suggestion? Why do you answer as you do?

4. What evidence do you find in the poem that Blake was deeply serious in his sympathy for animals? If you have used the revised edition of *Adventure* of this series, compare Blake's mood, especially that expressed in lines 29–30, with Christopher Morley's mood

in his "Nursery Rhymes for the Tender-Hearted."

5. Suggest another victim of cruelty that Blake might have added to his list in the second stanza.

6. Select two or three of Blake's couplets that could be quoted as epigrams,* and learn them by heart.

Passages to be Explained

A Robin Redbreast in a cage
Puts all Heaven in a rage (ll. 5–6)
The strongest poison ever known
Came from Caesar's* laurel crown (ll. 55–56)
The soldier armed with sword and gun
Palsied strikes the summer's sun (ll. 59–60)

The Tiger

1. Have you ever seen a Royal Bengal tiger? If so, try to describe it.

2. In which stanza of "The Tiger" is the sound of the words harshest and grimmest? Explain.

3. Does the last stanza add a new idea to the rest of the poem? Explain your answer.

4. What thought in the poet's mind explains the answer to the question asked in line 20?

ROBERT BURNS[1] (1759–1796)

To a Mouse

"To a Mouse" is irresistible in its appeal. It is one of the most perfect expressions in English literature of romantic sympathy for the lower animals. Burns wrote the poem soon after turning up the nest of a field mouse with his plow. His lines are thus a spontaneous overflow of emotion in words, a characteristic of the best lyric poetry. The artistry, moreover, is well-nigh perfect, and the language, the dialect of Burns's native district in Scotland, is simple and admirably adapted to the sense. Here, as elsewhere in reading Burns's poetry, we should remember that the author was a native of Scotland, where some of the influences that led to the Romantic Period found expression earlier than they did in England.

[1] For biography see page 714.

WEE, sleekit,[1] cowrin, tim'rous
  beastie,
O, what a panic's in thy breastie!
Thou need na start awa sae hasty
      Wi' bickering brattle[2]!
I wad be laith to rin an' chase thee,
      Wi' murdering pattle[3]!

I'm truly sorry man's dominion[4]
Has broken Nature's social union,[5]

[1] Sleek.   [2] *bickering brattle.* Hurrying scamper.
[3] Paddle. It is said that the boy plowing along with Burns started after the mouse to kill it, but that Burns called him back.
[4] *man's dominion.* Genesis 1 : 26 says that God gave man dominion over all animals.
[5] *social union.* Romantic social thinkers taught that all creatures are brothers.

Galloway

The cottage at Ayr, Scotland, in which Burns was born

An' justifies that ill opinion
  Which makes thee startle 10
At me, thy poor, earth-born companion
  An' fellow-mortal!

I doubt na, whyles,[1] but thou may
  thieve[2];
What then? poor beastie, thou maun[3]
  live:
A daimen icker in a thrave[4]
  'S a sma' request;
I'll get a blessin wi' the lave,[5]
  An' never miss 't!

Thy wee-bit housie, too, in ruin!
Its silly wa's the win's are strewin[6]! 20
An' naething, now, to big[7] a new ane,
  O' foggage[8] green!

An' bleak December's win's ensuin,[1]
  Baith snell[2] an' keen!

Thou saw the fields laid bare an' waste,
An' weary winter comin fast,
An' cozie here, beneath the blast,
  Thou thought to dwell,
Till, crash! the cruel coulter[3] passed
  Out thro' thy cell. 30

That wee bit heap o' leaves an' stibble,[4]
Has cost thee monie a weary nibble!
Now thou's turned out, for a' thy
  trouble,
  But house or hald,[5]
To thole[6] the winter's sleety dribble,
  An' cranreuch[7] cauld!

[1] Sometimes. [2] Steal. [3] Must.
[4] *A daimen . . . thrave.* One head of rye out of two dozen sheaves. [5] Rest.
[6] *Its . . . strewin!* The winds are strewing its frail walls.
[7] Build.   [8] Coarse grass.

[1] Here, coming on.
[2] Bitter.
[3] A cutter on a plow.
[4] Stubble.
[5] *But . . . hald.* Without a home.
[6] Endure.
[7] Hoar frost.

But Mousie, thou art no thy lane,[1]
In proving foresight may be vain:
The best laid schemes o' mice an' men
      Gang aft agley,[2]   40
An' lea'e[3] us naught but grief an' pain,
      For promised joy!

Still thou art blest, compared wi' me!
The present only toucheth thee:
But och! I backward cast my e'e,
      On prospects drear!
An' forward, tho' I canna see,]
      I guess an' fear!

To a Mountain Daisy

"To a Mountain Daisy" expresses in highly appropriate language Robert Burns's emotions on uprooting a little daisy while he was plowing on a spring day. Like Burns's poem "To a Mouse," it is thoroughly romantic in its attitude toward nature: all created things, even plants, are embraced in the poet's affection. The poem is also romantic in that the poet, sad at his hard lot, sees his own misfortune reflected in that of the humble English daisy. The moralizing found in the concluding stanzas is quite in accord with the fondness for preaching that characterized much of the poetry written at the time. The human appeal of "To a Mouse" and "To a Mountain Daisy" does much to make them two of the most famous poems in English literature.

WEE, modest, crimson-tippèd flow'r,[4]
   Thou's met me in an evil hour;
For I maun[5] crush amang the stoure[6]
      Thy slender stem:
To spare thee now is past my pow'r,
      Thou bonnie gem.

Alas! it's no thy neebor sweet,
The bonnie lark, companion meet,[7]
Bending thee 'mang the dewy weet,
      Wi' spreckled breast!   10
When upward-springing, blythe, to greet
      The purpling east.

Cauld blew the bitter-biting north
Upon thy early, humble birth;
Yet cheerfully thou glinted forth
      Amid the storm,
Scarce reared above the parent-earth
      Thy tender form.

The flaunting flow'rs our gardens yield,
High shelt'ring woods and wa's[1] maun
      shield;   20
But thou, beneath the random bield[2]
      O' clod or stane,
Adorns the histie stibble-field,[3]
      Unseen, alane.

There, in thy scanty mantle clad,
Thy snawie bosom sunward spread,
Thou lifts thy unassuming head
      In humble guise;
But now the share[4] uptears thy bed,
      And low thou lies!   30

Such is the fate of artless maid,
Sweet flow'ret of the rural shade!
By love's simplicity betrayed,
      And guileless trust;
Till she, like thee, all soiled, is laid
      Low i' the dust.

Such is the fate of simple Bard,
On Life's rough ocean luckless starred!
Unskilful he to note the card[5]
      Of prudent lore,   40
Till billows rage, and gales blow hard,
      And whelm him o'er!

[1] *thou . . . lane.* You are not alone.
[2] *Gang aft agley.* Often go wrong. Remember this line; it is frequently quoted.
[3] Leave.
[4] *crimson-tippèd flow'r.* The flower here referred to is the English daisy, which is much smaller than our daisy and has either pink or white petals. See illustration on page 340.
[5] Must.
[6] Dust.
[7] Fitting. proper.

[1] Walls.
[2] Shelter.
[3] *histie stibble-field.* Barren field of stubble.
[4] Plowshare.
[5] Compass. chart.

Such fate to suffering Worth is giv'n,
Who long with wants and woes has
   striv'n,
By human pride or cunning driv'n
     To mis'ry's brink;
Till, wrenched of ev'ry stay but Heav'n,
     He, ruined, sink!

Ev'n thou who mourn'st the Daisy's
   fate,
That fate is thine — no distant date; 50
Stern Ruin's plough-share drives elate,
     Full on thy bloom,
Till crushed beneath the furrow's weight
     Shall be thy doom!

Auld Lang Syne

"Auld Lang Syne" is one of the most widely sung of all songs known to the English-speaking peoples. Its enormous popularity is due to its singing quality and to the universal appeal of the sentiment it expresses. As in the case of some others of Burns's poems, its subject was suggested by an old song, but the best part is Burns's own composition.

SHOULD auld acquaintance be forgot
  And never brought to mind?
Should auld acquaintance be forgot,
  And auld lang syne![1]

CHORUS

For auld lang syne, my dear,
  For auld lang syne,
We'll tak a cup o' kindness yet,
  For auld lang syne!

And surely ye'll be your pint-stowp,[1]
  And surely I'll be mine,   10
And we'll tak a cup o' kindness yet
  For auld lang syne!

We twa hae run about the braes,[2]
  And pu'd[3] the gowans[4] fine;
But we've wandered monie a weary foot
  Sin' auld lang syne.

We twa hae paidled i' the burn[5]
  Frae mornin' sun till dine[6];
But seas between us braid[7] hae roared
  Sin' auld lang syne.   20

And there's a hand, my trusty fiere,[8]
  And gie's a hand o' thine;
And we'll tak a right guid-willie waught,[9]
  For auld lang syne.

Sweet Afton

"Sweet Afton" is thoroughly romantic in its use of natural objects as a background for human emotions. The Afton is a stream in Burns's native Ayrshire, and the lady referred to is thought by some to be Burns's well-known sweetheart Highland Mary. Whatever the truth may be, the poem is an excellent example of Burns's lyric genius at its best.

FLOW gently, sweet Afton, among thy
  green braes[2]!
Flow gently, I'll sing thee a song in thy
  praise!

My Mary's asleep by thy murmuring
  stream —
Flow gently, sweet Afton, disturb not her
  dream!

[1] *auld lang syne.* Literally, old long since.
[2] Hill slopes.

[1] *ye'll . . . pint-stowp.* You'll be able to drink
  your pint measure of ale.
[2] Hill slopes.
[3] Pulled.
[4] Daisies.
[5] *paidled . . . burn.* Paddled (waded) in the
  brook.
[6] Dinnertime.
[7] Broad.
[8] Comrade.
[9] *guid-willie waught.* Friendly drink.

Thou stock-dove whose echo resounds
    thro' the glen,
Ye wild whistling blackbirds in yon
    thorny den,
Thou green-crested lapwing, thy scream-
    ing forbear —
I charge you disturb not my slumbering
    fair!

How lofty, sweet Afton, thy neighbouring
    hills,
Far marked with the courses of clear,
    winding rills!   10
There daily I wander, as noon rises high,
My flocks and my Mary's sweet cot[1] in
    my eye.

How pleasant thy banks and green val-
    leys below,
Where wild in the woodlands the prim-
    roses blow!

There oft, as mild Evening weeps over
    the lea,
The sweet-scented birk[1] shades my Mary
    and me.

Thy crystal stream, Afton, how lovely it
    glides,
And winds by the cot where my Mary
    resides!
How wanton thy waters her snowy feet
    lave,
As, gathering sweet flowerets, she stems
    thy clear wave!   20

Flow gently, sweet Afton, among thy
    green braes,
Flow gently, sweet river, the theme of
    my lays!
My Mary's asleep by thy murmuring
    stream —
Flow gently, sweet Afton, disturb not her
    dream!

John Anderson My Jo

In "John Anderson My Jo" an elderly wife expresses her affection for her bald and aging husband in words that will be recalled and loved as long as the English language is spoken.

JOHN ANDERSON my jo,[2] John,
    When we were first acquent,
Your locks were like the raven,
    Your bonnie brow was brent[3];
But now your brow is beld,[4] John,
    Your locks are like the snaw,

But blessings on your frosty pow,[2]
    John Anderson my jo!

John Anderson my jo, John,
    We clamb the hill thegither,   10
And monie a cantie[3] day, John,
    We've had wi' ane anither;
Now we maun totter down, John,
    And hand in hand we'll go,
And sleep thegither at the foot,
    John Anderson my jo!

Scots, Wha Hae wi' Wallace Bled

"Scots, Wha Hae wi' Wallace Bled" illustrates Burns's patriotic enthusiasm for the heroes of the Scottish struggle for independence. The words are supposed to be addressed by Robert Bruce to his army just before the battle of Bannockburn. Burns is said to have composed this song while galloping home in a storm.

    [1] Cottage.
    [2] Sweetheart, darling.
    [3] Unwrinkled.
    [4] Bald.

SCOTS, wha hae wi' Wallace[4] bled,
    Scots, wham Bruce[5] has aften led,
Welcome to your gory bed,
    Or to victorie!

[1] Birch.   [2] Head.   [3] Happy.
[4] A celebrated Scottish national hero (1274?–1305) who, after long resistance, finally was taken prisoner and executed by the English.
[5] Robert Bruce, a celebrated Scottish national hero, king of Scotland (1306–1329). He led his men to victory over the English at Bannockburn * in 1314.

Now's the day, and now's the hour:
See the front o' battle lour,
See approach proud Edward's[1] power —
    Chains and slaverie!

Wha will be a traitor knave?
Wha can fill a coward's grave?   10
Wha sae base as be a slave? —
    Let him turn, and flee!

Wha for Scotland's King and Law
Freedom's sword will strongly draw,

Freeman stand or freeman fa',[1]
    Let him follow me!

By Oppression's woes and pains,
By your sons in servile chains,
We will drain our dearest veins,
    But they shall be free!   20

Lay the proud usurpers low!
Tyrants fall in every foe!
Liberty's in every blow!
    Let us do, or die!

A Man's a Man for A' That

"A Man's a Man for A' That" is one of the most highly praised of Burns's songs. It expresses the conviction that the lowly may be fundamentally as noble as the great. Born in a liberty-loving country and of self-respecting peasant stock, Burns declares in unforgettable language that "the rank is but the guinea's stamp," whereas the true value of the coin lies in the gold of which it is made. When Burns wrote this poem, the American republic had recently been founded on the principle that all men are created free and equal, and the French revolutionists had shouted their battle cry of "Liberty, equality, fraternity."

IS THERE for honest poverty [1]
  That hings his head, an' a' that?[2]
The coward slave, we pass him by —
    We dare be poor for a' that!
For a' that, an' a' that,
    Our toils obscure, an' a' that,
The rank is but the guinea's stamp,
    The man's the gowd[3] for a' that.

What tho' on hamely fare we dine,
    Wear hodden-grey,[4] an' a' that?   10
Gie fools their silks, and knaves their
    wine —

A man's a man for a' that,
For a' that, an' a' that,
    Their tinsel show, an' a' that,
The honest man, tho' e'er sae poor,
    Is king o' men for a' that.

Ye see yon birkie[2] ca'd a lord,
    Wha struts, an' stares, an' a' that?
Tho' hundreds worship at his word;
    He's but a coof[3] for a' that.   20
For a' that, an' a' that,
    His ribband, star, an' a' that,
The man o' independent mind,
    He looks an' laughs at a' that.

A prince can mak a belted knight[4]
    A marquis, duke, an' a' that!
But an honest man's aboon[5] his[6]
    might —
    Guid faith, he mauna fa' that![7]
For a' that, an' a' that,
    Their dignities, an' a' that,
The pith o' sense an' pride o' worth
    Are higher rank than a' that.

---

[1] Edward II of England, whose army was defeated by Bruce at Bannockburn.*
[2] *Is . . . that?* Is there anyone who is ashamed (hangs his head) because of honest poverty and all that kind of thing?
[3] Gold.
[4] Coarse gray cloth.

[1] Fall.
[2] A conceited fop, a snob.
[3] Blockhead.
[4] *A prince . . . knight.* Knights were created by order of the king.
[5] Above.
[6] A prince's.
[7] *mauna fa' that.* May not accomplish that ("an honest man").

Then let us pray that come it may
  (As come it will for a' that)
That Sense and Worth o'er a' the earth
  Shall bear the gree[1] an' a' that!
For a' that, an' a' that,
  It's comin yet for a' that,
That man to man the warld o'er
  Shall brithers be for a' that.   40

Discussion Hints

To a Mouse

1. What similarity do you find between "To a Mouse" and any of Blake's poems (p. 325)?

2. Explain why Burns says that the mouse is more fortunate than he.

3. By reference to the footnotes and to the introduction to the Romantic Period (p. 313), explain lines 7–12.

To a Mountain Daisy

1. With what does Burns contrast the daisy (ll. 19–24)? To what does he compare its fate (ll. 31–48)? What contrast is brought out in the first and second stanzas?

2. Where does Burns's description of the daisy end and his moralizing begin?

3. Do you know of any benevolent organizations of the present day whose work is suggested by (1) "To a Mouse"? (2) "To a Mountain Daisy"? If so, name them and describe their purpose.

Words and Passages to be Explained

*Cauld blew the bitter-biting north
Upon thy early, humble birth* (ll. 13–14)
Such fate to suffering Worth is giv'n (l. 43)
elate (l. 51)

Auld Lang Syne

1. What common experiences unite the poet and his friend?

2. Explain
  "And gie's a hand o' thine" (l. 22)

---

[1] Reward.

Sweet Afton

Why does Burns mention the "echo" of the stock-dove, the "whistling" of the blackbirds, and the "screaming" of the lapwing? Explain your impression of these descriptions in relation to the rest of the poem.

John Anderson My Jo

1. An early picture illustrating the poem shows the old couple nodding and smiling over their long, happy life together instead of weeping over age. Does this suggest a different idea of the song from the one you had on first reading it? Explain your answer.

2. Which of the other poems of Burns given here might have been spoken by either of the characters in "John Anderson My Jo"?

3. Explain
  "We clamb the hill thegither" (l. 10)

Scots, Wha Hae wi' Wallace Bled

1. Note the meter of "Scots, Wha Hae wi' Wallace Bled." See "trochee."*

2. Give the historical facts on which this poem is based. What can you learn about the Scottish struggle for independence from England? See "Bannockburn,"* "Culloden,"* "Old Pretender,"* and "Young Pretender."*

A Man's a Man for A' That

1. "A Man's a Man for A' That" has been well called the greatest expression of democracy in poetry. How does this fact connect the poem with the Romantic Period? with the American ideal?

2. Explain
  "The man's the gowd for a' that" (l. 8)

General Discussion Hints on Burns's Lyric Poetry

1. Point out passages in the introduction to the Romantic Period (p. 313) that are illustrated by the lyric poetry of Burns. Write a theme of one hundred words on Burns's attitude toward democracy.

2. Do you know that the fourth edition of Webster's Collegiate Dictionary has a special "Glossary of Scottish Words and Phrases"? In the fifth edition (1936) these are arranged alphabetically throughout the main vocabulary.

3. The following lyrics by Burns are available in recordings by the RCA (Victor) Manufacturing Company, Inc.: "Sweet Afton" and "Scots, Wha Hae wi' Wallace Bled" (No. 4083); "Auld Lang Syne" and "Ye Banks and Braes o' Bonnie Doon" (No. 22082); "Comin' thro the Rye" (No. 1146). If possible get these records and play them in class.

Suggestions for Reading

"O A' the Airts the Wind Can Blow!"
"Green Grow the Rashes"
"Highland Mary"
"Bonnie Doon"
"Ae Fond Kiss"
"My Heart's in the Highlands" (given, with tune, in the revised edition of *Achievement* of this series)
"To Mary in Heaven"

WILLIAM WORDSWORTH[1] (1770–1850)

Both in theory and in practice Wordsworth was a literary radical. (1) Poetry, according to Wordsworth's theory, should deal, not with aristocratic ideas and situations, but with everyday happenings, and should give to them the charm of novelty and romance. (2) It should also treat of these simple events in the language of common men, not in the far-fetched, high-flown phrases that had characterized most of the poetry of the Age of Classicism (see page 214). In his own poetry he succeeded, even with these limitations, in throwing around ordinary persons and things an atmosphere of romance and mystery that lifted them out of the commonplace and made them truly poetic.

(3) True poetry is not so much the expression of intense emotions as the memory of such emotions after the first disturbing gust of feeling has passed and only a pleasant recollection remains. To Wordsworth, poetry arose from "emotion recollected in tranquillity." He first illustrated his poetical theories in the *Lyrical Ballads* (1798) and defended them in the preface to the 1800 edition, which has been called the "declaration of independence of the romantic movement" (p. 313). In Wordsworth's poetry, nature plays a much larger part than it does in the work of his predecessors. To him nature is a spiritual reality which reveals to us the beauty and goodness of God and binds us in love to our fellow men.

We Are Seven

"We Are Seven" owes its place in English literature not so much to music or rhythm or imagery as to its stark simplicity and its underlying theme, the inability of a little child to comprehend death. Its very simplicity charms us.

To the student of literature it is interesting because it illustrates several of Wordsworth's ideas of how poetry should be written. (1) It takes an ordinary scene among humble folk and, by emphasizing the little girl's replies, reveals her conviction that her dead brother and sister are still alive. (2) It is written in words chosen from the language of everyday life. Thus, including as it does several characteristics of the new poetry combined with Wordsworth's imaginative interpretation of ordinary life, it is a truly romantic poem.

"We Are Seven" first appeared in the *Lyrical Ballads*.

—— A SIMPLE child,
That lightly draws its breath,
And feels its life in every limb,
What should it know of death?

I met a little cottage[1] girl:
She was eight years old, she said;
Her hair was thick with many a curl
That clustered round her head.

She had a rustic, woodland air,
And she was wildly clad: 10
Her eyes were fair, and very fair;
— Her beauty made me glad.

---

[1] For biography see page 715.

[1] Living in a cottage; hence, poor and humble.

Dove Cottage at Grasmere, in the English Lake Region, where Wordsworth and his sister lived from 1799 to 1813

"Sisters and brothers, little maid,
How many may you be?"
"How many? Seven in all," she said,
And wondering looked at me.

"And where are they? I pray you tell."
She answered, "Seven are we;
And two of us at Conway dwell,
And two are gone to sea.   20

"Two of us in the church-yard lie,
My sister and my brother;
And, in the church-yard cottage, I
Dwell near them with my mother."

"You say that two at Conway dwell,
And two are gone to sea,
Yet ye are seven! — I pray you tell,
Sweet maid, how this may be."

Then did the little maid reply,
"Seven boys and girls are we;   30
Two of us in the church-yard lie,
Beneath the church-yard tree."

"You run about, my little maid,
Your limbs they are alive;
If two are in the church-yard laid,
Then ye are only five."

"Their graves are green, they may be
    seen,"
The little maid replied,
"Twelve steps or more from my mother's
    door,
And they are side by side.   40

"My stockings there I often knit,
My kerchief there I hem;
And there upon the ground I sit,
And sing a song to them.

"And often after sunset, sir,
When it is light and fair,
I take my little porringer,[1]
And eat my supper there.

"The first that died was sister Jane;
In bed she moaning lay,   50
Till God released her of her pain;
And then she went away.

"So in the church-yard she was laid;
And, when the grass was dry,
Together round her grave we played,
My brother John and I.

"And when the ground was white with
        snow,
And I could run and slide,
My brother John was forced to go,
And he lies by her side."   60

"How many are you, then," said I,
"If they two are in heaven?"
Quick was the little maid's reply,
"O master! we are seven."

"But they are dead; those two are dead!
Their spirits are in heaven!"
'Twas throwing words away; for still
The little maid would have her will,
And said, "Nay, we are seven!"

Lucy Gray

In "Lucy Gray" Wordsworth took a simple
story of a tragedy among humble countryfolk
and, by applying his characteristic poetical
method, sought to throw around it an atmosphere of mystery and romance. Because the
story is of the sort that might have formed the
subject of a popular ballad (p 57), the
author composed his poem in a stanza form
somewhat like that common in the ballads.
To appreciate the poem fully, you should
realize how difficult it is to tell of simple
things in simple language as Wordsworth
does

OFT I had heard of Lucy Gray:
    And, when I crossed the wild,[2]
I chanced to see at break of day
The solitary child.

No mate, no comrade Lucy knew;
She dwelt on a wide moor,
— The sweetest thing that ever grew
Beside a human door!

You yet may spy the fawn at play,
The hare upon the green;   10
But the sweet face of Lucy Gray
Will never more be seen.

"To-night will be a stormy night —
You to the town must go;
And take a lantern, Child, to light
Your mother through the snow."

"That, Father! will I gladly do:
'Tis scarcely afternoon —
The minster-clock[1] has just struck two,
And yonder is the moon!"   20

At this the Father raised his hook,
And snapped a faggot-band[2];
He plied his work; — and Lucy took
The lantern in her hand.

Not blither is the mountain roe:
With many a wanton stroke
Her feet disperse the powdery snow,
That rises up like smoke.

The storm came on before its time:
She wandered up and down;   30
And many a hill did Lucy climb:
But never reached the town.

---

[1] A child's shallow bowl.
[2] Here, open, uninhabited country.

[1] Church clock.
[2] A band for binding the faggots (bundles of
   twigs) which the father was gathering.

The wretched parents all that night
Went shouting far and wide;
But there was neither sound nor sight
To serve them for a guide.

At day-break on a hill they stood
That overlooked the moor;
And thence they saw the bridge of wood,
A furlong from their door.   40

They wept — and, turning homeward,
cried,
"In heaven we all shall meet";
— When in the snow the mother spied
The print of Lucy's feet.

Then downwards from the steep hill's edge
They tracked the footmarks small;
And through the broken hawthorn hedge,
And by the long stone-wall;

And then an open field they crossed:
The marks were still the same;   50
They tracked them on, nor ever lost;
And to the bridge they came.

They followed from the snowy bank
Those footmarks, one by one,
Into the middle of the plank;
And further there were none!

— Yet some maintain that to this day
She is a living child;
That you may see sweet Lucy Gray
Upon the lonesome wild.   60

O'er rough and smooth she trips along,
And never looks behind;
And sings a solitary song
That whistles in the wind.

She Dwelt among the Untrodden Ways

In the unadorned language that characterizes Wordsworth's best work, "She Dwelt among the Untrodden Ways" paints, or rather suggests, an exquisite picture of young English girlhood. Wordsworth's Lucy poems are a famous group of lyrics, and this one is probably the best of them all.

SHE dwelt among the untrodden ways
Beside the springs of Dove,
A Maid whom there were none to praise
And very few to love:

A violet by a mossy stone
Half hidden from the eye!
— Fair as a star, when only one
Is shining in the sky.

She lived unknown, and few could
know
When Lucy ceased to be;   10
But she is in her grave, and, oh,
The difference to me!

A Slumber Did My Spirit Seal

"A Slumber Did My Spirit Seal" is another of Wordsworth's Lucy poems. It is one of the finest expressions in literature of tragic grief made all the more terrible because it is expressed in a few simple, compressed phrases.

A SLUMBER did my spirit seal;
I had no human fears:
She seemed a thing that could not
feel
The touch of earthly years.

No motion has she now, no force;
She neither hears nor sees;
Rolled round in earth's diurnal[1] course,
With rocks, and stones, and trees.
[1] Daily.

Val Doone

A scene in the English Lake Region, where Wordsworth lived for many years and where he wrote some of his best poetry

To the Daisy

© A. W. Kerr

English daisies

In his poem "To the Daisy" Wordsworth takes the modest roadside daisy and, by letting his poetic imagination play upon it, makes the little flower smile and glow in its country setting. The poem thus becomes a piece of true romantic art, a picture of something simple and real glorified by imagination and genius. The English daisy, we should remember, is a pink or white flower with a much shorter stem than the American flower of the same name.

WITH little here to do or see
  Of things that in the great world
    be,
Sweet Daisy! oft I talk to thee,
    For thou art worthy,
Thou unassuming Commonplace
Of Nature, with that homely face,
And yet with something of a grace
    Which Love makes for thee!

Oft on the dappled turf at ease
I sit and play with similes,[1]   10

[1] In the general sense of "comparisons."

Loose types of things through all degrees,
    Thoughts of thy raising;
And many a fond and idle name
I give to thee, for praise or blame
As is the humour of the game,
    While I am gazing.

A nun demure, of lowly port;
Or sprightly maiden, of Love's court,
In thy simplicity the sport
    Of all temptations;   20
A queen in crown of rubies drest;
A starveling in a scanty vest;
Are all, as seems to suit thee best,
    Thy appellations.

A little Cyclops,* with one eye
Staring to threaten and defy,
That thought comes next — and in-
    stantly
    The freak is over,
The shape will vanish, and behold!
A silver shield with boss[1] of gold   30
That spreads itself, some faery bold
    In fight to cover.

I see thee glittering from afar —
And then thou art a pretty star,
Not quite so fair as many are
    In heaven above thee!
Yet like a star with glittering crest,
Self-poised in air thou seem'st to rest;—
May peace come never to his nest
    Who shall reprove thee!   40

Sweet Flower! for by that name at
    last
When all my reveries are past
I call thee, and to that cleave fast,
    Sweet silent Creature!
That breath'st with me in sun and
    air,
Do thou, as thou art wont, repair
My heart with gladness, and a share
    Of thy meek nature!

[1] Here, the round center of the daisy.

My Heart Leaps Up When I Behold

To Wordsworth nature was not merely a thing of beauty to be enjoyed with the senses; it was a gentle but powerful spiritual influence which, on the one hand, helps to bind us in deeper affection to our fellow men and, on the other, unites us to God, who is the perfection of beauty and goodness.

MY HEART leaps up when I behold
 A rainbow in the sky:
So was it when my life began;
So is it now I am a man;
So be it when I shall grow old,

Or let me die!
The Child is father of the Man;
And I could wish my days to be
Bound each to each by natural
 piety.

She Was a Phantom of Delight

"She Was a Phantom of Delight," addressed to Mrs. Wordsworth, was, as the poet tells us, "written from . . . [his] heart." It is thus a spontaneous tribute by a poet to his wife. She was an ideal wife for a poet, tranquil, energetic, practical, and loving. The poem also illustrates Wordsworth's idea that poetry should treat of everyday affairs in everyday language. In this case the words are shaped into charming imagery* and beautiful verse.

SHE was a Phantom of delight
 When first she gleamed upon my
  sight;
A lovely Apparition,[1] sent
To be a moment's ornament;
Her eyes as stars of Twilight fair;
Like Twilight's, too, her dusky hair;
But all things else about her drawn
From May-time and the cheerful Dawn;
A dancing Shape, an Image gay,
To haunt, to startle, and waylay. 10

I saw her upon nearer view,
A Spirit, yet a Woman too!
Her household motions light and free,
And steps of virgin-liberty;
A countenance in which did meet
Sweet records, promises as sweet;
A Creature not too bright or good
For human nature's daily food;
For transient sorrows, simple wiles,
Praise, blame, love, kisses, tears, and
 smiles. 20

And now I see with eye serene
The very pulse of the machine,[1]
A Being breathing thoughtful breath,
A Traveller between life and death;
The reason firm, the temperate will,
Endurance, foresight, strength, and skill;
A perfect Woman, nobly planned,
To warn, to comfort, and command;[2]
And yet a Spirit still, and bright
With something of angelic light. 30

The Solitary Reaper

The original idea of "The Solitary Reaper" was suggested to Wordsworth while he was on a walking tour through the Highlands of Scotland in 1803. To the poet's imagination the peasant girl reaping grain on a lonely mountain side was an appealing object, and her song, which he did not understand because she sang in Gaelic, her native language, brought to his mind a host of suggestions from medieval legends and from the folk poetry of

his own day. He carried away the memory of the song in his heart and later, recollecting it "in tranquillity," turned it into poetry. The romantic suggestions with which the poem abounds and the beautiful imagery* in which these suggestions are expressed make "The Solitary Reaper" one of the best poems of the Romantic Period.

[1] The whole organization of the household.
[2] *A perfect . . . command.* Commit to memory these two famous lines.

[1] Here, sight, object.

BEHOLD her, single in the field,
　Yon solitary Highland Lass!
Reaping and singing by herself;
Stop here, or gently pass!
Alone she cuts and binds the grain
And sings a melancholy strain;
Oh listen! for the vale profound
Is overflowing with the sound.

No nightingale did ever chaunt
More welcome notes to weary bands 　10
Of travellers in some shady haunt,
Among Arabian sands:
A voice so thrilling ne'er was heard
In spring-time from the cuckoo-bird
Breaking the silence of the seas
Among the farthest Hebrides.*

Will no one tell me what she sings? —
Perhaps the plaintive numbers flow
For old, unhappy, far-off things,[1]
And battles long ago: 　20
Or is it some more humble lay,
Familiar matter of to-day?
Some natural sorrow, loss, or pain,
That has been, and may be again?

Whate'er the theme, the maiden sang
As if her song could have no ending;
I saw her singing at her work,
And o'er the sickle bending; —
I listened, motionless and still;
And, as I mounted up the hill, 　30
The music in my heart I bore,
Long after it was heard no more.

SONNETS

Wordsworth composed more than five hundred sonnets,* many
of unsurpassed beauty. Among the best are those printed below.

It Is a Beauteous Evening

Aside from its simple, dignified, and appropriate language, the sonnet* "It Is a Beauteous Evening" illustrates Wordsworth's passionate love of humanity and nature as revelations of beauty and of God. In it the poet's delight in the lovely, calm evening reminds him that young people, because of their closeness to nature, are constantly nearer to God.

IT IS a beauteous evening, calm and free,
　The holy time is quiet as a Nun
Breathless with adoration; the broad sun
Is sinking down in its tranquillity;
The gentleness of heaven broods o'er the
　Sea:

Listen! the mighty Being is awake,
And doth with his eternal motion make
A sound like thunder — everlastingly.
Dear Child[2]! dear Girl! that walkest with
　me here,
If thou appear untouched by solemn
　thought, 　10
Thy nature is not therefore less divine:
Thou liest in Abraham's bosom all the
　year;[3]
And worship'st at the Temple's inner
　shrine,
God being with thee when we know it
　not.

London, 1802

In the sonnet* "London, 1802" the poet calls upon Milton, with his free, bold spirit, to come back to life and recall England from artificiality and corruption to her ancient

state of "inward happiness." To the English romanticists Milton stood for an earlier freeing of the human spirit from tradition and prejudice.

[1] Note the haunting suggestiveness of this and the succeeding line. They are regarded as one of the best expressions of romanticism in English literature.
[2] Wordsworth's daughter Caroline.
[3] *Thou . . . year.* Thou art always close to God.

MILTON![1] thou shouldst be living at this hour:
England hath need of thee: she is a fen[2]
Of stagnant waters: altar, sword, and pen,
Fireside, the heroic wealth of hall and bower,
Have forfeited their ancient English dower
Of inward happiness. We are selfish men;
Oh! raise us up, return to us again;
And give us manners, virtue, freedom, power.
Thy soul was like a Star, and dwelt apart:
Thou hadst a voice whose sound was like the sea: 10
Pure as the naked heavens, majestic, free,
So didst thou travel on life's common way,
In cheerful godliness; and yet thy heart
The lowliest duties on herself did lay.

The World Is Too Much with Us

Wordsworth, like many other writers of the Romantic Period, was convinced that the increasing complications of human life resulting from commercialism and the desire to "get and spend" blinded men to the beauties of nature, and thus tended to destroy the art of happy living. The ancient pagans, he implies, saw more of the true beauty of nature than the civilized people of England in his day.

THE World is too much with us; late and soon,
Getting and spending, we lay waste our powers:
Little we see in Nature that is ours;
We have given our hearts away, a sordid boon!
This Sea that bares her bosom to the moon;
The winds that will be howling at all hours,
And are up-gathered now like sleeping flowers;
For this, for everything, we are out of tune;
It moves us not. — Great God! I'd rather be
A Pagan suckled in a creed outworn;   10
So might I, standing on this pleasant lea,[3]
Have glimpses that would make me less forlorn;
Have sight of Proteus* rising from the sea;
Or hear old Triton* blow his wreathèd horn.

[1] For biography see page 702.   [2] Marsh, bog.
[3] Meadow. Here, a meadow by the sea.

Discussion Hints

We Are Seven

1. Which stanza gives the theme of the poem?

2. Who was right, after all: the poet or the little girl?

3. What foot is most commonly used in this poem? Point out exceptions.

Lucy Gray

1. In what ways does this poem remind you of the old ballads (p. 57)?

2. A friend and sympathetic interpreter of Wordsworth said that in "Lucy Gray" the poet's object was "to exhibit poetically entire *solitude,* and he represents the (country) child as observing the day moon, which few town or village girls would ever notice." What features of the poem help to emphasize the solitude?

3. What was Lucy's purpose in going?

4. What fate befell her?

5. What supernatural elements does the poem contain?

6. Have you ever seen the moon in the daytime?

She Dwelt among the Untrodden Ways

1. Memorize this poem. It is one of the most simple and beautiful in the whole range of English literature.

2. The last two lines furnish a good example of economy in language, profound, almost in-

expressible emotion set forth in few words. Other examples are to be found in *Macbeth*, III, iv, 50–51 (p. 119), and in Landor's "Rose Aylmer" (p. 348). Do you feel that more is meant than is expressed in words?

A Slumber Did My Spirit Seal

1. What do the first two lines mean, and what is the connection between them and the third and fourth lines? Express in prose the thought set forth in the third and fourth lines.

2. What takes place between the two stanzas?

To the Daisy

1. Rewrite the first, fourth, and sixth stanzas, using the natural order of prose sentences.

2. What does the poet say in the second stanza?

3. Make a list of the metaphors* in the poem.

4. List the comparisons that Wordsworth uses to describe the daisy. Which do you regard as most appropriate? Do any seem to you inappropriate? Give reasons for your answer.

5. Compare this poem with Burns's "To a Mountain Daisy" (p. 330). What thoughts suggested to Burns by the daisy are not referred to in Wordsworth's poem? How do you explain the difference?

My Heart Leaps Up When I Behold

1. Write a précis (summary) of this poem.

2. Memorize the poem.

3. In the light of the definition of "epigram"* explain line 7.

4. Compare your thoughts when you see a rainbow with those that occurred to Wordsworth. What differences do you find, if any? Do you, for example, think of beauty, or of the old superstition that a pot of gold is to be found at the end of a rainbow?

She Was a Phantom of Delight

1. Do you get a clear picture of Mrs. Wordsworth from this poem?

2. If you had been Mrs. Wordsworth, should you have been pleased with the poem?

3. Which of the metaphors* that Wordsworth uses to describe his wife do you like best?

The Solitary Reaper

1. What does the poet think may have been the subject of the girl's song? If the poet met a mountain girl in our country today, what kind of songs on the same subjects might he hear her sing (see page 57)?

2. Explain how this poem illustrates Wordsworth's theories of poetry (p. 335).

3. Paraphrase the second stanza, bringing out clearly the two different scenes described.

4. Memorize the first and third stanzas.

SONNETS

It Is a Beauteous Evening

1. What contrast is there between the idea of the first five lines and that of the next three?

2. Sum up in one sentence the idea of the octave of this sonnet*; of the sestet.

3. In which of Wordsworth's other lyrics does the poet compare something to a nun? State the comparison.

4. Write a theme comparing Wordsworth's sonnet with Collins's "Ode to Evening" (p. 296). What features characteristic of the Age of Classicism are used by Collins but omitted by Wordsworth?

London, 1802

1. Write a précis (summary) of this sonnet.

2. What facts in the life of Milton would suggest to Wordsworth that Milton was a distinguished example of a man who believed in freedom, in simple living, and in noble ideals?

The World Is Too Much with Us

1. State in simple prose each idea expressed in the sonnet.

2. What did Wordsworth think was the matter with England in his day? What did he believe was the cure? Judging by this poem, what do you think his attitude was toward the Industrial Revolution (p. 319).

3. Write out the rhyme* scheme of each of Wordsworth's sonnets.* Are they Italian or are they English? Are they regular or irregular as to rhyme scheme?

4. Which of the sonnets do you prefer? Give reasons for your answer.

5. Memorize the sonnet that you like best.

General Discussion Hints on Wordsworth's Lyric Poetry

1. Which of Wordworth's lyrics illustrate most fully his theories of poetry (p. 335)? Explain your answer.

2. What evils of society referred to in Wordsworth's lyrics exist or are believed to exist today?

3. Do you feel that your reading of the lyrics has revealed to you either (1) aspects of nature which you previously had not observed or (2) new emotional experiences? Illustrate your answer by quotations from the poems.

4. Wordsworth, who liked simplicity in theme and language, has been charged with being at times so simple as to be commonplace and unpoetical. In the poems by Wordsworth that you have read, do you find any cases where his fondness for simple themes or simple language has led him to be prosaic, commonplace, and unpoetical? If so, quote the passages in point and discuss in class.

Suggestions for Reading

"Lines Written in Early Spring"
"Lines Composed a Few Miles above Tintern Abbey"
"Three Years She Grew in Sun and Shower"
"To the Cuckoo"
"To a Skylark"
"I Wandered Lonely as a Cloud" (in the revised edition of *Achievement* of this series)
"Ode to Duty"
"Ode: Intimations of Immortality from Recollections of Early Childhood"
"Scorn not the Sonnet; Critic, You Have Frowned"
"Yarrow Revisited"

ROBERT SOUTHEY[1] (1774–1843)

The Cataract of Lodore

How would a romanticist describe a picturesque and noisy waterfall? Southey answers in "The Cataract of Lodore." We read the poem purely for the sound of the words and the images they bring to our minds. It shows us a poet experimenting with the sound effects of words. It is one of the best examples of sustained onomatopoeia* in the English language. Read it aloud, for only so can you get the full effect. Another famous example of onomatopoeia is Edgar Allan Poe's "Bells."[2]

How does the water
Come down at Lodore?"[3]
My little boy asked me
Thus once on a time;
And moreover he tasked me
To tell him in rhyme.

Anon at the word
There first came one daughter
And then came another
To second and third   10
The request of their brother
And to hear how the water
Comes down at Lodore
With its rush and its roar,
As many a time
They had seen it before.
I told them in rhyme,
For of rhymes I had store:
And 'twas in my vocation
For their recreation   20
That so I should sing;
Because I was Laureate[1]
To them and the King.

From its sources which well[2]
In the tarn[3] on the fell[4];

---

[1] For biography see page 716.
[2] In the revised edition of *American Writers* of this series.
[3] The waterfall of Lodore (lŏ dōr′) is on the Derwent River in Cumberland, a county in the north of England where Southey lived for many years.

[1] Southey was appointed poet laureate* in 1813.
[2] Spring up.
[3] Lake.
[4] A treeless upland, or moor.

From its fountains
In the mountains,
Its rills and its gills;
Through moss and through brake,[1]
It runs and it creeps 30
For awhile, till it sleeps
In its own little lake.
And thence at departing,
Awakening and starting,
It runs through the reeds
And away it proceeds,
Through meadow and glade,
In sun and in shade,
And through the wood-shelter,
Among crags in its flurry, 40
Helter-skelter,
Hurry-scurry.
Here it comes sparkling,
And there it lies darkling;
Now smoking and frothing
Its tumult and wrath in,
Till in this rapid race
On which it is bent,
It reaches the place
Of its steep descent. 50

The cataract strong
Then plunges along,
Striking and raging
As if a war waging
Its caverns and rocks among:
Rising and leaping,
Sinking and creeping,
Swelling and sweeping,
Showering and springing,
Flying and flinging, 60
Writhing and ringing,
Eddying and whisking,
Spouting and frisking,
Turning and twisting,
Around and around
With endless rebound!
Smiting and fighting,
A sight to delight in;
Confounding, astounding,
Dizzying and deafening the ear with its
sound. 70

[1] Fern.

Collecting, projecting,
Receding and speeding,
And shocking and rocking,
And darting and parting,
And threading and spreading,
And whizzing and hissing,
And dripping and skipping,
And hitting and splitting,
And shining and twining,
And rattling and battling, 80
And shaking and quaking,
And pouring and roaring,
And waving and raving,
And tossing and crossing,
And flowing and going,
And running and stunning,
And foaming and roaming,
And dinning and spinning,
And dropping and hopping,
And working and jerking, 90
And guggling and struggling,
And heaving and cleaving,
And moaning and groaning;
And glittering and frittering,
And gathering and feathering,
And whitening and brightening,
And quivering and shivering,
And hurrying and skurrying,
And thundering and floundering;

Dividing and gliding and sliding, 100
And falling and brawling and sprawl-
ing,
And driving and riving and striving,
And sprinkling and twinkling and
wrinkling,
And sounding and bounding and round-
ing,
And bubbling and troubling and dou-
bling,
And grumbling and rumbling and tum-
bling,
And clattering and battering and shat-
tering;

Retreating and beating and meeting and
sheeting,
Delaying and straying and playing and
spraying,

The cataract of Lodore

Advancing and prancing and glancing
  and dancing, 110
Recoiling, turmoiling and toiling and
  boiling,
And gleaming and streaming and steaming and beaming,
And rushing and flushing and brushing
  and gushing,
And flapping and rapping and clapping
  and slapping,
And curling and whirling and purling and
  twirling,
And thumping and plumping and bump-
  ing and jumping,
And dashing and flashing and splashing
  and clashing;
And so never ending, but always descending,
Sounds and motions for ever and ever are
  blending,

All at once and all o'er, with a mighty up-
  roar; 120
And this way the water comes down at
  Lodore.

Discussion Hints

1. What circumstance, according to Southey, led to the writing of the "Cataract of Lodore"? What bearing does your answer have upon the playfully experimental char- acter of the verse?

2. Point out passages in which the language shows that the stream moves progressively from slow to rippling to turbulent, or the reverse.

3. Point out passages that illustrate Southey's interest in alliteration. *

4. Point out passages in which the poet, by his choice of words, suggests the various im- pressions made by the cataract upon (1) the eye; (2) the ear. Which are more numerous?

WALTER SAVAGE LANDOR[1] (1775–1864)

Rose Aylmer

"Rose Aylmer" is one of the most famous poems of the Romantic Period. It owes its place in literature to the fact that it expresses profound emotion (1) in few words, yet (2) in beauti- ful and unforgettable language. Rose Aylmer was a lovely girl of whom Landor was fond.

AH WHAT avails the sceptred race,[2]
  Ah what the form divine!
What every virtue, every grace!
  Rose Aylmer, all were thine.

Rose Aylmer, whom these wakeful eyes
  May weep, but never see,
A night of memories and of sighs
  I consecrate to thee.

On His Seventy-fifth Birthday

"On His Seventy-fifth Birthday" not only is one of the best of Landor's short poems, but it also gives a thumbnail sketch of the poet's artistic creed. Except for the first line (Landor was always quarreling with some- body) the poem is literally true.

I STROVE with none, for none was worth
  my strife,
Nature I loved, and next to Nature, Art;
I warmed both hands before the fire of life,
  It sinks, and I am ready to depart.

• For biography see page 717.
‡ Rose came of a noble family, or "sceptred race," the scepter being the sign of royalty.

Discussion Hints

1. State in logical form the reasoning in- volved in the first stanza of "Rose Aylmer." What answer to the question regarding "every virtue, every grace" (l. 3) is im- plied?

2. Give an example of what Landor may have meant in the poem "On His Seventy- fifth Birthday" by loving "Nature" first and "next to Nature, Art." If you cannot an- swer, you may get help from the introduc- tions to "The Transition from Classicism to Romanticism" (p. 289) and to "The Romantic Period" (p. 313).

THOMAS MOORE[1] (1779–1852)

The Harp That Once through Tara's Halls

Like many other of Thomas Moore's poems, "The Harp That Once through Tara's Halls" is marked by its singing quality. Moore is at his best when, as in this case, he is writing of Ireland's past, of the glorious days when she was famous for culture, learning, poetry, and religion. The words of the poem express a mournful longing often found in Irish poetry and sometimes called "Celtic melancholy."

THE harp[2] that once through Tara's[3]
  halls
  The soul of music shed,
Now hangs as mute on Tara's walls,
  As if that soul were fled. —

So sleeps the pride of former days,
  So glory's thrill is o'er,
And hearts, that once beat high for
    praise,
  Now feel that pulse no more!

No more to chiefs and ladies bright
  The harp of Tara swells;   10
The chord alone, that breaks at night,
  Its tale of ruin tells.
Thus Freedom now so seldom wakes,
  The only throb she gives,
Is when some heart indignant breaks,
  To show that still she lives.

'Tis the Last Rose of Summer

"'Tis the Last Rose of Summer," perhaps better than any other song by Thomas Moore, expresses a gently pleasing and softly sentimental theme in musical language. Like several of Moore's other melodies, it has been sung and admired by thousands.

'TIS the last rose of summer
  Left blooming alone;
All her lovely companions
  Are faded and gone;
No flower of her kindred,
  No rose-bud is nigh,
To reflect back her blushes,
  Or give sigh for sigh.

I'll not leave thee, thou lone one!
  To pine on the stem;   10
Since the lovely are sleeping,
  Go, sleep thou with them.
Thus kindly I scatter
  Thy leaves o'er the bed,
Where thy mates of the garden
  Lie scentless and dead.

So soon may *I* follow,
  When friendships decay,
And from Love's shining circle
  The gems drop away.   20
When true hearts lie withered,
  And fond ones are flown,
Oh! who would inhabit
  This bleak world alone?

Discussion Hints

The Harp That Once through
Tara's Halls

1. Moore once wrote
"Dear Harp of my Country! in darkness I
    found thee,
  The cold chain of silence had hung o'er thee
    long,
When proudly, my own Island Harp, I un-
    bound thee,
  And gave all thy chords to light, freedom
    and song."

What does this imply as to the importance of "The Harp That Once through Tara's Halls" and Moore's significance as a song-writer?

2. Explain
"The chord alone, that breaks at night,
  Its tale of ruin tells" (ll. 11–12)

[1] For biography see page 717.
[2] Here, the spirit of Irish poetry.
[3] Tara (tä′rä) was the capital of the ancient kings of Ireland.

'Tis the Last Rose of Summer

1. Why should a poet be moved to write a poem on the last rose of summer?

2. Passages to be explained:

a. To pine on the stem (l. 10)
b. Go, sleep thou with them (l. 12)
c. thy mates of the garden (l. 15)

3. The following lyrics by Moore are available in recordings by the RCA (Victor) Manufacturing Company, Inc.: "The Harp That Once through Tara's Halls" (No. 1553), "'Tis the Last Rose of Summer" (No. 1355), "Believe Me, if All Those Endearing Young Charms" (Nos. 1238 and 22081). If possible get these records and play them in class.

LEIGH HUNT[1] (1784–1859)

Abou Ben Adhem

Leigh Hunt is remembered principally for the two short poems printed here. Because of its humanitarian sentiment, "Abou Ben Adhem" is worthy of a place in anyone's collection of literary gems. The fourteenth line is in harmony with one of the cardinal principles of the Romantic Period, namely, that all men are brothers in the great family of humanity.

ABOU BEN ADHEM[2] (may his tribe
  increase!)
Awoke one night from a deep dream of
    peace,
And saw, within the moonlight in his
    room,
Making it rich, and like a lily in bloom,
An angel writing in a book of gold:
Exceeding peace had made Ben Adhem
    bold,
And to the presence in the room he said,
"What writest thou?" — The vision
    raised its head,

And, with a look made of all sweet ac-
    cord,
Answered, "The names of those who love
    the Lord."   10
"And is mine one?" said Abou. "Nay,
    not so,"
Replied the angel. Abou spoke more
    low,
But cheery still; and said, "I pray thee,
    then,
Write me as one that loves his fellow-
    men."[1]
  The angel wrote, and vanished. The
    next night
It came again, with a great wakening
    light,
And showed the names whom love of God
    had blessed, —
And lo! Ben Adhem's name led all the
    rest.

Jenny Kissed Me

The Jenny of this charming little poem is Jane Welsh Carlyle, the wife of Thomas Carlyle.[3] She was noted for her wit and beauty. It is said that the celebrated kiss expressed her delight when Hunt told her that a publisher had accepted her husband's *History of Frederick the Great*.

JENNY kissed me when we met,
  Jumping from the chair she sat in;
Time, you thief, who love to get
  Sweets into your list, put that in:
Say I'm weary, say I'm sad,
  Say that health and wealth have missed
    me,
Say I'm growing old, but add,
  Jenny kissed me.

[1] For biography see page 718.
[2] *Abou Ben Adhem* (ä′bōō bĕn ä′dĕm).
[3] The famous essayist and author of *The French Revolution*, which helped to inspire Dickens to write *A Tale of Two Cities*.

[1] *Write . . . fellow-men.* A line often quoted. It is carved on Hunt's tombstone.

Discussion Hints

Abou Ben Adhem

1. State in one sentence the message of "Abou Ben Adhem."

2. Abou Ben Adhem, here represented as a wise and loving ancient Hebrew philosopher, is purely imaginary. The name seems to mean "Father, son of Adam." What bearing have these facts on the message of the poem?

Jenny Kissed Me

1. Tell what episode in the life of Thomas Carlyle helps to explain "Jenny Kissed Me."

2. Why should Time be called a "thief" (l. 3)?

3. Why does Time "love to get Sweets" into his "list" (ll. 3–4)?

GEORGE GORDON, LORD BYRON[1] (1788–1824)

Maid of Athens, ere We Part

"Maid of Athens" is one of the best-known of Byron's shorter lyrics. It illustrates the poet's extraordinary skill in composing light, musical, metrically perfect verses on slight occasion. The poem is supposed to have been addressed to Theresa Macri, a lady in whose house Byron lodged on his first visit to Athens.

Ζώη μου, σᾶς ἀγαπῶ [2]

MAID of Athens, ere we part,
Give, oh, give me back my heart!
Or, since that has left my breast,
Keep it now, and take the rest!
Hear my vow before I go,
Ζώη μου, σᾶς ἀγαπῶ.[2]

By those tresses unconfined,
Woo'd by each Aegean wind;

By those lids whose jetty fringe
Kiss thy soft cheeks' blooming tinge; 10
By those wild eyes like the roe,
Ζώη μου, σᾶς ἀγαπῶ.

By that lip I long to taste;
By that zone-encircled[1] waist;
By all the token-flowers that tell
What words can never speak so well;
By love's alternate joy and woe,
Ζώη μου, σᾶς ἀγαπῶ.

Maid of Athens! I am gone:
Think of me, sweet! when alone, 20
Though I fly to Istambol,[2]
Athens holds my heart and soul:
Can I cease to love thee? No!
Ζώη μου, σᾶς ἀγαπῶ.

From "Adieu, Adieu!"

"Adieu, Adieu!" owes its popularity to its vivid portrayal of Byron's feelings when, stung by criticism which he felt to be unjust, he left England never to return (see page 719). It illustrates also the poet's fondness for making himself the hero of his poems and for indulging in sentimental self-pity.

ADIEU, adieu! my native shore
Fades o'er the waters blue;
The night-winds sigh, the breakers roar,
And shrieks the wild sea-mew.[3]

Yon sun that sets upon the sea
We follow in his flight;
Farewell awhile to him and thee,
My native land — Good night!

A few short hours, and he will rise,
To give the morrow birth; 10
And I shall hail the main [3] and skies,
But not my mother earth.
Deserted is my own good hall,
Its hearth is desolate;
Wild weeds are gathering on the wall,
My dog howls at the gate.

[1] For biography see page 718.
[2] Ζώη μου, σᾶς ἀγαπῶ (zō′ē mōō′, säs ä gä pō′). Greek for "My life, I love you."
[3] A sea gull.

[1] Encircled by a girdle, or belt.
[2] Constantinople.   [3] Open sea.

And now I'm in the world alone,
  Upon the wide, wide sea;
But why should I for others groan,
  When none will sigh for me?   20
Perchance my dog will whine in vain,
  Till fed by stranger hands;
But long ere I come back again
  He'd tear me where he stands.

With thee, my bark, I'll swiftly go
  Athwart the foaming brine;
Nor care what land thou bear'st me to,
  So not again to mine.
Welcome, welcome, ye dark blue waves!
  And when you fail my sight,   30
Welcome, ye deserts, and ye caves!
  My native land — Good night!

From *Childe Harold's Pilgrimage*

THE EVE OF WATERLOO

The following passages are selected from *Childe Harold's Pilgrimage*, one of Byron's longer poems, which did more, perhaps, than any other of his works to make the author famous. In it Childe[1] Harold, who is really Byron himself, wanders through Europe seeking romantic scenes and sentimental situations in keeping with his somber and sometimes morbid character. Scattered throughout the narrative are numerous lyric or descriptive passages that have long been greatly admired. Most of the poem is written in the Spenserian* stanza. To get the full effect of the lines, you should read aloud the following passages, as well as the other selections from Byron.

In "The Eve of Waterloo" Byron, while describing a ball at Brussels shortly before the great battle of Waterloo,* heightens the romantic effect by contrasting the careless revelry of youth and beauty at the ball with the wholesale slaughter that was to follow, and, with equal skill, brings each individual stanza, as well as the whole passage, to an effective close in the last line.

THERE was a sound of revelry by night,[2]
  And Belgium's capital had gather'd
    then
  Her Beauty and her Chivalry, and
    bright
The lamps shone o'er fair women and
    brave men;
A thousand hearts beat happily; and
    when

Music arose with its voluptuous swell,
Soft eyes look'd love to eyes which
  spake again,
And all went merry as a marriage
  bell;
But hush! hark! a deep sound strikes like
  a rising knell!

Did ye not hear it? — No; 'twas but
  the wind,   10
Or the car[1] rattling o'er the stony
  street;
On with the dance! let joy be uncon-
  fined;
No sleep till morn, when Youth and
  Pleasure meet
To chase the glowing Hours with flying
  feet. —
But hark! that heavy sound breaks in
  once more,
As if the clouds its echo would repeat;
And nearer, clearer, deadlier than
  before!
Arm! Arm! it is — it is — the cannon's
  opening roar!

Within a window'd niche of that high
  hall
Sate Brunswick's fated chieftain[2]; he
  did hear   20
That sound the first amidst the festival,
And caught its tone with Death's prophetic ear,

[1] Here, as in the old ballads, *Childe* is used as a kind of title meaning a youth of noble birth.
[2] *revelry by night.* The Countess of Richmond gave a ball in Brussels on the evening preceding the battle of Quatre Bras, three days before Waterloo.*

[1] Here, a horsecart.
[2] *Brunswick's fated chieftain.* Frederick William, Duke of Brunswick, who was killed in the next day's fighting.

*But hush! hark! a deep sound strikes
like a rising knell!*

FROM A PAINTING BY HAROLD SICHEL

And when they smiled because he
deem'd it near,
His heart more truly knew that peal
too well
Which stretch'd his father on a bloody
bier,
And roused the vengeance blood alone
could quell.
He rush'd into the field, and, foremost
fighting, fell.

Ah! then and there was hurrying to
and fro,
And gathering tears, and tremblings of
distress,
And cheeks all pale, which but an hour
ago   30
Blush'd at the praise of their own
loveliness;
And there were sudden partings, such
as press
The life from out young hearts, and
choking sighs
Which ne'er might be repeated: who
could guess
If ever more should meet those mutual
eyes,
Since upon night so sweet such awful
morn could rise!

And there was mounting in hot haste:
the steed,
The mustering squadron, and the clattering car,
Went pouring forward with impetuous
speed,
And swiftly forming in the ranks of
war;   40
And the deep thunder peal on peal
afar;
And near, the beat of the alarming
drum
Roused up the soldier ere the morning
star;
While throng'd the citizens with terror
dumb,
Or whispering with white lips — "The
foe! They come! they come!"

D

And wild and high the "Cameron's
Gathering" rose,
The war-note of Lochiel, which Albyn's
hills
Have heard, and heard, too, have her
Saxon foes;
How in the noon of night that pibroch[1]
thrills
Savage and shrill! But with the
breath which fills   50
Their mountain pipe, so fill the moun-
taineers
With the fierce native daring which
instils
The stirring memory of a thousand
years,
And Evan's, Donald's[2] fame rings in
each clansman's ears!

And Ardennes[3] waves above them her
green leaves,
Dewy with Nature's tear-drops, as
they pass,
Grieving, if aught inanimate e'er
grieves,
Over the unreturning brave, — alas!
Ere evening to be trodden like the grass
Which now beneath them, but above
shall grow   60
In its next verdure,[4] when this fiery
mass
Of living valour, rolling on the foe,
And burning with high hope, shall
moulder cold and low.

Last noon beheld them full of lusty
life,
Last eve in Beauty's circle proudly
gay,
The midnight brought the signal-sound
of strife,

[1] Scottish bagpipe music, used to sound the call
to arms.
[2] *Evan's, Donald's.* The reference is to Donald
Cameron, who fought at Culloden,* and his
famous ancestor Sir Evan Cameron.
[3] A wooded district of northern France. Byron
mentions it for contrast, since the ancient
forest of Ardennes was associated with peace.
[4] Greenness of spring.

The morn the marshalling in arms —
the day
Battle's magnificently stern array!
The thunder-clouds close o'er it, which
when rent

The earth is cover'd thick with other
clay,   70
Which her own clay shall cover,
heap'd and pent,
Rider and horse — friend, foe, — in one
red burial blent!

APOSTROPHE TO ROME

The "Apostrophe[1] to Rome" is famous as a piece of vivid description charged with intense feeling and expressed in thunderous verse. The poignant grief for departed glories is typically romantic.

O ROME! my country! city of the soul!
The orphans of the heart must turn
to thee,
Lone mother of dead empires! and
control
In their shut breasts their petty misery.
What are our woes and sufferance?
Come and see
The cypress,[2] hear the owl, and plod
your way
O'er steps of broken thrones and
temples, — Ye!
Whose agonies are evils of a day —
A world is at our feet as fragile as our
clay.

The Niobe* of nations! there she stands,
Childless and crownless, in her voice-
less woe;   11
An empty urn within her wither'd
hands,
Whose holy dust was scatter'd long ago;

The Scipios'[1] tomb contains no ashes
now;
The very sepulchres lie tenantless
Of their heroic dwellers: dost thou flow,
Old Tiber! through a marble wilder-
ness[2]?
Rise, with thy yellow waves, and mantle
her distress.

The Goth, the Christian, Time, War,
Flood, and Fire,
Have dealt upon the seven-hill'd city's[3]
pride: 20
She saw her glories star by star ex-
pire,
And up the steep barbarian monarchs
ride,
Where the car climb'd the Capitol; far
and wide
Temple and tower went down, nor left
a site: —
Chaos of ruins! who shall trace the
void,
O'er the dim fragments cast a lunar
light,[4]
And say, "Here was, or is," where all is
doubly night?

MAN AND NATURE

"Man and Nature" is typically lyrical, typically Byronic, and typically romantic. The poem shows Byron's characteristic attitude toward nature. Byron sought nature as an escape from man. Note also his complete abandonment of himself to emotional moods and his rapturous devotion to the object present at the moment to his mind. These are traits that mark many of the more exalted flights of romantic poetry in general. In all these respects Byron's poetry represents a reaction against the accepted standards of the Age of Classicism (p. 213).

[1] *Scipios' tomb.* An ancient Roman burial place associated with the Scipios, a family some of whom were famous for their patriotism.
[2] A typical bit of Byronic imagery.*
[3] *seven-hill'd city's.* Rome was built on seven hills.
[4] *lunar light.* Light as of the moon.

[1] Address.
[2] A symbol of funerals.

[The desert.]

OH THAT the Desert were my dwell-
　　ing-place,
With one fair Spirit for my minister,
That I might all forget the human race,
And, hating no one, love but only her!
Ye Elements!—in whose ennobling stir
I feel myself exalted — can ye not
Accord me such a being? Do I err
In deeming such inhabit many a spot,
Though with them to converse can rarely
　　be our lot?

[The forest.]

There is a pleasure in the pathless
　　woods,   10
There is a rapture on the lonely shore,
There is society where none intrudes,
By the deep Sea, and music in its roar:
I love not man the less, but Nature
　　more,
From these our interviews, in which I
　　steal
From all I may be or have been before,
To mingle with the Universe, and feel
What I can ne'er express, yet cannot all
　　conceal.

[The ocean.]

Roll on, thou deep and dark blue
　　Ocean — roll!
Ten thousand fleets sweep over thee in
　　vain;   20
Man marks the earth with ruin — his
　　control
Stops with the shore; — upon the
　　watery plain
The wrecks are all thy deed, nor doth
　　remain
A shadow of man's ravage,[1] save his
　　own,
When, for a moment, like a drop of
　　rain,
He sinks into thy depths with bubbling
　　groan,
Without a grave, unknell'd, uncoffin'd,
　　and unknown.

　　　　　[1] Desolation, ruin.

His steps are not upon thy paths — thy
　　fields
Are not a spoil for him — thou dost
　　arise
And shake him from thee; the vile
　　strength he wields   30
For earth's destruction thou dost all
　　despise,
Spurning him from thy bosom to the
　　skies,
And send'st him, shivering in thy play-
　　ful spray,
And howling, to his Gods, where haply
　　lies
His petty hope in some near port or
　　bay,
And dashest him again to earth — there
　　let him lay.

The armaments which thunderstrike
　　the walls
Of rock-built cities, bidding nations
　　quake
And monarchs tremble in their capi-
　　tals,
The oak leviathans,[1] whose huge ribs
　　make   40
Their clay creator[2] the vain title take
Of lord of thee, and arbiter[3] of
　　war,
These are thy toys, and, as the snowy
　　flake,
They melt into thy yeast of waves,
　　which mar
Alike the Armada's* pride or spoils of
　　Trafalgar.*

Thy shores are empires, changed in all
　　save thee —
Assyria, Greece, Rome, Carthage, what
　　are they?
Thy waters washed them power while
　　they were free,
And many a tyrant since; their shores
　　obey

[1] Here, ships. The leviathan is a great sea
　monster.
[2] *Their clay creator.* Man.
[3] Judge, lord.

The stranger, slave, or savage; their
  decay   50
Has dried up realms to deserts : — not
  so thou,
Unchangeable save to thy wild waves'
  play;
Time writes no wrinkle on thine azure
  brow;
Such as creation's dawn beheld, thou
  rollest now.

Thou glorious mirror, where the Al-
  mighty's form
Glasses itself in tempests : in all
  time,
Calm or convulsed — in breeze, or
  gale, or storm,
Icing the pole, or in the torrid clime
Dark-heaving; — boundless, endless,
  and sublime[1] —   59
The image of Eternity — the throne
Of the Invisible; even from out thy
  slime
The monsters of the deep are made;
  each zone
Obeys thee; thou goest forth, dread,
  fathomless, alone.

And I have loved thee, Ocean! and my
  joy
Of youthful sports was on thy breast
  to be
Borne, like thy bubbles, onward : from
  a boy
I wanton'd with thy breakers — they
  to me
Were a delight; and if the freshening
  sea
Made them a terror — 'twas a pleasing
  fear,   69
For I was as it were a child of thee,
And trusted to thy billows far and
  near,
And laid my hand upon thy mane — as
  I do here.

[1] *Dark-heaving . . . sublime.* Byron was fond of
lines composed of sonorous adjectives.

Discussion Hints

Maid of Athens

1. Why does Byron use Greek instead of
English in the refrain of "Maid of Athens"?
See his biography (p. 718).

2. Express in simple language "jetty fringe"
(l. 9).

3. Explain

a. token-flowers (l. 15)

b. love's alternate joy and woe (l. 17)

From "Adieu, Adieu!"

1. In what respects does this poem appear
to be connected with Byron's life?

2. Explain

a. stranger hands (l. 22)

b. Athwart the foaming brine (l. 26)

c. fail my sight (l. 30)

From *Childe Harold's Pilgrimage*

THE EVE OF WATERLOO

1. Show how lines 1–18 work up to a
climax.

2. Point out passages that illustrate the
contrast indicated in the last paragraph of the
headnote.

3. What differences in sound are there between the sixth and seventh stanzas?

4. Which stanza do you think a survivor of
the battle might read with greatest feeling?
Why?

5. Put into simple language

a. Death's prophetic ear (l. 22)

b. the noon of night (l. 49) ¶

c. Nature's tear-drops (l. 56)

d.   *this fiery mass*
Of living valour, rolling on the foe
(ll. 61–62)

e. Beauty's circle (l. 65)

f. The earth is cover'd thick with other clay,
Which her own clay shall cover (ll. 70–71)

g. blent (l. 72)

APOSTROPHE TO ROME

1. Point out passages that illustrate the
trait brought out in the last sentence of the
headnote.

2. What argument is implied in lines 1–9?

3. What influences, according to Byron, caused the changes in Rome?

4. Which line makes you see most clearly a picture? What is the picture?

5. Explain the symbolism* of "empty urn" and "wither'd hands" (l. 12).

6. Explain

a. The Niobe of nations (l. 10)

b. marble wilderness (l. 17)

c. mantle her distress (l. 18)

MAN AND NATURE

1. Point out passages that illustrate Byron's fondness for nature as an escape from man.

2. What fact regarding Byron's youthful amusements do you learn from the last stanza (see page 356)?

3. Point out several illustrations of Byron's fondness for high-sounding adjectives.

4. Write a précis (summary) of lines 37–45.

5. Read again the introduction to the Romantic Period (p. 313), and then list the features that make "Man and Nature" romantic.

6. Explain

a. steal (l. 15)

b. unknell'd, uncoffin'd, and unknown (l. 27)

c.   thy fields
Are not a spoil for him (ll. 28–29)

d. Thy shores are empires, changed in all save
thee (l. 46)

e. Thou glorious mirror, where the Almighty's form
Glasses itself in tempests (ll. 55–56)

Suggestions for Reading[1]

"Sonnet on Chillon"

"Know Ye the Land Where the Cypress and Myrtle"

"She Walks in Beauty" (in the revised edition of *Achievement* of this series)

"So, We'll Go No More a Roving"

"When We Two Parted"

"Fare Thee Well"

PERCY BYSSHE SHELLEY[1] (1792–1822)

Ozymandias[2]

Shelley happened to read an account of the fragments of a gigantic statue found lying in the Egyptian desert and bearing this inscription: "I am Ozymandias, king of kings." The idea of a monarch once so powerful, but now remembered only by a broken statue, inspired the poet to write "Ozymandias," one of the best English poems on the futility of human greatness. Aside from its lyric beauty, it emphasizes the truth that even the greatest and most powerful may be forgotten.

I MET a traveller from an antique land[3]
  Who said: Two vast and trunkless legs of stone
Stand in the desert. Near them, on the sand,
Half sunk, a shattered visage lies, whose frown,
And wrinkled lip, and sneer of cold command,

Tell that its sculptor well those passions read
Which yet survive,[2] stamped on these lifeless things,
The hand that mocked them[3] and the heart[4] that fed:
And on the pedestal these words appear:
"My name is Ozymandias, king of kings: 10
Look on my works, ye Mighty, and despair!"
Nothing beside remains. Round the decay
Of that colossal wreck, boundless and bare
The lone and level sands stretch far away.

---

[1] For biography see page 719.
[2] *Ozymandias* (ŏz ĭ măn'dĭ ás).
[3] *antique land*. Egypt.

[1] For suggestions for reading in Byron's narrative poetry see page 410.
[2] Are expressed in the face of the statue.
[3] The passions.
[4] The heart of the king.

Ode to the West Wind

The "Ode to the West Wind," one of Shelley's most intense lyrics, is the outcome of two contrasting influences, one within the poet's own heart, and the other outside of him in the world of nature. The inner influence was Shelley's mood of weakness and discouragement. He felt out of touch with the world, heartsick and hopeless over his own career as a poet. He spent the day in the woods beside the river Arno, near Florence, Italy. The month was October, and a fierce storm was coming up from the west, accompanied by rushing winds, black clouds, and thunder and lightning. This storm was the second influence, and suggested the idea for the poem.

The poet watches the resistless onset of the rushing autumn wind and views the tempest as a mighty destroyer and preserver in one, working its will successively upon leaf and seed (stanza I), upon cloud (stanza II), and upon wave (stanza III). In stanza IV the poet wishes he were leaf, cloud, or wave to feel through his weakness and passiveness the might and power of the wind. In stanza V his mood kindles and rises to the hope of a more active partnership with the tempest. Beyond the storm and beyond the winter that it ushers in, he sees life and hope and spring:

"O Wind,
If Winter comes, can Spring be far behind?"

I

O WILD West Wind, thou breath of
 Autumn's being,
Thou, from whose unseen presence the
 leaves dead
Are driven, like ghosts from an enchanter
 fleeing,

Yellow, and black, and pale, and hectic[1]
 red,
Pestilence-stricken multitudes! O thou
Who chariotest to their dark wintry bed

The wingèd seeds, where they lie cold and
 low,
Each like a corpse within its grave, until
Thine azure sister[2] of the Spring shall
 blow

[1] Feverish.
[2] The gentle west wind of spring.

Her clarion o'er the dreaming earth and
 fill   10
(Driving sweet buds like flocks to feed
 in air)
With living hues and odours plain and
 hill:

Wild Spirit, which art moving everywhere;
Destroyer and Preserver; hear, oh hear!

II

Thou on whose stream, 'mid the steep
 sky's commotion,
Loose clouds like earth's decaying leaves
 are shed,
Shook from the tangled boughs of heaven
 and ocean,

Angels of rain and lightning! there are
 spread
On the blue surface of thine airy surge,
Like the bright hair uplifted from the
 head   20

Of some fierce Maenad,* ev'n from the
 dim verge
Of the horizon to the zenith's height —
The locks of the approaching storm.
 Thou dirge

Of the dying year, to which this closing
 night
Will be the dome of a vast sepulchre,
Vaulted with all thy congregated might

Of vapours, from whose solid atmosphere
Black rain, and fire, and hail, will burst:
 Oh hear!

III

Thou who didst waken from his sum-
 mer-dreams   29
The blue Mediterranean, where he lay,
Lull'd by the coil[1] of his crystalline
 streams,

[1] Murmurous windings.

Beside a pumice isle[1] in Baiae's bay,[2]
And saw in sleep old palaces and towers
Quivering within the wave's intenser day,

All overgrown with azure moss, and
flowers
So sweet, the sense faints picturing them!
Thou
For whose path the Atlantic's level powers

Cleave themselves into chasms, while far
below
The sea-blooms and the oozy woods
which wear
The sapless foliage of the ocean, know 40

Thy voice, and suddenly grow gray with
fear
And tremble and despoil themselves: Oh
hear!

IV

If I were a dead leaf thou mightest
bear;
If I were a swift cloud to fly with thee;
A wave to pant beneath thy power, and
share

The impulse of thy strength, only less
free
Than Thou, O uncontrollable! If even
I were as in my boyhood, and could be

The comrade of thy wanderings over
heaven,
As then, when to outstrip thy skiey speed
Scarce seem'd a vision, — I would ne'er
have striven 51

As thus with thee in prayer in my sore
need.
Oh! lift me as a wave, a leaf, a cloud!
I fall upon the thorns of life! I bleed!

A heavy weight of hours has chain'd and
bow'd
One too like thee — tameless, and swift,
and proud.

V

Make me thy lyre, ev'n as the forest is:
What if my leaves are falling like its own!
The tumult of thy mighty harmonies

Will take from both a deep autumnal
tone, 60
Sweet though in sadness. Be thou, Spirit
fierce,
My spirit! be thou me, impetuous one!

Drive my dead thoughts over the universe,
Like wither'd leaves, to quicken a new
birth;
And, by the incantation of this verse,

Scatter, as from an unextinguish'd hearth
Ashes and sparks, my words among
mankind!
Be through my lips to unawaken'd earth

The trumpet of a prophecy! O Wind,
If Winter comes, can Spring be far behind? 70

The Indian Serenade

"The Indian Serenade" is deservedly famous as one of the most beautiful and delicately passionate love lyrics that have ever
been written.

[1] *pumice isle.* An island made of pumice stone,
a volcanic substance.
[2] *Baiae's bay.* A bay in the south of Italy, near
Naples. Baiae was the leading Roman water-
ing place in the time of Augustus and Nero.

I ARISE from dreams of thee
In the first sweet sleep of night,
When the winds are breathing low,
And the stars are shining bright;
I arise from dreams of thee,
And a spirit in my feet
Hath led me — who knows how?
To thy chamber window, sweet!

The wandering airs, they faint
On the dark, the silent streams; 10
The champak[1] odours fail
Like sweet thoughts in a dream;
The nightingale's complaint,
It dies upon her heart,
As I must die on thine,
Oh, belovèd as thou art!

Oh, lift me from the grass!
I die! I faint! I fail!
Let thy love in kisses rain
On my lips and eyelids pale. 20
My cheek is cold and white, alas!
My heart beats loud and fast,
Oh! press it close to thine again,
Where it will break at last.

The Cloud

"The Cloud" is a charming lyric written in exquisitely beautiful and melodious language. It is also an excellent illustration of what is ordinarily called Shelley's "myth-making" ability; that is, the faculty of personifying* inanimate objects so as to make them "real spiritual presences." In Shelley's verses the cloud and the moon become alive and take part in stories resembling the beautiful myths of ancient times. No modern poet has revealed the myth-making ability as perfectly as Shelley has.

I BRING fresh showers for the thirsting
    flowers,
  From the seas and the streams;
I bear light shade for the leaves when laid
  In their noonday dreams.
From my wings are shaken the dews that
    waken
  The sweet buds every one,
When rocked to rest on their mother's
    breast,
  As she dances about the sun.
I wield the flail of the lashing hail,
  And whiten the green plains under, 10
And then again I dissolve it in rain,
  And laugh as I pass in thunder.

I sift the snow on the mountains below,
  And their great pines groan aghast;
And all the night 'tis my pillow white,
  While I sleep in the arms of the blast.
Sublime on the towers of my skiey bowers,
  Lightning my pilot sits;
In a cavern under is fettered the thunder,
  It struggles and howls at fits; 20

[1] A tree with sweet-smelling blossoms, somewhat like the magnolia.

Over earth and ocean, with gentle motion,
  This pilot is guiding me,
Lured by the love of the genii[1] that move
  In the depths of the purple sea;
Over the rills, and the crags, and the hills,
  Over the lakes and the plains,
Wherever he dream, under mountain or
    stream,
  The Spirit he loves remains;
And I all the while bask in Heaven's blue
    smile,
  Whilst he is dissolving in rains. 30

The sanguine Sunrise, with his meteor
    eyes,
  And his burning plumes outspread,
Leaps on the back of my sailing rack,[2]
  When the morning star shines dead,
As on the jag of a mountain crag,
  Which an earthquake rocks and swings,
An eagle alit one moment may sit
  In the light of its golden wings.
And when Sunset may breathe, from the
    lit sea beneath,
  Its ardours of rest and of love, 40
And the crimson pall of eve may fall
  From the depth of Heaven above,
With wings folded I rest, on mine airy
    nest,
  As still as a brooding dove.

That orbèd maiden with white fire laden,
  Whom mortals call the Moon,
Glides glimmering o'er my fleece-like floor,
  By the midnight breezes strewn;

[1] Spirits.   [2] Thin, flying mist.

And wherever the beat of her unseen feet,
  Which only the angels hear,   50
May have broken the woof of my tent's
    thin roof,
  The stars peep behind her and peer;
And I laugh to see them whirl and flee,
  Like a swarm of golden bees,
When I widen the rent in my wind-built
    tent,
  Till the calm rivers, lakes, and seas,
Like strips of the sky fallen through me
    on high,
  Are each paved with the moon and
    these.

I bind the Sun's throne with a burning
    zone,   59
  And the Moon's with a girdle of pearl;
The volcanoes are dim, and the stars reel
    and swim,
  When the whirlwinds my banner un-
    furl.
From cape to cape, with a bridge-like
    shape,
  Over a torrent sea,
Sunbeam-proof, I hang like a roof, —
  The mountains its columns be.

The triumphal arch through which I
    march
  With hurricane, fire, and snow.
When the Powers of the air are chained
    to my chair,
  Is the million-coloured bow;   70
The sphere-fire above its soft colours
    wove,
  While the moist Earth was laughing
    below.

I am the daughter of Earth and Water,
  And the nursling of the Sky;
I pass through the pores of the ocean
    and shores;
  I change, but I cannot die.
For after the rain when with never a
    stain
  The pavilion of Heaven is bare,
And the winds and sunbeams with their
    convex gleams
  Build up the blue dome of air,   80
I silently laugh at my own cenotaph,[1]
  And out of the caverns of rain,
Like a child from the womb, like a ghost
    from the tomb,
  I arise and unbuild it again.

To a Skylark

Nearly all readers consider "To a Skylark" one of the loveliest lyrics that have ever been composed. The admirable verse form, the appropriate imagery,* the perfect melody and rhythm,* the intense emotion, and the human interest, all unite to make the poem supremely beautiful. Many thousands of American readers who have never heard an English skylark sing have, with the poet Shelley, been imaginatively thrilled by this divine flood of rapture.

The setting in which Shelley heard this particular skylark sing is worthy of the poem. Mrs. Shelley tells us: "It was on a beautiful summer evening, while wandering near the lanes whose myrtle hedges were the bowers of fireflies, that we heard the caroling of the lark which inspired one of the most beautiful of his [Shelley's] poems."

[Six stanzas of lyric outbursts of delight at the beauty of the skylark's song.]

HAIL to thee, blithe Spirit!
  Bird thou never wert,
That from Heaven, or near it,
  Pourest thy full heart
In profuse strains of unpremeditated art.

  Higher still and higher
    From the earth thou springest
  Like a cloud of fire;
    The blue deep thou wingest,
And singing still dost soar, and soaring
    ever singest.   10

[1] An empty tomb erected in memory of a person who is buried elsewhere.

In the golden lightning
  Of the sunken sun,
O'er which clouds are bright'ning,
  Thou dost float and run;
Like an unbodied joy whose race is just
    begun.

The pale purple even
  Melts around thy flight;
Like a star of Heaven,
  In the broad daylight
Thou art unseen, but yet I hear thy
    shrill delight,   20

Keen as are the arrows
  Of that silver sphere,[1]
Whose intense lamp narrows
  In the white dawn clear
Until we hardly see — we feel that it is
    there.

All the earth and air
  With thy voice is loud,
As, when night is bare,
  From one lonely cloud
The moon rains out her beams, and
    Heaven is overflowed.   30

[Six stanzas of lyric comparisons between
the skylark's song and other forms of joyous
    beauty.]

What thou art we know not;
  What is most like thee?
From rainbow clouds there flow not
  Drops so bright to see
As from thy presence showers a rain of
    melody.

Like a Poet hidden
  In the light of thought,
Singing hymns unbidden,
  Till the world is wrought
To sympathy with hopes and fears it
    heeded not: 40

[1] Probably the morning star.

Like a high-born maiden
  In a palace-tower,
Soothing her love-laden
  Soul in secret hour
With music sweet as love, which over-
    flows her bower:

Like a glow-worm golden
  In a dell of dew,
Scattering unbeholden
  Its aëreal hue
Among the flowers and grass which screen
    it from the view!   50

Like a rose embowered
  In its own green leaves,
By warm winds deflowered,[1]
  Till the scent it gives
Makes faint with too much sweet those
    heavy-wingèd thieves:[2]

Sound of vernal showers
  On the twinkling grass,
Rain-awakened flowers,
  All that ever was
Joyous, and clear, and fresh, thy music
    doth surpass: 60

[Six stanzas contrasting the bird's song of
complete and perfect happiness with human
music and its constant undertone of unful-
    filled longing and sadness.]

Teach us, Sprite or Bird,
  What sweet thoughts are thine:
I have never heard
  Praise of love or wine
That panted forth a flood of rapture so
    divine.

Chorus Hymeneal,[3]
  Or triumphal chant,
Matched with thine would be all
  But an empty vaunt,
A thing wherein we feel there is some
    hidden want.   70

[1] Robbed.
[2] The "warm winds" of line 53.
[3] *Chorus Hymeneal.* Wedding song.

The Art Institute of Chicago, Henry Field Memorial Collection

The song of the lark

From a painting by Jules Breton

What objects are the fountains
　Of thy happy strain?
What fields, or waves, or mountains?
　What shapes of sky or plain?
What love of thine own kind? what igno-
　　rance of pain?

With thy clear keen joyance
　Languor cannot be:
Shadow[1] of annoyance
　Never came near thee:
Thou lovest — but ne'er knew love's sad
　　satiety.[2]　　　　　　　　　　80

Waking or asleep,
　Thou of death must deem
Things more true and deep
　Than we mortals dream,
Or how could thy notes flow in such a
　　crystal stream?

We look before and after,[3]
　And pine for what is not:
Our sincerest laughter
　With some pain is fraught;
Our sweetest songs are those that tell of
　　saddest thought.　　　　　　90

[Three stanzas of appeal in which the poet
desires the bird's skill and gladness, but fears
that they are beyond his reach.]

Yet if we could scorn
　Hate, and pride, and fear;
If we were things born
　Not to shed a tear,
I know not how thy joy we ever should
　　come near.

Better than all measures
　Of delightful sound,
Better than all treasures
　That in books are found,
Thy skill to poet were, thou scorner of
　　the ground!　　　　　　100

Teach me half the gladness
　That thy brain must know,
Such harmonious madness
　From my lips would flow,
The world should listen then — as I am
　　listening now.

Music, When Soft Voices Die

A theme that has been expressed very often
in poetry is that beauty fades and vanishes. In
"Music, When Soft Voices Die" Shelley shows
us the silver lining to this dark fact; namely,
that beauty, even in its passing, leaves an
afterglow of loveliness in our memories.

MUSIC, when soft voices die,
　Vibrates in the memory;

Odours, when sweet violets sicken,
Live within the sense they quicken.

Rose leaves, when the rose is dead,
Are heaped for the belovèd's bed;
And so thy thoughts,[1] when thou art
　　gone,
Love itself shall slumber on.

One Word Is Too Often Profaned

If for no other reason, "One Word Is Too
Often Profaned" is worth reading because
lines 13 and 14 have been so often quoted.

[1] "Shadow" is the important word in this line.
　Emphasize it in your reading.
[2] State of having had too much.
[3] It has been said that mankind suffers each
　affliction three times: once in prospect,
　once in reality, and once in retrospect, or
　memory.

ONE word is too often profaned
　For me to profane it,
One feeling too falsely disdain'd
　For thee to disdain it.
One hope is too like despair
　For prudence to smother,
And pity from thee more dear
　Than that from another.

　　[1] thy thoughts. Thoughts of thee.

I can give not what men call love;
But wilt thou accept not   10
The worship the heart lifts above
And the Heavens reject not:
The desire of the moth for the star
Of the night for the morrow,
The devotion to something afar
From the sphere of our sorrow?

Discussion Hints

Ozymandias

1. What is the message of the poem?

2. Does the rhyme scheme follow exactly either the Italian or the English form of the sonnet?* Write out the rhyme scheme and explain your answer.

3. Explain *shattered visage* (l. 4).

Ode to the West Wind

1. What figure of speech does Shelley use most often throughout the poem? Give examples.

2. Make a list of the color words used in the poem.

3. Explain how the west wind is both "Destroyer and Preserver" (l. 14).

4. Where in the poem does Shelley turn the thought to himself? Explain in connection with the poet's life (p. 719).

5. What do "Autumn," "Spring," and "Winter" represent symbolically?

6. Note that in this poem Shelley uses with great success *terza* rima, a rare and difficult verse form borrowed from Italian poetry of the Middle Ages. Why should a poet of the Romantic Period borrow from such a source?

7. Do you like the comparison of "sweet buds" to "flocks" (such as sheep) (l. 11)? Explain your answer.

8. Explain

  a. chariotest to their dark wintry bed (l. 6)
  b. the steep sky's commotion (l. 15)
  c.   *dirge*
  Of the dying year (ll. 23–24)

The Indian Serenade

1. Do any sounds or odors increase the romantic appeal of the poem for you? If so, which ones?

2. Memorize the first stanza.

The Cloud

1. To which of the five senses does Shelley appeal most in the poem? Illustrate your answer.

2. In lines 17–30 Shelley thinks of the lightning as the pilot of the cloud, who is lured by the love of the sea genii. In line 30 he speaks of the lightning as dissolving in rains. What should you expect to dissolve in rain?

3. If you were going to make one illustration in color for this poem, what lines would you choose? Justify your answer.

4. Point out how line 81 is both beautiful and true.

5. Compare "The Cloud" with lines 67–72 of Milton's "Il Penseroso" (p. 194). Explain the difference in imagery.* Which, if either, do you prefer?

6. Show that the meter of "The Cloud" is partly iambic,* partly anapaestic.*

7. How does the poem illustrate Shelley's myth-making ability?

8. Memorize the fourth stanza. Many persons consider it the most musical in English poetry.

To a Skylark

1. Shelley uses four famous similes* to describe the skylark. What are they? Which of the four do you like best? Give reasons for your answer.

2. Comment on *unbodied* (l. 15). What word would you use instead?

3. Do you agree with what Shelley says in the stanza beginning with line 86? Be prepared to defend your answer.

4. Memorize the last two stanzas of the poem.

5. Compare the last stanza of "To a Skylark" with the last stanza of Poe's "Israfel" (in the revised edition of *American Writers* of this series).

6. Explain
a. *profuse strains of unpremeditated art* (l. 5)
b. *shrill delight* (l. 20)
c. *the world is wrought
  To sympathy* (ll. 39–40)
d. *unbeholden* (l. 48)
e. *vernal showers* (l. 56)
f. *With thy clear keen joyance
  Languor cannot be* (ll. 76–77)
g. *annoyance* (l. 78)
h. *measures* (l. 96)

Music, When Soft Voices Die

The poet reminds us that the odor of violets "remains" even after the violets fade. What other pleasant experiences can you think of that linger long afterward in your memory?

One Word Is Too Often Profaned

1. What is the word that is "too often profaned"?
2. Commit to memory the last four lines of the poem.

Suggestions for Reading

"Lines Written among the Euganean Hills, October 1818"
"I Fear Thy Kisses, Gentle Maiden"
"To Night"
"Adonais: an Elegy on the Death of John Keats" (especially stanzas I–VIII and stanza LII)

JOHN KEATS[1] (1795–1821)

Ode on a Grecian Urn

In his "Ode on a Grecian Urn" Keats reveals his passionate devotion to beauty, especially the beautiful things of Greece. Indeed, the poem is almost Greek in its artistic perfection and in the brightness and clearness of the pictures portrayed. It is also thoroughly romantic. Deeply impressed with the loveliness of the object before him, Keats allows his imagination to play around the idea until the silent figures on the vase turn into actual shepherds wooing and entire communities worshiping. The chief idea of the poem is the permanence of all these beautiful forms and hence the permanence of their delight and quiet happiness, as contrasted with the shortness of human pleasures and the cloying of human passion that wins to its goal.

Interpretative Outline

This urn was carved with a succession of beautiful scenes and figures. In Keats's eyes they take on life, and we learn what they are like from the emotions and reflections they produce in him.

The urn presents two main scenes: (1) the throng of fleeing maidens and pursuing men of lines 8–10; (2) the sacrificial procession of lines 31–37. The youth piping beneath the trees (l. 15) and the bold lover (l. 17), who has almost caught the maiden, are apparently

[1] For biography see page 720.

details of the first scene; and the little town of silent streets (ll. 38–39) is obviously not in the picture, but only inferred by the poet from the crowd that follows the priest and the sacrificial victim to the forest altar, which also is not visible except to the imagination.

THOU still unravished[1] bride of quietness,
  Thou foster-child[2] of silence and slow time,
Sylvan historian, who canst thus express
  A flowery tale more sweetly than our rhyme:
What leaf-fringed legend haunts about thy shape
Of deities or mortals, or of both,
  In Tempe* or the dales of Arcady*?
What men or gods are these? What maidens loth?
  What mad pursuit? What struggle to escape?
    What pipes and timbrels? What wild ecstasy?   10

[1] Preserving its beauty and purity.
[2] The urn is called a foster-child of silence and slow time because it represents a silent picture which time, in its slow progress, has preserved ("fostered").

John Keats's house in Hampstead, London

Heard melodies are sweet, but those un-
 heard
 Are sweeter;[1] therefore, ye soft pipes,
  play on;
Not to the sensual ear, but, more endeared,
 Pipe to the spirit ditties of no tone:
Fair youth, beneath the trees, thou
 canst not leave
 Thy song, nor ever can those trees be
  bare;
  Bold Lover, never, never canst thou
   kiss,
Though winning near the goal — yet,
 do not grieve;
 She cannot fade, though thou hast not
  thy bliss,
  For ever wilt thou love, and she be
   fair! 20

Ah, happy, happy boughs! that cannot
 shed

Your leaves, nor ever bid the Spring
 adieu;
And, happy melodist, unwearièd,
 For ever piping songs for ever new;
More happy love! more happy, happy
  love!
 For ever warm and still to be enjoyed,
  For ever panting, and for ever
   young;
All breathing human passion far above,
 That leaves a heart high-sorrowful
  and cloyed,
  A burning forehead, and a parching
   tongue. 30

Who are these coming to the sacrifice?
To what green altar, O mysterious
 priest,
Lead'st thou that heifer lowing at the
 skies,
And all her silken flanks with garlands
 drest?

[1] *Heard . . . sweeter.* Learn this line; it is often quoted.

What little town by river or sea shore,
　Or mountain-built with peaceful cita
　　del,
　　Is emptied of this folk, this pious
　　　morn?
And, little town, thy streets for evermore
　Will silent be; and not a soul to tell
　　Why thou art desolate, can e'er re-
　　　turn.   40

O Attic[1] shape! Fair attitude! with
　brede[2]
　Of marble men and maidens over-
　　wrought,

With forest branches and the trodden
　weed;
　Thou, silent form, dost tease[1] us out of
　　thought
As doth eternity: Cold Pastoral*!
　When old age shall this generation
　　waste,
　　Thou shalt remain, in midst of other
　　　woe
Than ours, a friend of man, to whom thou
　say'st,
　"Beauty is truth, truth beauty,"—
　　that is all
　　Ye know on earth, and all ye need
　　　to know.   50

La Belle Dame sans Merci

"La Belle Dame sans Merci"[3] ("The
Beautiful Lady without Mercy") is a ballad
based on a theme common in medieval romance (p. 32). A knight wins a faërie love
only to find that he has fallen under the spell
of a beautiful, merciless witch. Keats is here
a genuine romanticist: he uses an adaptation
of the old ballad stanza (see page 58), he
derives his inspiration from medieval literature, and he allows his imagination to play
around the theme until he makes it something
strange and beautiful. The poem should be
read slowly aloud.

O WHAT can ail thee, knight-at-arms,
　Alone and palely loitering?
The sedge is wither'd from the lake,
　And no birds sing.

O, what can ail thee, knight-at-arms,
　So haggard and so woe-begone?
The squirrel's granary is full,
　And the harvest's done.

I see a lily on thy brow
　With anguish moist and fever dew, 10
And on thy cheeks a fading rose
　Fast withereth too.

"I met a lady in the meads,
　Full beautiful — a faery's child:
Her hair was long, her foot was light,
　And her eyes were wild.

"I made a garland for her head,
　And bracelets too, and fragrant zone[2];
She look'd at me as she did love,
　And made sweet moan.   20

"I set her on my pacing steed,
　And nothing else saw all day long,
For sideways would she lean, and sing
　A faery's song.

"She found me roots of relish sweet,
　And honey wild, and manna-dew,
And sure in language strange she said —
　'I love thee true.'

"She took me to her elfin grot,[3]
　And there she wept and sigh'd full
　　sore,   30
And there I shut her wild, wild eyes,
　With kisses four.

[1] See "Athens."*
[2] Decoration.
[3] La Belle Dame sans Merci (là běl dàm säṅ
　měr sē').

[1] Intrigue.
[2] Girdle, belt.
[3] Grotto, cave.

La Belle Dame sans Merci

"And there she lullèd me asleep,
　And there I dream'd — ah! woe be-
　　tide! —
The latest dream I ever dream'd
　On the cold hill's side.

"I saw pale kings and princes too,
　Pale warriors, death-pale were they all;
They cried — 'La Belle Dame sans Merci
　Hath thee in thrall!'　　　　　40

"I saw their starved lips in the gloom,
　With horrid warning gapèd wide;
And I awoke, and found me here
　On the cold hill's side.

"And this is why I sojourn here,
　Alone and palely loitering,
Though the sedge is wither'd from the
　　lake,
　And no birds sing."

Ode to a Nightingale

In the spring of 1819 Keats was visiting a friend in whose garden a nightingale was building her nest. He was deeply moved by the sweetness and gladness of the nightingale's singing. One morning, on leaving the break-fast table, he went into the garden, took his seat under a tree, and several hours later came back to the house with the "Ode to a Night-ingale" written off on two half sheets of paper. The tone of sadness that pervades the poem is probably due to the recent death from tuberculosis of Keats's loved brother, Tom; to Keats's own danger from the same disease; and to his hopeless love for the lady of his heart, Fanny Brawne.

The poem has won universal praise because of its melody, its rich imagery,* and its per-fect combination of beauty and sadness. It is no exaggeration to say that lines 65–70 have brought home the mystery and magic of poetic beauty to more readers than has any other passage in English poetry.

[The poet, listening to the song of the nightingale, is moved almost to tears at its beauty and gladness.]

MY HEART aches, and a drowsy numbness pains
My sense, as though of hemlock[1] I had drunk,
Or emptied some dull opiate[2] to the drains
One minute past, and Lethe*-wards had sunk:
'Tis not through envy of thy happy lot,
But being too happy in thine happiness, —
That thou, light-wingèd Dryad* of the trees,
In some melodious plot
Of beechen green, and shadows numberless,
Singest of summer in full-throated ease.   10

[He longs for a magical draft that will enable him to leave the world and to follow the bird.]

O for a draught of vintage! that hath been
Cooled a long age in the deep-delvèd earth,
Tasting of Flora* and the country green,
Dance, and Provençal song,[3] and sunburnt mirth!
O for a beaker full of the warm South,
Full of the true, the blushful Hippocrene,*
With beaded bubbles winking at the brim,
And purple-stainèd mouth;
That I might drink, and leave the world unseen,
And with thee fade away into the forest dim: 20

[1] A drug made from hemlock, a poisonous herb.
[2] A drink causing sleep.
[3] *Provençal* (prô vän säl') *song.* Here accented on the second syllable. The songs of the troubadours* of southern France.

[And thus forget the fever, fret, and sadness of life.]

Fade far away, dissolve, and quite forget
What thou among the leaves hast never known,
The weariness, the fever, and the fret
Here, where men sit and hear each other groan;
Where palsy shakes a few, sad, last gray hairs,
Where youth grows pale, and spectre-thin, and dies;
Where but to think is to be full of sorrow
And leaden-eyed despairs,
Where Beauty cannot keep her lustrous eyes,
Or new Love pine at them beyond tomorrow.   30

[Not wine, but his poetic imagination enables him to join the nightingale in the forest of his desire.]

Away! away! for I will fly to thee,
Not charioted by Bacchus* and his pards,[1]
But on the viewless[2] wings of Poesy,
Though the dull brain perplexes and retards:
Already with thee![3] tender is the night,
And haply the Queen-Moon is on her throne,
Clustered around by all her starry Fays,[4]
But here there is no light,
Save what from heaven is with the breezes blown
Through verdurous glooms and winding mossy ways.   40

[1] Leopards.
[2] Invisible.
[3] What the poet means to say is that the charm of "the viewless wings of Poesy" has been effective and that he is now with the bird.
[4] Fairies.

[In the soft moonlit night the poet recognizes the flowers around him by their odors.]

I cannot see what flowers are at my feet,
Nor what soft incense hangs upon the boughs,
But, in embalmèd[1] darkness, guess each sweet
Wherewith the seasonable month endows
The grass, the thicket, and the fruit-tree wild;
White hawthorn, and the pastoral eglantine[2];
Fast fading violets covered up in leaves;
And mid-May's eldest child,
The coming musk-rose, full of dewy wine,
The murmurous haunt of flies on summer eves.   50

[As he listens in imagination in the dark, even death seems richer and sweeter.]

Darkling I listen; and, for many a time
I have been half in love with easeful Death,
Called him soft names in many a musèd rhyme,
To take into the air my quiet breath;
Now more than ever seems it rich to die,
To cease upon the midnight with no pain,
While thou art pouring forth thy soul abroad
In such an ecstasy!
Still wouldst thou sing, and I have ears in vain —   59
To thy high requiem[3] become a sod.

[The bird's song is immortal, and charmed those of old as it is now charming the poet.]

Thou wast not born for death, immortal Bird!
No hungry generations tread thee down;

1 Filled with sweet odors.
2 Probably the woods honeysuckle.
3 A hymn in honor of the dead.

The voice I hear this passing night was heard
In ancient days by emperor and clown[1]:
Perhaps the self-same song that found a path
Through the sad heart of Ruth,* when, sick for home,
She stood in tears amid the alien corn[2];
The same that oft-times hath
Charmed magic casements, opening on the foam
Of perilous seas, in faery lands forlorn.[3]   70

[Even his poetic imagination ("fancy") is not strong enough to enable him to follow the nightingale farther, and as the bird's music grows more and more distant the poet's heart returns upon himself, and he wonders whether it may not have been all "a vision, or a waking dream."]

Forlorn! the very word is like a bell
To toll me back from thee to my sole self!
Adieu! the fancy cannot cheat so well
As she is famed to do, deceiving elf.
Adieu! adieu! thy plaintive anthem fades
Past the near meadows, over the still stream,
Up the hill-side; and now 'tis buried deep
In the next valley-glades:
Was it a vision, or a waking dream?
Fled is that music: — Do I wake or sleep?   80

1 Peasant.
2 Grain; here, barley.
3 *Charmed . . . forlorn.* These are two of the five lines that Kipling refers to in his well-known criticism: "Remember that in all the millions permitted there are no more than five — five little lines — of which one can say: 'These are the magic; these are the vision; the rest is only poetry.'" Memorize them. The other three lines he refers to are lines 14–16 in Coleridge's "Kubla Khan" (p. 394).

SONNETS

Keats's sonnets* rank among the best in English literature. In spite of the difficult and exacting verse form, the poet succeeded in expressing perfectly the passionate love of beauty and the other tumultuous feelings that often filled his soul.

On First Looking into Chapman's Homer

"On First Looking into Chapman's Homer" is worth reading, not only because of its beauty, but also because of its interest in connection with the life of the author. Keats never went to college and did not know Greek. The only school he attended was the preparatory school at Enfield, where he formed a close friendship with Charles Cowden Clarke, son of the headmaster. Keats was fond of reading, and Cowden Clarke used to lend him books. In 1816, when Keats was in his twenty-first year, young Clarke got hold of a copy of Chapman's famous translation of Homer and brought it to Keats. The two friends became so interested in it that they read together nearly all one night. Clarke went home about daybreak, leaving Keats still absorbed in the book. That same morning, about ten o'clock, Clarke received this sonnet* from Keats. Keats had struck it off in the intensity of his enthusiasm at reading Homer in Chapman's vigorous translation.

Some critics consider it the finest sonnet in the English language.

MUCH have I travelled in the realms
of gold,[1]
And many goodly states and kingdoms
seen;
Round many western islands have I been
Which bards* in fealty to Apollo* hold.[2]
Oft of one wide expanse had I been told
That deep-browed Homer* ruled as his
demesne[3];
Yet did I never breathe its pure serene
Till I heard Chapman[4] speak out loud
and bold:
Then felt I like some watcher of the skies
When a new planet swims into his ken;
Or like stout Cortez[5] when with eagle
eyes   11
He stared at the Pacific — and all his
men
Looked at each other with a wild sur-
mise —
Silent, upon a peak in Darien.[6]

Bright Star! Would I Were Steadfast as Thou Art

This lovely sonnet,* sometimes known as Keats's "last sonnet," sprang from a mood of intense sadness. In 1820 Keats was far gone with tuberculosis. As a last resort he decided to try the mild climate of Italy, though he felt that he would never return to England or see his sweetheart, Fanny Brawne, again. On shipboard he saw the evening star, pure, radiant, alone; and his love of England, of Fanny Brawne, and of universal beauty combined to wring from his heart this poignant lyric cry of grief and yearning.

BRIGHT Star! would I were steadfast
as thou art —
Not in lone splendour hung aloft the
night,
And watching, with eternal lids apart,

Like Nature's patient sleepless Eremite,[7]
The moving waters at their priestlike task
Of pure ablution[8] round earth's human
shores,
Or gazing on the new soft fallen mask
Of snow upon the mountains and the
moors: —

[1] *Much . . . gold.* I have read much beautiful literature.
[2] *Round . . . hold.* I have read much of the poetry of the British Isles.   [3] Domain, kingdom.
[4] George Chapman (1559–1634), an English poet and dramatist.
[5] Keats incorrectly makes Cortez instead of Balboa the discoverer of the Pacific Ocean, but this slight mistake does not affect the excellence of the poetry.
[6] The Isthmus of Panama.
[7] Hermit.   [8] A washing or cleansing.

No — yet still steadfast, still unchange-
 able,
Pillow'd upon my fair Love's ripening
 breast,   10
To feel forever its soft fall and swell,
Awake forever in a sweet unrest;
Still, still to hear her tender-taken breath,
And so live ever, — or else swoon to
 death.

Discussion Hints

Ode on a Grecian Urn

1. How many and what scenes are actually depicted on the urn? What other scenes does Keats imagine? Which scene would you choose as the best illustration for the poem?

2. Why does Keats call the vase a "Sylvan historian" (l. 3)? Pick out lines throughout the poem to show that the adjective "sylvan" is appropriate.

3. Write a précis (summary) of the second stanza.

4. Memorize the second stanza and the last two lines of the poem.

5. Explain line 28 by putting it into prose order.

6. Why will the streets of the little town forevermore be silent (ll. 38–39)?

7. What does "Cold Pastoral"* mean (l. 45)?

8. Explain
a. dales (l. 7)
*b. Heard melodies are sweet, but those un-
   heard
   Are sweeter* (ll. 11–12)
*c. Ah, happy, happy boughs! that cannot
   shed
   Your leaves* (ll. 21–22)
d. cloyed (l. 29)

La Belle Dame sans Merci

1. Who do you think is questioning the knight? Where in the poem does the knight's answer begin?

2. What season of the year is it? Show that the season fits well with other elements in the poem.

3. Why are the lady's eyes "wild" (l. 16)?

4. In the romances of the Middle Ages knights sometimes encounter lovely fairy ladies in mysterious castles, where they spend the night, only to discover next morning that all has disappeared and they are alone on a hillside or in an open field. How does this help to explain lines 43–44?

5. What traits show that the poem belongs to the Romantic Period?

6. How does the poem resemble the old ballads (p. 57)?

7. The poem is full of pictures and has often been illustrated. If you can find any of the illustrations, bring them to class. If you were an artist, which stanza would you select to illustrate?

8. Explain
a. I see a lily on thy brow (l. 9)
b. She look'd at me as she did love (l. 19)
c. Hath thee in thrall! (l. 40)

Ode to a Nightingale

1. To which of the five senses does Keats appeal most in this poem? Prove your answer.

2. What is the "draught of vintage" (l. 11) that will transport the poet?

3. What sorrows has the nightingale "never known" (l. 22)? How do these suggest Keats's real reason for writing the poem?

4. Lines 41–50 have been praised as especially beautiful in their portrayal of nature. Do you agree?

5. Whom had the song of the nightingale (or, rather, his ancestors) charmed in the past?

6. What kind of window is a casement (l. 69)?

7. Write a paraphrase of the stanza beginning with line 61.

8. Explain.
a. Lethe-wards (l. 4)
b. deep-delvèd (l. 12)
c. sunburnt mirth (l. 14)
d. charioted (l. 32)
e. fancy . . . deceiving elf (ll. 73–74)

On First Looking into Chapman's Homer

1. After reading the headnote and the biography of Keats (p. 720), explain why, in your opinion, Keats would be especially thrilled on reading Homer* for the first time. You will be able to give a better answer if you have read any of Homer. A selection from the Odyssey is given in the revised edition of *Adventure* of this series.

2. Keats refers to Homer as a king ruling over a great domain. What is Homer's "demesne" (l. 6)? If you do not know, reread page 18 and, if possible, the headnote to "Ulysses and the Cyclops" in the revised edition of *Adventure* of this series.

3. Write out the rhyme scheme of this sonnet. Is it an Italian sonnet or an English sonnet*?

4. Write a paraphrase of the sonnet.

5. Memorize the poem.

6. If you have used the revised edition of *Adventure* of this series, reread Richard Halliburton's "Upon a Peak in Darien," a fascinating account of how the author climbed to the top of the very peak from which Balboa first beheld the Pacific Ocean.

Bright Star! Would I Were Steadfast as Thou Art

1. Sum up in one sentence the meaning of the octave of this sonnet.* Summarize in the same way the sestet.

2. Does Keats represent the star as coldly detached from earthly affairs or as deeply interested in them? Point out words or phrases that support your answer.

3. What is the object of "watching" (l. 3)?

General Discussion Hints on Keats's Lyric Poetry

1. Quote lines from poems by Keats to show that the author was acquainted with names or themes from Greek literature or that he considered Greece the source of ideal beauty.

2. Quote lines from Keats's poems to show that the author believed that we can best find relief from reality by a worship of beauty.

Suggestions for Reading[1]

"To Autumn"
"Ode on the Poets"
"Lines on the Mermaid Tavern"
"On the Grasshopper and the Cricket"
"Ode on Melancholy"
"The Terror of Death"

General Discussion Hints on the Lyric Poetry of the Romantic Period

1. Which of the lyric poems of the Romantic Period do you like best? Give reasons for your answer.

2. What poets of the Romantic Period deal with nature? Distinguish between their attitudes toward nature.

3. What poets of the Romantic Period deal with freedom or democracy? Illustrate from their poems the attitude of each.

4. What poets of the Romantic Period derive inspiration (1) from ancient classical tradition? (2) from the Middle Ages?

5. What famous mistake does a well-known poet of the Romantic Period make with regard to the discoverer of the Pacific Ocean? Name the poet and the poem in which he makes the mistake. Quote the passage in question.

[1] For suggestions for reading in Keats's narrative poetry see page 420.

ESSAYS

CHARLES LAMB[1] (1775–1834)

From "A Dissertation upon Roast Pig"

[From Essays of Elia]

Lamb's *Essays of Elia*,[2] fifty-three in all, represent the high-water mark of the familiar essay (p. 173) in English literature. Gentle and delicate in humor, simple, unconventional, and, at times even chatty in style, they lead the reader on and on without once making him feel the immense store of learning upon which they are based or the painstaking care with which they were composed. The essays are filled with quotations from earlier writers. Beaumont, Fletcher, Shakespeare, and Milton, whose works Lamb knew almost by heart, appear frequently in them. Lamb has been called an Elizabethan born out of his time. In his love of old literature and old things he is a romanticist.

Lamb's style is charming, but it is extremely difficult to imitate. Though his chief models are Addison (p. 261) and Steele (p. 255), he uses many words and expressions derived from his wide reading in earlier English literature, a fact that often gives his style a peculiarly antiquated flavor. Pupils desirous of improving their style will do well to familiarize themselves with Lamb's works, but they should not try to imitate the style of the *Essays of Elia*.

"A Dissertation upon Roast Pig" illustrates the qualities that have endeared Lamb to five generations of readers. Students must not take the story too seriously, however. It is, first of all, a laughter-provoking story. Secondly, it is a bit of fun poked at those who were busy "discovering" old manuscripts[3]

which "revealed" almost everything imaginable. Thirdly, it is a bit of satire* upon the easily observable human propensity for putting forth a great effort to achieve small results. Lamb, for instance, thought the gains were entirely too trifling to compensate for the disturbances caused by the revolutions and other social upheavals at the end of the eighteenth century.

MANKIND, says a Chinese manuscript, which my friend M—— was obliging enough to read and explain to me, for the first seventy thousand ages ate their meat raw, clawing or biting it from the living animal, just as they do in Abyssinia[1] to this day. This period is not obscurely hinted at by their great Confucius[2] in the second chapter of his Mundane Mutations, where he desig- 10 nates a kind of golden age by the term Cho-fang, literally the Cooks' Holiday. The manuscript goes on to say, that the art of roasting, or rather broiling (which I take to be the elder brother) was accidentally discovered in the manner following. The swine-herd Ho-ti, having gone out into the woods one morning, as his manner was, to collect mast[3] for his hogs, left his cottage in the care of 20 his eldest son Bo-bo, a great lubberly

---

[1] For biography see page 721.

[2] "Elia" is merely a pen name adapted from that of one of the clerks in the South Sea House, where Lamb was employed for several years. The clerk's real name was Ellia.

[3] Percy's "folio manuscript," the basis of Percy's *Reliques*,* was discovered in 1763; *Beowulf* was rediscovered, and was printed in 1815;

and other works, some of them supposed to be ancient but really modern forgeries, were brought to light during the Transition and Romantic periods.

[1] A country in Africa of which little was known in Lamb's day but wild rumors.

[2] A noted Chinese philosopher.

[3] Nuts, acorns, etc. used as food for hogs.

boy, who being fond of playing with fire, as younkers[1] of his age commonly are, let some sparks escape into a bundle of straw, which kindling quickly, spread the conflagration over every part of their poor mansion, till it was reduced to ashes. Together with the cottage (a sorry antediluvian [2] makeshift of a build-30 ing, you may think it), what was of much more importance, a fine litter of new-farrowed [3] pigs, no less than nine in number, perished. China pigs have been esteemed a luxury all over the East, from the remotest periods that we read of. Bo-bo was in the utmost con-sternation, as you may think, not so much for the sake of the tenement,[4] which his father and he could easily 40 build up again with a few dry branches, and the labour of an hour or two at any time, as for the loss of the pigs. While he was thinking what he should say to his father, and wringing his hands over the smoking remnants of one of those untimely sufferers, an odour as-sailed his nostrils, unlike any scent which he had before experienced. What could it proceed from? Not from 50 the burnt cottage: he had smelt that smell before; indeed this was by no means the first accident of the kind which had occurred through the negli-gence of this unlucky young fire-brand. Much less did it resemble that of any known herb, weed, or flower. A pre-monitory moistening at the same time overflowed his nether lip. He knew not what to think. He next stooped down 60 to feel the pig, if there were any signs of life in it. He burnt his fingers, and to cool them he applied them in his booby fashion to his mouth. Some of the crumbs of the scorched skin had come away with his fingers, and for the first time in his life (in the world's life in-deed, for before him no man had known

it), he tasted *crackling*[1]! Again he felt and fumbled at the pig. It did not burn him so much now, still he licked his fin- 70 gers from a sort of habit. The truth at length broke into his slow understanding, that it was the pig that smelt so, and the pig that tasted so delicious; and surrendering himself up to the new-born pleasure, he fell to tearing up whole handfuls of the scorched skin with the flesh next it, and was cramming it down his throat in his beastly fashion, when his sire entered amid the smoking rafters 80 armed with retributory cudgel,[2] and finding how affairs stood, began to rain blows upon the young rogue's shoul-ders as thick as hail-stones, which Bo-bo heeded not any more than if they had been flies. The tickling pleasure which he experienced in his lower regions[3] had rendered him quite callous to any in-conveniences he might feel in those re-mote quarters. His father might lay. 90 on, but he could not beat him from his pig, till he had fairly made an end of it, when, becoming a little more sensible of his situation, something like the fol-lowing dialogue ensued: —

"You graceless whelp, what have you got there devouring? Is it not enough that you have burnt me down three houses with your dog's tricks, and be hanged to you! but you must be eating 100 fire, and I know not what. What have you got there, I say?"

"O father, the pig, the pig! do come and taste how nice the burnt pig eats."

The ears of Ho-ti tingled with horror. He cursed his son, and he cursed himself that ever he should beget a son that should eat burnt pig.

Bo-bo, whose scent was wonderfully sharpened since morning, soon raked out 110 another pig, and fairly rending it asunder, thrust the lesser half by main force into

[1] Youths.
[2] Here, exceedingly ancient.
[3] Newly born. [4] Dwelling.

[1] The crisp roasted skin or fat of pork.
[2] *retributory cudgel*. Vengeance-taking stick. An illustration of Lamb's quaint, humorous dic-tion. [3] *lower regions*. Stomach.

He fell to tearing up whole handfuls of the scorched skin

the fists of Ho-ti, still shouting out, "Eat, eat, eat the burnt pig, father, only taste — O Lord!" — with such-like barbarous ejaculations, cramming all the while as if he would choke.

Ho-ti trembled in every joint while he grasped the abominable thing, wavering 120 whether he should not put his son to death for an unnatural young monster, when the crackling scorching his fingers, as it had done his son's, and applying the same remedy to them, he in his turn tasted some of its flavour, which, make what sour mouths he would for a pretence, proved not altogether displeasing to him. In conclusion (for the manuscript here is a little tedious), both father 130 and son fairly sat down to the mess, and never left off till they had despatched all that remained of the litter.

Bo-bo was strictly enjoined not to let the secret escape, for the neighbours would certainly have stoned them for a couple of abominable wretches, who could think of improving upon the good meat which God had sent them. Nevertheless, strange stories got about. It was 140 observed that Ho-ti's cottage was burnt down now more frequently than ever. Nothing but fires from this time forward. Some would break out in broad day, others in the night-time. As often as the sow farrowed, so sure was the house of Ho-ti to be in a blaze; and Ho-ti himself, which was the more remarkable, instead of chastising his son, seemed to grow more indulgent to him than ever. At 150 length they were watched, the terrible mystery discovered, and father and son summoned to take their trial, at Pekin, then an inconsiderable assize town.[1] Evidence was given, the obnoxious food itself produced in court, and verdict about to be pronounced, when the foreman of the jury begged that some of the burnt pig, of which the culprits stood accused, might be handed into the box. He han- 160 dled it, and they all handled it; and burn-

ing their fingers, as Bo-bo and his father had done before them, and nature prompting to each of them the same remedy, against the face of all the facts, and the clearest charge which judge had ever given, — to the surprise of the whole court, townsfolk, strangers, reporters, and all present — without leaving the box, or any manner of consultation whatever, they brought in a simultaneous 170 verdict of Not Guilty.

The judge, who was a shrewd fellow, winked at the manifest iniquity of the decision: and, when the court was dismissed, went privily and bought up all the pigs that could be had for love or money. In a few days his lordship's town house was observed to be on fire. The thing took wing, and now there was nothing to be seen but fires in every di- 180 rection. Fuel and pigs grew enormously dear all over the district. The insurance offices, one and all, shut up shop. People built slighter and slighter every day, until it was feared that the very science of architecture would in no long time be lost to the world. Thus this custom of firing houses continued, till in process of time, says my manuscript, a sage arose, like our Locke, who made a discovery 190 that the flesh of swine, or indeed of any other animal, might be cooked (*burnt*, as they called it), without the necessity of consuming a whole house to dress it. Then first began the rude form of a gridiron. Roasting by the string or spit[1] came in a century or two later, I forget in whose dynasty. By such slow degrees, concludes the manuscript, do the most useful, and seemingly the most obvi- 200 ous, arts make their way among mankind.

Discussion Hints

1. Point out illustrations of Lamb's humor.
2. What is the "terrible mystery" referred to in lines 150–151?

---

[1] *assize town.* Town where a law court is held.

[1] A large fork or iron rod used for roasting meat over an open fire.

3. Describe in your own words the trial and acquittal of Ho-ti and Bo-bo.

4. Tell in your own words what was in the manuscript referred to on page 375, ll. 1–2.

5. If you have read Della T. Lutes's "Little Runt,"[1] compare it with Lamb's essay (1) in regard to style; (2) in regard to the attitude

toward pigs. Which do you prefer: **Lamb's** essay or Mrs. Lutes's sketch?

6. Explain
a. untimely sufferers (p. 376, l. 46)
b. A premonitory moistening . . . overflowed his nether lip (p. 376, ll. 56–58)
c. barbarous ejaculations (p. 378, ll. 115–116)
d. inconsiderable (p. 378, l. 153)
e. manifest iniquity (p. 378, l. 173)

Dream Children; A Reverie

[From *Essays of Elia*]

"Dream Children" is one of the most touching of several essays by Lamb on family relationships. It illustrates the author's sympathetic and understanding attitude toward children. This is all the more interesting in view of certain facts in Lamb's life. He was at least twice in love, and he liked to attend weddings, of which he wrote, "On these occasions I am sure to be in a good humor for a week or two after, and enjoy a reflected honeymoon"; yet he never married. He longed for a home and he loved children; but his domestic life was largely confined to caring for an afflicted sister in a childless household. Lamb's children and their dead mother are truly the offsprings of a tender, romantic dream, but the essay is even more charming than Lamb's essays usually are, perhaps on this very account.

CHILDREN love to listen to stories about their elders, when *they* were children; to stretch their imagination to the conception of a traditionary great-uncle, or grandame, whom they never saw. It was in this spirit that my little ones crept about me the other evening to hear about their great-grandmother Field,[2] who lived in a great house in Norfolk[3] (a
10 hundred times bigger than that in which they and papa lived) which had been the scene — so at least it was generally believed in that part of the country — of the tragic incidents which they had lately become familiar with from the

ballad of the Children in the Wood. Certain it is that the whole story of the children and their cruel uncle was to be seen fairly carved out in wood upon the chimney-piece of the great hall, the whole 20 story down to the Robin Redbreasts[1]; till a foolish rich person pulled it down to set up a marble one of modern invention in its stead, with no story upon it. Here Alice put out one of her dear mother's looks, too tender to be called upbraiding. Then I went on to say, how religious and how good their great-grandmother Field was, how beloved and respected by everybody, though she 30 was not indeed the mistress of this great house, but had only the charge of it (and yet in some respects she might be said to be the mistress of it too) committed to her by the owner, who preferred living in a newer and more fashionable mansion which he had purchased somewhere in the adjoining county; but still she lived in it in a manner as if it had been her own, and kept up the dignity of the great 40 house in a sort while she lived, which afterward came to decay and was nearly pulled down, and all its old ornaments stripped and carried away to the owner's other house, where they were set up, and looked as awkward as if some one were to carry away the old tombs they

[1] In the revised edition of *Adventure* of this series.
[2] Lamb's grandmother, a Mrs. Field, who was housekeeper in an English country mansion.
[3] Norfolk County, England.

[1] At the end of the story the children starve to death in the wood, and robin redbreasts cover their bodies with leaves.

had seen lately at the Abbey, and stick them up in Lady C.'s tawdry[1] gilt draw-
50 ing-room. Here John smiled, as much as to say, "that would be foolish indeed." And then I told how, when she came to die, her funeral was attended by a concourse of all the poor, and some of the gentry too, of the neighborhood for miles round to show their respect for her memory, because she had been such a good and religious woman; so good indeed that she knew all the Psaltery[2] by heart,
60 ay, and a great part of the Testament besides. Here little Alice spread her hands. Then I told what a tall, upright, graceful person their great-grandmother Field once was; and how in her youth she was esteemed the best dancer — here little Alice's right foot played an involuntary movement, till, upon my looking grave, it desisted — the best dancer, I was saying, in the county, till
70 a cruel disease, called a cancer, came, and bowed her down with pain, but it could never bend her good spirits, or make them stoop, but they were still upright, because she was so good and religious. Then I told how she was used to sleep by herself in a lone chamber of the great lone house; and how she believed that an apparition of two infants was to be seen at midnight glid-
80 ing up and down the great staircase near where she slept, but she said "those innocents would do her no harm;" and how frightened I used to be, though in those days I had my maid to sleep with me, because I was never half so good or religious as she — and yet I never saw the infants. Here John expanded all his eyebrows and tried to look courageous. Then I told how good she was to all her
90 grandchildren, having us to the great house in the holy-days, where I in particular used to spend many hours by myself in gazing upon the old busts of the twelve Caesars, that had been Emperors of Rome, till the old marble heads

would seem to live again, or I to be turned into marble with them; how I never could be tired with roaming about that huge mansion, with its vast empty rooms, with their worn-out hangings, 100 fluttering tapestry, and carved oaken panels, with the gilding almost rubbed out — sometimes in the spacious old-fashioned gardens, which I had almost to myself, unless when now and then a solitary gardening man would cross me — and how the nectarines and peaches hung upon the walls, without my ever offering to pluck them, because they were forbidden fruit,[1] unless now and then — 110 and because I had more pleasure in strolling about among the old melancholy-looking yew-trees or the firs, and picking up the red berries, and the fir-apples which were good for nothing but to look at — or in lying about upon the fresh grass with all the fine garden smells around me — or basking in the orangery till I could almost fancy myself ripening too, along with the oranges and the limes 120 in that grateful warmth, or in watching the dace[2] that darted to and fro in the fish-pond, at the bottom of the garden, with here and there a great sulky pike hanging midway down the water in silent state, as if it mocked at their impertinent friskings. I had more pleasure in these busy-idle diversions than in all the sweet flavors of peaches, nectarines, oranges and such-like common baits of children. 130 Here John slyly deposited back upon the plate a bunch of grapes, which, not unobserved by Alice, he had meditated dividing with her, and both seemed willing to relinquish them for the present as irrelevant. Then, in somewhat a more heightened tone, I told how, though their great-grandmother Field loved all her grandchildren, yet in an especial manner she might be said to love their 140 uncle John L——[3], because he was so

[1] See Genesis 2 : 16–17.   [2] A kind of small fish.
[3] John Lamb, brother of the author. He had died shortly before this essay was written.

Showy but worthless.   [2] The Book of Psalms.

handsome and spirited a youth, and a king to the rest of us; and instead of moping about in solitary corners, like some of us, he would mount the most mettlesome[1] horse he could get, when but an imp no bigger than themselves, and make it carry him half over the county in a morning, and join the hunters 150 when there were any out — and yet he loved the old great house and gardens too, but had too much spirit to be always pent up within their boundaries — and how their uncle grew up to man's estate as brave as he was handsome, to the admiration of everybody, but of their great-grandmother Field most especially, and how he used to carry me upon his back when I was a lame-footed boy — 160 for he was a good bit older than me — many a mile when I could not walk for pain; and how in after life he became lame-footed too, and I did not always (I fear) make allowances enough for him when he was impatient and in pain, nor remember sufficiently how considerate he had been to me when I was lame-footed; and how when he died, though he had not been dead an hour, it seemed 170 as if he had died a great while ago, such a distance there is betwixt life and death; and how I bore his death as I thought pretty well at first, but afterward it haunted and haunted me; and though I did not cry or take it to heart as some do, and as I think he would have done if I had died, yet I missed him all day long, and knew not till then how much I had loved him. I missed his 180 kindness, and I missed his crossness, and I wished him to be alive again, to be quarreling with him (for we quarreled sometimes), rather than not have him again, and was as uneasy without him, as he, their poor uncle, must have been when the doctor took off his limb. Here the children fell a-crying, and asked if their little mourning which they had on was not for Uncle John, and they looked up, and prayed me not to go on about 190 their uncle, but to tell them some stories about their pretty dead mother. Then I told how for seven long years, in hope sometimes, sometimes in despair, yet persisting ever, I courted the fair Alice W——n[1]; and as much as children could understand, I explained to them what coyness, and difficulty, and denial, meant in maidens — when suddenly 200 turning to Alice, the soul of the first Alice looked out at her eyes with such a reality of re-presentment,[2] that I became in doubt which of them stood there before me, or whose that bright hair was; and while I stood gazing both the children gradually grew fainter to my view, receding, and still receding, till nothing at last but two mournful features were seen in the uttermost distance, which, without speech, strangely impressed upon me the 210 effects of speech: "We are not of Alice, nor of thee, nor are we children at all! The children of Alice call Bartrum[3] father. We are nothing, less than nothing, and dreams. We are only what might have been, and must wait upon the tedious shores of Lethe[*] millions of ages before we have existence and a name" — and immediately awaking, I found myself quietly seated in my bachelor arm- 220 chair, where I had fallen asleep, with the faithful Bridget[4] unchanged by my side — but John L. (or James Elia) was gone forever.

Discussion Hints

1. Although Lamb's "dream children" are purely imaginary, a few references in the essay suggest certain real experiences of the author. After reading the essay consult the footnotes, read Lamb's biography (p. 721), and then see

---

[1] High-spirited.

[1] Probably Ann Simmons, a blue-eyed, fair-haired cottage girl with whom Lamb fell in love while he was still in his teens, but whom he never married.

[2] Reincarnation, rebirth.

[3] Ann Simmons married a man named Bartrum (or Bartram).

[4] Lamb's literary name for his sister Mary.

what actual personages and events you think are referred to.

2. Do you know anything about the ballad of the "Children in the Wood"? If not, ask some of your older relatives or neighbors, who may have read or heard it, for it was popular throughout most of the eighteenth and nineteenth centuries. See if you can find a copy in some old collection of poetry in your community.

General Discussion Hints

1. Pick out examples of Lamb's gentle humor.

2. Pick out illustrations of his quaint use of words.

3. Compare his style with Addison's (p. 261). Which is more direct? Which is easier to follow? Which uses more words that are archaic or otherwise unusual?

4. Write a paragraph describing Lamb's personality as seen in these two essays.

Suggestions for Reading

1. Essays:

"Witches, and Other Night-Fears"

"Blakesmoor in H——shire"

"Christ's Hospital Five and Thirty Years Ago"

"Poor Relations"

"A Chapter on Ears"

2. Poetry:

One of the best-known of Lamb's poems is "The Old Familiar Faces," two stanzas of which end with the haunting line "All, all are gone, the old familiar faces." It is reprinted in *Century Readings for a Course in English Literature* (D. Appleton-Century Company, Inc.).

In connection with Lamb's "Dream Children" read, if possible, Rudyard Kipling's "They" (in *Traffics and Discoveries*), a well-known story about imaginary children.

NARRATIVE POETRY

ROBERT BURNS[1] (1759–1796)

The Cotter's Saturday Night

Inscribed to Robert Aiken, Esq.

"The Cotter's Saturday Night" is one of Burns's best-loved poems. Its appeal is historic as well as literary. First, the poem illustrates the growing romantic interest in the lives of simple folk, an interest that prompted the poet to write it, and a host of readers to read it. Secondly, it echoes the romantic declaration that the greatness of a state depends, not on the nobles, but on the peasants. Thirdly, it emphasizes the truth that honesty, sobriety, and piety are personal characteristics rather than duties. Fourthly, it pleads for a personal patriotism, the kind that loves the "rocks and rills," the "woods and templed hills" of one's native land, not for the feudal patriotism that bound a vassal to his lord during the Middle Ages. Lastly, and best of all, it gives a vivid picture of the "plain living and high thinking" that characterized Scottish farm life in Burns's day.

Though the main thread of the poem is narrative, the poet frequently takes occasion to introduce passages that are essentially reflective or lyric in purpose. In this respect also "The Cotter's Saturday Night" is romantic in mood as well as in method of treatment. "The Cotter's Saturday Night" is written in the Spenserian * stanza.

Let not Ambition mock their useful toil,
  Their homely joys, and destiny obscure;
Nor Grandeur hear, with a disdainful smile,
  The short and simple annals of the poor.
GRAY

My LOVED, my honoured, much respected friend![2]
  No mercenary bard[3] his homage pays;
With honest pride, I scorn each selfish end,
  My dearest meed,[1] a friend's esteem and praise:
To you I sing, in simple Scottish lays,
  The lowly train in life's sequestered scene;[2]
The native feelings strong, the guileless ways;
  What Aiken in a cottage would have been;
Ah, tho' his worth unknown, far happier there I ween!

November chill blaws loud wi' angry sugh[3];   10
  The short'ning winter-day is near a close;
The miry beast retreating frae the pleugh[4];
  The black'ning trains o' craws[5] to their repose:
The toil-worn Cotter frae his labour goes, —
  This night his weekly moil[6] is at an end, —
Collects his spades, his mattocks, and his hoes,
  Hoping the morn in ease and rest to spend,
And weary, o'er the moor, his course does hameward bend.

---

[1] For biography see page 714.
[2] Robert Aiken, an Ayrshire lawyer.
[3] *mercenary bard.* A poet who expects a reward from a patron.*

[1] Reward.
[2] *The lowly . . . scene.* Humble people amid isolated surroundings.
[3] Wail.   [4] Plow.   [5] Crows.
[6] Labor.

At length his lonely cot appears in view,
　Beneath the shelter of an agèd tree:
Th' expectant wee-things, toddlin,
　stacher through[1]　　　　　　　　21
　　To meet their dad, wi' flichterin'[2] noise
　　and glee.
His wee bit ingle,[3] blinkin bonilie,
His clean hearth-stane, his thrifty wifie's
　smile,
The lisping infant, prattling on his knee,
Does a' his weary kiaugh[4] and care be-
　guile,
And makes him quite forget his labour
　and his toil.

Belyve,[5] the elder bairns[6] come drapping
　in,
　At service out, amang the farmers
　roun';
Some ca'[7] the pleugh, some herd, some
　tentie[8] rin　　　　　　　　　　30
A cannie[9] errand to a neebor town[10]:
Their eldest hope, their Jenny, woman-
　grown,
In youthfu' bloom, love sparkling in her
　e'e,[11]
Comes hame; perhaps, to shew a braw[12]
　new gown,
Or deposite her sair-won penny-fee,[13]
To help her parents dear, if they in hard-
　ship be.

With joy unfeigned, brothers and sisters
　meet,
　And each for other's weelfare kindly
　spiers.[14]
The social hours, swift-winged, unnoticed
　fleet;
　Each tells the uncos[15] that he sees or
　hears.　　　　　　　　　　　　40
The parents partial eye their hopeful
　years;
Anticipation forward points the view;

[1] *stacher through.* Stagger out.　　[2] Fluttering.
[3] Fireplace.　　[4] Fretting.　　[5] Soon.
[6] Children.　　[7] Drive.　　[8] Heedful.
[9] Careful.　　[10] *neebor town.* Adjoining farm.
[11] Eye.　　[12] Fine.
[13] *sair-won penny-fee.* Hard-won wages.
[14] Asks.　　[15] Strange things.

The mother, wi' her needle and her
　sheers,
Gars auld claes[1] look amaist as weel's the
　new;
The father mixes a' wi' admonition due.

Their master's and their mistress's com-
　mand
　The younkers a' are warnèd to obey;
And mind their labours wi' an eydent[2]
　hand,
　And ne'er, tho' out o' sight, to jauk[3] or
　play:
"And O be sure to fear the Lord alway,
And mind your duty, duly, morn and
　night;　　　　　　　　　　　　51
　Lest in temptation's path ye gang
　astray,
Implore His counsel and assisting might:
They never sought in vain that sought
　the Lord aright."

But hark! a rap comes gently to the door;
　Jenny, wha kens the meaning o' the
　same,
Tells how a neebor lad came o'er the
　moor,
　To do some errands, and convoy her
　hame.
The wily mother sees the conscious
　flame
Sparkle in Jenny's e'e, and flush her
　cheek;　　　　　　　　　　　　60
　With heart-struck anxious care, en-
　quires his name,
While Jenny hafflins[4] is afraid to speak;
Well-pleased the mother hears, it's nae
　wild, worthless rake.

With kindly welcome, Jenny brings him
　ben[5];
　A strappin' youth, he takes the
　mother's eye;
Blythe Jenny sees the visit's no ill taen;[6]
　The father cracks[7] of horses, pleughs,
　and kye.

[1] *gars auld claes.* Makes old clothes.
[2] Diligent.　　[3] Trifle.　　[4] Partly.　　[5] Inside.
[6] *no ill taen.* Not ill taken; that is, not badly
　received.　　　　　　[7] Tells.

The youngster's artless heart o'erflows
  wi' joy,
But blate[1] and laithfu',[2] scarce can weel
  behave;
The mother, wi' a woman's wiles, can
  spy   70
What makes the youth sae bashfu' and
  sae grave;
Weel-pleased to think her bairn's respected like the lave.[3]

O happy love! where love like this is
  found:
  O heart-felt raptures! bliss beyond
  compare!
I've pacèd much this weary, mortal
  round,
  And sage experience bids me this declare: —
  "If Heaven a draught of heavenly
  pleasure spare,
One cordial in this melancholy vale,
  'Tis when a youthful, loving, modest
  pair,
In other's arms, breathe out the tender
  tale   80
Beneath the milk-white thorn[4] that scents
  the evening gale."

Is there, in human form, that bears a
  heart,
  A wretch! a villain! lost to love and
  truth!
That can, with studied, sly, ensnaring
  art,
  Betray sweet Jenny's unsuspecting
  youth?
  Curse on his perjured arts! dis-
  sembling, smooth!
Are honour, virtue, conscience, all exiled?
  Is there no pity, no relenting ruth,
Points to the parents fondling o'er their
  child?
Then paints the ruined maid, and their
  distraction wild?   90

[1] Bashful.
[2] Shy.
[3] Rest.
[4] Hawthorn.

D

But now the supper crowns their simple
  board,
  The healsome parritch,[1] chief o' Scotia's food;
The soupe[2] their only hawkie[3] does
  afford,
  That 'yont the hallan[4] snugly chows
  her cood;
  The dame brings forth, in compli-
  mental mood,
To grace the lad, her weel-hained keb-
  buck, fell;[5]
  And aft[6] he's prest, and aft he ca's it
  guid;[7]
The frugal wifie, garrulous, will tell,
How 'twas a towmond[8] auld, sin' lint
  was i' the bell.[9]

The chearfu' supper done, wi' serious
  face,   100
  They, round the ingle, form a circle
  wide;
The sire turns o'er, wi' patriarchal grace,
  The big ha'-Bible,[10] ance his father's
  pride.
  His bonnet rev'rently is laid aside,
His lyart haffets[11] wearing thin and bare;
  Those strains that once did sweet in
  Zion[12] glide,
He wales[13] a portion with judicious care,
And "Let us worship God!" he says,
  with solemn air.

They chant their artless notes in simple
  guise,
  They tune their hearts, by far the
  noblest aim;   110
Perhaps "Dundee's" wild-warbling measures rise,

[1] Porridge.   [2] Milk.   [3] Cow.
[4] 'yont the hallan. On the other side of the
  partition.
[5] weel-hained . . . fell. Well-preserved, strong
  cheese.   [6] Often.
[7] ca's it guid. Calls it good.
[8] Twelvemonth.
[9] sin' . . . bell. Since flax was in blossom.
[10] Hall Bible, family Bible.
[11] lyart haffets. Gray side-locks.
[12] Jerusalem.
[13] Selects.

Or plaintive "Martyrs," worthy of the
name;
Or noble "Elgin"[1] beets[2] the heaven-
ward flame,
The sweetest far of Scotia's holy lays:
Compared with these, Italian trills[3]
are tame;
The tickled ears no heart-felt raptures
raise;
Nae unison hae they, with our Creator's
praise.

The priest-like father reads the sacred
page,
How Abram was the friend of God on
high;   119
Or Moses bade eternal warfare wage
With Amalek's ungracious progeny;[4]
Or, how the royal Bard[5] did groaning
lie
Beneath the stroke of Heaven's avenging
ire;
Or Job's pathetic plaint, and wailing
cry;
Or rapt Isaiah's wild, seraphic fire;
Or other holy Seers that tune the sacred
lyre.

Perhaps the Christian volume[6] is the
theme:
How guiltless blood[7] for guilty man
was shed;
How He, who bore in Heaven the second[8]
name,

Had not on earth whereon to lay His
head;   130
How His first followers and servants
sped;[1]
The precepts[2] sage they wrote to many a
land:
How he, who lone in Patmos[3] ban-
ishèd,
Saw in the sun a mighty angel stand,
And heard great Bab'lon's doom[4] pronounced by Heaven's command.

Then kneeling down to Heaven's Eternal
King,
The saint, the father, and the husband
prays:
Hope "springs exulting on triumphant
wing,"
That thus they all shall meet in future
days,   139
There ever bask in uncreated rays,
No more to sigh or shed the bitter tear,
Together hymning their Creator's
praise,
In such society, yet still more dear;
While circling Time moves round in an
eternal sphere.

Compared with this, how poor Religion's
pride,
In all the pomp of method, and of art;
When men display to congregations wide
Devotion's ev'ry grace except the
heart!
The Power, incensed, the pageant will
desert,
The pompous strain, the sacerdotal
stole[5];   150
But haply, in some cottage far apart,
May hear, well-pleased, the language of
the soul,
And in His Book of Life the inmates
poor enroll.

[1] *Dundee . . . Martyrs . . . Elgin.* Well-known
Scottish hymn tunes.
[2] Kindles.
[3] *Italian trills.* Trills of Italian opera.
[4] *Amalek's . . . progeny.* The descendants of
Amalek, a heathen tribe with whom, according to the Old Testament, the Hebrews
were often at war.
[5] *royal Bard.* King David,* who was a poet and
who is said to have composed many of the
Psalms. He suffered a long remorse for his
sins.
[6] New Testament.
[7] *guiltless blood.* Jesus was crucified for the sins
of mankind.
[8] The Christ, the second person of the Trinity
(Father, Son, and Holy Ghost).

[1] *How . . . sped.* What success or fortune the
followers of Jesus had. Told in the Acts of
the Apostles.   [2] Here, the Epistles.
[3] Saint John was imprisoned on the isle of Patmos.
[4] *Bab'lon's doom.* Told in the Book of Revelation.
[5] *sacerdotal stole.* Priestly robe.

Then homeward all take off their sev'ral
    way;
The youngling cottagers retire to rest:
The parent-pair their secret homage pay,
    And proffer up to Heaven the warm
      request,
    That He who stills the raven's clam'-
      rous nest,[1]
And decks the lily fair in flow'ry pride,
    Would, in the way His wisdom sees the
      best,   160
For them and for their little ones provide;
But, chiefly in their hearts with Grace
    Divine preside.

From scenes like these old Scotia's[2] gran-
    deur springs,
    That makes her loved at home, revered
      abroad:
Princes and lords are but the breath of
    kings,
    "An honest man's the noblest work of
      God";[3]
    And certes, in fair Virtue's heavenly
      road,
The cottage leaves the palace far behind;
    What is a lordling's pomp? a cum-
      brous load,
Disguising oft the wretch of human kind,
Studied in arts of Hell, in wickedness
    refined!   171

O Scotia! my dear, my native soil!
    For whom my warmest wish to Heaven
    is sent!
Long may thy hardy sons of rustic toil
    Be blest with health, and peace, and
    sweet content!
    And O may Heaven their simple lives
    prevent
From Luxury's contagion, weak and vile!
    Then, howe'er crowns and coronets be
    rent,
A virtuous populace may rise the while,
And stand a wall of fire around their
    much-loved Isle.   180

[1] See Job 38: 41 (p. 162).   [2] Scotland's.
[3] *An honest . . . God.* Quoted from the poet
Pope.

O Thou, who poured the patriotic tide,
    That streamed thro' Wallace's[1] un-
    daunted heart,
Who dared to, nobly, stem tyrannic
    pride,
    Or nobly die, the second glorious part:
    (The patriot's God, peculiarly Thou
    art,
His friend, inspirer, guardian, and re-
    ward!)
O never, never Scotia's realm desert;
But still the patriot, and the patriot-bard,
In bright succession raise, her ornament
    and guard!

Discussion Hints

1. Pick out lines that illustrate especially
well aspects of home life; of religious life; of
love; of patriotism.

2. How many different scenes would you
use if you were writing a scenario of this
poem? What scene would be the most impressive? the most amusing?

3. Come to class prepared to read aloud
any one of the selections from the Bible
which the father read.

4. Which of Thomas Gray's poems is the
source of the stanza given at the head of "The
Cotter's Saturday Night"? Why is the quotation appropriate?

5. What social or political doctrines set
forth in the poem remind you of beliefs associated with the establishment of a republic in
America?

6. Part of the poem is written in standard
English, part in the dialect of Scotland. Pick
out some of the best passages written in Scottish.

7. What occupations do the cotter's
children follow?

8. What, according to the poem, is the
essence of true religion? See especially lines
145–153.

9. Do you agree with what is said about
luxury in the stanza beginning with line 172?
What poet of the Transition Period (p. 289)
especially admired simple country people?

[1] Wallace was a Scottish leader of the beginning
of the fourteenth century. Read Burns's
"Scots, Wha Hae wi' Wallace Bled" (p. 332).

10. Point out passages that illustrate the various romantic traits listed in the headnote.

11. Scan the first stanza to show that it is Spenserian.* Why should Burns use this stanza form, invented by a poet two centuries previously? See the introduction to the Romantic Period.

12. What figures of speech do you find in lines 163–171?

13. Words and passages to be explained:

a. weary, o'er the moor, his course does hameward bend (l. 18)

b. beguile (l. 26)

c. The parents partial eye their hopeful years[1] (l. 41)

d. I've pacèd much this weary, mortal round (l. 75)

e. youngling (l. 155)

f. hardy sons of rustic toil (l. 174)

Tam o' Shanter

This inimitable tale is a favorite among all lovers of Burns. It combines masterly description, vivid narration, rich humor, excellent characterization, and skillful use of the horrible and grotesque. Carlyle called it "the best day's work done in Scotland since Bannockburn," and Burns himself said, "I look on 'Tam o' Shanter' to be my standard performance in the poetical line." The story told in the poem was based on legends familiar to Burns from childhood. He was born less than a mile from the ruins of old Alloway Kirk and the bridge over the river Doon (see illustration on page 391). Shanter was the name of a farm not far away.

Burns composed "Tam o' Shanter" in a happy burst of inspiration. Jean Armour, the poet's wife, has described the occasion. She says her husband had spent most of the day outdoors by the river. When she went to join him in the afternoon with the two children, she noticed that he was busily engaged in crooning verses over to himself, and hence she did not interrupt him. A little later he seemed to be overcome with joy, began to move his arms about wildly, and recited very loudly, with tears rolling down his cheeks, the lines he had just composed:

"Now Tam, O Tam! had thae been queans, A' plump and strapping in their teens!"

"I wish ye had seen him," said she; "he was in such ecstasy that the tears were happing [hopping] down his cheeks."

The Story of the Poem

Burns himself wrote out for a friend the following prose account of the story upon which "Tam o' Shanter" is based: "On a market day, in the town of Ayr, a farmer from Carrick, and consequently whose way lay by the very gate of Alloway Kirk-yard, in order to cross the river Doon at the old bridge, which is about two or three hundred yards farther on than the said gate, had been detained by his business, till by the time he reached Alloway it was the wizard hour, between night and morning.

"Though he was terrified with a blaze streaming from the Kirk, yet, as it is a well-known fact, that to turn back on these occasions is running by far the greatest risk of mischief, he prudently advanced on his road. When he had reached the gate of the Kirk-yard, he was surprised and entertained, through the ribs and arches of an old Gothic window, which still faces the highway, to see a dance of witches merrily footing it round their old sooty blackguard master, who was keeping all alive with the power of his bagpipe. The farmer, stopping his horse to observe them a little, could plainly descry the faces of many old women of his acquaintance and neighborhood. How the gentleman was dressed tradition does not say, but that the ladies were all in their smocks; and one of them happening unluckily to have a smock which was considerably too short to answer all the purposes of that piece of dress, our farmer was so tickled that he involuntarily burst out, with a loud laugh, 'Weel looppen, Maggy wi' the short sark!' and, recollecting himself, instantly spurred his horse to the top of his speed. I need not mention the universally known fact, that no diabolical power can pursue you beyond the middle of a running stream. Lucky it was for the poor farmer that the river Doon was so near, for, notwithstanding the speed of his horse, which was a good one, against he reached the middle of the arch of the bridge, and consequently

[1] Note that "parents" is the subject of the verb "eye."

the middle of the stream, the pursuing, vengeful hags were so close at his heels, that one of them actually sprang to seize him; but it was too late; nothing was on her side of the stream but the horse's tail, which immediately gave way at her infernal grip, as if blasted by a stroke of lightning; but the farmer was beyond her reach. However, the unsightly, tailless condition of the vigorous steed was, to the last hours of the noble creature's life, an awful warning to the Carrick farmers not to stay too late in Ayr markets."

WHEN chapman billies[1] leave the street,
And drouthy[2] neebors neebors meet;
As market-days are wearing late,
An' folk begin to tak the gate[3];
While we sit bousing at the nappy,[4]
An' getting fou[5] and unco[6] happy,
We think na on the lang[7] Scots miles,
The mosses, waters, slaps,[8] and stiles,
That lie between us and our hame,
Whare sits our sulky, sullen dame,[9]   10
Gathering her brows like gathering storm,
Nursing her wrath to keep it warm.
    This truth fand[10] honest Tam o' Shanter,
As he frae Ayr ae[11] night did canter:
(Auld Ayr, wham ne'er a town surpasses,
For honest men and bonnie lasses).
    O Tam, had'st thou but been sae wise,
As taen thy ain wife Kate's advice!
She taul thee weel thou was a skellum,[12]
A blethering,[13] blustering, drunken blellum[14];   20
That frae November till October,
Ae market-day thou was nae[15] sober;

That ilka melder[1] wi' the miller,
Thou sat as lang as thou had siller;[2]
That ev'ry naig[3] was ca'd a shoe on,[4]
The smith and thee gat roaring fou on;
That at the Lord's house, even on Sunday,
Thou drank wi' Kirkton Jean[5] till Monday.
She prophesied, that, late or soon,
Thou would be found deep drowned in Doon,   30
Or catched wi' warlocks[6] in the mirk[7]
By Alloway's auld, haunted kirk.[8]
    Ah! gentle dames, it gars me greet,[9]
To think how monie counsels sweet.
How monie lengthened, sage advices
The husband frae the wife despises!
    But to our tale: Ae market-night,
Tam had got planted unco right,
Fast by an ingle,[10] bleezing[11] finely,
Wi' reaming swats,[12] that drank divinely;
And at his elbow, Souter[13] Johnie,   41
His ancient, trusty, drouthy cronie:
Tam lo'ed him like a very brother;
They had been fou for weeks thegither.
The night drave on wi' sangs and clatter;
And ay the ale was growing better:
The landlady and Tam grew gracious
Wi' secret favours, sweet and precious:
The Souter tauld his queerest stories;
The landlord's laugh was ready chorus:
The storm without might rair and rustle,
Tam did na mind the storm a whistle.
    Care, mad to see a man sae happy,
E'en drowned himsel amang the nappy.
As bees flee hame wi' lades[14] o' treasure,
The minutes winged their way wi' pleasure:

[1] *chapman billies.* Peddler fellows.
[2] Thirsty.
[3] Road.
[4] *bousing . . . nappy.* Drinking the ale.
[5] Full; that is, drunk.
[6] Very.
[7] A Scottish mile is three hundred feet longer than an English mile.
[8] Gaps (or gates) in the fences.   [9] Wife.
[10] Found.   [11] One.   [12] Rogue.
[13] Idle-talking.
[14] Babbler. Note how the sound of the line imitates the scolding woman.   [15] Not.

[1] *ilka melder.* At each grinding.
[2] *sat . . . siller.* Sat drinking as long as your money (*siller,* silver) lasted.
[3] Nag.   [4] *ca'd . . . on.* Shod.
[5] *Kirkton Jean.* Jean from Kirkton, or Kirkoswald (a place).
[6] Witches or wizards.
[7] Dark.   [8] Church.
[9] *gars . . . greet.* Makes me weep.
[10] Fireplace, fire.
[11] Blazing.
[12] *reaming swats.* Foaming ale.
[13] Shoemaker.   [14] Loads.

Kings may be blest but Tam was glorious,
O'er a' the ills o' life victorious!

But pleasures are like poppies spread:
You seize the flow'r, its bloom is shed;
Or like the snow falls in the river,   61
A moment white — then melts forever;
Or like the borealis race,
That flit ere you can point their place;
Or like the rainbow's lovely form
Evanishing amid the storm.[1]
Nae man can tether time or tide;
The hour[2] approaches Tam maun[3] ride:
That hour, o' night's black arch the key-
    stane,
That dreary hour Tom mounts his beast
    in;   70
And sic a night he taks the road in,
As ne'er poor sinner was abroad in.

The wind blew as 'twad blawn its
    last;
The rattling showers rose on the blast;
The speedy gleams the darkness swal-
    lowed;
Loud, deep, and lang the thunder bel-
    lowed:
That night, a child might understand,
The Deil[4] had business on his hand.

Weel mounted on his gray mare Meg,
A better never lifted leg,   80
Tam skelpit[5] on thro' dub[6] and mire,
Despising wind, and rain, and fire;
Whiles[7] holding fast his guid blue bonnet,
Whiles crooning o'er some auld Scots
    sonnet,
Whiles glow'ring round wi' prudent cares,
Lest bogles[8] catch him unawares:
Kirk-Alloway[9] was drawing nigh,
Whare ghaists and houlets[10] nightly cry.

By this time he was cross the ford,
Whare in the snaw the chapman
    smoored[11]:   90
And past the birks[12] and meikle[13] stane,
Whare drunken Charlie brak's neck-
    bane;

And thro' the whins,[1] and by the cairn,[2]
Whare hunters fand the murdered bairn[3];
And near the thorn, aboon the well,
Whare Mungo's mither hanged hersel.
Before him Doon pours all his floods;
The doubling storm roars thro' the
    woods;
The lightnings flash from pole to pole;
Near and more near the thunders roll:
When, glimmering thro' the groaning
    trees,   101
Kirk-Alloway seemed in a bleeze:
Thro' ilka bore[4] the beams were glancing,
And loud resounded mirth and dancing.

Inspiring bold John Barleycorn,[5]
What dangers thou canst make us scorn!
Wi' tippenny,[6] we fear nae evil;
Wi' usquebae,[7] we'll face the Devil!
The swats sae reamed in Tammie's
    noddle,   109
Fair play, he cared na deils a boddle,[8]
But Maggie stood, right sair astonished,
Till, by the heel and hand admonished,
She ventured forward on the light;
And, wow! Tam saw an unco[9] sight!

Warlocks and witches in a dance:
Nae cotillion,[10] brent new[11] frae France,
But hornpipes, jigs, strathspeys,[12] and
    reels,
Put life and mettle in their heels.
A winnock-bunker[13] in the east,   119
There sat Auld Nick, in shape o' beast;
A tousie tyke,[14] black, grim, and large,
To gie them music was his charge:
He screwed the pipes[15] and gart them
    skirl,[16]
Till roof and rafters a' did dirl.[17]

---

[1] Brush.   [2] A pile of stones.   [3] Child.
[4] Crack.   [5] *John Barleycorn*. Whisky.
[6] Twopenny ale.   [7] Whisky.
[8] *The swats . . . boddle*. The ale so foamed in
    Tammie's head that you can bet he didn't
    care a halfpenny for devils.
[9] Very strange.   [10] A fashionable dance.
[11] *brent new*. Brand-new.
[12] *hornpipes, jigs, strathspeys*. Lively Scottish
    dances.
[13] *winnock-bunker*. Window seat.
[14] *tousie tyke*. A shaggy dog.
[15] *screwed . . . pipes*. Played the bagpipes.
[16] *gart . . . skirl*. Made them scream.   [17] Ring.

---

[1] *But pleasures . . . storm*. The similes * in these
    eight lines are famous.   [2] Midnight.
[3] Must.   [4] Devil.   [5] Splashed.
[6] Puddle.   [7] Sometimes.   [8] Spooks.
[9] Alloway church.   [10] Owls.
[11] Smothered.   [12] Birches.   [13] Big.

Taylor

The bridge over the river Doon

Coffins stood round, like open presses,[1]
That shawed the dead in their last dresses;
And, by some devilish cantraip sleight,[2]
Each in its cauld hand held a light:
By which heroic Tam was able
To note upon the haly table,[3]   130
A murderer's banes,[4] in gibbet-airns[5];
Twa span-lang, wee, unchristened bairns[6];
A thief, new-cutted frae a rape —
Wi' his last gasp his gab[7] did gape;
Five tomahawks wi' bluid red-rusted;
Five scimitars wi' murder crusted;
A garter which a babe had strangled;
A knife a father's throat had mangled —
Whom his ain son o' life bereft —
The gray-hairs yet stack to the heft[8];
Wi' mair of horrible and awefu',   141
Which even to name wad be unlawfu'.

  As Tammie glowered, amazed, and
    curious,
The mirth and fun grew fast and furious;
The piper loud and louder blew,
The dancers quick and quicker flew,
They reeled, they set, they crossed, they
    cleekit,[9]
Till ilka carlin[10] swat and reekit,[11]
And coost her duddies[12] to the wark,[13]
And linket at it in her sark![14]   150
  Now Tam, O Tam! had thae been
    queans,[15]
A' plump and strapping in their teens!
Their sarks, instead o' creeshie flannen,[16]
Been snaw-white seventeen-hunder
    linen[17]! —
Thir breeks[18] o' mine, my only pair,
That once were plush, o' guid blue hair,

I wad hae gi'en them off my hurdies[1]
For ae blink o' the bonnie burdies[2]!
  But withered beldams, auld and droll,
Rigwoodie[3] hags wad spean[4] a foal,   160
Louping[5] and flinging on a crummock,[6]
I wonder didna turn thy stomach!
  But Tam kend what was what fu'
    brawlie[7]:
There was ae winsome wench and wawlie,[8]
That night enlisted in the core,[9]
Lang after kend on Carrick shore
(For monie a beast to dead she shot,
An' perished monie a bonnie boat,
And shook baith meikle corn and bear,[10]
And kept the country-side in fear).   170
Her cutty sark, o' Paisley harn,[11]
That while a lassie she had worn,
In longitude tho' sorely scanty,
It was her best, and she was vauntie.[12]
Ah! little kend thy reverend grannie,
That sark she coft[13] for her wee Nannie,
Wi' twa pund Scots[14] ('twas a' her riches),
Wad ever grac'd a dance of witches!
  But here my Muse her wing maun
    cour,[15]
Sic flights are far beyond her power:
To sing how Nannie lap and flang[16]   181
(A souple jad[17] she was and strang),
And how Tam stood like ane bewitched,
And thought his very een[18] enriched;
Even Satan glowered, and fidged fu'
    fain,[19]
And hotched[20] and blew wi' might and
    main;
Till first ae caper, syne[21] anither,
Tam tint[22] his reason a' thegither,

---

[1] Cupboards.
[2] *cantraip sleight.* Magic trick.
[3] *haly table.* Holy table, Communion table.
[4] Bones.   [5] Gallows irons.   [6] Babies.
[7] Mouth.
[8] *stack . . . heft.* Stuck to the handle.
[9] Joined hands.   [10] Old woman.   [11] Steamed.
[12] Duds; that is, clothes.
[13] *coost . . . wark.* Cast her clothing off for the work.
[14] *linket . . . sark.* Tripped lightly in her shirt.
[15] Young girls.
[16] *creeshie flannen.* Greasy flannel.
[17] *seventeen-hunder linen.* Very fine linen.
[18] *thir breeks.* These breeches.

[1] Hips.   [2] Damsels.   [3] Withered.
[4] Wean (by disgust).   [5] Leaping.
[6] A staff with a crooked head.
[7] Well.   [8] Goodly.   [9] Company.
[10] *shook . . . bear.* Shook down wheat (or rye) and barley out of the ear, thus spoiling it.
[11] *cutty . . . harn.* Short shirt of coarse linen made in the town of Paisley.
[12] Proud of it.   [13] Bought.
[14] *twa pund Scots.* Worth much less than two pounds in English money.
[15] Fold.   [16] Kicked.
[17] *souple jad.* Agile wench.   [18] Eyes.
[19] *fidged . . . fain.* Fidgeted very eagerly.
[20] Jerked about.   [21] Afterward.   [22] Lost.

And roars out: "Weel done, Cutty-
    sark[1]!"
And in an instant all was dark;   190
And scarcely had he Maggie rallied,
When out the hellish legion sallied.
    As bees bizz out wi' angry fyke,[2]
When plundering herds assail their
    byke[3];
As open[4] pussie's[5] mortal foes,
When, pop! she starts before their
    nose;
As eager runs the market-crowd,
When "Catch the thief!" resounds aloud:
So Maggie runs, the witches follow,   199
Wi' monie an eldritch[6] skriech and hollo.
    Ah, Tam! ah, Tam! thou'll get thy
    fairin[7]!
In heil they'll roast thee like a herrin!
In vain thy Kate awaits thy comin!
Kate soon will be a woefu' woman!
Now, do thy speedy utmost, Meg,
And win the key-stane[8] of the brig[9];
There, at them thou thy tail may toss,
A running stream they dare na cross!
But ere the key-stane she could make,
The fient a tail[10] she had to shake: 210
For Nannie, far before the rest,
Hard upon noble Maggie prest,

And flew at Tam wi' furious ettle[1];
But little wist she Maggie's mettle!
Ae spring brought off her master hale,[2]
But left behind her ain gray tail:
The carlin[3] claught[4] her by the rump,
And left poor Maggie scarce a stump.
    Now, wha this tale o' truth shall read,
Ilk man, and mother's son, take heed:
Whene'er to drink you are inclined,   221
Or cutty sarks run in your mind,
Think! ye may buy the joys o'er dear:
Remember Tam o' Shanter's mare.

Discussion Hints

1. How much of the poem is devoted to introductory explanations? What facts given in this part are important later in the story?

2. Describe one of Tam's companions.

3. Which of the prophecies of Tam's wife is nearly fulfilled in the poem?

4. What hour is the keystone of "night's black arch" (l. 69)?

5. Did you ever hear or read any stories of haunted houses used by witches for midnight revels? If so, tell some of the stories in class.

6. Enumerate the things Tam saw on the "haly table." Compare the list with the contents of the witches' caldron in *Macbeth*, IV, i (p. 125).

SAMUEL TAYLOR COLERIDGE[11] (1772–1834)

Kubla Khan

"Kubla Khan" is only a fragment; but, brief and unfinished as it is, it is a masterpiece of romantic dream magic and word magic. Coleridge explained to friends the way the poem came to him. In an Elizabethan travel book, *Purchas his Pilgrimage*, he was reading a description of Kubla* Khan and his beautiful palace, when he fell fast asleep. He remained in a deep sleep, he tells us, for about three

hours, and with no conscious effort on his part composed in his sleep several hundred lines of poetry picturing the scenes and images that came thronging vividly into his imagination. Upon awaking he took pen, ink, and paper and began eagerly to write down the poem. When he had finished only fifty-four lines, there came a knock on his door and "a person on business from Porlock" (a small town near by) interrupted him and stayed for more than an hour. After the person from Porlock had gone, Coleridge tried to continue the poem, but in vain. The dream magic had faded; and never again, though he attempted to do so several times, could he add even a single line to the wonderful fragment as we

[1] Short shirt.   [2] Fuss.   [3] Hive.
[4] Give tongue, begin to bark.
[5] "Puss" is the regular hunting term for a hare or rabbit.   [6] Unearthly.
[7] Reward.   [8] Keystone, center.
[9] Bridge. A witch cannot cross running water, and hence has to stop at the center of a bridge.   [10] *fient a tail*. Devil a tail.
[11] For biography see page 721.

[1] Aim.   [2] Whole.   [3] Witch.   [4] Clutched.

have it. Even in its present form "Kubla Khan" is one of the most perfect examples of purely romantic imagery * in literature.

IN XANADU¹ did Kubla* Khan
A stately pleasure-dome decree:
Where Alph, the sacred river, ran
Through caverns measureless to man
    Down to a sunless sea.
So twice five miles of fertile ground
With walls and towers were girdled round:
And there were gardens bright with sinu-
    ous rills,
Where blossomed many an incense-
    bearing tree;
And here were forests ancient as the hills,
Enfolding sunny spots of greenery.   11

But oh! that deep romantic chasm which
    slanted
Down the green hill athwart a cedarn
    cover!²
A savage place! as holy and enchanted
As e'er beneath a waning moon was
    haunted
By woman wailing for her demon-lover!³
And from this chasm, with ceaseless tur-
    moil seething,
As if this earth in fast thick pants were
    breathing,
A mighty fountain momently was forced:
Amid whose swift half-intermitted burst
Huge fragments vaulted like rebounding
    hail,   21
Or chaffy grain beneath the thresher's
    flail:
And 'mid these dancing rocks at once
    and ever
It flung up momently the sacred river.

¹ *Xanadu* (zăn′à dōō). The residence of Kubla Khan.
² *cedarn cover.* A thicket of cedar trees.
³ *A savage . . . demon-lover!* These are three of the five lines that Kipling refers to in his well-known criticism: "Remember that in all the millions permitted there are no more than five — five little lines — of which one can say: 'These are the magic; these are the vision; the rest is only poetry.'" The other two lines he refers to are lines 69 and 70 in Keats's "Ode to a Nightingale" (p. 371).

Five miles meandering¹ with a mazy
    motion
Through wood and dale the sacred river
    ran,
Then reached the caverns measureless to
    man,
And sank in tumult to a lifeless ocean:
And 'mid this tumult Kubla heard from
    far
Ancestral voices prophesying war!   30
    The shadow of the dome of pleasure
    Floated midway on the waves;
    Where was heard the mingled measure
    From the fountain and the caves.
It was a miracle of rare device,
A sunny pleasure-dome with caves of ice!
    A damsel with a dulcimer²
    In a vision once I saw:
    It was an Abyssinian³ maid,
    And on her dulcimer she played,   40
    Singing of Mount Abora.³
    Could I revive within me
    Her symphony and song,
    To such a deep delight 'twould win me,
That with music loud and long,
I would build that dome in air,
That sunny dome! those caves of ice!
And all who heard should see them there,
And all should cry, Beware! Beware!
His flashing eyes, his floating hair!   50
Weave a circle round him thrice,
And close your eyes with holy dread,
For he on honey-dew hath fed,
And drunk the milk of Paradise.

Discussion Hints

1. Give in your own words a picture of the "caverns measureless to men" and the "sunless sea" (ll. 4–5).

2. What do you think an "incense-bearing tree" (l. 9) might look like? Such a tree is referred to in Shelley's "Indian Serenade,"

¹ Winding.
² A kind of stringed musical instrument played by hand.
³ *Abyssinian, Mount Abora.* These are merely words that had stuck in Coleridge's mind from his reading and came to his memory in his sleep because they suggest remoteness and romance.

l. 11 (p. 360). Can you give an example from your own experiences?

3. At what place in this poem do you feel least sure of your footing, or, in other words, where is the fantasy most noticeable? Do you like this part?

4. Who was Kubla* Khan? What long narrative poem by Coleridge deals with marvels in far-off places?

5. Another poem, given earlier in *English Writers*, is said to have been composed in a dream. Find it and describe the circumstances under which it is said to have been composed. Some of you may have had the experience of composing verse while you were asleep, or you may know someone who has had that experience. If so, tell the class about it.

6. Memorize lines 37–54.

Words and Passages to be Explained

> *athwart* (l. 13)
> *with ceaseless turmoil seething* (l. 17)
> *in fast thick pants* (l. 18)
> *momently* (l. 19)

From "Christabel"

"Christabel" is one of the most beautiful of the English romantic poems inspired by themes borrowed from the Middle Ages. The same love of weird dreams and supernatural marvels that led Coleridge to write "The Rime of the Ancient Mariner"[1] led him also to choose as the central theme of "Christabel" the ancient belief that witches and other demonic creatures can disguise themselves as women with lovely faces in order to do evil to their victims. "Christabel" portrays the struggle between the innocent heroine and such a creature in the form of Geraldine, whose character is hinted at rather than specifically described. By his hints, as well as by the ghostly background of dark forest and gloomy castle, the poet makes us feel both the horror and the fascination of the supernatural world. Coleridge composed the first part of "Christabel" in 1797–1798, when his genius was at its best. He tried several times to finish the story, but never did so successfully. As it is, "Christabel," like "Kubla Khan," remains a splendid fragment.

The verse form of "Christabel" is new. Nearly all the lines have four accented syllables, but the number of unaccented syllables varies. In general the variations correspond to changes in the musical or imaginative effect that the poet desired to produce. Note also that the lines do not rhyme with perfect regularity and that the stanzas vary in length. Thus, in the matter of meter,

[1]Given in the revised edition of *Achievement* of this series.

"Christabel" is a long way from the perfectly regular heroic* couplet of the Age of Classicism (p. 216).

PART THE FIRST

'TIS the middle of the night by the castle clock,
And the owls have awakened the crowing cock;
Tu-whit! — Tu-whoo!
And hark, again! the crowing cock,
How drowsily it crew.

Sir Leoline, the Baron rich,
Hath a toothless mastiff bitch;
From her kennel beneath the rock
She maketh answer to the clock,
Four for the quarters, and twelve for the hour;   10
Ever and aye, by shine and shower,
Sixteen short howls, not over loud;
Some say, she sees my lady's shroud.[1]

Is the night chilly and dark?
The night is chilly, but not dark.
The thin gray cloud is spread on high,
It covers but not hides the sky.
The moon is behind, and at the full;
And yet she looks both small and dull.
The night is chill, the cloud is gray: 20
'Tis a month before the month of May,
And the Spring comes slowly up this way.

[1] The shroud of Christabel's mother, who is dead.

The lovely lady, Christabel,
Whom her father loves so well,
What makes her in the wood so late,
A furlong from the castle gate?
She had dreams all yesternight
Of her own betrothèd knight;
And she in the midnight wood will pray
For the weal of her lover that's far away.

She stole along, she nothing spoke,   31
The sighs she heaved were soft and low,
And naught was green upon the oak
But moss and rarest mistletoe:
She kneels beneath the huge oak tree,
And in silence prayeth she.

The lady sprang up suddenly,
The lovely lady, Christabel!
It moaned as near, as near can be,
But what it is, she cannot tell. —   40
On the other side it seems to be,
Of the huge, broad-breasted, old oak tree.

The night is chill; the forest bare;
Is it the wind that moaneth bleak?
There is not wind enough in the air
To move away the ringlet curl
From the lovely lady's cheek —
There is not wind enough to twirl
The one red leaf, the last of its clan,
That dances as often as dance it can,   50
Hanging so light, and hanging so high,
On the topmost twig that looks up at the
    sky.[1]
Hush, beating heart of Christabel!
Jesu, Maria, shield her well!
She folded her arms beneath her cloak,
And stole to the other side of the oak.
  What sees she there?

There she sees a damsel bright,
Drest in a silken robe of white,   59
That shadowy in the moonlight shone:
The neck that made that white robe wan,
Her stately neck, and arms were bare;
Her blue-veined feet unsandal'd were;

And wildly glittered here and there
The gems entangled in her hair.
I guess, 'twas frightful there to see
A lady so richly clad as she —
Beautiful exceedingly!

"Mary, mother, save me now!"
(Said Christabel) "and who art thou?"
The lady strange made answer meet,[1]   71
And her voice was faint and sweet: —
"Have pity on my sore distress,
I scarce can speak for weariness:
Stretch forth thy hand, and have no
    fear!"
Said Christabel, "How camest thou
    here?"
And the lady, whose voice was faint and
    sweet,
Did thus pursue her answer meet: —

"My sire is of a noble line,
And my name is Geraldine: 80
Five warriors seized me yestermorn,
Me, even me, a maid forlorn:
They choked my cries with force and
    fright,
And tied me on a palfrey [2] white.
The palfrey was as fleet as wind,
And they rode furiously behind.
They spurred amain, their steeds were
    white:
And once we crossed the shade of night.[3]
As sure as Heaven shall rescue me,
I have no thought what men they be;
Nor do I know how long it is   91
(For I have lain entranced I wis[4])
Since one, the tallest of the five,
Took me from the palfrey's back,
A weary woman, scarce alive.
Some muttered words his comrades
    spoke:
He placed me underneath this oak;
He swore they would return with haste;
Whither they went I cannot tell —
I thought I heard, some minutes past,
Sounds as of a castle bell.   101

---

[1] *The one . . . sky.* Note the change in rhythm * at line 49 to correspond to the movement of the leaf.

[1] Fitting.   [2] A lady's riding horse.
[3] *once . . . night.* We traveled one whole night.
[4] *I wis.* Surely; literally, I know.

There she sees a damsel bright

Stretch forth thy hand" (thus ended
    she)
"And help a wretched maid to flee."

Then Christabel stretched forth her
    hand,
And comforted fair Geraldine:
"O well, bright dame! may you com-
    mand
The service of Sir Leoline;
And gladly our stout chivalry [1]
Will he send forth and friends withal
To guide and guard you safe and free
Home to your noble father's hall."   111

She rose: and forth with steps they passed
That strove to be, and were not, fast.
Her gracious stars the lady blest,
And thus spake on sweet Christabel:
"All our household are at rest,
The hall as silent as the cell;
Sir Leoline is weak in health,
And may not well awakened be,
But we will move as if in stealth,   120
And I beseech your courtesy,
This night, to share your couch with me."

They crossed the moat, and Christabel
Took the key that fitted well;
A little door she opened straight,
All in the middle of the gate;
The gate that was ironed within and
    without,
Where an army in battle array had
    marched out.
The lady sank, belike through pain,
And Christabel with might and main
Lifted her up, a weary weight,   131
Over the threshold* of the gate:
Then the lady rose again,
And moved, as she were not in pain.

So free from danger, free from fear,
They crossed the court: right glad they
    were.
And Christabel devoutly cried
To the lady by her side,

"Praise we the Virgin all divine
Who hath rescued thee from thy dis-
    tress!"   140
"Alas, alas!" said Geraldine,
"I cannot speak [1] for weariness."
So free from danger, free from fear,
They crossed the court: right glad they
    were.

Outside her kennel, the mastiff old
Lay fast asleep, in moonshine cold.
The mastiff old did not awake,
Yet she an angry moan did make!
And what can ail the mastiff bitch? [2]
Never till now she uttered yell   150
Beneath the eye of Christabel.
Perhaps it is the owlet's scritch [3]:
For what can ail the mastiff bitch?

They passed the hall, that echoes still,
Pass as lightly as you will.
The brands were flat, the brands were
    dying,
Amid their own white ashes lying;
But when the lady passed, there came
A tongue of light, a fit of flame; [4]
And Christabel saw the lady's eye,   160
And nothing else saw she thereby,
Save the boss [5] of the shield of Sir Leoline
    tall,
Which hung in a murky [6] old niche in the
    wall.
"O softly tread," said Christabel,
"My father seldom sleepeth well."
Sweet Christabel her feet doth bare,
And jealous of the listening air
They steal their way from stair to stair,
Now in glimmer, and now in gloom,
And now they pass the Baron's room,

[1] *I . . . speak.* Like witches and other demonic
    creatures, Geraldine cannot pray and hence
    excuses herself by saying she is too weak to
    speak.
[2] *what . . . bitch.* According to an old belief ani-
    mals instinctively feel the presence of super-
    natural creatures.
[3] Screech.
[4] See "threshold." *
[5] The knob at the center of the shield.
[6] Dark.

[1] Here, knights.

As still as death, with stifled breath! 171
And now have reached her chamber door;
And now doth Geraldine press down
The rushes[1] of the chamber floor.

The moon shines dim in the open air
And not a moonbeam enters here.
But they without its light can see
The chamber carved so curiously,
Carved with figures strange and sweet,
All made out of the carver's brain, 180
For a lady's chamber meet:
The lamp with twofold silver chain
Is fastened to an angel's feet.
The silver lamp burns dead and dim;
But Christabel the lamp will trim.
She trimmed the lamp, and made it bright,
And left it swinging to and fro,
While Geraldine, in wretched plight,
Sank down upon the floor below.

"O weary lady, Geraldine, 190
I pray you, drink this cordial wine!
It is a wine of virtuous powers;
My mother made it of wild flowers."

"And will your mother pity me,
Who am a maiden most forlorn?"
Christabel answered — "Woe is me!
She died the hour that I was born.
I have heard the gray-haired friar tell
How on her death-bed she did say,
That she should hear the castle-bell 200
Strike twelve upon my wedding day.
O mother dear! that thou wert here!"
"I would," said Geraldine, "she were!"

But soon, with altered voice, said she —
"Off, wandering mother! Peak and pine![2]
I have power to bid thee flee."[3]
Alas! what ails poor Geraldine?
Why stares she with unsettled eye?
Can she the bodiless dead espy? 209
And why with hollow voice cries she,
"Off, woman, off! this hour is mine —

[1] During the Middle Ages floors were often covered with rushes instead of carpets.
[2] *Peak and pine.* Waste away and languish.
[3] *Off . . . flee.* Geraldine, by her evil power, can for the time being drive away Christabel's guardian spirit, her mother.

Though thou her guardian spirit be,
Off, woman, off! 'tis given to me."

Then Christabel knelt by the lady's side,
And raised to heaven her eyes so blue —
"Alas!" said she, "this ghastly ride —
Dear lady! it hath wildered[1] you!"
The lady wiped her moist cold brow,
And faintly said, "'Tis over now!" 219

Again the wild-flower wine she drank:
Her fair large eyes 'gan glitter bright,
And from the floor whereon she sank,
The lofty lady stood upright:
She was most beautiful to see,
Like a lady of a far countrée.

And thus the lofty lady spake —
"All they who live in the upper sky,
Do love you, holy Christabel!
And you love them, and for their sake
And for the good which me befell, 230
Even I in my degree will try,
Fair maiden, to requite you well.
But now unrobe yourself; for I
Must pray, ere yet in bed I lie."

Quoth Christabel, "So let it be!"
And as the lady bade, did she.
Her gentle limbs did she undress,
And lay down in her loveliness.

But through her brain, of weal and woe,
So many thoughts moved to and fro,
That vain it were her lids to close; 241
So half-way from the bed she rose,
And on her elbow did recline,
To look at the lady Geraldine.

Beneath the lamp the lady bowed,
And slowly rolled her eyes around;
Then drawing in her breath aloud,
Like one that shuddered, she unbound
The cincture[2] from beneath her breast:
Her silken robe, and inner vest, 250
Dropt to her feet, and full in view,
Behold! her bosom and half her side —
A sight to dream of, not to tell![3]
O shield her! shield sweet Christabel!

[1] Bewildered.   [2] Girdle, belt.
[3] *her bosom . . . tell.* See "threshold." *

Yet Geraldine nor speaks nor stirs;
Ah! what a stricken look was hers!
Deep from within she seems half-way
To lift some weight with sick assay,[1]
And eyes the maid and seeks delay;
Then suddenly, as one defied,   260
Collects herself in scorn and pride,
And lay down by the Maiden's side! —
And in her arms the maid she took,
     Ah wel-a-day!
And with low voice and doleful look
These words did say:
"In the touch of this bosom there work-
     eth a spell,
Which is lord of thy utterance, Christabel!
Thou knowest to-night, and wilt know
     to-morrow,
This mark of my shame, this seal of my
     sorrow;   270
     But vainly thou warrest,
       For this is alone in
       Thy power to declare,
       That in the dim forest
       Thou heard'st a low moaning,
And found'st a bright lady, surpassingly
     fair;
And didst bring her home with thee in
     love and in charity,
To shield her and shelter her from the
     damp air."

[Sir Leoline, on learning that Geraldine is
the daughter of his old friend Lord Roland
de Vaux (vô), sends Bracy the bard to summon
Lord Roland, meanwhile keeping Geraldine
at his own castle in spite of the objections of
Christabel, who fears her. Here Coleridge
stops.]

Discussion Hints

1. It is not certain that Coleridge, at the
time he wrote Part the First of "Christabel,"
knew just how he would finish the story, but
presumably he intended to give it a happy
ending. Try finishing the story, and compare
your results with those of other members of
the class.

---

[1] *sick assay*. Such an effort that it makes her feel
    sick.

2. What unusual occurrences mark the
progress of Christabel and Geraldine toward
the castle, beginning with line 123? Do you
form an idea of Geraldine's nature at this
time?

3. Point out the suggestions of Geraldine's
supernatural character.

4. Notice the description of Christabel's
room. What other examples of brief, striking
description do you find in the poem?

5. What descriptions of eyes do you find
in the poem? How do some of these descriptions differ from others?

6. What echoes of the popular ballads
(p. 57) do you find in "Christabel"?

7. How does Coleridge make you feel that
there is a mystery involved? Where does the
mystery seem deepest?

8. What part does Christabel's dead
mother play in the poem? Who is addressed
in lines 211–213?

9. If "Christabel" were set to music and
made into an opera, at what places should you
expect to find the same kinds of musical
themes or motifs?

10. While you are reading the poem aloud,
try to discover why the rhythm changes at
various points.

11. In lines 43–57 find illustrations of what
is said in the headnote regarding the verse
form of the poem.

Words and Passages to be Explained

The one red leaf, the last of its clan,
That dances as often as dance it can (ll. 49–50)
unsandal'd (l. 63)
forth with steps they passed
That strove to be, and were not, fast (ll. 112–113)
straight (an adverb) (l. 125)
That vain it were her lids to close (l. 241)

Suggestions for Reading

"The Rime of the Ancient Mariner" (in
the revised edition of *Achievement* of this
series). You will do well to read some of
Coleridge's lyric poetry; for example: "Love,"
"Frost at Midnight," "Hymn before Sun-
Rise, in the Vale of Chamouni," "Time Real
and Imaginary," and "Youth and Age."

SIR WALTER SCOTT[1] (1771–1832)

Lochinvar

Of all Scott's many imitations of popular ballads (p. 57), "Lochinvar" is one of the best. Its spirited story, its lilting rhythm, and its pictures of the lovely bride, the craven bridegroom, and the gallant young Lochinvar have long made it a favorite.

Scott loved folk ballads, collected them all his life, and knew by heart a large number of them. His *Minstrelsy of the Scottish Border* (p. 317) is one of the best ballad collections ever made. It was only natural, therefore, that he should seek to imitate ballads in his own poetry. This he did with astonishing success. "Lochinvar" is based directly on an old folk ballad which Scott had first published in the *Minstrelsy*. He used "Lochinvar" as a song in *Marmion*, one of his long narrative poems.

O H! YOUNG Lochinvar[2] is come out
    of the west,
Through all the wide Border[*] his steed
        was the best;
And save his good broadsword he weap-
        ons had none,
He rode all unarmed and he rode all alone.
So faithful in love and so dauntless in war,
There never was knight like the young
        Lochinvar.

He stayed not for brake[3] and he stopped
        not for stone,
He swam the Eske river where ford
        there was none;
But ere he alighted at Netherby[4] gate,
The bride had consented, the gallant
        came late: 10
For a laggard in love and a dastard in war
Was to wed the fair Ellen of brave
        Lochinvar.

So boldly he entered the Netherby Hall,
Among bridesmen, and kinsmen, and
        brothers, and all:

Then spoke the bride's father, his hand
        on his sword
(For the poor craven bridegroom said
        never a word),
"Oh! come ye in peace here, or come ye
        in war,
Or to dance at our bridal, young Lord
        Lochinvar?"

"I long wooed your daughter, my suit
        you denied;
Love swells like the Solway,[1] but ebbs
        like its tide —   20
And now am I come, with this lost love
        of mine,
To lead but one measure, drink one cup
        of wine.
There are maidens in Scotland more
        lovely by far,
That would gladly be bride to the young
        Lochinvar."

The bride kissed the goblet: the knight
        took it up,
He quaffed off the wine, and he threw
        down the cup.
She looked down to blush, and she looked
        up to sigh,
With a smile on her lips and a tear in her
        eye.
He took her soft hand ere her mother
        could bar, —
"Now tread we a measure!" said young
        Lochinvar.   30

So stately his form, and so lovely her
        face,
That never a hall such a galliard[2] did
        grace;

[1] For biography see page 722.
[2] *Lochinvar* (lŏk ĭn vär').   [3] Thicket.
[4] All the places and families named in the poem are famous in Border[*] tales.

[1] Solway Firth, a bay on the west coast of Scotland, noted for its rushing tides.
[2] A lively dance.

D

While her mother did fret, and her father
    did fume,
And the bridegroom stood dangling his
    bonnet and plume;
And the bride-maidens whispered,
    "Twere better by far,
To have matched our fair cousin with
    young Lochinvar."

One touch to her hand and one word in
    her ear,
When they reached the hall-door, and
    the charger[1] stood near;
So light to the croupe[2] the fair lady he
    swung,
So light to the saddle before her he
    sprung!   40

"She is won! we are gone, over bank,
    bush, and scaur[1];
They'll have fleet steeds that follow,"[2]
    quoth young Lochinvar.

There was mounting 'mong Graemes of
    the Netherby clan;
Forsters, Fenwicks, and Musgraves, they
    rode and they ran:
There was racing and chasing on Can-
    nobie Lee,
But the lost bride of Netherby ne'er did
    they see.
So daring in love and so dauntless in
    war,
Have ye e'er heard of gallant like young
    Lochinvar?

Jock of Hazeldean

"Jock of Hazeldean" resembles "Lochinvar" in using the ancient theme of the
abducted bride, but it contains more features
of the popular ballads (p. 57) than "Lochinvar" does. This is due in part to the fact
that it contains one whole stanza taken from
an old ballad. Yet Scott had learned so perfectly how to imitate early English popular
poetry that no one could tell from a casual
reading what part of the poem he himself
wrote (the final three stanzas).

WHY weep ye by the tide, ladie?
    Why weep ye by the tide?
I'll wed ye to my youngest son,
    And ye sall be his bride:
And ye sall be his bride, ladie,
    Sae comely to be seen" —
But aye she loot[3] the tears down fa'
    For Jock of Hazeldean.

"Now let this wilfu' grief be done,
    And dry that cheek so pale;   10
Young Frank is chief of Errington
    And lord of Langley-dale;

His step is first in peaceful ha',[3]
    His sword in battle keen" —
But aye she loot the tears down fa'
    For Jock of Hazeldean.

"A chain of gold ye sall not lack,
    Nor braid to bind your hair;
Nor mettled hound, nor managed hawk,
    Nor palfrey[4] fresh and fair;   20
And you, the foremost o' them a',
    Shall ride our forest queen." —
But aye she loot the tears down fa'
    For Jock of Hazeldean.

The kirk[5] was decked at morning-tide,
    The tapers glimmered fair;
The priest and bridegroom wait the
    bride,
    And dame and knight are there.
They sought her baith by bower and
    ha';
    The ladie was not seen!   30
She's o'er the Border* and awa'
    Wi' Jock of Hazeldean.

---

[1] War horse.
[2] The place behind the saddle.
[3] Let.

[1] Bare hillside.
[2] To catch us they'll have to have swift horses.
[3] Hall.   [4] Here, a lady's riding horse.   [5] Church.

"She is won! we are gone, over bank, bush, and scaur."

Galloway

Sir Walter Scott's house, Abbotsford

Proud Maisie

So brief is this poem, so simple in words and pictures, and so melodious in verse that one scarcely realizes at first how grim and ironical* are the robin's replies to the proud lady who asks him to tell her fortune.

"Proud Maisie" is sung by the crazed and dying Madge Wildfire, a character in *The Heart of Midlothian*, one of Scott's best-known novels.

Pᴿᴼᵁᴰ Maisie is in the wood,
  Walking so early;
Sweet Robin sits on the bush,
  Singing so rarely.

"Tell me, thou bonny bird,
  When shall I marry me?"

"When six braw¹ gentlemen
  Kirkward² shall carry ye."

"Who makes the bridal bed,
  Birdie, say truly?"
"The gray-headed sexton
  That delves the grave duly.

"The glow-worm o'er grave and stone
  Shall light thee steady;
The owl from the steeple sing
  'Welcome, proud lady.'"

10

¹ Handsome.
² Churchward.

The Outlaw

"The Outlaw" is based on a common and much-loved ballad theme, the fair lady who is captivated by the graceful manners and the dashing spirit of an outlaw. It exemplifies several traits taken from the old ballads: the setting of castle and greenwood, the repeated ideas and phrases, and the singing quality. It shows how completely Scott caught the spirit of early-English popular poetry.

O BRIGNALL banks are wild and fair,
  And Greta woods are green,
And you may gather garlands there
  Would grace a summer queen.
And as I rode by Dalton-Hall
  Beneath the turrets high,
A Maiden on the castle wall
  Was singing merrily:
"O Brignall banks are fresh and fair,
  And Greta woods are green;   10
I'd rather rove with Edmund there
  Than reign our English queen."

"If, Maiden, thou wouldst wend with me,
  To leave both tower and town,
Thou first must guess what life lead we
  That dwell by dale and down.[1]
And if thou canst that riddle read,[2]
  As read full well you may,
Then to the greenwood shalt thou speed
  As blithe as Queen of May."   20
Yet sung she, "Brignall banks are fair,
  And Greta woods are green;
I'd rather rove with Edmund there
  Than reign our English queen.

"I read[3] you, by your bugle horn
  And by your palfrey[4] good,
I read you for a ranger sworn
  To keep the king's greenwood."

"A Ranger, lady, winds his horn,
  And 'tis at peep of light;   30
His blast is heard at merry morn,
  And mine at dead of night."[1]
Yet sung she, "Brignall banks are fair,
  And Greta woods are gay;
I would I were with Edmund there
  To reign his Queen of May!

"With burnish'd brand[2] and musketoon[3]
  So gallantly you come,
I read you for a bold Dragoon
  That lists[4] the tuck[5] of drum."   40
"I list no more the tuck of drum,
  No more the trumpet hear;
But when the beetle sounds his hum[6]
  My comrades take the spear.
And O! though Brignall banks be fair
  And Greta woods be gay,
Yet mickle must the maiden dare
  Would reign my Queen of May!

"Maiden! a nameless life I lead,
  A nameless death I'll die;   50
The fiend whose lantern lights the mead[7]
  Were better mate than I!
And when I'm with my comrades met
  Beneath the greenwood bough, —
What once we were we all forget,
  Nor think what we are now."

Chorus

"Yet Brignall banks are fresh and fair,
  And Greta woods are green,
And you may gather garlands there
  Would grace a summer queen."   60

[1] The speaker means that he is an outlaw who is abroad at night.
[2] Sword.
[3] An old-fashioned short-barreled gun.
[4] Listens to.   [5] Beat.
[6] *when . . . hum.* When night comes.
[7] *The fiend . . . mead.* The will-o'-the-wisp, or jack-o'-lantern. See Milton's "L'Allegro," p. 192, l. 104.

[1] *dale and down.* Valley and hill.
[2] Interpret.
[3] Recognize.
[4] A riding horse.

The Lay of Rosabelle

"The Lay of Rosabelle" is considered by many readers as Scott's best short narrative poem. Like the popular ballads (p. 57) it begins abruptly, moves directly and swiftly through the action, and relates a tragic tale effectively and impressively. Our interest is increased by the art with which Scott selected details that heighten the effect, and the skill with which he turned the story into swinging, musical verse.

It is sung by a character in *The Lay of the Last Minstrel*, one of Scott's best-known longer narrative poems.

Interpretative Outline

I. The minstrel appeals for attention and announces the nature and subject of his song (ll. 1–4).
II. The vain efforts of Rosabelle's attendants to persuade her not to tempt the rising storm (ll. 5–16) and her protests, which suggest the real reason for her going (ll. 17–24).
III. The blazing portents above the castle and chapel of Roslin, signifying tragedy (ll. 25–44).
IV. The fate of Rosabelle (ll. 45–52).

O LISTEN, listen, ladies gay!
  No haughty feat of arms I tell;
Soft is the note, and sad the lay,
  That mourns the lovely Rosabelle.

"Moor, moor the barge, ye gallant crew!
  And, gentle ladye, deign to stay!
Rest thee in Castle Ravensheuch,
  Nor tempt the stormy firth [1] to-day.

"The blackening wave is edged with
  white: 9
To inch [2] and rock the sea-mews [3] fly;
The fishers have heard the Water Sprite, [4]
  Whose screams forbode that wreck is
  nigh.

[1] A firth, or frith, is the Scottish name for a narrow arm of the sea.
[2] Island.
[3] Sea gulls.
[4] A kelpie, or water spirit. It was said to scream before an approaching calamity.

"Last night the gifted Seer [1] did view
  A wet shroud swathed round ladye gay;
Then stay thee, Fair, in Ravensheuch:
  Why cross the gloomy firth to-day?"

" 'Tis not because Lord Lindesay's heir
  To-night at Roslin leads the ball,
But that my ladye-mother there
  Sits lonely in her castle-hall.   20

" 'Tis not because the ring they ride, [2]
  And Lindesay at the ring rides well,
But that my sire the wine will chide, [3]
  If 'tis not fill'd by Rosabelle."

O'er Roslin all that dreary night
  A wondrous blaze [4] was seen to gleam;
'Twas broader than the watch-fire's light,
  And redder than the bright moonbeam.

It glared on Roslin's castled rock,
  It ruddied all the copse-wood glen; 30
'Twas seen from Dryden's groves of oak,
  And seen from cavern'd Hawthornden. [5]

Seem'd all on fire that chapel proud,
  Where Roslin's chiefs uncoffin'd lie,
Each Baron, for a sable shroud,
  Sheathed in his iron panoply. [6]

Seem'd all on fire, within, around,
  Deep sacristy [7] and altar's pale;
Shone every pillar foliage-bound, [8]
  And glimmer'd all the dead men's
    mail.   40

[1] *gifted Seer*. In Scotland certain persons were believed to be gifted with "second sight," the ability to foresee the future.
[2] *ring they ride*. In one form of tournament a knight riding at full speed attempted to thrust his lance through a suspended ring and bear the ring away.
[3] Complain of, blame.
[4] A supernatural light which was believed to foretell disaster.
[5] A place famous for its caves.
[6] *for . . . panoply*. Buried in his armor.
[7] The part of the church in which the sacred vessels are kept.
[8] Surrounded by foliage carved in the stone.

Galloway

Dryburgh Abbey, the ruins of a medieval monastery, where Scott is buried

Blazed battlement and pinnet [1] high,
 Blazed every rose-carved buttress
  fair —
So still they blaze when fate is nigh
 The lordly line of high St. Clair.[2]

There are twenty of Roslin's barons
 bold
 Lie buried within that proud chapelle;
Each one the holy vault doth hold —
 But the sea holds lovely Rosabelle!

And each St. Clair was buried there,
 With candle, with book, and with
  knell;   50
But the sea-caves rung, and the wild
 winds sung
 The dirge of lovely Rosabelle.

Discussion Hints

Lochinvar

1. Tell the story of the ballad. Do you
know of any other stories in which a bride
elopes on her wedding day with a man who is
not the bridegroom and is the enemy of her
family?

2. In what respect do the last two lines of
the first stanza and the last two lines of the
ballad resemble each other? What do you
think was Scott's reason for making them
do so?

3. In lines 23–24 is Lochinvar sincere?
What is his real purpose in making the assertion?

4. Quote passages that give a picture of
the bridegroom.

5. Read your favorite passages aloud to
illustrate the lilting, galloping rhythm of the
poem.

6. "Katherine Jaffray" is the old ballad
on which "Lochinvar" is based. It is printed
in *English and Scottish Popular Ballads*,
edited by Helen C. Sargent and G. L. Kittredge
(Houghton Mifflin Company). If you have
access to a copy, compare Scott's poem with
the original. Which do you prefer? Give
reasons for your answer.

[1] Pinnacle
[2] *lordly . . . St. Clair.* The family of Roslin Castle.

7. Explain:
a. laggard (l. 11)
b. craven (l. 16)
c. quaffed (l. 26)
d. clan (l. 43)

Jock of Hazeldean

1. The headnote tells you that "Jock of
Hazeldean" contains more features of the
popular ballads (p. 57) than "Lochinvar"
does. Point out some of them.

2. When Scott wrote the ballad, he knew
only the first stanza. If you knew only as
much as that, how would you finish the
story?

3. "Jock of Hazeldean" is available in
recording No. 4083, by the RCA (Victor)
Manufacturing Company, Inc. If possible
play it in connection with your study of the
poem.

Proud Maisie

1. During the Middle Ages pride was regarded as the worst possible sin. What does
this fact suggest regarding Maisie's attitude
toward her lovers and her marriage?

2. What do you find that is grim or ironical*
in the poem?

3. How does Maisie differ from the heroines
of "Lochinvar" and "Jock of Hazeldean"
(pp. 401 and 402)? What is the reason for the
difference?

The Outlaw

1. Point out passages in the poem which
suggest that the maiden is captivated by an
outlaw.

2. Who utters the speech beginning with
line 13?

3. Why does the lover say what he does in
lines 49–50?

4. What false impressions does the lady
derive from the lover's disguise? How does
he try to correct them?

5. What difficulties does the lover suggest
in answering the lady's proposal to share his
fate?

6. Give examples of parallelism.*

7. Explain lines 51–52 and 55–56.

The Lay of Rosabelle

1. In lines 17–24 Rosabelle gives two reasons for crossing the bay, and she rejects two other reasons. Discuss her answers in class.

2. Lines 25–44 are unusually musical and sonorous. Practice reading the passage aloud several times at home to get its full effect.

3. Make a list of the events, natural or supernatural, that seem to foretell disaster to Rosabelle.

4. "Lochinvar" (p. 401), "Proud Maisie" (p. 404), and "The Lay of Rosabelle" are all

musical and all effectively written, but they are all entirely different. Try to describe their differences briefly. Which of the three do you like best?

Suggestions for Reading

The Lady of the Lake (given in part in the revised edition of *Adventure* of this series), *The Lay of the Last Minstrel*, and *Marmion*, especially Canto VI.

You will also like some of Scott's lyric poetry; for example: "Soldier, Rest! Thy Warfare O'er" (from *The Lady of the Lake*) and "Hunting Song" (given, together with the tune, in the revised edition of *Achievement* of this series).

GEORGE GORDON, LORD BYRON[1] (1788–1824)

The Destruction of Sennacherib

"The Destruction of Sennacherib"* has long been a favorite poem for recitation by reason of the fine swing of the verse and the boldness of the imagery.* The "tripping" effect of the rhythm is produced by the use of anapaestic* feet:

"The Ás syr|ian came down | like the wolf | on the fold."

The poem is based upon the story told in 2 Kings 19 : 35.

THE Assyrian came down like the wolf on the fold,
And his cohorts [2] were gleaming in purple and gold;
And the sheen of their spears was like stars on the sea,
When the blue wave rolls nightly on deep Galilee.

Like the leaves of the forest when Summer is green,
That host with their banners at sunset were seen:

[1] For biography see page 718.
[2] Bands of warriors.

Like the leaves of the forest when Autumn hath blown,
That host on the morrow lay withered and strown.

For the Angel of Death spread his wings on the blast,
And breathed in the face of the foe as he passed;   10
And the eyes of the sleepers waxed deadly and chill,
And their hearts but once heaved, and for ever grew still!

And there lay the steed with his nostril all wide,
But through it there rolled not the breath of his pride;
And the foam of his gasping lay white on the turf,
And cold as the spray of the rock-beating surf.

And there lay the rider distorted and pale,
With the dew on his brow, and the rust on his mail:

The widows of Ashur are loud in their wail

And the tents were all silent, the banners
    alone,
The lances unlifted, the trumpet un-
    blown.   20

And the widows of Ashur [1] are loud in
    their wail,
And the idols are broke in the temple of
    Baal [2];
And the might of the Gentile, unsmote
    by the sword,
Hath melted like snow in the glance of
    the Lord!

Discussion Hints

1. Does "The Destruction of Sennacherib"
affect you most strongly through your appreciation of color or of sound or of the story?
What stanza or stanzas in particular determine your answer?

[1] Assyria.
[2] The supreme god of the Assyrians and certain
other Oriental peoples.

2. Look up in the Bible the account referred to in the headnote and read the whole
chapter in which it occurs. What important
matters, if any, are referred to in the Biblical
account but are omitted in the poem? Why
did only one verse fire Byron's poetic
imagination? Give five details that he adds
to the story.

3. Write out four lines and mark the
scansion so as to show that the meter is
anapaestic.*

4. Words to be explained:

a. sheen (l. 3)
b. waxed (l. 11)

Suggestions for Reading

"The Prisoner of Chillon" (in the revised
    edition of *Achievement* of this series)
Childe Harold's Pilgrimage. (Read especially
    Canto V, ll. 10–117.)
"Mazeppa"

JOHN KEATS[1] (1795–1821)

The Eve of St. Agnes

"The Eve of St. Agnes" owes its popularity to (1) its theme, two youthful lovers united in spite of difficulties; (2) its use of medieval and popular traditions; (3) its dreamy, melodious verse.

According to an old folk belief a girl can find out who her future husband is to be if she will do certain things on Saint Agnes's Eve. She must fast all day, must speak to no one on retiring, must not look behind her, and must lie on her back in bed with her hands under her head. If she does these things, her true love will come to her in a dream, kiss her, and spread a feast for her.

With the story of Saint Agnes and this folk belief as a foundation, Keats invented the tale of two lovers who were separated by the enmity of their families, but who nevertheless succeeded in finding happiness in each other. The scene is laid during the Middle Ages, when, according to the old ballads, bold and resourceful lovers often won fair ladies. The thread of the story is simple, but it serves effectively to hold together the succession of beautiful, glowing pictures that Keats paints in soft, musical Spenserian* stanzas. Especially famous are the first stanza and lines 208–225 and 262–270. Read these aloud slowly several times to get their rich word-music.

[The setting.]

ST. AGNES' Eve [2] — Ah, bitter chill it was!
The owl, for all his feathers, was a-cold;
The hare limped trembling through the frozen grass,
And silent was the flock in woolly fold:
Numb were the Beadsman's [3] fingers, while he told
His rosary, and while his frosted breath,
Like pious incense from a censer [4] old,

---

[1] For biography see page 720.
[2] Saint Agnes's Day is January 21; hence Saint Agnes's Eve falls on January 20.
[3] A beadsman was one who was paid to say prayers ("tell his beads") for others.
[4] A vessel to burn incense in.

Seemed taking flight for heaven, without a death,
Past the sweet Virgin's picture,[1] while his prayer he saith.

His prayer he saith, this patient, holy man;   10
Then takes his lamp, and riseth from his knees,
And back returneth, meagre, barefoot, wan,
Along the chapel aisle by slow degrees:
The sculptured dead, on each side, seem to freeze,
Emprisoned in black, purgatorial[2] rails[3]:
Knights, ladies, praying in dumb[4] orat'ries,[5]
He passeth by; and his weak spirit fails
To think how they may ache in icy hoods and mails.[6]

Northward he turneth through a little door,
And scarce three steps, ere Music's golden tongue   20
Flattered to tears this agèd man and poor;
But no — already had his deathbell rung:
The joys of all his life were said and sung:
His was harsh penance on St. Agnes' Eve:
Another way he went, and soon among
Rough ashes sat he for his soul's reprieve,
And all night kept awake, for sinners' sake to grieve.

That ancient Beadsman heard the prelude soft;
And so it chanced, for many a door was wide
From hurry to and fro. Soon, up aloft,
The silver, snarling trumpets 'gan to chide: 31
The level chambers, ready with their pride,

---

[1] The Beadsman was saying his prayers before the picture.   [2] Expiatory.   [3] Garments.
[4] Silent.   [5] Alcoves for prayer.
[6] *icy hoods and mails.* The cold stone hoods and suits of armor of the recumbent statues.

Were glowing to receive a thousand guests:
The carvèd angels, ever eager-eyed,
Stared, where upon their heads the cornice rests,
With hair blown back, and wings put crosswise on their breasts.

[Madeline and the legend of Saint Agnes's Eve.]

At length burst in the argent[1] revelry,
With plume, tiara, and all rich array,
Numerous as shadows haunting faerily
The brain, new stuffed, in youth, with triumphs gay   40
Of old romance. These let us wish away,
And turn, sole-thoughted, to one Lady there,
Whose heart had brooded, all that wintry day,
On love, and winged St. Agnes' saintly care,
As she had heard old dames full many times declare.

They told her how, upon St. Agnes' Eve,
Young virgins might have visions of delight,
And soft adorings from their loves receive
Upon the honeyed middle of the night,
If ceremonies due they did aright;   50
As, supperless to bed they must retire,
And couch supine their beauties, lily white;
Nor look behind, nor sideways, but require
Of Heaven with upward eyes for all that they desire.

Full of this whim was thoughtful Madeline:
The music, yearning like a God in pain,
She scarcely heard: her maiden eyes divine,
Fixed on the floor, saw many a sweeping train

Pass by — she heeded not at all: in vain
Came many a tiptoe, amorous cavalier,
And back retired; not cooled by high disdain,   61
But she saw not: her heart was otherwhere:
She sighed for Agnes' dreams, the sweetest of the year.

She danced along with vague, regardless eyes,
Anxious her lips, her breathing quick and short:
The hallowed hour was near at hand: she sighs
Amid the timbrels,[1] and the thronged resort
Of whisperers in anger, or in sport;
'Mid looks of love, defiance, hate, and scorn,
Hoodwinked with faery fancy; all amort,[2]   70
Save to St. Agnes and her lambs[3] unshorn,
And all the bliss to be before to-morrow morn.

[Porphyro, the lover, comes.]

So, purposing each moment to retire,
She lingered still. Meantime, across the moors,
Had come young Porphyro,[4] with heart on fire
For Madeline. Beside the portal doors,
Buttressed from moonlight, stands he, and implores
All saints to give him sight of Madeline,
But for one moment in the tedious hours,
That he might gaze and worship all unseen;   80
Perchance speak, kneel, touch, kiss — in sooth such things have been.

[1] Tambourines.
[2] Deadened, dazed.
[3] The symbol of Saint Agnes was a lamb. On her day two unshorn lambs were dedicated to her.
[4] *Porphyro* (pôr'fĭ rō).

[1] Here, gay and beautiful. Literally, made of silver.

He ventures in: let no buzzed whisper
    tell:
All eyes be muffled, or a hundred swords
Will storm his heart, Love's fev'rous
    citadel:
For him, those chambers held barbarian
    hordes,
Hyena foemen, and hot-blooded lords,
Whose very dogs would execrations[1]
    howl
Against his lineage[2]: not one breast af-
    fords
Him any mercy, in that mansion foul,
Save one old beldame, weak in body and
    in soul.   90

Ah, happy chance! the agèd creature
    came,
Shuffling along with ivory-headed wand,
To where he stood, hid from the torch's
    flame,
Behind a broad hall-pillar, far beyond
The sound of merriment and chorus
    bland:
He startled her; but soon she knew his
    face,
And grasped his fingers in her palsied
    hand,
Saying, "Mercy, Porphyro! hie thee
    from this place:
They are all here to-night, the whole
    bloodthirsty race!

Get hence! get hence! there's dwarfish
    Hildebrand;   100
He had a fever late, and in the fit
He cursèd thee and thine, both house and
    land:
Then there's that old Lord Maurice, not
    a whit
More tame for his gray hairs — Alas me!
    flit!
Flit like a ghost away." — "Ah, Gossip
    dear,
We're safe enough; here in this arm-
    chair sit

And tell me how" — "Good Saints! not
    here, not here;
Follow me, child, or else these stones will
    be thy bier."

He followed through a lowly archèd way,
Brushing the cobwebs with his lofty
    plume,   110
And as she muttered "Well-a — well-a-
    day!"
He found him in a little moonlight room,
Pale, latticed, chill, and silent as a tomb.
"Now tell me where is Madeline," said he,
"O tell me, Angela, by the holy loom
Which none but secret sisterhood may see,
When they St. Agnes' wool[1] are weaving
    piously."

"St. Agnes! Ah! it is St. Agnes' Eve —
Yet men will murder upon holy days:
Thou must hold water in a witch's sieve,[2]
And be liege-lord of all the Elves and
    Fays,   121
To venture so: it fills me with amaze
To see thee, Porphyro! — St. Agnes' Eve!
God's help! my lady fair the conjuror
    plays
This very night: good angels her de-
    ceive!
But let me laugh awhile, I've mickle[3]
    time to grieve."

Feebly she laugheth in the languid moon,
While Porphyro upon her face doth look,
Like puzzled urchin on an agèd crone
Who keepeth closed a wond'rous riddle-
    book,   130
As spectacled she sits in chimney nook.
But soon his eyes grew brilliant, when she
    told
His lady's purpose; and he scarce could
    brook[4]
Tears, at the thought of those enchant-
    ments cold,
And Madeline asleep in lap of legends old.

[1] Curses.
[2] Family, descent.

[1] *St. Agnes' wool.* Saint Agnes's wool was woven
    only by chosen nuns.
[2] *hold . . . sieve.* Hold water in a sifter, as witches
    were believed to have the power of doing.
[3] Much.   [4] Hold back.

[Porphyro's plan.]

Sudden a thought came like a full-blown
    rose,
Flushing his brow, and in his painèd heart
Made purple riot: then doth he propose
A stratagem, that makes the beldame
    start:
"A cruel man and impious thou art: 140
Sweet lady, let her pray, and sleep, and
    dream
Alone with her good angels, far apart
From wicked men like thee. Go, go! — I
    deem
Thou canst not surely be the same that
    thou didst seem."

"I will not harm her, by all saints I
    swear,"
Quoth Porphyro: "O may I ne'er find
    grace
When my weak voice shall whisper its
    last prayer,
If one of her soft ringlets I displace,
Or look with ruffian passion in her face:
Good Angela, believe me by these tears;
Or I will, even in a moment's space, 151
Awake, with horrid shout, my foemen's
    ears,
And beard them, though they be more
    fanged than wolves and bears."

"Ah! why wilt thou affright a feeble
    soul?
A poor, weak, palsy-stricken, churchyard
    thing,
Whose passing-bell[1] may ere the mid-
    night toll;
Whose prayers for thee, each morn and
    evening,
Were never missed." — Thus plaining,[2]
    doth she bring
A gentler speech from burning Porphyro;
So woeful, and of such deep sorrowing,
That Angela gives promise she will do
Whatever he shall wish, betide her weal
    or woe. 162
Which was, to lead him, in close secrecy,

    [1] A bell rung when one is dying.
    [2] Complaining.

Even to Madeline's chamber, and there
    hide
Him in a closet, of such privacy
That he might see her beauty unespied,
And win perhaps that night a peerless
    bride,
While legioned faeries paced the coverlet,
And pale enchantment held her sleepy-
    eyed.
Never on such a night have lovers met,
Since Merlin* paid his Demon all the
    monstrous debt.[1] 171

"It shall be as thou wishest," said the
    Dame:
"All cates[2] and dainties shall be storèd
    there
Quickly on this feast-night: by the tam-
    bour frame[3]
Her own lute thou wilt see: no time to
    spare,
For I am slow and feeble, and scarce dare
On such a catering trust my dizzy head.
Wait here, my child, with patience; kneel
    in prayer
The while: Ah! thou must needs the
    lady wed,
Or may I never leave my grave among
    the dead." 180

So saying, she hobbled off with busy fear.
The lover's endless minutes slowly
    passed;
The dame returned, and whispered in his
    ear
To follow her; with agèd eyes aghast
From fright of dim espial.[4] Safe at last,
Through many a dusky gallery, they gain
The maiden's chamber, silken, hushed,
    and chaste;

[1] *Merlin . . . debt.* Merlin was the son of a demon,
and according to one tradition finally disappeared in a violent storm by the magic of a
beautiful enchantress to whom he had taught
the spell which overcame him. In this way
he paid the "monstrous debt" he owed in
return for his supernatural gifts.
[2] Delicacies.
[3] *tambour frame.* A drum-shaped embroidery
frame.
[4] *dim espial.* Being seen in the dim light.

Where Porphyro took covert, pleased
amain.[1]
His poor guide hurried back with agues
in her brain.

[Madeline's retirement.]

Her falt'ring hand upon the balustrade,
Old Angela was feeling for the stair, 191
When Madeline, St. Agnes' charmèd
maid,
Rose, like a missioned[2] spirit, unaware:
With silver taper's light, and pious care,
She turned, and down the agèd gossip led
To a safe level matting. Now prepare,
Young Porphyro, for gazing on that bed;

She comes, she comes again, like ring-
dove frayed[3] and fled. 198
Out went the taper as she hurried in;
Its little smoke, in pallid moonshine, died:
She closed the door, she panted, all akin
To spirits of the air, and visions wide:
No uttered syllable, or, woe betide!
But to her heart, her heart was voluble,
Paining with eloquence her balmy side;
As though a tongueless nightingale[4]
should swell
Her throat in vain, and die, heart-stifled,
in her dell.

A casement high and triple-arched there
was,
All garlanded with carven imag'ries
Of fruits, and flowers, and bunches of
knot-grass, 210
And diamonded with panes of quaint
device,
Innumerable of stains and splendid dyes,
As are the tiger-moth's deep-damasked
wings;
And in the midst, 'mong thousand herald-
ries,
And twilight saints, and dim emblazon-
ings,
A shielded scutcheon blushed with blood
of queens and kings.

Full on this casement shone the wintry
moon,
And threw warm gules[1] on Madeline's
fair breast,
As down she knelt for heaven's grace and
boon;
Rose-bloom fell on her hands, together
prest, 220
And on her silver cross soft amethyst,
And on her hair a glory, like a saint:
She seemed a splendid angel, newly drest,
Save wings, for heaven:— Porphyro
grew faint:
She knelt, so pure a thing, so free from
mortal taint.

Anon his heart revives: her vespers done,
Of all its wreathèd pearls her hair she frees;
Unclasps her warmèd jewels one by one;
Loosens her fragrant bodice; by degrees
Her rich attire creeps rustling to her
knees: 230
Half-hidden, like a mermaid in sea-weed,
Pensive awhile she dreams awake, and
sees,
In fancy, fair St. Agnes in her bed,
But dares not look behind, or all the
charm is fled.

Soon, trembling in her soft and chilly
nest,
In sort of wakeful swoon, perplexed she
lay,
Until the poppied warmth of sleep oppressed
Her soothèd limbs, and soul fatigued
away;
Flown, like a thought, until the morrow-
day;
Blissfully havened both from joy and
pain; 240
Clasped[2] like a missal where swart Paynims pray;[3]

[1] Greatly.
[2] What was Madeline's special mission at this
time?
[3] Frightened. [4] See "Philomel."

[1] Red color (a term in heraldry).
[2] Closed as if with clasps.
[3] *a missal . . . pray.* A prayer book ("missal")
adorned with figures of black ("swart") pagans ("Paynims") at prayer. Missals with
such decorations were common in the Middle
Ages.

Blinded alike from sunshine and from
     rain,
As though a rose should shut, and be a
     bud again.

Stol'n to this paradise, and so entranced,
Porphyro gazed upon her empty dress,
And listened to her breathing, if it
     chanced
To wake into a slumberous tenderness;
Which when he heard, that minute did he
     bless,
And breathed himself: then from the
     closet crept   249
Noiseless as fear[1] in a wide wilderness,
And over the hushed carpet, silent, stept,
And 'tween the curtains peeped, where,
     lo! — how fast she slept.

[Madeline's vision.]

Then by the bed-side, where the faded
     moon
Made a dim, silver twilight, soft he set
A table, and, half anguished, threw
     thereon
A cloth of woven crimson, gold, and
     jet: —
O for some drowsy Morphean amulet![2]
The boisterous, midnight, festive clarion,
The kettle-drum, and far-heard clarinet,
Affray his ears, though but in dying
     tone: —   260
The hall door shuts again, and all the
     noise is gone.

And still she slept an azure-lidded sleep,
In blanchèd linen, smooth and laven-
     dered,
While he from forth the closet brought a
     heap
Of candied apple, quince, and plum, and
     gourd;
With jellies soother[3] than the creamy
     curd,
And lucent syrups, tinct[4] with cinnamon;
Manna and dates, in argosy[5] transferred

From Fez[1]; and spicèd dainties, every
     one,
From silken Samarcand[2] to cedared
     Lebanon.[3]   270

These delicates he heaped with glowing
     hand
On golden dishes and in basket bright
Of wreathèd silver: sumptuous they
     stand
In the retirèd quiet of the night,
Filling the chilly room with perfume
     light. —
"And now, my love, my seraph fair,
     awake!
Thou art my heaven, and I thine ere-
     mite[4]:
Open thine eyes, for meek St. Agnes' sake,
Or I shall drowse beside thee, so my soul
     doth ache."

Thus whispering, his arm, unnervèd arm
Sank in her pillow. Shaded was her
     dream   281
By the dusk curtains: — 'twas a mid-
     night charm
Impossible to melt as icèd stream:
The lustrous salvers[5] in the moonlight
     gleam;
Broad golden fringe upon the carpet lies:
It seemed he never, never could redeem
From such a stedfast spell his lady's eyes;
So mused awhile, entoiled in woofèd[6]
     phantasies.

Awakening up, he took her hollow lute,
Tumultuous, — and, in chords that ten-
     derest be,   290
He played an ancient ditty, long since
     mute,
In Provence called, "La belle dame sans
     merci,"[7]

[1] A city in northern Africa.
[2] A city in Turkestan.
[3] A mountain range in Syria noted for its beau-
     tiful cedars.   [4] Hermit.
[5] Trays.   [6] Here, woven.
[7] "La belle . . . merci." A love poem by Alain
     Chartier, a fifteenth-century French poet.
     The title was used by Keats for one of his
     best-known poems (p. 368).

[1] A person in fear.
[2] Morphean amulet. Sleep-producing charm. See
     "Morpheus."*   [3] Smoother.
[4] Delicately flavored.   [5] A large merchant vessel.

He played an ancient ditty, long since mute

Close to her ear touching the melody; —
Wherewith disturbed, she uttered a soft
  moan:
He ceased — she panted quick — and
  suddenly
Her blue affrayèd eyes wide open shone:
Upon his knees he sank, pale as smooth-
  sculptured stone.

Her eyes were open, but she still beheld
Now wide awake, the vision of her sleep:
There was a painful change, that nigh
  expelled   300
The blisses of her dream so pure and
  deep;
At which fair Madeline began to weep,
And moan forth witless words with
  many a sigh;
While still her gaze on Porphyro would
  keep;
Who knelt, with joinèd hands and piteous
  eye
Fearing to move or speak, she looked so
  dreamingly.

"Ah, Porphyro!" said she, "but even now
Thy voice was at sweet tremble in mine
  ear,
Made tuneable with every sweetest vow;
And those sad eyes were spiritual and
  clear: 310
How changed thou art! how pallid, chill,
  and drear!
Give me that voice again, my Porphyro,
Those looks immortal, those complain-
  ings dear!
Oh leave me not in this eternal woe,
For if thou diest, my Love, I know not
  where to go."

Beyond a mortal man impassioned far
At these voluptuous accents, he arose,
Ethereal, flushed, and like a throbbing
  star
Seen mid the sapphire heaven's deep
  repose;   319
Into her dream he melted, as the rose
Blendeth its odour with the violet, —
Solution sweet: meantime the frost-
  wind blows

Like Love's alarum pattering the sharp
  sleet
Against the window-panes; St. Agnes'
  moon hath set.

'Tis dark: quick pattereth the flaw-
  blown [1] sleet:
"This is no dream, my bride, my Madeline!"
'Tis dark: the icèd gusts still rave and
  beat:
"No dream, alas! alas! and woe is mine!
Porphyro will leave me here to fade and
  pine. —
Cruel! what traitor could thee hither
  bring?   330
I curse not, for my heart is lost in
  thine,
Though thou forsakest a deceivèd
  thing; —
A dove forlorn and lost with sick un-
  prunèd wing."

"My Madeline! sweet dreamer! lovely
  bride!
Say, may I be for aye thy vassal blest?
Thy beauty's shield, heart-shaped and
  vermeil [2] dyed?
Ah, silver shrine, here will I take my
  rest
After so many hours of toil and quest,
A famished pilgrim, — saved by miracle.
Though I have found, I will not rob thy
  nest   340
Saving of thy sweet self; if thou think'st
  well
To trust, fair Madeline, to no rude
  infidel.

"Hark! 'tis an elfin-storm from faery
  land,
Of haggard seeming,[3] but a boon indeed:
Arise — arise! the morning is at hand; —
The bloated wassaillers [4] will never
  heed: —

[1] Wind-blown.
[2] Vermilion.
[3] *haggard seeming.* Wild appearance.
[4] Revelers.

Let us away, my love, with happy speed;
There are no ears to hear, or eyes to
   see, —
Drowned all in Rhenish [1] and the sleepy
   mead [2]:
Awake! arise! my love, and fearless be,
For o'er the southern moors I have a
   home for thee."   351

[The lovers' escape.]

She hurried at his words, beset with
   fears,
For there were sleeping dragons [3] all
   around,
At glaring watch, perhaps, with ready
   spears —
Down the wide stairs a darkling way they
   found. —
In all the house was heard no human
   sound.
A chain-drooped lamp was flickering by
   each door;
The arras,[4] rich with horseman, hawk,
   and hound,
Fluttered in the besieging wind's uproar;
And the long carpets rose along the gusty
   floor.   360

They glide, like phantoms, into the wide
   hall;
Like phantoms, to the iron porch, they
   glide;
Where lay the Porter, in uneasy sprawl,
With a huge empty flagon by his side:
The wakeful bloodhound rose, and shook
   his hide,
But his sagacious eye an inmate owns:[5]
By one, and one, the bolts full easy
   slide: —
The chains lie silent on the footworn
   stones; —
The key turns, and the door upon its
   hinges groans.   369

[1] Wine from the vineyards along the river Rhine.
[2] A fermented drink made from honey.
[3] Dragoons, soldiers.
[4] Tapestry hung on the walls.
[5] *his . . . owns.* The intelligent watchdog recognizes Madeline and does not bark.

And they are gone: aye, ages long ago
These lovers fled away into the storm.
That night the Baron dreamt of many a
   woe,
And all his warrior-guests, with shade
   and form
Of witch, and demon, and large coffin-
   worm,
Were long be-nightmared. Angela the old
Died palsy-twitched, with meagre face
   deform;
The Beadsman, after thousand aves[1] told,
For aye unsought for slept among his
   ashes cold.

Discussion Hints

1. As you read the poem notice which of the five senses Keats appeals to most. Make a list under the headings "Sight," "Hearing," "Smell," "Taste," and "Feeling." Be prepared to report in class.

2. It is not easy to give the impression of intense cold. Keats gives four evidences that the Eve of St. Agnes was cold. What are they? What details would a newspaper reporter give in order to bring out the effects of an especially cold spell?

3. If you were dramatizing this poem, how many scenes would you have? Where would each be laid?

4. In the first four stanzas enumerate all the details that make clear where the scene is laid.

5. What do lines 20–21 mean?

6. Explain the meaning of the stanza beginning with line 82.

7. Compare the description in lines 208–216 with the description in lines 178–183 of Coleridge's "Christabel" (p. 399). Point out the rich beauty of detail as an example of romantic description.

8. What colors should you need to make a colored illustration for the three stanzas beginning with line 253?

9. Contrast the part played by the dog in "The Eve of St. Agnes" with the part played by the mastiff in lines 145–151 of Coleridge's "Christabel" (p. 398).

[1] The beads of a rosary which are counted ("told") as the aves (ā'vēz), or prayers to the Virgin Mary, are said.

10. Compare the porter (ll. 363–364) with the porter in *Macbeth*, II, iii, 1–28 (p. 106). In what respect are they alike?

11. Point out passages in which commonplace things are made to glow by the magic of Keats's treatment.

12. In what respect does the theme suggest the old ballads?

13. In what other poems in *English Writers* does a bold lover attract or win a lady?

14. In what stanza form is the poem written? What other poems earlier in the book are written in the same stanza form?

Words and Phrases to be Explained

for all his feathers (l. 2)
sculptured (l. 14)
tiara (l. 38)

supine (l. 52)
hallowed (l. 66)
sooth (l. 81)
Made purple riot (l. 138)
betide her weal or woe (l. 162)
diamonded with panes of quaint device (l. 211)
wakeful swoon (l. 236)
havened (l. 240)
lucent (l. 267)
entoiled in woofèd phantasies (l. 288)
witless (l. 303)

Suggestions for Reading

"Lamia"
"Isabella, or The Pot of Basil"
Endymion, Book I

THOMAS HOOD[1] (1799–1845)

Faithless Sally Brown

Hood was a friend of Lamb's,[2] and, like Lamb, was known as a punster. He is still remembered for his humorous verse, of which "Faithless Sally Brown" is a fair sample. If some of the puns seem stale, remember that they are at least a century old.

YOUNG Ben he was a nice young man,
  A carpenter by trade;
And he fell in love with Sally Brown,
  That was a lady's maid.

But as they fetch'd a walk one day,
  They met a press-gang crew[3];
And Sally she did faint away,
  Whilst Ben he was brought to.[4]

The Boatswain swore with wicked words,
  Enough to shock a saint,   10

That though she did seem in a fit,
  'Twas nothing but a feint.

"Come, girl," said he, "hold up your head,
  He'll be as good as me;
For when your swain is in our boat,
  A boatswain he will be."

So when they'd made their game of her,
  And taken off her elf,[1]
She roused, and found she only was
  A-coming to herself.   20

"And is he gone, and is he gone?"
  She cried, and wept outright:
"Then I will to the water side,
  And see him out of sight."

A waterman came up to her,
  "Now, young woman," said he,
"If you weep on so, you will make
  Eye-water in the sea."

[1] For biography see page 723.
[2] For biography see page 721.
[3] During a large part of the eighteenth century, sailors for the English navy were drafted by press gangs instead of being allowed to enlist voluntarily.
[4] *brought to.* A pun on the double meaning of *brought to,* whose nautical sense is "stopped."

[1] Here, companion, sweetheart.

"Alas! they've taken my beau Ben
   To sail with old Benbow[1];"   30
And her woe began to run afresh,
   As if she'd said Gee woe!

Says he, "They've only taken him
   To the Tender ship,[2] you see;"
"The Tender ship," cried Sally Brown,
   "What a hard-ship that must be!

"O! would I were a mermaid now,
   For then I'd follow him;
But Oh!— I'm not a fish-woman,
   And so I cannot swim.   40

"Alas! I was not born beneath
   The Virgin and the Scales,[3]
So I must curse my cruel stars,
   And walk about in Wales."

Now Ben had sail'd to many a place
   That's underneath the world;
But in two years the ship came home,
   And all her sails were furl'd.

But when he call'd on Sally Brown,
   To see how she got on,   50
He found she'd got another Ben,
   Whose Christian name was John.

[1] A famous English admiral of the seventeenth century.
[2] *Tender ship.* A ship where new recruits were kept until they were ready for service in the navy.
[3] *beneath . . . Scales.* Under auspicious circumstances. The Virgin and the Scales, or Balance, are signs of the zodiac.

"O Sally Brown, O Sally Brown,
   How could you serve me so?
I've met with many a breeze before,
   But never such a blow."

Then reading on his 'bacco-box,
   He heaved a bitter sigh,
And then began to eye his pipe,
   And then to pipe his eye.[1]   60

And then he tried to sing "All's Well,"
   But could not though he tried;
His head was turn'd, and so he chew'd
   His pigtail till he died.

His death, which happen'd in his berth,
   At forty-odd befell:
They went and told the sexton, and
   The sexton toll'd the bell.

Discussion Hints

1. "Faithless Sally Brown" is not a poem for study. One reads it, laughs, and reads it again to laugh some more.

2. Try to interpret the puns, but do not carry the study so far that you lose the joy of the mere reading.

3. Hood humorously called "Faithless Sally Brown" an "old ballad." In what respects does it resemble the popular ballads (p. 57)?

4. Some of Hood's humor results from the fact that certain words with different meanings are pronounced alike. Give illustrations from the poem.

5. The last two lines are the best-known in the poem. Have you ever heard them? Why might they be regarded as funny?

[1] *pipe his eye.* Weep.

1832-1892

❀

The
Victorian Period

Many an evening by the waters did we watch the stately ships (p. 466, l. 57)

THE Victorian Period covers roughly the years between the death of Scott in 1832 and the death of Tennyson in 1892. It is called Victorian to indicate that Queen Victoria, who came to the throne in 1837 and died in 1901, was the ruler of England during most of its extent.

HUMANITARIANISM

Many influences which had been at work during the Transition Period and the Romantic Period continued, though often in new ways, during the Victorian Period. In 1834 a sweeping reform in the English system of electing members of Parliament extended the franchise and placed hitherto unheard-of power in the hands of the voters. This movement was accompanied by an increase in popular education. More schools were established and more people read books than ever before. The interest of the romanticists in mankind ripened into modern social sympathy for the lowly and the oppressed. In 1833 Great Britain abolished slavery in her colonies. The next year pauperism was checked by a new Poor Law. People felt more responsibility for their neighbors' morals and welfare. As a result of this humanitarian, or philanthropic, attitude there came into existence a large number of organizations which made it their business to do their fellow mortals good by lightening their physical or their spiritual burdens. Thus modern social service began to be an active force in society. Laymen as well as clergymen were constantly trying to make evil appear repulsive, and virtue and goodness attractive. The new attitude of moral responsibility found expression in all sorts of writings. Many poems, dramas, and novels of the period draw some kind of "helpful" and "uplifting" moral or attack some sort of evil.

CAPITAL AND LABOR

As a result of the Industrial Revolution (p. 319), machines, such as the steam engine, completely transformed industry, and England was changed from an agricultural country into a manufacturing one. Many people abandoned farming and small businesses in order to work in factories. The manufacture of cotton goods, made out of raw material imported from America and other countries, became a major industry. Wealth increased by leaps and bounds. Large cities with crowded slums grew up. Poverty and discontent increased among the laboring classes. The conflict between capital and labor, or between riches and poverty, came to be a frequent cause of disturbance, and there were serious riots. Social protest of various kinds was expressed in English literature during the Victorian Period; for example, in Tennyson's "Locksley Hall" (p. 465) and in Elizabeth Barrett Browning's "Cry of the Children" (p. 487).

SCIENCE

The nineteenth century was also marked by a great advance in scientific investigation and theory. Gigantic strides were made in chemistry, physics, astronomy, and geology (p. 540). Invention flourished. The marvels accomplished by machinery, electricity, and the telegraph turned so many dreams into realities that human achievement through science seemed almost unlimited. During the Victorian Period scientific theories and discoveries influenced literature more profoundly than ever before.

CHANGE

The classicists had been generally satisfied with things as they are (p. 214); the Victorians, on the other hand, believed that the world and its inhabitants are constantly changing and progressing. Impressed by the idea of change in the universe, Tennyson[1] wrote

> This world was once a fluid haze of light
> Till toward the centre set the starry tides
> And eddied into suns, that wheeling cast
> The planets.

So too in the portrayal of human character, writers began to feel that human beings cannot pass through the world without changing for better or for worse as the result of environment or of love, hate, joy, sorrow, and other experiences. It became the fashion for writers of fiction to make the personages they created gradually improve as the result of courage and self-sacrifice, or grow worse because of selfishness and sin. To George Eliot (p. 434) and other writers human character was the outcome of a moral struggle between a person's will to do good and the temptation to do evil. Other writers, however, were fatalists, who believed that human will power had little or no effect in changing human character. To them, changes in human character result, not from personal effort, but from constant and irresistible outward forces. They believed that the individual is powerless to alter his life or change his fate. Hence, though much Victorian literature is optimistic in tone, the later literature of the period frequently expresses pessimism at mankind's supposed helplessness in his struggle against fate, environment, or heredity. Matthew Arnold,

[1] For biography see page 726.

instead of being soothed and cheered, as Wordsworth would have been, by the beauty of a moonlight night, was filled with sadness (p. 496); Swinburne (p. 499) thanked "whatever gods may be" for the "eternal" sleep of death; and Thomas Hardy,[1] both in his novels and in his poetry, looked upon mankind as the victim of cruel and irresistible laws of nature.

Among those who sought to escape from the modern world, with its machinery and its lack of idealism, was a group of artists and social theorists, including Rossetti [2] and Morris,[3] who loved the Middle Ages and who wished to revive in painting and in literature the simplicity of early Italian art before the time of Raphael. They are called Pre-Raphaelites.* Others still, of whom Cardinal Newman [4] was the greatest, tried to restore to religion the mysticism and charm which they saw in the life of the Middle Ages.

EMPHASIS UPON LAW AND ORDER

As the Victorian Period advanced, many English people began to feel that the tendency of the Romantic Period toward unlimited self-expression might result in excess and anarchy. Hence a reaction set in. The English, always conservative at heart, began to feel the importance of law, order, and self-control. People became convinced that it was undesirable, even indecent, to give completely free rein to all our desires. Patience, unselfishness, and self-restraint came to be highly praised virtues in society, morals, and religion. Of all the Victorian poets, Tennyson was perhaps most strongly impressed with the importance of law and moderation. We get an excellent idea of the difference between the young poet filled with romantic enthusiasm and the older, more conservative man in his two poems entitled "Locksley Hall" (p. 465) and "Locksley Hall Sixty Years After." In the former Tennyson portrays a high-minded and impatient youth who complains of social injustice, and sees visions of rapid change and almost limitless human progress, till even war shall cease and all men live happily as in a great "federation of the world"; in the latter, written more than forty years later, the poet, speaking through the same character, now an old man, feels that improvement will come, not from unlimited self-expression and violent revolution, but from self-control and gradual "change" through the slow operation of law and order. He is convinced that there must be many disappointing delays before wisdom and science can make the world perfect:

Forward then, but still remember, how the course of Time will swerve,
Crook and turn upon itself in many a backward streaming curve.

[1] For biography see page 741.   [2] For biography see page 733.
[3] For biography see page 734.   [4] For biography see page 732.

Contrasted with the freedom of literature and of life today the social and moral standards of the Victorian Period often seem unduly conventional. Yet, unlike many modern idealists, the later Victorians did not hope for too speedy perfection, and hence were not so disappointed as many of us are when things do not turn out exactly as we expect.

POETRY

In spite of limitations and restraints Victorian writers treated artistically many phases of life, and produced many kinds of literature, some of them new, some of them developments and expansions of older forms. Essays (p. 508), biographical writings, and novels (p. 436) especially increased in number and improved in quality. Among the most important new literary forms were the "dramatic monologue" (p. 502) and the short story (p. 547), the latter continuing to develop after the close of the period. Along with older verse forms, such as blank* verse, the heroic* couplet, the sonnet,* and the ode,* an unusually large number of new verse forms and metrical devices were used.

The Victorian Period produced two of our most famous English poets, Tennyson[1] and Browning,[2] as well as a host of lesser writers who found poetic material in a greater variety of subjects than any of their predecessors had done. Poets not only wrote of nature and the past, two stock themes of the romanticists, but succeeded in getting inspiration even out of science, astronomy, evolution, and poverty, low wages, and other problems of capital and labor. Tennyson was particularly fond of introducing into his poetry references to scientific discoveries and other matters interesting to the people of his day. Though some later Victorian writers were pessimistic regarding society, most of the greater writers leave us, as Browning does, with a larger sympathy for our fellow man and a stronger hope for the future.

Toward the close of the period English poetry showed a tendency to degenerate into mere prettiness. Many poets wrote delicate, charming verse, and Swinburne has left a few poems of almost incredible sweetness and beauty, but in general the poetry of the late Victorian Period is imitative rather than original and hence lacks vitality. The signs already pointed toward the need of new sources of strength and inspiration. Because of its supposedly light and frivolous tone the decade from 1890 to 1900 has been called the Gay Nineties.

[1] For biography see page 726.   [2] For biography see page 727.

PROSE

Although poetry showed a tendency to decline during the late Victorian Period, prose advanced steadily. There was a great improvement in the quality and a marked increase in the variety and extent of prose-writing, especially of imaginative prose. Much of the prose of the Victorian Period is picturesque and stimulating. Macaulay (p. 513) wrote in a clear, carefully balanced style that has exercised a tremendous influence upon later writers. An excellent example of Victorian prose at its best is furnished by the vivid, picturesque writing of Cardinal Newman (p. 508) and Robert Louis Stevenson (pp. 509 and 549). In general the prose of the Victorian Period resembles the simple, direct language of everyday speech more than the literary language of the past.

THE ESSAY

One of the forms of prose literature that flourished especially during the Victorian Period was the essay. The familiar essay broadened in scope, and the formal essay was often used to explain scientific theories or discoveries to the general public, as in the case of the famous lecturer and writer Huxley (p. 540). The essays of Cardinal Newman (p. 508) are noted for their cultivated tone and their clear, polished style, and both in style and in content Stevenson's essays (p. 509) occupy a unique position among English familiar essays.

Correlation of English Literature with Historical Events during the Victorian Period

HISTORICAL EVENTS		*LITERARY LANDMARKS*
	1800	MACAULAY *born. Died 1859*
	1801	NEWMAN *born. Died 1890*
	1806	ELIZABETH BARRETT BROWNING *born. Died 1861*
	1809	TENNYSON *born. Died 1892*
	1811	THACKERAY *born. Died 1863*
	1812	BROWNING *born. Died 1889*
		DICKENS *born. Died 1870*
	1819	GEORGE ELIOT *born. Died 1880*
	1822	ARNOLD *born. Died 1888*
	1825	HUXLEY *born. Died 1895*
	1828	MEREDITH *born. Died 1909*
		ROSSETTI *born. Died 1882*
	1832	*Death of* SCOTT
Abolition of SLAVERY	1833	
SYSTEM *of* NATIONAL EDUCATION *begun; pauperism reduced by new* POOR LAW	1834	MORRIS *born. Died 1896*
	1836	DICKENS, Pickwick Papers
Reign of VICTORIA 1837–1901	1837	SWINBURNE *born. Died 1909*
Establishment of PENNY POSTAGE	1840	HARDY *born. Died 1928*
First ELECTRIC TELEGRAPH	1843	
	1847	THACKERAY, Vanity Fair
		ELIZABETH BARRETT BROWNING, Sonnets from the Portuguese
	1848	MACAULAY, History of England, Volumes I and II
	1849	DICKENS, David Copperfield
	1850	STEVENSON *born. Died 1894*
		TENNYSON, In Memoriam *and poet laureate*
	1852	THACKERAY, Henry Esmond
CRIMEAN* WAR 1854–1856		
Battle of BALAKLAVA 1854		
Rebellion in INDIA 1857–1859		
	1859	TENNYSON, Idylls of the King (first series)
		GEORGE ELIOT, Adam Bede
		DICKENS, A Tale of Two Cities
	1860	GEORGE ELIOT, The Mill on the Floss
War Between the States in the UNITED STATES 1861–1865		
	1861	GEORGE ELIOT, Silas Marner
	1863	*Death of* THACKERAY
Assassination of PRESIDENT LINCOLN	1865	KIPLING *born. Died 1936*
		YEATS *born. Died 1939*
First TRANSATLANTIC CABLE *laid*	1866	

War between FRANCE *and* GERMANY	1870	
First public TELEPHONE	1875	
	1878	HARDY, The Return of the Native
		MASEFIELD *born*
	1881	CARLYLE *died. Born 1795*
	1883	STEVENSON, Treasure Island
	1885	MEREDITH, Diana of the Crossways
	1886	STEVENSON, Kidnapped
	1891	HARDY, Tess of the D'Urbervilles
QUEEN VICTORIA, *Diamond Jubilee*	1897	KIPLING, Recessional
Death of VICTORIA	1901	

The Victorian Period also includes the work of Arthur Hugh Clough (1819–1861), Charles Kingsley (1819–1875), and Christina Rossetti (1830–1894). Note that the Romantic and Victorian periods overlap.

THE VICTORIAN PERIOD IN SONG AND STORY

POETRY

HARTE, BRET. "Dickens in Camp" (in the revised edition of *Achievement* of this series).

KIPLING, RUDYARD. "The Explorer" (in the revised edition of *Adventure* of this series), "The Liner She's a Lady," "A Song of the English," "England's Answer," "The Native-Born," "The White Man's Burden," and "Tommy." (All are given in *Verse: Inclusive Edition, 1885–1932*.) Doubleday, Doran & Company, Inc.

LANDOR, WALTER SAVAGE. "To Robert Browning."

NEWBOLT, SIR HENRY. "The Little Admiral," "Ode for Trafalgar Day, 1905," and "Victoria Regina." (All are given in *Poems: New and Old*.) John Murray.

VAN DYKE, HENRY. "Robert Browning" and "Tennyson, in Lucem Transitus, October, 1892." (In *Works*, Vol. X.) Charles Scribner's Sons.

WHITTIER, JOHN GREENLEAF. "The Pipes of Lucknow."

PROSE

BARRIE, JAMES M. "R.L.S." (Robert Louis Stevenson). (In the revised edition of *Adventure* of this series.)

GALSWORTHY, JOHN. *The Man of Property* and *In Chancery*. Charles Scribner's Sons.

KIPLING, RUDYARD. *Stalky & Co.* Doubleday, Doran & Company, Inc.

LUCAS, FRANK LAURENCE. *Eight Victorian Poets*. The Macmillan Company. (Popular radio talks.)

STRACHEY, G. LYTTON. *Queen Victoria.* Harcourt, Brace and Company, Inc.

WOOLF, VIRGINIA. *Flush.* (A biography of Elizabeth Barrett Browning's cocker spaniel.) Harcourt, Brace and Company, Inc.

THE NOVEL[1]

THE novel, as contrasted with other forms of narrative literature, developed relatively late. In English literature it appeared first during the Age of Classicism (p. 219) in answer to the demands of the common people, who wished for stories better suited to their tastes than the old romances (pp. 32 and 166) were. The modern novel may be defined as a long connected narrative that depends for its appeal not so much upon thrilling plot or romantic setting as upon characters taken from real life.

Between 1700 and 1725, Daniel Defoe, a political writer who knew how to make fiction read like fact, wrote *Robinson Crusoe* (1719) (p. 265) and other long narratives which depicted realistically the lives of characters drawn from the lower classes. Defoe was followed by Samuel Richardson, a commonplace London printer with a gift for making narratives of contemporary life convincing. Richardson's *Pamela* (1740), the story of a virtuous, prudent, and fortunate servant girl, has been called the first real English novel. *Clarissa Harlowe*, generally regarded as his masterpiece, depicts for lowly readers the tragic career of a heroine of the upper classes. Richardson makes his novels more convincing by presenting them in the form of intimate letters supposed to be exchanged between the characters and written in a very sentimental style popular at the time.

As a reaction against the sentimentalism and overdone morality of Richardson's novels, Henry Fielding, a broad-minded gentleman who knew all classes of society well, wrote a number of novels in which he gave a frank and honest portrayal of English life, both high and low, as it existed in his day. His *Joseph Andrews* (1742), begun as a burlesque on Richardson's *Pamela*, is one of the most effective early English novels. *Tom Jones*, often regarded as his masterpiece, makes the hero far more human and convincing than are Richardson's chief characters.

The next important writer of English fiction, Laurence Sterne, appeared during the Transition Period (p. 293). His *Tristram Shandy* (1759) is famous for its broken sentences and other queer devices of style, its whimsical characters based on real life, and its tendency to become sentimental over matters that are unworthy of deep emotion. During the Transition Period there also appeared many novels intended to illustrate various social habits and customs of the day and known as novels of manners. Here too belong the earliest of the so-called Gothic romances,

[1] For an account of the development of the novel in America, see the revised edition of *American Writers* of this series.

romantic narratives which portrayed sentimental characters against such medieval settings as haunted castles, moldering dungeons, and crumbling ruins.

During the Romantic Period (p. 318) English novels increased greatly both in number and in variety of treatment. Sir Walter Scott [1] adopted some of the popular features of the Gothic romances and, combining them with more convincing characters and with romantic descriptions of natural scenery, produced a series of novels which may be regarded as the crowning achievement of the period. His *Waverley* (1814) and others of his historical novels, especially those that deal with the Middle Ages, became enormously popular and were widely imitated not only in England but also on the Continent and in America. Though Scott is best known for his romantic plots and settings, he was also successful in depicting Scottish peasants and in introducing touches of local color.

Especially important among Scott's contemporaries was Jane Austen, whose novels, published between 1811 and 1818, portray with painstaking and convincing realism middle-class English life in small communities, which she knew well from personal experience. In the simple, unadorned language of everyday life she satirizes with gentle humor the society life of small English towns and the supersentimentalism 'and unreality of the popular fiction of her youth. She is regarded as one of the greatest writers of English realistic* fiction.

Though the writing of romantic novels by no means ceased with the close of the Romantic Period, the most marked trait of English fiction since the beginning of the Victorian Period has been the increase in realism as opposed to romanticism. Charles Dickens published a long series of novels with many characters and elaborate plots. In accordance with the general movement toward social reform which characterized the nineteenth century, he used the novel as a social force directed against unjust laws, the school system, and other institutions that seemed to need reform. He defended the poor and the lowly against injustices which he attributed to the rich and the proud. His portrayal of human life and character is clear, simple, and realistic. Dickens's novels combine pathos, sentimentalism, and humor more successfully than had ever been done before. Among his best-known works are *The Pickwick Papers* (1836), a loosely connected series of sketches of English middle-class and lower-class life; and *David Copperfield* (1849) (p. 436), a biographical novel which includes a touching picture of life among the lowly and of the sorrows of childhood amid the poverty and misery of the London slums. In what is probably his most generally popular work, *A Tale of Two Cities* [2] (1859), he portrays against a realistic background the miseries of the French lower classes that led to the horror of the French Revolution. Humanitarian novels

[1] For biography see page 722.   [2] In the revised edition of *Achievement* of this series.

D

more or less like those of Dickens continued to be written until by the end of the nineteenth century almost every sort of social abuse had been attacked in fiction.

Along with Dickens ranks another great realistic novelist of the Victorian Period, William Makepeace Thackeray. Thackeray's novels, unlike those of Dickens, are not sentimental and have no special humanitarian purpose. They are, however, striking pictures of English society, with its struggle between goodness and vice, its sham sentiment, and its hypocrisy. Against the background of the Napoleonic Wars, Thackeray in *Vanity Fair* (1847) represents the English people at home as frittering away their lives for things of no value, like the citizens of Bunyan's Vanity * Fair. Perhaps his best work is *Henry Esmond* (1852) (p. 447), a historical novel in which the author succeeds in making the people of the eighteenth century live again so that we feel ourselves transported back to the days of Addison and Steele. Unlike the historical novels of Scott, Thackeray's historical novels treat war, not as a gorgeous and romantic spectacle, but as a background for the commonplace and often sordid life of the English people who stayed at home while their sons, husbands, and brothers died on the field of battle; that is, Thackeray combines the historical novel with a realistic portrayal of life. His view of war has been intensified by many later writers.

Another great novelist who introduced a new element into English fiction during the Victorian Period was Mary Ann Evans, who wrote under the pen name of "George Eliot." George Eliot portrayed with infinite care the life of small English communities which she knew well; but she was not content to describe only what she saw with her eyes: she tried to get at the inner forces by which her characters were controlled. She sought to discover the psychological forces that make character. Like Dickens, she was a realist with a purpose; but her purpose was, not to reveal some evil of the social system around her, but to emphasize the importance of duty and of the great part that individual character plays in human life. From the lives of many of her characters we may draw the lesson that we should do right, however painful it may be, because by so doing we develop our own personalities and help our fellow men. Among George Eliot's best-known works are *Adam Bede* (1859), *The Mill on the Floss* (1860), and *Silas Marner* (1861).

George Meredith,[1] who also wrote during the Victorian Period, was both a poet (p. 505) and a novelist. He possessed a rich and powerful imagination and great originality. He wrote more than a dozen novels. Like George Eliot, he was a psychological realist; that is, he went behind the outward actions of his characters to get at their hidden motives, but his analysis is more profound and his style more subtle than those of George

[1] For biography see page 731.

Eliot. In his *Diana of the Crossways* (1885) he portrayed for the first time in English fiction a healthy, athletic woman of independent spirit in contrast to the old-fashioned delicate, sentimental heroine.

Thomas Hardy[1] began his work as a novelist a generation before the close of the Victorian Period, and he lived long enough to feel the full effect of the intensely realistic forces at work during the Recent and Contemporary Period (p. 567). Though he wrote poetry and short stories of great merit, he is best known as a novelist. Among his best novels are *Far from the Madding Crowd* (1874), *The Return of the Native* (1878), and *Tess of the D'Urbervilles* (1891). In general his work reflects the pessimism and doubt that found expression in much late Victorian and more recent literature. He treats of such matters as sex, love, and general morality with a greater frankness than earlier novelists, and he leaves us with a feeling that human beings are the victims of environment or of a cruel and relentless fate. He knew well and described realistically the Wessex country of England, where most of his scenes are laid. Although his plots are not always well worked out and his view of human character is gloomy, his most popular prose writings are completely modern in their tone and rank among the greatest in English realistic fiction.

During the late nineteenth and the early twentieth century many readers, weary of the moral restraints of Victorian life, craved literature in which they could lose themselves and so escape from the conventional and commonplace world around them and from the growing commercialism which, they feared, might stifle romance. Such readers hailed with delight the writings of Robert Louis Stevenson.[2] Stevenson wrote delightful essays (p. 509), short stories (p. 549), and novels as well as poems (pp. 499 and 537). Like Scott, he wrote romantic novels of adventure; but though he used threadbare themes of romantic storytelling, such as fighting, pirates, and buried treasure, he made them fresh and fascinating. Stevenson was too great an artist to depend entirely upon romantic adventures for his effects. He made his characters real human beings, not the conventional good men and bad men, heroes and villains, of most other romantic fiction; that is, in his work we have romantic plots and romantic settings accurately described, but the characters are realistic. His writings are also important for their polished but simple style. Noteworthy among his novels is *Kidnapped* (1886), a fascinating story of adventure by land and sea; but his masterpiece is *Treasure Island*.[3]

In spite of the return to romanticism in Stevenson's work, most writers of recent fiction have tried to tell the whole truth about human life and behavior. They have usually portrayed life with a greater regard for accuracy than Dickens and other writers of the Romantic and Victorian periods.

[1] For biography see page 741.   [2] For biography see page 730.
[3] In the revised edition of *Adventure* of this series.

In other words, the general tendency of recent and contemporary English novels, as well as short stories (p. 547), is toward greater realism. Many English novels of today reveal new effects in plot or in setting; but the most important difference between the new fiction and the old is caused by the attempt of the authors to discover the profound and often complicated forces that determine human character and explain human action. Authors are no longer content to offer love, hate, jealousy, selfishness, and other apparently simple emotions as completely satisfactory explanations of human behavior. They regard these as merely the superficial evidences of forces that lie much deeper in the human mind. In their tireless efforts to get to the very bottom of human character they examine the world about them with the uncompromising eye of the scientist. Some modern novelists derive from anthropology the theory that man is essentially a primitive being covered with a thin veneer of culture; others make much of recent investigations in the influence of environment in forming human character; still others utilize the methods of psychoanalysis in explaining the conflicting emotions and actions of their characters. Recent realistic fiction, especially novels and short stories composed under the influence of the disillusionment that swept over society after the World War (1914–1918), often leaves us with a pessimistic or even hopeless impression of human life. Fortunately, however, not all contemporary novelists carry realism to such discouraging lengths. There are numerous English novelists of today who, like Galsworthy,[1] seek to avoid extremes and so to present life without either sentimentalism or bitterness. Barrie,[2] in his best works, combines Victorian sentimentalism with just enough modern realism to make the whole irresistibly appealing. Eric Knight's *This above All* is one of the most touching novels so far to come out of World War II.

CHARLES DICKENS[3] (1812–1870)

From *David Copperfield*

You will read with greater interest the selection from *David Copperfield* given here when you learn that Dickens is often said to be the most widely read writer of fiction in the English language, and that *David Copperfield* is his masterpiece. The selection illustrates Dickens at his best. (1) It is based on the author's own experiences. As a boy Dickens knew the sordid life of the London warehouses, streets, and pawnshops, and as a newspaper reporter he knew the dangers of the English roads in the neighborhood of London. (2) It exemplifies Dickens's seemingly simple but actually difficult method of

---

[1] For biography see page 745.   [2] For biography see page 747.   [3] For biography see page 724.

making his characters seem real and individual by emphasizing, even exaggerating, some habit of speech, some gesture, or some other trait until it is so impressed upon the reader as to be unforgettable. We remember Mr. Micawber because he is an optimistic gentleman who is always expecting "something to turn up," and Miss Trotwood as an elderly lady who, though really benevolent, is outwardly brusque and has a hatred of donkeys. (3) It exemplifies Dickens's gift for presenting the life and emotions of children. (4) Even so serious a narrative as *David Copperfield* exemplifies Dickens's famous gift as a humorist. From beginning to end our selection is marked by illustrations of the author's rich, characteristic humor.

[The story is told in the first person by the hero, David Copperfield. He was born after his father's death in Blunderstone, a village in the east of England. His father's aunt, Miss Betsey Trotwood, who was present at David's birth, regarded his mother as a mere "wax doll," was offended with his father for marrying her, and was disappointed that David was not a girl. As a child David went to visit the family of "Peggotty," his nurse, who lived in an old boat at Yarmouth, on the east coast. Here he met "little Em'ly," of whom he became very fond. While David was a small boy his mother married a handsome but domineering and cruel man named Murdstone, whose gloomy, ill-natured sister became a member of the household. The Murdstones made Mrs. Copperfield unhappy, abused David, and when he rebelled sent him to a boarding school, where he was ill treated and badly taught. Here he became the friend of the handsome rake Steerforth. His mother died of a broken heart and he was placed by Mr. Murdstone in a London warehouse, where, during long hours, he was forced to wash and label wine bottles under humiliating conditions. During this period he boarded with the poverty-stricken Micawber family, whose misery he shared without approving of their incurable optimism. When the Micawbers decided to leave London, he abandoned the warehouse, and after being robbed of his small supply of cash, set out in despair on foot in search of Miss Betsey Trotwood, who, he had heard, lived somewhere near Dover, on the southeast coast, and who, he feared, might not welcome him. On the way he slept in out-of-the-way places and lived miserably. He finally arrived at Dover.]

FROM CHAPTER XIII

The Sequel of My Resolution

I INQUIRED about my aunt among the boatmen first, and received various answers. The shopkeepers, not liking my appearance, generally replied, without hearing what I had to say, that they had got nothing for me. I felt more miserable and destitute than I had done at any period of my running away. My money was all gone, I had nothing left to dispose of; I was hungry, thirsty, and 10 worn out; and seemed as distant from the end as if I had remained in London.

The morning had worn away in these inquiries, and I was sitting on the step of an empty shop at a street corner, near the market-place, deliberating upon wandering towards those other places which had been mentioned, when a fly[1]-driver, coming by with his carriage, dropped a horse cloth. Something good- 20 natured in the man's face, as I handed it up, encouraged me to ask him if he could tell me where Miss Trotwood lived; though I had asked the question so often, that it almost died upon my lips.

"Trotwood," said he. "Let me see. I know the name, too. Old lady?"

"Yes," I said, "rather."

"Pretty stiff in the back?" said he, making himself upright. 30

"Yes," I said, "I should think it very likely."

"Carries a bag?" said he, "bag with a good deal of room in it; is gruffish, and comes down upon you sharp?"

My heart sank within me as I acknowledged the undoubted accuracy of this description.

"Why then, I tell you what," said he. "If you go up there," pointing with his 40 whip towards the heights, "and keep right on till you come to some houses facing the sea, I think you'll hear of her. My opinion is, she won't stand anything, so here's a penny for you."

[1] *fly.* A fly is a light carriage.

I accepted the gift thankfully, and bought a loaf with it. Despatching this refreshment by the way, I went in the direction my friend had indicated, and walked on a good distance without coming to the houses he had mentioned. At length I saw some before me; and approaching them, went into a little shop, and inquired if they would have the goodness to tell me where Miss Trotwood lived. I addressed myself to a man behind the counter, who was weighing some rice for a young woman; but the latter, taking the inquiry to herself, turned around quickly.

"My mistress?" she said. "What do you want with her, boy?"

"I want," I replied, "to speak to her, if you please."

"To beg of her, you mean," retorted the damsel.

"No," I said, "indeed." But suddenly remembering that in truth I came for no other purpose, I held my peace in confusion, and felt my face burn.

My aunt's handmaid, as I supposed she was from what she had said, put her rice in a little basket and walked out of the shop, telling me that I could follow her, if I wanted to know where Miss Trotwood lived. I needed no second permission; though I was by this time in such a state of consternation and agitation, that my legs shook under me. I followed the young woman, and we soon came to a very neat little cottage with cheerful bow-windows; in front of it, a small square gravelled court or garden full of flowers, carefully tended, and smelling deliciously.

"This is Miss Trotwood's," said the young woman. "Now you know, and that's all I have got to say." With which words, she hurried into the house, as if to shake off the responsibility of my appearance; and left me standing at the garden-gate, looking disconsolately over the top of it towards the parlour-window, where a muslin curtain partly undrawn in the middle, a large round green screen or fan fastened on to the window-sill, a small table, and a great chair, suggested to me that my aunt might be at that moment seated in awful[1] state.

The unbroken stillness of the parlour-window leading me to infer, after a while, that she was not there, I lifted up my eyes to the window above it, where I saw a florid, pleasant-looking gentleman, with a grey head, who shut up one eye in a grotesque manner, nodded his head at me several times, shook it at me as often, laughed, and went away.

I had been discomposed enough before; but I was so much the more discomposed by this unexpected behaviour, that I was on the point of slinking off, to think how I had best proceed, when there came out of the house a lady with her handkerchief tied over her cap, and a pair of gardening gloves on her hands, wearing a gardener's pocket like a tollman's apron,[2] and carrying a great knife. I knew her immediately to be Miss Betsey, for she came stalking out of the house exactly as my poor mother had so often described her stalking up our garden at Blunderstone Rookery.

"Go away!" said Miss Betsey, shaking her head, and making a distant chop in the air with her knife. "Go along! No boys here!"

I watched her, with my heart at my lips, as she marched to a corner of her garden, and stooped to dig up some little root there. Then, without a scrap of courage, but with a great deal of desperation, I went softly in and stood beside her, touching her with my finger.

"If you please, ma'am," I began.

She started and looked up.

"If you please, aunt."

"Eh?" exclaimed Miss Betsey, in a

[1] Inspiring awe or respect.

[2] *tollman's apron.* An apron with a pocket, worn by tollmen, employees appointed to collect tolls (fees) from travelers along the highways.

tone of amazement I have never heard
140 approached.

"If you please, aunt, I am your nephew."

"Oh, Lord!" said my aunt. And sat flat down in the garden-path.

"I am David Copperfield, of Blunderstone, in Suffolk, where you came on the night I was born, and saw my dear mama. I have been very unhappy since she died. I have been slighted, and
150 taught nothing, and thrown upon myself, and put to work not fit for me. It made me run away to you. I was robbed at first setting out, and have walked all the way, and have never slept in a bed since I began the journey." Here my self-support gave way all at once; and with a movement of my hands, intended to show her my ragged state, and call it to witness that I had suffered something, I
160 broke into a passion of crying, which I suppose had been pent up within me all the week.

My aunt, with every sort of expression but wonder discharged from her countenance, sat on the gravel, staring at me, until I began to cry; when she got up in a great hurry, collared me, and took me into the parlour. Her first proceeding there was to unlock a tall press, bring
170 out several bottles, and pour some of the contents of each into my mouth. I think they must have been taken out at random, for I am sure I tasted aniseed water, anchovy sauce, and salad dressing. When she had administered these restoratives, as I was still quite hysterical, and unable to control my sobs, she put me on the sofa, with a shawl under my head, and the handkerchief from her own head
180 under my feet, lest I should sully the cover; and then, sitting herself down behind the green fan or screen I have already mentioned, so that I could not see her face, ejaculated at intervals, "Mercy on us!" letting these exclamations off like minute guns.

After a time she rang the bell.

"Janet," said my aunt, when her servant came in. "Go upstairs, give my compliments to Mr. Dick, and say I wish to 190 speak to him."

Janet looked a little surprised to see me lying stiffly on the sofa (I was afraid to move lest it should be displeasing to my aunt), but went on her errand. My aunt, with her hands behind her, walked up and down the room, until the gentleman who had squinted at me from the upper window came in laughing.

"Mr. Dick," said my aunt, "you have 200 heard me mention David Copperfield? Now don't pretend not to have a memory, because you and I know better."

"David Copperfield?" said Mr. Dick, who did not appear to me to remember much about it. "*David* Copperfield? Oh yes, to be sure. David, certainly."

"Well," said my aunt, "this is his boy, his son. He would be as like his father as it's possible to be, if he was not so 210 much like his mother, too."

"His son?" said Mr. Dick. "David's son, indeed!"

"Yes," pursued my aunt, "and he has done a pretty piece of business. He has run away. Now, here you see young David Copperfield, and the question I put to you is, what shall I do with him?"

"What shall you do with him?" said 220 Mr. Dick, feebly, scratching his head. "Oh! do with him?"

"Yes," said my aunt, with a grave look, and her forefinger held up. "Come! I want some very sound advice."

"Why, if I was you," said Mr. Dick, considering, and looking vacantly at me, "I should —" The contemplation of me seemed to inspire him with a sudden idea, and he added, briskly, "I should 230 wash him!"

"Janet," said my aunt, turning around with a quiet triumph, which I did not then understand, "Mr. Dick sets us all right. Heat the bath!"

Janet had gone away to get the bath

ready, when my aunt, to my great alarm, became in one moment rigid with indignation, and had hardly voice to cry out, "Janet! Donkeys![1]"

Upon which, Janet came running up the stairs as if the house were in flames, darted out on a little piece of green in front, and warned off two saddle-donkeys, lady-ridden, that had presumed to set hoof upon it; while my aunt, rushing out of the house, seized the bridle of a third animal laden with a bestriding child, turned him, led him forth from those sacred precincts, and boxed the ears of the unlucky urchin in attendance who had dared to profane that hallowed ground.

To this hour I don't know whether my aunt had any lawful right of way over that patch of green; but she had settled it in her own mind that she had, and it was all the same to her. The one great outrage of her life, demanding to be constantly avenged, was the passage of a donkey over that immaculate spot. In whatever occupation she was engaged, however interesting to her the conversation in which she was taking part, a donkey turned the current of her ideas in a moment, and she was upon him straight. Jugs of water, and watering-pots, were kept in secret places ready to be discharged on the offending boys; sticks were laid in ambush behind the door; sallies were made at all hours; and incessant war prevailed. Perhaps this was an agreeable excitement to the donkey-boys; or perhaps the more sagacious of the donkeys, understanding how the case stood, delighted with constitutional obstinacy in coming that way. I only know that there were three alarms before the bath was ready; and that on the occasion of the last and most desperate of all, I saw my aunt engage, single-handed, with a sandy-headed lad

of fifteen, and bump his sandy head against her own gate, before he seemed to comprehend what was the matter. These interruptions were the more ridiculous to me, because she was giving me broth out of a table-spoon at the time (having firmly persuaded herself that I was actually starving, and must receive nourishment at first in very small quantities), and, while my mouth was yet open to receive the spoon, she would put it back into the basin, cry, "Janet! Donkeys!" and go out to the assault.

The bath was a great comfort. For I began to be sensible of acute pains in my limbs from lying out in the fields, and was now so tired and low that I could hardly keep myself awake for five minutes together. When I had bathed, they (I mean my aunt and Janet) enrobed me in a shirt and a pair of trousers belonging to Mr. Dick, and tied me up in two or three great shawls. What sort of bundle I looked like, I don't know, but I felt a very hot one. Feeling also very faint and drowsy, I soon lay down on the sofa again and fell asleep.

It might have been a dream, originating in the fancy which had occupied my mind so long, but I woke with the impression that my aunt had come and bent over me, and had put my hair away from my face, and laid my head more comfortably, and had then stood looking at me. The words "Pretty fellow," or "Poor fellow," seemed to be in my ears, too; but certainly there was nothing else, when I awoke, to lead me to believe that they had been uttered by my aunt, who sat in the bow-window gazing at the sea from behind the green fan, which was mounted on a kind of swivel, and turned any way.

We dined soon after I awoke, off a roast fowl and a pudding; I sitting at table not unlike a trussed bird[1] myself

---

[1] Donkeys intended for the use of visitors are a common sight at many English seaside resorts, such as Dover.

[1] *trussed bird.* A bird with its wings made fast to its body preparatory to cooking it.

My aunt, with every sort of expression
but wonder discharged from her countenance,
sat on the gravel, staring at me

FROM A PAINTING BY HAROLD SICHEL

330 and moving my arms with considerable difficulty. But as my aunt had swathed me up, I made no complaint of being inconvenienced. All this time I was deeply anxious to know what she was going to do with me; but she took her dinner in profound silence except when she occasionally fixed her eyes on me sitting opposite and said, "Mercy upon us!" which did not by any means relieve 340 my anxiety.

After tea, we sat at the window — on the look-out, as I imagined, from my aunt's sharp expression of face, for more invaders — until dusk, when Janet set candles, and a backgammon[1]-board, on the table, and pulled down the blinds.

FROM CHAPTER XIV

My Aunt Makes Up Her Mind about Me

On going down in the morning, I found my aunt musing so profoundly over the breakfast-table, with her elbow on the tray, that the contents of the urn[2] had overflowed the teapot and were laying the whole table-cloth under water, when my entrance put her meditations to flight. I felt sure that I had been the subject of her reflections and was more 10 than ever anxious to know her intentions towards me. Yet I dared not express my anxiety, lest it should give her offence.

My eyes, however, not being so much under control as my tongue, were attracted towards my aunt very often during breakfast. I never could look at her for a few moments together but I found her looking at me — in an odd, thoughtful 20 manner, as if I were an immense way off, instead of being on the other side of the small round table. When she had finished her breakfast, my aunt very deliberately

---

[1] A game played by two persons on a specially made board, with pieces, or men, a dice box, and dice.

[2] Here, a vessel with a faucet, used to heat water for making tea.

leaned back in her chair, knitted her brows, folded her arms, and contemplated me at her leisure, with such a fixedness of attention that I was quite overpowered by embarrassment. Not having as yet finished my own breakfast, I attempted to hide my confusion by 30 proceeding with it; but my knife tumbled over my fork, my fork tripped up my knife, I chipped bits of bacon a surprising height into the air instead of cutting them for my own eating, and choked myself with my tea, which persisted in going the wrong way instead of the right one, until I gave in altogether, and sat blushing under my aunt's scrutiny. 40

"Hallo!" said my aunt, after a long time.

I looked up and met her sharp bright glance respectfully.

"I have written to him," said my aunt.

"To ——?"

"To your father-in-law,[1]" said my aunt. "I have sent him a letter that I'll trouble him to attend to, or he and I will 50 fall out, I can tell him!"

"Does he know where I am, aunt?" I inquired, alarmed.

"I have told him," said my aunt, with a nod.

"Shall I — be — given up to him?" I faltered.

"I don't know," said my aunt. "We shall see."

"Oh! I can't think what I shall do," 60 I exclaimed, "if I have to go back to Mr. Murdstone!"

"I don't know anything about it," said my aunt, shaking her head. "I can't say, I am sure. We shall see.

"I wish you'd go up-stairs," said my aunt, as she threaded her needle, "and give my compliments to Mr. Dick, and I'll be glad to know how he gets on with his Memorial." 70

I rose with all alacrity, to acquit myself

---

[1] Stepfather.

of this commission, thinking as I went, that if Mr. Dick had been working at his Memorial long, at the same rate as I had seen him working at it, through the open door, when I came down, he was probably getting on very well indeed. I found him still driving at it with a long pen, and his head almost laid upon the paper. 80 He was so intent upon it, that I had ample leisure to observe the large paper kite in a corner, the confusion of bundles of manuscript, the number of pens, and, above all, the quantity of ink (which he seemed to have in, in half-gallon jars by the dozen), before he observed my being present.

"Do you recollect the date," said Mr. Dick, looking earnestly at me, and 90 taking up his pen to note it down, " when King Charles the First had his head cut off?"

I said I believed it happened in the year sixteen hundred and forty-nine.[1]

"Well," said Mr. Dick, scratching his ear with his pen, and looking dubiously at me. "So the books say; but I don't see how that can be. Because, if it was so long ago, how could the people about 100 him have made that mistake of putting some of the trouble out of *his* head, after it was taken off, into *mine*?"

I was very much surprised by the inquiry; but could give no information on this point.

"It's very strange," said Mr. Dick, with a despondent look at his papers, and with his hand among his hair again, "that I can never get that quite right. I never 110 can make that perfectly clear. But no matter, no matter!" he said cheerfully, and rousing himself, "there's time enough! My compliments to Miss Trotwood, and I am getting on very well indeed."

"Well, child," said my aunt, when I went downstairs. "And what of Mr. Dick this morning?"

I informed her that he had sent her

his compliments, and was getting on 120 very well indeed.

"What do you think of him?" said my aunt.

I had some shadowy idea of endeavouring to evade the question by replying that I thought him a very nice gentleman.

"Is he — is Mr. Dick — I ask because I don't know, aunt — is he at all out of his mind, then?" I stammered; for I 130 felt I was on dangerous ground.

"Not a morsel," said my aunt.

"Oh, indeed!" I observed faintly.

"If there is anything in the world," said my aunt, with great decision and force of manner, "that Mr. Dick is not, it's that."

I had nothing better to offer than another timid "Oh, indeed!"

"He has been *called* mad," said my 140 aunt. "I have a selfish pleasure in saying he has been called mad, or I should not have had the benefit of his society and advice for these last ten years and upwards."

"So long as that?" I said.

"And nice people they were, who had the audacity to call him mad," pursued my aunt. "Mr. Dick is a sort of distant connexion of mine; it doesn't matter 150 how; I needn't enter into that. If it hadn't been for me, his own brother would have shut him up for life. That's all."

"Is it a Memorial about his own history that he is writing, aunt?"

"Yes, child," said my aunt, rubbing her nose. "He hasn't been able to draw it up yet, but it doesn't signify[1]; it keeps him employed."   160

"I say again," said my aunt, "nobody knows what that man's mind is except myself; and he's the most amenable and friendly creature in existence. If he likes to fly a kite sometimes, what of that? Franklin used to fly a kite. He was a Quaker, or something of that sort,

_____
[1] Is this date correct?   [1] Matter.

if I am not mistaken. And a Quaker flying a kite is a much more ridiculous
170 object than anybody else."

If I could have supposed that my aunt had recounted these particulars for my especial behoof,[1] and as a piece of confidence in me, I should have felt very much distinguished, and should have augured favourably from such a mark of her good opinion. But I could hardly help observing that she had launched into them, chiefly because the question
180 was raised in her own mind, and with very little reference to me, though she had addressed herself to me in the absence of anybody else.

At the same time, I must say that the generosity of her championship of poor harmless Mr. Dick, not only inspired my young breast with some selfish hope for myself, but warmed it unselfishly towards her. I believe that I began to know that
190 there was something about my aunt, notwithstanding her many eccentricities[2] and odd humours, to be honoured and trusted in. Though she was just as sharp that day as on the day before, and was in and out about the donkeys just as often, and was thrown into a tremendous state of indignation, when a young man, going by, ogled Janet at a window (which was one of the gravest misdemeanours[3] that
200 could be committed against my aunt's dignity), she seemed to me to command more of my respect, if not less of my fear.

The anxiety I underwent, in the interval which necessarily elapsed before a reply could be received to her letter to Mr. Murdstone, was extreme. My aunt was a little more imperious and stern than usual, but I observed no other token of her preparing herself to receive
210 the visitor so much dreaded by me. She sat at work in the window, and I sat by, with my thoughts running astray on all possible and impossible results of Mr. Murdstone's visit, until pretty late in the afternoon. Our dinner had been

[1] Benefit.   [2] Peculiarities.   [3] Offenses.

indefinitely postponed; but it was growing so late, that my aunt had ordered it to be got ready, when she gave a sudden alarm of donkeys, and to my consternation and amazement, I beheld Miss
220 Murdstone, on a side-saddle, ride deliberately over the sacred piece of green, and stop in front of the house, looking about her.

"Go along with you!" cried my aunt, shaking her head and her fist at the window. "You have no business there. How dare you trespass? Go along! Oh! you bold-faced thing!"

My aunt was so exasperated by the
230 coolness with which Miss Murdstone looked about her, that I really believe she was motionless, and unable for the moment to dart out according to custom. I seized the opportunity to inform her who it was; and that the gentleman now coming near the offender (for the way up was very steep, and he had dropped behind) was Mr. Murdstone himself.

"I don't care who it is!" cried my
240 aunt, still shaking her head, and gesticulating anything but welcome from the bow-window. "I won't be trespassed upon. I won't allow it. Go away! Janet, turn him round. Lead him off!" and I saw, from behind my aunt, a sort of hurried battle-piece, in which the donkey stood resisting everybody, with all his four legs planted different ways, while Janet tried to pull him round by
250 the bridle, Mr. Murdstone tried to lead him on, Miss Murdstone struck at Janet with a parasol, and several boys, who had come to see the engagement, shouted vigorously.

Miss Murdstone, during the latter portion of the contest, had dismounted, and was now waiting with her brother at the bottom of the steps until my aunt should be at leisure to receive them.
260 My aunt, a little ruffled by the contest, marched past them with great dignity, and took no notice of their presence, until they were announced by Janet.

"Shall I go away, aunt?" I asked, trembling.

"No, sir," said my aunt. "Certainly not!"

Mr. Murdstone seemed afraid of a re-270 newal of hostilities, and began:

"Miss Trotwood!"

"I beg your pardon," observed my aunt, with a keen look. "You are the Mr. Murdstone who married the widow of my late nephew, David Copperfield?"

"I am," said Mr. Murdstone.

"You'll excuse my saying, sir," returned my aunt, "that I think it would have been a much better and happier 280 thing if you had let that poor child alone."

"I so far agree with what Miss Trotwood has remarked," observed Miss Murdstone, bridling,[1] "that I consider our lamented Clara to have been, in all essential respects, a mere child."

"It is a comfort to you and me, ma'am," said my aunt, "who are getting on in life, and are not likely to be made 290 unhappy by our personal attractions, that nobody can say the same of us."

"No doubt!" returned Miss Murdstone, though, I thought, not with a very ready or gracious assent. "And it certainly might have been, as you say, a better and happier thing for my brother if he had never entered into such a marriage. I have always been of that opinion."

300 "I have no doubt you have," said my aunt. "Janet," ringing the bell, "my compliments to Mr. Dick, and beg him to come down."

Until he came, my aunt sat perfectly upright and stiff, frowning at the wall. When he came, my aunt performed the ceremony of introduction.

"Mr. Dick. An old and intimate friend. On whose judgment," said my 310 aunt, with emphasis, as an admonition to Mr. Dick, who was biting his forefinger and looking rather foolish, "I rely."

[1] Tossing her head.

Mr. Dick took his finger out of his mouth, on this hint, and stood among the group, with a grave and attentive expression of face. My aunt inclined her head to Mr. Murdstone, who went on:

"Miss Trotwood. On the receipt of your letter, I considered it an act of greater justice to myself, and perhaps 320 of more respect to you —"

"Thank you," said my aunt, still eyeing him keenly. "You needn't mind me."

"To answer it in person, however inconvenient the journey," pursued Mr. Murdstone, "rather than by letter. This unhappy boy who has run away from his friends and his occupation —"

"And whose appearance," interposed 330 his sister, directing general attention to me in my indefinable costume, "is perfectly scandalous and disgraceful."

"Jane Murdstone," said her brother, "have the goodness not to interrupt me. This unhappy boy, Miss Trotwood, has been the occasion of much domestic trouble and uneasiness; both during the lifetime of my late dear wife, and since. He has a sullen, rebellious spirit; a vio- 340 lent temper; and an untoward, intractable disposition. Both my sister and myself have endeavoured to correct his vices, but ineffectually. And I have felt — we both have felt, I may say; my sister being fully in my confidence — that it is right you should receive this grave and dispassionate[1] assurance from our lips."

"It can hardly be necessary for me to 350 confirm anything stated by my brother," said Miss Murdstone; "but I beg to observe, that, of all the boys in the world, I believe this is the worst boy."

"Strong!" said my aunt, shortly.

"But not at all too strong for the facts," returned Miss Murdstone.

"Ha!" said my aunt. "Well, sir?"

"I have my own opinions," resumed Mr. Murdstone, whose face darkened 360

[1] Unprejudiced.

more and more, the more he and my aunt observed each other, which they did very narrowly, "as to the best mode of bringing him up; they are founded, in part, on my knowledge of him. It is enough that I place this boy under the eye of a friend of mine, in a respectable business; that it does not please him; that he runs away from it; makes him-370 self a common vagabond about the country; and comes here, in rags, to appeal to you, Miss Trotwood."

"But about this respectable business first," said my aunt. "If he had been your own boy, you would have put him to it, just the same, I suppose?"

"If he had been my brother's own boy," returned Miss Murdstone, striking in, "his character, I trust, would have 380 been altogether different."

"Or if the poor child, his mother, had been alive, he would still have gone into the respectable business, would he?" said my aunt.

"I believe," said Mr. Murdstone, with an inclination of his head, "that Clara would have disputed nothing which myself and my sister were agreed was for the best."

390 Miss Murdstone confirmed this with an audible murmur.

"Humph!" said my aunt. "Unfortunate baby!"

Mr. Dick, who had been rattling his money all this time, was rattling it so loudly now, that my aunt felt it necessary to check him with a look, before saying:

"The poor child's annuity[1] died with 400 her?"

"Died with her," replied Mr. Murdstone.

"And there was no settlement of the little property — the house and garden — upon her boy?"

"It had been left to her, unconditionally, by her first husband," Mr. Murdstone began, when my aunt caught him

[1] An amount of money received yearly.

up with the greatest irascibility and impatience. 410

"Left to her unconditionally! Of course it was left to her unconditionally. But when she married again — when she took that most disastrous step of marrying you, in short," said my aunt, "to be plain — did no one put in a word for the boy at that time?"

"My late wife loved her second husband, ma'am," said Mr. Murdstone, "and trusted implicitly in him." 420

"Your late wife, sir, was a most unworldly, most unhappy, most unfortunate baby," returned my aunt, shaking her head at him. "That's what *she* was. And now, what have you got to say next?"

"Merely this, Miss Trotwood," he returned, "I am here to take David back; to take him back unconditionally, to dispose of him as I think proper, and 430 to deal with him as I think right. I am here, for the first and last time, to take him away. Is he ready to go? If he is not, my doors are shut against him henceforth, and yours, I take it for granted, are open to him."

"And what does the boy say?" said my aunt. "Are you ready to go, David?"

I answered no, and entreated her not to let me go. 440

"Mr. Dick," said my aunt; "what shall I do with this child?"

Mr. Dick considered, hesitated, brightened, and rejoined, "Have him measured for a suit of clothes directly."

"Mr. Dick," said my aunt triumphantly, "give me your hand, for your common sense is invaluable." Having shaken it with great cordiality, she pulled me towards her and said to Mr. Murd- 450 stone:

"You can go when you like; I'll take my chance with the boy. If he's all you say he is, at least I can do as much for him then, as you have done. But I don't believe a word of it."

"Miss Trotwood," rejoined Mr. Murdstone, shrugging his shoulders, as he rose, "if you were a gentleman —"

460 "Bah! Stuff and nonsense!" said my aunt. "Don't talk to me!"

"How exquisitely polite!" exclaimed Miss Murdstone, rising. "Overpowering, really!"

"Good day, sir," said my aunt, "and good bye! Good day to you, too, ma'am," said my aunt, turning suddenly upon his sister. "Let me see you ride a donkey over *my* green again, and as sure 470 as you have a head upon your shoulders, I'll knock your bonnet off, and tread upon it!"

It would require a painter, and no common painter, too, to depict my aunt's face as she delivered herself of this very unexpected sentiment, and Miss Murdstone's face as she heard it. But the manner of the speech no less than the matter, was so fiery, that Miss Murd-480 stone, without a word in answer, discreetly put her arm through her brother's, and walked haughtily out of the cottage; my aunt remaining in the window looking after them; prepared, I have no doubt, in case of the donkey's reappearance, to carry her threat into instant execution.

No attempt at defiance being made, however, her face gradually relaxed, and became so pleasant, that I was embold-490 ened to kiss and thank her; which I did with great heartiness, and with both my arms clasped round her neck. I then shook hands with Mr. Dick, who shook hands with me a great many times, and hailed this happy close of the proceedings with repeated bursts of laughter.

"You'll consider yourself guardian, jointly with me, of this child, Mr. Dick," said my aunt.

500 "I shall be delighted," said Mr. Dick, "to be the guardian of David's son."

"Very good," returned my aunt, "*that's* settled. I have been thinking, do you know, Mr. Dick, that I might call him Trotwood?"

"Certainly, certainly. Call him Trot-wood, certainly," said Mr. Dick. "David's son Trotwood."

"Trotwood Copperfield, you mean," returned my aunt. 510

"Yes, to be sure. Yes. Trotwood Copperfield," said Mr. Dick, a little abashed.

My aunt took so kindly to the notion, that some ready-made clothes, which were purchased for me that afternoon, were marked "Trotwood Copperfield," in her own handwriting, and in indelible marking-ink, before I put them on; and it was settled that all the other clothes 520 which were ordered to be made for me (a complete outfit was bespoke that afternoon) should be marked in the same way.

Thus I began my new life, in a new name, and with everything new about me.

Discussion Hints

1. Give some of the events in Dickens's early life (p. 724) that are reflected in the selection from *David Copperfield*.

2. What is your impression of Miss Trotwood? Give reasons for your answer.

3. Why does Miss Trotwood ask Mr. Dick's opinions?

4. What is your estimate of the characters of Mr. and Miss Murdstone? On what evidence do you base your answer?

5. What evidence of Dickens's humor do you find in the selection given here?

6. Dickens was greatly interested in the drama and was an accomplished amateur actor; hence the scenes in his novels are often marked by their dramatic character. What episode in the selection given here would, in your opinion, be most effective if presented on the stage? Give reasons for your answer.

7. State in simpler language:

a. *I acknowledged the undoubted accuracy of this description* (p. 437, ll. 36–37)
b. *rigid with indignation* (p. 440, ll. 238–239)
c. *constitutional obstinacy* (p. 440, ll. 276–277)
d. *performed the ceremony of introduction* (p. 444, ll. 306–307)

8. Explain

a. *destitute* (p. 437, l. 7)
b. *consternation* (p. 438, l. 78)
c. *proceeding* (p. 439, l. 168)
d. *sallies* (p. 440, l. 271)
e. *meditations* (p. 441, l. 7)
f. *dubiously* (p. 442, l. 96)
g. *ogled* (p. 443, l. 198)
h. *hostilities* (p. 444, l. 270)
i. *admonition* (p. 444, l. 310)
j. *audible* (p. 445, l. 391)

Suggestions for Reading

David Copperfield
The Pickwick Papers
Dombey and Son
Bleak House
Great Expectations
A Tale of Two Cities[1]
Our Mutual Friend

WILLIAM MAKEPEACE THACKERAY[1] (1811-1863)

From *The History of Henry Esmond*

The History of Henry Esmond is one of the greatest historical novels ever written. Unlike the historical novels of Scott,[2] it is realistic* rather than romantic (see "romance"*), and, unlike the novels of Dickens,[3] it is not a novel with a definite social purpose. In its pages Thackeray attempts to reproduce English life of the late seventeenth and early eighteenth centuries: Jacobite* plots to restore to the throne the son of the exiled James II (see page 213); London society and court intrigue during the reign of Queen Anne (see page 213); and such famous personages of the Age of Classicism as Addison,[4] Steele,[5] Swift,[6] and Fielding (p. 219). Even the imaginary characters, such as the noble, unselfish hero, Henry Esmond, his jealous, loving patron, Lady Castlewood, the fascinating but selfish Beatrix Esmond, and Lord Frank Castlewood are as real as persons of Thackeray's own day. The selection that is given here is an especially good example of Thackeray's method of writing historical fiction. James II's unwise and imprudent son, later known as the Old Pretender,* made two separate attempts to secure the throne: one in 1708, six years before the death of Queen Anne; the other in 1715, a year after her death. These two attempts were connected with Scotland rather than with England; yet Thackeray, in writing *Henry Esmond*, combines features from both so skillfully that for the moment we are willing

to accept as facts the purely fictitious events which our selection represents as taking place in or near London.

Though *The History of Henry Esmond* contains many digressions, the main plot is comparatively simple. The author makes the story more convincing (1) by introducing many realistic details from the past; (2) by allowing the hero, who is represented as living at the time, to tell his own story; and (3) by having him tell his story in the third person as though he were an unprejudiced reporter. Thus the novel illustrates the important fact that Thackeray's realism is that of an observer who writes what he sees and knows.

The style also is unusual. It probably owes something to the influence of Addison, Steele, and other writers of the early eighteenth century; yet it is Thackeray's own in that it has a rhythmic cadence which haunts us long after we lay the book aside.

[Here, as in Dickens's *David Copperfield* (p. 436), the hero tells his own story, but, unlike David Copperfield, he tells it in the third person. The supposed author, the noble-minded Henry Esmond, grew up an orphan in the family of his cousins, the Castlewoods, who owned an estate in the country and a town house in London, and who were ignorant of the fact that he is the rightful heir to the property. Esmond is the family name; Castlewood is the title to which the cousins had succeeded. At Castlewood, Henry became infatuated with his cousin Beatrix, a beauti-

[1] For biography see page 725.
[2] For biography see page 722.
[3] For biography see page 724.
[4] For biography see page 709.
[5] For biography see page 709.
[6] For biography see page 711.

[1] In the revised edition of *Achievement* of this series.

ful but spoiled and heartless coquette; and
he was also devoted to Frank, the supposed
Lord Castlewood, and to the widowed Lady
Castlewood, their mother, who exemplified
all that is kind and virtuous in woman.
Frank went abroad, where he married, became a Roman Catholic, and remained for
a number of years. Meantime the family
had become involved in a Jacobite* plot to
place on the throne the Old Pretender,* son
of James II and brother of Queen Anne.
When the following chapter opens, Frank,
the supposed Lord Castlewood, is about to
return home from the Continent. He is accompanied by a mysterious "French gentleman," who is known as Monsieur Baptiste
(really the Old Pretender in disguise). Lord
Castlewood is to be met by Henry Esmond at
Rochester, a shipping port about twenty-five
miles southeast of London. The following
selection gives a graphic picture of English
politics in a dangerous period and of a daring, though futile, attempt to gain the English
throne.]

BOOK III. FROM CHAPTER IX

The Original of the Portrait Comes to England

'TWAS announced in the family that
my Lord Castlewood would arrive,
having a confidential French gentleman
in his suite,[1] who acted as secretary to
his Lordship, and who, being a Papist,[2]
and a foreigner of a good family, though
now in rather a menial place, would have
his meals served in his chamber, and not
with the domestics of the house. The
10 Viscountess[3] gave up her bed-chamber
contiguous to her daughter's, and having
a large convenient closet[4] attached to
it, in which a bed was put up, ostensibly
for Monsieur Baptiste, the Frenchman;
though, 'tis needless to say, when the
doors of the apartment were locked, and
the two guests retired within it, the

young Viscount[1] became the servant of
the illustrious Prince whom he entertained, and gave up gladly the more 20
convenient and airy chamber and bed to
his master.

The company in the servants' hall
never for a moment supposed that these
preparations were made for any other
person than the young Viscount, the
lord of the house, whom his fond mother
had been for so many years without
seeing.

Taking horse, Colonel Esmond rode 30
rapidly to Rochester, and there awaited
the King in that very town where his
father[2] had last set his foot on the English shore. A room had been prepared
at an inn there for my Lord Castlewood
and his servant; and Colonel Esmond
timed his ride so well that he had scarce
been half-an-hour in the place, and was
looking over the balcony into the yard
of the inn, when two travellers rode in at 40
the inn gate, and the Colonel running
down, the next moment embraced his
dear young lord.

My Lord's companion acting the part
of a domestic,[3] dismounted, and was
for holding the Viscount's stirrup; but
Colonel Esmond, calling to his own man,
who was in the court, bade him take the
horses and settle with the lad who had
ridden the post along with the two 50
travellers, crying out in a cavalier[4] tone
in the French language to my Lord's
companion, and affecting to grumble
that my Lord's fellow was a Frenchman,
and did not know the money or habits of
the country: — "My man will see to the
horses, Baptiste,[5]" says Colonel Esmond:
"do you understand English?" "Very
leetle." "So, follow my Lord and wait
upon him at dinner in his own room." 60

---

[1] *having . . . suite.* Having, among his attendants, a French gentleman who was in his
confidence.   [2] A Roman Catholic.
[3] The widowed Lady Castlewood.
[4] A small private room; not, as now, a space for
storing clothing, etc.

[1] *Viscount* (vī'kount). A title of nobility equivalent to "lord"; here applied to Frank
Castlewood.
[2] James II.   [3] A servant.
[4] Here, offhand, haughty.
[5] One of the assumed names of the Old Pretender.*

The landlord and his people came up presently bearing the dishes; 'twas well they made a noise and stir in the gallery,[1] or they might have found Colonel Esmond on his knee before Lord Castlewood's servant, welcoming his Majesty to his kingdom, and kissing the hand of the King.

[On leaving Rochester the Pretender, Lord Castlewood, and Henry Esmond set out for London.]

Mr. Esmond's servant was left behind 70 at Rochester, to take care of the tired horses, whilst we had fresh beasts[2] provided along the road. And galloping by the Prince's side the Colonel explained to the Prince what his movements had been; who the friends were that knew of the expedition; whom, as Esmond conceived, the Prince should trust; entreating him, above all, to maintain the very closest secrecy until the time should 80 come when his Royal Highness should appear. The town[3] swarmed with friends of the Prince's cause; there were scores of correspondents with St. Germain[4]; Jacobites * known and secret; great in station and humble; about the Court and the Queen; in the Parliament, Church, and among the merchants in the City. The Prince had friends numberless in the army, in the Privy Council, and 90 the Officers of State. The great object, as it seemed, to the small band of persons who had concerted that bold stroke, who had brought the Queen's brother[5] into his native country, was, that his visit should remain unknown till the proper

time came, when his presence should surprise friends and enemies alike; and the latter should be found so unprepared and disunited, that they should not find time to attack him.   100

The party reached London by nightfall, leaving their horses at the Posting-House over against[1] Westminster, and being ferried over the water, where Lady Esmond's coach was already in waiting. In another hour we were all landed at Kensington,[2] and the mistress of the house had that satisfaction which her heart had yearned after for many years, once more to embrace her son, who, on 110 his side, ever retained a most tender affection for his parent.

She did not refrain from this expression of her feeling, though the domestics were by, and my Lord Castlewood's attendant stood in the hall. Esmond had to whisper to him in French to take his hat off. Monsieur Baptiste was constantly neglecting his part with an inconceivable levity; more than once on the ride 120 to London, little observations of the stranger, light remarks, and words betokening the greatest ignorance of the country the Prince came to govern, had hurt the susceptibility of the two gentlemen forming his escort; nor could either help owning in his secret mind that they would have had his behaviour otherwise, and that the laughter and the lightness, not to say license, which charac- 130 terized his talk, scarce befitted such a great Prince, and such a solemn occasion. Not but that he could act at proper times with spirit and dignity. He had behaved, as we all knew, in a very courageous manner on the field. Esmond had seen a copy of the letter the Prince had writ with his own hand when urged by his friends in England to abjure his re-

---

[1] The passageway outside the door.
[2] Here, horses.
[3] London.
[4] *St. Germain* (săn zhĕr măn'). A fashionable part of Paris, the French headquarters of the Jacobites * and the seat of the royal family of France before the French Revolution.
[5] It is important to remember that the Old Pretender was the brother of Anne, who was queen of England at the time of the story.
D

[1] *over against.* Opposite to; here, on the south side of the Thames.
[2] At the time of the story a suburb of London where the royal palace and the town house of the Castlewood family were located.

140 ligion, and admired that manly and magnanimous reply by which he refused to yield to the temptation. Monsieur Baptiste took off his hat, blushing at the hint Colonel Esmond ventured to give him, and said, "Tenez, elle est jolie, la petite mère. Foi de Chevalier! Elle est charmante; mais l'autre, qui est cette nymphe, cet astre qui brille, cette Diane qui descend sur nous?"[1] And he started 150 back, and pushed forward, as Beatrix was descending the stair. She wore the diamonds Esmond gave her; it had been agreed between them, that she should wear these brilliants on the day when the King should enter the house, and a Queen she looked, radiant in charms, and magnificent and imperial in beauty.

Castlewood himself was startled by that beauty and splendour; he stepped 160 back and gazed at his sister as though he had not been aware before how perfectly lovely she was, and I thought blushed as he embraced her. The Prince could not keep his eyes off her; he quite forgot his menial part, though he had been schooled to it, and a little light portmanteau[2] prepared expressly that he should carry it. He pressed forward before my Lord Viscount. 'Twas lucky the servants' eyes 170 were busy in other directions, or they must have seen that this was no servant, or at least a very insolent and rude one.

Again Colonel Esmond was obliged to cry out, "Baptiste," in a loud imperious voice, "have a care to the valise!" at which hint the wilful young man ground his teeth together with something very like a curse between them, and then gave a brief look of anything but pleasure to 180 his Mentor.[3] Being reminded, however,

he shouldered the little portmanteau, and carried it up the stair, Esmond preceding him, and a servant with lighted tapers. He flung down his burden sulkily in the bedchamber: — "A Prince that will wear a crown must wear a mask," says Mr. Esmond in French.

Esmond's man, honest John Lockwood, had served his master and the family all his life, and the Colonel knew 190 that he could answer for John's fidelity as for his own. John returned with the horses from Rochester betimes the next morning, and the Colonel gave him to understand that on going to Kensington, where he was free of the servants' hall, and indeed courting Miss Beatrix's maid, he was to ask no questions, and betray no surprise, but to vouch stoutly that the young gentleman he should see in a red 200 coat[1] there was my Lord Viscount Castlewood, and that his attendant in grey[2] was Monsieur Baptiste the Frenchman.

The secretary of the night previous was now the Viscount; the Viscount wore the secretary's grey frock;[3] and John Lockwood was instructed to hint to the world below stairs that my Lord being a Papist, and very devout in that religion, his attendant might be no other 210 than his chaplain from Bruxelles[4]; hence, if he took his meals in my Lord's company there was little reason for surprise. Frank was further cautioned to speak English with a foreign accent, which task he performed indifferently well, and this caution was the more necessary because

[1] *young gentleman . . . red coat.* Really the Pretender.

[2] *his attendant . . . grey.* Really Viscount Castlewood.

[3] Now that the Pretender has arrived at the Castlewoods' town house, it is felt that he will be able to communicate with the conspirators more safely if he abandons the disguise of Baptiste and assumes the personality of the Viscount, who in turn acts the part of the secretary. This deception is possible only because the two men resemble each other.

[4] Brussels, the capital of Belgium (formerly a part of Holland), where Frank Castlewood has been living.

[1] *Tenez . . . nous?* French for "Indeed, the little mother is pretty, by my word as a gentleman! She is charming; but the other, who is this nymph, this shining star, this Diana who descends upon us?" The Pretender uses the high-sounding, complimentary language popular in court circles at the time.

[2] A traveling bag or case.   [3] A counselor.

He started back, and pushed forward, as Beatrix was descending the stair

the Prince himself scarce spoke our language like a native of the island: and
220 John Lockwood laughed with the folks below stairs at the manner in which my Lord,[1] after five years abroad, sometimes forgot his own tongue and spoke it like a Frenchman. "I warrant," says he, "that with the English beef and beer, his Lordship will soon get back the proper use of his mouth"; and, to do his new Lordship justice, he took to beer and beef very kindly.

230 The Prince drank so much, and was so loud and imprudent in his talk after his drink, that Esmond often trembled for him. His meals were served as much as possible in his own chamber, though frequently he made his appearance in Lady Castlewood's parlour and drawing-room, calling Beatrix "sister," and her Ladyship "mother" or "madam," before the servants. And, choosing to act en-
240 tirely up to the part of brother and son, the Prince sometimes saluted Mistress Beatrix and Lady Castlewood with a freedom which his secretary did not like, and which, for his part, set Colonel Esmond tearing with rage.

The Bishop of Rochester,[2] and other gentlemen engaged in the transaction which had brought the Prince over,[3] waited upon his Royal Highness, con-
250 stantly asking for my Lord Castlewood on their arrival at Kensington, and being openly conducted to his Royal Highness in that character, who received them either in my Lady's drawing-room below, or above in his own apartment; and all implored him[4] to quit the house as little as possible, and to wait there till the

signal should be given for him to appear. The ladies entertained him at cards, over which amusement he spent many hours 260 in each day and night. He passed many hours more in drinking, during which time he would rattle and talk very agreeably, and especially if the Colonel was absent, whose presence always seemed to frighten him; and the poor "Colonel Noir"[1] took that hint as a command accordingly, and seldom intruded his black face upon the convivial hours of this august young prisoner.[2] 270

As for Lady Castlewood, although she scarce spoke a word, 'twas easy to gather from her demeanour, and one or two hints she dropped, how deep her mortification was at finding the hero whom she had chosen to worship all her life (and whose restoration had formed almost the most sacred part of her prayers), no more than a man, and not a good one. She thought misfortune might have 280 chastened him; but that instructress had rather rendered him callous[3] than humble. His devotion, which was quite real, kept him from no sin he had a mind to. His talk showed good-humour, gaiety, even wit enough; but there was a levity in his acts and words that shocked the simplicity and purity of the English lady, whose guest he was.

FROM CHAPTER X

We Entertain a Very Distinguished Guest at Kensington

In expectation of the stroke that was now preparing, the Irish regiments in the French service were all brought round about Boulogne[4] in Picardy, to pass over

[1] *my Lord.* Really the Pretender, who, having been brought up in France, is unable to imitate perfectly the speech of Lord Castlewood.

[2] *Bishop of Rochester.* Francis Atterbury (1662–1732), a well-known English Tory * and Jacobite * who was bishop of Rochester in 1713. He was afterward banished for his Jacobite sympathies.

[3] *transaction . . . over.* The conspiracy to gain the throne.

[4] The Pretender.

[1] *Colonel Noir. Noir* is French for "black." Here applied by the Pretender * to Henry Esmond because Esmond's looks show disapproval of the Pretender's behavior.

[2] The Pretender was required to remain indoors as though he were a prisoner.

[3] Hardened, unfeeling.

[4] A seaport in France opposite the coast of England.

if need were with the Duke of Berwick[1];
the soldiers of France no longer, but subjects of James the Third of England and
Ireland King.[2] The fidelity of the great
mass of the Scots was notoriously un-
10 shaken in their King. A very great body
of Tory* clergy, nobility, and gentry,
were public partisans of the exiled Prince;
and the indifferents might be counted on
to cry King George or King James, according as either should prevail. The
Queen, especially in her latter days, inclined towards her own family.[3] The
Prince was lying[4] actually in London,
within a stone's-cast of his sister's pal-
20 ace; the first Minister[5] toppling to his
fall, and so tottering that the weakest
push of a woman's finger would send him
down; and as for Bolingbroke,* his successor, we know on whose side his power
and his splendid eloquence would be on
the day when the Queen should appear
openly before her Council and say: —
"This, my Lords, is my brother; here is
my father's heir, and mine after me."
30 During the whole of the previous year
the Queen had had many and repeated
fits of sickness, fever, and lethargy, and
her death had been constantly looked
for by all her attendants. The Elector of
Hanover[6] had wished to send his son, the
Duke of Cambridge — to pay his court
to his cousin the Queen, the Elector said;
— in truth, to be on the spot when death
should close her career. Frightened, per-

haps, to have such a *memento mori*[1] under 40
her royal eyes, her Majesty had angrily
forbidden the young Prince's coming into
England. Either she desired to keep the
chances for her brother open yet; or the
people about her did not wish to close
with[2] the Whig* candidate[3] till they
could make terms with him. The quarrels of her Ministers before her face at
the Council board, the pricks of conscience very likely, the importunities of 50
her Ministers, and constant turmoil and
agitation round about her, had weakened
and irritated the Queen extremely; her
strength was giving way under these continual trials of her temper, and from day
to day it was expected she must come to
a speedy end of them.

[The conspirators plan to have the Pretender
appeal in person to Queen Anne to assist him
in gaining the throne.]

The Court lady with whom our plan
was concerted, and who was a chief agent
in it, the Court physician, and the Bishop 60
of Rochester, who were the other two
most active participators in our plan,
had held many councils, in our house
at Kensington and elsewhere, as to the
means best to be adopted for presenting
our young adventurer to his sister the
Queen. The simple and easy plan proposed by Colonel Esmond had been
agreed to by all parties, which was that
on some rather private day, when there 70
were not many persons about the Court,
the Prince[4] should appear there as my
Lord Castlewood, should be greeted by
his sister-in-waiting,[5] and led by that

---

[1] *Duke of Berwick* (bĕr'ĭk) (1670–1734). A son
of James II, and a famous Jacobite* leader.
He fought against the English in Ireland and
in France.

[2] *James the Third . . . King.* The title which the
Old Pretender* would have assumed if he
had gained the English throne.

[3] *inclined . . . family.* That is, wished some member of her own family, such as the Old Pretender,* to be her successor on the throne.

[4] Here, living.

[5] Robert Harley (1661–1724), first Earl of Oxford, a prominent English statesman. He
began as a Whig,* later turned Tory,* and
was finally impeached for treason, but was
acquitted.

[6] *Elector of Hanover.* A German ruler who married a granddaughter of James I of England.

[1] *memento mori.* Latin for "Remember that you
must die."

[2] *close with.* Here, accept as Queen Anne's successor.

[3] *Whig candidate.* The son of the Elector of
Hanover. He became George I of England.

[4] The Old Pretender.*

[5] *his sister-in-waiting.* Beatrix Esmond, who is
actually one of the ladies in waiting to Queen
Anne and is also to play the part of the sister
of the supposed Lord Castlewood (who is
really the Pretender *).

other lady into the closet of the Queen. And according to her Majesty's health or humour, and the circumstances that might arise during the interview, it was to be left to the discretion of those 30 present at it, and to the Prince himself, whether he should declare that it was the Queen's own brother, or the brother of Beatrix Esmond, who kissed her royal hand. And this plan being determined on, we were all waiting in very much anxiety for the day and signal of execution.[1]

Two mornings after, it being the twenty-seventh day of July, the Bishop 90 of Rochester breakfasting with Lady Castlewood and her family, and the meal scarce over, Doctor A.'s[2] coach drove up to our house at Kensington, and the Doctor appeared amongst the party there, enlivening a rather gloomy company.

He asked for the guest; the guest was above in his own apartment: he bade *Monsieur Baptiste*[3] go up to his master instantly, and requested that *my Lord* 100 *Viscount Castlewood* would straightway put his uniform on, and come away in the Doctor's coach now at the door.

He then informed Madam Beatrix what her part of the comedy was to be :—— "In half-an-hour," says he, "Her Majesty[4] and her favourite lady will take the air in the Cedar Walk behind the new Banqueting-house. Her Majesty will be drawn in a garden chair,[5] Madam 110 Beatrix Esmond and *her brother*, *my Lord Viscount Castlewood*, will be walking in the private garden, and will come unawares upon the Royal party. The man that draws the chair will retire, and leave

the Queen, the favourite, and the Maid of Honour[1] and her brother[2] together; Mistress Beatrix will present her brother, and then! —— and then, my Lord Bishop will pray for the result of the interview, and his Scots clerk will say Amen! 120 Quick, put on your hood, Madam Beatrix: why doth not his Majesty come down? Such another chance may not present itself for months again."

The Prince was late and lazy, and indeed had all but lost[3] that chance through his indolence. The Queen was actually about to leave the garden just when the party reached it; the Doctor, the Bishop, the Maid of Honour, and her 130 brother, went off together in the physician's coach, and had been gone half-an-hour when Colonel Esmond came to Kensington Square.[4]

In half-an-hour more the coach returned; the Bishop descended from it first, and gave his arm to Beatrix, who now came out. His Lordship went back into the carriage again, and the Maid of Honour entered the house alone. We 140 were all gazing at her from the upper window, trying to read from her countenance the result of the interview from which she had just come.

She came into the drawing-room in a great tremor and very pale; she asked for a glass of water as her mother went to meet her, and after drinking that and putting off her hood, she began to speak: —— "We may all hope for the best," says 150 she; "it has cost the Queen a fit. Her Majesty was in her chair in the Cedar Walk, accompanied only by Lady ——, when we entered by the private wicket from the west side of the garden, and turned towards her, the Doctor following us. They waited in a side walk, hidden by the shrubs, as we advanced towards

[1] *of execution.* For carrying out the plan.
[2] Doctor A. is the court physician referred to on page 453, 1. 60, as one of the most active among the conspirators.
[3] Here and elsewhere in the text, italics are used to indicate that the names given are assumed; that is, *Monsieur Baptiste* is really "my Lord Viscount Castlewood," and *my Lord Viscount Castlewood* is really the Prince.
[4] Queen Anne.
[5] *garden chair.* A chair on wheels.

[1] *Maid of Honour.* Here, Beatrix.
[2] Here, the Pretender, who appears as her brother.
[3] *had . . . lost.* Came near losing.
[4] *Kensington Square.* The location of the Castlewood residence in London.

the chair. My heart throbbed so I scarce
160 could speak; but my Prince whispered,
'Courage, Beatrix,' and marched on with
a steady step. His face was a little
flushed, but he was not afraid of the
danger. He who fought so bravely at
Malplaquet[1] fears nothing.

"The Prince uncovered,"[2] Beatrix
continued, "and I saw the Queen turning round to Lady ——, as if asking who
these two were. Her Majesty looked very
170 pale and ill, and then flushed up; the
favourite made us a signal to advance,
and I went up, leading my Prince by the
hand, quite close to the chair: 'Your
Majesty will give my Lord Viscount your
hand to kiss,' says her lady, and the
Queen put out her hand, which the Prince
kissed, kneeling on his knee, he who
should kneel to no mortal man or woman.

"'You have been long from England,
180 my Lord,'[3] says the Queen; 'why were
you not here to give a home to your
mother and sister?'

"'I am come, madam, to stay now, if
the Queen desires me,' says the Prince,
with another low bow.

"'You have taken a foreign wife, my
Lord, and a foreign religion; was not
that of England good enough for you?'

"'In returning to my father's church,'[4]
190 says the Prince, 'I do not love my mother
the less, nor am I the less faithful servant
of your Majesty.'

"Here," says Beatrix, "the favourite
gave me a little signal with her hand to
fall back, which I did, though I died to
hear what should pass; and whispered
something to the Queen, which made her
Majesty start and utter one or two words
in a hurried manner, looking towards the

Prince, and catching hold with her hand
200 of the arm of her chair. He advanced
still nearer towards it; he began to
speak very rapidly; I caught the words,
'Father, blessing, forgiveness,' and then
presently the Prince fell on his knees;
took from his breast a paper he had there,
handed it to the Queen, who, as soon as
she saw it, flung up both her arms with
a scream, and took away that hand
nearest the Prince, and which he en-
210 deavoured to kiss. He went on speaking
with great animation of gesture, now
clasping his hands together on his heart,
now opening them as though to say: 'I
am here, your brother, in your power.'
Lady —— ran round on the other side
of the chair, kneeling too, and speaking
with great energy. She clasped the
Queen's hand on her side, and picked up
the paper her Majesty had let fall. The
220 Prince rose and made a further speech as
though he would go; the favourite on
the other hand urging her mistress, and
then, running back to the Prince,
brought him back once more close to the
chair. Again he knelt down and took the
Queen's hand, which she did not withdraw, kissing it a hundred times; my
Lady all the time, with sobs and supplications, speaking over the chair. This
230 while the Queen sat with a stupefied look,
crumpling the paper with one hand, as
my Prince embraced the other; then of
a sudden she uttered several piercing
shrieks, and burst into a great fit of
hysteric tears and laughter. 'Enough,
enough, sir, for this time,' I heard Lady
—— say: and the chairman,[1] who had
withdrawn round the Banqueting-house,
came back, alarmed by the cries. 240
'Quick,' says Lady ——, 'get some help,'
and I ran towards the Doctor, who, with
the Bishop of Rochester, came up instantly. Lady —— whispered the Prince
he might hope for the very best and to
be ready to-morrow; and he hath gone

---

[1] *Malplaquet* (màl plà kĕ'). A village in northern France where in 1709 the English (under
Marlborough *) and their allies defeated the
French in a famous battle. The Pretender
had fought on the side of the French.

[2] Took off his hat.

[3] The queen imagines her visitor to be Lord
Castlewood.

[4] Lord Castlewood's father had been a Roman
Catholic.

[1] The attendant who drew the garden chair (p. 454,
l. 113).

away to the Bishop of Rochester's house to meet several of his friends there. And so the great stroke is struck," says 250 Beatrix, going down on her knees, and clasping her hands. "God save the King! God save the King!"

[The Pretender becomes infatuated with Beatrix, who consequently is sent by her family to their country estate of Castlewood in order that she may be in safety until the attempt at the throne is completed]

FROM CHAPTER XI

Our Guest Quits Us as Not Being Hospitable Enough

Beatrix's departure took place within an hour, her maid going with her in the post-chaise, and a man armed on the coach-box to prevent any danger on the road.

[After her departure] we had a gloomy and silent meal; it seemed as if a darkness was over the house, since the bright face of Beatrix had been withdrawn from 10 it. In the afternoon came a message from the favourite to relieve us somewhat from this despondency. "The Queen hath been much shaken," the note said; "she is better now, and all things will go well. Let *my Lord Castlewood*[1] be ready against[2] we send for him."

The Prince came home shortly after the messenger who bore this billet had left the house. His Royal Highness was 20 so much the better[3] for the Bishop's liquor, that to talk affairs to him now was of little service. He was helped to the Royal bed; he called Castlewood familiarly by his own name; he quite forgot the part upon the acting of which his crown, his safety, depended. 'Twas lucky that my Lady Castlewood's servants were out of the way, and only those heard him who would not betray him.

[1] Here, the Old Pretender.
[2] In preparation for the time that.
[3] Is this ironical *?

He inquired after the adorable Beatrix, 30 with a Royal hiccup in his voice; he was easily got to bed, and in a minute or two plunged in that deep slumber and forgetfulness with which Bacchus * rewards the votaries of that god.[1]

The account of the previous evening was known all over the town early next day. A violent altercation had taken place before the Queen in the Council Chamber; and all the coffee-houses * had their 40 version of the quarrel. The news brought my Lord Bishop early to Kensington Square, where he awaited the waking of his Royal master above stairs, and spoke confidently of having him proclaimed as Prince of Wales and heir to the throne before that day was over. The Bishop had entertained on the previous afternoon certain of the most influential gentlemen of the true[2] British 50 party. His Royal Highness had charmed all, both Scots and English, Papists and Churchmen: "Even Quakers," says he, "were at our meeting; and, if the stranger[3] took a little too much British punch and ale, he will soon grow more accustomed to those liquors; and my Lord Castlewood," says the Bishop with a laugh, "must bear the cruel charge of having been for once in his life a little 60 tipsy.[4] He toasted your lovely sister a dozen times," says the Bishop. "Where is that charming nymph, and why does she not adorn your Ladyship's tea-table with her bright eyes?"

Her Ladyship said, drily, that Beatrix was not at home that morning;[5] my Lord Bishop was too busy with great affairs to trouble himself much about

[1] *that deep . . god.* Express in simpler language.
[2] Here, true to the Jacobite * cause and loyal to the Old Pretender.*
[3] The Old Pretender.
[4] *Lord Castlewood . . . tipsy.* The bishop implies that since the Pretender impersonated Lord Castlewood, the latter would have to bear the charge of intemperance.
[5] She had really been sent to the Castlewoods' country place. See note preceding Chapter XI.

70 the presence or absence of any lady, however beautiful.

We were yet at table when Dr. A. came from the Palace with a look of great alarm; the shocks the Queen had had the day before had acted on her severely; he had been sent for, and had ordered her to be blooded.[1]

No second visit could be paid to the Queen on that day at any rate; and 80 when our guest above gave his signal that he was awake, the Doctor, the Bishop, and Colonel Esmond waited upon the Prince's levée,[2] and brought him their news, cheerful or dubious. The Doctor had to go away presently, but promised to keep the Prince constantly acquainted with what was taking place at the Palace hard by. His counsel was, and the Bishop's, that as soon as ever the Queen's 90 malady took a favourable turn, the Prince should be introduced to her bedside; the Council summoned; the guard at Kensington and St. James's,[3] of which two regiments were to be entirely relied on, and one known not to be hostile, would declare for the Prince, as the Queen would before the Lords of her Council, designating him as the heir to her throne.

100 The Prince's meals were commonly served in the chamber which had been Beatrix's bedroom, adjoining that in which he slept. And the dutiful practice of his entertainers was to wait until their Royal guest bade them take their places at table before they sat down to partake of the meal. On this night only Frank Castlewood and his mother were in waiting when the supper was announced to 110 receive the Prince; who had passed the whole of the day in his own apartment, with the Bishop.

The Prince's countenance wore an ex-

pression by no means pleasant, when looking towards the little company assembled, and waiting for him, he did not see Beatrix's bright face there as usual to greet him. He asked Lady Esmond for his fair introducer of yesterday: her Ladyship only cast her eyes down, and 120 said quietly, Beatrix could not be of the supper that night; nor did she show the least sign of confusion, whereas Castlewood turned red, and Esmond was no less embarrassed.

Our guest swallowed his supper very sulkily; it was not till the second bottle his Highness began to rally. When Lady Castlewood asked leave to depart, he sent a message to Beatrix, hoping she 130 would be present at the next day's dinner, and applied himself to drink and to talk afterwards, for which there was subject in plenty.

The next day we heard from our informer at Kensington[1] that the Queen was somewhat better, and had been up for an hour, though she was not well enough yet to receive any visitor.

At dinner a single cover was laid for 140 his Royal Highness, and the two gentlemen[2] alone waited on him.

The Prince tried to cover his displeasure: he was but a clumsy dissembler at that time, and when out of humour could with difficulty keep a serene countenance; and having made some foolish attempts at trivial talk, he came to his point presently, and in as easy a manner as he could, saying to Lord Castlewood, 150 he hoped, he requested, his Lordship's mother and sister would be of the supper that night. As the time hung heavy on him, and he must not go abroad,[3] would not Miss Beatrix hold him company at a game of cards?

At this, looking up at Esmond, and taking the signal from him, Lord Castlewood informed his Royal Highness that

[1] Caused to bleed by opening a vein, an old-fashioned medical practice.

[2] A reception held by a prince or noble upon rising in the morning.

[3] An old palace in London where certain members of the royal family resided.

[1] That is, at the royal palace.

[2] Lord Castlewood and Henry Esmond.

[3] Out of doors.

160 his sister Beatrix was not at Kensington; and that her family had thought it best she quit the town.

"Not at Kensington!" says he. "Is she ill? she was well yesterday; wherefore should she quit the town? That which you do is unworthy, Monsieur; it is inhospitable — is, is lâche,[1] yes, lâche" (he spoke rapidly in French, his rage carrying him away with each phrase):
170 "I come to your house; I risk my life; I repose myself on your fidelity; I have no company but your Lordship's sermons or the conversation of that adorable young lady, and you take her from me! Merci, Monsieur![2] I shall thank you when I have the means; I shall know to recompense a devotion a little importunate, my Lord — a little importunate.[3] I enter your house, and you mis-
180 trust me. I will leave it, Monsieur; from to-night I will leave it. I have other friends whose loyalty will not be so ready to question mine. Bring me a coach and let me quit this place."

My Lord Castlewood replied to the Prince's tirade very nobly and simply.

"Sir," says he, "your Royal Highness is pleased to forget that others risk their lives, and for your cause. Very few
190 Englishmen, please God, would dare lay hands on your sacred person, though none would ever think of respecting ours. Our family's lives are at your service."

[Though the Prince's anger continues throughout the evening, he does not actually leave the house that night, as he had threatened to do.]

At an early hour next morning the Bishop arrived, and was closeted for some time with his master in his own apartment.

"I have soothed your guest," says he, coming out to the two gentlemen and the widow,[1] who had been made acquainted 200 with somewhat of the dispute of the night before. "But I think, all things considered, 'tis as well he should leave this house."

The Prince entered [the room] presently with a smile on his face, and if he felt any offence against us on the previous night, at present exhibited none. He offered a hand to each gentleman with great courtesy. "If all your bishops 210 preach so well as Doctor Atterbury," says he, "I don't know, gentlemen, what may happen to me. I spoke very hastily my Lords, last night, and ask pardon of both of you. But I must not stay any longer," says he, "giving umbrage[2] to good friends. My Lord Bishop hath found a safe place for me, hard by at a curate's house, whom the Bishop can trust. Where is my hostess, that I may bid her 220 farewell? to welcome her in a house of my own, soon, I trust, where my friends shall have no cause to quarrel with me."

FROM CHAPTER XII

A Great Scheme, and Who Balked It

From the conduct of my Lord Bolingbroke,* those who were interested in the scheme they had in hand saw pretty well that he was not to be trusted. Should the Prince prevail, it was his Lordship's gracious intention to declare for him; should the Hanoverian party[3] bring in their Sovereign, who more ready to go on his knee, and cry "God save King George"? 10

Our friends kept a pretty close watch upon his[4] motions, as on those of the brave and hearty Whig* party, that made little concealment of theirs. They would have in the Elector, and used

---

[1] Unworthy, cowardly.

[2] *Merci, Monsieur!* French for "Thanks, Sir!"

[3] *I shall know . . . importunate.* "I shall know how to recompense your devotion, which requires too much of me."

[1] The widowed Lady Castlewood.

[2] Offense.

[3] *Hanoverian party.* The political party that favored the future George I, who came from Hanover, Germany.

[4] Bolingbroke's.*

every means in their power to effect their end. My Lord Marlborough* was now with them. His expulsion from power by the Tories* had thrown that great cap-
20 tain at once on the Whig side. We heard he was coming from Antwerp[1]; and, in fact, on the day of the Queen's death, he once more landed on English shore. A great part of the army was always with their illustrious leader; even the Tories in it were indignant at the injustice of the persecution which the Whig officers were made to undergo. The chiefs of these were in London, and at
30 the head of them one of the most intrepid men in the world, the Scots Duke of Argyle,[2] whose conduct on the second day after that to which I have now brought down my history, ended, as such honesty and bravery deserved to end, by establishing the present Royal race on the English throne.

Meanwhile there was no slight difference of opinion amongst the councillors
40 surrounding the Prince, as to the plan his Highness should pursue. His female Minister at Court, fancying she saw some amelioration[3] in the Queen, was for waiting a few days, or hours it might be, until he could be brought to her bedside, and acknowledged as her heir. Mr. Esmond was for having him march thither, escorted by a couple of troops of Horse Guards, and openly presenting
50 himself to the Council. During the whole of the night of the 29th–30th July, the Colonel was engaged with gentlemen of the military profession, whom 'tis needless here to name; suffice it to say that several of them had exceeding high rank in the army, and one of them in especial was a General, who, when he heard the Duke of Marlborough* was coming on

the other side, waved his crutch over his head with a huzzah, at the idea that he 60 should march out and engage him. Of the three Secretaries of State, we knew that one was devoted to us. The Governor of the Tower[1] was ours; the two companies on duty at Kensington barrack were safe; and we had intelligence, very speedy and accurate, of all that took place at the Palace within.

At noon, on the 30th of July, a message came to the Prince's friends that the 70 Committee of Council was sitting at Kensington Palace. In an hour afterwards, hurried news was brought that the two great Whig* Dukes, Argyle[2] and Somerset,[3] had broke into the Council Chamber without a summons, and had taken their seat at table. After holding a debate there, the whole party proceeded to the chamber of the Queen, who was lying in great weakness, but still sensible, 80 and the Lords recommended his Grace of Shrewsbury[4] as the fittest person to take the vacant place of Lord Treasurer; her Majesty gave him the staff,[5] as all know. "And now," writ my messenger from Court, "*now or never is the time.*"

Now or never was the time indeed. In spite of the Whig* Dukes, our side had still the majority in the Council, and Esmond, to whom the message had been 90 brought (the personage at Court not being aware that the Prince had quitted his lodging in Kensington Square), and gallant young Frank Castlewood, putting on sword and uniform, took a brief leave of their dear lady,[6] who embraced and

[1] An important seaport of Belgium (formerly part of Holland).
[2] *Duke of Argyle.* John Campbell (1678–1743), second Duke of Argyle, a Scottish general who in 1715 suppressed a Jacobite* rebellion in favor of the Old Pretender.
[3] Here, improvement in health.

[1] The Tower of London, an important stronghold at that time.
[2] See column 1, note 2.
[3] Charles Seymour (1662–1748), a powerful Whig* politician and an opponent of the Old Pretender's claims to the throne.
[4] *his Grace of Shrewsbury.* Charles Talbot, Duke of Shrewsbury, a Whig* statesman who, as treasurer and Lord Justice of England, did much to prevent the accession of the Old Pretender* and ensure the accession of George I.
[5] The staff of office as Lord Treasurer.
[6] The widowed Lady Castlewood.

blessed them both, and went to her chamber to pray for the issue of the great event which was then pending.

100 Castlewood sped to the barrack to give warning to the captain of the Guard there; and then went to the "King's Arms" tavern at Kensington, where our friends were assembled, having come by parties of twos and threes, riding or in coaches, and were got together in the upper chamber, fifty-three of them; their servants, who had been instructed to bring arms likewise, being below in 110 the garden of the tavern, where they were served with drink. Out of this garden is a little door that leads into the road of the Palace, and through this it was arranged that masters and servants were to march; when that signal was given, and that Personage appeared, for whom all were waiting. There was in our company the famous officer next in command to the Captain-General of the Forces, his 120 Grace the Duke of Ormond,[1] who was within the Council. There were with him two more lieutenant-generals, nine major-generals and brigadiers, seven colonels, eleven Peers of Parliament, and twenty-one members of the House of Commons. The Guard was with us within and without the Palace; the Queen was with us; the Council; the day was our own; and with a beating 130 heart, Esmond walked rapidly to the Mall[2] of Kensington, where he had parted with the Prince on the night before. For three nights the Colonel had not been to bed; the last had been passed summoning the Prince's friends together, of whom the great majority had no sort of inkling of the transaction pending until they were told that he was actually on the spot, and were summoned to 140 strike the blow.

---

[1] *Duke of Ormond.* James Butler (1665–1745), an Irish statesman and general who in 1712 succeeded Marlborough* as chief of the English forces on the Continent.

[2] A level shaded walk.

[Henry Esmond now hastens to notify the Pretender that all is ready for him to appear in public as the acknowledged heir to the throne.]

[Esmond] ran to the curate's house in Kensington Mall, and asked for Mr. Bates, the name the Prince went by. The curate's wife said Mr. Bates had gone abroad very early in the morning in his boots, saying he was going to the Bishop of Rochester's house at Chelsey. But the Bishop had been at Kensington himself two hours ago to seek for Mr. Bates, and had returned in his coach to 150 his own house, when he heard that the gentleman was gone thither to seek him.

This absence was most unpropitious, for an hour's delay might cost a kingdom; Esmond had nothing for it but to hasten to the "King's Arms," and tell the gentlemen there assembled that Mr. George (as we called the Prince there) was not at home, but that Esmond would go fetch him; and taking a Gen- 160 eral's coach that happened to be there, Esmond drove across the country to Chelsey, to the Bishop's house there.

"Where is Mr. George?" says Mr. Esmond; "now is the time."

The Bishop looked scared. "I went to his lodging," he said, "and they told me he was come hither. I returned as quick as coach would carry me; and he hath not been here."   170

The Colonel burst out with an oath; ran down the stairs again, and bidding the coachman, an old friend and fellow-campaigner, drive as if he was charging the French — they were back at Kensington in half-an-hour.

Again Esmond went to the curate's house. Mr. Bates had not returned. The Colonel had to go with this blank[1] errand to the gentlemen at the "King's 180 Arms," that were grown very impatient by this time.

As we were looking out from the win-

---

[1] Fruitless.

dow in gloomy discourse, we heard presently trumpets blowing, and some of us ran to the window of the front room, looking into the High Street of Kensington, and saw a regiment of horse coming.

"It's Ormand's Guards," says one.

190 "No, it's Argyle's[1] old regiment!"[2] says my General, clapping down his crutch.

〕It was, indeed, Argyle's regiment that was brought from Westminster, and that took the place of the regiment at Kensington on which we could rely.

As we were talking, Castlewood entered the room with a disturbed air.

"What news, Frank?" says the Colo-200 nel. "Is Mr. George coming at last?"

"Look here!" said Castlewood, holding out a paper. "I found it in a book. It was directed to me, and I broke the seal and read it."

The whole assembly of officers seemed to swim away before Esmond's eyes as he read the paper; all that was written on it was: — "Beatrix Esmond is sent away to prison, to Castlewood, where 210 she will pray for happier days."

"Can you guess where he is?" says Castlewood.

"Yes," says Colonel Esmond. He knew full well; Frank knew full well: our instinct told whither that traitor had fled.

He had courage to turn to the company and say: "Gentlemen, I fear very much that Mr. George will not be here to-day: 220 something hath happened — and — and — I very much fear some accident may befall him, which must keep him out of the way. Having had your noon's draught, you had best pay the reckoning and go home; there can be no game where there is no one to play it."

Some of the gentlemen went away without a word, others called to pay their duty to her Majesty and ask for

her health. The little army disappeared 230 into the darkness out of which it had been called; there had been no writings, no paper to implicate any man. Some few officers and members of Parliament had been invited over night to breakfast at the "King's Arms" at Kensington; and they had called for their bill and gone home.

[The Pretender had gone to visit Beatrix and so, by yielding to a passing fancy, had lost his chance at the throne.]

Discussion Hints

1. *The History of Henry Esmond* includes historical events between the years 1690 and 1715. During what period represented in *English Writers* do these dates fall? What personages and events in that period are referred to in the selection given here?

2. Can you point out examples of Thackeray's rhythmic, haunting style in the selection given here?

3. Read again the headnote to the selection from *The History of Henry Esmond*, the footnotes, and the appropriate entries in the "Dictionary of Names and Phrases," and then be prepared to report on the chief historical references in the selection.

4. What friends, according to Colonel Esmond, may the Pretender count on at the beginning of the selection? Which of these fail him at the end?

5. Read again the passage describing Beatrix descending the stair (p. 450, ll. 150–163). It is famous as an example of Thackeray's ability to present a dramatic setting. See the illustration on page 451.

6. What part does John Lockwood play?

7. Point out passages that seem vague until we know that they refer to the plot designed to make the Old Pretender* king of England.

8. What was Lady Castlewood's reaction to the behavior of the Pretender while in her home? Illustrate your answer by quotations from the selection.

9. Write a theme of about a hundred words on the character of the Old Pretender* as revealed in the selection.

[1] See page 459, column 1, note 2.
[2] A regiment that was unfavorable to the cause of the Old Pretender.

Words and Phrases to be Explained

contiguous (p. 448, l. 11)
an inconceivable levity (p. 449, ll. 119–120)
convivial (p. 452, l. 269)
demeanour (p. 452, l. 273)
mortification (p. 452, ll. 274–275)
supplications (p. 455, ll. 229–230)
altercation (p. 456, l. 38)
importunate (p. 458, ll. 177–178)
tirade (p. 458, l. 186)
inkling (p. 460, l. 137)
unpropitious (p. 460, l. 153)

Suggestions for Reading

The History of Henry Esmond
The Virginians (sequel to *Henry Esmond*)
Vanity Fair
The Newcomes
The History of Pendennis

LYRIC POETRY[1]

ALFRED LORD TENNYSON[2] (1809–1892)

Break, Break, Break

When Tennyson, as a youth of eighteen, entered Cambridge University he met Arthur Hallam, who was two years younger. Between Hallam and Tennyson there quickly sprang up one of those rare and intimate college friendships which remain as cherished possessions in after years. Like David* and Jonathan in the Bible, they loved each other with a love "passing the love of women." An additional tie between them was formed later when Hallam became engaged to Tennyson's sister. Tennyson said of Hallam, "He was as near perfection as mortal man could be." In the fall of 1833, at the early age of twenty-two, Hallam died suddenly while on a trip to the Continent. The blow almost broke Tennyson's heart. He was stunned by it into grief-stricken silence. Then out of his sadness came first the cry of "Break, Break, Break"; next "Ulysses"; and, much later, growing and evolving with time, *In Memoriam* (p. 471).

BREAK, break, break,
 On thy cold grey stones, O Sea!
And I would that my tongue could utter
 The thoughts that arise in me.

O well for the fisherman's boy,
 That he shouts with his sister at play!
O well for the sailor lad,
 That he sings in his boat on the bay!

And the stately ships go on
 To their haven under the hill;   10
But O for the touch of a vanish'd hand,
 And the sound of a voice that is still![1]

Break, break, break,
 At the foot of thy crags, O Sea!
But the tender grace of a day that is dead
 Will never come back to me.

Ulysses

"Ulysses" is frequently considered Tennyson's greatest poem. Even readers who do not care greatly for his other poetry admire it. The distinguished critic Thomas Carlyle declared it was "Ulysses" that first convinced him Tennyson was a true poet. It is said that when in 1845 the British government had a vacant pension to bestow and Tennyson's name among others was being considered, a friend of Tennyson's got the prime minister to read "Ulysses," whereupon the pension was granted.

The poem takes up the story of Ulysses* where Homer* leaves off. The Iliad* deals with the close of the ten-year siege of Troy

by the Greeks, among whom Ulysses was a wise counselor and courageous chieftain. The Odyssey* relates Ulysses' thrilling adventures during his ten years of wandering from Troy to Ithaca, his island home in Greece. Arriving there after twenty years of absence, he slew the greedy suitors who were wasting his possessions and harassing his faithful wife Penelope (pĕ nĕl'ō pĕ). It is at this point that Tennyson takes up the tale.

He represents Ulysses as old and wise, but still stout-hearted and restless. The Greek chieftain has seen too much and has done too much to find contentment in his quiet island kingdom. He calls his loyal veterans around him and challenges them to follow him into

[1] For general discussion hints on the lyric poetry of the Victorian Period see page 501.
[2] For biography see page 726.

[1] *But . . . still!* These lines are famous. Remember them.

the unknown, to look again upon the bright face of danger, for he is resolved

"To strive, to seek, to find, and not to yield."

One reason for the poem's impressiveness is its underlying sincerity and intensity. Tennyson himself explained that it "was written soon after Arthur Hallam's death and gave my feeling about going forward and braving the struggle of life perhaps more simply than anything in *In Memoriam*." In other words, "Ulysses" may be read as an allegorical* poem depicting the incentive to look upon life as a great adventure and the need of braving the struggle no matter what obstacles we meet or what the end may be.

IT LITTLE profits that an idle king,
By this still hearth, among these
    barren crags,
Match'd with an agèd wife, I mete and
    dole[1]
Unequal laws unto a savage race,
That hoard, and sleep, and feed, and
    know not me.
I cannot rest from travel: I will drink
Life to the lees:[2] all times I have enjoy'd
Greatly, have suffer'd greatly, both with
    those
That loved me, and alone; on shore,
    and when   9
Thro' scudding drifts the rainy Hyades*
Vext the dim sea; I am become a name;
For always roaming with a hungry heart
Much have I seen and known; cities of
    men,
And manners, climates, councils, govern-
    ments,
Myself not least, but honour'd of them
    all;
And drunk delight of battle with my
    peers,
Far on the ringing plains of windy Troy.*
I am a part of all that I have met.
Yet all experience is an arch where-thro'
Gleams that untravell'd world, whose
    margin fades   20
Forever and forever when I move.

How dull it is to pause, to make an end,
To rust unburnish'd, not to shine in use!
As tho' to breathe were life. Life piled
    on life
Were all too little, and of one to me
Little remains: but every hour is saved
From that eternal silence, something
    more,
A bringer of new things; and vile it were
For some three suns to store and hoard
    myself,   29
And this grey spirit yearning in desire
To follow knowledge like a sinking star,
Beyond the utmost bound of human
    thought.
    This is my son, mine own Telemachus,*
To whom I leave the sceptre and the
    isle —
Well-loved of me, discerning to fulfil
This labour, by slow prudence to make
    mild
A rugged people, and thro' soft degrees
Subdue them to the useful and the good.
Most blameless is he, centred in the
    sphere
Of common duties, decent not to fail   40
In offices of tenderness, and pay
Meet[1] adoration to my household gods,
When I am gone. He works his work, I
    mine.
    There lies the port; the vessel puffs
    her sail:
There gloom the dark broad seas. My
    mariners,
Souls that have toil'd, and wrought, and
    thought with me —
That ever with a frolic welcome took
The thunder and the sunshine, and op-
    posed
Free hearts, free foreheads — you and I
    are old;
Old age hath yet his honour and his toil;
Death closes all: but something ere the
    end,   51
Some work of noble note, may yet be
    done,
Not unbecoming men that strove with
    Gods.

[1] *mete and dole*. Measure and deal out bit by bit.
[2] *I . . . lees*. I will experience all that life has to give. "Lees" means "last drop," "dregs."

[1] Fit, due.

The lights begin to twinkle from the rocks:

The long day wanes: the slow moon climbs: the deep

Moans round with many voices. Come, my friends,

'Tis not too late to seek a newer world.

Push off, and sitting well in order smite

The sounding furrows; for my purpose holds

To sail beyond the sunset, and the baths

Of all the western stars, until I die. 61

It may be that the gulfs will wash us down:

It may be we shall touch the Happy* Isles,

And see the great Achilles,* whom we knew.

Tho' much is taken, much abides; and tho'

We are not now that strength which in old days

Moved earth and heaven; that which we are, we are;

One equal temper of heroic hearts,

Made weak by time and fate, but strong in will 69

To strive, to seek, to find, and not to yield.

Locksley Hall

"Locksley Hall" is one of Tennyson's earliest and best-known poems. It is written in the form of a soliloquy supposed to be uttered by a thoughtful young man who, with little experience of the world, has returned, on a hunting trip, to his boyhood home, Locksley Hall. From memories of his earlier years the imaginary speaker passes to bitter musings on the fickleness of Amy, his cousin. She has rejected his love in order to marry a wealthy rival whose "grossness" of nature, he feels, will drag her down to his low level. Into this slender narrative the speaker weaves thoughts on such subjects as the evils of mercenary marriages, labor problems, democracy, civilization remade by science, world war, world peace, an international republic, woman's rights, and the relative advantages of primitive and civilized life. He ends by expressing the hope that, in spite of his disappointment, he may still renew his earlier inspiration by means of the new discoveries of science.

All the subjects treated interested Tennyson and his contemporaries, and they still interest many of us who feel that our civilization needs reform, that "social wants" often "sin against the strength of youth," and that something should be done to create a better understanding between the nations of the world. Even the speaker's more fanciful ideas, such as that of escaping from the evils of civilized society to primitive life on a far-off tropical isle, find echoes in some minds today. Taken as a whole, the poem is a noble poetic expression of youthful idealism.

D

In spite of numerous digressions the progress of the speaker's thought is clear and simple. Follow it carefully by means of the interpretative outline inserted in the text. Not least of the attractive features of the poem is the spirited, galloping meter. To get the best effects from "Locksley Hall," read it aloud.

[Recollections of earlier years when the speaker, looking at the past and the future, expected the wonders of science to revolutionize the world.]

COMRADES, leave me here a little, while as yet 'tis early morn:

Leave me here, and when you want me, sound upon the bugle-horn.

'Tis the place, and all around it, as of old, the curlews call,

Dreary gleams about the moorland flying over Locksley Hall;

Locksley Hall, that in the distance overlooks the sandy tracts,

And the hollow ocean-ridges roaring into cataracts.

Many a night from yonder ivied casement, ere I went to rest,

Did I look on great Orion[1] sloping slowly to the West.

[1] A prominent constellation, supposed to represent the giant Orion, a hero of Greek mythology.

Many a night I saw the Pleiads,[1] rising
    thro' the mellow shade,
Glitter like a swarm of fire-flies tangled
    in a silver braid.   10

Here about the beach I wander'd,
    nourishing a youth sublime
With the fairy tales of science, and the
    long result of Time;[2]

When the centuries behind me like a
    fruitful land reposed;
When I clung to all the present for the
    promise that it closed:

When I dipt into the future far as
    human eye could see;
Saw the Vision of the world, and all the
    wonder that would be. —

[The speaker has fallen in love with his cousin
Amy.]

In the Spring a fuller crimson comes upon
    the robin's breast;
In the Spring the wanton lapwing gets
    himself another crest;

In the Spring a livelier iris[3] changes on
    the burnish'd dove;   19
In the Spring a young man's fancy
    lightly turns to thoughts of love.[4]

Then her cheek was pale and thinner than
    should be for one so young,
And her eyes on all my motions with a
    mute observance hung.

[1] The Pleiades, or Seven Stars, one of the constellations.
[2] *the fairy . . . Time.* Tennyson and other Victorians were profoundly impressed by the
  great age of the earth and other marvels set
  forth by scientific writers during the nineteenth century. Huxley's "On a Piece of
  Chalk" (p. 540) is one of many nineteenth-
  century scientific writings that reveal the
  "fairy tales of science" and "the long result
  of Time."
[3] The rainbow-colored ring on the neck of the
  male pigeon.
[4] *In . . . love.* This is a famous line.

And I said, "My cousin Amy, speak,
    and speak the truth to me,
Trust me, cousin, all the current of my
    being sets to thee."

On her pallid cheek and forehead came a
    colour and a light,
As I have seen the rosy red flushing in
    the northern night.[1]

And she turn'd — her bosom shaken
    with a sudden storm of sighs —
All the spirit deeply dawning in the dark
    of hazel eyes —

Saying, "I have hid my feelings, fearing
    they should do me wrong";   29
Saying, "Dost thou love me, cousin?"
    weeping, "I have loved thee long."

Love took up the glass of Time, and
    turn'd it in his glowing hands;   31
Every moment, lightly shaken, ran itself
    in golden sands.

Love took up the harp of Life, and smote
    on all the chords with might;
Smote the chord of Self, that, trembling,
    passed in music out of sight.[2]

Many a morning on the moorland did
    we hear the copses[3] ring,
And her whisper throng'd my pulses
    with the fullness of the Spring.

Many an evening by the waters did we
    watch the stately ships,
And our spirits rush'd together at the
    touching of the lips.

[But Amy has jilted him for an unworthy
    rival preferred by her father.]

O my cousin, shallow-hearted! O my
    Amy, mine no more!
O the dreary, dreary moorland! O the
    barren, barren shore!   40

[1] *rosy . . . night.* The aurora borealis, or northern
  lights.
[2] The beautiful figure in this stanza was a favorite
  of Tennyson's.   [3] Thickets.

Falser than all fancy fathoms, falser than
    all songs have sung,
Puppet to a father's threat, and servile to
    a shrewish tongue!

[The lover predicts unhappy results from
    Amy's marriage.]

Is it well to wish thee happy? — having
    known me — to decline
On a range of lower feelings and a nar-
    rower heart than mine!

Yet it shall be: thou shalt lower to his
    level day by day,
What is fine within thee growing coarse
    to sympathise with clay.

As the husband is, the wife is: thou art
    mated with a clown,
And the grossness of his nature will have
    weight to drag thee down.

He will hold thee, when his passion shall
    have spent its novel force,
Something better than his dog, a little
    dearer than his horse.   50

What is this? his eyes are heavy: think
    not they are glazed with wine.
Go to him: it is thy duty: kiss him:
    take his hand in thine.

It may be my lord is weary, that his brain
    is overwrought:
Soothe him with thy finer fancies, touch
    him with thy lighter thought.

He will answer to the purpose, easy things
    to understand —
Better thou wert dead before me, tho' I
    slew thee with my hand!

Better thou and I were lying, hidden from
    the heart's disgrace,
Roll'd in one another's arms, and silent
    in a last embrace.

[Melancholy thoughts on social injustice,
which lead him back to Amy and her fate.]

Cursed be the social wants that sin
    against the strength of youth!

Cursed be the social lies that warp us
    from the living truth!   60

Cursed be the sickly forms that err from
    honest Nature's rule!
Cursed be the gold that gilds the strait-
    en'd forehead of the fool!

Well — 'tis well that I should bluster! —
    Hadst thou less unworthy proved —
Would to God — for I had loved thee
    more than ever wife was loved.

Am I mad, that I should cherish that
    which bears but bitter fruit?
I will pluck it from my bosom, tho' my
    heart be at the root.

Never, tho' my mortal summers to such
    length of years should come
As the many-winter'd crow that leads the
    clanging rookery home.

Where is comfort? in division of the
    records of the mind?
Can I part her from herself, and love her,
    as I knew her, kind?   70

I remember one that perish'd; sweetly
    did she speak and move;
Such a one do I remember, whom to look
    at was to love.

Can I think of her as dead, and love her
    for the love she bore?
No — she never loved me truly; love is
    love for evermore.

Comfort? comfort scorn'd of devils!
    this is truth the poet sings,
That a sorrow's crown of sorrow is re-
    membering happier things.[1]

Drug thy memories, lest thou learn it,
    lest thy heart be put to proof,
In the dead unhappy night, and when the
    rain is on the roof.

---

[1] *That . . . things.* This line is often quoted. It
comes ultimately from Dante.*

Like a dog, he hunts in dreams, and thou
    art staring at the wall,
Where the dying night-lamp flickers, and
    the shadows rise and fall.   80

Then a hand shall pass before thee, point-
    ing to his drunken sleep,
To thy widow'd marriage-pillows, to the
    tears that thou wilt weep.

Thou shalt hear the "Never, never,"
    whisper'd by the phantom years,
And a song from out the distance in the
    ringing of thine ears;

And an eye shall vex thee, looking ancient
    kindness on thy pain.
Turn thee, turn thee on thy pillow; get
    thee to thy rest again.

Nay, but Nature brings thee solace; for
    a tender voice will cry,
'Tis a purer life than thine, a lip to drain
    thy trouble dry.

Baby lips will laugh me down; my latest
    rival brings thee rest.
Baby fingers, waxen touches, press me
    from the mother's breast.   90

O, the child too clothes the father with a
    dearness not his due.
Half is thine and half is his; it will be
    worthy of the two.

O, I see thee old and formal, fitted to thy
    petty part,
With a little hoard of maxims[1] preaching
    down a daughter's heart.

"They were dangerous guides, the feel-
    ings — she herself was not exempt —
Truly, she herself had suffer'd" —
    Perish in thy self-contempt!

_____
[1] Wise sayings, proverbs.

[Some occupation would help to save him
from despair, but he lacks money to open the
    doors of opportunity.]

Overlive it — lower yet — be happy!
    wherefore should I care?
I myself must mix with action, lest I
    wither by despair.

What is that which I should turn to,
    lighting upon days like these?
Every door is barr'd with gold, and
    opens but to golden keys.   100

Every gate is throng'd with suitors, all
    the markets overflow.
I have but an angry fancy; what is that
    which I should do?

I had been content to perish, falling on
    the foeman's ground,
When the ranks are roll'd in vapour,
    and the winds are laid with sound.

But the jingling of the guinea helps the
    hurt that Honour feels,
And the nations do but murmur, snarling
    at each other's heels.

[Recollections of his earlier hopes for himself
    and his fellow men.]

Can I but relive in sadness? I will turn
    that earlier page.
Hide me from thy deep emotion, O thou
    wondrous Mother-Age!

Make me feel the wild pulsation that I
    felt before the strife,
When I heard my days before me, and
    the tumult of my life;   110

Yearning for the large excitement that
    the coming years would yield,
Eager-hearted as a boy when first he
    leaves his father's field,

And at night along the dusky highway
    near and nearer drawn,
Sees in heaven the light of London flaring
    like a dreary dawn:

And his spirit leaps within him to be
gone before him then,
Underneath the light he looks at, in
among the throngs of men:

[Progress by means of organized labor and
democracy.]

Men, my brothers, men the workers,
ever reaping something new:
That which they have done but earnest
of the things that they shall do:

For I dipt into the future, far as human
eye could see,
Saw the Vision of the world, and all the
wonder that would be;   120

[A vision of aviation, of world war, and of
world peace.]

Saw the heavens fill with commerce,
argosies[1] of magic sails,
Pilots of the purple twilight, dropping
down with costly bales;

Heard the heavens fill with shouting,
and there rain'd a ghastly dew
From the nations' airy navies grappling
in the central blue[2];

Far along the world-wide whisper of the
south-wind rushing warm,
With the standards of the peoples plung-
ing thro' the thunder-storm;

Till the war-drum throbb'd no longer,
and the battle-flags were furl'd
In the Parliament of man, the Federation
of the world.

There the common sense of most shall
hold a fretful realm in awe,
And the kindly earth shall slumber,
lapt[3] in universal law.   130

So I triumph'd ere my passion sweeping
thro' me left me dry,
Left me with the palsied heart, and left
me with the jaundiced eye;

[Science advances slowly, but according to
"one increasing purpose."]

Eye, to which all order festers, all things
here are out of joint:
Science moves, but slowly slowly, creeping on from point to point:

Slowly comes a hungry people, as a lion
creeping nigher,
Glares at one that nods and winks behind
a slowly-dying fire.

Yet I doubt not thro' the ages one increasing purpose runs,
And the thoughts of men are widen'd
with the process of the suns.

What is that to him that reaps not harvest of his youthful joys,
Tho' the deep heart of existence beat forever like a boy's?   140

Knowledge comes, but wisdom lingers,
and I linger on the shore,
And the individual withers, and the world
is more and more.[1]

Knowledge comes, but wisdom lingers,
and he bears a laden breast,
Full of sad experience, moving toward the
stillness of his rest.

[He is ashamed of his foolish passion for Amy.
After all, he thinks, women are inferior
creatures.]

Hark, my merry comrades call me,
sounding on the bugle-horn,
They to whom my foolish passion were a
target for their scorn:

---

[1] Fleets of ships laden with great riches.
[2] This is famous as an early poetic prophecy of
warfare in the air.
[3] Wrapped.

[1] As the tendency of men to organize in large
groups has increased, the significance of the
individual has decreased.

Shall it not be scorn to me to harp on such
  a moulder'd string?
I am shamed thro' all my nature to have
  loved so slight a thing.

Weakness to be wroth with weakness!
  woman's pleasure, woman's pain —
Nature made them blinder motions[1]
  bounded in a shallower brain :   150

Woman is the lesser man, and all thy
  passions, match'd with mine,
Are as moonlight unto sunlight, and as
  water unto wine —

[He longs to escape from civilization to primitive life in the Orient, where he was born.]

Here at least, where nature sickens, nothing. Ah, for some retreat
Deep in yonder shining Orient, where
  my life began to beat;

Where in wild Mahratta-battle[2] fell my
  father evil-starr'd ; —
I was left a trampled orphan, and a selfish
  uncle's ward.

Or to burst all links of habit — there to
  wander far away,
On from island unto island at the gate-
  ways of the day.

Larger constellations burning, mellow
  moons and happy skies,
Breadths of tropic shade and palms in
  cluster, knots of Paradise.   160

Never comes the trader, never floats an
  European flag,
Slides the bird o'er lustrous woodland,
  swings the trailer from the crag;

Droops the heavy-blossom'd bower,
  hangs the heavy-fruited tree —
Summer isles of Eden lying in dark-
  purple spheres of sea.

There methinks would be enjoyment
  more than in this march of mind,
In the steamship, in the railway, in the
  thoughts that shake mankind.

There the passions cramp'd no longer
  shall have scope and breathing
  space ;
I will take some savage woman, she shall
  rear my dusky race.

Iron-jointed, supple-sinew'd, they shall
  dive, and they shall run,
Catch the wild goat by the hair, and hurl
  their lances in the sun ;   170

Whistle back the parrot's call, and leap
  the rainbows of the brooks,
Not with blinded eyesight poring over
  miserable books —

[Instead of seeking to escape from the world,
he will try to regain from the wonders of
modern science the enthusiasm he had before
he fell in love with Amy.]

Fool, again the dream, the fancy! but I
  know my words are wild,
But I count the grey barbarian lower
  than the Christian child.

I, to herd with narrow foreheads, vacant
  of our glorious gains,
Like a beast with lower pleasures, like a
  beast with lower pains!

Mated with a squalid savage — what to
  me were sun or clime?
I the heir of all the ages, in the foremost
  files of time —

I that rather held it better men should
  perish one by one,
Than that earth should stand at gaze like
  Joshua's moon[1] in Ajalon!   180

---

[1] Beings.
[2] The battle in which the imaginary speaker's
  father was killed. The Mahrattas were a warlike and powerful people of central India.

[1] *Joshua's moon.* "And the sun stood still, and
  the moon stayed, until the people had
  avenged themselves upon their enemies"
  (Joshua 10 : 13).

Not in vain the distance beacons.[1] For-
    ward, forward let us range,
Let the great world spin forever down
    the ringing grooves of change.

Thro' the shadow of the globe we sweep
    into the younger day:
Better fifty years of Europe than a cycle
    of Cathay.[2]

Mother-Age (for mine I knew not), help
    me as when life begun:
Rift the hills, and roll the waters, flash
    the lightnings, weigh the Sun.

O, I see the crescent[3] promise of my
    spirit hath not set.

Ancient founts of inspiration well thro'
    all my fancy yet.

Howsoever these things be, a long farewell
    to Locksley Hall!
Now for me[1] the woods may wither, now
    for me the roof-tree fall.   190

Comes a vapour from the margin, black-
    ening over heath and holt,[2]
Cramming all the blast before it, in its
    breast a thunderbolt.

Let it fall on Locksley Hall, with rain or
    hail, or fire or snow;
For the mighty wind arises, roaring sea-
    ward, and I go.

The Splendour Falls

"The Splendour Falls" is deservedly one of
the best-known of Tennyson's lyrics. At first
glance it appears to be no more than a successful presentation in verse of a musical echo of
bugle notes which Tennyson once heard
across the Lakes of Killarney in Ireland, or, in
other words, an unusually good example of the
use of alliteration* and internal rhyme.* But,
on careful reading, it is much more than this:
the true purpose is brought out in the last
stanza.

"The Splendour Falls" is one of the lyrics
included by Tennyson in *The Princess*, a
long narrative poem dealing with woman's
rights and many other matters. It was one
of Tennyson's favorite readings. You too
should read it aloud.

THE splendour falls on castle walls
    And snowy summits old in story;
The long light shakes across the lakes,
    And the wild cataract leaps in glory.

Blow, bugle, blow, set the wild echoes
    flying,
Blow, bugle; answer, echoes, dying,
    dying, dying.

O, hark, O, hear! how thin and clear,
    And thinner, clearer, farther going!
O, sweet and far from cliff and scar   9
    The horns of Elfland faintly blowing!
Blow, let us hear the purple glens replying,
Blow, bugle; answer, echoes, dying,
    dying, dying.

O love, they die in yon rich sky,
    They faint on hill or field or river;
Our echoes roll from soul to soul,
    And grow for ever and for ever.
Blow, bugle, blow, set the wild echoes
    flying,
And answer, echoes, answer, dying, dying,
    dying.

From *In Memoriam*[4]

The following lyrics are taken from *In
Memoriam*, Tennyson's most spiritual and
best-loved work. *In Memoriam* is a collection

of a hundred and thirty-three poems composed
at various times during seventeen years and
intended to commemorate the death of
Arthur Hallam, Tennyson's most intimate
friend and the fiancé of Tennyson's sister
Emily. But *In Memoriam* is more than an

---

[1] Gleams like a beacon.
[2] China; here, any far-off land.
[3] Growing, increasing.
[4] *In Memoriam*. To the memory of.

[1] *for me*. So far as I am concerned.   [2] Wood.

elegy,* or lament. In it Tennyson sets forth his feelings about art, the scientific knowledge of the nineteenth century, politics, religion, and a host of other matters. Though the individual lyrics vary considerably in merit, the best of them are characterized by the rich, mellow verse, the painstaking care, and the high ideals that mark his best work. Several of the poems and scores of individual lines have become famous.

The poems are written in a special stanza form consisting of four-stress iambic* lines rhyming *abba*. It is known as the "*In Memoriam* stanza."

PROEM

Firm faith in the immortality of the soul in spite of every doubt is the subject of the "Proem."

STRONG Son of God, immortal Love,
　Whom we, that have not seen thy
　　face,
　By faith, and faith alone, embrace,
Believing where we cannot prove;[1]

Thine are these orbs of light and shade;[2]
　Thou madest Life in man and brute;
　Thou madest Death; and lo, thy foot
Is on the skull which thou hast made.[3]

Thou wilt not leave us in the dust:　9
　Thou madest man, he knows not why,
　He thinks he was not made to die;[4]
And thou hast made him: thou art just.

Thou seemest human and divine,
　The highest, holiest manhood, thou:
　Our wills are ours, we know not how:
Our wills are ours, to make them thine.

Our little systems[5] have their day;
　They have their day and cease to be:
　They are but broken lights[6] of thee,
And thou, O Lord, art more than they.

We have but faith: we cannot know;
　For knowledge is of things we see;　22
　And yet we trust it comes from thee,
A beam in darkness:[1] let it grow.

Let knowledge grow from more to more,
　But more of reverence in us dwell;
　That mind and soul, according well,
May make one music as before,[2]

But vaster. We are fools and slight;
　We mock thee when we do not fear:　30
　But help thy foolish ones to bear;
Help thy vain worlds to bear thy light.

Forgive what seem'd my sin[3] in me;
　What seem'd my worth since I began;
　For merit lives from man to man,
And not from man, O Lord, to thee.

Forgive my grief for one removed,
　Thy creature, whom I found so fair.
　I trust he lives in thee, and there
I find him worthier to be loved.　　40

Forgive these wild and wandering cries,
　Confusions of a wasted youth;
　Forgive them where they fail in truth,
And in thy wisdom make me wise.

RING OUT, WILD BELLS

"Ring out, Wild Bells," the most popular lyric of *In Memoriam*, calls upon the New Year's bells to ring out the old epoch of war, disease, and sin, and to ring in the new era of order, peace, Christian benevolence, and truth.

RING out, wild bells, to the wild sky,
　The flying cloud, the frosty light:
　The year is dying in the night;
Ring out, wild bells, and let him die.

Ring out the old, ring in the new,
　Ring, happy bells, across the snow:
　The year is going, let him go;
Ring out the false, ring in the true.

---

[1] *Strong . . . prove.* This stanza sets forth Tennyson's belief in victory over death.
[2] *orbs . . . shade.* Planets, with one side illumined and the other in darkness.
[3] *thy foot . . . made.* Thou hast supreme power over death.
[4] *He . . . die.* Man has an instinctive belief in immortality.　　[5] Systems of philosophy.
[6] *broken lights.* Bits of knowledge.

[1] *A beam in darkness.* Knowledge is like a beam of light in the midst of darkness.
[2] *as before.* As they did before modern skepticism separated mind and soul.
[3] Sorrow for Hallam.

Ring out the grief that saps the mind,
  For those that here we see no more;
  Ring out the feud of rich and poor,
Ring in redress[1] to all mankind.   12

Ring out a slowly dying cause,
  And ancient forms of party strife;
  Ring in the nobler modes of life,
With sweeter manners, purer laws.

Ring out the want, the care, the sin,
  The faithless coldness of the times;
 Ring out, ring out my mournful rhymes,
But ring the fuller minstrel[2] in.   20

Ring out false pride in place and blood,
  The civic slander and the spite;
  Ring in the love of truth and right,
Ring in the common love of good.

Ring out old shapes of foul disease;
  Ring out the narrowing lust of gold;
  Ring out the thousand wars of old,
Ring in the thousand years of peace.

Ring in the valiant man and free,   29
  The larger heart, the kindlier hand;
  Ring out the darkness of the land,
Ring in the Christ that is to be.

Flower in the Crannied Wall

"Flower in the Crannied Wall" is important because it embodies in a few memorable words one of Tennyson's most firmly fixed beliefs — God lives in all nature, and we live in God; hence a complete understanding of even "the meanest flower" would reveal to us both God and man.

FLOWER in the crannied wall,
I pluck you out of the crannies,
I hold you here, root and all, in my hand,
Little flower — but *if* I could understand
What you are, root and all, and all in all,
I should know what God and man is.

Merlin and the Gleam

"Merlin* and the Gleam" tells us in allegorical* form how Tennyson, an old man, felt about his art. It is a poetical biography of a poet. The unrhymed, irregular verse is used in imitation of Old English poetry of about the supposed time of King Arthur,* when the prophet Merlin is said to have lived. The pupil who will read the poem until he masters the rhythm* and the beautiful imagery* will not only have a literary treat, but also receive one of the bravest and most inspiring calls ever made to follow one's ideals.

I

O YOUNG Mariner,[3]
  You from the haven
Under the sea-cliff,
You that are watching
The gray Magician[4]

With eyes of wonder,
I am Merlin,
And *I* am dying,
I am Merlin
Who follow The Gleam.[1]   10

II

Mighty the Wizard[2]
Who found me at sunrise
Sleeping. and woke me
And learn'd[3] me Magic!
Great the Master,
And sweet the Magic,
When over the valley,
In early summers,
Over the mountain,
On human faces,   20
And all around me,
Moving to melody,
Floated The Gleam.

[1] Remedy, relief.
[2] *fuller minstrel.* Here, some greater poet or singer. See also "minstrel." *
[3] The youth of England.
[4] Merlin.* Here, Tennyson.

[1] Passion for beauty in art.
[2] Bleys.*   [3] Taught.

III

Once at the croak of a Raven who crost it,
A barbarous people,[1]
Blind to the magic
And deaf to the melody,
Snarl'd at and cursed me.
A demon vext me,
The light retreated,   30
The landskip darken'd,
The melody deaden'd,
The Master whisper'd
"Follow The Gleam."

IV

Then to the melody,
Over a wilderness
Gliding, and glancing at
Elf of the woodland,
Gnome of the cavern,
Griffin * and Giant,   40
And dancing of Fairies
In desolate hollows,
And wraiths of the mountain,
And rolling of dragons
By warble of water,
Or cataract music
Of falling torrents,
Flitted The Gleam.

V

Down from the mountain
And over the level,   50
And steaming and shining on
Silent river,
Silvery willow,
Pasture and plowland,
Innocent maidens,
Garrulous children,
Homestead and harvest,
Reaper and gleaner,
And rough-ruddy faces
Of lowly labour,   60
Slided The Gleam. —

[1] *A barbarous people.* My critics.

VI

Then, with a melody
Stronger and statelier,
Led me at length
To the city and palace
Of Arthur * the king;
Touch'd at the golden
Cross of the churches,
Flash'd on the tournament,
Flicker'd and bicker'd[1]   70
From helmet to helmet,
And last on the forehead
Of Arthur the blameless
Rested The Gleam.

VII

Clouds and darkness
Closed upon Camelot *;
Arthur had vanish'd
I knew not whither,
The king who loved me,
And cannot die;[2]   80
For out of the darkness
Silent and slowly
The Gleam, that had waned[3] to a wintry
        glimmer
On icy fallow[4]
And faded forest,
Drew to the valley
Named of the shadow,[5]
And slowly brightening
Out of the glimmer,   89
And slowly moving again to a melody
Yearningly tender,
Fell on the shadow,
No longer a shadow,
But clothed with The Gleam.

VIII

And broader and brighter
The Gleam flying onward,
Wed to the melody,

[1] Moved quickly and unsteadily.
[2] According to the oldest tradition Arthur did not
    die, but went off to fairyland. See Malory's
    Morte d'Arthur, p. 49.
[3] Grown pale.   [4] Uncultivated field.
[5] *valley . . . shadow.* The Valley of the Shadow
    of Death.

Sang thro' the world;
And slower and fainter,
Old and weary,　　　　　100
But eager to follow,
I saw, whenever
In passing it glanced upon
Hamlet or city,
That under the Crosses
The dead man's garden,[1]
The mortal hillock,[2]
Would break into blossom;
And so to the land's
Last limit I came —　　　　110
And can no longer,
But die rejoicing,
For thro' the Magic
Of Him the Mighty,
Who taught me in childhood,

There on the border
Of boundless Ocean,
And all but in Heaven
Hovers The Gleam.

IX

Not of the sunlight,　　　120
Not of the moonlight,
Not of the starlight!
O young Mariner,
Down to the haven,
Call your companions,
Launch your vessel,
And crowd your canvas,
And, ere it vanishes
Over the margin,
After it, follow it,　　　130
Follow The Gleam.

[1] Cemetery.
[2] Mound over the grave.

Crossing the Bar

A few years after Tennyson became famous and had been made poet laureate,* he bought a house, Farringford (see illustration on page 476), on the Isle of Wight. There he lived nearly all the rest of his life. Once, when he was over eighty years old, full of years and of honors, he was returning home with his son across the narrow strait that separates the Isle of Wight from England. It was on this occasion that the idea of "Crossing the Bar" came to him. His son has explained: "It was written in my father's eighty-first year, on a day in October when we came from Aldworth to Farringford. Before reaching Farringford he had the 'moaning of the bar' in his mind, and after dinner he showed me this poem written out. I said, 'This is the crown of your life's work.' He answered, 'It came in a moment.' He explained the 'Pilot' as 'that Divine and Unseen who is always guiding us.'"

The poem speaks simply and beautifully of sunset, twilight, evening bell and evening star, the moving tide, the Master and the Pilot. Not a word is said of old age and death; yet the real theme of the poem is, of course, Tennyson's calm, confident, Christian attitude toward approaching death. It is a triumph in poetic suggestion.

A few days before his death Tennyson directed that this poem should be placed at the end of all editions of his works.

SUNSET and evening star,
 And one clear call for me!
And may there be no moaning of the bar,[1]
 When I put out to sea.

But such a tide as moving seems asleep,
 Too full for sound and foam,
When that which drew from out the
  boundless deep
 Turns again home.[2]

Twilight and evening bell,
 And after that the dark!　　　10
And may there be no sadness of farewell,
 When I embark;

[1] moaning of the bar. A reference to the moaning of the rising surf on the bar at the mouth of a river or bay from which the poet thinks of himself as sailing out into the sea of Eternity. The moaning of the bar usually forebodes a storm.

[2] When . . . home. Tennyson himself said that line 7 means "the vital spark, life" and that line 8 means "goes back to God, its source." The two lines therefore mean simply "When I die."

© Frith & Co.

Farringford, Tennyson's home on the Isle of Wight

For tho' from out our bourne[1] of Time
   and Place
  The flood may bear me far,
I hope to see my Pilot face to face
  When I have crost the bar.

Discussion Hints

Break, Break, Break

1. What is the theme of the poem? What is the effect of the phrase "cold grey stones" (l. 2) in connection with it?

2. How do lines 5–8 serve to remind the poet of his own sorrow?

3. What other things serve to recall his sorrow?

4. Compare lines 15–16 with Wordsworth's "Slumber Did My Spirit Seal" (p. 338). From a comparison of the two passages which do you regard as the more sincere?

[1] Boundary.

Ulysses

1. Point out lines which in your opinion are allegorical.* Explain their significance.

2. Explain lines 19–21. Do you agree with Tennyson?

3. How do Ulysses' plans for his own future contrast with his plans for Telemachus? What contrast does this imply between the characters of the two men?

4. One critic has said that Ulysses, on returning home after his many exciting and romantic experiences, could hardly be expected to settle down to a commonplace existence with nothing more inspiring than "pork chops and Penelope." After reading Tennyson's poem do you feel that many thrilling adventures unfit a man for a quiet domestic life? Discuss in class.

5. Why should Ulysses refer to Achilles?

6. Ulysses intends to sail from Greece out through the Strait of Gibraltar. What "newer world" (l. 57) might he have found if he had continued to sail westward?

7. Memorize lines 62–70.

Phrases to be Explained

barren crags (l. 2)
To rust unburnish'd (l. 23)
that eternal silence (l. 27)
The sounding furrows (l. 59)

Locksley Hall

1. Pick out five passages in "Locksley Hall" which allude to social problems. To what problem does each passage allude?

2. Do you recognize any of the lines of "Locksley Hall" as often quoted? If so, which ones?

3. How does the attitude toward woman as reflected in the poem differ, if at all, from that of today? Quote lines to prove your answer.

4. What is the meaning of the stanza beginning with line 33?

5. What recent scientific discoveries and inventions would fill Tennyson with enthusiasm? In answering do not be satisfied with referring to aviation and the radio; correlate Tennyson's poem with what you have learned in school about such subjects as chemistry, physics, astronomy, and the social sciences. Write a theme of two hundred words on "Locksley Hall" as a prophecy of more recent scientific discoveries.

6. Look up trochee,* and describe the meter of the poem.

Passages to be Explained

her eyes on all my motions with a mute observance hung (l. 22)
Cursed be the gold that gilds the straiten'd forehead of the fool! (l. 62)
Baby lips will laugh me down (l. 89)
the nations do but murmur, snarling at each other's heels (l. 106)
that earth should stand at gaze like Joshua's moon in Ajalon! (l. 180)

The Splendour Falls

1. It has been said that "The Splendour Falls" deals with four worlds: (*a*) the world of medieval castles; (*b*) the world of wild nature; (*c*) the world of romantic folk lore, where the "horns of Elfland" faintly sound;

and (*d*) the world of the future in which the echoes of exalted love

"roll from soul to soul,
And grow for ever and for ever."

Point out the passages that illustrate each of these elements.

2. Point out lines in which the effect is due largely to the skillful use of alliteration.*

3. Point out examples of internal* rhyme.

From *In Memoriam*

PROEM

1. What, according to the stanza beginning with line 25, will make increased knowledge a blessing to mankind?

2. How are lines 37–40 connected with "Break, Break, Break" (p. 463)?

RING OUT, WILD BELLS

1. What contrasts do you observe between the things that Tennyson asks the bells to ring out and those that he asks them to ring in?

2. What hopes illustrative of Tennyson's optimism are expressed?

3. What political or social reforms are suggested?

4. Why does Tennyson write "The year is going, let him go" (l. 7)?

5. Memorize the first stanza of the "Proem" and any two stanzas of "Ring Out, Wild Bells."

Flower in the Crannied Wall

1. After reading this short poem read the first four lines of Blake's "Auguries of Innocence" (p. 325), and decide which you like better. Explain your answer.

2. What does "crannied" mean?

Merlin and the Gleam

1. What message has the poem for young people?

2. Have you a purpose in life which you wish, above all else, to achieve? If so, what is it? If you do not care to tell the class, tell your teacher or your best friend.

3. In what respect does "Merlin and the Gleam" resemble "Ulysses" (p. 463)? In what respect is it like "Gareth and Lynette" and "The Passing of Arthur"? (The two latter are given in the revised edition of *Achievement* of this series.)

4. In stanza IV Tennyson refers to his early poems, in stanza VI to his Arthurian poems (*The Idylls of the King*), and in stanza VIII to his later poems.

5. What is the allegorical* significance of the poem?

6. Explain

a. *landskip* (l. 31)
b. *Gnome* (l. 39)
c. *wraiths* (l. 43)
d. *Garrulous* (l. 56)
e. *Hamlet* (l. 104)

General Discussion Hints on Tennyson's Lyric Poetry

1. What passages refer to or were suggested by Tennyson's friendship for Arthur Hallam? Quote them.

2. What poems refer to the part played in human life by (*a*) love between men and women? (*b*) love of humanity?

3. Discuss, with illustrations from the poems, Tennyson's interest and faith in scientific discoveries and inventions.

4. Point out passages that illustrate his idealism. Memorize two.

Suggestions for Reading[1]

"Lady Clara Vere de Vere"
"The May Queen"
"The Lotus-Eaters"
"A Dream of Fair Women"
"Sir Galahad"
From *The Princess*: "Tears, Idle Tears, I Know Not What They Mean," "Sweet and Low, Sweet and Low," and "Home They Brought Her Warrior Dead"
From *In Memoriam*: I, XXVII, XXXIV, L, LXXXVI, CVI, and CXXX
From *Maud*: "Come into the Garden, Maud" and "Oh! That 't Were Possible"
"The Song of the Brook"
"To Virgil"
"Locksley Hall Sixty Years After"

ROBERT BROWNING[2] (1812–1889)

From *Pippa Passes*

Pippa Passes is one of Browning's earliest and most admired works. It was begun in 1835, when the poet was a young man, and it was continued and revised for more than fifty years, reaching its final form in 1888, not many months before his death. It is partly dramatic, partly lyrical. Aside from its poetic beauty, it is important for us chiefly because it illustrates Browning's theory that even an obscure person may leave a lasting impression upon others. It centers around Felippa, familiarly known as Pippa, a little factory girl from a silk mill in the Italian town of Asolo (ä'zō lō). As Pippa goes about on her only day off, her one holiday in the year, she sings, and by her singing she unconsciously touches the lives of various people and turns them from evil to good, saving them from despair or from sin. Several of her songs are given here.

Pippa's unconscious teaching through her songs is full of truth and beauty; her deep love for humanity helps to illuminate some of the greatest difficulties of life; and her gentle, kindly philosophy furnishes the most natural, easy, and simple solutions of our most pressing human problems, such as personal relations (including married love) and other social questions.

Nowhere in Browning's writings has he combined dramatic interest with more freshness, charm, and true humanitarianism. Pippa herself has been rightly called a "beautiful creation," a naturally spiritual, sweetly human girl who wishes well to all her fellow creatures, has faith in humanity, and proves her faith by her life. The dramatic elements are subordinate to the lyric poems and their effects.

Pippa Passes was Browning's favorite among his works, as it was also the favorite of his wife, Elizabeth (see page 487). The following lyrics are among the best-known of those sung by Pippa.

[1] For suggestions for reading in Tennyson's narrative poetry see page 525.
[2] For biography see page 727.

I

[Leaving her poor room to go forth on her only holiday of the year, Pippa thinks of some of the people of her native town, Asolo, who are, she imagines, happier than she; yet she says she will pass them without envying them, and concludes that though she might wish to be one of them, she prefers to reflect the love of God for all human beings. She remembers that we are all creatures of him who "trod Paradise" and that of "the mass of deeds which make up life," "All service ranks the same with God."]

ALL service ranks the same with God:
  If now, as formerly he trod
Paradise, his presence fills
Our earth, each only as God wills
Can work—God's puppets, best and worst,
Are we; there is no last nor first.

Say not "a small event"! Why "small"?
Costs it more pain that this, ye call
A "great event," should come to pass, 9
Than that? Untwine me[1] from the mass
Of deeds which make up life, one deed
Power shall fall short in or exceed![2]

II

[Pippa passes the garden house where are the two persons whom she regards as the happiest in Asolo: Ottima and her lover. She does not dream that they, that very night, have murdered Ottima's rich old husband, owner of the silk mill in which Pippa works. Pippa's song brings to them the realization of their guilt and, some readers think, a determination to pay the price of their crime in suicide.]

> The year's at the spring
> And day's at the morn;
> Morning's at seven;
> The hillside's dew-pearled;
> The lark's on the wing;
> The snail's on the thorn:
> God's in his heaven —
> All's right with the world!

[1] For me.
[2] *Untwine . . . exceed.* Pippa is thinking in terms of the silk mill: life a tangled skein of seemingly fragile, thread-like deeds, every one of which seems to her as important as every other in the completed, strong hank. Look up *skein* and *hank* in the dictionary.

III

[A hot-headed revolutionist named Luigi (loō ē'jē) is almost persuaded by his mother to desist from his patriotic purpose of killing an evil king; but when he hears Pippa's song about an ideal king in the golden* age, whom even serpents did not dare to harm, he thinks he hears God's voice and returns to his virtuous, though no doubt mistaken, purpose. He rushes from the tower, where he and his mother have been talking, just in time to escape the police, who have come to arrest him.

In this lyric Browning shows his ability to paint a picture with words, here a picture of life in an early time before the complications of modern civilization. It is idyllic* in its picture of a happy people ruled by a king who loved his subjects, cherished their rights, and rendered simple justice in public. It reminds us of King Arthur as he is depicted in Tennyson's *Idylls of the King* (in the revised edition of *Achievement* of this series).]

A king lived long ago,
In the morning of the world,
When earth was nigher heaven than now;
And the king's locks curled,
Disparting[1] o'er a forehead full
As the milk-white space 'twixt horn and
    horn
Of some sacrificial[2] bull —
Only calm as a babe new-born:
For he was got to a sleepy mood,
So safe from all decrepitude,   10
Age with its bane,[3] so sure gone by,
(The gods so loved him while he dreamed)
That, having lived thus long, there seemed
No need the king should ever die.

Among the rocks his city was:
Before his palace, in the sun,
He sat to see his people pass,
And judge them every one
From its threshold of smooth stone.
They haled him[4] many a valley-thief   20
Caught in the sheep-pens, robber-chief
Swarthy and shameless, beggar-cheat,
Spy-prowler, or rough pirate found
On the sea-sand left aground;
And sometimes clung about his feet,

[1] Parted.   [2] Intended for sacrifice.
[3] Here, weakness and sorrow.
[4] *haled him.* Brought before him (as judge).

With bleeding lip and burning cheek,
A woman, bitterest wrong to speak
Of one with sullen thickset brows:
And sometimes from the prison-house 29
The angry priests a pale wretch brought,
Who through some chink had pushed and
  pressed
On knees and elbows, belly and breast,
Worm-like into the temple, — caught
He was by the very god,
Who ever in the darkness strode
Backward and forward, keeping watch
O'er his brazen bowls, such rogues to
  catch!
These, all and every one,
The king judged, sitting in the sun.

His councillors, on left and right,   40
Looked anxious up, — but no surprise
Disturbed the king's old smiling eyes
Where the very blue had turned to white.
'Tis said, a Python scared one day
The breathless city, till he came,
With forky tongue and eyes on flame,
Where the old king sat to judge alway;
But when he saw the sweepy hair
Girt with a crown of berries rare   49
Which the god will hardly give to wear
To the maiden who singeth, dancing bare
In the altar-smoke by the pine-torch lights,
At his wondrous forest rites, —
Seeing this, he did not dare
Approach that threshold in the sun,
Assault the old king smiling there.
Such grace had kings when the world
  begun!

IV

[An aged bishop is tempted by an unscrupulous wretch to become a party to the undoing of the innocent daughter of his dead brother, a deed by which he may gain great riches. Now Pippa, quite ignorant of who her parents are, is that innocent child. As the great man is about to make the terrible decision, he hears Pippa's song and orders the tempter to be arrested. Pippa's song reveals her love of nature and her intimacy with it. In it she reviews her life. She has loved nature from her earliest childhood, and has studied it so carefully that she has come to perceive the hidden beauty of earth, has learned to recognize the stars, and has gazed at the moon so often that she "could all but understand" the reasons for its changes throughout the year. "But," she imagines, "just as I attained this knowledge of truth and beauty, I died" ("God took me"). No wonder her uncle was moved to spare her life.]

Overhead the tree-tops meet,
Flowers and grass spring 'neath one's feet;
There was naught above me, naught
  below,
My childhood had not learned to know:
For, what are the voices of birds
— Ay, and of beasts, — but words, our
  words,
Only so much more sweet?
The knowledge of that with my life
  begun.
But I had so near made out the sun,
And counted your stars, the seven and
  one,   10
Like the fingers of my hand:
Nay, I could all but understand
Wherefore through heaven the white
  moon ranges;[1]
And just when out of her soft fifty
  changes[2]
No unfamiliar face might overlook me —
Suddenly God took me.

All service ranks the same with God —
With God, whose puppets, best and
  worst,
Are we; there is no last nor first.

[1] *I had ... ranges.* Pippa says that as a child she has observed nature carefully, noticing such heavenly bodies and constellations as stand out plain, to be seen by anyone: the sun; the moon; the seven stars which form the Great Dipper; and the North Star, to which the outer edge of the Dipper points. The four stars that form the bowl of the Dipper are grouped together as are the four fingers of Pippa's hand; the North Star stands apart from the Dipper as her thumb stands apart from the four fingers.
[2] *soft ... changes.* The moon changes four times during each month of twenty-eight days; that is, fifty times a year. Pippa means that she watches and is acquainted with the moon throughout the year.

Marching Along

[From "Cavalier Tunes"]

This is one of three stirring songs intended by Browning to represent the gay, reckless loyalty of the Cavalier* adherents of King Charles* I (see page 186), and their contempt for his Puritan opponents. The songs are among Browning's most readable poems. We read "Marching Along" to enjoy its singing quality and its meter, which imitates the quick tread of marching soldiers. This enjoyment does not grow less if we know something about the personages of whom the poet writes. Here, as elsewhere in Browning's poetry, it is especially important to make full use of the footnotes; for Browning often writes of real persons and real places, and in his poetry sense is usually as important as sound.

KENTISH Sir Byng stood for his King,[1]
Bidding the crop-headed Parliament[2]
        swing:
And, pressing a troop unable to stoop
And see the rogues flourish and honest
        folk droop,
Marched them along, fifty-score strong,
Great-hearted gentlemen, singing this
        song.

God for King Charles! Pym and such
        carles[3]
To the Devil that prompts 'em their
        treasonous parles[4]!
Cavaliers, up! Lips from the cup,
Hands from the pasty,[5] nor bite take nor
        sup   10
Till you're —

[1] *Kentish . . . King.* Sir Byng (bǐng) has raised a force in the shire of Kent and is hurrying to join the main Royalist army.
[2] *crop-headed Parliament.* Cropped hair was worn by the Puritans, who made up most of the Parliament.
[3] *carles.* Common fellows, churls.
[4] *parles.* Conferences, talks.
[5] *pasty.* Here, food in general; originally, meat pie.

CHORUS

Marching along, fifty-score strong,
Great-hearted gentlemen, singing this
        song.

Hampden to hell, and his obsequies'
        knell.
Serve Hazelrig, Fiennes, and young
        Harry[1] as well!
England, good cheer! Rupert[2] is near!
Kentish and loyalists, keep we not here,[3]

CHORUS

Marching along, fifty-score strong,
Great-hearted gentlemen, singing this
        song?

Then, God for King Charles! Pym and
        his snarls   20
To the Devil that pricks on such pestilent
        carles!
Hold by the right, you double your
        might;
So, onward to Nottingham,[4] fresh for the
        fight,

CHORUS

March we along, fifty-score strong,
Great-hearted gentlemen, singing this
        song!

[1] *Pym . . Hampden . . . Hazelrig, Fiennes . . young Harry.* All were leaders of various ranks on the antiroyalist side. It is interesting to note that young Harry is Sir Henry Vane, who became governor of the Massachusetts Bay Colony.
[2] *Rupert.* A famous cavalry leader who was a nephew of Charles I and fought on the Royalist side.
[3] *keep . . . here.* Let us not remain here, but march on, to join forces with Rupert at Nottingham.
[4] A town in England where, in 1642, Charles gathered his army.

D

Galloway

Palazzo Rezzonico, on the Grand Canal, Venice, where Robert Browning died

Home-Thoughts from Abroad

"Home-Thoughts from Abroad" has been called "a song of homesickness." In simple yet musical language Browning here interprets for us the characteristic English love of England and the English countryside. He was living in Italy when he wrote the poem. The delights of springtime in England have been a favorite subject with poets ever since the Middle Ages, but few have treated the subject so personally or have added so many picturesque details as Browning.

OH, TO be in England
Now that April's there,
And whoever wakes in England
Sees, some morning, unaware,
That the lowest boughs and the brush-
    wood sheaf
Round the elm-tree bole[1] are in tiny leaf,
While the chaffinch sings on the orchard
    bough
In England — now!

        [1] Trunk, stem.

And after April, when May follows
And the white-throat builds, and all the
    swallows!   10
Hark, where my blossomed pear-tree in
    the hedge
Leans to the field and scatters on the
    clover
Blossoms and dewdrops — at the bent
    spray's edge —
That's the wise thrush: he sings each
    song twice over
Lest you should think he never could
    recapture
The first fine careless rapture!
And, tho' the fields look rough with
    hoary dew,
All will be gay when noontide wakes anew
The buttercups, the little children's
    dower
— Far brighter than this gaudy melon-
    flower!

My Star

"My Star" is an exquisite little lyric written about the time of Browning's marriage. The poem evidently refers to the poet's own "star," Elizabeth Barrett.

ALL that I know
Of a certain star
Is, it can throw
(Like the angled spar[1])
Now a dart of red,
Now a dart of blue;
Till my friends have said

They would fain see, too,
My star that dartles[1] the red and the
blue!
Then it stops like a bird; like a flower,
hangs furled: 10
They must solace themselves with the
Saturn above it.
What matter to me if their star is a
world?
Mine has opened its soul to me; there-
fore I love it.[2]

Evelyn Hope

"Evelyn Hope" is one of the most exquisite expressions in literature of a devotion that contains no earthly elements, but is purely spiritual. The speaker's love for Evelyn Hope will not reach its perfect fulfillment until he also is in the spirit world.

One can appreciate this poem much more fully if he tries to visualize the scene. The almost completely darkened room; the speaker, nearly fifty years old, gazing sadly at the beautiful girl of sixteen who has just died, both of them surrounded by the things that once were hers, — these form, indeed, a proper setting for the gentle and mature melancholy of the poem. The dominant thought is found in lines 25–32. God creates his works with the intention that they shall eventually be completed, either in this life or in another. Consequently Evelyn Hope's lover is serene in the certainty that his love will be rewarded, despite the fact that he must become perfected ("Through worlds I shall traverse") before he is united with his love.

Here, as elsewhere in Browning, read the poem aloud so as to understand how the thought and feeling are reflected in the words and meter.

BEAUTIFUL Evelyn Hope is dead!
Sit and watch by her side an hour.
That is her book-shelf, this her bed;
She plucked that piece of geranium-
flower,

Beginning to die too, in the glass;
Little has yet been changed, I think:
The shutters are shut, no light may pass
Save two long rays through the hinge's
chink.

Sixteen years old when she died!
Perhaps she had scarcely heard my
name;   10
It was not her time to love; beside,
Her life had many a hope and aim,
Duties enough and little cares,
And now was quiet, now astir,
Till God's hand beckoned unawares, —
And the sweet white brow is all of her.[3]

Is it too late then, Evelyn Hope?
What, your soul was pure and true,
The good stars met in your horoscope,
Made you of spirit, fire and dew[4] —
And, just because I was thrice as old 21
And our paths in the world diverged
so wide,
Each was naught to each, must I be told?
We were fellow mortals, naught be-
side?

[1] Darts repeatedly.
[2] *Then it stops . . . I love it.* When others try to see the star they see only Saturn, which, though a world, can be seen by everyone. The poet loves his star because he alone can see it.
[3] *All of her.* All that is left of her.
[4] *spirit . . . dew.* The finer elements.

[1] *angled spar.* The Iceland spar, or prism, which makes colors change according to the angle from which one looks through it.

No, indeed![1] for God above
  Is great to grant, as mighty to make,
And creates the love to reward the love:
  I claim you still, for my own love's
    sake!
Delayed it may be for more lives yet,
  Through worlds I shall traverse, not
    a few: 30
Much is to learn,[2] much to forget
  Ere the time be come for taking you.

But the time will come, — at last it will,
  When, Evelyn Hope, what meant (I
    shall say)
In the lower earth, in the years long
    still,
  That body and soul so pure and gay[3]?
Why your hair was amber, I shall divine,
  And your mouth of your own gera-
    nium's red —
And what you would do with me, in fine,[4]
  In the new life come in the old one's
    stead.   40

I have lived (I shall say) so much since
    then,
  Given up myself so many times,
Gained me the gains of various men,
  Ransacked the ages, spoiled the climes;[1]
Yet one thing, one, in my soul's full scope,
  Either I missed or itself missed me:
And I want and find you, Evelyn Hope!
  What is the issue? let us see!

I loved you, Evelyn! all the while,   49
  My heart seemed full as it could hold;
There was place and to spare for the
    frank young smile,
  And the red young mouth, and the
    hair's young gold.
So, hush, — I will give you this leaf to
    keep:
  See, I shut it inside the sweet cold
    hand!
There, that is our secret: go to sleep!
  You will wake, and remember, and
    understand.

Prospice[5]

"Prospice," written soon after the death
of Browning's wife, has been called "the most
original poem on death in English literature."
In unusually striking imagery* the poet expresses his desire to meet death bravely and
turn defeat into victory. The poem is written
in mingled iambic* and anapaestic* feet.

Fear death? — to feel the fog in my
    throat,
  The mist in my face,
When the snows begin, and the blasts
    denote
  I am nearing the place,

The power of the night, the press of the
    storm,
  The post of the foe;
Where he stands, the Arch Fear[2] in a visi-
    ble form,
  Yet the strong man must go:
For the journey is done and the summit
    attained,
  And the barriers fall,   10
Tho' a battle's to fight ere the guerdon[3]
    be gained,
  The reward of it all.
I was ever a fighter, so — one fight more,
  The best and the last!
I would hate that death bandaged my
    eyes, and forbore,
  And bade me creep past.

[1] *No, indeed!* This answers the question asked in
  line 17.
[2] *Much . . . learn.* There is much for me to
  learn.
[3] *When . . . gay?* When I shall say, "What did
  your body and soul so pure and gay mean
  when you lived on earth many years ago?"
[4] *in fine.* In short; in the end.
[5] *Prospice* (prŏs'pǐ sē). "Look forward."

[1] *spoiled the climes.* Had full experience of all
  parts of the universe.
[2] *Arch Fear.* Death.
[3] Reward.

No! let me taste the whole of it, fare like
   my peers[1]
   The heroes of old,
Bear the brunt,[2] in a minute pay glad
   life's arrears
   Of pain, darkness and cold.   20
For sudden the worst turns the best to
   the brave,
   The black minute's at end,

And the elements' rage, the fiend-voices
   that rave,
   Shall dwindle, shall blend,
Shall change, shall become first a peace
   out of pain,
   Then a light, then thy breast,
O thou soul of my soul![1] I shall clasp thee
   again,
   And with God be the rest!

Epilogue to *Asolando*

The "Epilogue to *Asolando*," written
shortly before Browning's death, expresses in
striking and forceful language the poet's desire to continue, even beyond the grave, his
career of strenuous optimism and endeavor.
Its message is in direct contrast to the calm
resignation of Tennyson's "Crossing the
Bar" (p. 475).

AT THE midnight in the silence of the
   sleep-time,
   When you set your fancies free,
Will they pass to where — by death, fools
   think, imprisoned —
Low he lies who once so loved you, whom
   you loved so,
      — Pity me?

Oh to love so, be so loved, yet so mistaken!
   What had I on earth to do
With the slothful, with the mawkish, the
   unmanly?
Like the aimless, helpless, hopeless, did I
   drivel
      — Being — who?   10

One who never turned his back but
   marched breast forward,
   Never doubted clouds would break,
Never dreamed, tho' right were worsted,
   wrong would triumph,
Held we fall to rise, are baffled to fight
   better,
     Sleep to wake.

No, at noonday in the bustle of man's
   work-time
   Greet the unseen[2] with a cheer!
Bid him forward, breast and back as
   either should be,
"Strive and thrive!" cry "Speed, —
   fight on, fare ever
      There as here!"   20

Discussion Hints

Pippa Passes

1. Asolo is an ancient and picturesque town
in northern Italy famous for its silk culture
and manufacture. It was familiar to Browning, who had many happy experiences there
among the simple, lovable Italian people.
Here he spent some of the last weeks of his
life. The name helped to suggest *Asolando*,
the title of the last collection of Browning's
poems published before his death. How
do these facts suggest his choice of an Asolo
factory girl as his ideal of simplicity, virtue,
and optimism?

2. Critics say that Browning can express a
volume of thought in few words. Can you find
examples of such condensation in these songs?
If you can, show how the thought might have
been expressed in more diffuse language by
making a paraphrase of the passage.

3. Select a few examples of Browning's
power of suiting the rhythm* to the thought
expressed.

4. Are these songs characterized by a singing quality or are they better adapted for
silent reading?

---

[1] Here, comrades, equals.
[2] Force of the attack.

[1] *soul of my soul.* The reference is to Mrs. Browning, who died in 1861, a few months before
the poem was written.
[2] *the unseen.* The poet himself after death.

5. Quote passages that reveal Browning's love of humanity.

6. Quote passages that reveal Browning's love of nature.

7. Compare lyric III, "A king lived long ago," with Keats's "Ode on a Grecian Urn (p. 366). In what way do they resemble each other?

Marching Along

1. Browning was especially interested in human beings, in the drama of human life. Even his imaginary characters are vital. How do Sir Byng's words characterize him?

2. What is the meter of the poem? Show that it fits the subject.

Home-Thoughts from Abroad

1. If possible read the headnote to Jesse Stuart's "My Land Is Fair for Any Eyes to See," in the revised edition of *American Writers* of this series.

2. Make a list of the words that appeal to the different senses. What sense predominates?

3. What details noted by the poet show that spring has come?

4. What does the poet say about the thrush?

5. Many poets before Browning had noticed with delight that the thrush sings a lilting little song which it repeats immediately; but only Browning suggests that it "sings each song twice over" in order to prove that though the "first fine careless rapture" seems inimitable, it is perfectly capable of singing its little lay a second time as perfectly as it did at first.

6. Point out personal touches and picturesque details that seem to show that Browning was thinking of some particular place or places rather than of England as a whole.

7. Several earlier lyrics in *English Writers* refer to spring or some particular time in spring. See, for example, pages 55 and 190. Write a theme comparing your findings with Browning's poem.

My Star

1. The poem expresses just such a compliment as an Elizabethan poet might have expressed in a sonnet* (see page 157). Is "My Star" a sonnet? Prove your answer.

2. Why cannot the poet's friends see his star?

Evelyn Hope

1. Do you think Evelyn Hope and the speaker were real people or only creations of Browning's imagination? Before giving your answer, read Browning's biography (p. 727).

2. Describe the circumstances under which Evelyn Hope appears.

3. What stanzas suggest that Browning believed in a future life?

4. Explain:
a. horoscope (l. 19)
b. diverged (l. 22)
c. the lower earth (l. 35)
d. divine (l. 37)

5. Other great poems depicting the sorrow of a lover for a dead sweetheart are "The Blessed Damozel," by Dante Gabriel Rossetti (p. 526), and "The Raven," by Edgar Allan Poe (in the revised edition of *American Writers* of this series). If possible compare them with "Evelyn Hope" and write a theme on the subject.

Prospice

1. What are the two most important thoughts you get from reading this poem?

2. What is the difference between the attitude of the poet in the first twenty lines of the poem and in the remaining lines?

Epilogue to *Asolando*

1. *Asolando* is the title of a volume of Browning's poems which appeared in 1889, on the day of the poet's death.

2. What is an "epilogue"?

3. Do you think Browning's description of himself in this poem is true?

4. How is the volume *Asolando* connected with *Pippa Passes* (p. 478)?

General Discussion Hints on Browning's Lyric Poetry

1. What specific evidence can you point out that Browning loved beauty?

2. In his poems Browning uses information from (*a*) England, (*b*) Italy, and (*c*) history. Illustrate from the poems given here.

3. Describe one of Browning's poems that refers (*a*) to England; (*b*) to Italy.

4. In which of the lyrics given here does Browning's personality as a man and a serious thinker become clearest to you? Explain your answer by specific references to the poems.

5. Which of the poems deals with England's past? Write a short theme on the historical events by which it was suggested.

Suggestions for Reading

"The Pied Piper of Hamelin" (in the revised edition of *Adventure* of this series)

"Incident of the French Camp" (in the revised edition of *Adventure* of this series)

"How They Brought the Good News from Ghent to Aix" (in the revised edition of *Adventure* of this series)

"Meeting at Night"

"Parting at Morning"

"The Lost Leader"

"A Woman's Last Word"

"The Last Ride Together"

"De Gustibus"

"Fra Lippo Lippi"

"Andrea del Sarto"

"Abt Vogler"

"Hervé Riel" (in the revised edition of *Achievement* of this series)

ELIZABETH BARRETT BROWNING[1] (1806-1861),

The Cry of the Children

"The Cry of the Children" reflects Elizabeth Barrett's intense indignation over child-labor conditions in the English factories and her deep sympathy with the child workers themselves. It is one of the best of the many poems of social protest written during the Victorian Period.

I

Do ye hear the children weeping
  O my brothers,
Ere the sorrow comes with years?
They are leaning their young heads
  against their mothers,
And *that* cannot stop their tears.
The young lambs are bleating in the
  meadows,
The young birds are chirping in the nest,
The young fawns are playing with the
  shadows,
The young flowers are blowing toward
  the west —
But the young, young children, O my
  brothers,
They are weeping bitterly!   10
They are weeping in the playtime of the
  others,
In the country of the free.

[1] For biography see page 728.

II

Do you question the young children in
  their sorrow
Why their tears are falling so?
The old man may weep for his to-morrow
  Which is lost in Long Ago;
The old tree is leafless in the forest,
  The old year is ending in the frost,
The old wound, if stricken, is the
  sorest,
  The old hope is hardest to be
    lost: 20
But the young, young children, O my
  brothers,
Do you ask them why they stand
Weeping sore before the bosoms of their
  mothers,
  In our happy Fatherland?

III

They look up with their pale and sunken
  faces,
  And their looks are sad to see,
For the man's hoary anguish draws and
  presses
  Down the cheeks of infancy;

"Your old earth," they say, "is very
   dreary,
Our young feet," they say, "are very
   weak;   30
Few paces have we taken, yet are weary —
   Our grave-rest is very far to seek:
Ask the aged why they weep, and not
   the children,
   For the outside earth is cold,
And we young ones stand without, in our
   bewildering,
   And the graves are for the old.

IV

"True," say the children, "it may
   happen
   That we die before our time:
Little Alice died last year, her grave is
   shapen
   Like a snowball, in the rime.[1]   40
We looked into the pit prepared to take
   her:
   Was no room for any work in the close
   clay!
From the sleep wherein she lieth none
   will wake her,
   Crying, 'Get up, little Alice! it is day.'
If you listen by that grave, in sun and
   shower,
   With your ear down, little Alice never
   cries;
Could we see her face, be sure we should
   not know her,
   For the smile has time for growing in
   her eyes:
And merry go her moments, lulled and
   stilled in
   The shroud by the kirk-chime.[2]   50
It is good when it happens," say the
   children,
   "That we die before our time."

V

Alas, alas, the children! they are seeking
   Death in life as best to have:
They are binding up their hearts away
   from breaking,

    [1] Frost.   [2] Chimes of the church bells.

   With a cerement[1] from the grave.
Go out, children, from the mine and from
   the city,
   Sing out, children, as the little thrushes
   do;
Pluck your handfuls of the meadow-
   cowslips pretty,
   Laugh aloud, to feel your fingers let
   them through!   60
But they answer, "Are your cowslips
   of the meadows
   Like our weeds anear the mine?
Leave us quiet in the dark of the coal-
   shadows,
   From your pleasures fair and fine!

VI

"For oh," say the children, "we are
   weary,
   And we cannot run or leap;
If we cared for any meadows, it were
   merely
   To drop down in them and sleep.
Our knees tremble sorely in the stoop-
   ing,
   We fall upon our faces, trying to
   go;   70
And, underneath our heavy eyelids
   drooping,
   The reddest flower would look as pale
   as snow,
For, all day, we drag our burden tiring,
   Through the coal-dark, underground;
Or, all day, we drive the wheels of
   iron
   In the factories, round and round.

VII

"For all day the wheels are droning,
   turning;
   Their wind comes in our faces,
Till our hearts turn, our heads with
   pulses burning,
   And the walls turn in their places: 80

    [1] Cloth used for wrapping dead bodies.

Turns the sky in the high window, blank
and reeling,
Turns the long light that drops adown
the wall,
Turn the black flies that crawl along the
ceiling:
All are turning, all the day, and we
with all.
And all day the iron wheels are droning,
And sometimes we could pray,
'O ye wheels,' (breaking out in a mad
moaning),
'Stop! be silent for to-day!'"

VIII

Ay, be silent! Let them hear each other
breathing
For a moment, mouth to mouth!   90
Let them touch each other's hands, in
a fresh wreathing
Of their tender human youth!
Let them feel that this cold metallic
motion
Is not all the life God fashions or re-
veals:
Let them prove their living souls against
the notion
That they live in you, or under you,
O wheels!
Still, all day, the iron wheels go onward,
Grinding life down from its mark;
And the children's souls, which God is
calling sunward,
Spin on blindly in the dark.   100

IX

Now tell the poor young children, O my
brothers,
To look up to Him and pray;
So the blessed One who blesseth all the
others,
Will bless them another day.
They answer, "Who is God that He
should hear us,
While the rushing of the iron wheels is
stirred?
When we sob aloud, the human creatures
near us

Pass by, hearing not, or answer not a
word.
And *we* hear not (for[1] the wheels in their
resounding)
Strangers speaking at the door: 110
Is it likely God, with angels singing round
Him,
Hears our weeping any more?

X

"Two words, indeed, of praying we re-
member;
And at midnight's hour of harm,
'Our Father,' looking upward in the
chamber,
We say softly for a charm.
We know no other words except 'Our
Father,'
And we think that, in some pause of
angels' song,
God may pluck them with the silence
sweet to gather,
And hold both within His right hand
which is strong.   120
'Our Father!' If He heard us, He would
surely
(For they call Him good and mild)
Answer, smiling down the steep world
very purely,
'Come and rest with me, my child.'

XI

"But no!" say the children, weeping
faster,
"He is speechless as a stone:
And they tell us, of His image is the
master
Who commands us to work on.
Go to!"[2] say the children, — "Up in
Heaven,
Dark, wheel-like, turning clouds are
all we find: 130
Do not mock us; grief has made us un-
believing:
We look up for God, but tears have
made us blind."

[1] Because of.
[2] An exclamation meaning about the same as
"Come, come!"

Do you hear the children weeping and
  disproving,
O my brothers, what ye preach?
For God's possible is taught by His
  world's loving,[1]
And the children doubt of each.

XII

And well may the children weep before
  you!
They are weary ere they run;
They have never seen the sunshine, nor
  the glory
Which is brighter than the sun.   140
They know the grief of man, without its
  wisdom;
  They sink in man's despair, without its
  calm;
Are slaves, without the liberty in Christ-
  dom,
  Are martyrs, by the pang without the
  palm:
Are worn as if with age, yet unretriev-
  ingly[2]
  The harvest of its memories cannot
  reap, —

Are orphans of the earthly love and
  heavenly.
  Let them weep! let them weep!

XIII

They look up with their pale and sunken
  faces,
  And their look is dread to see,   150
For they mind you of their angels in high
  places,
  With eye turned on Deity.[1]
"How long," they say, "how long, O
  cruel nation,
  Will you stand, to move the world, on
  a child's heart, —
Stifle down with a mailed heel its pal-
  pitation,[2]
  And tread onward to your throne amid
  the mart[3]?
Our blood splashes upward, O gold-
  heaper,
  And your purple shows your path!
But the child's sob in the silence curses
  deeper   159
  Than the strong man in his wrath."

From *Sonnets from the Portuguese*

Sonnets from the Portuguese is a volume of
poems recording the love story of Elizabeth
Barrett and her husband, the poet Robert
Browning (p. 478). The individual sonnets *
rank among the finest love lyrics in the English language. Their deep feeling, their soft
music, and their graceful turns of phrase en-
title them to a high place in literature.

The sonnets are not translations. Elizabeth Barrett was a pronounced brunette, and
once in jest Robert Browning called her
"my little Portuguese." She remembered this
nickname; and when she put her love sonnets together in book form, she called them
Sonnets from the Portuguese.

[1] God's power is revealed by the ability of human
  beings to express love.
[2] Without compensation or remedy.

XIV

If thou must love me, let it be for
  nought
Except for love's sake only. Do not
  say
"I love her for her smile — her look —
  her way
Of speaking gently, — for a trick of
  thought
That falls in well with mine, and certes[4]
  brought

[1] God.
[2] Beating.
[3] A place where public sales are carried on.
  Here, the business world.
[4] Certainly, truly.

A sense of pleasant ease on such a day"—
For these things in themselves, Belovèd,
    may
Be changed, or change for thee, — and
    love, so wrought,
May be unwrought so. Neither love me
    for
Thine own dear pity's wiping my cheeks
    dry, —   10
A creature might forget to weep, who bore
Thy comfort long, and lose thy love
    thereby!
But love me for love's sake, that evermore
Thou may'st love on, through love's
    eternity.

XLIII

How do I love thee? Let me count the
    ways.
I love thee to the depth and breadth and
    height
My soul can reach, when feeling out of
    sight
For the ends of Being and ideal Grace.
I love thee to the level of everyday's
Most quiet need, by sun and candlelight.
I love thee freely, as men strive for
    Right;
I love thee purely, as they turn from
    Praise.
I love thee with the passion put to use
In my old griefs, and with my child-
    hood's faith.   10
I love thee with a love I seemed to lose
With my lost saints, — I love thee with
    the breath,
Smiles, tears, of all my life! — and, if
    God choose,
I shall but love thee better after death.

Discussion Hints

The Cry of the Children

1. In connection with "The Cry of the Children" read again pages 425–426, of the introduction to the Victorian Period.

2. In "The Cry of the Children" notice how the use of the first and second persons (instead of the third) increases the vividness and the pathos.

3. Can the poem be correlated with any recent legislation, public discussions, or social movements? If so, which ones?

4. In stanza II what comparisons help to make the children's sorrow more bitter?

5. State in simple, logical form the argument implied in stanza III.

6. In stanzas V and VI why do the children decline the offer of "pleasures fair and fine"?

7. What is the effect of the repetition of the word *turn* in stanza VII?

8. Do you know the prayer beginning "Our Father," referred to in stanza X? If not, look it up in the Bible (Matthew 6 : 9–13).

9. What is the meaning of line 144? Remember that martyrs are often thought of as receiving a palm-branch, the symbol of victory, as a reward for their sacrifice (see Revelation 7 : 9).

Passages to be Explained

The old hope is hardest to be lost (l. 20)
Our grave-rest is very far to seek (l. 32)
cold metallic motion (l. 93)
They are weary ere they run (l. 138)
their look is dread to see (l. 150)

Sonnets from the Portuguese

1. What relations between Elizabeth Barrett Browning and her husband are reflected in these sonnets?

2. Mrs. Browning's sonnet XLIII, "How do I love thee?" has been called the greatest love lyric in English. Do you agree? If not, what poem would you rank above it?

3. What contrast do you find between the theme of sonnet XIV and that of sonnet XLIII?

4. Write out the rhyme scheme of sonnet XIV. Does it agree more closely with the Italian or with the Shakespearean form of the sonnet?*

Suggestions for Reading

"The Lady's Yes!"
"The Romance of the Swan's Nest"
"A Man's Requirements"
From *Sonnets from the Portuguese* : VII, **XIII,**
    XVII, XX, XXII, XXXV, XXXIX
"Life and Love"
"Question and Answer"
"A Musical Instrument"

ARTHUR HUGH CLOUGH[1] (1819-1861)

Say Not the Struggle Nought Availeth

"Say Not the Struggle Nought Availeth" should be read as an expression of Clough's indomitable courage in the conflict between faith and reason which involved the poet and many other thinkers of the Victorian Period. The language is well chosen, the imagery* varied but sustained, and the theme exalted, especially in the last two stanzas.

SAY not the struggle nought availeth,
    The labour and the wounds are
        vain,
The enemy faints not, nor faileth,
    And as things have been they remain.

If hopes were dupes,[2] fears may be
        liars;
    It may be, in yon smoke concealed,
Your comrades chase e'en now the fliers,
    And, but for you, possess the field.

For while the tired waves, vainly breaking,
    Seem here no painful inch to gain,   10
Far back, through creeks and inlets
        making,
    Comes silent, flooding in, the main.[1]

And not by eastern windows only,
    When daylight comes, comes in the
        light,
In front, the sun climbs slow, how slowly,
    But westward, look, the land is bright.

Discussion Hints

1. Each stanza has two meanings: an apparent meaning and a metaphorical* meaning. Point out both meanings for each stanza.

2. What change in the metaphorical* language used occurs between the second and third stanzas? between the third and fourth?

3. What conclusion does the poet reach?

MATTHEW ARNOLD[3] (1822-1888)

The Forsaken Merman

"The Forsaken Merman," one of Arnold's most admired poems, depends for its appeal chiefly upon the emotions it calls up and the pictures it paints. To produce his effects, the poet used an old, pathetic fairy tale of a merman deserted by his mortal wife. The wife, Margaret, has gone to visit her mortal kinsfolk at Easter and apparently has decided not to return to her watery home for fear she may lose her soul. Arnold presents the scene with remarkable clearness and pathos, and, by his poetic power, is able to choose the exact words that suit the sense and to vary the meter to accord with the action.

COME, dear children, let us away;
    Down and away below!
Now my brothers call from the bay,
Now the great winds shoreward blow,

Now the salt tides seaward flow;
Now the wild white horses[2] play,
Champ and chafe and toss in the spray.
Children dear, let us away!
This way, this way!

Call her once before you go —   10
Call once yet!
In a voice that she will know:
"Margaret! Margaret!"
Children's voices should be dear
(Call once more) to a mother's ear;
Children's voices, wild with pain —
Surely she will come again!
Call her once and come away;
This way, this way!
"Mother dear, we cannot stay!   20

---

[1] Clough (klŭf). For biography see page 728.
[2] A dupe is one who has been deceived.
[3] For biography see page 729.

[1] Ocean.
[2] white horses. Waves white with foam.

Come, dear children, let us away;
Down and away below!

The wild white horses foam and fret."
Margaret! Margaret!

Come, dear children, come away down;
Call no more!
One last look at the white-walled town,
And the little gray church on the windy
    shore,
Then come down!
She will not come though you call all day;
Come away, come away!

Children dear, was it yesterday   30
We heard the sweet bells over the bay?
In the caverns where we lay,
Through the surf and through the swell,
The far-off sound of a silver bell?
Sand-strewn caverns, cool and deep,
Where the winds are all asleep;
Where the spent lights quiver and gleam,
Where the salt weed sways in the stream,
Where the sea-beasts, ranged all round,
Feed in the ooze of their pasture ground;
Where the sea-snakes coil and twine,   41
Dry their mail[1] and bask in the brine;
Where great whales come sailing by,
Sail and sail, with unshut eye,
Round the world for ever and aye?
When did music come this way?
Children dear, was it yesterday?

Children dear, was it yesterday
(Call yet once) that she went away?
Once she sate with you and me,   50
On a red gold throne in the heart of the
    sea,
And the youngest sate on her knee.
She combed its bright hair, and she
    tended it well,
When down swung the sound of a far-off
    bell.
She sighed, she looked up through the
    clear green sea;
She said: "I must go, for my kinsfolk
    pray
In the little gray church on the shore
    to-day.

[1] Armorlike scales.

'Twill be Easter-time in the world — ah
    me!
And I lose my poor soul, Merman! here
    with thee."
I said: "Go up, dear heart, through the
    waves;   60
Say thy prayer, and come back to the
    kind sea-caves!"
She smiled, she went up through the surf
    in the bay.
Children dear, was it yesterday?

Children dear, were we long alone?
"The sea grows stormy, the little ones
    moan;
Long prayers," I said, "in the world they
    say;
Come!" I said; and we rose through the
    surf in the bay.
We went up the beach, by the sandy
    down
Where the sea-stocks bloom, to the
    white-walled town;
Through the narrow-paved streets, where
    all was still,   70
To the little gray church on the windy
    hill.
From the church came a murmur of folk
    at their prayers,
But we stood without in the cold blowing
    airs.
We climbed on the graves, on the stones
    worn with rains,
And we gazed up the aisle through the
    small leaded panes.
She sate by the pillar; we saw her
    clear:
"Margaret, hist! come quick, we are
    here!
Dear heart," I said, "we are long alone;
The sea grows stormy, the little ones
    moan."
But, ah, she gave me never a look,   80
For her eyes were sealed to the holy
    book!
Loud prays the priest; shut stands the
    door.
Come away, children, call no more!
Come away, come down, call no more!

Down, down, down.
Down to the depths of the sea.
She sits at her wheel in the humming
    town,
Singing most joyfully.
Hark what she sings: "O joy, O joy,
For the humming street, and the child
    with its toy! 90
For the priest, and the bell, and the holy
    well;
For the wheel where I spun,
And the blessed light of the sun!"
And so she sings her fill,
Singing most joyfully,
Till the spindle drops from her hand,
And the whizzing wheel stands still.
She steals to the window, and looks at
    the sand,
And over the sand at the sea;
And her eyes are set in a stare; 100
And anon there breaks a sigh,
And anon there drops a tear,
From a sorrow-clouded eye,
And a heart sorrow-laden,
A long, long sigh;
For the cold strange eyes of a little Mer-
    maiden
And the gleam of her golden hair.

Come away, away, children;
Come, children, come down!
The hoarse wind blows coldly; 110
Lights shine in the town.

She will start from her slumber
When gusts shake the door;
She will hear the winds howling,
Will hear the waves roar.
We shall see, while above us
The waves roar and whirl,
A ceiling of amber,
A pavement of pearl.
Singing: "Here came a mortal, 120
But faithless was she!
And alone dwell forever
The kings of the sea."

But, children, at midnight,
When soft the winds blow,
When clear falls the moonlight,
When spring tides are low;
When sweet airs come seaward
From heaths starred with broom,
And high rocks throw mildly 130
On the blanched sands a gloom;
Up the still, glistening beaches,
Up the creeks we will hie,
Over banks of bright seaweed
The ebb-tide leaves dry.
We will gaze, from the sand-hills,
At the white, sleeping town;
At the church on the hillside —
And then come back down.
Singing: "There dwells a loved one, 140
But cruel is she!
She left lonely forever
The kings of the sea."

Shakespeare

In his sonnet* "Shakespeare," Arnold expresses in a difficult verse form and in
choice, dignified diction his reverence for the
incomprehensible genius of the "Bard* of
Avon." According to Arnold, Shakespeare,
though far above the weaknesses and sorrows
of humanity, understood them and knew how
to give voice to feelings which common men
experience but cannot express.

OTHERS abide our question. Thou art
    free.[1]
We ask and ask — Thou smilest and art
    still,
Out-topping[2] knowledge. For the loftiest
    hill,
Who to the stars uncrowns his majesty,
Planting his steadfast footsteps in the sea,

[1] *Others . . . free.* Shakespeare, unlike other poets, is generally
    regarded as so great a genius that he is beyond criticism.
[2] Rising far above.

Making the heaven of heavens his dwell-
    ing-place,
Spares but the cloudy border of his base
To the foiled searching of mortality;[1]
And thou, who didst the stars and sun-
    beams know,
Self-schooled, self-scanned, self-honoured,
    self-secure,   10

Didst tread on earth unguessed at. —
    Better so!
All pains the immortal spirit must en-
    dure,
All weakness which impairs, all griefs
    which bow,
Find their sole speech in that victorious
    brow.

Requiescat[2]

Like many of Arnold's other lyrics, "Requiescat" is marked by unusual clearness of
diction. It is a beautiful expression of the
poet's characteristic world-weariness.

STREW on her roses, roses,[3]
    And never a spray of yew[4]!
In quiet she reposes;
    Ah, would that I did too!

Her mirth the world required;
    She bathed it in smiles of glee.

But her heart was tired, tired,
    And now they let her be.

Her life was turning, turning,
    In mazes of heat and sound.   10
But for peace her soul was yearning,
    And now peace laps her round.

Her cabined, ample spirit,
    It fluttered and failed for breath.
To-night it doth inherit
    The vasty hall of death.

Dover Beach[5]

In "Dover Beach" the calm of nature suggests to Arnold only the meaningless struggle
and want of faith which he imagines he sees
everywhere in the world around him. The
charm of the poem lies in its soft music, its
delicate imagery,* and its wistful sadness.
It opens with a beautiful picture of the calm
of nature. This suggests, by contrast, the
turbid ebb and flow of humanity. This in
turn leads to still sadder thoughts of the
incomprehensible waning of faith. Brought
almost to despair by these tragic musings, the
poet turns to his loved one as the only refuge
in a confused and ignorant world.

THE sea is calm to-night,
    The tide is full, the moon lies fair

Upon the straits[1]; — on the French
    coast the light
Gleams and is gone; the cliffs of England
    stand,
Glimmering and vast, out in the tranquil
    bay.

Come to the window, sweet is the night-
    air!
Only, from the long line of spray
Where the sea meets the moon-blanched
    land,
Listen! you hear the grating roar
Of pebbles which the waves draw back,
    and fling,   10
At their return, up the high strand,
Begin, and cease, and then again begin,
With tremulous cadence slow, and bring
The eternal note of sadness in.

[1] *foiled . . . mortality.* The fruitless searching of
    men.
[2] "May she rest [in peace]."
[3] Symbols of life and love.
[4] A symbol of death.
[5] *Dover Beach.* A well-known resort on the south-
    east coast of England.

[1] The English Channel, between Dover and
    France.

Sophocles* long ago
Heard it on the Aegean,* and it brought
Into his mind the turbid ebb and flow
Of human misery; we
Find also in the sound a thought,   19
Hearing it by this distant northern sea.

The Sea of Faith
Was once, too, at the full, and round
    earth's shore
Lay like the folds of a bright girdle
    furled.
But now I only hear
Its melancholy, long, withdrawing roar,
Retreating, to the breath
Of the night-wind, down the vast edges
    drear
And naked shingles¹ of the world.

Ah, love, let us be true
To one another; for the world, which
    seems   30
To lie before us like a land of dreams,
So various, so beautiful, so new,
Hath really neither joy, nor love, nor
    light,
Nor certitude, nor peace, nor help for
    pain;
And we are here as on a darkling plain
Swept with confused alarms of struggle
    and flight,
Where ignorant armies clash by night.

Discussion Hints

The Forsaken Merman

1. Point out the lines in which the merman's wife gives her reasons for wishing to return to the land of mortals.

2. Describe the submarine world where the merman lives, contrasting it with Margaret's feeling about her native town (ll. 89–93).

3. After reading lines 25–26 and 70–71, what picture do you get of the surroundings of the "little gray church"?

4. Why does Margaret not even look at her merman husband when he calls to her?

¹ Rounded stones forming the sea beach.

D

5. What contrast do you observe between the scene described at the beginning of the poem and that at the end?

6. It has been said that "The Forsaken Merman" is a "poem of picture and emotion, rather than of thought," and that Arnold has "his object clearly present in mind." Describe several pictures created by the poem. Show that they are clear. What emotions are depicted in the poem? Try to describe some of the emotions the poem arouses in you.

7. The clearness of Arnold's pictures results in part from the fact that he uses few similes* and metaphors.* Show that this is true of "The Forsaken Merman." Do you find any similes in the poem?

8. Pick out several examples of alliteration* in the poem.

Shakespeare

1. Is "Shakespeare" more like an Italian sonnet* or a Shakespearean sonnet?

2. In what respect is Shakespeare compared to the "loftiest hill"?

3. What is the subject of "Find" (l. 14)?

4. Compare Arnold's sonnet "Shakespeare" with Milton's poem on the same subject (p. 198). Which do you prefer? Why?

5. Pick out the two lines in "Shakespeare" that seem to you the greatest. Learn them by heart.

Requiescat

1. What picture of the dead person's character do you get from "Requiescat"?

2. Why is the phrase

    "doth inherit
The vasty hall of death" (ll. 15–16)

more poetical than "is dead"? What is the meaning of "inherit," and what words contribute particularly to the poetical quality of the phrase?

3. Explain lines 12–14. "Laps" here means "enfolds." "Cabined" means "confined by the duties and limitations of human life."

4. What line expresses most clearly Arnold's world-weariness?

5. Compare "Requiescat" with Landor's "Rose Aylmer" (p. 348) and Tennyson's "Break, Break, Break" (p. 463). Which seems to you to show the deepest feeling? Give reasons for your answer.

6. What evidence of Arnold's pessimism do you find in his poem?

Dover Beach

1. Using the outline given in the headnote, write a précis (summary) of the poem.

2. What would be your natural reaction upon hearing the waves washing the beach on a calm moonlight night amid pleasant surroundings? Compare your feelings with Arnold's.

3. In line 10 the word *fling* makes the line rush on to the next, like a wave flinging itself upon a beach. Show how also in lines 10–13 the words suggest the motion of the waves.

4. Do you think Browning would have agreed with the feelings that Arnold expresses in "Dover Beach"? Why?

5. Memorize lines 21–37.

6. What evidence of Arnold's pessimism do you find in his poem?

7. Explain

a. moon-blanched land (l. 8)

b.   *a darkling plain*
Swept with confused alarms of struggle and flight,
Where ignorant armies clash by night (ll. 35–37)

In passage *b* what words contribute most to the gloom of the picture?

Suggestions for Reading

"Sohrab and Rustum"
"To a Friend"
"A Picture at Newstead"
"Morality"
"The Future"
"Thyrsis" (an elegy on the death of Arthur Hugh Clough (p. 492))
"Rugby Chapel, November, 1857"
"Three Shadows"

CHRISTINA GEORGINA ROSSETTI[1] (1830–1894)

Remember Me When I Am Gone Away[2]

The sonnet* "Remember Me When I Am Gone Away" is characteristic of the author in its tender pathos, its simple language, and its delicate fancy. It is Christina Rossetti at her best.

REMEMBER me when I am gone away,
    Gone far away into the silent land[3];
When you can no more hold me by the hand,
Nor I half turn to go, yet turning stay.
Remember me when no more, day by day,
You tell me of your future that you planned:
Only remember me; you understand
It will be late to counsel then or pray.

Yet if you should forget me for a while
And afterwards remember, do not grieve:
For if the darkness and corruption leave
A vestige[1] of the thoughts that once I had,
Better by far you should forget and smile,
Than that you should remember and be sad.

Discussion Hints

1. Who do you think is speaking in the poem, a man or a woman? Do you think the speaker is Christina herself?

2. State the substance of the sonnet in one sentence.

3. Is the sonnet* English or Italian in form? What is the rhyme* scheme?

Passages to be Explained

Nor I half turn to go, yet turning stay (l. 4)
It will be late to counsel then or pray (l. 8)

---

[1] For biography see page 729.
[2] From Christina Rossetti's *Poetical Works*. By permission of The Macmillan Company and The Macmillan Company of Canada, Limited, publishers.
[3] *silent land.* Land of death.

[1] Trace.

Suggestions for Reading

"Song" ("When I am Dead, my Dearest")
"Song" ("Oh Roses for the Flush of Youth")
"A Summer Wish"

"A Wish"
"The First Spring Day"
"Yet a Little While"
"Spring"
"Summer"

ROBERT LOUIS STEVENSON[1] (1850–1894)

Requiem[2]

Stevenson's life was one long, heroic struggle against a painful and debilitating disease. This poem expresses in melodious verse a brave man's resignation to an untimely fate. The imagery of the closing lines is especially effective. The word *requiem* means a song in memory of the dead.

UNDER the wide and starry sky,
  Dig the grave and let me lie.
Glad did I live and gladly die,
  And I laid me down with a will.

This be the verse you grave for me[1]:
Here he lies where he longed to be;
Home is the sailor, home from sea,
  And the hunter home from the hill.

ALGERNON CHARLES SWINBURNE[3] (1837–1909)

The Garden of Proserpine[4]

"The Garden of Proserpine" is one of Swinburne's most admired poems. It illustrates (1) his rich imagery,* (2) the extraordinary melody of his verse, and (3) his fondness for themes drawn from classical antiquity. The imagery, though beautiful, is at times a little hard to grasp because of the excess of words and the long, involved sentences in which the images are expressed. But do not let either of these difficulties or the characteristic late-Victorian world-weariness of Swinburne's mood prevent you from enjoying to the full this beautiful poem. Many lovers of Swinburne consider the last six stanzas the most musical in the English language. They are certainly very lovely, as you will agree if you read them aloud.

Proserpine was the wife of Pluto* and hence queen of the underworld. Swinburne here conceives her as a pale, lovely figure ruling in the half light and half life of her domain and receiving as her due all the precious things that perish on the earth above: fruit, flowers, life, love, dreams, and beauty.

[1] For biography see page 730.
[2] *Requiem* (rē'kwĭ ĕm).
[3] For biography see page 731.
[4] *Proserpine* (prŏ sûr'pĭ nē). Here. prŏs'ẽr pĭn.

HERE, where the world is quiet;
  Here, where all trouble seems
Dead winds' and spent waves' riot
  In doubtful dreams of dreams;
I watch the green field growing
For reaping folk and sowing,
For harvest-time and mowing,
  A sleepy world of streams.

I am tired of tears and laughter,
  And men that laugh and weep;   10
Of what may come hereafter
  For men that sow to reap:
I am weary of days and hours,
Blown buds of barren flowers,
Desires and dreams and powers
  And everything but sleep.

Here life has death for neighbour,
  And far from eye or ear
Wan waves and wet winds labour,
  Weak ships and spirits steer;   20

[1] *grave for me.* Carve on my tombstone.

They drive adrift, and whither
They wot[1] not who make thither;
But no such winds blow hither,
   And no such things grow here.

No growth of moor or coppice,[2]
   No heather-flower or vine,
But bloomless buds of poppies,
   Green grapes of Proserpine,
Pale beds of blowing rushes,
Where no leaf blooms or blushes   30
Save this whereout she crushes
   For dead men deadly wine.

Pale, without name or number,
   In fruitless fields of corn,
They bow themselves and slumber
   All night till light is born;
And like a soul belated,
In hell and heaven unmated,
By cloud and mist abated
   Comes out of darkness morn.   40

Though one were strong as seven,
   He too with death shall dwell,
Nor wake with wings in heaven,
   Nor weep for pains in hell;
Though one were fair as roses,
His beauty clouds and closes;
And well though love reposes,
   In the end it is not well.

Pale, beyond porch and portal,   49
   Crowned with calm leaves, she[3] stands
Who gathers all things mortal
   With cold immortal hands;
Her languid lips are sweeter
Than love's who fears to greet her
To men that mix and meet her
   From many times and lands.

She waits for each and other,
   She waits for all men born;
Forgets the earth her mother,
   The life of fruits and corn;   60
And spring and seed and swallow
Take wing for her and follow
Where summer song rings hollow
   And flowers are put to scorn.

There go the loves that wither,
   The old loves with wearier wings;
And all dead years draw thither,
   And all disastrous things;
Dead dreams of days forsaken,
Blind buds that snows have shaken,   70
Wild leaves that winds have taken,
   Red strays of ruined springs.[1]

We are not sure of sorrow,
   And joy was never sure;
To-day will die to-morrow;
   Time stoops to no man's lure[2];
And love, grown faint and fretful,
With lips but half regretful
Sighs, and with eyes forgetful
   Weeps that no loves endure.   80

From too much love of living,
   From hope and fear set free,
We thank with brief thanksgiving
   Whatever gods may be
That no life lives forever;
That dead men rise up never;
That even the weariest river
   Winds somewhere safe to sea.

Then star nor sun shall waken,
   Nor any change of light: 90
Nor sound of waters shaken,
   Nor any sound or sight:
Nor wintry leaves nor vernal,[3]
Nor days nor things diurnal[4];
Only the sleep eternal
   In an eternal night.

Discussion Hints

1. In Proserpine's garden, poppies have buds, as they do on earth, but, unlike earthly poppies, they never bloom (l. 27). The grapes too never ripen (l. 28). In lines 1-40 what other contrasts do you find between conditions in the underworld and those on earth?

2. What is the antecedent of "They" (l. 35)?

3. What is the subject of "Comes" (l. 40)?

[1] Red . . . springs. Red leaves that have fallen into ruined springs.   [2] Enticement.
[3] Belonging to spring.
[4] Belonging to the daytime.

[1] Know.   [2] A clump of small trees.   [3] Proserpine.

Passages to be Explained

Dead winds' and spent waves' riot
In doubtful dreams of dreams (ll. 3–4)
They drive adrift, and whither
They wot not who make thither (ll. 21–22)
all dead years draw thither (l. 67)

Suggestions for Reading

Chorus from "Atalanta in Calydon" ("When the Hounds of Spring Are on Winter's Traces")
"Love at Sea"
"To Walt Whitman in America"
"The Oblation"
"Child's Song"
"William Shakespeare"
"Children"
"Étude Réaliste"
"On a Country Road"

General Discussion Hints on Lyric Poetry of the Victorian Period

1. What poem or poems reflect sorrow for the loss of a friend or a loved one? Was the event that caused the sorrow real or imaginary?

2. What poem or poems express hope? What poems express optimism in the face of obstacles and discouragements? Which ones express pessimism, world-weariness, or disillusionment?

3. What poem or poems reveal interest in social or industrial problems or in humanitarianism? Illustrate your answer.

4. What poem shows an interest in aviation?

5. What poem was inspired by an experience in Ireland?

6. What poem or poems draw inspiration from earlier English literature? Explain your answer.

7. In what poem or poems is the scene laid in Italy? in the time of King Arthur?

8. What poets who wrote sonnets during the Victorian Period are represented in *English Writers*?

9. What evidences of the scientific trend of the nineteenth century do you find in these lyrics?

10. What evidence of the introduction of machinery do you find in these lyrics?

11. What poem or poems express faith in the ultimate victory of right? Which one, in your opinion, is the most convincing? Explain your answer.

12. What poem or poems mirror the Englishman's love of the country?

13. How many of these lyric poets express satisfaction with life as they come to die? Quote specific passages to illustrate your answer.

DRAMATIC MONOLOGUES

A MONOLOGUE is a speech spoken by one person. Thus it differs from a dialogue in having one speaker instead of two. A "dramatic" monologue is a monologue that sketches a person's character and reveals that person's inmost thoughts and feelings and his response to the words or actions of some other person just as a drama does; but the words of the other person are not given, and we can guess at them only from what the speaker actually says or does. In other words, a dramatic monologue gives the words of only one of two characters who are conversing.

ROBERT BROWNING[1] (1812-1889)

My Last Duchess

Ferrara

"My Last Duchess" is one of Browning's best dramatic monologues. Since the dramatic monologue is a form especially associated with Browning's name and since "My Last Duchess" is unusually interesting for its own sake, you should read the poem with especial care. You will find it well worth the trouble you take in mastering it.

The scene of "My Last Duchess" is a magnificent palace at Ferrara, a city in northern Italy not far from Florence. The time is the Renaissance (p. 71) in Italy, when the Italian nobility were especially noted for their interest in art, their magnificence, and their haughty pride. In this poem a proud, cold, cruel Italian duke is speaking to the personal representative of a neighboring count concerning the duke's approaching marriage with the count's daughter. The two have left the rest of the company and have gone upstairs, where they can talk privately. There is a curtained portrait on the wall. The duke draws aside the curtain and reveals a lovely, vivid, girlish face reflecting innocence and beauty. The messenger turns to him with a questioning look, and the duke coldly remarks, "That's my last Duchess." They take seats facing the portrait, and the duke goes

on to explain wherein his former wife's conduct displeased him. She was a sweet, gentle girl, not the stately, haughty type of woman he wanted his wife to be. She was too kind-hearted and responsive to those around her. Then the duke says calmly and significantly to the messenger:

> "This grew[1]; I gave commands;
> Then all smiles stopped together."

The messenger understands, of course, that the cold, selfish duke will require a different standard of behavior from the count's daughter, who will be the next to wear his "nine-hundred-years-old name." Then, with a subtle reference to the large dowry he is expecting and a gracious word to the messenger, who is standing aside to let the duke pass out first, the duke links arms with the messenger, and they go down together to join the other guests.

The character of the former young duchess is clearly and delightfully drawn. Also, and this is the important thing, the duke reveals completely, though indirectly, his own nature as well. Notice that though the messenger makes gestures, the thoughts and remarks he must have made are not given. Thus we have a monologue that is truly dramatic.

[1] For biography see page 727.

[1] Her sweetness and gentleness increased.

My last Duchess

THAT'S my last Duchess painted on the wall,
Looking as if she were alive. I call
That piece a wonder, now: Frà Pandolf's[1] hands
Worked busily a day, and there she stands.
Will 't please you sit and look at her?
I said
"Frà Pandolf" by design: for never read
Strangers like you that pictured countenance,
The depth and passion of its earnest glance,
But to myself they turned (since none puts by
The curtain I have drawn for you, but I)
And seemed as they would ask me, if they durst,   11
How such a glance came there; so, not the first

Are you to turn and ask thus. Sir, 'twas not
Her husband's presence only, called that spot
Of joy into the Duchess' cheek: perhaps
Frà Pandolf chanced to say "Her mantle laps
Over my lady's wrist too much," or "Paint
Must never hope to reproduce the faint
Half-flush that dies along her throat": such stuff
Was courtesy, she thought, and cause enough   20
For calling up that spot of joy. She had
A heart — how shall I say? — too soon made glad,
Too easily impressed; she liked whate'er
She looked on, and her looks went everywhere.
Sir, 'twas all one! My favour at her breast,
The dropping of the daylight in the West,

---

[1] *Frà Pandolf's.* Brother (Frà) Pandolf is an imaginary painter.

The bough of cherries some officious fool
Broke in the orchard for her, the white
　mule
She rode with round the terrace — all and
　each
Would draw from her alike the approving
　speech,　　　　　　　　　　　　　30
Or blush, at least. She thanked men, —
　good! but thanked
Somehow — I know not how — as if she
　ranked
My gift of a nine-hundred-years-old
　name
With anybody's gift. Who'd stoop to
　blame
This sort of trifling? Even had you skill
In speech — (which I have not) — to
　make your will
Quite clear to such an one, and say, "Just
　this
Or that in you disgusts me; here you
　miss,
Or there exceed the mark" — and if she
　let
Herself be lessoned so, nor plainly set
Her wits to yours, forsooth, and made
　excuse,　　　　　　　　　　　　　41
— E'en then would be some stooping;
　and I choose
Never to stoop. Oh, sir, she smiled, no
　doubt,
Whene'er I passed her; but who passed
　without
Much the same smile? This grew; I
　gave commands;
Then all smiles stopped together. There
　she stands
As if alive. Will 't please you rise? We'll
　meet
The company below, then. I repeat,
The Count your master's known munifi-
　cence[1]　　　　　　　　　　　　49
Is ample warrant that no just pretence
Of mine for dowry will be disallowed;
Though his fair daughter's self, as
　avowed

　　　[1] Great liberality.

At starting, is my object. Nay, we'll go
Together down, sir. Notice Neptune,*
　though,
Taming a sea-horse, thought a rarity,
Which Claus of Innsbruck[1] cast in bronze
　for me!

Discussion Hints

1. What three examples does the duke give
to show how little his last duchess had valued
his "favour" (l. 25)?

2. Tell what words or action on the part of
the messenger called for the duke's reply in
lines 53–54:

　　　　"Nay, we'll go
　　　Together down, sir."

3. In what respects did Caesar Borgia*
resemble the duke?

4. Make a list of the characteristics (1) of
the duke; (2) of the duchess. What qualities
does the duke expect the second duchess to
possess? Do you blame the first duchess at all
for her conduct?

5. Point out details in the poem which indicate that Browning meant the poem to be a
description of life during the Renaissance.

6. Let one pupil read the poem aloud while
two other pupils carry out the action, indicating any change in position (getting up,
sitting down, walking, and so on) of the duke
and the representative of the count.

7. What are the meter and the rhyme*
scheme of the poem? Are you conscious of the
rhyme as you read the poem?

Passages to be Explained

*E'en then would be some stooping; and I choose
Never to stoop* (ll. 42–43)
　　　*This grew; I gave commands;
Then all smiles stopped together* (ll. 45–46)

Suggestions for Reading

　"Up at a Villa — Down in the City"
　"The Patriot"
　"The Italian in England"

　　　[1] *Claus of Innsbruck.* An imaginary artist.

GEORGE MEREDITH[1] (1828–1909)

The Last Words of Juggling Jerry

"The Last Words of Juggling Jerry" is a dramatic monologue (p. 502) which in directness of appeal and in vividness of characterization matches even Browning at his best (see the headnote to "My Last Duchess," p. 502). Jerry is dying. The time is the middle of May. The place is a little hill near a village common not far from where the old juggler Jerry was born. Around him are old familiar sights and sounds and smells: the thatched alehouse, the donkey, the sheep, the geese, the sweet-smelling wind blowing through the gorse, and, over all, the warm, golden sunlight. By his side is his faithful wife. The old juggler looks back upon his past life, but finds little to regret or bewail. He has lived straight according to his lights and has played the game fairly and squarely. He thinks of all life as a kind of juggling, and even death seems the Great Juggler that at last outjuggles all. His wife has always meant more to him than anything else in the world, and now the thought of leaving her is his chief regret. The old juggler's courage and affection shine through the poem and keep it from being mournful. The last stanza, however, can hardly be read without tears.

PITCH here the tent, while the old
   horse grazes:
  By the old hedge-side we'll halt a stage.
It's nigh my last above the daisies:
  My next leaf'll be man's blank page.
Yes, my old girl! and it's no use crying:
  Juggler, constable, king, must bow.
One[2] that outjuggles all's been spying
  Long to have me, and has me now.

We've travelled times to this old com-
   mon: 9
  Often we've hung our pots in the gorse.[3]
We've had a stirring life, old woman!
  You, and I, and the old gray horse.
Races, and fairs, and royal occasions,
  Found us coming to their call:
Now they'll miss us at our stations:
  There's a Juggler outjuggles all!

Up goes the lark, as if all were jolly!
  Over the duck-pond the willow shakes.
It's easy to think that grieving's folly,
  When the hand's firm as driven stakes!
Ay, when we're strong, and braced, and
   manful,   21
  Life's a sweet fiddle: but we're a batch
Born to become the Great Juggler's
   han'ful:
  Balls he shies[1] up, and is safe[2] to catch.

Here's where the lads of the village
   cricket[3];
  I was a lad not wide from here:
Couldn't I juggle the bail off the wicket?[4]
  Like an old world those days appear!
Donkey, sheep, geese, and thatched ale-
   house — I know 'em!
  They are old friends of my halts, and
   seem,   30
Somehow, as if kind thanks I owe 'em:
  Juggling don't hinder the heart's
   esteem.

Juggling's no sin, for we must have
   victual:
  Nature allows us to bait for the fool.[5]
Holding one's own makes us juggle no
   little;
  But, to increase it, hard juggling's the
   rule.
You that are sneering at my profession,
  Haven't you juggled a vast amount?
There's the Prime Minister, in one Ses-
   sion,[6]
  Juggles more games than my sins'll
   count.   40

---

[1] For biography see page 731.   [2] Death.
[3] A kind of wild, prickly shrub.

[1] Flings.   [2] Sure.   [3] Play cricket.*
[4] *juggle . . . wicket.* Knock the crosspieces (bails) off the top of the three parallel upright sticks forming the wicket. Jerry means that he was a good cricket-player.
[5] *bait . . . fool.* Here, furnish entertainment for people who are foolish enough to be entertained by juggling.
[6] Session of Parliament.

I've murdered insects with mock thunder:
Conscience, for that, in men don't quail.
I've made bread from the bump of wonder:[1]
That's my business, and there's my
tale.

Fashion and rank all praised the profes-
sor[2];
Ay! and I've had my smile from the
Queen:
Bravo, Jerry! she meant: God bless her!
Ain't this a sermon on that scene?

I've studied men from my topsy-turvy
Close, and, I reckon, rather true.   50
Some are fine fellows: some, right
scurvy;
Most, a dash between the two.
But it's a woman, old girl, that makes me
Think more kindly of the race:
And it's a woman, old girl, that shakes me
When the Great Juggler I must face.

We two were married, due and legal:
Honest we've lived since we've been
one.
Lord! I could then jump like an eagle:
You danced bright as a bit o' the sun.
Birds in a May-bush we were! right
merry!   61
All night we kissed, we juggled all day.
Joy was the heart of Juggling Jerry!
Now from his old girl he's juggled
away.

It's past parsons to console us;
No, nor no doctor fetch for me:
I can die without my bolus[3];
Two of a trade, lass, never agree!
Parson and Doctor! — don't they love
rarely,
Fighting the devil in other men's
fields!   70
Stand up yourself and match him fairly:
Then see how the rascal yields!

I, lass, have lived no gipsy, flaunting
Finery while his poor helpmate grubs:
Coin I've stored, and you won't be want-
ing:
You sha'n't beg from the troughs and
tubs.
Nobly you've stuck to me, though in his
kitchen
Duke might kneel to call you Cook!
Palaces you could have ruled and grown
rich in,
But your old Jerry you never for-
sook.   80

Hand up the chirper[1]! ripe ale winks in
it;
Let's have comfort and be at peace.
Once a stout draught made me light as a
linnet.
Cheer up! the Lord must have his
lease.
May be — for none see in that black hollow —
It's just a place where we're held in
pawn,
And, when the Great Juggler makes as[2]
to swallow,
It's just the sword-trick[3] — I ain't
quite gone.

Yonder came smells of the gorse, so
nutty,
Gold-like and warm: it's the prime of
May.   90
Better than mortar, brick, and putty,
Is God's house on a blowing day.
Lean me more up the mound; now I
feel it;
All the old heath-smells! Ain't it
strange?
There's the world laughing, as if to con-
ceal it!
But He's by us, juggling the change.

[1] Cheering cup.
[2] As if.
[3] A make-believe, as when a juggler pretends to
swallow a sword, but in reality does not
do so.

[1] made . . . wonder. Earned my living by satisfying people's liking for marvels.
[2] Expert in juggling.   [3] A large pill.

I mind it well, by the sea-beach lying,
   Once — it's long gone — when two
   gulls we beheld,
Which, as the moon got up, were flying
   Down a big wave that sparked and
   swelled.   100
Crack, went a gun; one fell: the second
   Wheeled round him twice, and was off
   for new luck:
There in the dark her white wing beck-
   oned; —
   Drop me a kiss — I'm the bird dead-
   struck!

Discussion Hints

1. What characteristics cause this poem to be classed as a dramatic monologue?

2. In Jerry's day juggling, like play-acting and other forms of worldly entertainment, was regarded by many people as sinful. In lines 33–40 Jerry attempts to justify his calling. He uses the word *juggling* in two different senses: (*a*) as referring to his own calling and (*b*) as referring to the juggling (compromising) with truth and honesty often practiced by human beings. The "you" addressed in line 37 is, of course, not Jerry's wife. Who is addressed?

3. What are some of the most extraordinary tricks you have ever seen performed by a magician?

4. In line 48 what conclusion ("sermon") do you think Jerry means to draw from the scene referred to?

5. What is Jerry's estimate of most of mankind? Who makes him think "more kindly of the race" (l. 54)?

6. What supposed characteristic of gypsies does Jerry look down upon?

7. In lines 77–78 Jerry claims that even an aristocrat such as a duke might well have paid respect to Jerry's wife, though she were only a cook in his kitchen. What other high compliments does Jerry pay his wife?

8. In connection with lines 89–96, what sights, sounds, and smells suggest the country in springtime most vividly?

9. Do you regard the comparison given in lines 97–104 as appropriate? Give reasons for your answer.

10. Compare lines 57–80 with Burns's "John Anderson My Jo" (p. 332).

11. Give the meaning of the phrase "lease on life" and then explain line 84.

12. Does the "Great Juggler," referred to in line 87, mean death? Explain your answer.

ESSAYS

JOHN HENRY NEWMAN[1] (1801-1890)

A Definition of a Gentleman

Cardinal Newman's "Definition of a Gentleman" is one of the best of his many admirable prose writings. It is marked by terse, clear, vigorous English. On the present subject, as on many others, the author felt strongly; yet here, as elsewhere in his writings, he never allows his feelings to obscure his clearness of vision or his appreciation for the right word in the right place. Though he was a classicist in his love of clarity and order, he was a true Victorian in his fondness for moral lessons and strict rules of right living.

IT IS almost a definition of a gentleman to say he is one who never inflicts pain. This description is both refined and, as far as it goes, accurate. He is mainly occupied in merely removing the obstacles which hinder the free and unembarrassed action of those about him; and he concurs with their movements rather than takes the initiative himself.
10 His benefits may be considered as parallel to what are called comforts or conveniences in arrangements of a personal nature; like an easy-chair or a good fire, which do their part in dispelling cold and fatigue, though nature provides both means of rest and animal heat without them.

The true gentleman, in like manner, carefully avoids whatever may cause a
20 jar or a jolt in the minds of those with whom he is cast, — all clashing of opinion, or collision of feeling, all restraint, or suspicion, or gloom, or resentment,— his great concern being to make everyone at their ease and at home. He has his eyes on all his company; he is tender toward the bashful, gentle toward the distant, and merciful toward the absurd; he can recollect to whom he is speaking; he guards against unseasonable allu- 30 sions, or topics which may irritate; he is seldom prominent in conversation and never wearisome.

He makes light of favors while he does them, and seems to be receiving when he is conferring. He never speaks of himself except when compelled, never defends himself by a mere retort; he has no ears for slander or gossip, is scrupulous in imputing motives [1] to those who interfere 40 with him, and interprets everything for the best.

He is never mean or little in his disputes, never takes unfair advantage, never mistakes personalities or sharp sayings for arguments, or insinuates evil which he dare not say out. From a longsighted prudence, he observes the maxim of the ancient sage, that we should ever conduct ourselves toward our enemy as 50 if he were one day to be our friend. He has too much good sense to be affronted at insults; he is too well employed to remember injuries, and too indolent to bear malice. He is patient, forbearing, and resigned, on philosophical principles; he submits to pain because it is inevitable, to bereavement because it is irreparable, and to death because it is his destiny.

If he engages in controversy of any 60 kind, his disciplined intellect preserves him from the blundering discourtesy

[1] *scrupulous . . . motives.* Careful not to judge motives wrongly.

[1] For biography see page 732.

of better, perhaps, but less educated minds, who, like blunt weapons, tear and hack instead of cutting clean, who mistake the point in argument, waste their strength on trifles, misconceive their adversary, and leave the question more involved than they find it. He may be 70 right or wrong in his opinion, but he is too clear-headed to be unjust; he is as simple as he is forcible, and as brief as he is decisive. Nowhere shall we find greater candour, consideration, indulgence: he throws himself into the minds of his opponents; he accounts for their mistakes. He knows the weakness of human reason as well as its strength, its province, and its limits.

Discussion Hints

1. Is the definition of a gentleman as "one who never inflicts pain" accurate?

2. How does Newman's idea of a gentleman compare with that in vogue today?

3. Pick out three or four of Newman's skillfully arranged climaxes.

4. Distinguish between "refined" and "accurate" as used in lines 3 and 4.

5. Explain the difference between "clashing of opinion," "collision of feeling," "restraint," "suspicion," "gloom," and "resentment" (p. 508, ll. 21–23).

6. Commit to memory the last twenty lines.

Words and Passages to be Explained

His benefits may be considered as parallel to what are called comforts or conveniences in arrangements of a personal nature (p. 508, ll. 10–13)
mean or little (p. 508, l. 43)
candour (p. 509, l. 74)
he throws himself into the minds of his opponents (p. 509, ll. 75–76)

ROBERT LOUIS STEVENSON[1] (1850–1894)

The Philosophy of Umbrellas[2]

In "The Philosophy of Umbrellas" Stevenson takes a common human trait and plays with it so delightfully that we are forced to laugh with him at our own absurdities. The essay is marked by the clear and easy, yet carefully polished, style characteristic of Stevenson's prose writings. Stevenson spoke his lines as he wrote, with the result that many of his essays are admirably adapted for reading aloud. "The Philosophy of Umbrellas" is one of these.

I T IS wonderful to think what a turn has been given to our whole Society by the fact that we live under the sign of Aquarius,* — that our climate is essentially wet. A mere arbitrary distinction,

like the walking-swords[1] of yore, might have remained the symbol of foresight and respectability, had not the raw mists and dropping showers of our island[2] pointed the inclination of Soci- 10 ety to another exponent of those virtues. A ribbon of the Legion of Honour[3] or a string of medals may prove a person's courage; a title may prove his birth; a professorial chair his study and acquirement; but it is the habitual carriage of the umbrella that is the stamp of respectability. The umbrella has become the acknowledged index of social position.

Robinson Crusoe presents us with a 20 touching instance of the hankering after them inherent in the civilised and edu-

[1] For biography see page 730.
[2] This paper was written in collaboration with James Walter Ferrier, and if reprinted this is to be stated, though his principal collaboration was to lie back in an easy-chair and laugh. — R. L. S., October 25, 1894

[1] A light sword formerly worn as part of a gentleman's costume.
[2] Remember what island Stevenson is referring to.
[3] *Legion of Honour*. In France an order of distinction and reward for civil or military services.

cated mind. To the superficial, the hot suns of Juan Fernandez[1] may sufficiently account for his quaint choice of a luxury; but surely one who had borne the hard labour of a seaman under the tropics for all these years could have supported an excursion after goats or a peaceful constitutional[2] arm in arm with the nude Friday.* No, it was not this: the memory of a vanished respectability called for some outward manifestation, and the result was — an umbrella. A pious castaway might have rigged up a belfry and solaced his Sunday mornings with the mimicry[3] of church bells; but Crusoe was rather a moralist than a pietist, and his leaf-umbrella is as fine an example of the civilised mind striving to express itself under adverse circumstances as we have ever met with.

It is not for nothing, either, that the umbrella has become the very foremost badge of modern civilisation — the Urim and Thummim[4] of respectability. Its pregnant symbolism has taken its rise in the most natural manner. Consider, for a moment, when umbrellas were first introduced into this country, what manner of men would use them, and what class would adhere to the useless but ornamental cane. The first, without doubt, would be the hypochondriacal,[5] out of solicitude for their health, or the frugal, out of care for their raiment; the second, it is equally plain, would include the fop, the fool, and the Bobadil.[6] Any one acquainted with the growth of Society,

and knowing out of what small seeds of cause are produced great revolutions and wholly new conditions of intercourse, sees from this simple thought how the carriage of an umbrella came to indicate frugality, judicious regard for bodily welfare, and scorn for mere outward adornment, and, in one word, all those homely and solid virtues implied in the term RESPECTABILITY. Not that the umbrella's costliness has nothing to do with its great influence. Its possession, besides symbolising (as we have already indicated) the change from wild Esau* to plain Jacob* dwelling in tents, implies a certain comfortable provision of fortune. It is not every one that can expose twenty-six shillings' worth of property to so many chances of loss and theft. So strongly do we feel on this point, indeed, that we are almost inclined to consider all who possess really well-conditioned umbrellas as worthy of the Franchise.[1] They have a qualification standing in their lobbies[2]; they carry a sufficient stake in the commonweal below their arm. One who bears with him an umbrella — such a complicated structure of whalebone,[3] of silk, and of cane, that it becomes a very microcosm[4] of modern industry — is necessarily a man of peace. A half-crown cane may be applied to an offender's head on a very moderate provocation; but a six-and-twenty shilling silk is a possession too precious to be adventured in the shock of war.

These are but a few glances at how umbrellas (in the general) came to their present high estate. But the true Umbrella-Philosopher meets with far stranger applications as he goes about the streets.

Umbrellas, like faces, acquire a certain sympathy with the individual who

---

[1] *Juan Fernandez.* An island in the Pacific Ocean, for four years the home of Alexander Selkirk,* on whose adventures Defoe based in part his *Robinson Crusoe.* See Defoe's *Robinson Crusoe* (p. 265) and Cowper's "Solitude of Alexander Selkirk" (p. 303).

[2] A walk for the benefit of one's health.

[3] Imitation.

[4] *Urim and Thummim.* Here, a mark of respectability; originally, sacred objects worn by the Jewish high priest as part of the breastplate.

[5] People morbidly anxious about their health.

[6] A boastful character in Ben Jonson's comedy *Every Man in His Humour.* Here, an affected braggart.

[1] The privilege of voting.

[2] We would say "front halls" or "entries."

[3] Strips of a horny substance from the upper jaw of a whale, formerly used for umbrella ribs.

[4] Little world, epitome.

carries them: indeed, they are far more capable of betraying his trust; for whereas a face is given to us so far ready-made, and all our power over it is in frowning, and laughing, and grimacing, during the first three or four decades of 110 life, each umbrella is selected from a whole shopful, as being most consonant[1] to the purchaser's disposition. An undoubted power of diagnosis rests with the practised Umbrella-Philosopher. O you who lisp, and amble, and change the fashion of your countenances[2] — you who conceal all these, how little do you think that you left a proof of your weakness in our umbrella-stand — that even now, as 120 you shake out the folds to meet the thickening snow, we read in its ivory handle the outward and visible sign of your snobbery, or from the exposed gingham of its cover detect, through coat and waistcoat, the hidden hypocrisy of the *dickey*[3]! But alas! even the umbrella is no certain criterion.[4] The falsity and the folly of the human race have degraded that graceful symbol to the ends 130 of dishonesty; and while some umbrellas, from carelessness in selection, are not strikingly characteristic (for it is only in what a man loves that he displays his real nature), others, from certain prudential motives, are chosen directly opposite to the person's disposition. A mendacious[5] umbrella is a sign of great moral degradation. Hypocrisy naturally shelters itself below a silk; while the 140 fast youth goes to visit his religious friends armed with the decent and reputable gingham. May it not be said of the bearers of these inappropriate umbrellas that they go about the streets "with a lie in their right hand"?

The king of Siam,[6] as we read, besides having a graduated social scale of um-brellas (which was a good thing), prevented the great bulk of his subjects from having any at all, which was cer-150 tainly a bad thing. We should be sorry to believe that this Eastern legislator was a fool — the idea of an aristocracy of umbrellas is too philosophic to have originated in a nobody, — and we have accordingly taken exceeding pains to find out the reason of this harsh restriction. We think we have succeeded; but, while admiring the principle at which he aimed, and while cordially recognising in 160 the Siamese potentate the only man before ourselves who had taken a real grasp of the umbrella, we must be allowed to point out how unphilosophically the great man acted in this particular. His object, plainly, was to prevent any unworthy persons from bearing the sacred symbol of domestic virtues. We cannot excuse his limiting these virtues to the circle of his court. We must only remem-170 ber that such was the feeling of the age in which he lived. Liberalism had not yet raised the war-cry of the working classes. But here was his mistake: it was a needless regulation. Except in a very few cases of hypocrisy joined to a powerful intellect, men, not by nature *umbrellarians*, have tried again and again to become so by art, and yet have failed — have expended their patrimony[1] in the 180 purchase of umbrella after umbrella, and yet have systematically lost them, and have finally, with contrite spirits, and shrunken purses, given up their vain struggle, and relied on theft and borrowing for the remainder of their lives. This is the most remarkable fact that we have had occasion to notice; and yet we challenge the candid reader to call it in question. Now, as there cannot be any *moral* 190 *selection* in a mere dead piece of furniture — as the umbrella cannot be supposed to have an affinity for individual men equal and reciprocal to that which men certainly feel towards individual

---

[1] Suitable.
[2] *lisp . . . countenances.* Adapted from *Hamlet*, III, i, 149–151.
[3] False shirt front.   [4] Standard of judgment.
[5] Lying.   [6] A kingdom in southeastern Asia.

[1] Inheritance.

umbrellas, — we took the trouble of consulting a scientific friend as to whether there was any possible physical explanation of the phenomenon. He was unable 200 to supply a plausible theory, or even hypothesis; but we extract from his letter the following interesting passage relative to the physical peculiarities of umbrellas: "Not the least important, and by far the most curious property of the umbrella, is the energy which it displays in affecting the atmospheric strata. There is no fact in meteorology better established — indeed, it is almost the 210 only one on which meteorologists are agreed — than that the carriage of an umbrella produces desiccation[1] of the air; while if it be left at home, aqueous[2] vapour is largely produced, and is soon deposited in the form of rain. No theory," my friend continues, "competent to explain this hygrometric law[3] has yet been given (as far as I am aware) by Herschel, Dove, Glaisher, Tait, Buchan,[4] or any 220 other writer; nor do I pretend to supply the defect. I venture, however, to throw out the conjecture that it will be ultimately found to belong to the same class of natural laws as that agreeable to which a slice of toast always descends with the buttered surface downwards."

But it is time to draw to a close. We could expatiate much longer upon this topic, but want of space constrains us 230 to leave unfinished these few desultory[5] remarks — slender contributions towards a subject which has fallen sadly backwards, and which, we grieve to say, was better understood by the king of Siam in 1686 than by all the philosophers of today. If, however, we have awakened in any rational mind an interest in the symbolism* of umbrellas — in any gen-

erous heart a more complete sympathy with the dumb companion of his daily 240 walk, — or in any grasping spirit a pure notion of respectability strong enough to make him expend his six-and-twenty shillings — we shall have deserved well of the world, to say nothing of the many industrious persons employed in the manufacture of the article.

Discussion Hints

1. In order to get the full flavor of Stevenson's humor in the first paragraph, we should recall that in Great Britain at the time of the essay umbrellas were generally carried by gentlemen of the well-to-do and upper classes.

2. Give in your own words the reason which, as Stevenson suggests, best accounts for Robinson Crusoe's using an umbrella. If you have read Daniel Defoe's *Robinson Crusoe* (see page 265), what, in your opinion, was Defoe's reason for representing Robinson Crusoe as using an umbrella? In what does the humor of Stevenson's explanation consist?

3. What does Stevenson mean by suggesting that the possession of an umbrella symbolizes "the change from wild Esau* to plain Jacob* dwelling in tents" (p. 510, ll. 73–74)?

4. Express in brief and simple form the extract from the letter of Stevenson's scientific friend (p. 512, ll. 204–226).

5. Choose from the essay a sentence and, taking it for a topic sentence, give a three-minute talk on the subject of the essay.

6. Point out and explain three illustrations of Stevenson's humor.

Words and Passages to be Explained

manifestation (p. 510, l. 33)
Its pregnant symbolism has taken its rise in the most natural manner (p. 510, ll. 46–48)
a very microcosm of modern industry (p. 510, ll. 89–90)
provocation (p. 510, l. 93)
An undoubted power of diagnosis rests with the practised Umbrella-Philosopher (p. 511, ll. 112–114)
prudential (p. 511, l. 135)
reciprocal (p. 511, l. 194)
conjecture (p. 512, l. 222)

---

[1] Drying out.
[2] Watery.
[3] *hygrometric law.* A law in physics relating to the amount of moisture in the air.
[4] *Herschel . . . Buchan.* Nineteenth-century authorities on science.
[5] Rambling.

THOMAS BABINGTON MACAULAY[1] (1800–1859)

From "England in 1685"[2]

[From The History of England]

The History of England is the greatest work of Lord Macaulay, the most famous English historian of the nineteenth century. It was widely read and admired in Macaulay's day. It is still admired, but as literature rather than history. In connection with your reading of the selection given below you should recall the following facts: (1) History, according to Macaulay, should be made as attractive as fiction; it should give to persons and events of the past the same vitality which fiction gives to persons and events that are purely imaginary. The author illustrates his theory admirably in The History of England. (2) Macaulay was an accomplished public speaker, and his literary style resembles that of the finished orator. It is simple and direct and is characterized by well-rounded, rhythmic sentences and by repetitions that make the course of his thought easy to follow. (3) The many details of his account are so carefully arranged that they give not only a clear and uniform picture, but also a distinctly dramatic effect. All are presented and arranged according to an orderly plan. In short, Macaulay's History is an outstanding example of the most important traits of good style — clarity and interest resulting from unity, coherence, and emphasis.

Though Macaulay, unlike our best historians of the present day, does not concern himself with the causes or philosophy of history, and though he has been accused of superficiality, inaccuracy, Whig* prejudice, and certain other faults, his history nevertheless remains a memorable example of classical English prose style at its best. The famous third chapter of the History, from which the following selection is taken, resembles in many respects some of Macaulay's well-known essays.

I INTEND, in this chapter, to give a description of the state in which England was at the time when the crown passed from Charles the Second to his brother.

[Since that period] the increase of the people has been great in every part of the kingdom, but generally much greater in the northern than in the southern shires.[1] In the north the air was inclement; the soil was generally such as required skillful and industrious cultivation; and there could be little skill or industry in a tract which was often the theatre of war, and which, even when there was nominal peace, was constantly desolated by bands of Scottish marauders. There was still a large class of mosstroopers,[2] whose calling was to plunder dwellings and to drive away whole herds of cattle. It was found necessary, soon after the Restoration,[3] to enact laws of great severity for the prevention of these outrages. The magistrates were authorised to raise bands of armed men for the defence of property and order; and provision was made for meeting the expense of these levies by local taxation. The parishes were required to keep bloodhounds for the purpose of hunting the freebooters. Yet, even with such auxiliaries, it was often found impossible to track the robbers to their retreats among the hills and morasses. For the geography of that wild country was imperfectly known. The seats of the gentry and the larger farmhouses were fortified. Oxen were penned at night beneath the overhanging battlements of the residence, which was known by the name of the

---

[1] For biography see page 732.

[2] "England in 1685" is merely a convenient title intended to include conditions in England during the reign of Charles II (1660–1685), the reign of James II (1685–1688), and, indeed, throughout the whole latter part of the seventeenth century and during the early part of the eighteenth.

D

---

[1] Counties.

[2] Bandits, so called because of the "mosses," or bogs, through which they found their way to and fro across the Border.*

[3] See page 213.

40 Peel. The inmates slept with arms at their sides. Huge stones and boiling water were in readiness to crush and scald the plunderer who might venture to assail the little garrison. No traveller ventured into that country without making his will.

In the drawings of English landscapes made in that age scarce a hedgerow is to be seen,[1] and numerous tracts, now rich
50 with cultivation, appear as bare as Salisbury Plain.[2] At Enfield, hardly out of sight of the smoke of the capital, was a region which contained only three houses and scarcely any enclosed fields. Deer wandered there by thousands. Wild animals of large size were far more numerous than at present. The last wild boars, indeed, which had been preserved for the royal diversion, had been slaugh-
60 tered by the exasperated rustics during the license[3] of the civil war. The last wolf that had roamed our island had been slain in Scotland a short time before the close of the reign of Charles the Second. But many breeds now extinct, or rare, both of quadrupeds and birds, were still common.

The progress of this great change can nowhere be more clearly traced than in
70 the number of enclosure acts passed since King George the Second came to the throne. The area enclosed under the authority of those acts exceeds, on a moderate calculation, ten thousand square miles. How many square miles which formerly lay waste have, during the same period, been fenced and carefully tilled by the proprietors, without any application to the legislature, can
80 only be conjectured. But it seems highly probable that a fourth part of England

has been, in the course of little more than a century, turned from a wild into a garden.

Great as has been the change in the rural life of England since the Revolution, the change which has come to pass in the cities is still more amazing. At present about a sixth part of the nation is crowded into provincial[1] towns of more 90 than thirty thousand inhabitants. In the reign of Charles the Second no provincial town in the kingdom contained thirty thousand inhabitants; and only four provincial towns contained so many as ten thousand inhabitants.

Next to London, but next at an immense distance, stood Bristol, then the first English seaport, and Norwich, then the first English manufacturing town. 100 Both have since that time been far outstripped by younger rivals; yet both have made great positive advances. The population of Bristol has quadrupled. The population of Norwich has more than doubled.

The position of London, relatively to the other towns of the empire, was, in the time of Charles the Second, far higher than at present. For at present 110 the population of London is little more than six times the population of Manchester or of Liverpool. In the days of Charles the Second the population was more than seventeen times the population of Bristol or Norwich. There is reason to believe that, in 1685, London had been, during about half a century, the most populous capital in Europe. The inhabitants, who are now at least 120 nineteen hundred thousand, were then probably little more than half a million. London had in the world only one commercial rival, now long ago outstripped, the mighty and opulent Amsterdam.[2] English writers boasted of the forest of

---

[1] The proportion of unenclosed country seems to have been very great. From Abington to Gloucester, for example, a distance of forty or fifty miles, there was not a single enclosure. — Note by MACAULAY

[2] See the appearance of Salisbury Plain around Stonehenge (p. 4).

[3] Unrestrained lawlessness.

---

[1] Here, lying outside the London area.

[2] The capital and chief seaport of Holland. The most important commercial city in Europe during the seventeenth century.

masts and yardarms which covered the river from the Bridge to the Tower,[1] and of the stupendous sums which were col-
130 lected at the Customs House in Thames Street. There is, indeed, no doubt that the trade of the metropolis then bore a far greater proportion than at present to the whole trade of the country; yet to our generation the honest vaunting of our ancestors must appear almost ludicrous. The shipping which they thought incredibly great appears not to have exceeded seventy thousand tons. This was,
140 indeed, then more than a third of the whole tonnage of the kingdom, but is now less than a fourth of the tonnage of Newcastle, and is nearly equalled by the tonnage of the steam vessels of the Thames. The customs of London amounted, in 1685, to about three hundred and thirty thousand pounds a year. In our time the net duty paid annually, at the same place, exceeds ten millions.
150   The coffee house* must not be dismissed with a cursory mention. The first of these establishments had been set up, in the time of the Commonwealth,[2] by a Turkey merchant,[3] who had acquired among the Mahometans a taste for their favourite beverage. The convenience of being able to make appointments in any part of the town, and of being able to pass evenings socially at a very small charge,
160 was so great that the fashion spread fast. Every man of the upper or middle class went daily to his coffee house to learn the news and to discuss it. Every coffee house had one or more orators to whose eloquence the crowd listened with admiration. Foreigners remarked that the coffee house was that which especially distinguished London from all other

cities; that the coffee house was the Londoner's home, and that those who[170] wished to find a gentleman commonly asked, not whether he lived in Fleet Street or Chancery Lane, but whether he frequented the Grecian or the Rainbow.[1] Nobody was excluded from these places who laid down his penny at the bar. Yet every rank and profession, and every shade of religious and political opinion, had its own head quarters. In general, the coffee rooms reeked with tobacco like [180] a guardroom; and strangers sometimes expressed their surprise that so many people should leave their own firesides to sit in the midst of eternal fog and stench. Nowhere was the smoking more constant than at Will's. That celebrated house, situated between Covent* Garden and Bow Street, was sacred to polite letters.[2] There talk was about poetical justice[3] and the unities of place and time.[4] One [190] group debated whether Paradise Lost[5] ought not to have been in rhyme. Under no roof was a greater variety of figures to be seen. There were Earls in stars and garters, clergymen in cassocks and bands,[6] pert Templars,[7] sheepish lads from the universities, translators and indexmakers in ragged coats of frieze. The great press[8] was to get near the chair where John Dryden[9] sate. In winter that [200] chair was always in the warmest nook by the fire; in summer it stood in the balcony. To bow to him, and to hear his opinion of a tragedy or of epic poetry,

[1] *The Grecian . . . the Rainbow.* Names of London coffeehouses.
[2] *polite letters.* Literature such as poetry, drama, and criticism.
[3] *poetical justice.* An ideal distribution of rewards and punishments, such as is common in literature but is seldom found in real life.
[4] *unities . . . time.* During the Age of Classicism (p. 213) critics maintained that the action of a drama should be confined to one place and one day.   [5] See page 187.
[6] *cassocks . . . bands.* Bands were strips of white cloth worn over the clergymen's long coats (cassocks).
[7] See "Temple,* the."   [8] Here, crowding.
[9] For biography see page 706.

[1] *from . . . Tower.* The part of the Thames between London Bridge and the Tower of London (about half a mile), formerly used as an anchorage for shipping.
[2] See pages 183 and 214.
[3] *Turkey merchant.* A merchant who imported goods from Turkey, one of the countries from which coffee was brought to Europe.

was thought a privilege. A pinch from his snuff box was an honour sufficient to turn the head of a young enthusiast. There were Puritan coffee houses where no oath was heard, and where lankhaired 210 men discussed election and reprobation[1] through their noses; Jew coffee houses where darkeyed money changers from Venice and from Amsterdam greeted each other.

These gregarious habits[2] had no small share in forming the character of the Londoner of that age. He was, indeed, a different being from the rustic Englishman. There was not then the inter-220 course which now exists between the two classes. Only very great men were in the habit of dividing the year between town and country. Few esquires came to the capital thrice in their lives. Nor was it yet the practice of all citizens in easy circumstances to breathe the fresh air of the fields and woods during some weeks of every summer. A cockney,[3] in a rural village, was stared at as much as if he 230 had intruded into a Kraal of Hottentots.[4] On the other hand, when the lord of a country manor appeared in London, he was easily distinguished from the resident population. His dress, his gait, his accent, the manner in which he gazed at the shops, stumbled into the gutters, ran against the porters, and stood under the waterspouts, marked him out as an excellent subject for the operations of 240 swindlers and banterers. Bullies jostled him into the kennel.[5] Thieves explored with perfect security the huge pockets of his horseman's coat. If he went into a shop, he was instantly discerned to be a fit purchaser of everything that nobody else would buy, of secondhand embroidery, copper rings, and watches that would not go. If he rambled into any fashionable coffee house, he became a mark for the insolent derision of fops and the grave 250 waggery of Templars. Enraged and mortified, he soon returned to his mansion, and there, in the homage of his tenants and the conversation of his boon companions, found consolation for the vexations and humiliations which he had undergone. There he was once more a great man.

The chief cause which made the fusion of the different elements of society so 260 imperfect was the extreme difficulty which our ancestors found in passing from place to place. In the seventeenth century the inhabitants of London were, for almost every practical purpose, farther from Reading[1] than they now are from Edinburgh,[2] and farther from Edinburgh than they now are from Vienna.[3]

It was by the highways that both travellers and goods generally passed 270 from place to place; and those highways appear to have been far worse than might have been expected from the degree of wealth and civilisation which the nation had even then attained. On the best lines of communication the ruts were deep, the descents precipitous, and the way often such as it was hardly possible to distinguish, in the dusk, from the unenclosed heath[4] which lay on both sides. 280 It was only in fine weather that the whole breadth of the road was available for wheeled vehicles. Often the mud lay deep on the right and the left; and only a narrow track of firm ground rose above the quagmire. At such times obstructions and quarrels were frequent, and the path was sometimes blocked up during a long time by carriers, neither of whom would break the way. It happened, al- 290

---

[1] *election. . . reprobation.* Theological terms referring to the salvation or condemnation of human souls. The Puritans (see page 183) were fond of theological discussions.

[2] *gregarious habits.* Habits of flocking together.

[3] A typical native Londoner.

[4] *Kraal . . . Hottentots.* A village of supposedly primitive South-African savages.

[5] An old name for a street gutter.

[1] About twenty miles away.

[2] About three hundred and fifty miles away.

[3] About eight hundred miles away.

[4] Open country covered with shrubs.

most every day, that coaches stuck fast, until a team of cattle[1] could be procured from some neighbouring farm, to tug them out of the slough. On the roads of Derbyshire, travellers were in constant fear of their necks, and were frequently compelled to alight and lead their beasts. The great route through Wales to Holyhead was in such a state that, in 300 1685, a viceroy,[2] going to Ireland, was five hours in travelling fourteen miles. The markets were often inaccessible during several months. It is said that the fruits of the earth were sometimes suffered to rot in one place, while in another place, distant only a few miles, the supply fell far short of the demand.

On the best highways heavy articles were, in the time of Charles the Second, 310 generally conveyed from place to place by stage waggons. In the straw of these vehicles nestled a crowd of passengers, who could not afford to travel by coach or on horseback, and who were prevented by infirmity, or by the weight of their luggage, from going on foot. The expense of transmitting heavy goods in this way was enormous. It was about fifteen pence a ton for every mile, more by a 320 third than was afterwards charged on turnpike roads, and fifteen times what is now demanded by railway companies. The cost of conveyance amounted to a prohibitory tax on many useful articles. Coal in particular was never seen except in the districts where it was produced, or in the districts to which it could be carried by sea, and was indeed always known in the south of England by the 330 name of sea coal.

On byroads, and generally throughout the country north of York and west of Exeter,[3] goods were carried by long trains of packhorses. A traveller of humble condition often found it con-venient to perform a journey mounted on a packsaddle between two baskets, under the care of these hardy guides. The expense of this mode of conveyance was small. But the caravan moved at a 340 foot's pace, and in winter the cold was often insupportable.

Whatever might be the way in which a journey was performed, the travellers ran considerable risk of being stopped and plundered. The mounted highwayman, a marauder known to our generation only from books, was to be found on every main road. The waste tracts which lay on the great routes near London were 350 especially haunted by plunderers of this class. Hounslow Heath, on the Great Western Road, and Finchley Common, on the Great Northern Road, were per-haps the most celebrated of these spots. Seamen who had just been paid off were often compelled to deliver their purses on Gadshill, celebrated near a hundred years earlier by the greatest of poets as the scene of the depredations of Falstaff.[1] 360 The public authorities seem to have been often at a loss how to deal with these enterprising plunderers.

It was necessary to the success and even to the safety of the highwayman that he should be a bold and skilful rider, and that his manners and appear-ance should be such as suited the master of a fine horse. He therefore held an aristocratical position in the community 370 of thieves, appeared at fashionable coffee houses and gaming houses, and betted with men of quality on the race ground. Sometimes, indeed, he was a man of good family and education. A romantic in-terest therefore attached, and perhaps still attaches, to the names of freebooters of this class. The vulgar eagerly drank in tales of their ferocity and audacity, of their occasional acts of generosity and 380 good nature, of their miraculous escapes, of their desperate struggles, and of their

[1] Here, horses.
[2] A royal governor of a dependent country.
[3] *north . . . Exeter.* That is, in the most unde-veloped parts of the kingdom.

[1] See Shakespeare's *Henry IV, Part I*, Act II, Scenes i, ii, and iv.

manly bearing at the bar and in the cart.[1]

In such anecdotes there is doubtless a large mixture of fable; but they are not on that account unworthy of being recorded, for it is both an authentic and an important fact that such tales, 390 whether false or true, were heard by our ancestors with eagerness and faith.

In the seventeenth century England abounded with excellent inns of every rank. The traveller sometimes lighted on a public house such as Walton[2] has described, where the brick floor was swept clean, where the walls were stuck round with ballads, where the sheets smelt of lavender, and where a blazing fire, a cup 400 of good ale, and a dish of trouts fresh from the neighbouring brook, were to be procured at small charge. At the larger houses of entertainment were to be found beds hung with silk, choice cookery, and claret equal to the best which was drunk in London. The innkeepers too, it was said, were not like other innkeepers. On the Continent the landlord was the tyrant of those who crossed the threshold. In 410 England he was a servant. Never was an Englishman more at home than when he took his ease in his inn.

To facilitate correspondence between one part of London and another was not originally one of the objects of the Post Office. But, in the reign of Charles the Second, an enterprising citizen set up, at great expense, a penny post, which delivered letters and parcels six or eight 420 times a day in the busy and crowded streets near the Exchange,[3] and four times a day in the outskirts of the capital. This improvement was, as usual, strenuously resisted. The porters[4] complained that their interests were attacked, and tore down the placards in which the

scheme was announced to the public. The utility of the enterprise was, however, so great and obvious that all opposition proved fruitless.   430

No part of the load which the old mails carried out was more important than the newsletters. In 1685 nothing like the London daily paper of our time existed, or could exist. [But not long afterward] many newspapers were suffered to appear. [A typical example was] the London Gazette, [which] came out only on Mondays and Thursdays. The contents generally were a royal proclamation, two 440 or three Tory* addresses,[1] notices of two or three promotions, an account of a skirmish between the imperial troops and the Janissaries on the Danube, a description of a highwayman, an announcement of a grand cockfight between two persons of honour, and an advertisement offering a reward for a strayed dog. The whole made up two pages of moderate size. Whatever was communicated re- 450 specting matters of the highest moment was communicated in the most meagre and formal style. The newswriter rambled from coffee room[2] to coffee room, collecting reports, squeezed himself into the Sessions House at the Old Bailey, if there was an interesting trial, nay, perhaps obtained admission to the gallery of Whitehall, and noticed how the King and Duke looked. In this way he gathered 460 materials for weekly epistles. At the seat of a man of fortune in the country, the newsletter was impatiently expected. Within a week after it had arrived it had been thumbed by twenty families.

The general effect of the evidence [of improvement] which has been submitted to the reader seems hardly to admit of doubt. But, in truth, there is constant improvement precisely because there is 470 constant discontent. If we were perfectly satisfied with the present, we should cease to contrive, to labour, and to save with a view to the future. And it is

---

[1] Criminals were carried to execution in a cart.
[2] For biography see page 704.
[3] Here, a place in London where businessmen, brokers, bankers, and the like meet to transact business.
[4] Porters carried messages as well as packages.

[1] Speeches, orations.   [2] See "coffeehouses." *

natural that, being dissatisfied with the present, we should form a too favourable estimate of the past.

Discussion Hints

1. How do the social disorder and the administration of justice in the northern counties of England during the late seventeenth century suggest those of frontier days in America? In what ways did they differ?

2. Can you give any examples of animals or birds that were once common in your district but have now become "extinct, or rare" (p. 514, l. 65)?

3. Do you know of any movement in America corresponding to the progress of enclosures in England?

4. Compare the population of London in 1685 with that in Macaulay's day and with that in recent years. In order to get the last figure, look up the word *London* in an encyclopedia or in the list of places at the end of a large dictionary.

5. In England in 1685 the freight rate per mile for heavy goods was fifteen pence (about thirty cents) a ton (p. 517, ll. 318–319); in Macaulay's day the rate by rail was about one penny (two cents) per ton per mile. Compare these with present-day American railroad freight rates on such materials as iron and coal.

6. Compare a seventeenth-century English inn as described by Macaulay with the one described by Goldsmith (p. 307, ll. 99–116).

7. What facts brought out connect "England in 1685" with "The Industrial Revolution" (p. 319)? As your teacher directs, write a theme on the subject, or discuss in class.

8. Point out "well-rounded, rhythmic" passages that would sound well when recited.

9. Explain
a. nominal (p. 513, l. 15)
b. exasperated (p. 514, l. 60)
c. vaunting (p. 515, l. 135)
d. waggery (p. 516, l. 251)

Suggestions for Reading

Macaulay's essays are models of clearness and style. Especially well-known essays are those on Milton, Johnson, Goldsmith, and Warren Hastings.

Lays of Ancient Rome (especially "Horatius," an old favorite).

NARRATIVE POETRY

ALFRED LORD TENNYSON[1] (1809–1892)

The Lady of Shalott

"The Lady of Shalott" (shă lŏt') is one of Tennyson's earliest poems dealing with a subject from the medieval romances of King Arthur*and the Knights of the Round*Table, material which he was to use later in *The Idylls of the King*.

"Sweet and dreamy melancholy" is the keynote of "The Lady of Shalott," and it is in this spirit that one must read it to appreciate it to the full. Of course the reader must not overlook the almost perfect adaptation of the sound to the sense, a characteristic of much of Tennyson's poetry.

INTERPRETATIVE OUTLINE

The poem may be divided into four parts. Each of the four gives one step in the development of the central theme.

Part I: In a castle overlooking the highway to Camelot* sits a mysterious lady.

Part II: Shut off from the outside world, she spends her time in weaving, knowing real things and people only through the reflection in a mirror, for she has heard it whispered that a curse will come upon her if she ever stops to look at the world outside the castle.

Part III: Catching in the mirror a glimpse of the handsome knight Sir Lancelot riding by, she leaves her task, goes to the window, and sees directly for the first time the world of reality, including Sir Lancelot, whom she loves at first sight. With the coming of reality and love into her life, the curse, symbolized by the breaking of the mirror, falls upon her.

Part IV: Finding a boat, she floats down the river, but dies before she reaches Camelot. Lancelot, although he knows not of her love, admires her beauty and breathes a prayer for her soul.

[1] For biography see page 726.

PART I

ON EITHER side the river lie
   Long fields of barley and of rye,
That clothe the wold[1] and meet the sky;
And thro' the field the road runs by
     To many-tower'd Camelot*;
And up and down the people go,
Gazing where the lilies blow
Round an island there below,
    The island of Shalott.

Willows whiten,[2] aspens quiver,   10
Little breezes dusk and shiver
Thro' the wave that runs for ever
By the island in the river
    Flowing down to Camelot.
Four gray walls, and four gray towers,
Overlook a space of flowers,
And the silent isle imbowers
    The Lady of Shalott.

By the margin, willow-veil'd
Slide the heavy barges[3] trail'd   20
By slow horses; and unhail'd
The shallop[4] flitteth silken-sail'd
    Skimming down to Camelot:
But who hath seen her wave her hand?
Or at the casement seen her stand?
Or is she known in all the land,
    The Lady of Shalott?

[1] Open, rolling country.
[2] The underside of the willow leaf is white; hence the leaves "whiten" when the undersides are turned upward by the breeze.
[3] A barge is a roomy, flat-bottomed boat used for freight. The poet is thinking of boats drawn by horses and used on canals.
[4] A light pleasure boat.

Only reapers, reaping early
In among the bearded barley,
Hear a song that echoes cheerly   30
From the river winding clearly,
        Down to tower'd Camelot:
And by the moon the reaper weary,
Piling sheaves[1] in uplands airy,
Listening, whispers "'Tis the fairy
        Lady of Shalott."

PART II

There she weaves by night and day
A magic web with colours gay.
She has heard a whisper say,
A curse is on her if she stay   40
        To look down to Camelot.
She knows not what the curse may be,
And so she weaveth steadily,
And little other care hath she,
        The Lady of Shalott.

And moving thro' a mirror clear
That hangs before her all the year,
Shadows of the world appear.
There she sees the highway near
        Winding down to Camelot: 50
There the river eddy whirls,
And there the surly village-churls,
And the red cloaks of market girls,
        Pass onward from Shalott.

Sometimes a troop of damsels glad,
An abbot on an ambling pad,[2]
Sometimes a curly shepherd-lad,
Or long-hair'd page[3] in crimson clad,
        Goes by to tower'd Camelot:
And sometimes thro' the mirror blue
The knights come riding two and two:
She hath no loyal knight and true,[4]   62
        The Lady of Shalott.

But in her web she still delights
To weave the mirror's magic sights,

1 Bundles of grain.
2 *abbot ... pad.* The head of a monastery* riding
    an easy-paced horse (pad).
3 A youth in training for knighthood.
4 *no loyal ... true.* No knight who loves her.

For often thro' the silent nights
A funeral, with plumes and lights
        And music, went to Camelot:
Or when the moon was overhead,
Came two young lovers lately wed;   70
"I am half sick of shadows," said
        The Lady of Shalott.

PART III

A bow-shot from her bower-eaves,
He rode between the barley-sheaves,
The sun came dazzling thro' the leaves,
And flamed upon the brazen greaves[1]
        Of bold Sir Lancelot.*
A red-cross knight[2] for ever kneel'd
To a lady in his shield,
That sparkled on the yellow field,   80
        Beside remote Shalott.

The gemmy[3] bridle glitter'd free,
Like to some branch of stars we see
Hung in the golden Galaxy.[4]
The bridle bells rang merrily
        As he rode down to Camelot:
And from his blazon'd baldric[5] slung
A mighty silver bugle hung,
And as he rode his armour rung,
        Beside remote Shalott.   90

All in the blue unclouded weather
Thick-jewell'd shone the saddle-leather,
The helmet and the helmet-feather
Burn'd like one burning flame together,
        As he rode down to Camelot.
As often thro' the purple night,
Below the starry clusters bright,
Some bearded meteor,[6] trailing light,
        Moves over still Shalott.   99

1 Armor for the legs below the knees.
2 *A red-cross knight.* The figure of a knight who
    symbolizes Saint* George as in Spenser's
    Faerie Queene (p. 166).
3 Set with gems.
4 The Milky Way, the broad path of light, formed
    of myriads of stars, which extends across the
    heavens.
5 *blazoned baldric.* A highly decorated belt that
    passed over the shoulder and under the op-
    posite arm.
6 *bearded meteor.* A shooting-star with a long train.

She floated down to Camelot

His broad clear brow in sunlight
    glow'd;
On burnish'd hooves his war-horse
    trode;
From underneath his helmet flow'd
His coal-black curls as on he rode,
    As he rode down to Camelot.
From the bank and from the river
He flash'd into the crystal mirror,
"Tirra lirra," by the river
    Sang Sir Lancelot.

She left the web, she left the loom,
She made three paces thro' the room, 110
She saw the water-lily bloom,
She saw the helmet and the plume,
    She look'd down to Camelot.
Out flew the web and floated wide;
The mirror crack'd from side to side;
"The curse is come upon me," cried
    The Lady of Shalott.[1]

[1] *She . . . Shalott.* Note the rapid action and the
forceful expression in these lines.

PART IV

In the stormy east-wind straining,
The pale yellow woods were waning,[1]
The broad stream in his banks com-
plaining,   120
Heavily the low sky raining
    Over tower'd Camelot;
Down she came and found a boat
Beneath a willow left afloat,
And round about the prow she wrote
    The Lady of Shalott.

And down the river's dim expanse
Like some bold seër in a trance,
Seeing all his own mischance —
With a glassy countenance   130
    Did she look to Camelot.
And at the closing of the day
She loosed the chain, and down she lay;
The broad stream bore her far away,
    The Lady of Shalott.

Lying, robed in snowy white
That loosely flew to left and right —
The leaves upon her falling light —
Thro' the noises of the night
    She floated down to Camelot; 140
And as the boat-head wound along
The willowy hills and fields among,
They heard her singing her last song,
    The Lady of Shalott.

Heard a carol, mournful, holy,
Chanted loudly, chanted lowly,
Till her blood was frozen slowly,
And her eyes were darken'd wholly,
    Turn'd to tower'd Camelot.
For ere she reach'd upon the tide   150
The first house by the water-side,
Singing in her song she died,
    The Lady of Shalott.

Under tower and balcony,
By garden-wall and gallery,
A gleaming shape she floated by,
Dead-pale between the houses high,
    Silent into Camelot.
Out upon the wharfs they came,
Knight and burgher,[1] lord and dame, 160
And round the prow they read her name,
    The Lady of Shalott.

Who is this? and what is here?
And in the lighted palace near
Died the sound of royal cheer;
And they cross'd themselves for fear,
    All the knights at Camelot:
But Lancelot mused a little space;
He said, "She has a lovely face;
God in his mercy lend her grace,   170
    The Lady of Shalott."

The Charge of the Light Brigade

"The Charge of the Light Brigade" is one of the most stirring poems in literature. It celebrates the heroism of a troop of light cavalry in the battle of Balaklava.* Six hundred and seventy-three rode into the charge; only one hundred and ninety-five returned.

The charm of the poem lies in the thrilling story of heroism that defies death and in the movement of the verse, which, Tennyson said, was suggested by the cadence of the tragic words "Someone had blundered" (l. 12).

HALF a league, half a league,
  Half a league onward,

All in the valley of death
  Rode the six hundred.
"Forward, the Light Brigade!
Charge for the guns!" he said:
Into the valley of death
  Rode the six hundred.

"Forward, the Light Brigade!"
Was there a man dismayed?   10
Not though the soldiers knew
  Some one[2] had blundered.

[1] *The pale . . . waning.* Note the change from midsummer to autumn.

[1] Citizen.

[2] In the original version the poet tells us that Nolan, the messenger who delivered the fatal order, was the "Some one."

Theirs not to make reply,
Theirs not to reason why,
Theirs but to do and die.
Into the valley of death
   Rode the six hundred.

Cannon to right of them,
Cannon to left of them,
Cannon in front of them   20
   Volleyed and thundered;
Stormed at with shot and shell,
Boldly they rode and well,
Into the jaws of death,
Into the mouth of hell
   Rode the six hundred.

Flashed all their sabers bare,
Flashed as they turned in air,
Sabring the gunners there,
Charging an army, while   30
   All the world wondered.
Plunged in the battery smoke,
Right through the line they broke;
Cossack* and Russian
Reeled from the saber stroke
   Shattered and sundered.
Then they rode back, but not —
   Not the six hundred.

Cannon to right of them,
Cannon to left of them,   40
Cannon behind them
   Volleyed and thundered;
Stormed at with shot and shell,
While horse and hero fell,
They that had fought so well
Came through the jaws of death,
Back from the mouth of hell,
All that was left of them,
   Left of six hundred.

When can their glory fade?   50
O the wild charge they made!
   All the world wondered.
Honor the charge they made!
Honor the Light Brigade!
   Noble six hundred.

Discussion Hints

The Lady of Shalott

1. Besides its apparent, superficial meaning, "The Lady of Shalott" has a secondary, or allegorical,* significance, the key to which, according to Tennyson's son, lies in lines 69–72. Tennyson explained these lines as follows: "The newborn love for something, for someone in the wide world from which she has been so long excluded, takes her out of the region of shadows into that of realities." Thus, as has been suggested, the poem might be called "The Soul's Awakening." With these hints in mind, find passages that seem to be allegorical and explain their allegorical significance.

2. Select six passages that express the "dreamy melancholy" of the poem.

3. Find at least four passages in which the sound fits the sense.

4. Point out three passages that owe their effectiveness to the use of alliteration.*

5. An excellent critic has said that lines 11–12 "describe exactly the effect of light puffs of air on flowing water." What do the words *dusk* and *shiver* suggest to your mind in this connection? What part of speech is *dusk* here? What part of speech is it usually?

6. Contrast the picture of nature given in lines 1–36 with that given in lines 118–126. Show that each passage forms a fit setting for the accompanying action.

7. What is the curse that threatens the Lady of Shalott? How does it affect her? Quote passages to prove your answer.

8. Do you find any passage that could be illustrated? If you like to draw, illustrate one of them.

9. What is the rhyme scheme of the poem? What foot is most common?

Words and Expressions to be Explained

   imbowers (l. 17)
   willow-veil'd (l. 19)
   bower-eaves (l. 73)
   trailing light (l. 98)

Charge of the Light Brigade

1. The meter is irregular. According to Henry van Dyke, "The general movement is trochaic* and dactylic* with three stresses to the longer lines and two stresses to the short lines."

2. Does the poem contain more monosyllabic or more polysyllabic words?

3. Compare the poem with Tennyson's "*Revenge*" (in the revised edition of *Adventure* of this series). Note especially the similarities.

4. Tennyson wrote the poem in a few minutes, after reading a newspaper account of the charge. Later he revised it somewhat. Line 10 was originally "No man was there dismayed." Do you prefer this or the line as it now stands? Justify your answer.

5. Each stanza contains a line intended to rhyme with the last line of the stanza. In which case or cases are these rhymes perfect; in which are they imperfect? Discuss in class.

6. Poets are fond of gaining emphasis by repeating words and phrases. Reread the repeated words and lines in this poem. Do they add to the effect?

7. Similar cases of soldiers ordered to charge against great odds have occurred in other wars. If you can learn of such a charge, tell the class about it. (Ask the teacher, your parents, or older friends.)

Suggestions for Reading[1]

"Lady Clare" (in the revised edition of *Adventure* of this series)
From *The Princess*: Parts I, II, and III
Maud
Enoch Arden
From *The Idylls of the King*: "Gareth and Lynette," "The Marriage of Geraint," "Geraint and Enid," "Lancelot and Elaine," and "The Passing of Arthur." ("Gareth and Lynette" and "The Passing of Arthur" are given in the revised edition of *Achievement* of this series)
"The *Revenge*" (in the revised edition of *Adventure* of this series)

CHARLES KINGSLEY[1] (1819–1875)

The Sands of Dee

Of Kingsley's small body of verse "The Sands of Dee" is still greatly admired for its pathetic theme, its haunting cadences, and its ballad-like simplicity.

O MARY, go and call the cattle home,
  And call the cattle home,
  And call the cattle home
Across the sands of Dee.[2]"
The western wind was wild and dank wi'
    foam,
  And all alone went she.

The western tide crept up along the sand,
  And o'er and o'er the sand,
  And round and round the sand,
As far as eye could see.　　　　　　10
The rolling mist came down and hid the
    land —
  And never home came she.

"Oh! is it weed, or fish, or floating hair —
  A tress o' golden hair,
  A drownèd maiden's hair
Above the nets at sea?
Was never salmon yet that shone so fair
  Among the stakes on Dee."

They rowed her in across the rolling
    foam,
  The cruel crawling foam,　　　　20
  The cruel hungry foam,
To her grave beside the sea:
But still the boatmen hear her call the
    cattle home
Across the sands of Dee!

Discussion Hints

1. "The Sands of Dee" resembles the popular ballads by reason of the fact that it tells in simple language of a tragic event in the lives of simple folk. Compare it with Words-

---

[1] For biography see page 733.
[2] A river flowing through parts of northern England and North Wales and emptying into the Irish Sea. At the mouth are broad flats which are covered with water at high tide.

[1] For suggestions for reading in Tennyson's lyric poetry see page 478.

worth's "Lucy Gray" (p. 337). In what respects do the stories of the two poems resemble each other? In what respects do they differ? Which is written in a stanza form more closely resembling that of the popular ballads (p. 58)?

2. Compare "The Sands of Dee" with Scott's "Lay of Rosabelle" (p. 406), also an imitation of the popular ballads. In what respects do the two poems resemble each other?

3. Among American poems that tell in the ballad manner tragic stories of maidens who are drowned, the most famous is Longfellow's "Wreck of the *Hesperus*" (in the revised edition of *Adventure* of this series). Compare Longfellow's poem with Kingsley's in regard both to similarities and to differences.

DANTE GABRIEL ROSSETTI[1] (1828–1882)

The Blessed Damozel

Rossetti was only nineteen years old when he composed "The Blessed Damozel." He had been thinking of writing a poem concerning the grief of a living lover for the loss of the loved one, but he read the American poet Edgar Allan Poe's "Raven" and felt that it described that kind of grief so perfectly that it was useless for anyone else to deal with the same theme. Accordingly, by a daring leap of the imagination, he transfers the scene of his poem from earth to heaven, and with great simplicity and reverence describes the grief and longing with which the loved one in heaven awaits the coming of her lover, who is still on earth.

The stanzas in quotation marks give the words of the Blessed Damozel herself as she leans over the parapet of heaven and yearns toward the tiny, far-distant earth where her lover is. The stanzas and sentences in parentheses give the unspoken thoughts of the lover on earth, who lost his sweetheart ten years before, and has been grieving for her ever since. The poem presents the Blessed Damozel's life in heaven in a series of beautiful, detailed pictures. Indeed, after reading the poem we are not surprised to learn that Rossetti was a painter as well as a poet. The clearness with which the author visualizes the unseen world suggests the work of the Pre-Raphaelite* group, of which Rossetti was a member.

THE Blessed Damozel[2] leaned out
　From the gold bar of Heaven;
Her eyes were deeper than the depth
　Of waters stilled at even;
She had three lilies in her hand,
　And the stars in her hair were seven.

Her robe, ungirt from clasp to hem,
　No wrought flowers did adorn,
But a white rose of Mary's gift,
　For service meetly[1] worn;　　　10
Her hair that lay along her back
　Was yellow like ripe corn.[2]

Herseemed[3] she scarce had been a day
　One of God's choristers;
The wonder was not yet quite gone
　From that still look of hers;
Albeit, to them she left, her day
　Had counted as ten years.

(To one, it is ten years of years.
　. . . Yet now, and in this place,　　20
Surely she leaned o'er me — her hair
　Fell all about my face. . . .
Nothing: the autumn fall of leaves.
　The whole year sets apace.)

It was the rampart of God's house
　That she was standing on;
By God built over the sheer depth
　The which is Space begun;
So high, that looking downward thence
　She scarce could see the sun.　　30

It lies in Heaven, across the flood
　Of ether, as a bridge.
Beneath, the tides of day and night
　With flame and darkness ridge
The void, as low as where this earth
　Spins like a fretful midge.[4]

---

[1] For biography see page 735.　　[2] Maiden.

[1] Suitably, fitly.　　[2] Grain (here, wheat).
[3] It seemed to her.　　[4] A gnat.

The Blessed Damozel

From a painting by Rossetti in the collection of C. W. Dyson Perrins

Around her, lovers, newly met
  'Mid deathless love's acclaims,
Spoke evermore among themselves
  Their heart-remembered names;   40
And the souls mounting up to God
  Went by her like thin flames.

And still she bowed herself and stooped
  Out of the circling charm;
Until her bosom must have made
  The bar she leaned on warm,
And the lilies lay as if asleep
  Along her bended arm.

From the fixed place of Heaven she saw
  Time like a pulse shake fierce   50
Through all the worlds. Her gaze still
    strove
  Within the gulf to pierce
Its path; and now she spoke as when
  The stars sang in their spheres.[1]

The sun was gone now; the curled moon
  Was like a little feather
Fluttering far down the gulf; and now
  She spoke through the still weather.
Her voice was like the voice the stars
  Had when they sang together.   60

(Ah sweet! Even now, in that bird's
    song,
  Strove not her accents there,
Fain to be hearkened? When those bells
  Possessed the mid-day air,
Strove not her steps to reach my side
  Down all the echoing stair?)

"I wish that he were come to me,
  For he will come," she said.
"Have I not prayed in Heaven? — on
    earth,
  Lord, Lord, has he not prayed?   70
Are not two prayers a perfect strength?
  And shall I feel afraid?

"When round his head the aureole[1] clings,
  And he is clothed in white,
I'll take his hand and go with him
  To the deep wells of light;
As unto a stream we will step down,
  And bathe there in God's sight.

"We two will stand beside that shrine,
  Occult,[2] withheld, untrod,   80
Whose lamps are stirred continually
  With prayer sent up to God;
And see our old prayers, granted, melt
  Each like a little cloud.

"We two will lie i' the shadow of
  That living mystic tree
Within whose secret growth the Dove[3]
  Is sometimes felt to be,
While every leaf that His plumes touch
  Saith His Name audibly.   90

"And I myself will teach to him,
  I myself, lying so,
The songs I sing here, which his voice
  Shall pause in, hushed and slow,
And find some knowledge at each pause,
  Or some new thing to know."

(Alas! We two, we two, thou say'st!
  Yea, one wast thou with me
That once of old. But shall God lift
  To endless unity   100
The soul whose likeness with thy soul
  Was but its love for thee?)

"We two," she said, "will seek the groves
  Where the lady Mary is,
With her five handmaidens, whose names
  Are five sweet symphonies,
Cecily, Gertrude, Magdalen,
  Margaret and Rosalys.[4]

"Circlewise sit they, with bound locks
  And foreheads garlanded;   110

---

[1] According to ancient astronomy the stars and other heavenly bodies are set in transparent spheres which, as they revolve, make music. See also Job 38 : 7 (p. 161).

[1] The golden ring of light represented in art as surrounding the heads of saints and heavenly beings.
[2] Secret.   [3] The Holy Ghost.
[4] *Cecily . . . Rosalys.* Christian saints.

Into the fine cloth white like flame
 Weaving the golden thread,
To fashion the birth-robes for them
 Who are just born, being dead.

"He shall fear, haply, and be dumb:
 Then will I lay my cheek
To his, and tell about our love,
 Not once abashed or weak:
And the dear Mother will approve
 My pride, and let me speak.   120

"Herself shall bring us, hand in hand,
 To Him round whom all souls
Kneel, the clear-ranged unnumbered
  heads
 Bowed with their aureoles:
And angels meeting us shall sing
 To their citherns and citoles.[1]

"There will I ask of Christ the Lord
 Thus much for him and me: —
Only to live as once on earth
 With Love, only to be,   130
As then awhile, for ever now
 Together, I and he."

She gazed and listened and then said,
 Less sad of speech than mild, —
"All this is when he comes." She ceased.
 The light thrilled towards her, filled
With angels in strong level flight.
 Her eyes prayed, and she smiled.

(I saw her smile.) But soon their path
 Was vague in distant spheres: 140
And then she cast her arms along
 The golden barriers,
And laid her face between her hands,
 And wept. (I heard her tears.)

Discussion Hints

1. How many of the details given in lines 1–6 can you identify in the illustration given on page 527?

2. For whom do Mary and her hand-maidens make garments?

3. The similes* in lines 35–36 and lines 55–57 are unusually effective. Why?

4. How does the poet create the impression that heaven is far away?

5. To what are the souls mounting to God compared?

6. Point out details that show Rossetti's remarkable gift of visualizing and depicting the unseen world.

7. What passages suggest that Rossetti was a painter as well as a poet?

8. What is the difference between "ether" (l. 32) and "either"?

9. Memorize the two consecutive stanzas that you like best, and be prepared to recite them in class.

10. If possible read Edgar Allan Poe's "Raven" and discuss Poe's and Rossetti's poems together. "The Raven" is given in the revised edition of *American Writers* of this series.

Suggestions for Reading

"The Ballad of Dead Ladies"
"The Sonnet"
From *The House of Life*: IV, XXVI, XXVII, XLIII
"Three Shadows"
"Chimes"
"Lost Days"
"A Superscription"

WILLIAM MORRIS[2] (1834–1896)

From "The Lady of the Land"

"The Lady of the Land" illustrates the fondness for medieval themes which Morris shared with the other Pre-Raphaelites.* The poem is a retelling of a story found in *The Travels of Sir John Mandeville*, famous among medieval travel books describing real or imaginary marvels of far-off lands. "The Lady of the Land" is contained in Morris's *Earthly Paradise*, a collection of narratives supposed to be told by a group of travelers, somewhat as in Chaucer's *Canterbury Tales* (p. 37). Like others of Morris's narrative poems, it is

---

[1] *citherns and citoles.* Ancient musical instruments.
[2] For biography see page 734.

D

written in a gently flowing, simple style, and it is a well-told story.

IT HAPPENED once, some men of Italy
Midst the Greek Islands went a sea-
    roving,
And much good fortune had they on the
    sea:
Of many a man they had the ransoming,
And many a chain they gat,[1] and goodly
    thing;
And midst their voyage to an isle they
    came,
Whereof my story keepeth not the name.

Now though but little was there left to
    gain,
Because the richer folk had gone away,
Yet, since by this of water they were fain,[2]
They came to anchor in a land-locked
    bay,   11
Whence in a while some went ashore to
    play,
Going but lightly armed in twos or threes,
For midst that folk they feared no
    enemies.

And of these fellows that thus went
    ashore,
One was there who left all his friends
    behind;
Who going inland ever more and more,
And being left quite alone, at last did find
A lonely valley sheltered from the wind,
Wherein, amidst an ancient cypress
    wood,   20
A long-deserted ruined castle stood.

[Here he finds a garden run wild and a temple
in ruins.]

Close to the temple was the castle-gate,
Doorless and crumbling; there our fel-
    low turned,
Trembling indeed at what might chance
    to wait

[1] The old form of "got."
[2] Desirous. The whole line means, "By this time they were very thirsty."

The prey entrapped, yet with a heart
    that burned
To know the most of what might there
    be learned,
And hoping somewhat too, amid his fear,
To light on such things as all men hold
    dear.

Noble the house was, nor seemed built
    for war,   29
But rather like the work of other days,
When men, in better peace than now
    they are,
Had leisure on the world around to
    gaze,
And noted well the past times' changing
    ways;
And fair with sculptured stories it was
    wrought,
By lapse of time unto dim ruin brought.

Now as he looked about on all these
    things,
And strove to read the mouldering his-
    tories,
Above the door an image with wide wings,
Whose unclad limbs a serpent seemed to
    seize,
He dimly saw, although the western
    breeze,   40
And years of biting frost and washing
    rain,
Had made the carver's labour well-nigh
    vain.

But this, though perished sore, and
    worn away,
He noted well, because it seemed to be,
After the fashion of another day,
Some great man's badge of war, or
    armoury[1];
And round it a carved wreath he seemed
    to see:
But taking note of these things, at the
    last
The mariner beneath the gateway passed.

[1] Coat of arms.

Therefrom unto the chambers did he
pass,   50
And found them fair still, midst of their
decay,
Though in them now no sign of man
there was,
And everything but stone had passed
away
That made them lovely in that vanished
day;
Nay, the mere walls themselves would
soon be gone
And nought be left but heaps of mouldering stone.

But he, when all the place he had gone
o'er,
And with much trouble clomb the broken
stair,
And from the topmost turret seen the
shore
And his good ship drawn up at anchor
there,   60
Came down again, and found a crypt[1]
most fair
Built wonderfully beneath the greatest
hall,
And there he saw a door within the wall,

Well-hinged, close shut; nor was there
in that place
Another on its hinges, therefore he
Stood there and pondered for a little
space,
And thought, "Perchance some marvel
I shall see,
For surely here some dweller there must
be,
Because this door seems whole, and new,
and sound,   69
While nought but ruin I can see around."

So with that word, moved by a strong
desire,
He tried the hasp, that yielded to his
hand,
And in a strange place, lit as by a fire
Unseen but near, he presently did stand;

¹ An underground chamber, or vault.

And by an odorous breeze his face was
fanned,
As though in some Arabian plain he stood,
Anigh the border of a spice-tree wood.

He moved not for awhile, but looking
round,
He wondered much to see the place so
fair,   79
Because, unlike the castle above ground,
No pillager or wrecker had been there;
It seemed that time had passed on other-
where,¹
Nor laid a finger on this hidden place,
Rich with the wealth of some forgotten
race.

With hangings, fresh as when they left
the loom,
The walls were hung a space above the
head,
Slim ivory chairs were set about the room,
And in one corner was a dainty bed,
That seemed for some fair queen ap-
parellèd;
And marble was the worst stone of the
floor,   90
That with rich Indian webs² was covered
o'er.

The wanderer trembled when he saw all
this,
Because he deemed by magic it was
wrought;
Yet in his heart a longing for some bliss,
Whereof the hard and changing world
knows nought,
Arose and urged him on, and dimmed the
thought
That there perchance some devil lurked
to slay
The heedless wanderer from the light of
day.

Over against him was another door
Set in the wall; so, casting fear aside,
With hurried steps he crossed the varied
floor,   101

¹ Elsewhere.   ² Rugs.

And there again the silver latch he tried
And with no pain the door he opened
    wide,
And entering the new chamber cautiously
The glory of great heaps of gold could
    see.

Upon the floor uncounted medals lay,
Like things of little value; here and
    there
Stood golden cauldrons,[1] that might well
    outweigh
The biggest midst an emperor's copper-
    ware,   109
And golden cups were set on tables fair,
Themselves of gold; and in all hollow
    things
Were stored great gems, worthy the
    crowns of kings.

The walls and roof with gold were
    overlaid,
And precious raiment from the wall hung
    down;
The fall of kings that treasure might have
    stayed,
Or gained some longing conqueror great
    renown,
Or built again some god-destroyed old
    town;
What wonder, if this plunderer of the sea
Stood gazing at it long and dizzily?

But at the last his troubled eyes and
    dazed   120
He lifted from the glory of that gold,
And then the image, that well-nigh
    erased
Over the castle-gate he did behold,
Above a door well wrought in coloured
    gold
Again he saw; a naked girl with wings
Enfolded in a serpent's scaly rings.

And even as his eyes were fixed on it,
A woman's voice came from the other
    side,
And through his heart strange hopes
    began to flit

[1] Large kettles.

That in some wondrous land he might
    abide   130
Not dying, master of a deathless bride,
So o'er the gold which now he scarce
    could see
He went, and passed this last door
    eagerly.

[Having passed the door, he finds himself in
a gorgeous apartment occupied by a lovely
woman holding in one hand a comb and in the
other a mirror. As he is about to address her,
she stops him with a look and then speaks.]

For now she spoke in gentle voice and
    clear,
Using the Greek tongue that he knew full
    well;
"What man art thou, that thus hast
    wandered here,
And found this lonely chamber where I
    dwell?
Beware, beware! for I have many a
    spell;
If greed of power and gold have led thee
    on,
Not lightly shall this untold wealth be
    won.   140

"But if thou com'st here, knowing of
    my tale,
In hope to bear away my body fair,
Stout must thine heart be, nor shall that
    avail
If thou a wicked soul in thee dost bear;
So once again I bid thee to beware,
Because no base man things like this may
    see,
And live thereafter long and happily."

"Lady," he said, "in Florence* is my
    home,
And in my city noble is my name;   149
Neither on peddling voyage am I come,
But, like my fathers, bent to gather fame;
And though thy face has set my heart
    a-flame
Yet of thy story nothing do I know,
But here have wandered heedlessly enow.[1]

[1] Enough.

"But since the sight of thee mine eyes
 did bless,
What can I be but thine? what wouldst
 thou have?
From those thy words, I deem from some
 distress
By deeds of mine thy dear life I might
 save;
O then, delay not! if one ever gave
His life to any, mine I give to thee; 160
Come, tell me what the price of love
 must be?

"Swift death, to be with thee a day and
 night
And with the earliest dawning to be
 slain?
Or better, a long year of great delight,
And many years of misery and pain?
Or worse, and this poor hour for all my
 gain?
A sorry merchant am I on this day,
E'en as thou willest so must I obey."

She said, "What brave words! nought
 divine am I, 169
But an unhappy and unheard-of maid
Compelled by evil fate and destiny
To live, who long ago should have been
 laid
Under the earth within the cypress shade.
Hearken awhile, and quickly shalt thou
 know
What deed I pray thee to accomplish
 now.

"God grant indeed thy words are not
 for nought!
Then shalt thou save me, since for many
 a day
To such a dreadful life I have been
 brought: 178
Nor will I spare with all my heart to
 pay
What man soever takes my grief away;
Ah! I will love thee, if thou lovest me
But well enough my saviour now to be.

"My father lived a many years agone
Lord of this land, master of all cunning,
Who ruddy gold could draw from out
 grey stone,
And gather wealth from many an un-
 couth thing;
He made the wilderness rejoice and sing,
And such a leech[1] he was that none could
 say
Without his word what soul should pass
 away.

[The lady then tells how she had been a priest-
ess of Diana,* but had offended the goddess.
She then proceeds with her story.]

"And then the doom foreseen upon me
 fell, 190
For Queen Diana* did my body change
Into a fork-tongued dragon, flesh and fell,[2]
And through the island nightly do I range;
Or in the green sea mate with monsters
 strange,
When in the middle of the moonlit night
The sleepy mariner I do affright.

"But all day long upon this gold I lie
Within this place, where never mason's
 hand
Smote trowel on the marble noisily; 199
Drowsy I lie, no folk at my command,
Who once was called the Lady of the
 Land;
Who might have bought a kingdom with
 a kiss,
Yea, half the world with such a sight as
 this.

"Wilt thou not save me? once in every
 year
This rightful form of mine that thou
 dost see
By favour of the goddess have I here
From sunrise unto sunset given me,
That some brave man may end my misery.
And thou — art thou not brave? can
 thy heart fail,
Whose eyes e'en now are weeping at my
 tale? 210

[1] Physician.   [2] Skin.

"Then listen! when this day is over-
past,
A fearful monster shall I be again,
And thou mayst be my saviour at the
last;
Unless, once more, thy words are nought
and vain.
If thou of love and sovereignty art fain,[1]
Come thou next morn, and when thou
seest here
A hideous dragon, have thereof no fear,

"But take the loathsome head up in
thine hands,
And kiss it, and be master presently　219
Of twice the wealth that is in all the lands
From Cathay [2] to the head of Italy;
And master also, if it pleaseth thee,
Of all thou praisest as so fresh and
bright,
Of what thou callest crown of all delight.

"Ah! with what joy then shall I see
again
The sunlight on the green grass and the
trees,
And hear the clatter of the summer rain,
And see the joyous folk beyond the seas.
Ah me! to hold my child upon my knees,
After the weeping of unkindly tears,　230
And all the wrongs of these four hundred
years.

"Go now, go quick! leave this grey
heap of stone;
And from thy glad heart think upon thy
way,
How I shall love thee — yea, love thee
alone,
That bringest me from dark death unto
day;
For this shall be thy wages and thy pay;
Unheard-of wealth, unheard-of love is
near,
If thou hast heart a little dread to bear."

[1] Here, desirous. Compare the use of the word in
line 10.
[2] An old name for China.

[The lady then gives the adventurer a valuable jewel and hurries from the room.]

Then at the doorway where her rosy
heel
Had glanced and vanished, he awhile did
stare,　240
And still upon his hand he seemed to
feel
The varying kisses of her fingers fair;
Then turned he toward the dreary crypt
and bare,
And dizzily throughout the castle passed,
Till by the ruined fane [1] he stood at last.

Then weighing still the gem within his
hand,
He stumbled backward through the
cypress wood,
Thinking the while of some strange
lovely land,
Where all his life should be most fair and
good;　249
Till on the valley's wall of hills he stood,
And slowly thence passed down unto
the bay
Red with the death of that bewildering
day.[2]

The next day came, and he, who all
the night
Had ceaselessly been turning in his bed,
Arose and clad himself in armour bright,
And many a danger he remembered;
Storming of towns, lone sieges full of
dread,
That with renown his heart had borne
him through,
And this thing seemed a little thing
to do.

So on he went, and on the way he
thought　260
Of all the glorious things of yesterday,
Nought of the price whereat they must
be bought,

[1] Temple.
[2] A poetical way of saying that the day, which
had been filled with bewildering adventures,
ended in a red sunset.

But ever to himself did softly say,
"No roaming now, my wars are passed
    away;
No long dull days devoid of happiness,
When such a love my yearning heart
    shall bless."

Thus to the castle did he come at last,
But when unto the gateway he drew
    near,
And underneath its ruined archway
    passed
Into a court, a strange noise did he hear,
And through his heart there shot a pang
    of fear;   271
Trembling, he gat his sword into his
    hand,
And midmost of the cloisters took his
    stand.

But for a while that unknown noise
    increased,
A rattling, that with strident roars did
    blend,
And whining moans; but suddenly it
    ceased,
A fearful thing stood at the cloister's end,
And eyed him for a while, then 'gan to
    wend [1]
Adown the cloisters, and began again
That rattling, and the moan like fiends in
    pain.   280

And as it came on towards him, with
    its teeth
The body of a slain goat did it tear,
The blood whereof in its hot jaws did
    seethe,
And on its tongue he saw the smoking
    hair;
Then his heart sank, and standing
    trembling there,
Throughout his mind wild thoughts and
    fearful ran,
"Some fiend she was," he said, "the
    bane [2] of man."

Yet he abode [1] her still, although his
    blood
Curdled within him: the thing dropped
    the goat,
And creeping on, came close to where he
    stood,   290
And raised its head to him, and wrinkled
    throat,
Then he cried out and wildly at her
    smote,
Shutting his eyes, and turned and from
    the place
Ran swiftly, with a white and ghastly
    face.

But little things rough stones and tree-
    trunks seemed,
And if he fell, he rose and ran on still:
No more he felt his hurts than if he
    dreamed,
He made no stay for valley or steep hill,
Heedless he dashed through many a
    foaming rill,
Until he came unto the ship at last   300
And with no word into the deep hold
    passed.

Meanwhile the dragon, seeing him clean
    gone,
Followed him not, but crying horribly,
Caught up within her jaws a block of
    stone
And ground it into powder, then turned
    she,
With cries that folk could hear far out at
    sea,
And reached the treasure set apart of old,
To brood above the hidden heaps of gold.

Yet was she seen again on many a day
By some half-waking mariner, or heard,
Playing amid the ripples of the bay,   311
Or on the hills making all things afeard,
Or in the wood, that did that castle gird,
But never any man again durst go
To seek her woman's form, and end her
    woe.

1 'gan to wend. Did go.
2 Curse, destroyer.

1 Waited for.

As for the man, who knows what things
    he bore?
What mournful faces peopled the sad
    night,
What wailings vexed him with reproaches
    sore,
What images of that nigh-gained delight!
What dreamed caresses from soft hands
    and white,   320
Turning to horrors ere they reached the
    best:
What struggles vain, what shame, what
    huge unrest?

No man he knew, three days he lay
    and raved,
And cried for death, until a lethargy[1]
Fell on him, and his fellows thought him
    saved;
But on the third night he awoke to die;
And at Byzantium* doth his body lie
Between two blossoming pomegranate
    trees,
Within the churchyard of the Genoese.

Discussion Hints

1. Why did the lone adventurer enter the ruined castle?

2. What caused him to conclude that the castle was not "built for war" (l. 29)?

3. What difference did he observe between the part of the castle which he entered at line 71 and the part which he had just left? How do you account for the difference (see lines 83–84)?

4. What conditions must the adventurer fulfill in order to win the lady? What will be the result if he has not the required qualifications?

    [1] Profound drowsiness.

5. How many doors does the adventurer open, and what wonders does he see after opening each?

6. Do you think you would have had the courage to kiss the dragon and thus break the spell, or would you have run away as the sailor did?

7. Morris uses a number of archaic words in order to give his narrative the flavor of medieval romance. Make a list of them and be prepared to explain what they mean.

8. What account does the adventurer give of himself and his character? Does his behavior bear out these claims?

9. What account does the lady give of her ancestry and of her own experiences?

10. Why is there no exact description of the dragon? Compare the description of Grendel (p. 21).

Words and Passages to be Explained

fair with sculptured stories it was wrought,
By lapse of time unto dim ruin brought
    (ll. 34–35)
for some fair queen apparellèd (l. 89)
The fall of kings that treasure might have stayed
    (l. 115)
strident (l. 275)
seethe (l. 283)

Suggestions for Reading

NARRATIVE POETRY

"Shameful Death"
"Atalanta's Race"
Sigurd the Volsung (See p. 24)

LYRIC POETRY

"The Sailing of the Sword"
"The Haystack in the Floods"
"An Apology" (from Prologue to *The Earthly Paradise*)
"L'Envoi" (from *The Earthly Paradise*)

ROBERT LOUIS STEVENSON[1] (1850–1894)

Heather Ale

Anyone who likes ballads will enjoy Stevenson's swinging version of the old Scottish legend told in "Heather Ale." It is the story plus the singing quality of the verse that gives the poem a place in literature.

FROM the bonny bells of heather
　They[2] brewed a drink long-syne,[3]
Was sweeter far than honey,
　Was stronger far than wine.
They brewed it and they drank it,
　And lay in a blessed swound[4]
For days and days together
　In their dwelling underground.

There rose a king of Scotland,
　A fell[5] man to his foes,　　　10
He smote the Picts in battle,
　He hunted them like roes.[6]
Over miles of the red mountain
　He hunted as they fled,
And strewed the dwarfish bodies
　Of the dying and the dead.

Summer came in the country,
　Red was the heather bell;
But the manner of the brewing
　Was none alive to tell.　　　20
In graves that were like children's
　On many a mountain head,
The Brewsters[7] of the Heather
　Lay numbered with the dead.

The king in the red moorland
　Rode on a summer's day;
And the bees hummed, and the curlews[8]
　Cried beside the way.
The king rode, and was angry,
　Black was his brow and pale,　　　30
To rule in a land of heather
　And lack the Heather Ale.

It fortuned[1] that his vassals,
　Riding free[2] on the heath,
Came on a stone that was fallen
　And vermin[3] hid beneath.
Rudely plucked from their hiding,
　Never a word they spoke:
A son and his aged father —
　Last of the dwarfish folk.　　　40

And the king sat high on his charger,
　He looked on the little men;
And the dwarfish and swarthy[4] couple
　Looked at the king again.
Down by the shore he had them;
　And there on the giddy brink —
"I will give you life, ye vermin,
　For the secret of the drink."

There stood the son and father;
　And they looked high and low;　　　50
The heather was red around them,
　The sea rumbled below.
And up and spoke the father,
　Shrill was his voice to hear:
"I have a word in private,
　A word for the royal ear.

"Life is dear to the aged,
　And honour a little thing;
I would gladly sell the secret,"
　Quoth the Pict to the King.　　　60
His voice was small as a sparrow's,
　And shrill and wonderful clear:
"I would gladly sell my secret,
　Only my son I fear.

"For life is a little matter,
　And death is nought to the young;
And I dare not sell my honour
　Under the eye of my son.

[1] For biography see page 730.
[2] The Picts. According to tradition they were a small, dark people of ancient Scotland who lived underground.　[3] Long ago.　[4] Swoon.
[5] Dangerous, fierce.　[6] Deer.　[7] Brewers.
[8] The curlew is a Scottish bird with a shrill, haunting cry.

[1] Happened.
[2] In the open, away from the road.
[3] The hated cave-dwelling Picts.
[4] Dark-skinned.

Rudely plucked from their hiding, . . .
Last of the dwarfish folk

Take *him*, O king, and bind him.
  And cast him far in the deep;   70
And it's I will tell the secret
  That I have sworn to keep."

They took the son and bound him,
  Neck and heels in a thong,
And a lad took him and swung him,
  And flung him far and strong,
And the sea swallowed his body,
  Like that of a child of ten; —
And there on the cliff stood the father,
  Last of the dwarfish men.   80

"True was the word I told you:
  Only my son I feared;
For I doubt the sapling courage
  That goes without the beard.
But now in vain is the torture,
  Fire shall never avail:
Here dies in my bosom
  The secret of Heather Ale."

Discussion Hints

1. What characteristics justify calling "Heather Ale" a ballad (p. 57)? Is the meter that of the popular ballads?

2. According to an old tradition the Picts were a small, dark people of ancient Scotland who took refuge in caves underground when they were persecuted by invaders of larger stature. How does this tradition throw light on Stevenson's poem? Have you ever heard any other stories about dwarfish or fairy people who live underground?

3. Heather is a common Scottish wild flower. Do you know of any other beverages made by country people from wild flowers?

4. Why does the Pict in the poem refuse to sell the secret of making heather ale?

5. How does Stevenson bring out the small size of the Picts?

6. Besides Stevenson, what poets of the Romantic and Victorian periods represented in *English Writers* wrote poems based on Scottish tradition?

7. What deception does the Pict use to hide his secret?

Words and Expressions to be Explained

bonny (l. 1)
giddy brink (l. 46)
   the sapling courage
That goes without the beard (ll. 83–84)

Suggestions for Reading

You will enjoy others of Stevenson's poems in the ballad style and, if you are not too old, some of the poems in his *Child's Garden of Verses.*

SCIENTIFIC PROSE

THOMAS HENRY HUXLEY[1] (1825–1895)

From "On a Piece of Chalk"

"On a Piece of Chalk," originally delivered as a popular lecture, was written to convince English workingmen that certain easily observable natural causes were operative in the formation of the great chalk beds of the world. Throughout its entire length the essay shows the results of keen observation and illustrates the passion for truth which is characteristic of the true scientist. It is only one of a large number of essays and addresses which brought the results of scientific research to the attention of the common people and which marked the rapid growth of popular education in England during the Victorian Period.

It is written in clear, simple, unadorned English. Seldom has science been presented in as truly literary form as it is in the writings of Huxley.

IF A WELL were to be sunk at our feet in the midst of the city of Norwich,[2] the diggers would very soon find themselves at work in that white substance, almost too soft to be called rock, with which we are all familiar as "chalk." Not only here, but over the whole county of Norfolk, the well-sinker might carry his shaft down many hundred feet without coming to the end of the chalk; and, on the sea-coast, where the waves have pared away the face of the land which breasts them, the scarped faces of the high cliffs are often wholly formed of the same material. Northward, the chalk may be followed as far as Yorkshire[3]; on the south coast it appears abruptly in the picturesque western bays of Dorset,[1] and breaks into the Needles of the Isle of Wight;[2] while on the shores of Kent[3] it supplies that long line of white cliffs to which England owes her name of Albion.*

Were the thin soil which covers it all washed away, a curved band of white chalk, here broader and there narrower, might be followed diagonally across England from Lulworth in Dorset to Flamborough Head in Yorkshire — a distance of over two hundred and eighty miles as the crow flies. From this band to the North Sea, on the east, and the Channel, on the south, the chalk is largely hidden by other deposits; but, except in the Weald[4] of Kent and Sussex,[5] it enters into the very foundation of all the south-eastern counties.

Attaining, as it does in some places, a thickness of more than a thousand feet, the English chalk must be admitted to be a mass of considerable magnitude. Nevertheless, it covers but an insignificant portion of the whole area occupied by the chalk formation of the globe, which has precisely the same general characters as ours, and is found in detached patches, some less and others more extensive than the English. Chalk

---

[1] For biography see page 735.
[2] A town in the eastern part of England where Huxley originally delivered "On a Piece of Chalk."
[3] A county in northeastern England.
[1] A county in southwestern England.
[2] *Needles . . . Wight.* Three white-pointed rocks of chalk, resting on dark-colored bases and rising abruptly from the sea to the height of a hundred feet. They are situated near the Isle of Wight in the English Channel.
[3] A county in southeastern England.
[4] A very old word meaning "forest." It is applied to an oval-shaped area in the south-eastern part of England.
[5] A county in southeastern England.

© Fox

The Needles of the Isle of Wight

occurs in northwest Ireland; it stretches over a large part of France, — the chalk which underlies Paris being, in fact, a continuation of that of the London basin; it runs through Denmark and Central Europe, and extends southward to North Africa; while eastward, it appears in the Crimea and in Syria, and may be traced as far as the shores of the Sea of Aral, in Central Asia. If all the points at which true chalk occurs were circumscribed, they would lie within an irregular oval about three thousand miles in long diameter, the area of which would be as great as that of Europe, and would many times exceed that of the largest existing inland sea — the Mediterranean.

Thus the chalk is no unimportant element in the masonry of the earth's crust, and it impresses a peculiar stamp, varying with the conditions to which it is exposed, on the scenery of the districts in which it occurs. The undulating downs[1] and rounded coombs,[2] covered with sweet-grassed turf, of our inland chalk country, have a peacefully domestic and mutton-suggesting prettiness, but can hardly be called either grand or beautiful. But on our southern coasts, the wall-sided cliffs, many hundred feet high, with vast needles and pinnacles standing out in the sea, sharp and solitary enough to serve as perches for the wary cormorant,[3] confer a wonderful beauty and grandeur upon the chalk headlands. And in the East, chalk has its share in the formation of some of

[1] Rolling uplands; here, the rolling treeless highland in the south and southeast of England.
[2] Valleys enclosed on all sides but one by cliffs.
[3] A kind of large, greedy sea bird.

the most venerable of mountain ranges, such as the Lebanon.

90 What is this widespread component of the surface of the earth? and whence did it come?

You may think this no very hopeful inquiry. You may not unnaturally suppose that the attempt to solve such problems as these can lead to no result, save that of entangling the inquirer in vague speculations, incapable of refutation and of verification. If such were really the case, I should have selected 100 some other subject than a "piece of chalk" for my discourse. But in truth, after much deliberation, I have been unable to think of any topic which would so well enable me to lead you to see how solid is the foundation upon which some of the most startling conclusions of physical science rest A great chapter in the history of the world is written in the chalk. Few passages 110 in the history of man can be supported by such an overwhelming mass of direct and indirect evidence as that which testifies to the truth of the fragment of the history of the globe which I hope to enable you to read, with your own eyes, tonight.

Let me add that few chapters of human history have a more profound significance for ourselves. I weigh my 120 words well when I assert that the man who should know the true history of the bit of chalk which every carpenter carries about in his breeches-pocket, though ignorant of all other history, is likely, if he will think his knowledge out to its ultimate results, to have a truer, and therefore a better, conception of this wonderful universe, and of man's relation to it, than the most learned 130 s udent who is deep read in the records of humanity and ignorant of those of Nature. The language of the chalk is not hard to learn, not nearly so hard as Latin, if you only want to get at the broad features of the story it has to tell; and I propose that we now set to work to spell that story out together.

[In the part of the essay omitted, Huxley explains that chalk is composed of carbonic acid and lime, in which are found numerous skeletons of tiny animals called *Globigerinae*[1] and resembling microscopic marine animals now living, called by the same name. He explains also that the ocean bottom between Ireland and Newfoundland is covered with soft mud filled with these same skeletons of *Globigerinae*. From the fact that this mud, now being slowly deposited, is similar in composition to chalk, he concludes that chalk was deposited as mud of the same kind as that which is now being laid down, and that the period of its formation — the Cretaceous Period[2] — was of great length.]

Thus not only is it certain that the chalk is the mud of an ancient sea-bottom; but it is no less certain that the 140 chalk sea existed during an extremely long period, though we may not be prepared to give a precise estimate of the length of that period in years. The relative duration is clear, though the absolute duration may not be definable. The attempt to affix any precise date to the period at which the chalk sea began, or ended, its existence, is baffled by difficulties of the same kind. But the 150 relative age of the cretaceous epoch may be determined with as great ease and certainty as the long duration of that epoch.

You will have heard of the interesting discoveries recently made in various parts of Western Europe of flint implements, obviously worked into shape by human hands, under circumstances which show conclusively that man is a very 160 ancient denizen[3] of these regions. It has been proved that the old populations of Europe, whose existence has been revealed to us in this way, consisted of savages, such as the Esquimaux are

[1] *Globigerinae* (glŏ bĭj ēr ĭ'nē).
[2] *Cretaceous Period*. The geological period, or epoch, in which chalk and coal deposits were formed.
[3] Inhabitant.

now; that, in the country which is now France, they hunted the reindeer, and were familiar with the ways of the mammoth and the bison. The physical 170 geography of France was in those days different from what it is now — the river Somme,[1] for instance, having cut its bed a hundred feet deeper between that time and this; and it is probable that the climate was more like that of Canada or Siberia than that of Western Europe.

The existence of these people is forgotten even in the traditions of the oldest historical nations. The name and fame 180 of them had utterly vanished until a few years back; and the amount of physical change which has been effected since their day renders it more than probable that, venerable as are some of the historical nations, the workers of the chipped flints of Hoxne[2] or of Amiens[3] are to them, as they are to us, in point of antiquity.

But if we assign to these hoar[4] relics 190 of long-vanished generations of men the greatest age that can possibly be claimed for them, they are not older than the drift, or boulder clay, which, in comparison with the chalk, is but a very juvenile[5] deposit. You need go no further than your own sea-board for evidence of this fact. At one of the most charming spots on the coast of Norfolk,[6] Cromer, you will see the boulder clay forming a 200 vast mass, which lies upon the chalk, and must consequently have come into existence after it. Huge boulders of chalk are, in fact, included in the clay, and have evidently been brought to the position they now occupy by the same agency as that which has planted blocks

of syenite[1] from Norway side by side with them.

The chalk, then, is certainly older than the boulder clay. If you ask how 210 much, I will again take you no further than the same spot upon your own coasts for evidence. I have spoken of the boulder clay and drift as resting upon the chalk. That is not strictly true. Interposed between the chalk and the drift is a comparatively insignificant layer, containing vegetable matter. But that layer tells a wonderful history. It is full of stumps of trees standing as they grew. 220 Fir-trees are there with their cones, and hazel-bushes with their nuts; there stand the stools[2] of oak and yew trees, beeches and alders. Hence this stratum[3] is appropriately called the "forest-bed."

It is obvious that the chalk must have been upheaved[4] and converted into dry land before the timber trees could grow upon it. As the boles[5] of some of these trees are from two to three feet in diam- 230 eter, it is no less clear that the dry land thus formed remained in the same condition for long ages. And not only do the remains of stately oaks and well-grown firs testify to the duration of this condition of things, but additional evidence to the same effect is afforded by the abundant remains of elephants, rhinoceroses, hippopotamuses, and other great wild beasts, which it has yielded to the 240 zealous search of such men as the Rev. Mr. Gunn.[6] When you look at such a collection as he has formed, and bethink you that these elephantine bones did veritably carry their owners about, and these great grinders crunch, in the dark woods of which the forest-bed is now the

---

[1] A river in northern France which flows into the English Channel.
[2] A town in eastern England where prehistoric flint implements have been found.
[3] A city in northern France where prehistoric flint implements have been found.
[4] Ancient.
[5] Young; here, deposited in comparatively recent times.
[6] A county in eastern England.

[1] A kind of massive granite rock.
[2] Stumps.
[3] Layer.
[4] That is, raised as the result of some elevation of the earth's crust.
[5] Trunks.
[6] Robert Campbell Gunn (1808–1881), a British naturalist who contributed many specimens of plants and animals to the British Museum.

only trace, it is impossible not to feel that they are as good evidence of the 250 lapse of time as the annual rings of the tree-stumps.

Thus there is a writing upon the walls of cliffs at Cromer, and whoso runs may read it. It tells us, with an authority which cannot be impeached, that the ancient sea-bed of the chalk sea was raised up, and remained dry land until it was covered with forest, stocked with the great game whose spoils have re-260 joiced your geologists. How long it remained in that condition cannot be said; but "the whirligig of time brought its revenges"[1] in those days as in these. That dry land, with the bones and teeth of generations of long-lived elephants hidden away among the gnarled roots and dry leaves of its ancient trees, sank gradually to the bottom of the icy sea, which covered it with huge masses of 270 drift and boulder clay. Sea-beasts, such as the walrus, now restricted to the extreme north, paddled about where birds had twittered among the topmost twigs of the fir-trees. How long this state of things endured we know not, but at length it came to an end. The upheaved glacial mud hardened into the soil of modern Norfolk. Forests grew once more, the wolf and the beaver replaced 280 the reindeer and the elephant; and at length what we call the history of England dawned.

Thus you have, within the limits of your own county, proof that the chalk can justly claim a very much greater antiquity than even the oldest physical traces of mankind. But we may go further and demonstrate, by evidence of the same authority as that which testi-290 fies to the existence of the father of men, that the chalk is vastly older than Adam * himself.

The Book of Genesis informs us that Adam, immediately upon his creation, and before the appearance of Eve,* was placed in the Garden of Eden.* The problem of the geographical position of Eden has greatly vexed the spirits of the learned in such matters, but there is one point respecting which, so far as I know, 300 no commentator has ever raised a doubt. This is, that of the four rivers which are said to run out of it, Euphrates * and Hiddekel[1] are identical with the rivers now known by the names of Euphrates and Tigris.* But the whole country in which these mighty rivers take their origin, and through which they run, is composed of rocks which are either of the same age as the chalk, or of later date. 310 So that the chalk must not only have been formed, but, after its formation, the time required for the deposit of these later rocks, and for their upheaval into dry land, must have elapsed before the smallest brook which feeds the swift stream of "the great river, the river of Babylon," * began to flow.

Thus, evidence which cannot be rebutted, and which need not be strength-320 ened, though if time permitted I might indefinitely increase its quantity, compels you to believe that the earth, from the time of the chalk to the present day, has been the theater of a series of changes as vast in their amount as they were slow in their progress. The area on which we stand has been first sea and then land, for at least four alternations[2]; and has remained in each of these conditions for a 330 period of great length. Nor have these wonderful metamorphoses[3] of sea into land, and of land into sea, been confined to one corner of England. During the chalk period, or "cretaceous epoch," not one of the present great physical features of the globe was in existence. Our great mountain ranges, Pyrenees, Alps,

---

[1] *whirligig . . . revenges.* "And thus the whirligig of time brings in his revenges." — SHAKE-SPEARE, *Twelfth Night*

[1] A river mentioned in Genesis 2 : 14 as flowing out of the Garden of Eden.

[2] Exchanges, shifts.

[3] *metamorphoses* (mĕt á môr'fō sēz). Changes.

Himalayas, Andes, have all been up-340 heaved since the chalk was deposited, and the cretaceous sea flowed over the sites of Sinai and Ararat. All this is certain, because rocks of cretaceous, or still later, date have shared in the elevatory movements which gave rise to these mountain chains; and may be found perched up, in some cases, many thousand feet high upon their flanks. And evidence of equal cogency[1] demonstrates 350 that, though in Norfolk the forest-bed rests directly upon the chalk, yet it does so, not because the period at which the forest grew immediately followed that at which the chalk was formed, but because an immense lapse of time, represented elsewhere by thousands of feet of rock, is not indicated at Cromer.

I must ask you to believe that there is no less conclusive proof that a still more 360 prolonged succession of similar changes occurred before the chalk was deposited. Nor have we any reason to think that the first term in the series of these changes is known. The oldest sea-beds preserved to us are sands, and mud, and pebbles, the wear and tear of rocks which were formed in still older oceans.

But, great as is the magnitude of these physical changes of the world, they have 370 been accompanied by a no less striking series of modifications[2] in its living inhabitants. All the great classes of animals, beasts of the field, fowls of the air, creeping things, and things which dwell in the waters, flourished upon the globe long ages before the chalk was deposited. Very few, however, if any, of these ancient forms of animal life were identical with those which now live. Certainly not one of the higher 380 animals was of the same species as any of those now in existence. The beasts of the field, in the days before the chalk, were not our beasts of the field, nor the fowls of the air such as those which the eye of man has seen flying, unless his antiquity

[1] Force, convincingness.
[2] Changes.

dates infinitely further back than we at present surmise. If we could be carried back into those times, we should be as one suddenly set down in Australia before it was colonized. We should see mam- 390 mals, birds, reptiles, fishes, insects, snails, and the like, clearly recognizable as such, and yet not one of them would be just the same as those with which we are familiar, and many would be extremely different.

From that time to the present, the population of the world has undergone slow and gradual, but incessant changes. There has been no grand catastrophe[1] — no destroyer has swept away the forms of 400 life of one period and replaced them by a totally new creation; but one species has vanished and another has taken its place; creatures of one type of structure have diminished, those of another have increased, as time has passed on. And thus, while the differences between the living creatures of the time before the chalk and those of the present day appear startling if placed side by side, we 410 are led from one to the other by the most gradual progress if we follow the course of Nature through the whole series of those relics of her operations which she has left behind.

And it is by the population of the chalk sea that the ancient and the modern inhabitants of the world are most completely connected. The groups which are dying out flourish side by side with the 420 groups which are now the dominant forms of life. Thus the chalk contains remains of those strange flying and swimming reptiles, the pterodactyl, the ichthyosaurus, and the plesiosaurus, which are found in no later deposits, but abounded in preceding ages. The chambered shells called ammonites and belemnites, which are so characteristic of the period preceding the cretaceous, in like manner die 430 with it. But amongst these fading remainders of a previous state of things are some very modern forms of life, looking

[1] *catastrophe* (kă tăs'trō fê). Sudden calamity.

D

like Yankee peddlers among a tribe of Red Indians. Crocodiles of modern type appear; bony fishes, many of them very similar to existing species, almost supplant the forms of fish which predominate in more ancient seas; and many kinds of 440 living shell-fish first become known to us in the chalk. The vegetation acquires a modern aspect. A few living animals are not even distinguishable as species from those which existed at that remote epoch. The *Globigerina* of the present day, for example, is not different specifically from that of the chalk; and the same may be said of many other *Foraminifera*.[1] I think it probable that critical and un-450 prejudiced examination will show that more than one species of much higher animals have had a similar longevity; but the only example which I can at present give confidently is the snake's-head lamp-shell (*Terebratulina caput serpentis*), which lives in our English seas and abounded (as *Terebratulina striata* of authors)[2] in the chalk.

The longest line of human ancestry 460 must hide its diminished head before the pedigree of this insignificant shell-fish. We Englishmen are proud to have an ancestor who was present at the Battle of Hastings.[3] The ancestors of *Terebratulina caput serpentis* may have been present at a battle of *Ichthyosauria* in that part of the sea which, when the chalk was forming, flowed over the site of Hastings. While all around has changed, this *Tere-*470 *bratulina* has peacefully propagated its species from generation to generation, and stands, to this day, as a living testimony to the continuity of the present with the past history of the globe.

[1] *Foraminifera* (fō răm ĭ nĭf'ēr ä). A kind of small animal living in shells with minute holes.
[2] *Terebratulina . . . authors.* That is, referred to by this name by authors.
[3] Fought in 1066.

Discussion Hints

1. Look up on a map the various districts of England which are associated in the essay with chalk deposits.

2. According to Huxley what animals existed in Europe in prehistoric times?

3. What is the "forest-bed" (p. 543, l. 247)?

4. Find out from a chemistry book or from the teacher of chemistry in your school some of the facts about carbonic acid, lime, and chalk. Perhaps the chemistry teacher will consent to give the class a short talk on chalk, putty, lime, marble, coral, and other substances containing calcium carbonate. In any case you should try to correlate with Huxley's essay what you know or can learn about chalk. Write a theme of two hundred words describing the formation of the chalk beds of the world.

5. Chalk has been said to lie at the basis of all life. If you know a doctor ask him to tell you what part chalk (or calcium) plays in the human body.

6. Huxley calls his address a "lecture to workingmen." Do you know of any recent book or books written for the purpose of informing common people about the progress of science? Several interesting and instructive essays or selections from popular books on science are given in the revised editions of *Adventure*, *Achievement*, and *American Writers* of this series.

7. Huxley's essay is carefully organized. In order to study the organization, make an outline showing the various headings under which he presents his material.

Expressions to be Explained

the scarped faces (p. 540, l. 13)
the masonry of the earth's crust (p. 541, ll. 68–69)
mutton-suggesting (p. 541, l. 76)
vague speculations, incapable of refutation and of verification (p. 542, ll. 97–98)
the annual rings of the tree-stumps (p. 544, ll. 250–251)
Sinai and Ararat (p. 545, l. 342)
a similar longevity (p. 546, l. 452)

THE SHORT STORY

THE short story was one of the last of the important literary types to appear in English literature. It is a form of short prose narrative and, as such, can be understood best if we consider it in relation to other short prose narratives. Short prose narratives have existed in English literature from the Middle Ages to the present day. Medieval literature abounds in humorous episodes and romantic or pious tales, which range all the way from a few hundred to several thousand words in length. Great collections of pious tales were made during the Middle Ages and were widely used by medieval preachers as illustrations in sermons. The most famous medieval collection of short prose narratives is Boccaccio's *Decameron*, written originally in Italian, in which a group of ladies and gentlemen are represented as telling each other stories in order to while away the time.

We also find many short narratives in the pastoral* and other romances of the late Middle Ages and the Renaissance. These little stories are usually represented as being told by the characters who figure in the main plot of the romance. The practice of introducing short independent stories into longer prose narratives continued until late in the history of English fiction. Short narratives also appeared occasionally in *The Tatler,** The Spectator,** and other early periodicals. As the English periodicals grew in number and in popularity there was an increasing call for short prose stories, until today many magazines publish nothing but brief fictional narratives.

In spite of their number and popularity, however, the older short prose narratives in English literature have little in common with the modern short story. The modern short story developed first in America,[1] about a century after the modern novel [2] had begun to take form in England. It would have developed independently in England; but the development would probably have been slower and the history of the short story in English literature would undoubtedly have been different if Poe, Hawthorne, and other early writers in the United States had not laid down the principles of the new form and illustrated their theories by actual practice.

The short prose narratives in early English literature usually emphasize plot at the expense of everything else. Many of them, it is true, have excellent plots; but the development of the plots is often slow, and the

---

[1] For a discussion of the short story in America, see the revised edition of *American Writers* of this series.   [2] Page 219.

reader is left almost entirely to imagine for himself just what the characters are like and what the setting is. Even in those cases where the characters are at all individualized and the surroundings are described, the authors seem to have known little of how to combine plot, characters, and setting in such a way as to produce a harmonious effect. The modern short story, like the modern one-act play, deals with a single situation rather than with a chain of events; it focuses the reader's attention upon one single flashing moment or emotional crisis; it reveals human character rather than shows how character develops; it can be read in approximately half an hour; and it concentrates all its elements, plot, character, dialogue, and setting, upon one single effect.

Though the general trend of the modern short story in England, like that of other literary types in recent years, has been toward realism,* the realism has generally been less intense than in the case of the short story in America. Many excellent short stories of a romantic[1] tone have appeared in recent English literature.

One of the earliest modern English short stories, as opposed to stories that are merely short, was Stevenson's "Sire de Malétroit's Door" (p. 549), which appeared in 1878 and which illustrates both Stevenson's romantic plots and his realistic method of making characters as well as scenes convincing. The exquisite nicety with which the setting is fitted to the plot and to the characters — the gallant hero, the cruel uncle, and the scornful, weeping, and finally melting maiden — creates a perfect balance and a unity of emotional effect that mark the whole as a true short story rather than merely a condensed novel or a padded episode.

Since the days of Stevenson, English writers of short stories have multiplied. There are Kipling, Galsworthy, Knight, "Saki," H. G. Wells, to mention only a few. "Rikki-tikki-tavi" (p. 642) is typical of Kipling's work; for the scene is laid in India, it has animal characters more interesting than human ones, and it is at the same time a story excellent in structure and in style. Galsworthy's "Quality" (p. 653), like his plays and novels, not only makes its reader acquainted with a most interesting person, but arouses his sympathy for one unfairly treated by a hardhearted world. In "Cockles for Tea" (p. 657) Eric Knight describes in a delightfully humorous manner the experiences of a young Englishman who returns to his native village after having settled in America. "Saki" (H. H. Munro) is as successful a maker of short stories as the old bachelor in his "Story-Teller" (p. 668). In them are to be found in abundance Saki's unfailing wit and charm and mockery. H. G. Wells's "Man Who Could Work Miracles" (p. 671) illustrates the fantastic ideas suggested by science, which the author so often uses as the central themes of his writings.

[1] See "romance."*

The short stories given here illustrate only a few of the various effects produced by modern short-story writers. The ways of writing short stories are almost numberless; but all good short stories are alike in one respect: they blend plot, character, dialogue, and setting so as to produce a single effect which was in the mind of the author before he began to write.

ROBERT LOUIS STEVENSON[1] (1850–1894)

The Sire de Malétroit's Door

"The Sire de Malétroit's Door" is one of Robert Louis Stevenson's most delightful stories of romantic adventure, stories of which it has been said that they have added more to the stock of English romantic fiction than those of any other man since Scott. The setting, the characters, the incidents, all alike shimmer in the magic of the gifted author's imagination and glowing style. There is not a dull page in the entire story from the moment we meet Denis, escaping after midnight from the watchmen in the dangerous, wind-swept streets of a fifteenth-century French town, to the dawn of day, when, after a nerve-racking night, he and Blanche, now betrothed sweethearts, together turn to bid good morning to Blanche's shrewd old uncle, the Sire de Malétroit.[2]

Much of the charm of the story comes from the French setting. Be careful to pronounce correctly the beautiful French names. A distinguished critic has said that "no story in the world reads better aloud than 'The Sire de Malétroit's Door.'" Try it.

D ENIS DE BEAULIEU[3] was not yet two-and-twenty, but he counted himself a grown man, and a very accomplished cavalier into the bargain. Lads were early formed in that rough, warfaring epoch; and when one has been in a pitched battle and a dozen raids, has killed one's man in an honourable fashion, and knows a thing or two of strategy and
10 mankind, a certain swagger in the gait is surely to be pardoned. He had put up his horse with due care, and supped with due deliberation; and then, in a very agreeable frame of mind, went out to pay a visit in the gray of the evening. It was not a very wise proceeding on the young man's part. He would have done better to remain beside the fire or go decently to bed. For the town was full of troops of Burgundy and England[1] under a
20 mixed command; and though Denis was there on safe-conduct, his safe-conduct was like to serve him little on a chance encounter.

It was September, 1429; the weather had fallen sharp; a flighty, piping wind, laden with showers, beat about the township; and the dead leaves ran riot along the streets. Here and there a window was already lighted up, and
30 the noise of men-at-arms, making merry over supper within, came forth in fits and was swallowed up and carried away by the wind. The night fell swiftly; the flag of England, fluttering on the spire top, grew even fainter and fainter against the flying clouds, — a black speck like a swallow in the tumultuous, leaden chaos of the sky. As the night fell the wind rose and began to hoot under archways
40 and roar amid the tree-tops in the valley below the town.

Denis de Beaulieu walked fast and was soon knocking at his friend's door; but though he promised himself to stay only a little while and make an early return, his welcome was so pleasant, and he

---

[1] For biography see page 730.

[2] *Sire de Malétroit* (sēr dĕ mȧl ȧ trwȧ'). "Sire" means "lord."

[3] *Denis de Beaulieu* (dĕ nē' dĕ bō lyû').

---

[1] The Duke of Burgundy, though himself French, was at this time an ally of England.

found so much to delay him, that it was
already long past midnight before he
said good-bye upon the threshold. The
wind had fallen again in the meanwhile;
the night was as black as the grave; not
a star, nor a glimmer of moonshine,
slipped through the canopy of cloud.
Denis was ill acquainted with the in-
tricate lanes of Château Landon[1]; even
by daylight he had found some trouble
in picking his way; and in this absolute
darkness he soon lost it altogether. He
was certain of one thing only, — to keep
mounting the hill; for his friend's house
lay at the lower end, or tail, of Château
Landon, while the inn was up at the head,
under the great church spire. With this
clew to go upon he stumbled and groped
forward, now breathing more freely in
the open places where there was a good
slice of sky overhead, now feeling along
the wall in stifling closes.[2] It is an eerie
and mysterious position to be thus submerged in opaque blackness in an almost
unknown town. The silence is terrify-
ing in its possibilities. The touch of cold
window bars to the exploring hand
startles the man like a touch of a toad;
the inequalities of the pavement shake
his heart into his mouth; a piece of
denser darkness threatens an ambuscade
or a chasm in the pathway; and where
the air is brighter, the houses put on
strange and bewildering appearances,
as if to lead him further from his way.
For Denis, who had to regain his inn
without attracting notice, there was real
danger as well as mere discomfort in the
walk, and he went warily and boldly at
once, and at every corner paused to make
an observation.

He had been for some time threading
a lane so narrow that he could touch a
wall with either hand, when it began to
open out and go sharply downward.
Plainly this lay no longer in the direction

of his inn, but the hope of a little more
light tempted him forward to recon-
noitre.[1] The lane ended in a terrace with
a bartizan wall,[2] which gave an outlook
between high houses, as out of an em-
brasure,[3] into the valley lying dark and
formless several hundred feet below.
Denis looked down, and could discern a
few tree-tops waving and a single speck
of brightness where the river ran across a
weir.[4] The weather was clearing up, and
the sky had lightened, so as to show the
outline of the heavier clouds and the
dark margin of the hills. By the uncertain glimmer the house on his left hand
should be a place of some pretensions;
it was surmounted by several pinnacles
and turret-tops; the round stern of a
chapel, with a fringe of flying buttresses,[5]
projected boldly from the main block,
and the door was sheltered under a deep
porch carved with figures and overhung
by two long gargoyles.[6] The windows
of the chapel gleamed through their in-
tricate tracery with a light as of many
tapers, and threw out the buttresses and
the peaked roof in a more intense blackness against the sky. It was plainly the
hotel[7] of some great family of the neighbourhood, and as it reminded Denis of a
town house of his own at Bourges,[8] he
stood for some time gazing up at it and
mentally gauging the skill of the archi-
tects and the consideration[9] of the two
families.

There seemed to be no issue to the
terrace but the land by which he had
reached it; he could only retrace his

---

[1] Look carefully about.
[2] *bartizan wall.* An overhanging wall for lookout
　　or defense.
[3] An opening with sides flaring outward in a wall.
[4] Dam.
[5] A flying buttress is a structure in masonry to
　　brace a roof or an arch. See illustration in an
　　unabridged dictionary.
[6] A gargoyle is a waterspout, often grotesquely
　　carved, jutting from the roof gutter.
[7] In the French sense of "mansion."
[8] *Bourges* (bōōrzh). A city in France.
[9] Importance, or consequence.

[1] *Château Landon* (shä tō′ läN dôN′).　A small
　　town southeast of Paris.
[2] Narrow passages.

steps, but he had gained some notion of his whereabouts, and hoped by this means to hit the main thoroughfare and speedily regain the inn. He was reckoning without that chapter of accidents which was to make this night memorable above all others in his career; for he had not gone back above a hundred yards before he saw a light coming to meet him, and heard loud voices speaking together in the echoing narrows of the lane. It was a party of men-at-arms going the night round with torches. Denis assured himself that they had all been making free with the wine-bowl and were in no mood to be particular about safe-conducts or the niceties of chivalrous war. It was as like as not that they would kill him like a dog and leave him where he fell. The situation was inspiriting but nervous. Their own torches would conceal him from sight, he reflected; and he hoped that they would drown the noise of his footsteps with their own empty voices. If he were but fleet and silent, he might evade their notice altogether.

Unfortunately, as he turned to beat a retreat, his foot rolled upon a pebble; he fell against the wall with an ejaculation, and his sword rung loudly on the stones. Two or three voices demanded who went there — some in French, some in English; but Denis made no reply, and ran the faster down the lane. Once upon the terrace, he paused to look back. They still kept calling after him, and just then began to double the pace in pursuit, with a considerable clank of armour and great tossing of the torchlight to and fro in the narrow jaws of the passage.

Denis cast a look around and darted into the porch. There he might escape observation, or — if that were too much to expect — was in a capital posture whether for parley[1] or defence. So thinking, he drew his sword and tried to set his back against the door. To his surprise it yielded behind his weight and, though

he turned in a moment, continued to swing back on oiled and noiseless hinges until it stood wide open on a black interior. When things fall out opportunely for the person concerned, he is not apt to be critical about the how or why, his own immediate personal convenience seeming a sufficient reason for the strangest oddities and revolutions in our sublunary[1] things; and so Denis, without a moment's hesitation, stepped within and partly closed the door behind him to conceal his place of refuge. Nothing was further from his thoughts than to close it altogether; but for some inexplicable reason — perhaps by a spring or a weight — the ponderous mass of oak whipped itself out of his fingers and clanked to, with a formidable rumble and a noise like the falling of an automatic bar.

The round,[2] at that very moment, debouched[3] upon the terrace and proceeded to summon him with shouts and curses. He heard them ferreting in the dark corners; the stock of a lance even rattled along the outer surface of the door behind which he stood; but these gentlemen were in too high a humour to be long delayed, and soon made off down a corkscrew pathway which had escaped Denis' observation, and passed out of sight and hearing along the battlements of the town.

Denis breathed again. He gave them a few minutes' grace for fear of accidents, and then groped about for some means of opening the door and slipping forth again. The inner surface was quite smooth, — not a handle, not a moulding, not a projection of any sort. He got his finger-nails round the edges and pulled, but the mass was immovable. He shook it, it was as firm as a rock. Denis de Beaulieu frowned and gave vent to a little noiseless whistle. What ailed the door, he wondered. Why was it open?

---

[1] Conference.
[1] Literally, "under the moon"; that is, earthly.
[2] The party of soldiers making the night round.
[3] Marched out.

How came it to shut so easily and so effectually after him? There was something obscure and underhand about all this, that was little to the young man's fancy. It looked like a snare, and yet who could suppose a snare in such a quiet by-street and in a house of so prosperous and even noble an exterior? And yet — snare or no snare, intentionally or unintentionally — here he was, prettily trapped; and for the life of him he could see no way out of it again. The darkness began to weigh upon him. He gave ear; all was silent without, but within and close by he seemed to catch a faint sighing, a faint sobbing rustle, a little stealthy creak — as though many persons were at his side, holding themselves quite still, and governing even their respiration[1] with the extreme of slyness. The idea went to his vitals with a shock, and he faced about suddenly as if to defend his life. Then, for the first time, he became aware of a light about the level of his eyes and at some distance in the interior of the house, — a vertical thread of light, widening toward the bottom, such as might escape between two wings of arras[2] over a doorway.

To see anything was a relief to Denis; it was like a piece of solid ground to a man labouring in a morass[3]; his mind seized upon it with avidity,[4] and he stood staring at it and trying to piece together some logical conception of his surroundings. Plainly there was a flight of steps ascending from his own level to that of this illuminated doorway, and indeed he thought he could make out another thread of light, as fine as a needle and as faint as phosphorescence, which might very well be reflected along the polished wood of a handrail. Since he had begun to suspect that he was not alone, his heart had continued to beat with smothering violence, and an intolerable desire for action of any sort had possessed itself of his spirit. He was in deadly peril, he believed. What could be more natural than to mount the staircase, lift the curtain, and confront his difficulty at once? At least he would be dealing with something tangible; at least he would be no longer in the dark. He stepped slowly forward with outstretched hands, until his foot struck the bottom step; then he rapidly scaled the stairs, stood for a moment to compose his expression, lifted the arras, and went in.

He found himself in a large apartment of polished stone. There were three doors, one on each of three sides, all similarly curtained with tapestry. The fourth side was occupied by two large windows and a great stone chimney-piece, carved with the arms of the Malétroits. Denis recognised the bearings and was gratified to find himself in such good hands. The room was strongly illuminated, but it contained little furniture except a heavy table and a chair or two, the hearth was innocent of fire, and the pavement was but sparsely strewn with rushes clearly many days old.

On a high chair beside the chimney, and directly facing Denis as he entered, sat a little old gentleman in a fur tippet.[1] He sat with his legs crossed and his hands folded, and a cup of spiced wine stood by his elbow on a bracket on the wall. His countenance had a strong masculine cast, — not properly human, but such as we see in the bull, the goat, or the domestic boar, — something equivocal[2] and wheedling, something greedy, brutal, and dangerous. The upper lip was inordinately[3] full, as though swollen by a blow or a toothache; and the

---

[1] Breathing.
[2] A screen, or hangings, of tapestry.
[3] Swamp.
[4] Extreme eagerness.

[1] A scarf, or muffler.
[2] Shifty.
[3] Excessively, unusually.

smile, the peaked eyebrows, and the small, strong eyes were quaintly and almost comically evil in expression. Beautiful white hair hung straight all round his head, like a saint's, and fell in a single curl upon the tippet. His beard and moustache were the pink of venerable sweetness. Age, probably in consequence of inordinate precautions, 10 had left no mark upon his hands; and the Malétroit hand was famous. It would be difficult to imagine anything at once so fleshy and so delicate in design; the taper, sensual fingers were like those of one of Leonardo's* women; the fork of the thumb made a dimpled protuberance[1] when closed; the nails were perfectly shaped, and of a dead, surprising whiteness. It rendered his 20 aspect tenfold more redoubtable[2] that a man with hands like these should keep them devoutly folded like a virgin martyr, — that a man with so intent and startling an expression of face should sit patiently on his seat and contemplate people with an unwinking stare, like a god, or a god's statue. His quiescence seemed ironical and treacherous, it fitted so poorly with his looks.

30 Such was Alain,[3] Sire de Malétroit.

Denis and he looked silently at each other for a second or two.

"Pray step in," said the Sire de Malétroit. "I have been expecting you all the evening."

He had not risen, but he accompanied his words with a smile and a slight but courteous inclination of the head. Partly from the smile, partly from the strange 40 musical murmur with which the sire prefaced his observation, Denis felt a strong shudder of disgust go through his marrow. And what with disgust and honest confusion of mind, he could scarcely get words together in reply.

"I fear," he said, "that this is a double accident. I am not the person you suppose me. It seems you were looking for a visit; but for my part, nothing was further from my thoughts — 50 nothing could be more contrary to my wishes — than this intrusion."

"Well, well," replied the old gentleman indulgently, "here you are, which is the main point. Seat yourself, my friend, and put yourself entirely at your ease. We shall arrange our little affairs presently."

Denis perceived that the matter was still complicated with some misconcep- 60 tion,[1] and he hastened to continue his explanations.

"Your door," he began.

"About my door?" asked the other, raising his peaked eyebrows. "A little piece of ingenuity." And he shrugged his shoulders. "A hospitable fancy! By your own account, you were not desirous of making my acquaintance. We old people look for such reluctance 70 now and then; when it touches our honour, we cast about until we find some way of overcoming it. You arrive uninvited, but believe me, very welcome."

"You persist in error, sir," said Denis. "There can be no question between you and me. I am a stranger in this countryside. My name is Denis, damoiseau[2] de Beaulieu. If you see me in your house it is only —" 80

"My young friend," interrupted the other, "you will permit me to have my own ideas on that subject. They probably differ from yours at the present moment," he added with a leer, "but time will show which of us is in the right."

Denis was convinced he had to do with a lunatic. He seated himself with a shrug, content to wait the upshot, and a pause ensued, during which he thought 90 he could distinguish a hurried gabbling as of a prayer from behind the arras

---

[1] A bulging; a swelling.
[2] To be feared.
[3] *Alain* (à lăn').

[1] Misunderstanding.
[2] *damoiseau* (dà mwà zō'). A young noble not yet made a knight.

immediately opposite him. Sometimes there seemed to be but one person engaged, sometimes two; and the vehemence of the voice, low as it was, seemed to indicate either great haste or an agony of spirit. It occurred to him that this piece of tapestry covered the entrance to the chapel he had noticed from without.

10   The old gentleman meanwhile surveyed Denis from head to foot with a smile, and from time to time emitted little noises like a bird or a mouse, which seemed to indicate a high degree of satisfaction. This state of matters became rapidly insupportable; and Denis, to put an end to it, remarked politely that the wind had gone down.

The old gentleman fell into a fit of
20 silent laughter, so prolonged and violent that he became quite red in the face. Denis got upon his feet at once, and put on his hat with a flourish.

"Sir," he said, "if you are in your wits, you have affronted me grossly. If you are out of them, I flatter myself I can find better employment for my brains than to talk with lunatics. My conscience is clear; you have made a fool
30 of me from the first moment; you have refused to hear my explanations; and now there is no power under God will make me stay here any longer; and if I cannot make my way out in a more decent fashion, I will hack your door in pieces with my sword."

The Sire de Malétroit raised his right hand and wagged it at Denis with the fore and the little fingers extended.
40   "My dear nephew," he said, "sit down."

"Nephew!" retorted Denis, "you lie in your throat"; and he snapped his fingers in his face.

"Sit down, you rogue!" cried the old gentleman, in a sudden, harsh voice, like the barking of a dog. "Do you fancy," he went on, "that when I had made my little contrivance for the door I had

stopped short with that? If you prefer to 50 be bound hand and foot till your bones ache, rise and try to go away. If you choose to remain a free young buck, agreeably conversing with an old gentleman — why, sit where you are in peace, and God be with you."

"Do you mean I am a prisoner?" demanded Denis.

"I state the facts," replied the other. "I would rather leave the conclusion to 60 yourself."

Denis sat down again. Externally he managed to keep pretty calm, but within, he was now boiling with anger, now chilled with apprehension.[1] He no longer felt convinced that he was dealing with a madman. And if the old gentleman was sane, what, in God's name, had he to look for? What absurd or tragical adventure had befallen him? What coun- 70 tenance was he to assume?

While he was thus unpleasantly reflecting, the arras that overhung the chapel door was raised, and a tall priest in his robes came forth, and, giving a long, keen stare at Denis, said something in an undertone to Sire de Malétroit.

"She is in a better frame of spirit?" asked the latter.

"She is more resigned, messire," re- 80 plied the priest.

"Now, the Lord help her, she is hard to please!" sneered the old gentleman. "A likely stripling — not ill-born — and of her own choosing, too! Why, what more would the jade have?"

"The situation is not usual for a young damsel," said the other, "and somewhat trying to her blushes."

"She should have thought of that be- 90 fore she began the dance! It was none of my choosing, God knows that; but since she is in it, by our Lady, she shall carry it to the end." And then addressing Denis, "Monsieur de Beaulieu," he asked, "may I present you to my niece? She has been waiting your arrival, I may

[1] Fear.

say, with even greater impatience than myself."

Denis had resigned himself with a good grace — all he desired was to know the worst of it as speedily as possible; so he rose at once, and bowed in acquiescence. The Sire de Malétroit followed his example and limped, with the assistance of the chaplain's arm, toward the chapel door. The priest pulled aside the arras, and all three entered. The building had considerable architectural pretensions. A light groining [1] sprung from six stout columns, and hung down in two rich pendants from the centre of the vault. The place terminated behind the altar in a round end, embossed and honeycombed with a superfluity of ornament in relief, and pierced by many little windows shaped like stars, trefoils, [2] or wheels. These windows were imperfectly glazed, so that the night air circulated freely in the chapel. The tapers, of which there must have been half a hundred burning on the altar, were unmercifully blown about; and the light went through many different phases of brilliancy and semi-eclipse. On the steps in front of the altar knelt a young girl richly attired as a bride. A chill settled over Denis as he observed her costume; he fought with desperate energy against the conclusion that was being thrust upon his mind; it could not—it should not—be as he feared.

"Blanche," [3] said the sire, in his most flute-like tones, "I have brought a friend to see you, my little girl; turn round and give him your pretty hand. It is good to be devout; but it is necessary to be polite, my niece."

The girl rose to her feet and turned toward the newcomers. She moved all of a piece; and shame and exhaustion were expressed in every line of her fresh young body; and she held her head down and kept her eyes upon the pavement, as she came slowly forward. In the course of her advance her eyes fell upon Denis de Beaulieu's feet — feet of which he was justly vain, be it remarked, and wore in the most elegant accoutrement even while travelling. She paused — startled, as if his yellow boots had conveyed some shocking meaning — and glanced suddenly up into the wearer's countenance. Their eyes met; shame gave place to horror and terror in her looks; the blood left her lips; with a piercing scream she covered her face with her hands and sank upon the chapel floor.

"That is not the man!" she cried. "My uncle, that is not the man!"

The Sire de Malétroit chirped agreeably. "Of course not," he said; "I expected as much. It was so unfortunate you could not remember his name."

"Indeed," she cried, "indeed, I have never seen this person till this moment — I have never so much as set eyes upon him — I never wish to see him again. Sir," she said, turning to Denis, "if you are a gentleman, you will bear me out. Have I ever seen you — have you ever seen me — before this accursed hour?"

"To speak for myself, I have never had that pleasure," answered the young man. "This is the first time, messire, that I have met with your engaging niece."

The old gentleman shrugged his shoulders.

"I am distressed to hear it," he said. "But it is never too late to begin. I had little more acquaintance with my own late lady ere I married her; which proves," he added, with a grimace, "that these impromptu marriages may often produce an excellent understanding in the long run. As the bridegroom is to have a voice in the matter, I will give him two hours to make up for lost time before we proceed with the ceremony." And he turned toward the door, followed by the clergyman.

---

[1] The angle formed by the meeting of arched vaults to form a roof. See illustration in an unabridged dictionary.

[2] An ornament made up of three divisions, or leaves.

[3] *Blanche* (blänsh).

The girl was on her feet in a moment. "My uncle, you cannot be in earnest," she said. "I declare before God I will stab myself rather than be forced on that young man. The heart rises at it; God forbids such marriages; you dishonour your white hair. Oh, my uncle, pity me! There is not a woman in all the world but would prefer death to such a nuptial.[1] Is it possible," she added, faitering — "is it possible that you do not believe me — that you still think this" — and she pointed at Denis with a tremor of anger and contempt — "that you still think *this* to be the man?"

"Frankly," said the old gentleman, pausing on the threshold, "I do. But let me explain to you once for all, Blanche de Malétroit, my way of thinking about this affair. When you took it into your head to dishonour my family and the name that I have borne, in peace and war, for more than threescore years, you forfeited, not only the right to question my designs, but that of looking me in the face. If your father had been alive, he would have spat on you and turned you out of doors. His was the hand of iron. You may bless your God you have only to deal with the hand of velvet, mademoiselle. It was my duty to get you married without delay. Out of pure good-will I have tried to find your own gallant for you. And I believe I have succeeded. But before God and all the holy angels, Blanche de Malétroit, if I have not, I care not one jackstraw. So let me recommend you to be polite to our young friend; for, upon my word, your next groom may be less appetizing."

And with that he went out, with the chaplain at his heels; and the arras fell behind the pair.

The girl turned upon Denis with flashing eyes.

"And what, sir," she demanded, "may be the meaning of all this?"

"God knows," returned Denis, gloomily. "I am a prisoner in this house, which seems full of mad people. More I know not; and nothing do I understand."

He told her as briefly as he could. "For the rest," he added, "perhaps you will follow my example, and tell me the answer to all these riddles, and what, in God's name, is like to be the end of it."

She stood silent for a little, and he could see her lips tremble and her tearless eyes burn with a feverish lustre. Then she pressed her forehead in both hands.

"Alas, how my head aches!" she said, wearily, "to say nothing of my poor heart! But it is due to you to know my story, unmaidenly as it must seem. I am called Blanche de Malétroit; I have been without father or mother for — oh! for as long as I can recollect, and indeed I have been most unhappy all my life. Three months ago a young captain began to stand near me every day in church. I could see that I pleased him; I am much to blame, but I was so glad that anyone should love me; and when he passed me a letter, I took it home with me and read it with great pleasure. Since that time he has written many. He was so anxious to speak with me, poor fellow! and kept asking me to leave the door open some evening that we might have two words upon the stair. For he knew how much my uncle trusted me." She gave something like a sob at that, and it was a moment before she could go on. "My uncle is a hard man, but he is very shrewd," she said at last. "He has performed many feats in war, and was a great person at court, and much trusted by Queen Isabeau[1] in old days. How he came to suspect me I cannot tell; but it is hard to keep anything from his knowledge; and this morning, as we came from mass, he took my hand in his, forced it open, and read

[1] Wedding.

[1] *Isabeau* (ē zà bō').

my little billet,[1] walking by my side all the while.

"When he finished, he gave it back to me with great politeness. It contained another request to have the door left open; and this has been the ruin of us all. My uncle kept me strictly in my room until evening, and then ordered me to dress myself as you see me — a hard mockery for a young girl, do you not think so? I suppose, when he could not prevail with me to tell him the young captain's name, he must have laid a trap for him; into which, alas! you have fallen in the anger of God. I looked for much confusion; for how could I tell whether he was willing to take me for his wife on these sharp terms? He might have been trifling with me from the first, or I might have made myself too cheap in his eyes. But truly I had not looked for such a shameful punishment as this! I could not think that God would let a girl be so disgraced before a young man. And now I tell you all; and I can scarcely hope that you will not despise me."

Denis made her a respectful inclination.

"Madam," he said, "you have honoured me by your confidence. It remains for me to prove that I am not unworthy of the honour. Is Messire de Malétroit at hand?"

"I believe he is writing in the salle[2] without," she answered.

"May I lead you thither, madam?" asked Denis, offering his hand with his most courtly bearing.

She accepted it, and the pair passed out of the chapel, Blanche in a very drooping and shamefast[3] condition, but Denis strutting and ruffling[4] in the consciousness of a mission, and the boyish certainty of accomplishing it with honour.

The Sire de Malétroit rose to meet them with an ironical obeisance.

"Sir," said Denis, with the grandest

possible air, "I believe I am to have some say in the matter of this marriage; and let me tell you at once, I will be no party to forcing the inclination of this young lady. Had it been freely offered to me, I should have been proud to accept her hand, for I perceive she is as good as she is beautiful; but as things are, I have now the honour, messire, of refusing."

Blanche looked at him with gratitude in her eyes; but the old gentleman only smiled and smiled, until his smile grew positively sickening to Denis.

"I am afraid," he said, "Monsieur de Beaulieu, that you do not perfectly understand the choice I have offered you. Follow me, I beseech you, to this window." And he led the way to one of the large windows which stood open on the night. "You observe," he went on, "there is an iron ring in the upper masonry, and reeved[1] through that a very efficacious rope. Now, mark my words: if you should find your disinclination to my niece's person insurmountable, I shall have you hanged out of this window before sunrise. I shall only proceed to such an extremity with the greatest regret, you may believe me. For it is not at all your death that I desire, but my niece's establishment in life. At the same time, it must come to that if you prove obstinate. Your family, Monsieur de Beaulieu, is very well in its way, but if you sprung from Charlemagne,* you should not refuse the hand of a Malétroit with impunity — not if she had been as common as the Paris road — not if she was as hideous as the gargoyle over my door. Neither my niece nor you, nor my own private feelings, move me at all in this matter. The honour of my house has been compromised; I believe you to be the guilty person, at least you are now in the secret; and you can hardly wonder if I request you to wipe out the stain. If you will

---

[1] Note. [2] Hall. [3] Shamefaced. [4] Swaggering.

[1] Passed

not, your blood be on your own head! It will be no great satisfaction to me to have your interesting relics kicking their heels in the breeze below my windows, but half a loaf is better than no bread, and if I cannot cure the dishonour, I shall at least stop the scandal."

There was a pause.

10 "I believe there are other ways of settling such imbroglios[1] among gentlemen," said Denis. "You wear a sword, and I hear you have used it with distinction."

The Sire de Malétroit made a signal to the chaplain, who crossed the room with long, silent strides and raised the arras over the third of the three doors. It was only a moment before he let it fall again; but Denis had time to see a 20 dusky passage full of armed men.

"When I was a little younger, I should have been delighted to honour you, Monsieur de Beaulieu," said Sire Alain; "but I am now too old. Faithful retainers are the sinews of age, and I must employ the strength I have. This is one of the hardest things to swallow as a man grows up in years, but with a little patience even this becomes habitual. 30 You and the lady seem to prefer the salle for what remains of your two hours; and as I have no desire to cross your preference, I shall resign it to your use with all the pleasure in the world. No haste!" he added, holding up his hand, as he saw a dangerous look come into Denis de Beaulieu's face. "If your mind revolt against hanging, it will be time enough two hours hence to throw 40 yourself out of the window or upon the pikes of my retainers. Two hours of life are always two hours. A great many things may turn up in even as little a while as that. And, besides, if I understand her appearance, my niece has something to say to you. You will not disfigure your last hours by a want of politeness to a lady?"

Denis looked at Blanche, and she made him an imploring gesture.   50

It is likely that the old gentleman was hugely pleased at this symptom of an understanding, for he smiled on both and added sweetly, "If you will give me your word of honour, Monsieur de Beaulieu, to await my return at the end of the two hours before attempting anything desperate, I shall withdraw my retainers and let you speak in greater privacy with mademoiselle."   60

Denis again glanced at the girl, who seemed to beseech him to agree.

"I give you my word of honour," he said.

Messire de Malétroit bowed and proceeded to limp about the apartment, clearing his throat the while with that odd musical chirp which had already grown so irritating in the ears of Denis de Beaulieu. He first possessed himself of 70 some papers which lay upon the table; then he went to the mouth of the passage and appeared to give an order to the men behind the arras; and lastly he hobbled out through the door by which Denis had come in, turning upon the threshold to address a last smiling bow to the young couple, and followed by the chaplain with a hand-lamp.

No sooner were they alone than 80 Blanche advanced toward Denis with her hands extended. Her face was flushed and excited, and her eyes shone with tears.

"You shall not die!" she cried, "you shall marry me after all."

"You seem to think, madam," replied Denis, "that I stand much in fear of death."

"Oh, no, no," she said, "I see you are 90 no poltroon.[1] It is for my own sake — I could not bear to have you slain for such a scruple."

"I am afraid," returned Denis, "that you underrate the difficulty, madam. What you may be too generous to refuse,

---

[1] *imbroglios* (ĭm brōl'yōz). Quarrels.

[1] Coward.

He hobbled out . . ., turning . . . to address a last . . . bow to the young couple

I may be too proud to accept. In a moment of noble feeling toward me, you forget what you perhaps owe to others."

He had the decency to keep his eyes on the floor as he said this, and after he had finished, so as not to spy upon her confusion. She stood silent for a moment, then walked suddenly away, and falling on her uncle's chair, fairly burst out sobbing. Denis was in the acme of embarrassment. He looked round, as if to seek for inspiration, and seeing a stool, plumped down upon it for something to do. There he sat, playing with the guard of his rapier, and wishing himself dead a thousand times over, and buried in the nastiest kitchen-heap in France. His eyes wandered round the apartment, but found nothing to arrest them. There were such wide spaces between the furniture, the light fell so badly and cheerlessly over all, the dark outside air looked in so coldly through the windows, that he thought he had never seen a church so vast, nor a tomb so melancholy. The regular sobs of Blanche de Malétroit measured out the time like the ticking of a clock. He read the device upon the shield over and over again, until his eyes became obscured; he stared into shadowy corners until he imagined they were swarming with horrible animals; and every now and again he awoke with a start, to remember that his last two hours were running, and death was on the march.

Oftener and oftener, as the time went on, did his glance settle on the girl herself. Her face was bowed forward and covered with her hands, and she was shaken at intervals by the convulsive hiccough of grief. Even thus she was not an unpleasant object to dwell upon, so plump and yet so fine, with a warm brown skin, and the most beautiful hair, Denis thought, in the whole world of womankind. Her hands were like her uncle's; but they were more in place at the end of her young arms, and looked infinitely soft and caressing. He remembered how her blue eyes had shone upon him, full of anger, pity, and innocence. And the more he dwelt on her perfections, the uglier death looked, and the more deeply was he smitten with penitence at her continued tears. Now he felt that no man could have the courage to leave a world which contained so beautiful a creature; and now he would have given forty minutes of his last hour to have unsaid his cruel speech.

Suddenly a hoarse and ragged peal of cockcrow rose to their ears from the dark valley below the windows. And this shattering noise in the silence of all around was like a light in a dark place, and shook them both out of their reflections.

"Alas, can I do nothing to help you?" she said, looking up.

"Madam," replied Denis, with a fine irrelevancy, "if I have said anything to wound you, believe me, it was for your own sake and not for mine."

She thanked him with a tearful look.

"I feel your position cruelly," he went on. "The world has been bitter hard on you. Your uncle is a disgrace to mankind. Believe me, madam, there is no young gentleman in all France but would be glad of my opportunity, to die in doing you a momentary service."

"I know already that you can be very brave and generous," she answered. "What I *want* to know is whether I can serve you — now or afterward," she added, with a quaver.

"Most certainly," he answered, with a smile. "Let me sit beside you as if I were a friend, instead of a foolish intruder; try to forget how awkwardly we are placed to one another; make my last moments go pleasantly; and you will do me the chief service possible."

"You are very gallant," she added, with a yet deeper sadness "— very gallant — and it somehow pains me. But draw nearer, if you please; and if you find anything to say to me, you will at least make certain of a very friendly listener. Ah! Monsieur de Beaulieu," she broke forth — "ah! Monsieur de Beaulieu, how can I look you in the face?" And she fell to weeping again with a renewed effusion.

"Madam," said Denis, taking her hand in both of his, "reflect on the little time I have before me, and the great bitterness into which I am cast by the sight of your distress. Spare me, in my last moments, the spectacle of what I cannot cure even with the sacrifice of my life."

"I am very selfish," answered Blanche. "I will be braver, Monsieur de Beaulieu, for your sake. But think if I can do you no kindness in the future — if you have no friends to whom I could carry your adieus. Charge me as heavily as you can; every burden will lighten, by so little, the invaluable gratitude I owe you. Put it in my power to do something more for you than weep."

"My mother is married again, and has a young family to care for. My brother Guichard[1] will inherit my fiefs[2]; and if I am not in error, that will content him amply for my death. Life is a little vapour that passeth away, as we are told by those in holy orders. When a man is in a fair way and sees all life open in front of him, he seems to himself to make a very important figure in the world. His horse whinnies to him; the trumpets blow and the girls look out of windows as he rides into town before his company; he receives many assurances of trust and regard, — sometimes by express in a letter, sometimes face to face, with persons of great consequence falling on his neck. It is not wonderful if his head is turned for a time. But once he is dead, were he as brave as Hercules* or as wise as Solomon,* he is soon forgotten. It is not ten years since my father fell, with many other

[1] *Guichard* (gē shär').
[2] Lands that are a part of a family estate.
D

knights around him, in a very fierce encounter, and I do not think that any one of them, nor as much as the name of the fight, is now remembered. No, no, madam, the nearer you come to it, you see that death is a dark and dusty corner, where a man gets into his tomb and has the door shut after him till the judgment day. I have few friends just now, and once I am dead shall have none."

"Ah, Monsieur de Beaulieu!" she exclaimed, "you forget Blanche de Malétroit."

"You have a sweet nature, madam, and you are pleased to estimate a little service far beyond its worth."

"It is not that," she answered. "You mistake me if you think I am easily touched by my own concerns. I say so because you are the noblest man I have ever met, — because I recognise in you a spirit that would have made even a common person famous in the land."

"And yet here I die in a mousetrap, with no more noise about it than my own squeaking," answered he.

A look of pain crossed her face, and she was silent for a little while. Then a light came into her eyes, and with a smile she spoke again.

"I cannot have my champion think meanly of himself. Anyone who gives his life for another will be met in paradise by all the heralds and angels of the Lord God. And you have no such cause to hang your head. For — Pray, do you think me beautiful?" she asked, with a deep flush.

"Indeed, madam, I do," he said.

"I am glad of that," she answered, heartily. "Do you think there are many men in France who have been asked in marriage by a beautiful maiden — with her own lips — and who have refused her to her face? I know you men would half despise such a triumph; but believe me, we women know more of what is precious in love. There is nothing that should set a person higher in his own esteem; and we women would prize nothing more dearly."

"You are very good," he said; "but you cannot make me forget that I was asked in pity and not for love."

"I am not so sure of that," she replied, holding down her head. "Hear me to an end, Monsieur de Beaulieu. I know how you must despise me; I feel you are right to do so; I am too poor a creature to occupy one thought of your mind, although, alas! you must die for me this morning. But when I asked you to marry me, indeed, and indeed, it was because I respected and admired you, and loved you with my whole soul, from the very moment that you took my part against my uncle. If you had seen yourself, and how noble you looked, you would pity rather than despise me. And now," she went on, hurriedly checking him with her hand, "although I have laid aside all reserve and told you so much, remember that I know your sentiments toward me already. I would not, believe me, being nobly born, weary you with importunities[1] into consent. I too have a pride of my own; and I declare before the holy Mother of God, if you should now go back from your word already given, I would no more marry you than I would marry my uncle's groom."

Denis smiled a little bitterly.

"It is a small love," he said, "that shies at a little pride."

She made no answer, although she probably had her own thoughts.

"Come hither to the window," he said with a sigh. "Here is the dawn."

And indeed the dawn was already beginning. The hollow of the sky was full of essential daylight, colourless and clean; and the valley underneath was flooded with a gray reflection. A few thin vapours clung in the coves of the forest or lay along the winding course of the river. The scene disengaged[2] a surprising effect of stillness, which was hardly interrupted when the cocks began once more to crow among the steadings.[1] Perhaps the same fellow who had made so horrid a clangour in the darkness, not half an hour before, now sent up the merriest cheer to greet the coming day. A little wind went bustling and eddying among the tree-tops underneath the windows. And still the daylight kept flooding insensibly out of the east, which was soon to grow incandescent and cast up that red-hot cannon-ball, the rising sun.

Denis looked out over all this with a bit of a shiver. He had taken her hand, and retained it in his almost unconsciously.

"Has the day begun already?" she said; and then, illogically enough: "the night has been so long! Alas! what shall we say to my uncle when he returns?"

"What you will," said Denis, and he pressed her fingers in his.

She was silent.

"Blanche," he said, with a swift, uncertain, passionate utterance, "you have seen whether I fear death. You must know well enough that I would as gladly leap out of that window into the empty air as to lay a finger on you without your free and full consent. But if you care for me at all, do not let me lose my life in a misapprehension, for I love you better than the whole world; and though I will die for you blithely, it would be like all the joys of paradise to live on and spend my life in your service."

As he stopped speaking a bell began to ring loudly in the interior of the house, and a clatter of armour in the corridor showed that the retainers were returning to their post, and the two hours were at an end.

"After all that you have heard?" she whispered, leaning toward him with her lips and eyes.

"I have heard nothing," he replied.

"The captain's name was Florimond de Champdivers,"[2] she said in his ear.

---

[1] Pleas, requests.

[3] Here, produced.

[1] Farm buildings.

[2] *Florimond de Champdivers* (flŏ rē môn' dĕ shän dē vâr').

"I did not hear it," he answered, taking her supple body in his arms, and covered her wet face with kisses.

A melodious chirping was audible behind, followed by a beautiful chuckle, and the voice of Messire de Malétroit wished his new nephew a good morning.

Discussion Hints

1. Describe the setting of the story. (Setting includes time as well as place.)

2. What is the "one single flashing moment or emotional crisis" revealing human character (p. 548) that is brought out in this story?

3. In what respects does the character of the Sire de Malétroit suggest that of the Italian duke in Browning's "My Last Duchess" (p. 502)? In what respects do the two seem to differ?

4. What effect does the "dimpled protuberance" of the "fork of the thumb" (p. 553, ll. 16–17), combined with the "dead, surprising whiteness" of the nails (p. 553, ll. 18–19), have upon your estimate of the Sire de Malétroit?

5. To what "double accident" (p. 553, l. 47) does Denis refer?

6. Tell the story that explains why the Sire de Malétroit's door was left unlocked.

7. How do Blanche's hands as described on page 560, ll. 47–50, contrast with those of her uncle (p. 553, ll. 8–19)?

8. Point out examples of humor.

9. Explain

a. strategy (p. 549, l. 9)
b. canopy (p. 550, l. 7)
c. opaque (p. 550, l. 24)
d. inspiriting but nervous (p. 551, l. 20)
e. ejaculation (p. 551, l. 29)
f. inordinate precautions (p. 553, l. 9)
g. sensual (p. 553, l. 14)
h. quiescence (p. 553, l. 27)
i. obeisance (p. 557, l. 47)
j. impunity (p. 557, l. 86)

10. Subjects for themes:

a. Blanche's life before the beginning of the story.

b. The hero's life before the beginning of the story.

Suggestions for Reading

Dr. Jekyll and Mr. Hyde
"The Merry Men"
"A Lodging for the Night"
"Markheim"
The New Arabian Nights

1892-

❀

Recent
and Contemporary
Literature

She shrugs and turns again to the muskroses (p. 625, ll. 161-162)

ENGLAND TODAY

BEFORE the year 1900 new forces were at work, forces destined, in the twentieth century, to produce marked changes in the world itself and consequently in the world of literature. Most striking were the changes wrought by science, changes which revolutionized living and profoundly shook the world of ideas. In England, as elsewhere, the standard of living rose. In the twentieth century England found herself an industrial rather than an agricultural land, a condition that inevitably, it seemed, led to difficulties between capital and labor. Yet many reforms were brought about in the early years of the century, such reforms as the establishment of old-age pensions, workingmen's compensation, and improvement in child health. An England no longer agricultural found herself dependent on distant lands not only for raw materials for her industries, but also for food.

It is true that for centuries England had been the center from which ships had gone out to all the world; but transportation in a new era of steam and electricity became increasingly easy and swift. The laying of the Pacific cable, the invention of the airplane, the opening of the Panama Canal, all were important in the long procession of events that brought distant parts of the British Empire closer and closer together. Tied to England in an easy but strong net of common interest, her colonies became, one by one, self-governing dominions. And seldom, despite the rush of changing life, was the truth lost sight of, that the advance in ideas and ideals must keep pace with science and invention. The radio, for instance, with its far-reaching voice, has brought the news of the world and the treasures of music and literature into the cottages of the humblest workers. The movies (the cinema, the English would say) have made thousands of persons acquainted with literary characters and themes of which ordinary readers never would have heard. Improved methods of printing have made books and magazines more plentiful, public libraries have brought the best literature to the Englishman's door, and even the daily papers contain sections devoted to literature, art, and culture.

Yet early in our twentieth century, almost unrecognized, trouble was brewing, world trouble. Though there was much talk of peace and of international understanding, yet at the same time nations were rivals in commerce and in colonial ambitions. Armies and navies were built up on a large scale. Alliances were made. Back in 1887 Germany, Austria, and Italy had formed a Triple Alliance between northern, central, and southern Europe. In 1907 England, France, and Russia formed a Triple Entente which allied eastern and western Europe. Moreover, though there was no great war anywhere, there were wars of minor importance going on in the world: before 1900 the Spanish-American War and the Boer War in South Africa; after 1900, wars in the Balkans and in Manchuria. The guns were being tried out.

In 1914 began the First World War, that colossal catastrophe which threatened to destroy the very foundations of modern civilization. It was a machine war in which mankind turned its scientific knowledge against itself, a form of human suicide not possible before the twentieth century. Into war's gaping, never-satisfied jaws poured wealth and life: billions of dollars, millions of men. The United States was in the war only about a year and a half; yet the country is, and will long continue to be, affected by the dreadful struggle. The effect on England, so close to the Continent, and involved in the war from beginning to end, was, of course, immensely greater. Submarines lay in wait for English ships; air raids on London were numbered by scores. Over 1,000,000 Englishmen were killed; over 2,000,000 were wounded. No wonder labor, suffragist, and Irish troubles were lost sight of as the English, man and boy, woman and girl, stood shoulder to shoulder in the fight. Not only were England and the British Isles involved; over 1,500,000 colonial troops joined the mother country in the war.

Since the Civil War of the seventeenth century the English have preferred slow and steady progress rather than revolution. They have kept to this tradition despite the instabilities which were the results of the First World War: the wiping out of whole families, the shift of wealth, the upset of classes. Women, ahead of their sisters in the United States, gained the right to vote. The centuries-old Irish problem was met by the forming of the Irish Free State (Eire) and a separate state for north Ireland. A general strike was settled without guns (would you be interested to know that London policemen are unarmed?). In fact, British leadership, whether Labor or Conservative, has been notably sane and able.

The England of the 1930's continued, as did the United States, her democratic beliefs and practices: freedom of speech and of the press, respect for humanity and for the individual. She continued her belief in self-discipline and in the welfare of all being bound up in the welfare of each. There was genuine concern at the failure of the League of Nations in the settling of disputes, and an insistence that its machinery be kept well oiled for that time when the conscience of the world shall change. Meanwhile England would have avoided war if she could; she would, if possible, have lived peaceably alongside her neighbors.

Finally, at long last, England joined France in declaring war against Germany, or rather, to use the words of Prime Minister Chamberlain, "against force, bad faith, injustice, oppression, and persecution." Once again, not only England, but other parts of the British Empire, were involved in a world war. One after another, the neutral countries of Europe were invaded by a Germany bent on conquest. There came a time when Great Britain stood alone between warring Europe and the rest of the world. There came a time when Germany turned on Russia, her former ally. There came, too, a memorable Sunday morning when Japan, partner of Germany and Italy, attacked American territory "without warning." Once again the United States was unable longer to remain neutral. This time, however, with Great Britain, she set about waging total warfare, resolved to win, not only the victory but the peace as well. Aided by refugees from the invaded European democracies and by many of the American republics as well, the great English-speaking democracies formed an alliance and fought a world civil war, a war between the aggressor nations and men of good will everywhere.

After six years of bitter conflict, the Allies were victorious, only to discover that the victors as well as the vanquished had lost. England's cities were in ruins, her man power was depleted, and her debts were increased enormously. But her courage never failed. A Labor government replaced the more conservative government led by the popular war hero, Winston Churchill. The Labor government helped to improve the working conditions and to raise the wages of laboring men and women, and all Englishmen united in the hope that the United Nations, a union of freedom-loving peoples the world around, would finally succeed in truly ending war and in making the world "safe for democracy."

On this outcome depends the survival of freedom of the individual everywhere. On this outcome depends the future of English and of American literature, for only with the survival of free individual expression in England, in America, and everywhere, can there be a literature at all.

All these events and changes have led, of course, to changes in literature itself. Early in our century came a reaction against Victorianism. Many Englishmen began to doubt whether their civilization was as sound, their moral standards as reliable, as they had been taught to believe. Since 1900 there has grown up both in England and in America a whole generation which maintains that questions of marriage, of morality, and of religion should be discussed openly and frankly instead of being hushed up and glossed over. In their efforts to be what they call "frank," some modern writers treat subjects never before discussed in public or on the printed page.

In general the greatest change in literature has been in the direction of realism* as opposed to romanticism.[1] For the modern realist the first and sometimes the only question is, Is this true to life? In his earnest striving after truth he examines the world about him, its men and its women, with

---

[1] For the meaning of "romanticism" see introduction to "The Romantic Period," p. 313.

an uncompromising gaze. He looks at life through no glamour, no glitter, no rose light of sentimental fancy. He does not exclude from his picture the ugly, the sordid, or the evil if, by including them, he thinks he can make his work "true to life." Everything that is part of life is suitable material for his pen. This new realism reflects life and, in turn, affects practically every department of literature. However, as you read the writings of recent realists you should never forget that even the realist must pick and choose the material he presents in his books, and that no writer, however gifted, can tell all there is in life. Whether romantic or realistic, literature is art; it can never be, like a photograph, a direct presentation of reality and life.

English writers of the twentieth century are remarkably versatile. The typical English author of today writes novels, short stories, poetry, and plays—all with facility and often with success.

POETRY

After the death of Tennyson there followed a pause in poetry, a short period during which little good verse was written and no important new poet appeared. Similar pauses took place after the other creative periods in English literature; for example, after the Elizabethan and Romantic periods. But about 1900 a new poetic wave began to rise rapidly, a movement that had many similarities to the new realism in America. Poets on both sides of the Atlantic wished to get away from the forms and fashions of the past and to discover fresh subjects and new patterns of their own.

In this attitude the American and English writers were in agreement. The English movement, however, differed in several ways from the American movement.[1]

In the first place, English poets reacted more directly than did American poets against Tennyson and what he had come to stand for in their minds. They objected to his romantic, idealistic subjects, which they condemned as false and unreal. Then, too, they did not approve of Tennyson's poetic technique: his extreme care in choosing and polishing his verse forms, his use of traditional rhymes and stanzas, and his great preference for the iambic* beat, or rhythm. Of course we now see that the revolt against Tennyson went too far, and that, after all, it was directed against the worst and weakest elements in Victorian poetry instead of against the best and strongest.

Yet despite their revolt against Victorianism, English poets are not so radical and extreme as American poets. The English poetic tradition is much older and greater than the American. Then, too, because the past and its precedents have a stronger hold in England than in America, the English

---

[1] For a discussion of realism in recent American poetry, see the revised edition of *American Writers* of this series.

movement has been quieter and less revolutionary. Free verse, for example, never gained the foothold in Great Britain that it did in America. The English avoided some of the freakishness and faddishness that showed itself here. In form, at least, English poetry followed the traditional patterns more closely than did American poetry. In general, however, it became more realistic* and more vital than it had been during the Victorian Period.

Though the general tendency of English literature today is toward realism and though some poets, like the American-British T. S. Eliot, still experiment with new forms and are hard to understand, others follow their predecessors in the exquisite polish and technical perfection of their verse. English poetry of today also shows occasional flashes of romanticism, and one English poet, Stephen Spender, suggests that English poetry is already entering a new Romantic Period.

There were many other influences which led up to and, at least in part, brought about the new poetry movement. Among them was the reaction against using literature to preach a moral or to teach a lesson, as had often been the case during the Victorian Period. This reaction, which took as its motto "Art for Art's sake," was first fostered in England by Oscar Wilde (p. 633) and his followers. Next came the robust, original influence of William Ernest Henley (p. 577) and Rudyard Kipling (pp. 608 and 628), who, while they differed in all else, were alike in their freshness, power, and realism. In Ireland arose what is now called the Celtic revival. Under its impetus Irish poets and playwrights stopped writing like Englishmen and went back to Irish history, Irish legend and folklore, and Irish peasant life and speech for their subjects and for the spirit of their work. Leaders in this movement were chiefly William Butler Yeats (pp. 581 and 632) and John Millington Synge, and after them many younger poets, including Padraic Colum (p. 585), James Stephens (p. 601), and others. The effect of the First World War was at first to stun poetry with horror and then to quicken it and direct it into two opposite channels. Many English poets sought to strip away the glitter and glamour of war and reveal its underlying bloodiness, horror, stench, and ghastly futility; others reflected a mood of heart-longing for quiet, for home, and for the lovely English countryside.

In contemporary British poetry certain names stand out above the rest: A. E. Housman (p. 579), William Butler Yeats (pp. 581 and 632), Walter de la Mare (p. 603), Wilfred Wilson Gibson (p. 604), and John Masefield (p. 611). All are represented in the following section. It will be interesting to read their lyric and narrative poems and then to read "The New Poetry" section in the revised edition of *American Writers* of this series, and compare the British and American fields. Their differences are summed up as follows by Louis Untermeyer, a leading American critic and poet: "Modern American verse is sharp, vigorously experimental, full of youth and its occasional—and natural—crudities. English verse is smoother, more matured and, molded by centuries of literature, richer in associations and surer in artistry."

Probably the greatest new name that has arisen recently in English poetry is that of John Masefield. A few years before the First World War he astonished the critical world by producing a series of long, brilliant narrative poems which for realistic vigor and power have not been equaled in this generation: *The Everylasting Mercy, The Widow in the Bye Street,* and *Dauber.* Besides these he has written many beautiful and intense lyrics of the sea, of the call of the open road and of far places, and of the innate nobility of common life. It is fitting that such a one should be the poet laureate of democratic England.

THE ESSAY

In the twentieth century the essay has flowered luxuriantly. Increased public interest in literature, science, and history has led to the writing of many formal and informal essays of a critical, scientific, or biographical character. In fact, almost any human theme, grave or gay, is now considered a fit subject for an essay in which the author approaches his material in a familiar and interesting manner. It is no exaggeration to say that the essay now rivals poetry, fiction, and drama in importance and in popularity. The essays presented here are varied in subject, in approach, and in style, but are alike in that all are well written and readable.

THE SHORT STORY AND THE NOVEL

The short story, which took form in the United States about a century ago,[1] but did not appear in England until later, has flourished abundantly in recent and contemporary literature. Not only do more and more short stories appear in answer to the demand of the public for literature in small doses, but the contemporary short story has broadened so greatly in its scope that today many aspects of human life and character are depicted in the short stories that crowd the pages of English and American periodicals. Though they often lack the unity of effect necessary for perfection in this form of literature, many of them show a tremendous advance in construction and rapidity of action over the short narratives of earlier English literature.

Many recent writers of short stories are also novelists, and some, notably Thomas Hardy, began their literary careers during the Victorian Period; but in the case of Hardy we have a modern born out of time, a writer who, though living for sixty years of his long life in a period when people refused to call a spade a spade, painted humanity with a frankness and an undisguised realism that have scarcely been surpassed by even the most advanced moderns.

[1] The development of the short story is discussed in various places in the revised edition of *American Writers* of this series.

Eric Knight (p. 657), H. G. Wells (p. 671), and John Galsworthy (p. 653), three of the short-story writers represented in this section, are all well known as novelists. Knight, though probably best known in America for his famous dog story *Lassie Come-Home*, wrote short stories of great merit. Wells depends largely upon his knowledge of science and of contemporary life in England. John Galsworthy, who wrote numerous short stories that resemble essays in their intimate, personal tone, is, many think, the most distinguished novelist of his generation. All three are consummately skillful writers of short stories.

In fact, every writer whose work is represented here has done excellent writing of other sorts. Rudyard Kipling's (p. 642) name is a mighty one on the roll of the poets as well as on the roll of the writers of short stories. And "Saki" (p. 668), whom one thinks of particularly as a writer of short stories, wrote a novel.

In a one-volume anthology that would cover English literature at all adequately it is impossible to include a full-length recent or contemporary novel.[1] It is possible to represent the work of the modern novelists by their poems and essays and, particularly, by their short stories. See, however, the "Suggestions for Reading" after the individual short stories (pp. 642–684), and "Suggestions for Further Reading in the Short Story and the Novel" (p. 684).

THE DRAMA

In our twentieth century the moving and talking pictures and the radio seemed for a time to threaten the sure position of the theater. Worry over that possibility was, and is, a sheer waste of effort; for the widespread interest in movie and radio has only increased general interest in plays, be they the modern one-act plays or the more conventional full-length plays, be they given on the stages of school auditoriums or in the "little theaters" or the commercial theaters. From small beginnings the famous Abbey Theater in Dublin has grown to fame and has made many Irish plays well known in America.

Movie and radio audiences are not always discriminating or exacting, but year by year they are becoming more so. As they supplement their movie-going and radio-listening with flesh-and-blood drama they come to realize more and more that drama, on the screen or on the air or (best of all, because most real) on the stage itself, is an art, the art of human conduct.

To meet the general interest in the theater, there has been an immense output of plays by the best English writers (see "Suggestions for Further Reading in the Drama," p. 695). The play given here is by one of the greatest modern playwrights, Sir James M. Barrie, whose plays are popular in America as well as in England. It is an unfinished mystery whose very incompleteness tends to heighten curiosity and suspense.

[1] For selections from earlier novels see pages 265, 436, and 447.

Correlation of English Literature with Historical Events during the Modern Period

HISTORICAL EVENTS		LITERARY LANDMARKS
	1901	KIPLING, Kim
		WELLS, First Men in the Moon
Reign of EDWARD VII 1901–1910		
	1902	MASEFIELD, Salt-Water Ballads
BRITISH PACIFIC CABLE	1903	SHAW, Man and Superman
WRIGHT BROTHERS' *first airplane flight*		BARRIE, Peter Pan
	1904	*Opening of the* ABBEY THEATER
RUSSO-JAPANESE WAR 1904–1905		
	1905	MEREDITH *awarded the Order of Merit*
WORKMEN'S COMPENSATION ACT	1906	
TRIPLE ENTENTE	1907	KIPLING *awarded the Nobel prize*
		FRANCIS THOMPSON *died. Born 1859*
	1909	MEREDITH, SWINBURNE, SYNGE *died*
Reign of GEORGE V 1910–1936		
War between ITALY *and* TURKEY 1911–1912		
	1913	BRIDGES *poet laureate*
Opening of the PANAMA CANAL	1914	
WORLD WAR I 1914–1918		
	1915	RUPERT BROOKE *died. Born 1887*
	1916	"SAKI" *died. Born 1870*
RUSSIAN REVOLUTION; *entrance of the* UNITED STATES *into* WORLD WAR I	1917	
WOMAN SUFFRAGE	1918	SASSOON, Counter-Attack
TREATY OF VERSAILLES	1919	
LEAGUE OF NATIONS	1920	WELLS, Outline of History
IRISH FREE STATE; MUSSOLINI, *dictator of* ITALY	1922	GALSWORTHY, Forsyte Saga
		STRACHEY, Queen Victoria
		BARRIE, Shall We Join the Ladies?
	1923	YEATS *awarded the Nobel prize*
		BARRIE *awarded the Order of Merit*
Death of WOODROW WILSON	1924	CONRAD *died. Born 1857*
First Labor government		
	1925	SHAW *awarded the Nobel prize*
LINDBERGH'S *flight to* PARIS	1927	
Inauguration of SOVIET RUSSIA'S *first* FIVE-YEAR PLAN	1928	HARDY *died. Born 1840*
	1930	BRIDGES *died. Born 1844*
		MASEFIELD *poet laureate*
	1931	BENNETT *died. Born 1867*
	1932	GALSWORTHY *awarded Nobel prize*
		STRACHEY *died. Born 1880*
FRANKLIN D. ROOSEVELT, *President of the* UNITED STATES; HITLER, *dictator of* GERMANY	1933	GALSWORTHY *died. Born 1867*
Abdication of EDWARD VIII; GEORGE VI; ITALY'S *conquest of* ETHIOPIA	1936	A. E. Housman, Kipling, Chestertor *died*
	1937	BARRIE *died. Born 1860*

MUNICH CONFERENCE: *English hope for "peace in our time"*

1938 E. V. LUCAS *died. Born 1864*

GEORGE VI *and* QUEEN ELIZABETH *visit* CANADA *and the* UNITED STATES; GERMANY *and* RUSSIA *partition* POLAND; *beginning of* WORLD WAR II

1939 YEATS *died. Born 1865*
LAURENCE HOUSMAN, My Brother, A. E. Housman
WELLS, Fate of Man

GERMANY *invades* DENMARK, NORWAY, HOLLAND, BELGIUM, *and* FRANCE; CHURCHILL *made prime minister*; DUNKIRK; *Battle of* BRITAIN

1940 BELLOC, Silence of the Sea
McFEE, Watch Below
WELLS, All Aboard for Ararat

ITALY *invades* GREECE; GERMANY *attacks* RUSSIA; AMERICAN *Lend-Lease Bill*; ATLANTIC CHARTER; JAPAN *attacks the* UNITED STATES; UNITED STATES *declares war on* JAPAN, GERMANY, *and* ITALY; *the 26* UNITED NATIONS *pledge to fight*

1941 LAURENCE HOUSMAN, Ways and Means
MASEFIELD, Some Memories of W. B. Yeats *and* The Nine Days' Wonder
WELLS, Guide to the New World
ERIC KNIGHT, This above All
COWARD, Blithe Spirit
MME. CHIANG KAI-SHEK, China Shall Rise Again

JAPAN *overruns* MALAYA, NETHERLANDS INDIES, BURMA, *and the* PHILIPPINES; RUSSIA *stops* NAZIS *on* VOLGA

1942 WELLS, Conquest of Time
GUEDALLA, Liberators
ERIC KNIGHT, Lassie Come-Home

AMERICANS *in* NORTH AFRICA; CASABLANCA CONFERENCE; *Siege of* STALINGRAD *lifted*; CAIRO CONFERENCE: ROOSEVELT, CHURCHILL, *and* CHIANG KAI-SHEK; TEHERAN CONFERENCE: ROOSEVELT, CHURCHILL, *and* STALIN

1943 ERIC KNIGHT *killed. Born 1897*
LAURENCE HOUSMAN, Palestine Plays
MASEFIELD, Wonderings
EVE CURIE, Journey among Warriors

ALLIED FORCES *in* ITALY; *Invasion of the* PHILIPPINES; *liberation of* FRANCE

1944 CHURCHILL'S *war speeches*, Onward to Victory

Invasion of GERMANY; LLOYD GEORGE, ROOSEVELT, MUSSOLINI *died*; UNITED NATIONS CONFERENCE *on International Organization*; *Atomic bomb, surrender of* JAPAN; *surrender of* GERMANY; *Occupation of* BERLIN *by* ALLIES

1945 GABRIELA MISTRAL (*Chilean*), *Nobel prize for literature*

1946 H. G. WELLS *died. Born 1866*

MARSHALL PLAN *to aid* EUROPE; *Death of* JAN MASARYK (*Czechoslovakia*)

1948 T. S. ELIOT, *Nobel prize for literature*

NORTH ATLANTIC DEFENSE PACT; *Atomic explosion in* RUSSIA; WEST GERMAN REPUBLIC *established*

1949 MAURICE MAETERLINCK (*Belgian*) *died. Born 1862*

Independence of INDIA; *Building of headquarters*, UNITED NATIONS, NEW YORK

1950 WINSTON CHURCHILL, The Grand Alliance (Vol. III of The Second World War)
SHAW'S *plays revived in United States*

LYRIC POETRY

I. POETS OF TRADITION

CLASSIFYING modern poets is a difficult business and one likely to cause disagreement; however, in making the acquaintance of so many at once, there are advantages in grouping them.

Under the confines of the narrow heading "Poets of Tradition" are grouped four very different singers. All, of course, speak the language of today rather than that of Shakespeare or Milton. Some of them, like Bridges and Henley, experiment with old and new rhythms and verse patterns; but, on the whole, they are content with conventional verse forms and with traditional subjects for poetry. See if you can discover a different reason for each one's being termed a "poet of tradition."

ROBERT BRIDGES[1] (1844-1930)

Robert Bridges became poet laureate in 1913, the year of the death of Alfred Austin, who had succeeded Tennyson. Though it is true that Bridges was an experimenter in complicated meters, a poet painstaking in his art, it is his simpler poems that are most popular: the dainty "Triolet," for instance, or the simpler, descriptive "The Windmill."

The Windmill

THE green corn waving in the dale,
  The ripe grass waving on the hill:
I lean across the paddock pale [2]
  And gaze upon the giddy mill.

Its hurtling sails a mighty sweep
  Cut through the air: with rushing
    sound
Each strikes in fury down the steep,
  Rattles, and whirls in chase around.

Beside his sacks the miller stands
  On high within the open door: 10
A book and pencil in his hands,
  His grist and meal he reckoneth o'er.

His tireless merry slave the wind
  Is busy with his work to-day:
From whencesoe'er he comes to grind;
  He hath a will and knows the way.

He gives the creaking sails a spin,
  The circling millstones faster flee,
The shuddering timbers groan within,
  And down the shoot the meal runs
    free.

The miller giveth him no thanks,   21
  And doth not much his work o'er-
    look:
He stands beside the sacks, and ranks
  The figures in his dusty book.

[1] For biography see page 735.
[2] *paddock pale.* A paling surrounding a small enclosed space for horses.

576

Triolet

ALL women born are so perverse
No man need boast their love pos-
sessing.
If nought seem better, nothing's worse;
All women born are so perverse.
From Adam's wife, that proved a curse,
Though God had made her for a blessing,
All women born are so perverse
No man need boast their love possessing.

Discussion Hints

1. Wherein lies the chief charm of "The Windmill"? Which seems to be enjoying his work more: the miller or his "slave the wind"?

2. What facts about the operation of a windmill does the poet use? Learn what you can about windmills.

3. Consider the pattern of the triolet: its repetition and rhyme scheme. It is an old form. Look it up in a large dictionary.

4. Try writing a triolet. When the first two lines are written satisfactorily, the triolet is well on the way to completion.

5. Discuss the theme of "Triolet." Does woman's perversity add to her interest to man?

WILLIAM ERNEST HENLEY[1] (1849-1903)

Henley, like Bridges, experimented with verse forms, sometimes even going so far as to imitate the free verse of the American Walt Whitman.[2] Henley's rebel nature stood him in good stead, enabling him to battle an almost lifelong invalidism. The stirring message of "Invictus" is one of the most famous portrayals of a courageous soul in all literature. Yet both it and "The Blackbird," a charming, singing lyric, a striking contrast to the surging power of "Invictus," are written in the simplest of traditional verse forms.

Invictus[3]

OUT of the night that covers me,
Black as the Pit[4] from pole to
pole,
I thank whatever gods may be
For my unconquerable soul.

In the fell[5] clutch of circumstance
I have not winced nor cried aloud.
Beneath the bludgeonings of chance
My head is bloody, but unbowed.

Beyond this space of wrath and tears
Looms but the Horror of the shade, 10
And yet the menace of the years
Finds and shall find me unafraid.

It matters not how strait[1] the gate,
How charged with punishments the
scroll,
I am the master of my fate:
I am the captain of my soul.

The Blackbird

THE nightingale has a lyre of gold,[6]
The lark's is a clarion[7] call,

And the blackbird plays but a boxwood
flute,
But I love him best of all.

For his song is all of the joy of life,
And we in the mad, spring weather,
We two have listened till he sang
Our hearts and lips together.

[1] For biography see page 735.
[2] See the revised edition of *American Writers* of this series.
[3] A Latin word meaning "unconquered."
[4] Hell itself. [5] Cruel, ruthless.
[6] *lyre . . . gold*. Here, soft, sweet music like that of a lyre.
[7] A clear note, as if blown on a trumpet.

[1] Narrow.

D

Discussion Hints

1. Write a one-sentence précis of "Invictus."

2. "Invictus" is worth memorizing.

3. English birds are these in "The Blackbird." Compare American and English larks and blackbirds. But such matters are beside the point of the poem, which is the happy human result of the second stanza.

WILLIAM HENRY DAVIES[1] (1871–1940)

Not only did all things love Davies; he loved all things: had companionship with, and compassion for, the rain, the sun after the rain, sheep, the blind man who led him who could not see for the fog. Here are simple musical songs of nature that seem to flow spontaneously from the heart of the "super-tramp," as Davies called himself.

Nature's Friend

SAY what you like,
  All things love me!
I pick no flowers —
  That wins the Bee.

The Summer's Moths
  Think my hand one —
To touch their wings —
  With Wind and Sun.

The garden Mouse
  Comes near to play;   10
Indeed, he turns
  His eyes away.

The Wren knows well
  I rob no nest;

When I look in,
  She still will rest.

The hedge stops Cows,
  Or they would come
After my voice
  Right to my home.   20

The Horse can tell
  Straight from my lip,
My hand could not
  Hold any whip.

Say what you like,
  All things love me!
Horse, Cow, and Mouse,
  Bird, Moth and Bee.

The Rain

I HEAR leaves drinking rain;
  I hear rich leaves on top
Giving the poor beneath
  Drop after drop;
'Tis a sweet noise to hear
These green leaves drinking near.

And when the Sun comes out,
  After this rain shall stop,
A wondrous light will fill
  Each dark, round drop;   10
I hope the Sun shines bright;
'Twill be a lovely sight.

Sheep

WHEN I was once in Baltimore,
  A man came up to me and cried,
'Come, I have eighteen hundred sheep,
  And we will sail on Tuesday's tide.

'If you will sail with me, young man,
  I'll pay you fifty shillings down;
These eighteen hundred sheep I take
  From Baltimore to Glasgow town.'

[1] For biography see page 736.

He paid me fifty shillings down,
I sailed with eighteen hundred sheep;
We soon had cleared the harbour's
mouth,   11
We soon were in the salt sea deep.

The first night we were out at sea
Those sheep were quiet in their mind;

The second night they cried with fear —
They smelt no pastures in the wind.

They sniffed, poor things, for their green
fields,
They cried so loud I could not sleep:
For fifty thousand shillings down
I would not sail again with sheep.   20

The Fog

I SAW the fog grow thick,
Which soon made blind my ken;
It made tall men of boys,
And giants of tall men.

It clutched my throat, I coughed;
Nothing was in my head
Except two heavy eyes
Like balls of burning lead.

And when it grew so black
That I could know no place,   10
I lost all judgment then,
Of distance and of space.

The street lamps, and the lights
Upon the halted cars,
Could either be on earth
Or be the heavenly stars.

A man passed by me close,
I asked my way, he said,
'Come, follow me, my friend' —
I followed where he led.   20

He rapped the stones in front,
'Trust me,' he said, 'and come';
I followed like a child —
A blind man led me home.

Discussion Hint

May it be that all things loved Davies because he first loved them? Do the adjectives
simple, musical, spontaneous, describe Davies's
verse accurately? Add other adjectives or
descriptive terms.

ALFRED EDWARD HOUSMAN[1] (1859-1936)

Although Housman was a professor of
Latin at Cambridge* University, England,
there is in his poetry no classical mythology,
no *thee*, no *thou*, no *thy*. His sentences are as
simply made as the speech of ordinary folk,
but they are far more beautiful and melodious.
They are filled with meaning too, meaning
hidden in the many compact figures of speech.
"Loveliest of Trees" expresses with almost
childish simplicity two of Housman's favorite
themes, love of nature and regret at the passing of youth. "With Rue My Heart Is
Laden" repeats the second theme, as, in a
way, does "When I Was One-and-Twenty."
"Reveille" is the call of the poet to young
people to waken to the beauty of life while
there is yet time. Housman loved youth and
beauty and sorrowed over life's brevity and
over the waste that young people make of
their swiftly passing years.

Loveliest of Trees

LOVELIEST of trees, the cherry now
Is hung with bloom along the bough,
And stands about the woodland ride
Wearing white for Eastertide.

Now, of my threescore years and ten,
Twenty will not come again,

And take from seventy springs a score,
It only leaves me fifty more.

And since to look at things in bloom
Fifty springs are little room,   10
About the woodlands I will go
To see the cherry hung with snow.

[1] For biography see page 736.

With Rue My Heart Is Laden

WITH rue [1] my heart is laden
    For golden friends I had,
For many a rose-lipt maiden
    And many a lightfoot lad.

By brooks too broad for leaping
    The lightfoot boys are laid;
The rose-lipt girls are sleeping
    In fields where roses fade.

When I Was One-and-Twenty

WHEN I was one-and-twenty
    I heard a wise man say,
"Give crowns and pounds and guineas
    But not your heart away;
Give pearls away and rubies
    But keep your fancy free."
But I was one-and-twenty,
    No use to talk to me.

When I was one-and-twenty
    I heard him say again,   10
"The heart out of the bosom
    Was never given in vain;
'Tis paid with sighs a-plenty
    And sold for endless rue."
And I am two-and-twenty,
    And oh, 'tis true, 'tis true.

Reveille [2]

WAKE: the silver dusk returning
    Up the beach of darkness brims,
And the ship of sunrise burning
    Strands upon the eastern rims.

Wake: the vaulted shadow shatters,
    Trampled to the door it spanned,
And the tent of night in tatters
    Straws the sky-pavilioned land.

Up, lad, up, 'tis late for lying:
    Hear the drums of morning play;   10
Hark, the empty highways crying
    "Who'll beyond the hills away?"

Towns and countries woo together,
    Forelands beacon, belfries call;
Never lad that trod on leather
    Lived to feast his heart with all.

Up, lad: thews that lie and cumber
    Sunlit pallets never thrive;
Morns abed and daylight slumber
    Were not meant for man alive.   20

Clay lies still, but blood's a rover;
    Breath's a ware that will not keep.
Up, lad: when the journey's over
    There'll be time enough to sleep.

  [1] Sorrow, regret.   [2] *Reveille* (rĕ vāl'yĭ).

Discussion Hints

1. "Loveliest of Trees," which some of its admirers prefer to call "The Cherry Tree," is a gem that should be stowed away in the memory to be taken out again and again.

2. Compare the tiny "With Rue My Heart Is Laden" with the famous and much longer "Elegy Written in a Country Churchyard" (p. 298).

3. Use an unabridged dictionary to find the meaning of the following words used in "Reveille":

strands	thews
straws	cumber
pavilioned	pallets
forelands	ware

4. In "Reveille" how many times must stay-abeds be wakened? Is the poet a youth or an older person? Give a reason for your answer.

Suggestions for Reading in Poets of Tradition

Bridges has written some beautiful love poems: "My Delight and Thy Delight," "I Love All Beauteous Things," "I Will Not Let Thee Go"; the often-quoted "London Snow"; and the sonnet sequence "The Growth of Love."

After Henley's "Invictus," one of the most frequently reprinted poems in English, his "England, My England" follows close. His "Hospital Sketches" and "London Voluntaries" contain many beautiful lyrics.

Choosing from the poems by W. H. Davies is difficult. Perhaps best known of all he has written is "Leisure" (in the revised edition of *Achievement* of this series). Others are "The Example," "A Great Time," "A Child's Pet," and "Happy Wind."

Best from the slight output of A. E. Housman is his first slender volume, *A Shropshire Lad*, from which all the verses reprinted here are taken. You will like especially "Is My Team Plowing?" and "The Power of Malt."

Lyric poets who sing of England, their homeland, are many. Memorable among them are Sir William Watson and Sir Henry Newbolt. See especially Watson's "England My Mother" and Newbolt's "Drake's Drum." Alfred Noyes, popular in the United States as well as at home, writes also of his native land, as witness "When Spring Comes Back to England" and "A Song of Sherwood." Best loved, perhaps, of all his lilting lyrics is "The Barrel-Organ." Both the narrative verse and the lyric verse of Alfred Noyes are represented in the revised editions of *Adventure* and *Achievement* of this series.

Five different American publishers publish the verse of these five "poets of tradition": Oxford University Press, Robert Bridges; The Macmillan Company, William Ernest Henley; Bruce Humphries, Inc., William Henry Davies; Henry Holt and Company, Inc., Alfred Edward Housman; Frederick A. Stokes Company, Alfred Noyes.

II. IRISH POETS

The Irish poets are in one sense difficult to classify. Some of them write poetry that is definitely religious in tone, like Katharine Tynan's "Sheep and Lambs" (p. 584). Some of them have been identified in one way or another with the rise of the Irish drama, and are dramatic as well as lyric poets. This is especially true of Yeats,[1] who until his death was head of the Irish, or Celtic, movement, a revival of interest in Irish legend, language, drama, and poetry. In a sense all the Irish poets may be called poets of tradition; for their chief aim has been to express the beauty they found in ancient Irish legend and in common Irish life. Often they use English that is full of charming Gaelic turns of phrase.

But whether we note their religious tone, their dramatic bent, or their interest in traditional themes, the fact that they rejoice in Ireland as their common birthplace is their outstanding bond. They are Irish poets first, other sorts of poets afterward.

WILLIAM BUTLER YEATS[2] (1865-1939)

If Ireland had had a poet laureate, the title would, as a matter of course, have belonged to William Butler Yeats. A poet from boyhood, he was a lifelong lover of Irish folklore and ancient Irish legend and did more than any other one person to interpret his native Ireland and his people to England and to America.

"The Lake Isle of Innisfree" has the singing

[1] See also Winifred M. Letts, under "Poets of the World War," p. 594.
[2] For biography see page 736.

melody and the tender, wistful note characteristic of the best Irish poetry. Its music and yearning for home have endeared it to a host of readers.

Early folk tales and folk songs are full of references to the superstition that fairies sometimes induce human children to steal away from home and join them in fairyland. In "The Stolen Child" the call of the fairies is expressed in such a musical and alluring way that it is no wonder the child cannot resist it.

The Lake Isle of Innisfree[1]

I WILL arise and go now, and go to
   Innisfree,
And a small cabin build there, of clay and
   wattles [2] made;
Nine bean rows will I have there, a hive
   for the honey bee,
And live alone in the bee-loud glade.

And I shall have some peace there, for
   peace comes dropping slow,
Dropping from the veils of the morning
   to where the cricket sings;

There midnight's all a glimmer, and noon
   a purple glow,
And evening's full of the linnet's [1] wings.

I will arise and go now, for always night
   and day
I hear lake water lapping with low sounds
   by the shore;   10
While I stand on the roadway, or on the
   pavements grey,
I hear it in the deep heart's core.

The Stolen Child[1]

WHERE dips the rocky highland
   Of Sleuth Wood in the lake,
There lies a leafy island
Where flapping herons wake
The drowsy water rats;
There we've hid your faery vats,
Full of berries
And of reddest stolen cherries.
Come away, O human child!
To the waters and the wild   10
With a faery, hand in hand,
For the world's more full of weeping than
   you can understand.

Where the wave of moonlight glosses
The dim grey sands with light,
Far off by furthest Rosses
We foot it all the night,
Weaving olden dances,
Mingling hands and mingling glances
Till the moon has taken flight;
To and fro we leap   20
And chase the frothy bubbles,
While the world is full of troubles
And is anxious in its sleep.
Come away, O human child!
To the waters and the wild
With a faery, hand in hand,

For the world's more full of weeping than
   you can understand.

Where the wandering water gushes
From the hills above Glen-Car,
In pools among the rushes   30
That scarce could bathe a star,
We seek for slumbering trout
And whispering in their ears
Give them unquiet dreams;
Leaning softly out
From ferns that drop their tears
Over the young streams.
Come away, O human child!
To the waters and the wild
With a faery, hand in hand,   40
For the world's more full of weeping than
   you can understand.

Away with us he's going,
The solemn-eyed:
He'll hear no more the lowing
Of the calves on the warm hillside
Or the kettle on the hob
Sing peace into his breast,
Or see the brown mice bob
Round and round the oatmeal-chest.
For he comes, the human child,   50
To the waters and the wild
With a faery, hand in hand,
From a world more full of weeping than he
   can understand.

[1] From William Butler Yeats's *Early Poems and
   Stories.* By permission of the author's estate
   and The Macmillan Company, publishers.
[2] Woven twigs.

[1] The linnet is a songbird familiar in the British
   Isles.

Come away, O human child!

1. Read the first lyric until you notice the falling cadence* of the final line of each stanza.

2. How are this sad world and the happy "faery" world contrasted in "The Stolen Child"?

3. Is the change in the refrain of the final stanza appropriate? Why? What details of Irish cottage life are given in the final stanza?

4. Give examples of the effective use of sound and sight in the two poems.

EVA GORE-BOOTH[1] (1872-1926)

The Little Waves of Breffny

From the very beginning of English literature, lyrics that sing of a homeland have been sure of a wide reading. "The Little Waves of Breffny" is one of these songs. It is characterized by the tender, wistful note and simple imagery that make Irish poetry so appealing. Read again Yeats's poem "The Lake Isle of Innisfree" (p. 582), on a similar theme.

THE grand road from the mountains
  goes shining to the sea,
And there is traffic in it, and many a
  horse and cart,
But the little roads of Cloonagh are
  dearer far to me,
And the little roads of Cloonagh go
  rambling through my heart.

A great storm from the ocean goes shouting o'er the hill,
And there is glory in it and terror on
  the wind,

But the haunted air of twilight is very
  strange and still,
And the little winds of twilight are
  dearer to my mind.

The great waves of the Atlantic sweep
  storming on their way,
Shining green and silver with the hidden herring shoal,   10
But the Little Waves of Breffny have
  drenched my heart in spray,
And the Little Waves of Breffny go
  stumbling through my soul.

Discussion Hints

1. Copy one stanza of the poem, rearranging it in such a way as to show that the author is using the ballad pattern (p. 58) in disguise. In what respect, besides the line arrangement, does it not fit the ballad pattern?

2. What is the subject of each stanza? With what word does the third line of each stanza begin? Why?

3. Comment on the title.

KATHARINE TYNAN[2] (1861-1931)

Sheep and Lambs

"Sheep and Lambs" is a lyric poem beautiful in its religious devotion and simplicity. Its effectiveness lies in the delicacy with which the poet compares the real lambs, with their "weak, human cry," with Jesus, "the Lamb of God, which taketh away the sin of the world" (John 1:29)

ALL in the April evening,
  April airs were abroad;
The sheep with their little lambs
  Passed me by on the road.

The sheep with their little lambs
  Passed me by on the road;
All in an April evening,
  I thought on the Lamb of God.

[1] For biography see page 737.
[2] For biography see page 737.

The lambs were weary, and crying
 With a weak, human cry. 10
I thought on the Lamb of God
 Going meekly to die.

Up in the blue, blue mountains
 Dewy pastures are sweet;
Rest for the little bodies,
 Rest for the little feet.

Rest for the Lamb of God
 Up on the hill-top green,
Only a Cross of shame,[1]
 \ Two stark crosses between.[2] 20

All in the April evening,
 April airs were abroad;
I saw the sheep with their lambs,
 And thought on the Lamb of God.

Discussion Hints

1. *Compare* is a word which means in its widest sense to point out both resemblances and differences. Does Miss Tynan do both?

2. What line or lines seem to you most beautiful? What lines does the poet repeat most often, almost word for word?

PADRAIC COLUM[3] (1881-   )

"An Old Woman of the Roads" and "A Cradle Song" are illustrations of the work of Colum, one of the modern Irish poets who choose the life of the lowly as the theme of their verse. Colum writes of the soil, the hard earth, and the equally hard life of the peasant toilers. His poems, which are marked by simple language and wistful music, can be gay, can be sad, and they often have a twist peculiarly Irish.

An Old Woman of the Roads[4]

OH, TO have a little house!
 To own the hearth and stool and
  all!
The heaped-up sods upon the fire,
The pile of turf against the wall!

To have a clock with weights and
 chains
And pendulum swinging up and down,
A dresser filled with shining delph,[5]
Speckled and white and blue and brown!

I could be busy all the day
Clearing and sweeping hearth and floor, 10
And fixing on their shelf again
My white and blue and speckled store!

I could be quiet there at night
Beside the fire and by myself,
Sure of a bed and loath to leave
The ticking clock and the shining delph!

Och! but I'm weary of mist and dark,
And roads where there's never a house
 nor bush,
And tired I am of bog and road,
And the crying wind and the lonesome
 hush! 20

And I am praying to God on high,
And I am praying him night and day,
For a little house, a house of my own—
Out of the wind's and the rain's way.

---

[1] In Roman times crucifixion was considered the most shameful death.
[2] *Two . . . between.* Jesus was crucified between two thieves.
[3] For biography see page 737.
[4] From Padraic Colum's *Wild Earth and Other Poems.* By permission of The Macmillan Company, publishers.
[5] Glazed pottery for table use. The more usual spellings are "delft" and "delf."

A Cradle Song[1]

O MEN from the fields!
  Come softly within.
Tread softly, softly,
O men coming in!

Mavourneen [2] is going
From me and from you,
Where Mary [3] will fold him
With mantle of blue!

From reek of the smoke
And cold of the floor,   10
And the peering of things
Across the half-door.

O men from the fields!
Soft, softly come through —
Mary puts round him
Her mantle of blue.

Discussion Hints

1. Which lyric is in keeping with the spirit of a poet who writes for and of children?

2. In what way is each of the lyrics a commentary on Irish life?

3. Are the themes of the little poems Irish only?

4. Why is the phrase "lonesome hush" (l. 20) in "An Old Woman of the Roads" especially effective?

Suggestions for Reading in Irish Poets

To the fine tradition of poetry built up by such verse-makers as Thomas Moore (p. 349)

[1] From Padraic Colum's *Wild Earth and Other Poems*. By permission of The Macmillan Company, publishers.
[2] *Mavourneen* (mȧ voōr'nēn). Irish for my darling.
[3] The Virgin Mary.

and other lovers of Ireland's past, modern Irish poets belong. You will want to read more. Here are suggestions:

YEATS, WILLIAM BUTLER. Songs from *The Land of Heart's Desire*, and poems of love, such as "When You Are Old," "The Rose of the World," and "Never Give All the Heart." See "Suggestions for Further Reading" under "The Drama" (p. 695).

GORE-BOOTH, EVA. "The Harvest" and "The Weaver."

TYNAN, KATHARINE. "She Asks for New Earth," "The Making of Birds," and "The Desire." See "Suggestions for Reading" under "Poets Who Write on Religious Themes" (p. 592).

COLUM, PADRAIC. "The Fair Hills of Eire," "A Driver," and "The Plower."

The Macmillan Company publishes the verse of Colum, Katharine Tynan, and Yeats; Longmans Green & Co. that of Eva Gore-Booth.

The Irish poems of Winifred Letts (p. 594; E. P. Dutton & Co., Inc.) should also be mentioned, poems such as "In Service," "Boys," and "Quantity and Quality."

Should you wish to adventure further alone there is the inspired verse of Æ (the pen name of George Russell; The Macmillan Company) and of J. M. Synge (Random House, Inc.), Irish dramatist.

Collections of poetry which are concerned especially with Irish poets include the following:

Treasury of Irish Poetry, edited by Stopford Augustus Brooke and Thomas William Hazen (The Macmillan Company), which contains a final section of the work of the later Irish poets.

A Golden Treasury of Irish Verse, edited by Lennox Robinson (The Macmillan Company), which includes translations from the Gaelic by Lady Augusta Gregory.

III. POETS WHO WRITE ON RELIGIOUS THEMES

Today as in other days, especially in times of stress, poets turn to religious themes. Such a poem is Colum's "Cradle Song" (p. 586).

The poets represented in this particular group did not write exclusively on such themes, not even Alice Meynell, devout Roman Catholic. The many-sided Hilaire Belloc is an historian, a biographer, and an essayist, as well as a writer of verse sometimes light, sometimes serious, even religious in tone. Chesterton wrote narrative poetry (p. 636), essays,[1] and detective stories.[2] It happens, however, that in this brief section of lyrics the poems are all of a religious nature; and Francis Thompson, Alice Meynell, and Chesterton are noted for their religious verse.

Perhaps it should be added that though the first two, devoted friends, are sometimes thought of as Victorians, the verse of both is to be found in many modern anthologies. Moreover, though they were influenced by the writings of earlier poets, their work is definitely their own, definitely modern, definitely timeless. Be sure to read not only the brief accounts of Alice Meynell and Francis Thompson in the biographies at the back of the book, but also more detailed accounts, such as may be found in the Encyclopaedia Britannica.

FRANCIS THOMPSON[3] (1859–1907)

Thompson was a drifter and tramp who, somehow, had the awareness of nature we associate with Wordsworth and the awareness of the unseen possessed by the religious poets of the seventeenth century.

"Daisy," a song written by Thompson in honor of one of the Meynell[4] children, is marked by felicity of phrase and a singing music of rhyme and rhythm.

In "To a Snowflake" poet and snowflake exchange question and answer. Far from modern in point of view is Francis Thompson; but though his language is curious, even strange, his insight is clear and enlightening.

Daisy

WHERE the thistle lifts a purple crown
  Six foot out of the turf,
And the harebell shakes on the windy hill —
  O the breath of the distant surf!—

The hills look over on the South,
  And southward dreams the sea;
And, with the sea-breeze hand in hand,
  Came innocence and she.

Where 'mid the gorse the raspberry
  Red for the gatherer springs,   10
Two children did we stray and talk
  Wise, idle, childish things.

She listened with big-lipped surprise,
  Breast-deep mid flower and spine:
Her skin was like a grape, whose veins
  Run snow instead of wine.

[1] See "Suggestions for Further Reading in the Essay" (p. 626).

[2] See "Suggestions for Further Reading in the Short Story and the Novel" on page 684.

[3] For biography see page 737.

[4] Two of Alice Meynell's poems are given on page 589. She was the mother of the Meynell children referred to.

She knew not those sweet words she
   spake,
Nor knew her own sweet way;
But there's never a bird, so sweet a
   song   19
Thronged in whose throat that day!

Oh, there were flowers in Storrington
   On the turf and on the spray;
But the sweetest flower on Sussex hills
   Was the Daisy-flower that day!

Her beauty smoothed earth's furrowed
   face!
She gave me tokens three: —
A look, a word of her winsome mouth,
   And a wild raspberry.

A berry red, a guileless look,
   A still word, — strings of sand!   30
And yet they made my wild, wild heart
   Fly down to her little hand.

For standing artless as the air,
   And candid as the skies,
She took the berries with her hand,
   And the love with her sweet eyes.

The fairest things have fleetest end:
   Their scent survives their close,
But the rose's scent is bitterness
   To him that loved the rose!   40

She looked a little wistfully,
   Then went her sunshine way: —
The sea's eye had a mist on it,
   And the leaves fell from the day.

She went her unremembering way,
   She went and left in me
The pang of all the partings gone,
   And partings yet to be.

She left me marvelling why my soul
   Was sad that she was glad;   50
At all the sadness in the sweet,
   The sweetness in the sad.

Still, still I seemed to see her, still
   Look up with soft replies,
And take the berries with her hand,
   And the love with her lovely eyes.

Nothing begins, and nothing ends,
   That is not paid with moan;
For we are born in others' pain,
   And perish in our own.   60

To a Snow-flake

WHAT heart would have thought
   you? —
Past our devisal
(O filigree petal!)
Fashioned so purely,
Fragilely, surely,
From what Paradisal
Imagineless metal,
Too costly for cost?
Who hammered you, wrought you,
From argentine[1] vapour? —   10
"God was my shaper.
Passing surmisal,
He hammered, He wrought me,
From curled silver vapour,

       [1] Silver.

To lust of His mind: —
Thou could'st not have thought me!
So purely, so palely,
Tinily, surely,
Mightily, frailly,
Insculped and embossed,   20
With His hammer of wind,
And His graver of frost."

Discussion Hints

1. Compare "Daisy" with Wordsworth's
Lucy poems (p. 337), also a tribute from an
older person to a young English girl.

2. Note in "To a Snow-flake" the unusual
and interesting use of words: adjectives, ad-
verbs, verbs, and nouns. Comment on several
of them.

ALICE MEYNELL[1] (1850-1922)

Like many of Mrs. Meynell's best lyrics, "The Shepherdess" and "Parted" reveal her sincere attempts to explore religious experience, a field shunned, most unhappily, by some foolish persons. When read reverently and thoughtfully, they will lead the reader along the paths the author herself has trod. Mrs. Meynell's style is tender and delicate.

The Shepherdess

SHE walks — the lady of my delight —
  A shepherdess of sheep.
Her flocks are thoughts. She keeps them white;
  She guards them from the steep;
She feeds them on the fragrant height,
  And folds them in for sleep.

She roams maternal hills and bright,
  Dark valleys safe and deep.

Into that tender breast at night
  The chastest stars may peep.   10
She walks — the lady of my delight —
  A shepherdess of sheep.

She holds her little thoughts in sight,
  Though gay they run and leap.]
She is so circumspect and right;
  She has her soul to keep.
She walks — the lady of my delight —
  A shepherdess of sheep.

Parted

FAREWELL to one now silenced quite,
  Sent out of hearing, out of sight, —
My friend of friends, whom I shall
  miss.
He is not banished, though, for this, —
Nor he, nor sadness, nor delight.

Though I shall talk with him no more,
A low voice sounds upon the shore.
  He must not watch my resting-place,
  But who shall drive a mournful face
From the sad winds about my door?   10

I shall not hear his voice complain,
But who shall stop the patient rain?
  His tears must not disturb my heart,
  But who shall change the years, and
    part
The world from every thought of pain?

Although my life is left so dim,
The morning crowns the mountain-rim;

[1] For biography see page 738.

Joy is not gone from summer skies,
  Nor innocence from children's eyes,
And all these things are part of him.   20

He is not banished, for the showers
Yet wake this green warm earth of ours.
  How can the summer but be sweet?
  I shall not have him at my feet,
And yet my feet are on the flowers.

Discussion Hints

1. Which poem seems to have been written by a man?

2. In what respect is "The Shepherdess" allegorical?*

3. Is it possible to shepherd one's thoughts and keep them "white"? Is there any suggestion of the Virgin Mary in "The Shepherdess"?

4. What is meant by line 20 in "Parted"? Compare "Parted" with Wordsworth's "A Slumber Did My Spirit Seal" (p. 338). Is remembrance in any sense a sort of immortality?

HILAIRE BELLOC[1] (1870-   )

Courtesy

Hilaire Belloc, an Englishman with a French name, is a man of many interests: history, biography, religion. He is also a man of many moods: playful, serious, even belligerent. "Courtesy" is a charming example of his serious religious verse. As may be guessed from the poem, Belloc is an ardent Roman Catholic; so, it happens, were or are all the poets whose verse is included in this group.

O F COURTESY, it is much less
  Than Courage of Heart or Holiness,
Yet in my Walks it seems to me
That the Grace of God is in Courtesy.

On Monks I did in Storrington[2] fall,
They took me straight into their Hall;
I saw Three Pictures on a wall,
And Courtesy was in them all.

The first the Annunciation[3];
The second the Visitation[3];   10
The third the Consolation,[3]
Of God that was Our Lady's Son.

The first was of Saint Gabriel;
On Wings a-flame from Heaven he fell;
And as he went upon one knee
He shone with Heavenly Courtesy.

Our Lady out of Nazareth rode —
It was Her month of heavy load;
Yet was Her face both great and kind,
For Courtesy was in Her Mind.   20

The third it was our Little Lord,
Whom all the Kings in arms adored;
He was so small you could not see
His large intent of Courtesy.

Our Lord, that was Our Lady's Son,
Go bless you, People, one by one;
My Rhyme is written, my work is done.

Discussion Hints

Explain the meaning of Annunciation, Visitation, and Consolation. Read carefully the fourth, fifth, and sixth stanzas of "Courtesy" for suggestions.

GILBERT KEITH CHESTERTON[4] (1874-1936)

The Donkey

In "The Donkey" the grotesque and the holy are strikingly contrasted. The little poem is a good example of Chesterton's gift of taking an original view of a familiar object and saying altogether unexpected things about it.

The last stanza has a touch of genuine imaginative splendor.

W HEN fishes flew and forests walked
  And figs grew upon thorn,[5]
Some moment when the moon was blood
  Then surely I was born;

With monstrous head and sickening cry
  And ears like errant wings,
The devil's walking parody
  On all four-footed things.

The tattered outlaw of the earth,
  Of ancient crooked will;   10
Starve, scourge, deride me: I am dumb,
  I keep my secret still.

Fools! For I also had my hour;
  One far fierce hour and sweet:
There was a shout about my ears,
  And palms before my feet.[1]

[1] For biography see page 738.
[2] In this village, in Sussex, is a monastery devoted to the worship of the Virgin.
[3] Use the very old-fashioned pronunciation ti-on.
[4] For biography see page 739.
[5] When . . . thorn. An ancient time when the impossible might have happened. See Luke 6:44.

[1] Jesus made his triumphal entry into Jerusalem riding upon an ass. See John 12:12-15.

There was a shout about my ears,
And palms before my feet

From a painting by Benjamin Haydon in Mount Saint Mary Seminary

Discussion Hints

1. Is it true that donkeys are dumb even when they are starved and scourged and derided? Is the strong feeling of the last stanza suitable to one who is shamed yet proud? to one who has long been patiently silent? What is the donkey's secret?

2. Is "Lepanto" (p. 636) in any sense a religious poem?

Suggestions for Reading in Poets Who Write on Religious Themes

Choosing from the wealth of Francis Thompson's religious verse is difficult. "Ex Ore Infantium" and "In No Strange Land" are excellent examples. The puzzling, difficult ode "The Hound of Heaven" is his best-known single poem. Several American companies publish Thompson's poetry.

Of Alice Meynell's religious verse almost the same statement may be made. "The Lady Poverty," "Unto Us a Son Is Given," "Christ in the Universe," will make a good beginning. Mrs. Meynell's poems on nature and her sonnets are notable. See also "Sug-gestions for Reading in Poets of the World War" (p. 600). Charles Scribner's Sons publish the poetry of both Thompson and Mrs. Meynell.

Not always do the titles of religious poems suggest their nature. Those of Hilaire Belloc usually do; for example, "Noël," "Our Lord and Our Lady," "To Dives." The same author wrote humorous verses, even more widely known, with titles like "Jim" and "Matilda, Who Told Lies, and Was Burned to Death," in *Cautionary Tales for Children*. "A Christmas Carol," "The House of Christmas," and "A Hymn" by G. K. Chesterton are very fine. See "Lepanto" (p. 636). See also the revised edition of *Achievement* of this series. Dodd, Mead & Company, Inc., publish Chesterton's poetry.

Other single fine poems of a religious sort are Katharine Tynan's "Of an Orchard," Walter de la Mare's "Ballad of Christmas," Thomas Hardy's "Oxen," and John Masefield's "Laugh and Be Merry."

See the *Home Book of Modern Verse*, Burton Egbert Stevenson, compiler (Henry Holt and Company, Inc.), for some forty pages of modern religious verse.

IV. POETS OF THE WORLD WAR

The World War had a numbing, silencing effect on all sorts of ordinary folk. Soldiers on leave refused to talk about their experiences and changed the subject. Try out the truth of this statement. Ask any veteran of the World War to tell you about it. He will talk of his comrades in arms; he will talk of little, inconsequential matters; but of the horrors of modern warfare as he knew it in the trenches, under the sea, in the air, of these he will not talk. It is as though he could not.

The poets, like the rest, were struck dumb. Words simply could not describe the war. To the few, Winifred Letts and Rupert Brooke (who died in the Dardanelles), for instance, it was a challenge, a testing; but to them also it was sad beyond measure, for it could mean to many only the end of life in youth. To some, like Siegfried Sassoon (who served throughout the World War), it meant year-by-year, day-by-day devotion to the mission of keeping fresh the memory of the awfulness of war, in the vain hope that men might not repeat its futility and horror.

Aerofilms

I saw the spires of Oxford

D

Gilman and Soane

They left the peaceful river,
The cricket field, the quad

WINIFRED M. LETTS[1] (1887-   )

The Spires of Oxford

(Seen from a Train)

The melody and perfection of rhyme and rhythm and the emotional appeal of the theme, youth nobly responding to the call of duty, have made "The Spires of Oxford" famous. Its author, Irish rather than English, lives in Dublin.

I SAW the spires of Oxford[2]
  As I was passing by,
The grey spires of Oxford
  Against a pearl-grey sky;
My heart was with the Oxford men
  Who went abroad to die.

The years go fast in Oxford,
  The golden years and gay;
The hoary colleges look down
  On careless boys at play,   10

But when the bugles sounded — War!
  They put their games away.

They left the peaceful river,
  The cricket field, the quad,[1]
The shaven lawns of Oxford
  To seek a bloody sod.
They gave their merry youth away
  For country and for God.

God rest you, happy gentlemen,
  Who laid your good lives down,   20
Who took the khaki and the gun
  Instead of cap and gown.
God bring you to a fairer place
  Than even Oxford town.

---

[1] For biography see page 739.
[2] Oxford University, at Oxford, England.

[1] *quad.* Quadrangle, an open square or rectangle around which a college building at an English university is usually built.

Discussion Hints

1. Oxford, like many other older universities, was for centuries largely a religious institution; hence many Oxford colleges have towers or spires, as churches do. Do you know of any American colleges where the architecture resembles that of early English churches?

2. What is the meaning of "took the khaki and the gun" (l. 21)?

3. There is a tradition that the Duke of Wellington remarked, as he watched a cricket match at Eton, "The battle of Waterloo* was won here." What did he mean?

4. Wherein lies the appropriateness of the variation of the ballad stanza used here?

5. Just what is a Rhodes scholar?

RUPERT BROOKE[1] (1887–1915)

To Rupert Brooke the challenge of war brought inspiration; yet he, just as poignantly as did Keats, saw in war chiefly the approach of death, death in youth, when he himself wished so to live.

Alan Seeger's "I Have a Rendezvous with Death" (in the revised edition of *American Writers* of this series), John McCrae's "In Flanders Fields," and Rupert Brooke's "Soldier" are the three best-known poems written by soldiers in the World War. The tragic deaths of these soldier-poets add a peculiar poignancy to their poems.

"The Soldier" is in sonnet* form. Its quiet intensity breathes a patriotism too genuine to be noisy, and a love of home too deep to be clamorous.

"The Great Lover" makes no mention of war, but records rather the simple joys of peace.

The Soldier

IF I should die, think only this of me:
  That there's some corner of a foreign
      field
That is forever England.[2] There shall be
  In that rich earth a richer dust con-
      cealed;
A dust whom England bore, shaped,
      made aware,
  Gave, once, her flowers to love, her
      ways to roam,
A body of England's, breathing English air,
  Washed by the rivers, blest by suns of
      home.

And think, this heart, all evil shed
      away,
  A pulse in the eternal mind, no less 10
      Gives somewhere back the thoughts
        by England given;
Her sights and sounds; dreams happy as
      her day;
  And laughter, learned of friends; and
      gentleness,
    In hearts at peace, under an English
      heaven.

The Great Lover

I HAVE been so great a lover: filled my
  days
So proudly with the splendour of Love's
  praise,

The pain, the calm, and the astonishment,
Desire illimitable, and still content,
And all dear names men use, to cheat
  despair,
For the perplexed and viewless streams
  that bear
Our hearts at random down the dark of
  life.
Now, ere the unthinking silence on that
  strife

[1] For biography see page 739.

[2] *If . . . England.* Rupert Brooke never reached Gallipoli, for which the Royal Naval Division, in which he held a commission, had sailed. Instead, he died of blood-poisoning on a French hospital ship. He is buried in Scyros, a Greek island in the Aegean Sea.

Steals down, I would cheat drowsy Death
so far,
My night shall be remembered for a star
That outshone all the suns of all men's
days.   11
Shall I not crown them with immortal
praise
Whom I have loved, who have given me,
dared with me
High secrets, and in darkness knelt to
see
The inenarrable godhead of delight?
Love is a flame; — we have beaconed
the world's night.
A city: — and we have built it, these
and I.
An emperor: — we have taught the
world to die.
So, for their sakes I loved, ere I go hence,
And the high cause of Love's magnifi-
cence,   20
And to keep loyalties young, I'll write
those names
Golden for ever, eagles, crying flames,
And set them as a banner, that men may
know,
To dare the generations, burn, and blow
Out on the wind of Time, shining and
streaming. . . .

These I have loved:
        White plates and cups, clean-
gleaming,
Ringed with blue lines; and feathery,
faery dust;
Wet roofs, beneath the lamp-light; the
strong crust
Of friendly bread; and many-tasting
food;
Rainbows; and the blue bitter smoke of
wood;   30
And radiant raindrops couching in cool
flowers;
And flowers themselves, that sway
through sunny hours,
Dreaming of moths that drink them
under the moon;
Then, the cool kindliness of sheets, that
soon

Smooth away trouble; and the rough
male kiss
Of blankets; grainy wood; live hair
that is
Shining and free; blue-massing clouds;
the keen
Unpassioned beauty of a great machine;
The benison of hot water; furs to touch;
The good smell of old clothes; and other
such —   40
The comfortable smell of friendly fingers,
Hair's fragrance, and the musty reek
that lingers
About dead leaves and last year's
ferns. . . .
                        Dear names,
And thousand others throng to me!
Royal flames;
Sweet water's dimpling laugh from tap
or spring;
Holes in the ground; and voices that do
sing;
Voices in laughter, too; and body's
pain,
Soon turned to peace; and the deep-
panting train;
Firm sands; the little dulling edge of
foam
That browns and dwindles as the wave
goes home;   50
And washen stones, gay for an hour; the
cold
Graveness of iron; moist black earthen
mould;
Sleep; and high places; footprints in
the dew;
And oaks; and brown horse-chestnuts,
glossy-new;
And new-peeled sticks; and shining
pools on grass; —
All these have been my loves. And these
shall pass,
Whatever passes not, in the great hour,
Nor all my passion, all my prayers, have
power
To hold them with me through the gate
of Death.
They'll play deserter, turn with the
traitor breath,   60

Break the high bond we made, and sell
    Love's trust
And sacramental covenant to the dust.
—— Oh, never a doubt but, somewhere,
    I shall wake,
And give what's left of love again, and
    make
New friends, now strangers. . . .
                But the best I've
    known,
Stays here, and changes, breaks, grows
    old, is blown

About the winds of the world, and fades
    from brains
Of living men, and dies.
                  Nothing remains.

O dear my loves, O faithless, once again
This one last gift I give: that after men
Shall know, and later lovers, far-removed,
Praise you, "All these were lovely";
    say, "He loved."   **72**

Mataiea, 1914 [1]

Discussion Hints

1. Someone in the class should recite John McCrae's "In Flanders Fields" and Alan Seeger's "I Have a Rendezvous with Death."

2. Were you misled by the title of "The Great Lover" into expecting something else? Do you like the title? What verse form does Rupert Brooke use for "The Great Lover"? Note the long, rather involved introductory stanza and the final, shorter concluding one framework for the simpler central section.

3. Could Rupert Brooke have been homesick? There is no mention of things connected with the South Seas in the list of "Dear names."

4. Why does Brooke call the things he loved "faithless"? Make a list of your own of things that you love. Try putting it into verse.

SIEGFRIED SASSOON [1] (1886–   )

Siegfried Sassoon speaks with authority on war, for he himself spent four and a half years in the World War. He went to the front a gay young man, a lover of poetry and music and sports; he came from the front embittered by what he had lived through there. Not that he was not a good soldier: he was awarded the military cross for bravery at the front. That cross he proceeded to throw into the sea as a protest against the prolongation of the war; and that action he has followed up through the years by writing and continuing to write verse, bitter, dreadful verse, with but one end in view, keeping alive the memory of the horror, the futility of war.

Suicide in the Trenches

I KNEW a simple soldier boy
  Who grinned at life in empty joy,
Slept soundly through the lonesome dark,
And whistled early with the lark.

In winter trenches, cowed and glum,
With crumps [2] and lice and lack of rum,
He put a bullet through his brain.
No one spoke of him again.

 .   .   .   .

You smug-faced crowds with kindling
    eye
Who cheer when soldier lads march
    by,   **10**
Sneak home and pray you'll never know
The hell where youth and laughter go.

[1] For biography see page 740.
[2] Soldier slang for shells from heavy German guns.

[1] In 1913 and early 1914 Rupert Brooke traveled
    in America and the South Seas. Mataiea is
    a village on the south coast of Tahiti.

The Rear-Guard

(Hindenburg Line, April 1917)

GROPING along the tunnel, step by
step,
He winked his prying torch with patch-
ing glare
From side to side, and sniffed the unwholesome air.

Tins, boxes, bottles, shapes too vague to
know,
A mirror smashed, the mattress from a
bed;
And he, exploring fifty feet below
The rosy gloom of battle overhead.

Tripping, he grabbed the wall; saw
someone lie
Humped at his feet, half-hidden by a
rug,
And stooped to give the sleeper's arm a
tug.   10
"I'm looking for headquarters." No
reply.
"God blast your neck!" (For days he'd
had no sleep.)

"Get up and guide me through this
stinking place."
Savage, he kicked a soft, unanswering
heap,
And flashed his beam across the livid
face
Terribly glaring up, whose eyes yet
wore
Agony dying hard ten days before;
And fists of fingers clutched a blackening
wound.

Alone he staggered on until he found
Dawn's ghost that filtered down a shafted
stair   20
To the dazed, muttering creatures under-
ground
Who hear the boom of shells in muffled
sound.
At last, with sweat of horror in his hair,
He climbed through darkness to the
twilight air,
Unloading hell behind him step by
step.

Aftermath

Have you forgotten yet? . . .
For the world's events have rumbled on
        since those gagged days,
Like traffic checked awhile at the cross-
        ing of city ways:
And the haunted gap in your mind has
        filled with thoughts that flow
Like clouds in the lit heavens of life; and
        you're a man reprieved to go,
Taking your peaceful share of Time,
        with joy to spare.
But the past is just the same, — and War's
        a bloody game. . . .
Have you forgotten yet? . . .
Look down, and swear by the slain of the
        War that you'll never forget.

Do you remember the dark months you
        held the sector at Mametz,[1] — 10
The nights you watched and wired and
    dug and piled sandbags on parapets?
Do you remember the rats: and the
                            stench
Of corpses rotting in front of the front-
                        line trench —
And dawn coming, dirty-white, and chill
        with a hopeless rain?
Do you ever stop and ask, "Is it all
        going to happen again?"

[1] The village of Mametz, France, was captured
    by the British on July 1, 1916, the first day
    of the battle of the Somme, which lasted over
    four months.

Vandamm

A scene from the play "Journey's End," by Robert C. Sherriff

Do you remember that hour of din before
the attack, —
And the anger, the blind compassion that
seized and shook you then
As you peered at the doomed and hag-
gard faces of your men?
Do you remember the stretcher-cases
lurching back
With dying eyes and lolling heads, —
those ashen-gray 20
Masks of the lads who once were keen
and kind and gay?
Have you forgotten yet? . . .
*Look up, and swear by the green of the
Spring that you'll never forget.*

Discussion Hints

1. Compare "Suicide in the Trenches"
with "The Spires of Oxford" (p. 594).

2. Which of Sassoon's poems given here expresses the horror of war most completely?
Which poem depicts most vividly the pity of
war? In which poem does Sassoon voice a
challenge to those who lived through the
World War?

3. Why is Sassoon placed last in this group
of three poets? Why is "Aftermath" placed
last in this group of three poems?

Suggestions for Reading in Poets of the World War

There was scarcely a poet in England
during the World War who did not show its
influence. Suggestions for further reading
include:

"The Connaught Rangers" and "For England's Sake," by Winifred Letts.

"1914," a group of sonnets by Rupert Brooke.
"The Soldier" is one of these.

"Dreamers," "Remorse," and "Survivors,"
by Siegfried Sassoon.

"Battle," a group of poems by Wilfrid Wilson
Gibson.

"Nurse Edith Cavell," by Alice Meynell.

"The Man He Killed," by Thomas Hardy.

"Epitaphs of the War," by Rudyard Kipling.

"August, 1914," by John Masefield.

American publishers of the poets of the
World War whose work is represented here
are: E. P. Dutton & Co., Inc., Winifred
Letts; The Macmillan Company, Rupert
Brooke; The Viking Press, Siegfried Sassoon.

Anthologies of war poetry include:

The Red Harvest, a Cry for Peace, edited by
Vincent Godfrey Burns. The Macmillan
Company.

A Treasury of War Poetry (first and second
series), edited by George Herbert Clarke.
Houghton Mifflin Company.

V. POETS OF NEW THEMES

Styles in poetry, as in houses, in clothes, and in conversation, change
with the years. We of today dress more simply, build our houses with
less decoration, talk more frankly than did the men and women of a generation ago. Poetry too has been simplified.

The new poetry may be, and often is, as beautiful and imaginative as
the old, and it is very often thoughtful and serious. Especially is it likely
to deal with human values in a realistic way. And no theme, however
commonplace or prosaic, is considered unsuitable.

W. W. Gibson tells the story of what has happened to poetry in "Snug
in My Easy Chair" (p. 605), the story of the turning of the new poets from
fanciful imaginings to the realism of today, in work and sweat and the daily
grind.

The modern poet may use the old verse forms or may make for himself
new patterns, but he is likely to lean toward simple, condensed form.

JAMES STEPHENS[1] (1882-1950)

As children we have all many times held sea shells to our ears and listened to the sound of the waves within. James Stephens takes this common childhood experience and makes it the basis of the following effective poem. As the poet listens to the shell his imagination ranges to far-off arctic seas. He is held spellbound by the picture of desolation thus conjured up, and he welcomes the homely noise of the street that brings him back to reality.

The desperate loneliness and hopelessness of poverty-stricken old age have never been better suggested than in "Bessie Bobtail." The poem is a striking combination of the significant with the pitiful. We may smile in places as we read, but no one smiles at the last two impressive lines.

The Shell[2]

I

AND then I pressed the shell
Close to my ear,
And listened well.

And straightway, like a bell,
Came low and clear
The slow, sad murmur of far distant
seas

Whipped by an icy breeze
Upon a shore
Wind-swept and desolate.

It was a sunless strand that never bore
The footprint of a man,   11
Nor felt the weight

Since time began
Of any human quality or stir,
Save what the dreary_winds and waves
incur.

II

And in the hush of waters was the
sound
Of pebbles, rolling round;
For ever rolling, with a hollow sound:

And bubbling sea-weeds, as the waters
go,
Swish to and fro   20
Their long cold tentacles[1] of slimy grey;

There was no day;
Nor ever came a night
Setting the stars alight

To wonder at the moon:
Was twilight only, and the frightened
croon,
Smitten to whimpers, of the dreary wind

And waves that journeyed blind . . .
And then I loosed my ear — Oh, it was
sweet
To hear a cart go jolting down the street. 30

Bessie Bobtail[2]

AS DOWN the street she wambled[3]
slow,
She had not got a place to go:
She had not got a place to fall
And rest herself — no place at all!

She stumped along and wagged her pate;
And said a thing was desperate.

Her face was screwed and wrinkled tight
Just like a nut — and, left and right,
On either side, she wagged her head
And said a thing; and what she said   10

[1] For biography see page 740.
[2] From James Stephens's *Collected Poems*. By permission of the author, The Macmillan Company, Messrs. Macmillan and Company Limited, and The Macmillan Company of Canada Limited, publishers.
[3] Walked unsteadily, tottered.

[1] Long, slender arms, especially those of certain sea creatures such as the octopus. Here, the waving branches of seaweed.

Was desperate as any word
That ever yet a person heard.

I walked behind her for a while,
And watched the people nudge and
  smile:
But ever as she went, she said,
As left and right she swung her head,
— *O God He knows: And, God He knows,*
And, surely God Almighty knows!

Discussion Hints

1. What is the real theme of "The Shell"?
What lines express it best?

2. Has "The Shell" a stanza pattern? a
pattern of line? a pattern of rhyme?

3. Compare the humor and the pathos of
"Bessie Bobtail" with "The Last Leaf," the
familiar poem by Oliver Wendell Holmes.
See the revised edition of *American Writers*
of this series.

RALPH HODGSON[1] (1878-   )

Time, You Old Gipsy Man[2]

Hundreds of poets have besought Time to
stay his resistless flight, and, like Shakespeare,
have tried to "hold his swift foot back," but
no poet has addressed Time more delightfully
and musically than Hodgson does here.

The theme is an old one, but in the garish
light of today Time seems to march more
swiftly than ever before.

TIME, you old gipsy man,
  Will you not stay,
Put up your caravan[3]
  Just for one day?

All things I'll give you
Will you be my guest,
Bells for your jennet[4]
Of silver the best,
Goldsmiths shall beat you
A great golden ring,   10
Peacocks shall bow to you,
Little boys sing.
Oh, and sweet girls will
Festoon you with may,[5]
Time, you old gipsy,
Why hasten away?

Last week in Babylon,
Last night in Rome,
Morning, and in the crush
Under Paul's dome[1];   20
Under Paul's dial
You tighten your rein —
Only a moment,
And off once again;
Off to some city
Now blind in the womb,
Off to another
Ere that's in the tomb.

Time, you old gipsy man,
  Will you not stay,   30
Put up your caravan
  Just for one day?

Discussion Hints

1. Why is Time appropriately called a
"gipsy man"?

2. How long did Babylon last? How long
did Rome last? How long has London been
in existence? How long has New York been
in existence?

3. Compare A. E. Housman's "Loveliest of
Trees" (p. 579) and "Reveille" (p. 580).

[1] For biography see page 740.
[2] From Ralph Hodgson's *Eve and Other Poems.*
By permission of The Macmillan Company,
publishers.
[3] A house on wheels, a van.
[4] A small Spanish horse.
[5] *Festoon . . . may.* Adorn you with garlands of
hawthorn.

[1] The dome of St. Paul's Cathedral, London.

WALTER DE LA MARE[1] (1873-   )

One of the chief joys of reading is forgetting troubles and losing oneself entirely in the thrill of a story. Old Susan experiences this joy to the utmost. She is old; she is poor; she has to work hard; she isn't very well educated; but give her a book, and she is queen of the world. The poem about her is a character sketch, a portrait in words, which the delicate touch of de la Mare makes a thing of beauty.

"Peeping Tom" is about a little boy and another old woman, an old woman who has died. Her curious boy neighbor doesn't know about death, though he senses that something is amiss. He is full of questions: "why," "Yet . . .," "what." Though the story is told from the boy's point of view, there are many suggestions of the mystery of life and of death. Symbolism* is everywhere latent. Read carefully, or you will miss some of it.

Old Susan

WHEN Susan's work was done, she would sit,
With one fat guttering candle lit,
And window opened wide to win
The sweet night air to enter in.
There, with a thumb to keep her place,
She would read, with stern and wrinkled
    face,
Her mild eyes gliding very slow
Across the letters to and fro,
While wagged the guttering candle flame
In the wind that through the window
    came.   10
And sometimes in the silence she
Would mumble a sentence audibly,

Or shake her head as if to say,
"You silly souls, to act this way!"
And never a sound from night I would
    hear,
Unless some far-off cock crowed clear;
Or her old shuffling thumb should turn
Another page; and rapt and stern,
Through her great glasses bent on me,
She would glance into reality;   20
And shake her round old silvery head,
With — "You! — I thought you was in
    bed!" —
Only to tilt her book again,
And rooted in Romance remain.

Peeping Tom

I WAS there — by the curtains —
    When some men brought a box:
And one at the house of
    Miss Emily knocks:

A low *rat-tat-tat*.
The door opened — and then,
Slowly mounting the steps, stooped
    In the strange men.

Then the door darkly shut,
And I saw their legs pass,   10
Like an insect's, Miss Emily's
    Window-glass —

Though why all her blinds
Have been hanging so low
These dumb foggy days,
    I don't know.

Yes, only last week
I watched her for hours,
Potting out for the winter her
    Balcony flowers.   20

And this very Sunday
She mused there a space,
Gazing into the street, with
    The vacantest face:

[1] For biography see page 741.

Then turned her long nose,
And looked up at the skies —
One you would not have thought
    Weather-wise!

Yet . . . well, out stepped the men —
One ferrety-fair—   30
With gentlemen's hats, and
    Whiskers and hair;

And paused in the porch.
Then smooth, solemn, grey,
They climbed to their places,
    And all drove away

In their square varnished carriage,
The horse full of pride,
With a tail like a charger's:
They all sate outside.   40

Then the road became quiet;
Her house stiff and staid —
Like a Stage while you wait
    For the Harlequinade[1]. . .

But what can Miss Emily
Want with a box
So long, narrow, shallow,
    And without any locks?

Discussion Hints

1. Just who is the "You" of "Old Susan"? Why is "You" not in bed? How late is it?

2. What is the significance of the title "Peeping Tom"? Prove that the picture Tom sees is a vivid one. How does the punctuation indicate Tom's puzzlement?

3. Had Miss Emily expected to live the winter through?

4. What does de la Mare think of funerals? How does Tom describe a coffin?

WILFRID WILSON GIBSON[1] (1878–   )

W. W. Gibson, as he is usually called, is a past master of the use of contrast and unexpected climax. He might have been (in fact, was) in his early days like Tennyson in his writing of decorative, imaginative verse. He still writes such verse, not for its own sake, but to set off the stark reality of poverty and labor. Actual living for a time in a London slum among the toilers made Gibson abandon "amber woodland streaming," and seek poetry in the "streaming shoulders stark" of "the man who hews the coal to feed my fire."

From the time of that London sojourn to the present Gibson has been seeing beauty and nobility in the struggles of the world's toilers.

Sight[2]

By the lamplit stall I loitered, feasting my eyes
On colours ripe and rich for the heart's
    desire —
Tomatoes, redder than Krakatoa's[3] fire,

Oranges like old sunsets over Tyre,*
And apples golden-green as the glades of
    Paradise.

And as I lingered, lost in divine delight,
My heart thanked God for the goodly
    gift of sight
And all youth's lively senses keen and
    quick . . .   8
When suddenly, behind me in the night,
I heard the tapping of a blind man's stick.

[1] For biography see page 741.

[2] From Wilfrid Wilson Gibson's *Collected Poems, 1905–1925*. By permission of the author, The Macmillan Company, Messrs. Macmillan and Company Limited, and The Macmillan Company of Canada Limited, publishers.

[3] The greatest of modern volcanic eruptions was that of Krakatao, or Krakatoa, west of Java, in 1883.

[1] Last scene of old English pantomime, in which the leading part is taken by the clown Harlequin, who wears particolored clothes and amuses the onlookers with his droll tricks.

The Ice-Cart[1]

PERCHED on my city office-stool,
I watched with envy, while a cool
And lucky carter handled ice. . . .
And I was wandering in a trice,[2]
Far from the grey and grimy heat
Of that intolerable street,
O'er sapphire berg and emerald floe,
Beneath the still, cold, ruby glow
Of everlasting Polar night,
Bewildered by the queer half-light,   10
Until I stumbled, unawares,
Upon a creek where big white bears
Plunged headlong down with flourished
    heels
And floundered after shining seals
Through shivering seas of blinding blue.
And as I watched them, ere I knew,
I'd stripped, and I was swimming, too,
Among the seal-pack, young and hale,
And thrusting on with threshing tail,
With twist and twirl and sudden leap   20

Through crackling ice and salty deep —
Diving and doubling with my kind,
Until, at last, we left behind
Those big, white blundering bulks of
    death,
And lay, at length, with panting breath
Upon a far untravelled floe,
Beneath a gentle drift of snow —
Snow drifting gently, fine and white,
Out of the endless Polar night,
Falling and falling evermore   30
Upon that far untravelled shore,
Till I was buried fathoms deep
Beneath that cold white drifting sleep —
Sleep drifting deep,
Deep drifting sleep. . . .

The carter cracked a sudden whip:
I clutched my stool with startled grip,
Awakening to the grimy heat
Of that intolerable street.

Snug in My Easy Chair[1]

SNUG in my easy chair,
I stirred the fire to flame.
Fantastically fair,
The flickering fancies came,
Born of heart's desire:
Amber woodland streaming;[3]
Topaz islands dreaming;
Sunset-cities gleaming,
Spire on burning spire;
Ruddy-windowed taverns;   10
Sunshine-spilling wines;
Crystal-lighted caverns

Of Golconda's[1] mines;
Summers, unreturning;
Passion's crater yearning;
Troy, the ever-burning;
Shelley's lustral pyre;[2]
Dragon-eyes, unsleeping;
Witches' cauldrons leaping;
Golden galleys sweeping   20
Out from sea-walled Tyre:
Fancies, fugitive and fair,
Flashed with singing through the air;
Till, dazzled by the drowsy glare,
I shut my eyes to heat and light;
And saw, in sudden night,
Crouched in the dripping dark,
With streaming shoulders stark,
The man who hews the coal to feed my
    fire.

[1] From Wilfrid Wilson Gibson's *Collected Poems,
1905–1925*. By permission of the author,
The Macmillan Company, Messrs. Macmillan and Company Limited, and The
Macmillan Company of Canada Limited,
publishers.
[2] Instant.
[3] From this line to line 23 the poet names over
the various ideas and images that poets have
been accustomed to weave into their verses.
Then, in the last six lines, comes the picture
that for him blots out all other pictures.

[1] Golconda was once a famous center of the diamond trade in India.
[2] Shelley (p. 719) was drowned off the shore of
Italy, and his body was burned on a funera'
pyre by his friends.

Discussion Hints

1. Compare the "lamplit stall" of "Sight" with McFee's "Market" (p. 623). Compare the polar regions of "The Ice-Cart" with James Stephens's "Shell" (p. 601).

2. Note the poet's imaginative picture of far-off places in "Sight" and the contrast of heat and cold in "The Ice-Cart." Note how Gibson uses the stuff of the old poetry and contrasts it with the new in "Snug in My Easy Chair."

3. Reread aloud the final, memorable two lines of "Sight" and the final four lines of each of the other two poems.

Suggestions for Reading in Poets of New Themes

Of the type of James Stephens's "Bessie Bobtail," but more fanciful, are "In the Poppy Field" and "Seumas Beg." "The Snare" and "Little Things" are brief verses that dwell thoughtfully but not sentimentally on wild life. Stephens wrote some charming poems of love, poems such as "Green Weeds" and "Deirdre." The Macmillan Company publishes his verse.

A mere single example of the verse of Ralph Hodgson calls for more. There are gemlike little poems, such as "The Bells of Heaven" and "The Hammers." There are the thoughtful "Three Poems," "The Bird-catcher," and "Thrown." There are verses of a religious slant: "Song of Honor" and "The Mystery."

And there are fine symbolic poems that mean far more than they say, poems such as the brief "Stupidity Street" and the longer poem "The Bull." The Macmillan Company publishes Hodgson's verse also.

Other poetic studies of interesting characters by de la Mare include "Old Ben," an old man whose children have all gone away; "Miss Loo," dreamer over the tea tray; "Martha," the storyteller; and "Nicholas Nye," a mule.

Of another sort are poems in which, as in "Peeping Tom," de la Mare touches on the mysteries of life and of death. Such are "The Sleeper," of a child that comes upon her mother asleep in her chair; "The Familiar," of a poet who meets his own ghost; and "The Listeners," of a house peopled by those who, dead, are still somehow there.

Do not forget that de la Mare is famous for his verse for and about children (see the revised edition of *Adventure* of this series). See also "Suggestions for Reading in Poets Who Write on Religious Themes" (p. 592). Henry Holt and Company, Inc., is the chief American publisher of de la Mare's poetry.

Scores of other poetic character sketches by W. W. Gibson are to be had: poems like "Merry Eye," "Betty Riddle," and "The Ragged Stone." Longer poems, dedicated to the common man, are "The Stone" and "The Ovens" from *Fires*. Gibson's excellent war poems must not be forgotten (see page 600). Again, it is The Macmillan Company that publishes in America the verse of an English poet.

VI. A TRIUMVIRATE

Three great poets, Thomas Hardy, Rudyard Kipling, John Masefield, defy grouping with others of less importance. Although they are very different from each other, they are here grouped together. Both Hardy and Kipling wrote in the nineteenth century. The Victorians knew Hardy as a novelist. The twentieth century knows him also as a poet. Kipling, like Hardy, is frequently spoken of as a Victorian, although, again like Hardy, he lived well into the twentieth century. Like the Victorians, Kipling loved the British Empire; like the English of today, he loved democracy. Both Kipling and Hardy wrote most of their verse before the World War (1914–1918).

John Masefield, poet laureate and member of the Order of Merit, appropriately concludes and brings to a climax this whole section. From a youth who knew poverty and hardship and manual labor, he came to a maturity honored above his fondest dreams. The subject matter of his lyrics is modern: the common man, the laborer, the poor. His verse form is more conventional than his material: the ballad, the sonnet,* the rhyming couplet* that Chaucer loved. John Masefield unites new material and old form.

THOMAS HARDY[1] (1840–1928)

Thomas Hardy has been called the "dean of modern poets." The title is suggestive of his priority and of his influence. Readers of Hardy think of him, and rightly, as serious, even somber. His chief joy was in nature. In "Weathers" he describes the miserable day so as to make it almost as attractive as the beautiful one.

"In Time of 'The Breaking of Nations'"

is a war poem, but it is strangely unlike other war poems. The poet's heart is dark with despair, full of horror and fears at the thought of a war-torn world. Yet, when he looks out over the peaceful English countryside, he sees that the great, simple, primal things in life and nature are going on the same yesterday, today, and forever: seedtime and harvest, youth and love.

Weathers[2]

THIS is the weather the cuckoo likes,
    And so do I;
When showers betumble the chestnut
    spikes,
    And nestlings fly:
And the little brown nightingale bills his
    best,
And they sit outside at "The Travellers'
    Rest,"[3]
And maids come forth sprig-muslin drest,
And citizens dream of the south and west,
    And so do I.

This is the weather the shepherd shuns,
    And so do I;   11
When beeches drip in browns and
    duns,
    And thresh, and ply;
And hill-hid tides throb, throe[1] on
    throe,
And meadow rivulets overflow,
And drops on gate-bars hang in a
    row,
And rooks in families homeward go,
    And so do I.

In Time of "The Breaking of Nations"[2]

I

ONLY a man harrowing clods
    In a slow silent walk
With an old horse that stumbles and
    nods
Half asleep as they stalk.

II

Only thin smoke without flame
    From the heaps of couch grass;
Yet this will go onward the same
    Though Dynasties pass.

III

Yonder a maid and her wight[2]
    Come whispering by;   10
War's annals will fade into night
    Ere their story die.

[1] For biography see page 741.
[2] From Thomas Hardy's *Collected Poems.* By permission of the author's Executors, The Macmillan Company, Messrs. Macmillan and Company Limited, and The Macmillan Company of Canada Limited, publishers.
[3] *The Travellers' Rest.* An English inn.

[1] A convulsive movement, as if in pain.
[2] Man, sweetheart.

Discussion Hints

Discussion Hints

1. Which stanza of "Weathers" is your favorite? What typically English details does Hardy use? Describe the weather you like best; the weather you shun.

2. What is the significance of the title of the second poem? Since the World War (1914–1918) what dynasties have passed?

3. What seem to Hardy more noteworthy, more eternal: wars and rulers, or seedtime and harvest and simple human life? Why?

RUDYARD KIPLING[1] (1865-1936)

Rudyard Kipling, many thought, should have been appointed poet laureate* after Tennyson. It was Queen Victoria who appointed Alfred Austin instead. She could not quite approve of a young poet who spoke of her familiarly as "Missis Victorier" and "the widow of Windsor." Kipling seems to have borne no grudge. He wrote "Recessional" (one of the most famous poems ever written for a special occasion) in 1897 for the queen's Diamond Jubilee.* It is said that when Victoria read it she was moved to tears.

"Recessional" is a prayer, a prayer for the welfare of England, a prayer that England may be humble just at the time when the whole world is ringing with her honor and glory. The poem shows the striking use of words and figures of speech characteristic of

much of Kipling's writing. In its use of Biblical figures it is thoroughly English. Its stately music and deep reverence unite to produce a most impressive effect. It is deservedly one of Kipling's best-known poems.

"Mandalay" is almost as famous as "Recessional." It belongs to that part of Kipling's work which, with great sympathy and vividness, interprets to England the life of the British soldier in the strange, faraway East. The "I" of the poem is a returned soldier who, in the fog and smoke of London, recalls happier days "in a cleaner, greener land" and wishes he were back again with his regiment in Mandalay. Kipling reproduces with rare skill both the soldier's mood and his cockney dialect. When read aloud, the singing lilt of the lines is irresistible.

Recessional

GOD of our fathers, known of old,
   Lord of our far-flung battle-line,
Beneath whose awful Hand we hold
   Dominion over palm and pine —
Lord God of Hosts, be with us yet,
Lest we forget — lest we forget!

The tumult and the shouting dies;
   The Captains and the Kings depart:
Still stands Thine ancient sacrifice,
   An humble and a contrite heart.   10
Lord God of Hosts, be with us yet,
Lest we forget — lest we forget!

Far-called, our navies melt away;
   On dune and headland sinks the fire:
Lo, all our pomp of yesterday
   Is one with Nineveh* and Tyre*!

[1] For biography see page 742.

Judge of the Nations, spare us yet,
   Lest we forget — lest we forget!

If, drunk with sight of power, we loose
   Wild tongues that have not Thee in
     awe,   20
Such boastings as the Gentiles use,
   Or lesser breeds without the Law —
Lord God of Hosts, be with us yet,
Lest we forget — lest we forget!

For heathen heart that puts her trust
   In reeking tube and iron shard,[1]
All valiant dust that builds on dust,
   And, guarding, calls not Thee to guard,
For frantic boast and foolish word —
Thy mercy on Thy people, Lord!   30

[1] *reeking tube . . . iron shard.* Here by metonymy,* military force.

There's a Burma girl a-settin', and I know she thinks o' me

Mandalay

BY THE old Moulmein Pagoda,[1] lookin'
    eastward to the sea,
There's a Burma girl a-settin', and I
    know she thinks o' me;
For the wind is in the palm-trees, and the
    temple-bells they say:
"Come you back, you British soldier;
    come you back to Mandalay!"
    Come you back to Mandalay,
    Where the old Flotilla[2] lay:
    Can't you 'ear their paddles
      chunkin' from Rangoon[3] to
      Mandalay?
    On the road to Mandalay,
    Where the flyin'-fishes play,
    An' the dawn comes up like
      thunder outer China 'crost the
      Bay!   10

'Er petticoat was yaller an' 'er little cap
    was green,
An' 'er name was Supi-yaw-lat — jes' the
    same as Theebaw's Queen,
An' I seed her first a-smokin' of a whack-
    in' white cheroot,
An' a-wastin' Christian kisses on an
    'eathen idol's foot:
    Bloomin' idol made o' mud —
    Wot they called the Great Gawd
      Budd —
    Plucky lot she cared for idols
      when I kissed 'er where she
      stud!
    On the road to Mandalay . . .

When the mist was on the rice-fields
    an' the sun was droppin'
    slow,
She'd git 'er little banjo an' she'd sing
    "*Kulla-lo-lo!*"   20
With 'er arm upon my shoulder an' 'er
    cheek agin my cheek

[1] *Moulmein* (mōl mān') *Pagoda.* A temple in
  Moulmein, near the west coast of Burma,
  not far from Rangoon.
[2] Fleet of river boats.
[3] A large city near Moulmein.

D

We useter watch the steamers an' the
    hathis[1] pilin' teak.[2]
    Elephints a-pilin' teak
    In the sludgy, squdgy creek,
    Where the silence 'ung that 'eavy
    you was 'arf afraid to speak!
    On the road to Mandalay . . .

But that's all shove be'ind me — long
    ago an' fur away,
An' there ain't no busses runnin' from
    the Bank[3] to Mandalay;
An' I'm learnin' 'ere in London what the
    ten-year soldier tells:
"If you've 'eard the East a-callin,
    you won't never 'eed naught
    else."   30
    No! you won't 'eed nothin' else
    But them spicy garlic smells,
    An' the sunshine an' the palm-
    trees an' the tinkly temple-
    bells;
    On the road to Mandalay . . .

I am sick o' wastin' leather on these
    gritty pavın'-stones,
An' the blasted English drizzle wakes
    the fever in my bones;
Tho' I walks with fifty 'ousemaids outer
    Chelsea[4] to the Strand,[5]
An' they talks a lot o' lovin', but wot do
    they understand?

[1] *hathis* (hä′tēz). An Indian word meaning
    "elephants."
[2] A tall East Indian tree valued for its hard,
    durable wood.
[3] The Bank of England, in the heart of London.
[4] An aristocratic section of west London where
    almost everyone would have one servant or
    more.
[5] The busiest thoroughfare in all London.

Beefy face an' grubby 'and —
Law! wot do they understand?
I've a neater, sweeter maiden in a
    cleaner, greener land!   41
On the road to Mandalay . . .

Ship me somewheres east of Suez,[1] where
    the best is like the worst,
Where there aren't no Ten Command-
    ments an' a man can raise a
    thirst;
For the temple-bells are callin', an' it's
    there that I would be —
By the old Moulmein Pagoda, looking
    lazy at the sea;
    On the road to Mandalay,
    Where the old Flotilla lay,
    With our sick beneath the awnings
    when we went to Mandalay!
    O the road to Mandalay,   50
    Where the flyin'-fishes play,
    An' the dawn comes up like thun-
    der outer China 'crost the Bay!

Discussion Hints

1. Why is the first poem called "Recessional"? "Lest we forget" what? Put into
words the answer which Kipling suggests in
every stanza. Turn to the Psalms of David
in the Bible, and find one that "Recessional"
is reminiscent of. Reginald De Koven has
set "Recessional" to music (John Church
Company).

2. "Mandalay" should certainly be read
aloud. It may be sung also, for it has been
effectively set to music by Oley Speaks (John
Church Company). See the Reinald Wer-
renrath Victor record No. 6638.

3. Compare the lyric poems given here
with the songs from "Rikki-tikki-tavi"
(pp. 642 and 652). See also "The Ballad of
East and West" (p. 628).

[1] At the end of the Suez Canal, on the way to the
    Orient.

JOHN MASEFIELD[1] (1878-   )

"A Consecration" is prefixed to the collected poems of England's poet laureate. With great power it sets forth Masefield's purpose to sing, not about the powerful, the rich, and the successful, but about "the scorned — the rejected," "the man with too weighty a burden, too weary a load."

There are two moods that are frequently and beautifully voiced in poetry: one is the home call to peace, to quiet, and to rest, the mood of Yeats's "Lake Isle of Innisfree" (p. 582) and Eva Gore-Booth's "Little Waves of Breffny" (p. 584); the other is the mood of "Sea-Fever" and "Tewkesbury Road," the gypsy call of the open road to wander in far places, whether by land or by sea. In "Sea-Fever" Masefield, sailor-poet, voices with especial effectiveness the call of ships and the sea.

The sadness of vanishing youth and oncoming old age has been sung hundreds of times in poetry, but never more poignantly and nobly than in "On Growing Old," the greatest sonnets,* some think, in contemporary poetry.

A Consecration [2]

Not of the princes and prelates with periwigged[3] charioteers
Riding triumphantly laurelled to lap the fat of the years, —
Rather the scorned — the rejected — the men hemmed in with the spears;

The men of the tattered battalion which fights till it dies,
Dazed with the dust of the battle, the din and the cries,
The men with the broken heads and the blood running into their eyes.

Not the be-medalled Commander, beloved of the throne,
Riding cock-horse to parade when the bugles are blown,
But the lads who carried the koppie[4] and cannot be known.

Not the ruler for me, but the ranker, the tramp of the road,   10

The slave with the sack on his shoulders pricked on with the goad,
The man with too weighty a burden, too weary a load.

The sailor, the stoker of steamers, the man with the clout,[1]
The chantyman bent at the halliards[2] putting a tune to the shout,
The drowsy man at the wheel and the tired lookout.

Others may sing of the wine and the wealth and the mirth,
The portly presence of potentates[3] goodly in girth; —
Mine be the dirt and the dross, the dust and scum of the earth!

Theirs be the music, the colour, the glory, the gold;
Mine be a handful of ashes, a mouthful of mould.   20
Of the maimed, of the halt and the blind in the rain and the cold —
Of these shall my songs be fashioned, my tales be told.

[1] For biography see page 742.
[2] From John Masefield's *Salt-Water Ballads*. By permission of The Macmillan Company, publishers.
[3] Wearing wigs.
[4] A South African word usually spelled "kopje," and meaning "small hill." The reference is to the events of the war between Great Britain and the Boers of South Africa in 1899–1902.

[1] A cloth, a rag.
[2] *chantyman . . . halliards*. A sailor who leads the chorus, singing as he handles the ropes that raise or lower the sails.
[3] The powerful ones of earth.

Tewkesbury Road[1]

IT IS good to be out on the road, and
going one knows not where,
Going through meadow and village,
one knows not whither nor why;
Through the grey light drift of the dust,
in the keen cool rush of the air,
Under the flying white clouds, and the
broad blue lift of the sky.

And to halt at the chattering brook, in
the tall green fern at the brink
Where the harebell grows, and the gorse,
and the foxgloves purple and white;

Where the shy-eyed delicate deer troop
down to the brook to drink
When the stars are mellow and large
at the coming on of the night.

O, to feel the beat of the rain, and the
homely smell of the earth,
Is a tune for the blood to jig to, a
joy past power of words;   10
And the blessed green comely meadows
are all a-ripple with mirth
At the noise of the lambs at play and
the dear wild cry of the birds.

Cargoes[2]

QUINQUIREME[3] of Nineveh from dis-
tant Ophir
Rowing home to haven in sunny Pales-
tine,
With a cargo of ivory,
And apes and peacocks,
Sandalwood, cedarwood, and sweet white
wine.

Stately Spanish galleon coming from the
Isthmus,[4]
Dipping through the Tropics by the
palm-green shores,

With a cargo of diamonds,
Emeralds, amethysts,
Topazes, and cinnamon, and gold moi-
dores.[1]   10

Dirty British coaster with a salt-caked
smoke stack
Butting through the Channel[2] in the
mad March days,
With a cargo of Tyne coal,
Road-rail, pig-lead,
Firewood, iron-ware, and cheap tin
trays.

Sea-Fever[1]

I MUST go down to the seas again, to
the lonely sea and the sky,
And all I ask is a tall ship and a star to
steer her by,
And the wheel's kick and the wind's song
and the white sail's shaking,
And a grey mist on the sea's face and a
grey dawn breaking.

I must go down to the seas again, for the
call of the running tide
Is a wild call and a clear call that may not
be denied;
And all I ask is a windy day with the
white clouds flying,
And the flung spray and the blown
spume,[3] and the sea-gulls crying.

[1] From John Masefield's *Salt-Water Ballads.* By permission of The Macmillan Company, publishers.
[2] From John Masefield's *Collected Poems.* By permission of The Macmillan Company, publishers.
[3] A large ancient seagoing vessel with five banks of oars.   [4] The Isthmus of Panama.

[1] *moidores* (moi'dōrz). Former Portuguese and Brazilian gold coins worth about $6.75. Note that for purposes of meter the accent falls on the last syllable here.
[2] The English Channel.
[3] Flying foam.

I must go down to the seas again

I must go down to the seas again to the
vagrant gypsy life,
To the gull's way and the whale's way
where the wind's like a whetted
knife;   10

And all I ask is a merry yarn from a
laughing fellow-rover,
And quiet sleep and a sweet dream when
the long trick's over.

On Growing Old[1]

BE WITH me, Beauty, for the fire is
dying;
My dog and I are old, too old for roving.
Man, whose young passion sets the
spindrift[2] flying,
Is soon too lame to march, too cold for
loving.
I take the book and gather to the fire,
Turning old yellow leaves; minute by
minute
The clock ticks to my heart. A withered
wire,
Moves a thin ghost of music in the spinet.[3]
I cannot sail your seas, I cannot wander
Your cornland, nor your hill-land, nor
your valleys   10
Ever again, nor share the battle yonder
Where the young knight the broken
squadron rallies.
Only stay quiet while my mind remem-
bers
The beauty of fire from the beauty of
embers.

Beauty, have pity! for the strong have
power,
The rich their wealth, the beautiful their
grace,
Summer of man its sunlight and its
flower,
Spring-time of man all April in a face.
Only, as in the jostling in the Strand,
Where the mob thrusts or loiters or is
loud,   20
The beggar with the saucer in his hand
Asks only a penny from the passing
crowd,

So, from this glittering world with all its
fashion,
Its fire, and play of men, its stir, its
march,
Let me have wisdom, Beauty, wisdom
and passion,
Bread to the soul, rain where the summers parch.
Give me but these, and, though the
darkness close
Even the night will blossom as the rose.

Discussion Hints

1. Compare "A Consecration" with the
final lines of W. W. Gibson's "Snug in My
Easy Chair" (p. 605). Compare also "Scum
o' the Earth," by Robert Haven Schauffler
(in the revised edition of *Achievement* of this
series).

2. In "Sea-Fever" there are many feet of
this unusual long swinging pattern, × × ′ ′,
suggestive of the slow-swinging seas. See
how many you can find of this sort.

3. "A Consecration" gains greatly from the
strong dactylic* rhythm and the skillfully
handled trios of rhymes. "Cargoes" is full of
beautiful onomatopoetic* effects that will
repay close study.

4. Compare "On Growing Old" with Li-
zette Woodworth Reese's "Tears" (in the
revised edition of *American Writers* of this
series), which many consider the most beautiful sonnet written by an American poet.

Suggestions for Reading in
A Triumvirate

The poetry of Thomas Hardy, taken as a
whole, is not easy reading; but that fact is no
reason for not reading more of it now, and
much more later: poems such as "The Two
Houses." "Waiting Both," and "'For Life I

[1] From John Masefield's *Enslaved*. By permission of The Macmillan Company, publishers.
[2] Spray from the waves.
[3] A kind of small, old-fashioned piano.

Never Cared Greatly,'" which comment on life; or "We Sat at the Window" and "'Ah, Are You Digging on My Grave?'" on love; "Snow in the Suburbs" and "Wagtail and Baby," on nature. For Hardy's religious verse see page 592; for his short stories and fiction see page 684.

A list of the poems by Kipling that it is taken for granted everyone knows would be a long one. "Danny Deever," "Fuzzy Wuzzy," "Boots," "Tomlinson," "When Earth's Last Picture is Painted," "Mother o' Mine," should certainly be included. There are songs of wanderlust, like "The Feet of the Young Men"; of the sea, like "The Liner She's a Lady"; of England, like "Sussex"; of English history, like "The Looking-Glass." The verse headings of chapters in books like *Just-So Stories* and *The Jungle Books* are delightful.

See suggestions for reading under "Poets of the World War" (p. 600), the "Short Story" (p. 652), and "Narrative Poetry" (p. 631). See also the revised editions of *Adventure* and *Achievement* of this series.

Masefield has written a great deal about the sea in verse, in essay, and in story. Titles of poems that come to mind are "Sea-Change," "'Port of Many Ships,'" and "Roadways." "A Creed" is reminiscent of "A Consecration." Masefield has written many beautiful sonnets besides "On Growing Old." Like those of Shakespeare, they are known by their opening lines:

"I never see the red rose crown the year,"
"Is there a great green commonwealth of thought?"
"Let that which is to come be as it may."

See suggestions for reading under "Poets Who Write on Religious Themes" (p. 592) and under "Poets of the World War" (p. 600). See also the revised editions of *Adventure* and *Achievement* of this series.

Suggestions for Further Reading in Lyric Poetry[1]

The easiest and perhaps the only practical way to suggest readings in modern British poetry is to refer you to a few of the many excellent anthologies of recent poetry. There you can browse to your heart's content.

COOPER, ALICE C. (ED.). *Poems of Today.* Ginn and Company.

GORDON, MARGERY, and KING, MARIE BURNADETTE (Compilers). *Verse of Our Day,* an anthology of modern American and British poetry with studies in poetry. D. Appleton-Century Company, Inc.

MERRILL, A. MARION, and SPRAGUE, GRACE ELIOT WINTHROP (EDS.). *Contemporary Verse.* Little, Brown & Company.

MONROE. HARRIET, and HENDERSON, ALICE CORBIN (EDS.). *The New Poetry:* an anthology of twentieth-century verse in English. The Macmillan Company.

RITTENHOUSE, JESSIE BELLE (Compiler). *A Little Book of Modern British Verse:* one hundred poets since Henley. Houghton Mifflin Company.

STEVENSON, BURTON EGBERT. *The Home Book of Modern Verse:* an extension of *The Home Book of Verse,* being a selection from American and English poetry of the twentieth century. Henry Holt and Company, Inc.

UNTERMEYER, LOUIS (ED.). *Modern British Poetry:* a critical anthology (1830–1930). Harcourt, Brace and Company, Inc.

WILKINSON, MARGUERITE OGDEN. *New Voices:* an introduction to contemporary poetry. The Macmillan Company.

YEATS, W. B. *Oxford Book of Modern Verse, 1892–1935.* The Oxford University Press.

[1] This list, with the exception of the single final addition, is taken in its entirety from *Highroad to English Literature* (Ginn and Company), by Elizabeth Collette.

ESSAYS

A. P. HERBERT[1] (1890-   )

On Drawing

The dignified title "On Drawing" leads the reader to expect a treatise written by an expert on the subject. Therein lies part, at least, of the humor; for Herbert, who knows no more about drawing than does the average untalented and untrained person, speaks throughout with authority. At the same time that A. P. H. (so he signs his articles for *Punch* and his letters to the London *Times*) is, with mock seriousness, discussing one of the arts, he is satirizing the slow and uninteresting meeting of almost any committee. All this is done in language seemingly simple but artistically clear and exact. Of its light, entertaining, merry sort, "On Drawing" can scarcely be improved upon.

IT IS commonly said that everybody can sing in the bathroom; and this is true. Singing is very easy. Drawing, though, is much more difficult. I have devoted a good deal of time to Drawing, one way and another; I have to attend a great many committees and public meetings, and at such functions I find that Drawing is almost the only Art one 10 can satisfactorily pursue during the speeches. One can seldom sing during the speeches; so as a rule, I draw. I do not say that I am an expert yet, but after a few more meetings I calculate that I shall know Drawing as well as it can be known.

The first thing, of course, is to get on to a really good committee; and by a good committee I mean a committee 20 that provides decent materials. An ordinary departmental committee is no use: generally they only give you a couple of pages of lined foolscap and no white blotting-paper, and very often the pencils are quite soft. White blotting-paper is essential. I know of no material the spoiling of which gives so much artistic pleasure — except perhaps snow. Indeed, if I was asked to choose between making pencil-marks on a sheet of white 30 blotting-paper and making foot-marks on a sheet of white snow I should be in a thingummy.[1]

Much the best committees from the point of view of material are committees about business which meet at business premises — shipping offices, for choice. One of the Pacific Lines has the best white blotting-paper I know; and the pencils there are a dream. I am sure the 40 directors of that firm are Drawers; for they always give you two pencils, one hard for doing noses, and one soft for doing hair.

When you have selected your committee and the speeches are well away, the Drawing begins. Much the best thing to draw is a man. Not the chairman, or Lord Pommery Quint, or any member of the committee, but just A Man. Many 50 novices make the mistake of selecting a subject for their Art before they begin. Usually they select the chairman; and when they find it is more like Mr. Gladstone* they are discouraged. If they had waited a little it could have been Mr. Gladstone officially.

[1] Thingumbob, thingumabob. An indefinite word used in the place of a precise word which one cannot at the moment remember. Here used humorously for, perhaps, "dilemma."

[1] For biography see page 743.

As a rule I begin with the forehead and work down to the chin (Fig. 1).

When I have done the outline I put in the eye. This is one of the most difficult parts cf Drawing; one is never

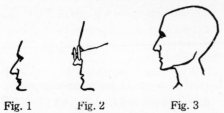

Fig. 1   Fig. 2   Fig. 3

quite sure where the eye goes. If, however, it is not a good eye, a useful tip is to give the man spectacles; this generally makes him a clergyman, but it helps the eye (Fig. 2).

Now you have to outline the rest of the head, and this is rather a gamble. Personally, I go in for *strong* heads (Fig. 3).

I am afraid it is not a strong neck; I expect he is an author, and is not well fed. But that is the worst of strong heads; they make it so difficult to join up the chin and the back of the neck.

The next thing to do is to put in the ear; and once you have done this the rest is easy. Ears are much more difficult than eyes (Fig. 4).

I hope that is right. It seems to me to be a little too far to the southward. But it is done now. And once you have put in the ear you can't go back: not

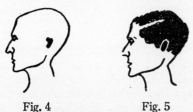

Fig. 4   Fig. 5

unless you are on a *very* good committee which provides india-rubber as well as pencils.

Now I do the hair. Hair may either be very fuzzy and black, or lightish and thin. It depends chiefly on what sort of pencils are provided. For myself I prefer black hair, because then the parting shows up better (Fig. 5).

Until one draws hair, one never realizes what large heads people have. Doing the hair takes the whole of a speech, usually, even one of the chairman's speeches.

This is not one of my best men; I am sure the ear is in the wrong place. And I am inclined to think he ought to have spectacles. Only then he would be a clergyman, and I have decided that he is Sir Philip Gibbs[1] at the age of twenty. So he must carry on with his eye as it is.

I find that all my best men face to the west; it is a curious thing. Sometimes I draw two men facing each other; but the one facing east is always a dud.[2]

Fig. 6   Fig. 7

There, you see (Fig. 7)? The one on the right is a Bolshevik[3]; he has a low forehead and beetling brows — a most unpleasant man. Yet he has a powerful face. The one on the left (Fig. 6) was meant to be another Bolshevik, arguing with him. But he has turned out to be a lady, so I have had to give her a "bun."[4] She is a lady solicitor[5]; but I don't know how she came to be talking to the Bolshevik.

When you have learned how to do Men, the only other things in Drawing are Perspective and Landscape.

[1] A well-known English journalist and novelist.
[2] A shell that fails to explode. Here, a failure.
[3] Here, one who is discontented with the present organization of society. In the comic papers Bolsheviks are usually pictured with whiskers, more or less like those in Mr. Herbert's drawing.
[4] Here, a roll of hair at the back of the head.
[5] Lawyer.

Perspective is great fun: the best thing to do is a long French road with telegraph poles (Fig. 8).

I have put in a fence as well. Unstable, I fear.

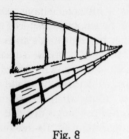

Fig. 8

Landscape is chiefly composed of hills and trees. Trees are the most amusing,
130 especially fluffy trees.

Here is a Landscape (Fig. 9).

Somehow or other a man has got into this landscape; and, as luck would have

Fig. 9

it, it is Napoleon. Apart from this it is not a bad landscape.

But it takes a very long speech to get an ambitious piece of work like this through.

There is one other thing I ought to
140 have said. Never attempt to draw a man front-face. It can't be done.

Discussion Hints

1. What does Herbert mean by a "good" committee?

2. What does he consider the best subject for a drawing?

3. What determines the type of hair?

4. How do the cuts, numbered and referred to in the text as if it were a scientific article, add to the humor?

5. What terms appropriate to maps does Herbert use in speaking of his little drawings?

6. What seems to be wrong with Fig. 8?

7. Does the man in Fig. 9 really look like Napoleon?

8. What words not usually capitalized are capitalized in the essay? Why?

9. What little touches do you like best?

Suggestions for Reading

1. There is much variety in the writing of A. P. Herbert. His gay little essays, many of which are reprinted from *Punch*, come first. They are often about London or at least about matters definitely British. His latest book (1937) is entitled *Sip! Swallow!* (Doubleday, Doran & Company, Inc.).

2. True, A. P. H. has never practiced law, but he has used his training in the law to good effect in Parliament and in books which ridicule the defects and absurdities of English courts. *Misleading Cases in the Common Law* (G. P. Putnam's Sons) has run into several editions.

3. A. P. Herbert writes entertaining, well-made verse, such as *Ballads for Broadbrows and Others* (Doubleday, Doran & Company, Inc.).

H. M. TOMLINSON[1] (1873–   )

The Master

"The Master" is at one and the same time narration, description, and character study. The story is told simply, and, for the convenience of the average reader, from the point of

---

[1] For biography see page 743.

view of a landsman from the city. Tomlinson did not take this angle from necessity; for from the time that he was a mere lad he has known ships and their ways intimately. Here, however, it is not ships nor "that large vacancy, the sea," which holds his attention and ours, so much as a certain young man, a seaman, whom we gradually come to know. As with the sea, on which he spent so much time, there is a mystery about him.

All this is accomplished with an informality suitable to a tale told before an open fire. Do not be misled by the seeming ease of the telling. Tomlinson's rhythmical, cadenced prose is the work of a master craftsman, an artist, if you please. Can you tell just what you enjoy about "The Master," and why?

THIS master of a ship I remember first as a slim lad, with a shy smile, and large hands that were lonely beyond his outgrown reefer jacket. His cap was always too small for him, and the soiled frontal badge of his line[1] became a coloured button beyond his forelock. He used to come home occasionally — and it was always when we were on the point of forgetting him altogether. He came with a huge bolster[2] in a cab, as though out of the past and nowhere. There is a tradition, a book tradition, that the boy apprenticed to the sea acquires saucy eyes, and a self-reliance always ready to dare to that bleak extreme the very thought of which horrifies those who are lawful and cautious. They know better who live where the ships are. He used to bring his young shipmates to see us, and they were like himself. Their eyes were downcast. They showed no self-reliance. Their shyness and politeness, when the occasion was quite simple, were absurdly incommensurate even with modesty. Their sisters, not nearly so polite, used to mock them.

As our own shy lad was never with us for long, his departure being as abrupt and unannounced as his appearance, we could willingly endure him. But he was extraneous to the household. He had the impeding nature of a new and superfluous piece of furniture which is in the way, yet never knows it, and placidly stays where it is, in its wooden manner, till it is placed elsewhere. There was a morning when, as he was leaving the house, during one of his brief visits to his home, I noticed to my astonishment that he had grown taller than myself. How had that happened? And where? I had followed him to the door that morning because, looking down at his cap which he was nervously handling, he had told me he was going then to an examination. About a week later he announced, in a casual way, that he had got his master's ticket. After the first shock of surprise, caused by the fact that this information was an unexpected warning of our advance in years, we were amused, and we congratulated him. Naturally he had got his certificate as master mariner. Why not? Nearly all the mates we knew got it, sooner or later. That was bound to come. But very soon after that he gave us a genuine surprise, and made us anxious. He informed us, as casually, that he had been appointed master to a ship; a very different matter from merely possessing the licence to command.

We were even alarmed. This was serious. He could not do it. He was not the man to make a command for anything. A fellow who, not so long ago, used to walk a mile with a telegram because he had not the strength of character to face the lady clerk in the post office round the corner, was hardly the man to overawe a crowd of hard characters gathered by chance from Tower Hill,[1] socialize them, and direct them successfully in subduing the conflicting elements of a difficult enterprise. Not he. But we said nothing to discourage him.

---

[1] *frontal . . . line* A badge worn on the front of a sailor's cap to identify the line of vessels by which he is employed.

[2] Here, a canvas bag resembling a bolster and used by sailors for carrying their belongings. Commonly called a duffle bag.

[1] A poor district of old London, near the famous Tower of London, where many sailors have their homes.

80　Of course, he was a delightful fellow. He often amused us, and he did not always know why. He was frank, he was gentle, but that large vacancy, the sea, where he had spent most of his young life, had made him — well, slow. You know what I mean. He was curiously innocent of those dangers of great cities which are nothing to us because we know they are there. Yet he was always on 90 the alert for thieves and parasites. I think he enjoyed his belief in their crafty omnipresence ashore. Proud of his alert and knowing intelligence, he would relate a long story of the way he had not only frustrated an artful shark, but had enjoyed the process in perfect safety. That we, who rarely went out of London, never had such adventures, did not strike him as worth a thought or two. He never 100 paused in his merriment to consider the strange fact that to him, alone of our household, such wayside adventures fell. With a shrewd air he would inform us that he was about to put the savings of a voyage into an advertised trap which a country parson[1] would have stepped over without a second contemptuous glance.

He took his ship away. The affair was not discussed at home, though each of us 110 gave it some private despondency. We followed him silently, apprehensively, through the reports in the *Shipping Gazette*. He made point after point safely — St. Vincent, Gibraltar, Suez, Aden — after him we went across to Colombo, Singapore, and at length we learned that he was safe at Batavia. He had got that steamer out all right. He got her home again, too. After his first 120 adventure as master he made voyage after voyage with no more excitement in them than you would find in Sunday walks in a suburb. It was plain luck; or else navigation and seamanship were greatly overrated arts.

A day came when he invited me to go with him part of his voyage. I could leave the ship at Bordeaux. I went. You must remember that we had never seen his ship. And there he was, walking 130 with me to the dock from a Welsh railway station, a man in a cheap mackintosh, with an umbrella I will not describe, and he was carrying a brown paper parcel. He was appropriately crowned with a bowler[1] hat several sizes too small for him. Glancing up at his profile, I actually wondered whether the turmoil was now going on in his mind over that confession which now he was bound to 140 make; that he was not the master of a ship, and never had been.

There she was, a bulky modern freighter, full of derricks and time-saving appliances, and her funnel lording it over the neighbourhood. The man with the parcel under his arm led me up the gangway. I was not yet convinced. I was, indeed, less sure than ever that he could be the master of this huge community 150 of engines and men. He did not accord with it.

We were no sooner on deck than a man in uniform, grey-haired, with a seamed and resolute face, which anyone would have recognized at once as a sailor's, approached us. He was introduced as the chief officer. He had a tale of woe: trouble with the dock-master, with the stevedores, with the cargo, with many 160 things. He did not appear to know what to do with them. He was asking this boy of ours.

The skipper began to speak. At that moment I was gazing at the funnel, trying to decipher a monogram upon it; but I heard a new voice, rapid and incisive, sure of its subject, resolving doubts, and making the crooked straight. It was the man with the brown paper 170 parcel. It was still under his arm — in fact, the parcel contained pink pyjamas, and there was hardly enough paper. The respect of the mate was not lessened by this.

[1] Country preachers are supposedly easy marks.

[1] Americans would say stiff hat or derby.

Burton Holmes, from Galloway

There she was, a bulky modern freighter

The skipper went to gaze down a hatchway. He walked to the other side of the ship, and inspected something there. Conned her length, called up in a 180 friendly but authoritative way to an engineer standing by an amidship rail above. He came back to the mate, and with an easy precision directed his will on others, through his deputy, up to the time of sailing. He beckoned to me, who also, apparently, was under his august orders, and turned, as though perfectly aware that in this place I should follow him meekly, in full obedience.

190 Our steamer moved out at midnight, in a drive of wind and rain. There were bewildering and unrelated lights about us. Peremptory challenges were shouted to us from nowhere. Sirens blared out of dark voids. And there was the skipper on the bridge, the lad who caused us amusement at home, with this confusion in the dark about him, and an immense insentient[1] mass moving with him at 200 his will; and he had his hands in his pockets, and turned to tell me what a cold night it was. The pier-head search-light showed his face, alert, serene, with his brows knitted in a little frown, and his underlip projecting as the sign of the pride of those who look direct into the eyes of an opponent, and care not at all. In my berth that night I searched for a moral for this narrative, 210 but went to sleep before I found it.

Discussion Hints

1. What do you think is the relationship of the author to the lad who became "the master"?

[1] Without feeling, unconscious.

2. Follow the new "master" on his first command. Locate every port.

3. What detail makes the young seaman seem most incompetent ashore? What makes him most competent aboard ship?

4. Contrast the untrue picture of the young seaman drawn in the first part of the essay with the real young man you come to know at the end.

5. What do you think is the moral of the tale?

6. Are you acquainted with anyone who, like Tomlinson's young seaman, appears to change his character as soon as he shoulders real responsibility? He may be a clerk or a mechanic, or of any other calling. If you do, write a sketch about him, and try to imitate Tomlinson's method.

Suggestions for Reading

1. Of Tomlinson's books of essays and sketches, *London River* (from which "The Master" is taken), the earlier *Old Junk*, and the more recent *Out of Soundings* stand out. The first two were published by Alfred A. Knopf, Inc. All other books referred to here are published by Harper & Brothers.

2. In his essays, with their sea-worthy titles, Tomlinson is seldom far from water. In his books of travel, *The Sea and the Jungle* (across the Atlantic and up the Amazon), *Tide Marks* ("to the beaches of the Moluccas and the forest of Malaya"), and *South to Cadiz* (to lovely Spain), ocean and river play a big part.

3. Besides essays and travel Tomlinson has written several novels. Especially fine are *Gallion's Reach*, a tale of an accidental murderer whose wanderings take him to the Malaya, and the recent *Pipe All Hands*, a story of a tramp steamer and her crew.

WILLIAM McFEE[1] (1881-   )

The Market

To most persons who know his work, William McFee and the sea not only rhyme but are synonymous; for immediately there come to mind his essays and sketches, his tales and novels, many of which have ships and the sea for their setting. Although it is true that he was born at sea and served as a seagoing engineer for years, yet William McFee knows something of the world besides the rolling deep. Our sea-born author grew up in a London suburb. He knows many lands at which his ships have touched, especially in the Central-American and South-American countries which the liners of the United Fruit Company serve. McFee belongs very definitely to North America too; for in 1922 he settled in Westport, Connecticut, and has since married an American woman. In interesting fashion "The Market," a short seven-paragraph descriptive essay, touches on many phases of McFee's experiences.

In 1908, while he was preparing for an engineering examination, McFee lived in chambers (so the English call rooms once occupied by law students) in ancient Clifford's Inn ("Inn" is another ancient term applied to buildings once used as law students' quarters). Now Clifford's Inn, situated in Fleet Street, the newspaper row of modern London, bore over its ancient archway the date 1472.[2] Within sight, from its deep-set windows, was the Strand, one of the busiest thoroughfares in the world. Out from that ancient gate sauntered William McFee early one bright summer morning with a young woman companion dressed in what we should call fancy dress, to visit the London produce market; when, presto! in his vivid, fresh prose he whisks us off with him to banana-land, Colombia, that northernmost country of South America, whose mountain peaks lazily overlook the blue Caribbean. Not only has McFee unusual skill in expression, but he has many worth-while things to say.

THERE is a sharp, imperative rap on my outer door; a rap having within its insistent urgency a shadow of delicate diffidence, as though the person re- sponsible were a trifle scared of the performance and on tiptoe to run away. I roll over and regard the clock. Four-forty. One of the dubious by-products of continuous service as a senior assistant at sea is the habit of waking automati- cally about four A.M. This gives one several hours, when ashore, to meditate upon one's sins, frailties, and (more rarely) triumphs and virtues. Because a man who gets up at say, four-thirty, is regarded with aversion ashore. His family express themselves with superfluous vigour. He must lie still and meditate, or suffer the ignominy of being asked when he is going away again.

But this morning, in these old Chambers in an ancient Inn buried in the heart of London City,[1] I have agreed to get up and go out. The reason for this momentous departure from a life of temporary but deliberate indolence is a lady. "Cherchez la femme,"[2] as the French say with the dry animosity of a logical race. Well, she is not far to seek, being on the outside of my heavy oak door tapping, as already hinted, with a sharp, insistent delicacy. To this romantic summons I reply with an inarticulate growl of acquiescence, and proceed to get ready. To relieve the anxiety of any reader who imagines an impending elopement it may be stated in succinct truthfulness that we are bound on no such desperate venture. We are going round the corner a few blocks up the Strand, to Covent* Garden Market, to see the arrival of the metropolitan supply of produce.

Having accomplished a hasty toilet, almost as primitive as that favoured by

---

[1] For biography see page 744.
[2] Clifford's Inn was torn down in 1935.

[1] The old city, once surrounded by a wall with a ditch and great gates, today quite swallowed up in greater London.
[2] Cherchez la femme. Find the woman.

gentlemen aroused to go on watch, and placating an occasional repetition of the tapping by brief protests and reports of 50 progress, I take hat and cane, and drawing the huge antique bolts of my door, discover a young woman standing by the window looking out upon the quadrangle of the old inn. She is a very decided young woman, who is continually thinking out what she calls "stunts" for articles in the press. That is her profession, or one of her professions — writing articles for the press. The other 60 profession is selling manuscripts, which constitutes the tender bond between us. For the usual agent's commission she is selling one of my manuscripts. Being an unattached and, as it were, unprotected male, she plans little excursions about London to keep me instructed and entertained. Here she is attired in the flamboyant finery of a London flower-girl. She is about to get the necessary copy 70 for a special article in a morning paper. With the exception of a certain expectant flash of her bright black Irish eyes, she is entirely businesslike. Commenting on the beauty of an early summer morning in town, we descend, and passing out under the ponderous ancient archway, we make our leisurely progress westward down the Strand.

London is always beautiful to those 80 who love and understand that extraordinary microcosm; but at five of a summer morning there is about her an exquisite quality of youthful fragrance and debonair freshness which goes to the heart. The newly hosed streets are shining in the sunlight as though paved with "patins of bright gold."[1] Early 'buses rumble by from neighbouring barns where they have spent the night. And,

as we near the new Gaiety Theatre, 90 thrusting forward into the great rivers of traffic soon to pour round its base like some bold Byzantine[1] promontory, we see Waterloo Bridge thronged with wagons, piled high. From all quarters they are coming, past Charing Cross the great wains are arriving from Paddington Terminus,[2] from the market-garden section of Middlesex and Surrey.[3] Down Wellington Street come carts laden with 100 vegetables from Brentwood and Coggleshall;[4] and neat vans packed with crates of watercress which grows in the lush lowlands of Suffolk and Cambridgeshire;[5] and behind us are thundering huge four-horse vehicles from the docks,[6] vehicles with peaches from South Africa, potatoes from the Canary Islands, onions from France, apples from California, oranges from the West Indies, pineapples 110 from Central America, grapes from Spain and bananas from Colombia.

We turn in under an archway behind a theatre and adjacent to the stage-door of the Opera House.[7] The booths are rapidly filling with produce. Gentlemen in long alpaca coats and carrying formidable marbled note-books walk about with an important air. A mountain range of pumpkins rises behind a hill of 120 cabbages. Festoons of onions are being suspended from rails. The heads of barrels are being knocked in, disclosing purple grapes buried in cork-dust.

---

[1] Patins are the little flat plates used in the Communion service of certain churches. The quotation is taken from a famous passage in Shakespeare's *Merchant of Venice* (V, i, 58). See also "Nature," by Margaret Deland, in the revised edition of *Adventure* of this series.

[1] Byzantium* was the old name for Constantinople, or Istanbul, on the Golden* Horn, through which the trade of two continents passed.

[2] A railway station.

[3] *Middlesex . . . Surrey*. Level midland counties on the Thames, not far from London.

[4] *Brentwood . . . Coggleshall*. Towns in the market-garden country northeast of London and close to it.

[5] *Suffolk . . . Cambridgeshire*. Flat, swampy counties northeast of London.

[6] On the river Thames, which accommodates ocean liners as well as smaller craft.

[7] For many years there has been a famous flower market on the south side of the Covent Garden Opera House.

Pears and figs, grown under glass for wealthy patrons, repose in soft tissue-lined boxes. A broken crate of Tangerine oranges has spilled its contents in a splash of ruddy gold on the plank run-130 way. A wagon is driven in, a heavy load of beets, and the broad wheels crush through the soft fruit so that the air is heavy with the acrid sweetness.

We pick our way among the booths and stalls until we find the flowers. Here is a crowd of ladies — young, so-so, and some quite matronly, and all dressed in this same flamboyant finery of which I have spoken. They are grouped about 140 an almost overpowering mass of blooms. Roses just now predominate. There is a satisfying solidity about the bunches, a glorious abundance which, in a commodity so easily enjoyed without ownership, is scarcely credible. I feel no desire to own these huge aggregations of odorous beauty. It would be like owning a harem, one imagines. Violets, solid patches of vivid blue in round baskets, 150 eglantine[1] in dainty boxes, provide a foil to the majestic blazonry of the roses and the dew-spangled forest of maiden-hair fern near by.

"And what are those things at all?" demands my companion, diverted for a moment from the flowers. She nods toward a mass of dull-green affairs piled on mats or being lifted from big vans. She is a cockney[2] and displays surprise 160 when she is told those things are bananas. She shrugs and turns again to the musk-roses, and forgets. But to me, as the harsh, penetrating odour of the green fruit cuts across the heavy perfume of the flowers, comes a picture of the farms in distant Colombia or perhaps Costa Rica. There is nothing like an odour to stir memories. I see the timber pier and the long line of rackety open-slatted cars

jangling into the dark shed, pushed by a 170 noisy, squealing locomotive. I see the boys lying asleep between shifts, their enormous straw hats covering their faces as they sprawl. In the distance rise the blue mountains; behind is the motionless blue sea. I hear the whine of the elevators, the monotonous click of the counters, the harsh cries of irresponsible and argumentative natives. I feel the heat of the tropic day, and see the gleam 180 of the white waves breaking on yellow sands below tall palms. I recall the mysterious, impenetrable solitude of the jungle, a solitude alive, if one is equipped with knowledge, with a ceaseless warfare of winged and crawling hosts. And while my companion is busily engaged in getting copy for a special article about the Market, I step nimbly out of the way of a swarthy gentleman from Calabria,[1] 190 who with his two-wheeled barrow is the last link in the immense chain of transportation connecting the farmer in the distant tropics and the cockney pedestrian who halts on the sidewalk and purchases a banana for a couple of pennies.

Discussion Hints

1. Find several comments which suggest that McFee is woman-shy.

2. What are the two professions of McFee's companion?

3. Does McFee actually carry a cane at 4.30 in the morning? How do you explain such seeming foppishness?

4. In *The Century Cyclopedia of Names*, Volume XI of the Century Dictionary and Cyclopedia, or in some special book dealing with London, look up such items as the following: the Strand, Covent* Garden, Covent Garden Market, Covent Garden Theatre, Charing Cross. Report your findings on these topics to the class.

5. Locate all the countries which McFee mentions as sources of food for London. Is he correct in each case?

---

[1] The sweetbrier, the European wild rose, which has single pink flowers.
[2] A born Londoner. Here, one who has seldom, if ever, been outside of London.

D

[1] Southwestern Italy, the toe of the boot.

6. From your home refrigerator or pantry or kitchen cupboard list some two dozen articles. Tell where each probably came from. Or account for every item on the dinner table tonight.

7. "There is nothing like an odor to stir memories." Prove this statement true from your own experience.

Words and Phrases to be Explained

frailties (p. 623, l. 13)

ignominy (p. 623, l. 19)

the dry animosity of a logical race (p. 623, ll. 29–30)

an inarticulate growl of acquiescence (p. 623, ll. 34–35)

flamboyant (p. 624, ll. 67–68)

debonair (p. 624, l. 84)

acrid (p. 625, l. 133)

aggregations of odorous beauty (p. 625, ll. 146–147)

irresponsible and argumentative natives (p. 625, ll. 178–179)

cockney pedestrian (p. 625, ll. 194–195)

Suggestions for Reading

1. Most often read of McFee's volumes of essays and sketches are *Harbours of Memory*, from which "The Market" is taken, and its companion volume, *More Harbours of Memory*. Especially interesting to Americans are the dedication of the first to Christopher Morley, whom McFee calls "my first pilot into the ports of American journalism," and "On Living in America," in the second.

2. Illuminating to readers of "The Market" is *Sunlight in New Granada*, sketches of banana-land, where steamers of the United Fruit Company, in which McFee served, often made port. New Granada was the name of the old viceroyalty, rechristened Colombia when the country became a republic. *Swallowing the Anchor* is still another collection, essays mostly on literary subjects and books.

3. A good supplement to McFee's essays is furnished by his novels *Casuals of the Sea* and *Command*. Doubleday, Doran & Company, Inc., publish McFee's books.

Suggestions for Further Reading in the Essay

1. There is scarcely an English writer of importance in any field who has not done some writing of essays or biography. Take, for instance, the prefaces to Bernard Shaw's plays and the personal comments that Barrie sprinkles so generously through his plays. Take too these excursions into biography: Arnold Bennett's *Journal of Arnold Bennett* (The Viking Press, Inc.), Joseph Conrad's *Personal Record* (Doubleday, Doran & Company, Inc.), Rudyard Kipling's *Something of Myself: for My Friends Known and Unknown* (Doubleday, Doran & Company, Inc.), and H. G. Wells's *Experiment in Autobiography* (The Macmillan Company).

2. More truly essays are Conrad's *Mirror of the Sea* (Doubleday, Doran & Company, Inc.) and John Galsworthy's *Inn of Tranquillity* (Charles Scribner's Sons).

3. G. K. Chesterton, poet, writer of mystery stories, and biographer, was an essayist first of all. Among his titles are *All Is Grist*, *All I Survey*, and *Fancies Versus Fads* (Dodd, Mead & Company, Inc.).

4. In England the writing of E. V. Lucas is published by Methuen & Co., Ltd., a concern of which he was the distinguished head. See *Who's Who* (before 1939, since he died in 1938) for the list of his works. Several publishers have brought out his books in the United States. *Slowcoach* and the Wanderer Series, *Wanderer in Florence*, *Wanderer in Holland*, and *Wanderer in Venice*, are publications of The Macmillan Company. E. P. Dutton & Co., Inc., publish *A Rover I Would Be*, *At the Shrine of St. Charles*, *Stray Papers on Lamb*, and *Turning Things Over*; and J. B. Lippincott Company publish *All of a Piece*, *London Afresh*, and *Only the Other Day*.

5. The list of English essayists is a long one. Here there is space for the titles of only a very few books of essays by the following:

BEERBOHM, MAX. *Seven Men* (Alfred A. Knopf, Inc.).

BELLOC, HILAIRE. *Selected Essays* (J. B. Lippincott Company), *Essays of a Catholic* (The Macmillan Company), and *The Path to Rome* (G. P. Putnam's Sons).

BENSON, EDWARD FREDERIC. *As We Are* (Longmans, Green & Co.).

HUDSON, WILLIAM HENRY. *Afoot in England, Birds and Man* (Alfred A. Knopf, Inc.), and *The Purple Land* (E. P. Dutton & Co., Inc.).

See also "Suggestions for Reading in the Light Essay" in the revised edition of *Achievement* of this series.

6. In biography you may go far by merely following the lead provided by Strachey's *Queen Victoria* (Harcourt, Brace and Company, Inc.). Read everything you can lay hands on by Strachey or on Victoria. Three other twentieth-century Englishmen who stand out as biographers are:

BELLOC, HILAIRE. *Marie Antoinette* and *Robespierre* (G. P. Putnam's Sons); *Cromwell: A Biography* and *Charles the First: King of England* (J. B. Lippincott Company).

CHESTERTON, G. K. *Robert Browning* (The Macmillan Company) and *Charles Dickens* (Dodd, Mead & Company, Inc.).

GUEDALLA, PHILIP. *Wellington* (Harper & Brothers).

7. Excellent prose is written in other fields. Philip Guedalla, in *The Hundred Years* (1837– 1936) (Doubleday, Doran & Company, Inc.), takes a long view of a century of history. H. G. Wells called himself a journalist, meaning that he wrote for his age, not for the future. *The Shape of Things to Come* and the widely read *Outline of History* (The Macmillan Company) are two of his many titles. Sir Philip Gibbs is more widely read in England than in the United States. His *European Journey* and *Ordeal in England* (Doubleday, Doran & Company, Inc.) have American publishers also.

8. With the advent of the radio the speech has assumed new importance. Barrie and Shaw will be hard to beat as after-dinner speakers. Besides "Courage," Barrie's best-known speech, there is easily available "The Entrancing Life," the address delivered by Barrie on his installation in 1930 as chancellor of the University of Edinburgh. Charles Scribner's Sons.

Preachers who hail from Great Britain may be heard at the turn of the dial. British leaders in many fields speak to their American cousins as well as to the world-wide British Empire.

NARRATIVE POETRY

RUDYARD KIPLING[1] (1865-1936)

The Ballad of East and West

Some like "The Ballad of East and West" for its swinging, striding meter; some, for its vigorous diction, its daring imagery; some, for the swiftness of its heroic narrative. Its theme, which Kipling announces in the last two lines of the opening stanza, a stanza repeated at the end, has been a favorite in English poetry since the days of *Beowulf* (p. 20).

Lovers of Kipling's verse find here the Indian flavor his poems and stories often have; for the tale is laid in the distant North-West Frontier Province of India, on the borders of Afghanistan. There, as you will remember, is the famous Khyber Pass, an ancient mountain gateway by which for centuries, through a thirty-three-mile defile, trade has passed between Afghanistan and the West, and India and the East. The pass begins just a little over ten miles west of Peshawur, the capital of the British-controlled North-West Frontier Province. Twice a week caravans pass through, guided by expert Afghan horsemen and marksmen under British command, and thus protected against raids from hostile robber bands. In this stupendous and difficult frontier country, where the high valley of Peshawur abruptly stops, and steep gray mountains rise from its edge, our story takes place, a story fine enough, big enough, not to be dwarfed by its setting.

O*H, EAST is East, and West is West,*
* and never the twain shall meet,*
Till Earth and Sky stand presently at
* God's great Judgment Seat;*
But there is neither East nor West, Border,
* nor Breed, nor Birth,*
When two strong men stand face to face,
* though they come from the ends of the*
* earth!*

[1] For biography see page 742.

Kamal[1] is out with twenty men to raise
  the Border side,
And he has lifted[2] the Colonel's mare that
  is the Colonel's pride.
He has lifted her out of the stable-door
  between the dawn and the day,
And turned the calkins[3] upon her feet,
  and ridden her far away.
Then up and spoke the Colonel's son
  that led a troop of the Guides:
"Is there never a man of all my men can
  say where Kamal hides?"   10
Then up and spoke Mahommed Khan,
  the son of the Ressaldar[4]:
"If ye know the track of the morning-
  mist, ye know where his pickets
  are.
"At dusk he harries the Abazai[5] — at
  dawn he is into Bonair,
"But he must go by Fort Bukloh to his
  own place to fare.
"So if ye gallop to Fort Bukloh as fast as
  a bird can fly,
"By the favour of God ye may cut
  him off ere he win to the Tongue of
  Jagai.
"But if he be past the Tongue of Jagai,
  right swiftly turn ye then,
"For the length and the breadth of that
  grisly plain is sown with Kamal's
  men.

[1] *Kamal* (kä'mǎl). A leader of a robber tribe.
[2] Stolen.
[3] *turned the calkins.* Reversed the shoes. The calkins are the turned-down points on the back of a horseshoe which raise the horse's heels from the ground.
[4] *Ressaldar* (rĕs ǎl där'). Native commander of a troop of Indian cavalry.   [5] An enemy tribe.

"There is rock to the left, and rock to the right, and low lean thorn between,
"And ye may hear a breech-bolt[1] snick where never a man is seen." 20
The Colonel's son has taken horse, and a raw rough dun was he,
With the mouth of a bell and the heart of Hell and the head of a gallows-tree.
The Colonel's son to the Fort has won, they bid him stay to eat —
Who rides at the tail of a Border thief, he sits not long at his meat.
He's up and away from Fort Bukloh as fast as he can fly,
Till he was aware of his father's mare in the gut of the Tongue of Jagai,
Till he was aware of his father's mare with Kamal upon her back,
And when he could spy the white of her eye, he made the pistol crack.
He has fired once, he has fired twice, but the whistling ball went wide.
"Ye shoot like a soldier," Kamal said. "Show now if ye can ride!" 30
It's up and over the Tongue of Jagai, as blown dust-devils go,
The dun he fled like a stag of ten,[2] but the mare like a barren doe.
The dun he leaned against the bit and slugged[3] his head above,
But the red mare played with the snaffle-bars,[4] as a maiden plays with a glove.
There was rock to the left and rock to the right, and low lean thorn between,
And thrice he heard a breech-bolt snick tho' never a man was seen.
They have ridden the low moon out of the sky, their hoofs drum up the dawn,
The dun he went like a wounded bull, but the mare like a new-roused fawn.

The dun he fell at a water-course — in a woeful heap fell he,
And Kamal has turned the red mare back, and pulled the rider free. 40
He has knocked the pistol out of his hand — small room was there to strive,
"'Twas only by favour of mine," quoth he, "ye rode so long alive:
"There was not a rock for twenty mile, there was not a clump of tree,
"But covered a man of my own men with his rifle cocked on his knee.
"If I had raised my bridle-hand, as I have held it low,
"The little jackals that flee so fast were feasting all in a row.
"If I had bowed my head on my breast, as I have held it high,
"The kite that whistles above us now were gorged till she could not fly."
Lightly answered the Colonel's son: "Do good to bird and beast,
"But count who come for the broken meats[1] before thou makest a feast. 50
"If there should follow a thousand swords to carry my bones away,
"Belike the price of a jackal's meal were more than a thief could pay.
"They will feed their horse on the standing crop, their men on the garnered grain.
"The thatch of the byres[2] will serve their fires when all the cattle are slain.
"But if thou thinkest the price be fair, — thy brethren wait to sup,
"The hound is kin to the jackal-spawn, — howl, dog, and call them up!
"And if thou thinkest the price be high, in steer and gear and stack,
"Give me my father's mare again, and I'll fight my own way back!"

[1] Part of the loading mechanism of a breech-loading rifle.
[2] stag of ten. A stag with ten tines, or points. on his antlers.
[3] Jerked, struck with.
[4] The small bars of iron that are joined with a ring to make a bit which moves easily in a horse's mouth.

[1] broken meats. Fragments of food. The whole line means "Consider those who come after the feast is over; that is, count the cost."
[2] Cow sheds.

Two strong men stand face to face

Kamal has gripped him by the hand and
    set him upon his feet.   59
"No talk shall be of dogs," said he,
    "when wolf and grey wolf meet.
"May I eat dirt if thou hast hurt of me
    in deed or breath;
"What dam of lances brought thee forth
    to jest at the dawn with Death?"
Lightly answered the Colonel's son: "I
    hold by the blood of my clan:
"Take up the mare for my father's gift —
    by God, she has carried a man!"
The red mare ran to the Colonel's son,
    and nuzzled against his breast;
"We be two strong men," said Kamal
    then, "but she loveth the younger
    best.
"So she shall go with a lifter's dower,[1]
    my turquoise-studded rein,
"My 'broidered saddle and saddle-cloth,
    and silver stirrups twain."
The Colonel's son a pistol drew, and held
    it muzzle-end,

"Ye have taken the one from a foe,"
    said he. "Will ye take the mate
    from a friend?"   70
"A gift for a gift," said Kamal straight;
    "a limb for the risk of a limb.
"Thy father has sent his son to me, I'll
    send my son to him!"
With that he whistled his only son, that
    dropped from a mountain-crest —
He trod the ling[1] like a buck in spring,
    and he looked like a lance in rest.
"Now here is thy master," Kamal said,
    "who leads a troop of the Guides,
"And thou must ride at his left side as
    shield on shoulder rides.
"Till Death or I cut loose the tie, at
    camp and board and bed,
"Thy life is his — thy fate it is to guard
    him with thy head.
"So, thou must eat the White Queen's
    meat, and all her foes are thine,
"And thou must harry thy father's hold
    for the peace of the Border-line. 80

[1] *lifter's dower*. Thief's gift. See line 6.

[1] Heather.

"And thou must make a trooper tough
and hack thy way to power —
"Belike they will raise thee to Ressaldar
when I am hanged in Peshawur."

They have looked each other between the
eyes, and there they have found no
fault.
They have taken the Oath of the Brother-
in-Blood on leavened bread and salt:
They have taken the Oath of the Brother-
in-Blood on fire and fresh-cut sod,
On the hilt and the haft of the Khyber[1]
knife, and the Wondrous Names of
God.
The Colonel's son he rides the mare and
Kamal's boy the dun,
And two have come back to Fort Bukloh
where there went forth but one.
And when they drew to the Quarter-
Guard, full twenty swords flew clear—
There was not a man but carried his feud
with the blood of the mountaineer.
"Ha' done! ha' done!" said the
Colonel's son. "Put up the steel at
your sides!   91
"Last night ye had struck at a Border
thief — to-night 'tis a man of the
Guides!"

*Oh, East is East, and West is West, and
never the twain shall meet,*
*Till Earth and Sky stand presently at God's
great Judgment Seat;*
*But there is neither East nor West, Border,
nor Breed, nor Birth,*
*When two strong men stand face to face,
though they come from the ends of the
earth!*

Discussion Hints

1. Why did Kamal turn the calkins?
2. What particular birds and beasts are
referred to in line 49?
3. What does the colonel's son daringly
call Kamal in line 56? What does Kamal
call himself and the colonel's son in line 60?
4. Who is the "White Queen"?
5. Note the metaphors and similes in lines

[1] Here, Afghan.

22, 32, 34, and 38. Which ones seem particularly appropriate to this poem?
6. What lines of Mahommed Khan's are
repeated later in the poem? Why?
7. What is the antecedent of "his," in line
90? What does the line mean?
8. Exactly where is the crisis, or turning
point, of the story?
9. What is it that Kamal admires so in
the colonel's son? How does he prove his
admiration?
10. How much time does this story cover?
11. Just why does Kipling repeat the introductory stanza at the end? Is its meaning any
clearer after you have read the story of Kamal
and the colonel's son? As the world gets
smaller and the East and West rub elbows does
the truth of Kipling's famous stanza become
more evident? Memorize the stanza.
12. In what respects does the language of
the poem suggest the popular ballad (p. 57)?
13. How does the underlying theme of the
poem suggest *Beowulf* (p. 20)?

Suggestions for Reading

1. "The Ballad of East and West" is an excellent point of departure into the realm of
Kipling's India. See especially the *Departmental Ditties* and *Barrack Room Ballads.*
Kipling's collected poetry may be had best in
*Rudyard Kipling's Verse, Inclusive Edition,
1885–1932.* Doubleday, Doran & Company,
Inc., are Kipling's American publishers. See
also "Gunga Din" in the revised edition of
Adventure of this series, and "If" in the revised edition of *Achievement* of this series.
2. For Kipling's fiction laid in India turn to
Soldiers Three, to "Wee Willie Winkie," a
story of the Border country; to his Jungle
Books (see "Rikki-tikki-tavi," p. 642); and
to *Kim,* which, in the story of a white boy who
thought he was brown, pictures India from
the English, native, Hindoo, and secret-service
angles.
3. In addition, there are several interesting
books of travel laid in the Indian Frontier
country:

SINCLAIR, GORDON. *Foot-loose in India.*
Farrar & Rinehart, Inc.
THOMAS, LOWELL. *Beyond Khyber Pass.*
Grosset & Dunlap.
TRINKLER, EMIL. *Through the Heart of
Afghanistan.* Houghton Mifflin Company.

WILLIAM BUTLER YEATS[1] (1865–1939)

The Ballad of the Foxhunter[2]

Narrative poems often stretch to great length. "The Ballad of the Foxhunter," with its touching picture of an old hard-riding, sport-loving Irish squire, tells only of his death, yet suggests much of the years that went before : his love of life, of the outdoors, of his horse and dogs, of huntsmen and servants, and of their devotion to him. Such compression, such use of description to suggest events not told, is artistry of the finest sort.

L AY me in a cushioned chair;
   Carry me, ye four,
With cushions here and cushions there,
To see the world once more.

'To stable and to kennel go;
Bring what is there to bring;
Lead my Lollard to and fro,
Or gently in a ring.

'Put the chair upon the grass:
Bring Rody and his hounds,   10
That I may contented pass
From these earthly bounds.'

His eyelids droop, his head falls low,
His old eyes cloud with dreams;
The sun upon all things that grow
Falls in sleepy streams.

Brown Lollard treads upon the lawn,
And to the armchair goes,
And now the old man's dreams are gone,
He smooths the long brown nose.   20

And now moves many a pleasant tongue
Upon his wasted hands,
For leading aged hounds and young
The huntsman near him stands.

'Huntsman Rody, blow the horn,
Make the hills reply.'

The huntsman loosens on the morn
A gay wandering cry.

Fire is in the old man's eyes,
His fingers move and sway,   30
And when the wandering music dies
They hear him feebly say,

'Huntsman Rody, blow the horn,
Make the hills reply.'
'I cannot blow upon my horn,
I can but weep and sigh.'

Servants round his cushioned place
Are with new sorrow wrung;
Hounds are gazing on his face,
Aged hounds and young.   40

One blind hound only lies apart
On the sun-smitten grass;
He holds deep commune with his heart:
The moments pass and pass;

The blind hound with a mournful din
Lifts slow his wintry head;
The servants bear the body in;
The hounds wail for the dead.

Discussion Hints

1. Notice how the twelve stanzas fall into groups of four. What is the theme or event that gives unity to each of these groups?

2. Prove that the old foxhunter has been ill for a long time.

3. For what is the foxhunter waiting in the fourth stanza? For what are they all waiting in the tenth stanza?

4. Why is it appropriate for lines 33–34 to repeat lines 25–26?

5. It is an ancient custom for sons and daughters to gather about the deathbed of the head of the family. Who make up the "family" of the old foxhunter?

6. Who is first to be aware of the foxhunter's death? Have you heard or read other

[1] For biography see page 736.
[2] From William Butler Yeats's *Early Poems and Stories*. By permission of the author's estate and The Macmillan Company, publishers.

Hounds are gazing on his face,
Aged hounds and young

FROM A PAINTING BY PAUL BROWN

stories that contain the idea of the keen perception of dogs in connection with their masters?

7. In what respects does the stanza form of the poem resemble that of the popular ballad (p. 57)? In what respects does it differ from it?

Suggestions for Reading

1. Yeats, who wrote for over half a century, beginning when he was a lad in his teens, has much poetry and many plays to his credit. For his lyrics see page 581. Of his plays, Irish folk tragedies and fairy plays most of them, the most famous is *The Land of Heart's Desire.* The Macmillan Company is his publisher.

2. *Reynard the Fox* is one of the most enjoyable of the longer poems of John Masefield, poet laureate. In Part I English countryfolk gather at the inn to watch the hunt get under way. In Part II Reynard the fox becomes the hero and manages to elude his pursuers. Of the same sort are *Right Royal,* a tale of a horse, and *King Cole,* a tale of a circus. All are published by The Macmillan Company.

3. There are several old English ballads that have to do with hunting: "Lord Randal" (p. 60), "Edward" (p. 64), "The Hunting of the Cheviot" (or "Chevy Chase," as it is sometimes called). The Robin Hood ballads (see the revised edition of *Adventure* of this series), laid in Sherwood Forest, are surrounded by the atmosphere of hunting in the greenwood. See page 68 of this book and page 89 of *Highroad to English Literature* (Ginn and Company), by Elizabeth Collette, for lists of collections of old English ballads.

OSCAR WILDE[1] (1856–1900)
From "The Ballad of Reading Gaol"

"The Ballad of Reading Gaol" is a poignant portrayal of the feelings of men in prison when one of them is condemned to be hanged. All the hopelessness and black despair of those deprived of liberty are revealed in its throbbing lines. With extraordinarily tragic effect the horror of the last day is depicted. So simply told as to seem artless and childlike, the poem is in reality white-hot with passionate and bitter irony.* Wilde spoke from experience, for he had been in prison, in Reading Gaol itself. "Out of the abundance of the heart the mouth speaketh."

I
[The first day.]

HE DID not wear his scarlet coat,
    For blood and wine are red,
And blood and wine were on his hands
    When they found him with the dead,
The poor dead woman whom he loved,
    And murdered in her bed.

He walked amongst the Trial Men
    In a suit of shabby grey;
A cricket cap was on his head,
    And his step seemed light and gay; 10
But I never saw a man who looked
    So wistfully at the day.

[1] For biography see page 744.

I never saw a man who looked
    With such a wistful eye
Upon that little tent of blue
    Which prisoners call the sky,
And at every drifting cloud that went
    With sails of silver by.

I walked, with other souls in pain,
    Within another ring,   20
And was wondering if the man had done
    A great or little thing,
When a voice behind me whispered low,
    "*That fellow's got to swing.*"

Dear Christ! the very prison walls
    Suddenly seemed to reel,
And the sky above my head became
    Like a casque of scorching steel;
And, though I was a soul in pain,
    My pain I could not feel.   30

I only knew what hunted thought
    Quickened his step, and why
He looked upon the garish day
    With such a wistful eye;
The man had killed the thing he loved,
    And so he had to die.

IV

[The last day.]

There is no chapel on the day
  On which they hang a man:
The Chaplain's heart is far too sick,
  Or his face is far too wan,   40
Or there is that written in his eyes
  Which none should look upon.

So they kept close till nigh on noon,
  And then they rang the bell,
And the Warders with their jingling keys
  Opened each listening cell,
And down the iron stairs we tramped,
  Each from his separate Hell.

Out into God's sweet air we went,
  But not in wonted way,   50
For this man's face was white with fear,
  And that man's face was grey,
And I never saw sad men who looked
  So wistfully at the day.

I never saw sad men who looked
  With such a wistful eye
Upon that little tent of blue
  We prisoners call the sky,
And at every careless cloud that passed
  In happy freedom by.   60

. . . .

The Warders strutted up and down,
  And kept their herd of brutes,
Their uniforms were spick and span,
  And they wore their Sunday suits,
But we knew the work they had been at,
  By the quicklime on their boots.

For where a grave had opened wide,
  There was no grave at all:
Only a stretch of mud and sand
  By the hideous prison-wall,   70
And a little heap of burning lime,
  That the man should have his pall.

For he has a pall, this wretched man,
  Such as few men can claim:
Deep down below a prison-yard,
  Naked for greater shame,
He lies, with fetters on each foot,
  Wrapt in a sheet of flame!

And all the while the burning lime
  Eats flesh and bone away,   80
It eats the brittle bone by night,
  And the soft flesh by day,
It eats the flesh and bone by turns,
  But it eats the heart alway.

. . . .

For three long years they will not sow
  Or root or seedling there:
For three long years the unblessed
    spot
  Will sterile be and bare,
And look upon the wondering sky
  With unreproachful stare.   90

They think a murderer's heart would
    taint
  Each simple seed they sow.
It is not true! God's kindly earth
  Is kindlier than men know,
And the red rose would but blow more
    red,
  The white rose whiter blow.

Out of his mouth a red, red rose!
  Out of his heart a white!
For who can say by what strange way,
  Christ brings His will to light,   100
Since the barren staff the pilgrim[1] bore
  Bloomed in the great Pope's sight?

But neither milk-white rose nor red
  May bloom in prison air;
The shard,[2] the pebble, and the flint,
  Are what they give us there:
For flowers have been known to heal
  A common man's despair.

[1] Probably a reference to the story of Tannhäuser,
a minstrel who, penitent for his prodigal life,
went on a pilgrimage to Rome. There Pope
Urban IV, who is depicted as an unforgiv-
ing man, declared his staff should blossom
sooner than pardon come for such sin as
Tannhäuser's. When, three days later, the
staff blossomed, the pilgrim was nowhere to
be found. Wilde varies the legend by making
the staff the pilgrim's, not the Pope's. See
"The Man Who Could Work Miracles,"
p. 671.

[2] Fragment of pottery.

So never will wine-red rose or white,
  Petal by petal, fall   110
On that stretch of mud and sand that lies
  By the hideous prison-wall,
To tell the men who tramp the yard
  That God's Son died for all.

. . . .

VI

In Reading gaol by Reading town
  There is a pit of shame,
And in it lies a wretched man
  Eaten by teeth of flame,
In a burning winding-sheet he lies,
  And his grave has got no name.   120

And there, till Christ call forth the dead,
  In silence let him lie:
No need to waste the foolish tear,
  Or heave the windy sigh:
The man had killed the thing he loved,
  And so he had to die.

And all men kill the thing they love,
  By all let this be heard,
Some do it with a bitter look,
  Some with a flattering word,   130
The coward does it with a kiss,
  The brave man with a sword!

Discussion Hints

1. What colors are contrasted in the first and second stanzas? Notice the effective use of high prison walls, small patch of blue sky, and "drifting cloud" to suggest that in Reading Gaol there is no liberty.

2. Find two metaphors and one simile in "The first day."

3. What is the significance of the roses, red and white?

4. Just what is the theme of "The first day"? of "The last day"? of the concluding stanzas?

5. Is it true that "all men kill the thing they love"? Give examples from literature and from life to prove the truth of your answer.

6. Is the death penalty lawful in your state? For what crimes may it be the penalty in the Federal courts?

7. Contrast prisons as Wilde describes them with prisons in our own democracy today.

8. Why may this poem be called a ballad (p. 57)?

Suggestions for Reading

1. Perhaps the other best-known poem on the identical theme of "The Ballad of Reading Gaol" is Kipling's "Danny Deever," with its refrain,

"They're hangin' Danny Deever in the mornin'."

2. In these days, when, except in the great democracies, freedom is too often valued lightly, the great poems of liberty written during the times of the French Revolution and of Napoleon take on new significance.

The liberty sonnets by William Wordsworth, some of the most noted of which are:

"Thought of a Briton on the Subjugation of Switzerland, 1807."
"In London, September 1802."
"London, 1802" (p. 342).
"Near Dover, September 1802."
"It Is Not to Be Thought of."
"On the Extinction of the Venetian Republic."

The Prisoner of Chillon, by Lord Byron (see the revised edition of *Achievement* of this series).

Prometheus Unbound, by Percy Bysshe Shelley, a magnificent choral poem of a Titan* who, crucified on a mountain-side, suffers most from his visions of the eternal sufferings of mankind.

3. Some of you have no doubt read or seen *Hurricane* (Little, Brown & Company), the book and moving picture by Charles Bernard Nordhoff and James Norman Hall. It is memorable for the terrific tropical storm; but it is pre-eminently a tale of Terangi, who became a legend in the South Sea Islands because he refused to be imprisoned.

4. There are many poems, tales, and plays by Oscar Wilde that you will enjoy. Why not read the whole of "The Ballad of Reading Gaol"? (It covers six weeks.) "The Birthday of the Infanta" is an excellent example of Wilde's stories and tales. *Lady Windermere's Fan* and *The Importance of Being Earnest,* the best known of his clever plays, are often performed by amateur groups. They make good reading too.

GILBERT KEITH CHESTERTON[1] (1874-1936)

Lepanto

We are accustomed to speak often of events that mark the beginnings of eras in history, events such as the discovery of America or the invention of the steam engine. We do not speak so often of events that close eras. The battle of Lepanto, fought one autumn day in 1571 just inside the strait which joins the Gulf of Corinth, or Lepanto, to the Mediterranean, was such an event; for it was the last great naval battle in which vessels propelled by oars were used on both sides. Over six hundred of these great ships took part in a terrific battle between Christian and Turk.

The Christian losses were great, some eight thousand killed and ten thousand wounded; but the Turkish fleet was almost completely destroyed. Besides the twenty-five thousand Turks killed, thousands of Christian prisoners who had been compelled to ply the oars of the Turkish galleys were freed.

In supreme command of the Christian fleet was Don John* of Austria, half brother to Philip II of Spain. Reared by humble village folk, John had no idea that his father was the famous Charles of Spain, who was also Charles V, Emperor of the Holy Roman Empire. But when the boy was thirteen his father, the great king and emperor, died, and in his will he acknowledged the boy as his. John was publicly recognized as a member of the royal family of Spain, but he had, of course, no throne. Intended for a monk, Don John, as the Spanish called him, preferred war. Three years before our story he had commanded a fleet of galleys against Algerian pirates. Two years before, he had fought against the rebellious Moors in Granada. In 1571 he won at Lepanto.

As poetry, "Lepanto" is marked by the irregular yet effective flow of its rhythm, by its use of vivid details, and by its picturesque imagery.* By all means read it aloud.

WHITE founts falling in the courts of the sun,
And the Soldan [2] of Byzantium [3] is smiling as they run;

[1] For biography see page 739.
[2] In the Middle Ages a ruler of a Mohammedan country, especially, as here, the Sultan of Turkey.
[3] The old name for Istanbul (Constantinople).

There is laughter like the fountains in that face of all men feared,
It stirs the forest darkness, the darkness of his beard,
It curls the blood-red crescent, the crescent of his lips,
For the inmost sea of all the earth is shaken with his ships.
They have dared the white republics up the capes of Italy,[1]
They have dashed the Adriatic round the Lion of the Sea,[2]
And the Pope has cast his arms abroad for agony and loss,
And called the kings of Christendom for swords about the Cross,   10
The cold queen of England [3] is looking in the glass;
The shadow of the Valois [4] is yawning at the Mass;
From evening isles fantastical rings faint the Spanish gun,
And the Lord [5] upon the Golden* Horn is laughing in the sun.

Dim drums throbbing, in the hills half heard,
Where only on a nameless throne a crownless prince [6] has stirred,

[1] *They . . . Italy.* Probably a reference to Albania (*alba* means "white"), which, while not a republic itself, was dominated by the Venetian republic in the fifteenth century. One after the other the cities of Albania had surrendered to the Turks, who must pass "the capes of Italy" to reach them.
[2] *Lion . . . Sea.* Venice.
[3] *cold queen . . . England.* Protestant Elizabeth had only a historic interest in the troubles of the Catholic countries.
[4] A French royal family who ruled for over two centuries. Their reign was almost over. The boy king, Charles IX, was in the hands of his mother, the unscrupulous Catherine de Medici, Duchess of Valois.
[5] The Sultan.
[6] Don John.

Metro-Goldwyn

A war galley of long ago

Where, risen from a doubtful seat and half attainted stall,
The last knight of Europe takes weapons from the wall,
The last and lingering troubadour* to whom the bird has sung,
That once went singing southward when all the world was young, 20
In that enormous silence, tiny and unafraid,
Comes up along a winding road the noise of the Crusade.*

Strong gongs groaning as the guns boom far,
Don John* of Austria is going to the war,
Stiff flags straining in the night-blasts cold
In the gloom black-purple, in the glint old-gold,
Torchlight crimson on the copper kettle-drums,
Then the tuckets,[1] then the trumpets, then the cannon, and he comes.

[1] Here, a signal with a drum.

Don John laughing in the brave beard
  curled,
Spurning of his stirrups like the thrones
  of all the world,   30
Holding his head up for a flag of all the
  free.
Love-light of Spain — hurrah!
Death-light of Africa![1]
Don John of Austria
Is riding to the sea.

Mahound* is in his paradise above the
  evening star,
(*Don John of Austria is going to the war.*)
He moves a mighty turban on the time-
  less houri's[2] knees,
His turban that is woven of the sunsets
  and the seas.
He shakes the peacock gardens as he
  rises from his ease,   40
And he strides among the tree-tops and
  is taller than the trees,
And his voice through all the garden is a
  thunder sent to bring
Black Azrael* and Ariel* and Ammon*
  on the wing.
Giants and the Genii,[3]
Multiplex of wing and eye,
Whose strong obedience broke the sky
When Solomon* was king.

They rush in red and purple from the
  red clouds of the morn,
From temples where the yellow gods
  shut up their eyes in scorn;
They rise in green robes roaring from
  the green hells of the sea   50
Where fallen skies and evil hues and eye-
  less creatures be;
On them the sea-valves cluster and the
  grey sea-forests curl,

Splashed with a splendid sickness, the
  sickness of the pearl;
They swell in sapphire smoke out of the
  blue cracks of the ground, —
They gather and they wonder and give
  worship to Mahound.
And he saith, "Break up the mountains
  where the hermit-folk can hide,
And sift the red and silver sands lest bone
  of saint abide,
And chase the Giaours[1] flying night and
  day, not giving rest,
For that which was our trouble comes
  again out of the west.
We have set the seal of Solomon on all
  things under sun,   60
Of knowledge and of sorrow and endur-
  ance of things done,
But a noise is in the mountains, in the
  mountains, and I know
The voice that shook our palaces —
  four hundred years ago[2]:
It is he that saith not 'Kismet'[3]; it is
  he that knows not Fate;
It is Richard,[4] it is Raymond,[5] it is God-
  frey[6] in the gate!
It is he whose loss is laughter when he
  counts the wager worth,
Put down your feet upon him, that our
  peace be on the earth."
For he heard drums groaning and he
  heard guns jar,
(*Don John of Austria is going to the war.*)
Sudden and still — hurrah!   70
Bolt from Iberia[7]!
Don John of Austria
Is gone by Alcalar.[8]

---

[1] *Giaours* (jourz; here, jä′ōōrz). A Turkish word
  for Christians and others who are not Mohammedans.
[2] When the crusades began.
[3] An Arabian word for "fate."
[4] Richard the Lion-Hearted, king of England,
  who was a leader in the Third Crusade.
[5] Raymond of Toulouse, a leader in the First
  Crusade.
[6] Godfrey de Bouillon, chief leader of the First Crusade, who captured Jerusalem.   [7] Spain.
[8] The site of John's university in Spain, not far
  from Madrid. This university was moved to
  Madrid a little over a century ago.

---

[1] John's first command was fought in Africa.
[2] The houri, a beautiful spirit in the Mohammedan paradise, is endowed with perpetual
  youth and perfect beauty.
[3] *Genii* (or *jinn*). In Mohammedan folklore and
  literature, creatures like men, but able to
  change their size and shape. They are usually
  spoken of as under the control of Solomon,*
  whose seal, on which was the ineffable name
  of God, gave him power over spirits.

St. Michael's on his mountain in the sea-roads of the north
(*Don John of Austria is girt and going forth.*)
Where the grey seas glitter and the sharp tides shift
And the sea folk labour and the red sails lift.
He shakes his lance of iron and he claps his wings of stone[1];
The noise is gone through Normandy[2]; the noise is gone alone;
The North is full of tangled things and texts and aching eyes   80
And dead is all the innocence of anger and surprise,
And Christian killeth Christian in a narrow dusty room,
And Christian dreadeth Christ that hath a newer face of doom,
And Christian hateth Mary that God kissed in Galilee,[3]
But Don John of Austria is riding to the sea.
Don John calling through the blast and the eclipse
Crying with the trumpet, with the trumpet of his lips,
Trumpet that sayeth ha!
  Domino gloria![4]
Don John of Austria   90
Is shouting to the ships.

King Philip[5]'s in his closet with the Fleece[6] about his neck
(*Don John of Austria is armed upon the deck.*)

The walls are hung with velvet that is black and soft as sin,
And little dwarfs creep out of it and little dwarfs creep in.
He holds a crystal phial[1] that has colours like the moon,
He touches, and it tingles, and he trembles very soon,
And his face is as a fungus of a leprous white and grey
Like plants in the high houses that are shuttered from the day,
And death is in the phial, and the end of noble work,   100
But Don John of Austria has fired upon the Turk.
Don John's hunting, and his hounds have bayed —
Booms away past Italy the rumour of his raid
Gun upon gun, ha! ha!
Gun upon gun, hurrah!
Don John of Austria
Has loosed the cannonade.

The Pope was in his chapel before day or battle broke,
(*Don John of Austria is hidden in the smoke.*)
The hidden room in man's house where God sits all the year,   110
The secret window whence the world looks small and very dear.
He sees as in a mirror[2] on the monstrous twilight sea
The crescent of his[3] cruel ships whose name is mystery;
They fling great shadows foe-wards, making Cross[4] and Castle[5] dark,
They veil the plumèd lions[6] on the galleys of St.* Mark;

[1] *St. Michael's . . . stone.* A reference to Mont-Saint-Michel (môn'săn mē shĕl'), an ancient French monastery, church, and fortress, a shrine of the archangel Michael, patron saint of high places. It is situated on a high, rocky isle off the coast of northern France. Although often attacked, the island has never been captured.
[2] Northwestern France.
[3] *The North . . . Galilee.* A reference to the troubles of the Reformation (see page 71) in northern Europe.
[4] *Domino gloria!* "Glory to the Lord!"
[5] King of Spain.
[6] The badge worn by the knights of the Order of the Golden Fleece.

[1] A small bottle for drugs. Philip was accused of poisoning Don John seven years later.
[2] *sees . . . mirror.* The story is that, while the battle of Lepanto was being fought, Pope Pius V had a vision that the battle was won.
[3] Mohammed's.   [4] The emblem of Aragon.
[5] The emblem of Castile.
[6] A winged lion was the emblem of St. Mark and of the Republic of Venice.

And above the ships are palaces of
brown, black-bearded chiefs,
And below the ships are prisons, where
with multitudinous griefs,
Christian captives sick and sunless, all a
labouring race repines
Like a race in sunken cities, like a nation
in the mines.
They are lost like slaves that swat,[1] and
in the skies of morning hung   120
The stair-ways of the tallest gods when
tyranny was young.
They are countless, voiceless, hopeless as
those fallen or fleeing on
Before the high Kings' horses in the
granite of Babylon.[2]
And many a one grows witless in his
quiet room in hell
Where a yellow face looks inward through
the lattice of his cell,
And he finds his God forgotten, and he
seeks no more a sign[3] —
(*But Don John of Austria has burst the
battle-line!*)
Don John pounding from the slaughter-
painted poop,
Purpling all the ocean like a bloody
pirate's sloop,
Scarlet running over on the silvers and
the golds,   130
Breaking of the hatches up and bursting
of the holds,
Thronging of the thousands up that
labour under sea
White for bliss and blind for sun and
stunned for liberty.
Vivat Hispania![4]
Domino gloria!
Don John of Austria
Has set his people free!

[1] Sweat.
[2] In ancient sculpture the king of Babylon * drives
his prisoners before him.
[3] *seeks . . . sign.* Seeking a sign from those who
declared that they spoke God's message was
common in Bible times. See Isaiah 7 : 10–14.
Does "finds his God forgotten" mean "finds
again his God whom he had forgotten" or
"finds that his God has forgotten him"?
[4] *Vivat Hispania!* "Long live Spain!"

Cervantes *[1] on his galley sets the sword
back in the sheath
(*Don John of Austria rides homeward
with a wreath.*)
And he sees across a weary land a straggling road in Spain,   140
Up which a lean and foolish knight[2] forever rides in vain,
And he smiles, but not as Sultans smile,
and settles back the blade. . . .
(*But Don John of Austria rides home
from the Crusade.**)

Discussion Hints

1. Read the notes with special care. Be
sure that you get also the full significance of
each word marked with an asterisk.

2. From the headnote and from the hints
given in the ballad and in the notes, tell what
happened in the battle of Lepanto.

3. Note the effectiveness of the italic lines
in parentheses. They suggest the plan of the
whole poem. Read them aloud thoughtfully.

4. What is particularly appropriate about
the use of Latin phrases in lines 89 and 134 and
135?

5. The poem is written in words suggestive,
significant, and poetic. Here are a few examples from the first stanza:
crescent (a symbol of Mohammedanism), l. 5
inmost sea (the Mediterranean), l. 6
cast his arms abroad (in the shape of a cross),
l. 9
cold queen (Elizabeth, uninterested in love
and not a Catholic), l. 11
evening isles (a poetic way of saying the
West), l. 13
Find one or more such suggestive, significant,
or poetic bits in each stanza.

6. Give your favorite line or lines descriptive of the Sultan; of Don John; of the
battle.

7. Pick out ten onomatopoetic* lines.

8. Find ten alliterative* lines.

9. Read your favorite passage over and
over, and see whether you do not find yourself
repeating it half unconsciously.

[1] Cervantes fought in the battle of Lepanto.
[2] Don Quixote, the hero of Cervantes' * famous
story of that name.

Suggestions for Reading

"Lepanto," perhaps more than any other selection in "Narrative Poetry," suggests varied avenues of interesting reading.

The Arabian Nights' Entertainments. Haroun-al-Raschid, who appears in this famous book, is a kindly sultan, very different from the Soldan in "Lepanto." See the revised edition of *Adventure* of this series for one story.

"The Birthday of the Infanta," by Oscar Wilde. Lines 94 and 95 of "Lepanto" might be its setting.

"The Pit and the Pendulum," by Edgar Allan Poe. Here are depicted the terrors of the Spanish Inquisition.

In the Palace of the King (The Macmillan Company), by F. Marion Crawford. A compact story of the court of the cruel Philip II. Don John of Austria is the chivalrous hero.

Ben-Hur, by Lew Wallace. The most famous of all stories about the galleys.

Don Quixote, by Miguel de Cervantes. Many think this book the finest outcome of chivalry, a book "forever" great.

For Chesterton's poetry see his *Collected Poems*. Very different are his detective stories, *The Father Brown Omnibus*. Both books are published by Dodd, Mead & Co., Inc.

Suggestions for Further Reading in Narrative Poetry

Besides the work in narrative poetry by Kipling, Yeats, Wilde, and Chesterton, that of Alfred Noyes (who at one time taught at Princeton) and of John Masefield (poet laureate,* who, years ago, before he ever dreamed of writing poetry, worked at all manner of odd jobs in the United States) stands out pre-eminent.

The titles of Noyes's volumes of narrative verse include *Forty Singing Seamen and Other Poems, Tales of the Mermaid Tavern, The Enchanted Island and Other Poems,* and *The Torchbearers.* Frederick A. Stokes Company publishes the poetry of Alfred Noyes.

Volumes by Masefield include *Story of a Round-House, and Other Poems* (sometimes called *Dauber*), his greatest sea poems; *Reynard the Fox*, one of the most delightful of his longer poems; *Right Royal*, a tale of a horse race; and *King Cole*, a tale of a circus. The Macmillan Company is Masefield's American publisher.

Narrative poetry by modern English authors is well represented in the earlier books of this series. See the revised editions of *Adventure* and *Achievement* of this series.

THE SHORT STORY

RUDYARD KIPLING[1] (1865–1936)

"Rikki-tikki-tavi"

The setting of this, our first story, is a little world in itself, a bungalow and garden in India. The birds, beasts, and snakes that are the chief characters seem, in Kipling's deft hands, more interesting and even more human than the persons who are officially the new tenants of the place. Some prove helpless or decorative only; but it is no exaggeration to say that no more villainous human villains could be conceived than the big cobras, Nag and Nagaina, and that no human hero ever fought more gallantly a single-handed fight against overwhelming odds than did Rikki-tikki-tavi. Thrilling climax follows thrilling climax in this "tooth and claw" struggle for mastery of the garden. No doubt about it, here is Kipling at his best; for here is his beloved India, here is a typical *Jungle Book* tale, and here, besides, is a short story excellent in structure and in style.

At the hole where he went in
Red-Eye called to Wrinkle-Skin.
Hear what little Red-Eye saith:
"Nag, come up and dance with death!"

Eye to eye and head to head,
   (*Keep the measure, Nag.*)
This shall end when one is dead;
   (*At thy pleasure, Nag.*)

Turn for turn and twist for twist —
   (*Run and hide thee, Nag.*)
Hah! The hooded Death has missed!
   (*Woe betide thee, Nag!*)

10

THIS is the story of the great war that Rikki-tikki-tavi fought single-handed, through the bath-rooms of the big bungalow in Segowlee cantonment.[2] Darzee,

[1] For biography see page 742.
[2] A military station, often connected in India with a native town.

the tailor-bird, helped him, and Chuchundra, the muskrat, who never comes out into the middle of the floor, but always creeps round by the wall, gave him advice; but Rikki-tikki did the real fighting. 20

He was a mongoose, rather like a little cat in his fur and his tail, but quite like a weasel in his head and his habits. His eyes and the end of his restless nose were pink; he could scratch himself anywhere he pleased, with any leg, front or back, that he chose to use; he could fluff up his tail till it looked like a bottle-brush, 30 and his war-cry as he scuttled through the long grass, was: "*Rikk-tikk-tikki-tikki-tchk!*"

One day, a high summer flood washed him out of the burrow where he lived with his father and mother, and carried him, kicking and clucking, down a roadside ditch. He found a little wisp of grass floating there, and clung to it till he lost his senses. When he revived, he was 40 lying in the hot sun on the middle of a garden path, very draggled indeed, and a small boy was saying: "Here's a dead mongoose. Let's have a funeral."

"No," said his mother; "let's take him in and dry him. Perhaps he isn't really dead."

They took him into the house, and a big man picked him up between his finger and thumb and said he was not dead but 50 half choked; so they wrapped him in cotton-wool, and warmed him, and he opened his eyes and sneezed.

"Now," said the big man (he was an

Englishman who had just moved into the bungalow); "don't frighten him, and we'll see what he'll do."

It is the hardest thing in the world to frighten a mongoose, because he is eaten 60 up from nose to tail with curiosity. The motto of all the mongoose family is, "Run and find out"; and Rikki-tikki was a true mongoose. He looked at the cotton-wool, decided that it was not good to eat, ran all round the table, sat up and put his fur in order, scratched himself, and jumped on the small boy's shoulder.

"Don't be frightened, Teddy," said 70 his father. "That's his way of making friends."

"Ouch! He's tickling under my chin," said Teddy.

Rikki-tikki looked down between the boy's collar and neck, snuffed at his ear, and climbed down to the floor, where he sat rubbing his nose.

"Good gracious," said Teddy's mother, "and that's a wild creature! I suppose 80 he's so tame because we've been kind to him."

"All mongooses are like that," said her husband. "If Teddy doesn't pick him up by the tail, or try to put him in a cage, he'll run in and out of the house all day long. Let's give him something to eat."

They gave him a little piece of raw meat. Rikki-tikki liked it immensely, 90 and when it was finished he went out into the veranda and sat in the sunshine and fluffed up his fur to make it dry to the roots. Then he felt better.

"There are more things to find out about in this house," he said to himself, "than all my family could find out in all their lives. I shall certainly stay and find out."

He spent all that day roaming over 100 the house. He nearly drowned himself in the bath-tubs, put his nose into the ink on a writing-table, and burned it on the end of the big man's cigar, for he climbed up in the big man's lap to see how writing was done. At nightfall he ran into Teddy's nursery to watch how kerosene lamps were lighted, and when Teddy went to bed Rikki-tikki climbed up too; but he was a restless companion, because he had to get up and attend to 110 every noise all through the night, and find out what made it. Teddy's mother and father came in, the last thing, to look at their boy, and Rikki-tikki was awake on the pillow. "I don't like that," said Teddy's mother; "he may bite the child." "He'll do no such thing," said the father. "Teddy's safer with that little beast than if he had a bloodhound to watch him. If a snake came into the 120 nursery now —"

But Teddy's mother wouldn't think of anything so awful.

Early in the morning Rikki-tikki came to early breakfast in the veranda riding on Teddy's shoulder, and they gave him banana and some boiled egg; and he sat on all their laps one after the other, because every well-brought-up mongoose always hopes to be a house-mongoose 130 some day and have rooms to run about in, and Rikki-tikki's mother (she used to live in the General's house at Segowlee) had carefully told Rikki what to do if ever he came across white men.

Then Rikki-tikki went out into the garden to see what was to be seen. It was a large garden, only half cultivated, with bushes as big as summer-houses of Marshal Niel[1] roses, lime and orange 140 trees, clumps of bamboos, and thickets of high grass. Rikki-tikki licked his lips. "This is a splendid hunting-ground," he said, and his tail grew bottle-brushy at the thought of it, and he scuttled up and down the garden, snuffing here and there

[1] The name of a world-famous rose sent out from France some seventy-five years ago, but derived from an original rose produced in Charleston, South Carolina, a half century earlier. Its large, fragrant yellow blossoms are especially effective in the South and in the tropics, where it is hardy.

till he heard very sorrowful voices in a thorn-bush.

It was Darzee, the tailor-bird, and his 150 wife. They had made a beautiful nest by pulling two big leaves together and stitching them up the edges with fibers, and had filled the hollow with cotton and downy fluff. The nest swayed to and fro, as they sat on the rim and cried.

"What is the matter?" asked Rikki-tikki.

"We are very miserable," said Darzee. "One of our babies fell out of the nest 160 yesterday and Nag ate him."

"H'm!" said Rikki-tikki, "that is very sad — but I am a stranger here. Who is Nag?"

Darzee and his wife only cowered down in the nest without answering, for from the thick grass at the foot of the bush there came a low hiss — a horrid cold sound that made Rikki-tikki jump back two clear feet. Then inch by inch out of 170 the grass rose up the head and spread hood of Nag, the big black cobra, and he was five feet long from tongue to tail. When he had lifted one-third of himself clear of the ground, he stayed balancing to and fro exactly as a dandelion-tuft balances in the wind, and he looked at Rikki-tikki with the wicked snake's eyes that never change their expression, whatever the snake may be thinking of.

180   "Who is Nag?" he said. "*I* am Nag. The great god Brahm[1] put his mark upon all our people when the first cobra spread his hood to keep the sun off Brahm as he slept. Look, and be afraid!"

He spread out his hood more than ever, and Rikki-tikki saw the spectacle-mark on the back of it that looks exactly like the eye part of a hook-and-eye 190 fastening. He was afraid for the minute; but it is impossible for a mongoose to stay frightened for any length of time, and though Rikki-tikki had never met a

[1] In Indian belief the spirit of the universe, the omnipotent one.

live cobra before, his mother had fed him on dead ones, and he knew that all a grown mongoose's business in life was to fight and eat snakes. Nag knew that too, and at the bottom of his cold heart he was afraid.

"Well," said Rikki-tikki, and his tail 200 began to fluff up again, "marks or no marks, do you think it is right for you to eat fledglings out of a nest?"

Nag was thinking to himself, and watching the least little movement in the grass behind Rikki-tikki. He knew that mongooses in the garden meant death sooner or later for him and his family; but he wanted to get Rikki-tikki off his guard. So he dropped his 210 head a little, and put it on one side.

"Let us talk," he said. "You eat eggs. Why should not I eat birds?"

"Behind you! Look behind you!" sang Darzee.

Rikki-tikki knew better than to waste time in staring. He jumped up in the air as high as he could go, and just under him whizzed by the head of Nagaina, Nag's wicked wife. She had crept up behind 220 him as he was talking, to make an end of him; and he heard her savage hiss as the stroke missed. He came down almost across her back, and if he had been an old mongoose he would have known that then was the time to break her back with one bite; but he was afraid of the terrible lashing return-stroke of the cobra. He bit, indeed, but did not bite long enough, and he jumped clear of the 230 whisking tail, leaving Nagaina torn and angry.

"Wicked, wicked Darzee!" said Nag, lashing up as high as he could reach toward the nest in the thorn-bush; but Darzee had built it out of reach of snakes, and it only swayed to and fro.

Rikki-tikki felt his eyes growing red and hot (when a mongoose's eyes grow red, he is angry), and he sat back on his 240 tail and hind legs like a little kangaroo, and looked all around him, and chat-

"Behind you! Look behind you!" sang Darzee

tered with rage. But Nag and Nagaina had disappeared into the grass. When a snake misses its stroke, it never says anything or gives any sign of what it means to do next. Rikki-tikki did not care to follow them, for he did not feel sure that he could manage two snakes at once. So 250 he trotted off to the gravel path near the house, and sat down to think. It was a serious matter for him.

If you read the old books of natural history,[1] you will find they say that when the mongoose fights the snake and happens to get bitten, he runs off and eats some herb that cures him. That is not true. The victory is only a matter of quickness of eye and quickness of foot, — 260 snake's blow against mongoose's jump, — and as no eye can follow the motion of a snake's head when it strikes, that makes things much more wonderful than any magic herb. Rikki-tikki knew he was a young mongoose, and it made him all the more pleased to think that he had managed to escape a blow from behind. It gave him confidence in himself, and when Teddy came running down the path, 270 Rikki-tikki was ready to be petted.

But just as Teddy was stooping, something flinched a little in the dust, and a tiny voice said: "Be careful. I am death!" It was Karait, the dusty brown snakeling that lies for choice on the dusty earth; and his bite is as dangerous as the cobra's. But he is so small that nobody thinks of him, and so he does the more harm to people.

280   Rikki-tikki's eyes grew red again, and he danced up to Karait with the peculiar rocking, swaying motion that he had inherited from his family. It looks very funny, but it is so perfectly balanced a gait that you can fly off from it at any angle you please; and in dealing with snakes this is an advantage. If Rikki-tikki had only known, he was doing a much more dangerous thing than fight-

ing Nag, for Karait is so small, and can 290 turn so quickly, that unless Rikki bit him close to the back of the head, he would get the return-stroke in his eye or lip. But Rikki did not know: his eyes were all red, and he rocked back and forth, looking for a good place to hold. Karait struck out. Rikki jumped sideways and tried to run in, but the wicked little dusty grey head lashed within a fraction of his shoulder, and he had to 300 jump over the body, and the head followed his heels close.

Teddy shouted to the house: "Oh, look here! Our mongoose is killing a snake"; and Rikki-tikki heard a scream from Teddy's mother. His father ran out with a stick, but by the time he came up, Karait had lunged out once too far, and Rikki-tikki had sprung, jumped on the snake's back, dropped his head far 310 between his fore legs, bitten as high up the back as he could get hold, and rolled away. That bite paralyzed Karait, and Rikki-tikki was just going to eat him up from the tail, after the custom of his family at dinner, when he remembered that a full meal makes a slow mongoose, and if he wanted all his strength and quickness ready, he must keep himself thin.   320

He went away for a dust-bath under the castor-oil[1] bushes, while Teddy's father beat the dead Karait. "What is the use of that?" thought Rikki-tikki. "I have settled it all"; and then Teddy's mother picked him up from the dust and hugged him, crying that he had saved Teddy from death, and Teddy's father said that he was a providence, and Teddy looked on with big scared eyes. Rikki- 330 tikki was rather amused at all the fuss, which, of course, he did not understand. Teddy's mother might just as well have petted Teddy for playing in the dust. Rikki was thoroughly enjoying himself.

That night, at dinner, walking to and

---

[1] *natural history.* The old-fashioned term for the study and description of plants and animals.

[1] The ordinary castor bean, which grows to be thirty or forty feet high in the tropics.

fro among the wine-glasses on the table, he could have stuffed himself three times over with nice things; but he remem-
340 bered Nag and Nagaina, and though it was very pleasant to be patted and petted by Teddy's mother, and to sit on Teddy's shoulder, his eyes would get red from time to time, and he would go off into his long war-cry of "*Rikk-tikk-tikki-tikki-tchk!*"

Teddy carried him off to bed, and insisted on Rikki-tikki sleeping under his chin. Rikki-tikki was too well bred to
350 bite or scratch, but as soon as Teddy was asleep he went off for his nightly walk round the house, and in the dark he ran up against Chuchundra, the muskrat, creeping round by the wall. Chuchundra is a broken-hearted little beast. He whimpers and cheeps all the night, trying to make up his mind to run into the middle of the room, but he never gets there.
360 "Don't kill me," said Chuchundra, almost weeping. "Rikki-tikki, don't kill me."

"Do you think a snake-killer kills muskrats?" said Rikki-tikki scornfully.

"Those who kill snakes get killed by snakes," said Chuchundra, more sorrowfully than ever. "And how am I to be sure that Nag won't mistake me for you some dark night?"
370 "There's not the least danger," said Rikki-tikki; "but Nag is in the garden, and I know you don't go there."

"My cousin Chua, the rat, told me —" said Chuchundra, and then he stopped.

"Told you what?"

"H'sh! Nag is everywhere, Rikki-tikki. You should have talked to Chua in the garden."

"I didn't — so you must tell me.
380 Quick, Chuchundra, or I'll bite you!"

Chuchundra sat down and cried till the tears rolled off his whiskers. "I am a very poor man," he sobbed. "I never had spirit enough to run out into the middle of the room. H'sh! I mustn't tell you anything. Can't you *hear*, Rikki-tikki?"

Rikki-tikki listened. The house was as still as still, but he thought he could just catch the faintest *scratch-scratch* in
390 the world, — a noise as faint as that of a wasp walking on a window-pane, — the dry scratch of a snake's scales on brickwork.

"That's Nag or Nagaina," he said to himself; "and he is crawling into the bath-room sluice. You're right, Chuchundra; I should have talked to Chua."

He stole off to Teddy's bath-room, but there was nothing there, and then
400 to Teddy's mother's bath-room. At the bottom of the smooth plaster wall there was a brick pulled out to make a sluice for the bath-water, and as Rikki-tikki stole in by the masonry curb where the bath is put, he heard Nag and Nagaina whispering together outside in the moonlight.

"When the house is emptied of people," said Nagaina to her husband, "*he* will
410 have to go away, and then the garden will be our own again. Go in quietly, and remember that the big man who killed Karait is the first one to bite. Then come out and tell me, and we will hunt for Rikki-tikki together."

"But are you sure that there is anything to be gained by killing the people?" said Nag.

"Everything. When there were no
420 people in the bungalow, did we have any mongoose in the garden? So long as the bungalow is empty, we are king and queen of the garden; and remember that as soon as our eggs in the melon-bed hatch (as they may to-morrow), our children will need room and quiet."

"I had not thought of that," said Nag. "I will go, but there is no need that we should hunt for Rikki-tikki afterward.
430 I will kill the big man and his wife, and the child if I can, and come away quietly. Then the bungalow will be empty, and Rikki-tikki will go."

Rikki-tikki tingled all over with rage and hatred at this, and then Nag's head came through the sluice, and his five feet of cold body followed it. Angry as he was, Rikki-tikki was very frightened as he saw the size of the big cobra. Nag coiled himself up, raised his head, and looked into the bath-room in the dark, and Rikki could see his eyes glitter.

"Now, if I kill him here, Nagaina will know; and if I fight him on the open floor, the odds are in his favour. What am I to do?" said Rikki-tikki-tavi.

Nag waved to and fro, and then Rikki-tikki heard him drinking from the biggest water-jar that was used to fill the bath. "That is good," said the snake. "Now, when Karait was killed, the big man had a stick. He may have that stick still, but when he comes in to bathe in the morning he will not have a stick. I shall wait here till he comes. Nagaina — do you hear me? — I shall wait here in the cool till daytime."

There was no answer from outside, so Rikki-tikki knew Nagaina had gone away. Nag coiled himself down, coil by coil, round the bulge at the bottom of the water-jar, and Rikki-tikki stayed still as death. After an hour he began to move, muscle by muscle, toward the jar. Nag was asleep, and Rikki-tikki looked at his big back, wondering which would be the best place for a good hold. "If I don't break his back at the first jump," said Rikki, "he can still fight; and if he fights — O Rikki!" He looked at the thickness of the neck below the hood, but that was too much for him; and a bite near the tail would only make Nag savage.

"It must be the head," he said at last; "the head above the hood; and, when I am once there, I must not let go."

Then he jumped. The head was lying a little clear of the water-jar under the curve of it; and, as his teeth met, Rikki braced his back against the bulge of the red earthenware to hold down the head.

This gave him just one second's purchase, and he made the most of it. Then he was battered to and fro as a rat is shaken by a dog — to and fro on the floor, up and down, and round in great circles; but his eyes were red, and he held on as the body cartwhipped over the floor, upsetting the tin dipper and the soap-dish and the flesh-brush, and banged against the tin side of the bath. As he held he closed his jaws tighter and tighter, for he made sure he would be banged to death, and, for the honour of his family, he preferred to be found with his teeth locked. He was dizzy, aching, and felt shaken to pieces when something went off like a thunderclap just behind him; a hot wind knocked him senseless and red fire singed his fur. The big man had been wakened by the noise, and had fired both barrels of a shot-gun into Nag just behind the hood.

Rikki-tikki held on with his eyes shut, for now he was quite sure he was dead; but the head did not move, and the big man picked him up and said: "It's the mongoose again, Alice; the little chap has saved *our* lives now." Then Teddy's mother came in with a very white face, and saw what was left of Nag, and Rikki-tikki dragged himself to Teddy's bedroom and spent half the rest of the night shaking himself tenderly to find out whether he really was broken into forty pieces, as he fancied.

When morning came he was very stiff, but well pleased with his doings. "Now I have Nagaina to settle with, and she will be worse than five Nags, and there's no knowing when the eggs she spoke of will hatch. Goodness! I must go and see Darzee," he said.

Without waiting for breakfast, Rikki-tikki ran to the thorn-bush where Darzee was singing a song of triumph[1] at the top of his voice. The news of Nag's death was all over the garden, for the sweeper had thrown the body on the rubbish-heap.

[1] See page 642, l. 1.

"Oh, you stupid tuft of feathers!" said Rikki-tikki, angrily. "Is this the time to sing?"

"Nag is dead — is dead — is dead!" sang Darzee. "The valiant Rikki-tikki caught him by the head and held fast. The big man brought the bangstick and Nag fell in two pieces! He will never eat 540 my babies again."

"All that's true enough; but where's Nagaina?" said Rikki-tikki, looking carefully round him.

"Nagaina came to the bath-room sluice and called for Nag," Darzee went on; "and Nag came out on the end of a stick — the sweeper picked him up on the end of a stick and threw him upon the rubbish-heap. Let us sing about the 550 great, the red-eyed Rikki-tikki!" and Darzee filled his throat and sang.

"If I could get up to your nest, I'd roll all your babies out!" said Rikki-tikki. "You don't know when to do the right thing at the right time. You're safe enough in your nest there, but it's war for me down here. Stop singing a minute, Darzee."

"For the great, the beautiful Rikki-560 tikki's sake I will stop," said Darzee. "What is it, O Killer of the terrible Nag?"

"Where is Nagaina, for the third time?"

"On the rubbish-heap by the stables, mourning for Nag. Great is Rikki-tikki with the white teeth."

"Bother my white teeth! Have you ever heard where she keeps her eggs?"

570 "In the melon-bed, on the end nearest the wall, where the sun strikes nearly all day. She had them there weeks ago."

"And you never thought it worth while to tell me? The end nearest the wall, you said?"

"Rikki-tikki, you are not going to eat her eggs?"

"Not eat exactly; no. Darzee, if you have a grain of sense you will fly off to 580 the stables and pretend that your wing

is broken, and let Nagaina chase you away to this bush! I must get to the melon-bed, and if I went there now she'd see me."

Darzee was a feather-brained little fellow who could never hold more than one idea at a time in his head; and just because he knew that Nagaina's children were born in eggs like his own, he didn't think at first that it was fair to kill them. 590 But his wife was a sensible bird, and she knew that cobra's eggs meant young cobras later on; so she flew off from the nest, and left Darzee to keep the babies warm, and continue his song about the death of Nag. Darzee was very like a man in some ways.

She fluttered in front of Nagaina by the rubbish-heap, and cried out, "Oh, my wing is broken! The boy in the house 600 threw a stone at me and broke it." Then she fluttered more desperately than ever.

Nagaina lifted up her head and hissed, "You[1] warned Rikki-tikki when I would have killed him. Indeed and truly, you've chosen a bad place to be lame in." And she moved toward Darzee's wife, slipping along over the dust.

"The boy broke it with a stone!" shrieked Darzee's wife. 610

"Well! It may be some consolation to you when you're dead to know that I shall settle accounts with the boy. My husband lies on the rubbish-heap this morning, but before night the boy in the house will lie very still. What is the use of running away? I am sure to catch you. Little fool, look at me!"

Darzee's wife knew better than to do that, for a bird who looks at a snake's eyes 620 gets so frightened that she cannot move. Darzee's wife fluttered on, piping sorrowfully, and never leaving the ground, and Nagaina quickened her pace.

Rikki-tikki heard them going up the path from the stables, and he raced for

[1] Nagaina is wrong: it was not Darzee's wife but Darzee who did the warning (see page 644, l. 214).

the end of the melon-patch near the wall. There, in the warm litter about the melons, very cunningly hidden, he found 630 twenty-five eggs, about the size of a bantam's eggs, but with whitish skin instead of shell.

"I was not a day too soon," he said; for he could see the baby cobras curled up inside the skin, and he knew that the minute they were hatched they could each kill a man or a mongoose. He bit off the tops of the eggs as fast as he could, taking care to crush the young cobras, 640 and turned over the litter from time to time to see whether he had missed any. At last there were only three eggs left, and Rikki-tikki began to chuckle to himself, when he heard Darzee's wife screaming:

"Rikki-tikki, I led Nagaina toward the house, and she has gone into the veranda, and — oh, come quickly — she means killing!"

650 Rikki-tikki smashed two eggs, and tumbled backward down the melon-bed with the third egg in his mouth, and scuttled to the veranda as hard as he could put foot to the ground. Teddy and his mother and father were there at early breakfast; but Rikki-tikki saw that they were not eating anything. They sat stone-still, and their faces were white. Nagaina was coiled up on the 660 matting by Teddy's chair, within easy striking distance of Teddy's bare leg, and she was swaying to and fro singing a song of triumph.

"Son of the big man that killed Nag," she hissed, "stay still. I am not ready yet. Wait a little. Keep very still, all you three. If you move I strike, and if you do not move I strike. Oh, foolish people, who killed my Nag!"

670 Teddy's eyes were fixed on his father, and all his father could do was to whisper, "Sit still, Teddy. You mustn't move. Teddy, keep still."

Then Rikki-tikki came up and cried: "Turn round, Nagaina; turn and fight!"

"All in good time," said she, without moving her eyes. "I will settle my account with *you* presently. Look at your friends, Rikki-tikki. They are still and white; they are afraid. They dare not 680 move, and if you come a step nearer I strike."

"Look at your eggs," said Rikki-tikki, "in the melon-bed near the wall. Go and look, Nagaina."

The big snake turned half round, and saw the egg on the veranda. "Ah-h! Give it to me," she said.

Rikki-tikki put his paws one on each side of the egg, and his eyes were blood-690 red. "What price for a snake's egg? For a young cobra? For a young king-cobra? For the last — the very last of the brood? The ants are eating all the others down by the melon-bed."

Nagaina spun clear round, forgetting everything for the sake of the one egg; and Rikki-tikki saw Teddy's father shoot out a big hand, catch Teddy by the shoulder and drag him across the little 700 table with the tea-cups, safe and out of reach of Nagaina.

"Tricked! Tricked! Tricked! *Rikk-tck-tck!*" chuckled Rikki-tikki. "The boy is safe, and it was I — I — I that caught Nag by the hood last night in the bath-room." Then he began to jump up and down, all four feet together, his head close to the floor. "He threw me to and fro, but he could not shake me 710 off. He was dead before the big man blew him in two. I did it. *Rikki-tikki-tck-tck!* Come then, Nagaina. Come and fight with me. You shall not be a widow long."

Nagaina saw that she had lost her chance of killing Teddy, and the egg lay between Rikki-tikki's paws. "Give me the egg, Rikki-tikki. Give me the last of my eggs, and I will go away and never 720 come back," she said, lowering her hood.

"Yes, you will go away, and you will never come back; for you will go to the rubbish-heap with Nag. Fight, widow!

The big man has gone for his gun! Fight!"

Rikki-tikki was bounding all round Nagaina, keeping just out of the reach of her stroke, his little eyes like hot coals. 730 Nagaina gathered herself together, and flung out at him. Rikki-tikki jumped up and backward. Again and again and again she struck, and each time her head came with a whack on the matting of the veranda and she gathered herself together like a watch-spring. Then Rikki-tikki danced in a circle to get behind her, and Nagaina spun round to keep her head to his head, so that the rustle of her tail 740 on the matting sounded like dry leaves blown along by the wind.

He had forgotten the egg. It still lay on the veranda, and Nagaina came nearer and nearer to it, till at last, while Rikki-tikki was drawing breath, she caught it in her mouth, turned to the veranda steps, and flew like an arrow down the path, with Rikki-tikki behind her. When the cobra runs for her life, she goes like a 750 whiplash flicked across a horse's neck.

Rikki-tikki knew that he must catch her, or all the trouble would begin again. She headed straight for the long grass by the thorn-bush, and as he was running Rikki-tikki heard Darzee still singing his foolish little song of triumph. But Darzee's wife was wiser. She flew off her nest as Nagaina came along, and flapped her wings about Nagaina's head. If 760 Darzee had helped they might have turned her; but Nagaina only lowered her hood and went on. Still, the instant's delay brought Rikki-tikki up to her, and as she plunged into the rat-hole where she and Nag used to live, his little white teeth were clenched on her tail, and he went down with her — and very few mongooses, however wise and old they may be, care to follow a cobra into its 770 hole. It was dark in the hole; and Rikki-tikki never knew when it might open out and give Nagaina room to turn and strike at him. He held on savagely, and struck out his feet to act as brakes on the dark slope of the hot, moist earth.

Then the grass by the mouth of the hole stopped waving, and Darzee said: "It is all over with Rikki-tikki! We must sing his death-song. Valiant Rikki-tikki is dead! For Nagaina will surely kill him 780 underground."

So he sang a very mournful song that he made up all on the spur of the minute, and just as he got to the most touching part the grass quivered again, and Rikki-tikki, covered with dirt, dragged himself out of the hole leg by leg, licking his whiskers. Darzee stopped with a little shout. Rikki-tikki shook some of the dust out of his fur and sneezed. "It is 790 all over," he said. "The widow will never come out again." And the red ants that live between the grass stems heard him, and began to troop down one after another to see if he had spoken the truth.

Rikki-tikki curled himself up in the grass and slept where he was — slept and slept till it was late in the afternoon, for he had done a hard day's work.

"Now," he said, when he awoke, "I 800 will go back to the house. Tell the Coppersmith, Darzee, and he will tell the garden that Nagaina is dead."

The Coppersmith is a bird who makes a noise exactly like the beating of a little hammer on a copper pot; and the reason he is always making it is because he is the town-crier to every Indian garden, and tells all the news to everybody who cares to listen. As Rikki-tikki went up the 810 path, he heard his "attention" notes like a tiny dinner-gong; and then the steady "*Ding-dong-tock!* Nag is dead — *dong!* Nagaina is dead! *Ding-dong-tock!*" That set all the birds in the garden singing, and the frogs croaking; for Nag and Nagaina used to eat frogs as well as little birds.

When Rikki got to the house, Teddy and Teddy's mother (she looked very 820 white still, for she had been fainting) and Teddy's father came out and almost cried over him; and that night he ate all that was given him till he could eat no more, and went to bed on Teddy's shoulder, where Teddy's mother saw him when she came to look late at night.

"He saved our lives and Teddy's life," she said to her husband. "Just think, he 830 saved all our lives."

Rikki-tikki woke up with a jump, for all the mongooses are light sleepers.

"Oh, it's you," said he. "What are you bothering for? All the cobras are dead; and if they weren't I'm here."

Rikki-tikki had a right to be proud of himself; but he did not grow too proud, and he kept that garden as a mongoose should keep it, with tooth and jump 840 and spring and bite, till never a cobra dared show its head inside the walls.

DARZEE'S CHAUNT

(Sung in honour of Rikki-tikki-tavi)

Singer and tailor am I —
    Doubled the joys that I know —
Proud of my lilt through the sky,
    Proud of the house that I sew —
Over and under, so weave I my music — so weave I the house that I sew.

Sing to your fledglings again,
    Mother, oh lift up your head!
Evil that plagued us is slain,
850   Death in the garden lies dead.
Terror that hid in the roses is impotent — flung on the dung-hill and dead!

Who hath delivered us, who?
    Tell me his nest and his name.
Rikki, the valiant, the true,
    Tikki, with eyeballs of flame.
Rik-tikki-tikki, the ivory-fanged, the hunter with eyeballs of flame.

Give him the Thanks of the Birds,
    Bowing with tail-feathers spread!
Praise him with nightingale words —
860   Nay, I will praise him instead.
Hear! I will sing you the praise of the bottle-tailed Rikki, with eyeballs of red!

(Here Rikki-tikki interrupted, and the rest of the song is lost.)

Discussion Hints

1. "Rikki-tikki-tavi" is a story of setting, a story of character, and a story of plot. Discuss all three statements. Which of the three seems to you to be of foremost importance?

2. Why is it so difficult to frighten a mongoose? What is the motto of the mongoose family? What is Rikki-tikki's war cry?

3. Find several comments on the animal, bird, and snake characters that make them seem especially human.

4. Do the songs which open and close the story add to its effectiveness? Was Kipling right in placing them as he did rather than in the story where Darzee sang them?

5. Just what seems to you most notable, even memorable, about "Rikki-tikki-tavi" as a story and about Rikki-tikki-tavi as a character?

Suggestions for Reading

1. There is no better introduction to the stories of Rudyard Kipling than *The Jungle Book* and *The Second Jungle Book* ("Rikki-tikki-tavi" is in the first), made up chiefly of tales of the boy Mowgli and his brothers of the jungle. Excellent also, and packed with wisdom, the practical wisdom of animals and of ancient human times, are *Just So Stories* (fables of men and beasts) and *Puck of Pook's Hill* and *Rewards and Fairies* (stories and verse about old England).

2. There are, besides, stories of life in India, such as *Soldier Stories* and *Plain Tales from the Hills*. Best of all the stories of India, many think, is *Kim*, a longer tale of a white boy who supposed he was brown. West and East meet again in *Kim*, but in a way different from that of "The Ballad of East and West" (p. 628).

3. You will like *Stalky & Co.* too, a story of English schoolboy life (Beetle is Rudyard Kipling himself), and *Captains Courageous* (Did you see Spencer Tracy in the moving picture?), a tale of the Gloucester fishing fleet.

For suggestions for reading from Kipling's verse see page 615; for his narrative verse see page 631. See also the revised editions of *Adventure* and *Achievement* of this series.

Doubleday, Doran & Company, Inc., are Kipling's American publishers.

JOHN GALSWORTHY[1] (1867-1933)

Quality

When Galsworthy first published "Quality," along with similar papers in book form, he called the collection *Studies and Essays.* However, when it appeared in his collected works, he spoke of it as a short story. Thus, judged by Galsworthy himself, "Quality" may be read either as an essay expressing sympathy for the underdog, or as a short story giving glimpses of the pathetic history of a conscientious old shoemaker. What we call it makes little difference. The important thing is that "Quality" illustrates one of Galsworthy's most important rules for writing short stories, a rule that may also be applied to the familiar, or personal, essay: "Write only what interests yourself."

I KNEW him from the days of my extreme youth, because he made my father's boots; inhabiting with his elder brother two little shops let into one, in a small by-street — now no more, but then most fashionably placed in the West End.[2]

That tenement had a certain quiet distinction; there was no sign upon its face that he made for any of the Royal Family — merely his own German name of Gessler Brothers; and in the window a few pairs of boots. I remember that it always troubled me to account for those unvarying boots in the window, for he made only what was ordered, reaching nothing down, and it seemed so inconceivable that what he made could ever have failed to fit. Had he bought them to put there? That, too, seemed inconceivable. He would never have tolerated in his house leather on which he had not worked himself. Besides, they were too beautiful — the pair of pumps, so inexpressibly slim, the patent leathers with cloth tops, making water come into one's mouth, the tall brown riding boots with marvellous sooty glow, as if, though new, they had been worn a hundred years.

Those pairs could only have been made by one who saw before him the Soul of Boot — so truly were they prototypes incarnating the very spirit of all footgear. These thoughts, of course, came to me later, though even when I was promoted to him, at the age of perhaps fourteen, some inkling haunted me of the dignity of himself and brother. For to make boots — such boots as he made — seemed to me then, and still seems to me, mysterious and wonderful.

I remember well my shy remark, one day, while stretching out to him my youthful foot:

"Isn't it awfully hard to do, Mr. Gessler?"

And his answer, given with a sudden smile from out of the sardonic redness of his beard: "Id is an Ardt!"

Himself, he was a little as if made from leather, with his yellow crinkly face, and crinkly reddish hair and beard, and neat folds slanting down his cheeks to the corners of his mouth, and his guttural and one-toned voice; for leather is a sardonic substance, and stiff and slow of purpose. And that was the character of his face, save that his eyes, which were grey-blue, had in them the simple gravity of one secretly possessed by the Ideal. His elder brother was so very like him — though watery, paler in every way, with a great industry — that sometimes in early days I was not quite sure of him until the interview was over. Then I knew that it was he, if the words, "I will ask my brudder," had not been spoken; and that, if they had, it was his elder brother.

When one grew old and wild and ran up bills, one somehow never ran them up with Gessler Brothers. It would not have seemed becoming to go in there and stretch out one's foot to that blue iron-

[1] For biography see page 745.
[2] The West End of London.

spectacled glance, owing him for more than — say — two pairs, just the comfortable reassurance that one was still his client.

For it was not possible to go to him very often — his boots lasted terribly,
80 having something beyond the temporary — some, as it were, essence of boot stitched into them.

One went in, not as into most shops, in the mood of: "Please serve me, and let me go!" but restfully, as one enters a church; and, sitting on the single wooden chair, waited — for there was never anybody there. Soon, over the top edge of that sort of well — rather dark, and
90 smelling soothingly of leather — which formed the shop, there would be seen his face, or that of his elder brother, peering down. A guttural sound, and the tiptap of bast slippers[1] beating the narrow wooden stairs, and he would stand before one without coat, a little bent, in leather apron, with sleeves turned back, blinking — as if awakened from some dream of boots, or like an owl surprised in day-
100 light and annoyed at this interruption.

And I would say: "How do you do, Mr. Gessler? Could you make me a pair of Russia leather boots?"

Without a word he would leave me, retiring whence he came, or into the other portion of the shop, and I would continue to rest in the wooden chair, inhaling the incense of his trade. Soon he would come back, holding in his thin,
110 veined hand a piece of gold-brown leather. With eyes fixed on it, he would remark: "What a beaudiful biece!" When I, too, had admired it, he would speak again. "When do you wand dem?" And I would answer: "Oh! As soon as you conveniently can." And he would say: "To-morrow fordnighd?" Or if he were his elder brother: "I will ask my brudder!"
120 Then I would murmur: "Thank you!

[1] *bast slippers.* Slippers made of bast, a kind of wood fiber.

Good-morning, Mr. Gessler." "Gootmorning!" he would reply, still looking at the leather in his hand. And as I moved to the door, I would hear the tiptap of his bast slippers restoring him, up the stairs, to his dream of boots. But if it were some new kind of foot-gear that he had not yet made me, then indeed he would observe ceremony — divesting me of my boot and holding it long in his 130 hand, looking at it with eyes at once critical and loving, as if recalling the glow with which he had created it, and rebuking the way in which one had disorganized this masterpiece. Then, placing my foot on a piece of paper, he would two or three times tickle the outer edges with a pencil and pass his nervous fingers over my toes, feeling himself into the heart of my requirements.   140

I cannot forget that day on which I had occasion to say to him: "Mr. Gessler, that last pair of town walking-boots creaked, you know."

He looked at me for a time without replying, as if expecting me to withdraw or qualify the statement, then said:

"Id shouldn'd 'ave greaked."

"It did, I'm afraid."

"You goddem wed before dey found 150 demselves?"

"I don't think so."

At that he lowered his eyes, as if hunting for memory of those boots, and I felt sorry I had mentioned this grave thing.

"Zend dem back!" he said; "I will look at dem."

A feeling of compassion for my creaking boots surged up in me, so well could 160 I imagine the sorrowful long curiosity of regard which he would bend on them.

"Zome boods," he said slowly, "are bad from birdt. If I can do noding wid dem, I dake dem off your bill."

Once (once only) I went absentmindedly into his shop in a pair of boots bought in an emergency at some large firm's. He took my order without show-

170 ing me any leather, and I could feel his eyes penetrating the inferior integument of my foot. At last he said:

"Dose are nod my boods."

The tone was not one of anger, nor of sorrow, not even of contempt, but there was in it something quiet that froze the blood. He put his hand down and pressed a finger on the place where the left boot, endeavouring to be fashionable, 180 was not quite comfortable.

"Id 'urds you dere," he said. "Dose big virms 'ave no self-respect. Drash!" And then, as if something had given way within him, he spoke long and bitterly. It was the only time I ever heard him discuss the conditions and hardships of his trade.

"Dey get id all," he said, "dey get id by adverdisement, nod by work. Dey 190 dake it away from us, who lofe our boods. Id gomes to this — bresently I haf no work. Every year id gets less — you will see." And looking at his lined face I saw things I had never noticed before, bitter things and bitter struggle — and what a lot of grey hairs there seemed suddenly in his red beard!

As best I could, I explained the circumstances of the purchase of those ill-200 omened boots. But his face and voice made so deep an impression that during the next few minutes I ordered many pairs. Nemesis* fell! They lasted more terribly than ever. And I was not able conscientiously to go to him for nearly two years.

When at last I went I was surprised to find that outside one of the two little windows of his shop another name was 210 painted, also that of a bootmaker — making, of course, for the Royal Family. The old familiar boots, no longer in dignified isolation, were huddled in the single window. Inside, the now contracted well of the one little shop was more scented and darker than ever. And it was longer than usual, too, before a face peered down, and the tip-

tap of the bast slippers began. At last he stood before me, and, gazing through 220 those rusty iron spectacles, said:

"Mr. ——, isn'd it?"

"Ah, Mr. Gessler," I stammered, "but your boots are really *too* good, you know! See, these are quite decent still!" And I stretched out to him my foot. He looked at it.

"Yes," he said, "beople do nod wand good boods, id seems."

To get away from his reproachful 230 eyes and voice I hastily remarked: "What have you done to your shop?"

He answered quietly: "Id was too exbensif. Do you wand some boods?"

I ordered three pairs, though I had only wanted two, and quickly left. I had, I do not know quite what feeling of being part, in his mind, of a conspiracy against him; or not perhaps so much against him as against his idea of boot. 240 One does not, I suppose, care to feel like that; for it was again many months before my next visit to his shop, paid, I remember, with the feeling: "Oh! well, I can't leave the old boy — so here goes! Perhaps it'll be his elder brother!"

For his elder brother, I knew, had not character enough to reproach me, even dumbly.

And, to my relief, in the shop there 250 did appear to be his elder brother, handling a piece of leather.

"Well, Mr. Gessler," I said, "how are you?"

He came close, and peered at me.

"I am breddy well," he said slowly; "but my elder brudder is dead."

And I saw that it was indeed himself — but how aged and wan! And never before had I heard him mention his 260 brother. Much shocked, I murmured: "Oh! I am sorry!"

"Yes," he answered, "he was a good man, he made a good bood; but he is dead." And he touched the top of his head, where the hair had suddenly gone as thin as it had been on that of his poor brother, to indicate, I suppose, the cause of death. "He could nod ged over losing 270 de oder shop. Do you wand any boods?" And he held up the leather in his hand: "Id's a beaudiful biece."

I ordered several pairs. It was very long before they came — but they were better than ever. One simply could not wear them out. And soon after that I went abroad.

ᵇ It was over a year before I was again in London. And the first shop I went to 280 was my old friend's. I had left a man of sixty, I came back to one of seventy-five, pinched and worn and tremulous, who genuinely, this time, did not at first know me.

"Oh! Mr. Gessler," I said, sick at heart; "how splendid your boots are! See, I've been wearing this pair nearly all the time I've been abroad; and they're not half worn out, are they?"

290 He looked long at my boots — a pair of Russia leather, and his face seemed to regain steadiness. Putting his hand on my instep, he said:

"Do dey vid you here? I'ad drouble wid dat bair, I remember."

I assured him that they had fitted beautifully.

"Do you wand any boods?" he said. "I can make dem quickly; id is a slack 300 dime."

I answered: "Please, please! I want boots all round — every kind!"

"I will make a vresh model. Your food must be bigger." And with utter slowness, he traced round my foot, and felt my toes, only once looking up to say:

"Did I dell you my brudder was dead?"

To watch him was painful, so feeble 310 had he grown; I was glad to get away.

I had given those boots up, when one evening they came. Opening the parcel, I set the four pairs out in a row. Then one by one I tried them on. There was no doubt about it. In shape and fit, in finish and quality of leather, they were

the best he had ever made me. And in the mouth of one of the Town walking-boots I found his bill. The amount was the same as usual, but it gave me quite a 320 shock. He had never before sent it in till quarter day.[1] I flew down-stairs, and wrote a cheque, and posted it at once with my own hand.

A week later, passing the little street, I thought I would go in and tell him how splendidly the new boots fitted. But when I came to where his shop had been, his name was gone. Still there, in the window, were the slim pumps, the 330 patent leathers with cloth tops, the sooty riding boots.

I went in, very much disturbed. In the two little shops — again made into one — was a young man with an English face.

"Mr. Gessler in?" I said.

He gave me a strange, ingratiating look.

"No, sir," he said, "no. But we can 340 attend to anything with pleasure. We've taken the shop over. You've seen our name, no doubt, next door. We make for some very good people."

"Yes, yes," I said; "but Mr. Gessler?"

"Oh!" he answered; "dead."

"Dead! But I only received these boots from him last Wednesday week."

"Ah!" he said; "a shockin' go. Poor 350 old man starved 'imself."

"Good God!"

"Slow starvation, the doctor called it! You see he went to work in such a way! Would keep the shop on; wouldn't have a soul touch his boots except himself. When he got an order, it took him such a time. People won't wait. He lost everybody. And there he'd sit, goin' on and on — I will say that for him — not a 360 man in London made a better boot!

[1] *quarter-day*. A day occurring once every three months and recognized in England as the day for paying the quarterly rent and settling other financial obligations.

But look at the competition! He never advertised! Would 'ave the best leather, too, and do it all 'imself. Well, there it is. What could you expect with his ideas?"

"But starvation ——!"

"That may be a bit flowery, as the sayin' is — but I know myself he was sittin' over his boots day and night, to 370 the very last. You see I used to watch him. Never gave 'imself time to eat; never had a penny in the house. All went in rent and leather. How he lived so long I don't know. He regular let his fire go out. He was a character. But he made good boots."

"Yes," I said, "he made good boots."

And I turned and went out quickly, for I did not want that youth to know 380 that I could hardly see.

Discussion Hints

1. What is the difference in the meaning of "boots" in England and in America? What is meant by makers of boots for the royal family?

2. What commentary does the story furnish on the statement that one's work marks him for its own? Compare the two brothers.

3. With what "beaudiful" material did Mr. Gessler work? Over whose boots was he working "day and night, to the very last"?

4. What is meant by "the Soul of Boot"?

"Id is an Ardt"? "essence of boot"? "dream of boots"?

5. What was the highest compliment paid both brothers?

6. What is the significance of the title "Quality"?

7. Is the old bootmaker a typical character or is he an individual? Give reasons for your answer.

Suggestions for Reading

1. Other short stories by the author of "Quality" may be found in *Caravan: The Assembled Tales of John Galsworthy* and in *On Forsyte 'Change*. The second title suggests at once the Forsytes, perhaps the best-known purely fictitious family of modern times. John Galsworthy tells their story in three great trilogies: *The Forsyte Saga*, the tale of three generations centered around Soames Forsyte, late Victorian, "the man of property"; *A Modern Comedy*, which, in three novels connected by two brief interludes, as in *The Forsyte Saga*, gives an account of the postwar generation; and *End of the Chapter*, in which the Forsytes of the 1920's and 1930's figure.

2. Galsworthy's essays may be sampled in *Castles in Spain and Other Screeds* and in *The Inn of Tranquillity*, studies and essays.

3. For Galsworthy's plays see page 695.

4. Galsworthy's *Collected Poems*, like all the books given above and many titles not mentioned here, are published by Charles Scribner's Sons.

ERIC KNIGHT[1] (1897-1943)

Cockles for Tea

Eric Knight, who was killed in an airplane crash during the Second World War, is usually regarded as a humorous writer, largely because of his accounts of Sam Small, the Yorkshireman who discovered that he could fly without a plane. Many stories by Knight, such as "Cockles for Tea," are unquestionably humorous, but beneath the fun is a shrewd analysis of people.

IT DIDN'T take long for the news to spread through the village of Polking-
D

thorpe Brig. After ten years in America, Walter Ashcroft was home for a visit! The lad had made his fortune, there was no doubt about it. But the way he was flinging his money about like a bloody millionaire was the chief subject of conversation. The womenfolk discussed it over the back fences, and the men argued 10 it over their evening pint of ale at The Spread Eagle.

[1]For biography see page 745.

Sitting in his room at the inn, Walter Ashcroft realized that the folk in the village didn't think much of him. But being a true Yorkshireman, he also realized that there was no way for him to explain to them that he had come back because he was homesick for the sound of their voices, because he wanted to taste a real Yorkshire pudding with the Sunday
10 roast, because of the intangible ties which drive a man to go and see how it is with the people among whom he was born.

However, he was puzzled by his own people. He could see that the village disapproved of his foreign habits. Yet he could not say to them that these habits were no longer foreign to him—the way he talked, the way he dressed, the way he spent his money. He knew that owning
20 his own home and a small automobile agency back in New Mexico was only a moderate success, judged by American standards, but he could not make this clear to the practical people of the village.

In their eyes Walter was a spendthrift. They were decided on that after the very first night he had appeared at The Spread Eagle. For he paid for a round of drinks out of turn—and did it not only once, but
30 twice! The shock of this was as nothing compared to his stubbornness about darts. In the evenings that followed he would go right on playing a game of darts for a round of drinks, even though it should have been clear to any man in his right senses that all the other lads could have shut both eyes and more than run him even.

"We never play at darts in the States,"
40 Walter would say, "so it's no wonder I'm badly out of practice."

When Sam Small, who had been in America—and not only that but all around the world, as everyone knows full well—said that it was true that they didn't play darts in America as far as he could ever find out, the men decided that Walter was a proper fool to play against them night after night.

"He may have been born in Yorkshire, 50 but ye'd never know it," said Gaffer Sitherthwick. "And he may have made a fortune in America, but he won't have it long the road he's going. Nay, a fool's soon parted from his brass—and a man soon parted from his brass is a fool."

"I notice tha's quite willing to get in on a dart game when he's playing, though," Sam Small commented sagely.

The Gaffer finished lighting his pipe, 60 and then cleared his throat. "Waste is sinful," he said. "And it's just as sinful to waste a good opportunity as owt else."

And that was the opinion of the entire village. It was sad to think that a lad from good stock like the Ashcrofts should have been turned by a foreign land into a fool, and him alone in the world, as you might say, without a relative to give him any good advice. Of the whole village, 70 perhaps the only lad who didn't believe the verdict was Sam Small.

But when even Sam heard about the wildest action of Walter, he strode angrily to the pub. His face red, from anger and the exertion of fast walking, he strode in and walked smack up to Walter.

"Young Walter Ashcroft," Sam said, in a clear voice, "I'm a chap o' few words. I knew thy father, and he were a good lad. 80 So I've felt I should keep a forbearing eye on thee. But now tha's capped the climax."

"Why, Mr. Small, what have I done?" asked the young man, cool as you please.

"What's tha done?" Sam echoed. "Eigh, lad, lad! 'Tis said tha's lent the loan of a shilling to Gommy Doakes, the Cockle[1] Man!"

At this, everybody looked at Walter in 90 horror, waiting for him to deny it. But Walter didn't.

"Oh," he said with a careless air, looking down into his pint. "I lent the poor old devil a bob. What's wrong with that?"

"Wrong?" choked old Gaffer Sitherthwick, getting in the discussion.

[1]Cockles are edible shellfish.

"Wrong? Why, doesn'ta know that the old miser has never ever paid nobody back owt that he borrowed i' all his life? That's why noan on us has ever lent him owt."

"If you never lent him anything, how could he pay you back?" Walter asked.

They all thought about this for a while.

"Come, come, now, ma lad," Gaffer Sitherthwick said, finally, "that's merely Yankee flim-flam. Gommy's that mishonest, tha can tell by looking at him that he'd never pay back."

"Oh, perhaps my trust in him will make him a reformed character, and he'll live up to his obligations."

"Obligations be jiggered," the Gaffer said scornfully. "Kiss thy bob good-by, because it's sixpence to a brass farthing tha'll never see it no more."

"You wouldn't like to make that bet an even half-sovereign,[1] would you?" the lad asked evenly.

At this there was many a gasp and whisper, with most men siding with Sam Small and counseling the Gaffer that it wouldn't be right to take advantage of the lad's innocence.

"Have done," the Gaffer shouted finally. "Now, the kindest thing a man can do in this hard life is to help young folk learn their lessons. So I'm not doing this to win his ten shillings, but more to teach him this is a cruel world he must live in. So I'll take that bet, my lad."

"Done," said Walter.

"And if tha wants to throw good brass after bad, I'd like a half-crown[2] on the same thing," Capper Wambley put in.

"And I'll take a shilling," Rowlie Helliker added.

Seeming fair crazed with recklessness, the young man took all bets, and before he could have had a chance to reckon up the score, he stood ready to be roundly beaten to the staggering tune of one pound, three shillings, and sixpence. Everyone there had bet against him but Sam Small. Sam, battling with himself, started from the inn. But he got only as far as the door. He struggled, and then came back.

"Lad," he said to Walter, "it's a crying shame to take advantage of thy weakness, but—well—put me down for two shillings on the same thing."

Now, of course, the whole village was all of an itch and a scratch, as you might say, over the famous bet that had been laid, and housewives and bairns were all peeping from behind curtains or over fences to report any latest move that might be made in the tremendous battle of wits that was sure to ensue. But did they have anything to report?

Not a bit of a thing, they did. For all Walter Ashcroft seemed to do was lead the veritable life of the grasshopper in the fable. Evenings he would sit in the pub and lose a round of drinks at darts, never seeming to get any better at the game. Especially did he seem a godsend to John Willie Braithwaite, who for years had been low man at the dart board. Daytimes he would moon around up the Green, and you can be sure all the neighbors wasted no time in reporting that the likely-looking lad was spending his time looking balmy at Gaffer Sitherthwick's lass, Barbara Alice.

Now it must be said that that, at least, was one sign of sense in Walter Ashcroft. For Barbara Alice was a right lass. Skin she had like May blossoms, and hair like burnished oak leaves, and her eyes were like nothing else if they weren't the very spit[1] of the bluebells that come in April up in the Duke of Rudling's woods, where no one is supposed to go because of the temptation that a fat rabbit might put before them.

There she was, all cream and gold, and now growing up to be twenty-three and

---

[1]Half a pound, or ten shillings.
[2]A crown is five shillings.

[1]Compare with the American slang expression, "spit and image."

never a man had spoken for her because of her ways.

And she had ways. For instance, she was uppy. It's hard to tell just how she was uppy, but it might be explained this way: Other women in the village always wore their weekday shawls over their heads with a bit of a twist back over one shoulder. Barbara Alice Sitherthwick always wore her shawl over her shoulders with her head bare—even on a rainy day you would see her going along that way, setting off for town over the moor with her head bare and her fine feet stepping down firmly. That's the kind of lass she was.

And there was Walter Ashcroft, passing away the precious hours talking to her at her front gate, instead of attending to his business of catching up with Gommy Doakes, the Cockle Man.

Now a right lad would have put himself on the trail of Gommy and with bulldog pertinacity would have made the Cockle Man's days a living misery over that shilling. But Walter seemed to do nothing at all. And there was no doubt about it that Gommy was playing a very proper game with Walter. Let Walter come down Green Lane, and Gommy would go ducking over the street and fade away down the Ginnel. Let Walter turn down the Ginnel, and Gommy would pop over the Widow Braithwaite's wall and slide like an eel down the Snicket and out by the alley. Walter didn't even seem to notice it, but everybody else did.

When word of Walter's attentions to Barbara Alice began to punctuate the nightly discussions at the pub, Gaffer Sitherthwick went home and faced his wife.

"I'll have ma say like any true Yorkshireman should," he orated to her, "and then I'll have done.

"Firstly, it's not that I wouldn't wish to see ma lass wed and having a houseful of bairns, as anyone knows is rightful and proper. Secondly, if yon lad is sparking our Barbara Alice, he's swinging on the wrong gate. For thirdly, I'd sooner have her on ma hands all the rest of her days than see her wed to a chap that squanders brass and that hasn't gumption enough to go out and collect what's properly and justly due him. Because thirdly, in ma opinion, such a chap would make a varry, varry poor sort of husband, and his ways would lead to nowt but indecent living. Now, has tha owt to say to that?"

"That's two thirdlys tha had, and take thy feet off ma fender[1]—I just polished it," Mrs. Sitherthwick said. "And besides, there's nowt to it. They haven't said a courting word to each other."

Of course the Gaffer's words got back to Walter—as they will in any village. But Walter only laughed at such talk. And anyhow, as Mrs. Sitherthwick had mentioned, nobody could say for certain if he really was sparking Barbara Alice.

The women in the neighboring cottages said—and it must be admitted it's terribly hard not to overhear what's being said under your front window, especially if the window is open a crack and you happen to be sitting near it—they said that Walter and Barbara Alice had the funniest sort of conversations you could ever wish to hear, with nothing but talk about the weather and such.

Actually, the weather didn't monopolize the conversation. Sometimes they'd talk of childhood and sometimes about America. To Barbara Alice, Walter felt he could explain about himself.

"It don't smell right out there, not like a home ought to," Walter would say.

"Smell right?"

"Aye, tha knows—the smell of bubbly soap and steam on washdays, and smell of bottom loaf cooling on bake days, and smell of a bit of a roast on Sundays, with gravy, like. You don't get them there."

"Who does thy cooking?" Barbara Alice asked.

[1]Low metal frame before a fireplace.

"Well, I eat mostly in the restaurant—it's handy to the business."

"Eigh, that's no sort of food for a man to be eating. No wonder tha looks poorly. I'll guarantee they couldn't make a Yorkshire pudding that wouldn't be sad as a bit of shoe leather."

"Yorkshire pudding! Why, lass, I haven't had a mouthful since I went away."

"Not in ten year!" she breathed. Barbara Alice stood aghast at the horror of it. "I should think a man would get heartsick."

"Nay, it's none so bad."

"But it is! I should think ye'd get heartsick."

So the women were right when they said Walter and Barbara Alice never spoke a courting word to each other. But there was one important feature they didn't report—Walter Ashcroft was beginning to talk Yorkshire again. The women of Polkingthorpe Brig knew that a man's born speech is needed for deep moments, for moments of intimacy, and they heard Walter Ashcroft use the dialect in talking to Barbara Alice Sitherthwick. But they didn't say anything about this to the men, for sometimes all women seem in league against the males of the world.

So there was Walter, draped over the Sitherthwick white picket fence, his voice becoming more and more Yorkshire as he talked to her of the weather and the garden; and all the time there was Gommy Doakes, sneaking around the village and making a high mock of the reputation that Walter should have had as a proper Yorkshireman.

Suddenly there were only three more days left for Walter's visit, and then it seemed as if he did wake up a bit—although most of the village, after proper discussion, decided that the encounter was accidental. Walter had seen Gommy Doakes shuffling down Green Lane. Gommy crossed the street quick as a snake. Walter crossed. Gommy slid into the Ginnel. Walter headed after him. With mad haste Gommy skimmed over the wall onto the Widow Braithwaite's midden tip[1], scurried through her yard, and shot back to Green Lane down the Snicket. And there he ran smack into the arms of Walter Ashcroft, who hadn't gone up the Ginnel at all.

"Hello, Gommy," Walter said.

"Glory be if it ain't Mr. Ashcroft. Nice mornin', ain't it," said Gommy, his feet going like mad.

But whereas his legs were going through the motions of running, Gommy wasn't getting anywhere, because Walter was holding him by the back of his coat collar, free from the ground.

"And ye're the varry man I wished to see," added Gommy, seeing he was getting nowhere and swiftly changing his tactics. "I've been looking for thee to tell thee about that there bob."

"Yes?"

"Aye. Ah, sad is the day, Mr. Ashcroft. A wife and nine starving bairns I have hoam, and not a soul in the house to addle a penny but me. Tha wouldn't rob a poor man—"

"Come, now, Gommy. You manage to make both ends meet and more."

"That's it, Mr. Ashcroft. When I make both ends meet, it leaves such a tarrible gap in th' middle, as tha might say."

And there was Gommy, wriggling and whining and weaseling to get out of paying his debt, with everyone in the village peeping through the shop windows, but keeping themselves politely hidden, and Walter looking at the watch on his wrist and saying,

"Talk fast, Gommy, for I have an appointment in the city today."

It was exciting news, for fair, and there was nothing else talked about that evening at The Spread Eagle. No one saw Walter the rest of that day. And no one

[1]*midden tip.* Rubbish pile.

saw him get off the bus from the city—
which was why he happened to walk into
the inn right while they were talking
about him. There was a silence, and then
Sam Small saw it was no good hiding the
topic.

"Us was just discussing, Walter lad,"
he said. "Us heard tha catched up wi'
Gommy Doakes. Did he pay thee?"

10 "Well," Walter said slowly, "as you
might say, he didn't; but in a manner of
speaking, he will."

"What dosta mean: 'as tha might say,'
and 'in a manner o' speaking'?" thundered the Gaffer. . .

"It's this way," Walter explained. "He
admitted he has nine shillings. But there's
a sack of cockles waiting at the railroad,
and he must pay ten shillings for 'em, or

20 they'll go bad. Now if he could get those
cockles, he'd make a few shillings' profit."

"So?" roared Gaffer Sitherthwick.

"So," Walter finished lamely, "I lent
him the other shilling."

The stunned silence that followed was
more eloquent than words. Those hor-
rified Yorkshiremen trooped from the
inn. The whole village soon had the unbelievable word that far from paying

30 back the shilling, Gommy Doakes had
weaseled another bob from that Walter
Ashcroft.

The next day was the last full one of
Walter Ashcroft's visit. But it was a
memorable one. For in mid-morning a
rumor came to the village that Gommy
Doakes had started over the moor at
dawn going as if headed for Scotland;
but that Walter Ashcroft had gone stroll-

40 ing after him not three minutes behind.

But the people shook their heads. For
there was no one for walking like Gommy
Doakes when he was headed away from a
debt. The way Gommy knew the moor,
and the twisting, turning tricks he had in
coming through near-by villages, would
shake off many a man who knew the country better than Walter. But in mid-
afternoon, amazing word came to the inn.

Gommy was streaking for home, but 50
Walter Ashcroft was swinging heel and
toe not fifty yards behind, unconcerned
as you please.

They all rushed out just in time to see
Gommy, panting wearily, come up by
the Green. And right by the inn, with a
dramatic gasp, he gave up and dropped to
the curb. Walter came up to the sitting
figure, cool as you please, and looked
surprised—just as if he'd noticed Gommy 60
for the first time that day.

"Good afternoon to you, Gommy
Doakes," he said.

Gommy held his chest and panted.
Anyone could see now that clearly it
was a case for skill, not endurance any
longer.

"Why, bless ma heart and sowl,"
Gommy came back, short on breath but
long on trickery. "If it ain't young Mr 70
Ashcroft! And, for one in this village, I
say long may he have a chair by his chimney, and coal for his grate when he's old
and poor and without a true-hearted
friend to aid him through stress and
strife, trial and tribulation, poverty and
want."

"Thankee, Gommy Doakes. But, to
put it in a nutshell, isn't it nigh time
you were off to get your cockles to be 80
selling this night?"

"Oh, sad's the day, Mr. Ashcroft!
And if I'd nobbut seen thee earlier this
day, I would have explained to thee."

"Why, what's up, Gommy?"

"Ma barrow, Mr. Ashcroft. Eigh,
broke it is, and so bad that not a foot
could ye push it, up hill nor down—and
no other one in this sad village but that
of Robbie Cobble the coal man. But it's 90
the cruel price of sixpence he'll be asking
for the lend of it. And here's poor me,
who's been walking all this day in solitude, as tha might say, just to try and
think out this problem. For if I spend
ma ten shillings for cockles, then I've no
sixpence left to rent a barrow to put 'em
in; while if I pay sixpence for a barrow,

then I've no ten shillings left for to get cockles to put in it. What can I do?"

"Eigh, it's a tale t'old miser is telling." Sam Small's voice put in from the crowd.

"Nay, it's truth, and may I have ma throat cut if it's not," Gommy protested. "Eigh, if I nobbut had another sixpence!"

Walter looked up, and you might almost have said that there was a bit of a nod passed between him and Barbara Alice, who was standing sedately away from the crowd.

"Oh, don't fret, Gommy Doakes. Here, lad. I'll lend you another sixpence. What's more, I'll even go with you and get the barrow and help you push it up to the station to get your cockles."

In dumbfounded amazement everyone stood aside and watched Gommy and Walter head up the street. Finally the crowd woke, and there rose a sort of muffled moan of anguish from those Yorkshiremen. Then they began to scatter, not speaking as they went. Only their faces left no doubt as to what they felt. Walter Ashcroft's Yankee wealth had surely driven him mad.

Walter Ashcroft, sitting in his room after dinner, heard the age-old sequence of sounds that meant the village was ending another day. The familiar routine filled him with the same feelings that had made him come so many miles. This was home.

The sounds claimed Walter and chained him to his Yorkshire youth. But there was an American side to him now. And it was the American side that made him rise when he heard the hum of voices beneath him as the men gathered in the public room. He straightened his tie. He had a job to do that was more than winning bets. He wanted to win the respect of the village in its own terms—and he felt American enough to do it.

"Good evening, all," said Walter as he went into the pub.

They did not answer.

"How about a game of darts for a round of ale?" Walter offered.

Sorely tempted as they were, they still made no answer. Only Sam Small spoke.

"Eigh, hasn't tha learned yet that it's always thee that pays?" he said, not unkindly.

"Well, seeing I go away tomorrow, I thought we might have a real farewell game," Walter explained. "Perhaps even for a half-crown a man—winner take all."

Now indeed they were sorely tried, and they made noises in their throats and shuffled their feet. Finally Gaffer Sitherthwick rose.

"Ba gum!" he exploded. "The lamb that hangs around the wolf's door deserves all he gets. Come on, lads."

So up they jumped, and each put up his money—nine half-crowns including Walter's—on the window sill. Winking to each other, they stood back while Walter took the three darts in his hand and toed the line.

There is no need to recount that game. If you want the details, you can drop in at The Spread Eagle Inn in Polkingthorpe Brig any day, and there'll be chaps there who can tell you point by point how Walter Ashcroft threw a perfect score, throwing with the unerring certainty of a master.

And as he picked up the half-crowns from the window sill, the admiring voice of Sam Small broke the dead silence:

"Lads! I begin to suspect we've been had."

"Tha can play darts," Gaffer Sitherthwick said accusingly.

"Just laying back for sucker bets," said Walter calmly.

"Eigh, there's summat varry funny going on," old Capper said slowly.

"Nay—just a Yankee trick," Walter explained. "What did you all think I've been buying drinks for, this last couple of weeks, except to learn the game?"

"Well, I'll be jiggered," old Sitherthwick said. "I feel it's downright cheating, almost, as tha might say. And—"

What Sitherthwick wanted to add was never heard, for Walter Ashcroft suddenly hissed, and stood silent, listening.

And then, faintly, they heard floating in from the night the doleful wail of Gommy Doakes, chanting his cockles. They could hear him coming along Green Lane, singing his call:

Cockles eelive, buy 'em eelive—oh.
Sixpence a quartern, thrupence half a quartern.
Any cockles eelive, buy 'em eelive?
  Fine big cockles!
  Great big cockles!
Buy 'em eelive, all eelive—oh.

Walter slipped the jingling silver coins into his pocket.

"You must pardon me," he said. "I've got another little matter."

With everyone at his heels, out he strode and planked himself right in the middle of the street before Gommy Doakes' cockle barrow, lit up with its lantern.

"Good evening to you, Gommy Doakes," cried Walter.

"Glory alive, if it ain't Mr. Ashcroft," said Gommy, dropping the shafts, now Walter barred his way. "Oh, sad is life. Here I were just saying to mysen that not a penny do I have and that good Mr. Ashcroft will be sailing away tomor't morn, and I'll never see him again so's I could pay him as I wish. Oh, ill is the luck."

"What, haven't you made any money yet, Gommy Doakes?"

"Not a penny—pushing ma weary way uphill and down with ma feet nigh walked to the ankles, and a chap can cry his lungs from his varry chest and not a cockle have I sold."

The waiting men stirred, for anyone could see that half the load of cockles was gone from Gommy's barrow.

"Well, happen business'll pick up,

Gommy," Walter said. "And I mustn't keep thee from thy work."

"Aye, I must be on ma weary road," Gommy said, delighted to have weaseled out of it. "So long."

"Nay, I'll go along with thee, Gommy."

"Tha'll what?"

"I'll go along with thee. A poor, comfortless chap like thee needs a trusting friend to walk a way with him on his weary rounds. Up with thy barrow, lad."

And before Gommy could say a word, Walter up with the shafts and off he went toward the Green with the Cockle Man trotting alongside and all the men following like a procession.

"Come on, Gommy Doakes," exhorted Walter. "Cry thy cockles, man!"

"But I been round t'Green once," Gommy protested, grabbing back the barrow shafts.

"Happen second time is better luck. Cry out, man!"

"Cockles eelive," Gommy chanted weakly, pushing as fast as he could in the hope of leaving Walter behind. But Walter stayed right by his side.

"There, tha sees how it is and all," Gommy said. "Not a soul to spend a meg on a poor old Cockle Man."

"Perhaps you don't cry loud enough, Gommy," Walter suggested.

"Glory be to the Black Prince," Gommy moaned. "Here's ma voice cried to a mere shadow of itself, as tha might say, and then the lad would have me cry louder."

Walter said nothing until they reached the corner of the Green. Then, suddenly, he roared in a voice that would have wakened old Wada, the Giant:

"Fine big cockles! Great big cockles!"

He made Gommy rest the barrow while he looked up and down the Green. Then a door opened, and out came none other than Barbara Alice Sitherthwick. And she was carrying a pail. Up she came, right to Walter.

"Oh, what champion cockles, Young

Mr. Cockle Man," she said. "I think I'll have a pailful."

"A pailful," groaned Gommy suspiciously.

"Fill it up, man. A customer," cheered Walter. "Here, I'll do it."

And he toppled and tippled in the cockles.

"How much?" asked Barbara Alice when he was done.

"Six quarterns," Walter reckoned. "That should be three shillings—but as it's almost wholesale business, as you might say, we'll call it a half-crown even."

Sweetly she passed over a shining half-crown to Walter. And Walter passed it to Gommy.

"Thank you, miss," Walter said. "Now Gommy Doakes, it just so chances you owe me a half-crown. Would you like to pay me now?"

Gommy shoved the coin in his slop pocket and put a protective hand over it. He looked at the circle of waiting faces. Then he looked at Walter's set jaw.

"Mr. Ashcroft," he moaned, "tha wouldn't be taking the bread and butter right out of the varry mouths of my wife and bairns?"

"Gommy Doakes, you mean old skinflint of a miser," Walter said. "I wouldn't be wanting to take thee by the heels and hold thee upside down so that all the shillings tha's made this night would come tumbling out to shame you. I wouldn't want to do that, because I'd rather have everyone in this village see thou art an honest man who is paying his debts of his own free will."

With a final cry of despair, Gommy passed over the money. "Well," he exploded. "Well! Ah never was so cheated in all ma born life!"

"Away wi' ye, ye weaseling mawngy old miser," called the men.

And away Gommy Doakes the Cockle Man went; muttering and bumbling nasty names on the entire family of Ashcroft, past, present, and future.

"Now, gentlemen," Walter said to the men, "I have collected from Gommy Doakes."

"And we've been beat," Sam Small cried. "But if there's one thing a Yorkshireman admits gladly, it's when he's fairly bested. So I'll pay up wi' a good heart. Let's see, it were a shilling I bet thee, weren't it?"

"It was not, Mr. Small," Walter said. "It were two shilling."

"Ba gum, he had thee there, Sam," Rowlie Helliker said. "So we'll pay up fairly."

And pay up they did—all until it came to the Gaffer, who was standing by his front gate. And he suddenly roared:

"Hold on a bit! I'm being right roundly done here somehow. He collected 'cause ma lass bought a pail o' cockles—I'm sure I don't want no pail o' cockles."

"Aye, we do, Feyther," Barbara Alice said. "For the party. Won't ye all step in and have a little summat?"

"Hold on," roared the Gaffer. "Us is not having no party."

"Oh, aye, us is," said Mrs. Sitherthwick, appearing at the door.

"May a man in his own house and home be allowed to ax just why he should be giving a party?" the Gaffer demanded.

Barbara Alice looked up quickly, and her eyes caught those of Walter Ashcroft, but she didn't say a word.

Mrs. Sitherthwick clicked her tongue as if to say she despaired of ever making some people see the light.

"Don't thee dit-dit-dit at me! I wean't have it!" the Gaffer thundered, poking his chin at her.

"I want to talk to thee, Harry Percival Sitherthwick," said his wife. "Come in! Barbara Alice, go in and fix them cockles! Widow Braithwaite—if tha wouldn't mind giving a hand wi' some sandwiches? The rest o' ye—if ye'll just wait a few minutes. Now, Harry Percival. Come!"

And in she stalked, with Gaffer Sither-thwick following her tiny figure obedi-ently. Through the kitchen she went, and into the bedroom.

"Sit down, Harry Percival," she said. "And not on ma new counterpane—over on that chair."

The Gaffer sat.

10 "Harry Percival Sitherthwick. Here us has a lass that's so funny and uppy, not a lad in the county comes courting, and her rising twenty-three—"

"Twenty-two," said Barbara Alice's voice.

"Go away from that door and stop lis-tening, Barbara Alice, or I'll skelp thee, big as tha is," Mrs. Sitherthwick said, without drawing a breath. "She's rising twenty-three, Harry. And now here 20 comes a likely lad, and I have a chance at last to get her off ma hands, and tha has to put thy big foot in it."

"Walter Ashcroft?" yelled the Gaffer, turning purple. "Ba gum, nay. I wean't have it!"

"What in the name o' goodness is thy objection?"

"It's his ways, lass! Flinging brass about. He's not—not practical! A lad 30 who wastes his shillings like yon does, well—he'd make a varry, varry poor sort of a husband for a daughter o' mine."

"Is that thy only objection?"

The Gaffer nodded.

"Indeed!" exploded Mrs. Sitherthwick. Then up she jumped and got paper and pencil from the chest of drawers. "I heard about that dart game tonight," she 40 said, looking sideways.

"What's that got to do wi' marriage?"

She did not answer. Instead she wrote busily for several minutes. Then she handed her husband a piece of paper.

"When tha's read that, come out and join the party," she said. Slowly the Gaffer took out his spectacles and read. The paper said:

To one bad debt		50
collected Gommy Doakes	.....	0.2.6[1]
To bets collected		
over Gommy's paying	....	1.3.6
To dart game, which you ninnies		
let him trick you into	....	1.0.0
Answer	.....	£2.6.0

Which just about pays his bill at the Inn. P.S. Now who's flinging whose brass about?

For a long time the Gaffer studied this, and then he rose. For the Gaffer was a 60 Yorkshireman, which means that he was a fair sportsman at heart. Firmly he stalked through the kitchen where the cockles were steaming and the women were as busy as hens, buttering bread and setting the table. He flung open the door and addressed the waiting people.

"Come in to ma house and hearth, all on ye," he roared.

And no one needed any second bidding. 70

"Now, Walter Ashcroft," boomed the Gaffer. "I hear tha wants to wed ma lass."

Barbara Alice blushed prettily and hid her face in a cloud of cockle-steam, while Walter opened his mouth.

"Drat ma buttons, don't interrupt," hollered the Gaffer. "Tak' her and bless ye, but on one condition. I don't believe in long courtships, so when can ye be 80 wed?"

"Well," Walter began hesitatingly, "you see, in America we move fast, and I've learned a lot of Yankee ways my-self—"

"I'll say tha has," Sam Small shouted. "Thy Yorkshire blood and thy Yankee training has combined to best every one on us in th' village. Hasn't it, lads?" 90

The men roared approval, but the Gaf-fer was a singleminded man.

"Never mind that," he boomed. "When's tha off to tak' this lass off ma hands?"

[1] The left-hand column represents pounds; the middle column, shillings; and the right-hand column, pence.

"I was coming to that. You see, there's so much to do these days what with passports and tickets and such, that it all couldn't be done at the last minute."

"So!" shouted the Gaffer.

"So," Walter said, "Barbara Alice and I got wed in the city yesterday."

For a moment the Gaffer looked like a turkey cock about to burst. Then he looked at his wife and cleared his throat.

"In such a case, there's only one thing to do," he said.

"And what would that be?" Mrs. Sitherthwick asked, sticking out her chin.

"Sit down and eat these here cockles," said the Gaffer.

Discussion Hints

1. Many short stories contain surprises, but a careful author makes the surprises seem plausible. As you look back over "Cockles for Tea," note how Knight carefully prepares for each surprise.

2. According to the citizens of Polkingthorpe Brig, what was "wrong" with Walter besides the fact that he lent a shilling to Gommy Doakes?

3. How, in the opinion of the village people, would a "right" lad have gone about collecting his debt from Gommy Doakes? Explain in your own language how Walter succeeded in doing it. What is meant by saying that Walter "wanted to win the respect of the village in its own terms" (p. 663, 1. 44)?

4. Which is the most interesting character, Walter, Barbara, Gaffer, Gommy, or someone else? Which one is most likable? least likable? Give your reasons.

5. What part does Sam Small, one of Knight's best-known characters, play in the story?

6. In what ways had Walter become a typical small businessman in an American town? Point out some of the respects in which he differs from a typical Yorkshireman.

7. If you had left home and lived for years in a foreign land, what "intangible ties" would cause you to return and "see how it is" with the people among whom you were born? What sights, sounds, or articles of food do you think would linger longest in your memory?

8. What fact about Barbara Alice's behavior made her seem "uppy" (p. 660, 1. 4)? What things about her besides her good looks do you think made her appeal to Walter? How do you explain the author's statement that "Walter and Barbara Alice never spoke a courting word to each other" (p. 661, 1. 19)?

9. What makes "Cockles for Tea" a humorous story? Explain the humor of: "If you never lent . . . back?" (p. 659, 1. 6); "That's two thirdlys tha had" (p. 660, 1. 61); "When I make . . . tha might say" (p. 661, 1. 81).

10. What proverb used in America means the same as "a fool's soon parted from his brass" (p. 658, 1. 54)? In what respect was "the grasshopper in the fable" (p. 659, 1. 69) thought to resemble Walter?

Suggestions for Reading

"Cockles for Tea" is only one of numerous delightfully amusing short stories by Eric Knight. Others which are sure to interest you are to be found in *The Flying Yorkshireman* and *Sam Small Flies Again* (Harper & Brothers). Both books contain stories about a man who discovered that he could fly without a plane. Knight's first novel, *Song on Your Bugles* (Harper), relates a Yorkshire tragedy. His appealing dog story, *Lassie Come-Home* (The John C. Winston Company), has become famous both in book form and as a motion picture. If you are not familiar with it, by all means make its acquaintance as soon as you can. *This Above All* (Grosset & Dunlap) is one of the most human books and one of the most touching novels to come out of the Second World War, during which, you recall, the author lost his life.

"SAKI"[1] (HECTOR HUGH MUNRO)[2] (1870-1916)

The Story-Teller

"The Story-Teller" is about an aunt. Hector Hugh Munro knew a lot on that subject, for he himself had been reared by strict spinster aunts. "The Story-Teller" is also about children. Munro knew a lot about children too. He had not forgotten being a child himself, and he had observed from his secluded bachelor corner the irritating, persistent-question-asking children of other people. In fact, the teller of the successful story is just such a bachelor as was Munro himself, a somewhat superior mocker, certain that he can do better whatever is being done. He tells a child's story to a child audience, but the story is not childish. It appeals to the very human dislike most of us, children and grownups too, have for persons who are "horribly good," and to the just as human delight we have when their goodness brings them an evil fate.

But "Saki" is decidedly better to read than to talk about. Characteristics such as wit and charm and the ability to coin the perfect phrase need not be discussed; they should, instead, be enjoyed, savored.

It was a hot afternoon, and the railway carriage was correspondingly sultry, and the next stop was at Templecombe, nearly an hour ahead. The occupants of the carriage were a small girl, and a smaller girl, and a small boy. An aunt belonging to the children occupied one corner seat, and the further corner seat on the opposite side was occupied by a 10 bachelor who was a stranger to their party, but the small girls and the small boy emphatically occupied the compartment. Both the aunt and the children were conversational in a limited, persistent way, reminding one of the attentions of a housefly that refused to be discouraged. Most of the aunt's remarks seemed to begin with "Don't," and nearly all of the children's remarks began 20 with "Why?" The bachelor said nothing out loud.

"Don't, Cyril, don't," exclaimed the aunt, as the small boy began smacking the cushions of the seat, producing a cloud of dust at each blow.

"Come and look out of the window," she added.

The child moved reluctantly to the window. "Why are those sheep being driven out of that field?" he asked.   30

"I expect they are being driven to another field where there is more grass," said the aunt weakly.

"But there is lots of grass in that field," protested the boy; "there's nothing else but grass there. Aunt, there's lots of grass in that field."

"Perhaps the grass in the other field is better," suggested the aunt fatuously.   40

"Why is it better?" came the swift, inevitable question.

"Oh, look at those cows!" exclaimed the aunt. Nearly every field along the line had contained cows or bullocks, but she spoke as though she were drawing attention to a rarity.

"Why is the grass in the other field better?" persisted Cyril.

The frown on the bachelor's face was 50 deepening to a scowl. He was a hard, unsympathetic man, the aunt decided in her mind. She was utterly unable to come to any satisfactory decision about the grass in the other field.

The smaller girl created a diversion by beginning to recite "On the Road to Mandalay."[1] She only knew the first line, but she put her limited knowledge to the fullest possible use. She repeated 60 the line over and over again in a dreamy but resolute and very audible voice; it seemed to the bachelor as though some one had had a bet with her that she could not repeat the line aloud two thou-

---

[1] Saki (sä'kĕ).
[2] For biography see page 746.

[1] See page 609.

sand times without stopping. Whoever it was who had made the wager was likely to lose his bet.

"Come over here and listen to a story," said the aunt, when the bachelor had looked twice at her and once at the communication cord.

The children moved listlessly towards the aunt's end of the carriage. Evidently her reputation as a story-teller did not rank high in their estimation.

In a low, confidential voice, interrupted at frequent intervals by loud, petulant questions from her listeners, she began an unenterprising and deplorably uninteresting story about a little girl who was good, and made friends with every one on account of her goodness, and was finally saved from a mad bull by a number of rescuers who admired her moral character.

"Wouldn't they have saved her if she hadn't been good?" demanded the bigger of the small girls. It was exactly the question that the bachelor had wanted to ask.

"Well, yes," admitted the aunt lamely, "but I don't think they would have run quite so fast to her help if they had not liked her so much."

"It's the stupidest story I've ever heard," said the bigger of the small girls, with immense conviction.

"I didn't listen after the first bit, it was so stupid," said Cyril.

The smaller girl made no actual comment on the story, but she had long ago recommenced a murmured repetition of her favourite line.

"You don't seem to be a success as a story-teller," said the bachelor suddenly from his corner.

The aunt bristled in instant defence at this unexpected attack.

"It's a very difficult thing to tell stories that children can both understand and appreciate," she said stiffly.

"I don't agree with you," said the bachelor.

"Perhaps *you* would like to tell them a story," was the aunt's retort.

"Tell us a story," demanded the bigger of the small girls.

"Once upon a time," began the bachelor, "there was a little girl called Bertha, who was extraordinarily good."

The children's momentarily-aroused interest began at once to flicker; all stories seemed dreadfully alike, no matter who told them.

"She did all that she was told, she was always truthful, she kept her clothes clean, ate milk puddings as though they were jam tarts, learned her lessons perfectly, and was polite in her manners."

"Was she pretty?" asked the bigger of the small girls.

"Not as pretty as any of you," said the bachelor, "but she was horribly good."

There was a wave of reaction in favour of the story; the word horrible in connection with goodness was a novelty that commended itself. It seemed to introduce a ring of truth that was absent from the aunt's tale of infant life.

"She was so good," continued the bachelor, "that she won several medals for goodness, which she always wore, pinned on to her dress. There was a medal for obedience, another medal for punctuality, and a third for good behaviour. They were large metal medals and they clicked against one another as she walked. No other child in the town where she lived had as many as three medals, so everybody knew that she must be an extra good child."

"Horribly good," quoted Cyril.

"Everybody talked about her goodness, and the Prince of the country got to hear about it, and he said that as she was so very good she might be allowed once a week to walk in his park, which was just outside the town. It was a beautiful park, and no children were ever allowed in it, so it was a great honour for Bertha to be allowed to go there."

"Were there any sheep in the park?" demanded Cyril.

"No," said the bachelor, "there were no sheep."

170 "Why weren't there any sheep?" came the inevitable question arising out of that answer.

The aunt permitted herself a smile, which might almost have been described as a grin.

"There were no sheep in the park," said the bachelor, "because the Prince's mother had once had a dream that her son would either be killed by a sheep or 180 else by a clock falling on him. For that reason the Prince never kept a sheep in his park or a clock in his palace."

The aunt suppressed a gasp of admiration.

"Was the Prince killed by a sheep or by a clock?" asked Cyril.

"He is still alive, so we can't tell whether the dream will come true," said the bachelor unconcernedly; "anyway, 190 there were no sheep in the park, but there were lots of little pigs running all over the place."

"What colour were they?"

"Black with white faces, white with black spots, black all over, grey with white patches, and some were white all over."

The story-teller paused to let a full idea of the park's treasures sink into 200 the children's imaginations; then he resumed:

"Bertha was rather sorry to find that there were no flowers in the park. She had promised her aunts, with tears in her eyes, that she would not pick any of the kind Prince's flowers, and she had meant to keep her promise, so of course it made her feel silly to find that there were no flowers to pick."

210 "Why weren't there any flowers?"

"Because the pigs had eaten them all," said the bachelor promptly. "The gardeners had told the Prince that you couldn't have pigs and flowers, so he decided to have pigs and no flowers."

There was a murmur of approval at the excellence of the Prince's decision; so many people would have decided the other way.

"There were lots of other delightful 220 things in the park. There were ponds with gold and blue and green fish in them, and trees with beautiful parrots that said clever things at a moment's notice, and humming birds that hummed all the popular tunes of the day. Bertha walked up and down and enjoyed herself immensely, and thought to herself: 'If I were not so extraordinarily good I should not have been allowed to come into this 230 beautiful park and enjoy all that there is to be seen in it,' and her three medals clinked against one another as she walked and helped to remind her how very good she really was. Just then an enormous wolf came prowling into the park to see if it could catch a fat little pig for its supper."

"What colour was it?" asked the children, amid an immediate quickening of interest. 240

"Mud-colour all over, with a black tongue and pale grey eyes that gleamed with unspeakable ferocity. The first thing that it saw in the park was Bertha; her pinafore was so spotlessly white and clean that it could be seen from a great distance. Bertha saw the wolf and saw that it was stealing towards her, and she began to wish that she had never been allowed to come into the park. She ran 250 as hard as she could, and the wolf came after her with huge leaps and bounds. She managed to reach a shrubbery of myrtle bushes and she hid herself in one of the thickets of the bushes. The wolf came sniffing among the branches, its black tongue lolling out of its mouth and its pale grey eyes glaring with rage. Bertha was terribly frightened, and thought to herself: 'If I had not been 260 so extraordinarily good I should have.

been safe in the town at this moment.' However, the scent of the myrtle was so strong that the wolf could not sniff out where Bertha was hiding, and the bushes were so thick that he might have hunted about in them for a long time without catching sight of her, so he thought he might as well go off and catch a little pig 270 instead. Bertha was trembling very much at having the wolf prowling and sniffing so near her, and as she trembled the medal for obedience clinked against the medals for good behaviour and punctuality. The wolf was just moving away when he heard the sound of the medals clinking and stopped to listen; they clinked again in a bush quite near him. He dashed into the bush, his pale grey 280 eyes gleaming with ferocity and triumph, and dragged Bertha out and devoured her to the last morsel. All that was left of her were her shoes, bits of clothing, and the three medals for goodness."

"Were any of the little pigs killed?"

"No, they all escaped."

"The story began badly," said the smaller of the small girls, "but it had a beautiful ending."

290 "It is the most beautiful story that I ever heard," said the bigger of the small girls, with immense decision.

"It is the *only* beautiful story I have ever heard," said Cyril.

A dissentient opinion came from the aunt.

"A most improper story to tell to young children! You have undermined the effect of years of careful teaching."

300 "At any rate," said the bachelor, collecting his belongings preparatory to leaving the carriage, "I kept them quiet for ten minutes, which was more than you were able to do."

"Unhappy woman!" he observed to himself as he walked down the platform of Templecombe station; "for the next six months or so those children will assail her in public with demands for an improper story!" 310

Discussion Hints

1. Whose favorite words are "Don't," "Why?" Who said "nothing out loud"?

2. In the first paragraph point out words or phrases that contribute to the satirical * effect.

3. Aunts and bachelors are, they say, much given to offering advice on the training of children. What is the aunt's chief aim in her storytelling? What is the bachelor's aim?

4. Do you like Bertha, whose "pinafore was so spotlessly white and clean that it could be seen from a great distance"? Why?

5. Why did the children approve so highly of the bachelor's story? Were they correct in their judgment?

Suggestions for Reading

"The Story-Teller" may be found, with a host of other good things, in *The Short Stories of Saki*, complete in one volume. The Viking Press publishes also *The Novels and Plays of Saki* (complete in one volume) and *The Westminster Alice*, "Saki's" political sketches. All are worth reading, but the short stories are pre-eminent. Be wary, however. Do not try to gulp them in one dose. They are strong medicine and should be read one at a time.

H. G. WELLS[1] (1866–1946)
The Man Who Could Work Miracles

H. G. Wells wrote numerous interesting stories about such odd things as life on Mars, negative gravity, and, as in the present story, a world in which all the natural laws of

space and time are turned upside down. From all his tales Wells chose "The Man Who Could Work Miracles" for inclusion in a collection of stories entitled *My Best Story*, for which each author chose his own favorite.

[1] For biography see page 746.

IT IS doubtful whether the gift was innate.[1] For my own part, I think it came to him suddenly. Indeed, until he was thirty he was a sceptic, and did not believe in miraculous powers. And here, since it is the most convenient place, I must mention that he was a little man, and had eyes of a hot brown, very erect red hair, a moustache with ends that he twisted up, and freckles. His name was George McWhirter Fotheringay — not the sort of name by any means to lead to any expectation of miracles — and he was clerk at Gomshott's. He was greatly addicted to assertive argument. It was while he was asserting the impossibility of miracles that he had his first intimation of his extraordinary powers. This particular argument was being held in the bar of the Long Dragon, and Toddy Beamish was conducting the opposition by a monotonous but effective "So *you* say," that drove Mr. Fotheringay to the very limit of his patience.

There were present, besides these two, a very dusty cyclist, landlord Cox, and Miss Maybridge, the perfectly respectable and rather portly barmaid of the Dragon. Miss Maybridge was standing with her back to Mr. Fotheringay, washing glasses; the others were watching him, more or less amused by the present ineffectiveness of the assertive method. Goaded by the Torres Vedras[2] tactics of Mr. Beamish, Mr. Fotheringay determined to make an unusual rhetorical effort. "Looky here, Mr. Beamish," said Mr. Fotheringay. "Let us clearly understand what a miracle is. It's something contrariwise to the course of nature done by power of Will, something what couldn't happen without being specially willed."

"So *you* say," said Mr. Beamish, repulsing him.

[1] Inborn, natural.
[2] *Torres Vedras* (tōr'rĕzh vä'thräsh). A town in Portugal, the site of a long, tiresome campaign between the Anglo-Portuguese and the French during the Napoleonic Wars.

Mr. Fotheringay appealed to the cyclist, who had hitherto been a silent auditor, and received his assent — given with a hesitating cough and a glance at Mr. Beamish. The landlord would express no opinion, and Mr. Fotheringay, returning to Mr. Beamish, received the unexpected concession of a qualified assent to his definition of a miracle.

"For instance," said Mr. Fotheringay, greatly encouraged. "Here would be a miracle. That lamp, in the natural course of nature, couldn't burn like that, upsy-down, could it, Beamish?"

"*You* say it couldn't," said Beamish.

"And you?" said Fotheringay. "You don't mean to say — eh?"

"No," said Beamish reluctantly. "No, it couldn't."

"Very well," said Mr. Fotheringay. "Then here comes some one, as it might be me, along here, and stands as it might be here, and says to that lamp, as I might do, collecting all my will — 'Turn upsy-down without breaking, and go on burning steady,' and — Hullo!"

It was enough to make any one say "Hullo!" The impossible, the incredible, was visible to them all. The lamp hung inverted in the air, burning quietly with its flame pointing down. It was as solid, as indisputable as ever a lamp was, the prosaic common lamp of the Long Dragon bar.

Mr. Fotheringay stood with an extended forefinger and the knitted brows of one anticipating a catastrophic smash. The cyclist, who was sitting next the lamp, ducked and jumped across the bar. Everybody jumped, more or less. Miss Maybridge turned and screamed. For nearly three seconds the lamp remained still. A faint cry of mental distress came from Mr. Fotheringay. "I can't keep it up," he said, "any longer." He staggered back, and the inverted lamp suddenly flared, fell against the corner of the bar, bounced aside, smashed upon the floor, and went out.

The lamp hung inverted in the air.

It was lucky it had a metal receiver, or the whole place would have been in a blaze. Mr. Cox was the first to speak, and his remark, shorn of needless excrescences, was to the effect that Fotheringay was a fool. Fotheringay was beyond disputing even so fundamental a proposition as that! He was astonished beyond measure at the thing that had occurred. The subsequent conversation threw absolutely no light on the matter so far as Fotheringay was concerned; the general opinion not only followed Mr. Cox very closely but very vehemently. Everyone accused Fotheringay of a silly trick, and presented him to himself as a foolish destroyer of comfort and security. His mind was in a tornado of perplexity, he was himself inclined to agree with them, and he made a remarkably ineffectual opposition to the proposal of his departure.

He went home flushed and heated, coat-collar crumpled, eyes smarting and ears red. He watched each of the ten street lamps nervously as he passed it. It was only when he found himself alone in his little bedroom in Church Row that he was able to grapple seriously with his memories of the occurrence, and ask, "What on earth happened?"

He had removed his coat and boots, and was sitting on the bed with his hands in his pockets repeating the text of his defence for the seventeenth time, "*I* didn't want the confounded thing to upset," when it occurred to him that at the precise moment he had said the commanding words he had inadvertently willed the thing he said, and that when he had seen the lamp in the air he had felt that it depended on him to maintain it there without being clear how this was to be done. He had not a particularly complex mind, or he might have stuck for a time at that "inadvertently willed," embracing, as it does, the abstrusest problems of voluntary action; but as it was, the idea came to him with a quite acceptable haziness. And from that, following, as I must admit, no clear logical path, he came to the test of the experiment.

He pointed resolutely to his candle and collected his mind, though he felt he did a foolish thing. "Be raised up," he said. But in a second that feeling vanished. The candle was raised, hung in the air one giddy moment, and as Mr. Fotheringay gasped, fell with a smash on his toilet-table, leaving him in darkness save for the expiring glow of its wick.

For a time Mr. Fotheringay sat in the darkness, perfectly still. "It did happen, after all," he said. "And 'ow I'm to explain it I *don't* know." He sighed heavily, and began feeling in his pockets for a match. He could find none, and he rose and groped about the toilet-table. "I wish I had a match," he said. He resorted to his coat, and there were none there, and then it dawned upon him that miracles were possible even with matches. He extended a hand and scowled at it in the dark. "Let there be a match in that hand," he said. He felt some light object fall across his palm, and his fingers closed upon a match.

After several ineffectual attempts to light this, he discovered it was a safety-match. He threw it down, and then it occurred to him that he might have willed it lighted. He did, and perceived it burning in the midst of his toilet-table mat. He caught it up hastily, and it went out. His perception of possibilities enlarged, and he felt for and replaced the candle in its candlestick. "Here! *you* be lit," said Mr. Fotheringay, and forthwith the candle was flaring, and he saw a little black hole in the toilet-cover, with a wisp of smoke rising from it. For a time he stared from this to the little flame and back, and then looked up and met his own gaze in the looking-glass. By this help he communed with himself in silence for a time.

"How about miracles now?" said Mr. Fotheringay at last, addressing his reflection.

The subsequent meditations of Mr. Fotheringay were of a severe but confused description. So far as he could see, it was a case of pure willing with him. The nature of his first experiences disinclined him for any further experiments except of the most cautious type. But he lifted a sheet of paper, and turned a glass of water pink and then green, and he created a snail, which he miraculously annihilated, and got himself a miraculous tooth-brush. Somewhen in the small hours he had reached the fact that his will-power must be of a particularly rare and pungent quality, a fact of which he had certainly had inklings before, but no certain assurance. The scare and perplexity of his first discovery was now qualified by pride in this evidence of singularity and by vague intimations of advantage. He became aware that the church clock was striking one, and as it did not occur to him that his daily duties at Gomshott's might be miraculously dispensed with, he resumed undressing, in order to get to bed without further delay. As he struggled to get his shirt over his head, he was struck with a brilliant idea. "Let me be in bed," he said, and found himself so. "Undressed," he stipulated; and, finding the sheets cold, added hastily, "and in my nightshirt — no, in a nice soft woollen nightshirt. Ah!" he said with immense enjoyment. "And now let me be comfortably asleep. . . ."

He awoke at his usual hour and was pensive all through breakfast-time, wondering whether his overnight experience might not be a particularly vivid dream. At length his mind turned again to cautious experiments. For instance, he had three eggs for breakfast; two his landlady had supplied, good, but shoppy, and one was a delicious fresh goose-egg, laid, cooked, and served by his extraordinary will. He hurried off to Gomshott's

in a state of profound but carefully concealed excitement, and only remembered the shell of the third egg when his landlady spoke of it that night. All day he could do no work because of this astonishingly new self-knowledge, but this caused him no inconvenience, because he made up for it miraculously in his last ten minutes.

As the day wore on, his state of mind passed from wonder to elation, albeit the circumstances of his dismissal from the Long Dragon were still disagreeable to recall, and a garbled account of the matter that had reached his colleagues led to some badinage.[1] It was evident he must be careful how he lifted frangible[2] articles, but in other ways his gift promised more and more as he turned it over in his mind. He intended among other things to increase his personal property by unostentatious[3] acts of creation. He called into existence a pair of very splendid diamond studs, and hastily annihilated them again as young Gomshott came across the counting-house to his desk. He was afraid young Gomshott might wonder how he had come by them. He saw quite clearly the gift required caution and watchfulness in its exercise, but so far as he could judge the difficulties attending its mastery would be no greater than those he had already faced in the study of cycling. It was that analogy, perhaps, quite as much as the feeling that he would be unwelcome in the Long Dragon, that drove him out after supper into the lane beyond the gas works, to rehearse a few miracles in private.

There was possibly a certain want of originality in his attempts, for apart from his will-power Mr. Fotheringay was not a very exceptional man. The miracle of Moses' rod came to his mind, but the night was dark and unfavourable to the proper control of large miraculous snakes. Then he recollected the story of

---

[1] *badinage* (băd ĭ näzh′). Raillery, banter.
[2] Easily breakable.
[3] Not showy, private.

"Tannhäuser"[1] that he had read on the back of the Philharmonic programme. That seemed to him singularly attractive and harmless. He stuck his walking-stick —a very nice Poona-penang-lawyer[2]— into the turf that edged the footpath, and commanded the dry wood to blossom. The air was immediately full of the scent of roses, and by means of a match he saw for himself that this beautiful miracle was indeed accomplished. His satisfaction was ended by advancing footsteps. Afraid of a premature discovery of his powers, he addressed the blossoming stick hastily: "Go back." What he meant was "Change back"; but of course he was confused. The stick receded at a considerable velocity, and incontinently came a cry of anger and a bad word from the approaching person. "Who are you throwing brambles at, you fool?" cried a voice. "That got me on the shin."

"I'm sorry, old chap," said Mr. Fotheringay, and then realizing the awkward nature of the explanation, caught nervously at his moustache. He saw Winch, one of the three Immering constables, advancing.

"What d'yer mean by it?" asked the constable. "Hullo! It's you, is it? The gent that broke the lamp at the Long Dragon!"

"I don't mean anything by it," said Mr. Fotheringay. "Nothing at all."

"What d'yer do it for then?"

"Oh, bother!" said Mr. Fotheringay.

"Bother, indeed! D'yer know that stick hurt? What d'yer do it for, eh?"

For the moment Mr. Fotheringay could not think what he had done it for. His silence seemed to irritate Mr. Winch. "You've been assaulting the police, young man, this time. That's what you done."

"Look here, Mr. Winch," said Mr. Fotheringay, annoyed and confused, "I'm very sorry. The fact is —"

"Well?"

He could think of no way but the truth. "I was working a miracle." He tried to speak in an offhand way, but try as he would he couldn't.

"Working a —! 'Ere, don't you talk rot. Working a miracle, indeed! Miracle! Well, that's downright funny! Why, you's the chap that don't believe in miracles. . . . Fact is, this is another of your silly conjuring tricks — that's what this is. Now, I tell you —"

But Mr. Fotheringay never heard what Mr. Winch was going to tell him. He realized he had given himself away, flung his valuable secret to all the winds of heaven. A violent gust of irritation swept him to action. He turned on the constable swiftly and fiercely. "Here," he said, "I've had enough of this, I have! I'll show you a silly conjuring trick, I will! Go to Hades! Go, now!"

He was alone!

Mr. Fotheringay performed no more miracles that night, nor did he trouble to see what had become of his flowering stick. He returned to the town, scared and very quiet, and went to his bedroom. "Lord," he said, "it's a powerful gift — an extremely powerful gift. I didn't hardly mean as much as that. Not really. . . . I wonder what Hades is like?"

He sat on the bed taking off his boots. Struck by a happy thought he transferred the constable to San Francisco, and without any more interference with normal causation went soberly to bed. In the night he dreamed of the anger of Winch.

The next day Mr. Fotheringay heard two interesting items of news. Someone had planted a most beautiful climbing

---

[1] In Wagner's opera *Tannhäuser* (tàn'hoi zĕr) the Pope's dry staff is represented as growing green and budding into life. See "The Ballad of Reading Gaol" (p. 634).

[2] A walking-stick with a bulbous head made from the stem of an Asiatic palm. Poona is a locality near Bombay; Penang, an island off the coast of the Malay Peninsula. The stick is jokingly called a "lawyer" because of its supposed use in settling disputes in the Straits Settlements.

rose against the elder Mr. Gomshott's private house in the Lullaborough Road, and the river as far as Rawling's Mill was to be dragged for Constable Winch.

Mr. Fotheringay was abstracted and thoughtful all that day, and performed no miracles except certain provisions for Winch, and the miracle of completing his day's work with punctual perfection in spite of all the bee-swarm of thoughts that hummed through his mind. And the extraordinary abstraction and meekness of his manner was remarked by several people, and made a matter for jesting. For the most part he was thinking of Winch.

On Sunday evening he went to chapel, and oddly enough, Mr. Maydig, who took a certain interest in occult matters, preached about "things that are not lawful." Mr. Fotheringay was not a regular chapel goer, but the system of assertive scepticism, to which I have already alluded, was now very much shaken. The tenor of the sermon threw an entirely new light on these novel gifts, and he suddenly decided to consult Mr. Maydig immediately after the service. So soon as that was determined, he found himself wondering why he had not done so before.

Mr. Maydig, a lean, excitable man with quite remarkably long wrists and neck, was gratified at a request for a private conversation from a young man whose carelessness in religious matters was a subject for general remark in the town. After a few necessary delays, he conducted him to the study of the Manse, which was contiguous to the chapel, seated him comfortably, and standing in front of a cheerful fire — his legs threw a Rhodian [1] arch of shadow on the opposite wall — requested Mr. Fotheringay to state his business.

At first Mr. Fotheringay was a little abashed, and found some difficulty in opening the matter. "You will scarcely

believe me, Mr. Maydig, I am afraid"— and so forth for some time. He tried a question at last, and asked Mr. Maydig his opinion of miracles.

Mr. Maydig was still saying "Well" in an extremely judicial tone, when Mr. Fotheringay interrupted again: "You don't believe, I suppose, that some common sort of person — like myself, for instance — as it might be sitting here now, might have some sort of twist inside him that made him able to do things by his will."

"It's possible," said Mr. Maydig. "Something of the sort, perhaps, is possible."

"If I might make free with something here, I think I might show you by a sort of experiment," said Mr. Fotheringay. "Now, take that tobacco-jar on the table, for instance. What I want to know is whether what I am going to do with it is a miracle or not. Just half a minute, Mr. Maydig, please."

He knitted his brows, pointed to the tobacco-jar, and said: "Be a bowl of vi'lets."

The tobacco-jar did as it was ordered.

Mr. Maydig started violently at the change, and stood looking from the thaumaturgist[1] to the bowl of flowers. He said nothing. Presently he ventured to lean over the table and smell the violets; they were fresh-picked and very fine ones. Then he stared at Mr. Fotheringay again.

"How did you do that?" he asked.

Mr. Fotheringay pulled his moustache. "Just told it — and there you are. Is that a miracle, or is it black art, or what is it? And what do you think's the matter with me? That's what I want to ask."

"It's a most extraordinary occurrence."

"And this day last week I knew no more that I could do things like that

---

[1] Like the Colossus * of Rhodes.

[1] *thaumaturgist* (thô má tûr'jïst). Miracle-worker magician.

than you did. It came quite sudden. It's something odd about my will, I suppose, and that's as far as I can see."

"Is *that* — the only thing? Could you do other things besides that?"

"Lord, yes!" said Mr. Fotheringay. "Just anything." He thought, and suddenly recalled a conjuring entertainment he had seen. "Here!" He pointed. "Change into a bowl of fish — no, not that — change into a glass full of water with goldfish swimming in it. That's better! You see that, Mr. Maydig?"

"It's astonishing. It's incredible. You are either a most extraordinary . . . But no —"

"I could change it into anything," said Mr. Fotheringay. "Just anything. Here! be a pigeon, will you?"

In another moment a blue pigeon was fluttering round the room and making Mr. Maydig duck every time it came near him. "Stop there, will you," said Mr. Fotheringay; and the pigeon hung motionless in the air. "I could change it back to a bowl of flowers," he said, and after replacing the pigeon on the table worked that miracle. "I expect you will want your pipe in a bit," he said, and restored the tobacco-jar.

Mr. Maydig had followed all these later changes in a sort of ejaculatory silence. He stared at Mr. Fotheringay and, in a very gingerly manner, picked up the tobacco-jar, examined it, replaced it on the table. "*Well!*" was the only expression of his feelings.

"Now, after that it's easier to explain what I came about," said Fotheringay; and proceeded to a lengthy and involved narrative of his strange experiences, beginning with the affair of the lamp in the Long Dragon and complicated by persistent allusions to Winch. As he went on, the transient pride Mr. Maydig's consternation had caused passed away; he became the very ordinary Mr. Fotheringay of everyday intercourse again. Mr. Maydig listened intently, the to-bacco-jar in his hand, and his bearing changed also with the course of the narrative. Presently, while Mr. Fotheringay was dealing with the miracle of the third egg, the minister interrupted with a fluttering extended hand —

"It is possible," he said. "It is credible. It is amazing, of course, but it reconciles a number of difficulties. The power to work miracles is a gift — a peculiar quality like genius or second sight — hitherto it has come very rarely and to exceptional people. But in this case . . . I have always wondered at the miracles of Mahomet, and at Yogi's miracles, and the miracles of Madame Blavatsky. But, of course! Yes, it is simply a gift! It carries out so beautifully the arguments of that great thinker" — Mr. Maydig's voice sank — "his Grace the Duke of Argyll.[1] Here we plumb some profounder law — deeper than the ordinary laws of nature. Yes — yes. Go on. Go on!"

Mr. Fotheringay proceeded to tell of his misadventure with Winch, and Mr. Maydig, no longer overawed or scared, began to jerk his limbs about and interject astonishment. "It's this what troubled me most," proceeded Mr. Fotheringay; "it's this I'm most mijitly in want of advice for; of course he's at San Francisco — wherever San Francisco may be — but of course it's awkward for both of us, as you'll see, Mr. Maydig. I don't see how he can understand what has happened, and I dare say he's scared and exasperated something tremendous, and trying to get at me. I dare say he keeps on starting off to come here. I send him back, by a miracle, every few hours, when I think of it. And of course, that's a thing he won't be able to understand, and it's bound to annoy him; and, of course, if

[1] Mr. Maydig (or perhaps H. G. Wells himself) is mistaken. *Dissertation on Miracles*, much admired in the eighteenth century, was written not by the Duke of Argyll, but by his distant relative, the Reverend George Campbell.

he takes a ticket every time it will cost him a lot of money. I done the best I could for him, but of course it's difficult for him to put himself in my place. I thought afterward that his clothes might have got scorched, you know — if Hades is all it's supposed to be — before I shifted him. In that case I suppose they'd have locked him up in San Francisco. Of course I willed him a new suit of clothes on him directly I thought of it. But, you see, I'm already in a deuce of a tangle —"

Mr. Maydig looked serious. "I see you are in a tangle. Yes, it's a difficult position. How you are to end it ..." He became diffuse and inconclusive.

"However, we'll leave Winch for a little and discuss the larger question. I don't think this is a case of the black art or anything of the sort. I don't think there is any taint of criminality about it at all, Mr. Fotheringay — none whatever, unless you are suppressing material facts. No, it's miracles — pure miracles — miracles, if I may say so, of the very highest class."

He began to pace the hearthrug and gesticulate, while Mr. Fotheringay sat with his arm on the table and his head on his arm, looking worried. "I don't see how I'm to manage about Winch," he said.

"A gift of working miracles — apparently a very powerful gift," said Mr. Maydig, "will find a way about Winch — never fear. My dear Sir, you are a most important man — a man of the most astonishing possibilities. As evidence, for example! And in other ways, the things you may do ..."

"Yes, *I've* thought of a thing or two," said Mr. Fotheringay. "But — some of the things came a bit twisty. You saw that fish at first? Wrong sort of bowl and wrong sort of fish. And I thought I'd ask some one."

"A proper course," said Mr. Maydig, "a very proper course — altogether the proper course." He stopped and looked at Mr. Fotheringay. "It's practically an unlimited gift. Let us test your powers, for instance. If they really *are* . . . if they really are all they seem to be."

And so, incredible as it may seem, in the study of the little house behind the Congregational Chapel, on the evening of Sunday, November 10, 1896, Mr. Fotheringay, egged on and inspired by Mr. Maydig, began to work miracles. The reader's attention is specially and definitely called to the date. He will object, probably has already objected, that certain points in this story are improbable, that if any things of the sort already described had indeed occurred, they would have been in all the papers a year ago. The details immediately following he will find particularly hard to accept, because among other things they involve the conclusion that he or she, the reader in question, must have been killed in a violent and unprecedented manner more than a year ago. Now a miracle is nothing if not improbable, and as a matter of fact the reader *was* killed in a violent and unprecedented manner a year ago. In the subsequent course of this story that will become perfectly clear and credible, as every right-minded and reasonable reader will admit. But this is not the place for the end of the story, being but little beyond the hither side of the middle. And at first the miracles worked by Mr. Fotheringay were timid little miracles — little things with the cups and parlour fitments, as feeble as the miracles of Theosophists, and, feeble as they were, they were received with awe by his collaborator. He would have preferred to settle the Winch business out of hand, but Mr. Maydig would not let him. But after they had worked a dozen of these domestic trivialities, their sense of power grew, their imagination began to show signs of stimulation, and their ambition enlarged. Their first larger enterprise was due to hunger and the negligence of Mrs. Minchin, Mr. Maydig's housekeeper. The meal to which the minister conducted Mr. Fotheringay was certainly ill-laid and uninviting as refreshment for two industrious miracle-workers; but they were seated, and Mr. Maydig was descanting in sorrow rather than in anger upon his housekeeper's shortcomings, before it occurred to Mr. Fotheringay that an opportunity lay before him. "Don't you think, Mr. Maydig," he said, "if it isn't a liberty, I —"

"My dear Mr. Fotheringay! Of course! No — I didn't think."

Mr. Fotheringay waved his hand. "What shall we have?" he said, in a large, inclusive spirit, and at Mr. Maydig's order, revised the supper very thoroughly. "As for me," he said, eying Mr. Maydig's selection, "I am always particularly fond of a tankard of stout and a nice Welsh rarebit, and I'll order that. I ain't much given to Burgundy," and forthwith stout and Welsh rarebit promptly appeared at his command. They sat long at their supper, talking like equals, as Mr. Fotheringay presently perceived with a glow of surprise and gratification, of all the miracles they would presently do. "And, by the bye, Mr. Maydig," said Mr. Fotheringay, "I might perhaps be able to help you — in a domestic way."

"Don't quite follow," said Mr. Maydig, pouring out a glass of miraculous old Burgundy.

Mr. Fotheringay helped himself to a second Welsh rarebit out of vacancy, and took a mouthful. "I was thinking," he said, "I might be able (*chum, chum*) to work (*chum, chum*) a miracle with Mrs. Minchin (*chum, chum*) — make her a better woman."

Mr. Maydig put down the glass and looked doubtful. "She's — She strongly objects to interference, you know, Mr. Fotheringay. And — as a matter of fact — it's well past eleven and she's probably in bed and asleep. Do you think, on the whole —"

Mr. Fotheringay considered these objections. "I don't see that it shouldn't be done in her sleep."

For a time Mr. Maydig opposed the idea, and then he yielded. Mr. Fotheringay issued his orders, and a little less at their ease, perhaps, the two gentlemen proceeded with their repast. Mr. Maydig was enlarging on the changes he might expect in his housekeeper next day, with an optimism that seemed even to Mr. Fotheringay's supper senses a little forced and hectic, when a series of confused noises from upstairs began. Their eyes exchanged interrogations, and Mr. Maydig left the room hastily. Mr. Fotheringay heard him calling up to his housekeeper and then his footsteps going softly up to her.

In a minute or so the minister returned, his step light, his face radiant. "Wonderful!" he said, "and touching! Most touching!"

He began pacing the hearthrug. "A repentance — a most touching repentance — through the crack of the door. Poor woman! A most wonderful change! She had got up. She must have got up at once. She had got up out of her sleep to smash a private bottle of brandy in her box. And to confess it too! . . . But this gives us — it opens — a most amazing vista of possibilities. If we can work this miraculous change in *her* . . ."

"The thing's unlimited seemingly," said Mr. Fotheringay. "And about Mr. Winch —"

"Altogether unlimited." And from the hearthrug Mr. Maydig, waving the Winch difficulty aside, unfolded a series of wonderful proposals — proposals he invented as he went along.

Now what those proposals were does not concern the essentials of this story. Suffice it that they were designed in a spirit of infinite benevolence, the sort of benevolence that used to be called postprandial.[1] Suffice it, too, that the problem of Winch remained unsolved. Nor is it necessary to describe how far that series got to its fulfilment. There were astonishing changes. The small hours found Mr. Maydig and Mr. Fotheringay careering across the chilly market-square under the still moon, in a sort of ecstasy of thaumaturgy, Mr. Maydig all flap and gesture, Mr. Fotheringay short and bristling, and no longer abashed at his greatness. They had reformed every drunkard in the Parliamentary division, changed all the beer and alcohol to water (Mr. Maydig had overruled Mr. Fotheringay on this point), they had, further, greatly improved the railway communication of the place, drained Flinder's swamp, improved the soil of One Tree Hill, and cured the Vicar's wart. And they were going to see what could be done with the injured pier at South Bridge. "The place," gasped Mr. Maydig, "won't be the same place to-morrow. How surprised and thankful every one will be!" And just at that moment the church clock struck three.

"I say," said Mr. Fotheringay, "that's three o'clock! I must be getting back. I've got to be at business by eight. And besides, Mrs. Wimms —"

"We're only beginning," said Mr. Maydig, full of the sweetness of unlimited power. "We're only beginning. Think of all the good we're doing. When people awake —"

"But — " said Mr. Fotheringay.

Mr. Maydig gripped his arm suddenly. His eyes were bright and wild. "My dear chap," he said, "there's no hurry. Look" — he pointed to the moon at the zenith — "Joshua!"

"Joshua?" said Mr. Fotheringay.

"Joshua," said Mr. Maydig. "Why not? Stop it."

Mr. Fotheringay looked at the moon. "That's a bit tall," he said after a pause.

"Why not?" said Mr. Maydig. "Of course it doesn't stop. You stop the rotation of the earth, you know. Time stops. It isn't as if we were doing harm."

"H'm!" said Mr. Fotheringay. "Well." He sighed. "I'll try. Here —"

He buttoned up his jacket and addressed himself to the habitable globe, with as good an assumption of confidence as lay in his power. "Jest stop rotating, will you," said Mr. Fotheringay.

Incontinently he was flying head over heels through the air at the rate of dozens of miles a minute. In spite of the innumerable circles he was describing per second, he thought; for thought is wonderful — sometimes as sluggish as flowing pitch, sometimes as instantaneous as light. He thought in a second, and willed. "Let me come down safe and sound. Whatever else happens, let me down safe and sound."

He willed it only just in time, for his clothes, heated by his rapid flight through the air, were already beginning to singe. He came down with a forcible, but by no means injurious, bump in what appeared to be a mound of fresh-turned earth. A large mass of metal and masonry, extraordinarily like the clock-tower in the middle of the market-square, hit the earth near him, ricochetted[1] over him, and flew into stonework, bricks, and masonry, like a bursting bomb. A hurtling cow hit one of the larger blocks and smashed like an egg. There was a crash that made all the most violent crashes of his past life seem like the sound of falling dust, and this was followed by a descending series of lesser crashes. A vast wind roared throughout earth and heaven, so that he could scarcely lift his head to look. For a while he was too breathless and astonished even to see where he was or what had happened. And his first movement was to feel his head and re-

---

[1] Literally "after-dinner"; that is, when one is feeling kindly after eating and drinking well.

[1] *ricochetted* (rĭk ŏ shĕt′ĕd). Skipped, rebounded.

assure himself that his streaming hair was still his own.

"Lord!" gasped Mr. Fotheringay, scarce able to speak for the gale, "I've had a squeak! What's gone wrong? Storms and thunder. And only a minute ago a fine night. It's Maydig set me on to this sort of thing. *What* a wind! If I go on fooling in this way I'm bound to have a thundering accident! Where's Maydig?"

"What a confounded mess everything's in!"

He looked about him so far as his flapping jacket would permit. The appearance of things was really extremely strange. "The sky's all right anyhow," said Mr. Fotheringay. "And that's about all that is all right. And even there it looks like a terrific gale coming up. But there's the moon overhead. Just as it was just now. Bright as midday. But as for the rest — Where's the village? Where's — where's anything? And what on earth set this wind a-blowing? *I* didn't order no wind."

Mr. Fotheringay struggled to get to his feet in vain, and after one failure, remained on all fours, holding on. He surveyed the moonlit world to leeward, with the tails of his jacket streaming over his head. "There's something seriously wrong," said Mr. Fotheringay. "And what it is — goodness knows."

Far and wide nothing was visible in the white glare through the haze of dust that drove before a screaming gale but tumbled masses of earth and heaps of inchoate [1] ruins, no trees, no houses, no familiar shapes, only a wilderness of disorder vanishing at last into the darkness beneath the whirling columns and streamers, the lightnings and thunderings of a swiftly rising storm. Near him in the livid glare was something that might once have been an elm tree, a smashed mass of splinters, shivered from boughs to base, and further a twisted

mass of iron girders — only too evidently the viaduct — rose out of the piled confusion.

You see, when Mr. Fotheringay had arrested the rotation of the solid globe, he had made no stipulation concerning the trifling movables upon its surface. And the earth spins so fast that the surface at its equator is travelling at rather more than a thousand miles an hour, and in these latitudes at more than half the pace. So that the village, and Mr. Maydig, and Mr. Fotheringay, and everybody and everything had been jerked violently forward at about nine miles per second [1] — that is to say, much more violently than if they had been fired out of a cannon. And every human being, every living creature, every house, and every tree — all the world as we know it — had been so jerked and smashed and utterly destroyed. That was all.

These things Mr. Fotheringay did not, of course, fully appreciate. But he perceived that his miracle had miscarried, and with that a great disgust of miracles came upon him. He was in darkness now, for the clouds had swept away together and blotted out his momentary glimpse of the moon, and the air was full of fitful struggling tortured wraiths of hail. A great roaring of wind and waters filled earth and sky, and peering under his hand through the dust and sleet to windward, he saw by the play of the lightnings a vast wall of water pouring toward him.

"Maydig!" screamed Mr. Fotheringay's feeble voice amid the elemental uproar. "Here! — Maydig!"

"Stop!" cried Mr. Fotheringay to the advancing water. "Oh, for goodness' sake, stop!"

"Just a moment," said Mr. Fotheringay to the lightnings and thunder. "Stop jest a moment while I collect my thoughts. . . . And now what shall I

---

[1] Recently begun, incomplete; here, shapeless.

[1] Wells meant *per minute.*

do?" he said. "What *shall* I do? Lord! I wish Maydig was about."

"I know," said Mr. Fotheringay. "And for goodness' sake let's have it right *this* time."

He remained on all fours, leaning against the wind, very intent to have everything right.

"Ah!" he said. "Let nothing what 10 I'm going to order happen until I say 'Off.' . . . Lord! I wish I'd thought of that before!"

He lifted his little voice against the whirlwind, shouting louder and louder in the vain desire to hear himself speak. "Now then! — here goes! Mind about that what I said just now. In the first place, when all I've got to say is done, let me lose my miraculous power, let my 20 will become just like anybody else's will, and all these dangerous miracles be stopped. I don't like them. I'd rather I didn't work 'em. Ever so much. That's the first thing. And the second is — let me be back just before the miracles begin; let everything be just as it was before the blessed lamp turned up. It's a big job, but it's the last. Have you got it? No more miracles, everything as it 30 was — me back in the Long Dragon just before I drank my half-pint. That's it! Yes."

He dug his fingers into the mold, closed his eyes, and said, "Off!"

Everything became perfectly still. He perceived that he was standing erect.

"So *you* say," said a voice.

He opened his eyes. He was in the bar of the Long Dragon, arguing about 40 miracles with Toddy Beamish. He had a vague sense of some great thing forgotten that instantaneously passed. You see, except for the loss of his miraculous powers, everything was back as it had been; his mind and memory therefore were now just as they had been at the time when this story began. So that he knew absolutely nothing of all that is told here, knows nothing of all that is

told here to this day. And among other 50 things, of course, he still did not believe in miracles.

"I tell you that miracles, properly speaking, can't possibly happen," he said, "whatever you like to hold. And I'm prepared to prove it up to the hilt."

"That's what *you* think," said Toddy Beamish, and "Prove it if you can."

"Looky here, Mr. Beamish," said Mr. Fotheringay. "Let us clearly under- 60 stand what a miracle is. It's something contrariwise to the course of nature done by power of Will. . . ."

Discussion Hints

1. What is the meaning of "the present ineffectiveness of the assertive method" (p. 672, ll. 32–33)?

2. Why does the author think that the concept "inadvertently willed" embraces "the abstrusest problems of voluntary action" (p. 674, ll. 47–48)?

3. Who are Mahomet, Yogi, and Madame Blavatsky (p. 678, ll. 64–66), and why does the author mention them together?

4. Have you ever thought what would happen if the earth suddenly stopped rotating on its axis? Read what Mr. Wells says about this (p. 682, ll. 52–70). What would happen if it stopped revolving around the sun? Discuss both matters in class or with the science teacher.

5. Describe the character of Mr. Fotheringay. Does Wells's choice of such a character as the central figure tend to make the story more surprising? more humorous? Give reasons for your answer.

6. In the ancient Greek myth of the "golden touch" King Midas receives the gift of turning whatever he touches to gold, but is ultimately sorry that he possesses this marvelous gift. Look up Midas in an encyclopedia or read the charming version of the story given by the American author Nathaniel Hawthorne in his *Tanglewood Tales*, and then compare the myth with Wells's story.

Suggestions for Reading

The work of H. G. Wells is as voluminous as it is vigorous. *Shape of Things to Come*

(The Macmillan Company), *The World Set Free* (E. P. Dutton & Co., Inc.), or *The War of the Worlds* (Harper & Brothers) should prove interesting introductions to his scientific romances.

Suggestions for Further Reading in the Short Story and the Novel

Here are mentioned only writers whose fiction is not represented in the group given above.

1. Best for an introduction to the novels and stories by Sir James M. Barrie is *The Little Minister*. A brief struggle with the Scottish dialect, and you are ready to proceed with *A Window in Thrums, Auld Licht Idylls*, and the rest. Charles Scribner's Sons are Barrie's publishers.

2. Reading *Buried Alive* is an interesting and surprising introduction to Arnold Bennett, but *The Old Wives' Tale* is a better book by far. Doubleday, Doran & Company, Inc., publish these and others of Bennett's novels. *The Old Wives' Tale* may be had in Modern Library, Inc., also.

3. "The Birthday of the Infanta" is perhaps the best-known of the short stories of Oscar Wilde. Others may be found in *The Happy Prince and Other Fairy Tales*.

4. Read Thomas Hardy in this order: *Under the Greenwood Tree, Far from the Madding Crowd, The Return of the Native*. Then go on to the other Wessex novels.

5. Katharine Mansfield, who died at thirty-five, was a master of the art of short-story writing. Alfred A. Knopf, Inc., publish *Stories by Katharine Mansfield* (selections) and *The Short Stories of Katharine Mansfield* (all she ever wrote).

6. The comical adventures of sailors in English shipping towns and in the "dockland" of the Thames, written by W. W. Jacobs, are favorites with many. Charles Scribner's Sons publish Jacobs's collected stories in a volume called *Snug Harbor*.

7. Leonard Merrick's American reading public should be larger than it is. E. P. Dutton & Co., Inc., publish his short stories and plays.

8. Americans know and enjoy Hugh Walpole. His Herries trilogy is fascinating, though long-drawn-out. The titles of the four novels, which carry his family through the eighteenth and nineteenth centuries, are *Rogue Herries, Judith Paris, The Fortress*, and *Vanessa*. *A Prayer for My Son*, a recent novel by Walpole, is a story of today. *Head in Green Bronze and Other Stories* is Walpole's latest volume of short stories. Doubleday, Doran & Company, Inc., are Walpole's publishers.

9. And then you may be hilarious at the expense of Psmith and Jeeves and the rest. P. G. Wodehouse, their creator, has fallen into the habit of spending half of each year in New York. Doubleday, Doran & Company, Inc., and Little, Brown & Company publish his fiction in the United States.

10. Detective stories, long and short, continue to come from the press in numbers on both sides of the Atlantic. Their devotees recommend especially the Dr. Fortune stories by Henry Christopher Bailey (Doubleday, Doran & Company, Inc.); the Father Brown stories by Gilbert Keith Chesterton (Dodd, Mead & Company, Inc.); those by Agatha Christie (Dodd, Mead & Company, Inc., and Grosset & Dunlap); and those by Dashiell Hammett, Earl Derr Biggers (the creator of Charlie Chan), and S. S. Van Dine (the creator of Philo Vance). Grosset & Dunlap, publish detective stories by Hammett, Biggers, and Van Dine.

11. The simplest way of procuring the detective stories by Conan Doyle is to borrow or, better, buy the recently published *Complete Sherlock Holmes* (Garden City Publishing Company, Inc.). This fourteen-hundred-page book contains fifty-six short stories and four novels. Christopher Morley has written the introduction. Harper & Brothers also publish *Adventures of Sherlock Holmes*, as well as several of Doyle's novels and stories of adventure.

12. Many libraries have some or all of the series The Best British Short Stories from 1926 and on, edited by Edward J. O'Brien. Dodd, Mead & Company, Inc., carry various volumes from 1926 through 1932; Houghton Mifflin Company, from 1933 on. Go to the card catalogue in the library and look up "Short Stories: Collections." You are likely to be surprised at what you find.

13. For suggestions for reading in the American short story, see the revised edition of *American Writers* of this series.

THE DRAMA[1]

JAMES M. BARRIE[2] (1860–1937)

Shall We Join the Ladies?

Shall We Join the Ladies? the first act of a play which was never completed, is, perhaps partly because of that very fact, one of the most famous of all mystery plays. The story goes that a friend of Barrie fished it out of the lower drawer of its author's big desk, where it had lain for a long time. Left to the tender mercies of its writer, it would probably never have been either produced or published.

Shall We Join the Ladies? proved exceedingly effective on the stage. Its original cast included such notable actors as Cyril Maude, Lady Tree, Sir Johnston Forbes-Robertson.

Shall We Join the Ladies? is exceedingly readable. Barrie has a way of taking his reader into his confidence, of putting in his oar now and then, like a novelist. Shakespeare would be amazed at the number and length of his stage directions. Truth to tell, the play, merely read, is much more thrilling than many so-called mystery thrillers.

For the past week the hospitable SAM SMITH *has been entertaining a country house party, and we choose to raise the curtain on them towards the end of dinner. They are seated thus, the host facing us.*

```
                     HOST
LADY JANE                    LADY WRATHIE
SIR JOSEPH                   MR. PREEN
MRS. PREEN     (  O  )       MISS VAILE
MR. VAILE                    MRS. BLAND
MR. GOURLAY                  CAPT. JENNINGS
                             MISS ISIT
             MRS. CASTRO
             BUTLER

               MAID
```

[1] For introduction to the drama in Recent and Contemporary Literature, see pages 85–86 and 573.
[2] For biography see page 747.

SMITH *is a little old bachelor, and sits there beaming on his guests like an elderly cupid. So they think him, but they are to be undeceived. Though many of them have not met until this week, they have at present that genial regard for each other which steals so becomingly over really nice people who have eaten too much.*

DOLPHIN, *the butler, is passing round the fruit. The only other attendant is a maid in the background, as for an emergency, and she is as interested in the conversation as he is indifferent to it. If one of the guests were to destroy himself,* DOLPHIN *would merely sign to her to remove the debris while he continued to serve the fruit.*

In the midst of hilarity over some quip that we are just too late to catch, the youthful LADY JANE *counts the company and is appalled.*

LADY JANE. We are thirteen, Lady Wrathie.

[*Many fingers count.*]

LADY WRATHIE. Fourteen.

CAPT. JENNINGS. Twelve.

LADY JANE. We are thirteen.

HOST. Oh dear, how careless of me. Is there anything I can do?

SIR JOSEPH [*of the city*]. Leave this to me. All keep your seats.

MRS. PREEN [*perhaps rather thankfully*]. I am afraid Lady Jane has risen. 10

[LADY JANE *subsides.*]

LADY WRATHIE. Joseph, you have risen yourself.

[SIR JOSEPH *subsides.*]

MRS. CASTRO [*a mysterious widow from Buenos Ayres*]. Were we thirteen all those other nights?

MRS. PREEN. We always had a guest or two from outside, you remember.

MISS ISIT [*whose name obviously needs to be queried*[1]]. All we have got to do is to make our number fourteen.

VAILE. But how, Miss Isit?

20   MISS ISIT. Why, Dolphin, of course.

MRS. PREEN. It's too clever of you, Miss Isit. Mr. Smith, Dolphin may sit down with us, mayn't he?

MRS. CASTRO. Please, dear Mr. Smith; just for a moment. That breaks the spell.

SIR JOSEPH. We won't eat you, Dolphin.

[*But he has crunched some similar ones.*]

HOST. Let me explain to him. You see, Dolphin, there is a superstition that 30 if thirteen people sit down at table something staggering will happen to one of them before the night is out. That is it, isn't it?

MRS. BLAND [*darkly*]. Namely, death.

HOST [*brightly*]. Yes, namely, death.

LADY JANE. But not before the night is out, you dear; before the year is out.

HOST. I thought it was before the 40 night is out.

[DOLPHIN *is reluctant.*]

GOURLAY. Sit here, Dolphin.

MISS VAILE. No, I want him.

MISS ISIT. It was my idea, and I insist on having him.

MRS. CASTRO [*moving farther to the left*]. Yes, here between us.

[DOLPHIN *obliges.*]

MRS. PREEN [*with childish abandon*]. Saved.

HOST. As we are saved, and he does not seem happy, may he resume his duties?

50   LADY WRATHIE. Yes, yes; and now we ladies may withdraw.

[1] Does Barrie mean to suggest that Isit is not her real name?

PREEN [*the most selfish of the company, and therefore perhaps the favourite*]. First, a glass of wine with you, Dolphin.

VAILE [*ever seeking to undermine* PREEN'S *popularity*]. Is this wise?

PREEN [*determined to carry the thing through despite this fellow*]. To the health of our friend Dolphin.

[DOLPHIN'S *health having been drunk, he withdraws his chair and returns to the sideboard. As* MISS ISIT *and* MRS. CASTRO *had made room for him between them exactly opposite his master, and the space remains empty, we have now a better view of the company. Can this have been the author's object?*]

SIR JOSEPH [*pleasantly detaining the ladies*]. One moment. Another toast. Fellow-guests, to-morrow morning, alas, this party has to break up, and I am sure you will all agree with me that we have 60 had a delightful week. It has not been an eventful week; it has been too happy for that.

CAPT. JENNINGS. I rise to protest. When I came here a week ago I had never met Lady Jane. Now, as you know, we are engaged. I certainly call it an eventful week.

LADY JANE. Yes, please, Sir Joseph.

SIR JOSEPH. I stand corrected. And 70 now we are in the last evening of it; we are drawing nigh to the end of a perfect day.

PREEN [*who is also an orator*]. In seconding this motion —

VAILE. Pooh. [*He is the perfect little gentleman, if socks and spats can do it.*]

SIR JOSEPH. Though I have known you intimately for but a short time, I already find it impossible to call you anything but Sam Smith. 80

MRS. CASTRO. In our hearts, Mr. Smith, that is what we ladies call you also.

PREEN. If I might say a word —

VAILE. Tuts.

SIR JOSEPH. Ladies and gentlemen, **is**

he not like a pocket edition of Mr. Pickwick?[1]

GOURLAY [an artist]. Exactly. That is how I should like to paint him.

MRS. BLAND. Mr. Smith, you love, we think that if you were married you could not be quite so nice.

SIR JOSEPH. At any rate, he could not be quite so simple. For you are a very simple soul, Sam Smith. Well, we esteem you the more for your simplicity. Friends all, I give you the toast of Sam Smith.

[The toast is drunk with acclamation, and DOLPHIN, who has paid no attention to it, again hovers round with wine.]

HOST [rising in answer to their appeals and warming them with his Pickwickian smile]. Ladies and gentlemen, you are very kind, and I don't pretend that it isn't pleasant to me to be praised. Tell me, have you ever wondered why I invited you here?

MISS ISIT. Because you like us, of course, you muddle-headed darling.

HOST. Was that the reason?

SIR JOSEPH. Take care, Sammy, you are not saying what you mean.

HOST. Am I not? Kindly excuse. I dare say I am as simple as Sir Joseph says. And yet, do you really know me? Does any person ever know another absolutely? Has not the simplest of us a secret drawer inside him with — with a lock to it?

MISS ISIT. If you have, Mr. Smith, be a dear and open it to us.

MRS. CASTRO. How delicious. He is going to tell us of his first and only love.

HOST. Ah, Mrs. Castro, I think I had one once, very nice, but I have forgotten her name. The person I loved best was my brother.

PREEN. I never knew you had a brother.

HOST. I suppose none of you knew. He died two years ago.

SIR JOSEPH. Sorry, Sam Smith.

MRS. PREEN [drawing the chocolates nearer her]. We should like to hear about him if it isn't too sad.

HOST. Would you? He was many years my junior, and as attractive as I am commonplace. He died in a foreign land. Natural causes were certified. But there were suspicious circumstances, and I went out there determined to probe the matter to the full. I did, too.

PREEN. You didn't say where the place was.

HOST. It was Monte Carlo.[1]

[He pauses here, as if to give time for something to happen, but nothing does happen except that MISS ISIT's wine-glass slips from her hand to the floor.]

Dolphin, another glass for Miss Isit.

LADY JANE. Do go on.

HOST. My inquiries were slow, but I became convinced that my brother had been poisoned.

MRS. BLAND. How dreadful. You poor man.

GOURLAY. I hope, Sam Smith, that you got on the track of the criminals?

HOST. Oh yes.

[A chair creaks.]

Did you speak, Miss Isit?

MISS ISIT. Did I? I think not. What did you say about the criminals?

HOST. Not criminals; there was only one.

PREEN. Man or woman?

HOST. We are not yet certain. What we do know is that my brother was visited in his rooms that night by some one who must have been the murderer. It was some one who spoke English and who was certainly dressed as a man, but it may have been a woman. There is

---

[1] Mr. Samuel Pickwick, eccentric but genial old English gentleman, founder of the Pickwick Club, in Charles Dickens's Pickwick Papers.

[1] Capital of Monaco, one of the smallest independent states of Europe, between France and the Mediterranean. It is famous for its gambling casino.

proof that it was some one who had been to the tables that night. I got in touch with every 'possible,' though I had to follow some of them to distant parts.

LADY WRATHIE. It is extraordinarily
170 interesting.

HOST. Outwardly many of them seemed to be quite respectable people.

SIR JOSEPH. Ah, one can't go by that, Sam Smith.

HOST. I didn't. I made the most exhaustive inquiries into their private lives. I did it so cunningly that not one of them suspected why I was so anxious to make his or her acquaintance; and then, when
180 I was ready for them, I invited them to my house for a week, and they are all sitting round my table this evening.

[*As the monstrous significance of this sinks into them, there is a hubbub at the table.*]

You wanted to know why I had asked you here, and I am afraid that in consequence I have wandered a little from the toast; but I thank you, Sir Joseph, I thank you all, for the too kind way in which you have drunk my health.

[*He sits down as modestly as he had risen, but the smile has gone from his face; and the curious — which includes all the diners — may note that he is licking his lips. In the babel that again breaks forth, DOLPHIN, who has remained stationary and vacuous for the speech, goes the round of the table refilling glasses.*]

PREEN [*the first to be wholly articulate*]. In the name of every one of us, Mr.
190 Smith, I tell you that this is an outrage.

HOST. I was afraid you wouldn't like it.

SIR JOSEPH. May I ask, sir, whether all this week you have been surreptitiously ferreting into our private affairs, perhaps even rummaging our trunks?

HOST [*brightening*] That was it. You remember how I pressed you all to show your prowess on the tennis courts and the golf links while I stayed at home? That
200 was my time for the trunks.

LADY JANE. Was there ever such a man? Did you — open our letters?

HOST. Every one of them. And there were some very queer things in them. There was one about a luncheon at the Ritz. 'You will know me,' the man wrote, 'by the gardenia I shall carry in my hand.' Perhaps I shouldn't have mentioned that. But the lady who got
210 that letter need not be frightened. She is married, and her husband is here with her, but I won't tell you any more.

MISS ISIT. I think he should be compelled to tell.

PREEN. Wrathie,[1] there are only two ladies here with their husbands.

SIR JOSEPH. Yours and mine, Preen.

LADY WRATHIE. Joseph, I don't need to tell you it wasn't your wife. 220

MRS. PREEN. It certainly wasn't yours, Willie.

PREEN. Of that I am well assured.

SIR JOSEPH. Take care what you say, Preen. That is very like a reflection on my wife.

GOURLAY. Let that pass. The other is the serious thing — so serious that it is a nightmare. Whom do you accuse of doing away with your brother, sir? Out 230 with it.

HOST. You are not all turning against me, are you? I assure you I don't accuse any of you yet. I know that one of you did it, but I am not sure which one. I shall know soon.

VAILE. Soon? How soon?

HOST. Soon after the men join the ladies to-night. I ought to tell you that I am to try a little experiment to-night, 240 something I have thought out which I have every confidence will make the guilty person fall into my hands like a ripe plum. [*He indicates rather horribly how he will squeeze it.*]

LADY JANE [*hitting his hand*]. Don't do that.

[1] Sir Joseph.

SIR JOSEPH [*voicing the general unrest*]. We insist, Smith, on hearing what this experiment is to be.

HOST. That would spoil it. But I can 250 tell you this. My speech had a little pit in it, and all the time I was talking I was watching whether any of you would fall into that pit.

MRS. PREEN [*rising*]. I didn't notice any pit.

HOST. You weren't meant to, Mrs. Preen.

PREEN. May I ask, without pressing the personal note, did any one fall into 260 your pit?

HOST. I think so.

CAPT. JENNINGS. Smith, we must have the name of this person.

LADY WRATHIE. Mrs. Preen has fainted.

[PREEN *hurries slowly to his wife's assistance, and there is some commotion.*]

MRS. PREEN. Why — what — who — I am all right now. Willie, go back to your seat. Why are you all staring at me so?

270 MISS ISIT. Dear Mrs. Preen, we are so glad that you are better. I wonder what upset you?

PREEN [*imprudently*]. I never knew her faint before.

MISS ISIT. I expect it was the heat.

PREEN [*nervous*]. Say it was the heat, Emily.

MRS. PREEN. No, it wasn't the heat, Miss Isit. It was Mr. Smith's talk of a 280 pit.

PREEN. My dear.

MRS. PREEN. I suddenly remembered how, as soon as that man mentioned that the place of the crime was Monte Carlo, some lady had let her wine-glass fall. That was why I fainted. I can't remember who she was.

LADY WRATHIE. It was Miss Isit.

MRS. PREEN. Really?

290 MISS ISIT. There is a thing called the law of libel. If Lady Wrathie and

D

Mrs. Preen will kindly formulate their charges —

GOURLAY. Oh, come, let us keep our heads.

HOST. That's what I say.

GOURLAY. What about a motive? Scotland Yard always seeks for that first.

HOST. I see two possible motives. If a woman did it — well, they tended to 300 run after my brother, and you all know of what a woman scorned is capable.

PREEN [*reminiscent*]. Rather.

HOST. Then, again, my brother had a large sum of money with him, which disappeared.

SIR JOSEPH. If you could trace that money it might be a help.

HOST. All sorts of things are a help. The way you are all pretending to know 310 nothing about the matter is a help. It might be a help if I could find out which of you has a clammy hand that at this moment wants to creep beneath the table.

[*Not a hand creeps.*]

I'll tell you something more. Murderers' hearts beat differently from other hearts. [*He raises his finger.*] Listen.

[*They listen.*]

Whose was it?

[*A cry from* MISS VAILE *brings her into undesired prominence.*]

MISS VAILE [*explaining*]. I thought I heard it. It seemed to come from across 320 the table.

[*This does not give universal satisfaction.*] Please don't think because this man made me scream that I did it. I never was on a yacht in my life, at Monte Carlo or anywhere else.

[*Nor does even this have the desired effect.*]

VAILE [*sharply*]. Bella!

MISS VAILE. Have I said — anything odd?

GOURLAY. A yacht? There has been no talk about a yacht. 330

MISS VAILE [*shrinking*]. Hasn't there?

HOST. Perhaps there should have been. It was on his yacht that my brother died.

MRS. CASTRO. You said in his rooms.

HOST. Yes, that is what I said. I wanted to find out which of you knew better.

LADY JANE. And Miss Vaile —

340 MISS VAILE. I can explain it all if — if —

MISS ISIT. Yes, give her a little time.

HOST. Perhaps you would all like to take a few minutes.

MISS VAILE. I admit that I was at Monte Carlo — with my brother — when an Englishman died there rather mysteriously on a yacht. When Mr. Smith 350 told us of his brother's death, I concluded that it was probably the same person.

VAILE. I presume that you accept my sister's statement?

MISS ISIT. Ab-sol-ute-ly.

HOST. She is not the only one of you who knew that yacht. You all admit having been at Monte Carlo two years ago, I suppose?

CAPT. JENNINGS. One of us wasn't. 360 Lady Jane was never there.

HOST [with beady eyes]. What do you say to that, Lady Jane?

[LADY JANE falters.]

CAPT. JENNINGS. Tell him, Jane.

HOST. Yes, tell me.

CAPT. JENNINGS. You never were there; say so.

LADY JANE. Why shouldn't I have been there?

CAPT. JENNINGS. No reason. But 370 when I happened to mention Monte Carlo to you the other day I certainly understood — Jane, I never forget a word you say, and you did say you had never been there.

LADY JANE. So you — you, Jack — you accuse me — you — me —

CAPT. JENNINGS. I haven't, I haven't.

LADY JANE. You have all heard that Captain Jennings and I are engaged. I 380 want you to understand that we are so no longer.

CAPT. JENNINGS. Jane!

[She removes the engagement ring from her finger and hesitates how to transfer it to the donor, who is many seats apart from her. The ever-resourceful DOLPHIN goes to her with a tray on which she deposits the ring, and it is thus conveyed to the unhappy JENNINGS. Next moment DOLPHIN has to attend to the maid, who makes an audible gurgle of sympathy with love, which is a breach of etiquette. He opens the door for her, and she makes a shameful exit. He then fills the Captain's glass.]

HOST [in one of his nicer moods]. Take comfort, Captain. If Lady Jane should prove to be the person wanted — mind you, perhaps she isn't — why, then the ring is a matter of small importance, because you would be parted in any case. I mean by the handcuffs. I forgot to say that I have them here. [He gropes at his 390 feet, where other people merely have a table-napkin.] Pass them round, Dolphin. Perhaps some of you have never seen them before.

PREEN. A pocket edition of Pickwick we called him; he is more like a pocket edition of the devil.

HOST. Please, a little courtesy. After all, I am your host.

[DOLPHIN goes the round of the table with the handcuffs on the tray that a moment ago contained a lover's ring. They meet with no success.]

Do take a look at them, Mrs. Castro; they are an adjustable pair in case they 400 should be needed for small wrists. Would you like to try them on, Sir Joseph? They close with a click — a click.

SIR JOSEPH [pettishly]. We quite understand.

[MRS. BLAND rises.]

MRS. BLAND. How stupid of us. We have all forgotten that he said the murderer may have been a woman in man's clothes, and I have just remembered that when we played the charade 410 on Wednesday he wanted the ladies to dress up as men. Was it to see whether one of us looked as if she could have passed for a man that night at Monte Carlo?

HOST. You've got it, Mrs. Bland.

SIR JOSEPH. Well, none of you did dress up, at any rate.

MRS. BLAND [distressed]. Oh, Sir Joseph. Some of us did dress up, in 420 private, and we all agreed that — of course there's nothing in it, but we all agreed that the only figure which might have deceived a careless eye was Lady Wrathie's.

PREEN. I say!

LADY WRATHIE. Joseph, do you sit there and permit this?

HOST. Now, now, there is nothing to be touchy about. Have I not been 430 considerate?

SIR JOSEPH. Smith, I hold you to be an impudent scoundrel.

HOST. May not I, who lost a brother in circumstances so painful, appeal for a little kindly consideration from those of you who are innocent — shady characters though you be?

PREEN. I must say that rather touches me. Some of us might have reasons for 440 being reluctant to have our past at Monte inquired into without being the person you are asking for.

HOST. Precisely. I am presuming that to be the position of eleven of you.

LADY WRATHIE. Joseph, I must ask you to come upstairs with me to pack our things.

MISS ISIT. For my part, after poor Mr. Smith's appeal I think it would be 450 rather heartless not to stay and see the thing out. Especially, Mr. Smith, if you would give us just an inkling of what your — little experiment — in the drawing-room — is to be?

HOST. I can't say anything about it except that it isn't to take place in the drawing-room. You ladies are to go this evening to Dolphin's room, where we shall join you presently.

[Even DOLPHIN is taken aback.]

MRS. PREEN. Why should we go 460 there?

HOST. Because I tell you to, Mrs. Preen.

LADY WRATHIE. I go to no such room. I leave this house at once.

MRS. PREEN. I also.

LADY JANE. All of us. I want to go home.

LADY WRATHIE. Joseph, come.

MRS. PREEN. Willie, I am ready. I 470 wish you a long good-bye, Mr. Smith.

[Their dignified advance upon the door is spoilt on opening it by their finding a policeman standing there. They glare at MR. SMITH.]

HOST. The ladies will now adjourn to Dolphin's room.

LADY WRATHIE. I say no.

MRS. CASTRO. Let us. Why shouldn't the innocent ones help him?

[She gives SMITH her hand with a disarming smile.]

HOST. I knew you would be on my side, Mrs. Castro. Cold hand — warm heart. That is the saying, isn't it?

[She shrinks.]

LADY WRATHIE. Those who wish to 480 leave this man's house, follow me.

HOST [for her special benefit]. My brother's cigarette case was of faded green leather, and a hole had been burned in the back of it.

[For some reason this takes the fight out of her, and she departs for DOLPHIN'S room, tossing her head, and followed by the other ladies.]

VAILE [seeing SMITH drop a word to MISS VAILE as she goes]. What did you say to my sister?

HOST. I only said to her that she isn't your sister. [The last lady to go is MISS ISIT.] So you never met my brother, 490 Miss Isit?

MISS ISIT. Not that I know of, Mr. Smith.

HOST. I have a photograph of him that I should like to show you.

MISS ISIT. I don't care to see it.

HOST. You are going to see it. [*It is in his pocket, and he suddenly puts it before her eyes.*]

MISS ISIT [*surprised*]. That is not — [*She checks herself.*]

HOST. No, that is not my brother. 500 That is some one you have never seen. But how did you know it wasn't my brother?

[*She makes no answer.*]

I rather think you knew Dick, Miss Isit.

MISS ISIT [*dropping him a curtsey*]. I rather think I did, Mr. Sam. What then?

> [*She goes impudently. Now that the ladies have left the room, the men don't quite know what to do except stare at their little host. Decanter in one hand and a box of cigarettes in the other, he toddles down to what would have been the hostess's chair had there been a hostess.*]

HOST. Draw up closer, won't you?

> [*They don't want to, but they do, with the exception of* VAILE, *who is studying a picture very near the door.*]

You are not leaving us, Vaile?

VAILE. I thought —

HOST [*sharply*]. Sit down.

510 VAILE. Oh, quite.

HOST. You are not drinking anything, Gourlay. Captain, the port is with you.

[*The wine revolves, but no one partakes.*]

PREEN [*heavily*]. Smith, there are a few words that I think it my duty to say. This is a very unusual situation.

HOST. Yes. You'll have a cigarette, Preen?

> [*The cigarettes are passed round and share the fate of the wine.*]

GOURLAY. I wonder why Mrs. Bland — she is the only one of them that there 520 seems to be nothing against.

VAILE. A bit fishy, that.

PREEN [*murmuring*]. It was rather odd my wife fainting.

CAPT. JENNINGS [*who has been a drooping figure since a recent incident*]. I dare say the ladies are saying the same sort of thing about us. [*He lights a cigarette — one of his own.* DOLPHIN *is offering them liqueurs.*]

PREEN [*sulkily*]. No, thanks. [*But he takes one.*] Smith, I am sure I speak for all of us when I say we would esteem it a favour if you ask Dolphin to withdraw. 530

HOST. He has his duties.

GOURLAY [*pettishly, to* DOLPHIN]. No, thanks. He gets on my nerves. Can nothing disturb this man?

CAPT. JENNINGS [*also refusing*]. No, thanks. Evidently nothing.

SIR JOSEPH [*reverting to a more hopeful subject*]. Everything seems to point to its being a woman — wouldn't you say, Smith?

HOST. I wouldn't say everything, Sir 540 Joseph. Dolphin thinks it was a man.

SIR JOSEPH. One of us here?

> [SMITH *nods, and they survey their friend* DOLPHIN *with renewed distaste.*]

GOURLAY. Did he know your brother?

HOST. He was my brother's servant out there.

VAILE [*rising*]. What? He wasn't the fellow who —?

HOST. Who what, Vaile?

PREEN. I say!

VAILE [*hotly*]. What do you say? 550

PREEN. Nothing [*doggedly*]. But I say!

> [*Though* DOLPHIN *is now a center of interest, no one seems able to address him personally.*]

GOURLAY. Are we to understand that you have had Dolphin spying on us here?

HOST. That was the idea. And he helped me by taking your finger-prints.

VAILE. How can that help?

HOST. He sent them to Scotland Yard.

SIR JOSEPH [*vindictively*]. Oh, he did, did he? 560

PREEN. What shows finger-marks best?

HOST. Glass, I believe.

PREEN [*putting down his glass*]. Now I see why the Americans went dry.

SIR JOSEPH. Smith, how can you be sure that Dolphin wasn't the man himself?

[MR. SMITH *makes no answer.* DOLPHIN *picks up* SIR JOSEPH'S *napkin and returns it to him.*]

PREEN. Somehow I still cling to the 570 hope that it was a woman.

VAILE. If it is a woman, Smith, what will you do?

HOST. She shall hang by the neck until she is dead. You won't try the benedictine, Vaile?

VAILE. No, thanks.

[*The maid returns with coffee, which she presents under* DOLPHIN'S *superintendence. Most of them accept. The cups are already full.*]

SIR JOSEPH [*in his lighter manner*]. Did you notice what the ladies are doing in Dolphin's room, Lucy?

MAID [*in a tremble, and wishing she* 580 *could fly from this house*]. Yes, Sir Joseph, they are wondering, Sir Joseph, which of you it was that did it.

PREEN. How like women!

GOURLAY. By the way, Smith, do you know how the poison was administered?

HOST. Yes, in coffee. [*He is about to help himself.*]

MAID. You are to take the yellow cup, sir.

HOST. Who said so?

590 MAID. The lady who poured out this evening, sir.

PREEN. Aha, who was she?

MAID. Lady Jane Wraye, sir.

PREEN. I don't like it.

GOURLAY. Smith, don't drink that coffee.

CAPT. JENNINGS [*in wrath*]. Why shouldn't he drink it?

GOURLAY. Well, if it was she — a 600 desperate woman — it was given in coffee the other time, remember. But stop, she wouldn't be likely to do it in the same way a second time.

VAILE. I'm not so sure. Perhaps she doesn't suspect that Smith knows how

it was given the first time. We didn't know till the ladies had left the room.

PREEN [*admiring him at last*]. I say, Vaile, that's good.

CAPT. JENNINGS. I have no doubt she 610 merely meant that she had sugared it to his taste.

VAILE [*smiling*]. Sugar!

PREEN [*pinning his faith to* VAILE]. Sugar!

GOURLAY. Couldn't we analyse it?

CAPT. JENNINGS [*the one who is at present looking most like a murderer*]. Smith, I insist on your drinking that coffee.

VAILE. Lady Jane! Who would have thought it!

PREEN [*become a mere echo of* VAILE]. Lady Jane! Who would have thought it! 620

CAPT. JENNINGS. Give me the yellow cup. [*He drains it to the dregs.*]

SIR JOSEPH. Nobly done, in any case. Look here, Jennings — you are among friends — it hadn't an odd taste, had it?

CAPT. JENNINGS. Not a bit.

VAILE. He wouldn't feel the effects yet.

PREEN. He wouldn't feel them yet.

HOST. Vaile ought to know.

PREEN. Vaile knows. 630

SIR JOSEPH. Why ought Vaile to know, Smith?

HOST. He used to practise as a doctor.

SIR JOSEPH. You never mentioned that to me, Vaile.

VAILE. Why should I?

HOST. Why should he? He is not allowed to practise now.

[*We now see that* VAILE *has unpleasant teeth.*]

PREEN. A doctor — poison — ease of access. [*His passion for* VAILE *is shat-* 640 *tered. He gives him back the ring, as* CAPT. JENNINGS *might say, and wanders the room despondently.*]

SIR JOSEPH. We are where we were again.

[DOLPHIN *escorts out the maid, who is not in a condition to go alone.*]

CAPT. JENNINGS. At any rate that fellow has gone.

GOURLAY [*the first to laugh for some time*]. Excuse me. I suddenly remembered that Wrathie had called this the end of a perfect day.

HOST. It isn't ended yet.

[MR. PREEN *in his wanderings toward the sideboard encounters a very large glass and a small bottle of brandy. He introduces them to each other. He swirls the contents in the glass as if hopeful that it may climb the rim and so escape without his having to drink it. This is a trick which has become so common with him that when lost in thought he sometimes goes through the motion though there is no glass in his hand.*]

PREEN [*communing with himself*]. I
550 feel I am not my old bright self. [*Sips.*] I can't believe for a moment that it was my wife. [*Sips.*] And yet — [*sips*] — that fainting, you know. [*Sips.*] I should go away for a bit until it blew over. [*Sips.*] I don't think I should ever marry again. [*Sips and sips, and becomes perhaps a little more like his old bright self.*]

GOURLAY. There is something shocking about sitting here, suspecting each other in this way. Let us go to that room and have it out.

660 HOST. I am quite ready. Nothing more to drink, anyone? Bring your cigarette, Captain.

SIR JOSEPH [*hoarsely*]. Smith — Sam — before we go, can I have a word with you alone?

HOST. Sorry, Joseph. And now, shall we join the ladies?

[*As they rise, a dreadful scream is heard from the direction of* DOL-PHIN'S *room — a woman's scream. Next moment* DOLPHIN *reappears in the doorway. He is no longer the imperturbable butler. He is livid. He tries to speak, but no words will come out of his mouth.* CAPT. JENNINGS *dashes past him, and the others follow.* DOLPHIN *looks*

at his master with mingled horror and appeal, and then goes. SMITH *sits down again to take one glass of brandy. Where he sits we cannot see his face, but his rigid little back is merciless. As he rises to follow the others the curtain falls on Act One.*]

Discussion Hints

1. What hints of approaching calamity are given as the play opens?

2. The names of which characters are appropriately chosen?

3. What is the climax to Smith's speech?

4. What do you think was the "little experiment" Sam Smith planned to try? Where was it to take place? Did it take place?

5. Who thinks the criminal to be a man? Does Smith think the criminal a man or a woman? What is your theory as to who committed the crime? Why?

6. What seems to you the most Barrie-like bit of all?

Suggestions for Reading

1. As with your favorite dessert, one taste of Barrie's plays leads to another and another. He has written excellent one-act plays besides *Shall We Join the Ladies? The Old Lady Shows Her Medals* and *The Twelve-Pound Look* are well-known examples. Of Barrie's ever-popular full-length plays the most popular, perhaps, are *The Little Minister, Peter Pan, The Admirable Crichton, What Every Woman Knows, Dear Brutus, Quality Street, Mary Rose.* Since Barrie's death *Boy David* has come from the press (Charles Scribner's Sons); rumor of its appearance had reached us on this side of the Atlantic for several years.

2. Barrie's plays may be read, they may be seen on the stage and at the movies, and they may be heard on the radio. Now that you have become aware of him you will stumble upon him wherever you turn. But it is in printed form that he is always available. Charles Scribner's Sons (Barrie's American publishers) print his plays in one volume, as does the Walter H. Baker Company. Both Baker and Samuel French, Inc., have, in inex-

pensive form for the use of actors, eight full-length plays and a dozen one-act plays. If you have a younger brother or sister or cousin, read him one of the various versions of *Peter Pan* for young people (Charles Scribner's Sons have seven different editions). And for yourself, if you have missed it, turn to Frank R. Stockton's "Lady or the Tiger," an unfinished short story, one of the most famous problem stories ever written.

3. G. P. Putnam's Sons and the Walter H. Baker Company publish several volumes of the delightful, often fantastic, plays of Lord Dunsany. *If, Plays of Gods and Men, Plays of Near and Far*, and *Seven Modern Comedies* are among them. Proof of the popularity of Lord Dunsany's works on the amateur stage is the fact that both Baker and Samuel French, Inc., have in print four full-length and eighteen one-act plays. Special favorites among his short plays are *Fame and the Poet, The Golden Doom*, and the hair-raising *A Night at an Inn*.

4. The plays of A. A. Milne are somewhat similar to those of Barrie and Lord Dunsany, though the work of each is definitely personal. As with Lord Dunsany, G. P. Putnam's Sons publish several volumes of Milne's plays, among them *The Ivory Door* and *Success*. French and Baker have in print over a dozen of his full-length plays and almost as many one-act plays. Outstanding among Milne's longer plays are *The Dover Road, The Truth about Blayds*, and *Mr. Pim Passes By*; among his short plays are *The Boy Comes Home, Wurzel-Flummery*, and *The Man in the Bowler Hat*.

Suggestions for Further Reading in the Drama

1. English storytellers, novelists, and poets of our day have written many excellent plays. Oscar Wilde's *The Importance of Being Earnest* and *Lady Windermere's Fan* are witty, clever comedies of manners. They may be had in *The Plays of Oscar Wilde* (Modern Library, Inc.) or in inexpensive editions (Samuel French, Inc., and the Walter H. Baker Company).

2. W. Somerset Maugham, well-known essayist and novelist, is as noted as a playwright. *The Breadwinner, The Constant Wife, The Circle*, are a few titles from the almost two dozen carried by the Walter H. Baker Company.

3. But John Galsworthy, among writers of fiction, has made for himself the surest place as a playwright. In *Loyalties, The Silver Box, Justice*, and over a score other long plays, he discusses, in dramatic form, current problems and opinions. Though Charles Scribner's Sons are Galsworthy's official American publishers, Samuel French, Inc., carries his plays, both long and short.

4. Among the poets who are also dramatists, John Masefield stands supreme. His plays are really semidramatic poems: recitations, scenes, tableaus. *Tristan and Isolt, End and Beginning*, and *King's Daughter* are a few (The Macmillan Company).

5. And then there are those who are dramatists first and foremost. The Irish group is headed by William Butler Yeats. Of his long plays, *The Countess Cathleen*, and of his one-act plays, *The Land of Heart's Desire*, are excellent examples. See his *Collected Plays* (The Macmillan Company).

6. Lady Augusta Gregory is still thought of as the chief patron of the Irish theater. *Spreading the News* and *The Rising of the Moon* are favorites among her plays (see *Seven Short Plays*, published by G. P. Putnam's Sons). No list of Irish playwrights would be complete without mention of John Millington Synge, whose *Riders to the Sea* is in many anthologies (see *The Complete Works of J. M. Synge*, published by Random House, Inc.). And then there are the more recent Irish playwrights: Sean O'Casey, *Juno and the Paycock* and *Within the Gates* (The Macmillan Company), and St. John Ervine, *Jane Clegg* and *John Ferguson* (The Macmillan Company).

7. Two amusing and puzzling gentlemen whose names are inseparably connected with the stage are George Bernard Shaw and Noel Coward, one an octogenarian, the other, by comparison, a gay young blade. Beneath his banter Shaw is and always has been the more serious of the two. *Androcles and the Lion* is an excellent introduction to Shaw. It may be followed by *Saint Joan* and *The Apple Cart*. Dodd, Mead & Company, Inc., publish Shaw's plays. Not only Shaw, but Galsworthy and Yeats, were recipients of the Nobel prize for literature.

A good beginning for Noel Coward is *Cavalcade* or *Tonight at 8:30* (Doubleday, Doran & Company, Inc.). Samuel French, Inc., and the Walter H. Baker Company publish for both Shaw and Noel Coward.

8. And then there is the unique work of Laurence Housman. First, of course, stands *Victoria Regina* (Charles Scribner's Sons), which is merely a collection of four volumes of little plays published earlier under the titles *Angels and Ministers, Palace Plays, The Queen's Progress,* and *Victoria and Albert,* with the addition of a single new play, *Aims and Objects.*

In the more recent *The Golden Sovereign* (also Charles Scribner's Sons) are some of the same plays and many others, again reprints of earlier small volumes: *Palace Scenes, Possession, Dethronements, Echo de Paris,* and *Cornered Poets.* Not all are concerned with Victoria; the last, for instance, is concerned with literary folk: the Carlyles, the William Blakes, Wordsworth and Lamb, Burns, and Gray.

Samuel French, Inc., publishes other plays by Laurence Housman, some long, some short. Representative titles are, among the longer plays, *The Chinese Lantern,* a costume comedy, and among the shorter ones, *Bird in Hand, A Likely Story, Lord of the Harvest,* and *The Snow-Man.*

9. Another English poet who has written snapshot plays successfully, but not so successfully as Laurence Housman does, is John Drinkwater. Houghton Mifflin Company publish his *Abraham Lincoln, Oliver Cromwell, Robert E. Lee,* and *Robert Burns,* all on historical characters. Americans have not yet recovered from their amazement at the understanding and grasp, the dignity and restraint, with which Drinkwater, an Englishman, wrote of Lincoln, most American of Americans.

10. For suggestions for reading in the American one-act play see the revised edition of *American Writers* of this series.

☆ ☆ ☆ ☆ ☆ ☆ ☆ ☆ ☆ ☆ ☆ ☆ ☆ ☆ ☆ ☆ ☆ ☆ ☆ ☆ ☆ ☆ ☆ ☆ ☆ ☆ ☆ ☆

Biographies

The Beginnings of English Literature (55 B.C.–1400 A.D.)

GEOFFREY CHAUCER

Chaucer was the son of a prosperous London wine merchant. As a young man he fought in the Hundred Years' War, was taken prisoner by the French, and was ransomed by the king. The next ten years of his life were spent for the most part at the brilliant court of Edward III, where he held various posts and wrote for the entertainment of his friends a number of courtly lyrics in the French manner. He also produced his first important work, *The Boke of the Duchesse,* an elegy on the death of the wife of the distinguished nobleman John of Gaunt, son of King Edward. This period of Chaucer's life and work is often called his first, or French, period.

British Museum

1340(?)–1400

For text see page 37

In his maturer years he occupied various responsible government positions, making several journeys to Flanders, to France, and to Italy on governmental missions. The first visit to Italy opened a new world to the young poet. Italy was then in the full glory of the Renaissance, and the work of its great writers, Dante,* Petrarch,* and Boccaccio,* made upon Chaucer a deep impression, which is reflected in the works of his second, or Italian, period. The most important of these is *Troilus and Criseyde* (trō′ĭ lŭs ; krĭ sā′dĕ), which, though the plot is based on an Italian novel by Boccaccio, is largely an original work in the treatment of the characters.

In the meantime Chaucer was gaining experience of life and adding by keen observation to his knowledge of human nature. His life at court and his contacts as a member of Parliament and government officer supplied him with a valuable fund of knowledge of the world and of human life. From this great storehouse he was to draw the material for his masterpiece, *The Canterbury Tales,* which is a true reflection of English life and is the product of his third, or English, period.

Chaucer was a gentleman of aristocratic training, but at the same time a kindly and sympathetic observer of the lower classes. His fame rests upon three facts : (1) he told many good stories well ; (2) his verse is musical and highly polished ; (3) his humor has never been surpassed. (The portrait is from a manuscript of the early fifteenth century.)

SIR THOMAS MALORY

[1430(?)–1471. For text see page 49]

Sir Thomas Malory was a knight, the descendant of an ancient family in the county of Warwickshire. As a young man he served in the French wars under Richard Beauchamp, Earl of Warwick, who was known as "the father of courtesy" because of his fondness for the customs and traditions of chivalry. Thus Malory was fitted by birth, education, and training to be the author of a great medieval romance. He proved his fitness by compiling the *Morte d'Arthur* ("Death of Arthur"), an extensive collection of legends about King Arthur and the knights of the Round* Table. It is the most famous

697

romance of the Middle Ages. Its author drew chiefly from French romances, but he also used English sources and made some original contributions. This work was the most ambitious effort in English prose made during the Middle Ages. It had a good deal of influence in the development of a simple, fluent, and flexible prose style in English. Many English poets, including Spenser and Tennyson, have been inspired by Malory's *Morte d'Arthur*.

The Elizabethan Period (1400–1616)

WILLIAM SHAKESPEARE

Little is known of Shakespeare's ancestry beyond the fact that he came of good yeoman stock. His father was a merchant of Stratford on Avon, in Warwickshire. His mother's family were prosperous, influential farmers. He was undoubtedly educated at the free grammar school of Stratford, where he studied principally the Latin language and literature. When he was about thirteen years of age, he left school, probably because his father was in financial difficulties. When he was only eighteen he married Anne Hathaway, a woman eight years older than he. Two daughters and a son were born to them. Within a few years he left his family in Stratford and went to London, one tradition ascribing his departure to a prosecution for a deer-stealing prank.

© National Portrait Gallery

1564–1616

For text see pages 86, 154, 159

He got work in London as an actor and member of one of the theatrical companies, which, under the leadership of the famous actor Richard Burbage, presented plays at the Globe and other London theaters. We know little of his life in London, except that he was an associate of the jolly group of literary men whose revels at the Mermaid * Tavern were almost as famous as their successes on the stage. He had a friend and patron in the young Earl of Southampton, to whom he dedicated some of his early poems. His dramatic work began when he was about twenty-seven and extended over a period of twenty years, making an average of two plays a year in addition to his poems. His dramas were popular, and Shakespeare became not only famous, but moderately rich. He returned, a successful man, to his native town, bought a large house, and retired when he was

about fifty to spend his few remaining years in tranquil comfort.

We do not know just when most of Shakespeare's plays were written; but we can estimate their respective dates from various sorts of evidence, especially differences in dramatic skill and in meter. The earliest dramas are simple comedies or tragedies, whereas the later ones have a complexity comparable with that of life itself, blending comedy with tragedy just as human sentiments and passions blend and shade into one another. The meter becomes more flexible and irregular, too, in the later plays. As he grew older Shakespeare also used blank verse more and more frequently in preference to rhyme.

Shakespeare's literary production has been conveniently divided into four periods. During the first, or period of experimentation (1590–1595), he wrote the two long poems "Venus and Adonis" and "The Rape of Lucrece," whose rich sensuousness makes them typical of the Renaissance, and tried his hand at several different types of drama ranging from the historical plays on Henry VI to the delightful romantic comedy *A Midsummer Night's Dream* and the love tragedy *Romeo and Juliet*. The work of the second period (1595–1600) consists of plays dealing with English history, such as *Henry IV* and *Henry V*, and a half-dozen delightful comedies and farces, including *As You Like It* (in the revised edition of *Adventure* of this series). To this period also belong Shakespeare's sonnets,* some of which are superior to all other efforts of their kind in the language. The third period (1600–1610) is marked by a note of tragedy expressed in cynical comedies and in the five great tragedies, *Julius Cæsar* (in the revised edition of *Achievement* of this series), *Hamlet*, *Macbeth*, *Othello*, and *King Lear*. Shakespeare's final mood, as expressed in the plays of the fourth and last period (1610–1616), was one of a serene thoughtfulness. The lovely romantic plays *Cymbeline*, *A Winter's Tale*, and *The Tempest* show an exquisite delicacy of touch and a supreme mastery of character portrayal which were reserved for these final utterances of the great dramatist.

In general Shakespeare did not invent his plots, but took them over from historical chronicles, from existing plays, or from popular legend, and remade them. In remaking them he transformed them into the most moving and powerful dramas in the English language.

CHRISTOPHER MARLOWE

[1564–1593. For text see page 153]

Christopher Marlowe, next to Shakespeare the greatest dramatist of the Elizabethan Period, was the son of a shoemaker who lived in Canterbury. He went to Cambridge University, where he studied the Latin classics. We do not know what he did next, but before long we find him in London leading a wild life and writing plays. He was a fearless rebel; he denounced the accepted religious ideas of his time so violently that the government finally ordered his arrest with the object of investigating charges of atheism against him. But the arrest was never made; for a few days before the warrant was served Marlowe was stabbed to death in a tavern brawl. He died at the early age of twenty-nine.

One of Marlowe's most important services to literature was to free blank* verse from the mechanical restraints which had resulted from imitation of the classics. His extravagant, sonorous verse, Marlowe's "mighty line," as Jonson called it, varies between sublimity and bombast. It had a great influence on other dramatists, notably Shakespeare. Marlowe is chiefly famous for his "blood and thunder" tragedies, in which he depicts heroic, elemental characters swayed by remorseless and superhuman ambition. Among the most famous of his tragedies are *Tamburlaine* and *The Tragedy of Doctor Faustus*. He also wrote lyric poems, of which "The Passionate Shepherd to His Love" is the best-known.

SIR WALTER RALEIGH

A little Devonshire boy named Walter Raleigh, who used to listen by the hour to the tales of sailors returned from foreign lands, was to grow up into one of the most daring and famous of English sea captains. Raleigh attended Oriel College, Oxford; saw military service on the sea against the Spaniards and in Ireland against the Irish; and became a courtier and favorite of Queen Elizabeth, who showered wealth and honors upon him. But he was an adventurer at heart, and refused to stay at home. He loved to organize expeditions to found colonies or search for gold in America, or even to plunder foreign vessels on the high seas. Under King James* I he was accused of treason and shut up in the Tower of London, where he did much of his writing. At last he was allowed to stake his life on the successful outcome of a voyage to South America; but he failed to bring back the storied gold of Orinoco, and in accordance with the agreement paid the forfeit with his head.

The writings of this literary courtier reflect for the most part his hours of misfortune and despondency. They are gloomy, even bitter, in tone, and are well described in the words of a critic of his day as "most lofty, insolent, and passionate." Raleigh's *History of the World* is one of the monuments of Elizabethan prose. "The Nymph's Reply to the Shepherd" is given in *English Writers* more because it is famous than because it is completely typical of Raleigh's most characteristic mood.

© National Portrait Gallery

Sir Walter Raleigh, 1552–1618
For text see page 153

© National Portrait Gallery

Ben Jonson, 1573(?)–1637
For text see page 154

© National Portrait Gallery

Sir Philip Sidney, 1554–1586
For text see page 157

BEN JONSON

"Rare Ben Jonson," as Shakespeare called him, somehow survived the hairbreadth escapes of his adventurous youth to become a dramatist, poet, and literary dictator. Jonson started life as a bricklayer's apprentice, but he soon ran away to Flanders to join the army. After fighting for a while in the war against Spain he returned to London, married a quarrelsome woman who made his life miserable, and began to write plays and to act. He spent some time in prison for killing a fellow-actor in a duel, and again for an allusion in one of his plays that was displeasing to the government; but his literary reputation does not seem to have suffered from these offenses. He wrote successful comedies and tragedies for the popular stage as well as elaborate masks* for the court, and counted both commoners and noblemen among his intimates. He was appointed poet laureate,* and became practically the dictator of the theatrical world. His favorite resort was the famous Mermaid* Tavern, where he gathered with a group of jolly companions whose names are now famous in the history of the Elizabethan drama.

Ben Jonson was both scholarly and talented. He was one of the writers who turned away from the extravagances of some of the Renaissance writers, and strove for a more restrained art modeled on the works of the Greek and Latin poets. Jonson and his followers, who imitated the ancient classics, became less popular than Shakespeare and other writers who cared little for classical rules of composition, but Jonson never acknowledged defeat; he held out for the supremacy of the Greek "unities"* to the end. One classical characteristic that is represented in Jonson's comedies had an important and permanent influence. This is the effort to portray life realistically, instead of attempting to escape from it through the fantastic creations of fancy. As a result, his comedies give us rapid, sparkling sketches of London life in one of the most brilliant and interesting periods of English history. *Volpone, or the Fox* is one of the most witty and gay of these plays. Other important realistic comedies by Jonson are *Every Man in His Humour*; *Epicene, or The Silent Woman*; and *The Alchemist*, the latter regarded by some critics as one of the best plays ever written in accordance with the principles of ancient classical drama. As a poet, Jonson lives in a few beautiful lyrics, such as the famous "To Celia" ("Drink to Me Only with Thine Eyes").

SIR PHILIP SIDNEY

Sir Philip Sidney, soldier, statesman, poet, and great Elizabethan gentleman, was the descendant of a noble family. He studied at Christ Church, Oxford, traveled on the Continent, and returned home to become a courtier and diplomat. His charm of manner, his perfect courtesy, and his varied accomplishments made him the darling of the court circle and a favorite of Queen Elizabeth, and his interest in art and letters gave him a place of honor in literary circles as well. He married Lady Frances Walsingham; but the great love of his life is commemorated by his *Astrophel and Stella*, a sonnet* sequence addressed to Lady Penelope Devereux. When Sidney died from a wound received while he was fighting with the English army in Holland, all England mourned his loss. The queen was inconsolable, and for months it was regarded as bad form for any gentleman in London to be seen gaily dressed. Sidney has gone down in history as the embodied ideal of English chivalry during the Renaissance.

Though Sidney's poetry is less remarkable than his life, his pastoral* romance* *Arcadia*, written in an elaborate, artificial style called euphuism,* had a great influence on other writers, and his *Astrophel and Stella* is one of the most beautiful sonnet sequences in the language.

EDMUND SPENSER

Spenser was born in London of a middle-class family. He was educated at the Merchant Taylors' School and at Pembroke Hall, Cambridge, where, in spite of poverty and ill health, he found time to establish many close friendships, of which the most notable was that with the critic Gabriel Harvey. Two years after taking his degree he went to London and became a member of the Earl of Leicester's household. This position brought him into contact with numerous prominent persons. Among his friends were Sir Philip Sidney and other literary notables. On the publication of his *Shepherd's Calendar* in 1579, Spenser was at once acknowledged to be the greatest living English poet. As a result his friends at court succeeded in getting him a place as secretary to Lord Grey de Wilton, who was about to leave for Ireland to take up his duties as lord deputy.

Spenser found Ireland uncongenial, but he remained for eight years. Then, on the advice of his friend Sir Walter Raleigh, he went to court to seek further preferment, taking with him the first three books of *The Faerie Queene*. Spenser and his poem were well received at court, and the queen gave him a pension, but he failed to receive a more attractive position. Bitterly disappointed, he returned to Ireland and settled down once more to an official life there. His disillusionment is expressed in his poem "Colin Clout's Come Home Again." In 1594 he married; his courtship is celebrated in a sonnet* sequence, the *Amoretti*, and his marriage in the beautiful "Epitha-

British Museum

1552(?)–1599

For text see pages 158 and 166

lamion." Spenser had just been appointed sheriff of Cork when a violent uprising of the Irish occurred. His castle at Kilcolman was burned over his head, and there is some reason to believe that one of his children perished in the flames. Sent with a report of the disaster to London, he fell ill there, and a month after his arrival he died. He is buried in Westminster Abbey.

The Shepherd's Calendar is a series of twelve pastoral* poems written in a peculiar diction which employs many archaic and rustic words. *The Faerie Queene* is an elaborate allegory* set forth in the form of a metrical romance.* The poet's intention was to divide it into twelve books, but of these only six were completed. Although the narrative is long and at times hard to follow, it contains frequent episodes that are rich in musical verse and in beautiful imagery.* *The Faerie Queene* has been imitated by many writers, and has exercised an immense influence on English literature.

Spenser was one of the most learned of English poets. His material was drawn from both classical and modern authors. In addition, his genius taught him how to create the illusion of a colorful and magical world, which he painted with the rich beauty characteristic of the Renaissance. Many modern poets have sought to acquire Spenser's gift for brilliant pageantry and his remarkable feeling for form, color, and sound; hence he is known as "the Poets' Poet." (The portrait is from an engraving by George Vertue.)

FRANCIS BACON

Son of a nobleman and court official, Francis Bacon was born in London, educated at Trinity College, Cambridge, and trained to practice law. After traveling to Paris as an attendant on the English ambassador, he became a courtier and statesman under Queen Elizabeth. In public life he allowed his official conduct to be influenced by his personal interests. The blackest mark against Bacon's memory is the part he played in helping to convict his patron and friend, the Earl of Essex, on a charge of treason, and in accepting a large sum from the confiscated estate of his executed friend. Bacon was appointed Lord Chancellor by King James* I, but was deprived of this office on being convicted of taking bribes. After his political downfall he occupied himself chiefly with writing and with scientific experiments. He died from the effects of a chill caught while gathering snow to stuff a fowl in order to determine the effect of cold upon its flesh.

Bacon regarded his philosophical and scientific writings in Latin as his most important contribution to thought. *The Advancement of Learning* and the *Novum Organum* emphasized the importance of the experimental method in scientific research. By insisting upon the value of practical experimentation as an aid to scientific inquiry, Bacon had a great influence on modern thought.

© National Portrait Gallery
1561–1626
For text see page 175

Today we think of Bacon's *Essays* as his most important literary achievement. On the other hand, he wrote them in English instead of Latin because he regarded them as unworthy of preservation in the scholarly tongue of his philosophical works. They are short, pithy discussions of a variety of subjects such as "Friendship," "Truth," "Studies," and "Adversity," written from a coldly practical point of view rather than from a strictly moral one. The *Essays* are still read for the sharply pointed maxims with which they are filled, as well as for their clear, crisp, and vigorous style, which has become a model for later writers of English prose. (The portrait is from a painting by Paul van Somer.)

The Puritan Period (1603–1660)

JOHN MILTON

John Milton, England's greatest epic poet, was born in London. His father, a scrivener (attorney), was a Puritan of culture and of some musical gifts. Milton received instruction from private tutors, then went to St. Paul's School and to Christ's College, Cambridge. At Cambridge he was a fellow student of two men who later became famous in America: John Harvard, the earliest benefactor of Harvard College; and Roger Williams, the founder of Rhode Island.

From boyhood Milton loved study, especially in foreign languages and in English literature. After a brief period during which he considered entering the church as a career, he determined to devote himself to literature.

This decision was not made lightly; for Milton believed himself called to be a poet of lofty themes, and determined to prepare himself for his great mission by leading a lofty life. He retired to the village of Horton, near London, where, in company with his father, he lived for several years studying mathematics, music, history, and the Greek and Latin classics, and communing with nature in the beautiful woods and meadows of the surrounding countryside. To this period belong a few perfect poems which combine an appreciation of nature with scholarly learning and produce an effect of flawless beauty. These are the shorter poems "L'Allegro," "Il Penseroso," "Lycidas," a few sonnets, and the exquisite mask* *Comus*. *Comus* was performed at Ludlow Castle before a distinguished company of courtiers in 1634.

At the close of his Horton period Milton traveled in Europe, where he met many distinguished persons. Then he took a quiet house in London, tutored a few pupils, and devoted himself to his studies.

Since Milton was a Puritan, it is not strange that he became involved in the theological controversies which were absorbingly interesting to almost everyone at that time. He wrote numerous pamphlets on religion and politics. The best-known of his prose works is the *Areopagitica*, opposing the censorship of the press, though with reservations. He was one of the warmest supporters of Cromwell* and the Puritan party. As secretary to the Puritan Commonwealth he labored so hard that he ultimately became blind. With the Restoration, Milton had to go into hiding. He was at length arrested, but was pardoned. Politics was now a closed career for him. He had lost his sight by writing too much during the period of his patriotic activity, and the London fire of 1666 destroyed most of his property.

Milton married three times. His first marriage, which took place in 1643, was unhappy, and Milton proceeded to write several pamphlets on divorce. After ten years of married

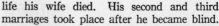

© National Portrait Gallery
1608–1674
For text see page 190

life his wife died. His second and third marriages took place after he became blind. His second wife, who died only fifteen months after her marriage, is the subject of his beautiful sonnet "On His Deceased Wife."

In spite of blindness, Milton, about 1658, began the writing of *Paradise Lost*, the epic which for years he had regarded as the great undertaking of his life. With the aid of friends and of his daughters, who wrote from his dictation, he brought the poem to completion after five years. For the finished work he is said to have received only a few pounds. No other poem in English approaches *Paradise Lost* in loftiness of theme, sublimity of conception, and dignity of expression. It is written in majestic and harmonious blank* verse, crowded with classical allusions that reveal the vastness of Milton's learning, and abounding in images and descriptions that give it an extraordinary impressiveness. It was followed after several years by *Paradise Regained*, which Milton regarded as his greatest work, but which is inferior to *Paradise Lost*, though it contains many magnificent passages. His last work, entitled *Samson Agonistes*, is a drama composed in the Greek manner and presenting a kind of allegory of Milton's own life.

The portrait is from an engraving by William Faithorne.

ROBERT HERRICK

[1591–1674. For text see page 200]

The son of a London goldsmith (jeweler), Herrick was educated at Cambridge University. He became a clergyman and settled in Devonshire, but disliked the loneliness of his parish, though much of his best poetry was written there. When he was ousted from his parish as a Royalist* at the time of the establishment of the Commonwealth, he said he would never return; but a few years spent in living on the charity of his friends proved still less to his taste, and with the Restoration he was glad to go back to his pulpit.

Herrick loved to describe the English country life which he had come to know during his residence among the Devonshire peasants. He wrote about love and nature in poems full of music and beautiful imagery.* A note of sadness runs through much of his verse. Sometimes he echoes Greek and Latin authors and writes in a pagan mood, but his characteristic note is one of sincere Christian piety. *Hesperides* and *Noble Numbers*, two collections of his poems, appeared in 1648.

RICHARD LOVELACE

The descendant of an ancient Kentish family, Lovelace was educated at the famous school known as the Charterhouse and at Gloucester Hall, Oxford. He went to court to make his fortune, was speedily recognized as the handsomest man there, and became a great social favorite. But he soon longed to conquer other fields than ladies' hearts, and gave up the career of a courtier to join the army. Here he distinguished himself by a chivalrous behavior that has caused him to be compared to Sir Philip Sidney (p. 157). His sympathy with the Royalists* got him into trouble that finally resulted in the loss of his fortune. He died in obscurity and in hopeless poverty.

Most of his verses are marred by far-fetched conceits,* but he lives as a true poet in a few exquisitely graceful lyrics. He belongs to the Cavalier* group of poets.

Dulwich College	© National Portrait Gallery	© National Portrait Gallery
Richard Lovelace, 1618–1658	Izaak Walton, 1593–1683	John Bunyan, 1628–1688
For text see page 200	For text see page 202	For text see page 205

IZAAK WALTON

Walton was born in London and spent his life there as a linen-draper (dry-goods merchant); but, like many other men who have given their lives to commonplace occupations, he had a hobby that gave him a chance to escape occasionally from the routine of business. He was an enthusiastic fisherman and spent his holidays in wandering through the fields and meadows with his fishing-rod in hand and his eyes open to the beauties of nature. At a time when most other Englishmen were in a state of turmoil over questions of religion and politics, Izaak Walton seems to have gone quietly about his business, untroubled by the disturbances in the world around him. His personal reminiscences and his observations on the habits of fishes and on country scenes he recorded in *The Complete Angler* (1653), one of the simplest and most charming books in the English language. (The portrait is from a painting by J. Huysmans.)

JOHN BUNYAN

John Bunyan, inspired preacher and author, was born in a little village in Bedfordshire, where his father carried on the trade of tinker, or mender of pots and kettles. After going to school for a short time, Bunyan helped his father in his trade, but his stepmother made life so miserable for him that he left home at the age of sixteen to become a soldier. At the close of the Civil War he returned to his native village, married, and took up his father's trade. His wife was as poor as he was; but she brought to her new home a few religious books which awakened Bunyan's spiritual nature and resulted in his becoming a devout member of a nonconformist (Puritan) congregation. He began to preach, gathering chance listeners about him in towns and fields and on highways wherever his trade of tinker took him.

After the Restoration nonconformist services became illegal, and Bunyan, who refused to give up his preaching, was arrested and sent to prison. There he read the Bible and Foxe's well-known *Book of Martyrs*, continued his preaching to his fellow prisoners and to visitors, and wrote books and tracts in his plain, forceful English. After twelve years he was released from prison. He at once became pastor of a nonconformist congregation, which held its simple services in a barn. His fame spread, and he received many offers of more influential positions; but he refused to leave his post, although he frequently traveled about preaching to vast crowds.

It is one of the great marvels of literature that this tinker, without any formal education, should have been able to compose a book which ranks with Spenser's *Faerie Queene* and the *Divine Comedy* of Dante as one of the great allegories* of literature. *The Pilgrim's Progress* (1678), written for the simple village people to whom Bunyan preached his sermons, has an appeal that is felt by Christians of all times and of all social classes. It is a true expression of the ideals of Christianity as understood by the common man. It is written in a picturesque, forceful, and often poetical style that has become one of the models of English prose. Like *Paradise Lost*, it is an epic of Puritanism; but it differs from Milton's great poem in that it is the expression of the inner and emotional phases of this great religious movement rather than of its outward and theological aspects. (The portrait is from a painting by Thomas Sadler.)

The Age of Classicism (1660–1744)

ALEXANDER POPE

The life of Pope is a triumph of great genius over tremendous handicaps. From early youth he suffered from poor health, which resulted in deformity, and he was barred by his Roman Catholic faith from the political career by which most of the literary men of the time sought fame and fortune. His religion unfortunately also kept him out of the universities. He attended two inferior schools and was tutored by several priests, but dug out most of his learning by himself through wide reading.

His first book of poems, published when he was twenty-one, had been written when he was only seventeen. His early efforts attracted attention at once. Several of the great poets of the day became enthusiastic about this frail boy, in whom they saw a poet destined to be one of Eng-

© National Portrait Gallery
1688–1744
For text see pages 223 and 230

land's greatest literary figures. Pope's popularity increased rapidly. In 1711 he published an exposition of the rules of the classical school in the form of a poem entitled *An Essay on Criticism*. The next year he showed what he could do at humorous poetry in a delightful mock epic, *The Rape of the Lock*. Soon he was the literary lion of London, the honored friend of great wits, poets, politicians, and painters. Among his patrons was Bolingbroke.* He was persuaded to bring out an edition of Shakespeare, though he felt himself unfitted for the task. He translated Homer in his characteristic flowing couplets, and the venture succeeded so well that he was enabled to buy a small estate at Twickenham, near London, where he lived a secluded life, entertaining a circle of literary friends. Unjust criticism by some of Pope's

D

meaner rivals, coupled with some malice on Pope's part, led to his writing *The Dunciad,* one of the greatest satires* ever penned. It successfully ridiculed his literary enemies, but thenceforth his life was full of bitter quarrels.

At his death he was universally acclaimed as England's greatest poet. His character was marred by his strong personal dislikes and perhaps by a tinge of unscrupulousness, but his generosity is evidenced by more than one instance. His aim was not so much novelty or emotional power as the expression of ideas in the most fitting and epigrammatic* language and the most melodious verse possible. He is remembered for his triumphant wit, for his knack of putting things clearly and unforgettably, and for his command of easy, flowing language. (The portrait is from a painting attributed to William Hoare.)

JOHN DRYDEN

John Dryden, the most prominent poet and dramatist of the Age of Classicism, was born in Northamptonshire of a well-to-do Puritan family. After attending Trinity College, Cambridge, he obtained a position in London and married Lady Elizabeth Howard. He began his literary career by writing comedies in which he was tremendously successful. More important however, were his heroic tragedies, in which the famous' actress Nell Gwyn appeared. He also rewrote Shakespeare's *Antony and Cleopatra* in an effort to bring it into conformity with the classical rules. The title of the new play was *All for Love, or The World Well Lost.*

© National Portrait Gallery

1631–1700
For text see page 226

Dryden wrote verse of various kinds; but he found his best field in the writing of satires,* of which some were political or religious in character, and others were directed against his literary enemies. Among his longer satirical poems are *Absalom and Achitophel* (à kĭt'ŏ fĕl) and *The Hind and the Panther.* Among his lyric poems some of his odes* are famous. He also wrote numerous critical works in prose. He took an active part in the feuds which were of common occurrence among the rival playwrights of the day, and on one occasion was actually beaten by ruffians in the pay of his enemies. In 1670 he was made poet laureate,* but he was later deprived of his office on political charges. As a result he wrote in poverty and ill health during his later years. But his ability was never questioned, in his old age he assumed the position of literary dictator, and might

be seen any evening lording it over a deferential circle at Will's Coffee-House.* He is buried in Westminster Abbey.

Dryden reflects better than any other writer the conditions of social life during the Restoration. He depended on the favor of the court for his living, a fact that explains his worldliness, his lack of deep moral feeling, and the instability of his political and religious ideas, which he altered to suit the changing fashions. He was at first a supporter of the Commonwealth, but later went over to the Royalist* side; he began as a Protestant, but in 1686 was converted to Roman Catholicism. He wrote verse about subjects which we today should consider suitable only for prose; but in Dryden's day poems dealing with the affairs of Church and State were accepted as normal. People admired and imitated the regularity and precision of his polished heroic* couplets. Some of his odes are still worthy of admiration. His literary criticism, which caused him to be regarded as the most eminent critic of the time, contains much sound advice, though its standards of judgment are not altogether those of modern readers. Dryden was the first great English writer to abandon the involved and artificial prose style of most of his contemporaries of the Classical School (p.214) and of his predecessors. In the order of his words and in the arrangement of his ideas he is the first great writer of modern prose.

The portrait is from a painting by Sir Godfrey Kneller.

SAMUEL PEPYS

Pepys lived a busy life in London during an age of change and disturbance. He was a man of affairs, occupying at various times important government positions in the navy department. During the Great Plague of 1665 he remained in London and continued his work. He also helped in checking the Great Fire (1666). He was interested in scientific research, was at one time president of the Royal* Society, and made a valuable collection of books, which was bequeathed to Cambridge University and still exists; in short, Pepys was a public-spirited and respected citizen.

Between 1660 (the year when Charles II was restored to the English throne) and 1669 Pepys kept a diary in secret writing, which was not deciphered for more than a century after the author's death. Pepys's *Diary* is important, because it gives us an intimate view of the life of a representative Englishman during one of the most interesting periods of English history. He tells us how he lived day by day, revealing his own most intimate affairs as well as the gossip and talk of the town. (The portrait is from a painting by Sir Godfrey Kneller.)

© National Maritime Museum
Samuel Pepys, 1633–1703
For text see page 233

© National Portrait Gallery
Samuel Johnson, 1709–1784
For text see pages 238 and 251

SAMUEL JOHNSON

Samuel Johnson was the son of a poor Lichfield bookseller. He studied at Pembroke College, Oxford, suffering greatly from poverty; then went to London, married a widow twenty years his senior, and supported himself precariously by tutoring, translating, and doing hack work for the magazines. Once he set up as a teacher of Latin and Greek; but his irritability, his unkempt appearance, and his strange, erratic habits frightened the pupils away. Many a night he walked the London streets, having no money to pay for a bed. At length he conceived the idea of the *Dictionary*, which is his greatest title to fame. This work he proposed to dedicate to Lord Chesterfield, thereby soliciting his patronage; but the nobleman treated him coldly, and

Johnson proceeded without his help. Later, when Johnson's writings began to attract public attention, Chesterfield became more gracious, but Johnson now proudly refused his favor in a letter which has become famous.

Johnson wrote numerous poems, the best one of which is "The Vanity of Human Wishes." In 1759 he composed his great allegorical* romance,* *Rasselas*, in one week in order to pay the expenses of his mother's funeral. His *Lives of the Poets*, written when Johnson was an old man, is composed in a simpler style than his earlier prose works.

His essays, poems, critical writings, and, above all, his great *Dictionary* at length won recognition, and he received a pension that made him independent. He was the founder of the famous Literary* Club, where he ruled as absolute monarch over a little court including, along with others, Goldsmith, Reynolds, Burke, and his biographer, Boswell.

He was almost as renowned for his conversational powers as for his literary works. Hour after hour he would talk on and on, and still his audience would listen enthralled by the utterances of this strange, uncouth man in slovenly dress.

Johnson was a profound scholar, a tireless worker, a faithful friend, and a dangerous foe. In spite of his melancholy and irritable temper he was kind to children, servants, poor people, and animals. His immense intellectual power, his high moral sense, and his shrewd gift of observation are illustrated by his works, though their interest is likely to be obscured for the modern reader by their ponderous style and the author's fondness for long, mouth-filling words of Latin origin. Johnson was one of the most influential of English literary men. He showed that it was possible for authors to earn their living by their pens without depending on charity. His *Dictionary* first set forth the principle, followed by later lexicographers. that the meaning of a word is to be sought in the way writers use it. Through his literary style he became a model for many other writers of English literature. (The portrait is from a painting by John Opie.)

JAMES BOSWELL

Boswell, the self-effacing worshiper of Samuel Johnson, is now more frequently read than the great man to whom he erected an enduring monument in the most famous of English biographies. A descendant of an old Scottish family, Boswell was educated at Edinburgh and Glasgow and began the study of law, but found it less congenial than the social life of London and Edinburgh. After two years of travel and study in Italy, he was admitted to the bar in 1766, but never made a financial success of his profession. Three years later he married his cousin, Margaret Montgomerie.

Boswell was never so happy as when conversing with prominent people. He managed to secure an introduction to Johnson, whom he had long admired from afar, and he followed up the acquaintance until it developed into the lifelong friendship which furnished the background for his *Life of Johnson*. In spite

© National Portrait Gallery

1740–1795

For text see page 244

of financial and domestic difficulties, Boswell for more than twenty years spent about two months of almost every year in London, seeking out the great man day after day and faithfully recording his doings and his conversations. After the death of Boswell's wife Boswell went to live in London, where he brought to completion and published his great work in 1791.

Though eccentric, vain, and touched with melancholy, Boswell was a pleasant companion and a loyal friend. He was an ideal hero-worshiper, but in spite of his admiration for Johnson he never surrendered his own independence of judgment. On the other hand, he did not intrude himself into the portrait. Vivacity of style, wealth of detail, and dramatic power of expression make the *Life of Johnson* one of the greatest biographies ever written. (The portrait is from a painting by Sir Joshua Reynolds.)

PHILIP DORMER STANHOPE, EARL OF CHESTERFIELD

Chesterfield was born of a noble family. After studying at Cambridge University and on the Continent he entered English politics, and rose eventually to be Secretary of State. He also became well known as an orator and a man of fashion. In 1748 he withdrew from politics and lived in ease and retirement until his death. His *Letters*, written to his son, and not intended for publication, teach a cold and selfish philosophy of life, but they contain one of the best expositions in the English language of fine, courtly manners. These *Letters* have become so popular that the adjective "Chesterfieldian" has been coined to describe manners which are polished and urbane. The *Letters* were published in 1774, after Chesterfield's death. (The portrait is from a painting by Allan Ramsay.)

© National Portrait Gallery
Earl of Chesterfield, 1694–1773
For text see page 253

© National Portrait Gallery
Richard Steele, 1672–1729
For text see page 255

RICHARD STEELE

Steele was born in Dublin, the son of a prosperous attorney, and was educated at the Charterhouse School in London. Here he began the lifelong friendship with Joseph Addison which was to result in one of the most famous of literary partnerships. He went with Addison to Oxford, but left, without taking a degree, to join the army. He rose to the rank of captain, but gave up military life to become a journalist in the interest of the Whigs.* He was rewarded by several government positions and became a member of Parliament, but was expelled for writing an offensive political pamphlet.

Careless, improvident, good-humored, he tried first one thing and then another: wrote for the papers, edited periodicals, wrote plays which were excessively moral in tone, and for a time even directed a theater. His greatest contribution to literature is found in the essays which he wrote for *The Tatler** and *The Spectator,** periodicals which he established and to which Addison contributed. In later life he quarreled with this old friend, who unfortunately died before a reconciliation could take place.

Steele's eager, warm-hearted nature was reflected in the sympathetic outlook and kindly humor of his essays. He wrote with natural lightness and ease. He was one of the first English authors to portray English domestic life sympathetically and was almost the only writer of his age to depict women without cynicism. The affection with which he is regarded is witnessed by the fact that he is often referred to familiarly as "Dick Steele." (The portrait is from a painting by Jonathan Richardson.)

JOSEPH ADDISON

Joseph Addison was a courteous, polished gentleman to whom literary elegance was so natural that he had to teach himself to write in the simpler, conversational style of his famous essays. He was born in Amesbury, Wiltshire, the son of a prominent clergyman.

He was educated at the Charterhouse School in London and at Oxford, where he acquired a reputation as a classical scholar and a writer of Latin poetry. After traveling in Europe he entered upon his combined political and literary career with a poem, "The Campaign," written in celebration of Marl-borough's* victory at Blenheim (1704). He was rewarded by a succession of political offices and finally was appointed Secretary of State (1717). He was married in 1716 to the Countess of Warwick.

Addison's great reputation as well as his sweetness of character and personal charm made him the center of a little circle of literary men, among them Richard Steele and Jonathan Swift, who used to gather at the London coffeehouses.* His fame in his own day rested upon his elegant, polished verse and his classically correct dramas, but today

no one would call Addison a great poet. For us he is admired as the author of the short familiar essays written during his association with Steele in *The Tatler** and in *The Spectator.**

The charm of these essays is chiefly due to their good-humored, conversational tone and to their clear and simple yet polished style. The essays of Addison and Steele were imitated by many writers of their own generation as well as by a host of later essayists both in England and in America. (The portrait is from a painting by Sir Godfrey Kneller in the Bodleian Library.)

Joseph Addison, 1672–1719
For text see page 261

© National Portrait Gallery
Daniel Defoe, 1661(?)–1731
For text see page 265

DANIEL DEFOE

Defoe was born in London, where his father, a retired butcher, saw to it that he received a good education. He thought of entering the church, but he gave up this plan and went into business. Before long he found himself bankrupt, perhaps because he paid more attention to politics than to his own affairs. He now supported himself as a journalist, writing for political papers, though not always writing on the same side of a question, since a journalist's fortunes in those days depended on his standing well with the political party that happened to be in power.

Defoe had a gift for writing imaginary histories with such minute and realistic* detail that everyone thought they were true. His *Journal of the Plague Year,* though largely imaginary, is so convincing that many people have mistaken it for the account of an eyewitness. *Robinson Crusoe* (1719) is almost

pure fiction based on a few historical facts; yet it contains so many circumstantial details that the reader is tempted to accept it as an account of actual events. It is one of the earliest pieces of English realistic fiction of the novel type.

Defoe also wrote several novels about rogues and other persons of low character. These stories have highly commendable morals; but the gusto with which they are told makes one suspect that the author may have been less interested in the moral lesson, which he dutifully presented, than in the scenes of roguery and vice with which his pages are filled.

Whatever his real motive, Defoe was the first English writer of fiction to portray scenes from actual life with anything like true realism.* Not till the novels of Fielding appeared did another author reproduce with any great success the life of the lower half of English society.

JONATHAN SWIFT

Swift was born in Ireland, though both his parents were English. Growing up in poverty, he became bitter, proud, and independent. He enrolled at Trinity College, Dublin, where he was considered extraordinarily dull. Then for a while he was secretary to a relative in England, a position which he heartily detested. During this time he took orders in the Church of England. In the meantime he had begun to exercise his gift for writing satire,* and soon afterward came an opportunity to put this dangerous talent to effective use.

1667–1745
For text see page 274

Most of the literary men of the time were members of one or the other of the two chief political parties of the day, the Whigs* and the Tories.* Swift's scornful genius was put at the service first of the Whigs and then of the Tories. His brilliant wit soon made him a powerful molder of public opinion, and spurred on by political ambition he found himself a power in the government. But his genius was always exerted in the service of men of less ability than himself, and he never won the political or ecclesiastical recognition he longed for. When his political hopes failed, he retired to Ireland with the somewhat disappointing reward of the deanship of St. Patrick's in Dublin. Characteristically defending the oppressed, he championed the cause of Ireland against England, and was acclaimed the hero of the Irish people.

With all his bitterness and his boasted hatred of mankind, which finally led to insanity, Swift had a most kindly nature, and all who knew him loved him. Though he never married, he was loved by two women, and his affection for one of them (Esther Johnson, whom he called Stella) is the most charming thing in his life. It was in his *Journal to Stella* that he used the playfully affectionate "little language" so often referred to by later writers. He is one of the greatest geniuses of the period and one of the most brilliant prose-writers in the English language. He struck at political scheming and dishonesty, religious sectarianism, literary squabbling, vice; wherever he saw shams and hypocrisy he aimed an unerring blow. The most famous of his works are *A Tale of a Tub* and *Gulliver's Travels*, two of the most brilliant allegorical* satires in literature. *The Battle of the Books*, another of his brilliant satires, deals with the comparative merits of ancient and modern authors. (The portrait is from a painting by Charles Jervas in the Bodleian Library.)

The Transition from Classicism to Romanticism
(1744–1798)

WILLIAM COLLINS

[1721–1759. For text see page 296]

Collins was the son of a respectable hatter who had been mayor of Chichester. He began to write poetry at an early age, and after leading a somewhat dissipated life at Oxford gave up a plan of entering the church and came to London to try literature. In London he made the acquaintance of Samuel Johnson as well as of many other distinguished literary figures. Collins's good temper, his charming conversation, and his knowledge of several languages, both ancient and modern, made him an interesting and entertaining companion. But he was an irresolute, despondent person, and in later life he became insane.

Though indolence and ill health prevented Collins from ever becoming a really great poet, he was one of the first of the new school that was beginning to protest against the rigid rules of the Classical School adhered to by Pope and his followers. His odes,* including his "Ode to Evening," show originality and sincerity. The "Ode on the Popular Superstitions of the Highlands" is an early example of a genuinely romantic treatment of ghostly beings and other supernatural creatures. His interest in solitude, twilight, the supernatural, and the Middle Ages helped to introduce into literature an element which was later to become very popular during the Romantic Period. His verse is especially beloved by poets for its sweetness and its delicate sensibility.

THOMAS GRAY

Gray was born in London of poor parents. He was one of twelve children. As a boy he was shy, took no part in athletics, and was regarded as effeminate. After attending Eton (a famous preparatory school) and Cambridge University he made the "grand tour" of Europe with his friend Horace Walpole, son of the prime minister. He then returned to Cambridge and studied law, but finding Greek literature much more absorbing he gave up the profession. He made his home in Cambridge for the rest of his life, studying, and enjoying quiet and congenial society, though he spent a part of each summer with his mother at Stoke Poges and occasionally made a summer tour in England or Scotland. He was appointed professor of modern history in Cambridge University, but delivered no lectures. He collected many notes, intending to write a history of English poetry, but the book was never written. In spite of the seeming ineffectiveness of his life he was interested in social and political matters, was a great reader, and was regarded as the most learned Englishman of his day.

© National Portrait Gallery
1716–1771

For text see page 298

He has left a small but precious body of writings. His poetry furnishes an interesting and instructive illustration of the changing temper of the Transition Period. His "Ode on a Distant Prospect of Eton College," written in 1742, is tinged with the artificialities characteristic of the poets of the Age of Classicism. The "Elegy in a Country Churchyard," begun the same year, but not completed till nearly ten years later, shows a combination of classical restraint and polish with features that foreshadow the Romantic Period. "The Fatal Sisters" and "The Descent of Odin," written in 1761, are thoroughly romantic in their language, in their meter, and in their imaginative treatment of themes from medieval Scandinavian tradition. Taken as a whole, Gray's poetry is marked by extremely careful workmanship and great imaginative power. (The portrait is from a painting by John Giles Eccardt.)

WILLIAM COWPER

Cowper was the son of a clergyman and was educated at Westminster School. He tried to practice law; but his timidity made him hate the profession, and he began to suffer from despondency, from which he found some relief in religion and in poetry. At one time he was so worried about an examination for a legal post that he tried to commit suicide. A period of insanity followed; and this malady continued to visit him at intervals through the rest of his life, with delusions often taking the form of religious fears. After the first attack he left London and went to live in the country among friends and relatives who did what they could to cheer and encourage him. Here, finding happiness in such simple occupations as caring for his rabbits, he continued to live and to write poetry.

Cowper is remembered chiefly for his letters, his *Task* (a long descriptive poem), a few of his hymns, and several of his shorter poems, such as "The Solitude of Alexander Selkirk," which has won fame partly because of its connection with Defoe's *Robinson Crusoe*.

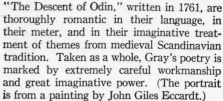

The poetry of this gentle and devout recluse reflects his sweet disposition and his fine moral perceptions. It shows tenderness and pathos relieved by playfulness, together with an exquisite appreciation of nature. (The portrait is from a painting by Lemuel Abbott.)

© National Portrait Gallery

William Cowper, 1731–1800
For text see page 303

© National Portrait Gallery

Oliver Goldsmith, 1728–1774
For text see page 305

OLIVER GOLDSMITH

Goldsmith is one of the few human beings who are universally beloved for their faults. He was born the son of a clergyman in a little village in Ireland. He was a dull student with a faculty for getting into mischief, but he began to compose verse almost before he could write. He struggled through Trinity College, Dublin, earning his living in a haphazard fashion, sometimes by writing and selling street ballads. He studied medicine but failed to pass the examination for a position, planned to go to America but missed his boat, and started back to Dublin to study law but spent all his money before reaching his destination.

He then tramped with his flute through most of the countries of Europe, finally arriving penniless in London, where he became a literary hack-writer. His genial, carefree temperament won him a place in the hearts of Samuel Johnson and other literary men; but his love of finery in dress, his complete impracticality in money matters, and his openhearted generosity kept the bailiffs (law officers) continually at his door.

Goldsmith's works show clearly that they belong to the Transition Period, when writers were not quite ready to abandon classical restraints upon feeling and form, but were beginning to make use of the English countryside and its rustic characters as material for literature. His poems, stories, and plays are stocked with the experience and characters of his own eventful life, but reality is always colored by his sentimental temperament and beautified by a rich romantic imagination. Thus his long poem "The Deserted Village," though written in the heroic* couplet of Pope and his Classical School, gives a sentimental cast to a charming picture of country scenes. His play She Stoops to Conquer is a delightful drama in which the world is seen through rose-colored glasses. His essays, many of which are included in The Citizen of the World, help to carry on the tradition of gentle humor and pleasant style which had been established by Steele and Addison in The Tatler* and The Spectator.* Optimism is Goldsmith's most characteristic trait; it is embodied in all its perfection in the character of the lovable and impractical hero of The Vicar of Wakefield, an idealized picture of the homely joys and sorrows of English family life, and one of the earliest examples of the modern novel.

The Romantic Period (1798–1832)

WILLIAM BLAKE

William Blake, poet, engraver, painter, mystic, and literary radical, was born in London. His father, a prosperous hosier, encouraged his artistic bent and sent him to drawing school at the age of ten. At twelve Blake began writing poetry, and at fourteen he was apprenticed to an engraver. When he was twenty-five he was happily married to Catherine Boucher, the daughter of a market gardener. His wife helped him to engrave and color copies of his own poems by a process revealed to him, he said, in a dream. These he published in exquisite little volumes now the delight of book-collectors, but then so poorly appreciated by the public that he died in poverty and comparative neglect.

Blake was a man of amazing energy and extraordinary imaginative gifts. He cultivated his remarkable creative imagination

© National Portrait Gallery
1757–1827
For text see page 325

until it became a strange visionary power which enabled him to see the creations of his fancy vividly enough to draw their "portraits" as if he had living models before him. His mystical view of life and nature is reflected in his verse, some of his later poems being almost unintelligible because of their mysticism; but other poems, such as the *Songs of Innocence* and the *Songs of Experience*, have a charming simplicity that reveals the childlike imagination of the author.

Blake was a lover of flowers and animals as well as of his fellow men. Many of his poems show an appreciation of nature that marks the poet as a romanticist. In his ability to see the mystery that lies behind the visible world, Blake somewhat resembles Wordsworth. (The portrait is from a painting by Thomas Phillips.)

ROBERT BURNS

Nothing better reveals the affection with which Robert Burns is regarded than the fact that throughout the English-speaking world he is usually referred to as "Bobbie Burns." Burns was born at Alloway, a tiny village near the town of Ayr, Scotland, in the two-room clay cottage where his father, a God-fearing peasant, struggled to support his family on the scanty produce of his small farm. Burns received little schooling, but read widely from borrowed books. His boyhood was spent in helping his father on the farm and hearing in his leisure moments from an old peasant woman, Betty Davison, folk legends which furnished him with some of the subjects later immortalized in his poems.

As a young man he got into bad company. After a succession of love affairs, which are commemorated in his poems, he decided to seek his fortune in Jamaica. In order to procure passage money, he published in 1786 his *Poems Chiefly in the Scottish Dialect*, but the

success of the volume was so great that he decided not to leave Scotland.

When he visited Edinburgh to arrange for a second edition of his poems, he was lionized in the most exalted social circles, but he did not give up his sturdy independence of spirit. On a second visit to the capital he paid court for some months to a society woman; but he later returned to a youthful sweetheart, Jean Armour, married her, and settled down as a farmer and collector of revenue. His health as well as his reputation had suffered, however, from the follies of his youth. In 1795 a severe illness weakened his constitution, and he contracted a rheumatic fever which caused his death at the early age of thirty-seven.

In his earlier years Burns was affectionate, genial, and witty. He was tall and dark, and had large, strong hands, eyes that glowed "like coals of fire" when he spoke, and a deep, musical voice.

As a song-writer few if any British poets approach Burns in combined strength, simplicity, and sweetness. He was both the brutal realist and the gentle lover. He has been called "a skylark incarnate in an Ayrshire plowboy." He used the Scottish dialect of his boyhood in most of his poetry, and wrote simply, freshly, and sincerely of country life, of nature, and, best of all, of love. In "The Cotter's Saturday Night" he pictures family life in a peasant household similar to that of his father's home. In "Tam o' Shanter" he draws upon popular legend for a subject, and treats his theme with inimitable

humor. Burns is best loved for his songs and lyrics, which pointed the way for English poetry to enter into its ancient heritage of deep and sincere feeling, of simple and natural tenderness, passion, joy, and sorrow.

Both in his life and in his literary work Burns represents an early radical reaction against the Classical School (see page 213), and exemplifies the new democratic independence, the enthusiastic treatment of simple scenes, and the use of ordinary language that characterized the Romantic Period. (The portrait is from a painting by Alexander Nasmyth.)

© National Portrait Gallery

Robert Burns, 1759–1796
For text see pages 328 and 383

© National Portrait Gallery

William Wordsworth, 1770–1850
For text see page 335

WILLIAM WORDSWORTH

Wordsworth was born in the north of England of a good family. His mother worried about the "stiff, moody, and violent temper" of the boy, and predicted for him a remarkable career for either good or evil. At school he read widely at his own pleasure, and took long, lonely walks. He entered St. John's College, Cambridge, and after taking his degree went abroad for a year, during which time he became an ardent sympathizer with the ideals of the French revolutionists. In the meantime his relatives were disgusted by his refusal to choose a profession. He had no money; and it seemed that he would be forced to take up some distasteful occupation when he was saved for literature by an unexpected legacy from a friend. He went to live with his talented and sympathetic sister, Dorothy, whose tender care helped him through the

painful period of disillusionment brought on by the Reign of Terror, in which the French Revolution culminated.

Wordsworth's friendship with Coleridge, which developed in 1796, marked an important period in the lives of both poets. Their association resulted in a book of poems, the *Lyrical Ballads*, published in 1798. For the second edition of this work Wordsworth wrote a preface in which he maintained that the language of poetry should be chosen from that of everyday life, and expressed other poetic theories markedly different from those of the classicists (see page 213). This famous preface is often referred to as the manifesto of the romantic movement. At the time it called forth the contempt of the critics; but the ideas of the romanticists gradually gained headway, and on Southey's death in 1843

Wordsworth was appointed poet laureate.* He married Mary Hutchinson, a gentle, sensible woman who had been a lifelong friend, and settled down with her and his sister in a little cottage at Grasmere in the beautiful Lake District, in the north of England (see illustration on page 336). Their peaceful life is described in an interesting journal kept by Dorothy Wordsworth. In his later years Wordsworth became conservative in his political opinions.

Wordsworth was wonderfully sensitive to the most trivial sights and sounds of nature. He collected his impressions with infinite patience and reproduced them with painstaking fidelity in simple and serene verse. In dealing with human nature his interest lies in the commonplace incidents of everyday life and the occupations and feelings of humble people. These familiar happenings and personages, he declared, should be treated in such a way as to give them the charm of novelty and romance. In spite of his realistic method he had an intensely mystical attitude toward nature. Between nature and man he sensed a mysterious bond. To him nature had the power to give joy and strength and consolation, to unite us on the one hand to God and on the other to our fellow men. The idea is carried to its highest imaginative point in Wordsworth's ode entitled "Intimations of Immortality from Recollections of Early Childhood."

In accordance with his theory of poetry Wordsworth purposely avoided high-flown, poetic diction and used words selected from the common language of peasants and other humble people. This avoidance of exalted language sometimes resulted in commonplace and prosaic expressions and even in clumsiness, and his lack of a sense of humor occasionally drew him into absurdity; but his best poems, his delight in nature, and his feeling for common life place him among the greatest English poets.

Wordsworth, Coleridge, and Southey are often spoken of as the Lake School because they spent so much time in the Lake District. (The portrait is from a painting by Benjamin Haydon.)

ROBERT SOUTHEY

Southey was born at Bristol, son of a linen-draper (dry-goods merchant). He attended Balliol College, Oxford, where he learned little but swimming and boating and where he formed with his friend Coleridge a project for an ideal colony in Pennsylvania. The colony was never founded, and Southey was forced to turn to more practical matters. He tried law, but disliked the profession and gave it up for poetry. He married and went to share a house with Coleridge at Keswick in the Lake District, where he also made the acquaintance of Wordsworth. The three poets are often spoken of together as the Lake School.

© National Portrait Gallery
1774–1843
For text see page 345

Contrary to his own honest belief, Southey was much less gifted than were his two friends Wordsworth and Coleridge. He did a great deal of literary hack work, wrote a number of long narrative poems, and also compiled several biographical works, including a life of Lord Nelson; but his writings are now little known, with the exception of a few ballads and lyrics, of which the "Battle of Blenheim" (see the revised edition of *Adventure* of this series) takes high rank among shorter poems in English for its terseness, simplicity, and irony. (The portrait is from a painting by Peter Vandyke.)

WALTER SAVAGE LANDOR

Landor, though probably best known as the author of the *Imaginary Conversations*, was also a poet of no mean rank. He was made miserable throughout his stormy career by a temper which he was unable to control. He entered Trinity College, Oxford, but had to leave because of his participation in a violent political demonstration. He withstood all efforts to induce him to enter a profession, married, and settled in Wales as a country gentleman.

Finding himself unable to get along with his neighbors, he took up his residence in France, where he quarreled with his landlady. He then moved to Florence, Italy, where, in spite of periodical disputes with the city authorities, he remained for several years, during which time he began his *Imaginary Conversations*, a series of imaginary dialogues between dead-and-gone notables of various past ages. This work finally appeared after several disagreements with the publishers. In a word, Landor quarreled with almost everybody with whom he came in contact.

In striking contrast to his stormy life, Landor's prose is calm, restrained, and dignified. His writings mark a reaction toward the ancient classical ideal at the very height of the Romantic Period. He wrote also numerous poems, among which a few, such as the famous lyric "Rose Aylmer," appear to have been composed in a single flash of inspiration. (The portrait is from a painting by William Fisher.)

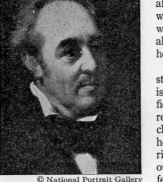

© National Portrait Gallery

1775–1864

For text see page 348

THOMAS MOORE

The national lyric poet of Ireland, as Moore is sometimes called, was born in Dublin, where his father was a grocer. While he was a student at Trinity College, Dublin, he won a reputation for wit and literary talent, and was popular for his ability in acting and singing. His social success continued in London, where he went to study law. He was in Bermuda for a time on a political appointment, went to New York, toured the United States, and then returned to London to continue his pleasant occupation of being a social favorite.

During a period of more than twenty-five years he published a series of songs known as *Irish Melodies*, which brought him fame and a considerable income. He also wrote some light but stinging satires* on public affairs. He finally married an actress and retired to the country, where he wrote *Lalla Rookh*, a metrical romance.* He was a friend of Lord Byron, and became Byron's official biographer.

Most of Moore's lyrics were written to be sung, many of them to music which he himself composed, and it is only as songs that they can fairly be judged. Like many Elizabethan lyrics (see page 153), they are remarkable for their singing quality. The best of them are gay, melodious, and graceful, with here and there an occasional touch of gentle melancholy. Especially popular are those dealing with love and with the ancient glories of Ireland.

© National Portrait Gallery

1779–1852

For text see page 349

LEIGH HUNT

Hunt is remembered chiefly for his friendships with literary men, most of his own works having been forgotten. As a boy he attended Christ's Hospital, where he met Lamb. Like Byron and Shelley, he was a radical and a revolutionary. Imprisoned for criticizing the government, he occupied himself with studying Italian poetry. He also interested his friend Keats in the Italian poets, whose influence was to affect Keats deeply. For years he struggled against poverty and ill fortune, but finally received a pension, which made his later life easier. Hunt wrote a long narrative poem and a large amount of critical and miscellaneous prose, notably essays upon actors and acting. Of his shorter poems, "Abou Ben Adhem" and "Jenny Kissed Me" are still popular. The latter is especially interesting because the celebrated kiss was given by Jane Welsh Carlyle, the gifted and beautiful wife of Thomas Carlyle, who was a friend of Hunt.

© National Portrait Gallery

Leigh Hunt, 1784–1859

For text see page 350

© National Portrait Gallery

Lord Byron, 1788–1824

For text see pages 351 and 409

GEORGE GORDON, LORD BYRON

To the popular mind Byron is one of the most romantic figures in English literature. His noble blood, his Apollo*-like physical appearance, his lonely but eventful life, his tumultuous passions, his spontaneous genius, and his disdain for the conventions of ordinary life have all contributed to his fame as a poet and man of letters. He has been both unduly praised and unduly blamed. Although he came of a noble family, he had a poor start in life; for his father was a scapegrace known as "Mad Jack," who had married Byron's mother for her money. Then, too, Byron was born lame, and this defect, aggravated by the unskillful treatment of medical quacks, probably helped to foster the despondent and cynical view of life which is reflected in many of his poems. He was educated at Harrow (a famous preparatory school) and at Cambridge University, where he led a wild life with the other young men of his rank, who spent their time in gaming, drinking, and shooting. In spite of physical handicaps he became an expert swimmer.

After graduating from college he made a two-year tour of Europe, in the course of which he visited Greece and swam the Hellespont in imitation of the fabled Leander. On his return to England he published the first part of *Childe Harold's Pilgrimage*, a long poem giving an account of the author's wanderings, interspersed with many lyrical passages of great beauty. With the publication of the first part of *Childe Harold's Pilgrimage* he suddenly found himself the possessor of both literary fame and social prominence, and he soon became the idol of the fashionable and sentimental world. The romantic beauty of his appearance increased his attractiveness. Scores of beautiful and fashionable women were anxious to console him for the mysterious sorrow which seemed to be preying upon his soul. In reality he was probably suffering, at least in part, from some of the strenuous diets (soda biscuits and vinegar was a favorite) by which he undermined his health in an effort to keep down a tendency to excessive fatness.

In 1815 he married Anne Isabella Milbanke, but the marriage was a failure. His wife was soon made unhappy by his selfishness, unkindness, and neglect. At last she divorced him; and Byron went in disgrace to Italy, where he defiantly plunged into a life of dissipation. We can say little in praise of Byron's life, but his death was truly noble. He had always been a rebel against injustice and tyranny and therefore welcomed the opportunity to take part in the Greek struggle for independence from Turkey. In 1816 he left England in disgust, never to return. A year after joining the Greek insurgents he became the commander in chief at Missolonghi, where, the climate of Greece proving too much for his weakened health, he contracted a fever and died.

Byron's literary work reveals his wild, discontented, uncontrollable nature. The strange, proud, inhumanly wicked, and melancholy heroes of his dramas *Manfred* and *Cain* reflect, in colors even darker than those of life, the moody, passionate character of their author. The spirit of revolt is also obvious in his long narrative poems, such as "The Prisoner of Chillon" (in the revised edition of *Achievement* of this series), "The Giaour," and "Mazeppa." *Don Juan* (dŏn jŏō'ăn), his greatest work, is a masterly satire* in verse on the corruption and hypocrisy of modern society. Byron had an intense feeling for wild beauty in nature, which he loved as an escape from society and which he described in sonorous, impressive verse with a magnificence that has scarcely been surpassed in English poetry. Through his personality, which caught and held the imagination of all Europe, and through his works, which place him in the highest rank of English poets, Byron exercised an immense influence on English literature and life. The "Byronic hero" is still a familiar type in literature. (The portrait is from a painting by or after Richard Westall.)

PERCY BYSSHE SHELLEY

Shelley came of a well-to-do family. At school he was a shy, sensitive lad who was tortured by the persecution of his schoolfellows. Perhaps the feelings aroused by this early suffering are responsible for the love of freedom and the spirit of resistance to oppression which dominated his whole life. Another trait he acquired at school was an interest in science, which was expressed in an attempt to call up the devil and in other imaginative escapades. His schoolmates used to call him "Mad Shelley" and "Shelley the atheist." He went to Eton and then to University College, Oxford, where his passion for experimentation and for spreading his revolutionary ideas kept him in continual conflict with the college officials. When he wrote and circulated a pamphlet called *The Necessity of Atheism,* the college authorities decided that he must leave the university.

© National Portrait Gallery

1792–1822

For text see page 357

Expelled from college, he took rooms in London and decided to study medicine. He renewed a former acquaintance with a young girl named Harriet Westbrook, who imagined herself the victim of persecution. Shelley's easily aroused sympathies finally resulted in an elopement and marriage; but the union had been based on compassion rather than on true affection or a community of interests, and neither party to it was happy.

In the meantime Shelley had found the real love of his life in Mary Godwin, the daughter of the radical economist and novelist William Godwin. Eventually Harriet and Shelley agreed upon a separation. As a result Harriet committed suicide, and Shelley went to France with Mary, whom he married. For a time the couple suffered from financial distress. Finally, however, their circumstances improved and they returned to England. Here, in his love for Mary, in his writing, and in the study of Greek literature, Shelley found peace of mind for the first time. Eventually they returned to Italy, where Shelley, at the early age of thirty, was drowned in a storm which overtook him while he was out in a sailboat.

Shelley is, above all else, a lyric poet. His period of poetic production covered little more than five years, during which he wrote incessantly. His most characteristic work, *Prometheus Unbound*, expresses his heroic passion for freedom and his spirit of revolt against tyranny. Its ethereal music and dreamlike imagery are repeated in his exquisite lyrics, which illustrate the perfect harmonizing of sound with mood. Shelley's longer works also include "Alastor, or the Spirit of Solitude"; *The Cenci* (chĕn'chē) and other romantic dramas; and "Adonais" (ăd ô nā'ĭs), a lament for the death of Keats, one of the greatest elegies* in English literature. *The Cenci* is regarded by some critics as the best tragedy since Shakespeare.

In contrast to Wordsworth's homely descriptions of nature, Shelley's poems seem to have been written in some strange world of lovely unreality. But this ghostlike loveliness created by the poet's art is as true and precious a possession of the English-speaking race as the simpler beauty that Wordsworth found in the fields and forests of reality. The keynote to Shelley's life and literary works is love, not a worldly affection, but a love that was too free, too ethereal, for the imperfect world of ordinary mortals. He has been called Ariel, after the well-known fairy character in Shakespeare's *Tempest*. Matthew Arnold called him "a beautiful, but ineffectual angel." (The portrait is from a painting by Amelia Curran.)

JOHN KEATS

Keats was born in a room above the place of business of his father, who kept a livery stable in London. He received no formal education except at a secondary school, where he became popular because he was loyal to his friends and "would fight anybody." As a boy he read everything he could lay his hands on. While he was at school someone gave him a copy of Spenser's *Faerie Queene* (see page 166). It opened to him a new world, and inspired him to write his first poetry. He studied surgery and practiced a little, but soon gave it up for poetry.

His first published poems were bitterly attacked by the critics; but in London he found congenial friends in Leigh Hunt, Shelley, Lamb, and other distinguished literary men, who encouraged him to keep on with his writing. Keats's love affair with the pretty and frivolous Fanny Brawne, who was not capable of appreciating him and who treated him capriciously, did much to increase the depression to which he had a natural tendency. Financial worries and the attitude of the critics added to his troubles and helped to

© National Portrait Gallery

1795–1821

For text see pages 366 and 411

undermine his health. Public recognition finally came, but it came too late. Acting under doctor's orders, he sailed for Italy in September, 1820, and died of tuberculosis in Rome, a few months later, at the early age of twenty-six.

To Keats the most important thing in the world was beauty. He gave to beauty the worship of a devotee or of a lover. He found the source of the purest beauty in ancient Greece, to which he turned for inspiration, following directly in the line of the great Elizabethan poets such as Chapman. This passion for beauty, working through a highly sensuous imagination, is expressed in poems so exquisite in their rich romantic color and their apparently effortless melody that the reader seems under the influence of some magic spell. His "Ode on a Grecian Urn" is one of the most perfect expressions of Greek beauty in English poetry. In his later poems, such as the "Ode to a Nightingale" and "The Eve of St. Agnes," he reaches a point of artistry that is very near perfection. Noteworthy among his other poems are "Endymion" (ĕn dĭm'ĭ ŏn), which is replete with beautiful imagery, and "Isabella," which, like "The Eve of St. Agnes," treats a theme from medieval literature. His mood, which varies from rapture to melancholy, from meditation to fantastic gaiety, is pictured in a thousand changing and exotic colors, but with unfailing good taste and restraint and with a classic sense of form. One of the highest tributes to Keats's lyric genius lies in the fact that he has been compared to Shakespeare. (The portrait is from a miniature by Joseph Severn.)

CHARLES LAMB

Charles Lamb, the most beloved of modern essayists, belonged to no aristocracy but that of the intellect. His father was a servant and later a clerk in the Temple*; his grand-mother, Elizabeth Field, was a housekeeper on a country estate. Lamb's life was one long struggle against poverty and insanity. He was edu-cated at a famous London charity school called Christ's Hospital, where he began a lifelong friendship with Cole-ridge. On leaving school he became a clerk, first in the South Sea House, and later in the famous old East India House, where he remained for thirty-three years. With great nobility of soul he undertook the care of his sister, Mary, who inherited a tendency to insanity. Giving up all thought of marriage, he made a home for her as long as he lived. Though shy and retiring, he liked good food and good company.

© National Portrait Gallery
1775–1834
For text see page 375

This gentle, whimsical, lovable writer is best known to us through his *Essays of Elia*. In the person of Elia,* Lamb talks to us delightfully and intimately of anything and everything: London streets, chimney-sweepers, his home life, his numerous literary friends, his memories and dreams. His style charms us by its appealing quaintness, pathos, and humor. Dear to the hearts of young and old are the summaries of Shake-speare's plays contained in *Tales from Shakespeare*, which he wrote jointly with his sister Mary. He delighted espe-cially in older English writers. His essays on Elizabethan dramatists opened to modern readers a field of English liter-ature which at that time was almost unknown. Under the influence of his depressing expe-riences he wrote his saddest and one of his best-known poems, "The Old Familiar Faces." (The portrait is after a painting by Henry Meyer.)

SAMUEL TAYLOR COLERIDGE

Coleridge was born of poor parents at Ottery Saint Mary (in the southwest of Eng-land), where his father taught school. The youngest of thirteen children, he was a preco-cious and imaginative boy who used to spend his time in daydreaming instead of playing active games with other children. He was educated at a famous London charity school called Christ's Hospital, where he became ac-quainted with Lamb, and at Cambridge Uni-versity, where his brilliant conversation won him many friends, but where he took no degree. At one time he ran away from college and joined the army under a false name, but was discovered and sent back. With some other unpractical persons, including the poet

Southey, he planned a colony to be estab-lished on the banks of the Susquehanna in Pennsylvania, but as none of the enthusiasts had any money the project died a natural death.

After leaving the university Coleridge lived with Southey, writing poetry and lecturing. Eventually the two friends married sisters. Coleridge tried editing a periodical, which was a failure, preached in Unitarian chapels, and finally settled at Nether Stowey (not far from Bristol), in the southwest of England, where the grant of an annuity by a rich friend enabled him to devote himself to writing. Wordsworth came to live near him and collaborated with him in the *Lyrical Ballads*,

D

which were published in 1798. In the same year Coleridge went to Germany with the Wordsworths, but left them in order to study German literature and philosophy at the University of Göttingen. On his return to England he settled in the Lake District not far from the Wordsworths' cottage at Grasmere. He continued to write for the papers and to lecture, but the charm of his conversation was so great that his friends were willing to help toward his support rather than see him waste his abilities on the hack work necessary to earn a living. In his later years depression and ill health drove him to the use of drugs. As a result he finally put himself under the care of a friend who lived in London. Here he spent the last sixteen years of his life, doing little writing, but delighting his friends by his charming discourse.

Coleridge was both a scholar and a poet of genius. He is almost the only English writer who is in the front rank of both poets and critics. His criticism, which shows a high degree of poetic sympathy and logical ability,

© National Portrait Gallery

1772–1834

For text see page 393

is still valuable. His best poetry is small in extent, but highly distinguished in character. One of his finest poems, "Kubla Khan," was composed in a dream; in fact, all his best poems might be regarded as waking dreams. They picture unearthly lands, in which phantasmal forms move weirdly through dimly visioned events and scenes. "The Ancient Mariner" (see revised edition of *Achievement* of this series), his masterpiece, gives a marvelous effect of spectral beauty so keenly realized as to give the illusion of reality. "Christabel" also is a strangely powerful compound of beauty and horror. Coleridge wrote in accordance with his literary theory that literature is not life but art, and that it ought to take us away from the sordidness and commonplace trivialities of real life into a world of supernaturalism and imagination, which, for the time being, we are led to accept as true.

Coleridge is sometimes spoken of as a member of the Lake School. (The portrait is from a painting by Peter Vandyke.)

SIR WALTER SCOTT

Scott was the son of an Edinburgh lawyer in whose veins flowed the blood of a warlike Border* clan. As a child he suffered from infantile paralysis and was sent to the country, where he was cared for by an aunt who told him romantic tales and read to him from the stirring ballads and legends of the Border* wars. When he grew a little older, he used to wander about the Highlands gathering more of these ancient traditions from the lips of peasants. He attended the University of Edinburgh and studied law, but soon afterward turned to literature. On one of his ballad-collecting expeditions to the English Lake country he saw a beautiful girl riding horseback. He secured an introduction and eventually married her. In 1802–1803 appeared his first important publication, *Minstrelsy of the Scottish Border*, which contains a large number of popular ballads. The colorful background of native tradition and superstition which Scott had accumulated proved

to be a treasure house of material for the poetry which he now began to compose. *The Lay of the Last Minstrel* (1805), *Marmion* (1808), and *The Lady of the Lake* (1810) (see the revised edition of *Adventure* of this series) are three of his vigorous narratives in verse that picture in a romantic spirit Scottish life during the Middle Ages.

It was not until he was forty-three years old that Scott began his career as a novelist. Thinking that public favor had shifted from him to the new poet, Byron, he turned from poetry to prose. From inexhaustible stores of Border legend, from historical sources, from medieval traditions, and from his own imagination he drew some of the most marvelous tales of adventure and romance that have ever been written. In 1814 he published *Waverley*, the first of a long series of novels that continued to appear almost until his death. *Waverley* became popular immediately. Among the other Waverley Novels (as they are called) *The Heart of Midlothian* (1818), *The Bride of Lammermoor* (1819), *Ivanhoe* (1820), and *The Talisman* (1825) are especially well known, though several others have been far above the average in popularity. It is by the Waverley Novels, rather than by his poetry, that Scott is remembered as a great author.

His fame as a writer was now safe, but his personal affairs were not progressing so well. He had invested heavily in a publishing firm whose financial condition went from bad to worse and finally ended in bankruptcy. Although Scott was not legally responsible, with great nobility of spirit he undertook in 1826 to help toward paying the company's debts with his pen. He spent his remaining years writing constantly in a desperate effort to see that all the creditors were paid. This effort at last cost him his life.

Both in his poetry and in his prose Sir

© National Portrait Gallery
1771–1832
For text see page 401

Walter Scott was a romanticist; that is, he treated his subjects with an enthusiastic idealism. He did much to cultivate the public taste for medieval themes both by his novels and by his imitations of early romances (see page 32) and ballads. In his pages the loves and adventures of brave knights and fair ladies appear with a fascination that has never failed to charm the reader.

In spite of all the romantic coloring which Scott gave to his novels, his minute descriptions of scenery and his realistic* portrayal of Scottish characters of the lower classes show that he was a keen and accurate observer. When he pictures a world that belonged to the past, he describes one that is real to him, and he paints it so clearly and graphically that to the reader also the romance of medieval England and Scotland becomes a living, breathing reality. (The portrait is from a painting by Sir Edwin Landseer.)

THOMAS HOOD

Thomas Hood was born in London, the son of a Scottish bookseller. After the death of his father when Thomas was twelve years old, the boy enjoyed a brief period of schooling, but he was soon put to work in a bank. However, this occupation injured his health, and he was sent to reside with his father's relatives in Dundee, Scotland. When he was nineteen he returned to London and studied engraving. This early training enabled him later to illustrate effectively many of his humorous writings. At the age of twenty-two he became assistant editor of *The London Magazine*, and thus came into contact with Charles Lamb, the essayist (see page 721), and other prominent literary men of the day. Although his earliest poems are serious

© National Portrait Gallery
1799–1845
For text see page 420

in tone, he is best known as a humorist. Some of his poems remind us of Keats's poems; others, such as "The Bridge of Sighs" and "The Song of the Shirt," reflect a social sympathy which resembles, to some extent, that of Charles Dickens and Elizabeth Barrett Browning. The public long neglected his serious works, but received with enthusiasm his humorous verse, which is characterized by striking puns, word juggling, and at times by brilliant phantasy. Among his best-known poems are "The Dream of Eugene Aram," "The Bridge of Sighs," "The Song of the Shirt," and "Miss Kilmansegg, and her Precious Leg."

Throughout much of his life Hood suffered from poverty and ill health.

The Victorian Period (1832–1892)

CHARLES DICKENS

Dickens put so many of his own experiences into his writings that it is especially important for us to know something of his life if we are to read his works with understanding and appreciation. He was born in a village on the southeast coast of England. His father and mother, who were the models for Mr. and Mrs. Micawber in *David Copperfield*, were constantly in debt. His father, like Mr. Micawber, spent some time in a debtor's prison, and his mother, like Mrs. Micawber, set up a "Boarding Establishment for Young Ladies." But, said Dickens, speaking in the person of David Copperfield, "I never found that any young lady had ever been to school there; or that any young lady ever came, or professed to come.... The only visitors I ever saw or heard of were creditors." Dickens, like David Copperfield, was forced to go out to work at an early age. When his father was imprisoned for debt, Charles, at the age of ten, was placed in a shoeblacking factory, where he was forced to paste labels on bottles at the pitifully small wage of six shillings (about one dollar and a half) a week. Like David Copperfield he too, during this period of his life, ate poor food and, in general, led a lonely, neglected existence. When his father was released from prison, Dickens received three years of schooling under an ignorant, tyrannical master whose school seems to have furnished some features of the boarding school to which David Copperfield was sent by the heartless Murdstones. At the age of sixteen he obtained a position in a solicitor's (lawyer's) office, where he began to acquire the intimate knowledge of the English legal system which he used later in some of his best-known novels, including *David Copperfield*. While he was employed as a law clerk he studied stenography at night, and soon became known as the best political newspaper reporter in London. As a reporter he traveled the London streets and the country roads at all hours,

thus gaining much knowledge of wayfaring life and the underworld, a knowledge which he afterward used in his writings. Again like David Copperfield, young Dickens fell in love with a silly, though attractive girl, somewhat like David Copperfield's Dora; but, unlike Copperfield, he did not marry her. He did, however, marry Catherine Hogarth, a daughter of one of his newspaper associates, —a woman whom he found childish and immature and whom he later divorced.

Shortly before this time he had begun writing little stories and character sketches for various periodicals. When he was twenty-four years old, some of these appeared in book form under the title *Sketches by Boz* (bōz). In 1837 *Sketches by Boz* was expanded and published as the famous *Pickwick Papers*. The *Pickwick Papers*, a series of humorous sketches depicting the activities of Mr. Pickwick, Sam Weller, and other imaginary characters, were widely read and made the author famous. About the same time Dickens published *Oliver Twist*. Later he wrote many novels and short stories, of which the following are especially well known: *Dombey and Son, Bleak House, David Copperfield, Great Expectations, A Tale of Two Cities* (in the revised edition of *Achievement* of this series), *Our Mutual Friend, A Christmas Carol*, and *The Cricket on the Hearth*.

For some unknown reason Dickens and his wife separated in 1857. For the next two years he was extremely unhappy. Just before the separation Dickens had purchased Gadshill, an estate not far from London, which he had admired as a boy and wished to own.

Dickens in 1853, after becoming famous, yielded to popular appeal and began giving public lectures and readings from his works. In this capacity he twice visited the United States. After his first visit he wrote *Martin Chuzzlewit*, which gives an unfavorable view of American life, but did little to injure his

Dickens House

1812–1870
For text see page 436

reputation in the United States. As a result of his restless activities his health failed, and he died in 1870. He is buried in Westminster Abbey.

In his writings Dickens always championed the cause of the lowly and the oppressed against the proud and the tyrannical. Many of his novels have as their purpose the correction of some evil in society. They attack the law courts for their slowness, the laws for their severity, the aristocracy for their pride and folly; in short, any social class or institution that appeared to him wasteful, insincere, or unjust.

Dickens had a keen sense of humor and was an untiring worker. He produced sixteen longer pieces of fiction besides shorter narra-tives. He created more than fifteen hundred distinct characters. One of his critics says, "It is hard to believe that so many characters were produced by one man." Moreover, Dickens's portrayal of English lowly life is based on personal experience. Mr. Pickwick, Sam Weller, Little Nell, Mr. and Mrs. Micaw-ber, Peggotty, and other characters in the *Pickwick Papers* and the novels are merely exaggerated characters taken from real life. In his works Dickens generally satirizes,* burlesques (makes fun of), or sentimentalizes his characters. The result is a combination of realism* and sentimentalism that is unique in English literature. (The portrait, showing Dickens at the age of eighteen, is from a mini-ature by Janet Barrow.)

WILLIAM MAKEPEACE THACKERAY

Thackeray was born of English parentage in India, where his father had won distinction in the service of the East India Company. When he was five years old his father died, and Thackeray was sent to England to be reared by an aunt. As a boy he attended the famous Charterhouse School, where he amused his schoolmates by writing clever little poems and parodies and where he had a fight which resulted in a broken nose. He entered Cambridge University when he was eighteen, but left a year later without tak-ing a degree. While he was at Cambridge he had joined a literary club which included Tennyson and other men who afterward became famous. After leaving the university he traveled on the Continent for several months and then came back to England to study law. He soon turned from law, however, to literature, a change due in part to natural inclination, in part to financial losses. While he was strug-gling to establish himself as a journalist he studied art, thus acquiring the skill which he afterward used in illustrating some of his own works (see "A Tragic Story" in the revised edition of *Adventure* of this series). In 1836, while he was receiving a very small income, Thackeray married. He became the father of three daughters, but his home was soon

National Portrait Gallery

1811–1863

For text see page 447

broken up by the mental derangement of his wife. Though sorrowful, he continued to work and in 1844 began to earn a good living by writing for the humorous journal *Punch* and other periodicals.

When he was thirty-seven years old, he published the novel *Vanity Fair*, which brought him immediate pop-ularity, especially among the upper classes, in spite of the fact that it satirizes* them. Two years later (in 1850) he brought out *Pendennis*, which, like Dickens's *David Copper-field*, reflects many of the au-thor's early experiences. This was followed by *Henry Es-mond* (1852) and *The New-comes* (1855). *Henry Esmond* is generally regarded as one of the best historical novels in English literature. Later Thackeray wrote other works, but none of them attained the literary level of *Vanity Fair* and its immediate successors.

Like Dickens, Thackeray became a public lecturer and paid two visits to the United States; but he was much more kindly in his judgment of Americans than Dickens was. In *The Virginians*, which represents Henry Esmond as settling in America and estab-lishing a family there, Thackeray gives a favorable picture of colonial life in the South.

After returning to England, Thackeray be-came a candidate for Parliament, but was defeated. As a result he continued his literary work; but his health began to fail, and in spite of the devoted care of his daughters he died on December 23, 1863.

Physically Thackeray was unusually impressive. He was over six feet tall, with a large body and head, and but for his broken nose he would have been handsome. He was kindly and lovable; but, because of his experiences, he was a keen critic of society. In his writings he attacked, not the great vices of mankind, but its petty follies. Judging him by his life, we cannot wonder that he was a great but sometimes bitter humorist. He was unlike Dickens in that he had no special theory of social betterment by reforms in the school system, in the law, or in the prisons; he only pleads for honesty and lack of pretense. (The portrait is from a painting by Samuel Laurence.)

ALFRED LORD TENNYSON

Tennyson was the son of a clergyman in a little village in north Lincolnshire. He was one of twelve brothers and sisters, two others of whom became poets of some distinction. He received his earliest education from his father, who was a man of broad literary interests. At the age of eight Tennyson began to write verse; but his initial poetic attempts were mostly imitative of the older poets and showed little promise of his future greatness. In his nineteenth year he entered Trinity College, Cambridge, where he found a number of congenial associates, among them Arthur Hallam, who remained his dearest friend until Hallam's death. His first important volume, containing "The Lady of Shalott" and other poems now familiar to all lovers of Tennyson, appeared in 1832, soon after his leaving the university. In spite of its merits the book was not well received by the critics, and for ten years the poet, though continuing to write verse, published nothing.

The death of Hallam in 1833 plunged Tennyson into deep grief, which profoundly affected the bent of his genius for many years afterward, and at length found expression in *In Memoriam*. In 1842 Tennyson published another collection of poems, which contained his "Morte d'Arthur," the first of a long series of Arthurian poems (most of them included in *The Idylls of the King*) (see the revised edition of *Achievement* of this series). The 1842 volume was so well received that he became recognized as the leading English poet of the

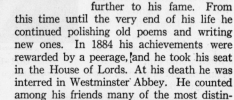

1809–1892
For text see pages 463 and 520

day. As the result of his success he received a pension from the government in 1845.

The year 1850 was a happy one for Tennyson; for in that year he married Miss Emily Sellwood (to whom he had been engaged for over ten years), and was appointed poet laureate.* In the same year he published *In Memoriam*, which established more firmly his reputation as the greatest poet of his period. After traveling on the Continent with his wife, he bought a house on the Isle of Wight, and settled down to the serious business of writing poetry. The first series of *The Idylls of the King*, which appeared in 1859, added still further to his fame. From this time until the very end of his life he continued polishing old poems and writing new ones. In 1884 his achievements were rewarded by a peerage, and he took his seat in the House of Lords. At his death he was interred in Westminster Abbey. He counted among his friends many of the most distinguished men of his day, and was held in high esteem by Queen Victoria and other members of the royal family.

In spite of his own rather retired existence Tennyson was deeply interested in the life of his time. He thought and wrote upon most of the burning questions of the nineteenth century: woman's rights, economics, politics, science, and religion. He reflects his age especially in his idealism and in his devotion to rather formal virtue. He was especially convinced that the greatness of a people depends upon the sacredness of home life.

Tennyson wrote seriously and with a high moral purpose; and although he seldom penetrates very deeply into the mysteries of life, he occasionally, as in "Locksley Hall," has a touch of prophetic vision that lifts him above the horizon of his time. He drew his materials from the ancient Latin and Greek classics, from medieval sources, and from contemporary life. He used a great variety of meters and nearly all the poetical types current in his day. He is, moreover, especially noteworthy for his conscientious and painstaking craftsmanship. His graceful and melodious lines have the finished beauty that results from flawless technique. Delicacy of phrase and felicity of language are among his most characteristic gifts. Readers whose minds are not open to refinements of language and whose ears are not responsive to beauty of expression will hardly enjoy Tennyson completely.

Though Tennyson wrote numerous short poems that deserve immortality, he is perhaps most generally known today for his two long poems *The Idylls of the King* and *In Memoriam*. In *The Idylls of the King*, which occupied much of his time for nearly half a century, he retold, with fine pictorial imagination, the famous legends of King Arthur* and the Round Table, reinterpreting these medieval stories in the light of Victorian ideals of character and morality. In *In Memoriam*, which he composed at various times over a period of seventeen years, he incorporated in simple yet exalted poetic language some of the most beautiful thoughts on death and immortality ever expressed by an English poet.

ROBERT BROWNING

Browning was born in a London suburb, of well-to-do parentage. He had no regular schooling, but studied under the direction of his father and of private tutors, and read widely. When he was fourteen years old, he chanced to pick up at a London bookstall a copy of Shelley's poems, which moved him to his first attempt at poetic creation. He began by writing a number of long poems, most of which display his artistic defects at their worst, though his real poetic ability was already manifest. In *Pippa Passes* (1841) he produced his first real masterpiece. He next wrote several dramas in verse and began the series of short poems known as dramatic monologues. In these poems his poetical powers found their most perfect expression. But his peculiar genius was slow to obtain recognition.

1812–1889
For text see pages 478 and 502

In 1846 he married Elizabeth Barrett, whose fame at that time was much greater than his. The two went to live in Italy, where they spent many happy years. Browning's *Men and Women*, a collection of poems in which he speaks through the mouth of various characters, appeared in 1855. In Italy he wrote *The Ring and the Book* (1868), often regarded as his greatest though by no means his simplest work. After his wife's death he lived chiefly in England, writing constantly. His later works show an increasing intellectual power, but diminishing poetic beauty. Fame did not reach him till he was an old man; but when it did, it came in abundance. He died in Venice at the age of seventy-seven. He is buried beside Tennyson in Westminster Abbey.

Browning, in contrast with Tennyson, was interested in the emotions of the individual rather than in universal law. Whereas Tennyson reflected the thought of the Victorian Period, Browning analyzed and interpreted its complex human life. He was chiefly interested in the "history of souls." Whether he was writing lyric or narrative poetry, drama, or dramatic monologue, he delighted in the subtle analysis of motive. He is best at presenting graphically a single dramatic situation with great compression and vividness. He treated such situations most successfully in the dramatic monologue, a form which he largely perfected and popularized. Of Browning's numerous dramatic monologues the best-known is "My Last Duchess."

Browning's philosophy is one of robust courage, optimism, and joy of life. He wrote with a moral purpose, pleading for faithfulness to human and divine love and believing that salvation comes through the exercise of the will. His peculiarly compressed style is often obscure and harsh; but when once his meaning is fathomed, the thought is indelibly impressed on the memory. And he could, and at times did, write simply as well as beautifully.

ELIZABETH BARRETT BROWNING

Elizabeth Barrett, daughter of Edward Moulton Barrett, was born in Durham. She was a precocious student. At the age of eight she could read Homer in the original and was writing poetry; but she led an active child's life until one day, in trying to saddle her pony, she fell and suffered an injury that made her a partial invalid for years. In spite of illness and family troubles she had achieved a considerable literary reputation by the time she was twenty. In 1846 she married the poet Browning and went with him to live in Florence, Italy, where her health improved and where their only son was born.

Mrs. Browning had an exquisite lyrical gift. Her best poems are often touched with mysticism and are full of intense emotion.

The beautiful *Sonnets from the Portuguese* (1847), written to her husband, are among the finest love poems in the English language. *Casa Guidi Windows*, a poem named from Casa Guidi (kä'sä gwē'dĕ), the house in Florence where she lived while writing it, appeared in 1851.

Some of Mrs. Browning's best poems were written in Italy, and many of these show how deeply she was interested in the struggle of her adopted country for freedom from oppression. Her reaction against social injustice in her own native land is reflected in "The Cry of the Children." In all of her poems she combines religious fervor with deep classical learning. (The portrait is from a painting by M. Gordigiani.)

© National Portrait Gallery

Elizabeth Barrett Browning, 1806–1861
For text see page 487

© National Portrait Gallery

Arthur Hugh Clough, 1819–1861
For text see page 492

ARTHUR HUGH CLOUGH

Clough was born in Liverpool of a good family. He studied at Oxford, where he went through a period of religious struggle resulting from the Oxford * Movement. After leaving Oxford he traveled in Europe, and later settled in London as head of University Hall, a dormitory for students at University College.

He suffered from financial difficulties and led a secluded life; but his lovable though diffident nature won him several distinguished friends, including Carlyle, Arnold, and Emerson. After a visit to the United States, where he taught for a while at Harvard University, he married and took up official work of various kinds in London. Ill health finally compelled him to travel in Greece and Italy. He died in Italy of a malarial fever.

Clough was not a prolific writer, and he never led a wholly detached literary life; yet his poetry is earnest and shows high moral feeling. His dauntless spirit in the face of his religious difficulties is reflected in "Say Not the Struggle Nought Availeth." (The portrait is from a sculpture by Thomas Woolner.)

MATTHEW ARNOLD

Matthew Arnold was the son of Dr. Thomas Arnold, a famous headmaster of Rugby School. He attended Oxford at a time when the university was deeply agitated by the religious revival known as the Oxford* Movement. At Oxford he became a friend of Clough. During almost all his life he held the position of inspector of schools, and during the latter part of this time he was also professor of poetry at Oxford. He lectured in the United States twice, in 1883 and 1886.

Arnold's activity as a poet belongs mainly to the earlier part of his life. In addition to "Sohrab and Rustum," a dignified and impressive epic based on Oriental tradition, his best poetical works include *Empedocles on Etna and Other Poems* (1853), which contains, besides the title poem, a collection of lyrics and a beautiful version of the medieval legend of Tristram and Isolt; "Rugby Chapel"; and "Thyrsis," a noble pastoral* elegy* on the death of Clough.

As he grew older he gave up writing poetry and turned to the practical work of reforming society through criticism of poetry, of society, and of religion. For the last twenty years of his life he was a leader in the field of prose criticism. Arnold's social message is the "gospel of ideas," by which he meant the

1822–1888
For text see page 492

pursuit of perfection in life through what he termed "culture" (that is, broadmindedness and openness to ideas). He was an uncompromising enemy of "Philistinism," by which he meant narrowmindedness, self-satisfaction, and vulgarity. His critical standards are high and pure. He felt that the function of the critic is primarily to select and interpret; to spread the knowledge of the best that is known and thought. To Arnold poetry is "a criticism of life" rather than "a thing of beauty." He believed that poetry, to be great, must possess what he called "high seriousness." His critical theories are set forth in *Essays in Criticism* (1865 and 1888), in *Culture and Anarchy* (1869), and in other volumes.

Arnold represents the period of transition between the earlier and later writers of the nineteenth century. He expressed the dejection and doubt of the time in the weary stoicism of his attitude toward life. He sought consolation in the intellect, but he too often neglected the consolation of the heart. Arnold's intellectual self-consciousness and his clear, pure style show his care for classical excellence. His combination of world-weariness with a romantic attitude toward the ancient classics is well illustrated in "Dover Beach."

CHRISTINA GEORGINA ROSSETTI

Christina Rossetti was the daughter of cultivated Italian parents who for political reasons left Italy and settled in England. She enjoyed the same educational advantages as her talented brother, Dante Gabriel Rossetti. Like him, she was precocious; but whereas he was essentially an artist, the keynote to her character was her devotion to religion. An unhappy love affair, in which the source of discord was a difference in religion, saddened her life and explains the melancholy and even morbid tone of much of her poetry. For a long time she was an invalid. She never perfectly recovered her health, and died after a prolonged illness.

Some of her best lyrics appeared in *The*

Germ (the official organ of the Pre-Raphaelite* group) in 1850–1851. Her fanciful *Goblin Market* appeared in 1862 and was received with enthusiasm. Her *Annus Domini* is a sequence of prayers for every day of the year. Her *Monna Innominata* is a series of beautiful love sonnets.* From 1881 until her death she produced little except religious prose.

Christina Rossetti's poetical work, which is poignant with experience and sacrifice, combines nature and art with the beautiful simplicity characteristic of the Pre-Raphaelite* group, of which she, like her brother, was a member. Her *Goblin Market* shows great imaginative power, and has a whimsicality and grace that make it one of the most beloved of her poems. Some of her sonnets and other lyrics are extremely simple and beautiful.

British Museum

Christina Georgina Rossetti, 1830–1894
For text see page 498

Robert Louis Stevenson, 1850–1894
For text see pages 499, 509, 537, and 549

ROBERT LOUIS STEVENSON

Robert Louis Stevenson was born in Edinburgh of a cultivated family. His delicate health prevented any regular schooling, and his education as a boy consisted chiefly in trips about Scotland and to the Continent for his health. In order to please his father, who was a distinguished civil engineer, he studied engineering and, later, law; but he practiced little.

During all this time, in spite of bad health, he wrote constantly, producing brilliant essays and descriptions of his travels. He was a lad of high spirits, Bohemian tastes, and charming personality. In France he fell in love with an American woman, Mrs. Osbourne, whom he eventually married. She proved to be a perfect companion and an ideal nurse during the following years, when Stevenson's health became steadily poorer. He tried the climate of California and other parts of the United States, and then went on a voyage to the South Seas, where his health improved to such an extent that he settled at Vailima in the Samoa Islands. Here he spent the rest of his life writing and working among the natives, who called him "Teller of Tales," and served him as a kind of beloved feudal lord. After his death they buried him, amid romantic surroundings, on the top of a lonely mountain.

Stevenson's personal charm is reflected in his works. His style is animated and graceful; yet he always wrote slowly and with great care. Believing that fiction should be an escape from life, he himself found relief from the ills of the body in composing glowing tales of romance and adventure such as those of the *New Arabian Nights*. His novels and tales usually combine romantic plots with characters and setting that are portrayed with realistic* detail. He ranks next to Sir Walter Scott as a writer of romantic prose fiction. His *Treasure Island* (see the revised edition of *Adventure* of this series), *Kidnapped*, and *The Master of Ballantrae* are masterpieces of modern romance. His *Dr. Jekyll and Mr. Hyde* is one of our best mystery stories. Of his numerous collections of essays perhaps the best-known is *Virginibus Puerisque* (vēr-jĭn′ĭ bŭs pū ĕr ĭs′kwĕ) ("To Youths and Maidens"). The poems contained in *A Child's Garden of Verses* rank among the best ever written for the very young. His short stories are marked by the same careful workmanship that characterizes all his other writings.

ALGERNON CHARLES SWINBURNE

Swinburne came of distinguished ancestry on both sides of his family. His father was an admiral, and his mother was the daughter of an earl. He was educated at Eton and at Oxford, where he became familiar with the ancient and Romance languages. After traveling for a while on the Continent he settled in London and became an associate of the distinguished writers and artists of the day. He was small of stature, and had sloping shoulders and a red head. As a result of ill health and indiscretions he grew old prematurely and produced little poetry during his later years.

His chief works include *Atalanta in Calydon* (1864) and other poetic dramas based on ancient classical models; *Songs before Sunrise* (1871), which contains some of his best lyrics; and *Tristram of Lyonesse* (1882), a poetic version of the legend of Tristram and Isolt. His best poems are lyrical. He also wrote a considerable amount of stimulating but often inaccurate prose criticism.

© National Portrait Gallery

1837–1909

For text see page 499

Swinburne was one of the writers who toward the end of the nineteenth century began to feel that the Victorians had taken life much too seriously, and that if the problems of existence cannot be solved, there is at least an escape from them in physical pleasures. Though some of Swinburne's poetry reflects this attitude, and though he has been called the last of the Pre-Raphaelites,* he is not always decadent. In sweeping, impetuous verse he wrote of freedom, of children, and of the sea, which he especially loved. He wrote of nature and of human life and death, usually from a melancholy point of view. His descriptions of nature, his portrayal of passion, his mastery of verse technique, and, above all, the music in his poetry place him in the front rank of English poets. (The portrait is from a painting by G. F. Watts.)

GEORGE MEREDITH

Meredith was born of mixed Welsh and Irish parentage. He was sent to school in Germany. On his return to England he became a journalist. At the age of twenty-one he married and went to live in the county of Surrey.

During the Italian war of 1866 he served as special correspondent for a London newspaper. Later he settled down to an uneventful scholarly life at Mickleham, in Surrey. Here he remained during long years of delayed recognition and hostile criticism, and from this quiet retreat, when old age and recognition came together, he ruled the world of letters with the genial, unspoiled kindliness of a benevolent monarch.

Meredith's style is a literary marvel. It is dazzling; sometimes it is witty; occasionally it is incomprehensible. He gives the impression that his brain is so crammed with brilliant ideas that they sometimes come tumbling forth in confusion and land topsy-turvy on the page. Meredith was a psychologist and also something of a moralist and a philosopher. His novels deal from a sophisticated point of view with psychological problems, treated in the kindly and genial spirit that animated his own life. He contended that the function of art was to portray, not the superficial truths of actual life, but the inner and spiritual truths of humanity. He tried to interpret these essential truths by means of typical rather than actual situations and characters. *The Ordeal of Richard Feverel* (1859) is his first great novel; *The Egoist* is generally accounted his best, though many readers prefer *Diana of the Crossways*. Meredith is chiefly famous for his novels; but his poetry, most of which is earlier in date than the novels, has long had appreciative readers and has grown constantly in popularity. It expresses much the same sensitiveness to the beauties of nature and of the human soul that his novels do.

© National Portrait Gallery
George Meredith, 1828–1909
For text see page 505

© National Portrait Gallery
John Henry Newman, 1801–
1890. For text see page 508

JOHN HENRY NEWMAN

Newman was born in London. He attended Oxford University, where he became profoundly interested in religious problems, and where he spent nearly half of his life engaged in various unselfish activities. In 1833 he became a leader in the Oxford* Movement. In 1845 he entered the Roman Catholic Church and later was made a cardinal. For a time he was rector of the Catholic university in Dublin, Ireland.

Cardinal Newman's charm and spirituality made him the object of a reverence and a love which are reserved for the truly great souls of this earth. His sermons won many followers for the cause which he advocated. He possessed a mysterious power to move multitudes.

Although Newman wrote primarily as an upholder of a special cause, his religious prose, novels, essays, poems, and especially his autobiography have high literary merit. His *Idea of a University* and his *Apologia pro Vita Sua, or History of My Religious Opinions*, are widely read, and his hymn "Lead, Kindly Light" is sung throughout Christendom. A remarkable clearness is his outstanding characteristic. His prose is also charmingly conversational in tone, and is marked by a melodious rhythm. Above all, it reflects his own ardent and fascinating personality.

THOMAS BABINGTON MACAULAY

Macaulay was of Scottish and Quaker ancestry. He showed extraordinary intellectual gifts as early as the age of three, when he had already begun to read voraciously and to talk in the language of books. At seven he was working on a universal history, and at eight he composed a treatise designed to convert the natives of Malabar to Christianity. He also showed at an early age the remarkable memory which enabled him to repeat word for word almost everything he had ever read. He was educated at Trinity College, Cambridge, where he won recognition as a writer and a debater. He studied law for a time, but gave it up for journalism and politics. Soon his essays, which were appearing in the periodicals, began to attract attention. At the same time he launched on a political career.

He was twice a member of Parliament, and held various offices in the government, one of which took him to India for several years. He was raised to the peerage in 1857.

Macaulay's political and literary careers naturally reacted upon each other. He spoke so well that an announcement of a speech by him is said to have been "like a trumpet-call to fill the benches" of Parliament. On the other hand, his political interests as a Conservative colored his writings. Essays, many of them dealing with subjects of literary or public significance, appeared throughout his political career. They are remarkable for their clear style, their balanced structure, and their effective narrative technique. Their style

shows the influence of ancient classical oratory. Among the best of his essays are those on "Warren Hastings," "Goldsmith," and "Samuel Johnson." His *Lays of Ancient Rome* celebrates in stately ballad verse the civic virtues admired by the ancient Romans. *The History of England*, Macaulay's masterpiece, is a fascinating story told with the picturesqueness and dramatic skill of the most absorbing novel, but it lacks the deep insight into the hidden causes of historical events that is necessary to a real understanding of the "philosophy of history." In this history Macaulay shows gratification and pride in England's material progress and prosperity. (The portrait is after a drawing by George Richmond.)

Thomas Babington Macaulay, 1800–1859
For text see page 513

© National Portrait Gallery

Charles Kingsley, 1819–1875
For text see page 525

CHARLES KINGSLEY

Kingsley was the son of a clergyman. He wrote poems and sermons at the age of four, and was a preacher and moral crusader all his life. He attended King's College, London, and Magdalen College, Cambridge; became a clergyman; married; and settled down to a busy life as a philosopher, professor, lecturer, and social worker. He found time, however,

to write a number of novels, including *Hypatia, Westward Ho,* and *Hereward the Wake,* which deal with historical themes and which became immensely popular. He wrote little verse, but some of his shorter poems are memorable. In some of his writings he suggests the work of Sir Walter Scott. (The portrait is from a painting by Lowes Dickinson.)

DANTE GABRIEL ROSSETTI

Rossetti was born in London. He was the son of an Italian poet, a political refugee from Naples, and he grew up in a literary and artistic atmosphere that combined the finest influences of the cultures of England and Italy. He entered King's College School, but left at the age of fourteen and continued his education by wide reading at home and by study at several art schools. Through his art teacher, Ford Madox Brown, he became acquainted with a group of young artists who, dissatisfied with the art of the time, wished to revive the mystic interpretation of nature and the elaboration of detail characteristic of early medieval art. Rossetti came to be one of the most ardent members of this group, which later was known as the Pre-Raphaelite* Brotherhood. He married the beautiful Elizabeth Siddal, who posed for many of his pictures of Dante's "Beatrice"; but she died within a short time, and Rossetti despairingly buried the manuscript of his poems in her grave. Here they remained for several years, until his friends at last persuaded him to dig them up and give them to the world.

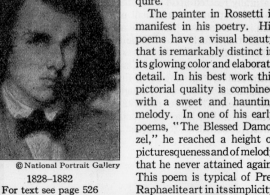

© National Portrait Gallery
1828–1882
For text see page 526

Rossetti became a famous and popular painter, making portraits of beauties from all ranks of society; but his health was poor, and the ill-advised kindness of a friend suggested his turning to the use of drugs as a relief from pain. He soon became enslaved, and the most distressing alterations took place in his character. But the poetic gift seemed more powerful than ever; and he continued up to the time of his death to produce poems which show the same originality, glowing color, and artistic sense as his paintings, together with a perfection of technique which as a painter he was too impatient to acquire.

The painter in Rossetti is manifest in his poetry. His poems have a visual beauty that is remarkably distinct in its glowing color and elaborate detail. In his best work this pictorial quality is combined with a sweet and haunting melody. In one of his early poems, "The Blessed Damozel," he reached a height of picturesqueness and of melody that he never attained again. This poem is typical of Pre-Raphaelite art in its simplicity and concreteness combined with spirituality. Among Rossetti's other short poems revealing his ability as a poet are "My Sister's Sleep" and "Sister Helen," the latter being based on a medieval practice connected with witchcraft. His versatility of emotion and his originality are illustrated in a wonderful sonnet sequence called *The House of Life*, which commemorates his tragic love. Noteworthy among his critical writings is *Dante and His Circle* (1873). (The portrait is from a drawing by Rossetti himself.)

WILLIAM MORRIS

This prolific poet and prose-writer, who preferred to be known as a "decorative artist," divided his interest between the making of artistic objects, such as furniture and books, and the invention of social theories, most of which have now gone out of fashion. He is best remembered as a poet and as a maker of beautiful books. Morris studied the art and literature of the Middle Ages at Oxford, and became a member of the Pre-Raphaelite* Brotherhood. He took up architecture, abandoned this for painting, and finally found his vocation in the designing and manufacture of furniture, wall paper, and textile fabrics, and still later in artistic printing and bookbinding. Morris's literary work was incidental to his other activities. He was convinced that modern commercialism was essentially wrong, and became an eager advocate of the brotherhood of man. Though he wrote much prose fiction, he was pre-eminently a poet. His early poems, such as "The Defence of Guenevere," deal with medieval subjects and attempt purely medieval treatment and psychology. *The Earthly Paradise* (1868–1870) consists of a series of narrative poems which, as in the case of Chaucer's *Canterbury Tales* (see page 37), are set in a frame. It contains some of the best narrative poetry written during the Victorian Period. *Sigurd the Volsung* (1876) is a long narrative poem dealing with Scandinavian mythology, a subject that interested Morris greatly and forms the theme of several of his other works. (The portrait is from a painting by G. F. Watts.)

© National Portrait Gallery   © National Portrait Gallery   Lafayette

William Morris, 1834–1896   Thomas Henry Huxley, 1825   Robert Bridges, 1844–1930
For text see page 529   1895. For text see page 540   For text see page 576

THOMAS HENRY HUXLEY

Huxley was the most active upholder and popularizer of the new theories that began to revolutionize science about the middle of the nineteenth century. After studying medicine at Charing Cross Hospital in London he went to the South Seas as ship's physician. On this expedition he spent his leisure time in studying the life forms that he found in the tropics. When he returned home he was appointed professor of natural history at the Royal School of Mines. Here he delivered a series of lectures entitled *Lay Sermons*, in which he tried to explain the mysteries of science to the general public. He also delivered instructive lectures in other parts of England. These lectures formed in part the basis for his famous book *Man's Place in Nature* (1863). Huxley is noted for his clever arguments, his forceful style, and his clear exposition of scientific theories in simple language. (The portrait is from a painting by the Honorable John Collier.)

Recent and Contemporary Literature (1892–   )

ROBERT BRIDGES

Robert Bridges, the late poet laureate* of England, is important chiefly in that he carried on a tradition that began in the Elizabethan Period. His chief interest was in the technical side of verse-writing. By his imitations and adaptations of classical meters and, particularly, by applying the principle of quantity to English verse, he added new resources to the technique of English poetry. In spite of the fact that in his poetry he makes use of stress rather than uniformity in the number of syllables, his verses are not lacking in restraint or purity. He is best known for his short, simple poems and for his poetical drama *The Return of Ulysses*. He was also a critic of distinction.

WILLIAM ERNEST HENLEY

The personality of Henley is more interesting than his work. He was a cripple who lay for a long time helpless in a hospital. His courageous spirit made him many friends and many enemies. He was a friend of Stevenson, with whom he collaborated occasionally. He was one of the few English poets who cared to imitate the free, wild style of Walt Whitman; but his adventurous spirit also led him to experiment with the most precise, highly formal kinds of verse. As an editor he greatly influenced literature by promoting the fortunes of some of the younger writers. He also wrote brilliant but rather dogmatic criticism.

© Elliott & Fry

William Ernest Henley, 1849–
1903. For text see page 577

© Elliott & Fry

William Henry Davies, 1871–
For text see page 578

© E. O. Hoppé

Alfred Edward Housman, 1859–
1936. For text see page 579

WILLIAM HENRY DAVIES

Davies was born in Wales and came to America as a young man. After many years spent in England, Canada, and the United States as a common tramp, years during which he picked up here and there a miscellaneous education, he finally yielded to a lifelong desire to write poetry. On losing a leg in a railroad accident in America, he returned to his native land and became a poet. His works include many volumes of verse, among them *A Poet's Pilgrimage* and *Later Days*. His *Autobiography of a Super-Tramp*, which appeared in 1906, helped to increase his reputation. His poetry is characterized chiefly by simplicity. He expresses directly and sincerely his feelings about nature and life as represented by the commonplace things which he sees about him. This interest in common things has caused him to be compared to Wordsworth.

ALFRED EDWARD HOUSMAN

Alfred Edward Housman was a professor of Latin at Cambridge University, and his poems occasionally show the influence of some of the great classic authors in their restraint, their artistic expression, their melancholy, and their universal appeal. He tried to express in language as simple as that of a plain country lad the fundamental emotions of mankind. His sentences are as unpretentious as those of the speech of the ordinary man, but they have an individual beauty and melody that few poets have approached. The emotions expressed are usually tragic, or at least colored with sadness. One of his most popular volumes of verse is *A Shropshire Lad*.

WILLIAM BUTLER YEATS

Yeats was born in the rugged west of Ireland, studied art and English literature, and played a prominent part in the Irish literary renaissance, especially in promoting the Irish drama. In this work he was associated particularly with Lady Gregory, Douglas Hyde, George Russell (Æ), and J. M. Synge, whom he also supported in their efforts to revive the ancient Gaelic language. With Lady Gregory he founded the Irish National Theater (also called the Abbey Theater). He received the Nobel prize for literature in 1923. Yeats devoted his life to interpreting and making popular in English the literature and legends of his native Ireland. Besides writing musical and highly imaginative poetry and plays, he encouraged and inspired many younger writers who love Irish literature. Notable among his poetical works are *The Wanderings of Oisin* (ŏsh'ĭn) and *Wind among the Reeds*; and, among his plays, *The Land of Heart's Desire* and *Deirdre of the Sorrows*.

William Butler Yeats, 1865–1939
For text see pages 581 and 632

Padraic Colum, 1881–
For text see page 585

EVA GORE-BOOTH

[1872–1926. For text see page 584]

Eva Gore-Booth, the third child of Sir Henry Gore-Booth, was born and spent her early years in the beautiful and romantic County Sligo, Ireland. In 1894 she traveled in the West Indies and in Canada. Throughout most of her later life she labored earnestly for the emancipation of women from political and social injustice. Though she was an enemy of oppression, she possessed a singularly sweet and deeply religious character. Her poetry reflects her love of nature, especially the scenes of her childhood. She was one of the most gifted poets associated with the Irish literary renaissance.

KATHARINE TYNAN

[1861–1931. For text see page 584]

Katharine Tynan was born in Dublin. She began writing at the age of seventeen and published many novels and volumes of verse. In her poetry she expresses religious feelings and a love of Ireland. In 1893 she married H. A. Hinkson, who died in 1919. She was one of the supporters of Irish nationalism and one of the leaders of the Irish literary renaissance.

PADRAIC COLUM

Padraic Colum (pä′drĭk kŏl′ŭm) was born in Ireland and was educated in local schools. He was one of the founders of the Irish National Theater and was associated with William Butler Yeats (p. 736) in the Irish literary renaissance. He was one of the founders of the *Irish Review* and was later its editor. The Hawaiian government invited him to make a survey of Hawaiian folklore, and he published a series of tales on this subject. He has published a great many poems and plays. His plays deal for the most part with the lives and problems of Irish country people. For some time he lived in the United States, where he delivered many lectures. He now lives in Dublin.

FRANCIS THOMPSON

After being educated at a Roman Catholic seminary, Thompson studied medicine for a time; then, dissatisfied with his progress, he abandoned his intended profession and wandered off to live a Bohemian life in the streets of London. After several years spent in this aimless manner, a chance poem of his attracted the attention of Wilfrid Meynell.

D

© Elliott & Fry   © Elliott & Fry   © E. O. Hoppé

Francis Thompson, 1859–1907   Alice Meynell, 1850–1922   Hilaire Belloc, 1870–
For text see page 587   For text see page 589   For text see page 590

Meynell made a search for the author, and found him at last, an unkempt tramp of the streets. Meynell invited the poet tramp to his home, where his wife, the poet Alice Meynell, won the wanderer back to himself. He continued unkempt; but became sober and industrious, composing his unusual verse and writing classic essays on literature and on men of letters.

Thompson represents a reaction from materialism to the Christian, especially to the Roman Catholic, point of view. His true literary ancestors were the mystical, religious poets of the Puritan Period (see page 183). Heavenly rather than earthly love is the theme of his most serious poems. "The Hound of Heaven" illustrates this theme and also furnishes a good example of Thompson's finished technique and his perfect adaptation of form to feeling. Though his diction and imagery are at times extravagant, he often writes with simple grace.

ALICE MEYNELL

Alice Meynell was born in London and educated principally in Italy. After her marriage to Wilfrid Meynell her London home became a literary center. All her verse is characterized by daintiness of thought and phrase and by an intense moral earnestness. She was a convert to Roman Catholicism, and she expressed in her poetry the Roman Catholic ideal of self-sacrifice and renunciation of life. Among her most characteristic poems are "After a Parting," "I Must Not Think of Thee," and "The Shepherdess." She was also the author of essays written in poetic prose.

HILAIRE BELLOC

Joseph Hilaire (hĭl'á rĭ) Pierre Belloc (bĕl'ŏk), or merely Hilaire Belloc, as he is usually called, is a very cosmopolitan literary personage. He was born in France, near Paris, the son of a French lawyer. He was educated at Oxford University, graduating with honors and a scholarship in history. His wife was an American, a native of California. Belloc himself became long ago a naturalized British citizen. He has even served two terms in Parliament; but he refused a third, because, he said, it was, for him, a waste of time.

Belloc is a big, sturdy, red-faced, serious man, a John Bull sort of person who likes to get things done. He began to write when he was young, and in the little over forty years since his first published work he has written over fifty books.

Belloc has two distinct sides. The most obvious is the belligerent side he shows in fighting for and against ideas and the persons who express those ideas. He detests the socialism of Bernard Shaw and the histories written by H. G. Wells, who, he believes, undervalues the importance of Roman Catholicism. For Belloc is not only a patriotic Englishman; he is, as was G. K. Chesterton, an ardent Roman Catholic. His serious writings include *A History of England* (four volumes), many biographies of English and French historical figures, such as Cromwell and Napoleon, and several volumes of Catholic essays; in fact, the serious Belloc has of late rather submerged the other Belloc, a Belloc who is whimsical, humorous, even nonsensical.

The humorous side, especially appealing to American readers, may be found in his *Path to Rome*, an account of a pilgrimage on foot to the Roman Catholic capital; in his volumes of essays, which rejoice in such delightful titles as *On Nothing, On Something*, and *Hills and the Sea*; and in his verse, such as the famous *Cautionary Tales for Children*.

© Hutchinson

Gilbert Keith Chesterton, 1874–1936. For text see pages 590 and 636

Winifred M. Letts, 1887– For text see page 594

Rupert Brooke, 1887–1915 For text see page 595

GILBERT KEITH CHESTERTON

Chesterton was born in London. After attending St. Paul's School he studied art and began his career by reviewing books on art. He produced many books: biography, criticism, fiction, poetry, and essays. Although much of his work was journalistic, in that it dealt with matters of only temporary interest, some of his writings enjoyed an unusually wide and long-continued popularity. He is noted for his striking, sometimes extravagant style, for his habit of saying things in new and unexpected ways, and for his delightfully whimsical humor. His stories of Father Brown are known to all lovers of detective fiction. His best verse, which is admirable, is published in his *Collected Poems*.

WINIFRED M. LETTS

Miss Letts is Irish and was educated at Alexandra College, Dublin. She married in 1926. Many of her contributions have appeared in English, Irish, and American magazines, and two of her plays were performed at the Abbey Theater, Dublin. She has published several books of poems and some children's books. She lives in Dublin.

RUPERT BROOKE

Brooke was the son of one of the teachers at the famous Rugby School. After spending some time in Germany, he traveled across America, going even as far as the South Seas. He entered the World War, but died on board ship in the harbor of Skyrós in 1915, when he was only twenty-eight years of age. He wrote some beautiful poetry; but probably his fame is due almost as much to his tragic fate as to the simple beauty of his verse and the promise it gave of further development.

SIEGFRIED SASSOON

In early August, 1914, Siegfried Sassoon, son of a Jewish father and an English mother, enlisted in the World War and went to the front. He was twenty-eight, no young stripling, but a mature man. He brought to the war not only maturity but cultivated sensibilities. He was a Cambridge man, an admirer of Thomas Hardy and Rupert Brooke. Moreover, his was a wholesome, hearty point of view; for he was a lover of sports, especially fox-hunting.

When, embittered by his war experience, he threw the military cross that had been given him for bravery in war into the sea as a protest against the continuance of what seemed to him to be a senseless and needless conflict, he was sent to a hospital for treatment instead of being court-martialed. Later on he returned to the trenches and was wounded. Sassoon knew the World War from beginning to end.

Since the armistice (1918) Sassoon has devoted himself, in verse and in autobiographical novels, to the self-appointed task of keeping fresh the memory of the horror of war and of rousing mankind against it. A notable volume of his verse appeared in 1918 under the title *A Counter Attack*.

© Howard Coster

Siegfried Sassoon, 1886–
For text see page 597

James Stephens, 1882–1950
For text see page 601

JAMES STEPHENS

James Stephens, Irish dreamer and poet, was working as a typist in a Dublin lawyer's office trying to support his family on less than seven dollars a week when another Irish poet, Æ (George W. Russell), discovered him there. Through the influence and encouragement of Æ, Stephens was drawn into the Irish literary renaissance, and gave up his position in the lawyer's office to devote his whole time to literature. His writings include several plays, a delightfully fanciful romance entitled *The Crock of Gold*, and a considerable body of poetry and short stories. His *Collected Poems* were published in 1926. Stephens loved to write about the beautiful and fantastic legends of early Ireland. His work is poetic, whether it is written in verse or in prose. It is full of that wistful, dreamlike beauty to which we sometimes give the name of "Celtic magic."

RALPH HODGSON

[1878–   . For text see page 602]

This man of varied interests was born in the north of England. He lived for a time in America, and lectured on English literature in Japan. He is a draftsman, and a great lover of animals, especially dogs, ranking as the greatest English authority on bull terriers. His first volume of poems did not appear till he was nearly forty. His verse is marked by purity, clearness, and that kind of simplicity which is an indication of high artistry.

WALTER DE LA MARE

De la Mare was born in Kent and was educated at St. Paul's School in London. He was engaged in business for some years and later became a reviewer of books. He is the author of both novels and poems which have been highly praised for their delicate and mysterious beauty. He has a remarkable power of looking at the world through the wondering eyes of a child and of making invisible presences real. His attitude toward the unseen world reminds us of Blake's earlier work and of Coleridge. The title of his *Songs of Childhood*, which appeared in 1902, indicates the theme of his best poetical work. He is also the author of *Stuff and Nonsense* and *Peacock Pie*, two of his most popular volumes.

© E. O. Hoppe

Walter de la Mare, 1873–
For text see page 603

© Elliott & Fry

Wilfred Wilson Gibson, 1878–
For text see page 604

© National Portrait Gallery

Thomas Hardy, 1840–1928
For text see page 607

WILFRED WILSON GIBSON

Gibson was born in the north of England and lived also in several other sections of the country. He began by imitating Tennyson; but he later reacted violently against Victorian prettiness, and wrote more in the manner of Masefield. He has also been compared to Wordsworth. He pictures the lives of the London poor in simple, almost prosaic but powerfully realistic, verse. He has written some deeply felt and finely expressed sonnets.* He introduced his poetry to the United States by a series of readings given in 1917.

THOMAS HARDY

First an architect, then a novelist, and last of all a poet, Thomas Hardy had a long and productive career. He is best known as a realistic novelist, and as a realist who generally sees the gloomy, hopeless side of life. But his descriptions of nature often reach the height of true poetry, and his characters are drawn with such a marvelous effect of truth that they seem ready to step out of the page into reality. Though his stories are sometimes carelessly constructed, they are always absorbingly interesting. Even if we do not agree with his belief that all effort is vain because our lives are determined by fate, we are willing to hear him expound his doctrine in stories that no one else could tell quite so well.

Among Hardy's best novels are *Tess of the D'Urbervilles*, *Far from the Madding Crowd*, and *The Return of the Native*. His recent achievements in the field of the new poetry have won for him a place among the first half-dozen poets of the last two decades. Both in his poetry and in his best fiction he is a modern, although he was born and lived most of his life during the Victorian Period. (The portrait is from a drawing by William Strang.)

RUDYARD KIPLING

Kipling led a varied and fascinating life, which is reflected in his numerous literary works. He was born in Bombay, India, and was educated in England. When he was seventeen years old, he returned to India to edit a newspaper. At the age of twenty-one he published his *Departmental Ditties*, followed in a few years by several volumes of short stories and his *Barrack-Room Ballads*. Both the volumes of verse became extremely popular. By the time Kipling was twenty-five he was an acknowledged master of the short story. His stories and poems opened up a new literary field, the life of the common soldier and sailor in Britain's possessions beyond the seas. His works, which are for the most part written in the language of the common people, made Kipling a genuinely popular writer. In 1894–1896 he produced the *Jungle Books*, two volumes of stories intended for children. He traveled widely in the Orient, in Africa, in South America, and in North America, where he lived for several years and where he married an American woman. In 1907 he received the Nobel prize for literature. Kipling's works are filled with the greatness of Britain and her far-flung domain. He was the poetic press-agent of the British Empire. His ballads have a fine singing quality that has helped to give them wide popularity. He is one of the greatest masters of the British short story.

© Elliott & Fry

1865–1936

For text see pages 608, 628, 642

JOHN MASEFIELD

From a wild, vagabond youth in all the four corners of the earth to an old age of honor and poetic reputation and even the laureateship of England is the story of John Masefield. He was born in Shropshire, in central England. As a boy he ran away from home and became a sailor. The sea always had glamour for him, and his love of it appears in his narratives and in his rousing sailor ballads. He worked in America for several years during his boyhood: at one time as farm hand; again as bartender and as factory laborer. His education, chiefly in English literature, he got for himself through reading for pleasure. Early in his career he began to write verse. Returning to England after his wanderings, he tried to make a living by journalism. He was encouraged by Yeats, who helped many young writers to find themselves, and he soon won a reputation for serious poetry. In one of his early poems he said that he wrote not of the great, the rich, the powerful, but of the sailors, the workers, the downtrodden, "the dregs of mankind." His poetry is always distinguished by realism in the interpretation of the minds and hearts of the masses. His fame is the reward of ability, sincerity, high purpose, and careful study. His highest honor came in 1930, when, on the death of Robert Bridges, he was appointed poet laureate.*

Masefield has written novels and plays as well as poems, but he is above all a poet. His poetical work falls into three groups. First come his ballads, dealing chiefly with the sea. To the second group belong his dramatic narrative poems, including *The Everlasting Mercy, The Widow in the Bye Street, Daffodil Fields*, and *Dauber*. To the third group belong his lyrical and most of his narrative poems.

© Foulsham & Banfield

1878–

For text see page 611

ALAN PATRICK HERBERT

A. P. Herbert, who had studied at Winchester School and at Oxford, was a soldier in France during the World War. Even before then he was writing for *Punch*, the leading English humorous journal. After the war he was admitted to the bar, but has never practiced. Instead, he has continued his writing for *Punch*, and has been on its editorial staff since 1924. He writes every day or so a letter to the London *Times* on some one of the numerous matters in which he is interested, and he has written many essays, novels, short plays, comic-opera librettos, verses, and sketches satirizing the English law courts. *Who's Who* lists thirty-three titles under the entry for Alan Patrick Herbert.

Besides all these accomplishments, Herbert has represented Oxford University in Parliament since 1935. He is an independent in politics, as one would expect. In public affairs this "reformer in motley," who is widely known as an excellent after-dinner speaker, is not humorous; but because he has been so labeled he has not always been taken seriously. In the House of Commons, where he is a frequent speaker, he often uses, with deadly purpose, his ability to make his side not "prissy" but amusing and the other side ridiculous. His brother members of Parliament, like his readers, have come to look for the common sense back of his foolery.

© Howard Coster

Alan Patrick Herbert, 1890–
For text see page 616

© Elliott & Fry

Henry Major Tomlinson, 1873–
For text see page 618

HENRY MAJOR TOMLINSON

He did not plan to write; it just happened, says H. M. Tomlinson, called sometimes a second Conrad. Be that as it may, he was born and bred among ships and, before he was in his teens, started earning his living doing clerical work connected with the old-time clippers. To get away from the routine of the work, he took refuge in books and in writing. True, he burned his early efforts, and did not publish his first book until he was thirty-eight. That was after Tomlinson, a man over thirty, had most unfortunately (he thought) lost his job. That happy event, however, led to his turning to full-time work on the (London) *Morning Ledger*, a

paper which assigned him to a two-thousand-mile journey from London up into the far reaches of the Amazon. The result of this jaunt was *The Sea and the Jungle*. When, shortly, the *Morning Ledger* consolidated with the *Daily News*, Tomlinson remained with the new setup and, beginning in August, 1914, served the united papers as war correspondent. A year later he became official correspondent at general headquarters of the British armies in France. Reporting the war was his job; but he found time to be a friend to all, a fine spirit in the midst of terror and ruin. Out of Tomlinson's war experience grew two books: *Waiting for Daylight*, based, apparently, on notes for a war diary; and *All Our Yesterdays*, a semi-autobiographical novel which emphasizes the futility of war.

After 1917 Tomlinson was for a time literary editor of the *Nation and Athenaeum*, but for fifteen years or more he has had no such definite connection with newspapers or magazines. Instead he has traveled and written as accident and impulse have led him. He is, first, a Londoner; secondly, a traveler, a lover of the sea and of the men to be found in ships and in strange lands. He does not travel to get away from himself, but takes himself along, a fact that makes his books of travel something apart from the run-of-the-mill sort. He collects more than souvenirs and oddities of information: yarns, scenes, which he recounts and describes in beautifully written prose. Over all plays his humorous, quiet, meditative mind. *Out of Soundings*, the title of one of his collections of essays, gives the clue to his work. On any subject Tomlinson sees more, feels more, than would the casual observer. There is more in his writing, be it book of travel, essay, or novel, than the casual reader will get.

WILLIAM McFEE

Back of William McFee lie two generations of English sea-captains. He himself was born on a ship homeward bound from India. While his seagoing father continued his work his Canadian mother lived with her small son in a London suburb. When the lad was grown, he studied engineering, and for several years he worked in an engineering plant in London. But at twenty-four he became junior engineer on one of his uncle's ships, and at sea he remained for more than fifteen years. During the World War he served on British ships, most of the time in the Mediterranean.

During all these years at sea McFee had for his avocation books, both their study and their writing. His cabin bookshelf was freshly stocked for every voyage. What with wide reading and wide travel and observation of places and people, the engineer became critic and philosopher as well. In his cabin was a typewriter, used for making out his engineering reports, not for his personal writing. That was never done by machine, but always by hand.

© E. O. Hoppé
1881–
For text see page 623

Now it happens that fame came to William McFee in the United States. Only later was he read and acclaimed in his native England. That fact may account partly for his settling in Connecticut when it was evident that he should give the greater part of his time to writing. Be that as it may, big blond blue-eyed "Mac" (as his friends call him) finds that "to keep in contact with reality" he must now and then motor, travel, put to sea. Back home in New England, he meditates on what he has seen, and writes on some phase of "the problem of human folly." Sometimes the new book is a group of tales; sometimes a group of essays; more often, of late, a novel.

McFee's essays and travel sketches are an excellent supplement to his fiction, and vice versa. Whatever the form, his style is easy, light, charming, touched with humor and sympathy.

Titles of his essays include *Harbours of Memory* and *More Harbours of Memory*; those of his novels, *Casuals of the Sea*, *Command*, and *The Beachcomber*.

OSCAR WILDE

The versatile Oscar Wilde was born in Dublin and educated there and at Oxford University. At Oxford he came under the influence of Pre-Raphaelitism* and of neo-paganism, a cult whose adherents tried to achieve beauty in life by modeling themselves on what they imagined to have been the lives of the ancient pagans. He preached the doctrine "Art for Art's sake," which means that the way a thing is done matters more than the thing itself. For a time Wilde was lionized by society; but in 1895 he was put in prison, quite deservedly, many thought. After his release he lived in obscurity in Paris until his death.

Wilde is typical of the writers of the end of the nineteenth century (the gay nineties) in his restless search for novelty. He wrote poetry, fiction, and drama. His style is brilliant, witty, sophisticated, and insincere in his early work; in later years, when he had experienced real suffering, he acquired a more human touch. His prison experiences are reflected in "The Ballad of Reading Gaol," one of the best of his poems. Some of his other poems are rich and refined in diction, but too often somewhat lacking in sincerity. He also wrote *Lady Windermere's Fan, The Importance of Being Earnest*, and other dramas marked by witty dialogue.

Downey
Oscar Wilde, 1856–1900
For text see page 633

© Underwood & Underwood
John Galsworthy, 1867–1933
For text see page 653

Curtis Brown, Ltd.
Eric Knight, 1897–1943
For text see page 657

JOHN GALSWORTHY

John Galsworthy was born in the south of England of an old Devonshire family. He was educated at the famous preparatory school of Harrow and at Oxford. He studied law, but gave it up and turned to writing. Few authors have so enthusiastic a group of admirers as Galsworthy. He is notable for his novels, his short stories, and his plays. He made little effort to gain a temporary hearing by being amusing, but wrote in a steady, straightforward manner with the assurance that the real worth of what he was saying would make his works permanently valuable. Much of his work has a social significance; it concerns itself with problems of modern society. His best novels compose a group called The Forsyte Saga, which includes *The Man of Property* and other novels. He also wrote essays of distinction. Galsworthy's writing is marked by closely knit dramatic construction, vivid characterization, and a charming style. He occupies a high place in recent literature.

ERIC KNIGHT

Eric Knight was a writer of fiction. Was he an Englishman or an American? He spent years in the United States, and at the time of his death in an airplane crash was a major in the United States Army. But he was born in England, spent his youth there, and in nearly all his fiction used Yorkshire as the background.

Eric's father died young; his widowed mother went to Russia as a governess to the children of a princess, but had to leave her sons behind. Eric lived with one relative after another. In a Yorkshire school he lost his "upperclass drawl," as he called it. When only twelve he began working in the mills. A few years later he headed for the United States.

Eric began working on newspapers, and

read hungrily to improve his meager education. He wrote his first novel, *Song on Your Bugles*, in 1936, scored a popular hit a few years later with his tales of Sam Small, the Flying Yorkshireman, and achieved even greater success with both young and old in his now beloved dog story *Lassie Come-Home*. In 1941 he wrote *This above All*, one of the most touching of the novels to come out of World War II.

"SAKI" (HECTOR HUGH MUNRO)

This very English author who wrote under the pen name "Saki," taken from that of the cupbearer in the "Rubáiyát" of Omar Khayyám, was born in Burma, India, where his father and grandfather before him had been in service. Because Burma is not a good place in which to bring up children, but especially because his mother had died when he was only two, the boy was sent to England, where he was reared in an English village by two very strict aunts, aided by a succession of governesses.

When he was seventeen a great change came about. His father, who had retired from service in India, took over his son's education, which became an interesting mixture of study, sports, and travel. After six years of this pleasant regime, young Munro was ready, at twenty-three, to go out in his turn to India, where his father had secured for him a place in the military police. But a succession of fevers, topped with malaria, caused him to resign; and two years later he was back in England, where he contracted double pneumonia. After undergoing all this he enjoyed good health, surprising as it may seem.

Munro began writing by contributing political sketches and humorous short stories to the *Westminster Gazette*. Then, for six years, he was foreign correspondent for the London *Morning Post* in the Balkans, in Russia, and in France, two years in each. In 1908 he settled in London, no more to travel,

Dorien Leigh

1870–1916
For text see page 668

but to write clever, somewhat cynical short stories, novels, sketches, plays, which appeared one after the other without attracting any very great attention. With 1914 came the World War. Munro enlisted at once, refusing a commission. In 1915 he was in France. In 1916 he was killed in the trenches. "Saki," mocking observer of politics and of life, had stepped into the background; H. H. Munro, with his "small and twisted face," lived and died in the war.

It would have amused him could he have known that belated fame came to him after the "tumult and the shouting died." Volumes of his unpublished work appeared. His short stories in particular became popular in the United States. In 1930 an omnibus volume, with an introduction by Christopher Morley, appeared. Some compared him to O. Henry, and not without reason. Like O. Henry, "Saki" is an excellent storyteller, given to the use of the surprise ending, adept in the felicitous use of English. Like O. Henry, too, he is typically native to his own country. The English find O. Henry difficult reading sometimes, because of his dyed-in-the-wool Americanism. Americans find difficult spots in the work of "Saki." The ability to read and enjoy him is, some say, an excellent test of an understanding of things English. It is, besides, an almost sure sign of a cultivated literary taste and of the possession of an unsentimental, objective* point of view.

HERBERT GEORGE WELLS

Wells was born of comparatively humble parents in a suburb of London. He was largely self-educated. He began his adult life as a dry-goods salesman; then he became a preparatory-school teacher; and at last, in 1893, after a physical breakdown, he turned to journalism, a profession which he followed, in a sense, until his death.

Wells wrote a great deal: fiction, history, essay, argument. He is noted especially for his novels and short stories. These may be divided into at least three groups: (1) those in which the author uses the discoveries of science as the basis for imaginative or fantastic romances; (2) those in which he tells a story for the purpose of expressing his views on politics, education, society, or religion; (3) realistic novels based upon the author's own experiences. In most of his works Mr. Wells is a journalist and a propagandist; that is, he ordinarily deals with problems of the present moment and has some cause to promote, some cure for some evil. His seriousness of purpose is, however, relieved by a sense of humor. He is, moreover, an optimist. In his famous *Outline of History* he uses the discoveries of historians and of archaeologists and other scientists as a basis for his own ideas about the past and future of mankind.

© Harris & Ewing

Herbert George Wells, 1866–1946. For text see page 671

Lizzie Smith

Sir James Matthew Barrie, 1860–1937. For text see page 685

SIR JAMES MATTHEW BARRIE

The story of James M. Barrie is not very different from that of many other men who have become famous. He was born in a tiny Scottish village, Kirriemuir by name, and was educated at Dumfries Academy and at the University of Edinburgh. Afterward he went into journalism, first in Nottingham, then in London, where he lived the rest of his life.

But when one looks beyond these events to what Barrie made of them, the resemblance ends. The little Scottish village where he was born, rechristened Thrums and used as the background of many of his books, made for him name and fame. No use, however, to go hunting in Kirriemuir for Barrie's Thrums. It is not there; in fact, it wasn't there even in his childhood. The Thrums he wrote of is the Kirriemuir of his mother's childhood, a quaint community seen down the softening vistas of two lifetimes. Those who wish to know Barrie's Thrums will find it awaiting them in *The Little Minister*, *Sentimental Tommy*, and *Tommy and Grizel*. He is perhaps best known as the creator of Peter Pan, the little boy who never grew up.

Barrie's mother, as have the mothers of many men, influenced her son's life enormously. He immortalized her in a delightful biography, *Margaret Ogilvy* (see the revised edition of *Adventure* of this series). When once her acquaintance has been made there, she will be recognized over and over in the heroines in Barrie's books, be they novels or plays.

Barrie, like Thomas Hardy, belongs both to the Victorian Period and to more recent times. Both Barrie and Hardy wrote novels in their earlier days; later both turned from the writing of fiction to other types of literature. Barrie's popularity in his later years is due chiefly to his plays. The dramatization of *The Little Minister* was a greater success than the novel itself had been. *Peter Pan* proved one of the most popular of plays for young or old. Play followed play with astounding success: *The Admirable Crichton, Dear Brutus,*

What Every Woman Knows, Shall We Join the Ladies? and the rest.

Once started, the little man who came out of Scotland found it very easy to concoct just the perfect mixture of everyday life with fairyland, a mixture seasoned with a dash of laughter and a suggestion of tears. Presto! another Barrie play was ready for the public. Barrie is difficult to classify. Novelist, dramatist, essayist, public speaker, he filled all roles with distinction. Gay, gentle, tolerant, kind, never superior, he preached in his novels and plays, as well as in his public addresses, the doctrine of courage. Come, says he, life is a game; let us play "till the whistle blows."

Small wonder that this great little man was knighted, was made a member of the distinguished Order of Merit, and received other high honors. Yet despite these honors and the signal success of his writing, the facts of his life story are few; it is the fancies of his books that are many.

Dictionary of Names and Phrases

KEY TO PRONUNCIATION. āle, châotic, câre, ădd, ŏccount, ărm, àsk, sofȧ; ēve, hēre, ĕvent, ĕnd, silĕnt, makĕr; īce, ĭll, charĭty; ōld, ōbey, ôrb, ŏdd, sŏft, cŏnnect; fōōd, fŏŏt; out, oil; cūbe, ŭnite, ûrn, ŭp, circŭs, ü *in French* lune; chair; go; sing; then, thin; natŭre, verdŭre; K = ch *in German* ich, ach; N *in French* boN; yet; zh = z *in* azure

accent. As applied to reading, the word *accent* means the stress, or emphasis, with which a syllable is pronounced. A syllable is accented when it is more strongly stressed than the neighboring syllables, which are usually unaccented, or unstressed. Though the musical effect of verse is generally dependent upon a regular recurrence of the accent, as in

A knight there was, and that a worthy man (p. 42, l. 1),

many lines of poetry owe their effect in part to slight irregularities in the placing of the accents, as in

On the topmost twig that looks up at the sky (p. 396, l. 52).

Acheron (ăk′ēr ŏn). In classical mythology, a dark river in the lower world. The souls of the dead had to wait on the shore of this river until Charon* came and ferried them over. The poets often refer to Acheron as "the river of sorrows."

Achilles (ȧ kĭl′ēz). The most celebrated legendary Greek hero of the Iliad,* which recounts events near the end of the war against Troy.* When he was an infant, his mother, Thetis, dipped him in the waters of the river Styx* and thus rendered him proof against injury in every part of his body except that part of his heel by which she held him. It was of a wound in the heel that he died. In the Iliad* he is described as impetuous, willful, swift, and brave. When Agamemnon took from him by force a beautiful captive girl, he sulked in his tent and refused to fight. Later, enraged by the death of his dear friend Patroclus, he re-entered the conflict and killed Hector,* the greatest of the Trojan warriors. In literature the name "Achilles" is sometimes used as a synonym for a handsome, brave young man.

Adam. According to the Bible, the first man whom God created. He and Eve* were placed in the beautiful Garden of Eden* and told to eat freely of all its fruits except of the fruit of the "tree of the knowledge of good and evil." Tempted by the serpent, they ate of the forbidden fruit, and were driven out of the garden. See Genesis 3.

Aegean (ē jē′ăn), **the.** The sea lying between Greece and Asia Minor. The origin of the name is uncertain. According to one Greek legend, it is said to have been named for King Aegeus, father of Theseus. Theseus, when he sailed to Crete to kill a monster called the Minotaur, promised his father that if he succeeded he would sail home with white sails, but if he was killed his ship would display black sails. Rejoicing in his victory, he forgot to hoist white sails. Aegeus, watching from the sea cliffs, saw the black sails, and threw himself into the water and was drowned.

Aeneid, the. See "Vergil."*

Aeschylus (ĕs′kĭ lŭs) **(525 B.C.–456 B.C.).** One of the three great Athenian tragic poets (the other two being Sophocles* and Euripides*) and in a real sense the founder of Greek drama. He wrote many plays, of which only seven are preserved. He fought against the Persians at Marathon, Salamis, and Plataea, and the epitaph on his tomb celebrated his bravery. The vigor and loftiness of his poetry reflect his part in the heroic events of Greek history.

Aesop. According to tradition, a Greek writer who lived between 620 B.C. and 560 B.C. He is said to have been a slave and is usually represented as a hunchback and a dwarf. To him is ascribed a noted collection of fables, stories which deal with animals but are intended to teach some lesson about human beings. Though few, if any, of the fables are actually the work of Aesop, the collection has long been popular under the title *Aesop's Fables.* This book forms the basis of most of the fable collections in modern European literature.

Albion. An ancient name for England. The name is possibly Celtic; but the Romans connected it with *albus* ("white"), referring to the chalk cliffs of Dover.

Alexander the Great (356–323 B.C.). The son of Philip, the king of Macedonia, and Olympias. He was educated by Aristotle.* He succeeded his father on the throne, and extended his dominion over most of the Eastern ancient world. According to one tradition, his father was Jove* (or the Egyptian god Ammon*), who is said to have visited Olympias in the form of a dragon. Alexander was a capable, vigorous leader and a ruthless conqueror. He led his victorious armies through Egypt, Persia, and on into India. He defeated the Persian army under Darius,* the last king of Persia, in the battle of Arbela in 331 B.C. There is a tradition that in the same year he set fire to the city of Persepolis, the capital of Persia, at the instigation of Thais.* He founded the city of Alexandria. Tradition says that after his victories he wept because there were no more worlds to conquer. In literature he is referred to as a great military genius, the typical world conqueror.

allegorical. See "allegory."*

allegorically. See "allegory." *

allegory (ăl'ē gŏ rĭ). A form of literature in which the words tell of one thing in such a way as to suggest another. An allegory may also be defined as an extended metaphor.* When we read a well-constructed allegory, we perceive not only that the writer tells a good story, which we understand at once, but that beneath the surface the narrative has a deeper, figurative meaning, usually moral, religious, or political. That is, an allegory has at least two meanings, one meaning being literal, the other symbolical or allegorical. Spenser's *Faerie Queene* and Bunyan's *Pilgrim's Progress* are allegories. Jesus, in his parables, told many simple stories that have allegorical meanings. In fables (see "Aesop"*) personified* animals are used allegorically to teach lessons of human conduct. Many pastoral* romances present real events and personages in the form of allegories.

alliteration (ă lĭt ēr ā'shŭn). A rhetorical device which consists in beginning two or more words near together with the same sound or similar sounds. Alliteration may be also defined as initial rhyme. It is a characteristic feature of Anglo-Saxon poetry, as "He

in the *m*ansion saw warriors *m*any" (*Beowulf*, p. 22, l. 22). Other examples are:

On! on! *o*ver *o*ceans he went. (Initial vowels alike)

*M*elancholy *m*arked him for her own. (Initial consonants alike)

*S*onorous *m*etal *m*aking *m*artial sounds. (Two alliterations in one line)

Alliteration was required in Anglo-Saxon poetry; in later literature poets have used it or not, as they desired.

alliterative. See "alliteration."*

Ammon (ăm'ŏn). In Egyptian mythology, a powerful god with some of the attributes of the Roman Jove* (Jupiter). According to one tradition he was the father of Alexander* the Great. In art he is pictured as a man with a ram's head.

anapaest (ăn'á pĕst). In poetry a metrical unit, or foot,* consisting of two unaccented syllables followed by one accented syllable, as in "to intend." Byron's "Destruction of Sennacherib" is written in anapaestic tetrameter.* Browning's "Prospice" also contains many anapaestic feet.

anapaestic (ăn á pĕs'tĭk). See "anapaest."*

Apollo. In classical mythology, the god of the sun, who shot arrows of sunbeams with his silver bow. He was leader and protector of the nine Muses,* and patron of music, poetry, and medicine. He was also the god of manly beauty and wisdom. With his music he delighted the ears of the immortal gods themselves.

apostrophe (á pŏs'trŏ fĕ). A figure of speech in which the writer or speaker addresses some absent person as if he were present, or some inanimate object as though it were alive (see "personification"*). Examples are Macbeth's address to the dagger (p. 103, ll. 33–49), Byron's lines beginning "Roll on, thou deep and dark blue Ocean" (p. 355, l. 19), and Burns's lines beginning "Ah, Tam! ah, Tam!" (p. 393, l. 201).

Aprille. April, being the month when nature awakes from her long winter sleep, when the flowers begin to bloom, and the birds mate, has long been celebrated by poets as the season of youth, happiness, and love. Because of its marked contrast with the long, gloomy months of winter the English spring seems particularly charming.

Aquarius (á kwā'rĭ ŭs) (the water-carrier). The eleventh sign (or division) of the zodiac, represented by a man pouring water from a vase. The sign Aquarius is occupied by the sun from about January 18 to February 16.

Araby (ăr′á bĭ) (**Arabie**). A poetical name for Arabia. Araby is sometimes referred to as "Araby the Blest," and is thought of merely as a far-off land of untold wealth, beauty, and romance.

Arcady (är′ká dĭ) (**Arcadia** (är kā′dĭ á)). A district of ancient Greece which was inhabited by a population of shepherds and hunters. Shut off by mountain ranges from easy communication with the rest of Greece, its people were supposed to lead a comparatively peaceful existence. In literature Arcady has come to signify an earthly paradise where people live a simple, idyllic,* pastoral* life.

Ariel (ā′rĭ ĕl). According to the Mohammedan faith, Ariel is one of the powerful angels who attend on God. In Shakespeare and generally in modern literature he is a bright and airy little sprite, the personification of freedom and happiness.

Aristotle (384–322 B.C.). The greatest philosopher of ancient Greece. He was born at Stagira (in Macedonia); hence he is sometimes referred to as the "Stagirite" (stăj′ĭ rīt). He was the pupil of Plato* and the instructor of Alexander* the Great. His works, which cover politics, literary criticism, and other subjects, were for centuries standard authorities, and they still command attention.

Armada (är mä′dá). The Spanish Armada, a fleet of about one hundred and thirty ships and nearly thirty thousand soldiers and sailors, sent by King Philip II of Spain against England in 1588. The Spaniards named it the Invincible Armada (armada is Spanish for a war fleet). It was beaten in a nine days' fight by an English fleet of about eighty vessels (more English ships coming in for the last two days), and was then utterly ruined by furious storms that came after the fighting. Barely fifty ships returned to Spain. This disaster helped to end Spain's supremacy on the sea and greatly stimulated the pride of the English people. In literature the fate of the Armada is frequently used as an illustration of the pride that goes before a fall.

Arthur. According to medieval tradition, a powerful king of Britain who ruled during the sixth century after Christ. He was the son of Uther Pendragon (ū′thĕr pĕn drăg′ŭn) and Ygerne (ē gĕrn′), the wife of Gorloïs (gôr′lŏ ĭs), Duke of Cornwall. He was the center of a brilliant court consisting of many fair and virtuous ladies and brave and loyal knights, the Knights of the Round* Table. From Camelot,* his chief seat, knights rode forth seeking adventures or righting wrongs. But sin entered the court and, with sin, unhappiness. While Arthur was abroad on the Continent engaged in a campaign, his nephew, Mordred (Modred), in whose hands he had left the kingdom, seized the royal power. Arthur returned to Britain and attacked and slew Mordred, but was grievously wounded and departed for Avilion* (Avalon) to be healed of his wounds. According to another tradition Arthur was actually killed and was buried at Glastonbury Abbey in Somersetshire. Many medieval romances deal with the adventures of Arthur's knights.

Athens. The capital and chief city of Greece. In literature the words "Athens" and "Attic," which means "Athenian," suggest perfection in art and in literary culture.

Aurora (ô rō′rá). In classical mythology, the goddess of the dawn. In art she appears as a winged maiden or as a maiden riding in a chariot drawn by winged horses preceding Helios, the sun.

Avilion (á vĭl′yŭn) (**Avalon, Avallon**). In Arthurian romance and in medieval Welsh literature, the happy Other World, or Island of Delight, an earthly paradise in the western seas. It is represented as a place of perpetual springtime, of feasting, and of love. Arthur* and other great heroes were carried thither instead of dying. It corresponds to the Land of Youth in Irish mythology. The word avallon means "place of apples."

Azrael (ăz′rá ĕl). In the Mohammedan religion, the angel that watches over the dead and separates the soul from the body.

Babylon (băb′ĭ lŏn). One of the most celebrated cities of antiquity, on the Euphrates,* in Mesopotamia. It came into prominence about 2300 B.C. and continued a powerful city until the sixth century before Christ, when, after being the capital of most of the civilized world, it was conquered by the Persians. Afterward its power declined, and now only ruins remain to tell the story of its greatness. As a result of the Babylonian Captivity (see "Babylonish* Captivity"), the Jews came to regard Babylon as a place of great wealth, power, and wickedness, and the name has kept this meaning in modern literature. Hence a great city such as London or New York may be referred to as "a modern Babylon." See also "Babylonia."*

Babylonia. A region between the Euphrates* and Tigris rivers and between Asia Minor and the Persian Gulf. The country took its name from Babylon,* the capital city. It had an extensive commerce and a highly developed culture, art, and literature.

Babylonish (Babylonian) Captivity. The period during which the Hebrews were kept in exile in Babylon,* usually said to have lasted 70 years. About 600 B.C. Nebuchadnezzar,* king of Babylon, made several attacks on Jerusalem, burned the city and Temple, and carried off much booty and many captives. In 536 B.C. Cyrus the Great, king of Persia, captured Babylon, and allowed those Jews to return who wished to do so.

Bacchus (băk′ŭs) (also called **Dionysus** (dī ō nī′sŭs)). In classical mythology, the beautiful and youthful god of vegetation, especially of the grapevine. He is said to have taught men the cultivation of the grape and the making of wine. Because of the numerous celebrations in his honor, he came to be associated with festivity and revelry. In literature he personifies wine, both in its good and in its bad qualities. In art he is sometimes represented as crowned with a wreath of vine or ivy leaves or as accompanied by leopards ("pards"). The adjective "Bacchanalian," derived from his name, suggests riotous festivity, usually inspired by alcoholic liquor.

Balaklava (băl á klä′vá). A notable battle fought during the Crimean* War.

Bannockburn (băn′ŭk bûrn). A battle fought on June 24, 1314, at Bannockburn, a village in Stirlingshire, Scotland, between the Scots (under Robert Bruce) and the English army. The English were attempting to relieve their countrymen at Stirling Castle, to which the Scottish forces had laid siege. Though greatly outnumbered by the English, the Scots were completely victorious.

bard. Among the ancient Celts, one who composed and sang, usually to the accompaniment of the harp, songs in honor of noble deeds and famous heroes. In modern times the name "bard" has come to be applied to any poet. David,* for example, is often referred to as the "Royal Bard."; Shakespeare, as the "Bard of Avon."

Bear. Two constellations (groups of stars) are known as the Bear. (1) The Great Bear (Ursa Major), the most conspicuous of the northern constellations, supposed in ancient times to resemble a bear with a long tail; it contains the stars which form Charles's Wain (wagon), or the Dipper, so named because of fancied resemblances to a wagon and to a dipper with a long handle. The two stars farthest from the handle of the Dipper point to the North Star. (2) Another constellation near the North Pole is called the Little Bear (Ursa Minor) and also Cynosura (Cynosure), "the dog's tail," because in ancient times the lower part of its tail marked the North Pole in the sky as the North Star, at the top of the tail, does now, so that the tail, on which sailors fixed their eyes to guide their course, was the important part to name it from.

bear-baiting. Bear-baiting and bull-baiting were popular amusements in England in the sixteenth and seventeenth centuries. The sport consisted in setting dogs to fight with captive bears or bulls. The bear was tied to a stake, and each attack of the dogs was called a "course." At the time when Shakespeare wrote *Macbeth* there was a famous bear-baiting establishment near the theater where the play was performed.

Beelzebub (bē ĕl′zē bŭb). Originally a heathen divinity referred to in the Old Testament. In the New Testament he is "the prince of the devils." In Milton's *Paradise Lost* he is next to Satan in power. In literature his name is often applied to Satan himself.

Billingsgate. The name of one of the ancient gates of the city of London and later of the fish market and wharf near it, which as early as the seventeenth century became noted for the foul and abusive language used by the fishwives (women who sold fish); hence the name came to be applied to that kind of language.

Birnam (bûr′năm) **Wood.** The wood that covered Birnam, in Scotland, formerly part of a royal forest referred to in *Macbeth*.

blank verse. Unrhymed verse, especially unrhymed iambic* pentameter,* the most common form of English blank verse. Blank verse is especially well suited to the more dignified forms of poetry, such as the epic and the tragic drama. It was used by Shakespeare in his plays, by Milton in *Paradise Lost*, by Tennyson in *The Idylls of the King*, and by other poets and dramatists both English and American.

Bleys (blās). A magician and seer named in Malory's *Morte d'Arthur* as the teacher of Merlin.*

Boccaccio (bōk kä′chō) (1313–1375). A celebrated Italian writer, best known in modern times as the author of a famous collection of tales called the *Decameron*. He presents these stories as if they were told by a group of people who were gathered at a country estate in order to escape from a plague in the city. In this use of a plot, or "framework," into which the individual tales are fitted, the *Decameron* is similar to the *Arabian Nights* and the *Canterbury Tales*. Boccaccio has been called the creator of modern Italian prose.

Bolingbroke (bŏl'ĭng brŏŏk). Henry St. John (1678–1751), Viscount Bolingbroke, a Tory* statesman and political writer who became Secretary of State of England, but who was regarded by many Tories as unreliable. He was helped to power by Marlborough,* whom he afterward betrayed. He was exiled in 1715 because of his Jacobite* sympathies. He was a friend of Pope (p. 223) and of Swift (p. 274).

Border, the. The parts of Scotland and England close to the boundary between the two countries. For hundreds of years the region was the scene of raids, war, and bloodshed. Out of the Border disturbances came many ballads, legends, and traditions that have been used often by British writers.

Borgia (bôr'jä), **Caesar.** A noted member of the notorious Italian family of Borgias in the fifteenth century. He was handsome in person, highly educated, a capable soldier, and a patron of art and learning, but was by nature proud, cruel, and treacherous, winning men to his cause by promises and then killing them when they had served his purpose. He finally died as he had lived, by violence. In literature his name is a symbol* of ruthless treachery and cruelty.

Burke, Edmund (1729–1797). A great statesman, orator, and author. He was graduated from Trinity College, Dublin, in 1748. He later became a member of Parliament, where he was noted for his convincing logic and his oratorical powers. He is especially famous in America because he sympathized with the colonies during the American Revolution. He attacked the French revolutionists for seeking to destroy completely the old aristocracy. Among his best-known works are his essay "On the Sublime and Beautiful," his "Speech on Conciliation with America," and his "Reflections on the Revolution in France."

burlesque. A kind of wit that ridicules small or trivial matters by treating them as though they were important or by treating dignified matters as though they were trivial. Burlesque resembles satire* in some respects, but is usually less bitter.

buskined. Originally a buskin was a thick-soled and high-heeled boot worn in ancient times by the actors of tragedy. Hence, by

D

metonymy,* "buskined" came to be connected with the tragic drama.

Byzantium (bĭ zăn'shĭ ŭm). An ancient Greek city on the Bosporus. The name sometimes stands for Constantinople (now Istanbul), which Constantine the Great built on the site of Byzantium.

cadence. A regular or agreeable succession of sounds, as in the rhythmical flow or modulation of the voice in reading or speaking. Cadence is usually another name for "rhythm."*

Caesar, Caius Julius. A celebrated Roman general, statesman, and author. He was born about 100 B.C. He early entered public life, in which he distinguished himself by taking the side of the common people. Being made governor of southern Gaul, he conquered the whole country, and invaded Britain in 55 and 54 B.C. By the year 46 B.C. he had become master of the Roman world. At the height of his power, in 44 B.C., he was assassinated by Brutus, Cassius, and others who professed to be his friends. Few names in history have been so frequently mentioned as Caesar's. In literature he is often referred to as a type of the world conqueror. As a victor he received a laurel crown. His fate is also used as an example of the result of ingratitude and envy. His *Commentaries* (part of which gives an account of his campaigns in Gaul) is remarkable for its clear style and has long been used as an elementary textbook in Latin.

Cain. According to the Bible, the first murderer. He was the eldest son of Adam* and Eve.* He slew his brother Abel. For his sin God condemned him to be a fugitive; hence the phrase "the curse of Cain." In literature his name is a synonym for a murderer. According to medieval tradition he was the ancestor of monsters such as Grendel.

Calvin, John (1509–1564). A Swiss reformer, scholar, and divine, a famous champion of the Reformation (p. 71). While a student in France he became an ardent supporter of the reformed doctrines which Martin Luther and others had already advanced. He soon became the leader of reformed thought in France. The danger of persecution led him to take refuge in Switzerland, where he wrote his famous book, *The Institutes of the Christian Religion*. He helped to establish at Geneva, Switzerland, a new form of city government in which the power lay largely in the hands of the church. The theology of Calvin exercised a great influence upon religious thought, especially on one form of Presbyterianism.

Cambridge. A town in England, famous because it is the seat of one of the two most ancient English universities, the other being Oxford. Both Oxford and Cambridge universities are divided into various colleges, such as Balliol, Trinity, King's, Emmanuel, etc.

Cambuscan (kăm bŭs'kăn). The king of Tartary in Chaucer's "Squire's Tale," one of the *Canterbury Tales*. The king of Arabia sends him a mirror, a ring, a magic sword, and a brazen horse. He is the father of two sons, Algarsife and Camballo (Camball), and a daughter, Canace. The story is unfinished, and ends by promising further adventures.

Camelot (kăm'ĕ lŏt). In the romances of the Middle Ages, the city where King Arthur* held court surrounded by the Knights of the Round* Table. It is sometimes represented as built on a mountain or beside a river. The place has not been identified.

Canaan (kā'năn). An ancient name for the Holy Land, a land "flowing with milk and honey." In literature the name "Canaan" is often applied to heaven.

Canterbury. An ancient town in England about fifty-five miles southeast of London. Thomas à Becket, a distinguished churchman at the court of Henry II (1154–1189), quarreled with the king, and as a result was murdered in the cathedral at Canterbury by four of the king's knights. Henry was blamed for the murder, and Thomas was worshiped as a martyr; that is, as one who had suffered death for Christianity. His tomb at Canterbury was the most famous shrine in medieval England. Hence it was natural that Chaucer should make it the object of the visit of his pilgrims in the *Canterbury Tales*. Thomas is the "holy blisful martir" referred to in line 17 of the Prologue. Canterbury, its beautiful cathedral, and Thomas à Becket are often alluded to in literature.

Cassiopeia (kăs ĭ ŏ pē'yà). In classical mythology, a beautiful queen of Ethiopia. She boasted that she was fairer than the sea nymphs and was punished for the sacrilege; but as a compensation she was "starred," that is, turned into a constellation (group of stars).

Cavalier. One of the court party in the time of Charles I. The Cavaliers favored the royal family of the Stewarts and hence were opposed to the adherents of Parliament, including the Puritans. They are sometimes referred to as Royalists.* After the dethronement of James II (p. 213) those in favor of the Stewart succession became known as Jacobites.* The Cavalier Poets were seventeenth-century English poets whose works reflect the gay and frivolous life of the court of Charles I. Among the best-known are Herrick and Lovelace.

Caxton, William (1422–1491). The first English printer. He learned the art of printing on the Continent, and then set up the first English printing-press in Westminster, in 1476. He printed numerous early English books.

Celestial City. The city to which Christian is journeying in Bunyan's *Pilgrim's Progress*. Allegorically* it stands for heaven. See also "Zion."*

Cephalus (sĕf'à lŭs). In Greek mythology, a beautiful youth of Attica who was fond of hunting and who was beloved by Aurora.* He accidentally slew his wife Procris while hunting.

Cerberus (sûr'bĕr ŭs). In classical mythology, a dog, usually described as three-headed, with a serpent's tail. It lived in a cave on the bank of the river Styx* and guarded the entrance to the land of the dead.

Cervantes (sĕr văn'tēz) (1547–1616). A celebrated Spanish writer. His famous romance entitled *Don Quixote* (dŏn kwĭk'sŏt or, *Spanish pronunciation*, dŏn kĕ hō'tā) satirizes* the high-flown knightly romances (p. 32) which were widely read in his day. The hero of the book is a kindly, middle-aged country gentleman whose brain is slightly addled by a too enthusiastic reading of romances. He tries to imitate the exploits of the knights of old in a very cold and practical modern world, and as a result gets into many amusing and ridiculous scrapes. The book made all Europe laugh, and attained such enduring fame that Don Quixote and his inimitable squire, Sancho Panza (săng'kō păn'zà or, *Spanish pronunciation*, sän'chō pän'thä), are still well known to many thousands of readers.

Charlemagne (shär'lĕ mān) (742?–814). Charles the Great. A famous king of medieval France and emperor of the vast territory afterward called the Holy Roman Empire. He was crowned emperor at Rome on Christmas Day in the year 800. As emperor he ruled over a large part of Europe. He did much to spread the teachings of the Church and was a great patron of learning, gathering many learned men from England and Ireland to his court, which thus became a center of art, science, and literature. Many romances and epics (see pages 32 and 18) were written about his exploits and those of his **Twelve** Peers, or warriors.

Charles I. King of England from 1625 to 1648. He became involved in a long dispute with Parliament over various questions of sovereignty, or royal rights. For eleven years he ruled without Parliament, meeting the expenses of government by forced loans and other illegal measures. He also offended many of his subjects, including the Puritans and the Scottish Presbyterians, by his religious intolerance as well as by his highhanded and autocratic methods of government. As a result the Civil War broke out. In 1642 Charles left London, and the four years' war between him and Parliament began. After he was made a prisoner he induced a Scottish army to invade England. Since Scotland was legally a foreign country, he was tried for treason, and was beheaded in 1649. The name of Oliver Cromwell* is third among the signers of his death warrant. Charles I was one of the Stewarts.*

Charon (kā′rŏn). In classical mythology, the son of Erebus (Nether Gloom) and Nox (Night). It was his duty to ferry the souls of the dead over the Styx* and the Acheron,* rivers in the lower world. In payment for this service he received a small coin, which had been placed in the mouth of the corpse.

cherubs (chĕr′ŭbz). In the Old Testament, winged spirits who attend upon Jehovah (God). The English plural of "cherub" is "cherubs"; the Hebrew plural, "cherubim." Among the heavenly beings the cherubim are the highest in rank except the seraphim (seraphs). Since they dwell very close to God, the source of all knowledge, they are often spoken of as examples of almost perfect wisdom. In painting and sculpture cherubs are generally represented as beautiful children or as children's heads with wings.

Cicero (sĭs′ĕr ō), **Marcus Tullius (106 B.C.–43 B.C.).** The greatest orator of ancient Rome, and one of her most illustrious statesmen and men of letters. He is famous for his eloquence, and his orations have been a model of polished style from his own day to the present.

Cimmerian (sĭ mēr′ĭ ăn). In Greek mythology, the Cimmerians were a people who lived in a land of perpetual mist and darkness, where the sun never shone. Hence "Cimmerian" is used in literature to mean "very dark and gloomy."

coffeehouses. Places of refreshment which served the same purpose in London during the late seventeenth and early eighteenth centuries as the taverns (see "Mer-

maid* Tavern") had done in Shakespeare's day and as clubhouses do now. The famous London coffeehouses, such as Will's, were open to all who could buy a cup of coffee; but each was frequented by a special group of visitors who were interested in some one subject, such as politics or literature. By acting as centers for discussion and the formation of popular opinion, they served somewhat the same purpose as our newspapers. The coffeehouses lost their importance late in the eighteenth century. (See also pages 515–516.)

Colmekill (kŏ′lŭm kĭl). A church on the island of Hy (Iona), off the west coast of Scotland, where many kings were buried. It is named for its founder, Columbkille (Saint Columba), the sixth-century Irish apostle to Scotland (see page 10).

Colossus (kō lŏs′ŭs). A gigantic statue, especially the Colossus of Rhodes, a huge bronze statue of Apollo on the island of Rhodes, in the eastern Mediterranean. It was one of the ancient Seven Wonders of the World. According to tradition it was more than a hundred feet tall and was placed at the mouth of a harbor, with one foot on each pier, or mole, so that ships under full sail passed between its legs. It was overthrown by an earthquake in 224 B.C.

conceit. In literature, an ingenious expression intended to be striking or poetical, but in many cases far-fetched or inappropriate. Conceits were apparently admired during the late sixteenth century and most of the seventeenth, but today many of them seem to us merely examples of bad taste. A seventeenth-century poet calls the weeping eyes of a saint

Two walking baths, two weeping motions,
Portable and compendious oceans.

It would be hard to find a more striking example of bad taste, and hence bad poetry, than these two lines. The trouble here, as with most conceits, is that the imagery,* instead of making the matter clearer, is so odd that it startles and offends the reader, and obscures the picture.

Cossack (kŏs′ăk). A name applied to certain military tribes living in southern and eastern Russia. The Cossacks are skillful and daring horsemen, and possess great strength and courage. They have often been employed as cavalry in the Russian armies.

couplet. Two consecutive rhyming lines. If the sense is completed at the end of the second line, the couplet is said to be closed. Pope was fond of using the closed couplet, but later poets often preferred couplets in which the sense continues without a break into the next line. The first line of such couplets is often referred to as "a run-on" line.

Covent (kŭv′ĕnt) **Garden.** A name applied to two places important in London life during the late seventeenth century and the eighteenth: (1) A square in London famous during the period for its taverns and coffee-houses* and for the fashionable people who gathered there. A part of the square was also used as a fruit and vegetable market till early in the nineteenth century. The space occupied by the square was once the garden of a convent; hence the name "Covent Garden." (2) A famous London theater. The original building was erected in 1731, but has been rebuilt several times. Many noted actors, including David Garrick,* the friend of Goldsmith and a member of the Literary* Club, have played in Covent Garden Theater.

cricket. An English outdoor game played with bats, ball, wickets, etc. between two sides of eleven players each.

Crimean (krī mē′ăn) **War.** A war (1854–1856) in which Russia fought against France, England, and Turkey. The cause of the war was the struggle of the Russians for free access to the Mediterranean and the determination of her opponents to prevent her from getting it. The war was marked by desperate fighting and terrible bloodshed on both sides. Among its most important events were the siege of Sebastopol and the battle of Balaklava, in 1854.

Cromwell, Oliver (1599–1658). A famous English Puritan leader. At the time of the rebellion against King Charles* I in 1642, Cromwell joined the army opposed to the king. He rose rapidly in power. After the death of the king and the establishment of the Commonwealth he became Lord Protector of England, Scotland, and Ireland, a position which he held until his death, ten years later. He showed that he was a great statesman by the moderation and tact with which he handled the perplexing problems of religion, government, and diplomacy that confronted England at that time.

crusaders. See "Crusades."*

Crusades. The Crusades were expeditions undertaken during the medieval period by the Christians of Europe for the purpose of recovering the Holy Land from the Mohammedans. There were several crusades. The first took place in 1096–1099. The Third Crusade (1189–1192) should be remembered

because one of its leaders was King Richard the Lionhearted of England. Of the thousands of soldiers who took part in the Crusades many were killed in battle or died of disease, but many returned, bringing with them marvelous tales that enriched the literature of England and the Continent. Numerous medieval romances and, later, several of Scott's novels, including *Ivanhoe* and *The Talisman*, tell of the Crusades, and many less well-known literary works owe their charm to plots in which brave knights leave wife or sweetheart and die fighting for the Cross in far-off Palestine, or return after years of privation and hardship to find the loved one at the altar about to become the bride of another.

Culloden (kŭ lŏd′ĕn *or* kŭ lō′dĕn). A famous battlefield in northern Scotland, where, in 1746, the army of Charles Edward Stewart, the Young Pretender,* was overwhelmed by the English army under the Duke of Cumberland. Because of the completeness of the defeat and the harsh measures adopted by Cumberland after the battle, the name "Culloden" suggests a national disaster.

Cupid (Greek **Eros**). In Roman mythology, the god of love, the son of Venus.* He is usually represented as a beautiful winged boy armed with a bow and a quiver full of arrows. His arrows are of two kinds: some are golden, and kindle love in the heart they wound; others are leaden, and cause dislike. His eyes are sometimes represented as covered, so that he acts blindly. He is often referred to as the little blind god. He is guilty of many tricks, some of which are cruel. He is sometimes represented as riding on a lion or a dolphin. He is the personification of love between man and woman.

curfew. A bell formerly rung at evening as a signal to the people that all fires must be covered and all lights extinguished.

Cyclops (sī′klŏps) ("Round-eye"). The proper form of the singular is "Cyclops"; of the plural, "Cyclopes" (sī klō′pēz). In Greek mythology, the Cyclopes were a race of giants who had but one eye, large and round, in the middle of the forehead. According to Homer they were gigantic and lawless shepherds who devoured human beings. (See "Ulysses and the Cyclops" in the revised edition of *Adventure* of this series.) According to other writers they were gigantic blacksmiths who lived under volcanoes, especially Mt. Etna in Sicily, and forged armor for gods and heroes.

Cynthia (sĭn′thĭ à). A name for the moon goddess, Diana, from her birthplace on Mt.

Cynthus, situated in one of the Greek islands. Milton speaks of her as riding in a chariot drawn by dragons, whereas according to mythology it was Ceres (see "Proserpine"*) who was drawn by dragons.

dactyl (dăk'tĭl). A poetical foot* of three syllables, one accented syllable followed by two unaccented syllables, as in "happily." The dactyl is chiefly important because dactylic hexameter* is the great measure of ancient classical epic poetry. Dactylic hexameter is not suitable for English, which is heavy with consonants.

dactylic. See "dactyl."*

Dante Alighieri (dän'tā ä lē gyâ'rē) **(1265–1321).** The greatest poet of Italy. His famous epic, *La Divina Commedia* (lä dē-vē'nä kŏm mě'dyä) (*The Divine Comedy*), gives him a place among the greatest poets of the world. The poem is a description of a journey through hell (see Inferno*), purgatory, and paradise, interspersed with comments on politics, religion, etc. It was the first great piece of literature to be written in the Italian language. Dante's name is frequently coupled with that of Beatrice, a lady whose beauty and goodness are celebrated in *La Vita Nuova* (lä vē'tä nwô'vä) (*The New Life*) and in part of *The Divine Comedy*.

Darius (dà rī'ŭs). A title given to several rulers of the ancient Persian Empire, especially to the following : (1) Darius III, the last king of Persia, who was defeated by Alexander* the Great in 331 B.C. While fleeing from Alexander he was abandoned by his friends and murdered. (2) Darius I, the great organizer of the Persian Empire, who reigned from 521 B.C. to 486 (?) B.C. To defend Persia against the wild tribes of the northern plains he led an army into Europe and across the Danube, expecting to take those tribes in the rear. During his reign began the wars between Persia and Greece; it was his army that was beaten in the famous battle of Marathon, 490 B.C.

David. The second and greatest of the ancient kings of Israel. In his youth he was a shepherd. He was invited to court to soothe the ailing king, Saul, by playing on his harp. While visiting the Hebrew army, he killed the Philistine giant, Goliath, with a stone from his sling (read 1 Samuel 17, or see the revised edition of *Adventure* of this series). When he was king, he extended the power of the Hebrews and refined their religious worship. He is noted as a warrior and as a musi-

cian. The Psalms are ascribed to him. He is often referred to as the "Royal Bard"* and as the "Sweet Singer of Israel." Literature also contains many references to the friendship between David and Jonathan, who loved David "as he loved his own soul."

Diana (Greek **Artemis** (är'tě mǐs)). In classical mythology, the twin sister of Apollo.* In art she is usually represented as tall and athletic, and armed with a bow, quiver, and arrows. She became the goddess of the chase, the huntress among the immortals. She is sometimes represented as accompanied by fawns or riding in a chariot drawn by stags. She was generally unmoved by love; but in later accounts she was identified with the goddess of the moon, who had a lover, Endymion. She sent plagues and sudden death, but she was also the protectress of wild animals, of women, and of children.

Douay. Douay (*or* Douai) (dōō ā') and Reims (rēmz, *or, in French,* răNs) are towns in France, where the Douay Bible, an English version translated from the Latin Vulgate, was published. The New Testament appeared at Reims in 1582 ; the Old Testament, at Douay in 1609–1610.

dryad (drī'ăd). In classical mythology, a nymph, or beautiful supernatural maiden, supposed to reside in trees and to preside over woods. Each tree, or at least each large tree, had its own dryad, who came into being with the tree and watched over its existence. The dryads were thought of as being exceedingly shy.

Duessa (dŭ ěs'à). An evil female character who is the enemy of the Faerie Queene in Spenser's *Faerie Queene*. Disguised as Fidessa, a young and beautiful woman, she nearly causes the ruin of the Redcross Knight, but is put to shame by Arthur. In literature Duessa appears as the personification of falsehood.

Dumferling (dŭm fěr'lǐng) **toune.** Dunfermline (dŭn fěrm'lǐn), a town in Scotland about fifteen miles from Edinburgh. Its fame is due to the fact that it was once a royal residence.

Eden. According to the Bible, the garden in which God placed Adam* and Eve.* God commanded them not to eat of the fruit of the "tree of the knowledge of good and evil." Eve, tempted by the serpent, ate of the fruit and gave some to Adam, "and he did eat." For this sin Adam and Eve were driven out of the Garden of Eden and never allowed to return (see Genesis 3). As the result of the Biblical tradition the term "Eden" has been often used to apply to any place where men are supposed to lead idyllic* lives under ideal conditions.

elegy. A lyric poem of a mournful or plaintive character, often on the death of some person. It ranges all the way from a single stanza on a tombstone (an epitaph) to such longer laments as Milton's "Lycidas," in which the poet's grief is expressed in the manner of a pastoral,* and Tennyson's *In Memoriam,* which may be regarded as a series of elegies mingled with other sorts of lyric poetry. In general the term "elegy" may be applied to any serious poem expressing gentle sadness as opposed to grief; for example, Gray's "Elegy," where the poet merely expresses his melancholy feelings concerning the lowly dead in the churchyard.

Elia (ē'lǐ à). The name of an Italian clerk who had formerly worked in the South Sea House, London, where Charles Lamb was for a time employed. Lamb whimsically adopted it as his own pen name when he began, in 1820, a series of essays which he called *Essays of Elia.*

Elysian. See "Elysium."*

Elysium (ē lǐzh'ǐ ŭm). In classical mythology, a place where winter never comes, and where favored heroes repose in bliss forever. Elysium was later thought of as a part of the lower world, the abode of the blessed dead. The Elysian Fields are sometimes said to be the same as the Islands of the Blessed, the Fortunate Islands, or the Happy* Isles, which poets placed in the Atlantic Ocean. The myth probably helped to inspire the idea of Atlantis, a mythical island in the Atlantic Ocean, where the inhabitants were said to have lived under ideal conditions.

epigram. A short saying in prose or verse, treating of only one thing, and expressing in witty or pointed language some striking or ingenious thought, such as "A little learning is a dangerous thing," "The child is father of the man." Many epigrammatic expressions are humorous or satirical.*

epigrammatic. See "epigram."*

Esau (ē'sô). In the Bible, the elder twin brother of Jacob,* and an unsettled and improvident hunter and rover. Coming from the fields hungry, he sold his birthright (right to inherit the headship of the family) to Jacob* for a mess of pottage (stew or thick soup) (Genesis 25 : 29–34). In literature his name frequently stands for barbarism or for unsuspecting honesty, as contrasted with sophisticated and suspicious civilized life.

Euphrates (û frā'tēz). A large river in Asia. It rises south of the Black Sea and flows southeast into the Persian Gulf. In the Bible (Genesis 15 : 18) it is referred to as the "great river."

Euphrosyne. See "Graces."*

euphuism (ū'fū ǐz'm). An affected style of writing popular in Shakespeare's day and named from Euphues (ū'fū ēz), the hero of a prose romance of the same name by John Lyly* (1554–1606), who did much to make euphuism popular. Its chief characteristics are an excessive use of antithesis and alliteration,* far-fetched similes and other conceits,* comparisons drawn from mythology and false natural history, and balanced constructions, as in the following: "Achilles' spear could as well heal as hurt; the scorpion though he sting, yet he stints the pain; though the herb Nerius poison the sheep, yet is a remedy to man against poison."

Euripides (û rǐp'ǐ dēz) **(484?–406 B.C.).** One of the three great ancient Athenian tragic poets. Although he is usually regarded as less great than Aeschylus* or Sophocles,* he was the product of the new Athens (the great intellectual center after the Persian War), and thus his dramas are extremely significant. Nearly twenty of his plays have come down to us.

Eurydice (û rǐd'ǐ sē). In classical mythology, the beloved wife of Orpheus.*

Eve. According to the Bible, the first woman created by God (see "Adam"*).

evil, the (the king's evil). Scrofula, called the king's evil because it was supposed to be healed by the touch of a king. Many kings have claimed the power of healing the evil by a touch. Among them were the English kings Edward the Confessor (ruled 1042–1066), James I (ruled 1603–1625), and Charles II (ruled 1660–1685). When Shakespeare, in *Macbeth,* represents Edward as touching for the king's evil, the audience at once thought of James I, the king who sat on the throne when the play was first given and who was proud of exercising his gift. The reference is therefore Shakespeare's compliment to the reigning sovereign.

Faustus. A character about whom there gathered during the fifteenth century a series of tales which credited him with the ability to perform great wonders by the help of evil spirits. The story is that he sold his soul to the devil in exchange for magic power. He is known in literature chiefly through Marlowe's *Doctor Faustus* and through Goethe's

Faust. The character of Faust is often used as a symbol of the sacrifice of Christian morality to worldly knowledge.

. **feudalism.** A social and legal system of the Middle Ages in which a person, in return for protection, became the vassal, or tenant, of a more powerful person, who thus became his lord. The vassal held his land by grant from his lord, and in return owed his lord homage and was obliged to render him military or other service as required.

Fielding, Henry (1707–1754). An important English playwright and novelist. His first success in the field of the novel came with the publication of *Joseph Andrews* (1742). This work was in part a burlesque* on *Pamela* (păm'ĕ là), a sentimental novel by Samuel Richardson.* The most famous of Fielding's works is *Tom Jones* (1749), which, both in plot and in characterization, is one of the best examples of the realistic novel ever written. His play *Tom Thumb the Great* is a successful burlesque on the more bombastic tragedies of the Age of Classicism.

Flora. In Roman mythology, the goddess of flowers and spring.

Florence. A city in Italy noted for its great collections of art and for the many famous artists and writers who have lived there. It took a leading part in the Renaissance.

foot. In poetry a division of a line, consisting of a group of syllables one of which is accented more strongly than the others. The most common type of foot used in English poetry is the iambus.* Other important feet are the trochee,* dactyl,* and anapaest.*

Friday. In Defoe's *Robinson Crusoe*, a black man whom Robinson Crusoe rescued from cannibals and educated. He became Robinson Crusoe's willing slave and constant attendant. Robinson Crusoe gave him the name of the day, Friday, on which the rescue took place. The term "man Friday" has come to mean valet, or personal attendant.

Furies. Also called Eumenides (û mĕn'-ĭ dēz) and Erinyes (ê rĭn'ĭ ēz). In classical mythology, avenging deities who pursue wrongdoers and drive them into misery and misfortune. Some writers limit their number to three and call them Tisiphone (tĭ sĭf'ŏ nĕ) (the Avenger), Alecto (the Unresting), and Megaera (mĕ jē'rȧ) (the Jealous). They were frightful in appearance, being represented as winged women clad in black garments, with serpents in their hair and with blood dripping from their eyes. In Dryden's "Alexander's Feast" the reference to the Furies implies that revenge is sought for the Greek soldiers slain by the Persians.

Garrick, David (1717–1779). A distinguished English dramatist, producer, and actor. He performed successfully both in Dublin and in London. He was remarkably versatile, being as gifted in farce and comedy as in tragedy. His repertory, which was very large, included seventeen Shakespearean plays, and he directed even more. He is often mentioned in Boswell's *Life of Johnson*. He is buried in Westminster Abbey, at the foot of the statue of Shakespeare.

Gladstone (glăd'stŭn), **William Ewart (1809–1898).** An eminent British orator and statesman. He was born in England, of Scottish parentage. Throughout his life he was noted for his endurance, industry, oratory, and courage. When he was only twenty-one, he entered Parliament, where his ability was recognized at once. During his career of sixty-one years in the House of Commons, Gladstone served as prime minister four times, an unprecedented record. He also held numerous other important governmental positions. In his early life he was a Conservative; later he became a Liberal, opposed to Disraeli (dĭz-rā'lĭ), who was more in favor with Queen Victoria than he. Gladstone was especially interested in national finance, in educational reforms, in the army, in the civil service, in the colonies, and in Ireland. He was well known as an advocate of Irish home rule. He also stood for liberty in religion and for free trade. Above all, he was the champion of the middle classes. At eighty-nine "the Grand Old Man," as he came to be called, died, and was buried with ceremony in Westminster Abbey. Gladstone had an unusually striking countenance, and his likeness was familiar to all readers of the public press of his day.

golden age. A fabled time in the past when there was no winter season, the earth bore fruit without cultivation, and men lived innocent, idyllic* lives without the need of government. There is also a tradition that during the golden age men lived much longer than they did in later times.

Golden Horn. The magnificent four-mile-long harbor of Constantinople (Istanbul), the inlet of the Bosporus, a strait which connects the Sea of Marmora with the Black Sea. It is called the Golden Horn because of its shape and because of the wealth of the trade that poured through it.

Gorgon. In classical mythology, one of

three sisters, with snaky hair and of terrible aspect, whose look turned the beholder to stone.

Graces. In classical mythology, the three divinities Euphrosyne (û frŏs'ĭ nē) (the Joyous), Aglaia (ȧ glā'yȧ) (the Brilliant), and Thalia (thȧ lī'ȧ) (the Blooming), goddesses of grace and of everything that lent charm and beauty to nature and human life. They were intimate with the Muses,* with whom they lived on Olympus. Sometimes they are spoken of as the daughters of Venus* and Bacchus,* or of Jove* and a goddess. Milton makes Euphrosyne (Joyousness, Mirth) the daughter of the West Wind and the Dawn Goddess.

griffin. A fabulous creature usually represented as having the head, wings, and claws of an eagle and the body and hindquarters of a lion.

Happy Isles (Fortunate Islands, or Islands of the Blessed). In literary tradition, a mythical earthly paradise beyond the sea where men led an idyllic* life. For many centuries European mariners seldom set sail on the Atlantic Ocean without feeling that by some chance they might discover these fabulous islands. According to some accounts these islands were the abode of departed spirits. The life of the inhabitants was much like that of the people of the golden* age. See "Elysium."*

Hebe (hē'bĕ). In Greek mythology, the goddess of youth and spring, originally the cupbearer of the gods. She had the power of restoring the gods to youth and beauty. In literature she often personifies* eternal and joyous youth.

Hebrides (hĕb'rĭ dēz) **(Western Isles).** A group of rocky islands off the northwest coast of Scotland. Until recent times the inhabitants had little contact with the mainland. Wordsworth, in "The Solitary Reaper," imagines that the sound of the cuckoo's call in spring would be especially charming amid such remote, lonely surroundings.

Hecate (hĕk'ȧ tē). In classical mythology, a goddess who is often referred to as the queen of ghosts and witches, being regarded as a deity of night and the lower world. Because of her identification with Diana, the moon goddess, she is sometimes called pale, and because of her identification with Proserpine* she is called black. Witches were said to make sacrifices to her; hence the references to "Hecate's [hĕk'ăts] offerings" (offerings made to Hecate) in *Macbeth*, II, i, 52.

Hector (hĕk'tĕr). In Homer's Iliad* the principal hero on the side of Troy* in the Trojan War. He was the son of Priam and Hecuba (hĕk' û bȧ) and the husband of Andromache (ăn drŏm'ȧ kê). He was killed by the Greek Achilles,* who, in his chariot, dragged Hector's body three times around the walls of Troy. Hector's father, Priam, persuaded Achilles to give back the body, and it was buried with great honor.

Helen. In Greek legend, the fairest of women, the wife of Menelaus (mĕn ĕ lā'ŭs), king of Sparta. Persuaded by Venus,* she eloped to Troy* with Paris,* son of Priam. The chieftains of Greece joined together to make war against Troy and bring Helen back. In literature she is often the symbol* of faithless beauty that causes destruction. Her elopement and the Trojan War form the background of the Iliad.*

Helicon (hĕl'ĭ kŏn). A mountain in Greece from the side of which flows the fountain Hippocrene.* In classical mythology Helicon is the home of Apollo* and the Muses,* and Hippocrene is sacred to them. Both Helicon and Hippocrene have come to be symbols of poetic or literary inspiration.

Hercules (hûr'cû lēz). A hero of Greek mythology, best known for his twelve labors, among the most famous of which are these: cleansing the Augean stables, in which three thousand cattle had been kept for many years; slaying the three-bodied Geryon; obtaining the golden apples from the garden of the Hesperides; and bringing the fierce dog Cerberus* from the lower world. Soon after finishing these tasks he died of poison absorbed from a cloak saturated with the blood of Nessus. "A labor of Hercules," or "a herculean task," has become a synonym for a stupendous piece of work. "Cleansing the Augean stables" has become a synonym for accomplishing a much-needed reform.

Heroic couplet. In poetry two successive iambic* pentameter* lines that rhyme; as,

$$\overset{\times}{\text{Be}} \overset{\prime}{\text{not}} \overset{\times}{\text{the}} \overset{\prime}{\text{first}} \overset{\times}{\text{by}} \overset{\prime}{\text{whom}} \overset{\times}{\text{the}} \overset{\prime}{\text{new}} \overset{\times}{\text{are}} \overset{\prime}{\text{try'd}},$$

$$\overset{\times}{\text{Nor}} \overset{\prime}{\text{yet}} \overset{\times}{\text{the}} \overset{\prime}{\text{last}} \overset{\times}{\text{to}} \overset{\prime}{\text{lay}} \overset{\times}{\text{the}} \overset{\prime}{\text{old}} \overset{\times}{\text{aside}} \text{ (p. 224,}$$
l. 33).

It derives its name from its use, during the Middle Ages, in composing certain kinds of heroic (epic) poetry. It was used frequently in the narrative poetry of Chaucer and of Spenser and in some of the dramatic writing of Shakespeare. During the Age of Classicism (see page 213) it came to be regarded as the accepted form of poetic expression; hence it is the most common meter in the poetry of Dryden, Pope, and other poets of the late seventeenth and early eighteenth centuries.

hexameter (hĕk săm'ĕ tēr). A line of poetry consisting of six feet (see "foot"*). The most common variety of hexameter is known as the dactylic* hexameter, because it is composed mostly of dactyls. The dactylic hexameter is the characteristic measure of Greek and Latin epic poetry.

Hippocrene (hĭp'ō krēn). In Greek mythology, a spring on Mount Helicon* sacred to the Muses.* It was fabled to have burst forth when the ground was struck by the hoof of the winged horse Pegasus.*

Homer. The great epic poet of ancient Greece to whom are ascribed the Iliad* and the Odyssey.* According to tradition he was poor and blind, and traveled from place to place, earning his living by reciting his poems. Seven cities claim to have been his birthplace.

Hours. In classical mythology the Hours (Horae, Seasons) were beautiful maidens, usually presented as three in number, who preside over the seasons, as well as the hours and other divisions of time, and are associated with youth, flowers, and fertility.

humours. According to the old physiology, a person's physical and mental qualities and disposition are determined by the proportions of certain animal fluids in the body. There are, as the old authorities believed, four "cardinal," or principal, humours: choler (kŏl'ēr) (yellow bile), which tends to make one choleric; melancholy (black bile), which tends to make one melancholic; phlegm, which tends to make one phlegmatic; and blood (Latin *sanguis*), which tends to make one sanguine. When no one humour predominates, the person has a well-balanced temperament. The humours were believed to be closely related to the four elements: earth (dry), water (moist), air (cold), and fire (hot). The use of the humours in creating literary characters was popularized by certain Elizabethan dramatists, notably by Ben Jonson in *Every Man in his Humour* and others of his comedies. Jaques, in Shakespeare's *As You Like It*, is a typical "humorous" character. His cynical outlook on life is determined by the fact that melancholy predominates in his system. The term "humour" gradually acquired the meaning of "characteristic peculiarity" or "affectation." It is in the first of these two senses that the word is used by Stevenson.

Hyades (hī'á dēz) (the rain nymphs). Nymphs of moisture and fruitfulness. They nursed the infant Bacchus,* and as a reward were placed among the stars near the head of the constellation of Taurus (the Bull). During the season when they rose at the same time as the sun, rainy weather might be expected.

Hymen (hī'mĕn). In classical mythology, the god of marriage. He is represented as a youth of delicate, girlish beauty, bearing a torch. In literature Hymen is sometimes represented as wearing a saffron robe.

iambic. See "iambus."*

iambic pentameter. A line of poetry consisting of five feet, all or most of which are iambic,* as in x / x / x / x / x /. Most of the lines in Chaucer's *Canterbury Tales*, Spenser's *Faerie Queene*, the verse in Shakespeare's plays, Milton's *Paradise Lost*, Pope's longer poems, and Tennyson's *Idylls of the King* are written in iambic pentameter.* Contrast the iambic with the trochaic* rhythm.* Iambic pentameter is the "heroic meter" of English poetry (see "heroic* couplet").

iambus (ī ăm'bŭs). In poetry an iambus is a foot* consisting of an unaccented syllable followed by an accented syllable, as in "invert," "compel," "accept." The iambic rhythm* is the most common in English poetry.

Ida. (1) A mountain near Troy where Paris, acting as a judge in a contest of beauty between Juno, Minerva, and Venus,* awarded the prize to Venus. In return for this decision Venus promised him the beautiful Helen* of Sparta. Mount Ida often appears in mythology and literature. (2) A lofty mountain in Crete, celebrated as the place where Zeus* was brought up.

idyll. A picturesque story, in prose or verse, describing any sort of simple, ideal life, such as that of the country people in Milton's "L'Allegro" (p. 190); the original inhabitants of "sweet Auburn" in Goldsmith's "Deserted Village" (p. 305); the family described in Burns's "Cotter's Saturday Night" (p. 383); the court of the king of "long ago" described in Browning's "Pippa Passes" (p. 478); and Tennyson's *Idylls of the King*, where even the king is not too great to mingle with his people and where such simple virtues as courage, loyalty, and truth are highly esteemed. Idylls are often associated with pastoral* scenes. Among the most famous early idylls are those of Theocritus* and Vergil.*

idyllic. See "idyll."*

Iliad. A famous epic poem of ancient Greece, attributed to Homer.* It tells of the events of a part of the last year of the siege of Troy* by the Greeks. The Greeks wished to redress the wrong done to Menelaus, king of Sparta, in the abduction of his wife, Helen,* by the Trojan prince Paris. Some of the chief episodes deal with the exploits of the Greek Achilles* and the Trojan Hector.*

imagery (ĭm′ĭj rĭ). In literature, devices by which a writer helps the reader to perceive poetical beauty by speaking of actions, things, moods, feelings, etc. in little pictures. When the dictionary-maker calls a daisy "one of the most familiar wild plants of Europe," he is not trying to make us see the poetical beauty of the flower. When the poet Wordsworth wishes to convey to the reader the poetical beauty which he perceives in the daisy, he allows his imagination to play around the flower and, using imagery, calls it "a nun demure," "a queen in crown of rubies drest," "a silver shield with boss of gold." The second stanza of Wordsworth's "She Dwelt among the Untrodden Ways" (p. 338) is an often-quoted example of imagery. Metaphor* and simile* are kinds of imagery.

Ind (Inde, Ynd). An old name for India, thought of as a far-off land of untold wealth, beauty, and romance.

Inferno. The first part of Dante's* *Divine Comedy*. It describes the visit of the poet, accompanied by Vergil,* to hell, and tells of the various kinds of punishment inflicted upon those who in their earthly lives had been morally weak or wicked.

inn. Early English hotels were called inns. They were usually named from their signs; as, for example, the "Blue Boar," the "Tabard," etc. In Shakespeare's day certain London inns (or taverns), especially the "Mermaid,"* were gathering places for literary men. As such they were succeeded later by coffeehouses,* which in turn were displaced by the modern clubs.

ironical. See "irony."*

irony. A figure of speech in which the meaning is the opposite of what is said. See the sentence beginning "Is not a Patron, my Lord," in Samuel Johnson's letter to Lord Chesterfield (p. 252, l. 44). The term "dramatic irony" is applied to a dramatic situation in which the audience, knowing facts not yet revealed to the characters, sees humor or tragedy of which the characters are unaware.

Jacob. In the Bible, the son of Isaac and Rebekah. With the help of his mother he cheated Esau,* his elder twin brother, out of his birthright. Read Genesis 25 and 27–35. He is spoken of as a "dweller in tents." In literature his name often symbolizes peaceful civilization and trade. In some cases his name suggests wily cunning.

Jacobite (jăk′ŏ bīt). One who favored the dethroned James II, his son (the Old Pretender*), and his grandson (the Young Pretender*) during the dispute over the crown of England in the seventeenth and eighteenth centuries. After William and Mary came to the throne in 1688 the Jacobites were in the minority in England; in Scotland they supported the Old Pretender in 1715, and later the Young Pretender at the battle of Culloden.* "Jacobite" comes from *Jacobus*, the Latin word for "James."

James I. King of England, Scotland, and Ireland from 1603 to 1625. He was also James VI of Scotland and son of Mary* Queen of Scots. At his command the revised translation of the Bible known as the King James Bible was made. It was the work of forty-seven of the most learned scholars available and was completed in 1611. The result was one of the finest pieces of English prose ever produced. Because of its simple yet dignified language, its clearness and simplicity of style, and its exalted subject, it has exercised a profound influence upon English prose composition and English thought.

John of Austria, Don. A celebrated Spanish general, son of Charles V (king of Spain under the title of "Charles I") and half brother to Philip II of Spain. On October 7, 1571, he attacked and decisively defeated a Turkish fleet on the west coast of Greece, near Lepanto.

Jove (Jupiter, Zeus). In classical mythology, the chief of all the gods, and ruler of the world. He was especially a divinity of the sky. He sent the rain, and his weapon was the thunderbolt. He was also the father of justice and law. Many great heroes of ancient Greece and Rome, both mortal and immortal, are said to be his sons by temporary alliances with mortal women. He often visited the earth in the form of a bull, dragon, swan, or some other animal. He was the son of the Titan* Cronus, whom he succeeded. As Cronus became identified with Saturn,* the ancient Roman god of culture and of the golden age, Milton represents Melancholy as being the daughter of the god of culture and as having been born in an age before the coming of sin and of Jove, the avenger of sin.

Jubilee, Diamond. The celebration in 1897 of Queen Victoria's sixty years as queen. It was celebrated in all parts of the empire. Representatives of the colonies came to England to pay homage to the queen. The significance of the widespread empire was manifest in the celebrations.

Jupiter. See "Jove."*

Knox, John (1505–1572). A stern, serious writer, preacher, and leader of the Reformation (p. 71) in Scotland, especially concerned with the organization of the Presbyterian Church. He opposed the Roman Catholic sympathies of Mary* Queen of Scots, whom he frequently, often dramatically, encountered. Knox's pulpit is one of the prized relics of the University of St. Andrews.

Kubla Khan (kōō′bla kän′) **(Kublai** (kōō′-blī) **Khan) (1216?–1294).** A great medieval emperor of the Mongol dynasty in China. He ruled not only China but also large portions of northern, southern, and western Asia and of Russia. Coleridge was reading Purchas's account of Kublai Khan's magnificent palace and gardens when he fell asleep and composed his famous poem.

Lancelot (Launcelot du Lac (dü lăk′), **"Lancelot of the Lake").** One of the most famous of King Arthur's* knights. Several medieval romances deal with his exploits. He received the name "du Lac" because, according to the oldest accounts, he was reared by a fairy woman who lived at the bottom of a lake. The main features of the romances about him are his guilty love for Guinevere and the war with Arthur in which he consequently became involved. He was the father of Sir Galahad.

laureate (lô′rê āt). The poet laureate of Great Britain is a poet appointed by the British government to give poetic expression to any great national event, such as a military victory or the death of a statesman.

Legion. Used, in Mark 5:9, not as the name of a devil, but to designate a group of devils whom Jesus cast out of a certain man and allowed to go into a herd of swine. The swine immediately ran down a precipice and were drowned. When Jesus asked the devil his name, the devil replied, "My name is Legion: for we are many." It was as if the devil had said, "You may call me Multitude, for there are many of us."

Leonardo da Vinci (lä ō när′dō dä vēn′-chē) **(1452–1519).** One of the greatest artists of Italy. He was a painter, musician, architect, sculptor, scientist, and inventor.

Lethe (lē′thē). The personification* of forgetfulness. In classical mythology it is also the name of a river in Hades, the abode of the dead. The souls of the departed drank of its water and thus forgot their former existence. "Lethe" does not mean "river," but "forgetfulness"; hence the expression "waters of oblivion."

Lister, Joseph. Sir Joseph Lister (1827–1912), a celebrated English surgeon, noted especially as the introducer of modern antiseptic methods in surgery. He was professor at King's College, London. He was created a baron in 1897.

Literary Club, the. A club formed by Samuel Johnson and others in 1764. It is still in existence, and has numbered among its members some of the most famous literary men of England. In Johnson's day its membership included James Boswell, the biographer of Johnson; David Garrick,* the actor; Sir Joshua Reynolds, the painter; Edmund Burke,* the orator; Oliver Goldsmith, the poet; and others.

Lucifer. A name applied to Satan. According to one tradition he was one of the brightest angels of heaven; but he rebelled against God and was cast down into hell. This is the tradition used by Milton in *Paradise Lost* (p. 240).

Lyly (lĭl′ĭ), **John (1554–1606).** A dramatist and fiction-writer of the Elizabethan Period. His best-known work is a long, wandering prose romance entitled *Euphues*, from which the style known as "euphuism"* is named. Lyly's comedies contain much clever, witty dialogue that served as a model for Shakespeare's early work.

Mab. In folklore, a mischievous but helpful fairy. Shakespeare, in *Romeo and Juliet* (I, iv, 53–92), calls her Queen Mab, and represents her as a mischievous, teasing sprite. Milton, in "L'Allegro," refers to her as eating the country dainties set out by the peasants to enlist her favor. In a mask by Ben Jonson she is said, like Robin Goodfellow, to help with the churning, to punish lazy housemaids and dairymaids, and to steal children.

Maenad (mē′năd). In ancient Greece one of the frenzied women who celebrated the rites of Dionysus (Bacchus*); a bacchante. "Maenad" means "madwoman."

Mahound (ma hound′). An old name for "Mohammed."*

Marlborough. John Churchill (1650–1722), first Duke of Marlborough, a famous English general and statesman. In 1692 he was imprisoned for Jacobite* activities; but he was soon pardoned and, to outward appearance, gave up the cause of the exiled Stewarts. He became a distinguished leader in the War of the Spanish Succession, which was opposed by the Tories* but was favored by the Whigs.* In his campaigns against the French he either won or helped to win several great battles, including Blenheim (pp. 217 and 221) and Malplaquet (p. 455, note 1, column 1). When the English people finally became weary of the war, Queen Anne appointed ministers of state who shared the popular feeling. As a result Marlborough lost his command and became apparently a Whig,* though he still favored the moderate Tories.* In spite of his many services to his country his old age was lonely and friendless.

Mary Queen of Scots. Mary Stewart* (1542–1587), only daughter of James V of Scotland, whom she succeeded on the throne. She married the heir to the throne of France, but on his death she returned to Scotland. She later was married twice, the first time to Lord Darnley, who was afterward murdered. On the death of Mary I ("Bloody Queen Mary") of England, she laid claim to the English throne, thereby incurring the enmity of the English. She was at last forced to resign the crown in favor of her son, afterward James VI of Scotland and James* I of England. She fled to England but was seized and imprisoned. She was later tried on the charge of conspiracy against Elizabeth, and was beheaded in 1587. She is one of the most romantic figures in the history of British royalty.

mask. A play accompanied by music and characterized by elaborate scenery and gorgeous settings, in which the characters represent fairies, gods, or demons, or abstract qualities such as mercy, truth, patriotism, etc. The purpose is often to present an idea rather than a story; for example, the triumph of virtue over vice. Masks were especially popular during the Elizabethan Period.

masque. See "mask."*

Mendelssohn-Bartholdy (mĕn′dĕl sŏn-bär tŏl′dĭ), **Jakob Ludwig Felix (1809–1847).** A famous German-Jewish musician and composer. He made his first public appearance at nine, and began to compose before he was twelve. When he was only sixteen he performed in Paris and, soon afterward, in England. He made nine more visits to England, where he became extremely popular. According to some authorities, he was as im-

portant as Handel in his influence on English music. He was a gifted conductor, reverent toward music as an art and toward the work of earlier composers. He composed between one hundred and two hundred works. *Elijah* is his most famous oratorio. The incidental music to *A Midsummer Night's Dream* is often considered to be his greatest work.

Merlin. According to medieval tradition, an ancient British prophet and magician, the friend and adviser of King Arthur.* His father was a demon. He became infatuated with the beautiful and unscrupulous Vivian (or Nimue) and taught her his magic. The accounts of his death vary. According to some stories Vivian met him in a romantic forest and beguiled him under a rock, where she shut him up by magic; according to others she entangled him in the branches of a thorn bush, where he still lies surrounded by a magic spell. According to still others, he disappeared during a storm. In any case, Merlin, as the result of his love affair with Vivian, may be said to have paid his debt to the demon from whom he derived his magic powers. Faustus,* we recall, also paid his debt to a demon.

Mermaid Tavern. A famous inn* in the London of Shakespeare's day. Here a company (what we now call a club) of literary men used to meet; many of them became famous.

metaphor (mĕt′à fẽr). In rhetoric, a figure of speech in which, for the purpose of emphasizing a particular quality, one thing is said to be something else which is well known for that quality. In the sentence "Adversity is the grindstone of life," adversity is compared to a grindstone because it is hard and rough and sharpens men. An extended metaphor is given in Psalm 23 (p. 163).

metaphorical. See "metaphor."*

metonymy (mê tŏn′ĭ mĭ). A figure of speech in which a word is put for another which it suggests. "Ophirs of fabulous ore" means places of great wealth, Ophir being a country referred to in the Bible as famous for its gold. "This dish is for you" means not the dish, but what is in it. "Do you like the theater?" means not the theater, but the plays given there.

minstrel. A singer and musician of the Middle Ages who traveled from place to place entertaining people with songs and ballads of love and war. He usually accompanied himself on the harp or the lute. Some minstrels were attached to the courts of kings or nobles.

Mohammed (mȯ hăm'ĕd). The founder of a religious system known as Mohammedanism or Islam (ĭs'lȧm). Its profession of faith is "There is no god but God, and Mohammed is God's messenger." Christians have often assumed that Mohammedans regard Mohammed, since his death, as a sort of secondary god possessing heavenly power or influence. There are various forms of the name "Mohammed."

monasteries. See "monastery."*

monastery. A religious establishment inhabited by monks (or friars), who spend their time in religious devotions and in work profitable to mankind, such as study, missionary work, and agriculture. See "monk."*

monk. The monks of the Middle Ages were men who, in order to escape temptation, formed themselves into societies, or orders, and shut themselves off from the world, living in accordance with a strict rule, or discipline. One of the oldest monastic rules, that of Saint Benedict, was brought to England about the time of the coming of Augustine the missionary in 597. The monks frequently conducted a school for the children of the community surrounding the monastery. They spent much time in copying books; some of the most beautiful manuscripts that have come down to us were written by monks. They were also great farmers. They cleared land, worked out better methods of fertilizing and tilling the soil, and improved the breeds of livestock. Chaucer's Monk was one of the men of business of his monastery. Besides being head of a "cell," or branch establishment, he was appointed to ride out and inspect the farms and other property belonging to his monastery.

Morpheus (môr'fūs or, more commonly, môr'fê ŭs). In classical mythology, the god of dreams. Popularly regarded as the god of sleep also.

Muses. In classical mythology, the goddesses who presided over song, the different kinds of poetry, and the other arts, and over the sciences. Clio was the Muse of history, Melpomene of tragedy, Thalia of comedy, Euterpe of music, Terpsichore of the dance, Polymnia of sacred lyric poetry, Erato of love poetry, Calliope of epic poetry and eloquence, and Urania of astronomy. They lived either on Mount Parnassus* or on Mount Olympus,* the dwelling place of the gods. See also Helicon* and Hippocrene.* In Milton's "Il Penseroso" they are thought of as singing around the altar of Jove,* who was their father. In literature the term "the Muses" is often used for poetic inspiration in general.

Nansen (nän'sĕn), **Fridtjof (1861–1930).** Norwegian arctic explorer, who went first to the Far North to observe arctic life there. His greatest expedition began in 1893, when he set out from Siberia in the *Fram*, a ship whose sides, two feet thick, were specially sloped to slip out of the ice when it pinched them. Nansen's hope of floating with the ice across the North Pole to Greenland was fulfilled. During the three years he was gone, he penetrated to within 272 miles of the pole, the farthest north anyone had succeeded in reaching at that time. Nansen was for years professor of zoology, and later of oceanography, at the University of Christiania (Oslo). He wrote several books on his explorations and on his favorite subject, oceanography. He was keenly interested in national and international affairs. During the World War (1914–1918) he was especially concerned over the plight of famine-stricken Russia. It was Nansen who aroused Herbert Hoover and, through him, the United States, to come to her aid. At one time he was Norwegian delegate to the League of Nations. When, in 1923, he was awarded the Nobel peace prize, he gave it to the model farms and demonstration estates in Russia.

Napoleon (1769–1821). A Corsican soldier whose astounding military and political achievements made him the most famous person of the modern world. In 1793 he was merely an officer in the French artillery. In 1804 he was emperor of France, and by 1807 he had subjugated nearly all Europe. He lost his power and was exiled; but in ten months he returned and regained his former position, only to go down in defeat before the allied armies at Waterloo,* in 1815. He died in exile on the island of St. Helena.

Nebuchadnezzar (nĕb û kȧd nĕz'ēr). A powerful king of Babylon* (about 600 B.C.), who carried off many Hebrews into captivity, destroyed their Temple, and seized its sacred vessels (see "Babylonish* Captivity"). As a punishment, according to the Bible, he "was driven from men, and did eat grass as oxen" (see Daniel 4 : 33).

Nemesis (nĕm'ê sĭs). An ancient goddess. She represented righteous anger and vengeance of the gods. The term has come to mean unavoidable penalty, inevitable result.

Neptune (nĕp'tūn) (also **Poseidon** (pȯ sī'dȯn)). In classical mythology, god of the seas; hence, often in literature, the sea.

Nereids (nē'rĕ ĭdz). In classical mythology, the daughters of Nereus. The Nereids were sea nymphs.* The chief of them, Thetis, was the mother of Achilles.*

Nineveh (nĭn'ĕ vĕ). The ancient capital of Assyria, destroyed by the Medes in 612 B.C. It was once a great and powerful city. Nothing remains now but two great mounds. The name is sometimes used in literature to suggest fallen grandeur.

Niobe (nī'ō bē). In Greek mythology, the daughter of Tantalus and wife of Amphion, king of Thebes. Proud of her numerous children, she compared herself to Leto (Latona), who had only two, Artemis (Diana*) and Apollo. To punish Niobe for her pride, Artemis and Apollo slew her children. Zeus turned her to stone, but she continued to weep for her children. In literature she often appears as the personification* of tearful sorrow.

Nottingham (or **Nottinghamshire**). A county in the north midland district of England. It contains the remains of Sherwood Forest, the traditional haunt of Robin* Hood and his merry men.

nun. Chaucer's Nun is a prioress; that is, the head of a convent. She is also the head of the convent school. As a model to her pupils, she cultivates exceedingly refined and ladylike manners, and speaks French. Chaucer does not, however, make fun of either her manners or her French accent. He simply means that she spoke French of the kind spoken at the large convent school situated at a place called Stratford-atte-Bowe.

nymph. In classical mythology, minor female divinities who presided over various objects in nature. The dryads* were associated with trees and forests; the Nereids,* with the sea; the oreads,* with mountains; etc.

objective. In literature, treating persons or things as they are rather than as interpreted by the reflections or feelings of the writer.

ode. The name "ode" may be applied to any lyric poem that is exalted in tone and deals with a single dignified theme. Two types of English odes should be remembered: (1) A few English odes are written in an elaborate but regular verse form imitated from the odes composed by the ancient Greek poet Pindar, and hence are called Pindaric. (2) The more common type, often known simply as English, is irregular in the arrangement and length of the lines and in the use of rhymes. Dryden's "Alexander's Feast" and Wordsworth's ode "Intimations of Immortality" are among the best English odes in our literature. Odes written for a particular occasion, such as the odes of Dryden, are called "occasional odes." Many odes were composed for singing.

Odyssey. A famous epic poem of ancient Greece. It celebrates the adventures of Odysseus (Ulysses*) during ten years of wandering, in repeated efforts to return to Ithaca, his native island, after the close of the Trojan War. The Odyssey contains many episodes describing Odysseus' thrilling experiences with giants, enchantresses, and strange people.

Olympus (ō lĭm'pŭs). A name applied in ancient times to several different mountains in Greece and Asia Minor. Olympus in Thessaly (northeastern Greece), 10,000 feet high, was, by popular belief from early times, the home of the gods.

onomatopoeia (ŏn ō măt ō pē'yȧ). A rhetorical device by which the sound of the words either resembles or suggests the thing referred to; for example, "And murmuring of innumerable bees." Southey's "Cataract of Lodore" is especially rich in onomatopoetic effects.

onomatopoetic (ŏn ō măt ō pō ĕt'ĭk). See "onomatopoeia."*

oread (ō'rē ăd). In classical mythology, one of the nymphs* of mountains and hills.

Orpheus (ôr'fūs or, more commonly, ôr'-fē ŭs). In classical mythology, a Greek poet and musician, the son of Apollo* or a Thracian river god and of Calliope (kȧ lī'ō pē), the Muse* of epic poetry. With his lyre he charmed wild beasts and made trees and rocks move. After the abduction of his beloved wife, Eurydice (ū rĭd'ĭ sē), by Pluto,* he sought her in the land of departed spirits. Pluto, entranced by the music of the poet's lyre, agreed to allow Eurydice to return to earth on condition that Orpheus should not look behind him until he reached the upper world; but at the entrance the singer looked back and saw Eurydice disappear forever. In his grief he returned to the mountains, where he was torn to pieces by a band of women who were celebrating the rites of Bacchus.* His head was thrown into the river Hebrus, and was carried, still sweetly singing, to Lesbos, where it was buried.

Ossianic (ŏsh ĭ ăn'ĭk). A term applied to any composition supposed to resemble the poetry attributed to Ossian (Oisin), an ancient Celtic bard* who is said to have lived in the third century after Christ. About 1760 James Macpherson, a young Scottish schoolmaster, published two epics and a number of shorter pieces of writing composed in musical prose which he falsely claimed were translations of ancient poems by Ossian. Macpherson's works are full of vague nature descriptions and laments for the departed glories of the past. They are also exceedingly gloomy in tone. They became popular all over Europe and exercised a great influence during the Transition and Romantic periods.

Oxford movement. A religious movement originating at Oxford University between 1833 and 1841 and growing out of a desire to restore to the Church of England the spiritual and mystical character of medieval Christianity. The resulting controversies caused much spiritual unrest.

palmer. See "pilgrim."*

parallelism. A rhetorical device which consists of a succession of statements having similar grammatical structure and expressing similar, contrasting, or supplementary ideas. Parallelism is often found in Hebrew poetry, as, "A wise son maketh a glad father; but a foolish son is the heaviness of his mother," and in the popular ballads, as, "A gude rede gie to mee . . . Now, brother, rede ye mee . . . Now, sister, rede ye mee" (p. 59, ll. 14, 22, and 34).

Paris. In classical mythology, the son of Priam, king of Troy.* He was the abductor of Helen.*

Parnassus (pär năs′ŭs). A mountain in central Greece, anciently sacred to Apollo and the Muses.* Hence the name "Parnassus" is often used figuratively as a name for the home of poets and poetry.

pastoral. A name applied to literature that deals with the lives of shepherds, idealizing them and picturing them as leading an innocent, happy life, untroubled by the worries and cares of the city; by extension, a poem or romance describing peaceful country scenes or life among such scenes. Some authors make the shepherds represent real persons, and thus give the pastoral the character of an allegory.* The Greek poet Theocritus,* who wrote famous poems idealizing the shepherds of Sicily, is often called the "father of pastoral poetry."

patron (pā′trŭn). One who assists an artist or author by giving him encouragement or financial aid. Before Johnson's time literary men usually assumed a subservient attitude toward the noblemen who patronized them.

Pegasus (pĕg′à sŭs). In classical mythology, a famous winged horse; according to the most common tradition the horse of the Muses.* From his hoofprint sprang the fountain Hippocrene.* In literature the name "Pegasus" often symbolizes* poetic ability or genius.

Pelops (pē′lŏps). In classical mythology, the son of Tantalus. He won his wife from her father, Oenomaus, in a chariot race, by the help of Myrtilus, Oenomaus's charioteer. When Myrtilus claimed his reward, Pelops threw him into the sea. His dying curse brought misfortune on the descendants of Pelops, including Agamemnon. These misfortunes have served as the subject of some of the greatest Greek tragedies.

pentameter (pĕn tăm′ē tĕr). A line of poetry having five accented syllables. The most common form of pentameter in English poetry is the iambic* pentameter.

personification. A figure of speech in which an inanimate object, an abstract quality, or one of the lower animals is spoken of as if it were a person. Examples of personification are evening in Collins's "Ode to Evening" (p. 296), a mouse and a daisy in Burns's poems (pp. 328 and 330), and a cloud in Shelley's poem (p. 360). In all except Shelley's poem the thing personified is also apostrophized (see "apostrophe"*). The poets of the Age of Classicism were especially fond of treating abstract ideas, such as truth, beauty, etc., as though they were living beings.

personify. See "personification."*

Petrarch (pē′trärk) **(1304–1374).** Francesco Petrarca, a great Italian poet and scholar who helped to start the Renaissance by recovering and praising many of the treasures of classical literature. His most famous poems are addressed to a certain lady named Laura, about whom almost nothing is known.

Philomel (fĭl′ō mĕl) *or* **Philomela** (fĭl ō-mē′là). In classical mythology, the daughter of Pandion, king of Athens. Her sister Procne, married to Tereus, king of Thrace, longed for Philomel and sent her husband after her. On the return voyage Tereus fell in love with Philomel, mistreated her, imprisoned her in a tower, cut out her tongue so that she could not tell the wrong she had suffered, and cut off her hands so that she could not write it. By way of recompense the gods transformed her into a nightingale, whose pathetic song was supposed to result from the sadness of the unfortunate Philomel.

Phoebus (fē′bŭs) *or* **Phoebus Apollo.** Another name for Apollo* in modern literature, especially for Apollo conceived as a sun god. The horses and chariot with which the sun god crosses the heavens are often referred to in literature.

pilgrim. During the Middle Ages one who made a journey to a shrine, or sacred place. Pilgrims who visited the tomb of Christ in Jerusalem and brought back palm branches as tokens were called palmers. In the ballad of "Johnie Cock" (p. 66) the palmer, like others of his class, is a great carrier of news and gossip. In modern times the word "pilgrim" may be applied to anyone who makes a journey to some spot of religious, historic, or literary interest.

Plato (427?–347 B.C.). A celebrated Greek philosopher and teacher of idealism whose doctrines have exercised a great influence on modern thought. He speaks of Socrates* not as a master, but as an older friend. His teachings are set forth in a series of dialogues, which have come down to us. He established the famous Academy, the first European institution for the systematic study of philosophy and science.

Platonic. According to the ancient Greek philosopher Plato,* abstract qualities such as virtue, truth, beauty, and love exist in their most perfect form in the mind of God, and when they appear on earth they are merely reflections of the divine original. Hence the term "Platonic love" came to be applied to pure affection unmixed with sensual desires.

Plautus (plô′tŭs) (254?–184 B.C.). A great comic dramatist of ancient Rome. He rose from humble station to prominence through the popularity of his plays. His influence on modern literature is widespread, and he has been imitated by many dramatists, including Shakespeare. Twenty of his plays are still in existence.

Plutarch (plŏo′tärk) (46?–120?). A Greek historian, famous as the author of forty-six lives of notable Greeks and Romans arranged in pairs. The book is usually referred to as Plutarch's *Lives*. Plutarch also wrote philosophical and other works.

Pluto (the Wealth-giver). In classical mythology, the god of the lower world. He ruled there with his wife Proserpina.* He was stern, pitiless, deaf to prayer or flattery. He carried off Eurydice, the wife of Orpheus.*

Pre-Raphaelite (prē-răf′ȧ ĭt). The Pre-Raphaelite movement was an attempt to purify art by going back to the simple manner and restoring the wonder, reverence, and awe of the medieval painters and craftsmen before the time of Raphael (Rafael*). The artists who fostered the movement came

to be known as the Pre-Raphaelite Brotherhood.

Pre-Raphaelitism (prē-răf′ȧ ĕl ĭt ĭzm). A theory of art adopted by the Pre-Raphaelites.*

Pretender, Old. James Francis Stewart (1688–1766), son of James II of England (see page 213) and father of the Young Pretender.* When James II fled from England, his son was sent to France, where he was brought up and where, in 1701, he was proclaimed James III of England. He later fought in the armies of France against England. In 1708, and again in 1715 after the death of Queen Anne, he attempted, with the help of the Jacobites,* to gain the English throne, but was foiled. After his failure in 1715 he fled to the Continent, where he lived during the remainder of his life. Queen Anne was actually succeeded by George I, Elector of Hanover in Germany, who was also a descendant of James I of England. The selection from *Henry Esmond* is based in part on the Old Pretender's efforts to gain the English throne. The word "pretender" here means claimant.

Pretender, Young. Charles Edward Stewart (1720–1788), son of the Old Pretender.* Both Pretenders were assisted by the French and the Scotch,. many of whom were Jacobites,* in their efforts to restore the Stewarts to the English throne. The Young Pretender won victories at first, but was decisively defeated at Culloden.*

Proserpine (prŏs′ẽr pĭn *or* pĕn *or* pĭn) *or* **Proserpina** (prŏ sûr′pĭ nȧ). In classical mythology, the wife of Pluto,* and queen of the underworld. She was the daughter of Ceres, the goddess of agriculture. One day her mother left her gathering flowers in a meadow, and Pluto* came and carried her away. In revenge Ceres put a blight on the earth, and nothing grew. To save the human race from starvation, Jupiter (Jove*) persuaded Pluto to let Proserpina return. But she had already eaten part of a pomegranate in the lower world, and hence, by the law of the supernatural realm, could not escape completely. Accordingly it was arranged that thereafter she should spend half of the year on earth and the other half in the gloomy land of shades.

Proteus (prō′tūs *or, more commonly,* prō′tē ŭs). In classical mythology, a sea divinity, shepherd of the flocks of the sea (seals etc.), and a great prophet. To be consulted, he had to be caught and bound, but this was difficult, because he could change himself into any number of shapes. In Wordsworth's sonnet

"The World Is Too Much with Us" he symbolizes* the poetic beauty seen in nature by pagans.

Rafael (răf'ȧ ĕl) *or* **Raphael** (**1483–1520**). One of the greatest painters of the Italian Renaissance, and said to be the most universally popular artist in history. In versatility and power he remains almost without a rival. Among his best-known paintings are the "Sistine Madonna" and his pictures in the Vatican (the Pope's palace at Rome), including "The Transfiguration." His personal beauty, his charm of manner, and his kindliness of heart endeared him to all who knew him.

Rambler, The. A journal published in London from 1750 to 1752 by Dr. Samuel Johnson, Of the same general character as *The Tatler** and *The Spectator.**

realism. In art and literature the attempt to present nature or life just as it is, without idealization. The realistic writer does not hesitate to introduce the commonplace, the ugly, or the unpleasant if he believes that by so doing he can make his work more nearly true to life.

realistic. See "realism."*

Reliques (rĕ lēks'), **Percy's.** The name usually given to the *Reliques of Ancient English Poetry*, published by Thomas Percy in 1765. It is one of the earliest and most famous modern collections of old ballads and poems, made under the influence of the fondness for medieval literature that developed during the Transition and Romantic periods.

rhyme, internal. A kind of rhyme in which a word not at the end of a line rhymes with another word, as,

> The splendour *falls* on castle *walls.*
>
> I cannot *tell* how it *befell*
> that he
> Came to her *door* as oft *before,*
> though she
> Day after *day* sent him *away*
> In place of me.

rhyme scheme. It is customary to describe a rhyming stanza* by using the letters of the alphabet to indicate the arrangement of the rhymes. Thus, when we wish to show that in a certain poem the stanzas consist of four lines, the first of which rhymes with the fourth, and the second with the third, we say that the scheme is *abba*, the rhyming lines being indicated by the same letter. If we wish to describe a four-line stanza in which only the second and fourth lines rhyme, we indicate

D

the fact thus: *abcb*, the unrhymed lines being indicated by two different letters.

rhythm. A measured or balanced movement, wherever found, as in poetry, music, dancing, and the like. In poetry the term "rhythm" is usually applied to the effects produced by the succession of accented and unaccented syllables. Prose is rhythmic if it gives a similar balanced effect of ebb and flow when read aloud. See also "cadence."*

Richardson, Samuel (**1689–1761**). An English writer, whose *Clarissa Harlowe* and other long prose narratives are among the earliest English novels.

Robin Goodfellow. In English folklore, an imp or elf who helped farmers with their work if he was rewarded with a bowl of milk or cream. He is sometimes regarded as a mischievous, playful fairy called Puck, and as such appears in Shakespeare's *Midsummer Night's Dream.*

Robin Hood. A legendary hero of the English popular ballads. He headed a band of brave and carefree yeomen who lived as outlaws in the greenwood (especially Sherwood Forest in Nottinghamshire*), killing the deer (which the king claimed the sole right to hunt) for food. With Little John, Will Scarlet, Friar Tuck, and the rest of his merry men, Robin Hood went about robbing the rich and proud and aiding the poor and oppressed. Robin Hood also figures in the early English drama (p. 83).

romance (rō măns'). (1) A narrative in which the interest lies not so much in the portrayal of real life or human character as in strange adventures, supernatural events, extraordinary behavior, or rapid changes of scene and fortune. The kind of romances that flourished especially during the Middle Ages, and hence are called medieval romances, usually tell of the exploits of knights and the loves of fair ladies. (2) The term "romance" is also applied to the real or commonplace made beautiful by imagination.

romantic. See "romance"* and page 313.

Roses, Wars of the. In English history, the long struggle between the rival families of Lancaster and York for supremacy, so called from the fact that the badge of the House of Lancaster was a red rose, that of the House of York a white rose. These wars began in 1455 and ended with the defeat and death of Richard III at Bosworth in 1485 and the accession of Henry VII, who, by marrying a princess of the House of York, united the warring families and brought peace. During the Wars of the Roses the people of England suffered much hardship and distress.

Round Table. (1) In Arthurian legend, a table made for Uther Pendragon (ū'thĕr pĕn drăg'ŭn), the father of King Arthur,* and afterward given to Arthur as a wedding present. It is said to have been made round so as to prevent quarrels over the right to sit at the head of the table. One seat was called the Siege (or Seat) Perilous, because it was death for any knight to sit in it unless it was certain he would achieve the adventure of the Holy Grail. (2) The Order of the Round Table was an institution, or fellowship, of knights founded by King Arthur at the advice of Merlin.* At first the Knights of the Round Table were all high-minded and noble, but sin gradually crept in. The Knights of the Round Table were nearly all slain in Arthur's last battle. The Round Table is often referred to in literature.

Royal Society, the. The Royal Society for the Advancement of Science, the oldest scientific society in Great Britain and one of the oldest in Europe. It was founded sometime before 1662, when the charter was granted. It has always numbered the leading British scientists among its members.

Royalist. A supporter or adherent of a king. In English history the name is applied especially to those who sympathized with Charles* I and the exiled Charles II during the Civil War and the Commonwealth (1642–1660). Later, after the abdication of James II (1689), the term "Royalist" was also applied to the Jacobites,* who sympathized with James and his descendants, the Old Pretender* and the Young Pretender.*

runes. The oldest form of Germanic writing, found in inscriptions on wood, metal, or stone over a large part of Europe. The runes came to be used for purposes of magic, a use which continued for a long time; and since they were found hard to decipher, the name "rune" has become almost a synonym for "a mysterious secret." The adjective "runic" has come to mean "rude and ancient" as well as "hard to understand."

Ruth. In the Bible, the leading character of the Book of Ruth. She was a young Moabitish widow who left her native country, Moab, and went with Naomi, her mother-in-law, to Bethlehem. Here, among strangers, she was gathering up the barley ("corn") left by the mowers in the field of a rich man named Boaz when Boaz saw and fell in love with her.

Later the two were married. She was an ancestor of David.*

Saint George. A legendary hero, the patron saint of England. During the Middle Ages he was known as the "Christian hero." According to tradition, he killed a terrible dragon to whom a beautiful virgin was about to be sacrificed. The story is often represented in art and referred to in literature. Plays dealing with Saint George were common in England during the late Middle Ages and the Renaissance.

Saint Mark. The patron saint of Venice, whose reputed relics were transported to Venice from Alexandria in 828.

Saint Nicholas. An early Christian saint. He came to be regarded as the patron saint of seafaring men, thieves, and children. According to tradition he saved three maidens from degradation by giving secretly to each a bag of gold as a marriage portion. The incident is said to be the origin of our Christmas custom of giving surreptitious gifts to children and attributing the gifts to Santa Claus (Saint Nicholas). During the Middle Ages periodical ceremonies were performed and plays were given in his honor.

Sarazin (săr'á zĭn) **(Saracen).** In medieval history and literature, a Mohammedan who was hostile to the crusaders. Often used, as in Spenser's *Faerie Queene*, for any despised and hated pagan.

satire (săt'īr). A literary composition, either in prose or in verse, in which public or private weaknesses, follies, or sins are ridiculed or rebuked. Some satires are inspired by a real desire to reform manners; others are merely the expression of prejudice, dislike, or hatred. The writer of satire may accomplish his purpose by the use of ridicule, derision, wit, sarcasm, burlesque,* or even abuse. One who makes use of satire is said to be satirical* and to satirize* the object of his attack.

satirical. See "satire."*

satirize. See "satire."*

Saturn (săt'ĕrn). In Roman mythology, an ancient divinity who was said to have introduced agriculture and civilization. He was thought of as having lived alone and having ruled the world in the golden* age before the coming of Jove* and the other Olympian gods.

schoolmen. A name applied to certain medieval philosophers who tried to solve religious problems by a strict system of logic. They were fond of making very delicate logical distinctions. They were called schoolmen because most of them were teachers in the schools.

Scone (skōōn). A place in Perthshire, Scotland, where from early times the kings of Scotland were crowned and had their residence. The Stone of Scone, or "Stone of Destiny," which formed part of the coronation chair at Scone, was carried to England in 1296 and now rests under the coronation chair in Westminster Abbey. It was said to have been brought originally from Ireland.

Selkirk, Alexander. A Scottish sailor who, in 1704, was set ashore on the island of Juan Fernández, off the western coast of South America, and remained there alone for four years. From the published accounts of Selkirk's experiences Daniel Defoe derived suggestions which he used in *Robinson Crusoe*.

Sennacherib (sĕ năk'ẽr ĭb) **(705–681 B.C.).** A great king of ancient Assyria who threatened to besiege Jerusalem with a mighty army, but, according to the Bible, was prevented by an act of God from taking the city. Read 2 Kings 19: 32–36.

simile (sĭm'ĭ lē). A figure of speech in which two very different things or ideas having, nevertheless, one or more characteristics in common are compared by means of some such word as "such," "like," or "as" applied to these characteristics: "He was like a lion in the fight"; " . . . he shall be like a tree planted by the rivers of water" (p. 163, Psalm 1: 3); Burns's "To a Mountain Daisy" (p. 330, ll. 31–48).

sock. Thin-soled, low-heeled footwear worn by actors in Roman comedy; hence a figure of speech for "comedy." See metonymy.*

Socrates (sŏk'rȧ tēz) **(470?–399 B.C.).** An Athenian philosopher and teacher. He was grotesque in appearance; but, as his friends knew, he was all-glorious within, the most righteous man of the whole age. His views eventually made him enemies, and he was unjustly accused of worshiping false gods and of corrupting the youth of Athens. He was convicted and sentenced to drink the poisonous hemlock. In his cell he chatted calmly with his disciples and then drank the poison and died. The description of his death given by his friend Plato* is one of the noblest and most affecting passages ever written. The Socratic (sŏ krăt'ĭk) method of teaching consisted in asking questions and thus making men use their own knowledge and reach their own conclusions.

Solomon. One of the most famous of the kings of Israel. He was the son of David.* Given the choice of all possible gifts, he asked for wisdom, and so became the wisest man in the world. Out of this wisdom grew the magnificence of his realm. He built the first Jewish temple, established peaceful relations with other great powers, and fostered learning and commerce. His wisdom and the famous visit of the Queen of Sheba are frequently alluded to in literature. Like Abraham, Solomon was appropriated by the Mohammedans, who considered him master of the demons that built, at his command, the temple in Jerusalem.

sonnet. A verse form that came into English from the Italian during the Elizabethan Period, and has been used ever since. The earliest English sonnets were those of Wyatt and Surrey, and were published in a volume, called Tottel's *Miscellany*, in 1557. Both in form and in substance the sonnet follows certain strict rules. A sonnet contains fourteen iambic* pentameter* lines.

There are two important varieties of sonnets in English poetry — the Italian form and the Shakespearean, or English, form.

The Italian form consists of two parts — an octave (the first eight lines) and a sestet (the last six lines). These two should correspond to a division of the thought, or substance, into two parts. The octave sketches a situation, and then, at the beginning of the sestet, the thought pauses and turns, the sestet applying the situation that the octave has sketched. For example, Wordsworth, in his sonnet "It Is a Beauteous Evening" (p. 342), describes the evening in the octave and then, in the sestet, applies the situation to his young companion. The rhyme* scheme of the Italian form is as follows: *abbaabba* (octave) and either *cdcdcd, cdecde*, or some other combination (sestet).

The English form, though consisting of fourteen lines, is divided into three quatrains, or groups of four lines, and ends with a couplet.* The rhyme scheme is as follows: *abab, cdcd, efef, gg*. Since the English form has no division into octave and sestet, the corresponding pause in the thought after the octave may be lacking. The English form was commonly used by Shakespeare and other Elizabethan poets. Notice especially that in the Italian form the last two lines usually do not rhyme, whereas in the English form they do. You can, in most cases, distinguish an Italian sonnet by the lack of rhyme in the last two lines. The greatest English sonnet-writers are Shakespeare (who wrote more than one hundred and fifty), Wordsworth (who wrote more than five hundred), Milton, and Keats.

Shakespeare used the English form, Milton and Wordsworth preferred the Italian form, and Keats was equally at home in either form.

Sophocles (sŏf'ŏ klēz) **(495?–406 B.C.).** One of the three great tragic poets of ancient Greece. He defeated Aeschylus* in a contest for the best tragedy in 468, and was defeated by Euripides* in 441. His dramas are regarded by many critics as the most perfect that the world has even seen. They are powerful, dignified, and lofty in tone. As great tragedies they may be said to deal with "the turbid ebb and flow of human misery," which, according to Arnold in "Dover Beach," was suggested to Sophocles by "the eternal note of sadness" in the sound of the Aegean* waves.

Spectator, The. A daily periodical, containing essays rather than news, published in London from 1711 to 1712. It followed *The Tatler** and contained articles by two famous English essayists, Richard Steele and Joseph Addison.

Spenserian stanza. A stanza form consisting of eight iambic* pentameter* lines followed by one line of iambic hexameter* (commonly called an Alexandrine) and having the rhyme* scheme *ababbcbcc.* It was invented by the poet Edmund Spenser, who used it in most of his poetry. Many later poets also have used it. In general the Spenserian stanza produces in the reader a musical, dreamy effect that keeps time to the harmony of fairyland.

squire. One who attended on a knight and bore his lance and shield; usually a young man who was himself preparing to be a knight. Squires were supposed to be particularly attentive to the service of ladies. *The Squire of Low Degree,* a famous medieval romance, tells of the sufferings which a squire endured for the love of his lady. Chaucer's Squire is a rather dandified young gentleman and an expert in the art of love ("a lovyer").

stanza. In poetry, a group of lines combined according to a typical scheme so as to form a unit.

Stewart (Stuart). A royal family of Scotland and England. Among many noble names the family includes Mary* Queen of Scots, and the Stewart sovereigns of England and Scotland jointly — James* I, Charles* I, Charles II, James II, Mary (the wife of William III), and Anne. Those who sympathized with the Stewarts and who, after the dethronement of James II in 1688, wished to see the Stewart line continued on the English throne were called Jacobites.*

Stygian (stĭj'ĭ ăn). Pertaining to the Styx*; dark, dismal.

Styx (stĭks). In Greek mythology, the principal river of the lower world, dividing the realm of the living from that of the dead.

subjective. In literature, treating persons or things not as they actually are, but as they are interpreted by the reflections or feelings of the writer.

symbol. See "symbolism."*

symbolism. The use of something, animate or inanimate, to stand for or represent something moral or intellectual. Thus a lamb may symbolize innocence; an olive branch, peace; the letter X, any unknown quantity. Stevenson humorously uses the umbrella as a symbol of British respectability.

symbolize. See "symbolism."*

Tarquins (tär'kwĭnz). The last line of Roman kings. They were licentious and cruel. Their name has become a synonym for cruelty and tyranny. Shakespeare, in *Macbeth,* refers to the story of how Tarquinius Sextus, one of the last of the Tarquins, visited the house of his cousin and grossly violated the laws of hospitality. As a result the people of Rome rose in rebellion and drove out the whole Tarquin family.

Tatler, The. A periodical published in London, by Richard Steele, from 1709 to 1711; one of the earliest ventures in magazine literature in English. See "*Spectator,* The."

Telemachus (tĕ lĕm'a kŭs). In Greek mythology, the son of Odysseus (Ulysses)* and Penelope. According to the Odyssey he helped his father to slay Penelope's suitors.

Tempe (tĕm'pē). A river valley in Thessaly, Greece, famous in ancient times for the beauty of its scenery. Tempe was regarded as sacred to the god Apollo.*

Temple, the. Anciently the seat, in London, of the Knights Templars. The present buildings of the Temple are used by societies of law students and lawyers, and are known as the Inns of Court and Chancery. The Temple and two of its divisions — namely, the Inner Temple and the Middle Temple — are often referred to in literature.

Terence (tĕr'ĕns) **(190?–159? B.C.).** A Roman comic dramatist. He is notable for the purity of his Latin. His work exercised a considerable influence upon later literature.

terza rima (tĕr'tsä rē'mä). A stanza form, or rather an arrangement of verse, according to which (1) in each group of three lines only the first and third lines rhyme, while (2) the second line rhymes with the first line of the next group of three, thus: *aba, bcb, cdc*, etc. Thus the groups are interlaced. Terza rima was used by Dante* in *The Divine Comedy*, and its use in English always marks Italian influence.

tetrameter (tĕt răm'ē tēr). A line of poetry having four accents.*

Thais (thā'ĭs). A famous beauty who was beloved by Alexander* the Great, and who accompanied him on his Asiatic campaigns. She is said to have induced him to set fire to the city of Persepolis.

Thebes (thēbz). A famous city of ancient Greece. Its mythical king Oedipus and his family were the subjects of certain famous tragic dramas and poems.

Theocritus (thē ŏk'rĭ tŭs) (flourished about 250 B.C.). A Greek poet who lived in Syracuse, in Sicily. He was the first known writer to compose poems dealing in romantic fashion with the life of shepherds; hence he is called the "father of pastoral* poetry."

Thomson, James (1700–1748). A Scottish poet. After studying at Edinburgh University he went to seek his fortune in London, where he supported himself as a tutor until he had made a name for himself by his poetry. His poem *The Seasons* marks a new era in English poetry. As one of the earliest poets to treat nature in a simple, a truthful, and yet a romantic spirit, he is the predecessor of Wordsworth and the other great romantic poets of nature.

threshold. In olden times it was the custom for the Church to bless the thresholds of dwellings, as it was believed that thus demons, witches, and other evil beings would be unable to enter. The fact that Geraldine has to be carried across the threshold of the castle gate by the innocent Christabel suggests Geraldine's true character. Another suggestion comes when the dying brands on the hearth flame up (p. 398, ll. 158–159) at the approach of a being so closely associated with the devil, the prince of the fiery regions. And again (p. 399, ll. 252–253), the fact that Geraldine is in part foul and ugly points to the old belief that demons and witches cannot transform themselves into creatures exactly like those made by the hand of God. "Christabel" contains still other hints of Geraldine's real nature; find them.

Tigris. A great river of western Asia, which, with the Euphrates,* bounds Mesopotamia.

Titan. In classical mythology, one of the most ancient divinities. Cronus, one of the chief Titans, swallowed five of his children, but was forced to disgorge them by his son Jove* (Zeus), who seized the kingship of the gods and imprisoned the Titans in an underworld. The Titans are sometimes confused with the giants, who are said to have piled mountains upon mountains in order to reach heaven. Hence the Titans became the types of lawlessness, gigantic size, and enormous strength.

Titian (tĭsh'ăn) **(Tiziano Vecelli) (1477–1576).** One of the greatest of Italian painters, also called "the divine." He was especially noted for his pictures of scenes from the life of Christ and the Holy Family.

Tolstoi. Count Leo Nikolaevich Tolstoi (1828–1910), a distinguished Russian novelist, social reformer, and religious thinker. During his early manhood he led the gay life of the upper classes, but he ultimately adopted a simpler way of living. During his later years he devoted himself to helping the peasants, working out his theories for the improvement of society, and writing on religious subjects. His best-known novel is *Anna Karenina*.

Tories. In English history, one of two powerful political parties that arose late in the seventeenth century. In matters of Church and State the Tories were conservatives and so were opposed to the Whigs.* They believed that the supreme power should belong to the king rather than to Parliament; many of them opposed the War of the Spanish Succession; some of them were Jacobites*; and some would have been glad to see Roman Catholicism, displaced during the Reformation, restored as the national religion. They represented the old aristocratic class as opposed to the new democracy. They may be regarded as the successors of the Cavaliers* and as the ancestors of the later Conservatives. The term was originally used as a nickname.

Trafalgar (trȧ făl'gēr). A naval battle fought between the British and the allied French and Spanish fleets, off the south coast of Spain near Cape Trafalgar, in 1805. It was the greatest British naval victory during the wars against Napoleon. The famous English naval commander Lord Nelson was slain in this battle.

trimeter (trĭm'ē tēr). A line of poetry having three accents.*

Triton (trī'tŏn). In Greek mythology, a son of Neptune,* god of the seas. He was represented with a human body down to the waist, but with a fish's tail instead of legs. He had a horn of twisted sea shell (conch) on which he blew to calm or raise the waves. Wordsworth uses him to symbolize* the poetic beauty which the ancient pagans saw in nature. In the plural the word is used to refer to lesser sea gods, half human, half fish or monster, who, like Triton, carried a conch shell.

trochaic (trŏ kā′ĭk). See "trochee."*

trochee (trō′kĕ). In poetry, a unit or "foot" consisting of an accented syllable followed by an unaccented syllable. In scanning poetry we usually indicate a trochaic foot thus: ̷ x. The following words are trochaic: "húndred," "ópen," "cóming." For examples of trochaic rhythm, see most of the lines spoken by the Witches in *Macbeth*, IV, i (p. 125); also Blake's "Piping down the Valleys Wild" (p. 325) and Burns's "Scots, Wha Hae wi' Wallace Bled" (p. 332). Contrast the trochaic rhythm with the iambic.* In American literature Poe's "Raven" and Longfellow's *Hiawatha* are both written in the trochaic rhythm.

troubadours. A class of lyric poets who flourished during the Middle Ages, chiefly in the south of France. They were mostly amateur poets of the aristocratic class. Their poems are complicated in meter and deal with romantic love.

Troy. An ancient city near the northwestern coast of Asia Minor. According to tradition, it was destroyed by the ancient Greeks after a famous siege lasting ten years. Episodes of the last year of the war are narrated in Homer's Iliad,* from which many European writers since have drawn inspiration. The Troy story also furnished subjects for several Greek dramas.

Turgenieff (Turgenev) (tōor gĕn′yĕf), **Ivan Sergyeevich (1818–1883).** A Russian poet, dramatist, and novelist, whose sympathy with the serfs and common people led to his leaving Russia. He was the first Russian author to be read and admired outside of his own country.

twelve good rules, the. The following rules were attributed to Charles I and were often printed below his portrait: 1. Urge no healths. 2. Profane no divine ordinances. 3. Touch no state matters. 4. Reveal no secrets. 5. Pick no quarrels. 6. Make no comparisons. 7. Maintain no ill opinions. 8. Keep no bad company. 9. Encourage no vices. 10. Make no long meals. 11. Repeat no grievances. 12. Lay no wagers.

Tyre. One of the oldest and most important cities in Phoenicia. It is on the Mediterranean Sea. It has been destroyed repeatedly, until today only an insignificant town marks the spot where the ancient city stood. The name suggests fallen grandeur.

Ulysses (ū lĭs′ēz) (in Greek, **Odysseus** (ŏ dĭs′ūs)). In literature, a Greek chieftain who appears as a wise and eloquent warrior in the Iliad* and as the hero of the Odyssey.* In the latter poem he is driven out of his way by storm while returning to his home, in Ithaca, from the siege of Troy.* His various adventures make up the material of the poem. He finally reaches home, slays the suitors who have been troubling his faithful wife Penelope, and resumes the government of his kingdom.

unities. A term applied to certain rules of dramatic composition followed by writers of several different periods in the history of literature. The three rules of the unities were these: (1) the plot of a play should have but one main action; (2) the scene of the action should be one place; (3) the time represented should not exceed twenty-four hours. These were falsely supposed to have been the rules followed by the ancient classical dramatists.

Vanity Fair. In Bunyan's *Pilgrim's Progress*, a perpetual fair or market at the town of Vanity, where the merchants dealt only in vain, worldly goods. In other literature "Vanity Fair" is often used to symbolize* the gaudy, empty pleasures of the world as contrasted with the more serious things of life.

Venus (Greek **Aphrodite**). In classical mythology, goddess of love and beauty. She sprang from the foam of the sea. Doves, swans, and sparrows were sacred to her.

Vergil (Virgil) (70–19 B.C.). Publius Vergilius Maro, the greatest poet of ancient Rome. His most famous work is the Aeneid, an epic which tells of the flight of Aeneas from burning Troy,* his later adventures, and his founding of Rome. This poem has been widely imitated by writers of epic poetry. Vergil also wrote pastoral* poetry.

Vesta. In the Roman religion, the goddess of the hearth and its fire, and hence of the preparation of food. She was the daughter of Saturn.* In literature she often personifies the quiet, retired atmosphere of the home.

Waterloo. A little village in Belgium, about nine miles south of Brussels. Here, in 1815, was fought the famous battle of Waterloo between the allied nations and the French under Napoleon.* The crushing defeat suffered by the great emperor in this battle has made the name of Waterloo synonymous with the ruin of ambitious plans; hence the common phrase "He met his Waterloo."

Wesley, John (1703–1791). An English clergyman, famous as the founder of Methodism. He was educated at Oxford. He went to Georgia as a missionary in 1735, returning to England in 1738. He was a powerful preacher. He also wrote extensively. His influence upon religious thought in England and America has been enormous. His brother Charles, also a clergyman, is famous as a hymn-writer.

Whigs. In English history, one of two powerful political parties that arose late in the seventeenth century. In matters of Church and State the Whigs opposed the Tories.* They wished to limit the power of the king by increasing the power of Parliament. They favored the revolution which drove out James II, and they preferred the supposedly moderate Elector of Hanover (George I) to the Old Pretender.* In general they were opposed to the Jacobites.* They represented the new democracy, which became historically influential during the Age of Classicism (p. 213). The Whigs, though headed by some of the greatest nobility, were for the most part either businessmen or members of one of the various religious sects opposed to the Church of England. They may be regarded as the successors of the more liberal Puritans (see page 183) and the less extreme members of the Church of England, and as the ancestors of the later Liberals.

Wyrd (Weird) (wẽrd). The Anglo-Saxon term for Fate, that which must be. Originally the idea was pagan; but after the introduction of Christianity early writers applied the name "Wyrd" not to an impersonal fatalism ruling the lives of men, but to the providence or will of the Christian God.

Zeus (zūs). See "Jove."*

Zion. A hill on which was situated the ancient city of Jerusalem; also the city of Jerusalem as a whole. Symbolically it is applied to the Church and to heaven. In Bunyan's *Pilgrim's Progress* it is the name of the Celestial* City.

Index

D

PRINTED IN THE UNITED STATES OF AMERICA

CÆDMON

CHAUCER

SPENSER

SHAKESPEARE

MILTON

JOHNSON

GRAY

1 ANGLO-SAXON GLEEMAN

2 MEDIEVAL MONK

6 COFFEEHOUSE

5 ELIZABETHAN THEATER

8 PHONOGRAPH

LITERATURE'S EVER—